Encyclopedia of
Paleontology

Encyclopedia of
Paleontology

Volume 2
M – Z

Editor
Ronald Singer
The R.R. Bensley Professor of Biology and Medical Sciences
University of Chicago

FITZROY DEARBORN PUBLISHERS
CHICAGO · LONDON

FITZROY DEARBORN PUBLISHERS
919 North Michigan Avenue, Suite 760
Chicago, IL 60611
USA

or

FITZROY DEARBORN PUBLISHERS
310 Regent Street
London W1R 5AJ
England

British Library and Library of Congress Cataloguing in Publication Data are available.

ISBN 1–884964–96–6

First published in the USA and UK 1999

Interior Design and Typeset by Print Means Inc., New York, New York

Printed by Edwards Brothers, Ann Arbor, Michigan

Cover design by Peter Aristedes, Chicago Advertising and Design, Chicago, Illinois

Cover illustration: Head reconstruction of *Pachychephalosaurus,* illustration by William Zucconi; body reconstruction of *Tanystropheus,* illustration by Matt Bonnan

CONTENTS

ALPHABETICAL LIST OF ENTRIES

THEMATIC OUTLINE OF ENTRIES

This outline is divided into the following 12 sections:

ANALYTICAL APPROACHES
BIOLOGY AND BEHAVIOR
EVOLUTIONARY CONCEPTS
GEOGRAPHY AND ENVIRONMENT
INDIVIDUALS
MORPHOLOGY
PALEONTOLOGY AS A DISCIPLINE
PATTERNS IN THE HISTORY OF LIFE
PRACTICAL APPROACHES
REGIONAL OVERVIEWS
STRATIGRAPHIC AND FOSSIL RECORD
TAXA

The section on taxa is further divided into subsections.

ANALYTICAL APPROACHES

Biomass and Productivity Estimates
Biomechanics
Comparative Anatomy
Functional Morphology
Statistical Techniques
Molecular Paleontology

BIOLOGY AND BEHAVIOR

Aerial Locomotion
Aquatic Invertebrates, Adaptive Strategies of
Aquatic Locomotion
Burrowing Adaptations in Vertebrates
Diet
Feeding Adaptations: Invertebrates
Feeding Adaptations: Vertebrates
Gastroliths
Growth, Postembryonic
Paleoethology
Reproductive Strategies: Plants
Reproductive Strategies: Vertebrates
Respiration
Terrestrial Locomotion in Vertebrates
Thermoregulation

EVOLUTIONARY CONCEPTS

Adaptation
Allometry
Coevolutionary Relationships
Diversity
Evolutionary Novelty
Evolutionary Theory
Evolutionary Trends
Extinction
Growth, Development, and Evolution
Heterochrony
Homology
Phyletic Dwarfism and Gigantism
Selection
Speciation and Morphological Change

Systematics
Variation

GEOGRAPHY AND ENVIRONMENT

Atmospheric Environment
Global Environment
Ocean Environment
Paleoclimatology
Plate Tectonics and Continental Drift
Seas, Ancient
Terrestrial Environment

INDIVIDUALS

Abel, Othenio
Agassiz, Jean Louis Rudolphe
Ameghino, Carlos
Ameghino, Florentino
Andrews, Roy Chapman
Anning, Mary

Australia: Vertebrate Paleontology
Canada and Alaska
China
Europe: Eastern Europe
Europe: Western Europe
Indian Subcontinent
Madagascar
Mexico and Central America
Oceanic Islands
Russia and the Former Soviet
    Union
South America
Southeast Asia
United States, Continental

STRATIGRAPHIC AND FOSSIL RECORD

Fossilization Processes
Fossil Record
Geological Timescale
Sedimentology
Seismic and Surface Activity
Taphonomy
Trace Fossils

TAXA
Non-Metazoans

Algae
Fungi
Lichens
Microbial Fossils, Precambrian
Skeletized Microorganisms: Algae
Skeletized Microorganisms: Protozoans
    and Chitozoans

(Plants)

Angiosperms
Bryophytes
Club Mosses and Their Relatives
Coniferophytes
Cycads
Ferns and Their Relatives
Forests, Fossil
Ginkgos
Gnetophytes
Gymnosperms
Horsetails and Their Relatives
Palynology
Plants: Overview
Problematic Plants
Progymnosperms
Seed Ferns
Vascular Plants, Earliest

Metazoans
(Non-Chordates)

Annelids
Anthozoans
Arthropods: Overview
Arthropods: Miscellaneous
    Arthropods
Bivalves
Brachiopods
Bryozoans
Cephalopods
Chelicerates
Coelenterates
Crustaceans
Echinoderms
Ediacaran Biota
Gastropods
Hemichordates
Insects and Other
    Hexapods
Metazoan Phyla, Minor
Molluscs: Overview
Molluscs: Minor Molluscan
    Classes
Myriapods
Problematic Animals: Overview
Problematic Animals: Phanerozoic
    Problematica
Problematic Animals: Poorly
    Characterized Problematica
Sponges and Spongelike
    Organisms
Superphyla
Trilobites
Urochordates

(Chordates)

Aardvarks
Acanthodians
Actinopterygians
Amniotes
Ankylosaurs
Aquatic Reptiles
Archosauromorphs
Artiodactyls
Bats
Birds
Carnivorans
Cephalochordates
Ceratopsians
Chondrichthyans
Chordates
Craniates
Creodonts
Crocodylians
Crocodylomorphs

Dermopterans
Dinosaurs
Glires
Gnathostomes
Hominids
Hyraxes
Ichthyosaurs
Insectivorans
Jawless Fishes
Lepidosauromorphs
Lepospondyls
Lissamphibians
Mammals, Mesozoic and
    Non-Therian
Marsupials
Mesonychids
Ornithischians
Ornithopods
Osteichthyans
Pachycephalosaurs
Palaeanodonts
Pangolins
Parareptiles
Pelycosaurs
Perissodactyls
Placentals: Overview
Placentals: Endemic South American
    Ungulates
Placentals: Minor Placental Orders of
    Large Body Size
Placentals: Minor Placental Orders of
    Small Body Size
Placoderms
Placodonts
Primates
Proboscideans
Pterosaurs
Sarcopterygians
Saurischians
Sauropodomorphs
Sauropsids
Sauropterygians
Sirenians
Stegosaurs
Synapsids
Tetrapods: Overview
Tetrapods: Basal Tetrapods
Tetrapods: Near-Amniote
    Tetrapods
Therapsids
Theropods
Tree Shrews
Turtles
Ungulates, Archaic
Whales
Xenarthrans

M

MADAGASCAR

Madagascar is the fourth largest island in the world, lying in the Indian Ocean some 400 kilometers off the southeast coast of Africa. It is home to one of the most unique biotas (collections of animals and plants) on Earth, including mammals such as lemurs and tenrecs, birds such as mesites, ground-rollers, and asities, and at least eight endemic families of plants. Approximately 85 percent of the living species are found nowhere else on Earth. One of the most fascinating unsolved mysteries of natural history revolves around how, when, and from where ancestral stocks of the various modern groups of plants and animals arrived on the island. The evidence to unravel that mystery, however, is in short supply since the Malagasy fossil record is very poor, arguably the poorest of any major landmass that once comprised the southern supercontinent of Gondwana.

Madagascar has an interesting geophysical history that bears directly on its biotic evolution (Coffin and Rabinowitz 1992). For the entire Paleozoic and much of the Mesozoic, it was sandwiched between Africa and the Indian subcontinent. Then, approximately 160 million years ago, in the Late Jurassic, Madagascar detached from Africa, opposite Kenya, Somalia, and Tanzania, and drifted south-southeastward along a fracture zone (area of tectonic activity) as part of a massive tectonic unit that included the Indian subcontinent, Antarctica, and Australia. Madagascar attained its current position opposite Mozambique in the Early Cretaceous, at approximately 120 to 130 million years ago. At the same time, connections between the Indo-Madagascar and Antarcto-Australia units were severed. Madagascar retained its connection with the Indian subcontinent until about 88 million years ago, when the latter rifted (broke away) from Madagascar's eastern margin and began its northeastward journey toward Eurasia.

The fossil record of Malagasy vertebrates is derived primarily from six periods: (1) Late Permian, (2) Early Triassic, (3) Late Triassic, (4) Early-Middle Jurassic, (5) Late Cretaceous, and (6) Late Pleistocene and Holocene.

The faunas of the Permian and Triassic periods have been recovered from Karoo sediments (a type of sediment that resembles water-borne rock strata located in the Karoo in South Africa). These sediments are dominantly of terrestrial origin (as opposed to sediments that accumulate in oceans) and are comprised of formations called the Sakoa, Sakamena, and Isalo Formations (or Groups). They also form the basal (lowest) sequences in the Morondava, Mahajanga, and Diego sedimentary basins along the western margin (edge) of Madagascar. In addition to a typical Gondwanan flora, including *Glossopteris* and *Thinnfeldia,* vertebrate fossils from the Late Permian, recovered largely from the lower Sakamena formation, include the atherstoniid (primitive ray-finned) fish *Atherstonia;* the amphibian *Rhinesuchus;* the procolophonoid cotylosaur *Barasaurus* (a parareptile); the primitive lizard ancestors *Acerosodontosaurus, Thadeosaurus,* and *Hovasaurus;* a primitive gliding lizard *Coelurosauravus;* and some fragmentary material of therapsids (mammal-like reptiles), including a nearly complete skull of the dicynodont *Oudenodon.* Some of these taxa (groups; singular, taxon) provide evidence that Madagascar was still annexed to Africa during this period. *Hovasaurus,* for instance, is very closely related to the South African *Tangasaurus,* and *Atherstonia, Rhinesuchus,* and *Oudenodon* are also found in South Africa. B. Battail and colleagues (1987), however, suggested that, since the terrestrial reptiles of South Africa are dominated by therapsids and therefore very different from that of Madagascar (which is dominated by a variety of aquatic and terrestrial diapsids), a water barrier already may have existed between the two landmasses by the Late Permian (for an alternative opinion, see Mazin and King 1991).

The Early Triassic record of fossil vertebrates, derived primarily from the middle Sakamena formation, contains abundant lagoonal and marine fish. There are early sharks, many primitive ray-finned fishes, primitive lobe-finned fishes, and lungfishes. Also found are as many as four large groupings of dominantly marine temnospondyl amphibians, very distant relatives of frogs and toads (Hewison 1996). The emphasis upon primarily marine vertebrate fauna is consistent with evidence that a sea had intruded into the area, serving as an effective barrier between Africa and Madagascar. In addition to these taxa, the nonmarine Early Triassic has yielded the earliest known remains of an aquatic, froglike amphibian, *Triadobatrachus,* which had not yet acquired jumping adaptations. *Triadobatrachus* provides the only known morphological link (link based upon physical shape and structure) between Paleozoic amphibians and frogs.

The Late Triassic vertebrate fauna of Madagascar is derived from the Isalo Formation and shares several taxa with Morocco but not with South Africa. The Malagasy fauna is not very diverse; it includes lungfish, a group of temnospondyl amphibians, phytosaurs (large, crocodile-like reptiles), and rhynchosaurs (heavy, barrel-shaped, plant-eating reptiles) (Buffetaut 1983; Battail et al. 1987).

Jurassic vertebrates from Madagascar are very poorly known. The long-snouted, marine teleosaurid crocodyliform *Steneosaurus* was found in deposits from the Early and Middle Jurassic (Buffetaut et al. 1981). The massive (possibly brachiosaurid) sauropod dinosaur *Bothriospondylus* was found in deposits from the Middle Jurassic part of the Isalo formation; it is a poorly known and taxonomically ambiguous form also found in the Late Jurassic deposits of England and France (McIntosh 1990).

Although the first Late Cretaceous nonmarine vertebrates from Madagascar were described over a century ago and, in the interim, numerous other specimens have been recovered, most of our knowledge has resulted from recent collecting efforts in the Maevarano formation in the Mahajanga Basin (Krause et al. 1997). These collections have more than quadrupled the previously known species diversity of Malagasy vertebrates from the Late Cretaceous. In addition to adding to the diversity of bony fishes, turtles, crocodyliforms, lizards, snakes, and sauropod (brontosaur-type) and theropod (bipedal, carnivorous) dinosaurs, the recent finds establish the first pre-Late Pleistocene Malagasy records of frogs, birds, and mammals. The bird specimens are particularly interesting since they represent the first skeletal remains of Mesozoic avians of a vast area, including mainland Antarctica, Africa, the Indian subcontinent, and Australia (Forster et al. 1996). The finds include at least four taxa of primitive birds, one of which is the sister-taxon (group most closely related) to *Archaeopteryx* and bears a number of features consistent with the hypothesis that birds evolved from theropod dinosaurs.

Similarly, the Late Cretaceous record of mammals, although currently based on only five isolated teeth, is tremendously important since it comprises the only record of Late Cretaceous mammals from Gondwana outside of South America and the Indian subcontinent. Interestingly, gondwanatherian mammals are represented, the first known from outside of Argentina's Late Cretaceous and Paleocene. Dinosaur specimens, including skulls and partial skeletons of theropods and sauropods, have been discovered in some abundance and reflect affinities with the dinosaurian faunas from the Late Cretaceous of India and South America. The first plesiosaurs (large marine reptiles) from Madagascar recently were reported from Campanian deposits in the western part of the island (Bardet and Termier 1990).

The record of Cenozoic vertebrates from the pre-Late Pleistocene is limited to a few incidental occurrences, in most cases poorly dated, that do not add significantly to knowledge of the evolutionary and biogeographic history of the modern Malagasy fauna. The meager Cenozoic fossil record is largely owing to the virtual lack of terrestrial rocks from the pre-Late Pleistocene. The earliest well-dated records of vertebrates from this interval go back only to about 26,000 years ago. As the fauna from the Late Creta-

ceous becomes better known, however, it appears that it did not contain the ancestors of many modern vertebrate fauna (e.g., frogs, birds, mammals). Since Madagascar already was fully isolated in the Indian Ocean at that time, it would appear that stock for those latest groups arrived during the Cenozoic by rafting, swimming, or flying.

The Late Pleistocene and Holocene record has revealed a diversity of extinct terrestrial animals, including an array of lemurs, an aardvarklike mammal called *Plesiorycteropus* (which recently has been placed in its own order, Bibymalagasia), dwarf hippopotami, giant tortoises, giant crocodiles, and enormous, flightless birds known as elephantbirds. Many of these remains have been recovered from cave deposits and sinkholes.

Some remains are subfossils—specimens that have not completed the fossilization process. Subfossil lemurs are among the most interesting of Madagascar's extinct vertebrates, and considerable work has been conducted on them recently. Included are 16 that have been grouped into nine genera, which have been further grouped into five families: *Pachylemur* (Lemuridae); *Archaeolemur* and *Hadropithecus* (Archaeolemuridae); *Palaeopropithecus, Archaeoindris, Babakotia,* and *Mesopropithecus* (Palaeopropithecidae); *Megaladapis* (Megaladapidae); and *Daubentonia* (Daubentoniidae) (Godfrey et al. 1997). Each extinct species of lemur is larger than its closest living relative. *Archaeoindris* is the largest fossil lemur, estimated to have been 160 to 200 kilograms, approximately as heavy as an adult male gorilla. Like extant (present-day) lemurs, some extinct forms exhibit adaptations for leaping and living and moving through trees on four feet. In addition, extinct lemurs include forms with slothlike suspensory adaptations *(Babakotia, Mesopropithecus, Palaeopropithecus)*—the joints in shoulders and hips may have enabled the animals to hang upside down in trees. Other forms probably incorporated substantial terrestrial adaptations into their lifestyle (e.g., *Archaeolemur, Hadropithecus*), and still other forms were slow-climbing and koala-like (e.g., Megaladapis).

Elephantbirds (Aepyornithiformes) survived at least until the tenth century and included the largest known birds, fossil or Recent. These ponderous, flightless, grazing forms grew to an estimated 3 meters in height and 450 kilograms in weight. Elephantbird eggs were larger than those of any known bird (or dinosaur), measuring 33 centimeters long and holding up to 9 liters of fluid—equivalent to 7 ostrich eggs or 12,000 hummingbird eggs. *Aepyornis* eggs have the distinction of being the largest known single cell. There are no confirmed reports of elephantbirds from anywhere other than Madagascar, and most current researchers speculate that their ancestors were flying forms that arrived on the island in the Neogene.

Over-hunting by humans, who appear to have inhabited the island approximately 2,000 years ago, is most frequently blamed for the extinction of elephantbirds and about two dozen other species of the terrestrial vertebrates, but other scholars have invoked such causes as the introduction of competitors, predators, hypervirulent diseases, and burning of forests, or a combination of all of these factors (Burney and MacPhee 1988).

DAVID W. KRAUSE

Works Cited

Bardet, N., and G. Termier. 1990. Première description des restes de Plesiodaure provenant de Madagascar (gisement de Berere, Campanian). *Comptes Rendus de l'Académie des Sciences,* ser. 2, 310:855–60.

Battail, B., L. Beltan, and J.M. Dutuit. 1987. Africa and Madagascar during Permo-Triassic time: The evidence of the vertebrate faunas. *In* G.D. McKenzie (ed.), *Gondwana Six: Stratigraphy, Sedimentology, and Paleontology.* Geophysical Monograph 41. Washington, D.C.: American Geophysical Union.

Buffetaut, E. 1983. Isalorhynchus genovefae, n. g. n. sp. (Reptilia, Rhynchocephalia), un nouveau Rhynchosaure du Trias de Madagascar. *Neues Jahrbuch für Geologie und Paläontologie, Monatschefte* 1983 (8):465–80.

Buffetaut, E., G. Termier, and H. Termier. 1981. A teleosaurid (Crocodylia, Mesosuchia) from the Toarcian of Madagascar and its paleobiogeographical significance. *Paläontologische Zeitschrift* 55:313–19.

Burney, D.A., and R.D.E. MacPhee. 1988. Mysterious island: What killed Madagascar's large native animals? *Natural History* 97:46–55.

Coffin, M.F., and P.D. Rabinowitz. 1992. The Mesozoic East African and Madagascan conjugate continental margins. *In* J.S. Watkins, F. Zhiqiang, and K.J. McMillen (eds.), *Geology and Geophysics of Continental Margins.* American Association of Petroleum Geologists Memoir 53. Tulsa, Oklahoma: American Association of Petroleum Geologists.

Forster, C.A., L.M. Chiappe, D.W. Krause, and S.D. Sampson. 1996. The first Cretaceous bird from Madagascar. *Nature* 382:532–34.

Godfrey, L.R., W.L. Jungers, K.E. Reed, E.L. Simons, and P.S. Chatrath. 1997. Subfossil lemurs: Inferences about past and present primate communities in Madagascar. *In* S.M. Goodman and B.D. Patterson (eds.), *Natural Change and Human Impact in Madagascar.* Washington, D.C. and London: Smithsonian Institute Press.

Hewison, R.H. 1996. The skull of Deltacephalus whitei, a lydekkerinid temnospondyl amphibian from the Lower Triassic of Madagascar. *Palaeontology* 39:305–21.

Krause, D.W., J.H. Hartman, and N.A. Wells. 1997. Late Cretaceous vertebrates from Madagascar: Implications for biotic change in deep time. *In* S.M. Goodman and B.D. Patterson (eds.), *Natural Change and Human Impact in Madagascar.* Washington, D.C. and London: Smithsonian Institution Press.

Mazin, J.M., and G.M. King. 1991. The first dicynodont from the Late Permian of Malagasy. *Palaeontology* 34:837–42.

McIntosh, J.S. 1990. Sauropoda. *In* D.B. Weishampel, P. Dodson, and H. Osmólska (eds.), *The Dinosauria.* Berkeley: University of California Press.

Further Reading

Battistini, R., and G. Richard-Vindard (eds.). 1972. *Biogeography and Ecology of Madagascar.* Hague: Junk.

Burney, D.A. 1993. Recent animal extinctions: Recipes for disaster. *American Scientist* 81:530–41.

Jolly, A., P. Oberlé, and R. Albignac (eds.). 1984. *Madagascar.* New York: Pergamon.

Lourenco, W. (ed.). 1996. *Biogeography of Madagascar.* Paris: Orstrom.

MacPhee, R.D.E. 1994. *Morphology, Adaptations, and Relationships of Plesiorycteropus, and a Diagnosis of a New Order of Eutherian Mammals.* Bulletin of the American Museum of Natural History, 220. New York: American Museum of Natural History.

Preston-Mafham, K. 1991. *Madagascar: A Natural History.* New York: Facts on File.

Sampson, S.D., D.W. Krause, and C.A. Forster. 1997. Madagascar's buried treasure. *Natural History* 106:24–27.

Simons, E.L., D.A. Burney, P.S. Chatrath, L.R. Godfrey, W.L. Jungers, and B. Rakotosamimanana. 1995. AMS 14C dates for extinct lemurs from caves in the Ankarana Massif, northern Madagascar. *Quaternary Research* 43:249–54.

MAMMALS, MESOZOIC AND NON-THERIAN

The fossil history of mammals is extremely well known for the Cenozoic era (65 million years to present), but this covers only about one-third of the total span of time during which mammals were in existence. The first two-thirds of mammalian history extends well back into the Mesozoic, at least into the Late Triassic, some 215 to 225 million years ago. Knowledge of Mesozoic mammals has long been extremely sketchy, being based almost exclusively on jaws and teeth, so little consensus has existed on the interrelationships of the major groups of mammals, including the living members. An enormous increase in understanding of early mammalian structure and phylogeny (evolutionary history) has occurred since about 1950, and especially since 1990, due to accelerating discoveries of skulls and postcranial skeletons.

Traditionally, the incomplete fossils of mammal-like forms from the Mesozoic were defined as members of the Mammalia on the basis of certain structural features. They were considered to be mammals if they possessed a jaw joint formed by a rounded condyle on the back of the dentary (the major, tooth-bearing element of the lower jaw) that fitted into a glenoid depression (shallow socket) on the squamosal. On the basis of this definition, extremely mammal-like cynodonts (the most mammal-like of the therapsids) like the tritheledontids and tritylodontids were excluded from the Mammalia because they possess only the "reptilian" articular-quadrate jaw joint. In recent years, however, the practice of defining taxa (groups; singular, taxon) on the basis of characters has given way to defining them on the basis of common ancestry relationships (Rowe and Gauthier 1992). Thus, Mammalia is now defined as the common ancestor of extant (present-day) mammals plus all extinct species descended from that common ancestor (Rowe 1988). In other words, Mammalia is the least inclusive clade of synapsids that includes the living monotremes (platypus and echidnas) and therians (marsupials and placentals). In our current understanding of mammalian phylogeny, Mammalia includes the following groups: Monotremata, Triconodonta,

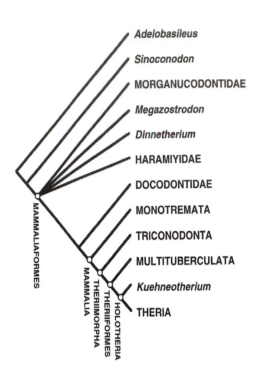

Figure 1. Cladogram of the major groups of mammaliaform and their two sequential outgroups. Detailed interrelationships of the early mammaliaforms are uncertain.

Multituberculata, and Holotheria (Figure 1). The last-named group comprises the Theria and those Mesozoic forms more closely related to therians than to the other taxa mentioned above.

Some well-known Mesozoic taxa traditionally classified as mammals on morphological grounds are now technically excluded from the Mammalia because they fall outside the clade stemming from the common ancestor of monotremes and therians. These include *Adelobasileus, Sinoconodon,* Morganucodontidae, *Dinnetherium, Megazostrodon,* Haramiyidae, and Docodontidae (Figure 1). These taxa, except for *Adelobasileus* and *Sinoconodon,* are included with Mammalia in the more inclusive taxon Mammaliaformes, which is defined as the common ancestor of *Morganucodon* and Mammalia and all of its descendants (Rowe 1988). *Sinoconodon* and the more primitive *Adelobasileus* appear to be sequential outgroups to Mammaliaformes.

This article deals with all of the above-mentioned taxa of Mesozoic age, as well as the post-Mesozoic members of the Monotremata and Multituberculata. More detailed treatment of marsupials and placentals occurs in separate articles.

History of Discovery of Mesozoic Mammals

The first-discovered Mesozoic mammals, found in about 1812, were two lower jaws of Middle Jurassic age from the Stonesfield Slate near Oxford, England (Desmond 1984). Though initially placed in the opossum genus *Didelphis,* one was eventually named *Amphitherium* (Blainville 1838), a primitive holothere,

and the other *Phascolotherium* (Owen 1838), an amphilestid triconodont. Beginning in the 1850s, a very large assemblage of early mammals was collected from the Late Jurassic Purbeck Beds of Dorsetshire, with smaller collections made from Early Cretaceous Wealden beds. These early mammals were reviewed by Sir Richard Owen (1871).

"The most diverse Mesozoic mammal assemblage yet known from the entire world" (Clemens et al. 1979) was discovered in 1877 at Como Bluff, southeastern Wyoming, in the Late Jurassic Morrison Formation. At least 23 genera and 40 species were named from this locality, principally by O.C. Marsh, although all are based on jaws and teeth (Simpson 1929). The first Late Cretaceous mammals were collected in the 1880s from the American West, mainly by John Bell Hatcher, who used a flour sifter to sort out teeth and small bones from the pebbles on anthills (Clemens et al. 1979).

The extensive studies of George Gaylord Simpson in the 1920s, published in a large number of short reports and culminating in two monographs on the European and American Mesozoic mammals respectively (Simpson 1928, 1929), were the final word on the subject for at least the next quarter century. Revitalization of the study of Mesozoic mammals came largely from discoveries by Walter Georg Kühne (1949, 1950, 1958; see also Kermack and Mussett 1958, 1959; Kermack et al. 1968) of very early mammaliaforms in fissure fills of South Wales and southwestern England of Late Triassic and Early Jurassic age. Equally important were near-contemporaneous discoveries of similar basal forms in Early Jurassic redbeds of southwestern China (Patterson and Olson 1961; Rigney 1963; Kermack et al. 1973, 1981). At the same time, discoveries of Early Cretaceous mammals from Texas were described by B. Patterson (1951, 1956), which contributed important information to our understanding of tooth cusp homologies in early holotherians. Kühne subsequently discovered important faunas of Late Jurassic and Early Cretaceous mammals in Portugal and Spain (Kühne 1961; Kühne and Crusafont-Pairó 1968).

Late Triassic and Early Jurassic mammals have since been discovered in western Europe, southern Africa, India, Mexico, and the American Southwest (Fraser and Sues 1994). Although Middle Jurassic mammals remain rare (Waldman and Savage 1972; Freeman 1979; Kermack et al. 1987), Late Jurassic mammals continue to be discovered in England and the American West, and earlier finds from Guimarota in Portugal continue to be described (Krusat 1980; Lillegraven and Krusat 1991; Krebs 1991). Especially important discoveries of skulls and postcranial skeletons have been made in the Early Cretaceous of the American West (Jenkins and Schaff 1988), Argentina (Bonaparte and Rougier 1987; Hopson and Rougier 1993; Rougier 1993), and China (Hu et al. 1997). Late Cretaceous mammalian faunas are now very well understood on the basis of thousands of teeth and jaws collected by screen-washing large quantities of fossil-bearing sediment. Well-preserved skeletons of multituberculates and early marsupials and placentals are being collected and described from Mongolia (Kielan-Jaworowska and Gambaryan 1994; Sereno and McKenna 1995; Rougier et al. 1996) and northern China (Miao 1988; Meng and Wyss 1995).

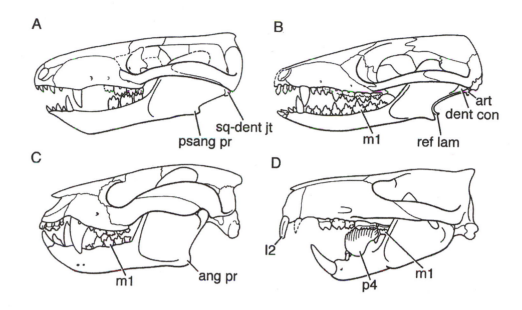

Figure 2. Skulls of early mammals: *A*, the Early Jurassic *Sinoconodon*; *B*, the Early Jurassic *Morganucodon*; *C*, the Early Cretaceous near-tribosphenidan holothere *Vincelestes*; *D*, the Paleocene multituberculate *Ptilodus*. Skulls not to scale. Abbreviations: *ang pr*, angular process; *art*, articular; *dent con*, dentary condyle; *I2*, second upper incisor; *m1*, first lower molar; *p4*, fourth lower premolar; *psang pr*, pseudangular process; *ref lam*, reflected lamina of the angular; *sq-dent jt*, squamosal-dentary jaw joint. After: A, Crompton and Sun (1985) and Crompton and Luo (1993); B, Kermack et al. (1981); C, Hopson and Rougier (1993); D, Krause (1982).

Adelobasileus, *Sinoconodon*, and Mammaliaformes

The animals described here are more mammal-like than cynodonts such as tritheledontids and tritylodontids in that they all possess a principal jaw joint formed by the dentary and squamosal. They also have cheek teeth with divided roots, an elongate cochlea of the inner ear housed in a bulbous promontorium, a sheet of membrane bone (the anterior lamina) forming about half the side wall of the braincase, and four rather than three incisors on each side of the lower jaw. Primitively, they tend to be much smaller than non-mammalian cynodonts. *Sinoconodon* and non-mammalian mammaliaforms all retain the full complement of reptilian postdentary bones in the lower jaw, albeit very reduced in size, and a functional articular-quadrate jaw joint lying medial to the dentary-squamosal joint. Also, a prominent, often slightly downturned, pseudangular process (Patterson 1956; Jenkins et al. 1983) lies anteroventral to (in front of and below) the articular condyle (Figure 2A). The pseudangular process is undoubtedly homologous with that of late cynodonts, but it is unlikely to be homologous with the true angular process of therians and most non-tribosphenic holotheres (Figure 2C) because it is absent in several more primitive outgroups—symmetrodont holotheres, multituberculates (Figure 2D), and triconodonts.

The oldest known fossil that appears to be closer to mammals than to tritheledontids or tritylodontids is *Adelobasileus cromptoni* from the early part of the Late Triassic of Texas (Lucas and Luo 1993). *Adelobasileus* is known at present only from an isolated braincase that shares numerous features with *Sinoconodon* and mammaliaforms. It is about 225 million years old, at least 10 million years older than any known mammaliaform.

Somewhat less primitive and much younger than *Adelobasileus* is *Sinoconodon* (Figure 2A) from the Early Jurassic (about 200 million years ago) of China (Patterson and Olson 1961; Crompton and Sun 1985; Crompton and Luo 1993). It is more primitive than contemporary mammaliaforms and resembles earlier cynodonts in lacking precise occlusion (meshing) between the molariform cheek teeth and having more than a single replacement of the incisors and canines.

Non-Mammalian Mammaliaforms

Mammaliaforms are characterized by having precise occlusion, with a consistent positional relationship between upper and lower molar cusps. In order to maintain the molars in proper alignment, adjacent teeth of early mammaliaforms have a tongue-and-groove interlocking arrangement formed by the posterior cusp of one tooth fitting into a notch between two cusps on the anterior (forward) face of the succeeding tooth (Figure 3A, 3B). Although the evidence is not clearcut (Crompton and Luo 1993), the molars were probably not replaced, and only a single replacement occurred in the more anterior teeth, as in living mammals. Limited tooth replacement is correlated with the acquisition of precise occlusion.

The molar cusps of early mammaliaforms (Figure 3) are conventionally designated by letters, upper case for the upper cusps and lower case for the lower (Crompton and Jenkins 1968). The main upper and lower cusps, homologous with the single reptilian cusp, are designated A and a, respectively. The anterior and

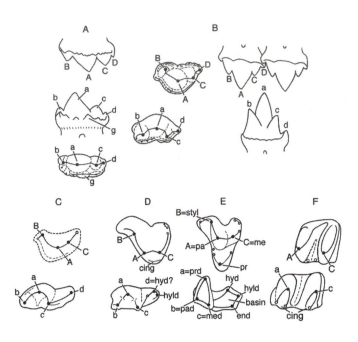

Figure 3. Evolution of the mammalian dentition: A, upper and lower molars of *Morganucodon* in lingual view and (below) lower molar in crown view, showing position of lower cusp a below the notch between upper cusps B and A; B, upper and lower molars of *Kuehneotherium* in crown view (left) and lingual view (right), showing lower cusp a below the notch between adjacent upper molars; C–F, upper and lower molars in crown view of: C, *Amphitherium*, D, *Peramus*, E, *Pappotherium*, and F, the monotreme *Obdurodon*. The upper molar of *Amphitherium* is hypothetical. Homologous cusps are indicated by upper case letters in the upper teeth, lower case letters in the lower teeth. The identity of cusp d as hypoconid or hypoconulid is uncertain. Abbreviations: *basin*, talonid basin; *cing*, cingulum; *end*, entoconid; *hyd*, hypoconid; *hld*, hypoconulid; *me*, metacone; *med*, metaconid; *pa*, paracone; *pad*, paraconid; *pr*, protocone; *prd*, protoconid; *styl*, stylocone. After: A, B, Crompton and Jenkins (1968) and Hopson and Crompton (1969); C–E, Crompton (1971); F, modified from Archer et al. (1993).

posterior accessory cusps are B/b and C/c, respectively. A small, consistently present, cingulum-derived posterior cusp is D/d. (A cingulum is a marginal ridge that partly or completely encircles the base of the crown.) Primitively, mammaliaforms possess both an external (labial or buccal) and internal (lingual) cingulum in the upper molars and an internal cingulum in the lowers (Figure 4A, 4B). The cingula provide the raw material in later mammaliaforms for new cusps that become important occlusal elements of the crown. An apparently primitive feature of the mammaliaform lower molar is an enlarged cingulum cusp, designated cusp g, lying internal to the notch between cusps a and c (Figure 3A).

Morganucodontids, Dinnetherium, *and* Megazostrodon

The interrelationships of the Late Triassic and Jurassic non-mammalian mammaliaforms are not well understood at present.

Morganucodon (Figure 2B) is by far the best described basal mammaliaform, being known from many complete skulls from the Lufeng beds of China and by thousands of beautifully preserved skeletal parts and teeth from fissure-fillings in Wales (Kermack et al. 1973, 1981; Jenkins and Parrington 1976; Crompton and Luo 1993). Other morganucodontids are known from England, western Europe, the southwestern United States, southern Africa, and Greenland. The family is characterized both by having the main lower molar cusp (a) occluding with the upper molar between cusps B and A, and by possession of a large g cusp (Figure 3A).

Dinnetherium from the Kayenta Formation (Early Jurassic) of Arizona (Jenkins et al. 1983) resembles morganucodontids in molar occlusal relations but differs in lacking cusp g and in the shape of its lower jaw. Whereas *Morganucodon* has a prominent pseudangular process, this structure is very reduced in *Dinnetherium*; furthermore, behind the process the lower border of the dentary is turned outward as a prominent lateral ridge that extends back to the condyle. This feature resembles the lateral ridge in triconodonts, multituberculates, and symmetrodonts, all of which lack both the pseudangular and true angular process.

Megazostrodon from the Early Jurassic of southern Africa is also very much like *Morganucodon*, including possession of a large cusp g, but here lower cusp a occludes in the notch between successive molars in the upper jaw rather than between B and A. This occlusal pattern is also seen in the basal holothere *Kuehneotherium*, and is suggested to occur in docodontids (Butler 1988). *Megazostrodon* may have a special relationship with docodonts, but clearly not with holotheres (Figure 1).

Haramiyidae

Until recently, haramiyids were known only from hundreds of isolated teeth with divided roots of Late Triassic and Early Jurassic age from Europe; it was not known with certainty that they were mammals or which teeth were premolars and molars or uppers and lowers. Functional studies (Sigogneau-Russell 1989; Butler and MacIntyre 1994) suggested that the upper molars are those known as *Haramiya* and the lowers those known as *Thomasia*. These studies also demonstrated that the lower molars moved backward as well as upward during occlusion, indicating a posterior movement of the lower jaw. The recent discovery in the Late Triassic of East Greenland of a new haramiyid with associated upper and lower jaws containing teeth (Jenkins et al. 1997) demonstrates that *Haramiya* indeed pertains to upper molars and *Thomasia* to lowers, with *Thomasia* being the older and therefore valid name (McKenna and Bell 1997).

The Greenland haramiyid, *Haramiyavia*, is the first to be known from cranial and postcranial remains. The lower jaw is very long and shallow and retains a large groove on the internal rear surface of the dentary for support of postdentary bones. It has four upper and lower incisors, the first three of which are forwardly inclined and the fourth greatly reduced and separated from the others by a diastema (gap). The first two lower incisors are large, spatulate, and strongly procumbent (forward-projecting). The small lower canine is followed by four premolars that increase in size toward the back. Both upper and lower molars consist of two longitudinal (fore-aft) rows of cusps enclosing an elongate basin between them. The internal row of upper cusps occluded within the central basin of the lower. *Haramiyavia* is less modified from the ancestral morganucodont than *Thomasia* in that it retains several enlarged external cingulum cusps on the upper molars, and, unlike *Thomasia*, it did not move the lower molars backwards across the uppers.

Haramiyids are often suggested as ancestors of the highly specialized, rodentlike multituberculates, but the pattern of molar occlusion differs between them and must have originated independently in the two groups. Haramiyids appear to represent an early mammaliaform experiment in herbivory that did not survive the Early Jurassic.

Docodontidae

Docodontids are a Middle and Late Jurassic group that retained postdentary bones in the lower jaw at a time when true mammals had freed these bones from the jaw to become the definitive mammalian middle ear ossicles. The molars of docodonts appear to be derived from those of morganucodonts by great enlargement of the internal cingula (Crompton and Jenkins 1968). In the uppers, a pair of large lingual cusps, called X and Y, occludes in a lower lingual basin bounded internally by an enlarged cusp g and a more anterior cingulum cusp h. The upper cusp B and the lower cusp c are lost.

The most primitive docodont, *Haldanodon* of the Upper Jurassic of Portugal (Krusat 1980; Lillegraven and Krusat 1991), is known from skulls and postcranial material. The skull is broad and heavily built. It has six upper incisors, two of which are in the maxilla (the main tooth-bearing element of the upper jaw), a robust two-rooted canine, three premolars, and five molars. The shoulder girdle and robust limb bones resemble those of monotremes.

More derived docodonts are known from the Middle Jurassic: *Borealestes* from Scotland (Waldman and Savage 1972) and *Simpsonodon* from England (Kermack et al. 1987). These genera and *Tegotherium* from the Late Jurassic of Mongolia (Tatarinov 1994) form a related group (Hopson 1995), characterized by lower molars with a greatly enlarged anterointernal basin bounded internally by a large h cusp. Quite distinct is *Docodon*, from the Late Jurassic of North America, in which an enlarged posterior (rear) basin is bounded internally by two large cusps, including cusp g. *Docodon* has a long lower jaw with seven or eight molars. Docodont molars are functionally convergent on advanced holotheres and were formerly considered to be close to dryolestoids; however, they are the latest surviving nonmammalian mammaliaforms.

Mammalia

Monotremes

The Monotremata is one of the two groups of living mammals, the other being the Theria. It consists of the duckbilled platypus (*Ornithorhynchus*, Family Ornithorhynchidae) and two genera of

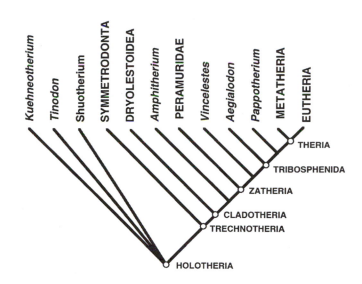

Figure 4. Cladogram of the major groups of Holotheria. Detailed interrelationships among *Kuehneotherium*, *Tinodon*, and *Shuotherium* are uncertain. Metatheria includes Marsupialia, and Eutheria includes Placentalia.

echidnas or spiny anteaters (*Tachyglossus* and *Zaglossus*, Family Tachyglossidae), of the Australian region. Monotremes retain many primitive amniote features in the reproductive system and skeleton that have been lost in marsupials and placentals (amniotes are tetrapods that lay shelled eggs, or whose ancestors did). Until recently, little basis for meaningful comparison between monotremes and other primitive mammals has existed because most Mesozoic mammals are known only from jaws and teeth, whereas echidnas are toothless and the platypus has vestigial teeth only in the juvenile. However, in recent years, as the skulls and postcranial skeletons of many groups of Mesozoic mammals have become increasingly known, it has become clear that monotremes are more derived than docodonts and the other mammaliaform taxa described above but more primitive than triconodonts, multituberculates, and holotherians.

The skull of monotremes is unusual, having a toothless bill formed by the premaxilla (upper jaw element at the tip of the snout) and a greatly enlarged septomaxilla (a bone that helps form the walls and floor of the nasal cavity, anteriorly); it is broad and ducklike in the aquatic platypus and narrow and pointed in the termite- or worm-eating echidnas. The vestigial cheek teeth of the young platypus are replaced in the adult by keratinous (horny) crushing plates. The zygomatic (cheek) arch is formed by a long process of the maxilla that meets the zygomatic process of the squamosal (a bone located at the rear corner of the skull); the jugal ("cheekbone") is reduced to a small process (prong) behind the orbit in the platypus and is absent in echidnas. In the side wall of the braincase, the anterior lamina is very large and the alisphenoid is reduced to a tiny vestige. In the lower jaw, the coronoid process (a projection to which jaw-closing muscles attach) is vestigial, and the angular, or pseudangular, process is reduced or absent.

Until 1975 monotremes lacked a pre-Pleistocene fossil record. However, in that year two functional teeth of a Middle Miocene platypus were described and named *Obdurodon insignis* (Woodburne and Tedford 1975). These teeth clarified the morphology of the ornithorhynchid molar and provided the basis for identification of the first Mesozoic mammal found in Australia, a jaw fragment containing three molars from the Early Cretaceous (Albian). The molars of this Mesozoic monotreme, called *Steropodon galmani* (Archer et al. 1985), show a pattern of ridges and cusps in the shape of a W, with the base of the W facing externally. They bear a close resemblance to the molars of *Obdurodon* (Figure 3F), but also show similarities to those of relatively primitive holotheres. This led Z. Kielan-Jaworowska and colleagues (1987) to argue for the derivation of monotremes from a nontribosphenic holothere similar to the Late Jurassic *Peramus* (Figure 3D). However, recent discoveries of cranial and postcranial remains of Mesozoic mammals have rendered this position untenable (Archer et al. 1992; Hopson 1994; Sereno and McKenna 1995; Rougier et al. 1996).

A recently described skull of the Miocene *Obdurodon* (Archer et al. 1992, 1993) is similar to that of *Ornithorhynchus* but is at least one-third longer, with a proportionally longer and broader bill. It has a fully functional cheek dentition, with two simple upper and lower premolars and two complex upper and lower molars, each with four to six roots, plus a small, single-rooted, third lower molar. The molar crowns are W-shaped, with the base of the W facing inward in the uppers and outward in the lowers, so that the opposing V's interlock (Figure 3F). The monotreme molar pattern most likely evolved from that of morganucodontids (Hopson and Crompton 1969) by the loss of the B/b cusps and gradual migration of the A/a and C/c cusps, lingually in the uppers and labially in the lowers, into the intercusp embrasures; eventually these embrasures became very deep and the crests joining the cusps formed acute-angled V's similar to those of advanced holotheres.

Among the most significant discoveries of fossil monotremes are a series of isolated teeth resembling those of *Obdurodon* from the Early Paleocene of Argentina. Appropriately named *Monotrematum sudamericum* (Pascual et al. 1992), this is the only monotreme known from outside the Australian region. It supports the notion of an Early Cenozoic land connection between South America and Australia via a route through Antarctica. Although the known teeth of *Monotrematum* and *Steropodon* resemble those of the undoubted platypus *Obdurodon*, there is no certainty that the former two taxa are also ornithorhynchids. This is because we have no idea when the echidnas branched from the basal monotreme stem. Tachyglossid fossils differing little from the living taxa, and indistinguishable from them at the generic level (McKenna and Bell 1997), are known only back to the Pliocene or possibly to the Late Miocene (Griffiths et al. 1991). Echidnas are considered to be more modified from the common ancestor of living monotremes than are ornithorhynchids, so it is probable that this common ancestor more closely resembled a platypus, at least dentally. Inasmuch as echidnas lack teeth, useful comparisons with the pre-Oligocene fossil monotremes are impossible; therefore, *Steropodon* and *Monotrematum* may predate the separation of echidnas from the ancestral monotreme stock.

Triconodonta

The remaining groups of mammals, Triconodonta, Multiutuberculata, and Holotheria, are grouped as Theriimorpha. They are clearly more derived than monotremes in postcranial features, particularly in the shoulder girdle, which has a supraspinous fossa (depression) on the scapula (major element of shoulder girdle), a greatly reduced coracoid, and lacks a procoracoid and interclavicle (the last three elements also belong to the shoulder girdle).

Triconodonts are a difficult group to characterize because their shared dental features are largely primitive. All have the main cusps aligned in a longitudinal row, but this feature also characterizes carnivorous cynodonts and basal mammaliaforms. Triconodonts are more derived than morganucodonts in having reduced molar cingula and in tending to make the molars symmetrical, with cusps b and c of near equal size. In addition, they lack a pseudangular process, the posteroventral border of the dentary curving smoothly up into the condyle. They also lack the internal trough that in primitive mammaliaforms held the postdentary bones; therefore, their ear ossicles were freed from the lower jaw. The postcranial skeleton, insofar as it is known in *Gobiconodon* and an undescribed triconodontid, has a therian-type shoulder girdle and other features more derived than those of monotremes (Jenkins and Crompton 1979; Jenkins and Schaff 1988). The ear region of triconodontids shows features that ally them with multituberculates and therians (Rougier et al. 1996).

Of the three well-known families of triconodonts, the Amphilestidae, from the Middle Jurassic Stonesfield Slate of England and the Late Jurassic Morrison Formation of North America, are the oldest. They are primitive in having four lower incisors, and cusp a higher than b and c. Lower cusp a appears to occlude between adjacent upper molars, as in *Megazostrodon*, but unlike *Morganucodon*.

Possibly closely related to the amphilestids are the Gobiconodontidae from the Early Cretaceous of Mongolia and North America. *Gobiconodon* is known from jaws and much of the postcranial skeleton (Jenkins and Schaff 1988). The North American species is very large for a Mesozoic mammal, being about the size of an American opossum *(Didelphis virginianus)*, although more robustly built. Its dentition is characterized by having a single caninelike lower incisor and two upper incisors, the second of which is also enlarged. The canines and premolars are small and simple. The five molars have large A/a cusps and symmetrically arranged, smaller B/b and C/c cusps similar to those of amphilestids. Also similar is the occlusion of cusp a between adjacent upper teeth. *Gobiconodon* is unusual among mammals in showing replacement of presumed molars, a therapsid-like condition.

The most diverse and long-lived family of triconodonts is the Triconodontidae, first known from the Late Jurassic Purbeck Beds of England and Morrison Formation of the United States and surviving into the Late Cretaceous of Canada. They are characterized by having very bladelike molars with the three main cusps about equal in height. As in *Morganucodon*, but unlike amphilestids and gobiconodontids, cusp a occludes between cusps B and A. Complete skulls and a partial postcranial skeleton of a triconodontid are known from the Early Cretaceous of Montana, but these have yet to be fully described (Crompton and Jenkins 1979; Jenkins and Crompton 1979; Crompton and Sun 1985; Crompton and Luo 1993). Jurassic triconodontids have two lower incisors, a robust canine, three or four premolars, and three or four molars. The undescribed Early Cretaceous triconodontid has one lower and two upper incisors and five molars. *Alticonodon,* the last known triconodontid, from the Late Cretaceous of Alberta, Canada, is remarkable for having very high-crowned molars (Fox 1969).

Multituberculates

Multituberculates were superficially rodentlike herbivorous mammals in which the dentition consists of enlarged grasping or cutting incisors separated by a diastema from the premolars. The premolars are specialized for holding (uppers) and cutting (lowers); the molars are specialized for grinding (Figure 2D). The earliest multituberculates occur in the middle part of the Late Jurassic (Kimmeridgian), and the group survived into the Late Eocene. Their decline in the Early Cenozoic appears to have been due to competitive exclusion by rodents (Krause 1986).

The earliest multituberculates have three upper incisors, the second of which is enlarged, and a single large lower incisor. In later taxa, the first upper incisor is reduced and eventually lost. In a few early taxa a multicusped upper canine is present, followed by up to five multicusped upper premolars. These teeth appear to have held and stabilized the food (with the aid of the tongue) so that it could be cut by the bladelike lower premolars. Primitively, a serrated cutting edge was spread over four lower premolars, but in derived (specialized) taxa of the Late Cretaceous the fourth premolar alone forms an enlarged cutting blade bearing 15 or more serrations; the third premolar, when present, forms a small single-rooted peg lying against the anterior root of the blade. The molars consist primitively of two longitudinal rows of cusps separated by a midline valley. The first molars occlude in expected fashion, with the outer row of upper cusps lying lateral to the outer row of lower cusps; this is just like the earlier haramiyids. The second upper molar is offset medially from the first so that its outer row lies directly behind the inner row of the first molar. Because the lower molar is not comparably offset, occlusion differs from that in the first molars in that the outer row of the upper occludes in the central groove of the lower. In more derived taxa, the upper molars add a third row of cusps, lingually in the first molar and labially in the second. Also, the cusps become more crescentic in shape, and the first molars tend to become much longer than the second.

The tooth row and secondary palate tend to be very long, while the skull base is short. In the zygomatic arch, the maxilla has a long posterior process that contacts the squamosal; the jugal, long thought to be absent, is a thin splint lying on the inner surface of the arch. The side wall of the braincase contains a large anterior lamina, a membrane bone fused to the petrosal (the bone that houses the inner ear), and the alisphenoid is usually greatly reduced. The articular glenoid on the squamosal is an elongated oval, which accommodates the longitudinal movement of the articular condyle of the lower jaw as it moves backward, drawing the lower molar cusps across those of the upper molars (Krause 1982).

The phylogenetic position of multituberculates has long been problematic, because, as with monotremes, their skulls and teeth are so modified from those of other mammals. The reduced jugal, increased size of the anterior lamina relative to the alisphenoid, and horizontally oriented ear ossicles have suggested a special relationship to monotremes (Kielan-Jaworowska 1971; Meng and Wyss 1995), but present evidence indicates that these resemblances are convergent. Derived postcranial similarities, especially in the shoulder girdle (Sereno and McKenna 1995), suggest that the multituberculates are the sister group of the Holotheria, forming the taxon Theriiformes.

The oldest multituberculates are the Paulchoffatiidae (Hahn 1969), a probable paraphyletic group with nearly subequal upper incisors 2 and 3 and only slightly smaller incisor 1, a probable upper canine, and up to five upper premolars. (A paraphyletic group is a grade, as opposed to a clade, or monophyletic group. While a paraphyletic group has a common ancestor, it fails to embrace its more specialized descendants.) The molar cusps are bulbous, lacking the crescentic shape of later taxa, which suggests little or no posterior movement of the lower molars over the uppers. More derived are the later Jurassic and earliest Cretaceous Plagiaulacidae (also paraphyletic), in which the molar cusps take on a more crescentic shape and wear facets indicate some horizontal movement of the lower molars.

Advanced multituberculates of primarily Late Cretaceous and Early Cenozoic age, often grouped as Cimolodonta, have lost the first upper incisor, reduced the number of lower premolars to two, with shear confined to the last premolar, and have increased the length of the first molar with respect to the second. This group includes the sister taxa Ptilodontoidea and Taeniolabidoidea, primarily North American and European groups, with the latter also occurring in the Early Cenozoic of Asia. Ptilodontoids show a tendency to enlarge the lower shearing blade (Figure 2D), whereas it tends to be reduced in taeniolabidoids. The latter have restricted the enamel covering on the incisors to the anterior face of the tooth, as in rodents.

Late Cretaceous multituberculates from Asia, originally considered to be taeniolabidoids (Kielan-Jaworowska 1971), form an endemic group, Djadochtatheria (Kielan-Jaworowska and Hurum 1997), distinct from the Cimolodonta (Rougier et al. 1997). They are characterized by having the third upper incisor lying well in from the margin of the palate, and, on the top of the skull, large frontals and short parietals separated by a U-shaped suture.

The fossil record of multituberculates was until recently entirely Laurasian (Laurasia was the northern supercontinent of the Mezoic; Gondwana, the southern). However, isolated teeth identified as those of multituberculates have been described from the Early Cretaceous of Morocco (Sigogneau-Russell 1991) and the Late Cretaceous and Paleocene of Argentina (Krause et al. 1992). The latter appear to form an endemic Gondwanan group, most of which are characterized by having extremely high-crowned molars bearing transverse ridges. They are placed in a new subgroup, Gondwanatheria (Krause and Bonaparte 1993). Similar teeth have recently been discovered in the Late Cretaceous of India and Madagascar (Krause et al. 1997).

Holotheria

Holotheria (Figure 4) is that group of mammals that includes as its most derived members the Metatheria (including marsupials) and Eutheria (including placentals). It is defined as the least inclusive clade that includes Theria and *Kuehneotherium* (Wible et al. 1995).

Holotheres are characterized by the possession of a specialized occlusal pattern, first seen in the Late Triassic/Early Jurassic *Kuehneotherium* (Figure 3B), in which the three main molar cusps and the shearing crests connecting them form a V, the apex of which points lingually in the upper molars and labially in the lowers. Thus the lower molars fit into the V-shaped embrasures between successive upper molars, the tooth row forming a zigzag cutting pattern much like that of pinking shears. This group was traditionally called the Theria, but this term is now reserved for the clade containing the common ancestor of marsupials and placentals and all of its descendants (Rowe 1988).

The fossil record of holotheres prior to the Late Cretaceous consisted until recently almost entirely of teeth and jaws, so that most of the phylogeny of the group has been based on molar crown morphology (Prothero 1981). Nearly complete skeletons are now known for the Late Jurassic dryolestoid *Henkelotherium* (Krebs 1991), and the Late Cretaceous symmetrodont *Zhangheotherium* (Hu et al. 1997) and near-tribosphenidan *Vincelestes* (Figure 2C; Rougier 1993); these discoveries of very modern skeletons in early holotheres demonstrate the great antiquity of therian postcranial specializations.

The oldest holothere, *Kuehneotherium,* is known only from isolated teeth and several jaw fragments that lack a pseudangular process but possess an internal trough for postdentary jaw bones (a feature also present in some other early holotheres). The latter feature implies that the jaw elements homologous with ear ossicles were not yet freed from the mandible in primitive holotheres. It also implies that the unknown early ancestors of monotremes, triconodonts, and multituberculates also retained the primitive condition of the postdentary jaw bones; thus, the middle ear ossicles would have become freed from the lower jaw at least four times in mammals.

Shuotherium from the Late Jurassic of China possesses a postdentary trough, but its lower molars are specialized beyond those of *Kuehneotherium* in having a large anterior basin, or pseudotalonid, into which a large internal upper cusp, the pseudoprotocone, occluded; these features are analogous to the posterior talonid and protocone of tribosphenidans (Chow and Rich 1982). The Late Jurassic *Tinodon* possesses molars very similar to those of *Kuehneotherium,* but it lacks a postdentary trough on the mandible. Also, from a *Kuehneotherium*-like dentition evolved, with relatively little change, the acute-angled molars of the Late Jurassic to Late Cretaceous symmetrodonts (Cassiliano and Clemens, 1979). The latter are grouped with more derived holotheres such as the Trechnotheria.

The Cladotheria contains, in addition to the derived clade Tribosphenida, the more primitive Jurassic to Cretaceous Dryolestoidea, *Amphitherium*, and Peramuridae, all formerly grouped in a paraphyletic "Eupantotheria." Peramurids show a number of resemblances to tribosphenidans, with which they are currently grouped as Zatheria.

Successive stages in the evolution of the tribosphenic molar pattern characteristic of living therians have been worked out in detail, beginning from the primitive condition seen in *Kuehneotherium* (Figure 3B; Crompton 1971). In *Amphitherium* of the Middle Jurassic (Figure 3C), the lower molar develops an enlarged heel, or talonid, bearing cusp d, which overlaps the succeeding tooth; it thus forms an embrasure with the three main cusps, called the trigonid, into which occluded the main upper cusp (A). In *Peramus* of the Late Jurassic (Figure 3D), the posterior upper cusp (C) lies more internally on the crown, on a level with cusp A; between them is a slight embayment into which occluded the main cusp of the lower molar heel, the probable homolog of cusp d, now called the hypoconid. A new posterior cusp, the hypoconulid, forms posteromedial to the hypoconid. *Peramus* possesses a narrow internal cingulum on the upper molars, which in the Early Cretaceous tribosphenidans (Figure 3D) becomes greatly enlarged to form an important new cusp, the protocone. Concomitantly, the central part of the lower heel develops a basin enclosed by the crests joining the hypoconid, hypoconulid, and a new internal cusp, the entoconid. The talonid basin acts as a pestle, receiving the upper protocone, which acts as a mortar, crushing food between the two surfaces.

This tribosphenic molar (with protocone and talonid basin) characterizes the Tribosphenida (Figure 4). The main cusps of the upper molar, forming a different triangle from that of basal holotheres, are the paracone (A) and metacone (C) externally and the protocone internally, the three forming the trigon. Cusp B, the stylocone, is usually reduced to a small anteroexternal accessory cusp. In the lower molars, the cusps of the trigonid are the external protoconid (a), the anterointernal paraconid (b), and the posterointernal metaconid (c); those of the talonid are the hypoconid (probably d), the hypoconulid, and the entoconid.

A basined molar is first seen in *Aegialodon,* known from a single lower molar from the Lower Cretaceous (Kermack et al. 1965), but better illustrated by *Pappotherium* from the late Early Cretaceous of Texas (Figure 3E; Butler 1990). Tribosphenic molars are extremely versatile because they combine the zigzagging cutting edges of the trigon (upper triangle) and trigonid (lower triangle) with the crushing action between the protocone and talonid basin. From this basic pattern evolved the enormous functional diversity of molars seen, for example, in modern carnivores, rodents, and ungulates.

A variety of early non-therian tribosphenidans are known primarily from isolated teeth of Cretaceous age (Cifelli 1993). The oldest member of the Theria is the eutherian *Prokennalestes* from the Early Cretaceous of Asia (Kielan-Jaworowska and Dashzeveg 1989). The oldest undoubted metatherian is *Pariadens* from the Late Cretaceous of North America (Cifelli and Eaton 1987). Deltatheroidans are a group of specialized carnivorous tribosphenidans, formerly of uncertain affinities but now known to be nonmarsupial metatherians (Rougier et al. 1998), which are confined to the Late Cretaceous of Asia.

JAMES A. HOPSON

See also Marsupials; Placentals; Synapsids; Teeth: Evolution of Mammalian Teeth

Works Cited

Archer, M., T.F. Flannery, and A. Ritchie. 1985. First Mesozoic mammal from Australia: An Early Cretaceous monotreme. *Nature* 318: 363–66.

Archer, M., F.A. Jenkins Jr., S.J. Hand, P. Murray, and H. Godthelp. 1992. Description of the skull and non-vestigial dentition of a Miocene platypus (*Obdurodon dicksoni* n. sp.) from Riversleigh, Australia and the problem of monotreme origins. *In* M.L. Augee (ed.), *Platypus and Echidnas.* Sydney: Royal Society of New South Wales.

Archer, M., P. Murray, S. Hand, and H. Godthelp. 1993. Reconsideration of monotreme relationships based on the skull and dentition of the Miocene *Obdurodon dicksoni*. *In* F.S. Szalay, M.J. Novacek, and M.C. McKenna (eds.), *Mammal Phylogeny: Mesozoic Differentiation, Multituberculates, Monotremes, Early Therians, and Marsupials.* New York and London: Springer-Verlag.

Blainville, H. de. 1838. Doutes sur le prétendu Didelphe fossile de Stonefield [sic]. *Compte Rendu Hebdominaire des Séances de l'Académie des Sciences* 7:402–18.

Bonaparte, J.F., and G.W. Rougier. 1987. Mamíferos del Cretacico Inferior de Patagonia. *IV Congreso Latinoamericano de Paleontológia, Bolivia* 1:343–59.

Butler, P.M. 1988. Docodont molars as tribosphenic analogues (Mammalia, Jurassic). *In* D.E. Russell, J.-P. Santoro, and D. Sigogneau-Russell (eds.), *Teeth Revisited: Proceedings of the VIIth International Symposium on Dental Morphology, Paris, 20–24 Mai, 1986.* Paris: Editions du Muséum.

———. 1990. Early trends in the evolution of tribosphenic molars. *Biological Reviews* 65:529–52.

Butler, P.M., and G.T. MacIntyre. 1994. Review of the British Haramiyidae (?Mammalia, Allotheria), their molar occlusion and relationships. *Philosophical Transactions of the Royal Society of London,* ser. B, 345:433–58.

Cassiliano, M.L., and W.A. Clemens. 1979. Symmetrodonta. *In* J.A. Lillegraven, Z. Kielan-Jaworowska, and W.A. Clemens (eds.), *Mesozoic Mammals: The First Two-Thirds of Mammalian History.* Berkeley and London: University of California Press.

Chow, M., and T.H. Rich. 1982. *Shuotherium dongi*, n. gen. and sp., a therian with pseudo-tribosphenic molars from the Jurassic of Sichuan, China. *Australian Mammalia* 5:127–42.

Cifelli, R.L. 1993. Theria of metatherian-eutherian grade and the origin of marsupials. *In* F.S. Szalay, M.J. Novacek, and M.C. McKenna (eds.), *Mammal Phylogeny: Mesozoic Differentiation, Multituberculates, Monotremes, Early Therians, and Marsupials.* New York and London: Springer-Verlag.

Cifelli, R.L., and J.G. Eaton. 1987. Marsupial mammal from the earliest Late Cretaceous of western US. *Nature* 325:520–22.

Clemens, W.A., J.A. Lillegraven, E.H. Lindsay, and G.G. Simpson. 1979. Where, when, and what: A survey of known Mesozoic mammal distribution. *In* J.A. Lillegraven, Z. Kielan-Jaworowska, and W.A. Clemens (eds.), *Mesozoic Mammals: The First Two-Thirds of Mammalian History.* Berkeley and London: University of California Press.

Crompton, A.W. 1971. The origin of the tribosphenic molar. *In* D.M. Kermack and K.A. Kermack (eds.), *Early Mammals,* supplement 1 to *Zoological Journal of the Linnean Society* 50:65–87.

Crompton, A.W., and F.A. Jenkins Jr. 1968. Molar occlusion in Late Triassic mammals. *Biological Reviews* 43:427–58.

———. 1979. Origin of mammals. *In* J.A. Lillegraven, Z. Kielan-Jaworowska, and W.A. Clemens (eds.), *Mesozoic Mammals: The First Two-Thirds of Mammalian History.* Berkeley and London: University of California Press.

Crompton, A.W., and Z. Luo. 1993. Relationships of the Liassic mammals *Sinoconodon, Morganucodon oehleri,* and *Dinnetherium. In* F.S. Szalay, M.J. Novacek, and M.C. McKenna (eds.), *Mammal Phylogeny: Mesozoic Differentiation, Multituberculates, Monotremes, Early Therians, and Marsupials.* New York and London: Springer-Verlag.

Crompton, A.W., and A.-L. Sun. 1985. Cranial structure and relationships of the Liassic mammal Sinoconodon. *Zoological Journal of the Linnean Society* 85:99–119.

Desmond, A. 1984. Interpreting the origin of mammals: New approaches to the history of paleontology. *Zoological Journal of the Linnean Society* 82:7–16.

Fox, R.C. 1969. Studies of Late Cretaceous vertebrates. Part 3, A triconodont mammal from Alberta. *Canadian Journal of Zoology* 6:1253–56.

Fraser, N.C., and H.-D. Sues (eds.). 1994. *In the Shadow of the Dinosaurs: Early Mesozoic Tetrapods.* Cambridge and New York: Cambridge University Press.

Freeman, E.F. 1979. A Middle Jurassic mammal bed from Oxfordshire. *Palaeontology* 22:135–66.

Gregory, W.K., and G.G. Simpson. 1926. Cretaceous mammal skulls from Mongolia. *American Museum Novitates* 225:1–20.

Griffiths, M., R.T. Wells, and D.J. Barrie. 1991. Observations on the skulls of fossil and extant echidnas (Monotremata: Tachyglossidae). *Australian Mammalogy* 14:87–101.

Hahn, G. 1969. Beitrage zur Fauna der Grube Guimarota Nr 3. Die Multituberculata. *Palaeontographica,* ser. A, 133:1–100.

Hopson, J.A. 1991. Systematics of the nonmammalian Synapsida and implications for patterns of evolution in synapsids. *In* H.-P. Schultze and L. Trueb (eds.), *Origins of the Higher Groups of Tetrapods: Controversy and Consensus.* Ithaca, New York, and London: Cornell University Press.

———. 1994. Synapsid evolution and the radiation of non-eutherian mammals. *In* D.R. Prothero and R.M. Schoch (eds.), *Major Features of Vertebrate Evolution.* Short Courses in Paleontology, no. 7. Knoxville, Tennessee: Paleontological Society.

———. 1995. The Jurassic mammal *Shuotherium dongi*: "Pseudo-tribosphenic therian," docodontid, or neither? *Journal of Vertebrate Paleontology* 15 (3, supplement):36A.

Hopson, J.A., and A.W. Crompton. 1969. Origin of mammals. *Evolutionary Biology* 3:15–72.

Hopson, J.A., and G.W. Rougier. 1993. Braincase structure in the oldest known skull of a therian mammal: Implications for mammalian systematics and cranial evolution. *American Journal of Science,* ser. A, 293:268–99.

Hu, Y., Y. Wang, Z. Luo, and C. Li. 1997. A new symmetrodont mammal from China and its implications for mammalian evolution. *Nature* 390:137–42.

Jenkins Jr., F.A., and A.W. Crompton. 1979. Triconodonta. *In* J.A. Lillegraven, Z. Kielan-Jaworowska, and W.A. Clemens (eds.), *Mesozoic Mammals: The First Two-Thirds of Mammalian History.* Berkeley and London: University of California Press.

Jenkins Jr., F.A., A.W. Crompton, and W.R. Downs. 1983. Mesozoic mammals from Arizona: New evidence on mammalian evolution. *Science* 222:1233–35.

Jenkins Jr., F.A., S.M. Gatesy, N.H. Shubin, and W.W. Amaral. 1997. Haramiyids and Triassic mammalian evolution. *Nature* 385:715–18.

Jenkins Jr., F.A., and F.R. Parrington. 1976. Postcranial skeleton of the Triassic mammals *Eozostrodon, Megazostrodon,* and *Erythrotherium. Philosophical Transactions of the Royal Society of London,* ser. B, 273:387–431.

Jenkins Jr., F.A., and C.R. Schaff. 1988. The Early Cretaceous mammal *Gobiconodon* (Mammalia Triconodonta) from the Cloverly Formation in Montana. *Journal of Vertebrate Paleontology* 6:1–24.

Kermack, D.M., K.A. Kermack, and F. Mussett. 1968. The Welsh pantothere *Kuehneotherium praecursoris*. *Journal of the Linnean Society (Zoology)* 47:407–23.

Kermack, K.A., A.J. Lee, P.M. Lees, and F. Mussett. 1987. A new docodont from the Forest Marble. *Zoological Journal of the Linnean Society* 89:1–39.

Kermack, K.A., P.M. Lees, and F. Mussett. 1965. *Aegialodon dawsoni,* a new trituberculosectorial tooth from the lower Wealden. *Proceedings of the Royal Society of London,* ser. B, 162:535–54.

Kermack, K.A., and F. Mussett. 1958. The jaw articulation of the Docodonta and the classification of Mesozoic mammals. *Proceedings of the Royal Society of London,* ser. B, 149:204–15.

———. 1959. The first mammals. *Discovery (London)* 20:144–51.

Kermack, K.A., F. Mussett, and H.W. Rigney. 1973. The lower jaw of *Morganucodon. Zoological Journal of the Linnean Society* 53:87–175.

———. 1981. The skull of *Morganucodon. Zoological Journal of the Linnean Society* 71:1–158.

Kielan-Jaworowska, Z. 1971. Results of the Polish-Mongolian Palaeontological Expeditions. Part 3, Skull structure and affinities of the Multituberculata. *Palaeontologia Polonica* 25:5–41.

Kielan-Jaworowska, Z., A.W. Crompton, and F.A. Jenkins Jr. 1987. The origin of egg-laying mammals. *Nature* 326:871–73.

Kielan-Jaworowska, Z., and D. Dashzeveg. 1989. Eutherian mammals from the Early Cretaceous of Mongolia. *Zoologica Scripta* 18:347–55.

Kielan-Jaworowska, Z., and P.P. Gambaryan. 1994. Postcranial anatomy and habits of Asian multituberculate mammals. *Fossils and Strata* 36:1–92.

Kielan-Jaworowska, Z., and J.H. Hurum. 1997. Djadochtatheria: A new suborder of multituberculate mammals. *Acta Palaeontologica Polonica* 42:201–42.

Krause, D.W. 1982. Jaw movement, dental function, and diet in the Paleocene multituberculate *Ptilodus. Paleobiology* 8:265–81.

———. 1986. *Competitive Exclusion and Taxonomic Displacement in the Fossil Record: The Case of Rodents and Multituberculates in North America.* Contributions to Geology, University of Wyoming, Special Paper 3. Laramie: University of Wyoming.

Krause, D.W., and J.F. Bonaparte. 1993. Superfamily Gondwanatherioidea: A previously unrecognized radiation of multituberculate mammals in South America. *Proceedings of the National Academy of Science* 90:9379–83.

Krause, D.W., Z. Kielan-Jaworowska, and J.F. Bonaparte. 1992. *Ferugliotherium windhauseni* Bonaparte, the first known multituberculate from South America. *Journal of Vertebrate Paleontology* 12:351–76.

Krause, D.W., G.V.R. Prasad, W. von Koenigswald, A. Sahni, and F.E. Grine. 1997. Cosmopolitanism among Gondwanan Late Cretaceous mammals. *Nature* 390:504–7.

Krebs, B. 1991. Das Skelett von *Henkelotherium guimarotae* gen. et sp. nov. (Eupantotheria, Mammalia) aus dem Oberen Jura von Portugal. *Berliner Geowissenschaftliche Abhandlungen,* ser. A, 133:1–110.

Krusat, G. 1980. Contribuição para o conhecimento da fauna do Kimeridgiano da Mina de Lignito Guimarota (Leira, Portugal). Part 4, *Haldanodon expectatus* Kühne and Krusat 1972 (Mammalia, Docodonta). *Memórias dos Serviços Geológicos de Portugal* 27:1–79.

Kühne, W.G. 1949. On a triconodont tooth of a new pattern from a fissure-filling in South Glamorgan. *Proceedings of the Zoological Society of London* 119:345–50.

———. 1950. A symmetrodont tooth from the Rhaeto-Lias. *Nature* 166:696–97.

———. 1958. Rhaetische Triconodonten aus Glamorgan, ihre Stellung zwischen Klassen Reptilia und Mammalia und ihre Bedeutung für die Reichert'she Theorie. *Paläontologische Zeitschrift* 32:197–235.

———. 1961. A mammalian fauna from the Kimmeridgian of Portugal. *Nature* 192:274–75.

Kühne, W.G., and M. Crusafont-Pairó. 1968. Mamíferos del Wealdiense de Uña, cerca de Cuenca. *Acta Geológica Hispanica* 3:133–34.

Lillegraven, J.A., and G. Krusat. 1991. *Cranio-Mandibular Anatomy of* Haldanodon exspectatus *(Docodonta; Mammalia) from the Late Jurassic of Portugal and Its Implications to the Evolution of Mammalian Characters.* Contributions to Geology, University of Wyoming, Special Paper 28. Laramie: University of Wyoming.

Lucas, S.G., and Z. Luo. 1993. *Adelobasileus* from the Upper Triassic of West Texas: The oldest mammal. *Journal of Vertebrate Paleontology* 13:309–34.

McKenna, M.C., and S.K. Bell. 1997. *Classification of Mammals above the Species Level.* New York: Columbia University Press.

Meng, J., and A. Wyss. 1995. Monotreme affinities and low-frequency hearing suggested by multituberculate ear. *Nature* 377:141–44.

Miao, D. 1988. *Skull Morphology of* Lambdopsalis bulla *(Mammalia, Multituberculata) and Its Implications to Mammalian Evolution.* Contributions to Geology, University of Wyoming, Special Paper 4. Laramie: University of Wyoming.

Owen, R. 1838. On the jaws of the *Thylacotherium prevostii* (Valenciennes) from Stonesfield. *Geological Society of London Proceedings* 3:5–9.

———. 1871. *Monograph of the Fossil Mammalia of the Mesozoic Formations.* Palaeontographical Society Monograph 2. London: Palaeontographical Society.

Pascual, R., M. Archer, E. Ortiz Jaureguizar, J.L. Prado, H. Godthelp, and S.J. Hand. 1992. The first non-Australian monotreme: An early Paleocene South American platypus (Monotremata, Ornithorhynchidae). *In* M. Augee (ed.), *Platypus and Echidnas.* Sydney: Royal Society of New South Wales.

Patterson, B. 1951. Early Cretaceous mammals from northern Texas. *American Journal of Science* 249:31–46.

———. 1956. *Early Cretaceous Mammals and the Evolution of Mammalian Molar Teeth.* Fieldiana, Geology, 13. Chicago: Natural History Museum.

Patterson, B., and E.C. Olson. 1961. A triconodontid mammal from the Triassic of Yunnan. *In International Colloquium on the Evolution of Lower and Non-Specialized Mammals (1960: Brussels, Belgium).* Brussels: Paleis des Academiën.

Prothero, D.R. 1981. New Jurassic mammals from Como Bluff, Wyoming, and the interrelationships of non-tribosphenic Theria. *Bulletin of the American Museum of Natural History* 167:277–326.

Rigney, H.W. 1963. A specimen of *Morganucodon* from Yunnan. *Nature* 197:1122–23.

Rougier, G.W. 1993. "*Vincelestes neuquenianus* Bonaparte (Mammalia, Theria): Un primativo mamífero del Cretacico Inferior de la Cuenca Neuquina." Thesis, Universidad Nacional de Buenos Aires.

Rougier, G.W., M.J. Novacek, and D. Dashzeveg. 1997. A new multituberculate from the Late Cretaceous Locality Ukhaa Tolgod, Mongolia: Considerations on multituberculate interrelationships. *American Museum Novitates* 3191:1–26.

Rougier, G.W., J.R. Wible, and J.A. Hopson. 1996. Basicranial anatomy of Priacodon fruitaensis (Triconodontidae, Mammalia) from the Late Jurassic of Colorado, and a reappraisal of mammaliaform relationships. *American Museum Novitates* 3183:1–38.

Rougier, G.W., J.R. Wible, and M.J. Novacek. 1998. Implications of *Deltatheridium* specimens for early marsupial history. *Nature* 396:459.

Rowe, T. 1988. Definition, diagnosis and origin of Mammalia. *Journal of Vertebrate Paleontology* 8:241–64.

Rowe, T., and J. Gauthier. 1992. Ancestry, paleontology, and definition of the name Mammalia. *Systematic Biology* 41:372–78.

Sereno, P.C., and M.C. McKenna. 1995. Cretaceous multituberculate skeleton and the early evolution of the mammalian shoulder girdle. *Nature* 377:144–47.

Sigogneau-Russell, D. 1989. Haramiyidae (Mammalia, Allotheria) en provenance du Trias Supérieur de Lorraine, France. *Palaeontographica*, ser. A, 206:137–98.

———. 1991. First evidence of Multituberculata (Mammalia) in the Mesozoic of Africa. *Neues Jahrbuch für Geologie und Paläontologie, Monatshefte* 1991:119–25.

Simpson, G.G. 1928. *A Catalogue of the Mesozoic Mammalia in the Geological Department of The British Museum: London.* London: Trustees of the British Museum (Natural History); as *A Catalogue of the Mesozoic Mammalia and American Mesozoic Mammalia,* New York: Arno, 1980.

———. 1929. *American Mesozoic Mammalia.* Peabody Museum (Yale University) Memoir, 3, Part 1. New Haven, Connecticut: Yale University Press.

Tatarinov, L.P. 1994. An unusual mammal tooth from the Jurassic of Mongolia. *Paleontological Journal* 28:121–31.

Waldman, M., and R.J.G. Savage. 1972. The first Jurassic mammal from Scotland. *Journal of the Geological Society* 128:119–25.

Wible, J.R., G.W. Rougier, M.J. Novacek, M.C. McKenna, and D. Dashzeveg. 1995. A mammalian petrosal from the Early Cretaceous of Mongolia: Implications for the evolution of the ear region and mammaliamorph relationships. *American Museum Novitates* 3149:1–19.

Woodburne, M.O., and R.H. Tedford. 1975. The first Tertiary monotreme from Australia. *American Museum Novitates* 2588:1–11.

Further Reading

Augee, M., and B. Gooden. 1993. *Echidnas of Australia and New Guinea.* Kensington: New South Wales University Press.

Grant, T. 1984. *The Platypus.* Kensington: New South Wales University Press; revised as *The Platypus: A Unique Mammal,* 1995.

Griffiths, M. 1978. *The Biology of the Monotremes.* New York and London: Academic Press.

Strahan, R. (ed.). 1995. *Mammals of Australia.* Washington, D.C.: Smithsonian Institution Press; as *A Photographic Guide to Mammals of Australia,* London: New Holland, 1995.

MARSH, OTHNIEL CHARLES

American, 1831–99

Othniel Charles Marsh was one of the foremost vertebrate paleontologists of nineteenth century America. He was the nephew of the industrialist and philanthropist George Peabody, who provided essential financial support first for his studies at Yale College and then for his career there as a vertebrate paleontologist. After his studies at Yale, Marsh left for Europe in 1862 and stayed there until 1865, studying paleontology in Berlin and visiting the Alps, France, and England. In 1866, when he returned to the United States, Yale created a chair of paleontology for him. (An allowance from George Peabody made up for the lack of a salary; it was not until 1896 that Marsh was finally placed on the university's payroll.) At the same time, Peabody donated $150,000 to Yale to found a Natural History Museum. Marsh went on to turn it into one of the leading paleontological institutions in the world.

Marsh's paleontological research began on the East Coast, where he studied reptiles from the Cretaceous of New Jersey, but he soon turned to the more promising fossil localities in the American West. In 1870, Marsh led a party of Yale students to the Eocene of the Bridger Basin of Wyoming and to the Late Cretaceous Chalk of western Kansas. Three more well-publicized student expeditions to the fossil beds of the West followed in 1871, 1872, and 1873.

Increasingly, Marsh came to rely on the services of hired collectors, at times having as many as 12 parties in the field simultaneously in various parts of the West. Some of these men, such as Samuel Wendell Williston and John Bell Hatcher, later became prominent paleontologists themselves. The field activities of Marsh and his collectors during the 1870s and 1880s produced impressive results, as testified by the large numbers of vertebrate fossils that the expeditions sent back to the Peabody Museum. The finds included giant pterosaurs, toothed birds, and marine reptiles from the Late Cretaceous Niobrara Chalk of Kansas; abundant mammals from various Tertiary basins in the Rocky Mountains; horned dinosaurs and mammals from the Late Cretaceous "Laramie Beds"; and dinosaurs and mammals from the Late Jurassic Morrison Formation, notably from the remarkable site at Como Bluff, Wyoming. This site was discovered in 1877 and worked for more than ten years. During this period, the competition over collecting between Marsh and the Philadelphia paleontologist E.D. Cope became increasingly fierce. Their parties spied on each other and tried to preempt each other's respective claims to new fossil localities, while their employers engaged in a bitter scientific feud over new discoveries, priority issues, and conflicting interpretations.

Once fossils were shipped to Yale, Marsh studied them with the help of a large staff of assistants. This resulted in numerous short papers, mainly in the *American Journal of Science,* and a series of great, profusely illustrated monographs, such as those on the Odontornithes (toothed birds) (1880), the Dinocerata (large, rhinoceros-like mammals) (1885), and the dinosaurs of North America (1896), which made Marsh's work famous among paleontologists all over the world.

Marsh was an early supporter of Charles Darwin's theory of evolution by natural selection, so he naturally interpreted his paleontological discoveries in evolutionary terms. Both his reconstruction of the genealogy of the horse, based on finds from the Tertiary of the western United States, and his discovery in the Chalk of Kansas of Cretaceous toothed birds, which in some respects were intermediate between reptiles and modern birds, were hailed by such authorities as Thomas Huxley and Darwin himself as highly significant evidence in favor of evolution.

In the late 1870s, as an influential member of the National Academy of Sciences, Marsh played a significant part in organizing the new United States Geological Survey. This organization replaced the various independent surveys that had been exploring the West during the previous decades. In 1882, Marsh became vertebrate paleontologist of the Federal Survey, a position that brought him into renewed conflict with Cope, who previously had held the position for the Hayden Survey. In 1890, Cope and journalist William H. Ballou launched a press campaign in the *New York Herald* against Marsh and the director of the U.S. Geological Survey, John Wesley Powell. Several of Marsh's former assistants turned against him, accusing him of denying them due credit for their scientific work. There was no clear winner, and both rivals suffered from the adverse publicity that their feud engendered.

Financial difficulties clouded Marsh's final years, but he continued publishing on fossil vertebrates until his death in 1899. His contributions to the knowledge of the fossil vertebrates of North America were equalled only by those of his arch-rival Cope. Marsh discovered an astounding array of extinct creatures, many of which were unknown at the time but now are among the most famous of fossil vertebrates—including the Jurassic dinosaurs *Diplodocus, Stegosaurus,* and *Allosaurus;* the Cretaceous toothed birds *Hesperornis* and *Ichthyornis;* the giant pterosaur *Pteranodon;* and the Cretaceous horned dinosaur *Triceratops.* He also brought forward a succession of early horses that has long been one of the best examples of reconstructing an evolutionary series on the basis of fossils (even though it was certainly not as linear as Marsh thought). In retrospect—regardless of the foibles revealed by his long-enduring feud with the equally remarkable and controversial Cope—Marsh clearly was one of the most influential paleontologists of the nineteenth century.

ERIC BUFFETAUT

Biography

Born in Lockport, New York, 29 October 1831. Received A.B., Yale College, 1860; M.A., Sheffield Scientific School, Yale, 1862; studied paleontology, Heidelberg, Berlin and Breslau, 1862–65. Professor of paleontology and director of the Peabody Museum, Yale, 1866–82; elected member (1874) and president (1883–95), National Academy of Sciences; recipient, Bigsby Medal, Geological Society of London, 1877; first vertebrate paleontologist, U.S. Geological Survey, 1882–92; recipient, Cuvier Prize, French Academy, 1897. Led expeditions to the west, 1870–73; described *Hesperornis* and *Ichthyornis,* 1872; described *Brontotherium,* 1873, *Mesohippus,* 1875; *Pteranodon,* 1876; *Allosaurus,* 1877; *Stegosaurus,* 1877; *Diplodocus,* 1878; *Triceratops,* 1889. Died 18 March 1899 in New Haven, Connecticut.

Major Publications

1874. Fossil horses in America. *American Naturalist* 8:288–94.
1876. Notice of a new sub-order of Pterosauria. *American Journal of Science* 11:507–9.
1877. Introduction and succession of vertebrate life in America. *American Journal of Science* 14:337–78.
1880. *Odontornithes: A Monograph on the Extinct Toothed Birds of North America.* Memoirs of the Peabody Museum, Yale College, 1. New Haven, Connecticut: Peabody Museum of Natural History.
1884. *Dinocerata: A Monograph of an Extinct Order of Gigantic Mammals.* Monographs of the U.S. Geological Survey, 10. Washington, D.C.: U.S. Government Printing Office.
1887. American Jurassic Mammals. *American Journal of Science* 33:327–48.
1891. On the gigantic Ceratopsidae, or horned dinosaurs, of North America. *American Journal of Science* 41:167–78.
1896a. The dinosaurs of North America. *16th Annual Report of the U.S. Geological Survey, 1894–95.* Washington, D.C.: U.S. Government Printing Office.
1896b. Vertebrate Fossils [of the Denver Basin]. *Monographs of the U.S. Geological Survey* 27:473–550.

Further Reading

Colbert, E.H. 1968. *Men and Dinosaurs.* New York: Dutton; London: Evans; 2nd ed., *The Great Dinosaur Hunters and Their Discoveries,* New York: Dover, 1984.
Howard, R.W. 1975. *The Dawnseekers.* New York: Harcourt Brace Jovanovich.
Lanham, U. 1973. *The Bone Hunters.* New York: Columbia University Press; rev. ed., New York and London: Constable, 1991.
McCarren, M.J. 1993. *The Scientific Contributions of Othniel Charles Marsh.* Peabody Museum of Natural History Special Publication, 15. New Haven: Peabody Museum of Natural History.
Ostrom, J.H., and J.S. McIntosh. 1966. *Marsh's Dinosaurs: The Collections from Como Bluff.* New Haven: Yale University Press.
Schuchert, C., and C.M. LeVene. 1940. *O.C. Marsh, Pioneer in Paleontology.* New Haven: Yale University Press; London: Milford.
Shor, E.N. 1974a. *The Fossil Feud between E.D. Cope and O.C. Marsh.* Hicksville, New York: Exposition.
———. 1974b. Marsh, O.C. *In* C.C. Gillispie (ed.), *Dictionary of Scientific Biography.* Vol. 9, New York: Scribner's.

MARSUPIALS

The higher order mammalian groups Metatheria and Eutheria are composed of what are customarily referred to as marsupial and placental mammals, respectively. Together, and in addition to the extinct Early Cretaceous Tribotheria, which may have had its beginnings in the Jurassic, these make up the "subclass" Theria (customarily all three are classified as infraclasses). While there are no problems distinguishing present-day marsupials and their similar fossil relatives from eutherian mammals, the more ancient and poorly known groups of the Cretaceous present some difficulties. Although the marsupial developmental and reproductive patterns (e.g., very immature newborns that develop further in the mother's pouch) are decidedly distinct from those of placentals, it is almost certain that not all therian lineages that cannot be classified as placentals were necessarily metatherians. Some may have been oviparous (egg-laying), similar to living monotremes, such as the duck-billed platypus.

Fossil metatherians carry few diagnostic features, making classification difficult. It is likely that the marsupial mode of reproduction (even if not identical to that of its most primitive living expression) was prevalent in the Tribotheria and even possibly among the earliest eutherian mammals (Figure 1). Here, an overview phylogenetic (evolutionary) hypothesis (Figure 2), and the classification of the marsupials to the family level will place the groups in a temporal and phylogenetic framework.

It appears that the hitherto least equivocal attribute of the first fossil metatherians (from here on, for vernacular convenience, referred to as marsupials) was the dental formula and tooth replacement pattern. Although the 5/4 incisor formula (i.e., 5 upper and 4 lower incisors) was probably a primitive therian trait, the marsupials replaced only the third premolars; the fourth premolar was not replaced and was transformed into the first of four permanent molars. As a result, having four molars in the protometatherian (prototype marsupial) is diagnostic. Also, living marsupials lack a stapedial artery (a branch off the internal carotid artery in the middle ear). This trait is difficult to substitute in fossils, however.

Tooth features previously thought to be diagnostic of all marsupials (e.g., enlarged metacone cusp of upper molars) may in fact not be and may simply characterize a more restricted subgroup.

A host of other attributes have been associated with marsupials but are not genuine diagnostic features. Instead, these are traits acquired at different times during the preceding stage of evolution. The following characteristics are only some of the traits that probably were present in the first metatherians and were almost certainly even more ancient: (a) an inflected angle of the mandible, (b) two windows in the wall enclosing the inner ear (round fenestra ovale and transversely elongate and elliptical fenestra rotunda) visible in the middle ear, (c) epipubic ("marsupial") bones, (d) jugal (cheekbone) extends back along cheek arch to the edge of the jaw joint, (e) "parafibula," as in the knee of the living Didelphidae. In living marsupials a "pseudovaginal canal" forms as the first young is born. The condition of the female reproductive tract in the protometatherian can only be guessed.

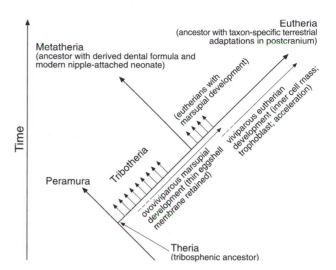

Figure 1. Connections between the three infraorders of the Theria. Included are diagnostic characters of the three groups (tribosphenic molars for Tribotheria, derived dental formula for Metatheria, and specific postcranial adaptations for Eutheria) and putative developmental attributes. Some groups included in eutherians may have had marsupial development as an ancestral attribute.

Lineage Multiplicity and Morphological Diversity of Metatherians

The known marsupials can be grouped in three major cohorts and five orders, a classification that reflects both their relationships and a classification that reflects both their relationships and their radiation (diversification) from a common ancestor (monophyly). Marsupials are not more diverse, nor do they have a greater number of lineages than the combined eutherian orders of the Insectivora, Carnivora, Primates, and Rodentia. Several recent experts on marsupials have elevated the splitting of lineages and modest diversifications to levels far beyond those discussed here, resulting in many more marsupial orders. (See Figures 3–7.)

Cohort Holarctidelphia

Cohort Holarctidelphia is the oldest of the three cohorts. It is also the most poorly known, consisting of only two orders and known only by a few species. The first order, the Cretaceous Deltatheroida, was an early lineage of carnivorous marsupials found primarily in Asia, although specimens have been recorded in North America. Deltatheroidans are difficult to evaluate because they combine, in an uncannily confusing manner, both primitive and advanced therian traits, and they are only known by skulls and teeth. The deltatheroidans stand out as significantly modified from pattern of a putative ancestor (one that is hypothesized to have existed) because their teeth have shearing (bladelike) edges. As a result, their phylogenetic relationships have been controversial for a long time.

Deltatheroida has been proposed to be the sister lineage (closest related group) of the South American carnivorous group Sparassodonta. It appears, however, that the proposed special similarities in the dentition and skull of the two groups are the result of convergent (independent) evolution. It has also been suggested that deltatheroidans supply evidence for the theory that marsupials originated from tribotherians independently from the placentals. These are as yet only uncorroborated hypotheses.

The second order is the Asiadelphia, represented by *Asiatherium* from the Late Cretaceous of Mongolia. This animal is relatively well known from cranial, dental, and postcranial (body) remains. This genus was a small insectivorous and probably also omnivorous animal. It is dentally unlike the deltatheroidans (which reduced the talonid [rear] basin of the lower molars and accentuated the shearing edges of all their molars). While on the surface the Holarctidelphia appears to be the least diverse of the three marsupial cohorts, this impression may turn out to be the result of the scant evidence in the fossil record. What we know now may be just the tip of a poorly known adaptive radiation. The Cretaceous of Asia is known exclusively from high-latitude dry country faunas, such as those recovered from Mongolia. The vast Asian tropics of that period may have been the home of numerous lineages of these marsupials.

Cohort Ameridelphia
Order Didelphida
The order Didelphida of the Cohort Ameridelphia contains four major radiations, classified in four suborders based on their suspected monophyletic or paraphyletic status (i.e., each group stems from a single lineage, although the lineage may not include all the descendants).

Suborder Archimetatheria
Suborder Archimetatheria is the oldest suborder. It probably had its beginnings in North America early in the Cretaceous, where the group's radiation is becoming increasingly better known from both Early and Late Cretaceous sediments. Archimetatheria consists largely of North American forms (and possibly one or two lineages in South America), although species of this group appear to have spread to Asia in the Cretaceous or Paleocene, traveled from there to Asia, Europe, and Africa, and then moved from Europe back to North America in the early Eocene.

Some of the Tertiary African marsupials discovered to date may not be parts of this archimetatherian assemblage but may represent some unknown African endemic Cretaceous radiation of marsupials. Although the various groups can be diagnosed, usually based on molar differences and some variation in the cranial morphology and foot bones (both still very poorly sampled), the Archimetatheria exhibit a modest degree of morphological diversity. While they were dentally diverse, they were restricted in size. One group, the Stagodontidae, was likely to be a malacophagous (shellfish-eating) and otterlike animal with swimming adaptations, whereas the other groups were the various omnivorous generalists (i.e., they had a varied diet) so familiar to students of living opossums.

Suborder Sudameridelphia
The first group of marsupials to invade South America after the latter became accessible in the latest Cretaceous was the stem group of the didelphidian suborder Sudameridelphia. This is the largest and most diverse group of Ameridelphia. Evidence from the Paleocene Tiupampa, Itaboraí, and Rio Chico faunas of Bolivia, Brazil, and Argentina, respectively, indicates that these ancestral sudameridelphians diversified rapidly into numerous lineages in what seems like a geological instant. With at least six families, the multiplicity of lineages displayed a great diversity of adaptations.

This spectacular adaptive radiation stemming from a newly immigrant stock (one of the best-documented ones in mammalian history) is grouped into three infraorders: Itaboraiformes, Polydolopimorphia, and Sparassodonta. The itaboraiforms, possibly the source of the other two infraorders, were represented by at least four subfamilies grouped in the Caroloameghiniidae of the Paleocene-Eocene and the Pucadelphydae of the Paleocene. While caroloameghiniids were relatively small omnivorous forms known primarily from their dentitions and a few foot bones, the rat-sized genus *Pucadelphys* is known from excellently preserved cranial and postcranial material. That genus, together with the equally splendidly preserved, small, weasel-sized borhyaenid *Myulestes,* which lived in the same area and time period, give us a very good estimate of the ancestral sudameridelphian skeletal morphology.

Infraorder Polydolopimorphia
The Polydolopimorphia comprises three distinct divisions that opted for a diet that probably relied primarily on plants. This required enlarged premolars, a reduction of the shearing edge of the lower molars, and construction of "bunodont" molars, which are molars with rounded cusps that are designed for crushing. The family Polydolopidae independently developed a short and broad daggerlike upper third premolar and a bladelike lower third premolar. (A similar type of development is seen in the glirimetatherian infraorder Paucituberculata, where a slicing pair of molars and premolars enlarge to become "carnassials," teeth that are designed for slicing.) Unlike the glirimetatherians, which have an enlarged incisor, prepidolopids, the stem group that probably gave rise to the Polydolopimorpha, are distinguished by enlarged, forward-angled, rodentlike canines. Also, the second and third premolars are enlarged, while the molars retain similarities to the ancestral condition. Foot bones allocated to the Polydolopidae suggest that these animals were terrestrial rather than arboreal.

Infraorder Sparassodonta
This group contains the radiation of the various predatory marsupials of South America that have shown carnivorous adaptations from the very beginning of the continent's Age of Mammals. The Borhyaenidae includes forms that ranged from weasel-sized to large-cat-sized, in addition to some large proborhyaenines that had skulls up to two feet in length. The Thylacosmilidae includes the saber-tooth marsupials, almost certainly descended from borhyaenids. These animals had enormous evergrowing canines,

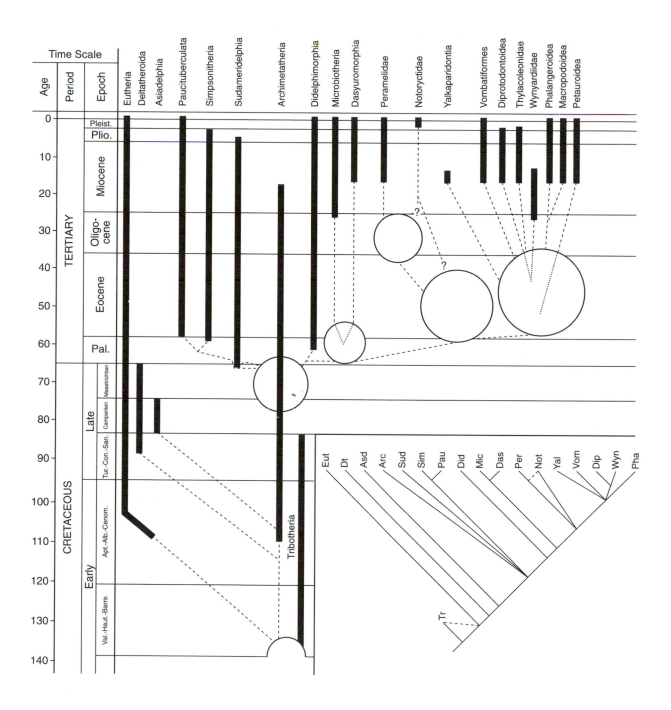

Figure 2. Phylogenetic tree of the Metatheria based on character analysis of morphological attributes.

with large bony flanges on the lower jaw to accommodate that tooth, and small cheek teeth behind the canine. At least four genera of these animals are known, species of which were the ecological equivalents of the saber-tooth cats. Eutherian carnivorous mammals entered South America in the Pliocene, and the last members of the Sparassodonta became extinct at the end of that epoch; this is perhaps one of the strongest cases that can be made in the fossil record for competitive exclusion (extinction owing directly to competition from another group).

Suborder Glirimetatheria

Glirimetatherians contain two very distinctive groups that are divergent from one another, yet both can be diagnosed by their enlarged incisors and reduced molar trigonids (front half of molar).

Infraorder Paucituberculata

The more primitive and perhaps more ancient of the two infraorders, the "diprotodont" Paucituberculata is represented by the Caenolestidae that still survives today in several largely terrestrial species. Today's forms inhabit cold, densely vegetated and wet forest habitats. These "shrew-opossums" appear to be rare; relatively few have been collected. They are relics of a once modestly diversified but flourishing radiation. Like almost all living marsupials (except kangaroos), caenolestids are nocturnal or crepuscular (active at dawn or dusk), and they feed on invertebrates, small vertebrates, and also some fruit and other vegetable material. They use their enlarged incisors in predation as effective stabbing tusks. They range from sea level to over 12,000 feet, but they prefer the alpine forests and adjacent meadows of the high, cold *paramos* of the Andes, from Colombia to Peru. The slightly distinct Chilean genus *Rhyncholestes* is more poorly known than the more northern species, which are classified in *Caenolestes*. The morphology retrieved from a fossil record extending from the Eocene suggests similar habits for a variety of extinct caenolestines, although the subfamilies Abderitinae and Palaeothentinae probably pursued a more vegetarian way of life than the caenolestines.

Infraorder Simpsonitheria

Infraorder Simpsonitheria is an assemblage of four families. The most primitive group may well be the Paleocene Gashterniidae, which is only known by scant dental remains. The best-known family is the Miocene-Pliocene Argyrolagidae, a group of rather amazing small marsupials that had a gerbil-like body and rabbit-like teeth. These ricochetal jumpers, with their extremely modified skull, dentition, and hind limb skeleton, were probably close relatives of the less well-known groberiids and patagoniids, which also had rodentlike and rabbitlike incisor and cheek tooth adaptations. In their skeletal morphology, these small animals, which survived into the Pleistocene, were some of the most highly derived of the known South American marsupials.

Suborder Didelphimorphia

The living Didelphidae occupy a historically and biologically important position in the study of the living marsupials. These opossums have served zoologists and paleontologists as models for the probable primitive marsupial condition for over 100 years. Yet, in spite of their undoubtedly numerous primitive metatherian attributes, the didelphids form a tightly knit monophyletic group that bear diagnostic testimony, particularly in their foot structure, that they are one of the numerous clade of the Ameridelphia. The family is ecologically diverse (75 species grouped in 11 genera), and it represents a distinct radiation among all sudameridelphians while retaining many primitive marsupial attributes. The shared derived morphology of all its known species clearly attests that the Didelphidae arose from a specialized sudameridelphian ancestor. The group is also important because it is unequivocally the source for the origin of the great australidelphian radiation.

Didelphids tend to be generalists in their diet (the omnivorous immigrant species *Didelphis* invaded North America, and rapidly spread into higher latitudes of the continent in the last hundred years), hence their relatively unmodified tooth morphology, which is far more conservative (unchanging) than many of

the sudameridelphian lineages. Their gestation period ranges from 12 to 14 days; they live from one to three years, although specimens in captivity have survived up to eight years. Their hand and foot structure shows advanced adaptations for arboreality (living in trees), a locomotor pattern that is more derived than their known relatives (Figures 6 and 7). Didelphids range in size from a head-body length of 3 to 20 inches (mouse- to cat-sized), most of them with prehensile (grasping) tails. Various species display either arboreal, terrestrial, or semiaquatic habits, or some combinations of these, although all are capable arborealists. The largely carnivorous water opossum *(Chironectes),* the only highly aquatic marsupial, has developed webbed hind feet and a pouch that can be closed watertight (both in males and females, in the former for the retracted scrotum).

Confusion exists over which dentitions are genuinely primitive and which are secondarily so (through evolutionary reversal). This confusion has resulted in mistaken allocations of unrelated taxa to the family Didelphidae. For example, peradectines or *Pucadelphys* and other taxa certainly lack the specific arboreal adaptations in their hands and feet that are found in all living didelphids. The family itself is divisible into two dentally distinct subfamilies, the Didelphinae and the Caluromyinae. Which of these is dentally more primitive is difficult to decide. One hypothesis, however, appears to be firmly corroborated, namely that the australidelphian Microbiotheriidae (with molar teeth not unlike those of the Caluromyinae) derived its unique ankle structure from a didelphid condition and not from any other group of sudameridelphians.

A probable member of the Didelphimorphia is the family Sparassocynidae of the Argentinean Late Miocene to Pliocene. The probably highly carnivorous and cranially badgerlike *Sparassocyon* (also convergent on the Tasmanian "devil," *Sarcophilus*) had adaptations that were so specialized that it is impossible to determine many of its potential links to other families, although it is unlikely to be a borhyaenid derivative. Knowledge of postcranial anatomy would undoubtedly facilitate understanding of its evolutionary relationships.

Ameridelphia, Incertae Sedis

One enigmatic group, the Necrolestidae, remains at least a geographic member (if not a proven relative) of the American assemblage. The Argentinean Miocene genus *Necrolestes,* a burrowing form that is suspected to have evolved from a borhyaenid, is still a puzzle. While the remains of its skull and front limbs attest to its subterranean adaptations, its phylogenetic status continues to be a mystery.

Cohort Australidelphia

There is little doubt that the orders Gondwanadelphia and Syndactyla represent a holophyletic (having a common ancestor) group of marsupials that originated in South America, spread to Antarctica, and today is largely restricted to Australasia (with the exception of the microbiotheriid *Dromiciops* in southern South America). Two ameridelphian families, the polydolopids and itaboraiforms, did reach Antarctica (Seymour Island) in the Eocene, but there is no

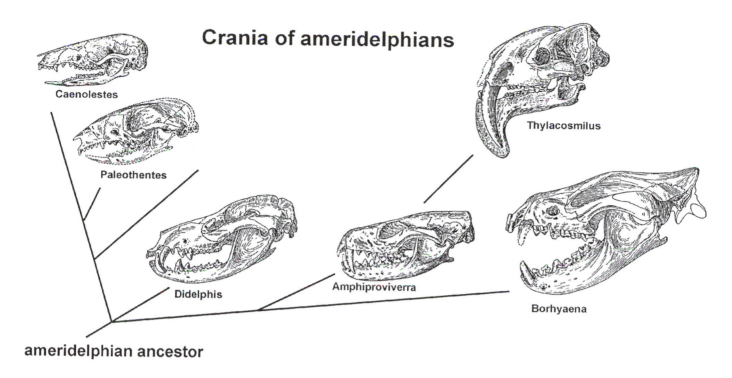

Crania of ameridelphians

Caenolestes

Paleothentes

Thylacosmilus

Didelphis

Amphiproviverra

Borhyaena

ameridelphian ancestor

Figure 3. Selected crania of some ameridelphians (not to scale). Connections of the genera shown represent the approximate evolutionary ties, in accordance with Figure 2. Crania modified after Gregory (1951).

evidence that any others reached this southern continent nor that any ameridelphian persisted here after this period.

Order Gondwanadelphia

The origins of the highly diverse Australidelphia can be traced clearly to an ancestor that was a modified didelphid, not another ameridelphian, contrary to several recent statements in the literature. Primitive australidelphians share with didelphids complex modifications of the tarsal bones and grasping mechanics of the foot, together with a modification of the wrist. These features are best exemplified in basal Gondwanadelphians. This first lineage of the order Gondwanadelphia was the source for both microbiotheres and dasyuromorphians, as suggested by their skeletal and incisor morphology.

Suborder Microbiotheria

A living link between didelphids and basal australidelphians is present in the sole surviving microbiotheriid, *Dromiciops*. The primarily arboreal "Monito del monte" lives in south-central Chile's cool, humid forests of southern beech trees *(Notophagus)* and bamboo thickets; there it hibernates during winter. This habitat probably characterized not only the southern reaches of South America but also southern and eastern Antarctica, the latter maintaining a persistent land bridge with Australia. Similar forests still persist in Tasmania. The family Microbiotheriidae, to which the monito belongs, is also known from the Patagonian fossil record.

Suborder Dasyuromorphia

It appears that the gondwanadelphian suborders Microbiotheria and the modified and largely terrestrial radiation of the Australasian Dasyuromorphia are each other's closest relatives. Dasyuromorphia is a diverse and largely insectivorous and carnivorous group with over 50 living species in at least 18 genera. The group's fossil record is known as far back as the Oligocene. Their incisor number is reduced to four upper and three lower incisors and so far are known by three families. The Dasyuridae are ferocious little predators that range from mouse- to large-cat-sized animals, all of which retain their ancestral ability to run up and down tree trunks (in spite of a reduced big toe), even if some, like *Sarcophilus,* are fully terrestrial. Their gestation period varies from 13 to 27 days. The termite-eating terrestrial numbat (Myrmecobiidae) is derived from a dasyurid. The recently extinct Tasmanian wolf (Thylacinidae), which was still known from live specimens in the 1920s, and which was specialized for running pursuit, also originated from a dasyurid. The extinction of the Tasmanian wolf was the result of a systematic extermination by European sheep ranchers. While thylacines had wolflike skulls and relatively long legs, mechanically they were not as efficient runners as most of the dog family.

Order Syndactyla

Some unknown gondwanadelphian that does not fit into either of the two known suborders was the ancestor of the great and complex adaptive radiation of Syndactyla. This ancestor initiated an adaptive radiation that includes such diverse forms as marsupial moles,

Crania of dasyurimorphians and peramelinans

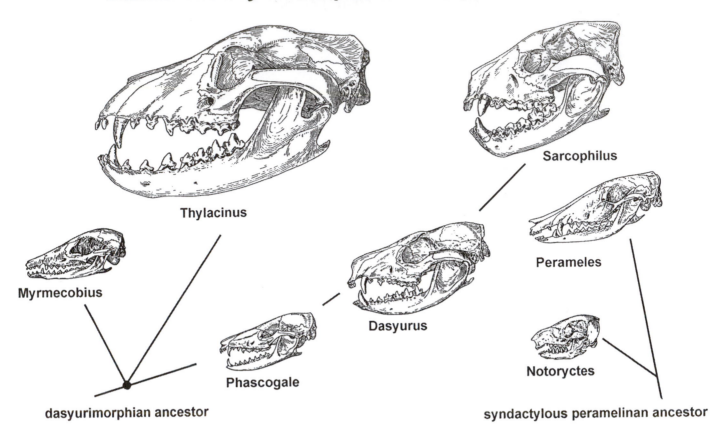

Figure 4. Selected crania of some dasyuromorphians and peramelinans (not to scale). Connections of the genera shown represent the approximate evolutionary ties, in accordance with Figure 2. Crania modified after Gregory (1951).

bandicoots, the various phalageriforms, and the diverse vombatiforms. The ancestor had a nearly full metatherian dental formula, a relatively primitive molar pattern with a W-shaped crest on the upper molars, a specialized temporal area, and a postcranial construction much like the living microbiotheriid—although the second and third rays of the foot are developmentally and functionally interconnected (the "syndactylous" condition). What makes phylogenetic assessment difficult for the beginnings of the syndactylan radiation is that scholars have not found fossils of intermediate or linking taxa (such as those between an early syndactylan and the very differently adapted bandicoots, notoryctids, and the early representatives of the diprotodontian superfamilies).

Semiorder Peramelina

In addition to the peramelid bandicoots (including the bilbies—or rabbit-bandicoots—as a separate subfamily), the enigmatic marsupial mole *Notoryctes* also may be a member of this group. Only the peculiar combination of specialized ankle structures, coupled with a hint of syndactyly in *Notoryctes,* supports grouping the two families together.

Family Peramelidae

The Peramelidae is represented today by 21 extant species. The group is a completely terrestrial, hind limb-dominated, running-bounding (but not hopping), nocturnal and omnivorous group with varying degrees of digging propensity. The bandicoot ancestor has evolved a number of interesting parallels with protoeutherians in its postcranial skeleton. The Peramelidae also independently developed a chorioallantoic placenta that only differs from the placental version in the absence of villi. The group's fossil record extends back to the beginnings of the Miocene. In spite of the retention of the nearly complete primitive marsupial dental formula, bandicoots are one of the more highly specialized australidelphian groups.

Family Notoryctidae

The single living species of the family Notoryctidae is the marsupial equivalent of the placental moles. Superbly adapted for digging and "swimming" just under the surface of the ground, it also burrows as deep as two to three meters underground. Its eyes are vestigial, the external ears are lost, and its entire external morphology and skeleton is a testimony to evolutionary adaptation and transformation

Crania of diprotodontians

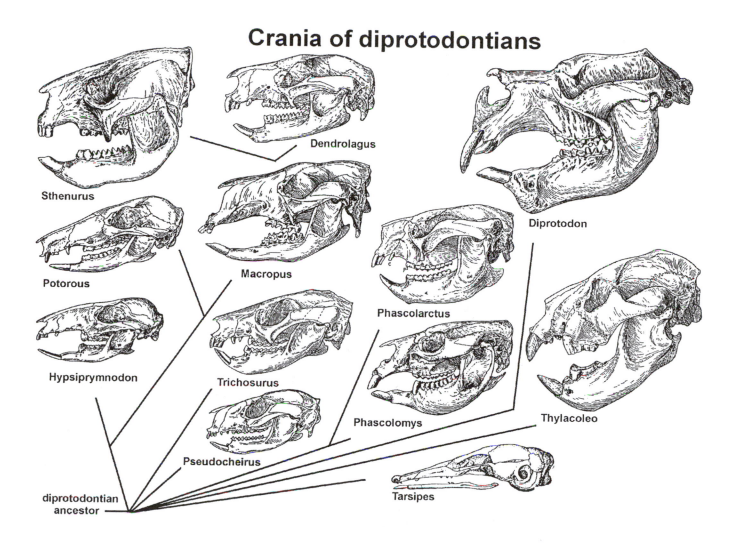

Figure 5. Selected crania of some diprotodontians (not to scale). Connections of the genera shown represent the approximate evolutionary ties, in accordance with Figure 2. Crania modified after Gregory (1951).

for its way of life. It closely resembles the placental Chrysochloridae—one of the outstanding examples of convergent evolution within the Mammalia. Tarsal evidence unequivocally ties this family to the rest of the Australidelphia, and there is a hint of the syndactylous ancestral condition on the foot (its second and third digits are webbed and of equal size). However, the extreme specializations for digging seen in this animal, which account for virtually all of the unique attributes of the skeleton, present major problems for a more precise classification, in spite of its tentative inclusion in Peramelina. The notoryctid fossil record goes back to the early Miocene.

Semiorder Diprotodontia

The last common ancestor of the Diprotodontia had the first of its three pairs of incisors enlarged, the third (last) premolar became more adapted for shearing, and the molars were perhaps more of the low-cusped variety than those seen in its immediate syndactylan ancestry. The carpus (wrist) still retained a crescent-shaped bone

(lunate), although it was probably as reduced as in the phalangeriforms. The arboreally adapted skeleton was opossum-like with a tarsal structure similar to the living microbiotheriid *Oromiciops*. In addition to a superficial thymus gland, the living forms have a connection between their two cerebral hemispheres that is convergent on a similar connection in placentals, the corpus callosum. The origin and adaptive radiation of the diprotodontians probably well predates their latest Oligocene–earliest Miocene appearance in the rich deposits of Riversleigh in Queensland, Australia.

Suborder Phalangeriformes

The Phalangeriformes encompasses the original arboreal radiation of the diprotodontians (e.g., phalangers, opossum-rats), along with other clades with a variety of dental specializations, and the phalangeroid-derived kangaroos. The phalangeriform ancestor was probably some petauroid- or phalangeroid-like species, although it is likely that on dental evidence this first phalangeriform would be

Carpal bone patterns in the major groups of marsupials to show probable paths of transformation

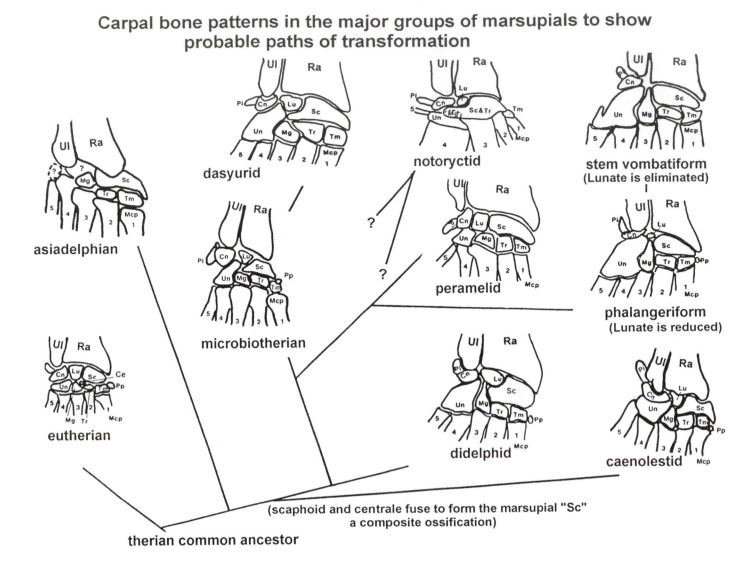

Figure 6. Representative arrangements in the pattern of wrist bones in selected groups of marsupials, shown in a phylogenetic perspective in accordance with Figure 2.

classified in a family separate from the known and extant groups of the Diprotodontia. From the tiny pygmy possums and honey possum to the six to seven kilogram cuscuses, the arboreal phalangeriforms are a fascinating primatelike group of marsupials among which gliding has evolved independently three times. In addition to the small insectivores, various subfamilies of phalangeroids and petauroids evolved impressive dental adaptations for what appears to be fairly obligate (i.e., exclusive) herbivory. During the wetter Miocene time in Australia, the rainforests, with a sprinkling of eucalyptus forests, extended not only from south to north on the eastern coast but also from the southeast quadrant of the continent into the interior. The variety of arboreal phalangeriforms recovered from the Riversleigh localities allows us to glimpse what must have been spectacularly active marsupial tree life—providing one could have watched them at dusk or at night.

The superb adaptations of kangaroo structure and function to terrestrial lifeways is well known; they are the most successful group of marsupials, competing exceptionally well with the placental herbivores introduced to Australia. Structurally conservative, and all taking advantage of the excellent ancestral adaptive package, the living species (probably well over 60) cover every conceivable habitat found in Australia and New Guinea. This includes the arboreal reinvasion of the rainforest canopy by the ancestors of today's tree kangaroos from their former terrestrial habitat. Yet the bulk of the modern radiation, the Macropodinae, did not begin its real success story until about five million years ago, when the disappearing rainforests gave way to grasslands and began to offer increasing opportunities for grazing. Until then the rat-kangaroos (Potoroinae) were showing spectacular evolutionary experimentation in the forest habitats, 12 to 13 million years before the grazing macropodines appear.

Evolution of the pes in some marsupials

(The plantar surface of the foot is shown to indicate such characters as hallux reduction and syndactyly of the second and third rays. The didelphid-microbiotheriid pattern, the only one where the pads are shown, is the most primitive one known. Derivations of the outlines of the foot of the major groups are shown from this structural ancestry.)

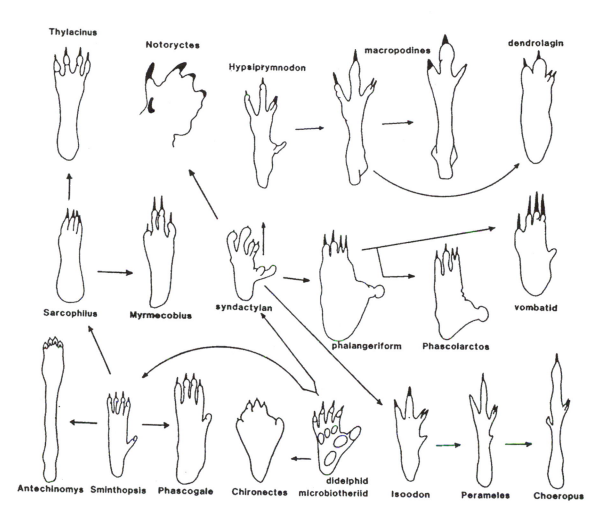

Figure 7. Patterns and evolution of the foot in marsupials.

The living musky rat-kangaroo is not a real potoroine but a member of probably the most ancient of macropodoid lineages, the Hypsiprymnodontidae. This terrestrial forest relic, with its prehensile tail but kangaroo-like locomotion, allows a glimpse at some aspects of the phalanger-macropodoid transition.

Suborder Vombatiformes
The two certainly monophyletic semisuborders included here may actually be an artificial group because their shared derived charac-

ters, such as (a) robust limbs, (b) the enlarged scaphoid bone in the wrist (Figure 6), and (c) loss of the lunate bone in the wrist, may well have evolved convergently. If true, then each taxon would merit subordinal rank.

Semisuborder Vombatimorphia
The ancestral vombatimorphian was probably terrestrial but had retained a grasping big toe. The extinct ilariids and the vombatid wombats, along with the koalas (Phascolarctidae), are what we

Marsupial paleobiogeography

(arrows show dispersal, broken arrows possible dispersal or vicariance, solid lines indicate barriers, and broken lines probable filter routes or sweepstakes dispersals)

(in the latest Cretaceous-Eocene only Metatheria and Monotremata are shown)

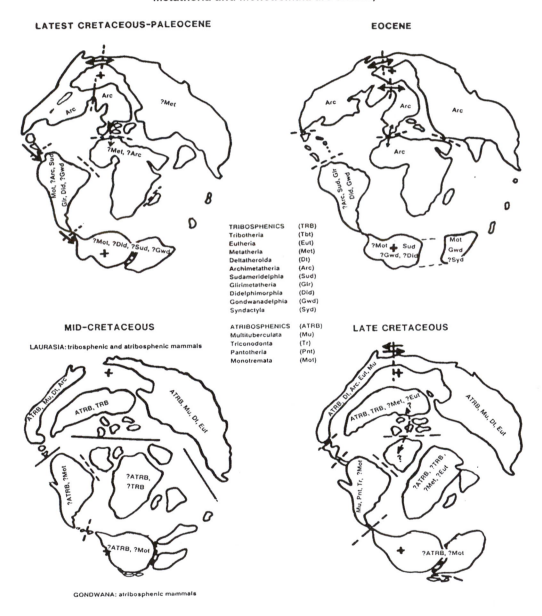

Figure 8. Marsupial paleobiogeography that appears to be the most corroborated of competing hypotheses on the basis of both phylogenetic analysis of fossil and extant taxa and known plate tectonic evidence.

Table 1.

Classification of Theria and Metatheria

Subclass **Theria** Parker and Haswell, 1897

Infraclass **Tribotheria** Butler, 1978
Order **Aegialodontia** Butler, 1978
Family **Aegialodontidae** Kermack, Lees, and Mussett, 1965
Order **Pappotherida** Butler, 1978
Family **Pappotheriidae** Slaughter, 1965
Infraclass **Eutheria** Gill, 1872
Infraclass **Metatheria** Huxley, 1880
Cohort **Holarctidelphia** Szalay, 1994
Order **Asiadelphia** Trofimov and Szalay, 1994
Family **Asiatheriidae** Trofimov and Szalay, 1994
Order **Deltatheroida** Kielan-Jaworowska, 1982
Family **Deltatheroididae** Kielan-Jaworowska, 1982
Family **Deltatheridiidae** Gregory and Simpson, 1926
Cohort **Ameridelphia** Szalay, 1982
Order **Didelphida** Szalay, 1982
Suborder **Archimetatheria** Szalay, 1994
Family **Stagodontidae** Marsh, 1889
Family **Pediomyidae** Simpson, 1927
Suborder **Sudameridelphia** Szalay, 1994
Infraorder **Itaboraiformes** Szalay, 1994
Family **Caroloameghiniidae** Ameghino, 1901
Family **Pucadelphydae** de Muizon, 1997
Infraorder **Polydolopimorphia** Ameghino, 1897
Family **Prepidolopidae** Pascual, 1981
Family **Polydolopidae** Ameghino, 1897
Family **Bonapartheriidae** Pascual, 1981
Infraorder **Sparassodonta** Ameghino, 1894
Family **Borhyaenidae** Ameghino, 1894
Family **Thylacosmilidae** Riggs, 1933
Suborder **Glirimetatheria** Szalay, 1994
Infraorder **Paucituberculata** Ameghino, 1894
Family **Caenolestidae** Trouessart, 1898
Infraorder **Simpsonitheria** Szalay, 1994
Family **Gashterniidae** Marshall, 1987
Family **Groberiidae** Patterson, 1982
Family **Argyrolagidae** Ameghino, 1904
Family **Patagoniidae** Pascual and Carlini, 1987

Classification of Theria and Metatheria (continued)

Suborder **Didelphimorphia** Gill, 1872
Family **Didelphidae** Gray, 1821
Family **Sparassocynidae** Reig, 1958
Cohort **Australidelphia** Szalay, 1982
Order **Gondwanadelphia** Szalay, 1994
Suborder **Microbiotheria** Ameghino, 1889
Family **Microbiotheriidae** Ameghino, 1887
Suborder **Dasyuromorphia** Gill, 1872
Family **Dasyuridae** Goldfuss, 1820
Family **Myrmecobiidae** Waterhouse, 1838
Family **Thylacinidae** Bonaparte, 1838
Order **Syndactyla** Wood-Jones, 1923–25
Semiorder **Peramelina** Gray, 1825
Family **Notoryctidae** Ogilby, 1892
Family **Peramelidae** Gray, 1825
Semiorder **Diprotodontia** Owen, 1866
Suborder **Phalangeriformes** Szalay, 1982
Superfamily **Phalangeroidea** Thomas, 1888
Family **Phalangeridae** Thomas, 1888
Superfamily **Petauroidea** Gill, 1872
Family **Petauridae** Gill, 1872
Family **Tarsipedidae** Gervais and Verreaux, 1842
Superfamily **Macropodoidea** Gray, 1821
Family **Hypsiprymnodontidae** Collett, 1877
Family **Macropodidae** Gray, 1821
Suborder **Vombatiformes** Woodburne, 1984
Semisuborder **Vombatomorphia** Aplin and Archer, 1987
Superfamily **Phascolarctoidea** Owen, 1839b
Family **Phascolarctidae** Owen, 1839b
Superfamily **Vombatoidea** Burnett, 1830
Family **Vombatidae** Burnett, 1830
Family **Ilariidae** Tedford and Woodburne, 1987
Semisuborder **Diprotodontiformes** Szalay, 1994
Superfamily **Wynyardioidea** Osgood, 1921
Family **Wynyardiidae** Osgood, 1921
Superfamily **Thylacoleonioidea** Gill, 1872
Superfamily **Diprotodontoidea** Gill, 1872
Family **Diprotodontidae** Gill, 1872
Family **Palorchestidae** Tate, 1948
Suborder **Yalkaparidontia** Archer et al., 1988
Family **Yalkaparidontidae** Archer et al., 1988

know of this once-major radiation of diprotodontians. There is strong evidence from comparative morphology that the tailless koalas with their backward opening pouches (both conditions resemble wombats) represent a group that returned to the trees but that acquired its predilection for vegetable matters in their earlier terrestrial ancestry. While the cheek teeth of the modern wombats are evergrowing, which means they do not wear out in the life of the animals, the Miocene vombatids did not show this adaptation.

Semisuborder Diprotodontiformes

The Diprotodontiformes contains some of the most spectacular marsupials that ever lived in Australia. It includes the poorly known and probably ancestral wynyardioids, the tapirlike vegetarian palorchestids with their huge claws (the last of which was a horse-sized animal that survived into the Pleistocene) and the diprotodontids, which ranged in size from a small sheep to a large hippopotamus. In fact, the last surviving giant *Diprotodon optatum* was the largest marsupial that ever lived. Both palorchestids and diprotodontids probably competed with kangaroos for ground vegetation. The diprotodonts were likely losing this race, and their large size, slow locomotion, and (probably) slow wits made them the easiest prey for the humans that entered Australia as far back as 50,000 years ago, in the late Pleistocene.

The spectacular Thylacoleoniodae was a carnivorous radiation of diprotodontiforms, with species ranging from cat- to leopard-sized animals. However, unlike placental felids (cats), thylecoleonids were not digitigrade—that is, they did not walk primarily on the toes, with the heel raised—therefore, thylecoleonids were not pursuit predators like some felids. Some rather esoteric attributes of the foot skeleton of these carnivores appear to link them with some of the other herbivorous diprotodontiforms, upon which they probably preyed.

Suborder *Yalkaparidontia*

The Yalkaparidontia, an odd group with an enlarged pair of front incisors and highly modified cheek teeth, is known from a phalangeroid-like skull. Allocation of the genus *Yalkapariodon* to the Diprotodontia is strongly corroborated by the way that the enlarged lower incisor meets with the unenlarged second and third upper incisors, much like the primitive diprotodontians.

Paleobiogeography and the Evolution of Marsupials

Distribution patterns of extinct and extant marsupial taxa partly reflect progressive isolation due to continental fragmentation and drift (vicariance biogeography). This isolation was periodically punctuated by dispersal events across ocean barriers, island chains, and other tenuous links.

The marsupials have been a puzzling and important group in discussions of biogeography and evolution because they seem to have been present at various times in virtually all continental landmasses (Figure 8).

The origins of metatherians can be safely dated probably at least 130 million years ago in the Early Cretaceous, perhaps the minimum time of the split between the Eutheria and Metatheria. We know unequivocally that marsupials were present during the Cretaceous in North America and Asia. The teeth and postcranial skeletons of metatherians that appear in the Eocene record of North America, Europe, Africa, and the Oligocene of Asia are from a stock that appears to be archimetatherian. Their exact origin is not well understood, but they are certainly not didelphids.

The South American Cretaceous record of marsupials is conspicuous by its complete absence in well-sampled vertebrate faunas (e.g., Los Alamitos fauna), where nontherian mammals were present in abundance without any of the typically tribosphenic molar teeth that signal the earliest therians. Nevertheless, either in the latest Cretaceous or earliest Paleocene, the marsupials appear there (along with condylarth and pantodontan immigrants), and their spectacular descendants, as seen in the Tiupampa, Itaboraí, and Rio Chico faunas, appear to have had a single source, judged from the dental and tarsal evidence. There is no other viable explanation but dispersal of a lineage (or at most several closely allied species) into South America.

The movement of marsupials into Australia (and undoubtedly the intervening Antarctica during the Paleogene) demands a similar explanation. All australidelphian groups can be traced back to an ancestry that is undoubtedly didelphid derived; and likewise, the modern family of opossums is also a derived group, compared to its Paleocene South American relatives. There are no other primitive groups in Australia that could replace the didelphids as a more likely source of the Australidelphia. This success story of dispersal continued as southeast Asia received its share of australidelphians up to "Wallace's line" (the one drawn passing south between Bali and Lombok) as the Australian plate drifted north and collided with the Philippine one. This tectonic movement created the New Guinea Highlands and provided the corridor (or filter) at varying times for a series of dispersal events from Australia toward southeast Asia.

FREDERICK S. SZALAY

See also Reproductive Strategies: Vertebrates

Work Cited

Gregory, W.K. 1951. *Evolution Emerging: A Survey of Changing Patterns from Primeval Life to Man.* Vols. 1 and 2. New York: Macmillan.

Further Reading

Archer, M., and G. Clayton (eds.). 1984. *Vertebrate Zoogeography and Evolution in Australasia: Animals in Space and Time.* Carlisle, Western Australia: Hesperian.

Marshall, L.G., C. de Muizon, and D. Sigoneau-Russell. 1995. Pucadelphys andinus (Marsupialia, Mammalia) from the early Paleocene of Bolivia. *Mémoires du Muséum d'Histoire Naturelle* 165:1–164.

Szalay, F.S. 1994. *Evolutionary History of the Marsupials and an Analysis of Osteological Characters.* New York and Cambridge: Cambridge University Press.

Szalay, F.S., and B.A. Trofimov. 1996. The Mongolian Late Cretaceous Asiatherium, and the early phylogeny and paleobiogeography of Metatheria. *Journal of Vertebrate Paleontology* 16 (3):474–509.

MATTHEW, WILLIAM DILLER

Canadian, 1871–1930

William Diller Matthew, one of the greatest of North American paleontologists, was born in St. John, New Brunswick on 19 February 1871. Matthew's father, George Frederic Matthew, an official in the Customs Service of Canada, spent his leisure hours studying the geology and paleontology of the Canadian maritime provinces. In the world of science he was an amateur; nonetheless, during his lifetime he published more than 200 scientific contributions, for which he was widely recognized. During his boyhood, Matthew accompanied his father on numerous geological field trips.

After graduating from the University of New Brunswick, Matthew went on to attend the School of Mines at Columbia, with every intention of becoming a mining geologist. During his time there he happened to take some graduate courses in vertebrate paleontology under Henry Fairfield Osborn. As a result, Matthew made a complete change in his scientific life, from hard rock geology to vertebrate paleontology. He received his doctorate in 1895. After Matthew completed his thesis, "The Effusive and Dyke Rocks near St. John, New Brunswick," Osborn, who was also curator at the American Museum of Natural History, appointed Matthew as assistant curator in the newly founded Department of Vertebrate Paleontology.

Matthew began his career at the American Museum collecting fossil reptiles. In the mid-1890s, he spent two miserably hot, humid summers in a North Carolina coal mine, vainly searching for Triassic mammals; instead, he found numerous reptilian fossils. In 1897 he was a member of the party collecting gigantic dinosaurs from the Bone Cabin quarry in the Morrison Formation in Wyoming.

Nonetheless, from that time on, Matthew devoted his field activities to the search for fossil mammals. For many seasons he worked in close collaboration with Walter Granger, obtaining Eocene faunas from the Bridger, Wasatch, and Wind River Bighorn basins of Wyoming. A series of classic papers by Matthew and Granger described these fossils. Matthew was also interested in very early mammalian faunas, which led to his huge monograph on the Paleocene mammals of the San Juan Basin, New Mexico. From more recent localities, he collected and described Miocene and Pliocene mammals from northeastern Colorado, from the famous Miocene quarries at Agate, Nebraska, and from the Miocene-Pliocene sediments at Snake Creek, Nebraska.

Matthew was a master of the study of rock strata, their formation, the succession of fauna that they revealed, and the chronological information contained therein. Yet he also gave much time and attention to various mammalian groups, notably the carnivores and the ungulates and particularly the horses. In these studies he emphasized "horizontal" relationships (those that lived together at the time), pointing out, for example, the relationships between Eocene perissodactyls (relatives of modern-day horses, rhinoceroses, and tapirs) or between early carnivores.

Matthew's studies of fossil mammals throughout the world led him to speculate on the origins and distributions of these vertebrates through geologic time. A result was his classic work, *Climate and Evolution,* which first appeared in 1915 and was reprinted in 1939. Matthew was writing before scholars' modern knowledge of plate tectonics, so the work reveals his firm belief in the permanence of continents. Therefore, his theory envisaged that mammalian (and other) vertebrates originated in northern latitudes, eventually spreading out to other continental regions along lines of present-day intercontinental connections. To explain certain faunal distributions, Matthew postulated that some vertebrates spread by means of natural rafts. Although such speculations are invalid today, they were a needed antidote at the time to the proliferating theories of immense transoceanic land bridges that had sunk to the oceanic depths in the distant past.

Matthew was a valued member of the American Museum scientific staff from 1895 until 1927. He then moved to the University of California at Berkeley, to take charge of the paleontological program there. He died there unexpectedly in 1930 of kidney failure.

Today, William Diller Matthew stands as one of the great students of the evolution and distribution of mammals and of mammalian faunas. His influence on modern students of mammalian evolution is widely felt, as it will be for years to come.

Matthew's career at the museum was a continuing story of outstanding paleontological field work and research that, over time, established him as a highly respected authority, particularly on fossil mammals, of international acclaim.

EDWIN H. COLBERT

Biography

Born in St. John, New Brunswick, 19 February 1871. Received B.A., University of New Brunswick, 1889; Ph.D. Columbia University, 1895. Member, curatorial staff of the American Museum of Natural History, 1895–1927; professor, University of California, Berkeley, 1927–30. Active collector and research student of fossil mammals, 1895–1930; published 352 scientific contributions in vertebrate paleontology. Died in San Francisco, California, 24 September 1930.

Major Publications

1909. *The Carnivora and Insectivora of the Bridger Basin, Middle Eocene.* Memoirs of the American Museum of Natural History, 9 (6). Cambridge, Massachusetts: Wheeler; Leiden: Brill.

1915. *Climate and Evolution.* Annals of the New York Academy of Sciences, 24 (6). New York: New York Academy of Sciences; 2nd ed., 1939.

1937. *Paleocene Faunas of the San Juan Basin, New Mexico.* Transactions of the American Philosophical Society, new ser., 30. Philadelphia: American Philosophical Society.

Further Reading

Colbert, E.H. 1992. *William Diller Matthew, Paleontologist. The Splendid Drama Observed.* New York: Columbia University Press.

MECHANORECEPTORS

See Lateral Line System

MESONYCHIDS

One of the most amazing stories in evolutionary biology is the origin of whales from land mammals. Archaic fossil whales first appeared in the Middle Eocene (approximately 50 million years ago) with a fully whalelike body, including a horizontal tail fluke, forelimbs modified into flippers, and no hind limbs. However, their distinctive triangular teeth provide a clue as to their origins: a group of hoofed mammals known as the mesonychids.

Mesonychids were the first group of mammals to become specialized meat-eaters, appearing in the middle Paleocene (approximately 62 million years ago), before more specialized carnivorous mammals (the creodonts and eventually the true carnivores) occupied that niche. Most mesonychids were the size and shape of large wolves or bears, although some were as small as foxes. Members of this group had a heavy robust skull armed with sharp canine teeth and huge round-cusped molar teeth, suitable not only for eating meat but also for crushing bone. The body was also very wolflike, with a long tail and limbs (Figure 1). Like many modern carnivores, mesonychids walked on the tips of their long toes, rather than flat-footed. Despite all these carnivorous adaptations, however, mesonychids were derived from hoofed mammals. The proof is in their toes, which had hooves rather than claws.

By the Early Eocene (approximately 55 million years ago), mesonychids had reached their peak of diversity, with wolf-sized beasts such as *Mesonyx* and *Harpagolestes* reigning as the largest carnivorous mammals of their time. However, they had to share their world with two other groups of carnivorous mammals: the creodonts (which soon surpassed them in size and diversity) and the true carnivores (which were still weasel-sized and which did not become large dog-sized or cat-sized predators until the Oli-

gocene (approximately 30 million years ago). By the Middle Eocene (approximately 50 to 47 million years ago), the mesonychids had declined rapidly in North America and Eurasia, where once they had dominated. The reasons for this decline are unclear. This period was a time of major climatic change, with global cooling and drying that destroyed the dense forests where mesonychids once had ruled. With the coming of open habitats, prey species became faster and more agile. Large, clumsy predators like mesonychids might have had difficulty finding cover to ambush their prey. In addition, some paleontologists speculate that mesonychids were less efficient at eating meat than creodonts or carnivorans, since the blunt, rounded cusps of mesonychid molars never developed the specialized, scissorlike shearing edges found in more specialized carnivorous mammals. For whatever reasons, in the late Middle Eocene the mesonychids were very rare. They disappeared from North America at the end of the Middle Eocene (approximately 37 million years ago) and from Asia in the Late Eocene (about 34 million years ago).

The last of the Asian mesonychids, however, was a truly spectacular beast known as *Andrewsarchus* (Figure 2). Only one specimen of this animal is known, but it is a skull almost a meter long, more than twice the size of any bear that has ever lived. If the rest of the animal were also bearlike, it would have been about four meters long, two meters high at the shoulder, and weighed almost four times as much as the largest known bear. It is possible that, since mesonychids were closely related to whales, the huge skull might just as easily have come from a whalelike body. However, the fossil was found in terrestrial deposits, so this seems less likely.

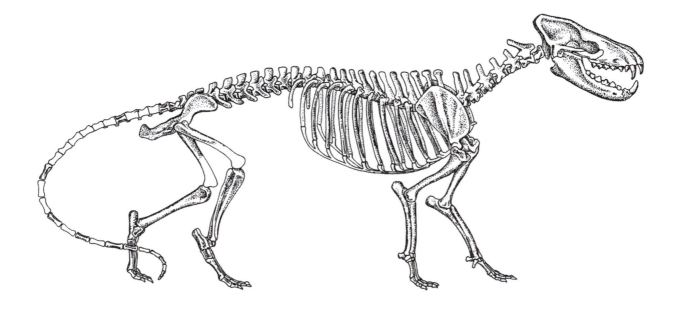

Figure 1. Skeleton of *Mesonyx*, a bear-sized mesonychid from the early Eocene of North America. From Scott (1888).

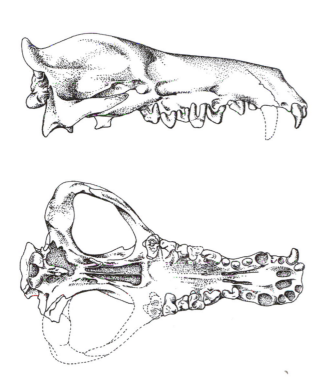

As the last of the mesonychids died out in the Late Eocene (approximately 34 million years ago), their close relatives, the whales, were already established in the oceans of the world. The connection between mesonychids and whales first was suggested by William Diller Matthew in 1937 and revived by Leigh Van Valen in 1968 and by Fred Szalay in 1969. The earliest whales have many features of the braincase and skull, and especially their distinctive, triangular-bladed teeth, that are very similar to the condition found in mesonychids. For years the oldest known whales of the early Middle Eocene (approximately 50 million years ago) were fully aquatic animals that lacked hind limbs and were very different from mesonychids. In the past few years, however, numerous transitional forms between whales and mesonychids have been found, dating from the Early Eocene of Africa and Asia. The most impressive of these is *Ambulocetus* from the early Eocene of Pakistan. Although it still has a mesonychid skull and teeth, its front and hind feet are both adapted for swimming. It does not yet have a tail fluke. Other fossil whales have even more specialized front flippers and have their hind limbs reduced to tiny vestiges and have a tail with a horizontal fluke. The transformation from a carnivorous hoofed mammal to a fully aquatic whale is now one of the best documented major evolutionary transitions in the fossil record.

DONALD R. PROTHERO

Figure 2. Meter-long skull of *Andrewsarchus,* the largest mesonychid ever found, from the late Eocene of Mongolia. From Osborn (1924).

See also Whales

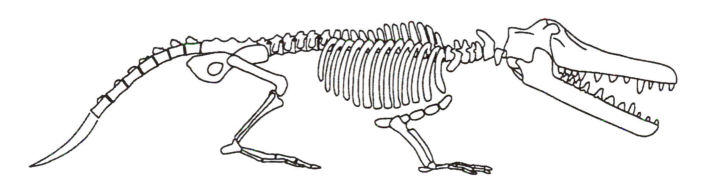

Figure 3. Reconstruction of *Abulocetus natans,* approximately 50 million years old, found in the Kala Chitta Hills of northern Pakistan. From Thewissen et al. (1996).

Further Reading

Carroll, R.L. 1988. *Vertebrate Paleontology and Evolution.* New York: Freeman.

Osborn, H.F. 1924. *Andrewsarchus,* giant mesonychid of Mongolia. *American Museum Novitates* 146:1–5.

Prothero, D.R., and R.M. Schoch. 1998. *Horns, Tusks, Hooves, and Flippers: The Evolution of Hoofed Mammals and Their Relatives.* Baltimore, Maryland: Johns Hopkins University Press; Princeton, New Jersey: Princeton University Press.

Savage, R.J.G., and M.R. Long. 1986. *Mammal Evolution: An Illustrated Guide.* London: British Museum (Natural History); New York: Facts-on-File.

Scott, E.B. 1888. On some new and little known creodonts. *Journal of the Academy of Natural Sciences of Philadelphia* 9:155–85.

Szalay, F.S. 1969. The Hapalodectinae and a phylogeny of the Mesonychidae. *American Museum Novitates* 2361:1–26.

Szalay, F.S., and S.J. Gould. 1966. Asiatic Mesonychidae (Mammalia, Condylarthra). *Bulletin of the American Museum of Natural History* 132:127–74.

Thewissen, J.G.M., S.I. Madar, and S.T. Hussain. 1996. *Ambulocetus natans,* an Eocene cetacean (Mammalia) from Pakistan. *Courier Forschungs-Institut Senckenberg* 190:1–86.

METAZOAN PHYLA, MINOR

It is beyond the scope of this discussion to provide a thorough discussion of the features of all those phyla (major groups; singular, phylum) with a minimal fossil record or those that are a minor component of most fossil assemblages. Instead, a brief description of their more distinctive morphological characters and fossil record is given, along with a table that summarizes some fundamental features of body organization (Table 1).

A characteristic of small and parasitic invertebrates is the absence of specialized structures for circulation, excretion, or gas exchange. The simplest form of metazoan (multicellular animals) body organization is diploblastic and is exemplified by the Cnidaria and Ctenophora. These have two layers of true tissue (or germ layers), an outer ectoderm, and inner endoderm. Between them is a gelatinous mesenchyme, which contains scattered unspecialized cells. More derived (specialized) groups have a third tissue layer, the mesoderm; hence, they are called triploblastic. The mesoderm may be a solid mass of tissue (as in the phylum Platyhelminthes, or flatworms), or incorporate a fluid-filled cavity (called a coelom) between the body wall and the gut. In true coelomates, a thin, cellular lining (peritoneum) derived from the mesoderm encloses the organs. Pseudocoelomates have no such membrane, and the organs lie free within what is really a persistent blastocoel (the cavity formed within the "hollow-ball" stage of very early embryonic development). A hypothesis of relationships between some of the phyla described here and other metazoan groups is illustrated in Figure 1.

Ctenophora

Comb-jellies are among the most primitive of the extant Metazoa. Many features of their body plan are similar to the cnidarians (symmetry, gelatinous mesenchyme, absence of a coelom, and a simple, reticulate—or netlike—nervous system), but these may be convergent (independently evolved) adaptations to a similar mode of life. However, the comb-jellies exhibit no alternation of generations, nor do they live any stage of their lives as sessile organisms, attached to the seafloor or any other surface. True muscle cells develop within the middle tissue layer (a character typical of triploblastic metazoans), but scholars disagree about whether the mesenchyme represents true mesoderm. The body of all Recent taxa (groups; singular, taxon) bears eight comb plates (ctenes), each bearing a single comb composed of a long, transverse (crosswise) band of fused cilia (short, hairlike structures), and controlled by a unique structure called an apical sense organ. The apical sense organ coordinates the movement of the cilia and plays a role in orientation of the animal in water. It appears that nervous impulses cause the cilia to beat sychronously. As adults, many species have a pair of prominent tentacles, one on each side of the body, emerging posteriorly (toward the rear of the body). The tentacles are embedded in a deep, ciliated pit, into which they may be withdrawn. Adhesive structures called colloblasts function to capture prey.

Being composed mostly of water, fossil ctenophores are rare. Two pyritized species (fossils formed of iron sulfide) similar to modern cydippids (commonly known as "sea gooseberries"), are known from the Devonian Hunsrück slate of southern Germany (Stanley and Stürmer 1987). Older ctenophores (*Xanioascus canadensis* and *Ctenorhabdotus capulus*) from the Middle Cambrian Burgess Shale of Canada differ from their modern counterparts, principally in terms of the number of comb rows per plate (a total of 24 rather than 8 comb rows). A third species, *Fasciculus vesanus,* from the same location, differs from Recent taxa more significantly (80 comb rows).

Platyhelminthes

The flatworms are among the most simply organized, triploblastic, bilaterally symmetrical animal groups. According to some hypotheses, flatworms represent the primitive body plan from which other triploblastic phyla may have been derived. The flattened body design provides a high surface area-to-volume ratio. In such cases, even the most internal cells can acquire gases and nutrients directly from the environment or neighboring cells; waste cells are also removed directly to the environment. As a result, flatworms have no need for specialized circulatory and gas exchange structures, although other organ systems are reasonably complex in nonparasitic groups. Two classes, the Trematoda (flukes) and Cestoda (tapeworms), are entirely parasitic and have no fossil record whatever. A third class, Turbellaria, is predominantly aquatic and includes free-living and endosymbiotic forms. Recent turbellarians may reach lengths of 60 millimeters or more, but most are in the region of 10 millimeters. Cocoons or fertilized egg capsules of tricladids have been found widely distributed in Pleistocene lake deposits in the Canadian Arctic, East Africa, Europe, and the United States. Three unnamed species have been found in petroliferous nodules in a Miocene lake in the Calico Mountains of California. Other possible body fossils (*Platypholinia* and *Vladimissa*) date from the Vendian of the White Sea region in far northwestern Russia and have been assigned to two unnamed families. However, like all Precambrian metazoans (with the exception of the Cnidaria), their affinities are uncertain.

Nemertea

"Ribbon worms" can reach lengths of nearly 30 meters, although most are very much shorter. The vast majority are marine (live in saltwater bodies), although there are some freshwater species, and a few terrestrial (land-based) forms are found in moist tropical habitats. Members of this group share several features with the platyhelminthes, including a similarly organized nervous system, similar types of sense organs, and a protonephridial excretory system (excretory tubules, ending blindly internally). Unlike the platyhelminthes, the gut is complete, and there is a well-developed circulatory system. It is uncertain whether nemerteans possess a coelom. While their bodies are relatively solid (and therefore functionally acoelomate), some blood vessels are thought to be the rudiments of a coelom.

Table 1:

Characters of Some Metazoan Phyla.

Notably	Overall Morphology	Organization of Body	Gut	Nervous System	Specialized Circulatory System	Specialized Gas Exchange Structures	Specialized Excretory Structures	Reproduction
Ctenophora	Biradially symmetrical. Body axis oral-aboral.	Diploblastic or triploblastic? Acoelomate. Ectoderm and endoderm separated by mesenchyme.	Gastrovascular cavity (gut) is the only body cavity. Intricately branched and complete.	Nerve net or plexus (more complex than cnidarians).	None except gut.	None except gut.	None except gut.	Most hermaphroditic.
Platyhelminthes	Bilaterally symmetrical. Usually dorsoventrally flattened.	Triploblastic. Acoelomate.	Complex though incomplete. Absent in some parasites.	Ladderlike. Anterior cerebral ganglion and (usually) longitudinal nerve cords connected by transverse commisures.	None except for small lymphatic channels in some flukes.	None.	Protonephridia.	Hermaphroditic, with complex reproductive systems.
Nemertea	Bilaterally symmetrical. Vermiform.	Triploblastic. Acoelomate or coelomate?	Gut complete. Unique proboscis apparatus dorsal to the gut, surrounded by a coelom-like hydrostatic chamber (rhynchocoel).	Lobed, supraenteric cerebral ganglion, and two or more longitudinal nerve cords connected by transverse commisures.	Closed circulatory system.	None.	Protonephridia.	Most gonochoristic.
Rotifera	Bilaterally symmetrical.	Triploblastic. Pseudocoelomate.	Complete and regionally specialized. Pharynx modified as a mastax, containing jaw-like elements.	Cerebral ganglion dorsal to mastax. Several tracts arise from this, some with small ganglia. Two major longitudinal nerves. Unique, retrocerebral ganglion.	None.	None.	None.	Males reduced or absent. Parthenogenesis common.

Table 1:

Characters of Some Metazoan Phyla. (Continued)

Notably	Overall Morphology	Organization of Body	Gut	Nervous System	Specialized Circulatory System	Specialized Gas Exchange Structures	Specialized Excretory Structures	Reproduction
Priapulida	Bilaterally symmetrical. Superficially annulated. Vermiform.	Triploblastic. Coelomate or pseudocoelomate. Body cavities not lined with peritoneum.	Gut complete.	Radially arranged and largely intraepidermal. No cerebral ganglion as such. Circumcentric nerve ring within epithelium of buccal tube gives rise to the main ventral nerve cord. This, in turn, gives off ring nerves and peripheral nerves along the body.	None. Amoebocytes and erythrocytes within coelomic fluid.	Many have unique caudal appendage that serves for gas exchange.	Numerous protonephridia associated with the gonads as a urogenital system.	Gonochoristic.
Sipuncula	Bilaterally symmetrical. Vermiform.	Triploblastic. Schizocoelomate.	Complete and U-shaped. Anus dorsal.	Nervous system on annelid-like plan, but simple and with no evidence of segmentation.	Compensation system associated with the tentacles. Coelomic fluid contains amebocytes and red blood cells.	Coelomic channels may extend through body wall muscles and into the epidermis, where they may function for gas exchange.	One pair of metanephridia. Coelomic fluid with specialized multicellular structures (urns) for waste collection.	Usually sexual and dioecious. Occasionally asexual by transverse fission and regeneration.
Echiura	Bilaterally symmetrical. Vermiform.	Triploblastic. Schizocoelomate.	Complete. Anus terminal.	Nervous system on annelid-like plan, but simple and with no evidence of segmentation.	Most with a simple, closed circulatory system. Blood is unpigmented, but red blood cells with hemoglobin occur in the coelomic fluid.	Muscles pump oxygenated water in and out of the hind gut (cloacal irrigation).	Metanephridia and anal vesicles.	Sexual and dioecious.

Table 1:

Characters of Some Metazoan Phyla. (Continued)

Notably	Overall Morphology	Organization of Body	Gut	Nervous System	Specialized Circulatory System	Specialized Gas Exchange Structures	Specialized Excretory Structures	Reproduction
Pogonophora/ Vestimentifera	Bilaterally symmetrical. Vermiform. Hind part of body metameric.	Triploblastic. Coelomate. Anterior body cavities not well developed in Vestimentifera.	Adult vestimentiferans lack a gut. Pogonophorans lack a gut at any stage in the life history.	Intraepidermal nervous system. Large adneural ganglion in prosoma gives rise to nerve ring and a single ventral nerve cord. Pogonophoran opisthosoma with three nerve cords, typically bearing ganglia. Vestimentiferan opisthosoma with single, unganglionated nerve cord.	Well developed and closed. Adneural and antineural blood vessels run almost the length of the body. Antineural vessel swollen anteriorly as a "heart." Similar to annelids.	Tentacles probably most important site of gas exchange.	Coelomoduct-like structures (protonephridia) from the coelom to the outside.	Sexual and dioecious.
Tardigrada	Bilaterally symmetrical. Metameric, homonomous (just four pairs of legs) and weakly cephalized.	Triploblastic. Coelomate, but greatly reduced. Confined to gonadal cavities in adults. Main body cavity is a hemocoel (as in arthropods).	Simple and complete.	Nervous system on annelid-like plan. Distinctly metamerous. Double, ventral nerve cord connects four ganglia associated with each pair of legs.	None.	None.	Malpighian tubules at mid-gut/hind-gut junction (possible osmoregulatory function). Some excretory products absorbed by gut or shed with molt.	Gonochoristic. Usually dioecious, though some hermaphroditic. Parthenogesis in some groups.
Onychophora	Bilaterally symmetrical. Metameric, homonomous. Variably cephalized (head quite well differentiated in modern taxa).	Triploblastic. Coelomate, but coelom greatly reduced. Confined to gonadal cavities in adults. Main body cavity is a hemocoel (as in arthropods).	Simple and complete.	Nervous system on annelid-like plan. Distinctly metamerous. Double, ventral nerve cord connects ganglia associated with each pair of legs.	Arthropod-like. Dorsal, tubular heart open at each end, with a pair of ostia in each segment. Open circulation within hemocoel.	Tracheae and spiracles.	Nephridia (probably modified metanephridia) in each segment.	Gonochoristic. Dioecious.

Table 1:

Characters of Some Metazoan Phyla. (Continued)

Notably	Overall Morphology	Organization of Body	Gut	Nervous System	Specialized Circulatory System	Specialized Gas Exchange Structures	Specialized Excretory Structures	Reproduction
Pentastomida	Bilaterally symmetrical. Metameric and weakly cephalized.	Triploblastic. Coelomate, but greatly reduced. Confined to gonadal cavities in adults. Main body cavity is a hemocoel (as in arthropods).	Simple and complete.	Nervous system on annelid-like plan. Distinctly metamerous, with up to five anterior ganglia.	None.	None.	None.	Gonochoristic. Dioecious.
Entoprocta	Bilaterally symmetrical. Vermiform.	Triploblastic. Area between gut and body filled with mesenchyme. Functionally acoelomate.	Complete and U-shaped.	Greatly reduced. Single sub-enteric ganglion giving rise to pairs of nerves.	None.	None.	One pair of protonephridia.	Most hermaphroditic. Some protandric. Some may be dioecious.
Phoronida	Bilaterally symmetrical. Vermiform. Trimeric.	Coelomate, but divided into three sections.	Gut U-shaped. Anus close to mouth.	Diffuse and lacks a distinct cerebral ganglion. Most nerves are intimately associated with the body wall.	Closed circulatory system. Large afferent and efferent vessels.	Lophophore and tentacles probably most important sites of gas exchange.	One pair of nephridia in each metasome.	Gonochoristic or hermaphroditic.
Chaetognatha	Bilaterally symmetrical. Streamlined and elongate. Trimeric.	Coelomate, but divided into three sections. Body cavities not lined with peritoneum.	Complete. Anus ventral at trunk-tail junction.	Large dorsal (cerebral) and ventral (subenteric) ganglia, connected by circumenteric connectives.	None.	None.	None.	Gonochoristic. Hermaphroditic. Asexual reproduction common.

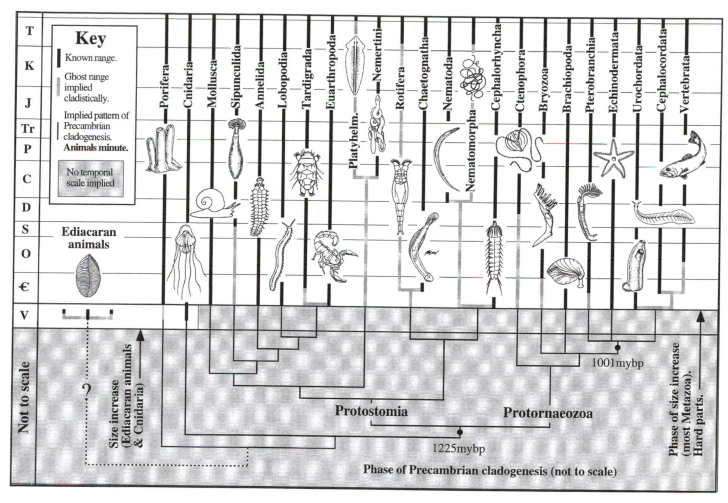

Figure 1. An evolutionary scenario for the Metazoa (not all phyla illustrated), allowing for extended divergence times. Skeletization (accompanied by an increase in size) marks the Cambrian-Precambrian boundary, 545 million years ago. The Cephalorhyncha contains the Priapulida, Loricifera, Kinorhyncha, and Gordiacea. Key: *V*, Vendian period, which preceded the Cambrian. From Fortey et al. (1997). Copyright © 1997 John Wiley and Sons, Inc., reprinted by permission of John Wiley and Sons, Inc., and Matthew A. Wills.

The most distinctive feature of nemerteans is a large proboscis (trunklike structure), which usually lies inside the body, within a specialized coelom-like, hydrostatic sac, the rhynchocoel. The entire structure can be rapidly everted (turned inside out) and wrapped around prey items. In the Class Anopla, the proboscis is unarmed but secretes a sticky, toxic fluid. In the Enopla the proboscis is also tipped with one or more nail-shaped stylets, which can be used to infiltrate the prey with toxins. Most nemerteans take small invertebrates, such as crustaceans and annelids, but some are oviparous (feed on eggs) or they feed on microbes within the mantle cavity of molluscs. Unsurprisingly for an almost entirely soft-bodied group, the fossil record of nemerteans is very sparse. Although the calcium phosphate stylets are likely candidates for fossilization, none have been reported to date. *Archisymplectes* from the Pennsylvanian Mazon Creek fauna of central Illinois (Carbondale Formation) was probably a nemertean, but only the outline of the animal is preserved. *Amiskwia,* from the Middle Cambrian Burgess Shale, resembles some aberrant deep-sea nemerteans, but the evidence for placing it in the group is minimal.

Rotifera

The rotifers are tiny Metazoa, some reaching lengths of three millimeters, but most not exceeding one millimeter. These animals assume a wide variety of life habits and body forms. Most live in fresh water, but a few are marine, and some live in damp soil or the water films on mosses (with striking cryptobiotic—camouflage—adaptations). Aquatic forms may swim, creep, or be sessile (fixed in place) on plants. Most are divided into a head, trunk, and foot. Anteriorly (toward the front) is a crown of cilia (corona), which, when active, gives the impression of a pair of rotating wheels (Rotifera means "wheel bearers"). The corona functions in locomotion and food gathering. The body is covered with a cuticle (lorica), which tends to be thinner and annulated (segmented) in errant forms to improve flexibility. The foot is often elongate and telescopic, armed at the far end with spines or a pair of "toes" through which pass ducts from adhesive pedal glands. The gut is complete, with a prominent, jawed pharynx (mastax) anteriorly. Only one convincing fossil rotifer is known, possibly a species of *Keratella,* from the lower Middle Eocene of North Maslin sands, near Adelaide, Australia.

Priapulida

Priapulids are cylindrical, vermiform (worm-shaped) animals, ranging in length from about 0.5 millimeters to 20 centimeters. All are marine and benthic (bottom-dwellers), and most are burrowers. The body comprises an introvert (or proboscis), a necklike collar, a trunk or abdomen, and posteriorly a caudal appendage, or tail (in some forms). Priapulids are bilaterally symmetrical but have a tendency to revert to radial symmetry. They may bear superficial annulations (segmentlike divisions), but they are not organized into body segments. In all modern priapulids, the entire proboscis (which bears the mouth on its tip) can be pulled back into the abdomen by muscles. The introvert itself bears small, conical or hooked projections (scalids) arranged in circles and longitudinal rows. The function of these projections is uncertain, but their form and arrangement are important for classification. The epidermis secretes a thin outer cuticle, which is periodically molted. Beneath the epidermis are layers of longitudinal and circular muscle, comprising a tube that also extends over the alimentary canal.

Caudal appendage(s) (where present) have a lumen (open bore) continuous with the body cavity and may serve for gas exchange. The nervous system is arranged radially and lies predominantly within the epidermis. The gut is complete. A buccal (inside of the mouth) tube armed with backward-pointing teeth leads into a highly muscular pharynx, variously armed with scalids and other elements. The buccal tube and anterior portion of the pharynx can be everted through the mouth to capture prey. The pharynx leads via the esophagus to the intestine, which has a thick epithelium and is bounded by a muscular tube of inner circular and outer longitudinal muscles. The intestine (the only part of the alimentary canal that derives from the endoderm) narrows to join the ectodermally lined rectum, while the anus is situated on the posterolateral (rear side) or posteroventral (rear belly) surface of the abdomen.

Modern priapulids tend to be restricted to harsh, marginal environments, but a comparatively rich Cambrian fossil record suggests that they were once a much more important constituent of faunas that lived in muddy-bottomed, sloped environments. Five fossil priapulid genera have been described from the Middle Cambrian Burgess Shale (*Ancalagon, Fieldia, Ottoia, Selkirkia,* and *Scolecofurca*) (Conway Morris 1977), and another from the Chengjiang fauna of the Yunnan Province in China (*Maotianshania*). These archaeopriapulids were able to evert the pharynx completely, whereas their Recent counterparts cannot. Other important differences concern the arrangement of the teeth and scalids and the location of the anus.

Another group of fossil worms, the Palaeoscolecida, were once thought to be annelids, but Recent evidence suggests they are probably also priapulids. Palaeoscolecidans have a fossil record extending from the Lower Cambrian to the Late Silurian; it includes the Chengjiang *Cricocosmia* and *Palaeoscolex* (Conway Morris 1997) and the Burgess Shale *Louisella* (Conway Morris 1977). The most recent fossil priapulid, *Priapulites,* from the Upper Carboniferous Francis Creek Shale (Schram 1973), is a member of the extant family Priapulidae.

Recent families appear to constitute a crown group (group containing extant, i.e., living members) in the evolutionary tree of priapulids, with the fossils branching off in two groups near the base. *Fieldia* and *Ancalagon* are the most primitive and anatomically least complex genera.

Sipuncula

"Peanut worms" have a body plan similar to annelids (segmented worms), but they lack any evidence of segmentation or chaetae (bristles). The coelom is well developed and fluid-filled, containing hemerythrocytes and free-floating clusters (ciliary urns) that collect waste. Circulatory and gas exchange systems are rudimentary and peripheral. The sausage-shaped body is divided into a retractable introvert and a thicker trunk. The mouth is situated anteriorly and is surrounded by rings of feeding tentacles (derived from the regions around the mouth and the nuchal organ, a ciliated sensory pit). The gut is complete but coiled and U-shaped; the anus is situated dorsally (on the back) near the junction of the introvert and the trunk (not terminally—at the very end—as in annelids).

Most sipunculids burrow into sand and mud, but some live in crevices in rocks or in empty shells. A minority are capable of boring into rock. Genera that lie with their tentacles at the interface of water and substrate (e.g., seabottom, coral surface, underwater rock shelf) are detritivores—they feed on dead material from animals and plants. Forms that burrow deeper into the substrate are direct deposit feeders—they ingest sediment and absorb nutrients from it within their guts. Those that burrow in calcareous substrates may use spines on their introverts to retrieve organic detritus.

While a close relationship of sipunculans to the annelids seems most likely, there are sipunculans that also have developmental similarities with the molluscs, both sharing a characteristic arrangement of cells in the embryo (the "molluscan cross"). The fossil record of sipunculans is suspect at best. *Skolithos* burrows found in Paleozoic rocks of all ages have been attributed to the group, but such traces could have been made equally well by any sedentary, vermiform animal. *Trypanites* from the lowest Devonian Bois Blanc Formation in Southern Ontario is the earliest, more characteristic trace fossil. Some hyoliths (conical shells with a coiled lid, usually classified in or with the molluscs) show traces of a looped, coiled gut, similar to that of sipunculans. Some extant (present-day) sipunculans secrete a calcified cuticular anal shield, and past relatives may have produced more elaborate shells. It is not impossible, therefore, that hyoliths (found throughout Paleozoic rocks) represent relatives of the sipunculans.

Echiura

Until recently, "spoon worms" were classified with the annelids and it still seems likely that they are close relatives. While echiurans have unsegmented bodies, their free-swimming trochophore larvae are very similar to those of polychaetes. Anteriorly, echiurans have an extensible proboscis, with tentacles derived from the region around the mouth (peripheral tentacles) and nuchal organ (nuchal tentacles). The mouth itself is situated at the bottom of a proboscis groove or gutter. The body may be smooth or warty and, like that of polychaetes, may bear chaetae. Posteriorly, there is a set of small hooks (echiurans means "spine-tails"). As in annelids, the gut is entire, and the anus is situated posteriorly. The nervous system is constructed on an annelid-like plan, but there is no evidence of segmentation. Blood is unpigmented, and flows within a system of closed vessels. Red blood cells with hemoglobin occur in the coelomic fluid.

Although there are only 150 species of living echiurans, they are relatively common in certain marine environments. Most burrow in sand and mud or live in surface detritus, but some may inhabit rock crevices. The majority feed on epibenthic (sea bottom) detritus, lying with the proboscis protruding from the sediment, and secreting a sticky mucous coating. The genus *Urechis* lives in a U-shaped burrow and catches food particles with an intricate mucous net, which it periodically ingests. U-shaped burrows are recorded as trace fossils throughout the Phanerozoic, but a number of other phyla may have produced them. The Recent family Echiuridae has a probable fossil representative (*Protechiurus edmonsi*) in the Precambrian (Glaessner 1979). Another Recent family, the Bonellidae, dates back to the Moscovian (*Coprinoscolex ellogimus* from the Moscovian Francis Creek Shale, Illinois; Jones and Thompson 1977).

Pogonophora and Vestimentifera

Pogonophorans (literally "beard-bearers") are a phylum exclusively restricted to the deep sea. Superficially, they resemble tube-dwelling polychaetes, but only the very hind part of the body is metameric (segmented) and bears chaetae. Notably, pogonophorans also lack any mouth, gut, or anus. The body is divided clearly into four regions. An anterior cephalic lobe bears from one to over 200 thin tentacles in a lophophore-like conformation (a horseshoe-shaped or coiled "beard"). Each tentacle has tiny side branches (pinnules). Behind this is a relatively short mesosoma (forepart), followed by the main trunk region (metasoma). Each of the first three body divisions has its own coelom. The worms fragment easily on collection, so until relatively recently, the segmented, terminal opisthosoma was unknown. Without this last section, pogonophorans superficially resemble deuterostomes (animals with, among other things, indeterminate cleavage); as a result, scholars speculated on an affinity with the hemichordates. A close relationship with the annelids now seems certain, borne out by observations on their ciliated, motile larvae, which closely resemble those of polychaetes.

In 1977 a new phylum of worms, the Vestimentifera, were discovered living in huge numbers around Pacific hydrothermal vents (in areas where sea floor is forming, rifts are characterized by those vents which extrude hot, inorganic-rich seawater). Vestimentiferans ("garment bearers") are giant pogonophoran-like animals reaching lengths up to 1.5 meters. The two phyla certainly are related closely, and the Vestimentifera are sometimes ranked as a class *within* the Pogonophora. Although adult vestimentiferans lack a gut, juveniles pass through a transitory phase with one. There are also some differences in the organization of the nervous system and the structure of the secreted tubes.

In the absence of a gut, the method of nutrition in pogonophorans and vestimentiferans is puzzling. It appears they are able to absorb dissolved nutrients directly from the seawater surrounding the tentacles and from the mud surrounding the body, without the aid of enzymes. Some species may be capable of epidermal pinocytosis and phagocytosis (the skin is manipulated to surround drops of liquid or particles of food, respectively, then draw the materials into the body). However, most nutrition in vestimentiferans (and a portion in pogonophorans) is provided by endosymbiotic bacteria, bacteria that live within the animal and absorb nutrients from it, often providing the host with nutrients. These live in a specialized organ, the trophosome, which develops from the embryonic gut. ATP is generated by sulphide oxidation; this reduces CO_2 to organic matter, which in turn can be used by the worm.

Some pogonophorans and vestiminiforms produce tubes around them. These tubes, or their impressions in the substrate, can be fossilized. Fossil tubes, once thought to be those of pogonophorans (e.g., *Sabellidites* and *Saarina*) are abundant in some Upper Precambrian and Lower Cambrian rocks, particularly in eastern Europe and Russia. Differences in ultrastructure between such tubes and those of modern pogonophorans cast doubt on this assignment. C.T.S. Little and colleagues (1997) described a hydrothermal-vent community, including pogonophorans, from the Silurian of the southern Urals, Russia. Other possible pogonophorans include those found in lowest Ordovician rocks from Poland (*Ivanovites* and *Sokolovites*), Oligocene shales from the Keasey Formation in Oregon (*Adekunbiella*), and Lower Pliocene concretions from the Antwerp Basin in Belgium (*Tasselia*).

Onychophora

"Velvet worms" superficially resemble giant caterpillars and are almost certainly close relatives of the euarthropods ("true" arthropods). Living representatives vary in length between 1.5 and 15 centimeters, and are confined to warm, humid, terrestrial, and almost exclusively tropical habitats. Onychophorans have an uncalcified and weakly sclerotized cuticle, so the body is soft and flexible. There are from 14 to 43 pairs of homonomous (similarly structured), lobopodous (short, unjointed, fleshy) walking legs down the belly side of the trunk in extant species. The legs have a stepping motion very similar to those of euarthropods. At the tips of the legs are sclerotized claws. Many scholars believe that lobopodia gave rise to the jointed limbs of euarthropods. In Recent onychophorans, the head, though not clearly demarcated from the trunk, bears several specialized appendages (although their precise similarities to the cephalic appendages of euarthropods is contentious). Anteriorly there is a pair of fleshy, annulated (made of ringlike segments) antennae. Behind these are a pair of heavily sclerotized, bladelike jaws, housed within a peribuccal (around the outside of the mouth) cavity and covered by fleshy lips. Flanking the jaws are a pair of oral papillae (or "slime" papillae), capable of firing jets of quick-drying cement to entangle prey items or aggressors. Paired salivary glands open into a groove on the underside of the jaws, and saliva can be worked into the body of the prey where the saliva begins to digest it. Then, semiliquid tissues are sucked into the mouth. The anus is located ventrally or terminally in the last body segment.

Several lobopod taxa are preserved as fossils, most notably from the Cambrian. Cambrian forms differ in several respects from modern Onychophora, particularly in the degree of cephalization (formation of a clearly separate head). Some have anterior limbs that are differentiated from those that follow, but none has true antennae, jaws, or slime papillae. There is uncertainty over whether these animals should be included within the Onychophora, or whether they represent close relatives. *Aysheaia* from the Burgess Shale is perhaps the best-known Cambrian lobopod (Whittington 1978). This animal had 10 pairs of walking legs down the annulated trunk, while the head bore a single pair of laterally directed, spine-bearing lobopod appendages. The anteriormost limbs could be flexed forwards and in toward the midline, bringing their tips within reach of the terminal, anteriorly directed mouth. The mouth itself was surrounded by a ring of papillae. Posteriorly, the trunk did not extend beyond the last pair of appendages (in contrast to modern Onychophora). There is evidence to suggest that *Aysheaia* fed on sponges.

Xenusion was a similar, basal (of ancestral stock) Cambrian form from the Baltic region (Hou and Bergström 1995). It had 21 pairs of spiny, lobopodous walking limbs, but no front appendages were specialized. There was a pair of "humps" on the back, opposite each pair of legs. These were armed with prominent, sclerotized spines. Similar spines are common as fossils in the lowest Paleozoic, and many of these may have belonged to lobopods (although the soft, body fossils are much rarer). The affinities of the Burgess Shale fossil *Hallucigenia*, for example, were once uncertain.

Originally, *Hallucigenia* was reconstructed walking on its long stiltlike spines, waving ten tentacle-like legs above it. Only more recently was it realized that this animal was a lobopod that in life had spines that were directed dorsally (above the back). *Microdictyon* from the Lower Cambrian of the Siberian Platform and Middle Cambrian of Utah bore dorsal plates (scalelike structures) rather than spines. The corresponding ten pairs of elongated, fleshy limbs are thought to have functioned in a sliding or swimming locomotion. A similar animal, *Luolishania*, has been described from the Yunnan province of China. None of these taxa appears to have had any specialized front appendages. *Helenodora*, from the Upper Carboniferous Mazon Creek biota, appears to have been related very closely, if not indistinguishable from, modern Onychophora. Uncertainty arises since the anterior and posterior extremities of the animal are poorly preserved.

Tardigrada

The "water bears" are a phylum of tiny (0.1 to 1.7 millimeters long), bean-shaped animals, probably closely related to the euarthropods. Most live in thin water films on terrestrial plants or plant litter, but a minority are freshwater or benthic marine. The body is covered in a thin, periodically molted, uncalcified cuticle, sometimes divided into a symmetrical arrangement of dorsal and lateral (very occasionally ventral) plates. The body bears four pairs of homonomous, ventrolateral (side belly) legs in all living taxa—short, hollow (occasionally telescopic) extensions of the body wall. These terminate in between one and a dozen "toes" that have adhesive pads or claws (similar to those of onychophorans).

Tardigrades are weakly cephalized, the head lacking true appendages but bearing an array of sensory cirri and chemosensory clavae. A pair of oral stylets, which can be extended some way from the mouth, are used to pierce cell walls, from which fluids are sucked. Most tardigrades feed on plants or bacteria (and have the mouth situated ventrally), but a minority take small prey items (and have a terminal mouth). The mouth leads into a short buccal tube, which in turn leads to a bulbous, muscular pharynx. A pair of large salivary glands flank the esophagus and are also responsible for producing a new pair of oral stylets at each molt.

Freshwater species have three or four large glandular structures at the intestine-hindgut junction. In some taxa, these Malpighian tubules may regulate fluid content in the body, but it is unclear whether they are homologous with the Malpighian tubules of euarthropods. Tardigrades are extremely rare as fossils. Phosphatized, ancestral representatives have been found from the Middle Cambrian of Siberia (Walossek et al. 1994). While there are many detailed anatomical similarities with living groups, all possess three rather than four pairs of legs. A freshwater species, *Beorn leggi*, has also been described from amber at Cedar Lake, Manitoba.

Pentastomida

The "tongue worms" are all parasites in the lungs and nasal passages of vertebrates, primarily reptiles. These animals have just two pairs of small, lobelike legs bearing terminal claws (not dissimilar from those of onychophorans and tardigrades) at the front of the belly; they use the claws to attach to their hosts. In some species, the legs are reduced such that only the claws remain. The mouth lacks jaws, and may be situated at the end of a snoutlike anterior projection. Together with the four legs, this projection gives the animal the appearance of having five snouts, which explains the group name: "penta," five; "stomida," mouths. The body musculature is similar to that of annelids, and the cuticle is thin and contains no chitin. Specialized circulatory, excretory, and gas exchange systems have been lost, which is typical of most metazoan endoparasites (parasites that live within the body of the host). However, the nervous system is constructed on the annelid/arthropod plan. Detailed examinations of pentastomid morphology (shape and structure) and larval development has demonstrated fairly conclusively that these creatures are actually highly modified crustaceans, forming a sister group to the fish lice (Branchiura, Maxillopoda). Similar conclusions have been drawn from phylogenetic (based on genealogical relationships) studies using 18s rRNA data (Abele et al. 1989). Phosphatized fossils thought to be marine, ancestral representatives of the pentastomids have been described from Late Cambrian limestones of Västergötland, Sweden (Walossek and Müller 1994), and the Cambrian-Ordovician boundary beds of Newfoundland, Canada (Walossek et al. 1994).

Entoprocta

Entoprocts (literally "inside anus") are solitary or colonial, predominantly sessile metazoans. All but one extant genus are marine. In many respects, they resemble ectoprocts (bryozoans) and hydroids. Each zooid (individual entopoct) has a cuplike body (calyx) supported by a stalk. The stalk attaches directly to the substrate in solitary forms, or to larger branches and horizontal stolons in colonial taxa. Although technically bilaterally symmetrical, in many respects zooids are functionally radially symmetrical. The calyx is surrounded by a whorl of ciliated tentacles (the tentacular crown), which serves to filter food particles (mostly phytoplankton) from the surrounding water. Both the mouth and the anus are located on the surface of the calyx, the latter elevated on a large papilla (the anal cone). Unlike ectoprocts, entoprocts appear to be acoelomate. The region between the epidermis and gut is packed with mesenchyme, but it is uncertain whether this is the primitive condition or if the entoprocts have a secondarily filled pseudocoelom. Some scholars still consider that entoprocts may be ancestral to the ectoprocts. There is only one fossil occurrence, *Barentsia* (a representative of the modern family Barentsiidae), from the Upper Jurassic of Humberside, England. This has been preserved as colonies attached to an oyster *(Deltoideum)*.

Phoronida

Phoronids, or "horseshoe worms," are among the smaller and least familiar of animal phyla, containing just two modern, exclusively marine genera (*Phoronis* and *Phoronopsis*). The body has three regions; a flaplike prosome, lophophore-bearing mesosome, and an elongate trunk or metasome. Each region has its own coelom, at least at some stage during development. The gut is U-shaped but uncoiled, with the anus emerging anteriorly. A chitinous tube is secreted, and the animal usually lives cemented to a hard substrate (typically in clusters) or else buried in sand or mud. A few species bore into shells or calcareous rocks, making distinctive holes. The lophophore is composed of a double row of ciliated tentacles (sometimes organized in a double spiral), with a narrow food groove between them. Phoronids are ciliary-mucous suspension feeders. Most scholars consider them to be close relatives of the ectoprocts and brachiopods, since all three phyla have a lophophore, U-shaped guts, peritoneal glands, metanephridia, and a tendency to secrete outer casings. (Metanephridia are absent in ectoprocts.) No phoronid body fossils are known. Agglutinated tubes of sediment have a reasonably high preservation potential, but it is all but impossible to distinguish phoronid tubes from those of annelids, arthropods, and other phyla. The oldest phoronid-like borings date from the Devonian *(Talpina)*.

Chaetognatha

"Arrow worms" are strictly marine, mostly streamlined, elongate or sacciform, pelagic (open waters) predators (although a few species are benthic). Their bodies are typically transparent and range in length from about 0.5 to 12 centimeters. The body is divided into a head, trunk, and postanal (after the anus) tail, separated from one another by transverse septa (membranes). The head has one coelom, while the trunk and tail have two. The body bears lateral and caudal (tail) fins, supported by "rays" of an uncertain origin. A ventral mouth is surrounded by sets of grasping spines and teeth and is located within a ventral vestibule in the head. The vestibule can be enclosed by an anterolateral fold of the body wall, the hood. The head also bears a pair of uniquely arranged eyes (which probably originated from cilia), and a unique ciliary loop

comprising two rings of ciliated epithelial cells (these possibly function in sensing chemicals). Ciliary fans on the body wall appear to detect water-borne vibrations. The gut is simple and complete, with the anus located at the trunk-tail junction. There are a few benthic species of chaetognath, but most are adapted as voracious, pelagic predators. There are no unequivocal chaetognath fossils. Some workers believe that the "conodont animal" was a close relative of the chaetognaths. More particularly, H. Szaniawski (1987) has described detailed histological similarities between Cambrian protoconodont elements and the grasping elements of chaetognaths. Therefore it seems probable that chaetognaths and conodonts have a common ancestor.

MATTHEW A. WILLS

See also Problematic Animals; Superphyla

Works Cited

Abele, L.G., W. Kim, and B.E. Felgenhauer. 1989. Molecular evidence for the inclusion of the phylum Pentastomida in the Crustacea. *Molecular Biology and Evolution* 6:685–91.

Conway Morris, S. 1977. Fossil priapulid worms. *Special Papers in Palaeontology* 20:1–155.

Fortey, R.A., D.E.G. Briggs, and M.A. Wills. 1997. The Cambrian evolutionary "explosion" recalibrated. *Bioessays* 19:429–34.

Glaessner, M.F. 1979. An echiurid worm from the late Precambrian. *Lethaia* 12:121–24.

Hou, X., and J. Bergström. 1995. Cambrian lobopodians: Ancestors of extant onychophorans? *Zoological Journal of the Linnean Society* 114:3–19.

Jones, D., and I. Thompson. 1977. Echiura from the Pennsylvanian Essex fauna of northern Illinois. *Lethaia* 10:317–25.

Little, C.T.S., R.J. Herrington, V.V. Maslennikov, N.J. Morris, and V.V. Zaykov. 1997. Silurian hydrothermal-vent community from the southern Urals, Russia. *Nature* 385:146–48.

Schram, F.R. 1973. Pseudocoelomates and a nemertine from the Illinois Pennsylvanian. *Journal of Paleontology* 47:985–89.

Stanley, G.D., and W. Stürmer. 1987. A new fossil ctenophore discovered by X-rays. *Nature* 328:61–63.

Szaniawski, H. 1987. Preliminary structural comparisons of protoconodont, paraconodont and euconodont elements. *In* R.J. Aldridge (ed.), *Paleobiology of Conodonts*. Chichester: Ellis Horwood; New York: Halstead Press.

Walossek, D., and K.J. Müller. 1994. Pentastomid parasites from the Lower Paleozoic of Sweden. *Transactions of the Royal Society of Edinburgh: Earth Sciences* 85:1–37.

Walossek, D., K.J. Müller, and R.M. Kristensen. 1994. A more than half a billion years old stem-group tardigrade from Siberia. *Sixth International Symposium on Tardigrada, Abstracts*.

Walossek, D., J.E. Repetski, and K.J. Müller. 1994. An exceptionally preserved parasitic arthropod, *Heymonsicambria taylori* n.sp. (Arthropoda incertae sedis: Pentastomida), from Cambrian-Ordovician boundary beds of Newfoundland, Canada. *Canadian Journal of Earth Sciences* 31:1664–71.

Whittington, H.B. 1978. The lobopod animal *Aysheaia pedunculata* Walcott, Middle Cambrian, Burgess Shale, British Columbia. *Philosophical Transactions of the Royal Society of London*, ser. B, 284:165–97.

Further Reading

Brusca, R.C., and J.G. Brusca. 1990. *Invertebrates*. Massachusetts: Sinauer.

Clark, R.B. 1979. Radiation of the Metazoa. *In* M.R. House (ed.), *The Origin of Major Invertebrate Groups*. London and New York: Academic Press.

Conway Morris, S., J.D. George, R. Gibson, and H.M. Platt (eds.). 1985. *The Origins and Relationships of Lower Invertebrates*. Systematics Association Special Volume 28. Oxford: Clarendon Press.

Dougherty, E.C. 1963. *The Lower Metazoa: Comparative Biology and Phylogeny*. Berkeley: University of California Press.

Harbison, G.R. 1985. On the classification and evolution of the Ctenophora. *In* S. Conway Morris, J.D. George, R. Gibson, and H.M. Platt (eds.), *The Origins and Relationships of Lower Invertebrates*. Systematics Association Special Volume 28. Oxford: Clarendon Press.

Hyman, L.H. 1951. *The Invertebrates*. Vol. 2, *Platyhelminthes and Rhynchocoela: The Acoelomate Bilateria*. New York: McGraw-Hill.

———. 1951. *The Invertebrates*. Vol. 3, *Acanthocephala, Aschelminthes and Entoprocta*. New York: McGraw-Hill.

———. 1959. *The Invertebrates*. Vol. 5, *Smaller Coelomate Groups*. New York: McGraw-Hill.

Nielsen, C. 1977. The relationship of Entoprocta, Ectoprocta, and Phoronida. *American Zoologist* 17:149–50.

———. 1985. *Animal Evolution: Interrelationships of the Living Phyla*. Oxford and New York: Oxford University Press.

Parker, S.P. (ed.). 1982. *Synopsis and Classification of Living Organisms*. 2 vols., New York: McGraw-Hill.

Roe, P., and J.L. Norenburg. 1985. Introduction to the symposium: Comparative biology of nemertines. *American Zoologist* 25:3.

Salvini-Plawen, L. von. 1986. Systematic notes on *Spadella* and on the Chaetognatha in general. *Zeitschrift für zoologische Systematik und Evolutionsforschung* 24:122–28.

Stephen, A.C., and S.J. Edmonds. 1972. *The Phyla Sipuncula and Echiura*. London: British Museum (Natural History).

Valentine, J.W. 1973. Coelomate superphyla. *Systematic Zoology* 22:97–102.

Wills, M.A. 1993. Miscellanea. *In* M.J. Benton (ed.), *The Fossil Record 2*. London and New York: Chapman and Hall.

MEXICO AND CENTRAL AMERICA

Pre-Nineteenth Century: Pre-Columbian Times and Early Works

In Central America and Mexico, the beginning of geological knowledge can be traced to pre-Columbian times. It is evident that the different indigenous groups had a utilitarian knowledge of rocks, minerals, and fossils. Fossils were used for ornaments such as those found in Mayan burial sites. Carved ornaments and artifacts were fashioned from jade, obsidian, shark teeth, fossil fishes, and bones of nonextinct mammals.

The arrival of the conquistadors began a new wave of exploration to satisfy the Spanish desire for precious metals. While prospecting in the new lands, early explorers encountered remains of animals and plants that no longer existed. Some of these encounters were mentioned in the explorer's early works. In his *Historia general de los hechos de los castellanos en las islas y tierra firme del mar océano*, Antonio de Herrera (1615) mentioned the presence of large bones (elephants) collected in Mexico. Also the Jesuit José Torrubia referred in his *Apartado para la Historia Natural de Espagnola* (1754) to fossils and minerals he collected in the New World. In a time when it was widely believed that fossils were tricks of nature, Torrubia was convinced of their organic origin.

In 1792, the Spanish crown founded the Real Seminario de Minería (School of Mines) in Mexico City, to protect its interests in the exploitation of the region's precious metals. The school trained mining engineers, who would be in charge of exploration and mining. The Spaniard Fausto de Elhuyar y de Zubice was the first Director. He invited well-known scientists to teach there, including Andrés Manuel del Río, who arrived in 1794. Del Río brought with him the neptunist geological concepts proposed by A.G. Werner and wrote numerous papers related to mineralogy. One of his most important works is *Elementos de Orictognosia; o, del conocimiento de los fósiles dispuestos según principios de A.G. Werner, para uso del Real Seminario de Minería de México* (1795).

The second half of the eighteenth century was characterized by the popularization of scientific discoveries. As a result, in the cities there was an explosion in the number of weeklies, newspapers, and journals, such as *Gaceta de México* (1784–1809). The oldest reports of vertebrate fossils recovered in Mexico were published in *Gaceta* (1790, 1799). In Central America the cultural movement was observed only in the capital cities of the countries. In Guatemala, *Gaceta de Goathemala* appeared in 1729, and the Sociedad Económica de Amigos del País was founded in 1791. Similar societies and newspapers appeared in the rest of the Central American countries.

Nineteenth Century: Pioneer Geological Investigations

By the late eighteenth century, new types of explorers began to arrive. They were geographers and natural historians who made the first scientific observations and descriptions of the region. During the nineteenth century a more extensive and systematic regional geological investigation in Central America was carried out, mainly by foreign naturalist explorers. Also, the first works by native investigators were published. A characteristic of this first period is the universality of the research conducted by individual explorers. In addition to gathering geological data, these scholars made important contributions to the knowledge of physical geography, flora and fauna, and even the ethnography of the countries they visited.

In 1839 Belgian geologist H. Galeotti published the results of his exploration in Mexico. He initiated the studies of historical geology based on the collected fossils. Another Belgian, H. Nyst in 1840 reported Jurassic fossils from Tehuacán, Mexico, and correlated them with those from the Old World. In 1840 H. von Meyer listed vertebrate fossils from the Valley of Mexico and Michoacán, and R. Owen (1846) published the description of vertebrate fossils from Darien, Panama.

In Mexico, long-held interest for the construction of an interoceanic canal in the Isthmus of Tehuantepec, in the southern part of the country, led the Mexican government to explore the region. As early as 1825, General Juan de Orbegoso carried on the investigations, and his results were part of the first scientific report on that zone: *Reconocimiento del istmo de Tehuantepec, hecho el año de 1825 por el ciudadano Juan de Obregoso* (1831).

In 1845 a significant improvement in the collecting, describing, and mapping of Mexican minerals and fossils occurred when Andrés Manuel del Río left his teaching position at the Colegio Nacional de Minería (which later became the Escuela Nacional de Ingenieros) and was replaced by Antonio del Castillo.

Antonio del Castillo was a former student of the School of Mines and, although he was a mining engineer, he devoted most of his teaching and researching to paleontology, stratigraphy, and field geology. He organized the most complete collection of Mexican minerals, rocks, and fossils thus far. Del Castillo also published the first descriptions of fossil mammals recovered from the Valley of Mexico: "Clasificación y datos sobre los mamíferos fósiles encontrados en el Valle de México" (1869) and "Adelantos de la paleontología y geología del Valle de México" (1879).

Thanks to the efforts of del Castillo, the Mexican Congress created the Comisión Geológica (Geological Commission) in 1886. This institution would be in charge of preparing and publishing the geological and mineralogical map of the republic, accompanied by a carefully written report. In 1888, the Congress approved the creation of the Instituto Geológico de México, which absorbed the Geological Commission. A paleontology section was included, as well as a fossil collection.

At the beginning, the commission's work was confined to preparing a general geologic map of the country, which was presented at the International Exposition of Paris in 1889. Del Castillo was the Institute director until his death, in 1895. That same year, the institution initiated a publication named Boletín del Instituto Geológico de México.

Another former student of the School of Mines, Mariano Bárcena (1842–99) was a naturalist who published numerous papers about the geology and paleontology of Mexico. Among his main paleontological contributions was *Datos para el estudio de las rocas mesozoicas de México y sus fósiles característicos* (Bárcena 1875), wherein he compiled all existing descriptions of Mexican invertebrates. His work signalled the beginning of stratigraphic and paleontological research in Mexico conducted by Mexican scholars.

During the French invasion of Mexico in 1864, led by Emperor Napoleon III, the French government organized a "Mission Scientifique au Mexique et dans l'Amérique Centrale" to explore the American lands. Among the academic personnel participating were the zoologist M. Milne-Edwards and geologists G. Tarayre, A. Dollfus, E. de Montserrat, and P. Pavie. All recorded their observations on the fossils they saw on their voyage to Mexico; these writings can be found in the three volumes of the *Archives de la Commission Scientifique du Mexique,* published in 1867.

Before their expedition to Mexico, A. Dollfus and E. de Montserrat spent some time in Central America, laying the foundations for most of our present-day geological knowledge of Guatemala and El Salvador. Their work *Voyage Geologique dans les Republiques de Guatemala et de Salvador* (1868), featured the first accounts of the stratigraphy and the first geological map of these areas.

The American invasion in the middle of the nineteenth century resulted in the loss of part of Mexico's territory. The U.S. government sent a commission to draw the new border between the two countries, under the lead of the Mayor Emory. This report, published in 1857, included the stratigraphic, petrographic, and paleontological contributions of J.R. Bartlett, J. Hall, A. Schott, and T. Conrad and marked the start of American geologic studies in Mexico. Toward the end of the century, the American contributions increased, because of the interest in Mexico's oil and mineral potential.

Mexico's paleontological promise became more widely known when E. Cope reviewed the collections at the Escuela Nacional de Ingenieros and described some important specimens, like the first rhinoceros collected in Toluca. Two of Cope's most important works are "Report on the coal deposits near Zacualtipan, in the State of Hidalgo, Mexico" (1885) and "The extinct mammalia of the Valley of Mexico" (1884).

Well into the middle of the nineteenth century, some geographers and geologists began to reside in or to conduct repeated expeditions in Central America. Their studies were no longer occasional but the result of an ample understanding of the environment through constant observations. The Germans quickly distinguished themselves as continuous and methodical observers of the geography and geology of Central America.

The American geologist and paleontologist William Gabb explored and described the geology of the Talamanca Mountains in Costa Rica. His geological map of the region, however, was never published. During 1860–70 Gabb worked in northern Mexico, describing Cretaceous and Tertiary fossils and establishing correlations based on paleontological evidence. The American J. Leidy described a *Mastodon* from Honduras (1859), and *Toxodon* and other fossils from Nicaragua (1886). Another American, F. Nason, published the description of vertebrate remains from Honduras in 1887.

As part of his work for the U.S. Geological Survey, geologist Robert Hill made some meaningful contributions to the geology of Panama and Costa Rica. He published his findings in "The Geological History of the Isthmus of Panama and Portions of Costa Rica" (1898). In some cases, Mexican scholars collected fossil material, then sent it abroad for their study. Such is the case of the description of the first Triassic plants from Honduras by J.S. Newberry (1888). C.G. Ehrenberg (1866–69) described fossil diatoms from Mexico. British geologists also made important contributions to the geology of Costa Rica (Attwood 1882) as well as Nicaragua. T. Belt (1874) wrote on some aspects of Nicaragua's geology; Crawford (1890) made the first systematic surveys of the geology of Nicaragua in "The Geological Survey of Nicaragua."

At the end of the nineteenth century, the great German geologist and naturalist Karl Sapper, considered the father of geology in Central America, undertook extensive investigations in Belize, Guatemala, southern Mexico, Honduras, and the Central American isthmus. His writings were gathered in his book *Mittelamerika* (1937), which is considered a classic in the geological literature of the region.

Sapper developed a conception of stratigraphy and structure, the basic principles of which are still valid even today. He recorded his findings in a great number of writings and maps (1890–1937). His pupil and successor, Franz Termer, wrote a biography of Sapper that was published first in Spanish (1956) and later also in German (1966). This text contains a bibliography of Sapper's works.

At the end of the nineteenth and early twentieth centuries, German contributions were important to the study of the ancient life and geology of Mexico. Among the best known are E. Böse, G. Boehm, C. Burckhardt, J. Felix, and H. Lenk. The last two, Felix and Lenk, later spent two years in Mexico (1887–88), and when they returned to Germany, they published their observations in *Beiträge zur Geologie und Paläeontologie der Republik Mexico,* where they described geology and fossils of the Valley of Mexico, Oaxaca, Puebla, and Estado de Mexico.

In 1888 and 1889 the German geologist R. Fritzgartner printed an English-language periodical in Tegucigalpa, Honduras: "Honduras Progress. A Paper of Mining, Commerce, Popular Science and General News." This periodical, which features notes on the fossil discoveries of the country, must be considered the oldest publication of its kind in Central America. Under Fritzgartner, the government of Honduras was the first in Central America to have an office dedicated solely to mining geology and assaying minerals. Elsewhere, all governments in the middle of the nineteenth century deposited their findings into one single, official department (Formento), in keeping with a general tradition throughout Spanish America.

The nineteenth century was also a time when natural history societies and national museums were founded, such as Sociedad Mexicana de Historia Natural (1868), with its official journal, "La Naturaleza," which was published from 1869 to 1914. In 1884 the Sociedad Científica Antonio Alzate was founded, which later became the Academia Nacional de Ciencias in Mexico. The Museo Nacional de México (National Museum of Mexico) was founded in 1825 and included a department of Natural History, which later became an independent institution.

Early Twentieth Century (1900–45): Major Oil Explorations, and the First University Studies

José Guadalupe Aguilera Serrano (1857–1941), another former student of the School of Mines, joined the Comisión Geológica to work with del Castillo. When del Castillo died in 1895, Serrano took his position as director until 1915. He organized the 10th Session of the International Geological Congress in 1906, which was held in Mexico City. Thirty-one field guidebooks were written for the Congress, and this event gave an important impetus to geological and paleontological research in Mexico. Aguilera Serrano is recognized as a promoter of all the disciplines of the Earth sciences: geology, mineral ores, seismology, paleontology, and meteoritic.

Exploration in preparation for construction of an interoceanic canal between the Atlantic and Pacific oceans gave a great impetus to geological investigations in Central America. When a French company attempted to build such a canal in Panama, new geological and paleontological materials were described by specialists, among them M. Bertrand, P. Zurcher, and R. Douvillé.

Under the direction of T. Vaughan, the Americans also investigated the geology and fossils of the canal zone, culminating in the publication, in 1919, of a wide review of the region's petrography, stratigraphy, and paleontology. Works by Brown and Pilsbry (1911–13) and in particular by W.P. Woodring (1957–64) are outstanding for their coverage. The studies laid the groundwork for understanding the Tertiary stratigraphy of this area.

The studies identified two routes for the interoceanic canal. One was through Nicaragua and took advantage of the country's navigable lakes and rivers; the other was through the Isthmus of Panama. Both routes were the subjects of deep geological investigations (on Nicaragua: C.W. Hayes 1899; on Panama: MacDonald 1919). Aware that the Nicaragua route passed near active volcanoes, and alarmed by the disastrous Mt. Pelée (Martinique) eruption of 1902, the U.S. Congress decided to build the interoceanic canal through the isthmus.

An important factor during the early twentieth century was the world's increasing demand for petroleum. Numerous oil companies undertook extensive exploration programs in Central America and Mexico. Unfortunately, much of the work done by oil company geologists has never been published. The use of fossilized foraminiferans for stratigraphic correlation, a technique pioneered by J. Cushman in the early 1930s, was important here.

The first attempt to compile existing geological knowledge of the Caribbean was made around 1930 by C. Schuchert (1935) in the *Historical Geology of the Antillean-Caribbean Region*. After years of experience in the region, R. Weyl (1915–88) compiled two books on the geology of Central America: *Die Geologie Mittelamerikas* (1961) and *Geology of Central America* (1980). Weyl's work is of interest because it heralded a shift in interest from stratigraphy to the tectonic problems of the region.

In Mexico, as in Central America, there was an impetus for foreign consultants and experts to explore oil reservoirs. Among the Germans was F. Müllerried, who arrived in 1922 and remained in Mexico until his death. He worked for several Mexican institutions, such as the Instituto Geológico, Instituto de Biología, Museo Nacional de Historia Natural, and was in charge of the Collections of Paleontology and Biology. His main work was done in the southeastern part of the country; later, the Pan-American Institution sent Müllerried to Central America.

After the oil expropriation of 1938, the Mexican government founded Petróleos Mexicanos (PEMEX), an institution in charge of the exploration, exploitation, and production of oil. A section for paleontology was also created; Díaz Lozano was one of the founders. By 1950, Maldonado-Koerdell (1908–72) began formal research on foraminiferans. During the 1960s, the Instituto Mexicano del Petróleo (IMP) was created, in order to support the activities of exploration of PEMEX. Micro- and macropaleontologists were moved from PEMEX to work at the IMP, initiating a tradition of micropaleontologists.

Later Twentieth Century (1945–99): Oil, Minerals, University Projects, and Regional Conferences

The increase in prosperity in Europe and North America after World War II created a demand for oil and minerals, and the relatively unexplored areas in the Caribbean, Central America, and Mexico seemed to be the obvious place to look. The region's countries were eager to participate in the postwar boom by exploiting their own mineral and natural resources. Ministries and bureaus of mines were established to deal with problems of mining legislation, to do geological work, and to encourage and monitor exploration by commercial concerns. Government institutions thus joined the universities and the oil and mineral companies as important agencies of geological investigation in the region. Universities of America and Europe performed vital research in the region, and a large number of unpublished master's and doctoral theses resulted in mapping programs.

A biological expedition conducted by the University of California to El Salvador (1941–42) discovered the Pleistocenic mammalian fauna of El Hormiguero. Another expedition sponsored by the University of Chicago and the Field Museum of Natural History (1937–38) to the Department of Gracias, Honduras, collected vertebrate fossils from Tertiary deposits. The Pan-American Institute of Geography and History sponsored cartographic and geographic works in the Central America Isthmus, forming the basis for a systematic geologic exploration for years to come. The institute also sent F. Müllerried to Guatemala, El Salvador, and Honduras. His findings were published in 1939 as *Investigaciones y exploracionos geográfico-geológicas en la porción noroeste de la America Central.* Later he published more specialized studies on those countries, most notably "Contribución a la Geología de México y Noroeste de América Central" (1945). As part of the U.S. Geological Survey, F. Whitmore and P. Stewart, geologists with the Panama Canal Company, described the important Miocene terrestrial vertebrate fauna of the La Cucaracha Formation in 1965.

The decades following the Second World War are marked by a great variety of foreign investigations in Central America. This period also is notable for the development of independent geological institutions in the countries of Central America. In the early twentieth century the countries of Central America already had initiated their own geological and paleontological studies. However, the work was hampered by the lack of Central American experts, so the governments were to contract the services of foreigners. Some conducted their research for more or less limited periods. Others, however, remained and became part of the national life.

In 1950 Jorge Lardé y Larin reorganized the Section of Paleontology of the National Museum "David Guzmán" in El Salvador and published *Palentología Salvadoreña: Indice Provisional de Regiones Fosilíferas de El Salvador.* In 1950 Dr. Helmut Meyer-Abich, a German geologist, began working for the Instituto Tropical de Investigación Científica of the Universidad de El Salvador, where he initiated geological research. In 1952, Lardé y Larin produced *Geología Salvadoreña,* in which he cataloged the main fossil sites in the country. And, in 1955, as a result of the efforts of Meyer-Abich, the government created the Servicio Geológico Nacional, an agency devoted to the study of the Salvadorian lands.

In 1954 the Nicaraguan government decided to conduct the systematic exploration of its mineral and petroleum resources through its Department of Economy. With the advice of the Pan-American Institute, the government contracted with Italian firms to initiate the geological work and supply equipment and technicians. The result was the Servicio Geológico de Nicaragua, created in 1956.

Nicaragua was also the site of the world's first marine drilling for entirely stratigraphic purposes, in 1963. The work was conducted on the Nicaraguan Rise, by the vessel Submarex. The year 1969 saw the first deep-sea drilling operations in the Caribbean. During the same year scholars began to seriously explore the implications of the new hypotheses about continental drift and plate tectonics. The tectonic evolution of the Caribbean still is among the least understood of any of the world's regions and is hotly debated.

In Mexico, the Instituto Nacional de Antropología e Historia (INAH) opened its Department of Prehistory in 1956. Then, the Pan-American Institute and the Geological Society of America sponsored Maldonado-Koerdell, a Mexican paleontologist, to compile the paleontological and geological information published about the region from Tehuantepec isthmus and Central America. His work was published in 1958. In 1963, INAH opened its Laboratory of Paleozoology, which is in charge of organizing the institution's fossil collection. Finally, in 1986, the federal law that protects the archaeological zones, historic, and artistic monuments was modified to include the paleontological sites as well, thus protecting the country's fossils and governing the loan of fossils for study outside the country.

In 1939 César Dandoli, an Italian, went to Costa Rica to work for the Centro Nacional de Agricultura. Within the Centro's framework he established the Departmento de Geología, Minas y Petróleo. Thirty years later, as a result of agreements among the Central American governments, the Escuela Centro Americana de Geología was founded at the University of Costa Rica. Opened in 1970, the institution is supported by UNESCO.

Today, the efforts of the individual countries are supported by a common institution, the Instituto Centroamericano de Investigaciones y Tecnología Industrial (ICAITI), whose main offices are located in Guatemala. It was the major force behind the establishment of the Central American Geological Conference, which began in 1965 and since then has been held approximately every three years.

Comments

The knowledge of the ancient life in Mexico and Central America is quite meager for many reasons. The scarcity of scholars, academic institutions, and financial resources are decisive factors. Another is the lack of an organized plan to survey adequately each country's natural resources. Basic geology and even topographic mapping at a scale required for detailed studies is unavailable. Most paleontological studies are only of reconnaissance nature, and if detailed, are very local and unrelated to the larger context of the region.

Paleontological research has been related mostly to geological works, yielding information to determine the age of rocks and correlating them with other regions of the world, as well as establishing paleogeography and paleoenvironments. Such work has often been conducted to foster petroleum exploration, not paleontological knowledge. Few studies have been done addressing only paleobiological aspects.

Foreign researchers were and continue to be important contributors, and, unfortunately, only small national groups participate in these efforts.

Overview: The Structure, Geologic History, and Paleogeography of Central America

In terms of geological history and structure, Central America can be divided into two large units, which differ completely from each other. These units were noticed by early investigators, and later workers have confirmed their existence. The northern part, also called "Nuclear Central America," comprises Guatemala, Honduras, El Salvador, and northern Nicaragua. The development of this area is related to Mexico and North America.

The southern part, also known as the "Isthmian Link," covers the area from southern Nicaragua to Panama. This area is one of the most complex of the entire Caribbean region, and its tectonic history has been the subject of many divergent interpretations.

Let's try to reconstruct just how Central America looked geographically through time and assess its relationship to both North and South America. At the beginning of the Mesozoic, the separation between North and South America, as well as the separation between both continents from Africa, was small, so the terrestrial animals probably would have had few barriers for dispersal from one landmass to another. During the Mesozoic and Cenozoic, the North and South Atlantic, the Gulf of Mexico, and the Caribbean Sea all gradually increased in size.

Different models are proposed to explain the origin of Central America. On the one hand, B.T. Malfait and M.G. Dinkelman (1972) suggest that during the expansion of the ocean basins, the Central American area was uplifted by the incursion of the Pacific crustal plate. Other workers (e.g., Gose and Scott 1979; Anderson 1978) identify a small number of crustal plates in the eastern Pacific and Caribbean area. These plates, they say, rotated relative to each other, leading to the Late Cenozoic aggregation that we know today as terrestrial Central America.

Even though it still is not clear which theory is correct, it is certain that from the latest Mesozoic until sometime in the Pliocene (5 to 6 million years ago), no terrestrial connection existed between North and South America—in other words, Central America did not exist. When the terrestrial connection was established (3.0 to 3.5 million years ago) the so-called Great American Faunistic Interchange started, and Central America played a crucial but often enigmatic role in this history.

The study of this event has produced numerous papers. The more "geological" studies focused upon microfossils and invertebrates in the Pacific and Caribbean sides. Some scholars conducted geochemical and isotopic studies. All this work concentrated upon determining the timing of the closure of the Bolivar trough (e.g., Keigwin 1978, 1982; Kaneps 1970). Scholars also have created models of how it happened (e.g., Gose 1985;

Savin and Douglas 1985) and the consequences, such as the changes in the circulation of the surface waters and the increase of salinity in the Caribbean Sea.

Scholars taking the "biological approach" analyzed the dynamics of the faunal interchange to determine which groups were involved, their distribution pattern, arrival times, results of competition, and the effect on speciation (Marshall et al. 1979, 1982; Patterson and Pascual 1972; Webb 1976, 1978, 1985, 1991).

The Central American Dispersal Route

Prior to the closure of the Isthmus of Panama, Central American mammalian faunas were composed of predominantly North American forms, as shown by the Miocene fossil mammals from La Cucaracha Formation (Panama), the Las Gracias Formation (Honduras), those from southeastern Mexico (El Gramal in Oaxaca and Ixtapa-Soyaló in Chiapas), and those from Central Mexico.

The paradox is that the modern biota (flora and fauna) of Central America has much stronger affinities with that of South America than with that of North America. The primary example of this is the angiosperms (flowering plants). Biogeographically, this area is today included within the Neotropical realm and joins the Neotropic of South America and the Nearctic of North America. It serves both as a corridor for terrestrial forms and as a barrier to marine forms attempting an east-west movement between the Caribbean–Gulf of Mexico region and the Pacific Ocean.

The basic outline of the exchange of terrestrial and freshwater biotas have been known for about a century but were given special vitality by Simpson's classic 1980 study of the interchange effects of the interchange on land mammals (*Splendid Isolation: The Curious History of South American Mammals*). In post-Simpson decades, the fossil record of land mammals in the Americas has increased greatly, especially through the use of screen-washing procedures that allow recovery of micromammal remains. Discovery of new localities in low latitudes and chronological precision has improved.

The major puzzle Simpson investigated was why more northern families of land mammals succeeded in South America than southern families succeeded in North America. He argued that since the South American mammalian fauna, made up primarily of marsupials, was isolated for so many million years, they were not competitive with the placental mammals from the north. Also, the marsupials were considered to be less "developed" than placentals.

Recently, S.D. Webb (1991) proposed an ecogeographic model to explain the asymmetrical interchange. It consists of two phases. During the humid interglacial phase, the tropics were dominated by rain forests, and the principal biotic movement was from Amazonia to Central America and southern Mexico. During the more arid glacial phase, savanna habitats extended through tropical latitudes. Because the temperate north was much larger than the south, northern immigrants outnumbered those from the south. Webb went on to suggest that before the interchange, North American taxa underwent a period of diversification in tropical latitudes that gave them a head start in adapting to conditions they would face in South America. Thus, Central America and southern Mexico played an important role as a center of origin for mammalian groups.

Unfortunately, very little is known of the small mammal faunas, plants, amphibians, and reptiles of Central America during the Cenozoic.

The Great American Interchange continues to arouse interest. The Smithsonian Tropical Research Institute is leading the "Panama Paleontology Project," which deals with the geological history of the rise and closure of the Panamanian Isthmus and its ecological and evolutionary consequences during the last 10 million years. By combining physical stratigraphy, biostratigraphy, paleomagnetics, and radiometric dating, this study will establish a highly detailed geological history of the last 10 million years, working in units of approximately 200,000 years. Also, new fossil collections recovered will allow analyses of rates of origination and extinction in the area during that time span. The answers to the understanding of this unique biogeographic phenomenon—the origin and composition of different faunas and floras—lie in the rocks of Mexico and Central America.

MARISOL MONTELLANO-BALLESTEROS

Works Cited

Anderson, T.H. 1978. Mesozoic crustal evolution of Middle America and the Caribbean: Geological considerations. *EOS* 59:404.

Attwood, G. 1882. On the geology of a part of Costa Rica, with an appendix (on the igneous rocks) by W.H. Hudleston. *Quarterly Journal of the Geolgical Society* 38:328–40.

Barcena, M. 1875. *Datos para el estudio de las rocas Mesozoicas de México y sus fósiles característicos.* Mexico City: Francisco Díaz de León.

Belt, T. 1874. Glacial phenomena in Nicaragua. *American Journal of Sciences and Arts,* 3rd ser., 7:594–95.

Brown, B. 1912. Brachyostracon: A new genus of Glyptodonts from Mexico. *Bulletin of the American Museum of Natural History* 31:167–77.

Commission Scientifique du Mexique. 1867. *Archives de la Commission Scientifique du Mexique.* 3 vols. Paris: Imprimerie Impériale.

Cope, E.D. 1884. *Extinct Mammalia of the Valley of Mexico: Read before the American Philosophical Society, May 15, 1884.* Philadelphia: American Philosophical Society.

———. 1885. *Report on the Coal Deposits near Zacualtipan, in the State of Hidalgo, Mexico.* n.p.

Crawford, J. 1890. The geological survey of Nicaragua. *American Geologist* 6:377–81.

de Herrera y Tordesillas, A. 1615. *Historia general de los hechos de los Castellanos en las Islas y Tierra Firme del Mar Oceano.* 9 vols. Madrid: Emplenta Real.

de Orbegoso, J. 1831. *Reconocimiento del Istmo de Tehuantepec, hecho el año de 1825 por el Ciudadano Juan de Orbegoso.* Jalapa: Impreso por Blanco y Aburto en al Oficina del Gobierno.

del Castillo, Antonio. 1869. Clasificación y datos sobre los mamíferos fósiles encontrados en el Valle de México. *Deutsche Geologische Gesellschaft, Zeitschrift* 21:479–80.

———. 1879. Adelantos de la paleontología y geología del Valle de México. *El Minero Mexicano* 6:484–85.

del Río, A.M. 1795. *Elementos de orictognosia; o, Del conocimiento de los fósiles dispuestos según los principios de A.G. Werner, para el uso del Real Seminario de Minería de México.* 2 vols. Mexico City: Zúñiga y Ontiveros.

Dollfus, A., and E. de Montserrat. 1868. *Voyage Géologique dans les Républiques de Guatemala et de Salvador.* Paris: Impremerie Nationale.

Ehrenberg, C.G. 1866. Ueber einen Phytolitharien-Tuff als Gebirgsart im Toluca-Thale von Mexiko. *Königlich-preussische Akademie der Wissenschaften zu Berlin,* Mber 1866:158–68.

———. 1869. *Ueber mächtige Gebirgs-Schichten vorherrschend aus microskopischen Bacillarien unter und bei der Stadt Mexiko.* Berlin: Kaiserliche Akademie der Wissenschaften zu Berlin, Abhandlungen.

Felix, J.P., and H. Lenk. 1890. *Beiträge zur geologie und paläontologie der republik Mexico.* 3 vols. Leipzig: Felix; Stuttgart: Schweizerbart'sche Verlagsbuchhandlung.

Galeotti, H. 1839. Mémoire sur les fougères du Mexique, et considérations sur la géographie botanique de cette contrée. Brussells: Hayez.

Gose, W.A. 1985. Caribbean tectonics from a paleomagnetic perspective. *In* F.G. Stehli and S.D. Webb (eds.), *The Great American Biotic Interchange.* New York: Plenum.

Gose, W.A., and G.R. Scott. 1979. The aggregation of Meso-America. *Abstracts of the Geological Society of America* 11:434.

Hayes, C.W. 1899. Physiography and geology of region adjacent to the Nicaragua Canal route. *Bulletin of the Geological Society of America* 10: 285–348.

Hill, R.T. 1898. *The Geological History of the Isthmus of Panama and Portions of Costa Rica: Based upon a Reconnaissance Made for Alexander Agassiz.* Bulletin of the Museum of Comparative Zoology at Harvard College, 28 (5). Cambridge, Massachussetts: Museum of Comparative Zoology.

Kaneps, A. 1970. Late Neogene biostratigraphy (planktonic foraminifera) biogeography and depositional history. Ph.D. diss., Columbia University.

Keigwin Jr., L.D. 1978. Pliocene closing of the Isthmus of Panama, based on biostratigraphic evidence from nearby Pacific Ocean and Caribbean Sea cores. *Geology* 6:630–34.

———. 1982. Isotopic paleoceanography of the Caribbean and east Pacific: Role of Panama uplift in Late Neogene time. *Science* 217:350–53.

Larde y Larin, J. 1950. *Paleontología Salvadoreña: Indice Provisional de las Regiones Fosiliferas de El Salvador.* San Salvador: Editorial Casa de la Cultura.

———. 1952. *Geologia Salvadoreña.* San Salvador: Ministerio de Cultura.

Leidy, J. 1859. On a mastodon tooth from Honduras. *Proceedings of the Academy of Natural Sciences of Philadelphia* 11:91.

———. 1886. Toxodon and other remains from Nicaragua, Central America. *Proceedings of the Academy of Natural Sciences of Philadelphia* 38:275–77.

MacDonald, D.F. 1919. The sedimentary formations of the Panama canal zone, with special reference to the stratigraphic relations of the fossiliferous beds. Washington, D.C.: U.S. Government Printing Office.

Maldonado-Koerdell, M. 1958. *Geological and Paleontological Bibliography of Central America.* Pan-American Institute of Geography and History Publication 204. Mexico City: Pan-American Institute of Geography and History.

Malfait, B.T., and M.G. Dikelman. 1972. Circum-Caribbean tectonic and igneous activity and the volution of the Caribbean Plate. *Bulletin of the Geological Society of America* 83:251–72.

Marshall, L.G., R.F. Butler, R.E. Drake, G.H. Curtis, and R.H. Tedford. 1979. Calibration of the Great American Interchange. *Science* 204:272–79.

Marshall, L.G., S.D. Webb, J.J. Sepkoski, and D.M. Raup. 1982. Mammalian evolution and the Great American Interchange. *Science* 215:1351–57.

Meyer, H. von. 1840. *Neue Gattungen Fossiler Krebse aus Gebilden vom Bunten Sandstein bis in die Kreide.* Stuttgart: Schweizerbart.

———. 1840. Über die Sammlung von Mexikanischen Antiquitäten, Mineralien und Petrefakten. *Neues Jahrbuch für Mineralogie, Geologie und Paläontologie* 1840:576–87.

Müllerried, F.K.G. 1939. *Investigaciones y exploraciones geográfico-geológicas en la porción noroeste de la America Central.* Instituto Panamericano de Geografía e Historia, 38. Mexico City: Instituto Panamericano de Geografía e Historia.

———. 1945. *Contribución a la geología de México y noroeste de la América Central.* Mexico City: Imprementa Universitaria.

Nason, F. 1887. On the location of some vertebrate fossil beds in Honduras, Central America. *American Journal of Science* 34:485–87.

Newberry, J.S. 1888. Rhaetic plants from Honduras. *American Journal of Sciences and Arts,* 3rd ser., 36:342–51.

Nyst, H. 1840. Sur quelques fossiles du calcaire jurassique de Tehuacan au Mexique. *Ac. R. Sc. Bruxelles,* ser. B, 7(2):212–21.

Olson, E.C., and P.O. McGrew. 1941. Mammalian fauna from the Pliocene of Honduras. *Bulletin of the Geological Society of America* 52:1219–44.

Orbegoso, Juan. 1831. *Reconocimiento hecho en el Istmo de Tehuantepec, de orden del Gobierno, por el General Orbegozo, en el año 1826.* N.p.

Owen, R. 1846. Observations on certain fossils from near Darien. *Proceedings of the Academy of Natural Sciences of Philadelphia* 1:93–96.

Patterson, B., and R. Pascual. 1972. The fossil mammal fauna of South America. *In* A. Keast, F.C. Erk, and B. Glass (eds.), *Evolution, Mammals and Southern Continents.* Albany: State University of New York Press.

Pilsbry, H.A. 1920. *Mollusca from Central America and Mexico.* Philadelphia: Academy of Natural Sciences of Philadelphia.

Sapper, K. 1937. *Mittelamerika. Handbuch der Regionalen Geologie.* Vol. 8, part 4A. Heidelberg: C. Winters universitätsbuchhandlung.

Savin, S.M., and R.G. Douglas. 1985. Sea level, climate, and the Central American land bridge. *In* F.G. Stehli and S.D. Webb (eds.), *The Great American Biotic Interchange.* New York: Plenum.

Schuchert, C. 1935. *Historical Geology of the Antillean-Caribbean Region, or the Lands Bordering the Gulf of Mexico and the Caribbean Sea.* New York: Wiley; London: Chapman and Hall.

Simpson, G.G. 1980. *Splendid Isolation: The Curious History of South American Mammals.* New Haven, Connecticut: Yale University Press.

Stirton, R.A., and W.K. Gealey. 1949. Reconnaissance geology and vertebrate paleontology of El Salvador, Central America. *Bulletin of the Geological Society of America* 60:1731–54.

Termer, F. 1956. *Carlos Sapper: Explorador de Centro America, 1866–1945.* Guatemala City: Asociación Guatemalteca de Historia

Natural; as *Karl Theodor Sapper, 1866–1945: Leben und Wirken eines deutschen Geographen und Geologen.* Leipzig: Barth, 1966.

Torrubia, J. 1754. *Apparato para la historia natural Espagnola: Contiene muches dissertaciones physicas especialmente sobre el Diluvio.* Vol. 1. Madrid: Jordejuela.

Vaughan, T.W. 1919. *Contributions to the Geology and Paleontology of the Canal Zone, Panama, and Geologically Related Areas in Central America and the West Indies.* Bulletin of the U.S. National Museum, 103. Washington, D.C.: Smithsonian Institution.

Webb, S.D. 1976. Mammalian faunal dynamics of the Great American Interchange. *Paleobiology* 2:216–34.

———. 1978. A history of Savanna Vertebrates in the New World. Part 2, South America and the Great Interchange. *Annual Review of Ecology and Systematics* 9:393–426.

———. 1985. Late Cenozoic mammal dispersals between the Americas. *In* F.G. Stehli and S.D. Webb (eds.), *The Great American Biotic Interchange.* New York: Plenum.

———. 1991. Ecogeography and the Great American Interchange. *Paleobiology* 17:266–80.

Weyl, R. 1961. *Die Geologie Mittelamerikas.* Beiträge zur regionalen Geologie der Erde, 1. Berlin: Borntraeger.

———. 1980. *Geology of Central America.* Beiträge zur regionalen Geologie der Erde, 15. 2nd ed., Berlin: Borntraeger.

Woodring, W.P. 1957–64. *Geology and Paleontology of Canal Zone and Adjoining Parts of Panama: Description of Tertiary Mollusks (Gastropods).* Washington, D.C.: U.S. Printing Office.

Further Reading

Aguilera, J.G. 1905. Reseña del desarrollo de la geología en México. *Boletín de la Sociedad Geológica Mexicana* 1:35–117.

de Cserna, Z. 1990. La evolución de la geología en México. *Universidad Nacional Autónoma de México, Revista del Instituto de Geología* 9:1–20.

Draper, G., and G. Dengo. 1990. History of geological investigation in the Caribbean region. *In* G. Dengo and J.E. Case (eds.), *The Caribbean Region,* vol. H of *The Geology of North America.* Boulder, Colorado: Geological Society of America; Lawrence: University of Kansas Press.

Müllerried, F.K.G. 1947. El mapa geológico de Centro América. *Anales de la Sociedad de Geografía e Historia de Guatemala* 23:143–65.

Rich, P.V., and T.H. Rich. 1983. The Central American dispersal route. *In* D.H. Janzen (ed.), *Costa Rican Natural History.* Chicago: University of Chicago Press.

Stehli, F.G., and S.D. Webb (eds.). 1985. *The Great American Biotic Interchange.* New York: Plenum.

Trabulse, E. 1989. *Historia de la ciencia en México.* Mexico City: Consejo Nacional de Ciencia y Tecnología/Fondo Cultura Económica.

MEYER, CHRISTIAN ERICH HERMANN VON

German, 1801–69

Christian Erich Hermann von Meyer was one of the leading German paleontologists of the middle part of the nineteenth century, although he never held a position as a professional paleontologist. Severely handicapped from birth by clubfeet, he still traveled to many parts of Germany and some other European countries to study fossil collections. After studying both finance and natural history at several German universities, von Meyer, who was independently wealthy, came back to his native city of Frankfurt and for several years devoted all his energy to paleontological research. In 1837 he became a controller in the financial administration of the German Parliament, but his paleontological work continued unabated in his spare time. In 1860 he was offered a position as professor of geology and paleontology at the University of Göttingen but rejected it because he felt such a post could threaten his scientific independence. He eventually became director of finances of the parliament in 1863.

Von Meyer never attempted to build his own fossil collection, but his reputation as a paleontologist quickly grew both in Germany and abroad, so he had easy access to both private and public collections. He was not a theorist (although he did oppose some of Georges Cuvier's sweeping generalizations about the laws of anatomical correlation), and apparently he was not an opponent of evolution. Von Meyer published several hundred papers, mostly characterized by detailed descriptions and beautiful illustrations (he drew the lithographic plates himself). Some of von Meyer's major contributions were published as a series of large monographs under the collective title *Zur Fauna der Vorwelt* (On the Fauna of the Prehistoric World). In 1846, together with Wilhelm Dunker, von Meyer founded *Palaeontographica,* which has remained one of the leading paleontological journals.

Von Meyer published on a wide range of paleontological topics, including fossil invertebrates and fishes, but he was mainly interested in fossil tetrapods. His most lasting contributions were in the field of paleoherpetology (ancient reptiles), although he also published on fossil mammals, including antracotheres (early relatives of hippopotami), proboscideans (the group including elephants), and rodents. He made a major contribution to paleornithology in 1861 when he described a single feather from the Solnhofen lithographic limestones as *Archaeopteryx lithographica,* a name later applied to the skeletal remains of the earliest known bird. In 1859 von Meyer had in fact described a fragmentary *Archaeopteryx* skeleton as *Pterodactylus crassipes,* a misidentification that was corrected only in 1970, when John Ostrom restudied the specimen in the Teyler Museum in Haarlem. Von Meyer's contribution to the study of pterosaurs, mainly based on specimens from the lithographic limestones of Bavaria, was nevertheless considerable: he erected the new genus *Rhamphorhynchus* (1846), and gave the first major review of Late Jurassic pterosaurs in his monograph on the fossil reptiles preserved in the lithographic limestones of Germany and France (1859–60). From those same Late Jurassic limestones, he also described turtles, sphenodontians (ancestors of tuataras), and pleurosaurs (ancient reptiles, that returned to aquatic life).

Von Meyer also described the first dinosaur from Germany in 1837: On the basis of some large bones from the Upper Triassic of the Stuttgart region, he erected the new genus *Plateosaurus,* with *P. engelhardti* as type species, and remarked that this giant reptile was related to *Iguanodon* and *Megalosaurus.* Interestingly, as early as 1830 he had recognized that gigantic Mesozoic terrestrial reptiles such as these could be placed in a group of their own, on the basis of their heavy limb bones, which were reminiscent of those of large mammals. In 1845, he called this group the Pachypoda. However, he proposed the name three years after Richard Owen gave the group the name Dinosauria, and Pachypoda never gained widespread acceptance.

Von Meyer's interest in Triassic vertebrates was not restricted to dinosaurs. He also studied phytosaurs (extinct crocodile-like reptiles) from the Keuper, and marine reptiles such as the long-necked nothosaurs and turtle-like placodonts from the Muschelkalk of southern Germany. In 1844, together with Theodor Plieninger, he published a major work on the Triassic vertebrates from Würtemberg, which was largely devoted to the labyrinthodonts, some of the first amphibians. His field of interest also extended to the Paleozoic, and he described amphibians and reptiles from the Carboniferous and the Permian Kupferschiefer of Germany.

Although von Meyer was not the first to study fossil vertebrates in Germany, he has been considered the real founder of vertebrate paleontology there. His intense activity and many publications certainly provided an impetus and a scientific basis from which a very active German school of vertebrate paleontology developed during the second half of the nineteenth century.

ERIC BUFFETAUT

Biography

Born in Frankfurt, 3 September 1801. Studied finance and natural history at Heidelberg, Munich, and Berlin; became a controller in the financial administration of the German Parliament in 1837. Proposed the name Pachypoda for giant Mesozoic terrestrial reptiles in 1845; founded the journal *Palaeontographica* in 1846; described *Plateosaurus engelhardti* in 1837, *Belodon plieningeri* in 1842, *Rhamphorhynchus gemmingi* in 1846, *Archaeopteryx lithographica* in 1861. Died in Frankfurt am Main, 2 April 1869.

Major Publications

1832. *Palaeologica, zur Geschichte der Erde und ihrer Geschöpfe.* Frankfurt: Schmerber.

1834. *Die fossilen Zähne und Knochen und ihre Ablagerung in der Gegend von Georgensgmünd in Bayern.* Frankfurt: Sauerlander.

1844. With T. Plieninger. *Beiträge zur Paläontologie Württembergs: Enthaltend die fossilen Wirbelthierreste aus den Triasgebilden mit besonderer Rücksicht auf die Labyrinthodonten des Keupers.* Stuttgart: Schweizerbart'sche.

1845a. *Zur Fauna der Vorwelt.* Vol. 1, *Fossile Säugethiere, Vögel und Reptilien aus dem Molasse-Mergel von Oeningen.* Frankfurt: Schmerber.

1845b. System der fossilen Saurier. *Neues Jahrbuch für Mineralogie, Geologie und Paläontologie* 278–85.

1846. *Pterodactylus (Rhamphorhynchus) gemmingi aus dem Kalkschiefer von Solenhofen. Palaeontographica* 1:1–20.

1855. *Zur Fauna der Vorwelt.* Vol. 2, *Die Saurier des Muschelkalkes, mit Rücksicht auf die Saurier aus buntem Sandstein und Keuper.* Frankfurt: Schmerber.

1856. *Zur Fauna der Vorwelt.* Vol. 3, *Saurier aus dem Kuperschiefer der Zechstein-Formation.* Frankfurt: Schmerber.

1856–59. Reptilien aus der Steinkohlen-Formation in Deutschland. *Palaeontographica* 6:59–219.

1860. *Zur Fauna der Vorwelt.* Vol. 4, *Reptilien aus dem lithographischen Schiefer des Jura in Deutschland und Frankreich.* Frankfurt: Keller.

1861a. *Archaeopteryx lithographica* (Vogel-Feder) und *Pterodactylus* von Solenhofen. *Neues Jahrbuch für Mineralogie, Geologie und Paläontologie* 678–79.

1861b. Reptilien aus dem Stubensandstein des obern Keupers. *Palaeontographica* 7:253–346.

1863. Der Schädel des *Belodon* aus dem Stubensandstein des oberen Keupers. *Palaeontographica* 10:227–46.
1867–70. Studien über das Genus Mastodon. *Palaeontographica* 17:1–72.

Further Reading
Probst, E., and R. Windolf. 1993. *Dinosaurier in Deutschland*. Munich: Bertelsmann.

Tobien, H. 1974. Meyer, Christian Erich Hermann von. In C.C. Gillispie (ed.), *Dictionary of Scientific Biography*. Vol. 9, New York: Scribner's.
Wellnhofer, P. 1991. *The Illustrated Encyclopedia of Pterosaurs*. London: Salamander; New York: Crescent.
Ziegler, B. 1986. *Der schwäbische Lindwurm*. Stuttgart: Theiss Verlag.
Zittel, C.A. 1870. *Denkschrift auf Christ. Erich Hermann von Meyer*. Munich: G. Franz.

MICROBIAL FOSSILS, PRECAMBRIAN

In Charles Darwin's time, the oldest accepted fossils known were the trilobites, brachiopods (shelled marine invertebrates), and other fossils of the Cambrian. The apparent absence of fossils in the extensive sedimentary rocks below the Cambrian system was a scientific conundrum: Darwin wrote, "To the question why we do not find records of these vast primordial periods, I can give no satisfactory answer" (Darwin 1859). Since then, a long stream of discoveries has extended the length and richness of the Precambrian fossil record far beyond anything Darwin could have foreseen. These discoveries show us a world deeply alien to our own experience—a world in which the vast majority of living organisms were microscopic in size. Yet the collective action of these microscopic organisms, over three billion years, literally made Earth what it is today.

Chemical Traces

Some of the most important Precambrian "fossils" are not fossils at all, at least not as the word is used generally. Various chemical traces in rocks and in the atmosphere, laid down in Precambrian time, signal some of the most important events in the history of life.

One such chemical signal may be the oldest geological evidence for life. Carbon exists in two stable isotopes, the lighter carbon-12 (^{12}C) and the heavier carbon-13 (^{13}C). (A third isotope, the well-known carbon-14, decays radioactively with a half-life of $5,730 \pm 40$ years; carbon-12 and carbon-13 do not decay.) The biochemical process of carbon fixation—the conversion of carbon dioxide to living matter—favors the use of ^{12}C over ^{13}C. Living tissues, or their fossil remains, are light isotopically: they contain less ^{13}C than would be expected from the relative abundances of these isotopes on Earth. In 1988, M. Schidlowski discovered that the 3.85-billion-year-old sedimentary rocks of Isua, West Greenland, contained an unexpectedly light mixture of carbon isotopes, a result that was confirmed recently (Mojzis et al. 1996). This should not be accepted without reservations; it is still possible that some kind of geochemical process, not life, created the light carbon ratio, since the rocks in question have been metamorphosed somewhat. However, given our current knowledge, the presence of life is the best explanation for this chemical trace.

Another "chemical fossil" of Precambrian life is Earth's first oxygen atmosphere. Early Earth had practically no free oxygen, and atmospheric oxygen built up slowly. Some of this oxygen probably was released by rock weathering or by other inorganic chemical processes, but much of it was released by photosynthetic microorganisms. These microorganisms used carbon dioxide, water, and light to make food and oxygen through photosynthesis. A number of independent geochemical indicators strongly suggest that between 2.2 and 2.0 billion years ago, the concentration of free oxygen in the atmosphere reached 1 percent of present-day levels. This concentration, called the "Pasteur point," is the lowest concentration of oxygen at which aerobic life can exist (Holland 1994). Since oxygen is toxic to many bacteria, this event has been dubbed "the first pollution crisis"; but oxygen was also a prerequisite for the evolution of more complex life.

Precambrian microbes also are implicated in the origins of certain mineral deposits, including commercially important ore deposits. Between 3.8 and 2.0 billion years ago, oxygen, produced at least in part by photosynthetic microbes, reacted with dissolved iron in the seas. This caused the formation of so-called banded iron formations. Today, these iron formations are important sources of low-grade iron ore. Microbial action also played a role in the formation of certain pyrite deposits (Schieber 1989). Some geologists have implicated Precambrian microbes in the formation of at least some types of gold ore (Hallbauer and van Warmelo 1974; Folinsbee 1982), manganese ore (Bandhopadhyay 1989), and lead-zinc and copper ores (Trudinger and Williams 1982), although universally this is not agreed upon.

Finally, organic matter in rocks can survive in altered but distinctive forms for billions of years. Much of this matter is in the form of hydrocarbons (molecules consisting primarily of carbon and hydrogen, such as the constituents of petroleum), graphite, or an insoluble, inert form called kerogen. But analysis of organic material from rocks as old as 1.7 billion years showed complex hydrocarbons such as steranes (similar to, and probably derived from, cholesterol) and phytanes (probably derived from other cell membrane components) (Ourisson 1994). Traces of carbohydrates also have been recovered from Precambrian rocks, even from those as old as 2.8 billion years (Swain et al. 1970; McKirdy and Hahn 1982). Some of these "molecular fossils," or "biomarkers," are restricted to certain groups of organisms and thus are important evidence for the evolution of these groups. For example, dinosteranes, compounds found almost exclusively in dinoflagellates (single-celled marine algae), have been isolated from Late Precambrian and Paleozoic rocks—up to 150 million years before the oldest known fossil dinoflagellate (Moldowan et al. 1996).

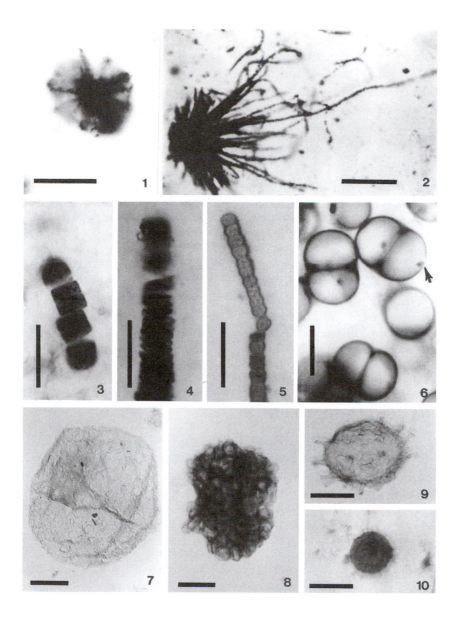

Figure 1. *Kakabekia*. Gunflint Chert, Ontario (approximately 2.0 billion years old). Scale bar, 10 microns. Courtesy of the University of California Museum of Paleontology (UCMP).

Figure 2. *Eoastrion,* a cluster of microbial filaments. Gunflint Chert, Ontario. Scale bar, 10 microns. Courtesy of the University of California Museum of Paleontology (UCMP).

Figure 3. *Oscillatoriopsis*. Bitter Springs Formation, Australia (approximately 850 million years old). Scale bar, 10 microns. Courtesy of the University of California Museum of Paleontology (UCMP).

Figure 4. Cyanobacterial filament cf. *Filiconstrictosus*. Bitter Springs Formation, Australia. Scale bar, 10 microns. Courtesy of the University of California Museum of Paleontology (UCMP).

Figure 5. *Anabaena,* a living filamentous cyanobacterium, for comparison. Taken from prepared slide. Scale bar, 10 microns. Courtesy of the University of California Museum of Paleontology (UCMP).

Figure 6. *Glenobotrydion,* a unicellular organism possibly of cyanobacterial affinity. Arrow, characteristic "nucleus." Scale bar, 10 microns. Courtesy of the University of California Museum of Paleontology (UCMP).

Figure 7. *Leiosphaeridia,* a simple acritarch. Late Precambrian, St. Petersburg region, Russia. Scale bar, 25 microns. Courtesy of the University of California Museum of Paleontology (UCMP).

Figure 8. *Sphaerocongregus,* a cluster of small acritarchs. Late Precambrian, St. Petersburg region, Russia. Scale bar, 25 microns. Courtesy of the University of California Museum of Paleontology (UCMP).

Figure 9. *Tylotopalla,* an acritarch ornamented with stout spines. Silurian, Indiana. Scale bar, 50 microns. Courtesy of the University of California Museum of Paleontology (UCMP).

Figure 10. *Polyancistrodorus,* an acritarch ornamented with slender processes. Middle Ordovician, Oklahoma. Scale bar, 50 microns. Courtesy of the University of California Museum of Paleontology (UCMP).

Precambrian Prokaryotes

The great American paleontologist Charles D. Walcott is known best today for his discovery of the remarkable Cambrian fossils of the Burgess Shale. Less well known, but no less groundbreaking, were Walcott's studies on stromatolites (sedimentary rocks formed mainly by photosynthetic bacteria), which he correctly perceived to be fossil algae of some kind. After cutting a Precambrian stromatolite into thin sections and viewing them under a microscope, Walcott saw fossilized bacteria inside the rock (Walcott 1915). Although a few scientists followed in Walcott's footsteps (e.g., Gruner 1923), others were skeptical of his claims (e.g., Seward 1933; Raymond 1935). It was not until the 1960s that the microfossils in Precambrian rocks were widely studied.

Microfossils now are known from nearly 400 sites, found on every continent and extending back 3.5 billion years. However, fossils are uncommon in rocks older than 2 billion years. These rocks are not only rare, but often are metamorphosed. Furthermore, even with careful study, it is easy to mistake artifacts of sample preparation, mineral grains, bubbles in the rock, or contaminants for fossils. For rocks older than 2 billion years, only a handful of the reported fossil finds have been confirmed and are accepted generally.

The oldest confirmed fossils are almost 3.5 billion years old, from rocks of the Warrawoona Group in northwestern Western Australia (Hofmann and Schopf 1983; Schopf 1992; Schopf and Packer 1987). Rocks of the same age or slightly younger, from the Onverwacht Group of South Africa, have yielded filaments and single sphere-shaped cells, although now some of these are considered doubtful (Schopf and Barghoorn 1967; Schopf and Packer 1987; Walsh and Lowe 1987). A few microfossil sites have been found that are between 3.5 and 2.0 billion years old, but most known Precambrian microfossils are younger than two billion years. Other well-known sites containing diverse microfossil assemblages include the Gunflint Chert of Ontario (1.9 to 2.0 billion years old) (Barghoorn and Tyler 1965); the Lakhanda Formation of the Khabarovsk region of Siberia (950 million years old); the Beck Spring Dolomite of the Death Valley region, California (850 million years old); the Bitter Springs Formation of Australia (850 billion years old) (Schopf 1968); the Svanbergfjellet and Draken Formations of Spitzbergen (700–800 million years old) (Butterfield et al. 1994); and the Skillogalee Dolomite of southern Australia (770 million years old). A recent review of these microfossils was completed by J.W. Schopf (1992).

Many of these microfossils resemble living cyanobacteria, or blue-green "algae." The resemblance between fossils and living species is often astonishingly close, not only in shape, but in growth form and ecology. Cyanobacteria evidently have evolved extremely slowly; the term "hypobradytely" has been coined for this extreme evolutionary stasis (Schopf 1994). Living cyanobacteria are quite rugged; species have been found that can withstand ultraviolet light, gamma radiation, desiccation (drying out), and extreme temperatures. Presumably, fossil cyanobacteria were similarly hardy, able to thrive under harsh, early Earth conditions.

There are Precambrian records of nonphotosynthetic bacteria as well (Figures 1, 2). Some resemble living filamentous iron bacteria, while *Kakabekia umbellata* (Figure 1), from the Gunflint Chert of Ontario, resembles certain living soil bacteria (Siegel et al. 1967). Filamentous bacteria similar to living actinomycetes (a type of bacteria) are known from Precambrian rocks in several places (e.g. Jackson 1967; Hallbauer and van Warmelo 1974; Gnilovskaya 1985). Noteworthy among these fossils are the bacterial filaments found in what were, 1.2 billion and 800 million years ago, terrestrial environments—today they are located in the southwestern United States (Horodyski and Knauth 1994). These filaments are the oldest, currently-known evidence of life on land, preceding land plants and land animals by as much as 750 million years (Figures 3, 4, 5).

Precambrian Eukaryotes

The German paleontologist Hans-Dieter Pflug (1978) described purported microfossils from the 3.8-billion-year-old rocks of the Isua Series of southwestern Greenland, including a yeastlike form that he called *Isuasphaera*. Most paleontologists who have studied the matter do not accept Pflug's findings as true fossils (Schopf and Walter 1983). A number of Precambrian microfossils have internal structures that resemble nuclei, notably *Glenobotrydion* from the Bitter Springs Formation of Australia (Figure 6). These fossils may be eukaryotes (organisms that have a membrane-bound nucleus), but many paleontologists now think that most or all of these fossils actually are cyanobacteria in which the cell contents contracted during fossilization (Horodyski et al. 1992). In any case, *Glenobotrydion* is not the oldest eukaryote.

The oldest fossils that generally are accepted as eukaryotic are not microbes, but coiled, ribbonlike fossils (up to 90 millimeters long) called *Grypania spiralis,* from 2.1-billion-year-old rocks of Michigan (Han and Runnegar 1992). These fossils are thought to be eukaryotic algae of uncertain types. Other fossils, as well as chemical evidence, point to the presence of eukaryotes about 1.9 billion years ago. It may be no coincidence that the time of origin of eukaryotes corresponds to the origin of an oxygenated atmosphere. Microscopic filaments that closely resemble eukaryotic algae are known from a number of Mid- to Late Precambrian sites (Butterfield et al. 1990, 1994).

Acritarchs

Acritarchs are hollow, organic-walled microscopic fossils that superficially look like pollen grains. The word "acritarch" is derived from the Greek for "uncertain origin," and in fact, acritarchs do not fit into any known biological taxon. They most closely resemble the cysts (thick-walled cells capable of surviving unfavorable conditions) made by various living eukaryotic algae, notably dinoflagellates and certain green algae (the Micromonadophyceae). Thus, most acritarchs are thought to represent single-celled eukaryotic algae of some sort. However, acritarchs generally lack the key characters that would link them with a living group of algae. It is possible that some acritarchs might be spores formed by multicellular algae, fungal cysts or zygotes, or even eggs of small invertebrate animals (Martin 1993; Vidal and Moczydlowska-Vidal 1997).

Whatever they were, acritarchs were dominant in the Precambrian oceanic plankton (microscopic aquatic plants and animals)—all known Precambrian species are marine. Acritarchs may range from 1 micrometer to 2 millimeters in diameter, although most are between 10 and 50 micrometers in size. They are usually more or less spherical, but some were oval, spindle-shaped, flask-shaped, polyhedral, or angular. Most acritarchs occurred singly, but some species formed clusters (Figure 8). The wall of an acritarch—composed of highly resistant carbohydrate polymers called "sporopollenin"—may be single or double, and its outer surface may be smooth or covered with bumps, wrinkles, spines, flanges, and/or long, slender filaments (Figures 9, 10). Most acritarchs, if not all, were resistant cysts that protected a living cell and eventually had to release that cell. To do this, many acritarchs simply split open, but some bore a specialized narrow opening (the pylome) for the cell to leave its cyst.

The earliest definite acritarchs appeared around 1,400 million years ago; less certain finds have been dated as old as 1,800 to 1,900 million years (Knoll 1992, 1994). These oldest acritarchs were simple, smooth-skinned forms (e.g., Figures 7, 8). About 1,100 to 1,200 million years ago, however, more complex forms began to appear (Knoll 1992; Martin 1993). Around 800 to 900 million years ago, spiny acritarchs increased in diversity. The latest Precambrian saw two periods of extinction, each followed by a burst of evolutionary diversification, in the ecosystems where acritarch lived throughout the world (Knoll 1994). Acritarchs were abundant and diverse in Cambrian through Devonian time (Figures 9, 10) but rapidly declined thereafter, their place being taken by other lineages of single-celled algae (Tappan 1980; Martin 1993).

Chitinozoans

Chitinozoans also are thought to represent eukaryotes of some kind. Like acritarchs, chitinozoans have walls of tough organic material. Unlike acritarchs, chitinozoans are sac-shaped or vase-shaped, with a single, relatively broad opening. Chitinozoans appeared and diversified around 800 to 900 million years ago (Knoll 1994). Chitinozoans also are somewhat problematic fossils. Usually they are considered to have been protists, probably feeding on algae and bacteria. Many resemble the organic armor, or "lorica," of a living group of ciliated protists abundant in today's oceans, called "tintinnids." However, some chitinozoans may have been algal in nature.

Mineralized Protists

The Cambrian was not only the period in which most of the mineralized animal groups appeared and diversified. Foraminiferans (tiny organisms that lived in calcium-based shells), radiolarians (deep-sea protozoans with a skeleton made of silica, a hard, glassy mineral), and several lineages of mineralized algae first appeared and increased in diversity and geographical spread during the Cambrian. One exception to this rule is the remarkable number of microfossils found in the Tindir Group of eastern Alaska and northwest Canada (Allison and Hilgert 1986). Originally, these rocks were described as Cambrian but later were dated as Late Precambrian, between 780 and 620 million years old (Kaufman et al.

1992). They have yielded fossils of remarkable silica scales of various shapes and sizes, resembling the scales and skeletons made by diatoms, certain algae, and certain amoebas. A few other finds of siliceous microfossils in the Precambrian hint at a long history for mineralized protists (e.g., Licari 1978).

BEN WAGGONER

See also Algae; Origin of Life; Skeletized Microorganisms

Works Cited

Allison, C.W., and J.W. Hilgert. 1986. Scale microfossils from the Early Cambrian of northwest Canada. *Journal of Palaeontology* 60:973–1015.

Bandhopadhyay, P.C. 1989. Proterozoic microfossils from manganese orebody, India. *Nature* 339:376–78.

Barghoorn, E.S., and S.A. Tyler. 1965. Microorganisms from the Gunflint Chert. *Science* 147:563–77.

Butterfield, N.J., A.H. Knoll, and K. Swett. 1990. A bangiophyte red alga from the Proterozoic of Arctic Canada. *Science* 250:104–7.

———. 1994. Paleobiology of the Neoproterozoic Svanbergfjellet Formation, Spitsbergen. *Fossils & Strata* 34:1–84.

Darwin, C. 1859. *On the Origin of Species*. London: Murray; New York: Humboldt.

Folinsbee, R.E. 1982. Variations in the distribution of mineral deposits with time. *In* H.D. Holland and M. Schidlowski (eds.), *Mineral Deposits and the Evolution of the Biosphere*. Berlin and New York: Springer-Verlag.

Gnilovskaya, M.B. 1985. Vendskie aktinomitsety i organizmy nejasnogo sistematicheskogo polozhenija. *In* B.S. Sokolov and A.B. Iwanowski (eds.), *Vendskaia sistema*. Vol. 1, Moscow: Nauka.

Gruner, J. 1923. Algae, believed to be Archaean. *Journal of Geology* 31:146–48.

Hallbauer, D.K., and K.T. van Warmelo. 1974. Fossilized plants in thucholite from Precambrian rocks of the Witwatersrand, South Africa. *Precambrian Research* 1:199–212.

Han, T.M., and B. Runnegar. 1992. Megascopic eukaryotic algae from the 2.1-billion-year-old Negaunee Iron-Formation, Michigan. *Science* 257:232–35.

Hofmann, H.J., and J.W. Schopf. 1983. Early Proterozoic microfossils. *In* J.W. Schopf (ed.), *Earth's Earliest Biosphere: Its Origin and Evolution*. Princeton, New Jersey: Princeton University Press.

Holland, H.D. 1994. Early Proterozoic atmospheric change. *In* S. Bengtson (ed.), *Early Life on Earth*. New York: Columbia University Press.

Horodyski, R.J., J. Bauld, J.H. Lipps, and C.V. Mendelson. 1992. Preservation of prokaryotes and organic-walled and calcareous and siliceous protists. *In* J.W. Schopf and C. Klein (eds.), *The Proterozoic Biosphere: A Multidisciplinary Study*. Cambridge and New York: Cambridge University Press.

Horodyski, R.J., and L.P. Knauth. 1994. Life on land in the Precambrian. *Science* 263:494–98.

Jackson, T.A. 1967. Fossil actinomycetes in middle Precambrian glacial varves. *Science* 155:1003–5.

Kaufman, A.J., A.H. Knoll, and S.M. Awramik. 1992. Biostratigraphic and chemostratigraphic correlation of Neoproterozoic sedimentary successions: Upper Tindir Group, northwestern Canada, as a test case. *Geology* 20:181–85.

Knoll, A.H. 1992. The early evolution of eukaryotes: A geological perspective. *Science* 256:622–27.

———. 1994. Neoproterozoic evolution and environmental change. *In* S. Bengtson (ed.), *Early Life on Earth*. New York: Columbia University Press.

Licari, G.R. 1978. Biogeology of the late pre-Phanerozoic Beck Spring Dolomite of eastern California. *Journal of Paleontology* 52:767–92.

Martin, F. 1993. Acritarchs: A review. *Biological Reviews* 68:475–538.

McKirdy, D.M., and J.H. Hahn. 1982. Composition of kerogen and hydrocarbons in Precambrian rocks. *In* H.D. Holland and M. Schidlowski (eds.), *Mineral Deposits and the Evolution of the Biosphere*. Berlin and New York: Springer-Verlag.

Mojzis, S., K.D. McKeegan, T.M. Harrison, A.P. Nutman, and G. Arrhenius. 1996. New evidence for life on Earth by 3870 Ma. *Origins of Life and Evolution of the Biosphere* 26:297–98.

Moldowan, J.M., J. Dalh, S.R. Jacobson, B.J. Huizing, F.J. Fago, R. Shetty, D.S. Watt, and K.E. Peters. 1996. Chemostratigraphic reconstruction of biofacies: Molecular evidence linking cyst-forming dinoflagellates with pre-Triassic ancestors. *Geology* 24:159–62.

Ourisson, G. 1994. Biomarkers in the Proterozoic record. *In* S. Bengtson (ed.), *Early Life on Earth*. New York: Columbia University Press.

Pflug, H.D. 1978. Yeast-like microfossils detected in oldest sediments of the earth. *Naturwissenschaften* 65:611–15.

Raymond, P.E. 1935. Pre-Cambrian life. *Bulletin of the Geological Society of America* 46:375–92.

Schidlowski, M. 1988. A 3,800-million-year isotopic record of life from carbon in sedimentary rocks. *Nature* 333:313–18.

Schieber, J. 1989. Pyrite mineralization in microbial mats from the mid-Proterozoic Newland Formation, Belt Supergroup, Montana, U.S.A. *Sedimentary Geology* 64:79–90.

Schopf, J.W. 1968. Microflora of the Bitter Springs Formation, Late Precambrian, central Australia. *Journal of Paleontology* 42:651–88.

———. 1992. Atlas of representative Precambrian microfossils. *In* J.W. Schopf and C. Klein (eds.), *The Proterozoic Biosphere: A Multidisciplinary Study*. Cambridge and New York: Cambridge University Press.

———. 1994. Disparate rates, differing fates: Tempo and mode of evolution changed from the Precambrian to the Phanerozoic. *Proceedings of the National Academy of Sciences of the United States of America* 91:6735–42.

Schopf, J.W., and E.S. Barghoorn. 1967. Alga-like fossils from the Early Precambrian of South Africa. *Science* 156:508–11.

Schopf, J.W., and B.M. Packer. 1987. Early Archean (3.3-billion to 3.5-billion-year-old) microfossils from Warrawoona Group, Australia. *Science* 237:70–72.

Schopf, J.W., and M.R. Walter. 1983. Archaean microfossils: New evidence of ancient microbes. *In* J.W. Schopf (ed.), *Earth's Earliest Biosphere: Its Origin and Evolution*. Princeton, New Jersey: Princeton University Press.

Seward, A.C. 1933. *Plant Life through the Ages*. 2nd ed., Cambridge: Cambridge University Press.

Siegel, S.M., K. Roberts, H. Nathan, and O. Daly. 1967. Living relative of the microfossil *Kakabekia. Science* 156:1231–34.

Swain, F.M., J.M. Bratt, and S. Kirkwood. 1970. Carbohydrates from Precambrian and Cambrian rocks and fossils. *Geological Society of America Bulletin* 81:499–504.

Tappan, H. 1980. *The Paleobiology of Plant Protists*. San Francisco: Freeman.

Trudinger, P.A., and N. Williams. 1982. Stratified sulfide deposition in modern and ancient environments. *In* H.D. Holland and M. Schidlowski (eds.), *Mineral Deposits and the Evolution of the Biosphere*. Berlin and New York: Springer-Verlag.

Vidal, G., and M. Moczydlowska-Vidal. 1997. Biodiversity, speciation, and extinction trends of Proterozoic and Cambrian phytoplankton. *Paleobiology* 23:230–46.

Walcott, C.D. 1915. Discovery of Algonkian bacteria. *Proceedings of the National Academy of Sciences of the United States of America* 1:256–57.

Walsh, M.M., and D.R. Lowe. 1987. Filamentous microfossils from the 3,500-Myr-old Onverwacht Group, Barberton Mountain Land, South Africa. *Nature* 314:530–33.

Further Reading

Margulis, L., and L. Olendzenski (eds.). 1992. *Environmental Evolution*. Cambridge, Massachusetts: MIT Press.

Schopf, J.W. (ed.). 1983. *Earth's Earliest Biosphere: Its Origin and Evolution*. Princeton, New Jersey: Princeton University Press

Schopf, J.W., and C. Klein (eds.). 1992. *The Proterozoic Biosphere: A Multidisciplinary Study*. Cambridge and New York: Cambridge University Press.

MICROPALEONTOLOGY, VERTEBRATE

The term "microvertebrates" refers to microfossils (fossil fragments) from vertebrates. Charles Moore, an English amateur paleontologist in the early nineteenth century, began the serious study of microvertebrates in the region of Bristol; as a young man at Cambridge, Fred McCoy undertook early histological work (studying microscopic structures) on early vertebrate scales (1853). C.H. Pander presented a definitive study of Baltic scales in 1856, but economic uses did not develop until after World War I, when petroleum companies began to finance applied micropaleontology, especially in the United States. Until recently, however, most microvertebrates, especially those of fishes, have been given scant regard in micropaleontological courses and text-books (e.g., Kummel and Raup 1965). D.J. Jones (1956) did devote four pages to vertebrate remains but they were dismissed as having no stratigraphic or environmental significance "except in local situations." (Stratigraphic studies analyze the characteristics of rock strata. One element studied is biological content; in fact, strata can sometimes be dated on the basis of the microorganisms they include.)

In the last few decades, however, much new information has been gained because of new techniques, such as acetic acid preparation and bulk sieving (e.g., McKenna in Kummel and Raup).

Animals from all the vertebrate groups, particularly juveniles, preserve well as microvertebrates. Consequent increase in ontogenetic (the developmental process), biogeographic, and biostratigraphic information comes from utilizing this fossil resource. In this essay we concentrate on fish microvertebrates, particularly in the Paleozoic era (570 to 250 million years ago). Knowledge has increased in great part due to the use of analytical and technical approaches pioneered by conodont scholars (conodonts are primitive chordates or vertebrates that are largely known from their abundant toothlike elements). These scholars traditionally use bulk sampling procedures and apply precise names to each conodont element (multielement terminology).

In the last decade an international research group was initiated to study Paleozoic vertebrate microfossils (see the newsletter *Ichthyolith Issues*, S. Turner ed.) From this sprung a UNESCO-IUGS International Geological Correlation Programme IGCP 328 Project: Paleozoic Microvertebrate Biochronology and Global Marine/Non-Marine Correlation, which operated from 1991 to 1996. The aims of this project were to coordinate research on microvertebrates, to integrate data, and to develop data bases of Paleozoic fishes. In addition, taxonomy (classification) of many early vertebrates has been clarified and nearly 1,000 publications have been produced (e.g., Turner and Blieck 1996; Arsenault et al. 1995; Lelièvre et al. 1995). By using fish microremains, the dating of rock strata on the basis of fossil content (biostratigraphy) has been investigated, allowing correlation of marine and nonmarine sequences. Data gathered have helped to solve other geological problems such as the nature of paleoenvironment, paleogeography and the distribution of taxa, and the impact of catastrophic events. One successful outcome has been production of biozonal schemes (systems organized according to biologically distinctive zones), in the first instance for Middle Paleozoic, and of correlation tables for all Paleozoic systems incorporating vertebrate zone fossils (those that signal a certain time period) (e.g., Turner 1995; Blieck and Turner 1997). The group and its IGCP project have revitalized work on microremains and shown their relevance to biostratigraphic studies, a field pioneered by Walter Gross (1936 et seq.) in Europe and by John W. Wells (1944) in America.

What Are Fish Microvertebrates?

Microfossils from fishes are referred to as microvertebrates, or sometimes "ichthyoliths." Generally, they are less than five millimeters in size, requiring a microscope to study them. Fine detail (micro-ornament and ultrastructure) is studied using a scanning electron microscope. The most common and abundant microvertebrates are teeth and scales (both simple and complex, some being "tesserae"—dermal armor—comprised of separate growing units united on a single base), modified forms ("denticles") such as clasper and tenaculae hooks (shark claspers), fin spines ("ichthyodorulites"), and various skeletal bone from all groups of fossil fishes. In addition, otoliths ("ear stones") may be preserved.

Although various fish bones, such as jawbones, ribs, and branchiostegal rays (bony rays that support the undersurface of the head of a fish) were thought to have little applied value in the past, slowly they are being found to have distinct characters that can aid

biostratigraphy. Other, rarer fossils include coprolites (fossilized feces) and calcified cartilage (e.g., in *McMurdodus whitei,* Turner and Young 1987). Coprolites are probably more common in some Mesozoic and Tertiary deposits, but they too can give much information on the microvertebrate component of a fauna and on the general biology of the fishes (e.g., McAllister 1996). Microvertebrates are fairly common (sometimes abundant) in marine and nonmarine sediments from Ordovician to Recent, occurring in general in shallow-water deposits. For instance, Jones (1956) and, more recently, I.J. Sansom and colleagues (1992) considered conodont elements to have been derived from fishes, but microvertebrate scholars have not accepted these structures as incontrovertibly vertebrate so far (e.g., Kemp and Nicoll 1996; Schultze 1996; Pridmore et al. 1997).

Scale and tooth patterns in various families and genera and the variation in scale or tooth shape and pattern over the skin or in the jaw of an individual fish are elucidated by examining articulated fossil specimens (those preserved in their original shape and organization) and modern fish (Figure 1). As used in biostratigraphy, specimens usually are identified in terms of familial or generic rank, and form or organ genera (generic names applied to isolated structures, rather than to whole animals) are used where association and identification with a particular fish are impossible to establish.

Scales

Louis Agassiz made an early classification of fossil fishes based on their scale type. Most of the principal groups of fishes possess distinctive types of scales. Agassiz defined "placoid," typical of some sharks; "ganoid," typical of actinopterygians (ray-finned fishes); "cycloid," with its characteristic circular outline and series of growth lines; and "ctenoid," with its circular outline modified posteriorly (at the rear) by a series of plications, which give a comblike, or serrate, edge. To Agassiz's list we might add "cosmoid" for sarcopterygian (includes fleshy-finned fishes, lungfish, and ceolacanths) scales, with their cosmine coating (a distinctive hard tissue with an enamel-like outer layer and deeper dentinal layer permeated by a "pore-canal system"). All types of modified scales are found as microfossils. Fin ray elements (lepidotrichiae) are confined to the osteichthyes (bony fishes) but have distinctive forms; fin spines are found in acanthodians and sharks; sexually dimorphic elements (those that differentiate between male and female) are found especially in Carboniferous-to-Recent sharks and holocephalans (a distinctive group of cartilaginous fishes that includes the living chimaeras or rat-fishes).

Teeth

Teeth are considered to be modified placoid scales (single crowns on a rhombic-shaped, nongrowing base, as in modern sharks) or dermal denticles. These structures vary greatly in shape: they can include simple, elongate cones; multiblade-like forms; discoidal; and conical-to-hemispherical "pavement" teeth in certain sharks. Scholars use features of the base and cusps as distinguishing tooth characters, along with micro-ornament on cusps or external tooth

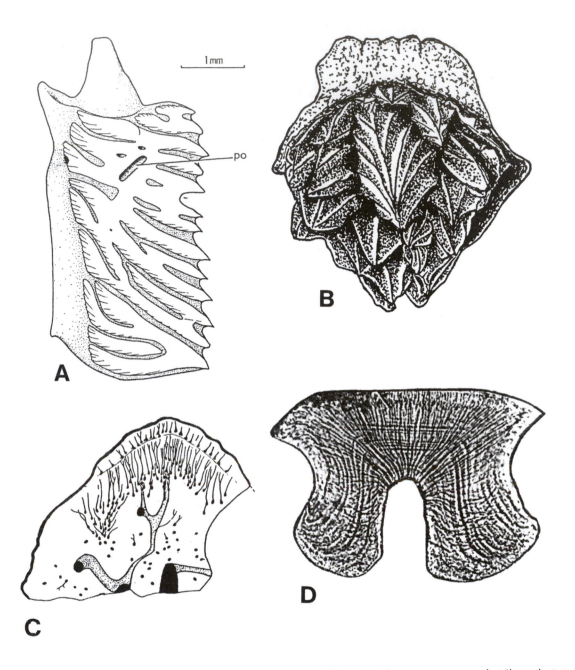

Figure 1. *A*, paleoniscoid scale, *Moythomasia durgaringa*, lateral line scale in lateral view; *po*, pore opening through ganoline layer. *B*, placoderm trunk scale from Lower Devonian acanthothoracid *Murrindalaspis wallacei*; scale, approximately ×3.5. *C*, characteristic placoderm hard tissue: semidentine with unipolar dentine tubules in upper layer. *D*, thelodont scale histological structure: sagittal section through *Thelodus parvidens*; scale ×150. From: *A*, Gardiner (1984), courtesy of Brian Gardiner; *B*, after Long and Young (1988); *C*, Gross (1947); *D*, after Märss (1986).

surface (e.g., Turner and Blieck 1995). Having several types of teeth ("heterodont dentition") is typical of several fish groups.

Otoliths

Calcifications in the fluid-filled inner ear are used by all gnathostomes (jawed vertebrates) for spatial orientation and to monitor vertical and horizontal acceleration and deceleration. These calcifications may take the form of large ear stones or otoliths. Otoliths are ovoid to lens-shaped and are usually composed of of calcium carbonate; a few taxa use calcium phosphate. Three types are formed in the labyrinth of the ear—a very small lapillus, the astericus, and the larger and most distinctive sagitta, which normally are found as microfossils. Sagitta are well-structured, with a scalloped edge, a median elongate sulcus (groove), and an accessory ventral (belly-side) furrow. They range in size from 0.1 to 3 millimeters in diameter. D. Nolf's (1985) Handbook is the "bible" on otolith identification up to the early 1980s and includes reference to Paleozoic otoliths found by V.N. Talimaa. Nolf has presented a cladistic classification, H.-P. Schultze (1990) has discussed otoliths from acanthodians (early jawed fishes called spiny sharks) and reviewed gnathostome occurrences in time, and J. Clack (1996) has discovered fossil coelacanth otoliths. To date, these structures have been most useful in biostratigraphy of Tertiary marine deposits, but, as more are discovered in the Paleozoic, they will surely be utilized.

What Use Are Fish Microvertebrates?

Microscopic remains are more abundant than complete fish fossils, and they possess distinctive shapes and structures. Also, they rarely are distorted during compaction. (The weight and pressure caused by accumulating sediments can compress—or compact—some structures.) However, microvertebrates can be broken or altered by heat. Preliminary work has been done on a Color Alteration Index for Microvertebrates, similar to one utilized in conodont study (e.g., Turner 1994). By their nature, microvertebrates can be found in small samples of rock such as borehole core (drilled during such activities as oil well prospecting). Teeth, scales, and other microremains also are often found in bonebeds in myriad numbers. And, because fish can swim in marine to fresh water, they are particularly important for correlating marine and nonmarine rocks in the absence of conodonts and, now, often in conjunction with palynological data (data from fossilized pollen and spores). As microvertebrates are more common in space and time than whole fossils, they can be used to investigate biostratigraphy, correlation of marine-nonmarine sequences, and controlling environmental factors and processes such as climate change, geographic change, and paleoenvironment adaptation.

Study of fish microremains also helps clarify taxonomy and biology of vertebrates. Microvertebrates allow a glimpse of the ontogeny and life histories of certain fishes because embryonic, larval, and juvenile structures are often preserved only as microfossils. Histological and ultrastructural study of scales, for instance, can aid in understanding the growth of individual animals (e.g., in thelodonts by Märss 1992; in placoderms by Upeniece and Upenieks 1992) and the evolution of hard tissues (e.g., Gross 1966; Reif 1982). Some groups and species are known only from microvertebrates (e.g., *Thrinacodus*), and we must use modern and fossil analogs (similar species or structures) to understand them.

One example of a biozonal scheme using microvertebrates is the Standard Silurian Microvertebrate Column (Märss et al. 1995). Using mainly thelodont scales, acanthodian scales, and one primitive osteichthyan (*Andreolepis*), Märss and colleagues proposed a series of zones for use in the Northern Hemisphere based particularly on research in the Baltic States and Britain. This is being tested in various northern regions and now in East Gondwana. Another success story of the UNESCO project is the utilization of phoebodont shark teeth as an efficient alternative to conodonts in marine Mid- to Late Devonian worldwide. M. Ginter and A. Ivanov (e.g., 1992, 1995) have contributed biostratigraphic schemes to the Standard Devonian Scheme being developed by the Subcommission on Devonian Stratigraphy.

Agnatha—The "Jawless Fishes"

Many agnathans provide microvertebrates. Microvertebrates form the oldest vertebrates known—Cambrian and Ordovician pteraspidomorphs—and their biostratigraphic use have been studied recently by G.C. Young (e.g., 1997) and Young and colleagues (1996). The Arandaspiformes, including *Arandaspis* from central Australia and *Sacabambaspis* from Bolivia and Australia, are known from scales, small plates, and pieces of ornamented bone. *Sacabambaspis* has distinctive oak-leaf style ornament. Astraspiformes in North America and Siberia also have distinctive tubercles (bony protrusions).

Heterostraci

Heterostracans proper (jawless fishes with separate but solid dorsal and ventral head shields and a single common gill opening on each side) are known from the Northern Hemisphere. The earliest heterostracans, such as *Athenaegis,* are Early Silurian in age and are found mostly in Arctic Canada. Dermal armor fragments and trunk scales made up of two or more dentine segments are typical heterostracan microvertebrates. The Silurian heterostracans fall into two groups, the cyathaspidiforms and the traquairaspidiforms. The cyathaspidiforms have simple ridged ornamentation. The traquairaspidiforms group with other "tessellate" taxa in having either pavement-style armor, armor decorated with oak leaf-patterned dentine tubercles, or a more flexible scale cover of separate tesserae (compound scales). At the end of the Silurian, there appeared "higher heterostracans" (anchipteraspidid pteraspidiforms), which were basic heterostracans of the Devonian with very taxon-specific dermal armor. By the end of Middle Devonian times through Late Frasnian, the only surviving heterostracans are the psammosteids (advanced heterostrachans), the scales of which have recently been studied by E. Mark-Kurik (1993). Dermal armor was also studied by her and L.B. Halstead (1964, 1965).

Thelodonti

Thelodont scales cover the entire body of the fish, as well as lining the area inside the mouth to the pharynx, in the manner of modern sharks. Generally, they range from 0.1 to 3 millimeters in size. Scales from the head, midthorax, and postpectoral body (behind the pectoral fin), and other areas, such as fins, are differently shaped. A scale is made of dentine in the crown and neck; a base of acellular bone or aspidin has spaces for "Sharpey's fibers," which held the scale in place. Study of the internal structure is important. Based on this histology, W. Gross (1967) defined two types, now regarded as orders, the Thelodontida, which has orthodentine (dentine with straight tubules) and one or a few openings into the pulp cavity, and Katoporida, which has numerous dentine canals opening into the pulp cavity. The Loganiida, an older (probably more primitive) group, have a simple dentine structure; some have no definite pulp canal. Typically, thelodont scales have a short-to-long anterior (front) anchoring device or a series of basal projections.

Thelodont scales have been used successfully for biostratigraphy for some three decades and, in some parts of the world, are often the only or the commonest fossils found in rocks that developed in shallow water of the late Silurian and Devonian. (For instance, this is the case with *Turinia* in Australia.) V.N. Talimaa (e.g., 1995) and S. Turner (1997) have defined thelodont biozones for the Northern and Southern Hemispheres.

Osteostraci and Anaspida

The oldest known, putative (alleged) osteostracan scales come from the Middle Ordovician Harding Sandstone in Colorado. Scales from the trunks of anaspids and cephalaspids (the latter members of the Osteostraci) are known as microvertebrates, but they have been studied little as yet for biostratigraphical purposes, although Märss (1986, 1989) has used them in Baltic biostratigraphy. O. Afanassieva (e.g., 1995) has investigated details of the micro-ornament on osteostracan armor and scales.

Other Agnathans

No systematic study has been made yet of the dermal ornaments and scales of endemic Chinese galeaspids and polybranchiaspids (unusual agnathans from China and North Vietnam), but Wang N.-Z. (1984) has described ornaments of the Early Silurian *Hanyangaspis* and P. Janvier (1990) has investigated the histological structure.

Acanthodians—First Jawed Predatory Fishes

The oldest microremains that are classified incontrovertibly as acanthodian are scales from the Early Silurian of Siberia (found by V. Karatajuté-Talimaa of Lithuania), although Sansom and colleagues (1995) claims to have found Mid-Ordovician scales from the Harding Sandstone. These generally small (less than 20 centimeters) bony fishes have an exoskeleton (skeleton on the outside of the body) of small to large (0.1 to 3 millimeters plus) rhomboid scales. The head, cheeks, and pectoral regions were covered with ornamented plates. Otoliths are also found. Fins were supported by spines formed of dentine, typically with ribbed ornamentation. The scales have no basal pulp cavity (as do thelodont and some shark scales) but may have neck canal openings for vascular strands. Acanthodian scales are distinguished, too, by their "box-in-box," or onionlike, growth zones. (This type of growth is called "superpositional.") However, this type of growth is not universal, and many taxa exhibit appositional (marginal) growth, either in scales from particular regions of the body or even in all scales.

A typical flank scale comprises a bony base with lamellae (layers) that parallel the basal surface and a dentinous crown with growth zones that parallel the outer surface. Radial, circular, and "ascending" vascular canals penetrate the crown, entering and leaving the scale via small openings in its "neck." Dentine tubules lead off from the vascular canals; each main tubule and its branches usually are confined to one growth zone. Two types of dentine are found in acanthodian scales. "Mesodentine" is characterized by a network of randomly oriented tubules that often has lacuna-like (resembling a bone cell chamber) widenings where the tubules coalesce. A special type, only found in climatiiforms (early,

presumed primitive, acanthodians), possesses a "Stranggewebe," which is characterized by parallel, thin, elongate lacunae that stretch between adjacent ascending canals. The other dentinous tissue is "orthodentine," characterized by long dentine tubules with limited branching.

The Acanthodii have been separated into Climatiiformes, Ischnacanthiformes, and Acanthodiformes. Microremains from members of the Climatiidae include head tesserae with apposed growth zones, fin spines with a short insertion zone (area that exists under the skin surface) and noded ornamentation, pectoral dermal plates, and multiple tooth whorls with flattened cusps (points on a tooth). The scales have *"Nostolepis"*-type microstructure, characterized by large circular and ascending vascular canals, bone cell lacunae in the base, and often also in the crown, and mesodentine (with or without Stranggewebe) forming the crown growth zones. Specialized scale types include "Pultschuppen," which are thought to be branchial (gill) scales, and umbellate scales (star-shaped or with a series of radiating ridges) that may have lined sensory canals. The well-preserved Arctic Canadian *Kathemacanthus* exhibits head tesserae, fin spines bearing longitudinal ridges, multiple tooth whorls with both conical and flattened cusps, and flank scales that were large, thin, unornamented, and overlapping. The histology of these scales is unknown. The specialized scales of *Kathemacanthus* include post-branchial "artichoke" scales and tectal tesserae, which both exhibit apposed growth zones.

Diplacanthids (Middle Devonian acanthodians) lacked teeth, and their microremains include large ornamented cheek plates, circumorbital bones, and fin spines with longitudinal ridges and a relatively long insertion zone. Their ornamented scales had *"Diplacanthus"*-type microstructure, characterized by vascular canals that penetrated both base and crown and no bone cell lacunae. The Gyracanthids (which include the largest acanthodians) had large, dentinous fin spines that bear a characteristic ornamentation of oblique, noded ridges; pectoral dermal plates; and scales with apposed growth zones in the crown.

The ischnacanthids (mostly predatory acanthodians) had head tesserae; probable sensory line scales also from the head, perhaps specialized branchial scales; symphyseal (at midline of lower jaw) tooth whorls; small, single or multicusped, isolated teeth; dentigerous jaw bones; "dentition cones"; and ornamented or smooth flank scales with *"Acanthodes"*- or *"Poracanthodes"*-type microstructure. Their true jaws had strong ankylosed (fused to bone) teeth whose morphology changed from front to back (heterodont dentition). In *Acanthodes*-type histology, the dentine tubules are long and have minimal branching, the bony base is formed of many thin lamellae and lacks lacunae, and crown growth zones are each capped by an enameloid layer. *Poracanthodes*-type histology includes both superpositional and appositional crown growth zones and is characterized by a system of canals (possibly mucus-filled) through the crown; these open out through pores on the crown surface.

Microremains from the oldest and least derived (most primitive) family of Acanthodiformes, the mesacanthids, include fin spines with longitudinal ridges and a short insertion zone, irregularly shaped head scales, mandibular (lower jaw) splints, branchiostegal rays, and smooth scales with *"Acanthodes"*-type microstructure. The cheiracanthids have slender fin spines with long insertion zones, small polygonal head scales, thin circumorbitals (bones around the eye socket), and scales with *"Acanthodes"*-type microstructure, which usually are ornamented with longitudinal or posteriorly converging ribs on the crown. Acanthodid microremains resemble those of the Mesacanthidae, but their fin spines have a long insertion zone.

The biostratigraphic use of acanthodian scales, in particular, has increased in the last two decades, pioneered especially by Lithuanian scholars, J. Valiukevicius (1979 et seq.), Märss (e.g., 1986), and J. Zajic (e.g., 1995).

Placoderms—Armor-Plated Jawed Fish

This complex group of extinct fishes had a dermal armor of bone and an internal cartilaginous skeleton. Placoderms had jaws with teeth fused together to form toothplates, and an exoskeleton of bony plates and scales, best seen in Lower Devonian placoderms. Many of these earlier placoderms (e.g., acanthothoracids and rhenanids) had almost a complete covering of platelets and body scales. The latter are small and cuboid with a rounded bony base and have a tubercular crown edged with a crimped fringe. Others are flattened and rhomboid. Tubercles and ornaments are made of primitive and derived types of dentine (mesodentine and semidentine). Small bones, including jawbones (gnathals) from juveniles, can be found complete in the microfauna (Figure 2).

Although most placoderm taxa are based on descriptions of dermal plates from the head and thoracic regions, partial or fully articulated specimens with plates and associated scales have been described from many groups. Dissociated scales occur commonly in the Early to Middle Devonian, particularly in China and Australia. Early Devonian primitive arthrodires (main group of placoderms) and acanthothoracids, petalichthyids, and rhenanids (three groups of primitive scale- or tesserae-bearing placoderms), bore dentinous, stellate tubercles on a lamellar bone base. Acanthothoracids (e.g., *Romundina* from the Arctic Canada and *Murrindalaspis* from Australia) have a micro-ornament of small nodes along the crests of the tubercular ridges, while in other groups (e.g., petalichthyids) the ridges apparently were smooth. Tubercles are composed of a dentinous tissue with lacunae sending off multiple processes similar to those in mesodentine. It is different from the latter in that distal (peripheral) dentine tubules arise from pear-shaped lacunae, each of which generally gives rise to a single process that is oriented perpendicular to the tubercle surface. T. Ørvig first recognized this specialized dentinous tissue, "semidentine," as a characteristic placoderm feature (1951).

Scales of many Middle and Upper Devonian placoderms (including antiarchs *Bothriolepis, Pterichthyodes,* and *Asterolepis*), and the ptyctodont *Campbellodus* (a member of a group of unusual Devonian placoderms with male claspers), lack an outer dentine layer (e.g., Ivanov et al. 1996). Loss of the outer layer, presumably to lighten the exoskeleton for more efficient swimming, seems to have occurred in most lineages, with total loss of scales in most taxa by the Late Devonian.

Chondrichthyes—The "Sharks," or Cartilaginous Fishes

The Chondrichthyes, a diverse group of jawed fishes that also includes the Holocephali (chimaeras or ratfishes), brings to mind sharp and aggressively used teeth, but early sharks seem not to have had recognizable teeth. Instead, they only had a covering of scales. Scales, which form a complex patterned squamation (scaly covering) in all but a few sharks, can be small or large, simple or complex. Like thelodonts (literally, "mammal-toothed," because the discrete scales covering the body have mammalian-like dentine), scales also coat the lining of the mouth, buccal (mouth) and pharyngeal (throat) cavities, and gill arches. Sometimes scales form complex branchial denticles (e.g., Nelson 1970). O.H. St. John and A.H. Worthen (1875) described these in Paleozoic sharks, naming them *"Stemmatodus,"* so that now the term stemmatodont is used for branchial scales, as in Carboniferous symmoriids. (This is a group of "cladodont" sharks from Late Devonian-Early Permian with teeth with large central cusps and smaller lateral ones.)

V. Karatajuté-Talimaa (1992) devised a morphogenetic classification of chondrichthyan scales based on differences between nongrowing and growing scales. She defined nine types. Quite complex *Mongolepis* and *Polymerolepis* types seem to be the oldest sharklike scales; *Elegestolepis* types are simple placoid scales, also of at least Early Silurian age; *Altholepis, Seretolepis,* and *Lugalepis* types appear by Early Devonian; *Protacrodus, "Heterodontus,"* and *Ctenacanthus* types appear later in the Devonian. Large complete sharks preserved in black shales from the Late Devonian to Carboniferous in North America (e.g., Zangerl and Case 1973; Williams 1985; Maisey 1989) enable us to study variations in teeth and squamation. Shark teeth come in many forms, all of which characterize different groups after the Late Silurian. Some, like the phoebodonts mentioned above, are now important for biostratigraphy. Some sharks also have dentinous fin spines, but only on unpaired fins; these are rarely found as microfossils.

Because sharks used internal fertilization and often had bizarre sexual habits, they have specialized mating structures called "claspers." Often, modified denticles and pelvic scales cover unusual claspers; these also are found in ptyctodont placoderms (e.g., Janvier 1996). Clasping devices on the head are modified from spines, like "tenaculae" in modern chimaeras. For instance, stethacanthid sharks (another cladodont group of sharks within symmoriids) have a dorsal brush (actually, a highly modified dorsal fin) capped by a layer of numerous denticles (originally named *Lambdodus*).

Osteichthyans, or Bony Fishes

The true bony fishes (actinopterygians and sarcopterygians) provide many microvertebrates after the Late Silurian, including scales, teeth, and numerous bones, including vertebrae (e.g., Schultze and Chorn 1986). Osteichthyans are characterized by fins with dermal fin ray elements, modified scales called "lepidotrichia" (Janvier 1996). In many Paleozoic bony fish, scales are ornamented with ganoine (see below) or cosmine (hard, dentine-like material that forms cosmoid scales). The type of scale appears to distinguish one group from another.

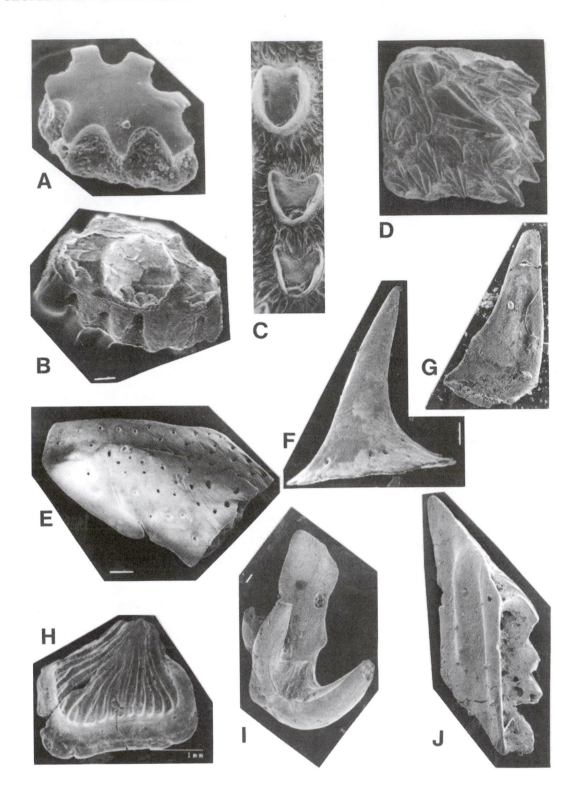

Figure 2. *A,* thelodont scale, crown view of *Thelodus* sp., Silurian; scale: approximately x100. *B,* protacrodont shark tooth, crown view of *Protacrodus* sp., Late Devonian; scale bar, 200µ. *C,* sarcopterygian scale ornament, crown view of tubercles of *Laccognathus,* Late Devonian; scale, approximately x45. *D,* shark scale, crown view of *Ohiolepis newberryi,* Middle Devonian; scale bar, 200µ. *E,* Sarcopterygian scale, surface view of cosmine, Middle Devonian; scale bar, 200µ. *F,* shark placoid denticle, lateral view, Late Devonian; scale bar, 200µ. *G,* sarcopterygian tooth, alter view of *Onychodus* sp., Early Devonian; scale, approximately x50. *H,* acanthodian scale, crown view of *Cheiracanthoides* sp., Middle Devonian; scale bar, 200µ. *I,* shark tooth, ventral view of *Thrinacodus ferox,* Late Devonian; scale bar, 200µ. *J,* paleoniscoid scale, ventral view of *Moythomasia?* sp., Late Devonian; scale, approximately x100. From: *B,* Turner (1982); *C,* after Vorobyeva and Panteleyev (1995); *F,* from Turner (1982); *I,* from Turner (1982).

Actinopterygii—Fin-Ray Fishes

The ancient members of the Actinopterygii were predatory, with ornamented bone on the dermal head plates, jawbones, tooth plates, and numerous small teeth. In all but the oldest genera, the teeth have a clear tip formed of a special tissue called "acrodin." Actinopterygians have rhomboidal or round scales. The former are usually referred to as "ganoid scales" because they have an outer covering of "ganoine," an enamel-like tissue. Ganoine is deposited by the basal layer of the epidermis, like true enamel, but is distinguished from the latter by the surface and ultrastructure (e.g., Schultze 1996). Paleozoic actinopterygians bore "palaeoniscoid scales," composed of an inner, lamellar (layered) bone layer; middle dentine layer; and outer ganoine layer. Modified "fulcral scales" sheathe the leading edge of midline fins in primitive actinopterygians. Fulcral scales vary at the specific and generic level with respect to morphology and position on the body.

The oldest actinopterygian is *Andreolepis*, from the Late Silurian of Gotland, Sweden. Its scales are typically palaeoniscoid, although only occasionally contain ganoine. Except for several early taxa—*Naxilepis* (Late Silurian, China), *Orvikuina* (Early Devonian, Baltic), and *Terenolepis* (Early Devonian, Australia)—Paleozoic palaeoniscoid flank scales are characterized by "peg and socket" articulation (jointing) (e.g., *Dialipina*, Early-Middle Devonian of Canada and Eurasia; and *Ligulalepis*, Early Devonian of Australia and China). A few rare taxa, including *Cheirolepis* (Middle-Late Devonian of Canada and Europe), *Tarrasius* (Early Carboniferous of Scotland), and *Yaomashania* (Upper Permian of China) have very small scales that are superficially similar to those of acanthodians. However, the histological structure of their scales is of "advanced" palaeoniscoid type, with superposed layers of ganoine.

Developmental trends in scale structure are notable, even within the same genus, with earlier taxa having bone cell lacunae in the base and minimal overlaying of ganoine. Later taxa lack lacunae but have multiple ganoine layers. They also usually have "Canals of Williamson" (which apparently had a vascular function). These structures penetrate the base and open out on the inner surface. In the younger lepidosteid type, scales usually lack the middle dentine layer. The number of actinopterygians increased dramatically during the Carboniferous, with scales of many taxa having very similar internal structure and ornament. B.G. Gardiner (1984), Schultze and D. Bardack (1987), and C. Burrow (1994) have dealt with squamation variation and ontogeny of scales in several early actinopterygians. D.N. Esin and colleagues (e.g., 1992) have applied the morphology of scales to biostratigraphic studies.

Sarcopterygians—Lobe-Finned Fishes

These small to enormous predatory fishes include onychodonts (Late Silurian-Devonian), porolepiforms, osteolepiforms, rhizodonts, and panderichthyids (all Paleozoic), coelacanths (Devonian-Recent), and dipnoi (lungfish) (Devonian-Recent). All are represented by ornamented bone, scales, and lepidotrichia (fin-ray scales), some with distinctive enamel-like "cosmine," which has numerous pores or pits in the surface. Most have jawbones armed with stabbing teeth and symphyseal tooth whorls. Sarcopterygian otoliths have definitely been found. Schultze (1977) reviewed the morphology of scales of osteichthyans.

Little work has been done as yet on sarcopterygian microvertebrates, but scholars are paying attention to histology and ornament details on scales and teeth. Such work has brought the nature of *Lophosteus superbus* as a stem group osteichthyan into doubt (Otto 1991, Burrow 1995).

Dipnoi

Lungfishes are specialized sarcopterygians typified by ridged and tuberculated tooth plates that are formed of a specialized dentine called "petrodentine." These fishes also have distinctive bone, rounded scales with ornamented cosmine, and sometimes "Westoll Lines," which indicate resorption during growth. N.J. Krupina (e.g., 1995) and A. Kemp (1997) have investigated microtooth plates of Devonian lungfishes. P.A. Pridmore and R.E. Barwick (1993) have investigated scale variation.

Tetrapoda

Early amphibian tetrapods in the late Devonian and early Carboniferous stayed fishlike and retained lepidotrichia and small dorsal and/or ventral flattened scutes or scales (e.g., Coates 1996). Such scales and teeth should be recognizable as microvertebrates.

SUSAN TURNER AND CAROLE J. BURROW

See also Chondrichthyans; Jawles Fishes; Teeth

Works Cited

Afanassieva, O. 1995. The structure of the exoskeleton of the Tremataspidoidei and its significance in the taxonomy of osteostracans (Agnatha). *In* H. Lelièvre, S. Wenz, A. Blieck, and R. Cloutier (eds.), *Premiers vertébrés et vertébrés inférieurs* (8th Congress. Intern, Paris, 4–9 Septembre 1995). *Géobios Mémoire Spécial* 19:13–18.

Agassiz, J.L.R. 1833–44. *Recherches sur les Poissons Fossiles*. Neuchâtel: Imprimerie de Petitpierre.

Arsenault, M., H. Lelièvre, and P. Janvier (eds.). 1995. *Études sur les Vertébrés inférieurs* (VIIᵉ Symposium International, Parc de Miguasha, Québec, 1991). *Bulletin du Muséum National d'Histoire Naturelle*, sec. C, ser. 4, 17 (1–4).

Blieck, A., and Turner, S. (eds.). 1997. *IGCP 328 Final Report*. Senckenberg: Courier Forschungsinstitut.

Burrow, C. 1994. Form and function in scales of *Ligulalepis toombsi* Schultze, a palaeoniscoid from the Early Devonian of Australia. Adelaide 1993 CAVEPS Symposium Volume. *Records of South Australia Museum* 27 (2):175–85.

——. 1995. A new lophosteiform (Osteichthyes) from the Lower Devonian of Australia. *In* H. Lelièvre, S. Wenz, A. Blieck, and R. Cloutier (eds.), *Premiers vertébrés et vertébrés inférieurs* (8th Congress. Intern, Paris, 4–9 Septembre 1995). *Géobios Mémoire Spécial* 19:327–34.

Clack, J. 1996. Otoliths in fossil coelacanths. *Journal of Vertebrate Paleontology* 16 (1):168–71.

Coates, M.I. 1996. The Devonian tetrapod *Acanthostega gunnari* Jarvik: Postcranial anatomy, basal tetrapod interrelationships and patterns of skeletal evolution. *Transactions of the Royal Society of Edinburgh (Earth Sciences)* 87:363–421.

Esin, D.N., V.N. Ustinov, I.I. Shatalov, and O.G. Saltykov. 1992. First finds of an ichthyofauna in Middle Carboniferous strata of the Tunguska Syneclise. *Transactions of the Academy of Science USSR* 314 (5):238–40.

Gardiner, B.G. 1984. The relationships of the palaeoniscid fishes, a review based on new specimens of Mimia and Moythomasia from the Upper Devonian of Western Australia. *Bulletin of the British Museum of Natural History, London (Geology)* 37:173–428.

Ginter, M., and A. Ivanov. 1992. Devonian phoebodont shark teeth. *Acta Palaeontologica Polonica* 37:55–75.

———. 1995. Middle/Late Devonian Phoebodont-based ichthyolith zonation. In H. Lelièvre, S. Wenz, A. Blieck, and R. Cloutier (eds.), *Premiers vertébrés et vertébrés inférieurs* (8th Congress. Intern, Paris, 4–9 Septembre 1995). *Géobois Mémoire Spécial* 19:351–56.

Gross, W. 1936. Histologische Studien am Aussenskelett fossiler Agnathen und Fische. *Palaeontographica* 83A:1–60.

———. 1938. Der histologische Aufbau der Anaspiden-Schuppen. *Norsk geollogisk tiddskrift* 17:191–96.

———. 1947. Die Agnathen und Acanthodier des obersilurischen Beyrichienkalks. *Palaeontographica* 96A:91–61.

———. 1966. Kleine Schuppenkunde. *Neues Jahrbuch für Geologie and Paläontologie, Abhandlungen* 125:29–48.

———. 1967. Über Thelodontier-Schuppen. *Palaeontographica* 127A:1–47.

Halstead, L.B. 1964. Psammosteiformes (Agnatha) a review with descriptions of new material from the Lower Devonian of Poland. 1, general part. *Palaeontologia Polonica* 13:1–135.

———. 1965. Psammosteiformes (Agnatha) a review with descriptions of new material from the Lower Devonian of Poland. 2, Systematic part. *Palaeontologica Polonica* 15:1–168.

Ivanov, A., E. Luksevics, and I. Upeniece. 1996. The squamous part of an asterolepid body. *Modern Geology* 20 (3):341–50.

Janvier, P. 1990. La structure de l'exosquelette des Galeaspida (Vertebrat). *Comptes rendus de l'Académie de Science Paris,* ser. 2, 310:655–69.

———. 1996. *Early Vertebrates.* Oxford Monographs on Geology and Geophysics, 33. Oxford: Clarendon; New York: Oxford University Press.

Jones, D.J. 1956. *Introduction to Microfossils.* New York: Harper.

Karatajuté-Talimaa, V. 1992. The early stages of the dermal skeleton formation in chondrichthyans. *In* E. Mark-Kurik (ed.), *Fossil Fishes as Living Animals.* Tallinn: Academy of Sciences of Estonia.

Kemp, A. 1997. *In* R.K. Jones and S. Turner (eds.), Late Devonian fauna from the Columbine Sandstone (Coffee Hill Member), Gap Creek, central New South Wales. *In* A. Blieck and S. Turner (eds.), *IGCP 328 Final Report.* Senckenberg: Courier Forschungsinstitut.

Kemp, A., and R.S. Nicoll. 1996. A histochemical analysis of biological residues in conodont elements. *Modern Geology* 20 (3):287–302.

Krupina, N.I. 1995. Comparison of the larval dentition developmental patterns in Devonian and Recent dipnoans. *In* S. Turner (ed.), *Palaeozoic Microvertebrates 1995 Report: Moscow-94 Workshop.* Ichthyolith Issues Special Publication 1. Socorro: J.J. Zidek Service.

Kummel, B., and D. Raup. (eds.). 1965. *Handbook of Paleontological Techniques.* San Francisco: Freeman.

Lelièvre, H., S. Wenz, A. Blieck, and R. Cloutier (eds.). 1995. *Premiers vertébrés et vertébrés inférieurs* (8th Congress. Intern, Paris, 4–9 Septembre 1995). *Géobios Mémoire Spécial* 19.

Long, J.A., and G.C. Young. 1988. Acanthothoracid remains from the Early Devonian of New South Wales, including a complete sclerotic capsule and pelvic girdle. *Memoirs of the Association of Australasian Palaeontologists* 7:65–80.

Maisey, J.G. 1989. *Hamiltonichthys mapesi,* g. and sp. nov. (Chondrichthyes; Elasmobranchii), from the Upper Pennsylvanian of Kansas. *American Museum of Natural History Novitates* 2931:1–42.

Mark-Kurik, E. 1993. Notes on the squamation in psammosteids. *Modern Geology* 18:1007–14.

Märss, T. 1986. Silurian Vertebrates of Estonia and West Latvia. *Fossilia Baltica.* Tallinn: Academy of Sciences of Estonia.

———. 1989. Vertebrates. *In* C.H. Holland, and M.G. Bassett (eds.), *A Global Standard for the Silurian System. National Museum of Wales, Geology Series,* 9:284–89.

———. 1992. The structure of growth layers of Silurian fish scales as a potential evidence of the environmental changes. *In* E. Mark-Kurik (ed.), *Fossil Fishes as Living Animals.* Tallinn: Academy of Sciences of Estonia.

Märss, T., D. Fredholm, V. Karatajuté-Talimaa, S. Turner, L. Jeppsson, and G. Nowlan. 1995. Silurian vertebrate biozonal scheme. *In* H. Lelièvre, S. Wenz, A. Blieck, and R. Cloutier (eds.), *Premiers vertébrés et vertébrés inférieurs* (8th Congress. Intern, Paris, 4–9 Septembre 1995). *Géobios Mémoire Spéciale* 19:369–72.

McAllister, J. 1996. Coprolitic remains from the Devonian Escuminac Formation. *In* H.-P. Schultze and R. Cloutier (eds.), *Devonian Fishes and Plants of Miguasha, Quebec, Canada.* Munich: Friedrich Pfeil.

McCoy, F. 1853. On the supposed Silurian fish remains. *Quarterly Journal of the Geological Society of London* 9:12–15.

Nelson, G.J. 1970. Pharyngeal denticles (Placoid scales) of sharks, with notes on the dermal skeleton of vertebrates. *American Museum of Natural History Novitates* 2 (415):1–26.

Nolf, D. 1985. Otolithi piscium. *In* H.-P. Schultze (ed.), *Handbook of Paleoichthyology.* Stuttgart and New York: Gustav Fischer.

Ørvig, T. 1951. Histologic studies on Placoderms and fossil Elasmobranchs. 1, The endoskeleton, with remarks on the hard tissues of lower vertebrates. in general. *Arkiv foer Zoologi* 2 (2):321–456.

Otto, M. 1991. Zur systematischen Stellung der Lophosteiden (Obersilur, Pisces inc. sedis). *Paläontologische Zeitschrift* 65:345–50.

Pander, C.H. 1856. *Monographie der fossilen Fische des silurischen Systems der russisch-baltischen Gouvernements.* St. Petersburg: Buchdruckerei die Kaiserlichen Akademie der Wissenschaften.

Pridmore, P.A., and R.E. Barwick. 1993. Post-cranial morphologies of the Late Devonian dipnoans, Griphognathus and Chirodipterus and locomotor implications. *Memoir of the Association of Australasian Palaeontologists* 15:161–82.

Pridmore, P.A., R.E. Barwick, and R.S. Nicoll. 1997. Soft tissue anatomy and the affinities of conodonts. *Lethaia* 29:317–28.

Reif, W.-E. 1982. Evolution of dermal skeleton and dentition in vertebrates: The odontode regulation theory. *In* M. Hecht, B. Wallace, and G. Prance (eds.), *Evolutionary Biology.* Vol. 15, New York and London: Plenum Press.

Sansom, I.J., M.P. Smith, H.A. Armstrong, and M.M. Smith. 1992. Presence of the earliest vertebrate hard tissues in conodonts. *Science* 256:1308–11.

Sansom, I.J., M.P. Smith, M.M. Smith, and P. Turner. 1995. The Harding Sandstone revisited: New look at some old bones. *In* H. Lelièvre, S. Wenz, A. Blieck, and R. Cloutier (eds.), *Premiers vertébrés et vertébrés inférieurs* (8th Congress. Intern, Paris, 4–9 Septembre 1995). *Géobios Mémoire Spécial* 19:57–60.

Schultze, H.-P. 1977. Ausgangsform und Entwicklung der rhombischen Schuppen der Osteichthyes (Pisces). *Paläontologische Zeitschrift* 51:152–68.

———. 1990. A new acanthodian from the Pennsylvanian of Utah, U.S.A., and the distribution of otoliths in gnathostomes. *Journal of Vertebrate Paleontology* 10:49–58.

———. 1996. Conodont histology: An indicator of vertebrate relationship? *Modern Geology* 20 (3):275–86.

Schultze, H.-P., and D. Bardack. 1987. Diversity and size changes in palaeonisciform fishes (Actinopterygii, Pisces) from the Pennsylvanian Mazon Creek fauna, Illinois, U.S.A. *Journal of Vertebrate Paleontology* 71:1–23.

Schultze, H.-P., and J. Chorn. 1986. Palaeoniscoid (Actinopterygii, Pisces) vertebrae from the Late Palaeozoic of central North America. *Journal of Paleontology* 60:744–57.

St. John, O.H., and A.H. Worthen. 1875. Descriptions of fossil fishes. Geological Survey of Illinois, 6 (2). *Palaeontology of Illinois* 1:245–488.

Talimaa, V. 1985. Otoliths piscium. *In* D. Nolf (ed.), *Handbook of Paleoichthyology.* Stuttgart and New York: Gustav Fischer.

Talimaa, V.N. 1995. Vertebrate complexes in the heterofacial Lower Devonian deposits of Timan-Pechora province. *In* S. Turner (ed.), *Palaeozoic Microvertebrates 1995 Report: Moscow-94 Workshop.* Ichthyolith Issues Special Publication 1. Socorro: Zidek Serv.

Turner, S. 1982. Middle Palaeozoic elasmobranch remains from Australia. *Journal of Vertebrate Paleontology* 2 (2):117–31.

———. 1994. Thermal alteration of vertebrate remains. *Ichthyolith Issues* 13:25–26.

———. 1997. Sequence of Devonian thelodont scale assemblages in East Gondwana. *In* J.G. Johanson, G. Klapper, M.A. Murphy, and J.A. Talent (eds.), *Paleozoic Sequence Stratigraphy, Biostratigraphy, and Biogeography: Studies in Honor of J. Granville ("Jess") Johnson.* Boulder, Colorado: Geological Society of America.

Turner, S. (ed.). 1995. *Palaeozoic Microvertebrates 1995 Report: Moscow–94 Workshop.* Ichthyolith Issues Special Publication 1. Socorro: Zidek Serv.

Turner, S., and A. Blieck. 1995. Conodont-vertebrate comparison and significance of micro-ornament. *In AUSCOS-1/Boucot Symposium Abstracts.* Sydney: Macquarie University.

———. 1997. The final flings of IGCP 328: Palaeozoic microvertebrate biochronology and global marine/non-marine correlation. *Episodes* 20 (1):48–52.

Turner, S., and A. Blieck (eds.). 1996. Gross symposium, volume I. *Modern Geology,* special issue, 20 (3–4):203–410.

Turner, S., and G.C. Young. 1987. Shark teeth from the Early-Middle Devonian Cravens Peak Beds, Georgina Basin, Queensland. *Alcheringa* 11:233–44.

Upeniece, I., and J. Upenieks. 1992. Young Upper Devonian antiarch (Asterolepis) individuals from the Lode Quarry, Latvia. *In* E. Mark-Kurik (ed.) *Fossil Fishes as Living Animals.* Tallinn: Academy of Sciences of Estonia.

Valiukevicius, J. 1979. Cheshooi akantodov iz eifeliskikh otlojenii Shpitsbergena. *Paleontological Journal* 13 (4):101–11.

———. 1992. First articulated Poracanthodes from the Lower Devonian of Severnaya Zemlya. *In* E. Mark-Kurik (ed.), *Fossil Fishes as Living Animals.* Tallinn: Academy of Sciences of Estonia.

Vorobyeva, E., and N. Panteleyev. 1995. Histological and SEM studies of Laccognathus scales. *In* S. Turner (ed.), *Palaeozoic Microvertebrates 1995 ReportL Moscow-94 Workshop.* Ichthyolith Issue Special Publication 1. Socorro: Zidek Serv.

Wang N.-Z. 1984. Thelodont, acanthodian, and chondrichthyan fossils from the Lower Devonian of southwest China. *Proceedings of the Linnean Society New South Wales* 107 (3):419–41.

Wells, J.W. 1944. Fish remains from the Middle Devonian bone beds of the Cincinnati Arch region. *Palaeontographica Americana* 3:103–60.

Williams, M.E. 1985. The "Cladodont level" sharks of the Pennsylvanian Black shales of Central North America. *Palaeontographica* 190A:83–192.

Young, G.C. 1997. Ordovician microvertebrate remains from the Amadeus Basin, central Australia. *Journal of Vertebrate Paleontology* 17:1–25.

Young, G.C., V.N. Karatajuté-Talimaa, and M.M. Smith. 1996. A possible Late Cambrian vertebrate from Australia. *Nature* 383:810–12.

Zajic, J. 1995. Some consequences of the recent investigations of the family Acanthodidae Huxley, 1861. *In* H. Lelièvre, S. Wenz, A. Blieck, and R. Cloutier (eds.), *Premiers vertébrés et vertébrés inférieurs* (8th Congress. Intern, Paris, 4–9 Septembre 1995). *Géobios Mémoire Spéciale* 19:167–72.

Zangerl, R., and G.R. Case. 1973. Iniopterygia, a new order of Chondrichthyan fishes from the Pennsylvanian of North America. *Fieldiana* 6:1–66.

Further Reading

Janvier, P. 1996. *Early Vertebrates.* Oxford Monographs on Geology and Geophysics, 33. Oxford: Clarendon; New York: Oxford University Press.

Jones, D.J. 1956. *Introduction to Microfossils.* New York: Harper.

Kummel, B., and D. Raup. (eds.). 1965. *Handbook of Paleontological Techniques.* San Francisco: Freeman.

Nolf, D. (ed.). 1985. *Handbook of Paleoichthyology.* Stuttgart and New York: Gustav Fischer.

Schultze, H.-P. (ed.). 1985. *Handbook of Paleoichthyology.* Stuttgart and New York: Gustav Fischer.

Turner, S. (ed.). 1988. *Ichthyolith Issues.* [Newsletter of International Research Group on Fish Microvertebrates.]

———. 1995. *Palaeozoic Microvertebrates 1995 Report: Moscow-94 Workshop.* Ichthyolith Issues Special Publication 1. Socorro: Zidek Serv.

MIDDLE EAST

See Africa: North Africa and the Middle East

MILLER, HUGH

Scottish, 1802–56

Hugh Miller is an obscure man today. The scientific and political crusades to which he devoted so much energy are no longer of much concern to us. Yet he was a major cultural figure in the early Victorian era, and his scientific writings were influential among scientists and the general public alike.

Miller was born in 1802, in Cromarty, a fishing village near the northwest Highlands of Scotland. After an indifferent public school education, Miller became an itinerant stonemason at the age of 18, traveling all over Scotland. Nonetheless, he read widely and aspired to a literary career. In 1829 he published a book of rather mediocre poetry, then began writing more successful prose articles and pamphlets on local folklore, culture, and politics. After becoming a bank accountant in 1835, he devoted more time to writing and to serious study of geology. His reputation grew in Scottish literary circles. In 1840 Miller moved to Edinburgh to publish *The Witness,* a newspaper devoted to the cause of the independence of the Church of Scotland from Parliamentary control. He wrote much of its copy, filling its pages with news, popular science, political commentary, and fierce invective. *The Witness* became one of the most influential newspapers in Scotland and established Miller as a leading journalist, a ferocious debater, and a force in shaping public opinion. On Christmas Eve of 1856, he committed suicide, after a period of extreme agitation, possibly brought on by overwork or mental disorder.

Miller's original contributions to science were modest; his editorial duties left him little time for geology. His notes and writings show him as a competent but hardly outstanding field geologist by the standards of his time (Oldroyd 1996). Miller's greatest contribution was his work on fossils from the Old Red Sandstone (now known to be Devonian) near Cromarty. The Old Red Sandstone was generally thought to lack fossils, but Miller discovered many, including some remarkable fossil fish. Miller reconstructed these fish (Figure 1) and worked out their mode of life. He sent his materials to leading paleontologists of the day, notably Louis Agassiz and Roderick Murchison. Later in his life, Miller published some interesting descriptions of Scottish fossil plants. His collections, now in the National Museum of Scotland, are still an important resource.

Miller was fortunate to be working during a great surge of public interest in geology, and his real importance came from his skill as a popularizer. His 1841 book *The Old Red Sandstone,* based partly on articles published in *The Witness,* fired the imagination of both scientists and the lay public. Miller had a gift for making the past come to life. One critic wrote, "His fossil fish swim and gambol as if they were creatures of today" (in Shortland 1995). He often used vivid metaphors from his stonemason days, comparing the bony plates on the back of one fish with a vaulted stone roof, the fin-rays of another with carved stone columns, and the shape of another with the angels carved on antique gravestones. Scientists like Agassiz, Murchison, and Buckland praised Miller's books highly: "There is in them a freshness of conception, a power of argumentation, a depth of thought, a purity of feelings, rarely met with in works of that character . . ." (Agassiz 1853).

A devout Christian, Miller adopted what would now be called "day-age creationism." In this interpretation, the six "days" of Creation were the six days on which the author of Genesis had seen six great visions of Creation, each day corresponding to a vast geological age. In each age, God had created new dominant life-forms—first fishes, then reptiles, then mammals, and finally humankind—and had placed the "highest" forms of each kind in a position of authority or domination. Later forms tended to "degenerate"; the fossil record showed nothing like evolutionary progress.

Miller would have no truck with the "development hypothesis," as evolutionary theory was called at the time; he saw it as both scientifically unsound and morally dangerous. He scoffed at Lamarck's theory of evolution, saying Lamarck "had a trick of dreaming when wide awake, and of calling his dreams philosophy" (Miller 1853). Incensed by the anonymous book *Vestiges of the Natural History of Creation* (1844), which presented a progressionist theory of evolution, he counterattacked with his 1849 book *Foot-Prints of the Creator,* in which he said *Vestiges* was "An ingenious but very unsolid work—full of images transferred not from the scientific field, but from the field of *scientific mind . . .* which, when passed current as the proper coin of philosophic argument, are really frauds on the popular understanding" (Miller 1853). Ironically, the author of *Vestiges* was Edinburgh publisher Robert Chambers, who had published some of Miller's early geological articles. As far as is known, Miller never suspected his friend and fellow publisher of having written *Vestiges.*

Yet Miller also took issue with Biblical literalists, who considered geology blasphemous. In his last book, *Testimony of the Rocks,* he wrote:

> [The history of the Earth] throughout the long geological ages—its strange story of successive creations, each placed in advance of that which had gone before . . . will be found in an equal degree more worthy of its Divine Author than that which would huddle the whole into a few days, and convert the incalculably ancient universe which we inhabit into a hastily run-up erection of yesterday (Miller 1857).

Miller's writings remained popular long after his death—even after Darwin published *The Origin of Species* in 1859 (Shortland 1995). New editions of his books and collected articles were in print for 50 years after his death, selling by the tens of thousands throughout the English-speaking world. Literary figures, including the novelist Charles Dickens and the historian Thomas Carlyle, admired Miller's prose. A memorial in the journal *Science* (Clarke 1902) summed up Hugh Miller's legacy: "When textbooks of geology were few and dull, Miller portrayed in most delightful tints the beauties of the science and the charm of its philosophy."

BEN WAGGONER

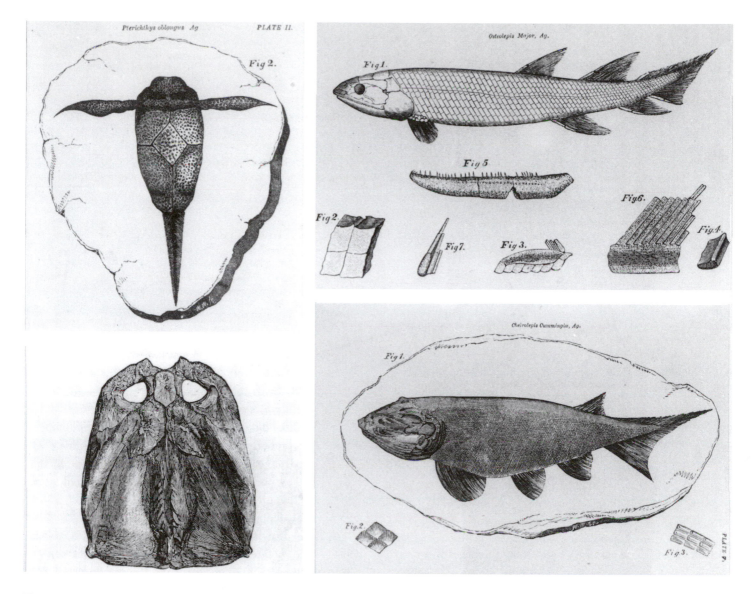

Figure 1. Hugh Miller's depiction of fossil fish of the Old Red Sandstone (Devonian). *Upper left,* reconstruction of the armored fish *Pterichthys* (now *Pterichthyodes* and classified in the order Placodermi); *lower left,* internal view of head-shield of the armored fish *Asterolepis* (now classified in the order Placodermi); *upper right,* reconstruction, jaw, fins, and scales of *Osteolepis* (now known to be one of the earliest lobe-finned fishes on the line leading to land vertebrates); *lower right,* reconstruction and scales of *Cheirolepis* (now considered one of the earliest true ray-finned fishes, Actinopterygii). Upper left, upper right, and lower right from Cromarty region, *The Old Red Sandstone* (1841); lower left from Orkney Islands, *Foot-Prints of the Creator* (1849).

Works Cited

Agassiz, L. 1853. Hugh Miller. *In* H. Miller, *The Foot-Prints of the Creator; or, The Asterolepis of Stromness.* 3rd ed., Boston: Gould and Lincoln.

Clarke, J. 1902. On the centenary of Hugh Miller. *Science* 15:631.

Miller, H. 1853. *The Foot-Prints of the Creator; or, The Asterolepis of Stromness.* 3rd ed., Boston: Gould and Lincoln.

———. 1857. *The Testimony of the Rocks; or, Geology in Its Bearings on the Two Theologies, Natural and Revealed.* Edinburgh: Constable.

Oldroyd, D. R. 1996. The geologist from Cromarty. *In* M. Shortland (ed.), *Hugh Miller and the Controversies of Victorian Science.* Oxford: Clarendon; New York: Oxford University Press.

Shortland, M. (ed.). 1995. *Hugh Miller's Memoir: From Stonemason to Geologist.* Edinburgh: Edinburgh University Press.

Biography

Born in Cromarty, Scotland, 10 October 1802. Educated in public schools; became apprentice stonemason, 1821; journeyman stonemason, 1824. Discovered fossil fish in the Old Red Sandstone (Devonian) of Scotland around 1830; began serious geological studies around 1834; first articles on geology published in 1838; newspaper editor, *The Witness,* Edinburgh, 1840; published his first book on geology, *The Old Red Sandstone*, 1841; elected president of Royal Physical Society of Edinburgh, 1852. Died in Edinburgh, 24 December 1856.

Major Publications

1841. *The Old Red Sandstone; or, New Walks in an Old Field*. Edinburgh: John Johnstone; New York: Virture and Yorston; rev. ed., New York: Hurst, 1858.

1849. *Foot-Prints of the Creator; or, The Asterolepis of Stromness*. London: Johnstone and Hunter; New York: Hurst, 1850.

1857. *The Testimony of the Rocks; or, Geology in Its Bearings on the Two Theologies, Natural and Revealed*. Edinburgh: Constable; New York: Virture and Yorston.

1858. *The Cruise of the Betsey; or, A Summer's Ramble among the Fossiliferous Deposits of the Hebrides*. Edinburgh: Constable; Boston: Gould and Lincoln.

1859. *Sketch-Book of Popular Geology*. Edinburgh: Constable; Boston: Gould and Lincoln.

1871. P. Bayne (ed.) *The Life and Letters of Hugh Miller*. 2 vols. London: Strahan; Boston: Gould and Lincoln.

Further Readings

Maisey, J.G. 1996. *Discovering Fossil Fishes*. New York: Holt.

Rosie, G. 1981. *Hugh Miller: Outrage and Order. A Biography and Selected Writings*. Edinburgh: Mainstream.

Rudwick, M.J.S. 1985. *The Great Devonian Controversy*. Chicago: University of Chicago Press.

Ruse, M. 1979. *The Darwinian Revolution*. Chicago: University of Chicago Press.

Shortland, M. 1996. *Hugh Miller and the Controversies of Victorian Science*. Oxford: Clarendon; New York: Oxford University Press.

MOLECULAR PALEONTOLOGY

The morphology (form and structure) of organisms provides a wealth of information about evolutionary history. However, additional information contained in molecules also can contribute to our understanding of past life. Molecular data are used to build phylogenetic trees (family trees based upon genetic information) and to estimate times of divergence. These data are especially useful for groups with relatively few morphological characters and poor fossil records (e.g., fungi, bacteria), although our knowledge of some well-known groups (e.g., vertebrates) also has increased greatly as a result of molecular studies. Some molecular characters (nucleotides and amino acids) have been conserved throughout the history of life and can be used to study ancient relationships. In some cases, molecular data have been obtained directly from fossil organisms.

Molecular Phylogenetics

A major advance in the field was the development of the polymerase chain reaction (PCR) in the 1980s (Mullis 1990). In this method, a region of interest in the genome, typically a portion of a gene that is 200 to 800 base pairs long, is amplified to a million or more copies in order to facilitate additional molecular analysis, such as DNA sequencing. The process is called a chain reaction because it involves repeated cycles of heating and cooling, during which the DNA fragments are split, short pieces of DNA (primers) are joined, and then new strands are created. Before PCR, DNA fragments were amplified by bacterial cloning, a much longer process.

The technique of PCR, combined with automated methods for sequencing DNA (determining the order of nucleotides and genes), has revolutionized evolutionary biology. A virtually unlimited number of characters can be obtained from a large number of species to address interesting systematic questions. The most popular molecule for study in animals has been the mitochondrial chromosome. This circular structure contains only a small proportion of genes (in animals, it is about 16 kilobases in length). Also, the greater technical ease and rapid rate of change of mitochondrial DNA, compared with typical nuclear genes, are responsible for its popularity in recent years. In plants, DNA contained in another organelle, the chloroplast, has been the primary source of sequence data for evolutionary studies.

A seemingly limitless number of nuclear genes also are available for tree-building. Unlike mitochondrial and chloroplast genes, which are tightly linked, nuclear genes used in estimating phylogeny usually are unlinked. One feature of nuclear genes in many eucaryotes (organisms with membrane-enclosed nuclei in their cells) is the presence of large amounts of noncoding DNA (introns) interspersed within regions that control the production of substances (coding regions). For example, a typical gene with only 900 base pairs of coding region (for a protein of 300 amino acids) may consist of 10,000 base pairs because of the presence of introns. While fast-evolving introns provide information for relationships of individuals or populations, they may not be useful in applications dealing with larger categories such as species phylogenies. In those cases, it is more informative to study only the coding region found in the messenger RNA (usually without introns) of that gene.

There are different methods of building evolutionary trees from molecular data (usually DNA or amino acid sequences). A common feature of all methods is that they minimize the amount of inferred change (substitutions of nucleotides or replacements of amino acids). Maximum likelihood methods seek the tree that matches the data set with highest probability, minimum evolution (neighbor-joining) searches for the tree with shortest overall length, and the maximum parsimony method tries to find the tree requiring fewest character-state changes. The groups of species defined within a tree can be evaluated by statistical tests to determine if they are significant. The most commonly used test is the bootstrap method, which involves sampling the sites randomly with replacement many times, constructing new trees at each cycle, and then determining the frequency that a particular group appears among the many bootstrap samples. For example, if 97 out of 100 bootstrap trees join human with chimpanzee, then we infer that the chimp-human relationship is supported with 97% confidence.

Molecular Clocks

For most groups in the fossil record, the time of divergence between two lineages is not known with accuracy. The minimum time of divergence is the date of the oldest fossil assigned to one of the two lineages. The actual divergence is assumed to have occurred even earlier. In those rare cases where the fossil record is excellent, the minimum age may be close to the divergence time. However, for most groups of organisms, an accurate time frame has yet to be established using data from fossils. For this reason, evolutionary biologists frequently turn to molecules to determine dates of divergence.

In groups for which molecular data can be obtained, such as all living and some fossil organisms, it is possible to estimate divergence times using a molecular clock. To do this, molecular divergence must be measured between the two taxa being compared and at least one additional taxon with a known or presumed time of divergence (for calibration). One requirement is that the rate of change along all lineages should not be significantly different. Although many of the molecular changes used for timing divergences probably do not result in a functional change in the protein or organism (i.e., are neutral), this is not a requirement of a molecular clock.

Sources of error in molecular clocks include the estimates of molecular divergence and the calibration time used. Calibrations are taken from the fossil record or from well-dated geologic (or climatic) events (if they are assumed to be the cause of the phylogenetic divergence). There is no "universal molecular clock" because different genes evolve at different rates. For instance, genes involved in the immune reaction must change rapidly to keep pace with a diversity of antigens (e.g., viruses), whereas genes involved in the most basic of cell functions rarely change because of their universal importance. However, a rapid rate of change in synonymous substitutions (those that do not cause changes in amino acids) is common to virtually all protein coding genes.

Genes that show strong positive selection in particular lineages are unlikely to behave as good molecular clocks. On the other hand, some genes, such as serum albumin in vertebrates, appear to evolve in a relatively clocklike fashion and have proven useful in dating evolutionary divergences. Ideally, divergence times should be estimated from a large number of genes in order to reduce the error of the time estimate (Hedges et al. 1996). The strong need to know times of divergence and the rapidly expanding databases of sequences have maintained a prominent role for molecular clocks in evolutionary biology.

Fossil Biomolecules

The possibility that proteins in the fossil record may have been preserved was suggested as early as the 1950s, when P.H. Abelson used techniques such as thin layer chromatography to identify organic components in fossils. The hypothesis also was supported by structures seen in electron microscopy. Researchers identified collagen-like fibers in fossil specimens from as long ago as the Early Paleozoic (545 million years ago), and these structures also were present in dinosaur bones of the Mesozoic era (251 to 65 million years ago).

Genetic information about the immune properties of proteins can be used to provide information on phylogenetic relationships. A small region of the whole protein molecule is all that is needed for a functional immune system to recognize an invader and form antibodies against it. A sequence of amino acids determines the shape of these three-dimensional regions, called epitopes. They are created by the complex folding of the protein molecule into its functional form. As few as five amino acids in the proper "shape" are enough for antibody recognition. Only small fragments of molecules are needed, and phylogenetic relationships can be inferred from the degree or strength of the bonds that bind the antibody and epitope together. Species that are more closely related usually have a greater number of antibody-epitope bonds.

Amino acid identification also was used very early to suggest the preservation of fossil proteins and continues to yield valuable information today. Individual proteins have been identified from fossil specimens, including the bone proteins (e.g., collagen, osteocalcin, and osteonectin). Proteins abundant in blood, such as albumin and hemoglobin, have been identified in several ancient specimens from as far back as the Mesozoic (Schweitzer et al. 1997). Using these preserved proteins as phylogenetic tools was suggested by J.M. Lowenstein and G. Scheuenstuhl (1991) through the application of immunological techniques, including Western blots and ELISA assays (tests). The degree of binding of antibodies to ancient protein fragments has been used to investigate the relationships of fossil taxa.

Variation in protein composition and structure also is useful in phylogenetic analysis. Researchers can study chemical content, hydrophobic characteristics, and amino acid composition, as well as the unique ways that proteins curve and fold into three-dimensional shapes, because these characteristics differ greatly between proteins and among the same proteins in different taxa. Additionally, while the phylogenetic information found in DNA is contained in the sequence of bases, phylogenetic information from proteins may be obtained indirectly from their three-dimensional structure as well as directly from their amino acid sequence. Finally, different classes of proteins can be determined by their function as well as by their constituent amino acids and the various ways that members of these classes are preserved.

The study of ancient DNA is a younger field, dating only to the early 1980s. Since then, several studies have successfully resolved relationships of extinct organisms, including the Tasmanian wolf (Krajewski et al. 1997). Others have reported finding ancient DNA in fossils, including those of dinosaurs and amber-encased insects, from as early as the Mid-Mesozoic. However, many of these studies have been received with caution, and no results have been replicated independently for fossils older than

100,000 years (Austin et al. 1997). Absolute time limits on molecular preservation have not yet been demonstrated under naturally occurring conditions, and, therefore, recovery of very ancient DNA remains a possibility. Authenticity and independent replication of results continue to be major concerns.

Problems with Contamination

Fossil bone and tissue have been exposed to many contaminants during decay, burial, and transformation into rock. In addition, human and laboratory contaminants can be introduced into samples despite the most careful controls. Also, the sensitivity of PCR greatly increases the potential for amplifying contaminant DNA molecules. Moreover, contaminant molecules may be more abundant and less damaged than ancient molecules within the same fossils (Austin et al. 1997). Thus, contamination is a major concern among researchers in this field.

Some contamination problems can be reduced through careful design of PCR primers. Primers can be designed to rule out amplification of the more common contaminant sources, such as microbial and human DNA. The chances of amplification of DNA from ancient sources successfully are increased by consideration of phylogenetic relationships among modern taxa. For example, in designing primers to amplify DNA from dinosaur bones, one would want to select DNA sequences unique to modern birds and modern crocodiles, the two living groups most closely related to the extinct dinosaurs.

Besides contamination, one may encounter other difficulties in working with ancient biomolecules. In the case of DNA, factors such as acids from organic humus may inhibit the action of the polymerase enzymes used in amplification attempts, or the DNA may be damaged enough to introduce misleading artifacts (artificial substances produced, inadvertently, by the process). Also, the ancient DNA may be degraded to strands that are too short for binding with PCR primers. Protein sequences obtained from ancient sources have not been reported in the literature and may be difficult to obtain, either because the minimal amounts of protein yield concentrations too low for sequencing or because modifications of binding sites make enzymatic degradation ineffective.

Molecular approaches have provided paleontology with new tools to answer old questions, and the result has been a revolution in our understanding of evolutionary history. In some instances, where molecular phylogenies have contrasted with long-standing views based on morphology, it might appear that information from fossils and morphology is no longer needed. On the contrary, molecular information is unlikely to replace the history of adaptations reflected in morphology and the fossil record. Molecular approaches will continue to complement classical approaches to paleontology in the foreseeable future.

S. BLAIR HEDGES AND MARY H. SCHWEITZER

Works Cited

Abelson, P.H. 1956. Paleobiochemistry. *Scientific American* 195:83–92.

Austin, J.J., A.J. Ross, A.B. Smith, R.A. Fortney, and R.H. Thomas. 1997. Problems of reproducibility: Does geologically ancient DNA survive in amber-preserved insects? *Proceedings of the Royal Society of London,* ser. B, 264:467–74.

Hedges, S.B., P.H. Parker, C.G. Sibley, and S. Kumar. 1996. Continental breakup and the ordinal diversification of birds and mammals. *Nature* 381:226–29.

Krajewski, C., L. Buckley, and M. Westerman. 1997. DNA phylogeny of the marsupial wolf resolved. *Proceedings of the Royal Society of London,* ser. B, 264:911–17.

Lowenstein, J.M., and G. Scheuenstuhl. 1991. Immunological methods in molecular palaeontology. *Philosophical Transactions of the Royal Society of London,* ser. B, 333:375–80.

Mullis, K.B. 1990. The unusual origin of the polymerase chain reaction. *Scientific American* (April):56–65.

Schweitzer, M.H., M. Marshall, K. Carron, D. Bohle, S. Busse, E. Arnold, D. Barnard, J. Horner, and J. Starkey. 1997. Heme compounds in dinosaur trabecular bone. *Proceedings of the National Academy of Sciences, USA* 94:6291–96.

Further Reading

Ambler, R.P., and M. Daniel. 1991. Proteins and molecular palaeontology. *Philosophical Transactions of the Royal Society, London,* ser. B, 333:381–89.

Herrmann, B., and S. Hummel (eds.). 1993. *Ancient DNA.* London: Springer-Verlag; New York: Springer-Verlag, 1994.

Li, W.H. 1997. *Molecular Evolution.* Sunderland, Massachusetts: Sinauer.

Pääbo, S. 1993. Ancient DNA. *Scientific American* (November):86–92.

MOLLUSCS: OVERVIEW

Although many features of evolution of the Mollusca are known in general terms, many issues remain unresolved regarding the early evolution of the phylum. Accordingly, emphasis will be placed on this early part of the record. A key point is that molluscs are probably more diverse today than at any time in the past, in contrast to the phylum brachiopoda, which are far better known in the fossil record. The phylum Mollusca is a biological concept, meaning that it is based on both exterior (hard shell) and interior (anatomy of soft parts) features. As a partial contrast, the class trilobita, ranging from the Cambrian to Permian, is placed within the Phylum Arthropoda, but all taxonomic divisions within that class are based on features of the hard parts.

There appears to be general agreement among most invertebrate zoologists that the Arthropoda, Annelida (segmented worms), and Mollusca are more closely related to one another within the Protostoma (animals in which mouth and anus develop from the same embryonic opening) than they are to other protostome phyla. As to determining which of the three is primitive and which is advanced, that depends on which authority is consulted. Likewise, what form gave rise to the Mollusca is unclear. For many years an organism resembling a living flatworm was favored. Although there has been a reaction against this concept, there is no clear notion of an alternative ancestor.

With respect to the fossil record, no undoubted reports of Mollusca in the Precambrian exist. A presumed aplacophoran impression (trail) from Australia has since been retracted. *Chuaria*, at one time considered a patellacean gastropod, is more convincingly placed as an organic-walled acritarch (microfossils of presumed algal affinities). *Kimberella*, which originally was assigned to the Cnidaria, was redescribed in 1996 as a mollusclike animal. While it has some of the features of the hypothetical ancestral mollusc proposed a century ago by E. Ray Lancaster, other features, such as the elaborate folding of the presumed mantle edge, are less convincing. It may be that the reason no Precambrian molluscs have been discovered so far is because there were none. A theoretical possibility at least worth considering is that the sudden development of hard parts within the Cambrian was particularly germane to the Mollusca; thus, from a paleontological aspect, the shell makes the mollusc, rather than vice versa.

A "thumbnail" description of the living Mollusca is a soft body within a hard shell. Key features are a radula (a feeding organ within the mouth) and a mantle to cover the body and, in most instances, to secrete a shell. A mantle is also a feature of Brachiopoda; in early classifications, this group was classified as a mollusc. Seemingly every generalization one can make concerning molluscs has exceptions, but to discuss them at each point would make an inordinately long article. The Mollusca, and particularly the Gastropoda, have developed a great variety of shells. Conversely, there is a trend within many of the extant classes toward reduction or loss of the shell. The reason that the soft-bodied Aplacophora are included within the Mollusca rests in large measure on their possession of a radula.

Because the shell is such a fundamental feature for paleontologists, there have been many studies of shell form and shell structure. To generalize, the molluscan shell is the exemplar of logarithmic growth. Each growth increment of the shell is basically like the preceding one except slightly larger. One of the prime, though not exclusive, features of Mollusca is the presence of growth lines, which may be subdued or prominent and may even give rise to elaborate external nodes and spines.

Thus, molluscs characteristically retain all growth stages. They have a growing edge at the anteriorward (front) margin of the shell, in marked contrast to the molting that characterizes the Arthropoda. This hard part (or parts) provides protection for the softer organs and allows for attachment of muscles. Because of this strong musculature, many molluscs can withdraw within their shell or cling tightly to the substrate on which they reside. The shell also provides protection from predators. In the early evolution of molluscs, protection from changes in the environment, such as sudden influxes of muddy water, may have been more fundamental than protection from predation. The original mechanism(s) for production of a shell are not obvious, but forming a shell out of calcium carbonate as a metabolic waste product seems the most plausible.

In living molluscs, the shell is formed atop an organic template. It is reasonable to assume that this mechanism was used throughout the history of the phylum. Although there are differences in shell details at all taxonomic levels, there is nevertheless an overall similarity. This may suggest that a small, simple organism developed a dorsal (back) organic covering; then many differentiated into the ancestors of the various classes. Members of the Polyplacophora (characterized by eight plates on the back) have calcareous spicules (spikes) surrounding the girdle, which holds the individual plates together; the shell-less Aplacophora has calcareous spicules within the body. It has been suggested that these isolated spicules combined to form a shell. This approach seemingly does not take into account the role of an organic template, and no convincing mechanism for the fusion of spicules has been proposed. This possible role of spicules is a major factor in the argument as to whether the Aplacophora are an ancestral form, or whether they are much younger and derived from a shelled group. I believe that the Aplacophora are derived from the shelled Polyplacophora.

With exceptions, the Mollusca are characterized by a shell of two primary layers, often supplemented by other layers. Crossed-lamellar structure is a feature unique to the Mollusca, but it is lost in some living classes. The shell generally is composed of aragonite, a less stable form of calcium carbonate than calcite, although there are exceptions. Among living molluscs, it is the shells of the sedentary and attached forms that are more commonly composed, either partially or entirely, of calcite. This generalization seems to hold throughout the geologic record.

Despite the fact that aragonite is a less stable mineral, there are places of exceptional preservation where apparently original shell structure has been found in fossil molluscs as old as Pennsylvanian. In many fossil occurrences, most mollusc shells are dissolved, but a few forms are well preserved. This is particularly apparent in Jurassic and younger beds where oysters, which have a calcite shell, occur.

In many limestones, the conversion of aragonite to calcite causes the shell to bond strongly to the matrix (the rock in which the shell is embedded). When discussing fossils, the words "cast" and "mold" are used in a variety of ways. Therefore, to avoid confusion, the terms "external mold" and "steinkern" (stone kernel) for the matrix-filled interior will be used. A pragmatic bit of advice for working with Early Paleozoic limestones is that when the rock is broken and the shell tends to adhere to the matrix, one is probably dealing with a mollusc; brachiopod shells are more likely to break free.

One difficulty is that molluscs may be represented by steinkerns, but it does not follow that all steinkerns are molluscs. Specimens that have been replaced by silica and are released from limestone by hydrochloric acid naturally have the shell structure replaced during mineralization but may retain several distinct layers and other features that allow them to be assigned to Mollusca with a fair degree of confidence. However, steinkerns that are phosphatic and are released from the matrix by the use of organic acids may preserve muscle scars and other features, but they give no data as to whether they can be confidently assigned to the Mollusca. An example is *Heraultipegma,* an Early Cambrian form that some scholars have identified as the oldest member of the extinct molluscan class Rostroconchia, and others have placed within the phylum Arthropoda. It should also be noted that the shape of a steinkern is a poor predictor of the external morphology; for example, two high-spired forms may belong to widely separate orders, yet have identical steinkerns.

This leads directly to the problem of homeomorphy (identical shapes in different species), commonly considered to be based on external features but comparable to the steinkern issue. Some coiled worm tubes resemble small gastropods, some calcareous worm tubes are remarkably similar to scaphopods, and some simple widely conical medusoids (freeswimming jellyfishes) mimic both patellacean gastropods and several genera of monoplacophorans.

The reverse of the homeomorphic issue is the morphologic limits to which a taxonomic group at any level of classification may be extended without coming into conflict with overall concepts of similarity and difference. Fossils commonly are assigned to the Mollusca if they resemble living forms to some extent. This practical approach works well in rocks as old as the Ordovician but is less satisfactory in the Cambrian. For example, gastropod shells are coiled, and the small Cambrian *Pelagiella* is coiled, but there is no agreement that this genus belongs within the Gastropoda. A more difficult issue, discussed in greater detail below, is whether the Hyolitha belong within the Mollusca or should be excluded.

Having considered some of the potential pitfalls paleontologists encounter, it is now possible to discuss the problems in classification. Although philosophers have argued for centuries whether taxonomic levels in a hierarchy are real in nature or a construct of the human mind, this argument will not be addressed here. By general agreement, the modern classification of animals began in 1758 with the publication of Linnaeus. Since that time, the number of levels of classification and the number at each level have increased dramatically. Some of this increase, which has aptly been termed "taxonomic inflation," came from finding living and fossil animals in areas unknown to Linnaeus, and some came from a more detailed examination of organisms and emphasis of features that separate rather than associate forms. As noted, Brachiopoda were separated from Mollusca. At the time of Linnaeus, there were no molluscs; it took about half a century until Lamarck differentiated that phylum from the Linnaean "Vermes." During the next three quarters of a century, various subdivisions were recognized within the living Mollusca, and one or two were even proposed to be of phylum rank. However, from about 1875 onward, both zoologists and paleontologists generally accepted that the Mollusca contained five classes. Three—Gastropoda, Pelecypoda, and Cephalopoda—were major, based on their diversity and abundance, and two—Polyplacophora and Scaphopoda—were minor in showing little diversity and relatively small total biomass.

Although various groups of Mollusca were used as raw material for evolutionary studies, this scheme remained unchanged until the work of J.B. Knight in 1952. He proposed that the Mollusca should be reduced to four classes. The Gastropoda were to be divided into two subclasses: the Anisopleura, containing essentially the Gastropoda, as recognized by zoologists, and the Isopleura.

Gastropoda undergo twisting, or torsion, of the soft parts, hence the subclass name. The Polyplacophora are bilaterally symmetrical and do not undergo torsion. To these Isopleura were added the Monoplacophora, a taxon proposed a decade earlier by W. Wenz. The Monoplacophora were exclusively known from fossil. They had a single shell in which there were multiple pairs of discrete muscle scars, suggesting that these forms were also bilaterally symmetrical and implying that they had not undergone torsion.

Five years later, H. Lemche's (1957) description of a living monoplacophoran astonished both paleontologists and zoologists working in malacology (study of molluscs). The ferment of ideas he produced has yet to subside. In very short order, both groups accepted Monoplacophora as a distinct sixth class within the Mollusca. Thereafter, some zoologists proposed that the shell-less Aplacophora be differentiated from the Polyplacophora as a seventh class of Mollusca. By appearing in many textbooks, this proposal seems to have overcome the prime hurdle of acceptance or rejection of a proposal at a high level of taxonomy.

In a 1963 abstract, E.L. Yochelson proposed that in a sense the evolution of the Mollusca was two-phased. An early diverse group of molluscs of class level rank appeared, all of which became extinct, followed by early representatives of the extant classes of the phylum. In earlier and subsequent works Yochelson proposed several classes based entirely on fossils. Although Yochelson did not view it as such at the time, this was a radical proposal. Extinct class-level taxa had never been proposed before within the Mollusca and were exceedingly rare in the literature on other phyla— except perhaps the Echinodermata—represented in the fossil record. Since then, other authors have made various proposals for class rank of extinct molluscan groups, and each proposal has been criticized or even vilified by still other authors.

In contrast to Yochelson's scheme, two scholars, jointly and independently, J. Pojeta Jr. and B. Runnegar, have argued that all extant classes extend far back in the fossil record, some to near the beginning of the Cambrian. They maintain that only one extinct class, the Rostroconchia, needs to be recognized. Defining class-level taxa based exclusively on fossils is a fundamental break with past concepts of molluscan classification.

As an ancillary point, Runnegar and Pojeta argued in 1974 that the reason molluscs are so poorly known in the Cambrian is that all specimens are small and therefore easily overlooked. This notion has some merit, especially when combined with the fact that remarkably few paleontologists have concentrated on studying the early record of the Mollusca compared to the number of scholars who have studied other groups of the same age. Notwithstanding this point, simple cap-shaped shells are known that are at least as large as a thumbnail. Attributing "average size" to specimens within a morphologically diverse group that has a 500-million-year record is a slippery concept to grasp. These thumbnail-sized specimens seem to approach the "average" size.

The concept of "largest" has in the distant past been used as one criterion for the peak of evolution within a group. Depending on how one measures the shell, the largest gastropods occur either in the Ordovician or in the Recent. The largest of the Pelecypoda (clams, mussels, oysters) is in the Cretaceous or the Recent. The largest known representative of the Scaphopoda occurs in the

Pennsylvanian, and the largest polyplacophoran occurs today. The largest shelled cephalopod occurs in either the Ordovician or the Jurassic, and the largest known mollusc, the giant squid *Architeuthis,* inhabits today's seas. Within the classes, the largest individuals of families and orders occur at varying times and positions throughout the ranges of these taxa. In may be misleading to use either overall increase in size through time for the phylum, or the rise and decline of smaller taxa measured by size, as an indication of evolutionary success.

Many specimens of Mollusca in the Early Cambrian are indeed small, but it is probable that at least two factors are involved. One may be the reliance on residues etched with organic acids. In the appropriate facies, these may produce phosphatic steinkerns of putative molluscs. As a general rule, phosphatic replacement or infilling occurs only in small specimens; silicification affects specimens of all sizes, but there is a dearth of Cambrian silicified molluscan faunas. A second more speculative factor concerns growth rates. In general, molluscs, particularly gastropods, continue to grow throughout their life span. Forms that show a change in maturity, such as a thickening of the aperture or closer spacing of growth lines, are the exceptions rather than the rule. Many molluscs have a life span of some years; any population that has been killed *in situ* (in its original position) and not transported will show a large number of small individuals and decreasing numbers of ever larger individuals. If, for physiological reasons, the "average" early mollusc grew more slowly than the average living mollusc, the record would be biased toward smaller size.

It may be simpler at this juncture to consider the record of the extant classes. Gastropoda is the most diverse class today and seems to have had that characteristic since these animals first appeared. Some orders extend far back into the Paleozoic, and others appear in the Mesozoic. To overgeneralize a bit, the Triassic gastropods resemble those in the Late Paleozoic, whereas the Cretaceous faunas are similar to the Recent. Unfortunately, the Jurassic gastropod faunas are not as well known as those that are either older or younger. As a general rule, Mollusca seem to have been less affected by the end-Permian extinction than most other phyla. Selected gastropods may be useful for age dating throughout their time range; they are the most important megafossils for this purpose within the Tertiary.

Some some discordance exists between the classification of living gastropods based on soft-part anatomical features and the paleontological classification, which must be based almost exclusively on the shell. In general, this issue is more relevant in determining the relationship of various orders to one another. Strictly speaking, it is impossible to definitively demonstrate that a particular fossil is a gastropod. The concept of Gastropoda is based on torsion of the soft parts, which begins in the larval stage and affects the subsequent growth of soft parts. Such twisting cannot be demonstrated in fossils known only from the shell. Because of this torsion, one might argue that the Gastropoda are the most advanced class within the Mollusca.

To speculate, one possible reason for the continued diversity of gastropod genera through time may lie in the twisting of the body. This has resulted in the development of a neck, thereby giving greater flexibility to the mouth and its contained radula. The living gastropods show a great variety of radulas, which in turn allowed for exploitation of a greater variety of food sources. A closure of the aperture is not unique to the gastropods, but they developed this feature more than any other class. This development allowed movement into habitats where intermittent deterioration of the environment may have been a serious problem. Perhaps the high development of the operculum (lid over the aperture) is partially related to the gastropods' ability to invade freshwater; the oldest forms that are known to have done so are in the Permian.

Gastropods also invaded the land habitat, but these groups lack an operculum, thereby weakening the above argument. On the other hand, fossil land snails occur in the Pennsylvanian (Late Carboniferous), so movement to land and freshwater may have been independent and unrelated events. At least some of the diversity within the land snails developed early, but these Pennsylvanian taxa are placed readily in living orders and superfamilies.

Bellerophontoidea shells, which are coiled but bilaterally symmetrical, occur within the Paleozoic. If these organisms have undergone torsion, they are to be classed with the gastropods, but if the soft parts are bilaterally symmetrical, they are to be classed with the Monoplacophora. The amount of literature on this point far exceeds the overall importance of the group. In the writer's view, most of these shells are gastropods, and only a few may belong to the Monoplacophora.

Fossils that are generally accepted to be gastropods occur in the late Late Cambrian. In the early Late Cambrian, coiled shells occur that are probably gastropods, yet all of these coil to the left, whereas almost all younger forms coil to the right. In the Middle and Early Cambrian, *Pelagiella,* a small coiled shell but with an atypical whorl profile, is present. W. Kier and R.M. Linsley have proposed the class Paragastropoda for gastropod-like shells, which on various morphologic grounds are judged not to have undergone torsion. This concept is not universally accepted.

The only living, externally shelled cephalopod is to be found in the well-known *Nautilus.* In external shape, the bilaterally symmetrical shell is remarkably similar to some members of the Bellerophontoidea. Internally, it differs in having curved partitions (septa) spaced in a logarithmic arrangement throughout most of the shell. Almost all of the soft parts are confined to the body chamber, occupying part of a whorl. Such internal partitions are not unique to the class; septa occur in gastropods and other classes. Indeed, they are widespread in the animal kingdom, presumably to strengthen a weaker part of a shell and perhaps to allow a hard part to be extended without creating an inordinate length to the soft parts.

What is unique to the Cephalopoda is that each septum is pierced by a hole through which a strand of soft parts (siphuncle) extends to the apical area (tip). As a consequence of this siphuncle, which is attached to the main portion of the soft body, the animal can withdraw water from a newly formed chamber and secrete gas into it, thereby permitting some control over its buoyancy. Presumably, most of the shelled cephalopods in the past had a similar physiological control.

Nautilus is an exception in modern seas, for all other cephalopods have either a small internal shell (cuttlefish) or no hard part at all. These animals also have developed different mechanisms to control their buoyancy and are remarkably mobile. Squid are exceedingly abundant, and the octopus has the most flexible body and best-developed eyes within the phylum. Because the octopus appears to be an intelligent animal capable of learning, some researchers consider it to be the most advanced of the Mollusca. The record of these soft-bodied creatures is woefully inadequate, but squid and octopus are known in rocks at least as old as the Jurassic. Objects which may be arm hooks of squid or belemnites (fossil cephalopods with bulletlike internal skeletons) occur in the Permian.

The belemnites are morphologically similar to the living cuttlefish because of their solid, straight, internal shell. They are well known in the Mesozoic and are useful in biostratigraphy; the belemnites may extend back into at least the Devonian. Because one is dealing with a predominately shelled group in the Paleozoic and a predominately soft-bodied group today, estimates of the number of genera through time are difficult to construct. In general, the living soft-bodied forms may have few genera but an enormous number of individuals, whereas the externally shelled forms have few individuals but much generic diversity.

The externally coiled forms are divided conveniently into two main groups: the nautiloids, allied to *Nautilus,* and the ammonoids, which began in the Devonian. Whereas the nautiloids have a simple curved septum, that of the ammonoids is wrinkled more complexly. The steinkern of a gastropod shows nothing of the shell, but in marked contrast the steinkern of a shelled cephalopod includes these septal walls. Most of the details of classification are based on the pattern of these internal features. It is a sobering thought that a well-preserved Paleozoic or Mesozoic cephalopod showing exquisite external detail is of less use in biostratigraphy than a steinkern. Although most shelled cephalopods are bilaterally symmetrical, ammonoids coiled in three dimensions are well known in the Cretaceous.

Within the Mesozoic, ammonoids are important guide fossils. They seem to have died out during the end-Cretaceous extinction. At the end-Permian extinction, all but a very few genera became extinct. In contrast, the coiled nautiloids, which show less morphologic diversity, were little affected by these extinction events. Coiled nautiloids are known from rocks as early as the Ordovician but are less common in the older parts of the Paleozoic.

The Early Paleozoic is the time when straight-shelled forms were at their greatest development. They are less common in the Late Paleozoic; however, recently a Cretaceous orthoconic (shaped like a straight, tapering cone) cephalopod was reported. A few gently curved forms are known from the Early and Middle Paleozoic, and one small group seems to have broken away the early part of the shell and floated, but these are exceptions. The largest known straight cephalopods occur in the Late Ordovician and can approach seven meters in length, resembling telephone poles. Some of the straight cephalopods had large siphuncles; because so much gas was generated, they compensated by depositing calcium carbonate in this tube. Isolated siphuncles and siphuncular deposits are difficult at first glance to associate with the Mollusca. It is difficult to associate them with the proper shell.

Calcified apertural coverings, called aptychi, are known from the Silurian through the Cretaceous. Like the record of gas-

tropod opercula, their preservation depends in large measure on secondary calcification. However, poorly calcified and even non-calcified coverings have been collected. Both living and fossil cephalopods have a strongly calcified two-part beak within the mouth. These may be preserved as fossils and arguments rage as to whether aptychi are actually beaks. This writer's view is that they function like the gastropod opercula to protect the soft part when retracted into the shell.

Based on observations of the living *Nautilus,* which has an organic hood to cover the aperture when the tentacles and head are withdrawn into the shell, the nautiloids are considered to be scavengers; rarely do they catch smaller organisms. The ammonoids, in contrast, have been judged to be faster swimmers and therefore are considered to have been predators. They are more commonly found in offshore than inshore deposits. The huge Ordovician orthoconic cephalopods and their smaller relatives are almost all characteristic of near shore, shallow water deposits. It seems implausible that such large animals could have been hunters or that they were able to scavenge enough material to sustain life. It seems more likely that the cephalopods were originally herbivores; the coiled shell allowed for increased ease of movement and may have led to a more carnivorous diet. Despite the predominance of straight forms in the Ordovician, the oldest known cephalopods are curved—neither coiled nor straight—and are first known in the late Late Cambrian.

The Pelecypoda (Bivalvia) are not as diverse as the Gastropoda but have a larger biomass and presumably have maintained that characteristic throughout their geologic history. While there is some discordance between zoological and paleontological subdivisions of this group, it is much less than that of the Gastropoda. Fossils with features that resemble the living *Nuculana* occur in the late Early Ordovician; by the Late Ordovician most of the major subdivisions of the pelecypods have appeared.

The pre-Ordovician record of the Pelecypoda presents another kind of problem encountered in dealing with fossils. The small, bivalved *Fordilla* is widespread and locally exceedingly abundant in the Early Cambrian. It is generally accepted as a mollusc and some scholars assign it to the Pelecypoda. A few rare, bivalved shells have been found in the Middle Cambrian, and even fewer are known from the Late Cambrian. Extinct organisms that are rare and restricted in habitat might be expected to show gaps in their fossil record. However, from the Middle Ordovician onward, pelerypods are both diverse and abundant. It is difficult to understand why there should be such a paltry record between *Fordilla* and Ordovician forms.

Presumably, the Pelecypoda were originally free-living, burrowing shallowly into the bottom. When closed, the two-part shell effectively sealed the soft parts safely within, aided by interlocking teeth and sockets along the hinge line. The development of siphons enabled deeper burrowing while allowing the shell to remain shut. Attachment on the surface, either by threads or by cementing the shell to a small, hard piece on an otherwise soft substrate was another significant trend in adaptive radiation of the class. In a sense, the Tertiary may well be described as the age of the oysters, based on the abundance of these cemented shells. Members of another closely allied group in the Jurassic were free-living but are still recognizable as oysters. Others increased in size and became strongly asymmetrical, superficially resembling giant horn corals. These rudistids were characteristic of Mesozoic tropical seas and did not survive the end of the Cretaceous extinction.

The extinct class Rostroconchia has been proposed for univalve shells, which in effect may be described as a folded sheet open at the anterior, posterior, and ventral surfaces. Whether these begin in the Early Cambrian is arguable, but they are well known in Late Cambrian and Early Ordovician rocks. The Rostroconchia are not known in post-Paleozoic rocks. How high they range into the Paleozoic is still not fully resolved. During the Silurian, the flattened forms of the Early Paleozoic are replaced by more inflated, ornamented forms that externally, at least, resemble more typical pelecypods.

The Pelecypoda may very well have developed from the Rostroconchia by the univalve shell splitting at the dorsum (back) to form a bivalve. However, if both Rostroconchia and Pelecypoda are both first observed in the fossil record in the Early Cambrian, this presumed relationship is more difficult to demonstrate. One great advantage of the fossil record is that the sequence in which forms appear is reasonably well known; although new collections may contribute additional knowledge, it is unlikely that after more than two hundred years of scientific collecting, the general sequence of occurrence will be greatly changed. The terms "primitive" and "advanced" carry with their usage a great deal of intellectual baggage. In one sense, the Rostroconchia may be primitive and the Pelecypoda are advanced. I prefer the terms "early" and "late" to indicate the facts of occurrence. If the first members of each class are coeval (occur at the same time) in geologic occurrence, derivation is less easy to accept. If the Pelecypoda began in the Ordovician and the Rostroconchia in the Cambrian, the facts of early and late occurrence would be in accord with the concepts of "primitive" and "advanced."

The soft-part anatomy of the Rostroconchia is unknown and can only be speculated on from features preserved on the interior of the shell and from paleoecological inferences. The anatomy of living Pelecypoda is known, and presumably this information can be applied with confidence to the indisputable early members of the class. If so, early pelecypods lacked both a head and a radula. For more than a century, it has generally been accepted from the evidence of larval forms that there is a closer relationship between the Pelecypoda and the Scaphopoda than between the Pelecypoda and other extant classes.

It is therefore reasonable to speculate that the Rostroconchia may have had a radula, for of all the groups of molluscs which appear early in the geologic record, they appear more like the Scaphopoda. If the rostroconch shell were to fuse ventrally (while remaining fused dorsally), the result would be a scaphopod-like shell with anterior and posterior openings. In my opinion, it is far more reasonable to suggest that the major changes in morphology came about as mutations, which affected the larval stage, than to look for intermediate forms among adult shells. In more general terms, the pronounced gaps between the high-level taxonomic categories may be real and not an artifact of an incomplete record.

Another unresolved issue is specifying when the scaphopods first appear in the fossil record. They may occur in the Middle Ordovician, or in the Devonian, but it is evident that by the Mississippian, indisputable scaphopod shells are present.

Just as the words "primitive" and "advanced" may cause difficulties, "generalized" and "specialized" are also slippery concepts. The scaphopods are specialized in their life habit. Throughout their known geologic record they show little morphologic diversity. In the Late Mesozoic, one order of this class moved into a deeper water habitat and modified the morphology, but otherwise the Paleozoic scaphopods are remarkably similar to the living ones.

On the other hand, specialized may also mean the greatest deviation from the presumed ancestral type. In that sense, the Gastropoda may be the most specialized because of the bizarre torsion of soft parts. One path out of this intellectual morass may be to consider simultaneously the features of anatomy, overall size of the group, geologic record, and ecology. It may be helpful to consider distinctiveness as meaning the fundamental morphologic difference between groups. Although this definition may apply at any level from genus and above, it is more intelligibly applied at the higher taxonomic levels. The Scaphopoda are distinct from the Pelecypoda and equally distinct from the Gastropoda. While there are a great many forms of gastropods and many forms of pelecypods, there are very few forms of scaphopods. Throughout their known history, the first two classes have been diverse whereas the scaphopods have never shown much diversity.

"Success" and "failure" also carry much intellectual baggage, clouding intelligent discussion. For example, were the Rostroconchia a failure because they no longer are extant, or were they a success because they may have given rise to one or possibly two classes of extant molluscs? Or, are the gastropods a success because there are so many kinds, and are the scaphopods a failure because there are so few kinds?

The Polyplacophora are germane to this argument. From the Pennsylvanian onward they show remarkably little change in major features and little diversity relative to the "major" classes of the Mollusca. The older part of their record is less easy to interpret. I believe that fossils of this class first appear at about the Cambrian-Ordovician boundary, whereas others would place them in older rocks of the Late Cambrian. Yu Wen has reported polyplacophoran plates from the Early Cambrian of China, but this record has been disputed, and there seems to be a growing consensus that these are pieces of a multipart animal that is not a mollusc.

The Polyplacophora and Scaphopoda show little change over time. The "major" classes of extant molluscs evolve visibly, although within each class there are selected lower-level groups which show little change. Perhaps "distinctiveness" is best defined as a fundamental morphologic development, such as would define a class-level taxonomic group, whereas "diversity"—conveniently measured by the number of genera within a class—is a measure of the extent to which this morphologic development permits the organism to move into various habitats. In other highly approximate terms, distinctiveness may be indicated by the ability of members of a class to survive in a particular ecological niche or lifestyle, and diversity may be thought of as a measure of this niche's width.

The Monoplacophora, the final extant class of shelled Mollusca, again illustrates the problem of a gap in the fossil record. In this instance, the gap between the Late Devonian and the Pleistocene is larger than any other considered above. Nevertheless, there seems to be a consensus that the Early and Middle Paleozoic forms and the living ones belong to the same class. This class also emphasizes the need to keep an open mind rather than accept a rigid scheme, for it shattered—there is no better word—the long-held basic concept of five classes of Mollusca. As J.B. Knight often repeated: "Say not that this is so, but this is how it seems to me to be as I now see the things I think I see."

Despite the small size of the class Monoplacophora, there is some morphologic diversity within the group. Some genera have a shape resembling the bowl of a spoon, other are slightly compressed and more hooklike, and still others are high, gently curved cones. *Knightoconus* is a high, gently curved form which has a multiple number of internal septae. E.L. Yochelson and colleagues (1973) suggested that this middle Late Cambrian genus may have been ancestral to the cephalopods. Although there has been debate over which suggested mechanism enables change from one class to another, there seems to be general agreement of a relationship between the Monoplacophora and Cephalopoda. If members of the most "primitive" class gave rise to members of the most "advanced" class, this may reinforce the notion that such concepts contribute little to our understanding.

During the last four decades, various scholars have assigned an increasing number of genera with a considerable range of morphologic diversity to the Monoplacophora. As a result, J.S. Peel has suggested that the term be abandoned altogether. He advocates erecting a more exclusive class, *Tergomya*, which would admit only a subset of all proposed monoplacophorans, according to a strict set of morphological criteria. Tergomya would be used in much the same way as Knight did in his seminal 1952 paper. While there is merit in this proposal, Monoplacophora has become so widely ingrained in the zoological and more general literature that it is unlikely to be abandoned.

Peel proposed the class Helcionelloida for Early and Middle Cambrian fossils as one step toward establishing the Tergomya. These fossils are more or less straight-sided and strongly compressed, have curved shells, and are much longer than they are wide at the aperture. They do not closely resemble the models of the hypothetical ancestral mollusc, which is generally shown as a simple, cap-shaped shell on the back. However, Helcionelloida are more of a generalized form than any of the molluscs discussed above and may indeed be the ancestral stock of the phylum. Whether they lived on the bottom or on other plants and animals is unknown. The occurrence of a prominent, open, siphonlike tube in some genera suggests that they could have been sedentary; the tube may have been used to expel deoxygenated water away from the gills. In his seminal 1952 paper, Knight suggested that torsion took place within this group; this supposition remains in question.

In the Early Cambrian of north Greenland, *Halkiera* (spinose fossils which heretofore had been known only as isolated pieces), recently were found attached to a soft-bodied form. Shells appear on the anterior and posterior ends of the animal; they are approximately the same shape as some geologically younger monoplacophorans. S. Conway Morris and J.S. Peel have suggested that these are earlier molluscs. The idea that these animals

are so morphologically distinct from all other forms as to constitute an extinct phylum seems not to have been considered.

During the nineteenth and first half of the twentieth century, the Mollusca were a dumping ground for Paleozoic fossils that did not fit easily into other recognized phyla. Some class rank names, such as Eopteropoda, were proposed but have never found general acceptance. Most, though by no means all, of these spurious forms have been removed from the Mollusca and with the exception of the halkierids, none have been added.

Proposals for two additional classes based on Cambrian fossils that are uncommon to rare, but that are probably molluscs, remain to be discussed. In the Late Cambrian, the genus *Matthevia* occurs as isolated, thick masses of calcium carbonate in which there are two deep cavities. Commonly, they occur near large stromatolites in beds that otherwise have a dearth of megafossils. Yochelson suggested that the pieces were anterior and posterior and were relatively heavy to allow the animal to remain in a moderately high energy environment (e.g., one with wave action). He suggested that there might have been intermediate plates; his theory appears to have been based on worm fragments, and he has since recanted. In contrast, Runnegar and others, in one paper, proposed that this genus was a member of the Polyplacophora. I am not convinced by their reconstruction with eight plates or by their hypothetical series leading to undoubted isolated polyplacophoran plates. However, in some sense the argument turns on the issue of how far a class-level proposal based on living organisms may be extended to forms known only from fossils. Yochelson remains convinced that there is an extinct class, Matth_eva, containing only the one genus, *Matthevia*. It is unlikely that this particular argument, in which there is at least partial agreement on morphology but no agreement on interpretation and reconstruction, will be readily resolved.

Yochelson also proposed the extinct class Stenotheca. About a year later, Akserina proposed the term Probivalvia for the same concept. Only two or three genera, all known from the Early and Middle Cambrian, are included in this concept. They are asymmetrical, elongate bivalves with an unusual shell morphology. Rather than having a hinge line, they have a tooth in one valve and a socket in the other at the apex. A series of internal grooves appear on either side of the curved central line of the shell.

Either the concept of Pelecypoda must be expanded dramatically to include these fossils, or they constitute a distinct class. Since the original class proposal, they have received little attention in phylogenetic studies. Runnegar and Pojeta have considered them to be partially torted, bivalved monoplacophorans; since monoplacophorans are characterized as bilaterally symmetrical univalves with paired muscles, their remarks are difficult to comprehend. If the class finds general acceptance, thereby establishing that bivalved molluscs other than Peleypoda occur early in the Cambrian, it could strengthen the case that *Fordilla* is not a pelecypod and that this class began in the Ordovician rather than the Cambrian.

The placement of the Hyolitha is a far more significant problem than the status of these two classes. This issue of placement once again involves the basic problem of the extent to which fossils may be used to modify the definition of a high-level taxon.

Yochelson maintains that they fall within the Mollusca. Runnegar and Pojeta insist that they are different enough to constitute an extinct phylum.

The hyoliths range from early Early Cambrian to the Permian, and are particularly abundant in the Cambrian. Thereafter they are increasingly uncommon. Most are assigned to two orders (or classes), but in the Permian, Peel and Yochelson place the giant specimens measuring up to a meter long in a third order. The Cambrian Hyolitha vary greatly in size, but specimens as large as 15 centimeters long are known. If these are Mollusca, they effectively end the argument that Cambrian molluscs are invariably tiny.

The shell of the Hyolitha is an elongate tube that expands gently from the closed apex. It may be straight or gently curved. The aperture is closed by an operculum. In one of the two main groups, the operculum may be retracted far into the tube. In the other, more common group, the operculum is hinged at the dorsum in a tooth and socket arrangement and may have elaborate muscle attachments on the interior. In this group, the sides of the operculum are bowed outward to allow the inner edges of two curved calcareous pieces, dubbed helens, to extend outward. These seem to have acted as stabilizing devices.

In the first group, the cross section of the tube is generally simple. It may be circular, oval, or kidney bean-shaped; unfortunately, there is a resemblance to worm tubes, and many genera may not be correctly assigned to this group. In the second group, the whorl profile is commonly triangular. It is generally agreed that the flat surface is ventral. Although various schemes have been proposed for their life habits, it is now generally accepted that they lived freely on the bottom and may have fed by processing detritus from the sediments.

Pojeta and Runnegar find that the Hyolitha differ from undoubted Mollusca. They suggest that they constitute an extinct phylum allied to the phoronid "worms," a rare phylum today, but one to which specimens from the Middle Cambrian Burgess Shale have been assigned.

Yochelson outlined a pragmatic definition of the Mollusca based more on the features of the hard parts. This led to his conclusion that the Hyolitha were Mollusca. The occurrence of crossed-lamellar shell structure reported by Runnegar and Pojeta may also be added to this list. No resolution has been reached on the systematic position of the Hyolitha, and it is unlikely to be clarified in the near future.

The primary purpose of this summary has been to emphasize the points of uncertainty facing paleomalacologists. Nevertheless, this emphasis on problems should not cloud the amount that has been learned during the last century about the evolution of Mollusca. They are important fossils throughout their long history, making them worthy of continued detailed study.

As a partial antithesis, Conway Morris has recently published on the Cambrian genus *Mobergella* and its allies. These are tiny fossils with several muscle scars on the interior. More importantly, the fossils are composed of calcium phosphate, not calcium carbonate. Traditionally, these commonly have been regarded as opercula of "worm" tubes. However, if these forms and *Halkeria* are accepted as molluscs, possibly related to the Monoplacopha, there would appear to be no morphologic limits as to what may be considered a fossil mollusc.

ELLIS YOCHELSON

See also Bivalves; Cephalopods; Gastropods; Molluscs: Minor Molluscan Classes

Works Cited

Knight, J.B. 1952. *Primitive Fossil Gastropods and Their Bearing on Gastropod Classification.* Smithsonian Miscellaneous Collections, 114 (13). Washington, D.C.: Smithsonian.

Lemche, H. 1957. A new living deep-sea mollusc of the Cambro-Devonian Class Monoplacophora. *Nature* 179:413–16.

Runnegar, B., and J. Pojeta Jr. 1974. Molluscan phylogeny: The paleontological viewpoint. *Science* 186:311–17.

Yochelson, E.L. 1963. *Problems of the Early History of the Mollusca.* Proceedings of the 16th International Congress on Zoology, Washington, D.C., August 20–26, 1963, 2, 187. Washington, D.C.: International Congress on Zoology.

Yochelson, E.L., R.H. Flower, and G.F. Webers. 1973. The bearing of the new Late Cambrian monoplacophoran genus *Knightoconus* upon the origin of the Cephalopoda. *Lethaia* 6:275–309.

Further Reading

Peel, J.S. 1991. Functional morphology of the Class Helcionelloida nov., and the early evolution of the Mollusca: 157–177. *In* A.M. Simonetta and S. Conway Morris (eds.), *The Early Evolution of Metazoa and the Significance of Problematic Taxa.* Cambridge and New York: Cambridge University Press.

Pojeta Jr., J., and B. Runnegar. 1976. *The Paleontology of the Rostroconch Molluscs and the Early History of the Phylum Mollusca.* U.S. Geological Survey Professional Paper 968. Washington, D.C.: International Congress on Zoology.

Taylor, J.D. (ed.). 1996. *Origin and evolutionary radiation of the Mollusca.* Oxford and New York: Oxford University Press.

Yochelson, E.L. 1979. Early radiation of Mollusca and mollusc-like groups. *In* M.R. House (ed.), *The Origin of the Major Invertebrate Groups.* Systematics Association Special Volume 12. Oxford: Clarendon Press.

MOLLUSCS: MINOR MOLLUSCAN CLASSES

The title of this article poses two obvious questions and at least one hidden one. The issue is one of nomenclature because the terms "minor" and "class" are ambiguous. The International Rules of Zoological Nomenclature specify standardized procedures for naming species, genera, and families. However, the names of higher taxa (groups; singular, taxon)—orders, classes, and phyla—are not covered specifically by these rules. The molluscan groups under consideration have been variously ranked, construed, and named by authors over the years. In an effort to provide some objectivity, the individual author's preferred usage will be noted.

The terms "minor" and "major" refer entirely to size as measured by the number of genera included in a molluscan class. Gastropoda, Pelecypoda (Bivalvia), and Cephalopoda are accepted conventionally as major classes. Scaphopoda are accepted conventionally as a minor class, and most authors, including K.A. Vaught (1989), treat Polyplacophora (Amphineura) as minor. However, J.E. Morton (1967), a recognized expert, considers it to be one of the "larger classes." The number of living genera, although a crude measure, suggests there is little variation in the basic morphology of the minor classes; by that standard the Polypacophora probably are minor.

"Class" is a far more complex notion, since it is based on morphologic distinctiveness (pertaining to shape and structure). The degree of significance ascribed to different features depends on the author. For example, in the 1870s, von Ihering differentiated a phylum Amphineura based in part on the ladderlike arrangement of the organism's nervous system. Contemporary and subsequent scholars lowered this taxon to class status and emphasized the multiple number of plates that cover the elongate, generally broad foot, hence the preferred class name Polyplacophora.

For approximately three-quarters of a century, the phylum Mollusca was conventionally treated as containing three major classes and two minor ones. In 1952 J.B. Knight studied the early fossil record and suggested that muscle scars (distinctive markings on the inner surface of a shell) within a few univalves (those with only one shell) indicated that the soft parts had not undergone torsion (been twisted). He expanded the Gastropoda to include two subclasses, the Anisopleura, more or less the conventional class, and the Isopleura, which contained two divisions: the bilaterally symmetrical, multishelled Polyplacophora and the univalved, presumed bilaterally symmetrical fossils, the Monoplacophora. Except for a mention in one textbook, this classification scheme generally was ignored.

Then, in 1957, the phylum Mollusca was expanded dramatically by the description of a modern monoplacophoran. Because the specimens had univalve shells with a bilateral arrangement of soft parts, the group was accepted immediately by malacologists as a sixth class within the Mollusca. Because Monoplacophora contains such a small number of genera, it is considered appropriately as a minor class.

As a consequence of its anatomical peculiarities, the Monoplacophora revolutionized the field of molluscan relationships. In

this sense, the acceptance of the class certainly was not minor. Different schemes of the relationships of the extant (present-day) classes appeared in the literature. The discovery of living examples also led to renewed interest in the fossil record of Monoplacophora and possible related forms.

The enigmatic relations of the Scaphopoda to the other molluscan classes remained essentially undisturbed by this new discovery, but the search for new relationships strongly affected the Polyplacophora. It had included some genera of shell-less forms, generally as a subclass. Within a few years, that perspective changed, and now it is accepted generally that the Aplacophora constitute a seventh class of living Mollusca.

In 1981, it was suggested that the Aplacophora actually constitutes two classes. During the mid-1990s, few persons actively studied the Aplacophora; two of the active scholars suggest that the Aplacophora should be divided into two classes while two others support subclass rank for these divisions. There is also disagreement on the names of these categories. According to Vaught (1989), the Chaetodermomorpha (Caudofoveata) contains nine genera. The Neomeniomorpha (Solenogasters) is more diverse, with three suborders and 22 families used for less than 70 genera. The more conservative approach recognizes a single class, but the new subclass names within the Aplacophora represent recent efforts to better understand these animals. As an indication of the great interest in this group, only one-third as many genera were recognized during the 1960s.

The Aplacophora live in marine waters of moderate to abyssal (extreme) depths. Most have a wormlike body, with a reduced mantle cavity and a reduced foot. The radula (a rasping mouthpart) within the mouth, is an important feature linking the Aplacophora to the more conventional molluscan classes; its bipartite form helps link the two subclasses, as does the absence of kidneys. The cuticle (outer protective coating) contains spicules (needles) formed of calcium carbonate. The Chaetodermomorpha process mud and ooze for contained organic detritus (dead plant and animal matter). The Neomeniomorpha live in close association with groups such as corals and anemones, feeding by sucking fluid from their tissues.

As might be anticipated when dealing with soft-bodied organisms, there is no authentic fossil record for the Aplacophora. A report based on a Precambrian trace has since been retracted. Isolated spicules have been identified in the Silurian, although it is unlikely that these are from Aplacophora. Whether this is an ancient group or one of more recent development is a puzzle. To quote one specialist, "The worm-like shape of the aculiferous (lacking a shell) Aplacophora is a derived state, yet the internal anatomy seems to be primitive" (Scheltma 1996).

The living representatives of the Polyplacophora are divided into three suborders and nine families. About 50 genera and 20 subgenera are recognized. Because the eight plates of the polyplacophorans are held together by soft tissue, most fossils occur in the form of isolated plates. In general, the geologically early plates are anteroposteriorly elongate, but most of the fossil plates are wider

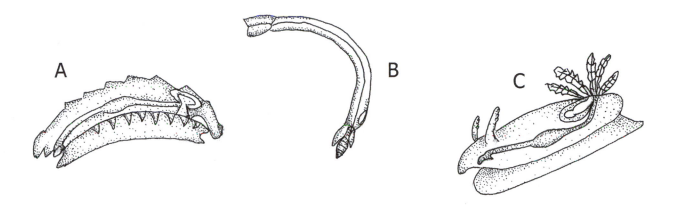

Figure 1. The minor molluscan classes. *A*, Amphineura, *Chiton; B*, Amphineura, *Chaetoderma; C*, Gastropoda, *Doris.* Illustration by Susan Lerner, after Morton (1967).

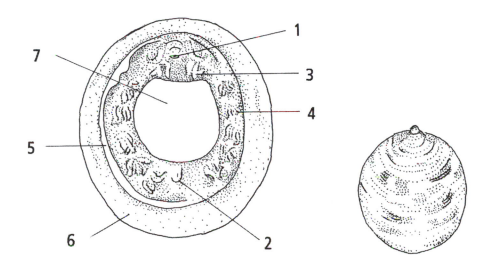

Figure 2. Simplified drawing of Neopilina galatheae, in ventral view (left) and the shell in dorsal view on a small scale. *1*, mouth; *2*, anus; *3*, palplike appendages; *4*, paired gill-like organs; *5*, mantle; *6*, shell rim; *7*, foot. Illustration by Susan Lerner, after Morton (1967).

than they are long. Most Paleozoic forms and one modern genus lack insertion plates (tiny, forward-facing extensions that allow for better articulation). One possible interpretation is that these forms did not cling to a hard substrate; the modern form commonly occurs on a soft bottom.

The age of the oldest polyplacophoran is in dispute. Early Cambrian forms reported from China are more likely pieces of an unrelated organism. Late Cambrian forms may belong in the class or represent an extinct class. Isolated plates generally accepted as polyplophorans occur in the latest Late Cambrian. Curiously, there are more fossil plates reported in the Palezoic than in the

Mesozoic, even though the Paleozoic precedes it. It is unlikely that a large number of genera occurred in the Paleozoic.

Despite the small number of genera in the Monoplacophora—probably less than two dozen—they have a long geologic history. Again, there is disagreement as to whether Early Cambrian forms are assigned correctly. Shells generally accepted as monoplacophorans occur in the Late Cambrian. Locally, they are abundant, but at most localities no specimens occur, and one may collect for years without finding a single example. They are most morphologically diverse in the Ordovician and Silurian but are exceedingly rare in the Devonian. Between the Devonian and the Pleistocene, no monoplacophorans have been found in the fossil record despite diligent search efforts for four decades. This absence is the most curious feature of their history.

The scaphopods are the most recent of the extant classes of molluscs to be found in the fossil record. Although they have been reported from the Ordovician, there is reason to believe that the fossils in question actually are calcerous worm tubes. Differentiating between these two unrelated types of fossils is exceedingly difficult. Occurrences in the Mississippian are certain, and they may extend into the Devonian. Paleozoic forms tend to be smooth and show little or no curvature. From the Cretaceous onward, forms with strong longitudinal ridges occur. Of all the minor groups, the fossil record of the scaphopods is the least known.

ELLIS L. YOCHELSON

See also Bivalves; Cephalopods; Gastropods; Molluscs: Overview

Works Cited

Ihering, H. von. 1876. *Die gehorneikzeue der mollusker.* Erlanger: Ihering.
Knight, J.B. 1952. *Primitive Fossil Gastropods and Their Bearing on Gastropod Classification.* Smithsonian Miscellaneous Collections, 117 (13). Washington, D.C.: Smithsonian Institution.
Scheltema, A.H. 1996. Phylogenetic position of Sipuncula, Mollusca and the progenetic Aplacophora. *In* J.D. Taylor (ed.), *Origin and Evolutionary Radiation of the Mollusca.* Oxford and New York: Oxford University Press.

Further Reading

Morton, J.E. 1967. *Molluscs.* London: Hutchinson University Press.
Taylor, J.D. (ed.). 1996. *Origin and Evolutionary Radiation of the Mollusca.* Oxford and New York: Oxford University Press.
Vaught, K.A. 1989. *A Classification of the Living Mollusca.* Melbourne, Florida: American Malacologists.

MORTALITY AND SURVIVORSHIP

Population structure can be studied by considering three important characteristics: the number of individuals surviving at any given time from a starting population; the mortality rate, or number that die or are removed from that population; and mean life expectancy of individuals remaining at any specific age. Graphs, referred to as survivorship curves, can be used to illustrate these relationships by plotting the number of living individuals at any given time on the y-axis as a function of their age (plotted on the x-axis). The data may represent a single population or several populations of a species. Understanding the basic life history of a particular species, its mode of life, and its reproductive habits are critical for interpreting data contained in survivorship curves. Three general types of survivorship curves can be recognized in natural populations (Figure 1) (Dodd and Scanton 1990). Concave upward curves (I) are characteristic of populations with high juvenile mortality and lower mortality later in life. This curve type is common among invertebrates that produce large numbers of larvae, most of which die early on, with few individuals living to maturity. A descending straight line (II) showing constant mortality throughout life applies to small mammals and some birds and invertebrate species. Convex upward curves (III) depict species such as human beings, with low juvenile mortality but which have an accelerated rate of death approaching maximum longevity.

The individuals that are removed from a living population generate a death assemblage, which, depending on a variety of physical, biological, and chemical processes (termed taphonomic processes), may result in a fossil assemblage. Environmental disturbances are usually the most important causes of mortality in many benthic (bottom-dwelling) invertebrates and thus produce variation in survivorship curves for a given species. Biological factors including disease and size-selective predation also can be important. Physical controls on burial, such as seasonal variations in the amount of sediment eroded or deposited in a continental shelf environment, can temporally alter the taxonomic composition, abundances, and sizes of individuals in the living community of bottom dwelling organisms and subsequently affect the nature of the shells available to be preserved (Cummins et al. 1986; Staff et al. 1986). Differential preservation also can modify survivorship curves. After death, the shells of small, thin-shelled species can disappear owing to dissolution after burial and expo-

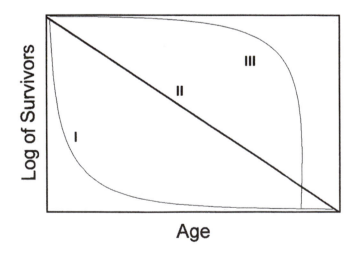

Figure 1. Schematic representation of three types of survivorship curves. *I,* mortality decreasing with increasing age; *II,* constant mortality rate; *III,* mortality increasing with age.

sure to acidic waters. The shells of these thin-shelled species are also more likely than ones with larger, more robust shells to be winnowed by currents and transported away after death instead of being buried and preserved.

Most fossil assemblages are thought to be formed by a combination of two processes. First, the gradual accumulation of preservable remains of individuals dying naturally produces a time-averaging of mortality patterns. Second, a catastrophic event such as an avalanche of sediment can result in sudden death of an entire population representing an occasional chance preservation (Kidwell and Bosence 1991). When examining a fossil assemblage, the paleontologist faces the question of whether all the specimens in a fossil assemblage were, in fact, preserved in the same environment as the original living community. Could some of them actually have originated from a contemporaneous but different environment and have been transported to that location by currents? Could some of the specimens have been derived from older weathered rocks? By using various kinds of physical evidence including sedimentologic, stratigraphic, or specimen structural features, it is possible to establish the likely predominate kind of mortality for a fossil assemblage and the possible origin of the specimens in the assemblage.

Specimens that are preserved in life position generally are thought to rule out the possibility that they were moved postmortem (Raup and Stanley 1978). Fossil mollusc shells that have been transported by currents from the site where they were originally located often can be recognized because they have been disarticulated or separated, they may be broken, show signs of wear, or they may be sorted by shell size (or weight). The presence of a disproportionately large number of specimens of a particular size with bore holes or shell breakage across the hinge area might indicate general or even size-selective predation by gastropods, crabs, or fish (Aller 1995). Postmortem changes owing to currents (or other dispersionary agents) can randomize dispersal patterns that originally were aggregated or uniform, or, sort and selectively concentrate shell debris.

It is important to understand that the occurrence of several species together in a fossil assemblage does not guarantee that they were members of the same community when they were alive or even that they were alive at the same time. Likewise, the appearance of random distributions does not necessarily mean that the distributions of the original species were not aggregated. An important strategy for interpreting fossil shelf environments

that are impacted by frequent and intense physical disturbances, and for judging how well they represent once-living patterns, is to compare the characteristics of recent death assemblages with those of the extant communities in that class of environments. Alternately, in environments with scant living populations, modern death assemblages can be examined to reconstruct the living community and understand factors that influence its structure (Aller 1995).

JOSEPHINE Y. ALLER

See also Fossilization Processes; Fossil Record; Paleoecology; Taphonomy

Works Cited

Aller, J.Y. 1995. Molluscan death assemblages on the Amazon Shelf: Implications for physical and biological controls on benthic populations. *Paleogeography, Paleoclimatology, Paleoecology* 118:181–212.

Cummins, H., E.N. Powell, R.J. Stanton Jr., and G. Staff. 1986. The rate of taphonomic loss in modern benthic habitats: How much of the potentially preservable community is preserved? *Paleogeography, Paleoclimatology, Paleoecology* 52:291–320.

Dodd, J.R., and R.J. Stanton Jr. 1990. *Paleoecology, Concepts and Applications.* 2nd ed., New York: Wiley.

Kidwell, S.M., and D.W.J. Bosence. 1991. Taphonomy and Time-Averaging of Marine Shelly Faunas. *In* P.A. Allison and D.E.G. Briggs (eds.), *Taphonomy.* New York: Plenum.

Raup, D.M., and S.M. Stanley. 1978. *Principles of Paleontology.* 2nd ed., San Francisco: Freeman.

Staff, G.M., R.J. Stanton Jr., E.N. Powell, and H. Cummins. 1986. Time-averaging, taphonomy, and their impact on paleocommunity reconstruction: Death assemblages in Texas bays. *Geological Society of America Bulletin* 97:428–30.

Further Reading

Dodd, J.R., and R.J. Stanton Jr. 1990. *Paleoecology, Concepts and Applications.* 2nd ed., New York: Wiley.

Kidwell, S.M., and D.W.J. Bosence. 1991. Taphonomy and Time-Averaging of Marine Shelly Faunas. *In* P.A. Allison and D.E.G. Briggs (eds.), *Taphonomy.* New York: Plenum.

Raup, D.M., and S.M. Stanley. 1978. *Principles of Paleontology.* 2nd ed., San Francisco: Freeman.

MURCHISON, RODERICK IMPEY

Scottish, 1792–1871

Roderick Impey Murchison was a pioneer of British geology, especially noted for his establishment of the Silurian System, which won him the Copley Medal. After his commission in the army in 1807, he had a short but illustrious military career, serving in the 36th Foot with the army in Spain and Portugal during the Peninsula Campaign, under Lord Wellington, and taking active part in several of the most important battles of the war. At the end of the

war in 1815, he married Charlotte, only daughter of General Francis Hugonin. She had interests in natural history and encouraged him to pursue his scientific interest in the subject of geology and actively supported him in his fieldwork and publications. This work was supported by Sir Humphrey Davy.

Murchison's first paper, in 1825, was on the geology of northwest Sussex and adjacent parts of Hampshire and Surrey. On

Dean Buckland's advice he examined the geology of Hereford-shire, Shropshire, and the Welsh borders, a project that culminated in his establishment of the system named after a pre-Roman tribe of the area known as the Silures (1839). He devoted his life to geology and traveled widely in Europe, where he studied the Devonian, Permian, and Laurentian systems (1846).

Murchison visited Russia in 1840 accompanied by M. de Verneuil. He named the Permian in honor of his studies in the province of Perm in Russia, where the strata of that system are extensively developed. He also established the theory of regional metamorphism and forecast the discovery of gold in Australia inferred by the analogy of rock formation there with gold-bearing strata in the Ural mountains. He served on a commission appointed to consider matters relating to the Coal Industry. The £6,000 he gave to found the Chair of Geology and Mineralogy in the University of Edinburgh was done so on condition that the government would supplement it with an annual grant of £200. This was duly endorsed. He published a very large number of monographs, papers, and reports (listed in the Royal Society's obituary of him) (1872) and a full account of his remarkable life has been published by the geologist A. Geikie (1875). Several fossil-type specimens (the first discovered fossils of new species or genera) bear his name. He died from bronchitis on 22 October 1871.

J.J. WYMER

Biography

Born in Tarradale, Scotland, 19 February 1792. Early education in grammar school at Durham; attended Royal Military College, Great Marlow, and a few months at the University of Edinburgh; commissioned, 1807; elected fellow (1825), secretary (1827–31), and president (1831–33, 1841–43), Geological Society of London; fellow of the Royal Society, 1826; president, Royal Geographic Society, 1844; president, British Association, 1846; received Copley Medal from Royal Society, 1849; director general of Geological Survey of Great Britain and Ireland and Royal School of Mines, 1855; created a knight commander of the Order of Bath, 1863; received Woolaston Gold Medal, 1864; created a baronet, 1866; founded Edinburgh Chair of Geology, 1870; he also received honorary degrees from the universities of Oxford, Cambridge, and Dublin, was a trustee of the British and Hunterian Museums, and a member of the Imperial Academy of Sciences and numerous other European academic institutions. Died 22 October 1871.

Major Publications

1829. On the coal-field of Brora in Sutherlandshire, and on some other stratified deposits in the north of Scotland. *Transactions of the Geological Society of London*, 2nd ser., 2 (2):293–326.

1932. With A. Sedgwick. A sketch of the structure of the eastern Alps. *Transactions of the Geological Society of London*, 2nd ser., 3 (2):301–420.

1839a. *The Silurian System, Founded on Geological Researches in the Counties of Salop, Hereford, Radnor, Montgomery, Caermarthen, Brecon, Pembroke, Monmouth, Gloucester, Worcester, and Stafford: With Descriptions of the Coal-Fields and Overlying Formations.* 3 vols. London: Murray.

1839b. With A. Sedgwick. Classification of the older rocks of Devonshire and Cornwall. *Philosophical Magazine* 14:242–60.

1842. With A. Sedgwick. On the classification and distribution of the older or Palaeozoic rocks of the north of Germany and of Belgium, as compared with formations of the same age in the British Isle. *Transactions of the Geological Society of London*, 2nd ser., 6 (2):221–302.

1845a. With É. de Verneuil and A. von Keyserling. *The Geology of Russia in Europe and the Ural Mountains.* 2 vols. London and Paris: Murray; 2nd ed., 1853.

1845b. On the Palaeozoic deposits of Scandinavia and the Baltic provinces of Russia, and their relations to Azoic or more ancient crystalline rocks: With an account of some great features of dislocation and metamorphism along their northern frontiers. *Quarterly Journal of the Geological Society of London* 1:467–94.

1847. On the meaning originally attached to the term "Cambrian system," and on the evidences since obtained of its being geologically synonymous with the previously established term "Lower Silurian." *Quarterly Journal of the Geological Society of London* 3:165–79.

1849. On the geological structure of the Alps, Apennines and Carpathians, more especially to prove a transition from secondary to tertiary rocks, and the development of Eocene deposits in southern Europe. *Quarterly Journal of the Geological Society of London* 5:157–312.

1854. *Siluria: The History of the Oldest Known Rocks Containing Organic Remains: With a Brief Sketch of the Distribution of Gold over the Earth.* London: Murray; 5th ed., 1872.

1859. On the succession of the older rocks in the northernmost counties of Scotland: With some observations on the Orkney and Shetland Islands. *Quarterly Journal of the Geological Society of London* 15:353–418.

Further Reading

1871. Sir Roderick Impey Murchison, Bart., K.C.B., LL.D., D.C.L., M.A., F.G.S., F.R.S. *Geological Magazine* 8(89):481–90.

1872. Obituaries of Fellows deceased: Sir Roderick Impey Murchison, Bart., K.C.B., & etc. *Proceedings of the Royal Society of London* 20:30–33

Geikie, A. (ed.). 1875. *Life of Sir Roderick Murchison, Bart.; K.C.B., F.R.S., sometime director-general of the Geological Survey of the United Kingdom: Based on His Journals and Letters with Notices of His Scientific Contemporaries and a Sketch of the Rise and Growth of Palaeozoic Geology in Britain.* 2 vols. London: Murray.

MYRIAPODS

Myriapods are many-legged, terrestrial arthropods whose bodies are divided into two major parts, a head and a trunk. The head bears a single pair of antennae, highly differentiated mandibles (or jaws), and at least one pair of maxillary mouthparts; the trunk region consists of similar "metameres," each of which is a functional segment that bears one or two pairs of appendages. Gas exchange is accomplished by tracheae—a branching network of specialized tubules—although small forms respire through the body wall. Malpighian organs are used for excretion, and eyes consist of clusters of simple, unintegrated, light-sensitive elements that are termed ommatidia. These major features collectively characterize the five major myriapod clades: Diplopoda (millipeds), Chilopoda (centipeds), Pauropoda (pauropods), Symphyla (symphylans), and Arthropleurida (arthropleurids). Other features indicate differences among these clades. For example, chilopods are opisthogoneate in that the genital openings occur in the penultimate trunk segment, while all other myriapods are progoneate by having the second abdominal segment housing the genital openings. Chilopods and symphylans possess a second pair of maxillary (or labial) mouthparts similar to hexapods (insects and parainsects), but these structures are absent in pauropods and diplopods. These and other unevenly distributed characters have made it difficult to unravel the evolutionary relationships of the higher groups of myriapods.

Myriapod Relationships

More contentious than internal myriapodan relationships is the relationship of myriapods to the rest of the Arthropoda, particularly the issue of whether they are phylogenetically close to the Hexapoda. Current thought on the relationship of myriapods to other arthropods can be characterized by five major hypotheses (Figure 1). The oldest currently held proposal (Figure 1A) consists of a Schizoramia clade that unites the Trilobita and Chelicerata (horseshoe crabs, spiders, and relatives), and a Mandibulata clade that contains the Crustacea and a more derived Tracheata clade that consists of the Myriapoda + Hexapoda (Weygolt 1979). (The Tracheata also are known as the Atelocerata or Antennata.) A second hypothesis envisions a clade that combines the Myriapoda + Hexapoda and another that unites the Trilobita and the Chelicerata + Crustacea, or a "TCC" clade (Figure 1B). This scheme maintains that the Myriapoda is a monophyletic clade, that is one with a single common ancestor, whose sister group, or closest relative, is the Hexapoda. Accordingly, this clade has very distant links to the rest of the Arthropoda (Briggs et al. 1992; Wheeler et al. 1993).

A third proposal, the uniramian hypothesis, was advocated by S.M. Manton (1977) and is based on functional analyses of the structure of arthropods, including myriapods. According to this view, because of functionally disparate mechanisms in walking, feeding, and other activities, major arthropodan clades are polyphyletic, indicating scant evidence of a common ancestor (Figure 1C). At a much coarser level, this hypothesis does distinguish four arthropod groups, the Trilobita, Chelicerata, Crustacea, and the Uniramia, the last consisting of the Myriapoda, Hexapoda, and Onychophora (velvet worms). However, subsequent structural and molecular evidence indicates that there are several characters uniting major arthropod taxa. Moreover, paleobiologic, embryologic, and other evidence demonstrates that myriapods and hexapods are fundamentally polyramous, having two major articulating appendages per embryological body segment, like other arthropods.

A fourth proposal (Figure 1D) suggests that myriapods are an ancient, basal arthropod lineage, and that the Hexapoda emerged as an independent, relatively recent clade from a rather terminal crustacean lineage, perhaps the Malacostraca, which contains lobsters and crabs (Ballard et al. 1992). Because few crustacean taxa were examined in this analysis, and due to the Cambrian age of many major crustacean lineages, it is possible that myriapods and hexapods are distinct lineages embedded within the Crustacea. Recently, an analysis by Friedrich and Tautz (1995) arrived at an unconventional conclusion that the Myriapoda is related closely, perhaps as a sister group, to the Chelicerata (Figure 1E), although support for this relationship was weak. Notably, there was lack of support for a Myriapoda-Hexapoda connection in two of these schemes.

Several conclusions have resulted from these and other studies of internal and external myriapod relationships. First, when analyses are limited to myriapods and hexapods, perhaps including some crustacean taxa, the Myriapoda is not sustained as a group defined by distinctive structures. The Symphyla becomes the sister group to the Hexapoda (Figure 2A), or the Chilopoda often becomes a paraphyletic taxon whose sister group is the rest of the Myriapoda and the Hexapoda (Figure 2B). Second, in more global analyses that include representatives from the other major arthropod groups, the Myriapoda + Hexapoda becomes disassembled, frequently radically so, leading to a conclusion that the several features that unite the Tracheata may have originated independently from convergence. Characters such as a single pair of antennae, tracheae, uniramy, and Malpighian tubules probably originated independently in both clades as adaptations to a terrestrial existence.

Taxonomic Characterization and Fossil History

Six major clades, or classes, of myriapods have been recognized, including two that are extinct (Kampecarida and Arthropleuridea) and an extant class that lacks a fossil record (Pauropoda). Kampecarids are poorly understood Late Silurian to Late Devonian myriapods with weakly coalesced segments, a head as wide or wider than body segments, large eyes with numerous ommatidia, and a medially divided sternum. Nothing is known of their mouthparts. Kampecarids are presumed to have been amphibious or even aquatic (Almond 1985). They probably were related to diplopods, whose major Paleozoic representatives were the giant, spiny euphoberiids (Figure 3) that bore prominent, rigid, and laterally positioned spines that were often forked.

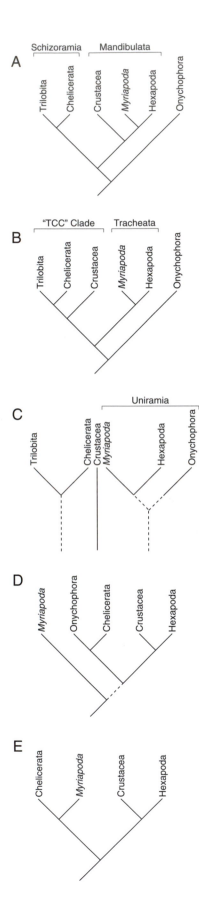

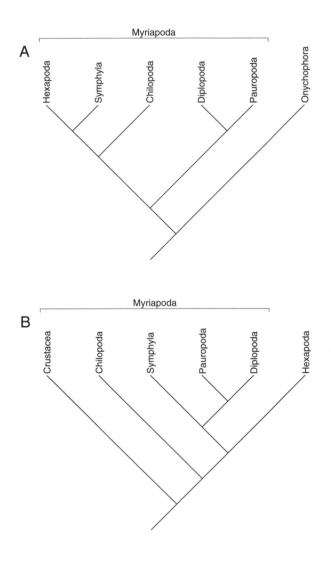

Figure 1. Summaries of five recent hypotheses indicating the relationship of myriapods to other major arthropod groups. All branch lengths are arbitrary; dotted lines indicate nodes that are theoretically inferred (c) or not statistically valid (others). This is not an exhaustive list. a, Schizoramia/Mandibulata Hypothesis; b, TCC/Tracheate Hypothesis, in which tracheates are recognized as a monophyletic clade but with the possibility of myriapods polyphyletic with respect to hexapods; some early Paleozoic subgroups, such as "trilobitoids," are not included; c, Uniramia Hypothesis, showing the polyphyletic origin of major arthropod clades from unspecified, lobopod ancestors; d, Basal Myriapod Hypothesis; e, Chelicerate/Myriapod Hypothesis. From: a, Weygolt (1979); b, Briggs et al. (1992), Wheeler et al. (1993); c, Manton (1977), see also Fryer (1996); d, Ballard et al. (1992); e, Turbeville et al. (1991).

Figure 2. Two recent hypotheses for the phylogenetic relationships of myriapod classes and hexapods, based on morphological data. a, Briggs et al. (1992); b, Kraus and Kraus (1994).

Figure 3. Structure of Carboniferous euphoberiid diplopods. *a,* dorsal view of trunk of *Amynilyspes wortheni* Scudder, from Mazon Creek, Illinois (from Hannibal 1984); note dorsal and lateral spines. *b,* ventral view of head of *?Myriacantherpestes* (from Hannibal 1997); note two laterally placed manibles at bottom of photograph, broad arcuate region above, and two lateral knobs for insertion of antennae above the labrum. Scale bars represent one cm. Both photographs were taken by Bruce Frumker, Cleveland Museum of Natural History, and are reproduced with permission.

Diplopods have a head narrower than trunk segment width. On the head are lateral eyes, eight-segmented antennae above a labrum, and mouthparts that include robust, highly toothed mandibles and maxillae modified into a special, multielement structure, the gnathochilarium (Figure 4b, c). The gnathochilarium is attached by membranes to a sternum and consists of a basal mentum and a pair of distal stipes. Their trunk segments are diplosomites, each consisting of a coalesced anterior prozonite and posterior metazonite that are fused or connected by membranes into a single functional segment that bears two pairs of segmented appendages (Figure 4a). These diplosomites are telescoped under the margin of the segment immediately in front of it, allowing some forms to curl or enroll completely. Modern diplopods are sluggish and range in length from two millimeters in the Julida to 26 centimeters in the Spirostrepsida, although Late Carboniferous euphoberiids were longer. Diplopods have the best fossil record of all myriapods, predominantly because of a relatively durable exoskeleton impregnated with calcium carbonate. Diplopod fossils are overwhelmingly represented in Baltic amber, from which the earliest occurrences of six of the 12 fossil orders are known (Table 1).

Pauropods are progoneate myriapods possessing nine pairs of legs, 11 body segments, and a terminal pygidium that forms a distinctive end segment. Reaching a maximum length of only two millimeters, pauropods lack tracheae and a circulatory system. They bear distinctive, two-branched antennae and have reduced mouthparts that lack a labial region. Pauropods lack a fossil record.

Symphylans are small, colorless, progoneate myriapods that exhibit a stereotyped combination of 12 leg-bearing segments ventrally and 15 or 22 dorsal sclerotized plates, plus a terminal segment bearing cercilike appendages homologous to walking legs. The head juts forward, bearing two simple antennae with beadlike segments, and well developed mandibular, maxillary, and labial mouthparts, imparting a distinctive insectan appearance. Described fossil symphylans are very rare; two of the three extant families are represented by single occurrences—a scolopendrellid from Late Eocene Baltic amber and a scutigerellid from Late Oligocene Dominican amber.

Chilopods are actively moving, opisthogoneate, tracheate myriapods that bear a single pair of appendages per functional segment (Figure 5a). With the exception of the presence of a second maxilla with a conspicuous palp (Figure 5b), the gross head structures and mouthparts of chilopods are similar to those of diplopods. The head is dorsoventrally flattened and is forwardly directed. The pair of appendages on the first trunk segment are walking legs modified into a poison claw, which contains an internal poison gland that releases toxin from an orifice at the appendage tip for immobilizing prey (Figure 5b, c). The trunk is elongate, flattened, and flexible, and each segment consists of an unmineralized, dorsal tergite, a ventral exoskeletal sternite, and up to several, complexly arranged, small exoskeletal pleurites on the body sidewall. Chilopods may reach lengths approaching 30 centimeters and are exclusively carnivorous, feeding extensively on other terrestrial arthropods. The chilopod fossil record extends to the Late Silurian. This and the occurrence of relatively advanced Middle Devonian fossils containing original cuticle (Shear and Bonamo

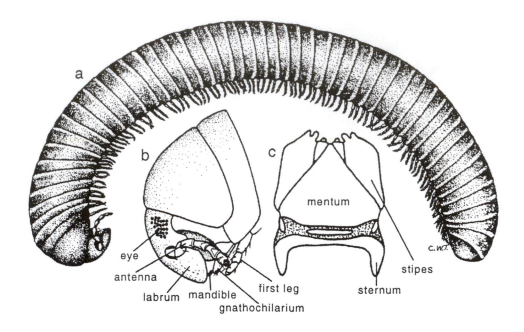

Figure 4. Major external features of the spirobolid milliped *Narceus,* representative of the myriapod class, Diplopoda. *a,* lateral view of the body; *b,* lateral view of head and first trunk segment; *c,* ventral view of the gnathochilarium. Figures from AN INTRODUCTION TO THE STUDY OF INSECTS, Sixth Edition by Donald J. Borror, Charles A. Triplehorn, and Norman F. Johnson, copyright © 1989 by Saunders College Publishing, reproduced by permission of the publisher.

1988) indicate that the initial radiation of chilopods probably was a Late Silurian event. Many chilopod fossils occur in Mid-Cenozoic Baltic amber, all assignable to modern families.

Arthropleurids are minute to gigantic myriapods up to two meters long, possibly slightly longer (Hahn et al. 1986), and are the largest terrestrial arthropods known (Figure 6). They are rare, occurring in two distinctive environments: Devonian *Eoarthropleura* is found in perimarine, early terrestrial deposits associated with diminutive and primitive vascular plants, whereas Late Carboniferous *Arthropleura* inhabited Late Carboniferous to Early Permian, equatorial, well-drained environments, especially seed-fern forests (Schneider and Barthel 1997). Segmentation consisted of two pairs of walking legs per functional segment (Briggs and Almond 1994), indicating that arthropleurids were anatomically close to diplopods. Arthropleurid cuticle was unmineralized and unusually thin, although it probably was sclerotized extensively (Rolfe 1969). The structure of the head is unknown, but it is inferred to have been significantly narrower than the total trunk width. The adult body consisted of at least 27 segments and probably a terminal telson; thoracic tergites were dorsolaterally expanded into anteriorly overlapping, trilobite-like structures. The tergites were ornamented by tubercles and blunt spines. Sternites were considerably complex, consisting of three major, characteristically shaped, ornamented plates. The limbs were comprised of eight to 10 tapering, imbricated segments, each bearing two spiny, ventral prongs. Arthropleurids probably were sluggish, yet capable of limited lateral and sinusoidal flexion. Late Carboniferous fossils of arthropleurids are associated with plants, and one specimen is known with club moss material filling its gut (Rolfe and Ingham

1967). These and other data indicate that arthropleurids lived on mineralic substrates and grazed on the forest floor.

Diversity

There are approximately 13,660 described species of extant myriapods (Borror et al. 1989). When compared to the extensive taxonomic diversity of other major terrestrial arthropod clades, namely the approximately 876,000 known hexapods and the 65,000 known arachnids (spiders, mites, and relatives) (Borror et al. 1989), myriapods are relatively undiverse. Of described extant species, 10,000, or 73 percent, are diplopods and 3,000, or 22 percent, are chilopods. Because myriapods are rarely of economic consequence, myriapodologists are significantly underrepresented when compared to the more economically applied fields of entomology and arachnology. This, in addition to major difficulties in recognizing genera and species of many myriapod groups, suggests that a significant hidden diversity probably exists for myriapods. As for past levels of diversity, the lack of a sufficiently diverse and abundant fossil record has prevented a robust evaluation. However, relative to insect diversity, documented myriapod diversity was greater during the Devonian and Early Carboniferous.

Biogeography

Myriapods have poor powers of dispersal, a reflection of several attributes, including an aversion to certain barriers such as deserts and the inability to fly. Consequently, myriapods, especially larger forms, have a high potential for delineating biogeographic pat-

Table 1.
Geochronologic Distribution of Myriapod Orders[1]

Order[2]	Common Name	First Occurrence[3]	Last Occurrence[3]
		Kampecarida	
Unnamed	kampecarids	Silurian (Pridoli)	Devonian (Lokhovian)
		Diplopoda	
Unnamed		Silurian (Pridoli)	Silurian (Pridoli)
Euphoberiida[4]	giant spined millipeds	Carboniferous (Moscovian)	Carboniferous (Kasimovian)
Polyxenida	bristly millipeds	Paleogene (Priabonian)	Recent
Glomerida	pill millipeds	Paleogene (Priabonian)	Recent
Amynilyspedida	pill millipeds	Carboniferous (Moscovian)	Carboniferous (Kasimovian)
Sphaerotheriida	sphaerotherids	Carboniferous (Moscovian)	Recent
Spirobolida	spirobolids	?Carboniferous (Moscovian)	Recent
Polyzoniida	polyzonids	Paleogene (Priabonian)	Recent
Julida	snake millipeds	Paleogene (Priabonian)	Recent
Spirostreptida	spirostreptids	?Carboniferous (Late)	Recent
Callipodida	callipodids	Paleogene (?Chattian)	Recent
Chordeumida	chordeumids	Paleogene (Priabonian)	Recent
Polydesmida	flatbacked millipeds	Paleogene (Priabonian)	Recent
[Uncertain]		Carboniferous (Moscovian)	
		Symphyla	
Scolopendrellida	scolopendrellids	Paleogene (Priabonian)	Recent
Scutigerellida	scutigerellids	Paleogene (Chattian)	Recent
		Chilopoda	
Devonobiomorpha	devonobiomorphs	Devonian (Givetian)	Devonian (Givetian)
Scutigeromorpha	scutigeromorphs	Silurian (Pridoli)	Recent
Lithobiomorpha	stone centipeds	Paleogene (Priabonian)	Recent
Geophilomorpha	soil centipeds	Paleogene (Priabonian)	Recent
Scolopendromorpha	scolopendromorphs	Carboniferous (Moscovian)	Recent
		Arthropleuridea	
Arthropleurida	arthropleurids	Devonian (Emsian)	Carboniferous (Kasimovian)

Notes

[1] This list is modified slightly from Ross and Briggs (1993). The Pauropoda lack a fossil record.

[2] The classification is from Hoffman (1969).

[3] Epoch and stage names are from Harland et al (1990).

[4] This is the Archipolypoda of some authors.

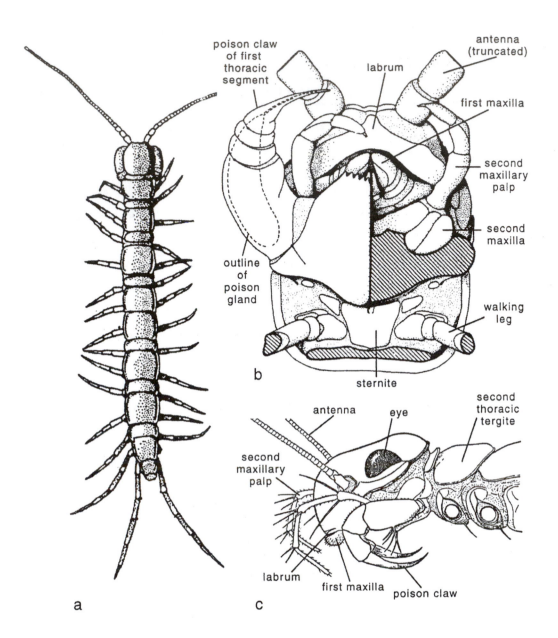

Figure 5. Major external features of the myriapod class, Chilopoda. *a*, dorsal view of the body of the lithobiomorph centiped *Lithobius*; *b*, ventral view of head and mouthparts of *Lithobius*; *c*, left lateral view of head and anterior trunk region of the scutigeromorph centiped, *Scutigera*. From: *a, b*, Lewis (1981), reprinting granted by Cambridge University Press, from J.G.E. Lewis, *Biology of Centipedes* (1981), Figs. 3 and 4; *c*, reprinted from Snodgrass (1952), copyright © 1952 by Cornell University Press, used by permission of the publisher, Cornell University Press.

terns. Myriapod biogeography is in its infancy, and only a small fraction of this potential has been explored, principally in the context of Late Cenozoic environmental change. Nevertheless, tentative conclusions can be made from the fossil record. For example, Late Silurian and Devonian kampecarids and eoarthropleurids are found only in several localities adjacent to marine deposits in Europe and North America, called Laurussia to indicate the single continent once encompassing both of these areas. These animals occur amid other early terrestrialized arthropods such as springtails, bristletails, trigonotarbid spiders, and mites. Kampecarids were probably connected to aquatic habitats, whereas eoar-

thropleurids were more terrestrialized. During the Late Carboniferous the presumed eoarthropleuriid descendants, the arthropleurids, are also found in Laurussia but apparently were confined to interior equatorial basins, amid vegetation rooted in mineralic substrates. One report records arthropleurids from the smaller paleocontinent of Kazakhstania, northeast of Laurussia, and at a more temperate latitude.

Gondwanaland was the major continent occupying the Southern Hemisphere at this time; it has since split into Africa, Antarctica, Australia, India, and South America. The Gondwanan distributional patterns of some extant myriapods provide evidence for Mesozoic taxa that still occur today. For example, the Spiro-streptidae occur in the tropics of Africa, Madagascar, and Central and South America, whereas the Harpagophoridae inhabit south-eastern Africa, Madagascar, Australia, New Zealand, and South-east Asia. These extant occurrences indicate broad Mesozoic distributions across Gondwanaland prior to its breakup during the Early Jurassic. One of the products of that breakup, India, formed the Himalaya Mountains as it became subducted under the south-ern margin of Eurasia. An analysis of the forest diplopod fauna of the Himalayas has revealed two fundamental biogeographic ele-ments that originated during the Early Cenozoic. One is a lowland diplopod fauna originating in the southeast, from western China and Indochina, and the other is a highland fauna emigrating from western Asia. Both immigrant faunal elements invaded the Hima-layas and subsequently diversified during the Pliocene and Pleis-tocene into the highly endemic fauna of today.

Functional Morphology

Myriapods derive their name from a multiplicity of trunk append-ages, and the role of these appendages in locomotion and copula-tion has inspired research in functional morphology—the analysis of form and its function. For example, biologists have speculated about the number of trunk walking legs in the ancestral myriapod. Suggestions have included a few pairs borne by short bodies to numerous pairs attached to long, winding bodies. An experimental solution to this question indicated that if the desirable trait was significant thrust involved in protracted burrowing, then numer-ous segments were necessary to gain purchase on the substrate for exertion of major physical forces. If rapid running is the optimized feature, then a small number of leg pairs is favored. However, it turns out that for a terrestrial running arthropod that has more than three pairs of walking legs, the answer is more complicated. Studies by Manton (1977) and others indicate that the distribu-tion of body weight across the pairs of legs is critical. Evidently, 13 pairs of legs is optimal, resulting in the fastest gaits.

Related to appendage number are the several gross specializa-tions of body form that characterize major myriapodan life habits. Combinations such as trunk segment number, a flattened or circular body cross section, and the length, articulation, segmentation, and musculation of the legs are important for determining how myria-pods feed, hunt prey, avoid prey, and seek shelter. In this context, the bulldozer life habit of julid diplopods is accomplished by a cylindri-cal body with numerous legs to provide forward thrust. In contrast, the geophilomorph centipede's burrowing life habit minimizes leg contact with the substrate but instead provides earthwormlike pro-pulsion by the interface of a flexible body surface with the soil sub-strate. The cursorial life habit of scolopendromorph and lithobiomorph centipedes, which rapidly run after and pursue other predators, is effected by numerous long legs and flattened bodies to penetrate narrow crevices. Scutigeromorph centipedes are active pursuit predators that modified this morphology by reducing leg pair number to an optimum for achieving high speed. The symphy-lan life habit of living among soil particles is conditioned by extreme trunk flexibility to achieve forward movement by twisting and turn-ing rather than by leg-directed thrust.

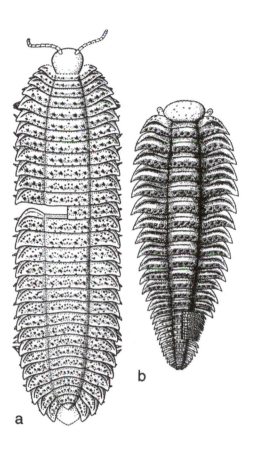

Figure 6. Dorsal views of adult and juvenile arthropleurids. *a*, dorsal view of adult *Arthropleura armata*; total body length approximately 1.8 meters; *b*, dorsal view of juvenile instar of *Arthropleura*; total body length approximately four centimeters. The reconstruction of the adult is shown with one pair of walking legs per functional segment, whereas recent data indicates that two walking legs occurred per functional segment, as illustrated in the juvenile. From: *a*, Rolfe and Ingham (1967), reprinted with permission from the *Scottish Journal of Geology*, volume 3, page 121; *b*, Briggs and Almond (1994).

Certain trunk appendages are modified for copulation, such as claspers, which males use for grasping the female during sperm transfer. Carboniferous euphoberiids have extensive spines along the sides and back of the trunk, rendering impossible the typical diplo-pod behavior of copulation through intertwining. However, it was found recently that a modified midtrunk segment with elongate legs was present in several Late Carboniferous euphoberiid taxa (Hanni-bal 1995). This structure was most likely a pair of clasping append-ages used by males to grasp females without becoming impaled.

Interactions with Other Organisms

Virtually all interactions of myriapods with other organisms involve feeding or the avoidance of being eaten. The dietary reper-toire of myriapods is broad, but unlike insects and mites, they rarely consume live plants and are largely confined to detritivory, a diet based upon the dead remains of other organisms, and to a lesser extent carnivory or the more eclectic spectrum of omnivory. Thus, myriapods are basically creatures of soil and litter. A few inhabit special habitats such as bark or fungi. Herbivory, the consumption of live plant tissue, has been documented only in a few diplopod species that consume roots or foliage, but such associations are either among rare detritivores or are confined to a handful of species. Most likely, myriapods never have had intimate or even diffuse associations with live plants during their evolutionary history. Myriapods typically are the prey of small vertebrates and large predatory arthropods.

Although we know the dietary spectra in detail for only a limited number of myriapod species, we can make broad characterizations. Diplopods are overwhelmingly detritivorous (Hopkin and Read 1992), although one family is insectivorous, and limited herbivory is known for a few pest species. Chilopods are almost exclusively carnivorous on other terrestrial arthropods and occasionally small vertebrates (Lewis 1981), indicated by the ubiquitous presence of poison glands on the first trunk segment (Figure 5). Depending on the higher-level taxon, chilopods are pursuit predators on the ground or will ambush prey in the soil or other cryptic habitats. Soil-inhabiting symphylans and pauropods are detritivorous on dead plants, but some will consume live rootlets (Snodgrass 1952; Eisenbeis and Wichard 1985). Arthropleurids were likely detritivores, as evidenced by the occurrence of macerated club-moss tissue in the gut of one specimen (Rolfe and Ingham 1967). It is highly likely that arthropleurids possessed symbiotic gut microbes to digest cellulose and perhaps lignin, similar to those documented in extant diplopods.

Fossil Record and History of Discovery

Five types of deposits account for virtually all myriapod fossils. In order of decreasing age, they are terrestrial deposits that border marine settings, ironstone nodules, bituminous coal and organic rich shales, amber, and mineral deposits associated with hot springs. These deposits represent relatively narrow windows of geologic time that preserve unique environments. No single deposit occurs throughout the 410-million-year-old myriapod fossil record, or even an appreciably long interval within it. Thus, what is presented are rare snapshots in time and space.

The earliest known deposits containing myriapods are Late Silurian and Devonian in age and are confined to the Old Red Sandstone continent of Laurussia, in water-lain deposits adjacent to major ocean basins. These clastic deposits have yielded kampecarids, eoarthropleurids, diplopods, and chilopods. During the Late Carboniferous to Early Permian, two fossilization modes are overwhelmingly responsible for preservation of myriapods. The first is ironstone nodules from better-drained clastic environments such as Mazon Creek (Illinois) and Montceau-les-Mines (France), which represent lowland deltaic and associated environments in the humid equatorial tropics. The second is coals and organic-rich shales such as those, respectively, from the bituminous Gaskohle Formation of the Czech Republic and the Anthracite Basin of Pennsylvania. These environments contain euphoberiid diplopods

and were associated with swamp forests. After a prolonged hiatus during the Late Permian to Eocene, in which myriapod fossils are very rare, the next most notable occurrence is that of Mid-Cenozoic Baltic amber, which has yielded the most diverse assemblage of fossil myriapods, including the earliest occurrences of many modern lineages (Table 1). Rivaling this diversity is somewhat younger Dominican amber, which recently has yielded a diverse assemblage of myriapods. During the Late Cenozoic several hot spring deposits, most in the southwestern United States and central Europe, have preserved myriapods in mineral deposits, presumably by rapid entombment of individuals by mineral-laden waters.

The two most important students of fossil myriapods were Samuel Scudder and Anton Fritsch. Scudder, who described and interpreted the life habits of many Late Carboniferous myriapods from Mazon Creek, was the first to reveal the taxonomic and structural diversity of Late Paleozoic myriapods. Fritsch complemented Scudder's work on Late Paleozoic myriapods, focusing on the exceptional deposits at Nyrany, in the Czech Republic, documenting similar Laurussian myriapods from another equatorial environment. Several, mostly German, researchers during the early and mid–twentieth century described myriapods from Baltic amber, although this work has been extensively supplemented by recently documented amber from the Dominican Republic (e.g., Santiago-Blay and Poinar 1992). By the late 1960s there was a sufficient myriapod fossil record that a major summary was provided by R.L. Hoffman (1969). Recently, new and exquisitely preserved chilopods from the Middle Devonian Gilboa site of New York state have been documented by W.A. Shear and P.A. Bonamo (1988).

Acknowledgments

Appreciation is extended to Finnegan Marsh, who formatted the figures accompanying this article. Thanks go to D. Briggs and J. Hannibal for excellent reviews of this manuscript. Financial support for this article was provided by the Scholarly Studies Program of the Smithsonian Institution. This is contribution no. 51 from the Evolution of Terrestrial Ecosystems Consortium at the National Museum of Natural History.

CONRAD C. LABANDEIRA

See also Terrestrialization of Animals

Works Cited

Almond, J.E. 1985. The Silurian-Devonian fossil record of the Myriapoda. *Philosophical Transactions of the Royal Society of London*, ser. B, 309:227–37.

Ballard, J.W.O., G.J. Olsen, D.P. Faith, W.A. Odgers, D.M. Rowell, and P.W. Atkinson. 1992. Evidence from 12S ribosomal RNA sequences that onychophorans are modified arthropods. *Science* 258:1345–48.

Borror, D.J., C.A. Triplehorn, and N.F. Johnson. 1989. *An Introduction to the Study of Insects*. Philadelphia: Saunders College.

Briggs, D.E.G., and J.E. Almond. 1994. The arthropleurids from the Stephanian (Late Carboniferous) of Montceau-les-Mines (Massif Central-France). *Mémoires de la Section des Sciences* 12:127–35.

Briggs, D.E.G., R.A. Fortey, and M.A. Wills. 1992. Morphological disparity in the Cambrian. *Science* 256:1670–73.

Eisenbeis, G., and W. Wichard. 1985. *Atlas on the Biology of Soil Arthropods.* New York and Berlin: Springer; as *Atlas zur Biologie der Bodenarthropoden,* Stuttgart: Fischer Verlag, 1985.

Friedrich, M., and D. Tautz. 1995. Ribosomal DNA phylogeny of the major extant arthropod classes and the evolution of myriapods. *Nature* 376:165–67.

Fryer, G. 1996. Reflections on arthropod evolution. *Biological Journal of the Linnean Society* 58:1–55.

Hahn, G., R. Hahn, and C. Brauckmann. 1986. Zur Kenntnis von Arthropleura (Myriapoda; Ober-Karbon). *Geologica et Palaeontologica* 20:125–37.

Hannibal, J.T. 1984. Pill millipeds from the Coal Age. *Field Museum of Natural History Bulletin* 55:12–16.

———. 1995. Modified legs (clasping appendages?) of Carboniferous euphoberiid millipeds (Diplopoda: Euphoberiida). *Journal of Paleontology* 69:932–38.

———. 1997. Myriapods and arthropleurids. *In* C.W. Shabica and A.A. Hay (eds.), *Richardson's Guide to the Fossil Fauna of Mazon Creek.* Chicago: Northeastern Illinois University Press.

Harland, W.B., R.L. Armstrong, A.V. Cox, L.E. Craig, A.G. Smith, and D.G. Smith. 1990. *A Geologic Time Scale: 1989.* Cambridge and New York: Cambridge University Press.

Hoffman, R.L. 1969. Myriapoda, exclusive of Insecta. *In* R.C. Moore (ed.), *Treatise of Invertebrate Paleontology.* Part R, *Arthropoda 4, 2.* Boulder, Colorado: Geological Society of America; Lawrence: University of Kansas.

Hopkin, S.P., and H.J. Read. 1992. *The Biology of Millipedes.* Oxford: Clarendon; New York: Oxford University Press.

Kraus, O., and M. Kraus. 1994. Phylogenetic system of the Tracheata (Mandibulata): On "Myriapoda"-Insecta interrelationships, phylogenetic age and primary ecological niches. *Verhandlungen des Naturwissenschaftlichen Vereins in Hamburg (N.F.)* 34:5–31.

Lewis, J.G.E. 1981. *The Biology of Centipedes.* Cambridge and New York: Cambridge University Press.

Manton, S.M. 1977. *The Arthropoda: Habits, Functional Morphology, and Evolution.* Oxford: Clarendon Press.

Rolfe, W.D.I. 1969. Arthropleurida. *In* R.C. Moore (ed.), *Treatise of Invertebrate Paleontology.* Part R, *Arthropoda 4, 2.* Boulder, Colorado: Geological Society of America; Lawrence: University of Kansas Press.

Rolfe, W.D.I., and J.K. Ingham. 1967. Limb structure, affinity, and diet of the Carboniferous "centipede" Arthropleura. *Scottish Journal of Geology* 3:118–24.

Ross, A.J., and D.E.G. Briggs. 1993. Arthropoda (Euthycarcinoidea and Myriapoda). *In* M.J. Benton (ed.), *The Fossil Record 2.* London and New York: Chapman and Hall.

Santiago-Blay, J.A., and G.O. Poinar Jr. 1992. Millipeds from Dominican amber, with the description of two new species (Diplopoda: Siphonophoridae) of Siphonophora. *Annals of the Entomological Society of America* 85:363–69.

Schneider, J., and M. Barthel. 1997. Eine Taphocoenose mit *Arthropleura* aus dem Rotliegend (?Unterperm) des Döhlen-Becken (Elbe-Zone, Sachsen). *Freiberger Forschungsheft,* ser. C, 466:193–223.

Shear, W.A., and P.A. Bonamo. 1988. Devonobiomorpha, a new order of centipeds (Chilopoda) from the Middle Devonian of Gilboa, New York State, USA, and the phylogeny of centiped orders. *American Museum Novitates* 2927:1–30.

Snodgrass, R.E. 1952. *A Textbook of Arthropod Anatomy.* Ithaca, New York: Cornell University Press.

Turbeville, J.M., D.M. Pfeifer, K.G. Field, and R.A. Raff. 1991. The phylogenetic status of arthropods, as inferred from 18S rRNA sequences. *Molecular Biology and Evolution* 8:669–86.

Weygolt, P. 1979. Significance of later embryonic stages and head development in arthropod phylogeny. *In* A.P. Gupta (ed.), *Arthropod Phylogeny.* New York: Van Nostrand Reinhold.

Wheeler, W.C., P. Cartwright, and C.Y. Hayashi. 1993. Arthropod phylogeny: A combined approach. *Cladistics* 9:1–39.

Further Reading

Borror, D.J., C.A. Triplehorn, and N.F. Johnson. 1954. *An Introduction to the Study of Insects.* New York: Rinehart; 6th ed., Philadelphia: Saunders College.

Gupta, A.P. (ed.). 1979. *Arthropod Phylogeny.* New York: Van Nostrand Reinhold.

Hopkin, S.P., and H.J. Read. 1992. *The Biology of Millipedes.* Oxford: Clarendon; New York: Oxford University Press.

Lewis, J.G.E. 1981. *The Biology of Centipedes.* Cambridge and New York: Cambridge University Press.

Manton, S.M. 1977. *The Arthropoda: Habits, Functional Morphology, and Evolution.* Oxford: Clarendon.

Moore, R.C. (ed.). 1969. *Treatise of Invertebrate Paleontology.* Boulder, Colorado: Geological Society of America; Lawrence: University of Kansas Press.

Snodgrass, R.E. 1952. *A Textbook of Arthropod Anatomy.* Ithaca, New York: Cornell University Press.

N

NEAR-AMNIOTE TETRAPODS
See Tetrapods: Near-Amniote Tetrapods

NON-GNATHOSTOME VERTEBRATES
See Jawless Fishes

NORTH AMERICA
See Canada and Alaska; Mexico and Central America; United States, Continental

NOVELTY, EVOLUTION OF
See Evolutionary Novelty

O

OCEAN ENVIRONMENT

The basic method for reconstructing past oceanic conditions from fossils is to assume that the environmental requirements and responses of ancient organisms were comparable to those of the most closely related living representatives. This is based on the principle of "uniformitarianism"—that the ecology of present organisms is the key to that of past organisms. Today's paleontologists employ biogeochemical analyses to aid in paleoenvironmental reconstructions, but uniformitarianism remains the guiding principle. Survival in the ocean is controlled by organisms' tolerances for temperature, salinity, depth, and availability of nutrient and oxygen, among other factors. By studying how these physical parameters impact the biogeochemistry of modern organisms, a paleontologist may be able to use biogeochemical data from fossils to determine the conditions under which ancient animals lived.

Changes in the Marine Environment over Time

There have been significant changes in oceanic conditions throughout time, apparently in cycles of larger and shorter periodicity. The longest of these cycles (300 to 500 million years) is controlled by convection of material deep within the Earth. These tectonic cycles are responsible for the movement of the continents, widening and narrowing of ocean basins, and other effects. These "supercycles" have been traced back as far as the Archean time period, but the last two of these cycles are known in the greatest detail (Fischer 1984). During the Late Proterozoic Eon, the continents were merged into one huge supercontinent known as Pangea I. In the early Paleozoic Era, rifting (breaking apart) of this continent began to occur, followed by the widening of oceans between the segments of land. Active seafloor spreading was accompanied by extrusions of hot material from inside the Earth into ocean basins, thereby displacing water and causing sea levels to rise and vast areas of continental crust to flood (creating "epeiric" seas). Increased volcanism released large amounts of carbon dioxide (CO_2) into the atmosphere. The carbon dioxide enhanced the trapping of solar radiation, which created a "greenhouse" climate and warmed the Earth, including the oceans. Warmer global temperatures melted much or all of the planet's ice sheets (like those

on Greenland and Antarctica today), which further increased sea level. This influx of fresh meltwater decreased the oceans' salinity. Biological productivity rose because the concentration of nutrients, such as nitrates and phosphates, increased. In general, nutrients derived from weathered continental rocks are more available when sea level is high. Also, organic material produced by photosynthesis in shallow, epeiric seas and on continental shelves is available to organisms for recycling.

The next phase was marked by the closing of oceans as the continents came together to form another supercontinent, Pangea II. Seafloor spreading and volcanism decreased, carbon dioxide levels dropped, and cooler global temperatures prevailed ("icehouse" conditions). Water was removed from the oceans as it built up as ice sheets again on the continents, thereby lowering global sea levels. Salinity increased as well: The ice was derived from precipitation, which in turn originated from evaporation of seawater, leaving the salt behind.

Much shorter cycles of sea level and temperature changes also have been documented. For example, during the last 2 million years (the Quaternary Period), the Earth has oscillated at least 20 times between ice ages and relatively warm climates, like today's. Causes for these fluctuations still are being debated. Theories include changes in incoming solar radiation owing to periodic changes in aspects of the Earth's orbit around the sun, concentration of CO_2 in the atmosphere, and changes in the patterns of ocean circulation. During glacial times, atmospheric and oceanic temperatures were lowered. Ice built up in areas at high latitudes, ocean salinity increased, productivity and nutrient availability decreased, and sea level dropped. The interglacial times featured higher temperatures, less ice, decreased salinity, greater concentrations of nutrients, and a rise in sea level. This alternating sequence of ice ages and interglacials has occurred quite recently (in geological terms) and and is considered by many to signify the start of the next icehouse supercycle.

The trends and cycles identified in the Earth's past have had a tremendous impact on the history of life. Major diversification of invertebrate life and an expansion in their numbers accompanied greenhouse conditions. Catastrophic extinctions can be tied to changes from one supercycle to another, with the creation of new niches for lifeforms and the destruction of others. The most intense biotic crisis (event affecting most or all of an ecosystem, usually negatively) in the history of life occurred at the end of the Permian period during the formation of Pangea II and the spread of glaciers over much of the continent.

Temperature

Effects on Life

Temperature is one of the most important factors in determining species distribution. The temperature range in the ocean varies geographically, usually from −2 degrees to higher than 40 degrees centigrade. Because surface temperatures are controlled basically by the input of solar energy, they tend to decrease with increasing latitudes. (Latitude numbering begins at zero at the equator and rises as one moves toward either pole. Thus, as latitude increases one moves into colder regions.) This pattern can be modified by ocean circulation as currents can carry warm water to the higher latitudes and cooler water toward the equator. Since cold seawater is more dense than warm water, there is also vertical thermal stratification, that is, temperature decreases with depth. Again, currents can modify this basic pattern, such as in areas of upwelling (a region in which bottom layers rise to the surface). As described above, ocean temperatures also have varied over time.

The rate of metabolism in poikilothermic (cold-blooded) organisms is roughly proportional to temperature: For each species there is an optimum temperature range within which biochemical reactions proceed smoothly. Beyond this optimum, rate extremes (too high or too low), rate imbalances, or breakdowns in biological materials occur. At greater fluctuations from the temperature optimum, death occurs. Temperature also affects reproduction. Larvae (immature stages of animals including some types of jellyfish, crustaceans, and fishes) are sensitive to temperature changes. Generally, they only can survive within a narrow temperature range. The temperature of reproduction in most species, therefore, is adjusted to the requirements of early ontogenetic (developmental) stages, which often lie near the warmer end of the temperature range of the adult.

Methods to Reconstruct Past Temperatures

The temperature of oceans in the past can be estimated in several different ways. A rigorous, quantitative approach employs the temperature distribution of modern planktic foraminifera (tiny zooplankton with shells). The precise mixture of species found at any particular temperature has been studied extensively and mathematical formulas (called transfer functions) have been developed to describe the assemblage (Imbrie and Kipp 1971). By examining an ancient sample as a mixture of different assemblages in different proportions, it is possible to determine the temperature at which the specimens in the sample lived.

Today, however, past temperatures often are ascertained by using geochemistry. Stable isotope analyses have proved especially useful (Hoefs 1987). Some elements, for example oxygen, exist in more than one form. Most oxygen atoms (99.8 percent) have eight

protons and eight neutrons and are designated ^{16}O. Some, however, have one or two extra neutrons (^{17}O and ^{18}O). These isotopes differ slightly in their rates of chemical reaction. When organisms such as molluscs, foraminifera, and corals construct their shells, the partitioning of the heavier isotope (i.e., the difference in the relative amount of ^{18}O in the shell as compared to the seawater) is determined at least partially by temperature. The relative amount of ^{18}O in a shell can be determined by a mass spectrometer, which detects the small difference in mass between isotopes and calculates their abundance in a sample. Once the relative amount of ^{18}O in a fossil shell (referred to as its "^{18}O value") is known, the temperature at which it was formed can be obtained through the use of equations relating temperature to ^{18}O (with a correction for salinity/ice volume effects as discussed below).

When organisms precipitate calcium carbonate ($CaCO_3$), it is never absolutely pure but contains trace amounts of foreign ions. The amount of "trace elements" in carbonates depends upon their concentration in the ambient seawater. For some ions, however, the numbers incorporated into shell material is also dependent on temperature (Kinsman and Holland 1969; Mucci 1987). Ions such as magnesium (Mg^{2+}) and strontium (Sr^{2+}) are about the same size as the calcium ion (Ca^{2+}), have the same charge (2+), and are abundant in seawater. Consequently, these foreign ions often replace Ca^{2+} in the carbonate molecule. That is, a structure composed primarily of $CaCO_3$ can have significant amounts of $MgCO_3$ and $SrCO_3$, the exact proportion of which is governed partially by the water temperature during precipitation (formation of a solid from liquid ingredients in a liquid environment. The crystals settle out of solution). Analyses of the trace element concentrations in fossil carbonates, therefore, can be used to ascertain the temperature at which the organisms lived. This can be done in several different ways: one method is to use an atomic absorption spectrophotometer, which burns a small sample of shell material. The particular spectrum of light energy released is characteristic of an individual element, enabling scholars to determine the precise composition of a sample.

Salinity

Effects on Life

Salinity is a measure of the concentration of dissolved salts in seawater, which includes ions of sodium, magnesium, calcium, potassium, strontium, chlorine, sulfate, bromine, and fluorine. It is expressed in terms of per mille (‰), or parts per thousand (ppt) of dissolved solids. Mean (average) global salinity has varied over time, as discussed above, depending how much freshwater was removed from the oceans to create ice sheets on land. Generally, during times without appreciable continental ice, the salinity of seawater was correspondingly lowered. At any given time, salinity can vary from place to place. Today, normal seawater has a salinity of approximately 35 parts per thousand. In areas of high evaporation, such as in restricted lagoons, in arid regions, or where continental runoff is sparse, salinity is increased (up to, perhaps, 100 parts per thousand). In regions with minimal evaporation, heavy precipitation, or with abundant runoff of fresh water from land, salinity is decreased (even reaching near zero).

The major effect of salinity is on the osmotic pressure across cell membranes within organisms. Inside the cells of an organism is a watery solution of a different salinity than the solution outside the cells. The two solutions are separated by a membrane that is permeable to the solvent (water), but not to the solute (particles). Solvent molecules flow from the less saline side of the membrane to the more saline side; the pressure necessary to prevent such flow is osmotic pressure. Organisms have evolved different physiological strategies for coping with internal/external salinity differences.

Methods to Reconstruct Past Salinities

Most marine invertebrates are tolerant of only a narrow salinity range (i.e., are stenohaline), so most can function only in the salinities found in the open ocean. In many cases, eggs and larvae are even more stenohaline than the adults. Among adult organisms that are not stenohaline, the ability to tolerate osmotic changes varies enormously. In the modern oceans, therefore, the greatest diversity (number of species) is found at normal, constant marine salinities. Diversity declines at both higher and lower salinities, and such regions include more euryhaline species (those able to tolerate a large salinity range). A paleontologist, using the principle of uniformitarianism (doctrine that physical processes observed today function in the same way as processes in the past), can examine a fossil assemblage, note the diversity and species present, and perhaps make an estimate of the salinity of the water in which the organisms lived.

Oxygen isotopes can also be used to reconstruct paleosalinities (Hoefs 1987). The lighter isotope (^{16}O) has a lower vapor pressure than ^{18}O. Evaporation of the ocean surface, therefore, preferentially removes ^{16}O, leaving the water enriched in the heavier isotope. Organisms growing in areas of high evaporation and elevated salinities have ^{18}O values higher than those living in normal marine salinities, even when temperatures are identical. Conversely, shells from regions with excessive continental runoff are relatively low in the heavy isotopes. Shells growing in oceans at times of significant buildup of continental ice will show a higher ^{18}O than an identical shell growing in water of the same temperature, but during a greenhouse phase—the water needed to make ice sheets originally was evaporated from the sea surface, leaving water enriched in ^{18}O behind. Consequently, if paleotemperatures can be assumed to be equal, variations in the ^{18}O values of fossil shells can be an indicator of salinity differences at the time the animals lived. Often, however, both temperature and salinity of paleoenvironments varied, so interpretations based solely on oxygen isotope differences must be tempered with caution.

Sea Level

Sea level has fluctuated throughout time (Vail et al. 1977). During times of active seafloor spreading, large portions of the ocean bottom are uplifted, which decreases ocean-basin volume. The amount of water in the basin does not change, but sea level is higher. During icehouse conditions, the buildup of glaciers on the continents removes water from the oceans, causing a drop in sea level. During Pleistocene glacial times, for example, sea level was more than 100 meters lower than today.

The ocean, of course, varies in depth at any one time. The continental margins—that is, the submerged portions of continental crust—account for about 14.5 percent of the Earth's surface. The boundary is defined as the two kilometer depth contour. About 33.2 percent of the Earth's surface comprise ocean basins, which are typically from four to six kilometers below sea level. The transition zones, called ocean rises, cover about 23.1 percent of the Earth's surface and are, on average, about 50 kilometers deep.

Water depth is a complex variable, and it is difficult to determine, unequivocally, the effect of depth on organisms. Many factors vary with depth: for example, pressure, light, temperature, salinity, and concentration of nutrients and dissolved gases. Most of the marine geologic record preserved on continents is from shallow habitats; more precise estimations of depth employ, again, the principle of uniformitarianism. The distribution of trace fossils (preserved tracks, trails, or burrows, all of which provide evidence of the activity of organisms on sediments) in modern settings has been shown to be a good indicator of depth because many aspects of animal behavior can be linked to a number of depth-related environmental parameters. Characteristic groupings of trace fossils, therefore, are used for making paleodepth reconstructions (Frey 1975). Foraminifera also vary in distribution and morphology with depth and have been used extensively for environmental reconstruction (Boltovskoy and Wright 1976). These data, although used successfully, are empirical, because the actual cause of depth-related variation in organisms often cannot be determined and probably is the result of a combination of factors.

Nutrients
Effects on Life

Primary productivity, the production of organic matter by photosynthesis, is controlled in large part by the availability of light and nutrients in the marine environment. Productivity is a large factor in the amount of living organic matter in a given area at any one time ("biomass"). In shallow water, sufficient light is nearly always available; it is the concentration of the nutrient elements nitrogen, phosphorous, and silicon that is the limiting factor for productivity. With increasing depth, the availability of light becomes progressively more of a limiting factor.

At the ocean surface, plants generally photosynthesize (produce chemical materials from light energy) faster than they respire (use those materials for growth and development), so they produce more organic material than they consume. With increasing depth, photosynthesis decreases but respiration does not; at some point, respiration exceeds photosynthesis and plants no longer can survive. However, in these lower depths animal respiration and inorganic oxidation continue: The destruction of organic matter allows nutrients to be released into the seawater again. Generally, then, there is a low concentration of nutrients at the sea surface, but that concentration increases with depth. There also is some geographical variation in nutrient availability: areas proximal to continents or where there are divergent currents or upwelling usually have the highest nutrient concentrations.

Methods to Reconstruct Past Nutient Concentrations

Estimates of past nutrient concentrations and paleoproductivity are difficult to make because, by definition, biomass refers to the organic portion of organisms, the portion that usually is not preserved in the fossil record. To estimate paleoproductivity and, hence, past nutrient concentrations, paleontologists often use biogeochemical proxies. Researchers have learned that the carbon isotopic composition of calcium carbonate in a skeleton reflects the productivity of the waters in which the organism lived (Hoefs 1987). Carbon has two stable isotopes, the common ^{12}C and the rarer ^{13}C. During photosynthesis, light carbon (^{12}C) is removed preferentially from the bicarbonate reservoir in the surrounding seawater. Consequently, the remaining bicarbonate has a greater $^{13}C / ^{12}C$ ratio (increased ^{13}C value) and so, the $^{13}C / ^{12}C$ ratio of shell material precipitated in this water will also increase. Therefore, high productivity and high nutrient concentrations will result in high ^{13}C values in shells, while low productivity and low nutrient concentrations will be reflected in low ^{13}C values. To a certain extent, researchers can use this technique to indicate the depth at which the fossil organism grew. Shells from more productive shallow waters usually have higher ^{13}C values than shells from unproductive deep water.

Cadmium (Cd) is another element that sometimes will replace calcium, in trace amounts, in the calcium carbonate skeleton of organisms such as corals, foraminifera, and molluscs. The Cd/Ca ratio in modern shelly material has been found to correlate closely with the phosphate concentration of the water in which the organism grew. Cd/Ca ratios in fossil shells have been used to estimate past phosphate levels and to infer paleoproductivities (Boyle 1988).

JODIE E. SMITH

See also Atmospheric Environment; Global Environment; Paleoclimatology; Paleoecology; Plate Tectonics and Continental Drift; Seas, Ancient; Sedimentology; Terrestrial Environment

Works Cited

Boltovskoy, E., and R. Wright. 1976. *Recent Foraminifera*. The Hague: Junk.

Boyle, E.A. 1988. Cadmium: Chemical tracer of deepwater paleoceanography. *Paleoceanography* 3:471–89.

Fischer, A.G. 1984. The two Phanerozoic supercycles. *In* W.H. Berggren and J.A. van Couvering (eds.), *Catastrophes in Earth History: The New Uniformitarianism*. Princeton, New Jersey: Princeton University Press.

Frey, R.W. 1975. *The Study of Trace Fossils*. New York: Springer-Verlag.

Hoefs, J. 1987. *Stable Isotope Geochemistry*. New York and Berlin: Springer-Verlag.

Imbrie, J., and N.G. Kipp. 1971. A new micropaleontological method for quantitative paleoclimatology: Application to a late Pleistocene Caribbean core. *In* R.F. Flint and K.K. Turekien (ed.), *The Late Cenozoic Glacial Ages*. New Haven, Connecticut: Yale University Press.

Kinsman, D.J.J., and H.D. Holland. 1969. The co-precipitation of cations with CaCO$_3$. Part 4, The co-precipitation of Sr^{2+} with aragonite between 16° and 96°C. *Geochimica et Cosmochimica Acta* 33:1–17.

Mucci, A. 1987. Influence of temperature on the composition of magnesian calcite overgrowths precipitated from seawater. *Geochimica et Cosmochimica Acta* 51:1977–84.

Vail, P.R., R.M. Mitchum, and S. Thompson. 1977. Seismic stratigraphy and global sea level. *In* C. Peyton (ed.), *Seismic Stratigraphy*. America Association of Petroleum Geologists Memoir 26:83–97.

Further Reading

Berggren, W.H., and J.A. van Couvering (eds.). 1976. *Catastrophes in Earth History: The New Uniformitarianism*. Princeton, New Jersey: Princeton University Press.

Bosence, D.W.J., and P.A. Allison (eds.). 1995. *Marine Paleoenvironmental Analysis from Fossils*. London: The Geological Society.

Hoefs, J. 1973. *Stable Isotope Geochemistry*. New York and Berlin: Springer; 4th ed., 1997.

Laporte, L. 1968. *Ancient Environments*. Englewood Cliffs, New Jersey: Prentice-Hall; 3rd ed., with C. Newton, 1989.

Valentine, J.W. 1973. *Evolutionary Paleoecology of the Marine Biosphere*. Englewood Cliffs, New Jersey: Prentice-Hall.

OCEANIC ISLANDS

Islands are isolated worlds. Usually, scholars distinguish between two types of islands, oceanic and continental (e.g., Williamson 1981). Nevertheless, from the point of view of biologists and paleontologists, it is useful to differentiate three types: oceanic, oceanic-like, and continental islands (Alcover et al. 1998). "Oceanic islands" are those that have never been connected by dry land to any continent. The faunas of these islands show a high rate of "endemicity" (species are unique to a particular island), the faunas are unbalanced (disharmonic) in comparison to continental faunas (i.e., with peculiar proportions of the ecological types, unlike the proportions found on the continents), and there are low degrees of diversity at the higher taxonomic levels (those that include large numbers of types).

"Oceanic-like" islands are those that previously have been connected to continents but have a fauna that is similar to those of oceanic islands. This characteristic may reflect several circumstances: The island-continent connection occurred in the distant past, was of short duration, or did not promote faunal transfer. Examples of oceanic-like islands are the greater part of the Mediterranean islands, which were joined to the surrounding continents during the Messinian (5.7 to 5.35 million years ago) but contacts between the areas were cut off because of saline deserts.

Later on, during the Pleistocene the islands were isolated by water. The Falkland Islands and Wrangle Island were joined to the continents during the Pleistocene, but glacial conditions produced very strong faunal filtering—that is, the number of groups that moved between regions was limited by glaciers (selective transfer). Some of the Mentawai Islands were joined to South Asia through Sumatra during glacial times, but the isthmus between them was narrow enough to act as a powerful filter.

Oceanic and oceanic-like islands vary greatly in area. West Anacapa Island is 2.3 square kilometers, and Little Swan Island is 3 square kilometers, but Madagascar is 580,000 square kilometers. The types of islands also vary in the degree to which they are isolated from mainlands, ranging from a few kilometers distance to over 2,000 kilometers in the case of the Hawaiian Islands. In contrast, "continental islands" have been broadly connected to continents, and this close connection is reflected in their faunas, which are subsamples of the continental faunas. In fact, the two faunas are mainly harmonic, with low levels of endemicity and a low degree of species diversity (species poorness). For this reason, this essay is concerned with only the fossil vertebrate faunas from oceanic and oceanic-like islands.

The global surface of oceanic and oceanic-like islands has been estimated at around 2 percent of the land surface, while recent estimates consider that they contain (or contained, until their discovery by humans) about 30 percent of the bird species and about 14 percent of the land mammals of the world. Also, these islands contain a high proportion of the reptile species of the world but only a very small percentage of the amphibians (no estimates are available for both groups). A considerable number of insular (island-based) species are known exclusively as fossils.

Studying fossil faunas ocasionally enables scholars to identify insular faunas in places that now are part of the mainland. Such cases are called "fossil islands." It is also possible to identify mainland fossil faunas on what currently are islands. These faunistic episodes indicate broad connections to mainland areas in the past. Thus, the fossil record eventually allows scholars to distinguish successive mainland and insular episodes of island history (Dermitzakis and Sondaar 1979).

The best-known "fossil islands" are Gargano and the Baccinello Basin, both in Italy. During the Pliocene, Gargano was an archipelago harboring gigantic owls (*Tyto gigantea*) and eagle-sized buteonini hawks (*Garganoaetus*) (Ballmann 1973), giant rodents (e.g., *Microtia*), the giant insectivore *Deinogalerix* (weighing approximately 14 kilogram), and the peculiar five-horned ruminant *Hoplitomeryx* (Freudenthal 1971, 1972; Leinders 1983). These fossil faunas display great similarities with the West Indian fossil faunas. At the Baccinello Basin (currently in Tuscany, mainland Italy), there were some insular episodes during the Upper Miocene. The most famous fossil of these faunistic episodes is *Oreopithecus*. Initially, this taxon (group; plural, taxa) was considered to be involved in human evolution, but now it is interpreted as a bipedal pongid (related to the mainland *Dryopithecus*) that evolved in an insular environment (Moyà-Solà and Köhler 1997). The fauna of Baccinello also includes dwarf artiodactyls of the endemic genus *Maremmia*, with highly derived (specialized) teeth, and some other species (Hurzeler 1976, 1983).

Insular species are frequently bizarre. A list of characteristic species would be long and complex: dwarf elephants, hippos, sloths, deer, giant rodents, dwarf and giant birds of prey, strange primates, "bibimalagasians," giant tortoises, marine iguanas, terrestrial otters, terrestrial crocodiles, walking bats, flightless ducks, rails, moa-nalos, moas, and dodos. All are known mainly or exclusively as fossils (Sondaar 1977; Olson 1989). In the past, the curious morphology (shape and structure) of insular species frequently was interpreted erroneously as "pathological" or "aberrant." Such interpretations have changed, because a huge amount of data now supports the notion that insular species are highly adapted to insular environments. In these environments pressures from predation and competition are structured in a very different way than on the mainland. On the more isolated islands, birds occupy practically all the guilds (segments of the ecosystem, including their relationship to each other). This situation contrasts sharply with the situation on the mainland (e.g., Alcover and McMinn 1994). The original (prehuman) structure of insular communities is known only through the study of fossils (James 1995).

One of the most peculiar insular faunas are the fossil faunas from the Hawaiian Islands (Olson and James 1982, 1991; James and Olson 1991). The prehuman fauna of the Hawaiian Islands includes two species of flightless ibises. Both belong to the endemic genus *Apteribis*, which apparently evolved only on the islands of Maui Nui ("big Maui," which consists of Maui and Molokai). (The only other flightless ibis—also known only as a fossil—is the very strange *Xenicibis* from Jamaica.) The moa-nalos, large flightless ducks occupying the guild (playing the role) of herbivorous mammals on continents or giant tortoises on other islands, are present at least on four of the Hawaiian Islands. As deduced from the analyses of coprolites (fossilized fecal material), the moa-nalos of the genus *Thambetochen* included a high amount of ferns in their diet. Another moa-nalo, *Chelychelynechen*, had a bill reminiscent of the bill of tortoises. At least seven species of flightless rails lived on the Hawaiian Islands until the arrival of humans. Other components of these faunas are a harrier (a type of hawk) of the genus *Circus* (which independently evolved a morphology similar to the hawks of genus *Accipiter*); an endemic genus of owl, *Gallistrix;* and more that 20 extinct passerines that exhibit a very wide range of shapes of bills.

Fossil faunas from the Pacific islands are known from different archipelagos (e.g., Marquesas, Society, Tuamotu, Cook, Pitcairn, and Tongan islands). They include a huge number of extinct flightless rails, pigeons, parrots, and some passerines, as well as enormous quantities of sea birds (mainly Procellariiformes) that recently became extinct (Steadman 1989a, 1989b).

A particular case is New Zealand. On these big islands there were no terrestrial mammals. Instead, some groups of birds occupied the terrestrial paleoguilds. Twelve species of moas are known (Millener 1982), some of them playing the role of terrestrial megaherbivores (very large plant-eaters, the size of a rhinoceros or Indian elephant). *Dinornis giganteus* was the tallest species, three meters in height. The extinct *Harpagornis*, a giant eagle, was the main predator on moas. The fossil record of New Zealand includes also the terrestrial flightless goose *Cnemiornis*, the strange gruiform-like *Aptornis* (probably the sister group of Galloanseres)

(Weber and Hesse 1995), and many other extinct bird species, as well as fossil geckos and frogs of the genus *Leiopelma* (Worthy 1987a, 1987b).

During the Pleistocene and Holocene, New Caledonia also had some strange endemic species (Balouet and Olson 1989; Buffetaut 1983), including the giant flightless *Sylviornis neocaledoniae* and the terrestrial crocodile *Mekosuchus inexpectatus*. Some authors have interpreted *Sylviornis* as a giant megapode (relative of the emu) that may be responsible for construction of the curious circular tumulus (mounds) of 40 meters in diameter present on the island (Mourer-Chauviré and Poplin 1985). Other interesting fossils endemic to this island are a megapode, some pigeons, and a large species of kagu, *Rhynochetos orarius*. On the neighboring island of Walpole (Île de Pins), the remains of the giant horned tortoise *Meiolania mackayi* have been found. Another extinct *Meiolania* species, *M. platyceps,* lived on Lord Howe Island, where the only native mammal was an extinct bat, *Nyctophilus howensis.*

The California Channel islands are typical oceanic islands situated near the mainland. The Upper Pleistocene deposits from these islands harbor remains of the dwarf mammoth *Mammuthus exilis* (Stock and Furlong 1928) and the giant mouse *Peromyscus nesodytes,* as well as two extinct species of birds (an endemic owl and a flightless duck).

The fossil fauna from the Galápagos, about 1000 kilometers away from mainland Ecuador, is known mainly from studies on Floreana (Steadman 1986) and, to a lesser extent, on Isabela. Three genera of rodents are present in the Upper Pleistocene/ Holocene deposits: *Megaoryzomys* (large, extinct rodents), *Nesoryzomys* (lava mice, with both extinct and extant species), and *Oryzomys* (still alive). Fossils of giant tortoises are found even on islands where they are now absent (e.g., Floreana). Deposits are mainly accumulations of pellets regurgitated by the endemic small barn owl *Tyto punctatissima,* but some caves also have acted as natural traps for tortoises, rodents, and snakes.

A clear parallel to the Galápagos Islands is found in the Canary Islands, about 100 kilometers from the mainland (Alcover and McMinn 1995). They have been the home of two extinct genera of rodents, the large *Canariomys* and *Malpaisomys* (lava mice), as well as extant (present-day) shrews, giant lizards (endemic genus *Gallotia*, with the extinct *G. maxima/goliath* about 1.4 meters long), geckos, skinks, small barn owls, and a variety of endemic passeriforms (including a flightless *Emberiza*), quails, and huge quantities of shearwaters. Some Miocene deposits contain bones and/or eggshells of tortoises, lizards, and Odontopterygiformes, giant sea birds with six-meter wingspans that were nesting on the coast of Famara and northern Lanzarote, and probably were living upon the stocks of fishes of the Canary-Sahara Upwelling.

On St. Helena and Ascension, very isolated Middle Atlantic islands, lived flightless rails of the genus *Atlantisia.* This genus includes one form still living on Inaccessible Island in the Tristan da Cunha group (Olson 1973). Other characteristic fossil birds from the Upper Pleistocene of St. Helena are a large terrestrial hoopoe *(Upupa antaios),* a cuckoo *(Nannococcyx psix),* and a probably flightless pigeon *(Dysmoropelia dekarchiskos)* (Olson 1975).

The West Indies display rich fossil faunas. The Greater Antilles, Cuba, Hispaniola, and Puerto Rico shared different families of mammals and birds, whereas Jamaica displayed a more differentiated fauna. In the first group, insectivores of the genus *Nesophontes* and *Solenodon* (the latter living only on Cuba and Hispaniola) were present. These primitive insectivores originated in North America. All species of *Nesophontes* became extinct, some after the arrival of Columbus, but two *Solenodon* species have survived to the present (one species on each island). Also, these islands shared sloths (12 described species from Upper Pleistocene/Holocene) and rodents. One family of rodents (Capromyidae) is endemic to Cuba, Hispaniola, Puerto Rico, the Bahamas, and the Swan Islands, whereas another family, Heptaxodontidae, expands its range even farther, through the Greater Antilles and some of the Lesser Antilles. One heptaxodontid, *Amblyrhiza inundata,* was a Quaternary species living on the islands of Anguilla and St. Martin, with an estimated weight of 50 to 200 kilograms. Fossil monkeys of the endemic family Xenothricidae inhabited Cuba *(Paralouatta),* Hispaniola *(Antillothrix),* and Jamaica *(Xenothrix)* (MacPhee 1996). In contrast to other islands of the world, early deposits from Oligocene and Miocene age are known from Cuba (Domo de Zaza), Hispaniola (e.g., La Toca), and Puerto Rico (Cibao Formation) (e.g., MacPhee and Iturralte-Vinent 1994). Among the early land vertebrates on the Greater Antilles were a sloth, a monkey, a *Nesophontds,* and a large bird. The pre-Pleistocene fossil record from the West Indies still is known very insufficiently. The fossil record of birds of the West Indies includes giant owls (e.g., *Bubo osvaldoi, Tyto riveroi,* and the huge *Ornimegalonix oteroi;* the latter is a long legged owl, 1.1 meters tall), giant buteonine hawks *(Tytanohierax)* (Arredondo 1976; Arredondo and Olson 1994), the strange Jamaican flightless ibis *Xenicibis xympithecus* (Olson and Steadman 1977), and two species of the flightless rail *Nesotrochis* (Olson 1974). Large tortoises have been described on Hispaniola. In the Lesser Antilles the fossil record includes several endemic species of *Oryzomys* as well as some birds, reptiles, and amphibians. There is a considerable debate about the origin of the faunas of the West Indies. Some scholars postulate overseas immigrations; others assume early land connections. The fossil faunas of these islands clearly displays the typical traits of insular faunas (endemicity, disharmony, and species poorness) (e.g., Woods 1990).

The fossil faunas from the Mediterranean islands are among the best known in the world. To a greater extent than in the West Indies, the knowledge of the land mammal assemblages is practically complete for the Upper Pleistocene. The faunistic successions on the Mediterranean islands are still insufficiently known. The faunas of these islands frequently include deer, hippos, and elephants, all of which colonized some of the islands by overseas immigration (Sondaar 1977). Some of the Mediterranean islands (e.g., Corsica, Sardinia, Mallorca, Menorca) originated as very small tectonic plates that separated from the mainland during the Lower Miocene. During the Messinian (5.7 to 5.35 million years ago), the Mediterranean dried up enough to allow the colonization of some islands (western and middle Mediterranean islands) through saline deserts.

The western Mediterranean islands are grouped in three archipelagos, each with different biogeographic histories. On Eivissa (Pityusic Islands) there is a succession of insular faunas from Miocene (Ses Fontanelles), Pliocene-Lower Pleistocene

(Cova de Ca Na Reia and other deposits), and Middle and Upper Pleistocene (Es Pouàs, which has furnished more than 150,000 bones, and other deposits). The faunas of the Upper Pleistocene of Eivissa are unique in the Mediterranean because of the absence of terrestrial mammals (Alcover et al. 1994). Instead, that period was populated by bats, a species of lizard, and huge quantities of birds, including some endemic species. The composition of the fossil communities of Eivissa display some parallels with their Hawaiian Islands counterparts.

In Corsica and Sardinia a succession of three insular faunas from the Miocene (Oschiri) through the Pleistocene has been recorded. The Upper Pleistocene faunas include endemic deer, fox, pika, mice, and voles, as well as a dwarf *Bubo* and a long-legged *Athene*. A supposed insular endemic species of *Homo* has been found in Grotta Su Corbeddu, Sardinia (Spoor and Sondaar 1986). On Mallorca and Menorca, three insular faunas also are known. The first one includes the largest known pika, *Gymnesicolagus gelaberti,* and three glirids. The second one, only represented in Menorca, is characterized by a highly derived giant hare. The last one includes *Myotragus balearicus,* a bizarre caprine (goat) 40 to 50 centimeters tall, and about 45 kilograms or more in weight, which lived until the arrival of humans. This species was managed and hunted by the first human settlers. One of the most peculiar derived traits of *Myotragus* is the presence of a solitary evergrowing incisor in each jaw. Other derived traits are in the postcranial (body) skeleton, ordinarily interpreted as adaptations for slow locomotion (Alcover et al. 1981). In the eastern Mediterranean, the dwarf hippo *Phanourios* from Cyprus is also bizarre. Its weight was about 200 kilograms (one-tenth of the African hippo), its teeth were designed for browsing (a diet of twigs and leaves), and, like *Myotragus,* it had anatomical adaptations to slow locomotion, with evident constraints on lateral (sideways) movements (Boekschoten and Sondaar 1972).

Madagascar is the biggest oceanic-like island. Isolated from Africa 50 million years ago, Madagascar is the home of very peculiar insular faunas (e.g., Woods and Eisenberg 1989). Primates (prosimians) radiated (diversified and spread) into at least 40 species. The larger are known only as fossils. A koala-like giant lemur *(Megaladapis),* some slothlike lemurs *(Babakotia, Palaeopropithecus),* and a baboonlike lemur *(Archaeolemur)* are among the most distinctive vanished prosimians. Other very strange components of the malagasy fossil fauna are a distinctive order of mammals, the bibymalagasians (genus *Plesiorycteropus*) (MacPhee 1994). Probably anteaters, practically all their skeleton is known except the rostral (snout) part of the skull. Other peculiar components of these faunas are the elephant-birds, Aepyornithidae, with *Aepyornis* weighing up to approximately 350 kilograms.

About 640 to 800 kilometers east of Madagascar are the Mascarene Islands, La Réunion, Mauritius, and Rodriguez. On Mauritius and Rodriguez lived two giant flightless columbiforms, which became extinct by the early eighteenth century. The dodo from Mauritius, *Raphus cucullatus,* was a terrestrial pigeon weighing 20 kilograms. The solitaire from Rodriguez, *Pezophaps solitaria,* was larger, up to 27 kilograms. Both are known through contemporany descriptions and illustrations, by some remains of captured birds (for the dodo), and by large

numbers of fossils of both species. On La Réunion no flightless pigeons were present. Instead, the historical descriptions of the Réunion solitaire probably reflects an endemic extinct ibis, *Threskiornis solitarius.*

Several islands of "Wallacea" (the intercontinental megarchipelago situated between the Australian and Oriental regions) contain fossil-rich vertebrate deposits. Dwarf stegodonts (primitive elephants) and giant rodents are known from Sulawesi and other islands (e.g., Musser 1983; Van Den Bergh 1997). On Timor a big varanid (lizard) could have preyed upon dwarf stegodonts. On the currently continental Java, during the Lower Pleistocene (Satir fauna, about 1.5 million years ago) there lived typical unbalanced fauna, with *Mastodon, Hexaprotodon,* Cervidae, and *Geochelone* (e.g., Vos et al. 1994).

JOSEP ANTONI ALCOVER

See also Oceanic Environment

Works Cited

Alcover, J.A., and M. McMinn. 1994. Vertebrate predators on islands. *BioScience* 44:12–18.

———. 1995. Fossil birds from the Canary Islands. *Courier Forschunginstitut Senckenberg* 181:207–13.

Alcover, J.A., M. McMinn, and C.R. Altaba. 1994. Eivissa: A Pleistocene oceanic-like island in the Mediterranean. *National Geographic Research and Exploration* 10:236–38.

Alcover, J.A., S. Moyà-Solà, and J. Pons-Moyà. 1981. Les Quimeres del Passat: Els Vertebrats fòssils del Plio-Quaternari de les Balears i Pitiüses. *Monografies Cientifiques, Memona Institucio Catalana d'Historia Natural,* II, 1:1–260.

Alcover, J.A., M. Palmer, and A. Sans. 1998. The extent of extinction of mammals on islands. *Journal of Biogeography* 25 (5):913.

Arredondo, O. 1976. The great predatory birds of the Pleistocene of Cuba. *Smithsonian Contributions to Paleobiology* 27:169–87.

Arredondo, O., and Olson, S.L. 1994. A new species of owl of the genus Bubo from the Pleistocene of Cuba. *Proceedings of the Biological Society of Washington* 107:436–44.

Ballmann, P. 1973. Fossile Vögel aus dem Neogen der Halbinsel Gargano. *Scripta Geologica* 17:1–75.

Balouet, J.C., and S.L. Olson. 1989. Fossil birds from Late Quaternary deposits in New Caledonia. *Smithsonian Contributions to Zoology* 469:1–38.

Boekschoten, G.J., and P.Y. Sondaar. 1972. On the fossil mammalia of Cyprus, parts 1 and 2. *Proceedings of the Koninglijke Nederlandse Akademie van Wetenschappen B, Palaeontology, Geology, Physics, and Chemistry* 75:306–38.

Buffetaut, E. 1983. Sur la persistance tardive d'un Crocodilien archaïque dans le Pleistocène de l'île des Pins (Nouvelle-Calédonie) et sa signification biogéographique. *Comptes-Rendus de Séances de l'Académie des Sciences,* sér. 2, 297:89–92.

Dermitzakis, M.D., and P.Y. Sondaar. 1979. The importance of fossil mammals in reconstructing paleogeography, with special reference to the Pleistocene Aegean archipelago. *Annales Géologiques des Pays Helléniques* 29:808–40.

Freudenthal, M. 1971. Neogene vertebrates from the Gargano Peninsula, Italy. *Scripta Geologica* 3:1–10.

———. 1972. Deinogalerix koenigswaldi nov. gen., nov. spec., a giant insectivore from the Neogene of Italy. *Scripta Geologica* 14:1–19.

Hurzeler, J. 1976. Les faunes de mammifères néogènes du bassin de Baccinello (Grosseto, Italie). *Comptes-Rendus de Séances de l'Académie des Sciences*, sér. D, 283:333–36.

———. 1983. Un alcelaphiné aberrant (Bovidé, Mammalia) des "lignites de Grossetto" en Toscane. *Comptes-Rendus de Séances de l'Académie des Sciences*, sér. 2, 256:497–503.

James, H.F. 1995. Prehistoric extinction and ecological changes on oceanic islands. *In* P.M. Vitousek, L.L. Loope, and H. Andersen (eds.), Islands: Biological Diversity and Ecosystem Function. *Ecological Studies* 115:87–102.

James, H.F., and S.L. Olson. 1991. Descriptions of thirty-two new species of birds from the Hawaiian Islands. Part 2, Passeriformes. *Ornithological Monograph* 45–46:1–88.

Leinders, J.J.M. 1983. Hoplitomerycidae fam. nov. (Ruminantia, Mammalia) from Neogene fissure fillings in Gargano (Italy). Part 1, The cranial osteology of Hoplitomeryx gen. nov. and a discussion on classification. *Scripta Geologica* 70:1–51.

MacPhee, R.D.E. 1994. *Morphology, Adaptations, and Relationships of Plesiorycteropus, and a Diagnosis of a New Order of Eutherian Mammals.* Bulletin of the American Museum of Natural History, 220. New York: American Museum of Natural History.

———. 1996. The Greater Antillean monkeys. *Revista de Ciències* 18:13–32.

MacPhee, R.D.E., and M.A. Iturralte-Vinent. 1994. *First Tertiary Land Mammal from Greater Antilles: An Early Miocene Sloth (Xenarthra, Megalonychidae) from Cuba.* American Museum Novitates, 3094. New York: American Museum of Natural History.

Millener, P.R. 1982. And then there were twelve: The taxonomic status of Anomalopteryx oweni (Aves: Dinornithidae). *Notornis* 29:165–70.

Mourer-Chauviré, C., R. Bour, and S. Ribes. 1995. Was the solitaire of Réiunion an ibis? *Nature* 373:568.

Mourer-Chauviré, C., and F. Poplin. 1985. Le mystère des tumulus de Nouvelle-Calédonie. *La Recherche* 16.

Moyà-Solà, S., and M. Köhler. 1997. The phylogenetic relationships of Oreopithecus bambolii Gervais, 1872. *Comptes-Rendus de Séances de l'Académie des Sciences*, sér. 2a, 324:141–48.

Musser, G.G. 1983. Identities of subfossil rats from caves in southwestern Sulawesi. *Modern Quarterly Research in Southeast Asia* 8:61–95.

Olson, S.L. 1973. Evolution of the rails of the South Atlantic islands (Aves: Rallidae). *Smithsonian Contributions to Zoology* 152:1–53.

———. 1974. A new species of Nesotrochis from Hispaniola, with notes on other fossil rails from the West Indies (Aves: Rallidae). *Proceedings of the Biological Society of Washington* 87:439–50.

———. 1975. Paleornithology of St. Helena Island, South Atlantic Ocean. *Smithsonian Contributions to Paleobiology* 23:1–49.

———. 1989. Extinction on islands: Man as a catastrophe. *In* D. Western and M.C. Pearl (eds.), *Conservation for the Twenty-First Century.* New York and Oxford: Oxford University Press.

Olson, S.L., and H.F. James. 1982. Prodromus of the fossil avifauna of the Hawaiian Islands. *Smithsonian Contributions to Zoology* 365:1–59.

———. 1991. Descriptions of thirty-two new species of birds from the Hawaiian Islands. Part 1, Non-Passeriformes. *Ornithological Monographs* 45:1–88.

Olson, S.L., and D.W. Steadman. 1977. A new genus of flightless ibis (Treskiornithidae) and other fossil birds from cave deposits in Jamaica. *Proceedings of the Biological Society of Washington* 90:447–57.

Sondaar, P.Y. 1977. Insularity and its effect on mammal evolution. *In* M.K. Hecht, P.C. Goody, and B.M. Hecht (eds.), *Major Patterns in Vertebrate Evolution.* New York: Plenum.

Spoor, C.F., and P.Y. Sondaar. 1986. Human fossils from the endemic island fauna of Sardinia. *Journal of Human Evolution* 15:399–408.

Steadman, D.W. 1986. Holocene vertebrate fossils from Isla Floreana, Galápagos. *Smithsonian Contributions to Zoology* 413:1–103.

———. 1989a. Extinction of birds in Eastern Polynesia: A review of the record, and comparisons with other Pacific island groups. *Journal of the Archaeological Society* 16:177–205.

———. 1989b. Fossil birds and biogeography in Polynesia. *Acta XIX Congressus Internationalis Ornithologici, Ottawa, 22–29, VI, 1986.* Ottawa: University of Ottawa Press.

Stock, C., and E.L. Furlong. 1928. The Pleistocene elephants of Santa Rosa Island, California. *Science* 68:140–41.

Van Den Bergh, G.D. 1997. The Late Neogene elephantoid-bearing faunas of Indonesia and their paleozoogeographic implications. Ph.D. diss., Universiteit Utrecht.

Vos, J. de, P.Y. Sondaar, G.D. Van Den Bergh, and F. Aziz. 1994. The Homo bearing deposits of Java and their ecological context. *Courier Forschungsinstitut Senckenberg* 171:129–40.

Weber, E., and A. Hesse. 1995. The systematic position of Aptornis, a flightless bird from New Zealand. *Courier Forschungsinstitut Senckenberg* 181:293–301.

Williamson, M. 1981. *Island Populations.* New York and Oxford: Oxford University Press.

Woods, C.A. 1990. The fossil and recent land mammals of the West Indies: An analysis on the origin, evolution and extinction of an insular fauna. *Atti Convegno Lincei* 85:641–80.

Woods, C.A., and J. Eisenberg. 1989. The land mammals of Madagascar and the West Indies: Comparison and analysis. *In* C.A. Woods (ed.), *Biogeography of the West Indies: Past, Present and Future.* Gainesville, Florida: Sandhill Crane.

Worthy, T.H. 1987a. Osteology of Leiopelma (Amphibia: Leiopelmatidae) and descriptions of three new subfossil Leipoelma species. *Journal of the Royal Society of New Zealand* 17:201–51.

———. 1987b. Palaeoecological information concerning members of the frog genus Leiopelma in New Zealand. *Journal of the Royal Society of New Zealand* 17:409–20.

ODOR AND PHEROMONE RECEPTORS

The olfactory system, or chemical sense of smell, is common to all animals, and most vertebrates have intricate and sensitive olfactory organs. In fish, the olfactory organs consist of paired capsules (membranes or sacs enclosing a body part) situated on the snout or inside the mouth. Bipolar olfactory neurons are protected within folds of epithelium (membranous cellular tissue) inside the capsule. A continuous flow of water is drawn into the capsule, and sensory information contained in the current of water is passed on to the brain. Vertebrates that breathe air have a similar arrangement of olfactory cells supported by epithelium, but to be able to sense particles of chemical in the air the sensory cells must be kept moist by the secretion of mucus. Therefore the olfactory epithelium of air breathing vertebrates includes increased numbers of mucous secreting cells as well as the bipolar olfactory cells and supporting epithelial cells (Hildebrand 1982).

The sensory cells in the olfactory epithelium synapse with neurons in the olfactory bulb, and these send axons down the olfactory tract or nerve to the brain. The size of the olfactory bulb and tract, and the amount of the forebrain devoted to the transmission and integration of olfactory stimuli, reflects the importance of the olfactory sense. The olfactory sense is reduced in most birds, although it is well developed in those that obtain their food by scavenging, such as vultures.

In derived (adapted) vertebrates such as mammals, the olfactory epithelium covers openings in the cribriform plate of the ethmoid bone, situated at the back of the roof of the nasal cavity. The size of the cribriform plate is correlated with the importance of the olfactory system to the animal. It is extensive in macrosmatic mammals (those with a good sense of smell), and small in microsmatic (those with a less developed sense of smell) primates such as humans.

Vertebrates are also able to sense pheromones that are produced by other members of the same species and influence sexual condition. Pheromones also have been implicated in prey capture in sharks. In fish there are no special sensory structures to receive these stimuli. In higher vertebrates, pheromones are sensed using the vomeronasal organ. This paired structure has its own nerve and accessory olfactory region in the brain. In some reptiles, the organ opens into the roof of the mouth. In other reptiles, and in mammals and amphibia, the organ is connected with the nasal cavity. Vomeronasal organs are reduced or absent in turtles, crocodiles, birds, aquatic mammals, and some primates. Certain members of the Squamata, particularly snakes, have bifid tongues that can be protruded, then inserted into the vomeronasal organ to sense adherent particles.

Traces of soft tissues are rarely preserved in fossils, and the structure and function of the olfactory system in fossils must be deduced from comparison with the olfactory system in living vertebrates. Important information also can be derived from endocranial casts, or impressions left by the brain and associated nerves within the cranial cavity of a fossil (Olson 1971).

In fish, the olfactory structures are enclosed in nasal capsules of cartilage or chondral bone. Fossil fishes such as the cephalaspids and anaspids and their living relatives, the lampreys, had single nasal capsules with single openings, but the sensory organ is paired (Olson 1971). Heterostracans, also fossil jawless fishes, have paired nasal capsules and paired openings (Olson 1971). In more derived vertebrates, the olfactory organ is paired. Except in sharks, which have single openings for the olfactory capsule, there is an incurrent and an excurrent opening.

In most bony fish, or osteichthyans, the olfactory capsule, with the incurrent and excurrent openings, is situated on the snout. In some osteichthyans, like the lungfish and the rhipidistians, the internal openings are in the roof of the mouth. The internal and external nares (nasal openings) or choanae (internal nasal openings) of amphibia, reptiles, birds, and mammals are derived from the openings of the olfactory organs of primitive fish. The incurrent and excurrent openings of this organ in the closest sister group of the early tetrapods, most probably a rhipidistian (Ahlberg and Milner 1994), developed the function of also transferring air from the environment to the lungs via the oral cavity. Subsequently, the nasal cavity became separated from the oral cavity by development of the hard palate.

The term hard, or secondary, palate, refers to the shelflike bony outgrowths from the premaxillary, maxillary, and palatal bones that form a secondary respiratory tube. A secondary palate is thought to have evolved more than once. Some turtles have a complete secondary palate, and crocodiles an exceptionally long one. Mammal-like reptiles have a short secondary palate involving the premaxilla and palatal bones, and mammals have a long and complex passage with rearrangement and development of the premaxilla, maxilla, and palatal bones (Hildebrand 1982).

In mammals, birds, and reptiles, the nasal cavity created by the secondary palate is divided into two channels by an internal nasal septum. This consists of processes from the ethmoid and vomerine bones, with associated cartilage and soft tissues. In amphibia, there is no secondary palate, and a cartilaginous septum separates the nasal capsules (Duellman and Trueb 1994). The external nares of tetrapods are primitively paired, but the two openings merge into a single median aperture in many taxa such as rhynchosaurs, turtles, crocodiles, and mammals.

Turbinate bones or conchae develop in the nasal cavities of mammals and are present in a rudimentary form in some mammal-like reptiles. These are delicate scrolls of bone, outgrowths of the maxillary, nasal, and ethmoid bones. The turbinates are covered with epithelium and function primarily to moderate the temperature and humidity of inspired air. They may include increased numbers of olfactory cells as well (Hildebrand 1982) or simply direct inspired air toward the olfactory organ at the back of the nasal cavity.

Understanding of the olfactory system of fossil vertebrates is based on knowledge of the system in living animals and is often speculative. In addition, evolutionary changes in the structure of the nasal cavity are linked not with the olfactory system but with respiration (Olson 1971) and are related to living on land. Despite these associated changes, the olfactory sense has retained the simple characteristics found in the earliest vertebrates.

ANNE KEMP

See also Sensory Capsules

Works Cited

Ahlberg, P., and A.R. Milner. 1994. The origin and early diversification of the tetrapods. *Nature* (London) 368:507–14.

Duellman, W.E., and L. Trueb. 1994. *Biology of the Amphibians.* 2nd ed. Baltimore, Maryland: Johns Hopkins University Press; 1st ed., New York: McGraw Hill, 1946.

Hildebrand, M. 1982. *Analysis of Vertebrate Structure.* 2nd ed. New York: Wiley; 1st ed., 1974; 4th ed., 1995.

Olson, E.C. 1971. *Vertebrate Paleozoology.* New York: Wiley.

Further Reading

Bone, Q., N.B. Marshall, and J.H.S. Blaxter. 1982. *The Biology of Fishes*. London and New York: Chapman and Hall; 2nd ed., 1995.

Kent, G.C. 1954. *Comparative Anatomy of the Vertebrates*. New York: McGraw; 8th ed., Dubuque, Iowa: Brown, 1997.

Romer, A.S. 1933. *Vertebrate Paleontology*. Chicago and London: University of Chicago Press; 3rd ed., 1966.

Wake, M.H. 1979. *Hyman's Comparative Vertebrate Anatomy*. Chicago: University of Chicago Press.

OLSON, EVERETT C.

American, 1910–93

Everett C. Olson pioneered the application of sedimentology (the study of strata deposited by water or wind), taphonomy (fossilization process), and statistical analysis of fossils to vertebrate paleoecology. His innovations in vertebrate paleoecology were accompanied by important contributions in graduate and undergraduate education, university administration, and professional service. The breadth of Olson's accomplishments reflect his extraordinary talent, formal training in geology and paleontology, and a life-long fascination with biology and foreign languages.

Olson's extraordinary talents were apparent at an early age. By age five, he had developed a passion for collecting and rearing butterflies, which he continued until college and resumed later in life. He was an excellent public school student, graduating class valedictorian. In 1928 Olson entered the University of Chicago, where he would remain as a student and member of the faculty for 41 years. After initial chemistry courses, he was attracted to geology, in which he eventually earned three degrees.

Olson's research in vertebrate paleontology began in 1933 as a graduate student of Alfred S. Romer at the University of Chicago. In 1936 he initiated fieldwork in the Permian deposits of north-central Texas, in the region around San Angelo, Abilene, and Wichita Falls. He started work in the Arroyo, Vale, and Choza formations of the Clearfork group and later moved westward into the overlying San Angelo Formation. This work filled an important gap between the Upper Carboniferous diversification of tetrapods (early reptiles) and appearance of synapsids (mammal-like reptiles) later in the Permian. The similarities Olson found between tetrapods from the Permian of Texas and those from southern Africa and Russia led him to make comparative studies of southern African material already in the Walker Museum of the University of Chicago and to visit Moscow six times to study Permian tetrapods from the Urals.

Olson's research yielded important insights into the early diversification of tetrapods, the emergence of the mammals, long-term paleoecological processes, and the influence of community ecology on the evolution of larger groups above the species level. Olson's study of tetrapods from long periods in the Permian of Texas incorporated information on growth patterns and the sediments in which the fossils were deposited. He also exploited aerial mapping to locate and correlate deposits. Based on Cold War era contacts with Soviet vertebrate paleontologist Ivan Antonovich Efremov, Olson applied the principles of taphonomy, the transformation of living populations into fossil assemblages, to problems in Permian vertebrate paleoecology, introducing this methodology to American paleontology. Olson coined the term "chronofauna" to describe fossil assemblages that represented communities that remained essentially stable for millions of years in the face of moderate environmental change and changes in species composition. He used statistical analysis and populational thinking to address problems in Permian paleoecology, accelerating the incorporation of these tools into paleontology. And he published more than 170 papers and eight books.

Olson also contributed to vertebrate paleontology through creation of the Committee on Paleozoology at the University of Chicago. This program provided an interdisciplinary framework that integrated biology and geology, and its graduates have made significant contributions to paleontology and related fields. Olson also trained graduate students at the University of California, Los Angeles (UCLA).

Olson's interdisciplinary approach and quick mind also made him a superb colleague for faculty in geology and biology, and he carefully nurtured the development of junior colleagues. Olson created intellectual and institutional ties between the University of Chicago and the Field Museum, and later played an important role in organizing the Center for the Study of Evolution and the Origin of Life at UCLA. At the time of his death, Olson was working on the molecular systematics of lepidoptera (butterflies, moths, and related groups), and was working on completing a book on the invasion of land by animals.

MICHAEL A. BELL

Biography

Born in Waupaca, Wisconsin, 6 November 1910. Received S.B. (1932), M.S. (1933), Ph.D. (1935), University of Chicago. Became vertebrate paleontologist, Department of Geology, University of Chicago, 1936–69; secretary (1945–57) and chair (1957–61), Department of Vertebrate Paleontology, University of Chicago; associate dean, Division of Physical Sciences, University of Chicago, 1948–60; chair, Interdivisional Committee on Paleozoology, 1948–69; professor (1969–78), chair (1971–72), and emeritus professor (1978–93), Department of Zoology, University of California, Los Angeles. Editor, *Evolution* (1953–58) and *Journal of Geology* (1962–67); board member, *The Quarterly Review of Biology* and *Palaeogeography, Palaeoclimatology, Palaeoecology.* Secretary-treasurer (1948) and president (1949–50), Society of Vertebrate Paleontology; president, Society for the Study of Evolution, 1964; president, Society of Systematic Zoology, 1979; elected to the National Academy of Sciences, 1980; recipient,

Paleontological Medal of Paleontological Society, 1980; recipient, first Romer-Simpson Distinguished Service Medal of the Society of Vertebrate Paleontology, 1987; member of numerous other scientific organizations including the Geological Society of America, the American Association for the Advancement of Science, and the National Academy of Sciences. Died in Los Angeles, 27 November 1993.

Major Publications

1952. The evolution of a Permian vertebrate chronofauna. *Evolution* 6:181–96.

1958a. Fauna of the Vale and Choza: 14. Summary, review and integration of the geology and faunas. *Fieldiana Geology* 10:397–448.

1958b. With R.L. Miller. *Morphological Integration*. Chicago: University of Chicago Press.

1966. Community ecology and the origin of mammals. *Ecology* 47:291–302.

1971. *Vertebrate Paleozoology*. New York: Wiley.

1990. *The Other Side of the Medal: A Paleobiologist Reflects on the Art and Serendipity of Science*. Blacksburg, Virginia: McDonald and Woodward.

Further Reading

Brunk, C.F., and J.W. Schopf. 1994. Everett C. Olson, 1910–1993, Professor of Biology, Emeritus, Los Angeles (Obituary). *In Memoriam*, 1994:196–99. Berkeley: University of California.

Hotton III, N. 1994. Both sides of the medal: A memorial to E.C. Olson (1910–1993). *Journal of Paleontology* 68:1166–68.

Rainger, R. 1993. Biology, geology, or neither, or both: Vertebrate paleontology at the University of Chicago, 1892–1950. *Perspectives on Science* 1:478–519.

———. 1997. Everett C. Olson and the development of vertebrate paleoecology and taphonomy. *Archives of Natural History* 24:373–96.

ORBIGNY, ALCIDE CHARLES VICTOR DESSALINES D'

French, 1802–57

Alcide Dessalines d'Orbigny was born on 6 September 1802 in Couëron, Loire-Atlantique, France. The son of a doctor and scientist, d'Orbigny often accompanied his father on scientific excursions along the Atlantic coast near their home. Given this exposure to science, d'Orbigny chose the natural sciences as a career and began, in 1819, the study of systematic zoology. His early scientific publications during this period were devoted to recent and Jurassic gastropods and the masticatory apparatus of the nautiluses, but the focus of his work from 1819 to 1826 was dedicated to recent and fossil Foraminifera. In 1826 d'Orbigny published the culmination of this work, *Tableau méthodique de la classe des Céphalopodes,* in which he separated the microscopic forms of protozoans into the Foraminifera based on the number and arrangement of the chambers of their shell. In this work, d'Orbigny classified the cephalopods into five classes, 53 genera, and 600 species and included extant forms from Antilles, the Canary Islands, Cuba, and South America and fossil forms from the Paris basin (Cretaceous) and the Vienna basin (Tertiary).

In 1826, commissioned by the Muséum d'Histoire Naturelle, d'Orbigny set out on an expedition that would last eight years and take him through the entire continent of South America. From 1826 to 1834, d'Orbigny conducted extensive scientific studies of the natural history, geology, geography, and people of South America. Upon his return to Paris, d'Orbigny published the findings of this expedition in the 10-volume work, *Voyage dans l'Amérique méridionale* (1834–47), which encompassed the anthropology, ethnography, geology, geography, paleontology, and zoology of the continent. The most exhaustive description of any continent then published, this work introduced the science of stratigraphical paleontology (biostratigraphy). Following his observations of the fossil bearing strata of the Paraná Basin, d'Orbigny concluded that the distinct layers of sedimentary rock had been deposited during successive periods of time, which could be dated according to the fossils found within each layer. D'Orbigny would continue to use this novel method of analysis in later works and is, thus, credited with founding stratigraphical paleontology. During this time, d'Orbigny also drew the most comprehensive map of South America (1842).

Throughout the publication of *Voyage dans l'Amérique méridionale,* d'Orbigny continued to publish works on cephalopods and foraminifera. From 1839 to 1848, he published, with Férussac as coauthor, *Histoire naturelle générale et particuliére de Céphalopodes acétabuliféres vivants et fossiles* and contributed sections on molluscs and Foraminifera to *Histoire naturelle des îles Canaries* (1839–40) and *Histoire naturelle de Cuba et des Antilles* (1839–43). At this time d'Orbigny also was busy developing new interests, having published a variety of papers on Cretaceous and Jurassic ammonites, belemnites, gastropods, Cretaceous rudists (a kind of bivalve), and Tertiary sepioideans (squid).

Returning to stratigraphical paleontology, d'Orbigny began work on his most ambitious work: *Paléontologie française,* in which he examined the paleontology and stratigraphic distribution of the known forms of brachiopods, bryozoans, echinoderms, and molluscs present in the Jurassic and Cretaceous deposits of France. Although never completed, this work is noted for its comprehensive survey of bryozoans, having classified the known extant (present-day) and extinct forms into 1,929 species. Following his death, the French Geological Society resumed work on this publication, but still, it was never completed. Nonetheless, during its time *Paléontologie française* served as a useful reference for geologists and stratigraphers.

In yet another work, d'Orbigny incorporated evolutionary theory into stratigraphical paleontology. With the publication of *Prodrome de paléontologie stratigraphique universelle* (1850–52), d'Orbigny arranged all the known fossil molluscs, as well as other invertebrates, according to their stratigraphic distribution. In doing so d'Orbigny created 27 different stages based on the characteristic fossils they contain and named these stages for the their locality or region (i.e., Silurian, Aptian, etc.). D'Orbigny's differentiation of stages also included the study of small marine fossils, pollen, grain, and spores for dating purposes, thus beginning the science of micropaleontology. Based on his observations of the fossil contents, d'Orbigny noted that most species present in a given stage would not be present in younger stages. He, therefore, concluded that older species were replaced by newer species during periods of destruction and creation. This theory paralleled Georges Cuvier's theory of catastrophism but differed from and was disproved by the theory of evolution set forth by Charles Darwin less than a decade later. Nonetheless, d'Orbigny established himself as a founder of biostratigraphy and micropaleontology.

Although he had tried to attain professorship in previous years, in 1853 d'Orbigny was finally appointed to the chair of paleontology at the Muséum d'Histoire Naturelle, a post created by a government decree particularly for d'Orbigny. For his contributions, he received the Wollaston Medal of the Geological Society of London twice and was a member of numerous scientific societies. However, given his novel methods and ideas, d'Orbigny faced considerable criticism from geologists and zoologists who did not accept his views on taxonomy, the stratigraphic distribution of animals, and the division of the Earth's history into stages. Rather than defend his ideas, however, d'Orbigny immersed himself in his work. His work ethic undermined his health to the point that he suffered from a fatal heart ailment during the final years of his life. Alcide d'Orbigny died on 30 June 1857 in Pierrefitte-sur-Seine, near Saint Denis, France.

EDOUARD L. BONÉ AND BRIAN CALLENDER

Biography

Born in Couëron, Loire-Atlantique, 6 September 1802. Traveled extensively through South America on a commission for the Muséum d'Histoire Naturelle, 1826–34; appointed chair of paleontology, Muséum d'Histoire Naturelle, 1853; member, Geological Society of France; awarded Wollaston Medal of the Geological Society of London; member of numerous scientific societies. Founder of biostratigraphy and micropaleontology. Died in Pierrefitte-sur-Seine, near Saint Denis, France, 30 June 1857.

Major Publications

1826. *Tableau méthodique de la classe des Céphalopodes.* Paris: Crochard.
1834–47. *Voyage dans l'Amérique méridionale.* 10 vols. Paris and Strasbourg: Bertrand and Pitois-Levrault.
1836–38. *Galérie ornithologique ou collection des oiseaux d'Europe.* Paris: Lamy.
1835–48. With Férussac. *Histoire naturelle générale et particulière des Céphalopodes acétabulifères vivants et fossiles.* Paris: Lacour.
1840. *Histoire naturelle générale et particulière des Crinoïdes vivants et fossiles: Comprenant la description zoologicale et géologique de ces animaux.* Paris: Chez L'auter.
1840–56. *Paléontologie française: Description zoologique et géologique de tous animaux mollusques et rayonnés fossiles de France.* 8 vols. Paris: Masson.
1849–52. *Cours élémentaire de paléontologie et de géologie stratigraphiques.* 3 vols. Paris: Masson.
1850–52. *Prodrome de paléontologie stratigraphique universelle des animaux mollusques et rayonnés.* 3 vols. Paris: Masson.
1856. *Notice analytique sur les travaux de géologie de paléontologie et de zoologie.* Corbeil: Crété.

Further Reading

Baulny, O. 1973. Alcide d'Orbigny, un grande americanista francese del sec. XIX. *Terra Ameriga* 29–30:57–68.
Fischer, P. 1878. Notice sur la vie et sur les travaux d'Alcide d'Orbigny. *Bulletin de la Société géologique de France* 3:434–53; also, Meulan: Masson.
Gaudant, J. 1984. Actualisme, antiprogressionnisme, catastrophisme et créationnisme dans l'oeuvre d'Alcide d'Orbigny (1802–1857). *Revue d'histoire des sciences* 37 (3–4):305–12.
Gaudry, A. 1859. Alcide d'Orbigny, ses voyages et ses travaux. *Revue des Deux Mondes,* 15 February; also, Paris: Claye.
Legré-Zaidline, F. 1977. *Voyage en Alcidie: À la dé'couverte d'Alcide d'Orbigny (1802–1857).* Paris: Société Nouvelle des Éditions Boubée.
Monty, C.L.V. 1968. D'Orbigny's Concepts of Stage and Zone. *Journal of Paleontology* 42:689–701.
Portlock, J.E. 1858. Obituary. *Quarterly Journal of the Geological Society of London* 14:123–29.

ORIGIN OF LIFE

Before we can ask "How did life evolve?" we must first ask "What is life?" Unfortunately, this deceptively simple question has no simple answer: a clear, unambiguous definition of life is elusive. Viruses, for instance, are not alive in the conventional sense but have some properties of living systems. Nevertheless, we can formulate a working definition of life with which most biologists would agree: A living organism is a self-contained, organized entity that uses matter and energy from its environment to grow, maintain itself, and replicate itself with heritable variation (Lazcano 1994a).

Paleontology, together with geochemistry and planetology, delineates the timing of life's appearance on Earth. The oldest accepted fossils are approximately 3.5 billion years old. They include several different bacteria-like forms, implying that life arose and began to diversify even earlier. In fact, there is indirect evidence that life was present 3.85 billion years ago, the age of the oldest surviving sedimentary rocks—implying that the Earth had a stable crust and liquid water at this time. The oldest rocks in the solar system—certain meteorites—are about 4.6 billion years old, and the consolidation of the proto-Earth was largely complete about 4.5 billion years ago. From the ages of cratered lunar regions, we know that until about 3.9 billion years ago, massive impacts were frequent enough to melt the Earth's crust and evaporate its oceans, sterilizing most or all of the Earth for several thousand years (Chyba 1993). This leaves, at most, a few hundred million years for life to have originated—not much time, from a cosmic perspective.

In the late nineteenth century, Charles Darwin speculated about life arising in "some warm little pond, with all sorts of ammonia and phosphoric salts, light, heat, electricity, etc., present. . . ." (Darwin 1887). Modern theories of the origin of life, however, began in the mid-1920s with the work of the Russian biochemist Aleksandr I. Oparin and the British geneticist J.B.S. Haldane. Each independently devised a similar theory of the origin of life. Oparin thought that the earliest atmosphere on Earth had been in a "reduced" (electron-rich) state, with carbon and nitrogen mostly present as methane (CH_4) and ammonia (NH_3). Heat, light, and other factors caused these gases and water to undergo a wide variety of chemical reactions, forming diverse new compounds. Describing this stage, Haldane (1929) coined a famous metaphor:

> Now, when ultra-violet light acts on a mixture of water, carbon dioxide, and ammonia, a vast variety of organic substances are made. . . . [B]efore the origin of life they must have accumulated till the primitive oceans reached the consistency of hot dilute soup.

Increasingly complex molecules, such as proteins and lipids, formed from these simpler precursors. Oparin (1938) proposed that these large molecules formed microscopic droplets, or *coacervates,* in the early ocean. The coacervates gave rise to the first cells.

A few scientists attempted to test the Oparin-Haldane theory, but strong support did not come until the early 1950s, with the experiments of Stanley L. Miller and Howard Urey at the University of Chicago. Miller filled a flask with liquid water and added a mixture of the gases methane, ammonia, and hydrogen. As the water was heated, the vapor and gases passed through a flask containing spark electrodes. The mixture then passed through a condenser, returned to the heating flask, and was reheated and recirculated. Within a week the water was full of organic molecules, including amino acids, the basic units of proteins (Miller 1953). Figure 1 illustrates the basic apparatus Miller and Urey used in their experiment.

Modern Theories of Biogenesis

Oparin-Haldane Hypothesis

Experiments like Miller's have been repeated time and again, using different energy sources (including heat, light, radiation, and shock) and different gas mixtures. As long as oxygen is excluded—and there are sound reasons for believing that there was virtually no oxygen in the earliest atmosphere—these experiments always form (polymerize) organic molecules, although the amounts and kinds vary (Miller and Urey 1959; Chang et al. 1983; Towe 1994). Spe-

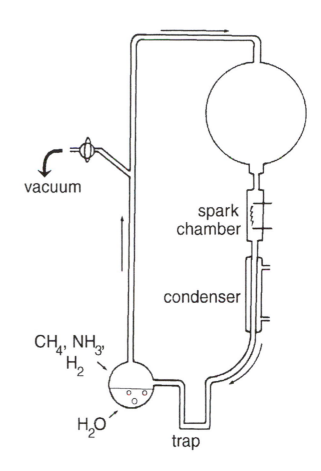

Figure 1. Diagram of Miller's original experiment. Modified from Miller 1953.

cific chemical reactions have been found to produce all the key building blocks of life. For instance, hydrogen cyanide (HCN) and cyanide derivatives can condense to form the nucleotide bases of DNA and RNA (Oró 1994). Hydrogen cyanide, aldehydes, and ammonia can form amino acids and even amino acid chains, while formaldehyde polymerization yields sugars (Figure 2).

A problem with the Oparin-Haldane hypothesis is that there was probably little methane or ammonia in the early Earth's atmosphere. Both are broken down by sunlight, and no known natural processes would have replenished them. It seems more likely that the atmosphere was a weakly reducing or neutral one consisting mainly of carbon dioxide, nitrogen, and water vapor that derived mostly from outgassing from the mantle (Levine et al. 1982; Chang et al. 1983). Miller-Urey experiments using gas mixtures like this produce far fewer organic molecules. The "primordial soup" oceans would have been quite dilute, and radiation, ultraviolet light, and heat would have broken down complex molecules as fast as they were formed. It seems unlikely that under such conditions simple molecules could assemble into anything like living organisms.

A number of alternatives to the Oparin-Haldane hypothesis have been proposed over the past twenty years. These scenarios are not mutually exclusive; the actual origin of life may well have owed something to several of them.

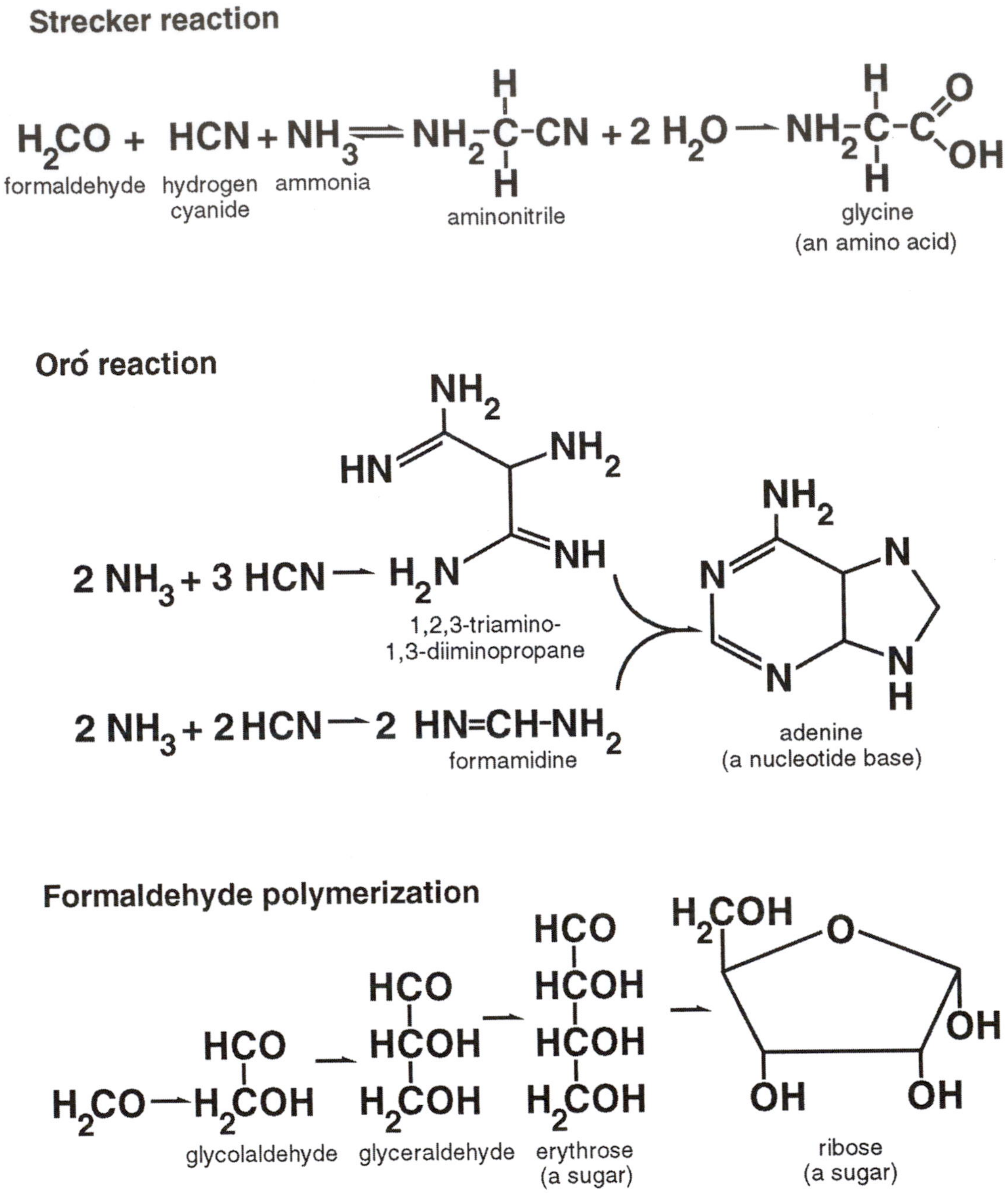

Strecker reaction

$$H_2CO + HCN + NH_3 \rightleftharpoons NH_2\text{-}\overset{H}{\underset{H}{\overset{|}{C}}}\text{-}CN + 2\,H_2O \longrightarrow NH_2\text{-}\overset{H}{\underset{H}{\overset{|}{C}}}\text{-}\overset{O}{\overset{\|}{C}}\text{-}OH$$

formaldehyde hydrogen ammonia
cyanide

aminonitrile

glycine
(an amino acid)

Oró reaction

$$2\,NH_3 + 3\,HCN \longrightarrow$$

1,2,3-triamino-
1,3-diiminopropane

adenine
(a nucleotide base)

$$2\,NH_3 + 2\,HCN \longrightarrow 2\,HN\text{=}CH\text{-}NH_2$$
formamidine

Formaldehyde polymerization

$$H_2CO \longrightarrow H_2COH \quad \longrightarrow \quad \longrightarrow$$

glycolaldehyde glyceraldehyde erythrose
(a sugar)

ribose
(a sugar)

Figure 2. Reactions that may have produced the "building blocks" of life. For simplicity, not all reaction intermediates are shown.

Origin from Space

The theory that life came to Earth from space is called *panspermia.* According to *directed panspermia* (e.g., Crick 1981), life was seeded on the early Earth by intelligent beings. *Random panspermia* (e.g., Hoyle and Wickramasinghe 1978) holds that life is common in the universe, even in interstellar space, and that it drifted onto the Earth by chance. It is true that many bacteria and some other organisms produce spores that survive interstellar conditions, at least for a short while (Weber and Greenberg 1985; Horneck 1993). The famous Martian meteorite ALH84001, with its controversial bacteria-like objects, suggests that meteorites conceivably could have transferred life between planets (Melosh 1988; McKay et al. 1996). But there are serious problems with panspermia. Unprotected spores would not survive the millions of years needed to cross interstellar distances, although shielding them in ice or dust increases their chances somewhat (Weber and Greenberg 1985; Horneck 1993). Practically all meteorites and comets (which could shield microbial passengers from radiation) originated from within the solar system at the time the Earth began to form or shortly thereafter. Random panspermia is thus unlikely, at least over interstellar distances. Directed panspermia avoids these problems, but it is practically impossible to test (unless the aliens who seeded the Earth contact us and admit it).

Nonetheless, key chemical precursors to life could have come from space, where they are surprisingly common. Comets and interstellar dust contain water, ammonia, cyanide, formaldehyde, alcohols, hydrocarbons, amino acids, and many other compounds (Chyba et al. 1990; Oró 1994). In fact, comets may have contributed a significant fraction of the water in the early oceans, as well as a large amount of the Earth's carbon (Chyba 1987; Chyba et al. 1990). Certain meteorites (the carbonaceous chondrites) contain even more complex organic compounds. For instance, the Murchison meteorite, which fell in Australia in 1969, contains 74 different amino acids, plus alcohols, aldehydes, purines and pyrimidines (DNA and RNA bases), hydrocarbons, and fatty acids (Cronin and Chang 1993; Deamer et al. 1994). Important raw materials for life could well have come from space, but the case for actual organisms coming from space is much less certain.

Origin in the Deep Sea

In 1981, J.B. Corliss and colleagues proposed that life first arose at hydrothermal vents—fissures in the ocean floor where superheated water, rich in dissolved gases, flows out into the ocean (Corliss et al. 1981). Complex organic compounds (and eventually living beings) formed in the sharp thermal gradient between the superheated vent water (approximately 350 degrees centigrade) and the cold ocean water (about 4 degrees centigrade). This hypothesis has an advantage: Complex molecules and/or early life forms would have been shielded from radiation and from the effects of large impacts, which could have destroyed them at shallower depths. Furthermore, according to some molecular phylogenies (evolutionary histories), the most archaic living organisms are *hyperthermophiles,* which live at extremely high temperatures (greater than 80 degrees centigrade). The common ancestor of all life may have been thermophilic (able to live in high temperatures) as well (Pace 1997).

However, the extremely high temperatures of the hotter hydrothermal vents rapidly break down most organic molecules (Miller and Bada 1988). The phylogeny of the earliest branches of life is still contentious (Pace 1997). In any case, the common ancestor of life today was not the first organism. Many evolutionary events happened between the origin of life and the common ancestry of the living domains of life (Lazcano 1994a). Still, at least key components of living systems may have arisen in milder deep-sea environments. Amino acids, for instance, may be formed today in deep-sea brine pools (Ingmanson and Dowler 1980) and in laboratory simulations of hydrothermal conditions (Hennet et al. 1992).

Genetic Takeover

A.G. Cairns-Smith has proposed that the earliest self-replicating entities were not organic at all, but mineral—specifically, the atomic layers on the surfaces of the microscopic crystals that make up clay minerals. A clay crystal grows when atoms from the surroundings bond to its outermost layer; thus, as the crystal grows, the complex arrangement of atoms in the crystalline structure of the clay is propagated from layer to layer. A layer can even "mutate" and pass "mutations" on to later layers. Also, the surfaces of clay grains are electrically charged, which enables them to bind with organic molecules. In a hypothetical process that Cairns-Smith calls "genetic takeover," various organic molecules were bound to clay organisms, eventually replacing the clay "genes" entirely (Cairns-Smith 1985).

The German scientist Gunter Wächtershäuser (1988, 1992) has proposed a somewhat similar theory, in which life began as a two-dimensional film of complex organic molecules bound to a layer of iron pyrite. A related theory has life arising from small vesicles of iron sulfides produced at hydrothermal vents. Similar vesicles can be observed growing and budding today. Over time, such vesicles would have accumulated more and more organic compounds, until they became wholly organic (Russell et al. 1993).

Even if clay layers were not the first "organisms," clay and/or pyrite may have been important in the origin of life. Both have surfaces that are electrically charged and bind organic molecules. Both have very ordered, regular structures; their orderliness may have made possible the formation of large, complex, ordered organic molecules. Some experimental results support these hypotheses: clay can catalyze the formation of short lengths of deoxyribonucleic acid (DNA) and ribonucleic acid (RNA) (Ferris and Ertem 1992) and of fairly long peptides (the basic building blocks of proteins) (Paecht-Horowitz 1977). Interestingly, both clays and pyrite are produced at hydrothermal vents, and clay minerals exist in carbonaceous chondrites. Much more experimental work is needed to assess these hypotheses fully.

The Next Steps

Life as we know it needs four things:

- a barrier between the organism and its environment, controlling the passage of substances into and out of the organism;
- sources of new matter and energy;
- catalysts, which drive the chemical reactions that the organism uses to obtain matter and energy; and
- the information needed to grow, repair itself, and reproduce.

How did the "building blocks" assemble into an organism with all these features? While the precise sequence of events that made the first cell may never be known, research is yielding plausible ways in which each of these requirements may have been fulfilled.

Oparin's coacervates are no longer thought to be good models for the earliest cells. However, if a solution of amino acids is dried out and then rewetted, the amino acids condense in a non-random order to form short chains called "proteinoids." In water, these proteinoids spontaneously form hollow spheres that behave in surprising ways. Under the right conditions, they can grow, divide, and catalyze certain chemical reactions. Perhaps more importantly, some microspheres are "selectively permeable"; they permit only certain molecules to pass in or out. Fatty acids and certain other long molecules—including the fatty acids in meteorites—also self-assemble into membrane spheres. These, too, can grow, divide, and selectively pick up smaller molecules (Morowitz et al. 1988; Deamer et al. 1994).

The standard Oparin-Haldane theory implies that the first organisms were "chemoheterotrophs": that is, they obtained both energy and new matter from taking in and breaking down chemical compounds already in the environment (Chang et al. 1983). Simply put, the first organisms acquired any compounds they needed directly from the "soup." As some compounds became depleted, proto-organisms that could manufacture the compounds internally had a selective advantage and survived; the end result was the evolution of complex metabolism. However, H.J. Morowitz and colleagues (1988) proposed that the first protocells could use light energy to convert nutrients into components; they were "photoheterotrophic." Wächterhäuser's theory radically differs from the others by implying that the first organisms were "lithoautotrophic": like living thermophiles, they fixed carbon dioxide using the energy from redox chemical reactions, such as the conversion of iron sulfide and hydrogen sulfide to pyrite. So far, experimental tests of the lithoautotrophic theory have not supported it (Keefe et al. 1995), but more work needs to be done.

Earth life uses proteins as catalysts in biochemical reactions (catalysis) and uses DNA for information storage, but protein synthesis is directed by the information in DNA. The question of "which came first, DNA or proteins?" is an old conundrum in origins research. Surprisingly, the answer may be "neither." Instead, the best candidate may be RNA. An amazing feature of RNA is that it can be used both to transmit genetic information and to catalyze reactions. RNA catalysts, called "ribozymes," are short lengths of RNA that can cut, splice, and even assemble other lengths of RNA. The "RNA world" hypothesis states that the earliest life forms used RNA for both information and for catalysis; DNA and protein enzymes came later. The earliest free-living organism might have looked like a bag of RNA molecules that could recombine in new arrangements, extract energy from the environment, and use it to drive the organism's collective replication (Gilbert 1986; Lazcano 1994b).

The ideal confirmation of this theory would be the synthesis of a self-replicating RNA molecule (or, much more plausibly, a set of such molecules). No one has accomplished this yet, and there are some difficulties with the theory: RNA molecules long enough to have interesting properties are unlikely to form spontaneously (Joyce 1991), and the sugar component of RNA, ribose, is both chemically unstable and hard to synthesize in quantity under prebiotic conditions (Shapiro 1986). RNA itself may have been derived from earlier polymers that did not use ribose; several plausible candidates have been proposed (Lazcano and Miller 1996).

It is possible to set up systems of ribozymes, protein enzymes, and DNA that replicate the ribozymes, with frequent mutations, for many generations. By artificial selection, more efficient ribozymes evolve, even ribozymes with new functions (Wright and Joyce 1997). It is even possible to evolve efficient, functional ribozymes from random RNA sequences (Ekland et al.

1995). This "test-tube Darwinism" may lead to solutions of some of the mysteries that still shroud the origin of life.

For Further Exploration

Origins research is a diverse and fast-changing field, and the published literature is huge, widespread, and growing rapidly. The best source for up-to-date information on origins research is the journal *Origins of Life and Evolution of the Biosphere,* published by the International Society for the Study of the Origin of Life (ISSOL). Books on the origin of life are plentiful but go out of date rapidly. The late Carl Sagan wrote some very accessible, if now somewhat dated, reviews of theories of the origin of life (Shklovskii and Sagan 1966; Sagan 1980), while the textbook edited by L. Margulis and L. Olendzenski (1992) includes a number of contributions by various leaders in origins research. A.G. Cairns-Smith (1985) has provided a very readable, nontechnical explanation of his theory of genetic capture. A fascinating topic, unfortunately beyond the scope of this article, is the mathematical theory behind the emergence of biological complexity: S.A. Kauffman's treatment (1993) is magisterial.

For those interested in the primary literature, the anthology *Origins of Life: The Central Concepts* (Deamer and Fleischaker 1992) is noteworthy for reprinting many of the classic papers in the field. Schopf (1983) and Bengtson (1994) are just two of many excellent compilations of technical papers and reviews. A recent U.S. government publication (National Research Council, Committee on Planetary Biology and Evolution 1990) both outlines the status of origins research and recommends further research programs, particularly in space exploration. Finally, Stan Miller's 1953 groundbreaking experiment is relatively easy to reproduce, even at home with simple equipment. See Stong (1970) for details.

BEN WAGGONER

See also Algae; Skeletized Microorganisms: Algae and Other Autotrophs

Works Cited

Bengtson, S. (ed.). 1994. *Early Life on Earth.* New York: Columbia University Press.

Cairns-Smith, A.G. 1985. *Seven Clues to the Origin of Life.* Cambridge and New York: Cambridge University Press.

Chang, S., D. DesMarais, R. Mack, S.L. Miller, and G.E. Strathearn. 1983. Prebiotic organic syntheses and the origin of life. *In* J.W. Schopf (ed.), *Earth's Earliest Biosphere: Its Origin and Evolution.* Princeton, New Jersey: Princeton University Press.

Chyba, C.F. 1987. The cometary contribution to the oceans of primitive Earth. *Nature* 330:632–35.

———. 1993. The violent environment of the origin of life: Progress and uncertainties. *Geochimica et Cosmochimica Acta* 57:3351–58.

Chyba, C.F., P.J. Thomas, L. Brookshaw, and C. Sagan. 1990. Cometary delivery of organic molecules to the early Earth. *Science* 249:366–73.

Corliss, J.B., J.A. Baross, and S.E. Hoffman. 1981. An hypothesis concerning the relationship between submarine hot springs and the origin of life on Earth. *Oceanologica Acta* 4 (supplement):59–69.

Crick, F. 1981. *Life Itself: Its Origin and Nature.* New York: Simon and Schuster; London: Macdonald.

Cronin, J.R., and S. Chang. 1993. Organic matter in meteorites: Molecular and isotopic analyses of the Murchison meteorite. *In* J.M. Greenberg, C.X. Mendoza-Gómez, and V. Pirrnello (eds.), *The Chemistry of Life's Origins.* NATO Advanced Studies Institute Series, ser. C., vol. 415. Dordrecht and Boston: Kluwer.

Darwin, F. 1887. *Life and Letters of Charles Darwin.* 3 vols. London: Murray; New York: Appleton.

Deamer, D.W., and G.W. Fleischaker. 1992. *Origins of Life: The Central Concepts.* Boston: Jones and Bartlett.

Deamer, D.W., E.H. Mahon, and G. Bosco. 1994. Self-assembly and function of primitive membrane structures. *In* S. Bengtson (ed.), *Early Life on Earth.* New York: Columbia University Press.

Ekland, E.H., J.W. Szostak, and D.P. Bartel. 1995. Structurally complex and highly active RNA ligases derived from random RNA sequences. *Science* 269:364–70.

Ferris, J.P., and G. Ertem. 1992. Oligomerization of ribonucleotides on montmorillonite: Reaction of the 5'-phosphorimidazolide of adenosine. *Science* 257:1387–90.

Gilbert, W. 1986. The RNA world. *Nature* 319:618.

Haldane, J.B.S. 1929. The origin of life. *The Rationalist Annual* 148:3–10.

Hennet, R.J.-C., N.G. Holm, and M.H. Engle. 1992. Abiotic synthesis of amino acids under hydrothermal conditions and the origin of life: A perpetual phenomenon? *Naturwissenschaften* 79:361–65.

Horneck, G. 1993. Responses of *Bacillus subtilis* spores to space environment: Results from experiments in space. *Origin of Life and Evolution of the Biosphere* 23:37–52.

Hoyle, F., and C. Wickramasinghe. 1978. *Lifecloud: The Origin of Life in the Universe.* London: Dent; New York: Harper and Row.

Ingmanson, D.E., and M.J. Dowler. 1980. Unique amino acid composition of Red Sea brine. *Nature* 286:51–52.

Joyce, G.F. 1991. The rise and fall of the RNA world. *New Biologist* 3:399–401.

Kauffman, S.A. 1993. *The Origins of Order: Self-Organization and Selection in Evolution.* Oxford and New York: Oxford University Press.

Keefe, A.D., S.L. Miller, G. McDonald, and J. Bada. 1995. Investigation of the prebiotic synthesis of amino acids and RNA bases from CO_2 using FeS/H_2S as a reducing agent. *Proceedings of the National Academy of Sciences of the USA* 92:11904–6.

Lazcano, A. 1994a. The transition from nonliving to living. *In* S. Bengtson (ed.), *Early Life on Earth.* New York: Columbia University Press.

———. 1994b. The RNA world, its predecessors, and its descendants. *In* S. Bengtson (ed.), *Early Life on Earth.* New York: Columbia University Press.

Lazcano, A., and S.L. Miller. 1996. The origin and early evolution of life: Prebiotic chemistry, the pre-RNA world, and time. *Cell* 85:793–98.

Levine, J.S., T.R. Augustsson, and M. Natarajan. 1982. The prebiological atmosphere: Stability and composition. *Origins of Life* 12:245–59.

Margulis, L., and L. Olendzenski (eds.). 1992. *Environmental Evolution.* Cambridge, Massachusetts: MIT Press.

McKay, D.S., E.K. Gibson Jr., K.L. Thomas-Keprta, H. Vali, C.S. Romanek, S.J. Clemett, X.D.F. Chillier, C.R. Maechling, and R.N. Zare. 1996. Search for past life on Mars: Possible relic biogenic activity in Martian meteorite ALH84001. *Science* 273:924–30.

Melosh, J.H. 1988. The rocky road to panspermia. *Nature* 332:687–88.

Miller, S.L. 1953. A production of amino acids under possible primitive Earth conditions. *Science* 117:528–29.

Miller, S.L., and J.L. Bada. 1988. Submarine hot springs and the origin of life. *Nature* 334:609–11.

Miller, S.L., and H.C. Urey. 1959. Organic compound synthesis on the primitive Earth. *Science* 130:245–51.

Morowitz, H.J., B. Heinz, and D.W. Deamer. 1988. The chemical logic of a minimum protocell. *Origins of Life and Evolution of the Biosphere* 18:281–87.

National Research Council, Committee on Planetary Biology and Chemical Evolution. 1990. *The Search for Life's Origins.* Washington, D.C.: National Academy Press.

Oparin, A.I. 1938. *The Origin of Life.* 2nd ed., New York: Macmillan.

Oró, J. 1994. Early chemical stages in the origin of life. *In* S. Bengtson (ed.), *Early Life on Earth.* New York: Columbia University Press.

Pace, N.R. 1997. A molecular view of microbial diversity and the biosphere. *Science* 276:734–40.

Paecht-Horowitz, M. 1977. The mechanism of clay catalyzed polymerization of amino acid adenylates. *Biosystems* 9:93–98.

Russell, M.J., R.M. Daniel, and A.J. Hall. 1993. On the emergence of life via catalytic iron-sulphide membranes. *Terra Nova* 5:343–47.

Sagan, C. 1980. *Cosmos.* New York: Random House; London: Macdonald, 1981.

Schopf, J.W. (ed.). 1983. *Earth's Earliest Biosphere: Its Origin and Evolution.* Princeton, New Jersey: Princeton University Press.

Shapiro, R. 1986. Prebiotic ribose synthesis: A critical analysis. *Origins of Life and Evolution of the Biosphere* 25:83–98.

Shklovskii, I.S., and C. Sagan. 1966. *Intelligent Life in the Universe.* San Francisco: Holden-Day; London: Pan Books, 1977; as *Vselennaia, zhizn, razum,* Moscow: Izd-vo Akademii nauk SSSR, 1962.

Strong, C.L. 1970. Experiments in generating the constituents of living matter from inorganic substances. *Scientific American* 222:130–39.

Towe, K.M. 1994. Earth's early atmosphere: Constraints and opportunities for evolution. *In* S. Bengtson (ed.), *Early Life on Earth.* New York: Columbia University Press.

Wächtershäuser, G. 1988. Pyrite formation, the first energy source for life: A hypothesis. *Systematic and Applied Microbiology* 10:207–10.

———. 1992. Order out of order: Heritage of the iron-sulfur world. *In* J. Trân Than Vân, K. Trân Than Vân, J.C. Mounoulou, J. Schneider, and C. McKay (eds.), *Frontiers of Life.* Gif-sur-Yvette; Éditions Frontières.

Weber, P., and J.M. Greenberg. 1985. Can spores survive in interstellar space? *Nature* 316:403–7.

Wright, M.C., and G.F. Joyce. 1997. Continuous in vitro evolution of catalytic function. *Science* 276:614–17.

Further Reading

Bengtson, S. (ed.). 1994. *Early Life on Earth.* New York: Columbia University Press.

Cairns-Smith, A.G. 1985. *Seven Clues to the Origin of Life.* Cambridge and New York: Cambridge University Press.

Deamer, D.W., and G.W. Fleischaker. 1992. *Origins of Life: The Central Concepts.* Boston: Jones and Bartlett.

Kauffman, S.A. 1993. *The Origins of Order: Self-Organization and Selection in Evolution.* New York and Oxford: Oxford University Press.

Margulis, L., and L. Olendzenski (eds.). 1992. *Environmental Evolution.* Cambridge, Massachusetts: MIT Press.

National Research Council, Committee on Planetary Biology and
    Evolution. 1990. *The Search for Life's Origins.* Washington, D.C.:
    National Academy Press.
Sagan, C. 1980. *Cosmos.* New York: Random House; London: Macdonald.
Schopf, J.W. (ed.). 1983. *Earth's Earliest Biosphere: Its Origin and
    Evolution.* Princeton, New Jersey: Princeton University Press.

Shklovskii, I.S., and C. Sagan. 1966. *Intelligent Life in the Universe.* San
    Francisco: Holden-Day; London: Pan, 1977; as *Vselennaia, zhizn,
    razum,* Moscow: Izd-vo Akademii nauk SSSR, 1962.
Strong, C.L. 1970. Experiments in generating the constituents of living
    matter from inorganic substances. *Scientific American*
    222:130–39.

ORNAMENTATION: INVERTEBRATES

When one refers to ornamentation of invertebrates, one refers to decorations on the surface of the invertebrate exoskeleton. The function of such ornamentation often is difficult to determine, but it commonly provides camouflage by masking the animal's contour or by providing a rough surface to which other invertebrates (e.g., anemones) can attach. In some cases, however, ornamentation is believed to inhibit the attachment of epifauna; the spiny shell of some productid brachiopods may serve this purpose (Muir-Wood and Cooper 1960). A lack of ornamentation does not necessarily imply a perfectly smooth surface. For example, unornamented brachiopod shells still display fine concentric growth lines.

Surface growth lines are present on invertebrates that have shells that grow in stages. The spiral shells of nautiloids and ammonoids have faint growth lines; each line represents the position of the shell aperture at some point in the life of the animal. These growth lines are not to be confused with suture lines, which mark the position of internal septa that wall off buoyancy-regulating chambers. In modern *Nautilus* the white conch is camouflaged by orange-brown stripes, and ornamental coloring undoubtedly characterized many fossil shells. Original color is rarely preserved, but pigmentation patterns are recorded from cephalopods and other groups (e.g., Foerste 1930). Ultraviolet light has been used to reveal the color patterns of bivalves, patterns that are not visible in normal light (Nuttall 1969).

In brachiopods and molluscan bivalve shells, small increments of shell are added during daylight hours, although they commonly can be detected only with a microscope (Williams 1968). In shells with fine growth lines, occasional strongly marked growth lines that indicate temporary cessations of growth may appear. These define "growth stages." Such cessations commonly reflect a fall in water temperature, which inhibits shell secretion and results in a thickening at the margin of the shell. A subsequent rise in temperature will revitalize metabolic activity, so that renewed outward growth results in a clearly defined growth stage (Figure 1A). The interval between such stages may be annual.

Many brachiopods show strong concentric ornaments that are controlled by genetics rather than seasons. These are referred to as fila, lamellae, imbrications, and frills. Each type confers increased strength to the shell and is produced by the retraction and readvance of the edge of the mantle. Typically, the small scale fila (Figure 1) are packed closely, with little extension away from the shell surface; they may be developed regularly *(Clitambonites)* or irregularly *(Raunites).* The thin layers of lamellose shells (e.g., *Glyptorthis*) are very clearly undercut, as are the more widely spaced imbrications *(e.g., Clitambonites).* Frills, well displayed by *Streptis* and the atrypides, are major extensions that develop away from the valve surface. Concentric undulations of the mantle edge produce a series of corrugations (rugae) on the surface, as in the pandemic Paleozoic *Leptaena.* Such shells commonly develop a major undulation or geniculation that permanently changes the growth direction of the adult shell and separates the visceral disc from the trail. This structure is interpreted as enabling the brachiopod to maintain contact with the water, while the majority of the shell is concealed by sediment (Grant 1966).

Radial undulations of the mantle edge produce radial ribbing. Ribs that originate at the umbones (shell apex or beak) are termed "costae"; those that arise in front of the larval shell, either by branching or, intercalation, are called "costellae"; very fine ribs are called "capillae." The last of these may either stand alone, as in *Grammoplecia,* or more commonly, be associated with existing ribs, as in *Orthis.* A major undulation will produce a fold (plication) in the shell's edge, with a corresponding depression (sulcus) in the opposite valve. In brachiopods a median plication more commonly develops on the upper valve, but it can occur on the lower valve. In a few forms, such as *Dicoelosia,* there is a sulcus in each valve. The undulations assist in segregating incoming water from outgoing water.

In shells with equal concentric and radial ornament, a reticulate (network) pattern develops, as in *Atrypa.* On ribbed lamellose shells such as *Spinorthis,* the sides of the ribs on the lamellae may join beneath to form a hollow spine protruding away from the valve surface.

Other spines are hollow and open into the valve interior and are represented particularly well by the cosmopolitan Upper Paleozoic group centered about *Productus.* These spines are lined with mantle epithelium, at least during growth (Williams and Rowell 1965). The spines are of diverse form and distribution, and they served various functions. Some spines may have anchored the lower valve to the sea floor or other reef substrate. Other spines may have clasped crinoid stems, elevating the brachiopod above the sea floor. Some brachiopods had horizontal balancing spines that functioned as outriggers, preventing the shell from turning over and facilitating a partly buried existence (Grant 1966). Researchers postulate that interlocking marginal spines formed a strainer for water entering the mantle cavity, while the spines of the minute, lingulate *Acanthambonia* appear additionally to have taken on the sensory function of setae, or tactile bristles (Wright and Nõlvak 1997).

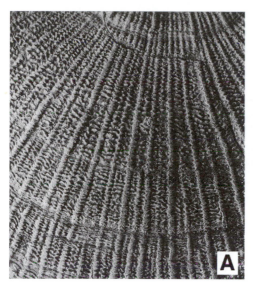

Figure 1. Basic brachiopod ornament. *A, Raunites* (×5), showing corrugated concentric fila and occasional growth stages crossing fine, intercalated radial costellae; *B, Clitambonites* (×6), showing costellae with sharp concentric fila and regular imbrications interrupting shell growth. From Wright and Rubel (1996), reproduced by permission of the Palaeontological Association.

Some brachiopods are characterized by definite pitted ornaments (Wright 1981) that are not simply the result of a reticulate pattern. The netlike ornament of *Dictyonella* is associated with a shell riddled with pores (endopunctuation), as is also the case with *Saukrodictya* and *Sarganostega,* although the strong radial ornaments of costellae and plications, respectively, produce quite different surface patterns. Netlike ornaments also occur in impunctate (having no pores) shells (e.g., *Punctolira*). Perforations arrayed along rib crests and directed toward the shell margin occur in both endopunctate and impuncate taxa. They are believed to have housed setae in life. Endopunctation itself may even be coarse enough to give an ornamentation to the shell surface.

Some molluscan bivalves are strikingly ornamented by a strong pattern of tubercles and ridges. Included among these are the trigoniids (brooch shells), a group in which most genera have a different ornament on flank and area. Oysters, like some brachiopods, may develop strong angular ribbing; this reflects a marked zigzag commissure (junction between the margins of the two valves), which serves to lengthen the commissure without enlarging the gape (the size of the opening when the shells are open). In scallops the ornament is one factor in swimming ability—the smooth forms are better swimmers than those with strong ribs. But the ribbed shells are stronger and, thus, better adapted to the shallower environments.

In general, the ammonoids had strong ornaments, unlike the coiled nautiloids. In addition to growth lines, which, as in the brachiopods and bivalves, may be variously accentuated, the radial ribs are distinctive. These may be variously spaced and positioned: simple or branching; straight, curved, sigmoidal, or sickle-shaped. The ridges may or may not be associated with rows of rounded or elongate tubercles, as in *Acanthoceras,* and occasionally develop into stout spines (*Eoderoceras*). Spiral ornament takes the form of lines or ridges, although this is not as common as in the gastropods. The ventral side of the ammonoid shell may be modified by a smooth or serrated keel that may be defined on either side by a sulcus (groove).

The shape of the ornament of a shell-bearing animal that attaches itself to another animal may be dictated not by the animal but by the host. This phenomenon, termed "xenomorphism," is displayed well by the brachiopod *Petrocrania,* a form that is cemented

Figure 2. *Marsupites* theca, with arms showing ornament of the plates (×1). From Rasmussen (1978).

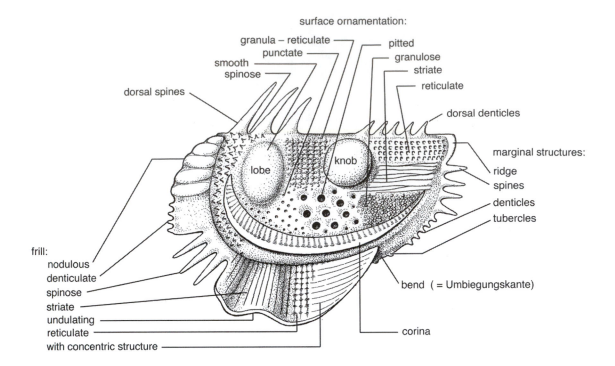

Figure 3. Composite diagram displaying ornamentation styles of palaeocope ostracodes. From Scott (1961), courtesy of the University of Michigan Museum of Paleontology.

to the host by the lower valve. The ornament mirrors that of its substrate, so that when it grows across a finely ornamented strophomenid, the fine details of the strophomenid ornament are traced by the growing edge and reproduced on the surface of the upper valve. Xenomorphic sculpture also commonly characterizes the bivalve oysters but is restricted to the umbonal region of the right valve, the ornament of the host disappearing as the developing left valve clears the substrate.

Growth lines do not characterize the surface of echinoids (e.g., sand dollars, sea urchins), as the test is composed of hundreds of small, separately formed calcite plates. However, the plates themselves grow and display growth lines. The plates are ornamented by tubercles (knobs) against the central boss. The boss fits the socket of a spine with a surrounding sheath of controlling muscles. The size of the tubercles reflects the size of the spines, from relatively few large tubercles in the regular urchins to densely distributed minute tubercles in the burrowing urchins. The ambulacral plates, which flank the tube feet, reflect the distribution of those feet. While they may be distinctive in individual species, their distinctiveness can hardly be construed as ornamentation. Similarly, the grooves and indentations found in heart urchins are related to the functions of burrowing and feeding, while deep notches or openings (lunules) of the flattened tests of sand dollars are related to their shallow burrowing habit.

As with the echinoid test, the thecae of pelmatozan echinoderms are modified by the water vascular system. One group, the cystoids, is subdivided according to whether the pore units are confined to one thecal plate (Diploporita) or shared by adjacent plates

(Rhombifera). These pores are commonly much more apparent than the surface ornament of the epitheca, which is thin and is often removed by weathering. The epitheca may be smooth, or it may be ornamented by concentric lines or by a network of ridges in concentric triangles (these triangles are shared by three adjacent thecal plates with the ridge junctions at the center of the plates).

The same pattern also occurs in another group, the eocrinoids, and among the camerate class of crinoids (e.g., *Glyptocrinus*). The thecal plates of crinoids may vary from smooth to finely granulose, pustulose (blistered), nodose (nodular), or spinose, in addition to ridges. The thecal plates of the Cretaceous *Marsupites* have narrow straight ridges or rows of granules arranged perpendicular to the edges of the plates (Figure 2). This pattern is related to the courses of nerve canals inside the plates. The same pattern is seen in the much earlier *Crotalocrinus* (Silurian) and in some species of the very highly ornamented cystoid *Echinoencrinites*. In the blastoids, the thecal plates farthest from the ambulacra again may be smooth, with growth lines, ridges, or rows of nodes.

Surface growth lines are not present in arthropods, which increase in size through molting. In trilobites, the basic surface relief of the shield is variously ornamented. In the illaenids the surface is relatively smooth, in the calymenids it is granular, while in the encrinurids it is typically coarsely tuberculate (covered with tubercles). In *Encrinurus* the cephalic tubercles may reach almost the size of the eye tubercles; this particular genus lacks tubercles on the thoracic segments, although different species display a range of patterns of pygidial (tail) tubercles. Pitted surfaces also occur and are best known from fringes around the heads of the harpids and trinucleids. The precise arrangement of the fringe pits in the trinucleids suggests a sensory array, possibly for determining the direction of the water current through contained sensory hairs in this predominantly blind group. The glabella (central head shield swelling) also may show much finer pitting, concentric ridges, or a reticulate pattern (Hughes et al. 1975).

Trilobites develop spines in a variety of forms, and researchers have proposed various functions for them. In the folded posture of the tiny *Agnostus,* spines at each corner serve to maintain balance within the water column (Müller and Walossek 1987). The widely developed genal spines of benthic polymerid trilobites may have a support function; three-dimensional reconstruction of *Leptoplastus crassicorne* shows that its long genal spines curve down and run beneath the body, thus raising the soft parts above a muddy substrate (Clarkson and Taylor 1995). In the odontopleurids, a series of small spines (denticles) occur around the cephalic margin in front of the genal spines, together with a pair of occipital spines; additionally, long spines are developed on each thoracic segment with further paired spines on the pygidium. Whatever the spines' primary functions—weight reduction, balance, floating adaptation—the exoskeleton would have formed a very prickly mouthful for any predator.

Terrace lines are commonly seen on the doublure of trilobites. These fine surface ridges roughly parallel the margin. Sensory pore canals open at the base of these ridges (Miller 1975), but the precise function is uncertain. The most impressive of the fossil chelicerates (a group of arthropods that includes extant horseshoe crabs and spiders), the eurypterids, may also have terrace lines on the thin cuticle, particularly around the border. The surface of the cuticle may be smooth or variously ornamented by tubercles or spines, but in particular by rows of scales that produce a very distinctive ornament (Størmer 1955), so much so that even small, fossilized fragments are recognizable immediately as being eurypterid.

Although ostracodes (tiny bivalved crustaceans) may have very smooth valves, those of the palaeocopes display an amazing diversity of surface ornament (Figure 3). Such ornamentation is superimposed on an already ornate surface of lobes and sulci that reflect the internal anatomy and is coupled with a very strong development of sexually dimorphic structures.

ANTHONY D. WRIGHT

See also Defensive Structures: Invertebrates; Exoskeletal Design; Feeding Adaptations: Invertebrates; Skeletized Organisms and Tissues: Invertebrates

Works Cited

Clarkson, E.N.K., and C.M. Taylor. 1995. The lost world of the olenid trilobites. *Geology Today* 11:147–54.

Foerste, A.G. 1930. The color pattern of fossil cephalopods and brachiopods, with notes on gastropods and pelecypods. *University of Michigan Museum Paleontological Contributions* 3:109–50.

Grant, R.E. 1966. Spine arrangement and life habits of the productoid brachiopod *Waagenoconcha. Journal of Paleontology* 40:1063–69.

Hughes, C.P., J.K. Ingham, and R. Addison. 1975. The morphology, classification and evolution of the Trinucleidae (Trilobita). *Philosophical Transactions of the Royal Society of London,* Ser. B, 272:537–607.

Miller, J. 1975. Structure and function of trilobite terrace lines. *Fossils and Strata* 4:155–78.

Muir-Wood, H.M., and G.A. Cooper. 1960. Morphology, classification and life habits of the Productoidea (Brachiopoda). *Memoirs of the Geological Society of America* 81:1–447.

Müller, K.J., and D. Walossek. 1987. Morphology, ontogeny and life habits of *Agnostus pisiformis* from the Upper Cambrian of Sweden. *Fossils and Strata* 19:1–56.

Nuttall, C.P. 1969. Coloration. *In* R.C. Moore (ed.), *Treatise on Invertebrate Paleontology,* part N, *Mollusca, 6, Bivalvia,* vol. 1. Boulder, Colorado: Geological Society of America; Lawrence: University of Kansas Press.

Rasmussen, H.W. 1978. Articulata. *In* R.C. Moore and C. Teichert (eds.), *Treatise on Invertebrate Paleontology.* Vol. 3, part T, *Echinodermata 2.* Boulder, Colorado: Geological Society of America; Lawrence: University of Kansas Press.

Scott, H.W. 1961. Shell morphology of Ostracoda. *In* R.C. Moore (ed.), *Treatise on Invertebrate Paleontology.* Part Q, *Arthropoda 3.* Boulder, Colorado: Geological Society of America; Lawrence: University of Kansas Press.

Størmer, L. 1955. Merestomata. *In* R.C. Moore (ed.), *Treatise on Invertebrate Paleontology.* Part P, *Arthropoda 2.* Boulder, Colorado: Geological Society of America; Lawrence: University of Kansas Press.

Williams, A. 1968. Evolution of the shell structure of articulate brachiopods. *Special Papers in Palaeontology* 2:1–55.

Williams, A., and A.J. Rowell. 1965. Morphology. *In* R.C. Moore (ed.), *Treatise on Invertebrate Paleontology.* Part H, *Brachiopoda 1.* Boulder, Colorado: Geological Society of America; Lawrence: University of Kansas Press.

Wright, A.D. 1981. The external surface of *Dictyonella* and other pitted brachiopods. *Palaeontology* 24:443–81.

Wright, A.D., and J. Nõlvak. 1997. Functional significance of the spines of the Ordovician lingulate brachiopod *Acanthambonia. Palaeontology* 40:113–19.

Wright, A.D., and M. Rubel. 1996. A review of the morphological features affecting the classification of clitambonitidine brachiopods. *Palaeontology* 39:53–75.

Further Reading

Benton, M.J., and D.A.T. Harper. 1997. *Basic Palaeontology.* Harlow: Longman.

Clarkson, E.N.K. 1979. *Invertebrate Palaeontology and Evolution.* London and Boston: Allen and Unwin; 3rd ed., London and New York: Chapman and Hall, 1993.

Moore, R.C. (ed.). 1965. *Treatise on Invertebrate Paleontology.* Part H, *Brachiopoda.* 2 vols. Boulder, Colorado: Geological Society of America; Lawrence: University of Kansas Press.

———. 1966. *Treatise on Invertebrate Paleontology.* Part U, *Echinodermata 3.* 2 vols. Boulder, Colorado: Geological Society of America; Lawrence: University of Kansas Press.

Moore, R.C., and C. Teichert (eds.). 1978. *Treatise on Invertebrate Paleontology.* Part T, *Echinodermata 2.* 3 vols. Boulder, Colorado: Geological Society of America; Lawrence: University of Kansas Press.

ORNAMENTATION: VERTEBRATES

Spines, horns, frills, and other ornamentation in vertebrates arise from the skin. The skin is a complex organ involved in protection, acting as a continuous barrier against microorganisms and mechanical injuries. It also produces one of the main vertebrate hard tissues, dermal bone. The skin also is involved in many other physiological functions: breathing, absorption, excretion, and behavior, through the production of color, scents, and pheromones.

The skin is formed of two sheets: the "epidermis" is the outer one, and the "dermis" the inner one. Those two sheets are independent but share functions that have changed over evolutionary time. One of these functions is protection, which the skin performs by producing keratin, a fibrous protein. In vertebrates, scales can be represented in two ways. One is a dermal formation, the bony scales of fishes; the second is an epidermal formation, the horny scales of reptiles, birds, and mammals.

In jawless fishes (agnathans), the epidermis is responsible for surface ornamentation. The designs of the ornamentation play a role in the hydrodynamic properties of the fish. In certain groups of advanced jawed fishes (gnathostomes), there is a trend toward reduced scale cover. Eels have minute scales deep in the dermis and some catfish have lost their scale cover completely. On the other hand, some groups have elaborated the scale cover into a heavy armor, such as some catfish or the sea horse.

The thin scales of higher bony fishes partially overlap from front to back. This "design" results in two types of scales: "cycloid" and "ctenoid" scales. Cycloid scales are more or less circular, with smooth rear edges. The surface of these scales is ornamented superficially with concentric ridges that record annual growth. The rear edge of ctenoid scales has minute points and ridges in numerous rows. The ornamentation on these scales can be used to differentiate between one species and another.

Some chondrichthyan fishes (cartilaginous fishes, including sharks and rays) show outgrowths on the head called "cephalic (head) spines," which are often spectacular. The name is misleading, because such spines do not originate from the head but from the dorsal fin. In most of these taxa, the spines have denticles (minute toothlike structures) and show a variety of shapes. In the most spectacular genera, the spines are hook-shaped or even broom-shaped. Such spectacular ornamentation is usually a sexual character limited to males. (When structures differentiate between males and females, scholars say the group exhibits "sexual dimorphism.") In one genus from the Carboniferous period of United States, *Falcatus,* one limestone slab shows many males around a single female. The various sizes of the spines suggest that the male with the largest probably would have been the one to reproduce with the female. In other taxa (groups; singular, taxon), the spine occurs in both sexes, so its function is still enigmatic.

In modern amphibians the skin usually is devoid of all scales. Some caecelians, a group limited to the tropics, possess cycloid scales embedded in the dermis. Early amphibians had a scale covering reminiscent of their aquatic ancestors.

In one group of amphibians, called "diplocaulids," the skull bones developed elaborate projections that gave the head a boomerang shape. The development of frills and spikes is also well documented in reptiles. This kind of ornamentation is characteristic of some dinosaur groups, such as the hadrosaurs, with their various head crests, or the pachycephalosaurs, which had a bulging head-dome, decorated across the occipital (the back of the skull) with a ridge of spikes. Some scholars have suggested that the skull was used in interspecific combats as a battering ram.

Comparisons with mammals often are used in interpreting the function of ornamental structures. Several studies have been done on the skull of ceratopsids (a dinosaurian group of which the best known is *Triceratops*). The variability in cranial morphology, particularly in brow horn cores, indicates sexual dimorphism (Ostrom and Wellnhofer 1990). In ceratopsids, males have larger skulls and horns, so males may have attained a larger body size. In the same way, evidence suggests that the horn cores (the basic structures that give rise to the horns) of adult females are shorter and have a smaller base area than those of adult males. Living bovids, which, like ceratopsians, have permanent horns, may provide a good living analogy. In antelopes and cattle the horns are used for defense, display, and interspecific (between members of different species) combat.

Besides cranial ornamentation, many reptiles are distinguished by ornamented bony plates called "osteoderms" or "scutes." In crocodilians the plates form armor over the animal's back and, in some species, belly. In reptiles, thickening and hardening of the epidermis results in the formation of horny scales (sometimes very large), also called "scutes." In crocodiles and turtles, scutes form a pattern of large flat scales. Commonly, these horny scales overlap and aid in the locomotion of lizards and snakes.

When the teeth are reduced or absent in tetrapods, the margins of the jaws often cornify (convert into horn) to produce a beak. On the end of the digits, horny claws, nails, and hoofs appear. In birds and mammals the most noticeable production of the epidermis are feathers and hair, respectively. All these horny productions are found rarely as fossils. However, they can be found as imprints in the rock, as is the case of the feathers of *Archeopteryx* (an early bird), or naturally preserved in ice, such as mammoth fur.

Ornamentation in mammals is based mainly on fur characteristics, but because this material is not often preserved, its character is not relevant in the case of fossils. However, one group, the ungulates, includes four well-known families that can be distinguished by the nature of their frontal appendages: Bovidae, Antilocapridae, Giraffidae, and Cervidae. The bovids are the only ones to have true horns. The structure consists of a conical bony horn core entrapped by a keratin sheath; these horns are never shed. The antilocaprids, represented today by the North American pronghorn antelope, have the same structures except that both the core and keratin sheath may be forked and the keratin horn is shed annually. Giraffes and okapi possess bony horn cores called "ossicones." An ossicone differs from the others by having a cover of skin rather than keratin. In living giraffes, the ossicone is a simple spike, but in extinct forms it may be forked or branched. The horn cores of bovids and giraffes develop as floating ossification centers (areas where bone builds up) that fuse to the skull. Cervids bear bony structures termed "antlers," which are shed annually and are characteristically forked. The antlers of cervids develop as outgrowths of the frontal bones (bones of the "forehead") of the skull. These antlers are attached to a permanent pedicel (slender base for growth) that extends from the skull. This pedicel is comparable to the ossicone of giraffes.

Antlers are true bony outgrowths of the frontal bones. They are sheathed in hairy, well-vasculated skin, which nourishes the growing bone. Antler growth diminishes and stops as the blood supply is cut off, except for the pedicels. The skin dries up and is shed, and the final antler consists of dead bone. Besides their function as a sexual ornament, the antlers are used as weapons. Shed annually after the mating season, the antlers are larger each successive year, so the age of the animal can be determined by the number of points. As a result, the antler morphology or size tells scholars much about an individual but very little about a species.

In bovids the horn sheath is responsible for the great variety of horn shapes and sizes. Because horn is rarely fossilized, such diversity is not very observable in the fossil record. In many bovids, head outgrowths show sexual dimorphism. Antlers usually are present only in male cervids. In giraffes the ossicone distinguishes between the male and the female. Variation in horn shape and size is evident in virtually all bovid species. That is true in both wild and domestic forms. Besides individual variation, shape and size reflect age and sexual differences.

Herding behavior, social structure, and sexual dimorphism are related in modern ungulates. Sexual dimorphism often is expressed in a polygamous breeding system. The characteristic creates a dynamism where females live in groups and males are selected on robustness for breeding. Some dinosaurs are believed to have exhibited a similar herding behavior. It has been argued (Farlow and Dodson 1975) that, besides driving away rival males or predators, ceratopsian frills and horns probably served primarily as visual recognition signs and as a way for males to attract females.

H. Bruhin (1953) classifies horn types into three groups based on anatomy and associated behaviors. The "bison type" is for horns that are similar in size and shape in both sexes and generally function as defensive weapons in interspecific combat against enemies. The "impala type" is for horns worn by animals that appear unable to fight predators and that serve for display and in intraspecific (between members of the same species) fighting. Finally, the "giraffe type" is for those horns that are never used as weapons and have a strictly ceremonial function.

PIERRE-YVES GAGNIER

See also Paleoethology; Reproductive Strategies: Vertebrates; Skeleton: Dermal Postcranial Skeleton; Skull; Vertebrate Hard Tissues

Works Cited

Bruhin, H. 1953. Zur Biologie der Stirnaufsältze bei Huftieren. *Physiologie Comparative et Oecologie* 3:63–127.

Farlow, J.O., and P. Dodson. 1975. The behavioral significance of frill and horn morphology in ceratopsion dinosaurs. *Evolution* 29:353–61.

Ostrom, J.H., and P. Wellnhofer. 1990. *Triceratops:* An example of flawed systematics. *In* K. Carpenter and P.J. Currie (eds.), *Dinosaur Systematics, Approaches and Perspectives.* Cambridge and New York: Cambridge University Press.

Further Reading

Romer, A.S. 1949. *The Vertebrate Body.* Philadelphia: Saunders; 6th ed., with T.S. Parsons, 1986.

Walker Jr., W.F. 1987. *Functional Anatomy of the Vertebrates: An Evolutionary Prospective.* Philadelphia: Saunders. 2nd ed., Fort Worth: Saunders, 1994.

ORNITHISCHIANS

Ornithischian dinosaurs are among the best-known dinosaurs. The very first dinosaur recognized by modern science was actually an ornithischian, discovered in the early nineteenth century by a medical doctor, Gideon Mantell, in the town of Lewes, about 15 kilometers south of London. One spring day in 1822, Dr. Mantell's wife brought to him an unusual fossil tooth. After several attempts to identify the piece, Dr. Mantell determined that it belonged to an unknown kind of herbivorous reptile. He proposed the name *Iguanodon* in a publication of *The Philosophical Transactions of the Royal Society of London* in 1825. After further discoveries in both Europe and North America, in 1887 Harry Govier Seeley distinguished between two basic types of dinosaurs, based upon the morphology (shape and structure) of the pelvic girdle (hip): saurischians (lizard-hipped) and ornithischians (bird-hipped).

Ornithischians are known as the "bird-hipped" dinosaurs because at first, the ornithischian pelvic girdle seems similar to that of birds. In both animals, the two lower pelvic bones (the pubis and the ischium) project strongly to the rear (Figure 1). Likely, these structures caused Seeley (1887) to create this name for the group (ornithischian from Greek, "bird-like hip"). At present, birds are considered to be feathered saurischian dinosaurs, completely unrelated to ornithischians.

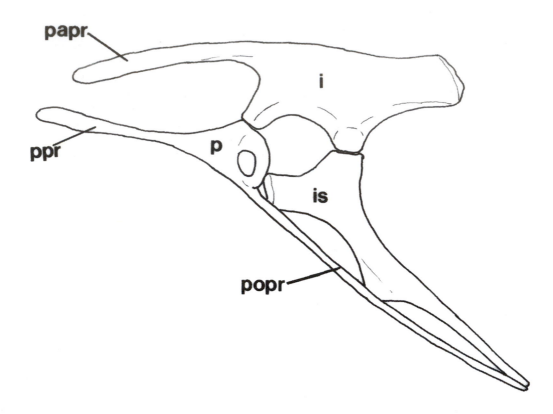

Figure 1. Ornithischian pelvis in lateral view. Abbreviations: *i*, ilium; *is*, ischium; *p*, pubis; *papr*, preacetabular process; *popr*, postpubis process; *ppr*, prepubis process.

Many mass-death accumulations of ornithischian dinosaurs are found all around the world. In the early twentieth century, coal miners found a huge accumulation of *Iguanodon* specimens at Bernissart, Belgium. Dr. Louis Dollo, from the Royal Museum in Brussels, studied the assemblage closely, making *Iguanodon* one of the better-known dinosaurs.

In 1922 Roy Chapman Andrews of the American Museum of Natural History led an expedition to the Gobi Desert, Mongolia. In an area the group members called Flaming Cliffs (now Bayn Dzak), they found the remains of *Protoceratops,* a small ceratopsian ornithischian that has a bony frill at the back of the neck. Since then, hundreds of *Protoceratops* skeletons, at different stages of growth, have been recovered. Another remarkable site with ornithischian remains—one that is many miles long—is in Alberta, Canada. There, at Provincial Park, bones of thousands of ceratopsians have been found.

Temporal Span

Ornithischians first appeared in the Early Upper Triassic and continued to diversify until their extinction in the Late Cretaceous. The oldest ornithischian is *Pisanosaurus mertii* from the Ischigualasto Formation in La Rioja Province, Argentina (Casamiquela 1967). Its age coincides with the origin of dinosaurs as a whole, but because dinosaurs exhibit such diversity already in existence at that time, it is possible that they actually originated earlier, perhaps in the Middle Trassic or even before. The major ornithischian orders originated during Jurassic times, including Ornithopoda, Ceratopsia, Ankylosauria, Pachycephalosauria, and Stegosauria. All of them continued on to the Cretaceous and became extinct with other dinosaurs, near the K-T boundary (the rock stratum that marks the shift from the Cretaceous to the Tertiary periods), about 65 million years ago.

Descriptive Morphology

The main anatomical features that distinguish ornithischians from saurischians include both cranial and postcranial (body) characters. In the cranium (skull), for instance, there is the presence of (1) a predentary bone that extends from the tip of the lower jaw, (2) the presence of cheeks, (3) a dentary with a dorsal coronoid process, and (4) a mandibular condyle of the quadrate (jaw joint) below the tooth row (Figure 2). Postcranial features include ossified tendons in sacral region and tail and bony projections at either end of the pubis (Figure 1). The most typical postcranial feature of ornithischians is a tetradiate pelvis. This kind of pelvic anatomy is retained, with very few variations, in all ornithischian dinosaurs. It is characterized by a relatively low iliac blade (the upper bone of the pelvis) with long preacetabular processes (projections in front of the hip joint) and another bony projection at the rear of the pubis, running back, all along the ischium.

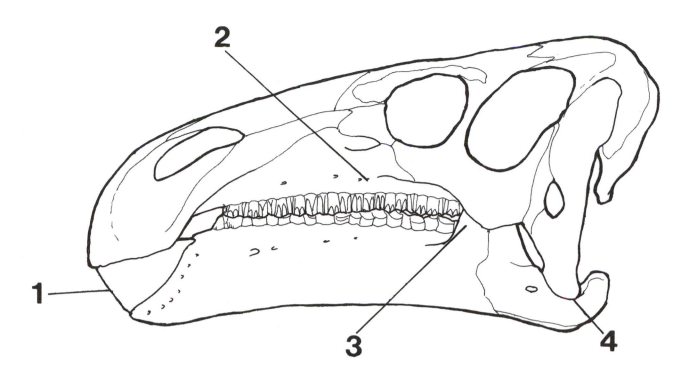

Figure 2. Major cranial features in the ornithischian skull. *1,* predentary bone; *2,* presence of "cheeks"; *3,* dentary with high coronoid process; *4,* quadrate mandibular articulation placed below the tooth row.

Taxonomic Diversity

During the last decade, scholars have used cladistics, a system based upon shared characteristics, to study ornithischians (Sereno 1986). It has provided a better idea about the evolutionary history of this group and the relationship between the smaller groups within it, as well as its complex taxonomic diversity. The main systematic scheme of ornithischians is shown in Figure 3. The most primitive ornithischians *(Lesothosaurus)* are the sister group of Genasauria, which includes the major and best-known groups. Within Genasauria, the Thyreophora (stegosaurs, ankylosaurs, and related forms) is the sister group of Cerapoda. The last contains the Ornithopoda (Heterodontosauria, Hypsilophodontia, iguanodonts, and hadrosaurs) and the Marginocephalia (Pachycephalosauria and Ceratopsia).

Evolutionary Relationships

The most primitive ornithischians are found at Triassic outcrops in South America (La Rioja Province, Argentina) and the Lower Jurassic levels of Africa (Lesotho, South Africa). Because of their primitive morphology, they do not fit within any of the major groups, which places them at the base of the cladogram (Figure 3).

For some authors (Bonaparte 1976), the most primitive ornithischian is *Pisanosaurus mertii* (Casamiquela 1967) from the Upper Triassic of La Rioja Province. Represented by only one incomplete specimen, it was a small, fast-running animal, characterized by leaf-shaped teeth and long, slender hind limbs. The phylogenetic (genetic history) relationships of this species are still controversial. Some authors think that *Pisanosaurus* is a heterodontosaurid, a group best represented by *Heterodontosaurus* (Santa Luca 1980). If so, the most primitive ornithischian would be the African *Lesothosaurus* (Sereno 1986). These old and primitive forms were small, bipedal, fast-running animals, a condition that is probably primitive for dinosaurs as a whole. During the Jurassic, the ornithischians evolved into their main groups, giving rise to the primitive forms of Thyreophora, Ornithopoda, and Marginocephalia (Sereno 1986).

Morphological Diversity

In comparison with its sister group, Saurischia, the ornithischians were much more diversified, seeming to have occupied many different ecological niches. Approximately 50 percent of the known dinosaur species are ornithischians, which include forms that are either bipedal (ornithopods, pachycephalosaurs) or quadrupedal (ankylosaurs, ceratopsians, stegosaurs).

Following the cladistic scheme of ornithischian relationships, *Lesothosaurus* and other poorly known forms are small bipedal animals that show some fast-running adaptations, such as long tails and hind limbs.

The Thyreophora are quadrupedal forms, and all of them bear body armor. The most primitive representatives *(Scutellosaurus, Scelidosaurus)* exhibit rows of keeled scutes (bony armor plates with a high center ridge) that lie parallel to the vertebral column.

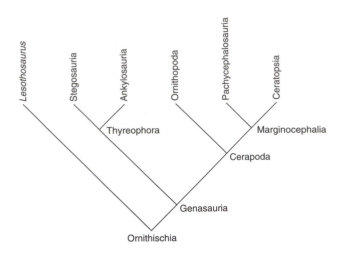

Figure 3. Cladogram showing the phylogenetic relationships among major ornithischians groups. After Sereno (modified), 1986.

This feature reaches a more sophisticated level in stegosaurs and ankylosaurs. Stegosaurs are one of the most familiar dinosaurs in popular imagination. Arranged along the back of these animals are two rows of alternating or parallel plates or spines. These elements run continuously from the neck to the middle of the tail and are graduated in size, with the smallest at either end and the largest at the dorsal section. Another peculiar characteristic is the two rows of spines at the end of the tail. Ankylosaurs, in contrast, have bony scutes and plates that cover the whole body and sometimes have a club at the tip of the tail.

The Ornithopoda includes both small (one to two meters long) and large (between five to seven meters long) bipedal forms, and they have no defensive structures. The most primitive ornithopods (*Heterodontosaurus, Hypsilophodon, Dryosaurus, Gasparinisaura*) retain the appearance of primitive ornithischians (short arms, long legs, single tooth-row), but the iguanodonts (*Tenontosaurus, Camptosaurus, Iguanodon*) and hadrosaurs are larger and have more sophisticated dental features. Among ornithopods, the hadrosaurs show the most diversity, with a wide variety of cranial features (*Saurolophus, Parasaurolophus, Carythosaurus*).

The pachycephalosaurs (*Stegoceras, Pachycephalosaurus*) are shaped very much like ornithopods. Perhaps their most distinguished feature is a dome-shaped skull roof formed by the very thick bones of the forehead and top of the skull.

The Ceratopsia includes both bipedal and quadrupedal forms, all of them featuring a parrotlike snout. The most primitive ceratopsians are the small-bodied, bipedal psittacosaurs (*Psittacosaurus*) from Mongolia. More derived (specialized) groups (*Protoceratops, Triceratops, Styracosaurus*) are all quadrupedal forms that have defensive features, such as horns above the nostrils and above the forehead, as well as neck frills.

Paleogeography

Ornithischian dinosaurs lived during the geological period when there were two large continents on Earth: Laurasia, which was in the northern hemisphere and included today's North America, Asia, and Europe; and Gondwanaland, which was in the southern hemisphere and included today's South America, Africa, Antarctica, Australia, and India. Ornithischian dinosaurs were distributed worldwide. Their fossils are found on every continent, including Antarctica and the Arctic. Laurasia was home to a more diversified ornithischian fauna than Gondwanaland, but scholars are not sure if these differences in distribution reflect more congenial environmental conditions in the northern hemisphere or an incomplete record in the south. This geographical distinction is even more marked in Cretaceous times. In that period, the herbivorous ecological niche in Laurasia was occupied mainly by ornithischians (hadrosaurs and ceratopsians). At the same time, in Gondwanaland the main herbivorous dinosaur fauna was saurischian. However, the distinctions may change. Recently, new localities with ornithischian remains have been discovered in South America, in Upper Cretaceous rocks from Patagonia, Argentina (Coria and Salgado 1996).

Biology and Behavior
Feeding Behavior

All ornithischians seem to have been herbivorous. Their teeth are relatively simple, most often consisting of a single row of leaf-shaped teeth. Only the latest hadrosaurs and ceratopsians developed massive dental batteries, consisting of hundreds of small teeth set close together. In these groups, the chewing mechanism was more complex than that of any other dinosaur. The way that the jaws are jointed suggests that these animals could move the lower jaws forward, which allowed food to go through some processing before swallowing, as in modern mammals.

Social Behavior

There is considerable evidence suggesting that ornithischians were gregarious (social). It is common to find many specimens at different growth stages buried together in a particular deposit. This is especially true of small ornithopods. They have been found in assemblages that are made up of only their species and were preserved at the same and in successive geologic levels. In such cases, it is logical to suppose that they represent remains of a pack or herd that lived in that area, and that the carcasses accumulated over time. Also, some findings support the idea that these animals exercised parental care for the young, at least for some types, since juvenile hadrosaurs have been found preserved in nests with hatchlings and eggs (Horner and Makela 1979).

Reproduction

The little information we have about dinosaur reproduction comes from ornithischians. Fossil eggs of different kinds have been found. Determining the identity of the fossil eggs is only possible when embryos are found inside them, and in a few samples, those conditions exist. So far scholars have identified eggs from the hadrosaur *Maiasaura,* the ceratopsian *Protoceratops,* and the hypsilophodontid *Orodromeus* (Coombs 1990). The shape of these eggs is regularly ovoid, with ornamented shells.

RODOLFO A. CORIA

See also Ankylosaurs; Ceratopsians; Ornithopods; Pachycephalosaurs; Stegosaurs

Works Cited

Bonaparte, J.F. 1976. *Pisanosaurus mertii* Casamiquela and the origin of the Ornithischia. *Journal of Paleontology* 50:808–20.

Casamiquela, R.M. 1967. Un nuevo dinosaurio ornitisquio Triásico (*Pisanosaurus mertii;* Ornithopoda) de la Formación Ischigualasto, Argentina. *Ameghiniana* 5:47–64.

Coria, R.A., and L. Salgado. 1966. A basal iguanodontian (Ornithischia: Ornithopoda) from the Late Cretaceous of South America. *Journal of Vertebrate Paleontology* 16:445–57.

Coombs Jr., W.P. 1990. Basal Thyreophora and Ankylosauria. *In* D.B. Weishampel, P. Dodson, and H. Osmólka (eds.), *The Dinosauria.* Berkeley: University of California Press.

Dodson, P., W.P. Coombs Jr., J.O. Farlow, and L.P. Tatarinov. Dinosaur paleobiology. *In* D.B. Weishampel, P. Dodson, and H. Osmólka (eds.), *The Dinosauria.* Berkeley: University of California Press.

Horner, J.R., and R. Makela. 1979. Nest of juveniles provides evidence of family structure among dinosaurs. *Nature* 282:296–98.

Santa Luca, A.P. 1980. The postcranial skeleton of *Heterodontosaurus tucki* from the Stormberg of South Africa. *Annals of the South African Museum* 79:159–211.

Seeley, H.G. 1887. On the classification of the fossil animals commonly named Dinosauria. *Proceedings of the Royal Society of London* 43:165–71.

Sereno, P.C. 1986. Phylogeny of the bird-hipped dinosaurs (Order Ornithischia). *National Geographic Research* 2:234–56.

Further Reading

Norman, D. 1985. *The Illustrated Encyclopedia of Dinosaurs.* New York: Crescent; London: Salamander.

Spinar, Z.V., and P.J. Currie. 1994. *The Great Dinosaurs.* London: Sunburst; Stamford, Connecticut: Longmeadow.

Weishampel, D.B., P. Dodson, and H. Osmólka (eds.), *The Dinosauria.* Berkeley: University of California Press.

ORNITHOPODS

The Ornithopoda, named by O.C. Marsh in 1881, consists of more than 80 species of herbivorous dinosaurs that demonstrate a great diversity of sizes and shapes. Their remains have been found all over the world, ranging from the Arctic to Antarctica, but they are especially abundant in North America, Europe, and China. Ornithopods spanned an enormous length of time. The first member of the group appeared in the Early Jurassic, approximately 210 million years ago, and the last ornithopods perished during the final extinction of the dinosaurs at the end of the Cretaceous, 65 million years ago. Although the term ornithopod means "bird foot," the feet of ornithopods are not particularly like those of birds.

Ornithopods were slender bipedal herbivores, unlike the large-bodied and quadrupedal stegosaurs, ankylosaurs, and ceratopsians. Their center of gravity lay over the hips, and their long tail counterbalanced the weight of their head and body. Body length in adults ranged from approximately 1.5 meters in early forms such as *Heterodontosaurus* to well over 10 meters in some of the later hadrosaurs such as *Edmontosaurus.* All ornithopods were likely bipedal when moving quickly, using hind limbs that were long (sometimes more than twice as long) and powerful relative to the forelimbs, but they could adopt a quadrupedal stance by resting their forelimbs on the ground while stationary or feeding. Larger ornithopods, such as *Iguanodon* and the hadrosaurs, have robustly constructed hands and probably indulged in quadrupedal motion more often than smaller members of the group.

The first ornithopod to be discovered was named *Iguanodon* (meaning "Iguana tooth") in 1825. Subsequent discoveries in the nineteenth century included more specimens of *Iguanodon* in England and Belgium, and the small English ornithopod, *Hypsilophodon.* As the nineteenth century progressed, dinosaur discoveries in the fertile Mesozoic deposits of the United States produced the iguanodontians *Camptosaurus* and *Dryosaurus,* and the first hadrosaurs, *Hadrosaurus* and *Claosaurus.* Twentieth-century discoveries of ornithopods began with several hadrosaurs, mostly in Canada, and continued with copious discoveries in China, Mongolia, and the United States, and many others in Australia, Kazakhstan, and South Africa. The most recent years have yielded interesting specimens especially in the United States and China. Throughout the last two centuries, ornithopods have attracted the attention of many of the world's foremost dinosaur authorities, including Marsh, B. Brown, L. Lambe, J.H. Ostrom, P.M. Galton, P. Dodson, D.B. Norman, and D.B. Weishampel.

Ornithopods are members of the clade Ornithischia and count among their numbers groups such as the heterodontosaurs, hypsilophodonts, iguanodonts, and hadrosaurs. Grouped together with the Marginocephalia (Ceratopsia and Pachycephalosauria), Ornithopoda constitute the Cerapoda clade (the group including all descendants of a common ancestor) within Ornithischia (Figure 1). The Ornithopoda is defined as all descendants of the common ancestor of the two major clades that make up the group, the Heterodontosauridae and the Euornithopoda. The clade Euornithopoda contains the majority of the ornithopods and is further subdivided into the Hypsilophodontidae and the Iguanodontidae (Figure 2).

The Heterodontosauridae (named by A.S. Romer in 1966 and meaning "different-toothed reptile") is defined as all the descendants of the common ancestor of two particular genera,

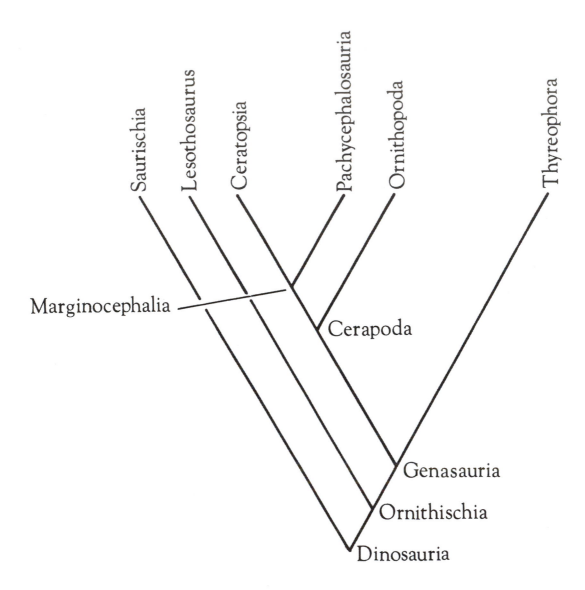

Figure 1. Cladogram of the Dinosauria illustrating the position of the Ornithopoda.

Heterodontosaurus and *Lanasaurus,* and consists of small, agile animals, no more than one to two meters long with an unusual pattern of dentition. Heterodontosaurids are Early Jurassic in age and known from South Africa and Lesotho, although fragmentary material has been reported from China and the United States. *Heterodontosaurus* and *Abrictosaurus* are the best-known members of the group. The cheek teeth of heterodontosaurids bear a high, chisel-shaped crown with small denticles, typical of herbivores' teeth. D.B. Weishampel and L.M. Witmer (1990) envisage heterodontosaurs as active herbivores, foraging on ground cover, and suggest that their forelimbs were structured for digging and tearing. Despite being restricted to herbivory because of their small, weak teeth, they possessed four large teeth that were similar in style, but not in function, to the canines of mammals (Figure 3a). The function of these caniniform teeth is not known, but it has been speculated that they may have been used for species recognition, intraspecific competition, or display (Molnar 1977).

Of the two clades that compose the Euornithopoda, the Hypsilophodontidae is smaller and much more exclusive, but it contains at least 10 monospecific genera (those with only a single species for each genus) that ranged through time from the mid-Jurassic to the end of the Cretaceous and the remains of which are found on four continents. The hypsilophodontids were small- to medium-sized animals two to four meters long and were similar to heterodontosaurids in body plan, but differed in the structure of the skull and dentition (Figure 3B). The group is named for the English form *Hypsilophodon* ("high ridged tooth"), first described by T.H. Huxley in 1869 and later in much greater detail by P.M. Galton (1974). The Hypsilophodontidae includes *Yandusaurus* (mid-Jurassic, China), *Othnielia* (Late Jurassic, United States), *Atlascopcosaurus* (Early Cretaceous, Australia), and *Thescelosaurus* (Late Cretaceous, North America). The hypsilophodonts have heterodont dentition, consisting of a number of simple, peglike teeth in the front of the jaw and more substantial, but laterally com-

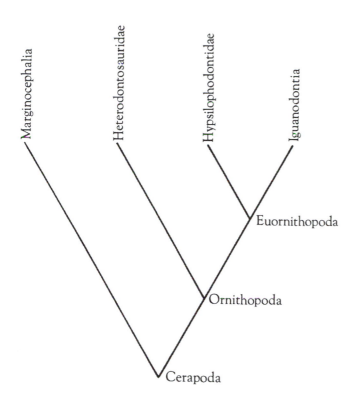

Figure 2. Cladogram of the Cerapoda illustrating the position of the Ornithopoda and Euornithopoda.

pressed, teeth at the back. Such dentition is well suited for herbivory. Galton (1974) noted the elongation of the lower portion of the hind limb in hypsilophodontids, and hypsilophodontids are envisaged as fast bipedal runners.

The Iguanodontia clade, not to be confused with the Family Iguanodontidae that is nestled within the Iguanodontia, seems at first glance to be nothing more than a grab bag of the many and diverse ornithopods not accounted for hitherto, but the members of the clade are united by many advanced skeletal features common to all. Its most conspicuous members are the hadrosaurs or "duckbills," many of whom are characterized by possession of an elaborate nasal crest on the skull. In addition to the hadrosaurs, the Iguanodontidae is also home to a wide array of large and famous ornithopods, such as *Tenontosaurus, Camptosaurus, Iguanodon,* and *Ouranosaurus* (Figures 3C, 3D). Opinion was divided as to whether *Tenontosaurus* is a large aberrant hypsilophodontid (Dodson 1980) or a primitive iguanodontid (Sereno 1986), but it is now regarded as the most primitive member of the Iguanodontidae (Figure 4). All other iguanodontians above *Tenontosaurus* belong in the Euiguanodontia, a taxon recently erected by R.A. Coria and L. Salgado (1996) to include the South American form *Gasparinisaura.* The Euiguanodontia consists of *Gasparinisaura* and the Dryomorpha, the collective taxon for all other iguanodontians above *Gasparinisaura.* Dryomorpha is named for *Dryosaurus,* the most primitive member of the group. Above *Dryosaurus,* all remaining members of the Dryomorpha are known collectively as the Ankylopollexia (Figure 4), literally the "fused thumbs." Members of the Ankylopollexia are characterized by a partial fusion of the wrist bones and development of a spiked thumb. This spike may have been used to rip open foodstuffs or possibly as a form of defense against rivals or predators. The character is not so well developed in *Camptosaurus,* the most primitive member of the clade, but it is prominent in all other members, including the numerous and diverse hadrosaurs.

The position of at least four genera within Iguanodontia is not certain. *Valdosaurus* is often regarded as a basal iguanodontian, as too is *Rhabdodon,* while *Muttaburrasaurus* and *Probactrosaurus* are likely nestled higher in the clade.

Within Iguanodontia, the most primitive member, *Tenontosaurus,* is an extraordinary animal with a tail composed of approximately 55 caudal vertebrae, which accounts for two-thirds of total body length (Ostrom 1970). The caudal vertebrae are surrounded by stiffened bony rods both above and below the main body of the vertebrae that help to keep the tail rigid and oriented horizontally to prevent it from dragging on the ground. This stiffening of a relatively long, muscular tail is a feature common to virtually all ornithopods, but *Tenontosaurus* is an extreme form.

Not surprisingly, the Iguanodontia contains the Early Cretaceous genus *Iguanodon,* one of first dinosaurs described and one of three used by British paleontologist Richard Owen to establish the Dinosauria in 1841. *Iguanodon* was known initially from fragmentary remains described by British medical doctor Gideon Mantell in 1825, but a spectacular discovery in 1878 allowed Louis Dollo to gain a thorough appreciation of the skeletal anatomy of this ornithopod. Miners working a coal seam in Bernissart, Belgium, encountered a clay-filled fissure that contained the remains of approximately 40 skeletons of *Iguanodon.* Material from his incredible find and subsequent discoveries have allowed David Norman (1980, 1986) to document *Iguanodon* as one of the most well known of all dinosaurs, including details of the musculature, blood vessels, and nerves.

Iguanodon, together with *Ouranosaurus,* an Early Cretaceous form from Niger first described by P. Taquet in 1976, are placed above *Camptosaurus* in the Ankylopollexia, but their exact position is not known for certain. D.B. Weishampel, D.B. Norman, and D. Grigorescu (1993) place them alongside Hadrosauridae.

The Hadrosauridae clade is comprised of the ornithopod dinosaurs that are commonly referred to as duckbills. The colloquial name reflects the condition of the front of the skull, where the premaxillary bones are expanded laterally to look something like the bill of a duck. Hadrosaurs were confined to the Late Cretaceous, spanning at least 20 million years. The great majority of hadrosaurs are North American, with notable exceptions found in China and Europe. Hadrosaurs offer a wealth of information on ornithopod biology and behavior. They have been found as mummies, in which soft tissues or the impressions of soft tissues are preserved, and there are even specimens in which the stomach contents have been preserved. The Hadrosauridae is composed of the Romanian genus *Telmatosaurus,* the most primitive member of the group, and all other hadrosaurs, known collectively as the Euhadrosauria. *Telmatosaurus* was first described under the name *Limnosaurus* in 1900 by the eccentric Transylvanian nobleman Franz Baron Nopcsa. He changed the name to *Telmatosaurus* in 1903. The Euhadrosauria is

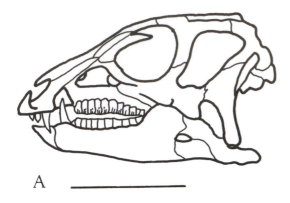

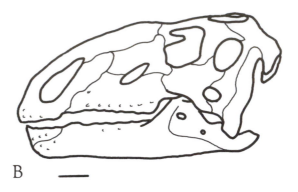

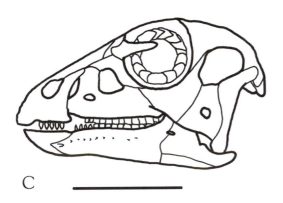

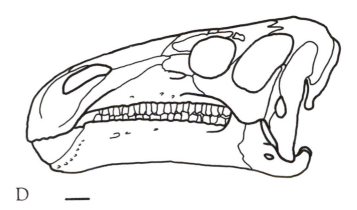

Figure 3. Skulls in left lateral view. A, *Heterodontosaurus*; B, *Hypsilophodon*; C, *Tenontosaurus*; D, *Iguanodon*. Scale bar = 5 cm.

further subdivided into the Hadrosaurinae and the Lambeosaurinae, the divisions reflecting the variation in the morphology of the narial region of the skull (Figure 5). Hadrosaurinae consists of all those forms that have no narial crest and a flat skull roof, such as *Edmontosaurus* (North America) and *Shantungosaurus* (China), or a solid crest, such as that seen in *Saurolophus* (Canada and Mongolia). The Lambeosaurinae consists of hollow-crested forms, such as the North American specimens *Corythosaurus, Parasaurolophus, Hypacrosaurus,* and *Lambeosaurus* (Figure 5).

The crests of hadrosaurs have attracted the attention of many workers over the last several decades. Virtually all the crests involve expansion of the nasal bones and the nasal cavity (although in many forms the premaxillary bones are enormously expanded), and this phenomenon, combined with the fact that many of the crests are chambered, often to a remarkable extent, has dictated many of the approaches adopted in attempting to elucidate the function of the structures. Explanations for the elaborate development of the crests have ranged from sexual display and visual mate recognition to a mechanism for the production of sound, the function of which also may have been mate recognition or warnings against the approach

of predators (Ostrom 1961; Hopson 1975; Weishampel 1981). In contrast to this, a recent discovery of a skull of *Parasaurolophus,* in which the elaborate crest is based in the frontal bones of the skull roof and not the nasal bones, has suggested to R.M. Sullivan and T.E. Williamson (1996) that the many hollow air passages whose presence is revealed by C-T scanning were more likely concerned with temperature regulation, rather than with the production of sounds. Whether primarily acoustic or visual signaling devices, or serving equally as both, it seems most likely that the crests of hadrosaurs were used for recognition, display, courtship, and other characteristics of the natural process of attracting and securing a mate (Hopson 1975). Similar reasoning probably lies behind the conspicuous bumps on the skull of *Ouranosaurus* and the expanded nasal region in the Early Cretaceous Australian genus, *Muttaburrasaurus.*

Ornithopods, from the small, primitive heterodontosaurs to the large, derived hadrosaurs, offer an opportunity to witness the evolution of teeth and feeding mechanisms that successive groups developed to exploit the available food source. Most ornithopods had a horny beak at the front of the mouth for nipping off leaves or twigs, teeth suitable for breaking down tough plant material,

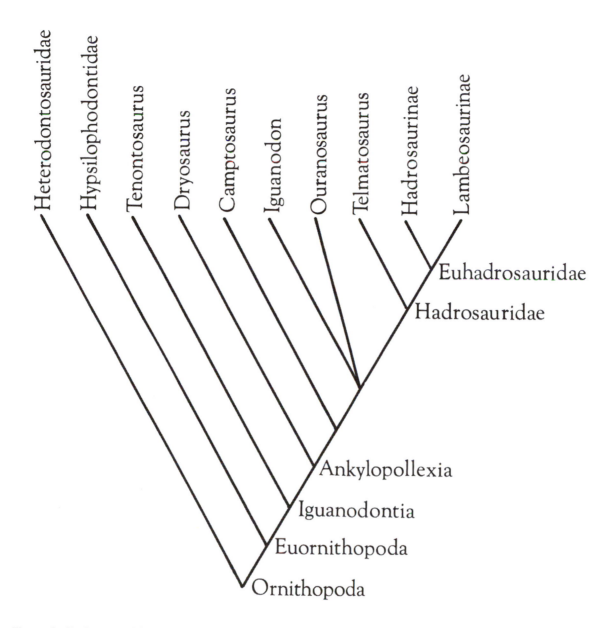

Figure 4. Cladogram of Ornithopoda illustrating the position of *Tenontosaurus*, Iguanodontia, and Ankylopollexia.

and well-developed muscles used to control the jaw and move the teeth against each other efficiently. Additionally, the tooth rows in ornithopods are located in the mouth in such a way as to suggest the presence of cheeks that would retain ingested food in the mouth as the tongue forced it between the tooth rows during chewing. As a supplement to these basic features, ornithopod groups developed specialized jaw movements to bring the opposing tooth rows together with great effectiveness. In heterodontosaurs a simple vertical movement with some rotation of the lower jaw allowed opposing single rows of teeth to move across each other and break up vegetation, whereas in hadrosaurs a highly specialized skull condition allowed portions of the upper jaw to actually hinge on one another and move sideways, allowing enormous

batteries of many hundreds of lozenge-shaped teeth to grind and pulverize any vegetable matter forced between them by the tongue. The evolution of such effective teeth and jaws in hadrosaurs is testimony to the tough nature of the woody vegetation that provided their food source in the Late Cretaceous.

The study of various ornithopods has revealed more about dinosaur biology than could possibly be derived from the study of any other dinosaurian group. The most spectacular information relates to parental care and the rearing of offspring. Based on studies of the hadrosaurine *Maiasaura* ("good mother reptile") from Montana, J.R. Horner (1984) has presented a vivid picture of previously unsuspected and sophisticated parental care and nesting behavior. Geological and paleontological evidence suggests that

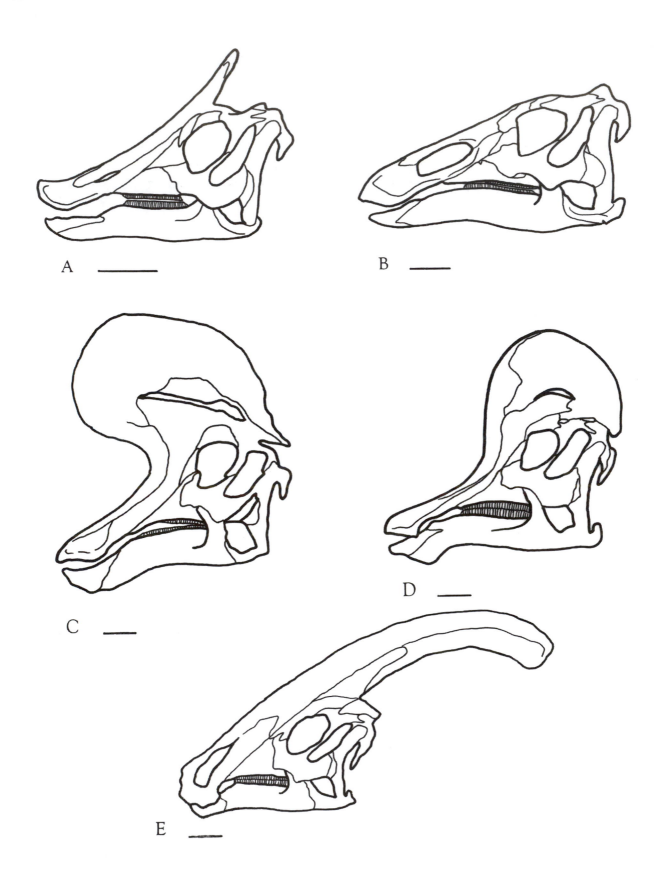

Figure 5. Skulls of members of the Hadrosaurinae and the Lambeosaurinae. Hadrosaurines are represented by *A, Saurolophus; B, Edmontosaurus.* Lambeosaurines are represented by *C, Lambeosaurus; D, Corythosaurus; E, Parasaurolophus.* Scale bar = 10 cm.

Maiasaura females nested in colonies, scooped out deep, protective nests, and brought food to their nestlings over a period of several weeks as the newborns matured and prepared to leave the nest, something that their incomplete limb bones prevented them from doing upon hatching. It is also suggested that *Maiasaura* gathered and traveled in huge herds, much as caribou or wildebeest do today, indicating a high level of sociality in this particular dinosaur. Comparable herding behavior has been proposed for other dinosaurs, such as many of the ceratopsians (see Dodson 1996).

Horner has used similar types of evidence pertaining to the hypsilophodontid *Orodromeus,* also from Montana, to imply a difference in the nesting behavior of the parents and the development of the hatchlings. Unlike those of *Maiasaura,* the limb bones of the *Orodromeus* hatchlings were fully formed and functional and there was no parental care, with the eggs abandoned after laying and the young left to fend for themselves.

The ornithopods, as befits such a large and well-studied group of animals, provide us with an array of insights into the evolutionary development, social behavior, and biology of a diverse group of dinosaurs. New specimens are being uncovered frequently and being described with increasing refinement with every passing decade, and new ornithopod species will probably allow us to further cultivate our picture of these dinosaurs as active, specialized herbivores with sophisticated behavioral repertoires and complex social interactions.

W. Desmond Maxwell

Works Cited

Coria, R.A., and L. Salgado. 1997. A basal iguanodontian (Ornithischia: Ornithopoda) from the Late Cretaceous of South America. *Journal of Vertebrate Paleontology* 16(3):445–57.

Dodson, P. 1980. Comparative osteology of the American ornithopods *Camptosaurus* and *Tenontosaurus. Mémoires de la Société Géologique de France* 139:81–85.

——. 1996. *The Horned Dinosaurs.* Princeton, New Jersey: University Press.

Galton, P.M. 1974. The ornithischian dinosaur *Hypsilophodon* from the Wealden of the Isle of Wight. *Bulletin of the British Museum (Natural History) Geology* 25:1–152.

Hopson, J.A. 1975. The evolution of cranial display structures in hadrosaurian dinosaurs. *Paleobiology* 1:21–43.

Horner, J.R. 1984. The nesting behavior of dinosaurs. *Scientific American* 250:130–37.

Molnar, R.E. 1977. Analogies in the evolution of display structure in ornithopods and ungulates. *Evolutionary Theory* 3:165–90.

Norman, D.B. 1980. On the ornithischian dinosaur *Iguanodon bernissartensis* from the Lower Cretaceous of Bernissart (Belgium).

Bulletin de l'Institut Royal de Science Naturelle de Belgique, Mémoire 178:1–103.

——. 1986. On the anatomy of *Iguanodon atherfieldensis* (Ornithischia: Ornithopoda). *Bulletin de l'Institut Royal de Science Naturelle de Belgique, Science de la Terre* 56:281–372.

Ostrom, J.H. 1961. Cranial morphology of the hadrosaurian dinosaurs of North America. *Bulletin of the American Museum of Natural History* 122:33–186.

——. 1970. Stratigraphy and paleontology of the Cloverly Formation (Lower Cretaceous) of the Bighorn Basin area, Wyoming and Montana. *Bulletin of the Peabody Museum of Natural History* 35:1–234.

Sereno, P.C. 1986. Phylogeny of the bird-hipped dinosaurs (Order Ornithischia). *National Geographic Research* 2:234–56.

Sullivan, R.M., and T.E. Williamson. 1996. A new skull of *Parasaurolophus* (long-crested form) from New Mexico: External and internal (CT scans) features and their functional implications. *Journal of Vertebrate Paleontology* 16 (3), Supplement 68A.

Weishampel, D.B. 1981. Acoustic analysis of potential vocalization in lambeosaurine dinosaurs (Reptilia: Ornithischia). *Paleobiology* 7:252–61.

Weishampel, D.B., D.B. Norman, and D. Grigorescu. 1993. *Telmatosaurus transsylvanicus* from the late Cretaceous of Romania: The most basal hadrosaurid dinosaur. *Paleontology* 36 (2): 3611–85.

Weishampel, D.B., and L.M. Witmer. 1990. Heterodontosauridae. *In* D.B. Weishampel, P. Dodson, and H. Osmolska (eds.), *The Dinosauria.* Berkeley: University of California Press.

Further Reading

Fastovsky, D.E., and D.B. Weishampel. 1996. Ornithopoda: The tushers, antelopes, and the mighty ducks of the Mesozoic. *In The Evolution and Extinction of the Dinosaurs.* Cambridge and New York: Cambridge University Press.

Horner, J.R., and J. Gorman. 1988. *Digging Dinosaurs.* New York: Workman.

Norman, D.B., and D.B. Weishampel. 1990. Iguanodontidae and Related Ornithopoda. *In* D.B. Weishampel, P. Dodson, and H. Osmolska (eds.), *The Dinosauria.* Berkeley: University of California Press.

Sues, H.-D., and D.B. Norman. 1990. Hypsilophodontidae, *Tenontosaurus,* and Dryosauridae. *In* D.B. Weishampel, P. Dodson, and H. Osmolska (eds.), *The Dinosauria.* Berkeley: University of California Press.

Weishampel, D.B. 1984. The evolution of jaw mechanics in ornithopod dinosaurs. *Advances in Anatomy, Embryology and Cell Biology* 87:1–110.

Weishampel, D.B., and J.H. Horner. 1990. Hadrosauridae. *In* D.B. Weishampel, P. Dodson, and H. Osmolska (eds.), *The Dinosauria.* Berkeley: University of California Press.

OSBORN, HENRY FAIRFIELD

American, 1857–1935

Henry Fairfield Osborn was born in Fairfield, Connecticut, on 8 August 1857 and spent his boyhood along the Hudson River highlands. In 1873 he entered Princeton University, at the time presided over by Dr. James McCosh, a dedicated Presbyterian who early on adopted the concept of evolution as expounded by Darwin. McCosh was very influential over young Osborn, and this determined the Deist-scientific philosophy that so characterized Osborn's outlook to the end of his days.

Osborn graduated from Princeton in 1877, and that summer he, with his close friends William Berryman Scott and Francis Speir Jr., spent several months in Wyoming and Colorado collecting fossil mammals. It was just a year after the Battle of the Little Bighorn; the young paleontologists found the summer exciting beyond the thrills of fossil collecting. Despite this early introduction to fieldwork and trips to fossil beds through the years, Osborn never became a field paleontologist. He left that aspect of paleontology to others.

In 1879 he and Scott went to England to follow postgraduate studies under Francis Maitland Balfour and Thomas Henry Huxley. Osborn was always proud of the fact that one day he met Darwin in Huxley's laboratory. On his return to Princeton in 1881, Osborn was appointed to the faculty and also was awarded the Sc.D. degree. When, in 1891, he was appointed as Da Costa Professor of Biology at Columbia University, Osborn supposed he was established for life.

His move to New York marked the beginning of a remarkably active scientific and administrative life. Simultaneously with his Columbia appointment, Osborn became curator on the scientific staff of the American Museum of Natural History. From that time until his death, he pursued two parallel careers, one at the university and the other at the museum. At the university he continued as a professor, training vertebrate paleontologists, many of whom became outstanding authorities in the paleontological world. From 1892 to 1895, he was the first Dean of the Faculty of Pure Science.

At the museum Osborn was very active in the promotion of research in natural history, in the development of modern exhibits, and in the sponsoring of public education. From 1908 to 1935 he was president of the museum, during which time the institution doubled in size, adding seven large buildings. He was especially proud of the Theodore Roosevelt Memorial building, which faces Central Park West and houses the grand entrance hall.

Despite these diverse activities, Osborn maintained a research schedule that resulted in more than 900 scientific papers and monographs, books, and miscellaneous publications. These totaled some 12,000 pages, of which more than 6,000 were devoted to paleontology. Although some papers covered various aspects of paleontology and evolution, perhaps Osborn's primary interest was in the evolution of mammals through geologic time. Particularly noteworthy was his massive two-volume monograph, *The Titanotheres of Ancient Wyoming, Dakota and Nebraska* (1929) and his even more massive two-volume monograph on the Proboscidea, extinct and modern-day animals with a long, fleshy, tube-like snout, such as elephants.

Henry Fairfield Osborn was a large, imposing man who liked large animals, large buildings, and large projects. A forceful person, he promoted his ideas and his projects with vigor and persistence. The American Museum of Natural History, the largest such museum in the world, is in many respects a monument to him and to his work.

EDWIN H. COLBERT

Biography

Born in Fairfield, Connecticut, 8 August 1857. Received B.S. (1877) and Sc.D. (1881), Princeton University. First field expedition of Wyoming and Colorado, 1877; lecturer and assistant professor of natural sciences (1881–83) and professor of comparative anatomy (1883–91), Princeton University; professor of biology (1891–96) and zoology (1896–35), Da Costa Professor (1891–1910), and dean, Faculty of Pure Science (1892–95), Columbia University; curator (1891–1910) and president (1908–35), American Museum of Natural History; vertebrate paleontologist (1900–24) and senior geologist (1924–35), U.S. Geological Survey. Recipient of numerous awards, including the Medal of the National Institute of Social Sciences, 1913; Hayden Memorial Geology Award, Academy of Natural Sciences of Philadelphia, 1914; Albert Gaudry Prize, Geological Society of France, 1918; Darwin Medal, Royal Society, 1918; Cullom Award, American Geological Society, 1919; Wollaston Medal, Geological Society of London, 1926; Daniel Giraud Elliot Medal, 1929. Member and officer of numerous scholarly and professional societies, including the American Academy of Arts and Sciences; American Geological Society; American Philosophical Society (vice president); American Society for the Advancement of Science; American Society of Naturalists (president); American Society of Paleontologists; French Academy of Sciences; New York Zoological Society (president, 1909–24); National Academy of Sciences (councilor); New York Academy of Sciences; Royal Society. Published more than 900 scientific papers, monographs, books, and miscellaneous contributions. Died at his home on the Hudson River in Garrison, New York, 6 November 1935.

Major Publications

1894. *From the Greeks to Darwin: An Outline of the Development of the Evolution Idea.* New York and London: Macmillan.

1907. *Evolution of Mammalian Molar Teeth to and from the Triangular Type.* New York: Macmillan.

1910. *The Age of Mammals in Europe, Asia and North America.* New York: Macmillan.

1915. *Men of the Old Stone Age: Their Environment, Life, and Art.* New York: Scribner's; London: Bell, 1916; 3rd ed., London: Bell, 1918; New York: Scribner's, 1919.

1916. Skeletal adaptations of Ornitholestes, Struthiomimus, Tyrannosaurus. *Bulletin of the American Museum of National History* 35:733–71.

1917. *The Origin and Evolution of Life: On the Theory of Action, Reaction, and Interaction of Energy.* New York: Scribner's; London: Bell, 1918.

1924. *Impressions of Great Naturalists: Reminiscences of Darwin, Huxley, Balfour, Cope, and Others.* New York: Scribner's; 2nd ed., as *Impressions of Great Naturalists: Darwin, Wallace, Huxley, Leidy, Cope, Balfour, Roosevelt, and Others,* New York and London: Scribner's, 1928.

1925. *The Earth Speaks to Bryan.* New York: Scribner's.

1926. *Evolution and Religion in Education: Polemics of the Fundamentalist Controversy of 1922 to 1926.* New York and London: Scribner's.

1929. *The Titanotheres of Ancient Wyoming, Dakota, and Nebraska.* 2 vols. U.S. Geographical Survey, Monograph 55. Washington, D.C.: U.S. Government Printing Office.

1930. *Fifty-two Years of Research, Observation, and Publication, 1877-1929: A Life Adventure in Breadth and Depth.* New York: Scribner's.

1931. *Cope: Master Naturalist*. Princeton, New Jersey: Princeton University Press; London: Oxford University Press.

1936-42. *Proboscidea: A Monograph of the Discovery, Evolution, Migration, and Extinction of the Mastodonts and Elephants of the World*. 2 vols. New York: American Museum Press.

Further Reading

Gregory, W.K. 1938. Biographical Memoir of Henry Fairfield Osborn 1857–1935. *National Academy of Sciences, Biographical Memoirs* 19:53–119.

OSTEICHTHYANS

Recent osteichthyans form the largest and most diverse group of vertebrates chiefly because of the diversity of actinopterygians (ray-finned fishes). Osteichthyans include the ray-finned fishes and the lobe-finned fishes (sarcopterygians). The four living groups of osteichthyans are the ray-finned fishes (29,000 species) and the three groups of sarcopterygians: the coelacanths (one species belonging to Actinistia), the lungfishes (six species of Dipnoi), and the land vertebrates (25,000 species of Tetrapoda). Although it is widely accepted among paleontologists and neontologists that actinopterygians are most closely related to sarcopterygians, the interrelationships among sarcopterygian groups are still debated (Schultze 1994; Cloutier and Ahlberg 1995).

The term "Osteichthyes," or bony fishes, was created by the English zoologist Thomas Henry Huxley in 1880, in opposition to the Chondrichthyes or cartilaginous fishes such as sharks, rays, and skates (batoids), and chimeras (holocephalians). The osteichthyans are referred to generally as the "true bony fishes." As originally defined, Osteichthyes includes only actinopterygians and the piscine sarcopterygians (those forms lacking limbs with digits and having gills throughout life). However, Osteichthes as a group comprises more than just fishes. It is a taxon inclusive of sarcopterygians, and therefore it encompasses all tetrapods, including humans. This broader, cladistic usage of the term was first suggested by the English systematist Peter L. Forey (1980) from The Natural History Museum, London. An alternative solution not adopted here is that of the Canadian ichthyologist Joseph S. Nelson (1994), from the University of Alberta, who proposed the usage of a new term—the Euteleostomi—in order to avoid using the well-known term Osteichthyes in a different way than its original definition.

In contrast to the etymology of the taxon name, the presence of bone is not a distinctive feature of the group because cellular bone is found also in other groups of primitive, non-osteichthyan vertebrates such as heterostracans, osteostracans, thelodonts, placoderms, and acanthodians. Endochondral bone, on the other hand, has been suggested as unique to osteichthyans. The endochondral bone does not only ossify superficially (perichondrally) but also internally (endochondrally). Endochondral bones have cartilaginous precursors during the early developmental stages of an animal. Based on the interpretation of certain paleoichthyologists including Forey, placoderms would have endochondral bones. However, in 1984, the French paleoichthyologist Daniel Goujet from the Muséum National d'Histoire Naturelle of Paris pointed out that endochondral-like ossification was observed only in one specimen of the placoderm *Dicksonosteus arcticus* from the Lower Devonian of Spitsbergen. The uncommon occurrence of endochondral bone in placoderms caused Goujet to question whether it is indeed homologous with osteichthyan endochondral bone.

At the moment, all known osteichthyans are classified exclusively within the two major taxonomic groups, the actinopterygians and the sarcopterygians. Osteichthyan origin dates to the Late Silurian, some 410 million years ago, where they are represented in the fossil record by isolated scales and bone fragments of actinopterygians (Schultze 1992) and sarcopterygians (Zhu and Schultze 1997). During the early Devonian, most major groups of bony fishes were differentiated, and before the end of the Devonian the first land animals had evolved from within the lobe-finned bony fishes.

The Late Silurian osteichthyan *Andreolepis hedei* is known from Sweden, the Baltic regions, Russia, Siberia, and South Wales; *Lophosteus superbus* is known from Saremaa, Estonia; and *Ligulalepis yunnanensis* and *Naxilepis gracilis* have been identified in eastern Yunnan in southern China. Originally described as lophosteiforms (with the exception of the newly described Chinese forms) by the German paleontologist Walter Gross, they were considered as the enigmatic ancestors of all bony fishes. The French paleoichthyologist Philippe Janvier (1978) from the Muséum National d'Histoire Naturelle of Paris suggested that the Lophosteiformes belong to the Actinopterygii or that they represent an unknown class of fishes. These earliest osteichthyans are now classified as actinopterygians by the German paleoichthyologist Hans-Peter Schultze (1992) from the Museum für Naturkunde in Berlin. However, the microvertebrate paleoichthyologist Carole J. Burrow (1995) from the University of Queensland in Australia has suggested some similarities between the ornamentation of the scales of the Lochkovian *Lophosteus incrementus* from central New South Wales and that of placoderm fishes; thus, she has kept the Lophosteiformes as a separate order with possible affinities to Placodermi. With the exception of *Andreolepis* (Janvier 1978) and *Dialipina* (Schultze 1992), these taxa are only known from isolated microscopic scales. The oldest complete bony fishes come from a locality in the district of Mackenzie in northwestern Canada that was recently discovered by Schultze and Steve L. Cumbaa (Canadian Museum of Nature, Ottawa). It has yielded numerous articulated specimens of the primitive actinopterygian *Dialipina* from the Early Devonian. Preceeding the discovery of *Dialipina*, the actinopterygian *Cheirolepis* (Middle Devonian *C. trailli* from Scotland and Late Devonian *C. canadensis* from eastern Canada) was considered to be the most primitive actinopterygian as well as the most primitive known osteichthyan (Pearson 1982).

Among sarcopterygians, the most primitive members are either the coelacanths or the onychodonts according to R. Cloutier and P.E. Ahlberg (1995), or the lungfishes according to Schultze (1994). In 1997, M. Zhu and Schultze described the oldest remains of sarcopterygian fish from the Upper Silurian of southern China. Only isolated cranial fragments and fin spines have been discovered in the Yulongsi and Xishancun Formations. This unnamed taxon is considered to be a phylogenetic intermediate between dipnoans and porolepiforms (Zhu and Schultze 1997). Slightly younger sarcopterygians include the dipnoiform *Powichthys* (Canadian Arctic), *Youngolepis* (China and Viet Nam), and *Diabolepis* and *Psarolepis* (China) from the Lochkovian (lowermost Lower Devonian).

Acanthodians or spiny fishes (Schaeffer 1968; Miles 1973; Pearson 1982, Lauder and Liem 1983, Véran 1988) and placoderms or armored fishes (Forey 1980; Gardiner 1984) are two likely candidates for consideration as the closest relatives to osteichthyans. Both phylogenetic hypotheses are based on the presence of only a few morphological characters that can be observed on basal (primitive) members of the two groups of fishes. Nevertheless, acanthodians are considered to be more closely related to osteichthyans than placoderms. These shared evolutionary novelties include, among other features, (1) the presence of a symplectic (Véran 1988), a small rodlike bone extending from the hyomandibular bone of the hyoid arch to the palatoquadrate and Meckel's bone, thus occupying an important function in jaw suspension; (2) the presence of dermal branchiostegal rays covering the gills laterally (Miles 1973); and (3) the presence of three pairs of otoliths (i.e., lagenar, saccular, and utricular) rather than statoconia, which are minuscule granules of calcite in the labyrinth of the inner ear. Acanthodians and osteichthyans form a large taxon referred to as the Teleostomi. The oldest acanthodians go as far back as the Lower Silurian (the late Llandoverian *Onchus clintoni* from Pennsylvania, U.S.A.). If acanthodians form a monophyletic group (i.e., a group composed of a common ancestor and all its descendants), osteichthyans are expected to be as old as the oldest acanthodians; thus, they must eventually be found in Lower Silurian sediments as well. The recent discoveries of isolated scales and scutes in the Middle Ordovician of central Australia (Young 1997) and from the famous Upper Ordovician Harding Sandstones of western U.S.A. (Sansom et al. 1996) suggest an Ordovician origin of the Chondrichthyes and possibly of other gnathostome (jawed-vertebrate) taxa. Although Ordovician osteichthyans have not been identified as such, their presence would not be too surprising given the presence of other non-osteichthyan gnathostomes.

Because approximately 98 precent of the living vertebrate diversity is composed of osteichthyans, it is difficult to generalize a morphological pattern shared by all extant and extinct species. Many osteichthyan evolutionary novelties are related to the bony structures of their head and gill arches (Schaeffer 1968; Forey 1980; Rosen et al. 1981; Lauder and Liem 1983; Véran 1988). Osteichthyans possess dermal skull bones with descending laminae attaching to the endocranium. These thin ossified blades brace the skull roof against the dorsal side of the braincase. Among the cranial bones, the parietals and postparietals (the two posterior pairs of skull roofing bones) are unique to this group; frequently, these bones are mistakenly referred to as frontals and parietals in the actinopterygian literature. In earlier literature (Pearson 1982) this roofing composition is frequently referred to as a mesomeric skull roof pattern in opposition to a micromeric pattern (meaning a skull covered by small dermal bones). According to the American vertebrate paleontologist Bob Schaeffer (1968), the evolutionary radiation at the base of the Osteichthyes was propelled by selective pressures on the feeding mechanism, which influenced skull architecture, jaw suspension, and breathing efficiency. The lower jaw includes a long dentary and a series of coronoids above the Meckel's cartilage (the latter being the original gnathostome lower jaw). The marginal teeth of the upper and lower jaws are attached to dermal bones located lateral to the palatoquadrate and dorsal to the Meckel's cartilage, respectively. Other cranial bones are unique to bony fishes, such as the premaxilla forming the anterior part of the upper dental arcade; the gill cover, including the operculum dorsally and the subopercula ventrally; and the gular plates bridging the two sides of the lower jaw. In 1983 G.V. Lauder and K.F. Liem suggested that acanthodians had dermal opercular plate(s) covering the gills laterally; however, such a large cheek plate or "opercular" plate is present only in rare advanced climatiid acanthodians from the Middle Devonian and most likely is not homologous to the osteichthyan operculum. Gill arches exhibit a series of changes that include the presence of new endoskeletal elements (e.g., hypohyals, suprapharyngobranchials), the presence of new processes on existing elements (e.g., a posterodorsal process on the ceratohyal articulating with the symplectic), and the reorganization of other branchial structures (e.g., forward orientation of infrapharyngobranchials, articulation of the first and second gill arches with the same basibranchial). In osteichthyans, the hyoid arch apparatus retains its dominant role in aquatic feeding, producing large and rapid volume changes of the oral cavity by means of posteroventral rotation.

Originally, the pectoral girdle of osteichthyans included five dermal bones (Schaeffer 1968; Lauder and Liem 1983)—posttemporal (dorsally), supracleithrum, cleithrum, clavicle, and interclavicle (ventrally)—some of which were lost during the evolution of the different groups. Fin webs are composed of lepidotrichia (segmented fin rays) that are originally composed of bone covered by dentine and enamel; this construction provides an increase in fin mobility and a greater maneuverability during locomotion. The radials of the fins, which are the supporting endochondral elements at the base of the lepidotrichia, never extend to the fin margin. The basal osteichthyan caudal fin was most likely heterocercal (notochord angled upward) without epichordal fin rays. The earliest osteichthyan vertebrae are composed of neural and haemal arches supported by the notochord. Subsequently, vertebrae ossified independently in various osteichthyan lineages; the composition of the centrum differs in various osteichthyan groups. The body of osteichthyans is covered with rhombic scales with a peg-and-socket articulation, in contrast to the more primitive placoid and acanthodian types of scales.

Among the features available for examination only in the living vertebrates, we count the presence of lungs and certain branchial muscles to be characteristic of bony fishes (Forey 1980; Rosen et al. 1981; Lauder and Liem 1983). A swim bladder—an internal organ of buoyancy—rather than a lung is frequently suggested to be a unique character for osteichthyans; however, a swim bladder, which is found exclusively within actinopterygians, is considered by most researchers to be a derivative of the lung. Living basal actinopterygians such as *Polypterus* have lungs.

RICHARD CLOUTIER

See also Actinopterygians; Sarcopterygians

Works Cited

Burrow, C.J. 1995. A new lophosteiform (Osteichthyes) from the Lower Devonian of Australia. *Geobios, mémoire spécial* 19:327–33.

Cloutier, R., and P.E. Ahlberg. 1995. Sarcopterygian interrelationships: How far are we from a phylogenetic consensus? *Geobios, mémoire spécial* 19:241–48.

Forey, P.L. 1980. *Latimeria:* A paradoxical fish. *Proceedings of the Royal Society of London*, ser. B, 208:369–84.

Gardiner, B.G. 1984. The relationships of the palaeoniscid fishes: A review based on new specimens of *Mimia* and *Moythomasia* from the Upper Devonian of Western Australia. *Bulletin of the British Museum (Natural History), Geology* 37:173–428.

Goujet, D. 1984. *Les poissons placodermes du Spitsberg: Arthrodires Dolichothoraci de la Formation de Wood Bay (Dévonien inférieur).* Cahiers de Paléontologie, Section Vertébrés. Paris: Editions du Centre national de la recherche scientifique.

Janvier, P. 1978. On the oldest known teleostome fish *Andreolepis hedei* Gross (Ludlow of Gotland), and the systematic position of the lophosteids. *Eesti NSV Teaduste Akadeemia Toimetised, Geoloogia* 27:88–95.

Lauder, G.V., and K.F. Liem. 1983. The evolution and interrelationships of actinopterygian fishes. *Bulletin of the Museum of Comparative Zoology* 150:95–197.

Miles, R.S. 1973. Relationships of acanthodians. *In* P.H. Greenwood, R.S. Miles, and C. Patterson (eds.), *Interrelationships of Fishes.*

Zoological Journal of the Linnean Society, vol. 53, supplement 1. London: Academic Press.

Nelson, J.S. 1994. *Fishes of the World.* 3rd ed., New York and Chichester: Wiley.

Pearson, D.M. 1982. Primitive bony fishes, with special reference to *Cheirolepis* and palaeonisciform actinopterygians. *Zoological Journal of the Linnean Society* 74:35–67.

Rosen, D.E., P.L. Forey, B.G. Gardiner, and C. Patterson. 1981. Lungfishes, tetrapods, paleontology and plesiomorphy. *Bulletin of the American Museum of Natural History* 167:159–276.

Samson, I.J., M.M. Smith, and M.P. Smith. 1996. Scales of thelodont and shark-like fishes from the Ordovician of Colorado. *Nature* 379:628–30.

Schaeffer, B. 1968. The origin and basic radiation of the Osteichthyes. *In* T. Ørvig (ed.), *Current Problems of Lower Vertebrate Phylogeny: Proceedings of the Fourth Nobel Symposium Held in June 1967 at the Swedish Museum of Natural History (Naturhistoriska riksmuseet) in Stockholm.* Stockholm: Almqvist and Wiksell; New York and London: Interscience.

Schultze, H.-P. 1992. Early Devonian actinopterygians (Osteichthyes, Pisces) from Siberia. *In* E. Mark-Kurik (ed.), *Fossil Fishes as Living Animals.* Tallinn: Academy of Sciences of Estonia.

———. 1994. Comparison of hypotheses on the relationships of sarcopterygians. *Systematic Biology* 43:155–73.

Véran, M. 1988. *Les éléments accessoires de l'arc hyoïdien des poissons téléostomes (Acanthodiens et Osteichthyens) fossiles et actuels.* Mémoires du Muséum national d'histoire naturelle, ser. C, vol. 54. Paris: Éditions du Muséum.

Young, G.C. 1997. Ordovician microvertebrate remains from the Amadeus Basin, central Australia. *Journal of Vertebrate Paleontology* 17:1–25.

Zhu, M., and H.-P. Schultze. 1997. The oldest sarcopterygian fish. *Lethaia* 30:293–304.

Further Reading

Maisey, J.G. 1996. *Discovering Fossil Fishes.* New York: Holt.

Paxton, J.R., and W.N. Eschmeyer (eds.). 1994. *Encyclopedia of Fishes.* San Diego, California: Academic Press.

OWEN, RICHARD

English, 1804–92

Richard Owen, the anatomist and paleontologist, was born 20 July 1804 in Lancaster and died 18 December 1892 in London. Owen's lifelong interest in the science of anatomy was sparked while he was apprenticed to a surgeon. His talents were quickly recognized while studying at Edinburgh University. He was directed to study and work in London, where he settled for the rest of his life. Although he initially established a practice as a surgeon, he soon was employed by the Royal College of Surgeons as assistant curator to their main collection of specimens. One of his noteworthy assignments during this period was that of acting as guide when the great French anatomist Georges Cuvier visited the museum in 1830. The following year, Owen reciprocated with a visit to Paris.

In 1836 Owen was appointed Hunterian professor of the Royal College of Surgeons, and also succeeding as conservator of the museum in 1842. He continued in these posts until 1856, when he assumed the position of superintendent of the natural history departments of the British Museum. Initially, these departments were designated as a sub-branch of the museum's premises in Bloomsbury. Eventually, however, owing to Owen's persuasion and the support he elicited from the prime minister William Gladstone, the departments were transferred to a new natural history museum he commissioned in South Kensington. In 1884 Owen retired. The recipient of many awards and honors, he died after a lengthy illness at his home in Richmond Park, in a lodge granted to him as a royal favor by Queen Victoria.

It is difficult, even today, to write in a neutral, let alone sympathetic, fashion about Richard Owen. It was his fate to be cast in the role of Beelzebub by the party that supported Charles Darwin, particularly by Darwin's chief lieutenant, his "bulldog," Thomas Henry Huxley. Owen and Huxley clashed violently many times, most notably in 1860 at the Oxford meeting of the British Association for the Advancement of Science. In Huxley's view, no motive was too base to ascribe to Owen, no act too vile to suppose that he committed. As a result, before addressing his scientific activities, it is important to understand Owen's character. Although he could be a difficult man to deal with, he had the capacity to establish lasting friendships. He worked diligently and garnered much respect. However his work may be judged—whether seminal or dated and of little lasting value—the fact is that he was a significant figure in his day and played a critical role in founding what is still today one of the most prominent museums in London.

Owen first drew attention in 1832 with a memoir published on the giant marine invertebrate, the Pearly Nautilus. In his analysis, Owen not only modified Cuvier's scheme for classifying living things; Owen also provided stimulating functional speculation about the ways in which the organism could control its depth and velocity through water. During this same time, he already was demonstrating the broad range of interests that were to characterize his activities throughout his long life. For example, he performed detailed dissections on all of the esoteric animals that died in the gardens of the London Zoological Society. His work yielded multiple benefits, notably through detailed studies of what were generally regarded as the most primitive of mammals—the monotremes (egg-laying mammals) and marsupials (mammals that rear their young in a pouch). Years of work on the Zoological Society specimens, supported by the study of many more specimens gathered by eager correspondents from around the world, enabled Owen to write major treatises on the nature and relations of these unusual animals.

Many other animals of all kinds and descriptions also came under Owen's knife. By the late 1830s Owen began to show considerable interest in the nature of the higher primates and their relationships to humans. He was able to use zoo specimens for these studies, as well as those frequently sent to him by African explorers. Owen acknowledged significant relationships between humans and apes; however, on anatomical grounds—grounds essentially concerning the brain—he argued for a taxonomic distinction between the two groups. This assertion formed the basis of his conflict with Huxley around the time that Darwin published *On the Origin of Species* (1859). Owen argued that the human brain is not only quantitatively different from the apes (the human brain is considerably larger), but that it is also qualitatively different. Owen contended that one part, a structure called the hippocampus minor, is distinctive of human brains. Huxley refuted Owen (correctly, as it would seem), saying that Owen had been misled by the preservation quality of the specimens on which he worked. An amusing account of this dispute appears in the children's story *The Water Babies* (1863) by Charles Kingsley. That this issue is featured comically in such a venue indicates how public and important these disputes were at the time.

Fossils, in themselves, were not Owen's primary interest, although with his midlife move to the British Museum, his inten-

tions and activities became more exclusively paleontological. This does not, however, deny his early involvement with the fossil record. He described in some detail many of the specimens that the young Darwin brought back from the *H.M.S. Beagle* voyage. (Until Huxley effectively severed all relations between Owen and the Darwinian party, Owen and Darwin had not only been reasonably friendly, but had demonstrated mutual professional respect. It is significant that the ambitious and knowledgeable Darwin had turned to Owen for aid instead of to a more established figure, like William Buckland, the professor of geology at Oxford.)

One of Owen's earliest interests in the fossil record was the nature of birds and their origins. He performed a remarkable anatomical inference after receiving a piece of broken bone from New Zealand. Owen declared that the piece represented a part of an extinct ostrich-type bird. Although editors accepted his essay for publication somewhat reluctantly, it was not until the early 1840s that he was vindicated completely—when whole specimens were unearthed and sent to England. Even within the time span of human settlement, New Zealand had been the home of huge birds (the most celebrated of which was the moa), that occupied the ecological niche filled elsewhere in the world by carnivorous mammals.

Owen's interest in reptiles matched that of birds, and he can be credited with distinguishing one group of these beasts that deserved a name to themselves. The "dinosaurs," as Owen called them, immediately grabbed the public imagination. Large dinosaur models were created for the Great Exhibition of 1851, and a celebrated dinner party was held in the bowels of the reconstruction of one of these prehistoric giants. It has been suggested, with some plausibility, that there was an ulterior motive in Owen's promotion of the dinosaurs, that he wanted to draw attention to the sophisticated nature of many extinct organic forms. His efforts were diametrically opposed to those thinkers who, even in the 1840s, argued for the "upward" progression in life from simple to complex forms, leading ultimately to the development of the human form, a process, perhaps fueled not by God's providence, but by unbroken law. In other words, dinosaurs were displayed as evidence against the theory of evolution!

Whether there is any truth in this suggestion will never be known. Although Owen equivocated about the progressive nature of the fossil record, especially in public, there is little doubt that he accepted the evidence for such a progression, as did most other thinkers of the day, except the geologist Charles Lyell. Indeed, as the years went by, Owen became more committed to this idea. Owen's position on the question of evolution is complicated and should not be prejudged. On the one hand, Owen was the great opponent of the Darwinians; on the other, his basic philosophy of nature, a philosophy that governed all of his biological activities, demonstrates the opposite.

Owen was given the honorary title of the "British Cuvier," and some of his triumphs in functional restoration (notably the giant birds of New Zealand) earned him the right to this title. However, the nineteenth-century German morphologists (those who studied shape and struction of organisms) influenced Owen even more. In particular, *Naturphilosophen,* written by the leading radical thinker Lorenz Oken, convinced Owen that certain transcendental archetypes (akin to Platonic forms) provide the basic design for all living organisms. The task of the anatomist is to discern, articulate, and present the nature of these archetypes. Owen believed that he had made considerable progress in unraveling the vertebrate archetype. His work not only demonstrated that there are isomorphisms ("homologies" or similarities, a word which Owen introduced) between the parts of individual bodies, but also that these isomorphisms exist between animals of different species—the arm of man, the foreleg of the horse, the flipper of the seal, the wing of the bat, the paw of the mole. Each of these appendages has a different function, yet all are built according to the same plan.

Although the theory of archetypical forms is rather static, a dynamic underpinning runs through *Naturphilosophen,* and for Owen, in his turn, the history of life is in some sense an unfurling, or development of the underlying idealistic forms of organic life. In this respect, the theory is "evolutionary" in a way. Although publicly Owen fed ammunition to the opponents of evolution (notably Cambridge geologist Adam Sedgwick and Cambridge philosopher William Whewell), privately he sent notes of encouragement and agreement to those who publicly supported evolution. Both the anonymous author of *Vestiges of the Natural History of Creation* (in actuality the Scottish publisher Robert Chambers) and the brazen Herbert Spencer (who had begun to argue publicly for evolution in the early 1850s) received friendly, positive letters. In another sense, however, the German position is far from evolution, insofar as evolution is understood in the material sense of the physical transformation of one set of organisms into another set of different organisms. According to *Naturphilosophen,* life was developmental; however, the actual fact of evolution was incidental and not truly significant. It was development of the *idea* that counted. Owen was clearly influenced by this line of thought. In a public lecture he gave in 1849, *On the Nature of Limbs,* Owen's vision of life's history focused primarily on the ever-greater manifestation of the archetype, regardless of how it came about:

> The archetypal idea was manifested in the flesh, under divers [sic] such modification, upon this planet, long prior to the existence of those animal species that actually exemplify it.
>
> To what natural laws or secondary causes the orderly succession and progression of such organic phaenomena [sic] may have been committed we as yet are ignorant. But if, without derogation [sic] of the Divine power, we may conceive the existence of such ministers, and personify them by the term 'Nature,' we learn from the past history of our globe that she has advanced with slow and stately steps, guided by the archetypal light, amidst the wreck of worlds, from the first embodiment of the Vertebrate idea under its old Ichthyic vestment, until it became arrayed in the glorious garb of the Human form. (Owen 1849)

The advent of Darwinism—the theory of evolution through natural selection—challenged Owen's idealism. Apparently, he was torn between the desire to repudiate the whole materialistic approach, arguing that idealism alone is adequate, and the inclination to accept the concept of material evolution. Indeed, Owen was not above suggesting that he had conceived the idea of natural selection before Darwin. It is interesting to speculate where he would have ended had he not been embroiled in controversy with the Darwinians. There were many reasons for the controversy. In part it was simply the result of Owen's personal rivalry with Huxley, especially for the desirable posts and other benefits in mid-Victorian science. Another factor was the idealism/materialism divide, which Owen proved very reluctant to cross all the way to a world explained by a fully natural mechanism such as selection. And part of the controversy may well be fictional. After the Darwinians seized power—as they did in organizations such as the Royal Society—the battles with Owen and his opposition to evolution probably grew in the telling.

Ultimately, Owen ended by sitting on the fence between idealism and material evolution. Ultimately, he slipped publicly onto the side of evolutionism. However, he did so with provisions that resulted in a version of evolutionism that today would be called "vitalism." (This theory explains that progressive change occurs through a basic life force that drives evolution "upward.") One can praise Owen for going so far in his thinking or condemn him for not going far enough. Nonetheless, he certainly should be recalled as the most important comparative anatomist in Britain in the nineteenth century, as well as the key figure in the founding of the great natural history museum of South Kensington.

MICHAEL RUSE

Biography

Born in Lancaster, 20 July 1804. Began surgeon's apprenticeship, 1820; began medical education at University of Edinburgh, 1824; transferred to St. Bartholomew's Hospital, London, 1825; qualified as a surgeon, Royal College of Surgeons, 1826. Became assistant conservator, Hunter Museum, Royal College of Surgeons, 1827; Hunterian Professor, Royal College of Surgeons, 1836–56; became conservator, Hunterian Museum, Royal College of Surgeons, 1842; appointed Fullerian Professor of Comparative Anatomy and Physiology, Royal Institution, 1858; superintendent, natural history departments, British Museum, 1856–84; helped found the Natural History Museum, South Kensington, 1871. Elected fellow, Royal Society of London, 1834; awarded Wollaston Medal, Geological Society of London, 1838; became member, French Académie des Sciences, 1839; awarded Royal Medal of the Royal Society of London, 1846; awarded Copley Medal of the Royal Society of London, 1851; awarded Prix Cuvier, French Académie des Sciences, 1857; became president, British Association for the Advancement of Science, 1858; created Knight of the Order of Bath, 1884. Died in London, 18 December 1892.

Major Publications

1834. On the generation of the marsupial animals, with a description of the impregnated uterus of the kangaroo. *Philosophical Transactions* 124:333–64.

[1837.] *The Hunterian Lectures in Comparative Anatomy, May and June 1837.* P.R. Sloan (ed.), Chicago: University of Chicago Press, 1992.

1840–45. *Odontography; or, A Treatise on the Comparative Anatomy of the Teeth.* London: Bailliére.

1846a. *Lectures on the Comparative Anatomy and Physiology of the Vertebrate Animals, Delivered at the Royal College of Surgeons of England, in 1844 and 1846.* London: Longman; 2nd ed., 1855.

1846b. *A History of British Fossil Mammals and Birds.* London: Van Voorst.

1848. *On the Archetype and Homologies of the Vertebrate Skeleton.* London: Taylor.

1849. *On the Nature of Limbs.* London: Van Voorst.

1849–84. *A History of British Fossil Reptiles.* 4 vols. London: Cassell.

1860. Darwin on the Origin of Species. *Edinburgh Review* 111:487–532. [Published anonymously.]

1866–68. *On the Anatomy and Physiology of Vertebrates.* 3 vols. London: Longman, Green.

1894. With R.S. Owen. *The Life of Richard Owen.* 2 vols. London: Murray; New York: Appleton; 2nd ed., London: Murray, 1895.

Further Reading

Desmond, A. 1989. *The Politics of Evolution: Morphology, Medicine and Reform in Radical London.* Chicago: University of Chicago Press.

Rupke, N.A. 1994. *Richard Owen: Victorian Naturalist.* New Haven, Connecticut: Yale University Press.

Ruse, M. 1979. *The Darwinian Revolution: Science Red in Tooth and Claw.* Chicago: University of Chicago Press.

P

PACHYCEPHALOSAURS

Pachycephalosaurs ("thick-headed reptiles") are a poorly known group of bipedal ornithischian (bird-hipped) dinosaurs found in Cretaceous deposits of Asia, North America, and Europe. Although remains of many ornithischian dinosaurs are frequently abundant, those of pachycephalosaurs are relatively rare and are composed largely of isolated skull domes. Most dinosaurs have a thin roof of bone (less than two centimeters) overlying the braincase. Pachycephalosaurs, however, tend to have thickened domes in this region, giving their skulls a distinctive rounded profile (Figure 1). These structures also give the illusion of increased brain volume, yet they are solid, composed of the fused bones at the top front and sides of the head, and brain size is small. The domes are frequently rimmed with spikes and nodules that, in some forms, extend onto the snout. The arrangement of the spikes and nodules varies according to species.

Pachycephalosaurs have small, leaf-shaped teeth with serrated margins (edges) that were probably used to slice plant material. The presence of large olfactory lobes (organs for sense of smell) may signify a heightened sense of smell (Maryanska 1990). Relatively short forelimbs and well-developed hind limbs indicate that dome-headed dinosaurs traveled on two legs. Limb proportions resemble those of bipedal ornithopods, and it is thought that at least the smaller pachycephalosaurs could run well. Dome-headed dinosaurs have long tails reinforced at the farthest point by a basketwork of ossified (bony) tendons; the tails probably served to counterbalance the head and trunk during locomotion.

Pachycephalosaurs range considerably in size, from smaller-bodied forms one to three meters in length (e.g., *Stegoceras, Prenocephale*) to the giant *Pachycephalosaurus,* from the Late Cretaceous of North America, approximately eight meters in length. Although relatively similar in overall morphology (shape and structure), pachycephalosaurs also show great variation in the size and shape of their skull domes and associated ornamentation, ranging from high-domed forms with large spikes, such as the North American *Stygimoloch,* to relatively flat-headed, unadorned species such as the Mongolian *Homalocephale.* The undisputed king of dome-heads, however, is *Pachycephalosaurus,* with a knob-studded skull dome more than 25 centimeters thick. Species for which multiple domes are represented (e.g. *Stegoceras validum*) demonstrate that there was a large degree of variation in the crania within the species as well, perhaps related to physical differences between males and females (Maryanska, 1990).

Owing in large part to a relative paucity of fossil material, the evolutionary relationships of dome-headed dinosaurs are enigmatic. The earliest known pachycephalosaur specimens were recovered in 1902 in Montana and placed in the category of the genus (group; plural, genera) *Troödon,* known only from isolated teeth. The first skull and partial skeleton of a pachycephalosaur were discovered about a quarter century later, and this find was also classified as *Troödon* (Gilmore 1924). It was not until the 1940s, with the discovery of more complete specimens, that investigators recognized *Troödon* to be a theropod dinosaur and therefore not closely related to pachycephalosaurs. Our knowledge of dome-headed dinosaurs, including their origins and relationships, remained sparse until the late 1970s, when several new genera were discovered in China and Mongolia (Maryanska 1990).

A number of features (e.g., presence of a bone at the tip of the lower jaw) clearly indicate that pachycephalosaurs are ornithischians, although various authors have argued that they are most closely allied with stegosaurs, ceratopsians, ankylosaurs, or (typically) ornithopods. Most recently, in the first comprehensive analysis of historical relationships within Ornithischia, P.C. Sereno (1986) united Pachycephalosauria and Ceratopsia in a new larger group, Marginocephalia, characterized by a bony shelf, or margin, composed of bones that project rearward from the skull.

Approximately 13 genera of pachycephalosaurs have been described, and these are generally subdivided into two types—flat-headed and dome-headed—that may or may not represent natural groups (Sues and Galton 1987; Maryanska 1990; Sereno 1986). The less derived (specialized) flat-headed forms (e.g., *Homalocephale*) retain two circular openings on top of the skull (supratemporal fenestrae) as do other ornithischians, whereas in dome-headed forms (e.g., *Pachycephalosaurus*) these openings are obscured or completely roofed over by the expansion of the dome to the rear.

Flat-headed pachycephalosaurs are thus far restricted to the Late Cretaceous of Mongolia and China. The more diverse dome-

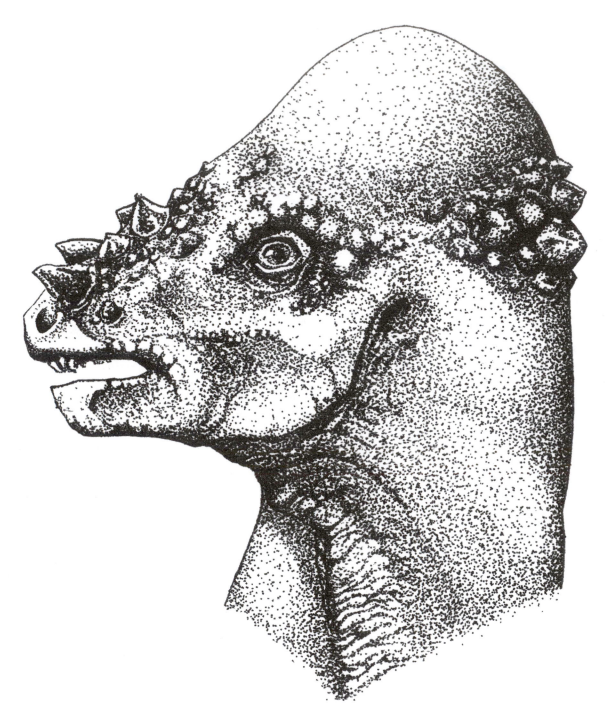

Figure 1. Head reconstruction of *Pachycephalosaurus*. Artwork by William Zucconi.

heads have a broader distribution over time, recognized from the Early to Late Cretaceous, and a broader geographic distribution, including Mongolia, China, western North America, and England (Sues and Galton 1987; Maryanska 1990). A single aberrant pachycephalosaur, *Majungatholus,* has been described from the Late Cretaceous of Madagascar on the basis of an isolated skull dome.

Recent discoveries, however, indicate conclusively that *Majungatholus* is in fact a theropod dinosaur, so once again there is no evidence that a pachycephalosaur lived in the southern hemisphere.

The massive skull roof of pachycephalosaurs has led investigators to speculate about its function as a shock absorber in head-to-head combat between members of the same species, probably in competition for mates (Galton 1970). Reconstructions of this head-butting behavior are now commonplace in popular books, television documentaries, and museum displays. However, such violent head-on confrontations are highly improbable, for at least two reasons. First, among living horned ungulates, head-to-head contests, particularly head-to-head ramming, are restricted to a relatively few, highly derived species. Far more common, and primitive, are confrontations to the side, in which the head is used to deliver blows to the flanks of an opponent. Second, and more significantly, pachycephalosaur skulls are poorly designed for head-to-head collisions since the rounded domes would tend to slip past each other on impact, potentially resulting in severe spinal cord injuries, as well as injuries of other types. During the evolutionary history of this group, the skull roof in at least some lineages became further enlarged and high-domed, which increased even more the likelihood of dangerous, glancing blows during head-on contests. Given these two points, it is much more probable that dome-headed dinosaurs engaged not in head-bashing but rather in flank-butting. The latter is supported by at least one pachycephalosaur specimen, which shows evidence of broken and rehealed ribs.

As with structures such as the horns and frills of ceratopsians and the crests of hadrosaurs, it is likely that the ornamented domes of pachycephalosaurs functioned in the competition for mates, acting as visual signals as well as weapons. If so, the great variation seen in these domes may be owing to evolutionary forces such as sexual selection operating to increase reproductive success. This would explain in part why each species tends to be characterized by its own specific type of dome and why we see a large degree of variability in these features within species.

SCOTT D. SAMPSON

Works Cited

Galton, P.M. 1970. Pachycephalosaurids: Dinosaurian battering rams. *Discovery* 6:23–32.

Gilmore, C.W. 1924. On *Troödon validus,* an ornithopodus dinosaur from the Belly River Cretaceous of Alberta, Canada. *University of Alberta Bulletin* 1:1–43.

Maryanska, T. 1990. Pachycephalosauria. *In* D.B. Weishampel, P. Dodson, and H. Osmolska (eds.), *The Dinosauria.* Berkeley: University of California Press.

Sereno, P.C. 1986. Phylogeny of the bird-hipped dinosaurs (Order Ornithischia). *National Geographic Society Research* 2:234–56.

Sues, H.-D., and P.M. Galton. 1987. Anatomy and classification of the North American Pachycephalosauria (Dinosauria: Ornithischia). *Palaeontographica* A 198:183–90.

Further Reading

Colbert, E.H. 1955. *Evolution of the Vertebrates.* New York: Wiley; 4th ed., New York: Wiley-Liss, 1991.

Fastovsky, D.E., and D.B. Weishampel. 1996. *The Evolution and Extinction of the Dinosaurs.* Cambridge and New York: Cambridge University Press.

Galton, P.M., and H.-D. Sues. 1983. New data on pachycephalosaurid dinosaurs (Reptilia: Ornithischia) from North America. *Canadian Journal of Earth Sciences* 20:462–73.

Maryanska, T., and H. Osmólska. 1974. Results of the Polish-Mongolian Expeditions. Part 5, Pachycephalosauria, a new suborder of ornithischian dinosaurs. *Palaeontologica Polonica* 30:45–102.

Sues, H.-D. 1978. Functional morphology of the dome in pachycephalosaurid dinosaurs. *Neues Jahrbuch für Geologie und Paläontologie, Monatshefte* 1978:459–72.

PALAEANODONTS

The palaeanodonts are an uncommon and highly unusual group of extinct small- to medium-sized mammals specialized for digging. Although known to occur in Europe, the group is predominantly North American, found in deposits ranging in age from Late Paleocene to Early Oligocene, approximately 55 to 30 million years ago (Rose and Emry 1993). Despite the relative rarity of palaeanodont fossils, the skeletal anatomy of the group is fairly well known. Those specimens that do exist are unusually well preserved, perhaps owing to the subterranean habits of these animals. Unfortunately, the anatomy of palaeanodonts is so unusual that it has been difficult to ally them with better-known groups of mammals.

The first fragmentary specimens were linked with the primates and the monotremes (egg-laying mammals such as the platypus) (Simpson 1931; Rose and Emry 1983). It also has been suggested that palaeanodonts derive from the Pantolestidae, a group of primitive mammals from the Paleocene of North America (Rose and Emry 1993). Since the early part of this century, however, most researchers have considered the palaeanodonts to

be related in some fashion to the Edentata, a group that includes members of two modern orders of digging mammals, the Xenarthra (the South American armadillos, sloths, anteaters, and their relatives) and the Pholidota (the pangolins of the Old World tropics). The precise nature of the relationship between Palaeanodonta and Edentata has never been clear and remains to this day a matter of considerable controversy. Some researchers advocate a close link between palaeanodonts and xenarthrans, some between palaeanodonts and pholidotans, and others have suggested that palaeanodonts are a distant relative to both groups (Rose and Emry 1993).

Although the higher-level affinities of the Paleanodonta remain shrouded in mystery, the relationships among the various members within the group are relatively well-understood. There are 12 described genera divided into two families: the Metacheiromyidae and the Epoicotheriidae. The only genus that does not fit neatly into either family is *Amelotabes*, the oldest and most primitive palaeanodont, represented by a single incomplete lower jaw from the Late Paleocene Polecat Bench Formation of

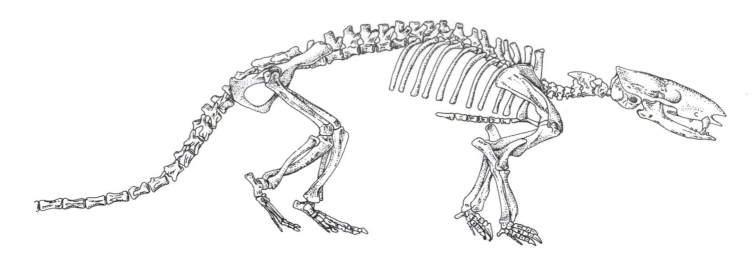

Figure 1. *Metacheiromys tatusia* (Mammalia, Palaeanodonta) skeletal reconstruction. From Simpson (1931), courtesy of the American Museum of Natural History.

Wyoming. *Amelotabes* displays the anatomical features that characterize palaeanodonts as a group: a large triangular canine tooth, simplified premolar and molar teeth with low cusps and thin tooth enamel, and a peculiar protuberance on the inside of the lower jaw, but it lacks the specializations of either the metacheiromyids or epoicotheriids (Rose et al. 1991).

The metacheiromyids were the first palaeanodonts to be described, and they remain the best-known family within the group. Their modifications for digging are less extreme than those of the epoicotheriids, but their dentition is more specialized. In the metacheiromyids, the teeth behind the canines are very simple, and the enamel layer and the tooth cusps are nearly or completely absent. These animals also tend to have a reduced number of premolars and molars, perhaps replacing the more posterior teeth with a horny pad like the one present in the modern duck-billed platypus (Simpson 1931; Rose et al. 1991). The family includes four genera. The oldest, *Propalaeanodon*, is Late Paleocene in age. The youngest, *Metacheiromys*, is found in middle Eocene deposits (Rose et al. 1991).

Metacheiromys is the best known palaeanodont, since it is represented by several complete skeletons (Figure 1). It was about 0.5 meters long, with a short neck, short robust limbs, and a long tail. Although specialized for digging, this animal was likely a burrower, resting and raising young below ground but foraging above ground. It may have been covered by scales, like an armadillo or a pangolin, but *Metacheiromys* was not armored like armadillos. The animal had large canines with distinctive cutting surfaces and a long tongue that could protrude a considerable distance from the mouth. There were only two postcanine teeth, but ridges on the upper and lower jaw indicate the presence of a large horny pad for crushing prey. The object of this distinctive feeding apparatus is not clear, although it may have

been used to acquire various types of invertebrates found in the soil and leaf litter. *Metacheiromys* was probably a fairly slow animal with poorly developed vision; it probably located its underground prey with a highly developed sense of smell (Simpson 1931).

The epoicotheriids are the more diverse of the two paleanodont families, including seven genera. They range in age from early Eocene to early Oligocene (Rose et al. 1991). Epoicotheriids are smaller than metacheiromyids and have a less specialized dentition that lacks the toothless regions in the back of the tooth row. However, these animals had among the most extraordinary skeletal specializations for digging known in any mammal living or extinct (Rose and Emry 1983).

The Oligocene epoicotheriids *Xenocranium* and *Epoicotherium* (Figure 2) were almost certainly subterranean, rarely if ever emerging above ground. They lacked functional eyes but had remarkable ear adaptations for hearing underground. Like some living golden moles from southern Africa, the tiny ear ossicles which transmit sound from the eardrum to the inner ear, were tremendously enlarged, enhancing their ability to perceive the low-frequency sounds that penetrate underground. *Xenocranium* and *Epoicotherium* had fused neck vertebrae, powerful neck muscles, and broad, flat, triangular skulls. It is likely that their broad snout was covered with a leathery pad. The heads of these animals were important digging tools, helping them not only to loosen soil but also to compact soil on the roof of their underground burrows. These two palaeanodonts also had huge bony crests on the shoulder blades and the bones of the forearm, indicating strongly muscled limbs. Enlarged claws on the forepaws were undoubtedly the primary digging tools. Stout hind limbs were used to push loosened soil from underneath to behind the body (Rose and Emry 1983).

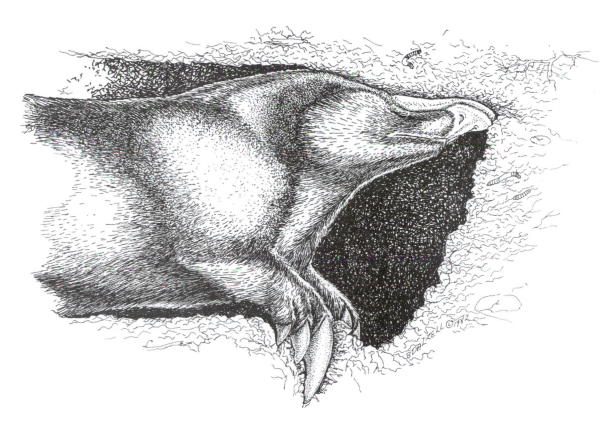

Figure 2. *Xenocranium* (Mammalia, Palaeanodonta) life restoration. From Rose and Emry (1983). Courtesy of Bonnie Dalzell, M.A.

For reasons that remain unknown, the metacheiromyids became extinct before the end of the Eocene. The epoicotheriids persisted longer. The youngest are contemporaneous with the oldest true moles, the proscalopines. However, while the true moles persist to the present day, epoicotheriids are unknown after the early Oligocene. It is possible that competition from these early moles led to the extinction of the epoicotheriids (Rose and Emry 1983) and with them, the final disappearance of palaeanodonts.

TIMOTHY J. GAUDIN

See also Burrowing Adaptations in Vertebrates; Pangolins; Xenarthrans

Works Cited

Rose, K.D., and R.J. Emry. 1983. Extraordinary fossorial adaptations in the Oligocene palaeanodonts *Epoicotherium* and *Xenocranium* (Mammalia). *Journal of Morphology* 175:33–56.

——. 1993. Relationships of Xenarthra, Pholidota, and fossil "edentates": The morphological evidence. *In* F.S. Szalay, M.J. Novacek, and M.C. McKenna (eds.), *Mammal Phylogeny*. New York and London: Springer-Verlag.

Rose, K.D., L. Krishtalka, and R.K. Stucky. 1991. Revision of the Wind River faunas, Early Eocene of Central Wyoming, Part 11, Paleanodonta (Mammalia). *Annals of the Carnegie Museum* 60:63–82.

Simpson, G.G. 1931. *Metacheiromys* and the Edentata. *Bulletin of the American Museum of Natural History* 59:295–381.

PALEOBIOGEOGRAPHY

Paleobiogeography is the study of the ancient geographic distribution of organisms and how they got to be where they are found today. Until recently, there was not much rigorous study or analysis of the methods of paleobiogeography. In the past, most paleobiogeography was done on a very casual, informal basis—the distribution of the organisms was mapped, and an explanation was concocted to explain this distribution. In recent years, the theory and methodology of biogeography has developed greatly, so now there are competing schools of theoretical biogeography as there are in systematics and other fields.

Such research begins with maps of biogeographic provinces. Some provinces, such as the realms recognized for terrestrial animals, correspond roughly to the boundaries of continents. Most of North America is the Nearctic Realm; South America is part of the Neotropical Realm; Eurasia makes up most of the Palearctic Realm; Australia comprises its own realm. The exceptions are areas of marked ecological change, such as the Sahara Desert, which separates the sub-Saharan Ethiopian Realm from North Africa (which is climatically more like the rest of the Mediterranean), or the tropical rain forests of Southeast Asia or Central America, which are distinct from the temperate regions of North America or Eurasia.

In the case of plant biomes, however, there are much finer-scale subdivisions. Plants are much more sensitive to variations in temperature and precipitation, so their biomes are subdivided into latitudinally defined climatic belts. For example, there are distinct regions of tundra, evergreen coniferous forest, deciduous forest, grasslands, deserts, and rain forest that correspond to certain latitudes, regardless of which continent they are found on. Clearly, the primary controlling factor is temperature, with the highest temperatures found in the tropics and the lowest found near the poles. Another important factor is precipitation, which is also latitudinally controlled.

Dispersalist Biogeography

Before the scientific understanding of plate tectonics, biogeographers looked at faunal and floral provinces as static entities on static continents. The chief problems were defining the province and its boundaries and determining how adjacent provinces had interacted and how organisms could disperse from one to another. This school of biogeography was later called dispersalism, since it assumes that land masses are relatively stable and that most biogeography can be explained by the dispersal abilities of organisms.

In dispersalist biogeography, the first task is to evaluate the similarity and/or differences between regions. For example, the mammals of North America are fairly similar across the continent, allowing for differences in climate and vegetation. At the ordinal level, 100 percent of the mammals in New York also occur in Oregon, and 83 percent of the mammals in Oregon also occur in New York. The similarity decreases slightly at the level of families, genera, and species (which are more restricted in geographic range), but it is clear that as a whole, temperate North America is faunally homogeneous, with few barriers to dispersal. This is called a corridor, since there are few or no barriers to dispersal, and organisms can move about freely within suitable habitats.

When one compares regions, however, the barriers to dispersal, such as oceans or mountain ranges, rapidly decrease the faunal similarity. For example, there are striking differences between the mammals of Eurasia and those of North America (separated by the Bering Sea) or between those of North and South America (connected only by the Isthmus of Panama). As we look at this pattern in the geologic past, the contrast is even more striking. For example, during the Ice Age, the Bering Strait was a major land bridge, allowing many "Old World" mammals (such as mammoths and bison) to migrate from Eurasia to North America,

and "New World" mammals (such as horses and camels) to migrate to Eurasia. However, the Bering route was not a freeway. For some reason, several Old World natives (such as woolly rhinos and pigs) never migrated to North America, even though woolly rhinos were just as cold-adapted as woolly mammoths. Likewise, some North American native animals (such as pronghorns and peccaries) never migrated to the Old World, although pronghorns live side by side with bison and other Old World immigrants. Such a selective route is called a filter bridge, since it allows some animals to pass, while others do not cross.

The most difficult route for dispersal is crossing major barriers, such as large oceans. In these cases, the probabilities of dispersal are very low, and any organism that manages to cross does so under unusual circumstances. The islands in the middle of the ocean are thousands of kilometers from land, so their only inhabitants are organisms that blew in on a major storm or rafted there on floating vegetation. Hawaii, for example, has no native mammals (except for bats) nor any reptiles, amphibians, or freshwater fishes, so all its land animals (especially birds, snails, and insects) were blown in by storms and have since evolved into a distinctive native fauna that is endemic (restricted) to Hawaii. Such a low-probability transport is called a sweepstakes route, since its odds of success are about the same as winning a sweepstakes or the lottery—it is highly improbable, but over the long span of geologic time it will happen sooner or later.

Biogeographers have documented many remarkable ways in which organisms can disperse across large barriers. Large rafts of floating vegetation with small mammals clinging to them have been found at sea, apparently launched when a major river flooded. These are capable of transporting small mammals across oceans, although the odds of success are decidedly low. Small land invertebrates, such as snails, have been known to be carried long distances in the mud on birds' feet. Land plants have remarkable ways of getting across oceans. Many different seeds float long distances or fly in the wind for thousands of kilometers. The coconut's hard seed is adapted for floating long distances to a new island, where the pounding of the surf finally cracks the shell and allows it to germinate near the beach. In addition to birds and bats, many other land animals also can cross enormous distances in the wind. Young spiders disperse from their mother's web by releasing strands of silk as a parachute or balloon and letting the wind carry them wherever it will.

In the marine realm, the problem of dispersal is the mirror image of that on land. What are considered bridges to land animals are barriers to the dispersal of marine life. For example, when the Panamanian land bridge closed in the Pliocene, it allowed mammals to migrate between the Americas, but it shut off the connection between Caribbean and Pacific marine faunas, which have since diverged. In addition, the ocean is not homogeneous but divided into provinces and water masses defined by temperature, salinity, and other properties. Nevertheless, most marine organisms have mechanisms for spreading over much of the ocean. Most have planktonic larvae that are released by the millions, allowing them to float wherever the currents take them and settle in any unoccupied spot. Others, such as jellyfishes, sea turtles, and bony fishes, can migrate or float huge distances across the ocean under the right circumstances. The principles of dispersal in the marine realm are similar to those on land, although there are also important differences.

South America provides an excellent example of many of these concepts. During most of the Cenozoic, this continent was isolated from the rest of the world. It had no direct land connection to North America until the Pliocene, and it had lost its supercontinent connection to Antarctica sometime in the Oligocene. Consequently, it has a highly endemic fauna of land mammals and large predatory birds, most of which are only distantly related to animals on other continents. Sometime in the Cretaceous it began to lose its faunal connection to the landmasses that had made up the supercontinent Gondwanaland, so it ended up with only a few native groups: the edentates (sloths, armadillos, anteaters, and their kin), marsupials (which evolved into the main carnivorous groups in the absence of placental carnivores, including remarkable hyenalike, wolflike, and saber-toothed marsupials), and archaic hoofed mammals (which evolved in parallel to resemble horses, hippos, camels, giraffes, antelopes, mastodonts, and many other ecological niches found on other continents). A few South American natives (such as the arctostylopids, an ungulate family) managed to get to North America and China, and a few North American taxa (groups; singular, taxon) (such as the pantodonts, an order of large, tusked herbivores) seemed to get from Asia and North America to South America in the Paleocene, so there was the possibility of some sweepstakes dispersal, or island hopping, during the Paleocene, but the continent was isolated through most of the early Cenozoic.

In the Oligocene two more mammalian groups appeared in South America: the New World monkeys and the caviomorph rodents (today represented by chinchillas, guinea pigs, capybaras, agoutis, cavies, and their kin). Both groups have their nearest relatives in Africa, so they must have rafted across the South Atlantic by some kind of sweepstakes route. South America's isolation continued until the Late Miocene, when mastodonts, raccoons, and some other North American groups apparently island-hopped across the Central American archipelago. Finally, the isolation ended in the mid-Pliocene with the completion of the Panamanian Isthmus, which became a filter bridge. Many North American natives (mastodonts, horses, camels, deer, and placental carnivores, such as bears, lions, and saber-toothed cats) moved south, but others (such as pronghorns) did not. Only a few of the South American natives (armadillos, ground sloths, and capybaras) managed to invade North America, while the majority stayed at home and may have died out in the face of competition from North American invaders.

Vicariance Biogeography

When the theory of plate tectonics became accepted in the 1960s and 1970s, some predicted that it would revolutionize biogeography. After all, what could be more fundamental than the overturning of the assumption that geographic regions were fixed? Paleontologists eagerly replotted their fossils on the new plate tectonic maps, and novel transport mechanisms were proposed.

One group of scientists, however, looked at biogeography in a wholly new light and found that plate tectonics fit their predic-

tions nicely. This school of thought is now known as vicariance biogeography, and in the 1970s it was embraced by the same scientists who had fought the wars over cladistics (a theory of systematics based on the possession of common traits and ancestry) a few years earlier. They argued that vicariance methods changed biogeography from the ad hoc, storytelling, untestable approach of dispersalist theory to something rigorous and testable. The battle between the vicariance and traditional biogeographers raged for years along many of the same battle lines that had been drawn between cladistic and traditional systematists: cladograms (branching diagrams of relationships, in this case of landmasses as well as organisms); formulation of testable hypotheses; and rejection of scenarios, storytelling, or anything considered untestable. Unlike the cladistic revolution in systematics, however, vicariance biogeography never quite caught on, and in recent years interest has declined to occasional papers in a few journals. Nevertheless, it has forced all scientists to be more careful about how they propose and test their biogeographic ideas.

The idea originated with an obscure Venezuelan botanist by the name of León Croizat, who spent decades documenting the geographic ranges of many different species of plants and animals. His approach was so unconventional, and his writing was so idiosyncratic, difficult to read, and quarrelsome that he was forced to publish his ideas privately at his own expense in three long monographs spanning more than 10,000 pages (the shortest of these is Croizat 1962). Thus, he was not widely read in the scientific community. For decades, his influence was so minor that George Gaylord Simpson never mentioned his work in print except in a footnote, a sure sign of obscurity. Then, when cladistics came along in the 1970s, Gary Nelson and Donn Rosen at the American Museum in New York saw how vicariance methods could be combined with cladistics to make biogeographic hypotheses that were more rigorous and testable. Suddenly, Croizat was rescued from obscurity and placed in the center of a noisy controversy, although he was unhappy with the way his ideas had been transformed. Before he died in 1982, he was at odds not only with his critics but even with supporters such as Nelson. He even hated the term "vicariance biogeography" for a concept that he originally had christened "panbiogeography."

What is vicariance biogeography, and why is it so controversial? Croizat rejected the central assumption of dispersalist biogeography: that organisms have a center of origin and they gradually spread from that point to their present range. Instead, Croizat argued that biogeographic ranges are initially large (in other words, he viewed dispersal as instantaneous rather than gradual), and that biogeographic patterns are determined more by the fragmentation (whether by plate movements, sea level changes, or mountain ranges) of formerly large ranges into smaller areas. In each of these areas, a vicar species represents a fragment of a formerly much larger range, hence the name "vicariance." (A "vicar" in Latin is a representative or replacement for something else, so we get vicarious thrills when we experience them for someone else; a vicar in the clergy is Christ's representative.) Croizat analyzed these fragmented ranges by drawing lines (tracks) between the remnants of a geographic distribution to show their original connections. When this was done for a variety of organisms, the tracks began to overlap and many had the same pattern, producing generalized tracks that show the biogeographic affinities of major regions. For example, Croizat was struck by the large number of tracks that connected South America and Africa, yet geologists insisted that there was no way the continents could have been connected. His ideas were developed before plate tectonics showed that Africa and South America had once been connected, so these ideas were at least a decade ahead of the geological discoveries that made them plausible.

When Croizat's ideas were embraced by Nelson, Rosen, and others, these scientists adapted them to cladistic methods and hypothesis testing. Instead of generalized tracks, they generated a cladogram of landmasses, based on their time of divergence. They would then analyze the cladistic relationships of a variety of different organisms found on those landmasses and see what patterns emerged. If the cladograms of landmasses and taxa were congruent, it suggested that the present distribution of those taxa resulted from the fragmentation of the region on which they originated, and did not result from recent dispersal from one place to another. For example, a number of animals have cladistic relationships that suggest that their distribution resulted from fragmentation of Gondwanaland. The flightless ratite birds—the ostrich in Africa, rhea in South America, emu and cassowary in Australia, kiwi and extinct moa in New Zealand, and extinct elephant bird *Aepyornis* in Madagascar—are all found on Gondwana fragments. (However, several scientists have argued that the ratite birds once were distributed worldwide, and today they just happen to survive on Gondwana continents.) This remnant Gondwanaland distribution is true of marsupial mammals, osteoglossine fishes, galliform birds, hylid frogs, and a variety of insects. When many different cladograms are congruent, it is no accident; it is statistically significant.

The primary appeal of vicariance biogeography, however, lies in its testability. If the cladograms of areas and taxa are congruent, then they provide a positive test of the hypothesis. If they are not, then the vicariance interpretation is falsified. Such cannot be said for the old school of dispersalist biogeography, which was dominated by storytelling rather than hypothesis testing. If the oldest fossil of a given taxon was found in area A, then the dispersalist said that it migrated from area A to area B; if another, older fossil was found in area B, then the direction of dispersal was arbitrarily reversed. There was no rigorous method of deciding where a taxon originated and when and in what direction dispersal had occurred. Just about any scenario could be made to fit the distributional data, so there was no criterion for deciding whether a given hypothesis had been falsified or not.

Vicariance biogeographers do not deny that dispersal occurs, only that hypotheses based on dispersalist ideas cannot be rigorously tested. Instead, they advocate doing the necessary systematic and cladistic analyses first to see if a vicariant pattern emerges, in which case there is no need to postulate dispersal at all. In their view, biographers for too long had been content to invoke easy dispersalist explanations without looking harder at systematic relationships to see if vicariant explanations fit better. Of course, if there is no vicariant pattern, then one can fall back to dispersalism by default, but it should not be the first step in the analysis.

One would think that vicariance explanations would be unnecessary in groups with good dispersal ability. Yet even in these cases, there are surprises. For example, young spiders can disperse hundreds of miles by ballooning with threads from their spinnerets. Yet N.D. Platnick (1976) analyzed the laroniine spiders and found their distribution could be explained entirely by vicariance. The first branch point on the cladogram separated Gondwana and Laurasian taxa, and then among the Laurasian taxa there was a clear split between Asian and North American clades, corresponding to the breakup of the supercontinent Laurasia.

So how does vicariance biogeography stand today? Clearly, for groups that have long histories (at least back to the Mesozoic, when the supercontinent Pangaea broke up), it is appropriate to look for vicariant distributions to see if dispersalism is unnecessary to explain them. However, it is just as clear that the distribution of organisms with very recent histories (especially of the late Cenozoic) cannot be explained by the slow pace of continental fragmentation and collision; such distribution requires dispersalist explanations (however untestable they are). No one argues that the Great American Interchange in the Pliocene or the migrations of Ice Age mammals are anything but dispersal. Similarly, most of the migrations of mammals during the Cenozoic are simply too rapid to be the result of anything but dispersal.

Still, the vicariance advocates refuse to give up easily, and they continue to find surprising new evidence in their favor. For example, biogeographers had long argued that the circum-Pacific distribution of many plants and animals required dispersal around the Pacific Rim. Unlike the Atlantic, the Pacific was not formed by continental fragmentation. However, A. Nur and Z. Ben-Avraham (1981) have postulated the existence of a "lost Pacifica continent" that once lay in the southwest Pacific. In their view, its fragments have since migrated across the Pacific and attached to various continents as exotic terranes. If this is true, then many circum-Pacific organisms may have gotten to their present location by floating on "Noah's Arks" (i.e., landmasses that rift away from one area and transport inhabitants to another) rather than by dispersal. However, this suggestion is still very controversial. It is not clear which if any of the exotic terranes on the Pacific Rim were once part of a "lost Pacifica continent." More importantly, if these fragments had drifted away from a former supercontinent, they would have sunk down the subsidence curve of the spreading seafloor and eventually become submerged, making it very hard for land animals to survive above water until they docked on some other continent.

It is hard to tell how important vicariance biogeography will be in the future. However, it generated a storm of controversy that had a positive effect in challenging many of the stale assumptions of traditional biogeography and forcing scientists to be more rigorous. No matter what the future of biogeography, that legacy was extremely important in the history of this science.

DONALD R. PROTHERO

See also Faunal and Floral Provinces; Global Environment; Ocean Environment; Paleoclimatology; Plate Tectonics and Continental Drift; Seas, Ancient; Terrestrial Environment

Works Cited

Croizat, L. 1962. *Space, Time, and Form, the Biological Synthesis*. Caracas: Croizat.

Nur, A., and Z. Ben-Avraham. 1981. Lost Pacifica continent: A mobilistic speculation. *In* G. Nelson and D.E. Rosen (eds.), *Vicariance Biogeography: A Critique*. New York: Columbia University Press.

Platnick, N.D. 1976. Drifting spiders or continents? Vicariance biogeography of the spider family Laroniinae (Araneae: Gnaphosidae). *Systematic Zoology* 24:101–9.

Further Reading

Croizat, L. 1962. *Space, Time, and Form, the Biological Synthesis*. Caracas: Croizat.

Darlington, P.J. 1957. *Zoogeography*. New York: Wiley.

Hallam, A. 1973. *Atlas of Palaeobiogeography*. Amsterdam and New York: Elsevier.

Humphries, C.J., and L.R. Parenti. 1986. *Cladistic Biogeography*. Oxford: Clarendon; New York: Oxford University Press.

Myers, A.A., and P.S. Giller (eds.). 1988. *Analytical Biogeography*. London and New York: Chapman and Hall.

Nelson, G., and N. Platnick. 1981. *Systematics and Biogeography, Cladistics and Vicariance*. New York: Columbia University Press.

Nelson, G., and D.E. Rosen (eds.). 1981. *Vicariance Biogeography: A Critique*. New York: Columbia University Press.

Nur, A., and Z. Ben-Avraham. 1981. Lost Pacifica continent: A mobilistic speculation. *In* G. Nelson and D.E. Rosen (eds.), *Vicariance Biogeography: A Critique*. New York: Columbia University Press.

Pielou, E.C. 1979. *Biogeography*. New York: Wiley-Interscience.

Platnick, N.D. 1976. Drifting spiders or continents? Vicariance biogeography of the spider family Laroniinae (Araneae: Gnaphosidae). *Systematic Zoology* 24:101–9.

PALEOCLIMATOLOGY

Paleoclimatology is the study of ancient climates. It is used to reconstruct past environments and the global position *(paleolatitude)* of rocks. The paleoclimatic record is invaluable for understanding how climates change and what factors cause changes. Such an understanding is becoming increasingly important for studies of today's weather patterns, and particularly, for predicting the effects of human activities on future climates.

A Definition of Climate

Daily forecasts record "weather" rather than "climate." Weather elements include temperature, precipitation, wind, sunshine, humidity, and cloud cover. Climate is the average weather for a part of the Earth over at least 30 years.

The Earth's weather patterns are caused by airflow in the atmosphere (winds) and ocean currents. Both are driven by the imbalance of the sun's heat on the Earth's surface. The Earth bulges around the equator, causing these latitudes to receive more solar heating, whereas at the poles, the sun's rays must travel through a greater thickness of air before reaching the ground. Generally, temperatures are higher nearer the equator. However, this general rule is complicated by winds and ocean currents interacting with geographical features: mountain belts, lowland plains, ocean deeps, and coastlines. Also, weather patterns change with the seasons as the Earth orbits the sun.

In 1918 Russian meteorologist Vladimir Köppen attempted a classification of modern global climates based on vegetation patterns and variations in temperature and precipitation. He identified five zones: tropical, equatorial, rainy climates with no cool season; dry, warm climates; rainy, midlatitude, temperate-to-subtropical climates with mild winters; rainy, midlatitude, temperate climates with cold winters; and frigid, polar climates with no warm season. Each of these zones can be further subdivided, depending upon seasonal rainfall and temperature.

Climate Change

In some ways, the Earth's climate appears to be remarkably stable. Air circulation always has been controlled by solar energy, and global surface temperatures have remained fairly stable throughout Precambrian and Phanerozoic times (Frakes 1979). However, there has also been continuous climate change, which still goes on today, but so slowly that it is difficult to measure.

Earth's paleoclimate was generally warm but was punctuated by periods of intense cold, when temperatures dropped up to 12 degree Celsius, called *ice ages*. Changes in surface temperatures are due to three variables: the energy emitted by the sun *(solar luminosity)*; the fraction of this energy reflected back into space *(albedo effect)*; and the *greenhouse effect*. In the last, atmospheric carbon dioxide (CO_2) combined with water vapor acts like a blanket around the Earth, absorbing heat radiated back from the surface and preventing it from escaping into space. The natural greenhouse effect keeps the world 30 degrees Celsius warmer than it would be otherwise and makes the world habitable. The proportion of CO_2 in the atmosphere has changed over time. CO_2 levels can be moderated as carbon is stored in soil, rocks, and seawater, and recycled by weathering. Living organisms can also store CO_2 and so affect the Earth's climate (Hsü 1992).

Another factor in climate change is the modification of air and ocean currents by continental drift. Mountain-building (orogeny) affects climate, because the seaward side of mountains captures moisture-bearing winds from the sea, causing a so-called "rain shadow" on the landward side. Times of rapid seafloor spreading produce buoyant midoceanic ridges, high sea levels, and higher levels of CO_2 in the atmosphere because of volcanism and reduced continental weathering. Such conditions produce a greenhouse climate, with no ice caps. Conversely, low tectonic activity affects low sea level, low CO_2, strong seasonality (i.e., large differences from season to season), and temperature variations between the poles and equator. During periods of great volcanic activity, dust and sulphate aerosols are thrown into the upper atmosphere. The sulphates induce acid rain, while the dust scatters the sun's rays, reducing the amount of heat reaching the surface, and lowering temperatures. This type of circumstance produces a *nuclear winter.*

Many extraterrestrial factors influence global climate changes: variations in solar heat output and distance between Earth and sun. Meteorite or comet impacts can produce global cooling by ejecting material into the atmosphere (Alvarez et al. 1980). Finally, in the nineteenth and twentieth centuries, human activities also have played their part in affecting climate change.

The Study of Palaeoclimates

The study of ancient climates can be viewed on three time scales: the last 11,000 years (Holocene); 11,000 years to two million years ago (Pleistocene); and the pre-Pleistocene record. In the first two intervals, the continents were in their present positions and polar areas were covered with permanent ice caps, so paleoclimate information can be compared directly with modern analogues. However, the farther back we go in time, the less certain we can be of the ages of the rocks and the time span they represent.

One way to study ancient climates is to find as much climatic information about one interval of geological time as possible. This might be a geological period or perhaps a worldwide event, such as the end-Cretaceous extinction. A second method involves studying continuous stratigraphic (rock strata) sections with numerous thin beds that record climatic change. This is known as a time-series study. If strata can be accurately dated and cross-correlated, then series of strata from different localities can be used.

Methods for Reconstructing Past Climates

Palaeoclimatic Indicators

The record of the Earth's paleoclimate has been laid down in the rocks of the continental and oceanic crusts. Clues for reconstructing past climates can be read from sedimentary rocks, fossilized plants and animals, and suites of minerals. The principal sedimentary indicators of palaeoclimate include the recognition of the following materials.

Glacial Deposits or Drift

The material left behind by ice sheets indicates development in polar regions or during a global ice age (Sellwood and Price 1993). Drift includes rock piles known as *moraines* (sands and gravels left behind by summer meltwater), large boulders (*erratics*) carried by ice sheets and left stranded when they melted, and wind-blown dust deposits (*loess*). Glaciers also leave evidence on the landscape by removing soil and gouging out *striae* marks (scratch marks or gouges) on the exposed bare rock. Certain types of pollen, insects, and fossil plants preserved in peat bogs suggest cold climates. Ice casts called *sand wedges* and a polygonal structure caused by frost cracking can be seen in fossil soils.

Evaporites

Deposits of salt or gypsum indicate arid paleoclimatic conditions with low rainfall and high evaporation of surface moisture (Parrish et al. 1982). The presence of high amounts of calcium carbonate as nodules or a *calcic horizon* in fossil soils also indicate dry conditions.

Coal Measures

Coals and lignites (intermediary in coal formation) suggest humid conditions with high precipitation; they support peat accumulation in permanently waterlogged mires (Parrish et al. 1982). Presently, peat forms in midlatitude, temperate, and equatorial wet climates. The preservation of organic matter is characteristic, as coal requires cool climates, rapid burial, or anoxic conditions.

Other useful sedimentary features include marine limestones, which suggest a warm, tropical sea, and marine storm deposits, or tempestites (Sellwood and Price 1993). Fossil soils can give information about regional climates (Retallack 1989): highly weathered deposits known as bauxites and laterites are formed under warm, humid climate conditions. Certain suites of clay minerals can also provide information on weathering regimes in soils (Hallam 1985).

The composition of fossil animal and plant communities may indicate certain climate regimes. For the Cenozoic and Late Cretaceous, plants are the best palaeoclimatic indicators because many fossils are similar to living taxa (Spicer 1990). Plants are exposed directly to the atmosphere, meaning that leaf morphology, size, and texture can be related to temperature and humidity levels. Wood anatomy also can provide paleotemperature information, since frost-sensitive plants, such as cycads, are anatomically different from frost-resistant types. Annual growth rings in fossil wood and carbonate concretions around fossil roots indicate seasonal temperature and rainfall variation. Charcoal deposits suggest the occurrence of storm-induced wildfires.

Not all fossils are useful indicators of paleoclimate: today's rhinoceroses and elephants live in tropical regions, but in the Pleistocene, their extinct relatives, the woolly mammoths and rhinoceroses, lived in arctic conditions, insulated from the cold by thick hair!

Paleoclimate information can be read from the stable isotopes of oxygen, carbon, and hydrogen (Faure 1986). Oxygen isotopes provide temperature and geochemical information for oceanic water. Isotopic measurements are made from well-preserved calcareous fossils (mainly foraminifera), phosphatic vertebrate fossils and rocks, carbonate rocks, cherts, clay minerals, and directly from the water within Holocene ice cores. Ancient temperatures are found by calculating the difference between the ratio of two isotopes of oxygen—oxygen-18 (^{18}O) to oxygen-16 (^{16}O)—in the sample and that of the water from which it precipitated. This difference is dependent on the temperature of the water.

Such comparisons can provide temperatures measured to within ±0.5 degrees Celsius, but have limitations. The isotopic ratio must not have been altered by geochemical diagenesis. The equation assumes that the mineral was precipitated in isotopic equilibrium with the water, but some organisms secrete their skeleton out of isotopic equilibrium. Finally, one of the unknowns in the oxygen isotope equation is the isotopic composition of ancient seawater (Hudson and Anderson 1989). Today's seawater has an isotopic composition of zero parts per million, but as ^{16}O is preferentially stored in ice, a world free of polar ice caps, such as in the Mesozoic era, would have a different value. The ratio also varies with evaporation, precipitation, and freshwater runoff.

Paleotemperature determinations through isotopic analyses are useful to detect relative changes in temperature and isotopic composition of oceans during the past, rather than absolute seawater temperatures. Seawater isotopic chemistry has been fairly consistent over time, varying no more than 2 to 3 percent and only over long time periods (Hudson and Anderson 1989).

Prediction: General Circulation Models

Paleoclimatic indicators can only record the climatic regime under which the sediments accumulated or organisms lived. In an attempt to discover global paleoclimate patterns, geologists have turned to prediction methods used by meteorologists and oceanographers. With a knowledge of how ancient landmasses were positioned and the paleotopography of the oceans, paleoclimatologists are using supercomputers to model atmospheric and ocean currents. These are known as general circulation models, or GCM (Price et al. 1995).

A simple GCM would have a flat, featureless sphere representing Earth, which can be modified by adding landmasses and other parameters. Large landmasses oriented along lines of latitude, like Eurasia, are cooler in winter than the surrounding ocean, and warmer in summer. In winter this contrast creates a high pressure cell within the continental interior, which causes a dry and cold wind. In summer, the opposite occurs, and a sea breeze laden with moisture is blown inland, giving rise to the monsoon.

Cenozoic and Mesozoic GCMs compare favorably with known distributions of climatically sensitive sediments (e.g., coals and evaporites) and have been used to find petroleum source-rocks (Price et al. 1995). The main weakness of these GCMs is the lack of precise information for the parameters needed in the modeling (e.g., sea surface temperatures, cloud behavior, and the topography of ancient continents).

Earth's Paleoclimatic Calendar
Precambrian
For the Precambrian, the most remote period of Earth's history, continental landmasses are difficult to define and position, even for younger Precambrian sequences. Also, many rock types may have been destroyed or rendered unrecognizable by changes that occurred after the sediments were deposited.

However, some statements about Earth's early climate can be made. For instance, the chemical compositions of the oceans and atmosphere were different from those of today. Oxygen isotope analyses of Archean cherts (rock laid down before the appearance of living things) suggest a different isotopic composition of

seawater or temperatures as high as 150 degrees Celsius. Banded iron formations (chert and iron ore) are found in sequences of around 2.2 to 1.8 billion years ago (Late Archean–Early Proterozoic) throughout the world. Atmospheric conditions to form these rocks are not present today. They suggest an atmosphere poor in oxygen, with almost double the amount of CO_2 than today. There was a greenhouse climate, even though the sun's luminosity was 30 percent less than its output today.

The evolution of life on Earth is linked to the evolution of the atmosphere. Excess carbon may have been fixed by early organisms, thinning out the atmospheric CO_2 (Hsü 1992). Plants evolved in the oceans about 2 to 2.5 billion years ago and began to liberate oxygen gas to the atmosphere through photosynthesis. Oxygen forms the ozone (O_3) layer in the upper atmosphere, which protects plants and animals from the sun's lethal ultraviolet radiation. Once oxygen increased to 1 percent in the atmosphere in the Late Proterozoic (1.5 billion years ago), multicellular organisms developed.

Glacial deposits dated between 2.0 to 2.5 billion years old occur throughout the world, indicating a major ice age. K.J. Hsü (1992) postulated that over-consumption of CO_2 from the atmosphere by stromatolite-building cyanobacteria (blue-green algae) caused the ice age and precipitated their own demise. However, the glaciation may have been caused by a massive meteorite impact, known as the Vredefort-Bushvelt structure in southern Africa and dated as 2.1 billion years old. A Late Precambrian glaciation occurred on nearly every continent around 900 to 600 million years ago. It is possible that the second cooling caused the Vendian mass extinction.

Paleozoic
Fossils and sediments provide reliable clues about the climate and climate change for the Paleozoic era. Following the Late Proterozoic glaciation, there was a warming trend through the Lower Paleozoic. Isotope records reveal that ocean temperatures could have been about 5 to 10 degrees Celsius higher than today for most of the Paleozoic (Hudson and Anderson 1989). The warming trend was punctuated by a Late Ordovician glaciation on southern continents, although contemporary marine carbonates indicate tropical conditions in equatorial latitudes.

The warming trend continued into the Late Paleozoic, although there may have been a minor glaciation at the end of the Devonian and Early Carboniferous. This may have been caused by a reduction of CO_2 in the atmosphere following the spread of land plants.

Perhaps the most important factor in Paleozoic climate change was the formation of the supercontinent Pangaea in Late Carboniferous–Early Permian times. At its greatest extent, in the Triassic, exposed land extended from 85 degrees north to 90 degrees south (Ziegler et al. 1982). The concentration of all landmasses in a single supercontinent halted the buffering effects of the ocean and increased the reflectiveness of the Earth's surface. The vastness of Pangaea, with large portions of it in low midlatitudes, and the position of the Tethys Ocean, a warm seaway that cut through equatorial regions, maximized summer heating.

The result of such conditions was more severe seasons and increased temperatures, especially in the continental interior, while tremendous storms occurred during a megamonsoon season along the Tethys Ocean coastline. The distribution of Pangaean coals and evaporites indicate weather patterns of humid and arid zones quite unlike modern Köppen zones. Pangaea in the Carboniferous experienced widespread peat formation in what is now North America and Europe, while drier conditions prevailed in the equatorial regions. At the end of the Carboniferous, peat formation shifted from low to high latitudes. The low latitudes became increasingly arid into the Permian, but with the development of a wet season, they grew into a monsoon climate. This change was probably the result of global warming that followed the disappearance of continental glaciation.

The greatest extent of continental glaciation began toward the end of the Late Carboniferous, when the south pole was located over southern Pangaea, or Gondwanaland. Widespread glaciation covered vast tracts of South America, Africa, Australia, Antarctica, and India. An alternative cause for the Carboniferous ice age is that large land plants removed too much CO_2 from the atmosphere (Hsü 1992). By mid-Permian times, the south pole became a marine environment and Gondwanaland was warm enough to support cold-blooded reptiles. Global warming continued into the Mesozoic.

Mesozoic

The Mesozoic worldwide climate was equable, with tropical and subtropical conditions spreading into present-day temperate belts and temperate conditions prevailing in polar regions. Fossil ferns intolerant to frost were found in Cretaceous sediments of Greenland (Vakhrameev 1991), and the presence of cold-blooded reptiles, such as crocodiles, at paleolatitudes of up to 60 degrees north (Colbert 1964) suggest much more equable conditions at high latitudes during the Mesozoic era than there are today. There was no equatorial wet-belt, and there is little evidence to suggest that there were permanent polar ice caps. The reason for the equable climate is not resolved. It may be related to the continental configuration at that time or to an increased amount of CO_2 in the atmosphere. The latter could induce the greenhouse effect.

Mesozoic continental configurations are reasonably well known. Pangaea persisted for much of the Triassic and Jurassic periods and moved northward. Land area was distributed evenly on either side of the equator, and the continental climate was again characterized by pronounced seasonal differences in temperature and precipitation. The megamonsoon reached its maximum extent in the Triassic, and continental interiors became drier: Redbeds, evaporites, and eolian sandstones occur in most continental sequences (Parrish 1993). Increased aridity in Late Triassic continental regions may be responsible for the extinction of Late Triassic land vertebrates and plants.

The southern Atlantic began to open up in the Late Triassic and Early Jurassic, and with the break-up of Pangaea in the Jurassic, the monsoon system broke down (Parrish 1993). By the Late Jurassic, coal deposition was replaced with evaporite deposition between 20 and 40 degrees north, and in Early Cretaceous times, lands at the edges of the newly opening central Atlantic and western Tethys experienced humid conditions. By the Late Cretaceous, there were restricted arid belts and a Köppen zonal climate pattern.

The geochemical constraints of Mesozoic oceans and ocean topography are not well known, meaning that pole-to-equator temperature gradients or humidity patterns are ambiguous. However, isotopic measurements of Mesozoic seawater do not differ greatly from those of Cenozoic oceans.

Dating from mid-Cretaceous times (100 million years ago), there are extensive deep-sea sediments from which cores have provided detailed paleontological and geochemical climatic information. Oxygen isotope temperatures from foraminifera have revealed that the global climate cooled over the last 100 million years, following a mid-Cretaceous maximum. The contrast in ocean temperatures from pole to equator also increased. Plant fossil evidence suggests that air temperatures declined through the Late Cretaceous. The conventional view of an ice-free Mesozoic was challenged recently by geological evidence for frequent polar glaciations (some stretching to 30 to 40 degree latitudes) in the Cretaceous (Frakes and Francis 1988). If polar ice caps waxed and waned through the Mesozoic, this would provide a ready explanation for the sea-level changes recorded in offshore rock sequences. A slight warming trend occurred in the Maastrichtian, and this did not change across the boundary between the Cretaceous and the Tertiary, so deteriorating temperatures cannot be blamed for the mass extinction.

Cenozoic

The configuration of Cenozoic continents and ocean basins can be reconstructed from seafloor paleomagnetic information, allowing for accurate general circulation modeling. A deep-sea sedimentary record yielding readings of calcium isotopes deposited in the form of planktonic and benthonic foraminifera has enabled the construction of surface-to-bottom gradients. Since angiosperm plants dominated the flora, more precise paleoclimate conclusions can be drawn for the Cenozoic than for the early paleobotanical record.

High latitude (above 60 degrees) plant fossils and warm oxygen isotope readings for the Paleocene and Early Eocene suggest that the climate in these upper regions was more equable than today (Hudson and Anderson 1989). However, in the mid-Eocene, waters began to cool, and at the Eocene–Oligocene boundary there was a dramatic fall in sea surface temperatures. Oligocene oxygen isotopes suggest significant storage of water in ice, and plants also show cooling in high latitudes, both of which suggest glaciation.

Late Cenozoic climate change can be blamed on the thermal isolation of Antarctica, which broke away from Gondwana and caused the formation of a new oceanic circum-Antarctic current system. Middle Miocene oxygen isotopes reflect the expansion of the Antarctic ice cap and a decrease in high latitude temperatures that has persisted until today. At the same time, there was warming in low latitudes, causing an increase in pole-to-equator temperature gradients. Cooling began around 2.37 million years ago in the Late Pliocene in the Northern Hemisphere, leading to the most well-known of all Earth's ice ages: the Pleistocene epoch.

Pleistocene Ice Age

Around 20,000 years ago, ice sheets reached their greatest extent, covering almost one-third of all land, including most of Britain, Scandinavia, Canada, parts of northern Europe, Siberia, and the United States. Temperatures throughout the rest of the world were generally cooler than they are today.

The Ice Age can be divided into glacial periods, which are prolonged periods of cold climate offset by interglacials, or prolonged warm periods, each lasting several thousand years. Briefer periods of warmth or coolness, lasting no more than a few hundred years, are called interstadials and stadials. The number of Pleistocene glacials varies, depending on where you look for evidence: Continental deposits suggest 21 full glacial episodes, but oxygen isotope studies of deep marine sediments indicate that there were many more. The alternating cool and warm periods (glacials and interglacials), occurred in cycles of 100,000 years. Stadials and interstadials occurred in a combination of 43,000 years, 24,000 years, and 19,000 years.

The reason for the cycles of glaciation is not well understood. One explanation was first suggested by Croll over a hundred years ago and later developed by the Yugoslavian scientist M. Milankovitch in the early 1920s (Milankovitch 1969). Known as the "Astronomical Theory," it suggests that the Earth's movements through space affect the amount of solar energy reaching its surface. The Earth's orbit around the sun wobbles between an ellipse (high eccentricity) and circular path (low eccentricity) every 96,000 years. When the Earth is in high eccentricity, it is much farther from the sun. Maximum eccentricity also increases and decreases through a 400,000-year cycle. The tilt of the Earth's axis changes between 21.8 and 24.4 degrees every 42,000 years. At the moment, the Earth is tilted at 23.5 degrees, and the pole tilted toward the sun receives more sunlight than the one pointed away. As the Earth rotates around the sun during a year, the hemispheres receive their seasons. When the Earth is at the minimum angle (21.8 degrees), seasonal changes are much less pronounced. Finally, the position of the equinox (the time when the Earth is closest to the sun) changes because of the wobble in the Earth's rotation. After 5,250 years, the equinox is roughly 90 degrees to the present, and 21,000 years from now it will be back to "normal."

A combination of these factors, linked with a high eccentricity, causes ice ages. Milankovitch believed that the strength of the sun at midlatitudes was the key to the growth and dissolution of ice sheets. Once summers become cool enough to retain snow cover in these regions, ice accumulates. Because ice increases the albedo effect, the system is self-perpetuating.

The Past 11,000 Years

Studies of the recent past are aided by the fact that we have historical records, instrument readings (reliable from the middle of the nineteenth century), and excellent proxies, such as ice core data, pollen distribution, and tree rings within timber from man-made structures and wood preserved in peat bogs.

Global temperature has increased by about 6 to 10 degrees Celsius since the end of the Pleistocene. However, the recovery was offset by 1 degree Celsius following the introduction of agriculture 8,000 years ago. This occurred because forests were replaced by plowed fields, increasing the Earth's albedo by 10 percent.

Fluctuations in temperature in the last millennium also have occurred. From around 1430 to 1850, Europe experienced the "Little Ice Age" caused by a reduction in the sun's activity. This was not a true glacial period, but a time of severe winters and storms.

Human activities over the past 200 years are altering the balance between the production of greenhouse gases (CO_2, methane, nitrous oxides, chlorofluorocarbons, or CFCs, and low-level ozone) and their absorption by forests and the oceans. CO_2 is produced by burning fossil fuel. Since the Industrial Revolution, atmospheric concentration of CO_2 has increased by 25 percent. Other contributing factors include tropical forest clearances, which has reduced CO_2 adsorption, increased the albedo effect, and reduced the amount of oxygen recycled into the atmosphere.

The consequence of the man-made greenhouse effect is global warming. The global temperature has risen by about 0.5 degrees Celsius since the mid–nineteenth century. Global warming could lead to unpredictable changes in the world's climate, including changes in wind and rainfall patterns, increased storminess, and a rise in sea level that could threaten global agriculture as well as coastal and island communities.

Studying paleoclimate is important for many reasons. Economically important minerals are produced by certain climatic conditions: gypsum, an evaporite, is used to make plasterboard. The coal deposits that yield gypsum derive from humid climates. Therefore, our ability to locate new resources is improved by understanding the Earth's paleoclimate. Climate also is closely linked to our agriculture and economy. It is in our interest to forecast how it changes. Studying ancient climates can give us a perspective on how stable the present climate might be and how fast climate responds to the changes we are wreaking today.

SARA J. METCALF

See also Atmospheric Environment; Global Environment; Ocean Environment; Plate Tectonics and Continental Drift; Sedimentology; Stable Isotope Analysis; Terrestrial Environment; Trace Element Analysis

Works Cited

Alvarez, L.W., W. Alvarez, F. Asaro, and H.V. Michel. 1980. Extraterrestrial cause for the Cretaceous-Tertiary extinctions: Experiment and theory. *Science* 208:1095–1108.

Colbert, E.H. 1964. Climatic zonation and terrestrial faunas. *In* A.E.M. Nairn (ed.), *Problems in Palaeoclimatology.* New York and London: Interscience.

Faure, G. 1986. *Principles of Isotope Geology.* 2nd ed., New York: Wiley.

Frakes, L.A. 1979. *Climates through Geologic Time.* Amsterdam and New York: Elsevier.

Frakes, L.A., and J.E. Francis. 1988. A guide to Phanerozoic cold polar climates from high-latitude ice-rafting in the Cretaceous. *Nature* 333:547–49.

Hallam, A. 1985. A review of Mesozoic climates. *Journal of the Geological Society of London* 142:433–45.

Hsü, K.J. 1992. Is Gaia endothermic? *Geological Magazine* 129:129–41.

Hudson, J.D., and T.F. Anderson. 1989. Ocean temperatures and isotopic compositions through time. *Transactions of the Royal Society of Edinburgh: Earth Sciences* 80:183–92.

Milankovitch, M. 1969. *Canon of Insolation and the Ice Age Problem.* Washington, D.C.: Israel Program for Scientific Translation for U.S. Department of Commerce and National Science Foundation; as *Kanon der Erdbestrahlung und seine Anwendung auf das Eiszeitenproblem,* Royal Serbian Sciences, Special Publication 132, Section of Mathematical and Natural Sciences 33, Belgrade: Royal Serbian Sciences, 1941.

Parrish, J.T. 1993. Climate of the supercontinent Pangea. *Journal of Geology* 101:215–33.

Parrish, J.T., A.M. Ziegler, and C.R. Scotese. 1982. Rainfall patterns and the distribution of coals and evaporites in the Mesozoic and Cenozoic. *Palaeogeography, Palaeoclimatology, Palaeoecology* 40:1–3, 67–101.

Price, G.D., B.W. Sellwood, and P.J. Valdes. 1995. Sedimentological evaluation of general circulation model simulations for the "greenhouse" Earth: Cretaceous and Jurassic case studies. *Sedimentary Geology* 100:2–22.

Retallack, G.J. 1989. *Soils of the Past: An Introduction to Paleopedology.* London: Unwin; Boston: Unwin Hyman, 1990.

Sellwood, B.W., and G.D. Price. 1993. Sedimentary facies as indicators of Mesozoic palaeoclimate. *Philosophical Transactions of the Royal Society of London,* ser. B, 341:225–33.

Spicer, R.A. 1990. Climate from plants. *In* D.E.G. Briggs and P.R. Crowther (eds.), *Palaeobiology: A Synthesis.* Oxford and Boston: Blackwell Science.

Vakhrameev, V.A. 1991. *Jurassic and Cretaceous Floras and Climates of the Earth.* N.F. Hughes (trans.). Cambridge and New York: Cambridge University Press; as *Iurskie i melovye flory klimaty zemli,* Moscow: Nauka, 1988.

Ziegler, A.M., C.R. Scotese, and S.F. Barret. 1982. Mesozoic and Cenozoic paleogeographic maps. *In* P. Brosche and J. Sündermann (eds.), *Tidal Friction and the Earth's Rotation II.* Berlin and New York: Springer-Verlag.

Further Reading

Allen, J.R.L., B.J. Hoskins, B.W. Sellwood, R.A. Spicer, and P.J. Valdes (eds.). 1994. *Palaeoclimates and Their Modelling: With Special Reference to the Mesozoic Era.* London and New York: Chapman and Hall.

Brenchley, P. (ed.). 1984. *Fossils and Climate.* Geological Journal Special Issue 11. Chichester and New York: Wiley.

Crowley, T.J., and G.R. North. 1991. *Paleoclimatology.* Oxford: Clarendon; New York: Oxford University Press.

Frakes, L.A., J.E. Francis, and J.I. Sykyus. 1992. *Climate Modes of the Phanerozoic.* Cambridge and New York: Cambridge University Press.

Hsü, K.J. (ed.). 1986. *Mesozoic and Cenozoic Oceans.* American Geophysical Union Geodynamic Series, 15. Washington, D.C.: American Geophysical Union; Boulder, Colorado: Geological Society of America.

Swart, P.K., K.C. Lohmann, J. McKenzie, and S. Savin (eds.). 1993. *Climate Change in Continental Isotopic Records.* American Geophysical Union Monograph, 78.

PALEOECOLOGY

Paleoecology is the ecology of the distant past. The field of ecology includes study of interactions between organism and the abiotic nonliving environments; interactions among organisms, both within species and between species; energy flow through food webs and biogeochemical cycles; organization of species in networks of various sizes—guilds, communities, and ecosystems; and geographic patterns of species richness and community organization. Studies range from the individual to the population, from single species to communities (all species that coexist in a defined area for a specified time interval), ecosystems, and the Earth as a whole. The time span of ecological studies is on the order of annual cycles, organism generations, up to the scales of decades and centuries of recent human history. Somewhere on the timescale between centuries and millions of years, ecology becomes paleoecology. There is a trade-off between ecology and paleoecology. Ecologists have access to virtually unlimited information about what happens to organisms in life assemblages but little historical depth about populations, communities, or the physical environment. Paleoecologists have long records of populations, species, communities, and paleoenvironments, but those records are fragmentary.

Distinctions between Ecology and Paleoecology

There are four main distinctions in subject and approach between ecology and paleoecology: age, time span, preservation biases, and accessibility of information about ecological interactions among individuals and species. "Age" refers to the geologic age of the subject matter. While most of the geologic past is remote in time, many Quaternary studies document trends in biotas and environments from the last ice age (about 10,000 years ago) up to the present time (e.g., Pielou 1991). From this perspective, many modern ecosystems are quite young and have not reached equilibrium in their composition.

The "time span" of paleoecological studies varies from the time of formation of a single catastrophic fossil assemblage (i.e., a mass death) to biotic change over many millions of years. The time resolution of paleontological data ranges from about 10^{-1} to 10^6 years, depending upon the ways that individual fossil assemblages were preserved and the types of dating methods available for fossils or stratigraphic sequences. Some fossil assemblages represent snapshots of living populations; other assemblages may be time-averaged during preservation over hundreds of thousands of years or more.

"Preservation biases" are the rule for paleoecological data: Original ecosystems are not preserved in their entirety. Agents of mortality do not uniformly select those species that are killed or consumed. Physical processes degrade or winnow organic remains selectively on the basis of body size. Biogeochemical processes selectively degrade organic remains according to chemical composition. A combination of these and other biotic and abiotic factors determine the size and composition of a fossil assemblage. Even *lagerstätten*—areas that are the preservational highlights of the fossil record, such as the Burgess Shale, Mazon Creek, and the Solnhofen Limestone—have experienced strong filtering processes. The most prevalent bias is simple physical location: only organisms that reside in, or are washed into, a depositional environment can contribute to the fossil record. Hence, the paleoecology of ancient river systems, large lakes, and continental shelves is fairly well known, but little is known of mountainous regions—except from patchy, middle-to-late Cenozoic cave or pond deposits that have built up over time and are currently eroding. A proliferation of taphonomic studies (which analyze events leading up to final burial), mostly in the last three decades, has illuminated the effects of preservation biases greatly (e.g., Allison and Briggs 1991). In some instances, taphonomic studies have demonstrated how to correct for the effects of particular biases and in other cases have provided reasonable limits to the inferences that paleoecologists can make based upon fossil evidence.

Because fossil assemblages represent snapshots of deceased organisms that may or may not have lived in the same period of time, the most serious limitation on paleoecological research is that most species interactions are not directly recorded. As a result, such things as competition, predation, mutualisms (interdependencies), social behavior, and other ecological interactions must be inferred on the basis of data such as the shape and possible function of feeding structures, the stable isotope composition of mineralized tissues, the repeated occurrences of certain taxa together, the damage patterns on fossil remains, and the population structure of fossil assemblages. Even interpreting whether individuals in a single fossil assemblage were alive together or occupied the same habitat is difficult to do. Scholars must evaluate the sedimentological and taphonomic context and consider alternative hypotheses about how the assemblage formed. For example, did individuals die and become buried in their life habitat, or were they transported, perhaps by a mountain river, from multiple sites of death to a setting that none of the individuals occupied while alive?

Paleoecological Techniques

Despite the daunting challenges posed by limited information, paleoecological studies do address research questions about species interactions over evolutionary time and across large biogeographic regions. For example, predatory gastropods (snails) may leave unambiguous drill holes on their molluscan prey. The carbon isotopic composition from a mammalian herbivore may signify that its diet consisted primarily of dry-season grasses (which use the C_4 photosynthetic pathway) instead of leafy shrubs (which use the C_3 photosynthetic pathway). Growth bands on mastodon tusks may indicate the time of year in which the individual died and, in combination with skeletal-damage patterns, indicate the likely process of mortality.

Since preservation bias, sample size, and taxonomic resolution are pervasive concerns for paleoecological research, there is strong emphasis on the design of field recovery methods, the effects of sampling on representation of taxa in datasets, the quantitative analytical methods, and the limits to paleoecological inference. (Reyment's 1971 text provides graphical and statistical approaches to paleoecological problems.) Nonetheless, the fossil record offers unique opportunities to study paleoenvironmental change at regional scales over millions of years and its effects on speciation, extinction, morphological evolution, and community structure (e.g., Vermeij 1987; Jablonski et al. 1996). Below, four general kinds of paleoecological research are described briefly.

Paleoenvironmental Reconstruction

This research ranges from reconstructing depositional environments of fossil assemblages to global paleoclimate. Classically, paleoenvironmental reconstruction involves inferring the sedimentary environment, reconstructing taphonomic events, and evaluating the properties of the original habitat. The last might include the texture of the soil substrate, unevenness of terrain (microtopography), or soil development. Sedimentological and microstratigraphic data are fundamental to inferring the general environment (e.g., lake, river, shallow marine), the more specific depositional environment within the sedimentary system (e.g., channel, forereef), and the mode by which fossil material accumulated (e.g., transport and winnowing in river channels, passive settling through a calm body of water). In continental settings, analysis of paleosol (ancient soil) development and the stable isotopic composition of paleosol and groundwater carbonates may indicate the scale of local environmental complexity, rates of soil formation, and the general nature of vegetation (e.g., C_3 vs. C_4 plants).

Taphonomic data may contribute to paleoenvironmental reconstruction in three respects. First, organic remains may act as sedimentary particles that are transported, preferentially positioned by agents of deposition, or sorted by size or shape, and thereby add information about depositional processes and environments. Second, certain preburial taphonomic features may be associated strongly with particular sedimentary environments—such as weathering features on bones or shells that indicate surface or near-surface exposure on floodplains or levees or heavy abrasion on skeletal material that indicates considerable time in fluvial channels. Third, heterogeneity of taphonomic features or of fossil assemblages may indicate habitat heterogeneity in the original ecosystem.

Climate is an important focus of paleoenvironmental reconstruction. Paleoclimatic data include sedimentological, geochemical, and biological indicators that may record local, regional, or global aspects of climate systems. Oxygen-isotope measurements from organic and inorganic carbonates in marine and terrestrial sequences have been particularly effective as a source of paleotemperature estimates (Broecker 1995). The taxonomic composition and abundance of faunal and floral assemblages have enabled scholars to make quantitative reconstructions of paleoclimatic conditions, especially for Quaternary sequences (e.g., Wright et al. 1993). Microinvertebrates, such as assemblages of foraminiferans (protists with mineralized casings), provide paleoceanographic climatic records, and tree pollen from lakes gives us continental climatic records. Many organisms reveal the influence of climate in their physical attributes, body size, geographic distribution, or isotopic composition of mineralized tissues.

Ecomorphological Characterization of Floras and Faunas

A growing interest in the nature of ecological communities over time has motivated approaches based on ecological adaptations of individual species, without consideration of evolutionary history or relationships. These methods are considered "taxon-free." Many groups of organisms are so ecologically diverse that simply knowing the taxonomic identity of an extinct species does little to narrow the range of its possible ecological specializations. Taxon-free approaches, well summarized for organisms in continental environments in Behrensmeyer et al. (1992), rely primarily on functional morphology to infer ecological attributes. The distribution of species among ecological categories or the frequency of particular ecomorphological attributes forms the basis for evaluating the ecological structure of the fossil assemblage or estimating a paleoenvironmental variable.

A classic example using ecological structure of mammalian faunas to infer the nature of paleovegetation is the work of P. Andrews and colleagues (1979). This work studied ecomorphological attributes of extant and Neogene mammalian faunas from East Africa. For each species in 23 modern faunas, they recorded taxonomic affiliation, body size, locomotor activity, and feeding habits. For each species of five Neogene faunas, they inferred ecological attributes from the size and morphological features of skeletal remains. From the frequency distributions of modern species with regard to such things as size classes and locomotor categories, Andrew's team distinguished five modern community types. The distributions for each paleofauna were compared to those of the modern faunas (Figure 1). Three of the five paleofaunas showed a strong resemblance to a modern community type, and two did not. One of the two that did not was considered to be a community type no longer present; the other was judged to be a mixture of species from two different community types.

A classic study based on ecomorphology of angiosperm leaves is that of J.A. Wolfe (1978). Wolfe noted that size, shape, margination (shape of leaf edges), and texture of the leaves of extant forest trees change in a regular manner with climatic conditions. Trees in areas of high annual temperature and high precipitation typically have large leaves with smooth margins, leathery texture, and drip tips. Trees in areas of low annual temperature and moderate precipitation typically have small leaves with toothed or lobed margins and lack drip tips. The percent of species with entire-margined leaves correlates so strongly with mean annual temperature among modern forests that numerous studies have used this relationship to estimate paleotemperatures from fossilized leaf assemblages (Figure 2). Using a dozen ecomorphological variables for modern and fossil leaf assemblages and seven climatic variables for the modern sites, Wolfe (1990) estimated paleoclimatic change across the Cretaceous-Tertiary boundary for sites in the western interior of North America. His results showed a substantial increase in mean annual temperature and in annual precipitation for 0.5 to 1.0 million years after the asteroid impact at the end of the Cretaceous.

Ecological Inferences for Single Taxa

A persistent goal in this field of study is the paleoecology of a particular species, often because its evolutionary significance is unusually great or its remains are unusually well preserved. For example, *Australopithecus afarensis* is the best-known of the earliest hominids. Remains of this species occur at several East African sites that date from the early Pliocene. Anatomical studies of dental, facial, cranial, and postcranial remains provide a basis for inferring posture, feeding behavior, body size, sexual dimorphism (physical distinctions between males and females), and whether or not this species was capable of making tools. The remarkable trackway site at Laetoli, Tanzania, preserves the footprints of *A. afarnsis* and many other animals. The footprints are highly diagnostic and provide a snapshot of life, and abundant ecological data, for the East Africa of 3.8 million years ago. Taken together, anatomical, taphonomic, and faunal-assemblage data indicate that this species was bipedal; sexually dimorphic, with males weighing about 27 to 36 kilograms and females 25 to 50 percent smaller; omnivorous, with a predominance of tough plants in the diet; lived in small family groups in a seasonally arid habitat similar to today's tropical African savannahs; was seasonally migratory, like many ungulates of modern savannah woodlands; and probably could not make tools like those of later hominids (Hay and Leakey 1982; Brown 1995).

Remarkably preserved dinosaur fossils from the Cretaceous of Montana are the basis for studies of nesting and social ecology of several ornithopod dinosaurs (Horner 1984; Fastovsky and Weishampel 1996). Skeletal remains of adults, nestlings, and hatchlings, along with eggs in nests of *Maiasaura, Hypacrasaurus,* and *Orodromeus,* all indicate that these dinosaurs nested in colonies. In the case of *Maiasaura,* up to 17 eggs were laid within a shallow hole dug in soft sediment. Nests were spaced about one adult body width apart, suggesting that adults tended the nests communally. After the young hatched, they remained in the nest for almost a year, fed by their parents, and grew at the rate of 12 centimeters per month in body length. In contrast, hatchlings of *Orodromeus* were precocial—they were born well-developed enough to leave the nest soon after birth and fend for themselves. Here, the combination of anatomical, ontogenetic, taphonomic, and sedimentological data provides a glimpse into the lives of dinosaur families.

Evolutionary Paleoecology

The long-term evolutionary consequences of ecological attributes and interactions are the subject of evolutionary paleoecology. Certain long fossil records enable scholars to study detailed taxonomic resolution, appropriate geographic coverage, and adequate sample sizes. Such records offer opportunities for testing hypotheses about evolutionary effects of species interactions, such as "arms races"

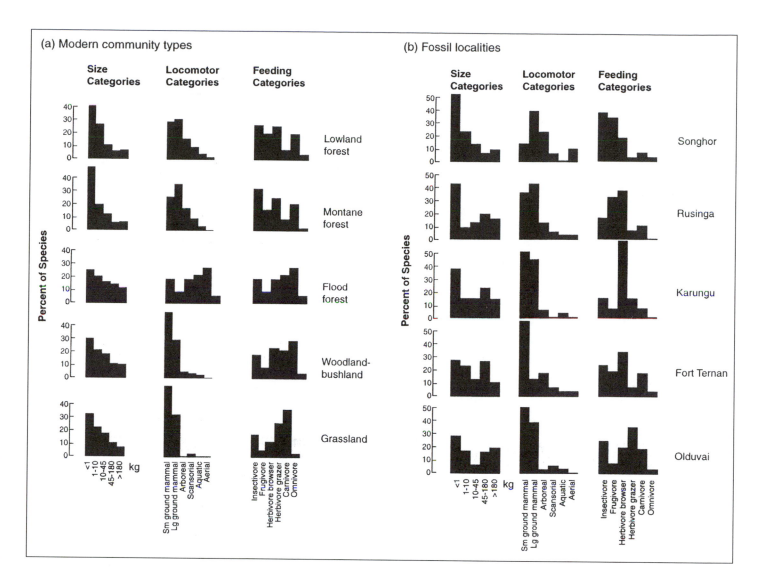

Figure 1. Reconstructing paleohabitat from the ecological diversity of mammalian assemblages, using the approach of Andrews et al. (1979). *a*, the average percent of species among size categories, locomotor categories, and feeding categories, from 23 modern faunas that represent live general community types; *b*, distribution of species among the same size, locomotor, and feeding categories, based on five fossil assemblages from the Neogene of East Africa. Key: Songhor represented lowland forest; Fort Ternan represented a woodland-bushland; Olduvai represented grassland; the other two sites did not resemble the modern community types.

between predators and prey, the effect of environmental changes on species mix and taxonomic profile, and ecosystem stability over geologic time.

A prominent paleoecological question concerns the causes of faunal or floral turnover—the replacement of species within a community through extinction, immigration, and speciation. The "Red Queen" model emphasizes the role of interspecific interactions (interactions between species) in maintaining persistent selective pressures for evolutionary change (phyletic evolution) and for species turnover within communities (Van Valen 1973). E.S. Vrba's contrasting idea is that external physical processes—notably episodes of climatic change—trigger changes in the size and continuity of species ranges, resulting in accelerated rates of speciation ("turnover pulses") accompanied by morphological evo-

lution, extinction, and dispersal. In the absence of extrinsic physical change, neither biotic turnover nor phyletic evolution are predicted to occur (Vrba 1995). While some records of paleoenvironmental change and faunal turnover meet the predictions of Van Valen's model, other records fit Vrba's model, such as the African mammalian record of the Plio-Pleistocene and the interchange of mammals between North and South America following the emergence of the Isthmus of Panama.

Another variant on the theme of biotic turnover is the subject of "coordinated stasis" of ecosystems (Brett et al. 1996). Here the emphasis is on long intervals of time in which there is little change in biotic composition or morphology, bounded by short episodes of rapid evolution and drastic changes in taxonomic composition. A corollary of this pattern is the long-term persistence (over millions

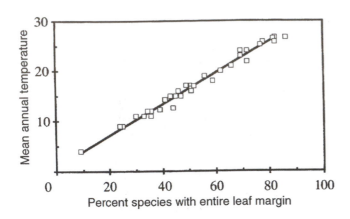

Figure 2. Estimating the mean annual temperature from fossil leaf assemblages, using Wolfe's approach (1978). The percent of dicot species with entire (smooth) margins in modern floras shows a close correlation with mean annual temperature (in degrees Centigrade) of the locality. Figure modified from Wing and Greenwood (1993) and Wolfe (1978).

of years) of ecological-evolutionary units resistant to invasion and change in guild structure. This pattern has been documented mainly for a number of Paleozoic marine sequences dominated by deep sea invertebrates, with some nonmarine examples, as well. The causes of stasis and turnover, as well as the generality of the pattern, are active subjects of research.

In conclusion, over the last few decades paleoecology has grown in research methods and in the scope of questions it engages. Clearly, some major paleoecological issues, such as causes of biotic turnover, cannot be addressed by studying modern eco-systems alone. Granted, there are limitations in trying to under-stand interactions among species and environments based on fossils and sedimentary rocks. However, paleoecological research is the primary way that the fossil record is brought to life.

CATHERINE BADGLEY

See also Atmospheric Environment; Biomass and Productivity Estimates; Global Environment; Ocean Environment; Paleoclimatology; Population Dynamics; Predation; Sedimentology; Stable Isotope Analysis; Terrestrial Environment; Trace Element Analysis; Trophic Groups and Levels

Works Cited

Allison, P.A., and D.E.G. Briggs. 1991. *Taphonomy: Releasing the Data Locked in the Fossil Record.* New York: Plenum.

Andrews, P., J.M. Lord, and E.M. Nesbit Evans. 1979. Patterns of ecological diversity in fossil and modern mammalian faunas. *Biological Journal of the Linnean Society* 11:177–205.

Behrensmeyer, A.K., J.D. Damuth, W.A. DiMichele, R. Potts, H.-D. Sues, and S.L. Wing. 1992. *Terrestrial Ecosystems through Time.* Chicago: University of Chicago Press.

Brett, C.E., L.C. Ivany, and K.M. Schopf. 1996. Coordinated stasis: An overview. *Palaeogeography, Palaeoclimatology, Palaeoecology* 127:1–20.

Broecker, W.S. 1995. *The Glacial World According to Wally.* Palisades, New York: Eldigio.

Brown, G.D., Jr. 1995. *Human Evolution.* Dubuque, Iowa: Brown.

Fastovsky, D.E., and D.B. Weishampel. 1996. *The Evolution and Extinction of the Dinosaurs.* Cambridge and New York: Cambridge University Press.

Horner, J.R. 1984. The nesting behavior of dinosaurs. *Scientific American* 250:130–37.

Jablonski, D., D.H. Erwin, and J.H. Lipps. 1996. *Evolutionary Paleobiology.* Chicago: University of Chicago Press.

Hay, R.L., and M.D. Leakey. 1982. The fossil footprints of Laetoli. *Scientific American* 246:50–57.

Pielou, E.C. 1991. *After the Ice Age: The Return of Life to Glaciated North America.* Chicago: University of Chicago Press.

Reyment, R.A. 1971. *Introduction to Quantitative Paleoecology.* Amsterdam and New York: Elsevier.

Van Valen, L. 1973. A new evolutionary law. *Evolutionary Theory* 1:179–229.

Vermeij, G.J. 1987. *Evolution and Escalation.* Princeton, New Jersey: Princeton University Press.

Vrba, E.S. 1995. On the connections between paleoclimate and evolution. *In* E.S. Vrba, G.H. Denton, T.C. Partridge, and L.H. Burckle (eds.), *Paleoclimate and Evolution with Emphasis on Human Origins.* New Haven, Connecticut: Yale University Press.

Wing, S.L., and D.R. Greenwood. 1993. Fossils and fossil climate: The case for equable continental interiors in the Eocene. *Philosophical Transactions of the Royal Society of London,* ser. B, 341:243–52.

Wolfe, J.A. 1978. A paleobotanical interpretation of Tertiary climates in the northern hemisphere. *American Scientist* 66:694–703.

———. 1990. Palaeobotanical evidence for a marked temperature increase following the Cretaceous/Tertiary boundary. *Nature* 343:153–56.

Wright, Jr., H.E., J.E. Kutzbach, T. Webb III, W.F. Ruddiman, F.A. Street-Perrott, and P.J. Bartlein (eds.). 1993. *Global Climates since the Last Glacial Maximum.* Minneapolis: University of Minnesota Press.

PALEOETHOLOGY

Traditionally, the fossil record has been used by paleontologists to systematically analyze and interpret the morphological characteristics of ancient life-forms. These data have been compiled primarily to reconstruct phylogenies (evolutionary classifications of life) and biostratigraphies (chronological sequences of life). Just as the fossil record can be used to construct a timetable for the evolution of groups of organisms, it also can reveal evolutionary patterns of behavior of long-extinct individuals, populations, and communities of organisms, thereby greatly expanding its biological utility. The study of such behavior is known as paleoethology.

Behavior can be broadly defined as any observable response of an organism to a stimulus. By this definition, nearly all conclusions about the behavioral patterns of extinct organisms are indirect. Direct determinations of behavioral patterns from the fossil record, so-called frozen behaviors (Boucot 1990), in which organisms have been preserved "in the act," are far less common. Indirect evidence of behavior ranges from highly reliable inferences based upon comparisons of the preserved anatomical characteristics of extinct organisms known to be functionally linked to behaviors, to a broad range of more speculative interpretations based upon scanty fossil evidence. The reliability of the first category of indirect evidence, based upon functional morphology, is greatly enhanced when fossil forms are represented by closely related living forms, thus providing observable models to test hypothetical behaviors of the extinct organisms.

Certain caveats are required when attempting to deduce behaviors of extinct organisms or groups of organisms. When interpreting behavioral patterns from the fossil record, it is crucially important to specify at which taxonomic level a behavior is being defined. That is to say, certain behaviors may be characteristic of highly inclusive groups of organisms (e.g., family level and above), whereas other behaviors may be exhibited only at lower levels of classification (i.e., genus or species). For example, all living members of the avian order Sphenisciformes (penguins), "fly" underwater in a fashion stereotypical for the order. Fossil penguins as far back as the Eocene period all shared with living penguins clear similarities in their anatomical adaptations related to this unique form of locomotion, therefore it is reasonable to assume that underwater "flying" is a primitive behavioral characteristic of the entire order (Simpson 1976). However, characteristic behaviors of extinct forms at lower taxonomic levels that are not tightly correlated to functional morphology, such as the unique and varied breeding patterns peculiar to different penguin species, are necessarily far more difficult to assess from the fossil record.

Similarly, the carnassial teeth (shearing, scissorlike premolars and molars) of many living carnivores (e.g., felids [cats] and canids [dogs]) are tightly linked with the feeding mechanisms of these mammals. The presence of carnassial teeth in fossil felids and canids is convincing evidence that extinct forms employed feeding behaviors similar to their living relatives, thus providing clues regarding the antiquity of these characteristic behaviors. Unfortunately, many other fossil groups are not represented by closely related living forms, and it is difficult to apply the laws of biological uniformity to such forms with as high a level of reliability.

Likewise, trace fossils (i.e., trackways, burrows, etc.) may be valuable as tools to determine ancient behaviors. The biological value of trace fossils is considerably enhanced if the organism that left the traces can be reliably confirmed. For example, a trilobite fossilized at the end of a set of tracks, a fossil crayfish within its burrow, or a bitch buried with her pups in a den are "frozen" behaviors and influence the reliability of the conclusions we may draw regarding other similar trace fossils.

Behaviors are not restricted within taxonomic groups or individual species; they also involve a variety of coevolutionary interactions between two or more unrelated species (that is, interspecific relationships that determine changes in gene frequencies and fitness). Examples of such behaviors may range from species-species interactions (such as predator-prey or host-parasite relationships) to the highly complex interplay that is probably typical at the organizational level of communities. The incomplete nature of the fossil record, coupled with the inherent complexities of community ecology, necessarily makes conclusions about coevolutionary aspects of behavior at these higher levels difficult to study.

It is far beyond the scope of this essay to attempt to list all known instances of fossil behavior (see Boucot 1990 for a more complete treatment of this issue); however, while keeping the conditions mentioned above in mind, several examples illustrating a range of behaviors are presented below.

Interspecific Behaviors

An elegant and highly informative study of predator-prey interactions comes from Late Cretaceous North American marine deposits. Mosasaurs, large (some 10 meters or larger) marine lizards related to modern-day monitor lizards, were dominant higher-order predators of the extensive warm, shallow, inland seas that covered much of the North American continent at that time. Equipped with streamlined, fusiform bodies (i.e., tapering at both ends), long, laterally compressed tails, and large heads with powerful, crushing jaws armed with single rows of sharply pointed "stabbing" teeth along the margins, these reptiles were predators potentially well-suited to dealing with a variety of large, mobile prey items. Ammonites, extinct shelled cephalopods morphologically similar to the modern-day chambered nautilus, were numerous and diverse in Late Cretaceous seas and an apparent favored prey of mosasaurs. Characteristic patterns of tooth marks from a number of fossil ammonite shells clearly matching mosasaur jaws and teeth suggest not only that ammonites were eaten, but also indicate the intricacies of mosasaurian feeding behavior (Figure 1). Mosasaurs apparently approached ammonites from their blind side, delivering a crippling bite to the gas-filled buoyancy chambers. Once disabled, other bite marks indicate that the ammonites were positioned quickly and dispatched by a bite, or bites, to the anterior living chamber, tearing out the soft parts for consump-

Figure 1. Fossil of a pelagic Late Cretaceous ammonite with characteristic pattern of mosasaur tooth marks suggesting distinctive predatory strategy. Maximum diameter of ammonite is 30 cm. Photo courtesy of A.J. Boucot.

tion. This specialized feeding pattern suggests not only familiarity with the prey but also perhaps a type of learned behavior on the part of mosasaurs (Kauffman and Kesling 1960).

Dinosaurs were one of the most successful lineages of extinct vertebrates and have attracted both public and scholarly attention. Dinosaurian evolutionary significance stems from their dominance of the terrestrial ecosystem for nearly 180 million years. The ecological importance of the dinosaurs has led to a great deal of speculation concerning their behavior. A dramatic example of predator-prey interactions is the fossil of the so-called "fighting dinosaurs" from the Gobi Desert. Two Late Cretaceous dinosaurs, a herbivorous ceratopsian, *Protoceratops andrewsi,* and a small meat-eating theropod, *Velociraptor mongoliensis,* died and were fossilized together while locked in the midst of an apparent battle. It has been suggested that this fossil may represent scavenging behavior on the part of *Velociraptor,* but the position of the theropod's forelimb within the beaklike mouth of the small ceratopsian dinosaur is a strong indication of active predation (Kielan-Jaworowska and Barsbold 1972; Unwin et al. 1995).

Additional examples of predatory behavior in dinosaurs have come out of China within recent years. Several exceptional fossils of a small compsognathid theropod, *Sinosauropteryx,* have been discovered with the remains of their last meals preserved in the gut. These dinosaurs had been preying upon small reptiles and mammals prior to their death, indicating a variety of prey items in their diet. Although fossils such as these and the "fighting dinosaurs" are spectacular, the information they provide regarding predatory behavior of dinosaurs is general and has limited evolutionary and biological utility (see Chin 1997 for a general treatment of dinosaur feeding behavior). All we can state with any

certainty is that the theropods possessed a number of anatomical features (serrated, recurved teeth, grasping hands, etc.) related to a predatory life history. Specific hunting strategies or favored prey are difficult, if not impossible, to verify.

Parasitic behavior differs from predation in that the parasite does not directly kill its host. The level of coevolutionary adaptation and anatomical and physiological specialization is extreme in most host-parasite situations. In fact, the parasite is dependent upon the host for many of its metabolic needs, and a high degree of pathogenicity (disease carrying) is evolutionarily counterproductive in parasites, usually resulting in the extinction of both partners (Noble et al. 1989). This level of dependency results in a remarkable level of behavioral stability over time in host and parasite. The antiquity of host-parasite behaviors has been chronicled in the fossil record for a number of organisms, particularly among marine invertebrates.

A representative example of parasitic interactions is between bopyrid isopods, highly specialized parasitic marine arthropods related to the common terrestrial "pill-bug," and their hosts, decapod crustaceans (e.g., crabs, shrimps). Some species of bopyrids attach themselves by their mouthparts within the gill cavity of the decapod host. The host responds to growth of the parasite underneath its exoskeleton by producing a characteristic bulge in the carapace directly above the point of attachment. Surveys of fossil crabs reveal characteristic deformations of the carapace indicating bopyrid parasitism as early as the Jurassic period, indicating a fixity of behavior between host and parasite that has lasted nearly 200 million years. Although the soft-bodied parasites do not fossilize, there is general agreement by experts (based upon extant host-parasite behavior and the characteristic morphology of parasitized decapods) about the source of the deformations seen in fossil crabs. In this and a number of other examples, the prevailing trend seems to be that highly specialized behaviors usually appear suddenly in the fossil record and then persist virtually unchanged from that point on.

Intraspecific Behaviors

Intraspecific behaviors, especially those involving reproductive behaviors, are of prime evolutionary importance. Functional morphology of structures, such as horns, tusks, and antlers, commonly associated with sexual selection, provide potential insight into the courtship and mating behaviors of extinct organisms. The antlers of living cervids (deer and elk) are used both in male-male combat as well as in sexual display. It is reasonable to conclude that the oversized antlers of the extinct Irish elk resulted from sexual selection on increased antler size, and that they probably were employed in a fashion similar to that of their living relatives.

A more compelling piece of fossil evidence for intraspecific combat is that of two male mammoths (*Mammuthus columbi*) that died when their tusks became inextricably locked together, most likely as the result of combat behavior (Figure 2). This extraordinary example of a frozen behavior is consistent with the typical fighting behavior of extant elephants, which use their tusks in violent battles, often over females.

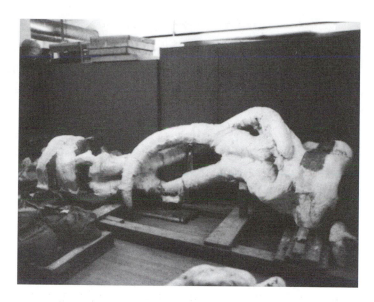

Figure 2. Skulls of two male mammoths (*Mammuthus columbi*) that died when their tusks became inextricably interlocked, probably while in combat over a female. Photo courtesy A.J. Boucot.

Conclusions

When properly analyzed, the fossil record can be a powerful tool in reconstructing behaviors of long-extinct organisms. Determination of behavioral patterns from fossils almost always involves interpretation of circumstantial evidence. The degree of reliability of that evidence depends on a number of factors. The highest category of reliability is in those relatively rare instances where organisms were preserved as examples of frozen behavior, that is, they died while actively engaged in a particular behavior. Fossil animals that possessed anatomical attributes tightly correlated to a specific behavior or behaviors rank next in terms of reliability, and that evidence becomes more compelling if closely related extant forms are available for comparison. Caution is advisable in instances where the fossil record is less informative, or when behaviors of extinct organisms cannot be modeled readily on any living group.

In those instances where ancient behaviors have been deduced with a relatively high level of confidence, several important trends are apparent. Evidence of behaviors usually appears suddenly in the fossil record, then tends to persist with no change over long spans of time. The implications of such stability and fixity of behavior are applicable not only to life of the past but are likely to have broad implications for existing biological systems, including human behavioral patterns. Studies of hominid handedness deduced from stone flakes produced in toolmaking indicate

that the percentage of left- to right-handed humans has remained the same for at least 1.4 to 1.9 million years (Toth 1985).

Few would dispute that many of our behaviors as a species are distasteful and often highly destructive, yet war, murder, and infanticide, among other traits, have remained consistent attributes of the human condition throughout our history. The fact that our species has been unable to purge such "undesirable" behaviors is not necessarily surprising when viewed from a paleontological perspective.

NICHOLAS R. GEIST

See also Reproduction; Trace Fossils

Works Cited

Boucot, A.J. 1990. *Evolutionary Paleobiology of Behavior and Coevolution.* New York and Amsterdam: Elsevier.

Chin, K. 1997. What did dinosaurs eat? Coprolites and other direct evidence of dinosaur diets. *In* J.O. Farlow and M.K. Brett-Surman (eds.), *The Complete Dinosaur.* Bloomington: Indiana University Press.

Kauffman, E.G., and R.V. Kesling. 1960. An Upper Cretaceous ammonite bitten by a mosasaur. *University of Michigan Museum of Paleontology Contributions* 15:193–248.

Kielan-Jaworowska, Z., and R. Barsbold. 1972. Narrative of the Polish-Mongolian Palaeontological Expeditions 1967–71. *Palaeontologica Polonica* 27:5–13.

Noble, E.R., G.A. Noble, G.A. Schad, and A.J. Macinnes. 1989. *Parasitology.* 6th ed., Philadelphia: Lea and Febiger.

Simpson, G.G. 1976. *Penguins, Past and Present, Here and There.* New Haven, Connecticut: Yale University Press.

Toth, N. 1985. Archaeological evidence for preferential right-handedness in the lower and middle Pleistocene, and its possible implications. *Journal of Human Evolution* 14:607–14.

Unwin, D.M., A. Perle, and C. Truman. 1995. *Protoceratops* and *Velociraptor* preserved in association: Evidence for predatory behavior in dromaeosaurid dinosaurs? *Journal of Vertebrate Paleontology* 15 (supplement to no. 3):57A–58A.

Further Reading

Boucot, A.J. 1990. *Evolutionary Paleobiology of Behavior and Coevolution.* New York and Amsterdam: Elsevier.

Chin, K. 1997. What did dinosaurs eat? Coprolites and other direct evidence of dinosaur diets. *In* J.O. Farlow and M.K. Brett-Surman (eds.), *The Complete Dinosaur.* Bloomington: Indiana University Press.

Noble, E.R., G.A. Noble, G.A. Schad, and A.J. Macinnes. 1961. *Parasitology: The Biology of Animal Parasites.* London: Kimpton; Philadelphia: Lea and Febiger; 6th ed. as *Parasitology,* Philadelphia: Lea and Febiger, 1989.

PALEOMAGNETISM

The Earth has a dense core composed mostly of iron. The outer portion of this core is a liquid, and the motion of this liquid produces a magnetic field, so the Earth behaves like a giant bar magnet. For unknown reasons, the magnetic field periodically reverses itself—the north and south poles switch positions. These reversals have occurred frequently but irregularly during Earth history. The process of reversal seems to take about 4,000 to 5,000 years. The current state of the magnetic field (in which a compass needle points toward the northern pole) has lasted for 700,000 years and is referred to as an interval of *normal polarity*. Geologists refer to periods when the poles had a switched position (so a compass needle would have pointed to the southern pole) as intervals of *reversed polarity*.

Most rocks contain minerals that are naturally magnetic, such as magnetite and hematite. Minute grains of magnetic minerals act like tiny bar magnets. When they are locked into rocks, these mineral grains can record the direction of the Earth's magnetic field. When lava flows cool, these magnetic minerals align themselves with the direction of the Earth's magnetic field. Magnetic mineral grains also align themselves with the magnetic field when they are deposited in sediments. These processes provide a record of the state of the magnetic field (normal or reversed polarity) when a rock is formed.

Beginning in the 1960s, geologists made a concentrated effort to decipher the history of the Earth's magnetic field. Because of plate tectonics and continental drift, the oldest seafloor preserved on Earth dates from the Middle Jurassic age, about 160 million years old. Geologists have determined the magnetic polarities of rocks from the seafloor, which are lavas for which some numerical ages have been calculated. This has allowed scientists to plot with fair accuracy the magnetic polarity history of the Earth back to the Middle Jurassic. Before that time, the polarity history is less well understood, although ongoing efforts are filling in our understanding of the Earth's polarity history at least as far back as 600 million years ago.

This polarity history is referred to as the geomagnetic polarity timescale. It provides a globally consistent pattern of normal and reverse polarity intervals that can be used to estimate the ages of rocks and the events they record. This age estimation is begun by first determining the magnetic polarity history of a local succession of rocks. Samples are collected in the field and oriented with a compass to the current magnetic field. They then are heated in a laboratory to remove the current magnetic signal and determine the original magnetic alignment at the time the rock formed.

Once the alignments have been determined for a succession of rock layers, its piece of geomagnetic polarity history has been determined. Now, this piece (preserved by a local rock succession) needs to be matched to a piece of the geomagnetic polarity timescale. This matching is termed "correlation."

In correlation, a signature is looked for—a distinctive pattern of magnetic polarity reversals—in order to establish a match. For example, during the Late Cretaceous, about 67 to 68 million years ago, the magnetic polarity timescale contains a very distinctive signature: two relatively long intervals of normal polarity split by a very short interval of reversed polarity. This signature in a local rock succession can readily be matched to the geomagnetic polarity timescale to conclude that the local succession is of Late Cretaceous age.

Unfortunately, not all local successions nor all portions of the geomagnetic polarity timescale contain such distinctive signatures. Some other idea of the general age of the local rock succession—either an index fossil or a numerical age—usually is needed to help narrow the possible correlation of magnetic reversal histories. This means that magnetic-polarity-based correlations are usually not an independent means of correlation, although once an index fossil or numerical age places our local slice of magnetic polarity history "in the ballpark," matching magnetic signatures often provide a more exact correlation than can fossils or numerical ages alone.

Some scientists have suggested that switches in magnetic polarity might have had an adverse affect on life and thus caused mass extinctions. However, no evidence supports this theory, because no clear correlation can be demonstrated between extinctions and magnetic polarity reversals. Dinosaur extinction provides a case in point. It took place during an interval of reversed polarity that lasted for 570,000 years, not at a reversal boundary. Indeed, none of the great extinctions in the history of life can be matched to a reversal boundary.

SPENCER G. LUCAS

See also Plate Tectonics and Continental Drift

Further Reading

Kennett, J.P. (ed.). 1966. *Magnetic Stratigraphy of Sediments*. Stroudsburg, Pensylvania: Dowden, Hutchinson and Ross.

McElhinny, M.W. 1973. *Paleomagnetism and Plate Tectonics*. Cambridge: Cambridge University Press.

Tarling, D.H. 1983. *Paleomagnetism*. London: Geological Society.

PALEONTOLOGY: OVERVIEW

Paleontology is the study of prehistoric life through its fossilized remains or the traces of its history in sediments. Fossils, the remains or traces of once-living organisms that are preserved in the sediments of the Earth's crust, provide the only direct evidence of life in the past.

As a scientific discipline, paleontology is the study of biological objects (fossils) in a geological context (the sediments in which they are preserved). Consequently, paleontology borders on, and draws from, two major branches of science. Paleontologists must be interdisciplinary in their interests and competent in both geology and biology. Some paleontologists find employment teaching geology in colleges or universities or working in geological jobs (such as in the oil or coal industries, or in governmental geological agencies), while others teach biology in colleges and universities, or anatomy in medical schools. Paleontological research is published in a wide variety of geological and biological journals, as well as in many specialized and interdisciplinary publications, so the relevant literature is often scattered among many books and journals.

Specialization

Most paleontologists specialize in a particular subdiscipline. Some subdisciplines are defined by the group of organisms that are studied. Vertebrate paleontologists study the remains of extinct backboned animals (vertebrates), including fishes, amphibians, reptiles, birds, and mammals. Invertebrate paleontologists study the remains of animals without backbones (such as arthropods, molluscs, echinoderms, brachiopods, bryozoans, corals, and sponges). Paleobotanists study the remains of ancient plants. Micropaleontologists specialize in a wide variety of different groups of organisms that are so tiny that they can only be studied with a microscope. These include microscopic plants (pollen, diatoms, calcareous algae), animals (ostracodes, conodonts, pteropods), and single-celled organisms that are neither plants nor animals (foraminifera, radiolaria, and many other protistans). Because micropaleontology is very useful in finding oil, the majority of micropaleontologists are employed by the petroleum industry. Paleontologists who study megascopic fossils, on the other hand, tend to be employed by colleges and universities because the benefits of their research are more academic in interest.

Paleontologists also may define themselves by areas of theoretical interest. Paleobiology describes any application of biological principles to the fossil record, and many paleobiologists study biological phenomena across many taxonomic groups (classifications). Paleobiogeography is the study of the past distribution of organisms in an attempt to understand their origin and dispersal around the world and sometimes to decipher the motions of continents and land bridges. Paleoecology is the study of ecological principles as they apply to the fossil record. Paleoecologists try to reconstruct ancient environments and the ecology of extinct organisms. Paleoclimatology is the study and reconstruction of ancient climates, a discipline that not only uses fossils as indicators of past environments but also uses information from geochemistry, climatic modeling, and many other fields. Biostratigraphy uses the distribution of fossils in stratified layers of rocks to correlate and date those rocks. Most paleontologists who are employed by oil and coal companies as economic paleontologists use their knowledge of the fossil record (especially biostratigraphy) to predict the location and the quality and quantity of future oil and coal resources.

The profession of paleontology itself has evolved and changed over last the century. The first people to study fossils were scholars who made their living in other professions. The Danish biologist Nicholaus Steno (also known as Niels Stenson) was a doctor, as was the American anatomist Joseph Leidy. Many eighteenth- and nineteenth-century paleontologists were professors of anatomy or mineralogy or were independently wealthy gentlemen who could study fossils as a hobby. Not until the mid-nineteenth century did it become possible for a scientist to earn a living as a paleontologist. A few were professional fossil collectors, but most were professors in universities or were employed by governmental geological surveys or museums. This employment pattern continued through much of the twentieth century, but by the 1920s and 1930s the explosive growth of the petroleum industry created an enormous demand for micropaleontologists, who were critical participants in the search for oil and gas. In the 1960s and 1970s the expansion of colleges and universities to cope with the "baby boom" generation meant that many more college geology and biology departments could employ paleontologists. Since the mid-1980s, however, the contraction of the oil industry, the decline in federal funding for science, and the change in priorities within academic departments have meant that employment opportunities for paleontologists are much worse than they were in the heyday of the 1960s. Paleontology now may be contracting to the smaller number of professional positions that it sustained before the oil and baby boom.

While many paleontologists study fossils because they are fascinated with prehistoric organisms and want to understand ancient life, there are also many practical reasons for studying paleontology.

Biostratigraphy

Fossils are the only practical means of telling time in geology. Radioisotopic decay methods, such as potassium-argon or uranium/lead dating, work only in rocks that have cooled down from a very hot state, such as igneous or metamorphic rocks. Most geological history is contained in sedimentary rocks, which cannot be dated by radioisotopes. Consequently, fossil studies are the only practical method of determining the age of rocks in most geological settings. For a long time, the major employers of paleontologists were oil companies, who relied heavily on biostratigraphers to tell them where to find oil. Modern civilization would have been impossible without these specialists. No matter what fads come and go in geology, there will always be a demand for paleontologists who can answer the basic question, "How old is it?"

Evolution

Fossils are the only direct record of the history of life. Although evolutionary biology has made enormous strides studying living organisms such as bacteria, fruit flies, and lab rats, these studies focus on evolution only within the thin slice of time known as the Recent epoch. Fossils provide the only direct evidence of 3.5 billion years of the history of life, and in many cases, they suggest processes that might not be explained by what is known from living organisms. Fossils provide a fourth dimension (time) to the biology of many living organisms. Many groups of organisms, such as conodonts (minute tooth-like fossils) and graptolites (widespread, floating, colonied animals), are extinct and are known only from the fossil record.

Paleoecology

Fossils can provide direct evidence of ancient environments. Although many sedimentary rocks deposited in different environments look very similar, the fossils and trace fossils found within them are often their most distinctive characteristic and provide a way to analyze conditions at the time sediments were deposited. (This process is called "diagnosis.") Fossils can be used to define the depositional environment more precisely than any other property of the sedimentary rock.

Paleogeography

Fossils can be critical to determining ancient continental positions and connections. Some of the earliest evidence for continental drift came from the similarities of fossils on different continents, and paleontological evidence is critical to any understanding of biogeography.

The Value of the Paleontological Perspective

Despite all these important reasons for understanding fossils, most paleontologists enter the profession because fossils and the extinct organisms they represent are fascinating, in and of themselves. The fossil record offers us a unique perspective on life that could never be appreciated from what is alive today. Without the fossil record, who would have imagined that the land was once ruled by such immense creatures as the dinosaurs and that the seas were ruled by equally impressive marine reptiles? Who would have dreamed of some of the bizarre creatures that are now extinct, from the trilobites (marine arthropods) and ammonites (shelled animals related to nautiluses) that once dominated the seas, to the incredible plants and animals of the land and air that once existed? Without the fossil record, who would have guessed that through 85 percent of life's history three billion years there were no organisms on this planet more sophisticated than bacteria, and no organic structures larger than algal mats?

Ecologists assume that the modern complexities of the food web and other principles of ecology are the norm, but the fossil record teaches us that such complex ecological relationships are a relatively recent innovation of life. Through most of life's history, much simpler ecological patterns prevailed. At one time, the land was not dominated by flowering plants, insects, mammals, and birds (which are all relatively late arrivals on this planet), but by simple plants and (if there were land animals at all) millipedes, spiders, and scorpions, and eventually by amphibians and reptiles. Today, the sea is the realm of fishes, clams, snails, and crustaceans, but in the past it was dominated by groups that are either extinct, or still alive but relatively rare in the modern ocean: trilobites, nautiloids, brachiopods, bryozoans, and crinoids. The air was inhabited by flying insects hundreds of millions of years before the first birds or bats, and even flying reptiles preceded the first birds. Without the fossil record, none of these insights into life of the past would have been possible, or would even have been predicted from our knowledge of life today.

DONALD R. PROTHERO

See also Micropaleontology, Vertebrate; Molecular Paleontology; Paleobiogeography; Paleoclimatology; Paleoecology; Paleoethology; Paleomagnetism; Paleontology: Careers for Paleontologists; Paleontology: History of Paleontology

Further Reading

Boardman, R.S., A.H. Cheetham, and A.J. Rowell (eds.). 1987. *Fossil Invertebrates*. Palo Alto, California: Blackwell Scientific.

Clarkson, E.N.K. 1979. *Invertebrate Palaeontology and Evolution*. London and Boston: Allen and Unwin; 3rd ed., London and New York: Chapman and Hall, 1993.

Colbert, E.H. 1955. *Evolution of the Vertebrates*. New York: Wiley; 4th ed., with M. Morales, 1991.

Cowen, R. 1976. *History of Life*. New York: McGraw-Hill; 2nd ed., Boston: Blackwell Scientific, 1990.

Lane, N.G. 1978. *Life of the Past*. Columbus, Ohio: Merrill; 3rd ed., New York: MacMillan.

Lipps, J. (ed.). 1993. *Fossil Prokaryotes and Protists*. Boston: Blackwell Scientific.

Nield, E.W., and V.C.T. Tucker. 1985. *Palaeontology: An Introduction*. Oxford and New York: Pergamon.

Prothero, D.R. 1998. *Bringing Fossils to Life: An Introduction to Paleobiology*. Boston: Brown/McGraw-Hill.

Raup, D.M., and S.M. Stanley. 1971. *Principles of Paleontology*. San Francisco: Freeman; 2nd ed., 1978.

Stearn, C.W., and R.L. Carroll. 1989. *Paleontology: The Record of Life*. New York: Wiley.

PALEONTOLOGY: HISTORY OF PALEONTOLOGY

Although the term "paleontology" (or palaeontology, from the Greek meaning the "study or science of ancient life") dates only to 1838, when it first was coined by the British geologist Sir Charles Lyell, the science of ancient life has much earlier roots. The fundamental objects of paleontological study are fossils, a term now used to denote the remains, impressions, or evidences of ancient life-forms preserved in rocks. The word "fossil," used long before there was a true science of paleontology, is derived from the Latin verb *fodere* ("to dig in the ground"), and the adjective *fossilis* originally was used to indicate objects dug from the ground; the noun *fossilium* (which became fossil in English) was such an object taken from the ground. Thus in the sixteenth century the category of fossils included not only fossils in the modern sense (that is, remains of once-living organisms) but also various rocks, minerals, crystals, gemstones, concretions, and even ancient human artifacts (such as stone tools).

A major step toward the modern science of paleontology was the collecting of the diverse entities known as fossils, the publication of illustrations and descriptions of the fossils (so that scholars from different countries could compare the materials they were finding), and the grouping of fossils into categories based on their appearances. In the sixteenth century it was clear to some naturalists, such as the Swiss scholar Conrad Gesner, that some fossils clearly resemble modern living organisms as well as other classes of objects (for instance, heavenly bodies such as the Sun, Moon, stars, and planets). Over the centuries the term fossil became progressively restricted in scope, ultimately referring only to those objects that resembled living organisms.

During the sixteenth and seventeenth centuries it was not immediately assumed that just because a fossil resembled a living organism it necessarily meant that it was the product of, or remains of, an actual once-living organism. Owing to the vagaries of fossil preservation, the diverse forms that minerals and concretions can take, and the finding of some fossilized remains of extinct organisms that have no close living relatives, sixteenth-century naturalists could view fossil petrifications (things made of stony material) as forming a gradational series from objects that very closely resembled known living organisms to obviously (at least to a modern eye) inorganic forms such as mineral crystals and gemstones. No matter how closely some fossils resembled living organisms, certain naturalists and philosophers could argue that such fossils never actually had been living organisms. Rather, the fossils were images or correspondences of organisms (as well as other objects) that had formed within the Earth by a molding force (following a Neo-Platonic philosophy). Or, some naturalists suggested, the fossils had grown in the rocks, either from seeds or by simple spontaneous generation (following a Neo-Aristotelian philosophy).

Even in the sixteenth and early seventeenth centuries, however, there were certain fossils that were viewed by some naturalists as clearly the remains of once-living organisms (what, in modern times, sometimes have been referred to as "easy fossils"). Such fossils included bones and shells that were only a few millions or tens of millions of years old, and were relatively unmodified in composition, were close or identical to the remains of living organisms, and in some cases were found close to the areas where similar modern organism still lived. A much publicized early example of such thinking is Leonardo da Vinci's conclusion, reached approximately 1508, that certain fossil mollusk shells were the remains of once-living organisms; da Vinci's conclusions went unpublished, however, and did little to influence the thinking of others. When such "easy fossils" were first generally recognized, they often were assumed to be the remains of organisms buried during the Biblical Noah's flood.

During the seventeenth century, a number of naturalists began to be convinced that a broad range of traditional fossils were of organic origin, and the term fossil became increasingly restricted to include only those remains of organisms that we now consider fossils in a modern sense. Two important contributors to this debate were the Danish scholar Niels Stensen (also widely known as Nicolas Steno) and the English naturalist Robert Hooke. Steno specifically argued that the class of objects then known as "tongue-stones" were actually the petrified teeth of once-living sharks, but he believed they were deposited in the rocks during the "Noachian" deluge. Hooke, speaking before the prestigious Royal Society of London (and also publishing his ideas in their *Philosophical Transactions*), argued for the interpretation of the wide range of fossil objects as once-living organisms, including ammonites (chambered mollusc shells) and other forms that have no close living relatives. Hooke also suggested that such fossils might have been placed at high altitudes on dry land by earthquakes that elevated what was once an ocean floor (a remarkably modern notion).

Still, many scholars doubted the explanations for fossils proposed by the likes of Steno and Hooke, preferring the older philosophical explanation. Throughout the seventeenth and eighteenth centuries a major stumbling block for some naturalists was the presence of many fossils that superficially appeared to be organic but did not closely resemble any known living organisms. The concept of extinction was unacceptable to many scholars for basic philosophical reasons. The deity was thought to have created a complete and perfect world; to suggest that some organisms had existed in the past, and then gone extinct, was to doubt this fundamental worldview.

The eighteenth century has been characterized as a period of systematic collection and detailed study of fossils (in the modern sense), with the continued recognition that more and more types of fossils were truly of organic origin. This work went hand-in-hand with the enthusiasm and increasing knowledge of organisms from all corners of the globe generally. The eighteenth century was the time of the great French naturalist Georges Buffon and the Swedish systematist Carolus Linnaeus, who founded the modern system of biological classification and did much to promote the discovery of new types of organisms around the world. Some of these newly discovered living organisms were found to be very similar to fossil objects. But toward the closing years of the century it also was becoming generally realized, as most of the world was being explored by naturalists, that extinction might be real.

By the end of the eighteenth and beginning of the nineteenth century, full-blown paleontology in the modern sense was being practiced by the French naturalist Georges Cuvier, often considered the father of vertebrate paleontology (the study of fossil animals with backbones, such as horses and humans). Cuvier was a brilliant comparative anatomist who reconstructed many fossil animals (mostly mammals) from their preserved bones. He clearly treated these animals as once-living organisms, and he cogently argued that the majority of the animals he was able to reconstruct were no longer alive—the species to which they belonged had gone extinct.

Cuvier, along with his colleague Alexandre Brongniart, was also establishing the fact that different fossils occur in different layers of rock: that is, the fossil faunas (and floras) occur in a definite sequence in the rock record. By the law of superposition, pioneered by Steno a century earlier, the oldest fossils occur in the bottom of the rock record and progressively younger fossils were deposited above. Cuvier recognized that, in general, progressively older fossils are more dissimilar to living organisms than are relatively younger fossils. Cuvier argued that life, and the Earth itself, had a significant history (not just a mere 6,000 years or so, as many people thought based on the Judeo-Christian Bible), and that life on Earth had gone through a series of "revolutions." Essentially, the history of the Earth could be seen as periods of relative "quiet" (such as the times in which we now live) interspersed with major "revolutions" or "catastrophes" that eliminated old local (and perhaps global) biotas, replacing them with new organisms. In the context of such a scheme the Noachian deluge could be viewed as the most recent revolution.

For Cuvier, extinction was real during such revolutions; it was not simply that the organisms migrated to some distant realms and were still alive in unexplored regions of the globe. Cuvier also rejected the notion that organisms somehow had transformed, metamorphosed (or in modern terms, evolved) over time from one sequential fauna to the next. Indeed, Cuvier's colleague Jean-Baptiste de Lamarck, working primarily with invertebrate fossils and their living counterparts, suggested just such a possibility. In the first decade of the nineteenth century, Lamarck was propounding a theory of evolution that, in his opinion, explained the apparent extinction of many ancient species. No organisms had gone extinct, they simply transformed or evolved through time into the species we see today. This evolution, according to Lamarck, could be traced through the sequential fossils preserved in the fossil record. Lamarck's ideas along these lines were only afforded serious consideration by most paleontologists after Charles Darwin's publication of his theory of evolution in 1859.

Cuvier and his colleagues in France were not the only researchers discovering the sequential nature of fossil assemblages in the rock record. Similar studies were being carried out in the early decades of the nineteenth century by such workers as Giovanni Battista Brocchi in Italy and, most famously, by William Smith in England.

Smith produced a geological map of England, Wales, and part of Scotland in 1815 that demonstrated the practical utility of fossils in correlating the strata (rock layers) in which they were embedded over a wide geographic area. Although not the earliest research on biostratigraphy, the work of Smith and others helped promote the study of fossils (especially the commonly preserved invertebrates, for example, mollusc shells) as a means of elucidating other issues in geology, such as the clear understanding of the geology of an area that in turn would bear on the location and exploitation of mineral and fossil fuel resources. The pragmatic application of knowledge about fossils has been a major theme in paleontology ever since. One important outgrowth of this work was the development of the geologic timescale, divided into sequential periods (systems) and finer subdivisions, based on the characteristic faunas and floras found in different superimposed layers of rocks. By the middle of the nineteenth century the terms Cambrian, Silurian, Devonian, Carboniferous, Permian, Triassic, Jurassic, Cretaceous, Tertiary, Quaternary, and Pleistocene were all in use among geologists and paleontologists.

The first half of the nineteenth century was also a time of fascinating paleontological discoveries, including the recognition of the animals eventually named the Dinosauria ("terrible lizards," dinosaurs) by the outstanding British anatomist and paleontologist Richard Owen in 1841. The first discoveries of these extinct giant "lizards" occurred in the 1820s in England when the husband-and-wife team of Gideon and Mary Ann Mantell collected fossils of *Iguanodon* and William Buckland published a monograph on *Megalosaurus* (1824). Also in the 1820s, William Conybeare was publishing reconstructions of the Mesozoic marine reptiles *Ichthyosaurus* and *Plesiosaurus.* By the 1830s reconstructed scenes of prehistoric times, including extinct animals on the land, in the oceans, and in the air (pterodactyls), were becoming increasingly popular and widely published. In the 1850s Richard Owen worked with sculptor Benjamin Waterhouse Hawkins to create life-sized reconstructions of fossil animals that were placed in a "theme park" on the grounds of the "Crystal Palace" (a huge glass-and-steel building used as an exhibition hall for the arts and sciences) in a suburb of London. Among the attractions was a giant sculpture of the *Iguanodon* dinosaur.

A major revolution in thinking among many biologists was engendered by the publication in 1859 of Charles Darwin's book espousing a theory of evolution: *On the Origin of Species by Means of Natural Selection, or the Preservation of Favored Races in the Struggle for Life.* Today it is sometimes popularly assumed that paleontologists were almost unanimously among the first and foremost proponents of evolution once it was proposed, but such is not the case.

The fossil record clearly demonstrated, in the minds of most paleontologists, some sort of one-way or linear history to life. The organisms of the various periods were distinctive, and one could even view the history of life as progressing from its distant origins (sometime prior to the ancient Cambrian fauna) to life on Earth today. There was a time, for instance, when vertebrates were extremely rare, and those present consisted only of fishes. There was a time dominated by reptiles, when mammals were an extremely minor constituent of the biota. And clearly, during much of geologic history, humans did not exist. Even if the history of life was, in the broadest sense, "progressive" and "linear," this did not necessarily support a notion of evolution.

Lamarck first proposed his theory of evolution around 1800, and in 1844 the Edinburgh publisher Robert Chambers anonymously authored a book entitled *Vestiges of the Natural History of Creation,* which espoused, among other things, the transmutation of organisms through time as they progressed to a higher state. These early theories of evolution were afforded little credit by most paleontologists. Overall, the fossil record did not document the slow, gradual transmutation of one species into another (as Lamarck predicted), and it did not include (at least to any great extent) intermediate organisms connecting major disparate groups of organisms (later often referred to as "missing links"). Rather, each major fossil biota was separate and distinct; and even though the organisms were different from those alive today, that did not necessarily mean they were less complex or well-adapted to their environment than extant species. William Buckland, for instance, could point out that the Silurian fauna—containing some of the oldest fossils then known, and very different modern faunas—contained extremely complex and well-adapted trilobites. Conversely, even today there are many "simple" or "primitive" organisms that appear to be at no risk of going extinct.

Given this context, it is perhaps easier to understand that when Darwin first published on evolution he viewed the paleontological record as more of stumbling block than a support for his ideas. Darwin would have to explain why the paleontological evidence was not more strongly in favor of his theory. In *Origin of Species,* Darwin includes a chapter "On the Imperfection of the Geological Record" (it should be remembered that Darwin was well versed in geology and made original contributions in the field) before moving to a discussion "On the Geological Succession of Organic Beings." But not all paleontologists were convinced that the fossil record was as incomplete and inadequate as Darwin suggested, although continuing work filled many gaps. Through the late nineteenth century more and more paleontologists adopted an evolutionary point of view, although many did not accept Darwin's mechanism of evolution (namely, natural selection). Instead, some paleontologists adopted various Neo-Lamarckian (inheritance of acquired characteristics) and orthogenetic (some sort of force that caused organisms to evolve, driving them toward predesignated ends) theories of evolution. It also is important to note that whether or not a particular paleontologist adopted a theory of evolution, in general it had little if any effect on the basic work of collecting, classifying, and stratigraphically correlating fossil organisms and the rocks in which they were found.

The British naturalist Thomas Henry Huxley, sometimes known as Darwin's bulldog, and other supporters of evolution searched the fossil record for support. *Archaeopteryx,* described by Owen in 1863, was interpreted by Huxley as an evolutionary link between birds and reptiles. The discovery by the American vertebrate paleontologist Othniel C. Marsh of additional fossil birds with teeth, announced in 1872, was used as further evidence of the truth of evolution. During the 1860s and 1870s in Europe, the vertebrate paleontologists Jean-Albert Gaudry and Ludwig Rutimeyer were constructing among the first tentative phylogenies (evolutionary histories of related organisms—in these early cases involving such animals as hyenas, elephants, rhinos, tapirs, and horses) based on fossil forms. In the 1870s Marsh reconstructed the presumed evolutionary record of horses in North America, dating back to the "dawn horse" *Eohippus* some tens of millions of years ago. This example quickly became a classic "proof" of evolution. Simultaneously in America, Edward Drinker Cope also was espousing a form of evolution (although more Lamarckian than Darwinian) and marshalling evidence from the vertebrate fossil record. Throughout the 1870s to the end of the century, support for evolutionary theories also was drawn from the invertebrate fossil record by such workers as Alphaeus Hyatt in America and Melchior Neumayr, Karl von Zittel, and Wilhelm H. Waagen in Europe.

However, throughout the latter half of the nineteenth century there were major obstacles to the use of the fossil record in advancing evolutionary theory. At best, the fossil record could be interpreted to demonstrate that evolution had occurred—at least among some groups of organisms. In hindsight, paleontology was unable to shed major light on the mechanism of evolutionary change. Darwin had promoted natural selection, Neo-Lamarckians advocated the direct influence of the environment on shaping organisms and the inheritance of acquired characteristics, and other theorists suggested that there was an inherent linear progression or driving force that caused evolutionary changes to occur.

The burning questions of how life arose and whether humans were the product of evolution also were left unanswered by paleontology at this time. The earliest known fossils were already quite complex and advanced. The pre-Cambrian reputed primitive single-celled "animal," *Eozoon,* which made scientific headlines in the 1860s and 1870s, was demonstrated to be based on nothing more than inorganic concretions in 1878. With regard to human evolution, the first recognized Neandertal skull had been uncovered in 1856 in Germany, the first Cro-Magnon man remains were recovered in France in 1868, and from the 1860s on there was increasingly solid evidence for the "Stone Age" and the greater antiquity of the human race. However, such evidence was far from convincing to those who doubted that humans had evolved from early ape-like creatures, as suggested by Huxley and the biologist Ernst Haeckel. Even the initial discovery of the fragmentary remains of Java Man (originally called *Pithecanthropus* but now referred to as *Homo erectus)* by Eugene Dubois in 1891 was greeted with skepticism by much of the public.

The last decades of the nineteenth century and first few decades of the twentieth century can be characterized as a period during which much of paleontology was somewhat divorced from cutting-edge research in mainstream biology and evolution. While experimental and laboratory techniques were embraced in such fields as genetics, developmental biology, and physiology, paleontologists continued to collect and classify fossils, working out tentative evolutionary phylogenies and ever refining the use of fossils in stratigraphic correlations. To general audiences of the time, perhaps the most public and exciting aspects of paleontology were the continuing discoveries of new dinosaurs, archaic mammals, and early human fossils. Such research often emanated from major natural history museums, such as the British Museum (Natural History) in London, the American Museum of Natural History in New York City (under the direction of the vertebrate paleontologist Henry Fairfield Osborn), the Smithsonian Institution in Washington, D.C., and the Peabody Museum at Yale University in New Haven, Connecticut.

Beginning in the late 1930s and into the 1940s, paleontology was in many ways reintegrated with developments in mainstream evolutionary biology. George Gaylord Simpson, one of the preeminent paleontologists of the twentieth century, was a major architect (along with the biologists Ernst Mayr, Julian Huxley, and Theodosius Dobzhansky) of the "modern synthesis" that combined recent work in genetics, paleontology, and evolutionary theory into an integrated neo-Darwinian whole. While Simpson's specialty was the evolution of fossil mammals, perhaps his most lasting contribution was the promotion of cross-fertilization between paleontology on the one hand and experimental genetic, evolutionary, and ecological studies of living organisms on the other hand. Simpson and colleagues argued that the fossil record is compatible with strict Darwinian evolutionary theory developed through the study of extant organisms—an idea doubted by many paleontologists previously. Simpson also promoted the use of statistical methods in classifying fossils and analyzing fossil assemblages.

The last half of the twentieth century witnessed renewed vigor and major advances in paleontology, but to a certain extent also a diversification and splintering of specialties and outlooks in the science. Paleontologists have never been a totally unified group, and there continues to be a fundamental dichotomy between paleontologists who approach the subject from a more strictly geological, biostratigraphic, and taxonomic standpoint, and those (often termed paleobiologists) who address fossil studies as an extension of neobiological studies. Paleoecological studies, analyses of faunal and population dynamics over time and space, functional morphological and paleophysiological studies, and certain types of paleobiogeographic, paleoenvironmental, evolutionary, and taphonomic (how fossils are preserved) research generally are considered more "paleobiological" in nature than strictly paleontological in the classic sense.

One also needs to remember that there are numerous group-oriented subdisciplines and specialties in paleontology; some paleontologists devote an entire career to the study of a single taxonomic group, such as dinoflagellates, scleractinian corals, or fossil rodents (to give just a few random examples). Among the broader subdisciplines in paleontology today are invertebrate paleontology, generally encompassing the study of macroscopic fossil animals, such as corals and molluscs, that lack backbones; vertebrate paleontology; paleobotany, the study of fossil plants; micropaleontology, which includes many further subdivisions, such as the study of the oldest known forms of life (essentially fossilized bacteria), single-celled and small multicellular marine fossils, microscopic elements of larger animals and plants, and palynology (the study of fossil pollen grains and spores); ichnology, the study of trace fossils, such as burrows, tracks, and trails; paleoanthropology, the study of fossil humans and their close relatives; and the newly emerging field of extraterrestrial paleontology (if the reputed microfossils from Mars announced in 1996 prove to be authentic remains of early Martian lifeforms). Each of these branches of paleontology has its own history.

Important developments in recent decades among paleontologists are quite numerous, and not all of the highlights can even be touched on here. In the 1960s and 1970s geology in general was subject to a major revolution in thinking with the introduction and general acceptance of a plate tectonic model of the Earth. Paleontological data played an important part in supporting this new theory, and in turn paleontological data could be interpreted in new ways within a plate tectonic context. Consequently, there has been renewed interest in paleobiogeographic analyses and paleoenvironmental reconstructions utilizing fossil data.

There has been continuing renewed interest in utilizing the fossil record to address questions relative to both the speed and mode or mechanism of evolutionary change, particularly with regards to macroevolutionary changes of a larger nature and over longer periods of time than can be studied in laboratories using bacteria or fruit flies. Such studies have been possible using ever more complete fossil sequences of selected taxonomic groups combined with more precise stratigraphic analyses and new techniques of dating fossils. One heated and highly heuristic (in that it generated many new studies and approaches) controversy of the 1970s and 1980s was whether or not evolution is characterized by continuous slow and gradual change, or if there are periods of stasis, when little evolution takes place, interspersed with periods of accelerated change (the so-called punctuated equilibrium model). This controversy appears to have become more refined as it was realized that not all groups of organisms necessarily evolve in the same manner, and whether one adopts a gradual or punctuated equilibrium model is often very much a matter of the scale and precision of the data one has available.

Dinosaur studies have surged forward as new interpretations of dinosaur physiology ("hot-blooded dinosaurs" rather than cold-blooded reptiles), anatomy, and complex social behavior (for instance, adults caring for the young) have been suggested. Also the 1979 suggestion that an asteroid or meteorite impact may have promoted the demise of the dinosaurs led to intensive new investigations into the nature and causes of mass extinctions in general. New methods and approaches toward the classification of organisms and the reconstruction of evolutionary relationships (for instance the methodology often referred to as "cladistics") have swept the field and led to both heated arguments and new insights. Continuing studies and fossil finds bearing on the evolution of humans have shed more light on the subject. It turns out that human evolution is not as simple and linear as many paleoanthropologists once thought; rather, the human evolutionary tree is characterized by many sidebranches and dead ends.

The field of paleontology remains vigorous. Classic taxonomic, systematic, stratigraphic, and evolutionary studies will surely remain important, but paleobiological and paleoecological studies may continue to proliferate. And certainly new types of studies, utilizing new methodologies undreamt of today, will be carried out.

ROBERT M. SCHOCH

See also Hoaxes and Errors; *biographies of particular paleontologists; geographical profiles of particular regions and countries*

Further Reading

Albritton, C.C., Jr. (ed.). 1963. *The Fabric of Geology.* Reading, Massachusetts: Addison-Wesley.

Bowler, P.J. 1984. *Evolution: The History of an Idea.* Berkeley: University of California Press; rev. ed., 1989.

Howard, R.W. 1975. *The Dawnseekers: The First History of American Paleontology.* New York: Harcourt Brace Jovanovich.

Rainger, R. 1996. History of paleontology. *In* E.J. Dasch (ed.), *Macmillan Encyclopedia of Earth Sciences.* Vol. 2, New York: Macmillan.

Rudwick, M.J.S. 1976. *The Meaning of Fossils.* London: Macdonald; New York: American Elsevier; rev. ed., Chicago: University of Chicago Press.

———. 1992. *Scenes from Deep Time.* Chicago: University of Chicago Press.

Schneer, C.J. (ed.). 1969. *Toward a History of Geology.* Cambridge, Massachusetts: MIT Press.

Schoch, R.M. (ed.). 1984. *Vertebrate Paleontology.* New York: Van Nostrand Reinhold.

———. 1994. Vertebrate Paleontology and Evolutionary Theory. *In* D.R. Prothero and R.M. Schoch (eds.), *Major Features of Vertebrate Evolution.* Knoxville: The Paleontological Society/University of Tennessee.

Simpson, G.G. 1983. *Fossils and the History of Life.* New York: Scientific American Books.

Zittel, K.A. von. 1901. *History of Geology and Paleontology to the End of* *the Nineteenth Century.* London: Walter Scott; New York: Scribner's; as *Geschichte der Geologie und Paläontologie bis Ende des 19. Jahrhunderts,* Munich and Leipzig: Oldenburg.

PALEONTOLOGY: CAREERS FOR PALEONTOLOGISTS

There is a diversity of careers in academic, research, and applied paleontology. The varied career specialties, which express the great significance that paleontology has to our society's knowledge and well-being, include economic paleontology, invertebrate paleontology, micropaleontology, paleobotany, paleoclimatology, paleoecology, palynology, vertebrate paleontology, and paleoanthropology.

Most paleontological career positions are at museums, universities and colleges, government agencies, and at mining and petroleum companies. Museums and universities may employ paleontologists of any sort, but usually in academic and research positions, whereas commercially oriented agencies and industries more typically offer employment for invertebrate paleontologists, palynologists, and micropaleontologists in applied positions. Paleontologists who hold academic positions usually teach and perform research, whereas those who hold other research positions usually do research and sometimes teach. Applied positions use paleontology as a tool, typically for commercial goals. Opportunities at most levels are competitive, and the level of employment depends on the employer's need and the employee's level of education, training, and experience.

Museums often require paleontological expertise at the levels of curator, collections manager, preparator, and artist. Curators do field and laboratory research, present their research at conferences, publish the results of their studies, apply for and administer grants that fund research and museum activities, have ultimate charge of the collections in their area, supervise and advise their assistants, advise staff in the exhibits and educational sections of the museum, and represent their museum to inform the public of activities in their area of expertise. They often affiliate with nearby colleges or universities, where they occasionally may teach specialty courses and mentor graduate students in paleontology.

Collections managers take direct charge of day-to-day operations in the collections area, where they manage the acquisition, cataloging, labeling, storage, and loaning of specimens. They usually are responsible to the curator of that collection, may supervise assistants, often participate in field collecting, and sometimes perform original research and publish the results.

Preparators make specimens ready for study or display by removing sediment from around them; by strengthening, reassembling, and repairing them; and by making molds and replicas. Preparators usually are responsible to one or more curators, may have assistants who they supervise directly, and may participate in field activities.

Paleontological artists are individuals who combine suffi-cient paleontological and artistic expertise that they can depict fossils accurately, make anatomically accurate reconstructions, and portray paleoenvironmental scenes in a variety of media. They often make illustrations to accompany research publications and reconstruct extinct animals as they looked in life, sometimes as three-dimensional models for display.

Academic positions in paleontology at universities and colleges usually are faculty positions, that is, academic professorships. Most are in departments of paleontology, geology, biology, zoology, anatomy, natural sciences, or anthropology. Such faculty almost always teach—often graduate courses in their research specialty and more general undergraduate courses in their department. Most mentor graduate students and advanced undergraduates (the latter especially in colleges without graduate programs) and participate in a variety of administrative activities through committee membership. Unless their teaching load is all consuming (as it may be in some smaller undergraduate colleges), most also apply for and administer grants, perform fieldwork and research, present the results of their research at conferences, and publish them in journals and books. Faculty paleontologists often affiliate with museums where they can study collections in their field and collaborate with museum paleontologists. The research of academic paleontologists may have practical intent or consequences.

Applied paleontologists work in positions that use paleontology as a tool for goals that extend beyond pure knowledge. Although some paleontologists may teach applied paleontology in universities, most applied paleontologists work for government or industry and do field, laboratory, or theoretical research that furthers the practical goals of the agency or enterprise for which they work. Governments may employ paleontologists of one or another specialty in divisions that administer affairs in natural resources, geology, minerals and mining, parks and recreation, and weather and aeronautics.

Because sedimentary rocks are the sources both for most fossils and for many of our most important natural resources, economic paleontologists can derive information from fossils that helps to find fossil fuels, such as coal and petroleum, and industrial minerals and metals. Economic paleontologists most likely specialize in invertebrate paleontology, palynology, or micropaleontology. Paleontologists may apply their special knowledge of ancient extinctions, oceans, atmosphere and climate, and geological and biotic events to understand the present and to predict the future. In practice then, they may help us to understand, prevent, or recover from changes in climate, oceanic stratification and circulation, volcanism, and other global events.

Most high-level careers in paleontology require a college education, typically through a masters or doctoral degree. As our society, knowledge, and technology increase in complexity, so do the job skills that paleontologists need. Broad interdisciplinary knowledge of the sciences, the ability to communicate well in writing and speaking, and substantial computer skills are becoming increasingly important to successful careers in paleontology.

RONALD G. WOLFF

PALYNOLOGY

Palynology is a branch of natural science dealing with the study of microscopic, decay-resistant remains of plants, mainly pollen and spores, or protists. These microremains (from about 5 to 200 micrometers in size), or "Palynomorphs," are highly resistant to destruction because of the chemical composition of their outer coatings: "Sporopollenin," a carotenoid-like polymer, characterizes pollen, spores, dinoflagellate cysts, and acritarchs, while "chitin," a polysaccharide, characterizes microforaminifera and chitinozoans. Palynomorphs are found in sediments or sedimentary rocks, which protect them from oxidation. Palynology has many applications, mainly in stratigraphical and evolutionary palynology and in Quaternary, environmental palynology. Mellisopalynology and aero- or agro-palynology are other specific applications of the study of modern and/or living pollen.

Definition of Pollen

Pollen is produced during the reproduction cycle of seed plants (angiosperms, or fruit-bearing plants, and gymnosperms). It is a male "microspore," resulting from a type of cell division that reduces the chromosome content by half (meiosis); the microspores are shed from pollen cones of gymnosperms or, in angiosperms, from a structure called the anthers. In either case, the role of pollen is to fertilize the female organ (the ovule) of the plant. All plants, go through two stages—the sporophyte and the gametophyte. Spores correspond to the resting and dispersal phase of the independent gametophyte generation of the cryptogams: ferns, algae, fungi, or mosses. Both pollen and spores are transported by wind or animals and develop a highly resistant wall layer of sporopollenin (the exine) around the living cell.

In flowering plants, the exine has a very complex structure where two thin layers, the endexine and the ektexine, are superimposed. The ektexine itself is divided into three layers: the inner layer or "foot-layer," the middle layer (composed of small columns or "columellae"), which supports the outer layer (tectum) (Figure 1). The different arrangements of these elements, as well as the ornamentation on the surface of the exine, differ considerably from one plant to another. A quick look at types of spores and pollen provides examples of this morphological variability (variability in shape and structure). There are basically two types of spores: Trilete spores have three scars that radiate from the proximal pole (the one closest to the point of attachment) of the spore; monoletes have only one scar. Pollen comes in many more varieties. Vesiculate has two air sacs. Composite pollen comes in tetrads—they are composed of four grains arranged in a tetrahedron. Polyplicate pollen has meridional grooves and a ridge. Colpate pollen has one, three, or more furrows. Colporate/colporoidate pollen has three furrows and pores; porate has one or more pores. Structure, sculpture, and the shape of the grain and the arrangement and number of its apertures (i.e., the thinning of the wall that serves, among other things, as an exit for a transport structure called the "pollen tube" during fertilization) are the many parameters used to determine fossil pollen grains.

Stratigraphy and Evolution

Spores, mainly trilete ones, are the first evidence of terrestrial plants, which appeared as early as the beginning of the Silurian period, approximately 435 million years ago (Figure 2). Spores experienced important differences in morphology since the Early Devonian (408 million years ago), with a maximum diversity reached during the Carboniferous (355 million years ago). During this period, different forms appeared: monosaccate pollen (Pteridospermales, Cordaitales), monolete spores, disaccates pollen (Coniferales), polyplicate pollen (Ephedrales), and monosulcate pollen (Cycadales). The wide development of pollen during the Permo-Triassic time interval (295 to 203 million years ago), in association with inaperturate pollen (Araucariaceae, Podocarpaceae) and *Classopolis* (all of which belonged to the gymnosperm group), was evolving at the same time as the progressive decrease of the spores. Gymnosperms dominated Jurassic times (203 to 135 million years ago) and decreased during the Cretaceous, when the first angiosperms appeared. The disappearance of *Classopolis* occurred at the same time (was coeval) as the appearance of triporate, Normapolle forms, probably related to the family Hamamelidaceae, at the end of the Cretaceous. The distribution and abundance of these main groups follows the timing of various periods so closely that when a type is found, it is a label for a time period. For example, suppose a fossil fish is found in a rock stratum that also includes a particular spore. If the age of the spore is known already, the date of the fish—indeed, of the stratum itself—also is known. Dating strata according to biological content is called biostratigraphy.

The history and phylogeny (evolutionary history) of the angiosperms have been elucidated by studies of long, well-dated geological records. The Potomac sequence of rock strata, studied by J.A. Doyle (1977), has revealed that the arrangement of the apertures of the angiosperms have changed during their evolution (Figure 3). The first angiosperm pollen grains dated from the Barremian-Aptian stages (117 to 108 million years ago) and were characterized by a single elongate aperture (a furrow). The structure of the exine was either granular (*Lethomasites*) or columellar (*Clavatipollenites*).

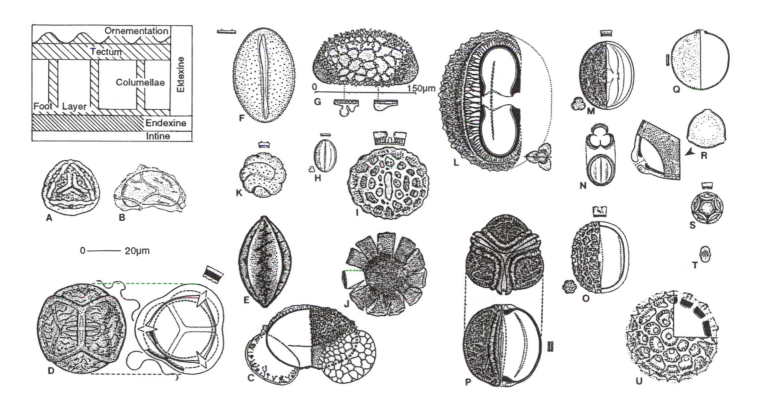

Figure 1. The great diversity in size, shape, structure, and sculpture of pollen grains and spores, which can be identified readily in terms of plant family, genus, or species. *Boxed insert*, schematic structure of the outer wall of the pollen grains: the exine is composed of two complex layers (endexine and ektexine) which overlie the "intine," the extra-cytoplasmic part of the pollen grain that usually is not fossilized—or is fossilized very seldom. *A–B*, variety in spores. *A*, trilete spores; *B*, monolete spores. *C–U*, variety in pollen grains. *C*, vesiculate pollen (Abietaceae); *D*, composite pollen *(Rhododendron)*; *E*, polyplicate pollen *(Ephedra)*; *F*, colpate pollen with one furrow *(Crinum)*; *G–K*, colpate pollen with three or more furrows: *G*, *Conanthera*; *H*, *Tamarix*; *I*, *Aprevalia*; *J*, *Josephinia*; *K*, *Eriocaulon*; *L–P*, colporate/colporoidate pollen, which has three furrows and pores: *L*, *Echinops sphaerocephalus*; *M*, *Nolana*; *N*, *Artemisia*; *O*, *Afzelia*; *P*, *Planchonia*; *Q–U*, porate pollen: *Q*, Gramineae; *R*, *Betula*; *S*, *Alternanthera*; *T*, *Cecropia*; *U*, *Tribulus*. Drawings from Erdtmann (1952); Reille in Pons (1970).

Later pollen grains, at the Aptian/Albian boundary (108 million years ago) developed three furrows *(Tricolpites)*, then, near the Albian/Cenomanian boundary (96 million years ago) a pore within each furrow *(Tricolporopollenites)*. Finally, pollen grains with three pores (the Normapolles complex: *Complexiopollis, Atlantopollis*) appeared during the Cenomanian. Additional analyses have been used to explore further the affiliation among the different families of the angiosperms, based upon deductions based upon the pollen forms and structures and comparisons with modern families (Doyle and Le Thomas, 1996). Uncertainties remain concerning the origin of the group. More fossil pollen data will be needed to resolve them. The origin probably traces back to the Late Triassic, about 90 million years ago, before the radiation of flowering plants that occurs during the Cretaceous.

Quaternary Environmental Palynology

Pollen analysis of Quaternary deposits, such as lake or peat sediments, has been developed since the end of the nineteenth century to such a degree that scholars now are able to reconstruct past flora, vegetation, and associated environmental conditions. The analysis is based on the specific characters of pollen grains and spores that (1) are extremely resistant and are preserved in deposits in which other types of microorganisms have been destroyed, conditions that produce good fossils; (2) display great diversity of forms and can be identified very specifically to their mother plants (sometimes to the species, more frequently to the genus level); (3) are produced in large quantities and dispersed regionally. When these conditions are met, pollen data can be treated statistically, and researchers can control quantitative variations linked to their production, dispersion, and deposition pattern.

Most pollen grains fall to the ground close to the plant from which they come. As a result, they give indications about the surrounding vegetation at the time when the deposit formed. Once scholars know which types of plants lived in the region, they also know those things the plants require to live. Therefore, scholars can infer related climate parameters such as annual or monthly temperature, rainfall, or precipitation/evaporation values. Interpretations of fossil pollen assemblages compare them with modern vegetation distribution and modern pollen rain and deposition.

GEOLOGICAL TIME SCALE

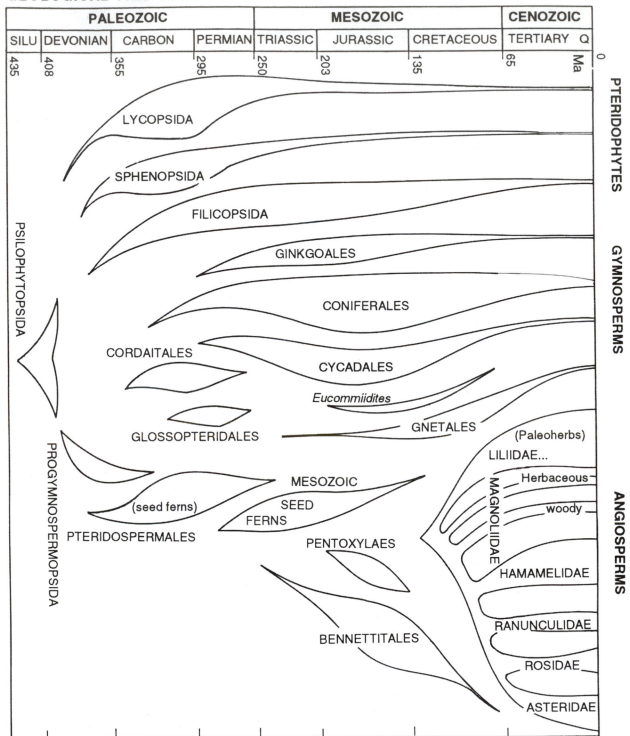

Figure 2. Stratigraphic distribution and changes in abundance (simplified) of major groups of vascular land plants. Names ending in *-opsida* are classes; *-idae,* subclasses; *-ales,* orders. Key: *Silur,* Silurian; *Carbon,* Carboniferous; *Q,* Quaternary (the last 2.5 million years). Scale: *ages,* million years. Drawn by M. Petzol, modified after Doyle (1977).

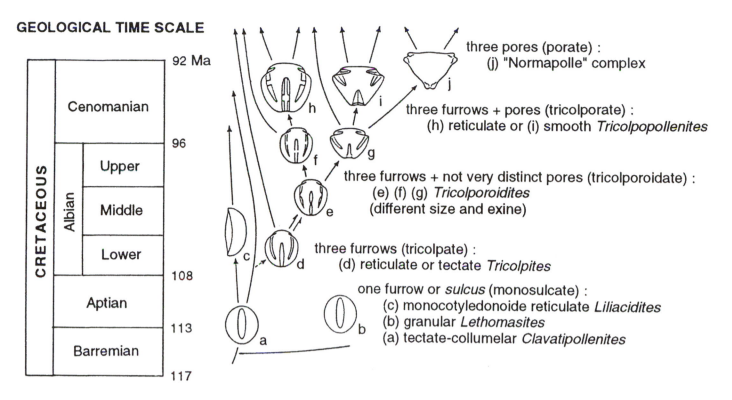

GEOLOGICAL TIME SCALE

three pores (porate) :
(j) "Normapolle" complex

three furrows + pores (tricolporate) :
(h) reticulate or (i) smooth *Tricolpopollenites*

three furrows + not very distinct pores (tricolporoidate) :
(e) (f) (g) *Tricolporoidites*
(different size and exine)

three furrows (tricolpate) :
(d) reticulate or tectate *Tricolpites*

one furrow or *sulcus* (monosulcate) :
(c) monocotyledonoide reticulate *Liliacidites*
(b) granular *Lethomasites*
(a) tectate-collumelar *Clavatipollenites*

Figure 3. Evolutionary relationships of major angiosperm pollen types in the Potomac sequence (Cretaceous). Symbol: *arrows,* proposed evolutionary lines. Modified from Doyle (1977).

Interpretations use multivariate statistical methods to test the relationships between pollen assemblages, vegetation, and climate, and to provide quantitative estimates of climate parameters. This approach is based mainly upon the assumption that the relationships between plants and their environment (mainly climatic conditions) were constant in time and that the modern observations contain all the necessary information to interpret fossil data.

Pollen grains also can be transported over long distances from their source zones. When this occurs, it provides additional indications of their means of transport (winds or currents) and related efficiency and path. Transported pollen grains are found, for instance, in marine or glacial deposits.

Method
To collect pollen samples from a sedimentary sequence (strata), samples of the soil are gathered at selected intervals (one centimeter or more) from the top to the base. Chemicals are used to separate the grains from the sediment. Then, all grains are identified and counted. In each level of a sedimentary sequence, samples from temperate regions, where pollen grains are mostly transported by winds, usually provide from 300 to 1000 grains; samples from tropical regions, where grains are transported by insects and other animals, usually provide from 1000 to 3000 grains. The percentage of pollen in a sample provides a "pollen spectrum." This data can be plotted as a function of time, producing a "pollen diagram."

Reconstruction of Past Vegetation and Climate
Figure 4 presents a pollen diagram of the Grande Pile region of Eastern France. It clearly illustrates the sequence of vegetation changes in the Northern Hemisphere temperate latitudes, sequences that have accompanied the approximately 100,000-year-long cycle of warm and cold climate states that have recurred for the past 2.5 million years. These variations can be depicted as follows:

Typically Glacial (Cold and Arid) Conditions
Glacial conditions are marked by the development of herbaceous steppes with Poaceae (grasses) and *Artemisia*. These plants lie close to the ground, spreading outward there. They prevailed during the last glacial period, from about 72 to 15 thousand years ago, and during the Riss glaciation.

The Transition to Warm, Interglacial Conditions
The transition to warmer conditions is marked mainly by rising and oscillating temperature and precipitations. Such conditions allow for the successive development of different types of forests. First, the progressive warming in summer was responsible for the development of pioneer taxa (groups; singular, taxon) from cold mixed forest such as *Juniperus* and *Betula* (juniper and birch) at the transition between the Riss glaciation and the "Eemian" interglacial, which occurred around 130 thousand years ago. After

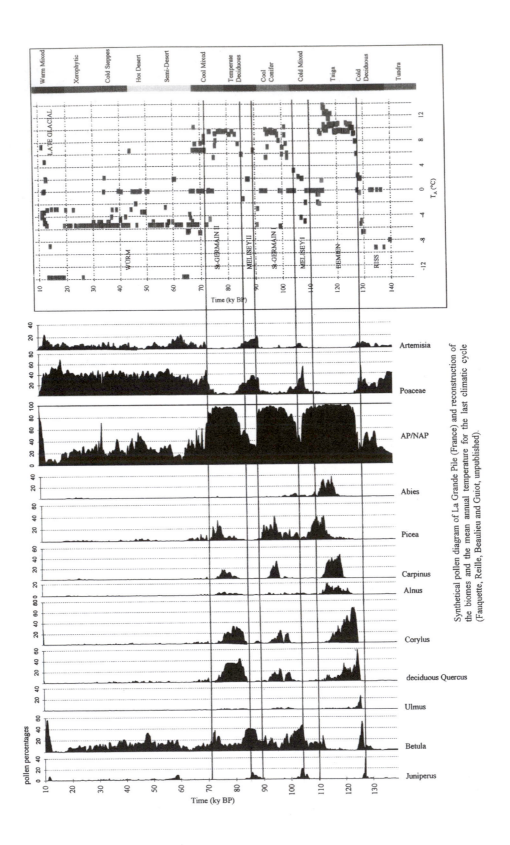

Figure 4. Synthetic pollen diagram for La Grande Pile showing, from left to right, the percentages of main taxa and inferred "biomes" as a function of the mean annual temperatures at the studied site. Diagram utilizes comparisons with modern analogs. Data are presented versus time. Scale: *kya,* thousands of years ago. From Fauquette et al. (unpublished), with the permission of the authors.

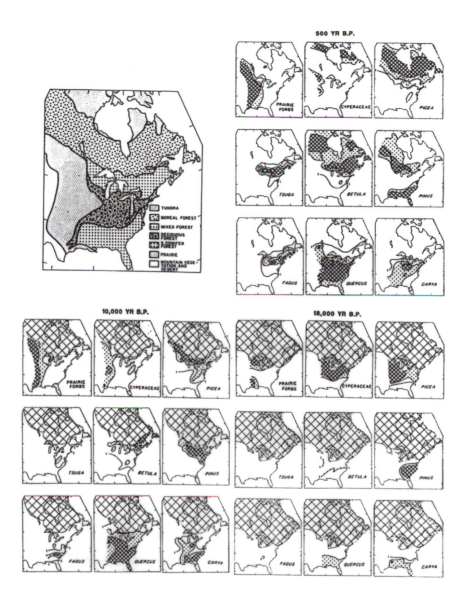

Figure 5. *Upper left,* generalized vegetation map for eastern North America; *upper right,* isopollen maps for 500 years ago for pollen for "forb" (5, 10 percent), Cyperaceae (1, 5, 10 percent), *Picea* (1, 5, 20 percent), *Tsuga* (1, 5, 10 percent), *Betula* (1, 10, 20 percent), *Pinus* (20, 40 percent), *Fagus* (1, 5, 10 percent), *Quercus* (1, 5, 20 percent), and *Carya* (1, 3, 6 percent). *Lower left,* isopollen maps for 10 thousand years ago; *lower right,* isopollen maps for the Last Glacial Maximum, 18 thousand years ago. Symbols: *white with black dots,* regions with intermediate percentages; *black with white circles,* high percentages; *cross-hatching,* location of the Laurentide ice-sheet. From Webb (1988), copyright © 1998 Kluwer Academic Publishers, reprinted with kind permission of Kluwer Academic Publishers.

approximately 124 thousand years ago, these groups were replaced by temperate deciduous taxa *Ulmus* (elm), deciduous *Quercus* (oaks), and *Corylus.* The change clearly points to a setting that featured oceanic conditions, with reduced seasonal amplitude of temperature and maximum precipitation in January.

Cooling Variations
At the end of the Eemian, after approximately 115 thousand years ago, the successive appearance of *Alnus* (alder) and *Carpinus* sug-

gests that climate conditions moved toward more continental influences, with increased variance in seasonal temperatures (with maximum July temperatures and decreasing winter temperatures) and the maximum period of precipitation shifting from winter to summer. Progressive cooling led to the complete replacement of deciduous forests by coniferous ones dominated by *Picea* and *Abies* (spruce and fur).

This progression repeated itself during the St.-Germain I period (approximately 104 to 95 thousand years ago) and St.-Germain II period (approximately 84 to 74 thousand years ago).

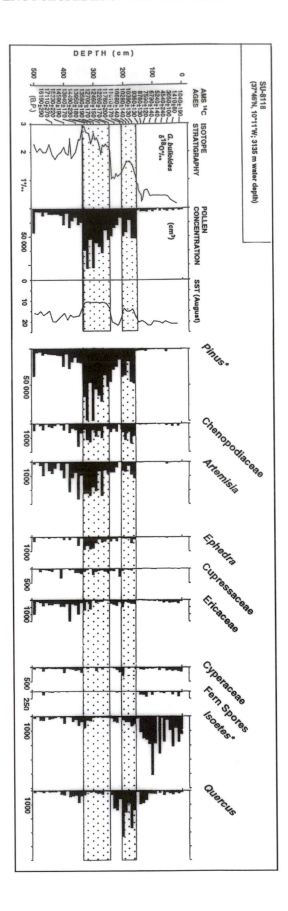

Figure 6 (left). Synthetic pollen diagram for core samples taken off Portugal, showing concentration values (per cubic centimeter of dry sediment) of selected taxa that represent the main vegetation association of the Iberian Peninsula: Steppes (Chenopodiaceae, *Artemisia*, *Ephedra*), coastal or montane vegetation (Ericaceae, Cupressaceae), thermo-philous forests (deciduous *Quercus*), humid ecosystems (Cyperaceae, fern spores, *Isoetes*, and *Pinus*). The pollen spectra are plotted versus depth. Isotope stratigraphy elaborated from the δ^{18}O measurement on *Globigerina bulloides*, and ^{14}C dates are from Bard et al. (1987). Symbol: *dotted areas*, periods of highest pollen influx of steppic taxa, interpreted as reflecting intense clockwise cyclonic circulation over the Eastern Atlantic during the dry and cold periods of the deglaciation. Modified from Lézine and Denèfle (1997).

Vegetation Mapping

Today, scholars can draw paleovegetation maps for selected periods of the recent past. Such maps are based on an important array of well-dated pollen series from a specific time period and are presented as isopollen maps (formed by synchronous lines delimiting areas with the same percentages of a certain species) (Figure 5). Such isopollen maps have been drawn for North America (Webb III 1988) and Europe (Huntley and Birks 1983). They allow us to see how the changing location, abundance, and association of individual taxa have produced different plant assemblages and influenced the modern vegetation patterns, and to observe rates and direction of broad-scale migration of taxa controlled by environmental changes, primarily in climate.

The primary role of climate in plant distribution has led paleoecologists to assign direct bioclimatic parameters to pollen assemblages and to set surface boundary conditions for paleoclimate model simulations on a global scale (Guiot et al. 1996).

Reconstruction of Past Atmospheric Circulation

Scholars also use pollen data to trace past exchanges between continents and ocean, as illustrated by the pollen record produced by core samples from the Eastern Atlantic (Lézine and Denèfle 1997) (Figure 6). First, samples are taken from the core sample. Then, scholars count the number of pollen grains per cubit centimeter of dry sediment in each sample to produce a "pollen influx diagram." The diagram records high amplitude variations in pollen distribution, which in turn reflect changes in wind trajectories during the last transition from a glaciated to a nonglaciated period.

Cold and Arid Episodes

Pollen analysis clearly reveals cold and arid episodes around 15 thousand years ago, then again during the Younger Dryas interval, around 10.3 thousand years ago. Such conditions are revealed by the presence of pollen from such plants as *Artemisia*, *Ephedra*, and Chenopodiaceae, all of which are herbaceous plants typical of cold and arid environments. Highest influx values (those that reveal the influx of pollen into an area from elsewhere) indicate the dominance of intense northeast-southwest circulation pattern in the atmosphere. This pattern is linked to enhanced clockwise air movements over the northern Atlantic. Cold and dry conditions on land occurred at the same time as low sea-surface temperatures.

Humid and Warm Episodes

Pollen that indicates the development of deciduous trees (*Quercus*) and taxa that grow primarily in humid conditions (Cyperaceae, fern spores) indicate humid and warm conditions. One such episode took place approximately 12.3 thousand years ago (during the Bölling/Alleröd interval), and another has been in place since 9.3 thousand years ago. Samples that show the lowest values of pollen influx testify to a much different atmospheric pattern than seen in cold and arid episodes. Here, patterns were dominated by the west-east direction of main air currents, as seen in our modern situation.

ANNE-MARIE LÉZINE

See also Dating Methods; Reproductive Strategies: Plants

Works Cited
Bard, E., M. Arnold, P. Maurice, J. Duprat, J. Moyes, and J.C. Duplessy. 1987. Retreat velocity of the North Atlantic polar front during the last deglaciation determined by ^{14}C accelerator mass spectrometry. *Nature* 328:791–94.

Doyle, J.A. 1977. Patterns of evolution in early angiosperms. *In* A. Haliam (ed.), *Patterns of Evolution as Illustrated by the Fossil Record*. New York and Amsterdam: Elsevier.
Doyle, J.A., and A. Le Thomas. 1996. Phylogenetic analysis and character evolution in Annonaceae. *Adansonia* 3–4:279–334.
Erdtmann, G. 1952. *Pollen Morphology and Plant Taxonomy: Angiosperms (An Introduction to Palynology I)*. Waltham, Massachusetts: Chronica Botanica.
Guiot, J., R. Cheddadi, I.C. Prentice, and D. Jolly. 1996. A method of biome and land surface mapping from pollen data: Application to Europe 6000 years ago. *Paleoclimates* 1:311–24.
Huntley, B., and H.J.B. Birks. 1983. *An Atlas of Past and Present Pollen Maps for Europe 0–13,000 Years Ago*. Cambridge and New York: Cambridge University Press.
Lézine, A.M., and M. Denèfle. 1997. Enhanced anticyclonic circulation in the eastern North Atlantic during cold intervals of the last deglaciation inferred from deep-sea pollen records. *Geology* 25 (2):119–22.
Pons, A. 1970. *Le pollen*. 2nd ed., Paris: Presses Universitaires de Paris, France.
Webb III, T. 1988. Eastern North America. *In* B. Huntley and T. Webb III (eds.), *Vegetation History*. Boston and Dordrecht: Kluwer.

Further Reading
Erdtmann, G. 1952. *Pollen Morphology and Plant Taxonomy: Angiosperms (An Introduction to Palynology I)*. Waltham, Massachusetts: Chronica Botanica; Stockholm: Almquist and Wiksell.
Huntley, B., and H.J.B. Birks. 1983. *An Atlas of Past and Present Pollen Maps for Europe 0–13,000 Years Ago*. Cambridge and New York: Cambridge University Press.
Huntley, B., and T. Webb III (eds.). 1988. *Vegetation History*. Boston and Dordrecht: Kluwer.

PANGOLINS

The living members of the order Pholidota, the pangolins or scaly anteaters, constitute a small, rather unfamiliar, and exceedingly unusual group of mammals. Their most noteworthy feature is an outer covering of large, horny, overlapping epidermal scales that causes them to appear somewhat like a four-legged pine cone. Like the true anteaters of the mammalian order Xenarthra, pangolins lack teeth. Similarly specialized for feeding on ants and termites, pangolins dig these insects out of their tunnels with powerful forelimbs and enlarged claws, then lap them up with a long, sticky tongue. The eight living pangolin species (placed by most specialists in a single genus, *Manis*) are distributed across sub-Saharan Africa, India, and southeast Asia. They range in body size from 0.5 to 1.5 meters long, including a long and robust tail, and consist of both arboreal and terrestrial forms. Pangolins may be found in either forested environments or more open grassy habitats, but wherever they are found, they occur in relatively low numbers (Kingdon 1971).

Because pangolins lack teeth (the hardest and most easily fossilized portion of the mammalian anatomy), and because their population sizes are typically small, the fossil record of the Pholidota is poor. However, a few nearly complete skeletons do exist, and they show that the group once enjoyed a much broader geographic distribution than they do today.

The oldest fossil pangolin is *Eomanis* from the famed middle Eocene Messel deposits of Germany (Storch 1978) (Figure 1). *Eomanis* is represented by several nearly complete skeletons that show it was more primitive than living pangolins. It retains a clavicle, has a relatively weak tail, and lacks the distinctive fissured terminal phalanges (the bones forming the base of the claws) of living pangolins. *Eomanis* also bears a strong resemblance both to the purported anteater from Messel, *Eurotamandua*, and to members of the extinct North American group Palaeanodonta (Rose and Emry 1993). However, there is little question that the toothless *Eomanis* is a true pangolin. Messel is famous for its preservation of soft tissues. And at Messel, preserved with one of the *Eomanis* skeletons, is an actual epidermal scale identical to those of modern pholidotans. Although no pangolins live in Europe today, the Pholidota has an extensive fossil record on the continent. Apart

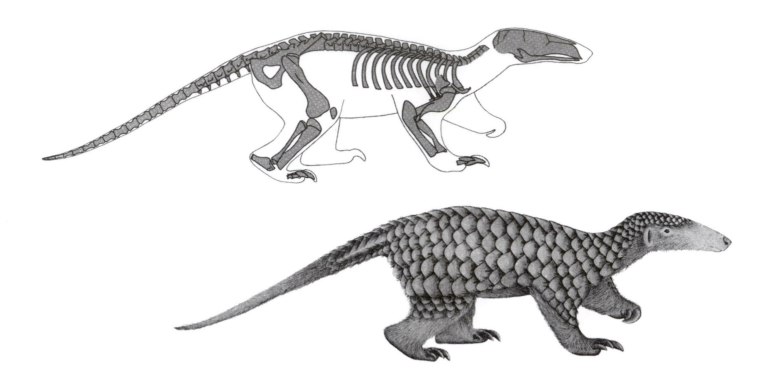

Figure 1. *Eomanis ealdi. Top*, skeletal reconstruction; *bottom*, life restoration. Redrawn by G. Storch after Storch (1978).

from *Eomanis,* isolated remains assigned to the genus *Necromanis* are known from numerous sites that range in age from Oligocene to Miocene. A single terminal phalanx shows that the Pholidota lived in Europe as recently as the Pliocene (Emry 1970).

Additional relatively complete pangolin skeletons date from late Eocene deposits in Mongolia (Rose and Emry 1993) and from early Oligocene sediments in North America (Emry 1970). Both live outside the geographic range of the Recent taxa. The Oligocene farm, *Patriomanis,* shares a number of detailed similarities with modern form, characters not found in *Eomanis* (e.g., fissured terminal phalanges, similarities in construction of the snout, wrist bones, and vertebrae). At the same time, *Patriomanis* retains primitive features in the ankle and in the bones surrounding the inner and middle ear.

In Africa and southern Asia, the domain of living pangolins, the fossil record of pholidota is still poorly known, due in part to a scarcity of paleontologists living and working in these areas. The record in Africa extends back to the Oligocene. Isolated skeletal elements have also been found in Pliocene and Pleistocene sediments of Africa (Emry 1970; Rose and Emry 1993). No pangolin fossils are found in southern Asia until the Pleistocene. Unlike the African record, the Asian fossils are comprised of some better preserved material, including relatively complete skeletons from Indonesia. They belong to the extinct species *Manis palaeojavan-*ica, the largest known pangolin, measuring nearly 2 meters in length (Emry 1970).

Relationships within the Pholidota and between pholidotans and other mammalian orders are somewhat obscure. There are suggestions that pholidotans bear some relationship to either the living mammalian order Xenarthra (armadillos, sloths, and anteaters) or to the extinct group Palaeanodonta, or both. However, these ideas remain controversial (Rose and Emry 1993).

TIMOTHY J. GAUDIN

See also Palaeanodonts; Vertebrate Hard Tissues: Keratinous Tissues; Xenarthrans

Works Cited

Emry, R.J. 1970. A North American Oligocene pangolin and other additions to the Pholidota. *Bulletin of the American Museum of Natural History* 142:459–510.

Kingdon, J. 1971. East African mammals. In *An Atlas of Evolution in Africa.* Vol. 1. London: Academic Press; Chicago: University of Chicago Press.

Rose, K.D., and R.J. Emry. 1993. Relationships of Xenarthra, Pholidota, and fossil "edentates": The morphological evidence. *In* F.S. Szalay,

M.J. Novacek, and M.C. McKenna (eds.), *Mammal Phylogeny.*
New York and London: Springer-Verlag.
Storch, G. 1978. *Eomanis waldi*, ein Schuppentier aus dem Mittel-Eozän
der "Grube Messel" bei Darmstadt (Mammalia: Pholidota).
Senckenbergiana lethaea 59:503–29.

Further Reading
Schaal, S., et al. 1992. *Messel: An Insight into the History of Life and of the
Earth.* Oxford: Clarendon; New York: Oxford University Press; as
Messel: Ein Schaufenster in der Geschichte der Erde und des Lebens,
Frankfurt am Main: Kramer.

PARAREPTILES

The name "parareptiles" originally denoted a mixed grouping of primitive amniotes and near-amniote tetrapods (limbed vertebrates) that are not closely related to each other (Olson, 1947). (Amniotes are tetrapods that lay shelled eggs, or whose ancestors did.) Recent scholars (Laurin and Reisz 1995; Lee 1995) have redefined the term to refer to a discrete monophyletic group (a group that consists of a common ancestor and all its descendants) containing turtles and related fossil reptiles. As currently recognized, the group Parareptilia includes turtles, pareiasaurs, procolophonoids, millerettids, and a few other minor groups. Within the amniotes, parareptiles appear to be the sister group to true reptiles (diapsids and related groups) (Laurin and Reisz 1995). Rieppel and deBraga (1996), however, disagree with this scheme and recently have proposed a heterodox arrangement, in which turtles are not "parareptiles" but have affinities with advanced diapsid reptiles.

Parareptiles first appeared in the mid-Permian and underwent an immediate radiation (diversification): pareiasaurs, procolophonoids, and millerettids formed a diverse and important constituent of Upper Permian terrestrial (land-based) ecosystems. However, of these, only procolophonoids survived past the Permo-Triassic boundary. Turtles are the most specialized parareptiles and the last group to appear. They have diversified steadily from the Late Triassic until the present day.

All parareptiles (except some aquatic turtles) are quadrupedal (four-footed), terrestrial animals with sturdy limbs and a sprawling gait. The skull is primitively anapsid (solid) in all groups. However, extensive cheek emarginations (notches) have evolved within turtles, and an opening in the cheek has evolved within milleretids. In all groups there is a distinct notch at the rear margin of the skull that presumably housed a tympanum (eardrum), but this feature is only weakly developed in pareiasaurs. Parareptiles are united by several derived (specialized) characters not found in other primitive reptiles (Laurin and Reisz 1995). The jaw joint is positioned anteriorly (forward), in front of the joint joining the skull and the neck; the prefrontal bone on the skull roof extends ventrally (downward) along the anterior (front) margin of the orbit (eye opening) to contact the palatine, one of the bones of the palate; the stapes (sound-transmitting bone) is rod-like, having lost the dorsal process; the anterior foramen (hole) on the lateral (outer) surface of the maxilla (main upper jaw bone) is enlarged; and a foramen just above the shoulder socket (supraglenoid foramen) is absent. Relationships within parareptiles, and some derived characters supporting this scheme, are depicted in Figure 1. Pareiasaurs appear to be the nearest relatives of turtles (Lee 1995), although there is conflicting evidence that unites procolophonids and turtles (Laurin and Reisz 1995).

Millerettids are small, superficially "lizard-like" forms, known only from the upper Permian of South Africa (Figures 2a, 2e). The skeleton is lightly built, with a slender trunk region, narrow vertebrae, and long gracile limbs. The skull is long and narrow, and the surface is weakly sculptured with an interwoven network of shallow grooves. In primitive forms the cheek is solid; however, derived forms have openings of variable sizes. This char-

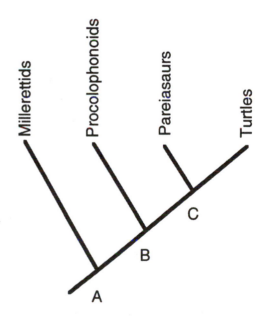

Figure 1. Cladogram of evolutionary relationships between the major groups of parareptiles. Derived characters diagnosing the indicated clades are as follows: *Clade A,* see text; *Clade B,* (1) tabular absent, (2) short cultriform process of the parasphenoid, (3) imperforate stapes, (4) notched anterior end of splenial, (5) coronoid process of lower jaw formed entirely by coronoid bone, (6) interclavicle with long, anteriorly grooved, lateral arms, (7) loss of centralia, and fifth distal tarsal, in the pes; *Clade C,* (1) dermal armor, (2) large palatal foramen (foramen palatinum posterius), (3) exoccipital with lateral flange, (4) twenty or fewer presacral vertebrae, (5) acromion process on anterior margin of shoulder girdle, (6) reduced fifth digit in the hindfoot. For alternative view of turtle relationships, see Rieppel and deBraga (1996). From Laurin and Reisz (1995) and Lee (1995).

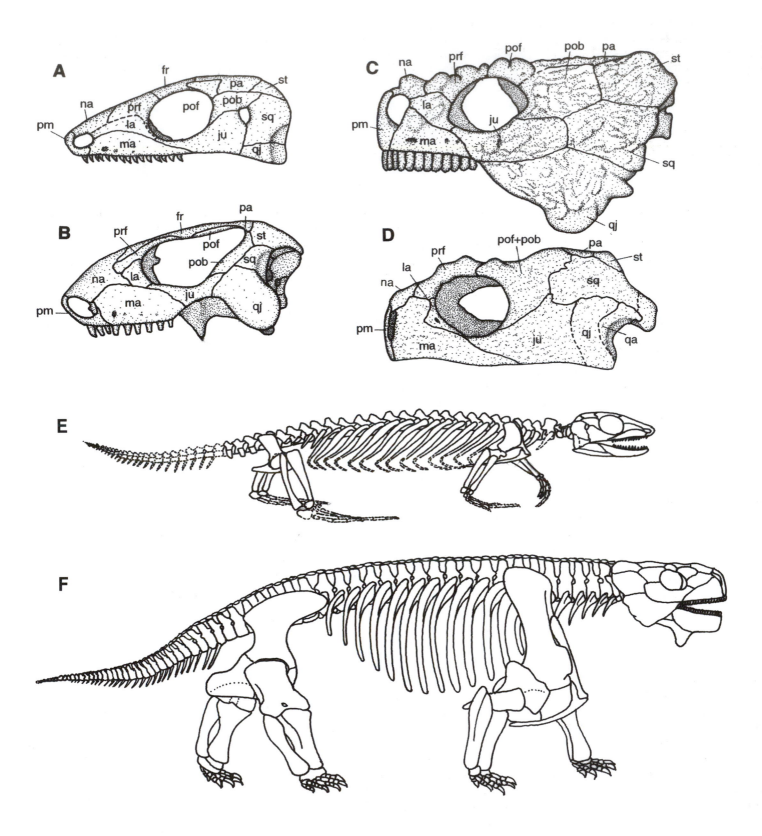

Figure 2. Representative parareptiles; skulls are in left lateral view. *a*, skull of a *Milleretta*, a millerettid; *b*, skull of a *Procolophon*, a procolophonoid; *c*, skull of a *Scutosaurus*, a pareiasaur; *d*, skull of a *Proganochelys*, a turtle; *e*, skeletal reconstruction of *Milleretta*, a millerettid; *f*, skeletal reconstruction of *Bradysaurus*, a pareiasaur. Abbreviations: *fr*, frontal; *ju*, jugal; *la*, lacrimal; *ma*, maxilla; *na*, nasal; *pa*, parietal; *pob*, postorbital; *pof*, postfrontal; *prf*, prefrontal; *qa*, quadrate; *qj*, quadratojugal; *sq*, squamosal; *st*, supratemporal.

acter is convergent with the lower temporal fenestra of diapsids and synapsids. Millerettids possess numerous simple conical teeth and presumably consumed insects and small vertebrates. Millerettids exhibit the following specializations, which are absent in other primitive reptiles: the second sacral rib is larger than first, the septomaxillae (bones lining the nasal cavities) are fused in the midline, and the contact between the prefrontal and palatine bones is mobile (Spencer 1994).

Procolophonoids range from the upper Permian to the Late Triassic and had a cosmopolitan (worldwide) distribution. They are unusual in possessing an orbit that is enlarged at the back; the resultant space behind the eye presumably helped accommodate jaw muscles (Figure 2b). The skull is short and broad. Primitive procolophonoids (e.g., *Owenetta*) are similar to millerettids, having small slender bodies, long gracile limbs, and numerous simple conical teeth. Scholars hypothesize that such physical similarities imply similar ecologies. Later forms of procolophonoids are larger and more robust, with shorter and stouter limbs. The teeth are modified—there are fewer of them, and those that remain are enlarged and bulbous. These procolophonoids presumably fed on slow-moving, hard-bodied invertebrates (Spencer 1994). Although the skull bones are always smooth, there is a general trend within the group to develop spines at the edges of the cheek bones. These spines, most highly developed in late forms such as *Hypsognathus,* project to the side and presumably helped deter predators. Procolophonoids exhibit the following specializations (Figure 2b): there is a posterior projection (formed by the prefrontal) on the anterior orbital margin; and the parietals (on the posterior skull roof) extend ventrally to form a vertical plate at the back of the skull.

Pareiasaurs are large bulky herbivores (up to 3 meters long, excluding tail) that are restricted to the upper Permian and had a cosmopolitan distribution (e.g., Ivachnenko 1987; Lee 1995). The skull is very short and wide and heavily ornamented with ridges and protuberances (Figure 2c). There are prominent bosses (rounded projections) on the posterior margin of the cheek and on the ventral surface of the lower jaw. The jaws are lined with later-ally compressed leaf-shaped teeth, which form a continuous shearing edge. The ribcage was capacious, indicating the presence of large fermentation chambers for storage and digestion of plant matter. The entire skeleton is heavily ossified and contains obvious weight-bearing adaptations (Figure 2f). The vertebrae are broadened from side to side; the limbs and digits are short and stout; and the pelvis is attached to the spine via four or five sacral ribs (rather than the usual two). Dermal armor is present along the midline of the back in the form of disc-shaped osteoderms. In some derived pareiasaurs, such as *Scutosaurus* and *Anthodon,* osteoderms cover the entire back as well as the limbs and may be fused together.

Scientists remain at odds over the position of turtles within Parareptilia, and some even question whether they are parareptiles at all. If they are parareptiles, turtles would represent the most diverse and important lineage—and the only group to survive beyond the Triassic (Figure 2D).

MICHAEL S.Y. LEE

See also Tetrapods: Near-Amniote Tetrapods; Turtles

Works Cited

Ivachnenko, M. 1987. Permian parareptiles of the USSR. *Trudy Paleontologicheskogo Instituta, Akademiia Nauk SSSR* 223:1–160.

Laurin, M., and R.R. Reisz. 1995. A reevaluation of early amniote phylogeny. *Zoological Journal of the Linnean Society* 113:165–223.

Lee, M.S.Y. 1995. Historical burden in systematics and the interrelationships of parareptiles. *Biological Reviews* 70:459–547.

Rieppel, O., and M. deBraga. 1996. Turtles as diapsid reptiles. *Nature* 384:453–55.

Olson, E.C. 1947. The family Diadectidae and its bearing on the classification of reptiles. *Fieldiana, Geology* 11:1–53.

Spencer, P.S. 1994. Morphology and interrelationships of basal Amniota. Ph.D. diss., University of Bristol.

PARKS, WILLIAM ARTHUR

Canadian, 1868–1936

William Arthur Parks was an eminent Canadian paleontologist and geologist of the early twentieth century, producing important work, particularly on dinosaurs, stromatoporoids, and building stones. He was associated professionally with the University of Toronto and the Royal Ontario Museum, in Ontario, Canada.

Born in Hamilton, Ontario, on 11 December 1868, Parks was the son of piano-maker George Dyer Parks and Mary Kate Snelgrove. In 1892 he graduated from the University of Toronto with distinction in natural sciences, and in 1900 he received the first doctorate in geology ever awarded in Canada. In 1892, Parks became a chemist for the Canadian Copper Company (later International Nickel). He discovered Ontario's Porcupine Gold area and learned to carry his own field samples after discovering that his native guides were dumping his specimens and refilling the bags with handy rocks at the end of the day.

In 1893 he joined the staff of the University of Toronto while studying for his Ph.D. In 1915 he became professor of paleontology and added the subject to the curriculum. By 1922, Parks became head of the geology department.

At the same time, Parks continued summer fieldwork in Ontario with the Geological Survey of Canada and the Ontario Bureau of Mines and became increasingly involved in paleontology, studying Paleozoic invertebrates and particularly stromatoporoids. He gathered fossil collections for the university and, as early as 1905, began urging establishment of a museum. In 1913 he and his colleagues gained approval to establish several museums. Parks volunteered to become director of the Royal Ontario Museum of Paleontology. When it opened in 1914, Parks saw the opportunity to exhibit dinosaur material. As early as 1912, Parks had sent out Alexander MacLean to collect dinosaurs in Alberta, and after World War I was over, Parks (at the age of 50) made the first of two expeditions to Alberta to collect dinosaurs. On the second, he was assisted by Levi Sternberg, the youngest son of eminent collector C.H. Sternberg. Levi Sternberg went on to lead expeditions for the museum almost every year until 1935, mainly to Alberta, but also to Saskatchewan and the United States. Thus, Parks was responsible for the early preeminence in dinosaur exhibition at what became the Royal Ontario Museum. By the end of 1932, the museum exhibition included 10 complete skeletons and more than 15 partial skeletons or skulls, prompting many to say it was "second only to New York."

During his career Parks undertook extensive research on paleontology and other geological topics, publishing more than 80 papers. Between 1907 and 1936 he produced a series of publications on stromatoporoids and between 1912 and 1917 brought out the five volumes of his *Building and Ornamental Stones of Canada.* Canadian dinosaurs already had been described by Lawrence Lambe and Barnum Brown, but the museum field expeditions produced many more discoveries, so between 1919 and 1935 Parks published more than 25 papers on dinosaurs and other Cretaceous vertebrates, making important contributions to the study of carnivores, ceratopsians (dinosaurs with a bony frill around the neck), and hadrosaurs (e.g., duck-billed hadrosaurs), and describing such important genera as *Arrhinoceratops, Centrosaurs, Kritosaurus,* and *Parasaurolophus.* With colleague Arthur Coleman, he also coauthored a text on Canadian geology, published in 1922.

In later life, Parks received extensive recognition. He was president of the Royal Society of Canada in 1926 and was elected to the Royal Society (U.K.) in 1934. He served on the executive committee for the 12th International Geological Congress, held in Toronto in 1913. In 1927 he was president of the Palaeontological Society of America. After his death, the dinosaur *Styracosaurus parksi* was named in his honor by B. Brown and E.M. Schlaijker.

Remembered as an "inspiring and forceful lecturer" by students and public, Parks took a great personal interest in his students, who included P.S. Warren, later at the University of Alberta, and Madeleine Fritz, who became his assistant at the museum and eventual biographer.

DAVID A.E. SPALDING

Biography

Born in Hamilton, Ontario, 11 December 1868. Received B.A., University of Toronto, 1892; Ph.D., University of Toronto, 1900; executive committee member, 12th International Geological Congress, 1913; founder and first director, Royal Ontario Museum of Paleontology, 1914; became professor of paleontology, University of Toronto, 1915; appointed head, geology department,

1922. President, Royal Society of Canada, 1926; president, Palaeontological Society of America, 1927; elected member, Royal Society, (London), 1934; received LL.D., University of Toronto, 1936. Did important work on Paleozoic fossils (especially stromatoporoids) and described a number of Cretaceous dinosaurs, including *Arrhinoceratops, Parasaurolophus.* Died in Toronto, 3 October 1936.

Major Publications

1919. The great fossil reptiles of Alberta. *Journal of the Proceedings of the Hamilton Association* 29:131–40.

1920a. *The Osteology of the Trachodont Dinosaur Kritosaurus incurvimanus.* University of Toronto Studies, Geological Series, 11. Toronto: University of Toronto Library.

1920b. Preliminary description of a new species of trachodont dinosaur of the genus *Kritosaurus, K. incurvimanus. Transactions of the Royal Society of Canada* Section 4 (Series 3), 13:51–59.

1921. The head and forelimb of a specimen of *Centrosaurus* [sic] *apertus. Trans. Roy. Soc. Can.* (3, 15 Section 4:53–64.

1922a. With A.P. Coleman. *Elementary Geology with Special Relevance to Canada.* London and Toronto: Dent and Sons.

1922b. A new genus and species of dinosaur from the Belly River beds of Alberta. *Science* New Series, 54:174.

1922c. *Parasaurolophus walkeri. A New Genus and Species of Crested Trachodont Dinosaur.* University of Toronto Studies, Geological Series, No. 13. Toronto: University Library.

1923. *Corythosaurus intermedius. A New Species of Trachodont Dinosaur.* University of Toronto Studies, Geological Series, 15. Toronto: University Library.

1924a. Dinosaurs of Alberta. *In Handbook of Canada.* Toronto: University of Toronto Press.

1924b. *Dyplosaurus acutosquameus. A New Genus and Species of Armoured Dinosaur; and Notes on a Skeleton of Prosaurolophus maximus.* University of Toronto Studies, Geological Series, 18. Toronto: University Library.

1924c. A new genus and species of horned dinosaur from the Cretaceous of Alberta. *Geological Society of America, Preliminary Lists* 36:226.

1925a. *Arrhinoceratops brachyops: A New Genus and Species of Ceratopsia from the Edmonton Formation of Alberta.* University of Toronto Studies, Geological Series No. 19. Toronto: University Library.

1925b. A new genus and species of horned dinosaur from the Cretaceous of Alberta. *Bulletin of the Geological Society of America* 36:226.

1926a. *Struthiomimus brevitertius*—a new species of dinosaur from the Edmonton Formation of Alberta. *Transactions of the Royal Society of Canada,* Section 4, 3, 20:65–70.

1926b. *Thescelosaurus warreni, a New Species of Orthopodous Dinosaur from the Edmonton Formation of Alberta.* University of Toronto Studies, Geological Series, 13. Toronto: University Library.

1927. *Champsosaurus albertensis, a New Species of Rhynchocephalian from the Edmonton Formation of Alberta.* University of Toronto Studies, Geological Series, 23. Toronto: University Library.

1928a. *Albertosaurus arctunguis, a New Species of Theropodous Dinosaur from the Edmonton Formation of Alberta.* University of Toronto Studies, Geological Series, 25. Toronto: University Library.

1928b. *Struthiomimus samueli, a New Species of Onithomimidae from the Belly River Formation of Alberta.* University of Toronto Studies, Geological Series, 26. Toronto: University Library.

1931. *A New Genus and Two New Species of Trachodont Dinosaurs from the Belly River Formation of Alberta.* University of Toronto Studies, Geological Series, 31. Toronto: University of Toronto Press.

1933a. Dinosaurs of the Red Deer Valley. *Discovery* 14:29–30.

1933b. New species of *Champsosaurus* from the Belly River Formation of Alberta, Canada. *Royal Society of Canada Transactions,* Section 4, Series 3, 27:121–38.

1933c. *New Species of Dinosaurs and Turtles from the Upper Cretaceous Formations of Alberta, with Notes on Other Species.* University of Toronto Studies, Geological Series, 34. Toronto: University of Toronto Press.

1935a. Dinosaurs in the Royal Ontario Museum. *University of Toronto Quarterly* 4 (2):179–299.

1935b. *New Species of Trachodont Dinosaurs from the Cretaceous Formations of Alberta, with Notes on Other Species.* University of Toronto Studies, Geological Series, 37. Toronto: University of Toronto Press.

1936. *Devonian Stromatoporoids of America.* University of Toronto Studies, Geological Series, 39. Toronto: University of Toronto Press.

Further Reading

Brown, B., and E.M. Schlaikjer. 1937. The skeleton of *Styracosaurus* with the description of a new species. *American Museum Novitates* 955.

Dickson, L. 1986. *The Museum Makers: The Story of the Royal Ontario Museum.* Toronto: Royal Ontario Museum.

Dodson, P. 1996. *The Horned Dinosaurs.* Princeton, New Jersey: Princeton University Press.

Fritz, M.A. 1971. William Arthur Parks, Ph.D., LL.D., F.R.S. 1868–1936. *Royal Ontario Museum, Life Science Miscellaneous Publications.* Toronto: Royal Ontario Museum.

Sarjeant, W.A.S. (comp.) 1996. *Geologists and the History of Geology: An International Bibliography from the Origins to 1978.* 3 vols. Malabar, Florida: Krieger.

Spalding, D. 1993. *Dinosaur Hunters: 150 Years of Extraordinary Discoveries.* Rocklin, California: Prima.

PELYCOSAURS

Paleozoic synapsids (also called mammal-like reptiles) are tetrapods—limbed vertebrates—that lay shelled eggs or had ancestors that once did so. They occupy a central position in amniote evolution. (Amniotes include lizards, snakes, crocodiles, turtles, mammals, and birds.) Paleozoic synapsids include some of the oldest known amniotes, and their fossil remains record the earliest successful adaptations of terrestrial vertebrates to herbivorous (plant-eating) and active predatory modes of life. During the Paleozoic, synapsids diversified greatly and became the most conspicuous terrestrial vertebrates of their time. Although both pelycosaurs and early therapsids are paraphyletic taxa at the base of the clade that includes advanced therapsids and mammals, these Paleozoic reptiles have played a pivotal role in considerations of synapsid evolution, including the origin of mammals. Recent cladistic analyses have shown that the synapsid clade (pelycosaurs, therapsids, and mammals) is the sister taxon (group; plural, taxa) of all other amniotes. Thus, an understanding of pelycosaurian evolution has implications to many broad problems of amniote evolution, including the origin and interrelationships of all higher vertebrates.

The oldest known mammal-like reptiles have been found in sediments of Early and Middle Pennsylvanian age in Nova Scotia. The remains of *Protoclepsydrops haplous,* retrieved from upright *Sigillaria* stumps from Joggins, Nova Scotia (Reisz 1972) are too fragmentary to provide any useful information; even the identification of these remains as a pelycosaur has been questioned (Reisz 1986; Reisz and Modesto 1996). By the Late Pennsylvanian pelycosaurs become the most common amniotes in North American sediments. The fossil record of this group is most extensive during the Early Permian, representing nearly 70 percent of all amniote finds of this time; by the Late Permian, however, pelycosaurs disappear from the fossil record. Instead, the early therapsids become the most diverse and common amniotes.

Pelycosaurs have been distinguished from other synapsids mainly on geological and geographical grounds. Although easily recognizable, and readily separated from more advanced synapsids, pelycosaurs represent a paraphyletic grade of basal synapsids that includes the ancestors of advanced synapsids (therapids and mammals). Nevertheless, it is worth discussing pelycosaurs as a group because they represent a major adaptive radiation that dominated the terrestrial landscape during the Late Pennsylvanian and Early Permian, and were replaced by the much more advanced therapsids only in the Late Permian. As primitive synapsids, pelycosaurs retain a number of characteristic features in the skull: the rear of the skull is inclined toward the front of the head; a small opening (post-temporal fenestra) at the back of the skull is bordered by three bones (supraoccipital, tabular, and opisthotic); there is a membrane-covered fenestra along the side and toward the rear of the skull (lateral-temporal fenestra), which is bordered by cheek bones (jugal and squamosal) and a bone behind the eye sockets (postorbital); and pillarlike bones border the nose (septomaxillae) with a broad base that straddles the suture between the upper jawbone (maxilla) and the bone that forms the tip of the snout (premaxilla). Pelycosaurs also retain a number of derived (specialized) features shared by all other amniotes, including therapsids. These features include the presence of broad, platelike bones (supratemporals) above the eyes, on the dorsal (back) surface of the skull; two coronoid bones that form the internal surface of the jaw; and a specialized bone in the ankle (medial centrale) in the foot (pes).

Recent phylogenetic studies of pelycosaurs have proposed that within this group six major clades (families) can be recognized (Figure 1): small insectivores (insect eaters) (Eothyrididae), two different types of large, bulky herbivores (plant eaters) (Caseidae and Edaphosauridae), and three different types of medium- to large-sized carnivores (meat eaters) (Varanopseidae, Ophiacodontidae, and Sphenacodontidae).

Family Eothyrididae

The Eothyrididae was erected as a provisional group by Romer and Price (1940) to house the small pelycosaur *Eothyris,* known

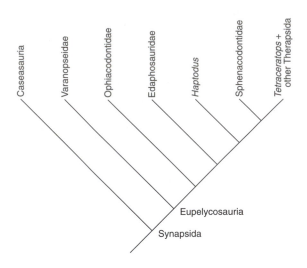

Figure 1. Phylogenetic relationships of pelycosaurs.

from a single skull from the Lower Permian of Texas, and for fragmentary remains of three large pelycosaurs. Subsequently, other fossils were placed within this family, but at present only two genera (general groupings; singular, genus)—*Eothyris,* from the Early Permian of Texas, and *Oedaleops,* from the Early Permian of New Mexico—can be assigned with confidence to the Eothyrididae. *Eothyris* still is known from only a single skull, whereas *Oedaleops* is represented by three partial skulls and some limb elements. Although fragmentary, these specimens have revealed that eothyridids were small amniotes. The teeth are simple conical structures, and there are distinct caninelike teeth. In most respects, eothyridids exhibit the most primitive known cranial morphology (skull shape and structure) of any pelycosaur. For example, in the skull roof, postparietal bones are paired and the supratemporal is broad. The postorbitals are large and extend far to the rear, the jugal bone of the cheek is not part of the lower margin of the skull, the parasphenoid sheathing the skull base is broad, the quadrate process at the back of the pterygoid (one of the bones that forms the roof of the mouth) has a ventral (bellyside) shelf, the bottom surface of the lower jaw is rounded, and there is no retroarticular process, or protrusion, at the rear of the jaw joint. There are, however, a few shared, derived traits (synapomorphies) that unite this family with caseids into the Caseasauria (Reisz 1986).

Family Caseidae

The caseids were a widespread and diverse group of herbivorous pelycosaurs, with a fossil record that extended from the Early Permian of North America and western Europe to the Late Permian of eastern Europe. Although ranging in size from one to nearly four meters in body length, caseids are surprisingly conservative in their skeletal anatomy and body proportions. The skulls are distinctive in the presence of relatively large temporal fenestrae, enormous external nares (nostrils), and large pineal foramen (opening

for the parietal, or "third eye"). The snout overhangs dramatically the tooth row to form a flexible structure somewhat like the snout (rostrum) of a pig. The external surface of the skull has unusual rounded deep pits and sometimes crevicelike depressions that form a distinctive sculpturing pattern. The marginal teeth have spatulate (spoon-shaped) crowns and are serrated along the edge, in some respects similar to the teeth of pariesaurs (Figure 3B). In contrast to most other pelycosaurs (except *Edaphosaurus*), there are neither caninelike teeth (caniniforms), nor a caniniform region on the maxilla. Instead, of those teeth that are along the edge of the jawbone, the largest are located at the front of both the upper and lower jawbones. (Like many early amniotes, pelycosaurs developed teeth, not only in the jawbone, but also as a cover on the bones on the roof of the mouth.) As a result, these front teeth are longer than all other marginal teeth, which gradually decrease in size as they move from front to back. Also, there is a general reduction in the number of marginal teeth in caseids, ranging from a minimum of 10 *(Ennatosaurus)* to a maximum of 20 *(Cotylorhynchus)* marginal cheek teeth.

All caseids, whether modest in size or enormous, are characterized by small cervical (neck) vertebrae; bulky, barrel-shaped bodies; and relatively massive limbs. The number of bones in the fingers and toes are reduced. Two distinct types of terminal phalanges (last finger and toe bones) can be found in caseids. In *Corylorhynchus* the claw-bearing element is very large and broad, with apparently sharp edges on the sides. In *Angelosaurus* the claw-bearing phalanges are also massive but more conservative in morphology, roughly triangular in outline.

Caseids and eothyridids share a number of derived characters associated with the morphology of the snout and external nares that support the hypothesis that these primitive pelycosaurs form a clade, the Caseasauria. These pelycosaurs share a significant number of primitive features that appear in derived form in all other pelycosaurs. All other pelycosaurs can be placed in the Eupelycosauria, a clade that also includes therapsids and mammals. Eupelycosaurs would be characterized by reduced width of the snout and supratemporal, increased contribution of the frontal bone to the upper edge of the orbit (eye socket), posterior location of the pineal foramen along the interparietal suture, and decreased length of the skull and the parietal relative to the length of the frontal.

Family Varanopseidae

The carnivorous Varanopseidae, which are of small to moderate size, are characterized by slender, lightly built skulls with highly specialized marginal teeth (Figure 2). All varanopseids have mediolaterally (side-to-side) flattened teeth with anterior and posterior cutting edges (along the front and back edges), much like knife blades, and are strongly recurved (curved toward the rear of the mouth). Both the premaxilla and maxilla are also highly modified: The tooth-bearing portion of the premaxilla is enlarged, and the maxilla is greatly elongated in association with the extension to the rear of the marginal dentition. Other diagnostic features of varanopseids include enlargement of the temporal fenestra and the reduction of the subtemporal arch (cheek arch or zygomatic arch)

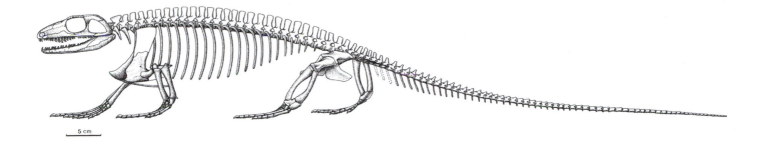

Figure 2. The varanopsid Aerosaurus. The large opening at the rear of the skull is the lateral temporal fenestra. From Reisz (1986).

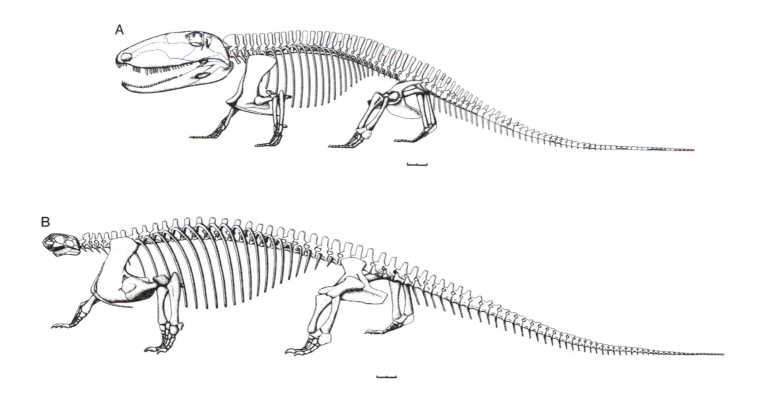

Figure 3. A, the ophiacodontid *Ophiacodon; B,* the caseid *Cotylorhynchus.* From Reisz (1986).

to a narrow bar. The lower jaw is slender, and the joint between left and right lower jaws (mandibular symphysis) is reduced in size. The postcranial (body) skeleton is also lightly built, giving varanopseids a sleek appearance, superficially similar to modern monitor lizards. Such a body shape makes it reasonable to suggest that varanopseid pelycosaurs were probably the most agile predators of their time.

Mycterosaurus longiceps is the most primitive member of the family. This small pelycosaur has the varanopseid features listed above, but lacks several derived traits (autapomorphies) of the advanced members of this family. The larger varanopseids—

Varanops, Aerosaurus, and *Varanodon*—are characterized by the presence of a massive external maxillary buttress above the caniniform region, a dramatic forward tilt of the occiput, and enlargement of the temporal fenestra. In these advanced varanopseids, the postfrontal (a bone that forms part of the orbit) is reduced in size, the pineal foramen is practically at the rear edge of the skull table, and the squamosal has a long process that reaches the dorsal process of the jugal (cheek bone), cutting the postorbital off from the margin of the temporal fenestra.

Varanopseids retain a number of primitive skeletal features that appear in derived form in all other eupelycosaurs, including the paired condition of the postparietals, the absence of a joint between the opisthotic (an inner ear bone) and the stapes (an ear ossicle), the retention of a nearly straight ventral skull margin, and the lack of a ventral keel on the angular (bone at the rear of the lower jaw).

The hypotheses of phylogenetic relationships of this group of pelycosaurs have changed dramatically as our knowledge of primitive synapsids has increased. In 1940, A.S. Romer and L.W. Price associated varanopseids with the advanced sphenacodontids as a group of primitive carnivorous sphenacodonts and even suggested that *Varanops* may have been close to the ancestry of sphenacodontids. The most recent hypothesis places varanopseids within the Eupelycosauria, as its most primitive member. Although retaining many primitive cranial and postcranial features that appear in derived form in edaphosaurs, ophiacodontids, and sphenacodontids, it is obvious that varanopseids developed a number of autamorphies (unique features), and the advanced members of this group outlasted all other carnivorous pelycosaurs as highly specialized, agile predators. *Varanodon* is one of the youngest known pelycosaurs, and there is strong evidence to indicate that *Elliotsmithia,* from the Upper Permian strata of South Africa, is also a varanopseid, making it the youngest known pelycosaur (Dilkes and Reisz 1996).

Family Ophiacodontidae

The oldest known pelycosaurs have been included in the Ophiacodontidae (Figure 3A). *Protoclepsydrops* from the Middle Pennsylvanian of Joggins, Nova Scotia has been placed within the Ophiacodontidae, but its identity and taxonomic status are uncertain, partly because the known skeletal remains are fragmentary. *Archaeothyris,* from slightly younger sediments near Florence, Nova Scotia, is the oldest known ophiacodontid.

Ophiacodontids include small to very large carnivorous pelycosaurs that have the following cranial characteristics in common: The posterotorsal process at the rear of the premaxilla is long, slender, and separated at the midline by an anterior process at the front of the nasal; the nasal is at least twice as long as the parietal; elongation of the snout is accompanied by the elongation of the lacrimal (bone bordering the front of the eye); the ossification of braincase elements is reduced, producing a lighter skull; and there is a well-developed opening on the side of the lower jaw (lateral mandibular fenestra). Among ophiacodontids there is a tendency toward an increase in the skull-to-trunk ratio, with larger taxa having unusually large, awkward-looking, elongate skulls. In the postcranium, ophiacodontids have relatively large, massive shoulder girdles, with broad scapulocoracoids ("shoulder blades") but small-headed interclavicles and clavicles ("collarbones").

Ophiacodon is the best-known member of the family, represented by an extensive fossil record in North America. This group has been subdivided, somewhat arbitrarily (based largely on stratigraphic position—position in the rock strata—and size) into six species. There appears to be extensive variation in morphology among the known specimens, even to the presence of two lateral temporal fenestrae on each side in larger specimens. In one particular specimen of *Ophiacodon retroversus,* the second opening

apparently is present on one side of the skull but not on the other. A particularly puzzling characteristic of the postcranial skeleton is its reduced level of ossification—the skeleton has a reduced amount of bone and an increased amount of cartilage—even in very large specimens. Another is the lack of sharp claws, as indicated by the truncated tip of the terminal phalanges. Largely because of these features, scholars have considered that *Ophiacodon* was amphibious. This hypothesis is supported by the location of the orbit high on the side of the face—this places the eyes above the water, a characteristic still seen in today's crocodiles. Nevertheless, it is difficult to imagine how this animal, with a tall skull, could be an effective aquatic predator.

Ophiacodontids, edaphosaurids, and sphenacodontids share a list of derived features that appear in primitive form in the other pelycosaurs: there is a distinct recess on the opisthotic for the dorsal process of the stapes, the ventral edge of the skull is concave in the postorbital region, the jugal contributes to the ventral edge of the skull, the nasal is longer than the parietal, and there is a well-developed ventral keel on the angular.

Family Edaphosauridae

One of the most striking features exhibited by several pelycosaurs is the great elongation of the neural spines. (As shown in Figure 4, these spines arise from the dorsal side of the vertebrae.) The poorly known Middle Pennsylvanian *Echinerpeton,* the Lower Permian pelycosaur *Lupeosaurus,* at least three distinct genera of sphenacodontids, and all the edaphosaurs have large sails supported by tall neural spines above the portion of the vertebral column that lies between the neck and pelvis. Among these, edaphosaurs have the most spectacular sail because the greatly elongated neural spines have cross projections along the side of each spine. Generally, it is accepted that this great elongation of neural spines must have occurred in independent groups at least three times among pelycosaurs. The presumed function of such elongation is to support the membrane that spanned the space between successive spines. By providing a surface for dispersing or absorbing heat, this membrane probably facilitated temperature control. The sail and its associated spines also may have served in display behavior in courtship or dominance rituals, and in edaphosaurs it may have also served as protection against predators. This last hypothesis is supported by the presence of the side tubercles, as well as by the orientation of the neural spines; anteriorly tilted cervical and thoracic spines and posteriorly tilted lumbar spines probably provided protection in the neck and thigh region, respectively.

Edaphosaurus and *Ianthasaurus* are the only pelycosaurs that can be placed with confidence in this family (Modesto and Reisz 1990; Modesto 1995). Both are characterized by the presence of greatly elongated neural spines that are rounded in cross section, and by the presence of well-developed lateral tubercles. The arrangement of these tubercles along the height of the spines is similar in the two taxa, the proximal lateral tubercles being not only the largest of the set, but also paired. Also, one distinctive cranial feature that is found in edaphosaurs is the loss of contact between the postorbital and supratemporal, probably because the posterior process of the postorbital is reduced in length.

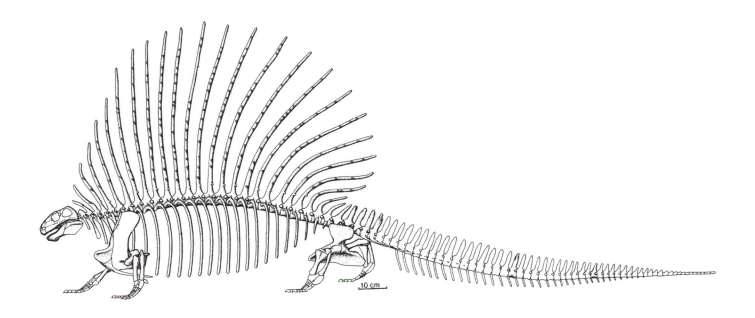

Figure 4. The edaphosaurid *Edaphosaurus*. From Reisz (1986).

Ianthasaurus is a small edaphosaur from the Upper Pennsylvanian that lacks many of the spectacular specializations seen in *Edaphosaurus*. For example, the marginal dentition of *Ianthasaurus* is similar to that of insectivorous reptiles, with slender conical teeth that are slightly recurved at the tips, and there is a slight development of a caniniform region. The teeth on the palate and the mandible are unspecialized, and there are no batteries of teeth for crushing of plant materials. This contrasts sharply with the cranial morphology of *Edaphosaurus,* where the palate has been modified greatly in order to carry a massive array of closely packed teeth that meet a similarly developed set of teeth on the mandible.

Edaphosaurus has other distinct characteristics. The modifications of the skull include reduction in its length, loss of the caniniform region, and the presence of a massive supraorbital shelf that probably formed a bony hood over the eyes. The lower jaws also are reduced in length but have become massive; they are especially deep where the large adductor muscles (those used to close the mouth) probably inserted.

The two edaphosaurs also are quite distinct from each other in their postcranial morphology. While *Ianthasaurus* appears lightly built and was probably quite agile, a combination of features in *Edaphosaurus* suggests that this animal was a heavy, relatively slow herbivorous reptile. For example, the cervical vertebrae are reduced in length in association with the reduced size of the skull, the dorsal (trunk) vertebrae are massive, the tail is deep, the limbs are short and robust, and the ribs form a wide ribcage. Nine species of *Edaphosaurus* have been described, ranging in size from small to very large, bulky animals. The largest species, *Edaphosaurus cruciger* and *Edaphosaurus pogonias,* have modified their cervical and anterior thoracic spines into massive, clublike, bony extensions.

It is not unreasonable to suggest that the small, insectivorous *Ianthasaurus* represents the primitive edaphosaur pattern from which the larger herbivorous *Edaphosaurus* may have been derived. *Ianthasaurus* shows many similarities in its cranial morphology to another relatively small pelycosaur, the primitive sphenacodont *Haptodus*. In fact, edaphosaurs and sphenacodonts share a surprisingly large number of derived cranial features that appear in primitive form in all other pelycosaurs. For example, in both edaphosaurs and sphenacodonts the subtemporal arch is formed by the jugal and the squamosal, the jugal contribution to the ventral edge of the skull is extensive, the anteroventral process of the quadratojugal is greatly reduced, on the palatal surface the parasphenoid wings lack the anterior spanning shelf, and the quadrate ramus of the pterygoid lacks the lateral shelf.

Family Sphenacodontidae

Haptodus is a relatively small pelycosaur that has been included in the family Sphenacodontidae, as a primitive member of that group (Laurin 1993). The better-known sphenacodontids include the large carnivores *Dimetrodon, Sphenacodon, Ctenospondylus,* and *Secodontosaurus* (Figure 5) (Reisz et al. 1992). These reptiles were the dominant predators of their time, and their fossil record extends from the Late Pennsylvanian throughout the Early Permian. The significance of this group, however, lies with its phylogenetic (evolutionary) relationships, because sphenacodontids generally are considered to be the nearest pelycosaurian relatives of therapsids. Sphenacodonts have a buttress on the medial (center) surface of the maxilla; the first premaxillary and second dentary teeth are greatly increased in size (similar in length to the enlarged canine); the slope of the ventral edge of

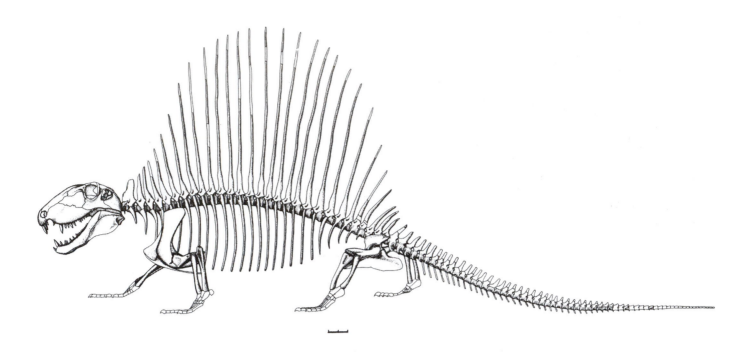

Figure 5. The sphenacodontid *Dimetrodon.* From Reisz (1986).

the premaxilla gives the snout a slightly hooked appearance; the supraorbital shelf terminates posteriorly on the concave lateral surface of the postorbital; the pineal foramen is located on a slightly raised area of the parietal, with a distinct ridge surrounding the foramen; and the ventral keel of the angular (one of the bones that support the rear section of the lower jaw) is deflected laterally from the long axis of the mandible. These synapomorphies (shared derived features) support the hypothesis that *Haptodus* and the large sphenacodontids are closely related. *Haptodus* has been found in the Late Pennsylvanian and Early Permian of North America and Europe. Both small- and medium-sized individuals have been discovered, ranging between about one and two meters in total length. Their morphology suggests that members of this genus probably were effective predators, able to feed on both arthropods and small vertebrates.

The better-known advanced sphenacodontids (*Dimetrodon, Sphenacodon, Secodontosaurus,* and *Ctenospondylus*) are all large to very large predators that have tall neural spines, strongly excavated vertebral centra and neural arches, and long limbs that make them relatively agile, fast-moving animals, especially when compared to their slower, bulkier herbivorous relatives. *Dimetrodon, Sphenacodon,* and *Ctenospondylus* all have similarly constructed, massive skulls with extremely large front incisors and canines. *Sphenacodon* and *Ctenospondylus* have bladelike neural spines, whereas *Dimetrodon* has greatly elongated rounded spines. *Secodontosaurus* is modified greatly from the pattern seen in the other large sphenacodontids: The skull roof is less wide and less deep, although the neural spine morphology of *Dimetrodon* is retained.

The cranial modifications of *Secodontosaurus* can only be interpreted as an adaptation to specialized feeding strategies, perhaps preying upon burrowing animals or feeding on tetrapods that tried to evade capture by hiding in crevices.

Origin of Therapsids

A major morphological gap exists between pelycosaurs, which are mostly Pennsylvanian and Early Permian synapsids from North America and Europe, and therapsids, which are Late Permian and Triassic advanced synapsids from South Africa and the former Soviet Union. Previous attempts at bridging this gap have not been successful. Among pelycosaurs, the haptodontine and sphenacodontine sphenacodontids have been proposed as the most likely candidates for sister-group status (the group related most closely) to therapsids. Romer and Price (1940) proposed that of all the known sphencodontids, *Haptodus* is the most likely ancestor of therapsids. More recently, however R.R. Reisz and colleagues (1992) have shown that the pattern of distribution of synapomorphies in haptodontines, sphenacodontines, and therapsids supports the hypothesis that sphenacodontines are the sister group of therapsids. The morphology of the reflected lamina of the angular provides the strongest evidence for the latter hypothesis: In both primitive therapsids and sphenacodontids the reflected lamina is a prominent feature of the lower jaw, whereas in haptodontines the reflected lamina, if present at all, is a modest, slightly developed ventral projection with little or no lateral displacement (Laurin 1993).

Recent studies of *Tetraceratops* indicate that this enigmatic fossil from the Early Permian of Texas bridges the morphological and temporal gaps between the pelycosaurian and earliest therapsids (Laurin and Reisz 1995). As the oldest known therapsid, this form shares with other early therapsids a number of derived cranial features, but retains numerous primitive features that are modified in derived form in all other therapsids. *Tetraceratops* is, therefore, the sister taxon to all other therapsids.

ROBERT REISZ

See also Mammals, Mesozoic and Non-Therian; Sauropsids; Synapsids; Therapsids

Works Cited

Dilkes, D.W., and R.R. Reisz. 1996. First record of a basal synapsid ("mammal-like reptile") in Gondwana. *Proceedings of the Royal Society of London,* ser. B, 263:1165–70.

Laurin, M. 1993. Anatomy and relationships of *Haptodus garnettensis,* a Pennsylvanian synapsid from Kansas. *Journal of Vertebrate Paleontology* 13:200–29.

Laurin, M., and R.R. Reisz. 1990. *Tetraceratops* is the oldest known therapsid. *Nature* 345:249–50.

———. 1995. The osteology and relationships of *Tetraceratops insignis,* the oldest known therapsid. *Journal of Vertebrate Paleontology* 16:95–102.

Modesto, S.P. 1995. The skull of the herbivorous synapsid *Edaphosaurus boanerges* from the Lower Permian of Texas. *Palaeontology* 38:213–39.

Modesto, S.P., and R.R. Reisz. 1990. A new skeleton of *Ianthosaurus hardestii,* a primitive edaphosaur (Synapsida: Pelycosauria) from the Upper Pennsylvanian of Kansas. *Canadian Journal of Earth Sciences* 27:834–44.

Reisz, R.R. 1972. Pelycosaurian reptiles from the Middle Pennsylvanian of North America. *Bulletin of the Museum of Comparative Zoology of Harvard* 144:27–61.

———. 1986. *Handbuch der Paläoherpetologie.* Vol. 17, *Pelycosauria.* Stuttgart and New York: Fischer Verlag.

Reisz, R.R., D.S. Berman, and D. Scott. 1992. The cranial anatomy and relationships of *Secodontosaurus,* an unusual mammal-like reptile (Synapsida: Sphenacodontidae) from the early Permian of Texas. *Zoological Journal of the Linnean Society* 104:127–84.

Reisz, R.R., and S.P. Modesto. 1996. *Archerpeton anthracos* from the Joggins Formation of Nova Scotia: A microsaur, not a reptile. *Canadian Journal of Earth Sciences* 33:703–9.

Romer, A.S., and L.W. Price. 1940. *Review of the Pelycosauria.* Geological Society of America Special Papers, 28. Boulder, Colorado: Geological Society of America; Lawrence: University of Kansas.

PERISSODACTYLS

The perissodactyls are the order of herbivorous "odd-toed" hoofed mammals that includes the living horses, zebras, asses, tapirs, rhinoceroses, and their extinct relatives (Figure 1). They are recognized by a number of unique specializations, but their most distinctive feature is their feet. Most perissodactyls have either one or three toes on each foot, and the axis of symmetry of the foot runs through the middle digit. The woodchuck-like hyraxes, or conies, are apparently closely related to perissodactyls, although there is still some controversy about their relationships. The perissodactyls (other than hyraxes) are divided into three groups: the Hippomorpha (horses and their extinct relatives), the Titanotheriomorpha (the extinct brontotheres), and the Moropomorpha (tapirs, rhinoceroses, and their extinct relatives).

Origins

Perissodactyls once were thought to have evolved in Central America from the phenacodonts, an extinct group of archaic hoofed mammals placed in the invalid taxon (group; plural, taxa) "Condylarthra." Then, in 1989 a specimen was recovered from deposits in China approximately 57 million years old. Described and named *Radinskya*, this specimen shows that perissodactyls originated in Asia approximately 57 million years ago and were unrelated to North American phenacodonts. *Radinskya* is very similar to the earliest relatives of the tethytheres (the proboscideans, or elephants, plus manatees, and their kin). This agrees with other evidence that perissodactyls are more closely related to tethytheres than to any other group of mammals.

By 55 million years ago, the major groups of perissodactyls had differentiated and migrated from Asia to Europe and North America. Before 34 million years ago, the brontotheres and the archaic tapirs were the largest and most abundant hoofed mammals in Eurasia and North America. After these groups became extinct, horses and rhinoceroses were the most common perissodactyls, with a great diversity of species and body forms. About five million years ago, both groups were decimated during another mass extinction, and today only five species of rhinoceros, four species of tapir, and a few species of horses, zebras, and asses cling to survival in the wild. The niches of large hoofed herbivores have been taken over by the ruminant artiodactyls, such as cattle, antelopes, deer, and their relatives.

Horses

From their Asian origin, the hippomorphs spread all over the northern continents. In Europe, the horselike palaeotheres substituted for true horses. North America became the center of evolution of true horses, which occasionally migrated to other continents. *Protorohippus* (once called *Hyracotherium* or *Eohippus*) was a terrier-sized horse with four toes on the front feet. It lived 55 to 50 million years ago, and its descendants evolved into many different lineages living side-by-side. Fossils of the collie-sized three-

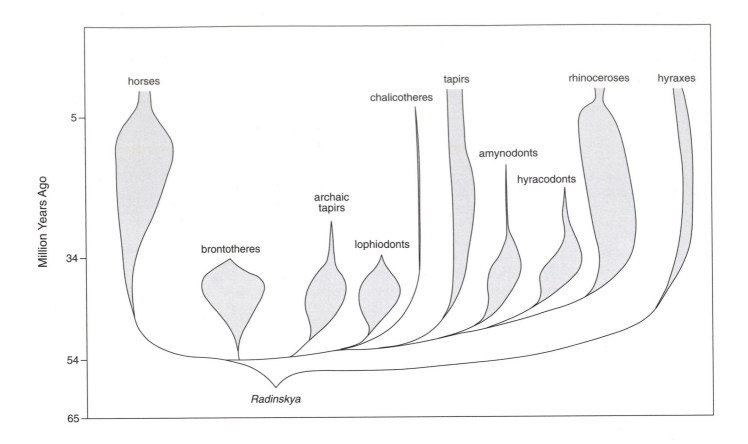

Figure 1. Family tree of the perissodactyls. Illustration by Catherine P. Sexton, after Prothero and Schoch, 1998.

toed horses *Mesohippus* and *Miohippus* (from rock strata, or layers, dated approximately 30 to 37 million years ago) once were believed to be sequential segments on the unbranched trunk of the horse evolutionary tree. However, these groups coexisted for millions of years, with five different species of the two genera (groups; singular, genus) living at the same time and place. From *Miohippus*-like ancestors, horses diversified into many different ecological niches. One major lineage, the anchitherines, retained low-crowned teeth, presumably for browsing soft leaves in the forests. Some anchitherines, such as *Megahippus,* were almost as large as the living horse. *Anchitherium* migrated from North America to Europe approximately 20 million years ago, the first true horse to reach Europe.

Approximately 15 million years ago, there were at least 12 different lineages of three-toed horses in North America, each with slightly different ecological specializations. This situation is analogous to the diversity of modern antelopes in East Africa. The ancestors of this great radiation (spread and diversity) of horses are a group of three-toed, pony-sized animals that long have been lumped into the "wastebasket" genus *Merychippus*. However, recent analyses have shown that the species of "*Merychippus*" are ancestral to many different lineages of horses. True *Merychippus* was a member of the hipparion lineage, a group of three-toed horses that developed highly specialized teeth and had a distinc-

tively concave bone on the front of the face. Hipparions were a highly diverse and successful group of horses, with seven or eight different genera spread not only across North America but also migrating to Eurasia. Merychippines also were ancestral to lineages such as *Calippus* (a tiny dwarf horse), *Protohippus,* and *Astrohippus.*

On two different occasions (*Pliohippus* and *Dinohippus*), three-toed horses evolved into lineages with a single toe on each foot. Approximately 5 million years ago, most of these three-toed and one-toed horse lineages became extinct, leaving only *Dinohippus* to evolve into the modern horse *Equus.* The main lineage of horses, known as the equines, survived the extinctions 5 million years ago. The living genus *Equus* first appeared approximately 3 million years ago and was widespread throughout the northern hemisphere. When the Isthmus of Panama rose approximately 2.5 million years ago, horses also spread to South America. There they evolved into the hippidions, distinctive horses with a short proboscis. At the end of the last Ice Age (approximately 10,000 years ago), horses became extinct in the New World. They were reintroduced to their ancestral homeland by Columbus in 1493. Wild horses that have escaped from domesticated stock are known as mustangs.

Most extinct horses were browsers that ate soft, leafy vegetation, but all living horses are grazers, using their sharp incisors and mobile lips to crop low-growing grasses. The only common wild horse, the plains zebra, lives in large herds (up to 100 individuals) and migrates over large areas of grasslands in search of food. Grevy's zebra, on the other hand, is a denizen of the African deserts, living in small herds, with a stallion guarding a small harem of mares. The mountain zebra is extremely scarce and is confined to the high elevations of southern Africa. The quagga, a partially striped zebra from southern Africa, became extinct in 1883.

The purpose of zebra stripes long has been a mystery. Plains zebras live on the open grasslands, not in the dense undergrowth where stripes might help camouflage the body (as do the stripes on a tiger). Zoologists now believe that when a herd of zebras stampede, their coloration creates a dizzying arrangement of moving stripes that makes it hard for a predator to single out its prey. However, the striped pattern is deeply engrained in the genes of all horses, and occasionally horses and asses are born with zebra stripes. Solid-colored horses and asses can be thought of as zebras that have lost their stripes.

In addition to the three living species of zebras, there also are three living species of wild asses, divided into a number of subspecies. They live in the rocky regions and deserts of southern Asia and northern Africa and have light tan coats to reflect the heat and blend into their backgrounds. Their long legs and ears help them shed heat in the desert, and the long ears also aid in long-range hearing to warn them of danger. Their narrow hooves are excellent for moving across rocky terrain without slipping. The onager, a common Asiatic ass, lives in deserts from Mongolia to Iran to Syria to Turkey. Tibet's high plateaus are home to the kiang, or Tibetan wild ass, which is adapted to the cold, harsh conditions in the Himalayan steppes between 13,000 and 16,000 feet. The African wild ass is found in the rocky deserts of Sudan, Ethiopia, and Somalia. The donkey or burro is a domesticated descendant of the wild ass. Its incredible ruggedness and ability to carry large loads over long distances are inherited from its ancestry among the desert-dwelling asses of Africa and Asia.

All living domesticated horses are thought to have descended from wild species once found in the steppes of central Asia. The only living relic of these wild horses is Przewalski's horse, fossils of which date as far back as the Ice Age, over 200,000 years ago. These horses have reddish brown coats, a short stiff mane, a light ring around the eyes and a dark stripe along the back. Around 6,000 years ago, prehistoric populations of Ukrainian nomads first began to domesticate the horse. Today, they are apparently extinct in the wild, although a number of zoos have specimens. Even though it is extinct in the wild, Przewalski's horse has many thousands of descendants in stables and also running wild as mustangs.

Brontotheres (Titanotheres)

The brontotheres began as pig-sized, hornless animals approximately 53 million years ago, and quickly evolved into multiple lineages of cow-sized animals with long skulls and no horns. In the late Middle Eocene (between 40 and 47 million years ago), there were six different lineages of brontotheres. Some had long skulls, while others had short snouts and broad skulls. Still others had a pair of tiny blunt horns on the tip of their noses. Between 37 and 34 million years ago, their evolution culminated with huge, elephant-sized beasts bearing paired blunt horns on their noses. Throughout their history, brontotheres were the largest animals in North America. They also appeared in Asia in the Late Eocene, where beasts such as *Embolotherium*, with a huge single "battering-ram" horn, evolved.

Because of their large size and spectacular appearance, brontotheres frequently have been illustrated in popular books, but much of what is said about them is wrong or badly out of date. In 1929, Henry Fairfield Osborn published an imposing two-volume monograph on brontotheres. Unfortunately, most of what Osborn wrote is wrong, and paleontologists have just begun to correct his mistakes. For example, he divided the North American brontotheres into dozens of genera in 12 subfamilies, but currently only 18 genera in 2 subfamilies are recognized. Osborn was a believer in "straight-line" evolution and showed brontothere evolution as a simple linear sequence of genera. Modern research, on the other hand, shows that multiple genera lived at the same time and adopts no linear evolutionary trend. Most of the names that appear in popular books, such as *Brontotherium*, *Titanotherium*, *Titanops*, *Diploclonus*, or *Menodus*, are no longer valid. Only three genera (*Megacerops*, *Menops*, and *Brontops*) are recognized for the huge brontotheres of the Late Eocene, with a pair of horns near the snout. Numerous paleontologists have compared the "battering ram" horns of brontotheres to those of sheep and goats, suggesting that brontotheres rammed head-to-head after lowering their horns and charging. However, this cannot be so, because the bone in the snout beneath the horn is very delicate and spongy and could not have survived a strong impact without shattering the skull. Instead, brontothere horns served mainly for display, fighting off predators, and low-impact wrestling and butting with other brontotheres. One brontothere specimen shows a healed fracture high in the rib cage, a wound most likely inflicted by the horn of another brontothere.

Finally, Osborn thought that brontotheres became extinct because of some internal forces during their evolution, or "racial senescence." Recent research has shown that the extinction of brontotheres approximately 34 million years ago was owing to a global climatic change (triggered by the first Antarctic glaciers) that caused worldwide cooling and drying of climates. This change decimated the forests of the temperate regions and eliminated most of the soft, leafy vegetation on which brontotheres fed.

Moropomorphs

The earliest moropomorphs, such as *Homogalax*, occur in rock strata approximately 55 million years old. They are virtually indistinguishable from the earliest horses, such as *Protorohippus*. From this unspecialized ancestry, a variety of archaic tapir-like animals diverged. Most retained the simple leaf-cutting teeth characteristic of tapirs, and like brontotheres they died out when their forest habitats shrank, approximately 34 million years ago. Only the modern tapir, with its distinctive long proboscis, still survives in the jungles of Central and South America (three species) and southeast Asia (one species). All are stocky, piglike beasts with short stout legs, oval hooves, and a short tail. They have no natural defenses against large predators (such as jaguars or tigers), so they are expert at fleeing through dense brush and swimming to make their escape.

Another moropomorph group, the horselike clawed chalicotheres, are closely related to some of these archaic tapirs. When chalicotheres were first discovered, paleontologists refused to believe that the claws belonged to a hoofed mammal related to horses and rhinos. However, many specimens have clearly shown that chalicotheres are an example of a hoofed mammal that evolved to regain its claws. There has been much speculation about the uses of chalicothere claws. Traditionally, they were considered useful for digging up roots and tubers, except that the fossilized claws show no sign of the characteristic scratches due to digging. Instead, chalicotheres apparently used their claws to haul down limbs and branches to eat leaves (much as ground sloths did), rather than for digging. *Chalicotherium* had such long forelimbs and short hind limbs that it apparently knuckle-walked like a gorilla, with its claws curled inward. In North America and Eurasia, chalicotheres were always rare; however, the animal did survive in Africa until the Ice Ages.

Rhinoceroses

The third group of moropomorphs, the rhinoceroses, have been highly diverse and successful throughout the past 50 million years. They have occupied nearly every niche available to a large herbivore, from dog-sized running animals, to several hippolike forms, to the largest land mammal that ever lived, *Paraceratherium*. Unlike the horns of cattle, sheep, and goats, rhino horns are made of cemented hair fibers. Having no bony core, they rarely fossilize. In fossils, the presence and size of the horn must be inferred from a roughened area on the top of the skull where the horn once attached. Most rhinoceroses were hornless. Even in species without horns, rhino fossils are easy to recognize by a number of anatomical features in the skeleton, skull, and braincase. One of the easiest to spot is the crests on the crowns of the upper molars, which look like the Greek letter "pi" (π).

The earliest rhinos, known as *Hyrachyus,* were widespread over Eurasia and North America approximately 53 million years ago and are even found in the Canadian Arctic. They apparently crossed back and forth between Europe and North America using a land bridge across the North Atlantic (before that ocean opened to its present width). From *Hyrachyus* three different families of rhino diverged. One family, the amynodonts, were hippolike amphibious forms, with stumpy legs and a barrel chest for living in ponds and rivers. They occupied this niche long before the hippo evolved. In addition, amynodonts are usually found in river and lake deposits. The last of the amynodonts, which had a short trunk like an elephant's, died out in Asia approximately 15 million years ago.

The second family was known as the hyracodonts, or "running rhinos," because they had unusually long slender legs compared to other rhinos. They were particularly common in Asia and North America between 42 and 34 million years ago. The last of the North American forms was *Hyracodon*, which was about the size and proportions of a Great Dane and survived until approximately 29 million years ago. The second group of hyracodonts were the

gigantic indricotheres, which were the largest mammals in Asia during the Late Eocene and Oligocene (approximately 40 to 30 million years ago). The biggest of all was *Paraceratherium* (once called *Baluchitherium* or *Indricotherium*), which was 6 meters tall at the shoulder and weighed 20,000 kilograms). It was so tall that it must have browsed leaves from the tops of trees, as giraffes do today. Despite its huge bulk, it did not have the massive limbs and short, compressed toes of most giant land animals, such as sauropod dinosaurs, brontotheres, or elephants. Instead, it reveals its heritage as a running rhino by retaining its long slender toes—even though it was much too large to run. Indricotheres were also the last of the hyracodonts, vanishing from Asia approximately 15 million years ago.

The third family is the true rhinoceroses, or family Rhinocerotidae. They first appeared in Asia and North America approximately 40 million years ago and lived side-by-side with the hyracodonts and amynodonts on both continents. Rhinocerotids can be distinguished from hyracodonts and amynodonts by their distinctive molars and by the development of a tusklike lower incisor which occluded against a chisel-like upper incisor. In the Late Eocene and Early Oligocene (approximately 37 to 28 million years ago), there were several different genera of rhinocerotids, including the primitive *Trigonias* and the common Badlands rhinocerotid, *Subhyracodon* (formerly called *Caenopus*). These cow-sized animals had low-crowned teeth for eating soft, leafy vegetation and probably lived in the more densely wooded parts of their habitat, unlike the running hyracodonts (which lived in open habitats) or the amphibious amyndonts (which occupied the rivers and lakes). When the brontotheres died out approximately 34 million years ago, rhinocerotids were the largest land mammals in North America, and they remained so until mastodonts arrived approximately 16 million years ago.

Until this point, all the rhinoceroses we have mentioned were hornless. Rhinos with horns first appeared approximately 28 million years ago; two different lineages independently evolved paired horns on the tip of the nose. Both of these groups became extinct approximately 18 million years ago, when two new subfamilies immigrated to North America from Asia: the browsing (leaf-eating) aceratherines, and hippolike grazing teleoceratines. Between 18 and 5 million years ago, browser-grazer pairs of rhinos were found all over the grasslands of Eurasia, Africa, and North America. The teleoceratine *Teleoceras* was remarkably similar to hippos, with its short limbs, massive barrel-shaped body, and high-crowned teeth for eating gritty grasses. We know these animals were aquatic because they are usually found in ancient lake or river sediments. Some extraordinary specimens buried in volcanic ash preserve the grass seeds of their last meal.

A mass extinction event that occurred approximately five million years ago wiped out North American rhinos and decimated most of the archaic rhino lineages (especially the teleoceratines and aceratherines) in the Old World. The surviving lineages diversified in Eurasia and Africa and even thrived during the Ice Ages. They included the gigantic, elephant-sized elasmotheres, which had a huge 2-meter-long horn in the center of their forehead. Elasmotheres were found from Spain to Siberia to China during the Ice Ages, as were the woolly rhinos and their relatives. Woolly rhinos are known from numerous mummified specimens that give us detailed information about their hair, tissues, and even stomach contents. Their two horns grew one in front of the other along the snout and were shaped like flattened blades resembling sabers. Scratches on the front edge show that they were used to scrape away snow in the search for food. Despite the great success of woolly rhinos all over Eurasia during the Ice Ages, for some reason they never crossed the Bering land bridge back into North America (even though the woolly mammoths and bison did). The only surviving descendant of the woolly rhino lineage is the endangered Sumatran rhinoceros. Only a few hundred individuals still live in the mountainous jungles of Sumatra.

Four other species of rhino survive in Asia and Africa. The Javan rhinoceros is rarely seen in the dense jungles of Java and Vietnam; fewer than 50 individuals may still be living in the wild. The Indian rhinoceros and the two African rhinos (the browsing black rhinoceros and the grazing white rhinoceros) inhabit grasslands, although they prefer to hide in dense vegetation. Rhinos have very poor eyesight but excellent senses of smell and hearing, so they can detect danger long before being seen by predators. Most live in small family groups of females with their calves; bull rhinos tend to be solitary.

All of the living species of rhinoceros are on the brink of extinction owing to heavy poaching for their horns. Rhino horn is widely used in Chinese folk medicine for reducing fevers and is also popular for the handles of the traditional dagger worn in the Arab states. As a result, the poaching has been particularly intense, because rhino horn is more valuable per ounce than gold or

cocaine. In the 1970s and 1980s, the slaughter was so severe that over 90 percent of the rhinos living in the wild (hundreds of thousands of animals) were killed, leaving only a few thousand in countries in Africa (such as South Africa and Zimbabwe) that have excellent game protection. Despite the international ban on the trade of rhino horn and protection as endangered species, rhinos are still being killed and their horn smuggled through the black market because the demand of Chinese apothecaries only increases as the horn becomes scarcer.

DONALD R. PROTHERO

Further Reading

Carroll, R.L. 1988. *Vertebrate Paleontology and Evolution.* New York: Freeman.

MacFadden, B.J. 1994. *Fossil Horses.* Cambridge and New York: Cambridge University Press.

Prothero, D.R. 1987. The rise and fall of the American rhino. *Natural History* 96:26–33.

Prothero, D.R., and R.M. Schoch (eds.). 1989. *The Evolution of Perissodactyls.* Oxford: Clarendon; New York: Oxford University Press.

———. 1998. *Horns, Tusks, Hooves, and Flippers: The Evolution of Hoofed Mammals and Their Relatives.* Baltimore, Maryland: Johns Hopkins University Press.

Savage, R.J.G., and M.R. Long. 1986. *Mammal Evolution: An Illustrated Guide.* London: British Museum (Natural History); New York: Facts-on-File.

PHANEROZOIC MICROFOSSILS

See Skeletized Microorganisms

PHANEROZOIC PROBLEMATICA

See Problematic Animals: Phanerozoic Problematica

PHARYNGEAL ARCHES AND DERIVATIVES

The pharynx, or throat region, of backboned (vertebrate) animals contains a series of skeletal bars called "pharyngeal arches." In fishes, these arches lie in the gills (the respiratory organs) and are separated by gill pouches, which originally opened to the outside at gill clefts (Figure 1). Early in the development of embryos of all vertebrates, the arches develop from a tissue called "neural crest," which forms next to the brain, then migrates into the pharyngeal wall between the pharyngeal pouches (gill pouches). The pharyngeal arches began as breathing structures, but during the half-billion year history of the vertebrates they have been modified for many other functions.

At first, two different series of arches—internal and external—probably existed in the pharynx (Mallatt 1996). The two form

the outer and the inner part of the gills, respectively (Figure 1). The external arches, which are unjointed, dominate in jawless fishes, including lampreys and the fossil jawless groups; jointed, internal arches dominate in jawed vertebrates. Bony fishes and the land vertebrates (tetrapods) have only internal arches. However, jawless hagfishes and jawed elasmobranchs (sharks, rays, and skates) have both external and internal series, which indicates that the ancestral vertebrates also probably had both. External and internal arches are seen together best in elasmobranchs, where the external arches are named "extrabranchial cartilages."

As shown in Figure 1D, the pharyngeal arches of fishes are sites of attachment for the breathing muscles. This reflects the

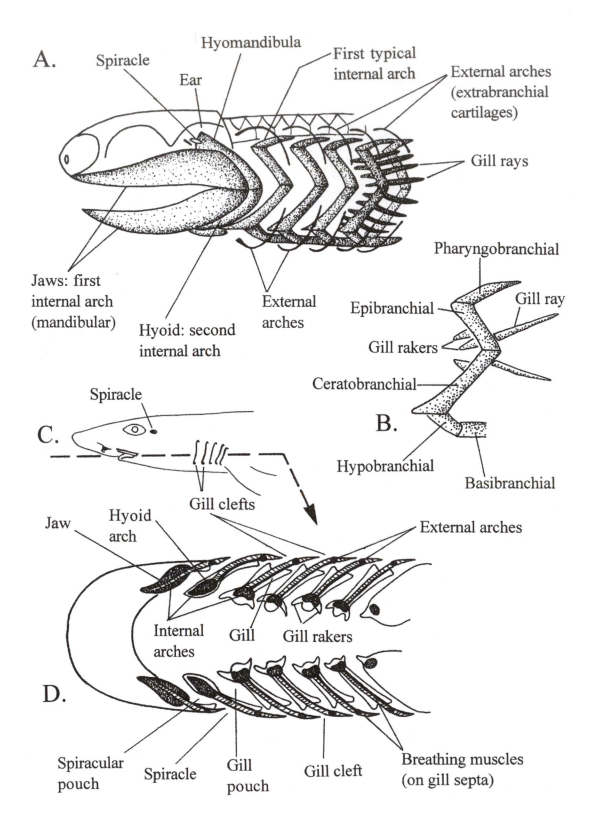

Figure 1. Pharyngeal arches in sharks, showing many ancestral features. *A*, skull and arches of a generalized shark, lateral view; note the internal (stippled) and external (clear) arches; gill rakers and gill rays (projecting anteriorly and posteriorly, respectively) are shown only on the fourth arch; *B*, enlargement of a typical internal arch (center right); *C*, leopard shark (side view), dashed horizontal line indicates the angle of cut for part *D*; *D*, shark pharynx (idealized horizontal cut), showing relationship between the pharyngeal arches, gills, and other structures; here, the spiracular (first) pouch is shown in the same section as the gill pouches, although it actually lies in a higher plane; shaded structures indicate breathing muscles. *D* is redrawn from Mallatt (1997).

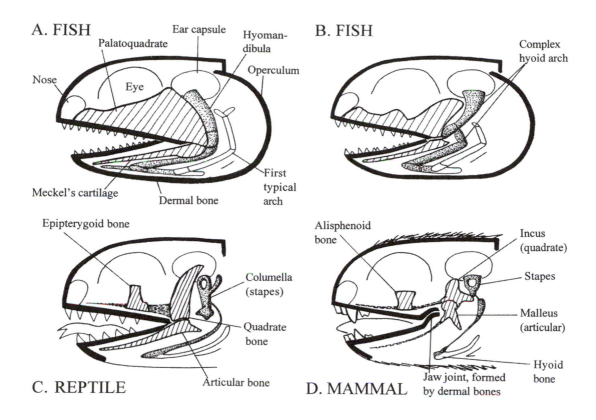

Figure 2. Evolutionary changes in the first two pharyngeal arches. *A*, condition in primitive bony fishes, such as certain fossil lobe-finned fishes (*Eusthenopteron*, Jarvik 1980); except for the covering of dermal bone (indicated by thick, black lines), this arrangement resembles the shark condition (Figure 1A); *B*, condition in primitive ray-finned fishes, showing that the hyoid arch has become more complex; *C*, reptile condition; *D*, mammal condition. Key: parallel lines indicate mandibular arch; stippling indicates hyoid arch. Modified and redrawn after Goodrich (1930).

original respiratory function of the arches, best seen in sharks among jawed fishes and in the larval developmental stage of lampreys among jawless fishes (Hughes 1974; Mallatt 1996). When these fishes exhale, the breathing muscles bend the arches, decreasing the size of the pharynx; this constriction pushes water backward, across the gills, and out the gill clefts. Then, during inhalation, the arches spring back (or are pulled back) to their original shape, enlarging the pharynx and drawing water in through the mouth.

Originally, the pharyngeal arches consisted of cartilage (gristle), as they still are in the present-day jawless fishes and cartilaginous fishes (sharks and their relatives). In bony fishes, by contrast, the internal arches ossify (bone replaces cartilage in these arches) early in life.

Internal arches are far more important to the history of vertebrates than are external arches, so only internal arches will be considered in the remainder of this essay. In almost all jawed fishes, there are five typical internal arches (Figure 1). As seen in cartilaginous fishes and in the acanthodians (fossil relatives of bony fishes), each of these arches originally had five joined elements (Figure 1B). From above to below, these are a pharyngobranchial, epibranchial, ceratobranchial, hypobranchial, and basibranchial (a basibranchial is often shared by several successive arches).

Attached to the outer side of the arch are long projections called "gill rays." These lie in a fibrous sheet (septum) in the center of the gill and help to support the gill's soft structures. Along the arch's inner side are cone-shaped projections called "gill rakers." These form a coarse screen that prevents food from entering the gill pouches when being swallowed through the pharynx. Gill rakers often are long and numerous in specialized fishes that feed by filtering tiny particles from the water (such as whale sharks and anchovies); in some manner not yet understood, such rakers strain the food particles (Sanderson and Wassersug 1993). Embedded in the soft, pink membrane that covers the inner surface of the arches are hard, toothlike elements (not illustrated). In elasmobranchs these are tiny, but in some bony fishes they form large plates for biting or crushing food deep within the pharynx (Nelson 1969; Galis and Drucker 1996).

In jawed vertebrates, the first internal (mandibular) arch is modified and enlarged, forming the jaws (Figure 1A). The upper jaw (palatoquadrate) is probably the epibranchial of the mandibular arch, and the lower jaw (Meckel's cartilage) is the ceratobranchial. There is no direct fossil evidence that jaws evolved from a pharyngeal arch. However, strong evidence for this adaptation comes from the way jaws look in embryos of living vertebrates, with the associated blood vessels and nerves and their musculature

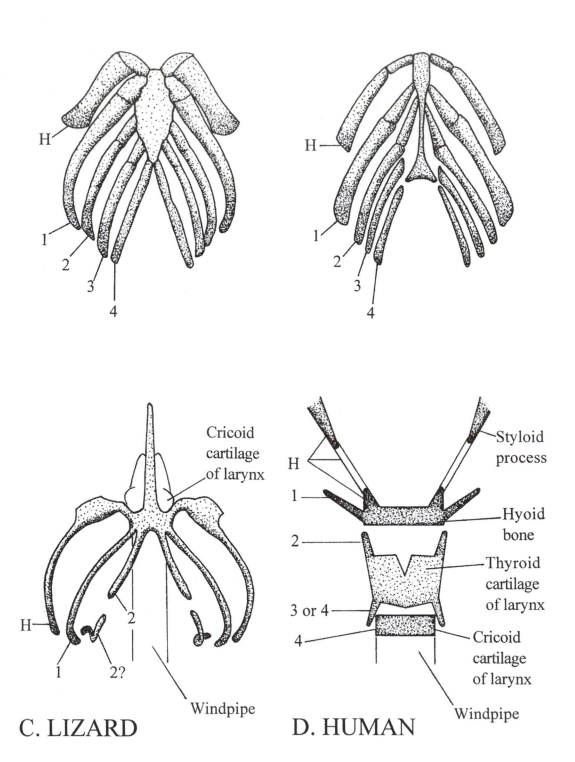

Figure 3. Pharyngeal arches of various vertebrates (viewed from below), mostly ceratobranchial, hypobranchial, and basibranchial elements (jaw arch not shown). *A,* bony fish *(Polypterus); B,* larval salamander *(Ambystoma); C,* lizard (reptile: *Lacerta); D,* human (mammal). Key: *H,* hyoid arch; *1, 2, 3, 4,* first to fourth typical arches. Redrawn after *A,* Nelson (1969), Reilly and Lauder (1988); *B,* Reilly and Lauder (1988); *C,* Goodrich (1930).

(Gegenbaur 1872; Goodrich 1930). At this stage, jaws resemble the other arches lying farther back. Additionally, the jaws of many fishes bear a gill-like structure (pseudobranch) and are associated with a "spiracular pouch" (Figure 1D), which is the structure that remains of the first gill pouch of the embryo. The spiracular pouch opens at the body surface through a modified gill cleft called a spiracle. From such evidence, we can infer that jaws did evolve from the first pharyngeal arch.

Some scientists have claimed that additional pharyngeal arches ("premandibular arches") once existed in front of the jaws, in the mouth region (Jarvik 1980). Many investigators now doubt this, however, because the mouth contains no evidence of gills or gill pouches in any known vertebrate nor in the closest relatives of vertebrates (such as amphioxus, a fishlike invertebrate).

How and why did jaws evolve from a pharyngeal arch? Although there is fossil evidence that jawed fishes had appeared by 460 million years ago (Sansom et al. 1996) and are related most closely to thelodonts (extinct jawless fishes with sharklike scales) (Turner 1993), fossils may never document the stages in jaw evolution. The ancestral pharyngeal arches were made of soft, watery cartilage, material that does not fossilize well. Still, scholars have proposed theories of jaw evolution, based on what is known about more recent vertebrates. The traditional hypothesis is that the mandibular arch became jaws for feeding (Stahl 1974) when early vertebrates changed from filter feeders (which strain small particles from the water) to predators (which feed on larger organisms). However, new evidence seems to go against this hypothesis because it indicates that the earliest (jawless) vertebrates already were predators. A survey of the entire animal kingdom reveals that only predators evolved complex sense organs for detecting things at a distance, such as the eyes of vertebrates (Northcutt and Gans 1983). Furthermore, conodonts (a very early group of fossil jawless vertebrates) were predators with toothlike elements in their pharynx for grabbing and shearing prey (Purnell 1995). Apparently, the appearance of jaws did not make vertebrates predators; they merely made predaceous vertebrates into better predators.

A newer theory (Mallatt 1996) argues that enlargement of the mandibular arch into jaws did not occur initially for feeding but for improved breathing or ventilation. Predation involves the pursuit of prey, which requires more energy than filter feeding. Therefore, as jawless, predaceous ancestors became more active, they breathed harder. These fishes evolved the ability to inhale more forcefully by opening their mouth wide and actively expanding their pharynx; they also gained the ability to close the mouth during strong exhalation so that water would not regurgitate forward out of the mouth (modern fishes do close and open their mouths like this while breathing). Closing and opening the mouth in this way involved bending and straightening the mandibular arch powerfully, which strengthened the structure into "breathing jaws." These ventilatory changes had a bonus—the fish could now suck in prey through the wide-open mouth, then close the jaws to grasp the prey so it could not escape. Thus, jaws attained their feeding function. In support of this "ventilatory" theory of jaw origin, most known jawed fishes are suction feeders, using their jaws to hold the prey as they inhale, rather than biting pieces from the prey.

Alternate theories propose other sources for jaws. For example, John Maisey has proposed that the mandibular arch was always different from the other pharyngeal arches and was always a feeding structure (1989). Peter Forey and Philippe Janvier have proposed that jaws evolved from a breathing flap called a velum, found at the front of the pharynx of present-day jawless fishes (1994). Neither of these theories, however, accounts for the many structural similarities between the jaws and the other pharyngeal arches.

Directly behind the jaw is the second internal ("hyoid") arch, which is also an atypical arch. In almost all jawed fishes, present-day and fossil, its epibranchial element (hyomandibula) is stout, bracing the palatoquadrate of the upper jaw against the braincase at the ear capsule (Figure 1A). According to the theory of Robert Denison (1961), in the earliest jawed fishes, the hyoid was a typical ventilatory arch. Then the jaws pushed back against it for support when the mouth opening enlarged to allow the entry of extremely large prey animals. A different interpretation (Maisey 1989) is that the hyoid always supported the mandibular arch, even before the latter enlarged into jaws—which would mean that the hyoid was never a ventilatory arch. There is, however, evidence against that interpretation. In some jawed fishes that have retained some primitive characteristics (ratfishes or chimaeroids and perhaps some of the extinct placoderms), the hyoid arch is a non-supportive, typical, ventilatory arch. Furthermore, in all jawed fishes the hyoid arch bears typical gill structures.

In all jawed fishes, the hyoid arch and its associated muscles participate more than the other arches in moving ventilatory water. In bony fishes and a few cartilaginous fishes (chimaeroids), the sheetlike septum of the hyoid gill is enlarged into an operculum (Figure 2A, B), a flap that helps pump water during both exhalation and inhalation (Hughes 1974). Outward and inward movements of the jaw and hyoid bone (the "suspensorium" of bony fishes) also contribute to the ventilatory pump (Lauder 1985).

In bony fishes, the head and pharynx are covered by dermal bones (bony plates in the surface skin), which encase the mandibular arch and contribute to the jaws (Figure 2). In tetrapods, the mandibular-arch elements are reduced, so that dermal bones form most parts of the jaw. But in amphibians, reptiles, and birds, the arch elements persist as the bones of the jaw joint (Figure 2C). At this joint, the quadrate bone of the upper jaw represents the back of the palatoquadrate, and the articular bone of the lower jaw represents the back of Meckel's cartilage. Another part of the palatoquadrate contributes to the base of the braincase as the epipterygoid bone (which in mammals is called the "alisphenoid," or greater wing of the sphenoid).

In tetrapods, the palatoquadrate is fused firmly to the braincase, so the hyomandibula is not needed for support. Instead, it has a role in hearing. In amphibians, reptiles, and birds, the hyomandibula runs from the ear capsule to the eardrum (a membrane covering the spiracle). Called a columella or stapes (Figure 2C), the hyomandibula transmits sound vibrations from the eardrum to the inner ear.

In mammals, the relation of the mandibular and hyoid arches to the ear region is especially interesting (Figure 2D). In the ancient reptile ancestors of mammals, the eardrum lay very near the jaw joint, and the quadrate and articular bones of that joint apparently transmitted sound through the stapes. Later, in the mammal-like reptiles, dermal bones of the skull joined the quadrate and articular to strengthen the jaw joint (possibly to withstand more powerful biting and chewing forces). Still later, in the earliest mammals, the brain and braincase enlarged, which pushed the ear capsule farther back in the skull. When this occurred, the quadrate and articular bones separated from the jaw and moved back with the ear. Because of this, the jaw joint of mammals is formed strictly by dermal bones, and the displaced quadrate and articular participate only in sound transmission. Sound vibrations travel from the eardrum through the articular bone (here named the "malleus") to the quadrate (here named the "incus") and stapes to reach the inner ear. This chain amplifies sound, so that soft sounds can be heard. It is possible to trace this evolutionary sequence by studying both the embryonic development of living mammals and a remarkably complete series of fossils from South Africa and other parts of the world (Allin 1975; Kemp 1982).

Having discussed the mandibular arch and hyomandibula, we should consider the evolution of the other arches in tetrapods (Figure 3). Most larval salamanders and frog tadpoles live in water and retain gills, so their arches resemble those of fishes (Figure 3B). In tadpoles, the ceratobranchial elements of the hyoid arch are broad plates shaped like ax heads. They move the pharyngeal floor down and up to pull in water and pump it across the gills (Sanderson and Wassersug 1993). In gill-less adult amphibians and other tetrapods, the pharyngeal arches are altered and reduced in size but still perform important functions, forming the hyoid apparatus and the skeleton of the larynx. The hyoid apparatus supports the tongue and provides attachment for muscles that move the tongue. For example, this apparatus allows some salamanders to project their tongue forward to capture prey far from the front of the mouth (Larsen et al. 1996). In tetrapods the windpipe and lungs evolved as an outpocketing of the pharyngeal floor, and some pharyngeal arches became the skeleton of the larynx, which lies at the entrance of the windpipe. The larynx keeps swallowed items from entering the lungs and allows for sound production (in humans, it is the "voice box," and its largest cartilage is the thyroid cartilage, our "Adam's apple"). Figure 3 shows the precise contributions of the different pharyngeal arches in various tetrapods.

The history of the pharyngeal arches demonstrates that evolution does not proceed in a straight, predestined, direction. Rather, structures can change their shapes and functions radically and unpredictably in response to different environmental conditions. Arches that originated for gill respiration in early fishes became a wide variety of structures in later vertebrates: jaws, bones for hearing, tongue supports, and the skeleton of the voice box.

JON MALLATT

See also Feeding Adaptations: Vertebrates; Gnathostomes; Respiration

Works Cited

Allin, E.F. 1975. Evolution of the mammalian middle ear. *Journal of Morphology* 147 (4):403–38.

Denison, R.H. 1961. Feeding mechanisms of agnatha and early gnathostomes. *American Zoologist* 1 (2):177–81.

Forey, P., and P. Janvier. 1994. Evolution of the early vertebrates. *American Scientist* 82:554–65.

Galis, F., and E.G. Drucker. 1996. Pharyngeal biting mechanics in centrarchid and cichlid fishes: Insights into a key evolutionary innovation. *Journal of Evolutionary Biology* 9:641–70.

Gegenbaur, K. 1872. *Untersuchungen zur vergleichenden Anatomie der Wirbelthiere. III. Das Kopfskelet der Selachier.* Leipzig: Engelmann.

Goodrich, E.S. 1930. *Studies on the Structure and Development of Vertebrates.* 2 vols. London: Macmillan; New York: Dover, 1958.

Hughes, G.M. 1974. *Comparative Physiology of Vertebrate Respiration.* 2nd ed., London: Heinemann.

Jarvik, E. 1980. *Basic Structure and Evolution of Vertebrates.* 2 vols. New York and London: Academic Press.

Kemp, T.S. 1982. *Mammal-like Reptiles and the Origin of Mammals.* New York and London: Academic Press.

Lauder, G.V. 1985. Aquatic feeding in lower vertebrates. *In* M. Hildebrand, D. Bramble, K.F. Liem, and D.B. Wake (eds.), *Functional Vertebrate Morphology.* Cambridge, Massachusetts: Harvard University Press.

Larsen, J.H., J.T. Beneski, and B.T. Miller, 1996. Structure and function of the hyolingual system in *Hynobius* and its bearing on the evolution of prey capture in terrestrial salamanders. *Journal of Morphology* 227:235–48.

Maisey, J.G. 1989. Visceral skeleton and musculature of a Late Devonian shark. *Journal of Vertebrate Paleontology* 9 (2):174–90.

Mallatt, J. 1996. Ventilation and the origin of jawed vertebrates: A new mouth. *Zoological Journal of the Linnean Society* 117:329–404.

Nelson, G.J. 1969. Gill arches and the phylogeny of fishes, with notes on the classification of vertebrates. *Bulletin of the American Museum of Natural History* 141 (4):475–552.

Northcutt, R.G., and C. Gans. 1983. The genesis of neural crest and epidermal placodes: A reinterpretation of vertebrate origins. *Quarterly Review of Biology* 58:1–28.

Purnell, M.A. 1995. Microwear on conodont elements and macrophagy in the first vertebrates. *Nature* 374:798–800.

Reilly, S.M., and G.V. Lauder. 1988. Atavisms and the homology of hyobranchial elements in lower vertebrates. *Journal of Morphology* 195:237–45.

Sanderson, S.L., and R. Wassersug. 1993. Convergent and alternative designs for vertebrate suspension feeding. *In* J. Hanken and B.K. Hall (eds.), *The Skull,* Vol. 3, *Functional and Evolutionary Mechanisms.* Chicago: University of Chicago Press.

Sansom, I.J., M.M. Smith, and M.P. Smith. 1996. Scales of thelodont and shark-like fishes from the Ordovician of Colorado. *Nature* 379:628–30.

Stahl, G.J. 1974. *Vertebrate History: Problems in Evolution.* New York: McGraw-Hill.

Turner, S. 1993. The thelodonti, an important but enigmatic group of Palaeozoic fishes. *Modern Geology* 18:125–40.

Further Reading

Alexander, R.M. 1975. *The Chordates.* London and New York: Cambridge University Press; 2nd ed., 1981.

Carroll, R.L. 1988. *Vertebrate Paleontology and Evolution.* New York: Freeman.

Goodrich, E.S. 1930. *Studies on the Structure and Development of Vertebrates.* 2 vols. London: Macmillan; New York: Dover, 1958.

Hughes, G.M. 1963. *Comparative Physiology of Vertebrate Respiration.* Cambridge, Massachusetts: Harvard University Press; London: Heinemann; 2nd ed., London: Heinemann, 1974.

Kardong, K.V. 1995. *Vertebrates: Comparative Anatomy, Function, Evolution.* Dubuque, Iowa and Oxford: Wm. C. Brown; 2nd ed., Dubuque, Iowa: McGraw-Hill/WBC, 1997.

Mallatt, J. 1996. Ventilation and the origin of jawed vertebrates: A new mouth. *Zoological Journal of the Linnean Society* 117:329–404.

Nelson, G.J. 1969. Gill arches and the phylogeny of fishes, with notes on the classification of vertebrates. *Bulletin of the American Museum of Natural History* 141 (4):475–552.

PHEROMONE RECEPTORS

See Odor and Pheromone Receptors

PHILLIPS, JOHN

English, 1800–74

The geologist John Phillips was born 25 December 1800 in Wiltshire, England and died 24 April 1874 in Oxford. Phillips was orphaned at an early age and raised by his paternal uncle, William Smith, the geologist, land surveyor, and author of the first detailed geological map of Britain. Although he had little formal education (he went to a school near Bath and spent a year under the instruction of the Reverend Benjamin Richardson of Farleigh Hungerford), Phillips received training from his uncle, and became one of England's few skilled lithographers. In return, Phillips concentrated on aiding his uncle in the production and illustration of his many reports.

In 1824 Phillips was appointed curator of the Yorkshire Philosophical Society's museum in York, a post that he held until 1840. During this period, Phillips became very involved in the organization of science in Britain. He was one of the primary instigators behind the formation of the British Association for the Advancement of Science, which held its first general meeting at York in 1831. Until 1859, Phillips served as the Association's executive officer and was instrumental in moving the annual assembly's venue to London. His involvement in the production of the Association's annual reports permitted his accession to a leading role in Britain's science community.

Phillips was a skilled and popular lecturer. He was appointed fellow of the Royal Society in 1834 and, at the same time, succeeded Charles Lyell as professor of geology at King's College, London. In 1840 he resigned both his position at York and the professorship at King's College to join the Geological Survey of Great Britain. This appointment lasted until he was invited to fill a post as deputy reader in geology at the University of Oxford in 1853. After the death of the geologist William Buckland in 1856, Phillips advanced to become reader, and subsequently, professor. He was a key figure in the building of the university's new museum and remained at Oxford until his accidental death (from a fall) in 1874.

Phillips was a practical field geologist, both by training and inclination. As a highly skilled illustrator of geological maps, his principle contribution to the science of geology was descriptive rather than theoretical. In his early years, Phillips concentrated on the stratigraphy and structure of geological formations in Yorkshire and introduced the term "Yoredale Series" for a succession of shales, sandstones, and limestones appearing in the uppermost zone of the carboniferous limestone series in the Yorkshire region. Later, Phillips studied the fossils of southwest England and coined the term "Mesozoic" to identify the geological era between the Paleozoic and Cenozoic eras (including the Triassic, Jurassic, and Cretaceous periods).

In the 1850s Phillips changed direction and assumed responsibility for executing the British Association's commission of new drawings and surveys of selected parts of the moon. Using the Earl of Ross' telescope, Phillips was the first to map the moon photographically. From the photographs, he used his lithographic skill to produce detailed drawings. He continued this work at Oxford several years later, using a telescope provided by the Royal Society. Phillips published his studies and drew analogies between the lunar landscape and the Earth's geological formations, calling on his intimate knowledge of many formations from his earlier investigations.

Phillips, as professor of geology at Oxford, naturally took great interest in the evolutionary debate sparked by the publication of Charles Darwin's *Origin of Species* (1859). Phillips and Darwin corresponded with each other; however, Phillips never accepted the Darwinian theory of transmutation (changes in shape and substance). Indeed, Phillips was one of the earliest critics of Darwin's use of geology to substantiate his theory. In particular, he challenged Darwin's attempts to develop a way to record absolute times through calculations based on the denudation of the Weald, the region in southeast England comprising the counties of Kent, Surrey, and Essex. Phillips demonstrated that Darwin's calculations were fallacious, which forced Darwin to refrain from using them in later editions of the *Origin.* Although Darwin respected Phillips' acuity, he was disappointed in Phillips' overall critical reaction and resistance to evolutionism. Understandably, Darwin frequently referred to Phillips in his correspondence in less than flattering terms.

Despite his noted skill, Phillips represented a vanishing breed by the time of his death. Formal training, not apprenticeship, had become a requirement to move up through the ranks in the scientific community. Although he was outdated by the time he retired from the scene, Phillips was one of the early nineteenth century's scientists who not only provided a detailed body of data on which his successors could build and elaborate, but who also contributed to transforming science into a professional discipline. His achievement allowed his successors, such as Thomas Henry Huxley, to generate the scientific advances that characterize the second half of the nineteenth century. Phillips may have been left behind during the day's greatest revolution, but his part in science was instrumental to further developments.

MICHAEL RUSE

Biography

Born in Marden, Wiltshire, 25 December 1800. Curator, Museum of Yorkshire Philosophical Society, 1826–40; professor of geology, King's College, London, 1834–41; member, Geological Survey of Great Britain, 1840–53; professor, Trinity College, Dublin, 1844–45; deputy reader of geology (1853–56), reader of geology (1856–60), professor of geology (1860–74), Oxford University. Fellow, Geological Society of London, 1828; founder and executive officer, British Association for the Advancement of Science, 1831–59; fellow, Royal Society of London, 1834; recipient, Wollaston Medal, Geological Society of London, 1845; president, Geological Society of London, 1858–60. Geologist best known for lithographic work documenting the fossil record and the surface of astronomical bodies such as the moon. Died in Oxford, 24 April 1874.

Major Publications

1829–36. *Illustrations of the Geology of Yorkshire; or, A Description of the Strata and Organic Remains.* 2 vols. Vol. 1, York: John Phillips, 1829; vol. 2 [with 2nd ed. of vol. 1], London: Murray, 1836; 3rd ed., London, 1875.

1834. *A Guide to Geology.* London: Longman; 5th ed., 1864.

1841. *Figures and Descriptions of the Paleozoic Fossils of Cornwall, Devon, and West Somerset, Observed in the Course of the Ordnance Geological Survey of that District.* London: Longmans.

1860. *Life on the Earth: Its Origin and Succession.* London: Macmillan.

1865. The planet Mars. *Quarterly Journal of Science* 2:369–81.

1868. Notices of some parts of the surface of the moon. *Philosophical Transactions of the Royal Society* 158:333–46.

Further Reading

Darwin, Charles. 1985–. *The Correspondence of Charles Darwin.* 9 vols. Cambridge and New York: Cambridge University Press.

Morrell, J., and A. Thackray. 1981. *Gentlemen of Science: Early Years of the British Association for the Advancement of Science.* Oxford: Clarendon; New York: Oxford University Press.

PHOLIDOTANS

See Pangolins

PHOTOGRAPHIC TECHNIQUES

Paleontological photography documents facts and ideas from paleontological investigations. Specimens, field sites, field and laboratory techniques, museum collections, paleontological illustrations, and even paleontologists are often subjects, usually for archives, research, displays, publications, posters, or lectures.

Radiant energy that an object absorbs or reflects produces the photographic image. Because they do not show all that we can perceive with our eyes, photographic images are only abstractions of the objects that they document: standard photographs are two dimensional; black-and-white images show no color; and no photograph can capture the great range of tones that our eyes can detect. Nonetheless, photographs usually extend our abilities to study a subject, because they clarify, emphasize, and enlarge the subject and make comparisons easier.

Paleontology demands photographs of high technical quality, both objective and subjective. High technical quality usually means the photograph faithfully reproduces tonal contrast; has high sharpness; clearly displays detail with high resolution; has unobtrusive grain; and has composition that communicates a simple, strong, and cohesive message.

Paleontology often requires standard, or scenic, photography (less than 0.05 magnification); close-up photography (0.05–1.0 magnification); photomacrography (1.0–10 magnification); or photomicrography (greater than 10 magnification). Only certain, not necessarily expensive, 35-millimeter, single-lens-reflex cameras offer the combination of compactness, portability, quality, and versatility that most paleontologists desire. Rangefinder, subminiature, twin-lens reflex, and nonfocusing cameras are the least desirable. Intermediate sized (e.g., 2 1/4–inch film) cameras are quite suitable and nearly as versatile, but more bulky. Plate-film view cameras are excellent for laboratory photography but are expensive and bulky and unwieldy in the field. Photographers prefer a sturdy camera that offers, at least as an option, manual exposure, manual focus, manual film-speed setting, interchangeable lenses, a through-the-lens exposure meter, a tripod socket, and off-camera flash capability. Macro lenses offer the most desirable capabilities of close-up to infinity focus, high quality, and light weight, and they may serve as the single lens of choice for laboratory and field. Less expensive but suitable are macro-tele extenders, which couple to a "standard" camera lens; extension tubes and bellows, which are versatile but less convenient; and "plus" lenses, which are lightweight but may produce somewhat lower image quality.

The photographer must chose an appropriate film, set up the background and lighting, and determine what special techniques or equipment may be necessary.

Untextured backgrounds distract less from the subject than those with texture. Black, white, or gray backgrounds best isolate and emphasize the subject in a black-and-white photograph, but white or light gray produce the best apparent specimen contrast in a published photograph.

Time-honored advice to improve composition and impact of a photograph is "Make it big, keep it simple." The best photographs include but a single specimen that fills the frame, which permits better control of focus, lighting, and composition. Audiences appreciate the simplicity and visibility of six or fewer specimens per slide. The best clarity requires a relatively low-speed film, an ISO speed of 25–100; a tripod for stability; and a small aperture, such as f/5.6 through f/11, or smaller.

A skillful person must prepare the specimen, clear away conservator's cement, and remove dust and lint to make the specimen presentable. Submerging some specimens in a liquid, such as water or alcohol, may enhance contrast and make details more visible. Mottled surfaces may benefit from the white coating of ammonium-chloride sublimate, which hides the mottling and better shows texture and shape.

Photographic lighting, a difficult but important element, is the only way to show significant details. The photographer must skillfully illuminate the specimen with one or more lights, diffusers, and reflectors. We evolved with one principal overhead light, the sun, and expect similar lighting in a photographic image. Other lights should be secondary so that shadows appear to come from the principal light. Correct shadows produce realistic perspective. Lighting direction affects the range of tones and so affects apparent clarity and detail. Low-angle lighting produces strong shadows that emphasize fine-scale texture.

Photographers recognize two extremes in lighting and surfaces: specular and diffuse. Specular lighting comes from relatively small or distant light sources and from reflection off shiny surfaces. Diffuse lighting comes from relatively large or nearby light sources and from reflection off dull surfaces. Specular lighting and surfaces increase image contrast; diffuse lighting and surfaces decrease contrast. Photographers often choose a small, bare-filament bulb to increase the contrast of a dull fossil; conversely, they may choose a larger light, perhaps a reflector or a "soft-box" diffuser, to decrease the contrast of a shiny fossil.

Photographers modify light quality to control reflections. Orienting a polarizer screen over each light and a polarizer filter over the lens helps eliminate reflections. A colored filter subdues

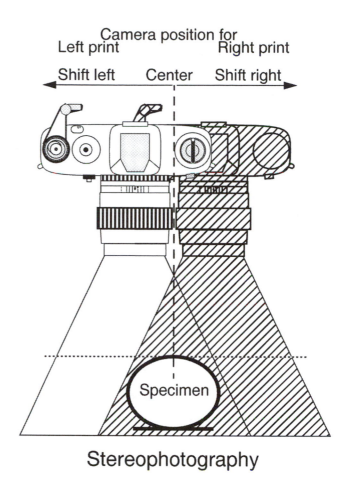

Figure 1. Stereophotography.

stains and mottling of the same color in black-and-white photography.

Stereophotography produces images that simulate three dimensions (3-D), which shows fossil specimens more realistically. The photographer makes a photograph for each eye, the same except for perspective. The photographer centers the camera over the specimen, then shifts it left about 32 millimeters (half the distance between the eyes) to make the left-eye photograph; re-centers the camera, then shifts the camera right about 32 millimeters to make the right-eye photograph. The photographer prints each no wider than twice the interocular distance (about 64 millimeters), then mounts them as a "stereopair" in the correct right-eye, left-eye positions, about 64 millimeters apart. As the eyes view the images through a stereo viewer, the brain fuses them into a realistic illusion of a three-dimensional object.

There are so many variables in photography, many of which are difficult to assess, that professional photographers often use a trial-and-error approach as they photograph challenging subjects. Experience with equipment, lights, and subjects promotes understanding that ultimately produces excellent results.

RONALD G. WOLFF

Further Reading

Blaker, A.A. 1977. *Handbook for Scientific Photography.* San Francisco: Freeman; 2nd ed. Boston: Focal Press, 1989.

Marsh, R.C., and L.F. Marsh. 1975. New techniques for coating paleontological specimens prior to photography. *Journal of Paleontology* 49 (3):565–66.

Scovil, J.A. 1996. *Photographing Minerals, Fossils, and Lapidary Materials.* Tucson, Arizona: Geoscience.

Stroebel, L., and R. Zakia. 1956. *The Focal Encyclopedia of Photography.* London and New York: Focal Press; 3rd ed., as *Encyclopedia of Photography.* Boston and Oxford: Focal Press, 1993.

PHYLETIC DWARFISM AND GIGANTISM

Phyletic dwarfism, or "nanism," is the phenomenon in which, over time, the body size of organisms in a lineage diminishes. Phyletic gigantism is generally not simply increase in body size, since this commonly occurs in many if not most lineages, but the phenomenon of some taxon (group; plural, taxa) becoming markedly (and perhaps rapidly) much larger than its ancestors and relatives. In other words, gigantism is a relative rather than absolute term.

For much of this century, phyletic dwarfism was considered fairly rare and dismissed almost totally as a possibility because of the almost-universal acceptance of Cope's Rule. This paleontological principle recognized that many lineages of animals increase in body size over time (Newell 1949). There are now many documented cases in the fossil record of size decrease over time, so the possibility of such a change no longer is doubted seriously. Since the term "phyletic dwarfism" is applied to any case of size decrease through time, other terms, in particular "miniaturization," have been suggested for instances of extreme size decrease. Miniaturization would be restricted to cases where size decrease has caused a "major change in the way an organism deals with its ancestral adaptive zone" (Hanken and Wake 1993). However, identifying cases of miniaturization that are distinct from simple phyletic size decrease (like identifying veritable "gigantism" from the background noise of normal phyletic size increase) is a fuzzy and often arbitrary distinction. What is a "major" change? What is "colossal," as opposed to just "pretty big"?

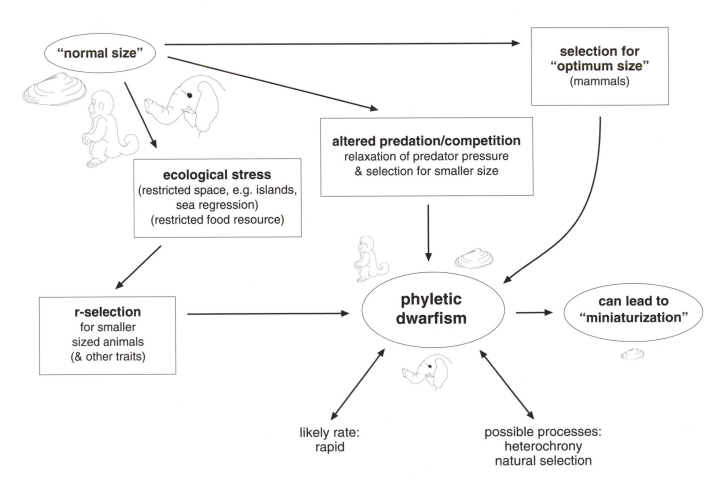

Figure 1. Phyletic dwarfism. Illustration by Catherine P. Sexton.

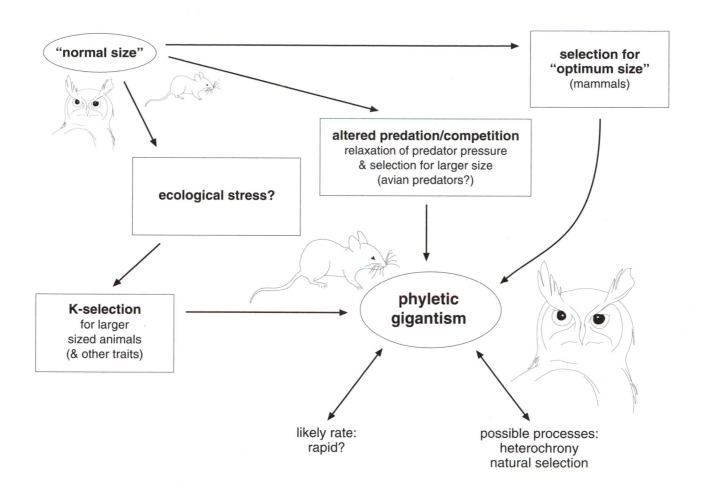

Figure 2. Phyletic gigantism. Illustration by Catherine P. Sexton.

Nonetheless, accepted examples of both phyletic dwarfism (including miniaturization) are widespread. They include invertebrates such as snails (Gould 1984) and other molluscs (Jablonski 1997), trilobites (Trammer and Kaim 1997), many fishes (Roberts 1986; Weitzman and Vari 1988), reptiles (Griffith 1990; Rieppel 1984) including dwarfed dinosaurs (Carroll 1990), hummingbirds (Rehkämper et al. 1991), and such mammals as rodents (Hafner and Hafner 1988; Moore 1959), rhinoceroses (Prothero and Sereno 1982), horses (Hulbert 1993; MacFadden 1992), primates (Ford 1980; Garber 1992; Shea 1992), and kangaroos (Marshall and Corruccini 1978). Gigantism has been shown more rarely, as in the Irish elk (Gould 1977). But perhaps the most striking examples come from many island faunas, where large mammals get small, including elephants, deer, hippopotamuses, tigers, porcupines, rhinoceroses, tapirs, and orangutans, while small animals get large (shrews and hedgehogs, mice and dormice, and owls), giving rise to what is known as the "island effect" (Ford 1986; Hooijer 1949; Lister 1989; Roth 1992; Sondaar 1986; Sondaar 1991).

Critical issues for paleobiology have been several. First, while paleontologists agree that phyletic dwarfism can occur, documenting any individual instance of dwarfism is difficult. Indeed,

Cope's rule generally holds true—most lineages have tended to increase in size through time, or at least, remain the same. Dwarfism appears to be the rarity and thus requires much supporting evidence ("when in doubt, assume it isn't so"). Yet the only true evidence is a dense, continuous fossil record documenting the episode of size decrease, and such evidence is seldom available. One recent study argues that lineages of Cretaceous molluscs decreased in body size as often as they increased, suggesting at least in these invertebrates, phyletic dwarfism is a common occurrence (Jablonski 1997). Second, for "miniaturization" or "gigantism" to be verified, it is important to identify some more radical alteration in the manner in which the animal adapted to its particular ecological niche. This can be particularly difficult to document because of the incompleteness of the fossil record, and differences of opinion easily arise about just how unique any *particular* evolutionary event of size increase or decrease actually is.

Stunning and peculiar as these dwarfs and giants are, of particular interest to paleontology are the broader questions of rate of change, cause, process, and effect, all of which surround instances of phyletic dwarfism and gigantism. Dwarfing, at least, may occur very rapidly; red deer on the Isle of Jersey reduced 5/6 in body weight in less than six thousand years (Lister 1989). Hypothesized causes of dwarfism and gigantism range from adaptations to local conditions to an evolutionary drift toward an "optimum" body size for energy capture, at least in mammals (Damuth 1993). Many have suggested that stressful environments with restricted resources, whether on islands or in regressing seas, select for animals capable of rapid turnover; such turnover requires early maturation and small body size (Ford 1980; Hallam 1990; Korn 1995); these animals are said to be "r-selected"—an ecological term for species that maximize the rate ("r") of population increase (Calder 1984). Size increase in lineages may be a reflection of the fact that founders most often are small (smaller animals more readily adapt to changing conditions with their shorter generation times and usually have a less specialized niche) (Arnold et al. 1995). Under these conditions, natural selection may favor phyletic dwarfism (Hallam 1990). Others have pointed to the special conditions of islands, where large carnivores are absent and food is less abundant (Masseti and Mazza 1996; Sondaar 1991). Freed from predator pressure, animals can adapt to needs for food acquisition, thermoregulation, and locomotion (Figures 1 and 2).

The processes leading to these changes may often be shifts in the timing of growth and maturation, or "heterochrony" (Gould 1977; Hanken and Wake 1993; McNamara 1982; Shea 1992; Shea et al. 1990). These shifts lead to different rates of growth and different adult ratios of various structures to size. Understanding these ratios and changes in specific features aids in understanding the evolution, as well as the ecology and behavior, of phyletically dwarfed and gigantic animals.

SUSAN M. FORD

See also Allometry; Evolutionary Trends; Growth, Development, and Evolution; Growth, Postembryonic; Heterochrony; Thermoregulation

Works Cited

Arnold, A.J., D.C. Kelly, and W.C. Parker. 1995. Causality and Cope's rule: Evidence from the planktonic foraminifera. *Journal of Paleontology* 69:203–10.

Calder III, W.A. 1984. *Size, Function, and Life History.* Cambridge, Massachusetts: Harvard University Press; London: Dover, 1996.

Carroll, R.L. 1990. A tiny microsaur from the Lower Permian of Texas: Size constraints in Palaeozoic tetrapods. *Paleontology* 33:893–909.

Damuth, J. 1993. Cope's rule, the island rule and the scaling of mammalian population density. *Nature* 365:748–50.

Damuth, J., and B.J. MacFadden (eds.). 1990. *Body Size in Mammalian Paleobiology: Estimation and Biological Implications.* Cambridge and New York: Cambridge University Press.

Ford, S.M. 1980. Callitrichids as phyletic dwarfs, and the place of the Callitrichidae in Platyrrhini. *Primates* 21:31–43.

——. 1986. Subfossil platyrrhine tibia (Primates: Callitrichidae) from Hispaniola: A possible further example of island gigantism. *American Journal of Physical Anthropology* 70:47–62.

Garber, P.A. 1992. Vertical clinging, small body size, and the evolution of feeding adaptations in the Callitrichinae. *American Journal of Physical Anthropology* 88:469–82.

Gould, S.J. 1977. *Ontogeny and Phylogeny.* Cambridge, Massachusetts: Harvard University Press.

——. 1984. Morphological channeling by structural constraint: Convergence in styles of dwarfing and gigantism in *Cerion,* with a description of two new fossil species and a report on the discovery of the largest *Cerion. Paleobiology* 10:172–94.

Griffith, H. 1990. Miniaturization and elongation in *Eumeces* (Sauria: Scincidae). *Copeia* 3:751–58.

Hafner, J.C., and M.S. Hafner. 1988. Heterochrony in rodents. *In* M.L. McKinney (ed.), *Heterochrony in Evolution: A Multidisciplinary Approach.* New York: Plenum Press.

Hallam, A. 1990. Biotic and abiotic factors in the evolution of early Mesozoic marine molluscs. *In* R.M. Ross and W.D. Allmon (eds.), *Causes of Evolution: A Paleontological Perspective.* Chicago: University of Chicago Press.

Hanken, J., and D.B. Wake. 1993. Miniaturization of body size: Organismal consequences and evolutionary significance. *Annual Review of Ecology and Systematics* 24:501–19.

Hooijer, D.A. 1949. Mammalian evolution in the Quaternary of southern and eastern Asia. *Evolution* 3:125–28.

Hulbert Jr., R.C. 1993. Late Miocene *Nannipus* (Mammalia: Perissodactyla) from Florida, with a description of the smallest hipparionine horse. *Journal of Vertebrate Paleontology* 13:350–66.

Jablonski, D. 1997. Body-size evolution in Cretaceous molluscs and the status of Cope's rule. *Nature* 385:250–52.

Korn, D. 1995. Paedomorphosis of ammonoids as a result of sealevel fluctuations in the Late Devonian Wocklumeria Stufe. *Lethaia* 28 (2):155–65.

Lister, A.M. 1989. Rapid dwarfing of red deer on Jersey in the last interglacial. *Nature* 342:539–42.

MacFadden, B.J. 1992. *Fossil Horses: Systematics, Paleobiology, and Evolution of the Family Equidae.* Cambridge and New York: Cambridge University Press.

Marshall, L.G., and R.S. Corruccini. 1978. Variability, evolutionary rates, and allometry in dwarfing lineages. *Paleobiology* 4:101–19.

Masseti, M., and P. Mazza. 1996. Is there any paleontological "treatment" for the "insular syndrome"? *Vie et Milieu* 46:355–63.

McNamara, K.J. 1982. Heterochrony and phylogenetic trends. *Paleobiology* 8:130–42.

Moore, J.C. 1959. Relationships among living squirrels of the Sciurinae. *Bulletin American Museum Natural History* 118:153–206.

Newell, N.D. 1949. Phyletic size increase—an important trend illustrated by fossil invertebrates. *Evolution* 3:103–24.

Prothero, D.R., and P.C. Sereno. 1982. Allometry and paleoecology of medial Miocene dwarf rhinoceroses from the Texas Gulf Coastal Plain. *Paleobiology* 8:16–30.

Rehkämper, G., K.L. Schuchmann, A. Schleicher, and K. Zilles. 1991. Encephalization in hummingbirds (Trochilidae). *Brain Behavior and Evolution* 37:85–91.

Rieppel, O. 1984. Miniaturization of the lizard skull: Its functional and evolutionary implications. *Symposium of the Zoological Society of London* 52:503–20.

Roberts, T.R. 1986. *Danionella translucida,* a new genus and species of cyprinid fish from Burma, one of the smallest living vertebrates. *Environmental Biology of Fishes* 16:231–41.

Roth, V.L. 1992. Inferences from allometry and fossils: Dwarfing of elephants on islands. *In* D. Futuyma and J. Antonovics (eds.), *Oxford Surveys in Evolutionary Biology.* Vol. 8. New York: Oxford University Press.

Shea, B.T. 1992. Ontogenetic scaling of skeletal proportions in the talapoin monkey. *Journal of Human Evolution* 23:283–307.

Shea, B.T., R.E. Hammer, R.L. Brinster, and M.J. Ravosa. 1990. Relative growth of the skull and postcranium in giant transgenic mice. *Genetical Research* 56:21–34.

Sondaar, P.Y. 1986. The island sweepstakes. *Natural History* 95 (9):50–57.

———. 1991. Island mammals of the past. *Science Progress* 75:249–64.

Stanley, S.M. 1973. An explanation for Cope's Rule. *Evolution* 27:1–26.

Trammer, J., and A. Kaim. 1997. Body size and diversity exemplified by three trilobite clades. *Acta Palaeontologica Polonica* 42:1–12.

Weitzman, S.H., and R.P. Vari. 1988. Miniaturization in South American freshwater fishes: An overview and discussion. *Proceedings of the Biological Society of Washington* 101:444–65.

Further Reading

Calder III, W.A. 1984. *Size, Function, and Life History.* Cambridge, Massachusetts: Harvard University Press; London: Dover, 1996.

Damuth, J., and B.J. MacFadden (eds.) 1990. *Body Size in Mammalian Paleobiology: Estimation and Biological Implications.* Cambridge and New York: Cambridge University Press.

Gould, S.J. 1977. *Ontogeny and Phylogeny.* Cambridge, Massachusetts: Harvard University Press.

Hanken, J., and D.B. Wake. 1993. Miniaturization of body size: Organismal consequences and evolutionary significance. *Annual Review of Ecology and Systematics* 24:501–19.

Sondaar, P.Y. 1986. The island sweepstakes. *Natural History* 95 (9):50–57.

PIVETEAU, JEAN

French, 1899–1991

Jean Piveteau was a researcher, a teacher, and a philosopher. He first taught paleobotany and invertebrate and vertebrate paleontology at the National School of Mines in Paris. In 1942, he became the first French professor of vertebrate paleontology at the Sorbonne (Paris). It later became University Paris 6, where he was active until his retirement in 1973.

Throughout his teaching years, Piveteau drew a varied audience of geology, biology, and philosophy students, as well as physicians, anthropologists, and prehistorians. All were attracted by the quality of his teaching. His lectures were characterized by their clarity, simplicity, and conciseness. During discussions with collaborators and students, he never tried to impose his views on others but was attentive to their remarks and respected them. Under his influence the field of vertebrate paleontology and paleoanthropology developed at French universities and research institutions, during the second half of the twentieth century. After World War II, Piveteau actively helped to end the isolation of French paleontology by reestablishing links with foreign colleagues that had been broken during the war. Convinced that both men and ideas benefited from confrontation, in 1947 he organized an international meeting entitled "Paleontology and Transformism," in which J.B.S. Haldane, G.G. Simpson, E. Stensiö, and D.M.S. Watson took part.

Piveteau was a dedicated evolutionist, continually in search of the underlying unity that lay below the apparent diversity of the living world, of which man is but a part. His aim was to make paleontology a science at the crossroads of geology and biology, integrating data from a number of fields—from genetics, embryology and histology (the study of minute biological structures) to stratigraphy (analysis of rock strata). Through the description of vertebrate fossils, his ability to synthesize diverse information led him to tackle fundamental aspects of evolution, such as organizational plans and unity of structural plan. He was influential in emphasizing the contribution of paleontology to our understanding of evolution.

Piveteau often was a precursor of new directions for investigations, either by encouraging new research, such as paleohistology and paleoneurology, or by putting forward hypotheses on the relationships and significance of some fossils, such as archaic *Homo sapiens* and neandertalians. He always emphasized the importance of methodological principles such as those of connection and correlation, which together with structures inherited from common ancestors, demonstrate the reality of evolution.

Piveteau's scientific works include several books, all of them published in French. From *Images des Mondes Disparus* (1951) to *La Main et l'Hominisation* (1991), his constant preoccupation emerges: a view of the human phenomenon as an "extension de la biogenèse [extension of the biological]" (1957), in the words of his friend Father P. Teilhard de Chardin, whose ideas exerted a strong influence on Piveteau's conception of man's place in nature.

However, Piveteau's major work, called "monumental" by American paleontologist E.H. Colbert, is undoubtedly the 10-volume "Traité de Paléontologie," published between 1952 and 1969. The *Traité* remains a standard reference work for paleontological knowledge in the mid-twentieth century. It was conceived in the same spirit as most of Piveteau's other publications: the aim was to reconstruct the history of the living world through evolution, adaptation, and environment. The text introduced two new topics—the evolution of the nervous system as reconstructed on the basis of endocranial casts, and the representations of vertebrates in Paleolithic art as an expression of the human mind. Both contributed to Piveteau's search for the living animal beyond the fossil remains. In later years, such approaches developed into the central theme of his reflections: conscious thought and hominization, a concept Piveteau helped to elucidate.

And because of the approaches he developed in his research, Piveteau naturally became interested in the history and philosophy of science, and especially in the works of the founders of paleontology, such as G. Cuvier, J.-B. Lamarck, G.-L. Buffon, and G. Saint-Hilaire.

BRIGITTE LANGE-BADRÉ

Biography

Born in Rouillac, Charentes, France, 23 September 1899. Doctor ès sciences naturelles, Paris, 1926; member, Academy of Sciences,

1956; received Albert Gaudry Prize for his body of work, 1961; Royal Academy of Belgium, 1962; Doctor Honoris Causa University of Laval, Québec, and University of Bâle (Switzerland); Officer Légion d'Honneur; Commandeur des Arts et des Lettres, Commandeur des Palmes académiques. Fieldwork in Madagascar, 1924; described *Hovasaurus boulei*, (1926); *Coelurosauravus elivensis*, 1926; *Parasemionotus labordei*, 1929; *Australosomus merlei*, 1930; *Watsonulus eugnathoides*, 1934; *Paracentrophorus madagascariensis*, 1939–40; *Protobatrachus massinoti*, 1937; mentioned the first therapsid dicynodont from the Permo-Trias of Madagascar; wrote more than 250 publications on vertebrate paleontology and history of science. Died in Paris, 7 March 1991.

Major Publications

1926. Amphibiens et reptiles permiens de Madagascar. Thèse Doctorat d'État ès sciences naturelles. *Annales de Paléontologie* 15.
1951. *Images des Mondes Disparus*. Paris: Masson.
1952–69. *Traité de Paléontologie*. Vol. 5, *Amphibiens, Reptiles, Oiseaux*; Vol. 6, *Origine des Mammifères*; Vol. 7, *Primates*. Paris: Masson.

1957. Les reptiles permotriasiques de Madagascar. *CR 3ᵉ Congrès de la PIOS*, Section C:229–32.
1963. *Des Premiers Vertébrés à l'Homme*. Paris: Albin Michel.
1991. *La Main et l'Hominisation*. Paris, Milan, and Barcelona: Masson.

Further Reading

Dechaseaux, C. 1991. Traité de Paléontologie-Précis de Paléontologie: Genèse, souvenirs. *Annales de Paléontologie* 77(4):260.
Devillers, C. 1991. Jean Piveteau et le Colloque international de 1947. *Annales de Paléontologie* 77(4):253–55.
Lange-Badré, B. 1991. Travaux et publications de Jean Piveteau. *Annales de Paléontologie* 77:271–84.
Lange-Badré, B., and L. de Bonis. 1991. Jean Piveteau enseignant. *Annales de Paléontologie* 77:246–48.
Taquet, P. 1991. Jean Piveteau. *Annales de Paléontologie* 77:227–29.
Taquet, P., and B. Badré. 1991. Hommage au Professeur Jean Piveteau. *Annales de Paléontologie* 77:227–86.
Vandermeersch, B. 1991. Jean Piveteau et la Paléontologie humaine. *Annales de Paléontologie* 77:266–70.

PLACENTALS: OVERVIEW

The extant (present-day) mammals include three clades or groups of species that have a common ancestor: the marsupials (kangaroos, opossums, and kin), the monotremes (duck-billed platypus and echidna), and the placentals. Of these, placental mammals account for the majority of living mammals, as well as many fossil groups. Placentals usually are subdivided into about 24 extinct and extant higher groups (traditionally denoted as orders). Placental diversification has produced lineages as varied as humans and their primate relatives; bats; whales; anteaters; pangolins; ardvarks; horned, antlered, and trunk-nosed herbivores (ungulates); as well as the diverse rats, mice, squirrels, beavers, and porcupines belonging to the Rodentia.

Such adaptive diversity, and the emergence of thousands of living and fossil species, apparently resulted from a radiation (diversification) beginning in the Cretaceous, between 90 and 110 million years ago (Novacek 1992a; Archibald 1996; Hedges et al. 1996). This explosive radiation (Figure 1) is one of the more intriguing chapters of vertebrate history, and the problem has attracted interest from unusually varied perspectives. As a result, placental mammals are known from a rapidly growing molecular database, as well as a wealth of morphological characters and a comparatively enriched fossil record. The interplay of molecular and morphological investigation is more apparent in the case of placental mammals that in any other vertebrates.

From the outset, it is important to address the issue of the formal names used to refer to the placental mammals. For many years the name "Eutheria" has been applied to this group. Because of some early confusion in use of this name, however, some have advocated abandoning it altogether, and using Placentalia to cover the modern orders of placental mammals and their near fossil relatives (e.g., McKenna and Bell 1997). A recent study (Novacek et al. 1997), however, clearly demonstrates that several Mongolian Cretaceous mammals are tied closely to the living placental groups, but split off as a basal branch before the latter clades diverged from a common ancestor. These authors propose retaining Eutheria as an inclusive group for both the Mongolian clade and the more modern clade. The name Placentalia then applies to the group that includes the common ancestor and all the descendants of the living placental mammal clades.

Placental Mammal History and Fossil Record

The placental mammals may have diverged in the Early Cretaceous, an interval old enough to reflect the influence of continental breakup on placental mammal diversification (Novacek 1990; Hedges et al. 1996). Nonetheless, records of placentals are sketchy before the Late Cretaceous, by which time several lineages are evident (see Archibald 1996; Novacek et al. 1997).

Clear fossil evidence for the marked diversification of placental mammals comes after the Cretaceous-Tertiary (K/T) extinction event. In North America mammalian diversity rose from 20 to 45 genera (groups of species; singular, genus) within 250,000 years of the K/T event, and by 2 million years into the Paleocene the number reached 70 genera (Archibald 1993). During the Paleocene, significant turnover is also evident in several mammalian families (Archibald 1993). Mammals during this interval were small and similar in body form. Many groups had specialized incisors (and other specialized teeth) that suggest adaptations for a variety of food items, including fruit, seeds, and small prey. Larger forms included heavy-bodied, stout-limbed pantodonts with generalized teeth suitable for a variety of vegetation sources. Special-

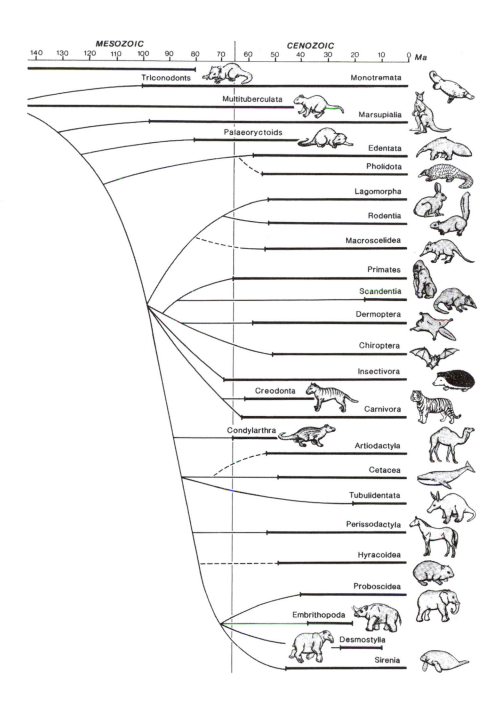

Figure 1. A phylogenetic tree showing relationships among the major mammalian clades. Key: *solid horizontal bars* indicate the age range of the clade, on the basis of dated first appearance in the fossil record; *solid lines* indicate the branching sequence, although the date of the actual splitting event can only be inferred from the relationships of the clades and their known ages; *dashed lines* indicate relatively more ambiguous relationships.

ized browsers—those who eat only leaves and twigs—were not part of these early faunas (Stucky 1990).

The Paleocene-Eocene transition was marked by the replacement of archaic placental groups by more modern forms (Rose 1984; Stucky 1990). The emergence of the rodents, a diverse group, occurred at least by the Late Paleocene. Many herbivorous groups with extant representatives—such as the even-toed artiodactyls (e.g., cattle and pigs) and the odd-toed perisso-

dactyls (horses, tapirs, rhinos, and many extinct lineages)—also appear in the fossil record during the Late Paleocene-Early Eocene interval. The radiation of these herbivorous groups involved a trend to larger body size.

Turnover and radiation in the Late Paleocene and thereafter can be related to major global climatic changes (Janis 1993). For example, the highest alpha-level (species- and genus-level) diversities in mammals were reached in the Late Paleocene and Early-to-

Middle Eocene, a period of high global temperatures and equability. In the Late Eocene, a decrease in temperature and humidity was accompanied by a shift toward more open savannah-like habitats (see review in Janis 1993). Concomitantly, mammalian herbivores showed further size increase, as well as accentuation of adaptations for browsing and grazing along with rapid locomotion in open habitats. During this interval there is evidence, at least in the North American record, for a decline in arboreal (tree-living) forms (Stucky 1990). A general correlation between the radiation of large herbivores and the loss of arboreal species is also apparent in South America and Europe (Marshall and Cifelli 1990; Legendre 1986).

Thus, the dominant groups of large herbivores, such as the perissodactyls and the artiodactyls, as well as many other more modern lineages of placentals, essentially were well-established by the Late Eocene. Even after the Late Eocene, there were several pulses of marked turnover in various placental mammal groups. These culminated in the mass extinction of many large mammals on several islands and continents during the Late Pleistocene, an event that possibly resulted from either (or both) climate change and expanding human populations and migrations.

Placental Mammal Phylogeny and Classification

The flourish of work on higher-level problems of placental mammal phylogeny is a comparatively modern development, one largely limited to the 1980s and 1990s. Prior to this period, much effort was focused on refining classifications within mammalian orders. Standard references for higher phylogeny and classification (Gregory 1910; Simpson 1945) were little embellished or modified. Cladistic studies (those that base classification upon shared characteristics) brought to light basic issues in mammalian phylogeny (McKenna 1975; Novacek 1980) that drew the attention of other scholars. An impressive number of case studies is covered in the multi-authored book *Mammal Phylogeny* (Szalay et al. 1993), and recent progress is documented in the new *Journal of Mammalian Evolution,* as well as several other journals on morphological and molecular research. A major compendium on mammalian classification by McKenna and Bell (1997) and other contributors covers both fossil and recent mammal taxa down to the generic level. This work should stand as the major source for such information in the same way Simpson's 1945 monograph served such a purpose for decades.

Morphology in both fossils and Recent taxa is the major basis for placental mammal phylogeny and classification. In general, tooth features have been used extensively in classification below the ordinal level, but their utility seems to diminish when one considers the early sequence of splitting among the higher placental mammal clades. The database for these relationships has greatly expanded to encompass skull, postcranial, neural, reproductive, developmental, and even behavioral data. The range of such data is showcased in edited volumes like Szalay and colleagues (1993).

Of course, skeletal and dental features are the only morphological evidence usually preserved in fossil mammals. Although fossils are often incomplete, when they preserve special combinations of features that cannot be extracted from extant taxa, they offer pivotal evidence (Donoghue et al. 1989; Novacek 1992b, 1992c). For example, inclusion of early fossil horses has a strong influence on identifying relationships of perissodactyls with other mammalian groups (Novacek 1992b, 1992c). (Fossils are likely to have this influence because there is a general correspondence between ancientness and primitiveness.) Although many groups do not show such correlation, such an equation is evident in the match between the first occurrence of taxa and their sequence in a cladogram (a branching diagram that illustrates relatedness). This has been shown independently in the morphology of horses and of certain other larger ungulates, where the paleontostratigraphic record is of high quality (Norell and Novacek 1992).

The molecular database for placental mammal relationships also has expanded dramatically. Early studies on protein immunological distances (Sarich 1969; Goodman and Moore 1971), DNA-DNA hybridization, and amino acid sequences in proteins (Goodman et al. 1982) have been succeeded by studies drawing on the burgeoning database of DNA sequences in selected genes (Irwin et al. 1991; Adkins and Honeycutt 1991), and even the whole mitochondrial genome (D'Erchia et al. 1996; Janke et al. 1997). Gene studies, especially those that treat a sufficient number of taxa, offer new evidence and insights for higher placental mammal phylogeny. There is, nonetheless, a rather intractable problem confronting molecular sampling. Despite some dramatic examples of gene identification in fossils (Golenberg et al. 1990; DeSalle et al. 1992), the fossil record is largely resistant to the recovery of such information. On the other hand, the character array provided by gene sequences is enormous. Molecular data potentially can recover all the heritable information, an attribute obviously not common to morphology or other phenotypic data.

Conflicting Studies on the Higher-Level Phylogeny of Placental Mammals

Despite the mass of both molecular and morphological information available, the current picture of placental mammal relationships (Figure 1) remains controversial. Notably, some recent results of gene studies clash with patterns suggested by morphology. Some of the major issues (see McKenna 1987; Novacek 1990, 1992a; Honeycutt and Adkins 1993; Simmons 1995; Allard et al. 1996; Miyamoto 1996) can be treated with respect to critical nodes (branching points) and branches shown in Figure 1.

Eutherians (including the Mongolian clade and the Placentalia) are associated with marsupials in the Theria. The monophyletic (group with a single ancestor) Theria split from a very early node that also branched in giving rise to the monotremes and certain Mesozoic and Early Cenozoic groups like the Multituberculata (Figure 1). Recent studies of the whole mitochondrial genome (Janke et al. 1997) show a surprising alternative to this long-recognized arrangement. The gene results closely associate monotremes and marsupials—but exclude eutherians. Nonetheless, despite the massive gene information, a marsupial-monotreme group does not seem compelling. The study needs to include more species, there should be less ambiguity concerning the clades used to root the tree (as acknowledged by Janke et al. 1997), and researchers need to clarify that the gene similarities between the monotremes and marsupials are not the result of parallel gene changes along two very ancient lineages (a bias known as "long branch attraction"). Moreover, the morphological case for Theria is bolstered by several extinct taxa (for example, multituberculates and symmetrodonts) that branched between Theria and monotremes (see Szalay et al. 1993). Importantly, these critical taxa are only known from fossils and are beyond the scope of molecular studies.

From Figure 1 it is apparent that poor resolution—as indicated by the branching of several clades from a single node (a polytomy)—affects a major basal area of the placental mammal radiation. Nonetheless, several higher clades are suggested. These include: (1) the grouping of South American edentates and the pangolins (pholidotes), (2) the exclusion of the edentate-pholidotes from all other modern eutherian clades (the epitheres), (3) the grouping of rodents plus lagomorphs (rabbits and pikas) and their aggregation with the African elephant shrews, (4) the linkage of dermopterans (flying lemurs) with bats, at the joining of that group with tree shrews and primates within the superorder Archonta, (5) a single node for the diversification of the medium-to-large herbivores including perissodactyls, artiodactyls, and even whales (Ungulata), and (6) a comblike sequence for the ungulates, culminating in a node joining the elephants and their fossil kin (Proboscidea) with the Sirenians (sea cows and manatees).

These higher groupings are controversial, as some of them are at odds with certain other molecular and morphological results. For example, the long-term geographic isolation of edentates (anteaters, sloths, and armadillos) in South America suggests their phylogenetic isolation from other placentals (McKenna 1975). Cladistic studies have endorsed such a view (Novacek and Wyss 1986), with the exception of one proposed alliance—a link between Old World pangolins (pholidotes) and the edentates, a proposal disputed by other authors (Rose and Emry 1993). With or without the alliance of pangolins, there is a case for the remote splitting of edentates from other placentals (epitheres), but the case is built on few lines of anatomical evidence (Novacek 1990). J.J. Gaudin and colleagues (1996) reanalyzed data provided by M.J. Novacek and A.R. Wyss (1986) and Novacek (1992c), adding several relevant morphological characters. The results of this study do not show a clear case for Epitheria. In fact, the tree that is slightly favored positions edentates as a branch near the ungulate clade. Interestingly, whole mitochondrial genome data suggest a close tie between edentates and carnivore-ungulate clade (Arnason et al. 1997). Unfortunately, this molecular study omits several higher placental taxa. Other molecular evidence on the edentate-epithere split is sketchy because of the lack of comprehensive sampling. A remote position for edentates in relation to epitheres has been supported by some studies of combined proteins (Miyamoto and Goodman 1986).

The sector of the placental tree drawing perhaps the most attention includes the primates and their putative relatives, Scandentia (tree shrews), Dermoptera (flying lemurs), and Chiroptera (bats). W.K. Gregory (1910) recognized this cluster of groups as "Archonta," based on shared adaptations for an arboreal lifestyle and, at later stages (in the case of bats and flying lemurs), gliding and powered flight. Currently, character evidence for Archonta is limited to a condition found in the male reproductive system (the pendulous penis) and tarsal (proximal foot) specializations that seem to indicate refinements for arboreal locomotion (Szalay 1977; Novacek and Wyss 1986).

In contrast, most of the newer findings on gene sequences (Adkins and Honeycutt 1991; Bailey et al. 1992; Ammerman and Hillis 1990; Stanhope et al. 1992) exclude bats from other archontans. The molecular results do, however, show some ambiguities, and combined analysis of molecular and morphological data returns bats to a monophyletic Archonta (Novacek 1994). Some fossil evidence (Beard 1993) also allegedly conflicts with the suggested tie between dermopterans and bats. These data instead suggest a close relationship between primates and dermopterans. Nonetheless, a recent review of the evidence (Simmons 1995) supports both the single origin for bats and a close chiropteran-dermopteran relationship.

Questions on archontan relationships have included the energetic debate over the origins of Chiroptera. Based on studies of the visual systems of bat brains, J.D. Pettigrew (1986; see also Pettigrew et al. 1989; Pettigrew 1991a, 1991b) raised the provocative notion that Megachiroptera (old world fruit bats) and echolocating Microchiroptera did not share a close common ancestry. If this is the case, it mandates that powered flight and numerous unique similarities in the wing evolved at least twice in mammals. This claim has been disputed on morphological grounds (Wible and Novacek 1988; Baker et al. 1991; Simmons et al. 1991; Simmons 1995). In addition, gene sequence data have offered resounding support for the single origin (monophyly) of bats (Mindell et al. 1991; Adkins and Honeycutt 1991; Bailey et al. 1992; Ammerman and Hillis 1992; Stanhope et al. 1992).

The relationships of rodents, the most diverse of the mammalian orders, has also been a subject of controversy. A strong morphological argument, summarized by W.P. Luckett and J.-L. Hartenberger (1985), links rodents with lagomorphs (the order that includes rabbits and pikas). Both protein analysis (Miyamoto and Goodman 1986) and some recent gene sequence studies (Stanhope et al. 1992) support this association, but not to the exclusion of primates. Molecular data also has supported the surprising claim that rodents are not monophyletic, as guinea pigs were shown to be a separate clade associated with a variety of other mammalian groups (Graur et al. 1991; D'Erchia et al. 1996). These studies, however, may be influenced by the inadequate samples of representative ingroups (closely related clades) and outgroups (distantly related clades) (Allard et al. 1991; Luckett and Hartenberger 1993).

Another major clade of placentals, represented by the herbivorous ungulates, apparently radiated within a collection of fossils vaguely denoted as "condylarths." For the most part, the cheek teeth of condylarths are low crowned and broad-basined, appropriate for chewing vegetation. The fossil record of "condylarths," as well as early members of the more modern ungulates, is extremely diverse and, from a phylogenetic standpoint, bewildering. This record includes the extraordinary radiation of South American ungulates, whose lineages show striking parallels to perissodactyls and other ungulates of the northern continents and the old world tropics.

At least two independent morphological studies (Novacek and Wyss 1986; Prothero et al. 1988) agree on several nodes of the ungulate sequence. Artiodactyls (pigs, hippos, giraffes, deer, camels, antelopes, and cattle) are perhaps the most remote of the extant ungulate clades. Through mesonychids and other fossil groups, artiodactyls may be related closely to whales. The connection between whales and terrestrial ungulates has been demonstrated dramatically by fossil evidence (Gingerich et al. 1990; Thewissean 1994). Recent molecular results point to an even more intimate association, suggesting that whales were actually a sub-branch of artiodactyls (Graur and Higgins 1994), possibly closely associated with hippos (Gatsey et al. 1996) or hippos and ruminant artiodactyls (Shimamura et al. 1997).

In another sector of the ungulate tree, Proboscidea, Sirenia (sea cows), and the fossil desmostylians are strongly associated in Tethytheria. Some authors argue that hyraxes represent the closest branch to tethytheres in the clade Paenungulata (Novacek and Wyss 1986; Novacek et al. 1988; Shoshani 1993), but others (Prothero et al. 1988) use morphological data to suggest that hyraxes are instead the closest lineage to perissodactyls. However, consideration of early fossil perissodactyls weakens the preference for a perissodactyl-hyrax grouping (Novacek 1992c). In this case, the molecular data clearly support the argument for Paenungulata, as demonstrated by studies of an eye lens protein alpha crystallin (McKenna 1992; De Jong et al. 1993), and ribosomal 12SrDNA genes (Springer and Kirsch 1993). A recent molecular study (Springer et al. 1997) draws a surprising alliance between paenungulates, aardvarks, and the endemic African insectivores (the golden moles and elephant shrews), but this result is based on very limited taxonomic sampling.

In sum, the contradictory results among diverse analyses underscore the difficulty in resolving the evolutionary relationships of the higher placental groups. This might be expected, given the known fossil history of placentals. The fossil record does suggest that the earliest members of various major clades appeared relatively closely in time. These early members often differ in very subtle details, even though their later relatives show marked divergence. These ancient and subtle branching patterns must be examined from the remote perspective of the present. However, scholars anticipate that the continuing expansion of the comparative database on morphology and molecules, as well as the marked improvement in the fossil evidence, will bring some clarity to the remaining questions concerning placental phylogeny and evolution.

MICHAEL J. NOVACEK

See also Marsupials; Placentals: Endemic South American Ungulates; Placentals: Minor Placental Orders of Large Body Size; Placentals: Minor Placental Orders of Small Body Size

Works Cited

Adkins, R.M., and R.L. Honeycutt. 1991. Molecular phylogeny of the superorder Archonta. *Proceedings of the National Academy of Sciences* 88:10317–21.

Allard, M.W., M.M. Miyamoto, and R.L. Honeycutt. 1991. Tests for rodent polyphyly. *Nature* 353:610–11.

Allard, M.W., B.E. McNiff, and M.M. Miyamoto. 1996. Support for interordinal eutherian relationships with an emphasis on primates and their archontan relatives. *Molecular Phylogenetics* 5 (1):78–88.

Ammerman, L.K., and D.M. Hillis. 1990. Relationships within archontan mammals based on 12S r RNA gene sequence. *American Zoology* 30:50A.

———. 1992. A molecular test of bat relationships: Monophyly or diphyly? *Systematic Biology* 41:222–32.

Archibald, J.D. 1993. The importance of phylogenetic analysis for the assessment of species turnover: A case history of Paleocene mammals in North America. *Paleobiology* 19:1–27.

———. 1996. Fossil evidence for a Late Cretaceous origin of "hoofed" mammals. *Science* 272:1150–53.

Arnason, U., A. Gullberg, and A. Janke. 1997. Phylogenetic analyses of mitochondrial DNA suggest a sister group relationship between Xenarthra (Edentata) and Ferungulates. *Molecular Biology and Evolution* 14 (7):762–68.

Bailey, W.J., J.L. Slightom, and M. Goodman. 1992. Rejection of the "flying primate" hypothesis by phylogenetic evidence from the epsilon-globin gene. *Science* 256:86–89.

Baker, R.J., M.J. Novacek, and N.B. Simmons. 1991. On the monophyly of bats. *Systematic Zoology* 40:216–31.

Beard, K.C. 1993. Phylogenetic systematics of Primatomorpha, with special reference to Dermoptera. In F.S. Szalay, M.J. Novacek, and M.C. McKenna (eds.), *Mammal Phylogeny*. Vol. 2, *Placentals*. New York and London: Springer-Verlag.

De Jong, W.W. 1982. Eye lens proteins and vertebrate phylogeny. In M. Goodman (ed.), *Macromolecular Sequences in Systematic and Evolutionary Biology*. New York: Plenum.

De Jong, W.W., A.M. Leunissen, and G.J. Wistow. 1993. Eye lens crystallins and the phylogeny of the placental mammal orders: Evidence for a macroscelid—paenungulate clade? In F.S. Szalay, M.J. Novacek, and M.C. McKenna (eds.), *Mammal Phylogeny*. Vol. 2, *Placentals*. New York and London: Springer-Verlag.

D'Erechia, A.M., C. Gissi, G. Pesole, C. Saccone, and U. Arnason. 1996. The guinea-pig is not a rodent. *Nature* 381:597–600.

DeSalle, R., J. Gatesy, W. Wheeler, and D. Grimaldi. 1992. DNA sequences from a fossil termite in Oligo-Miocene amber and their phylogenetic implications. *Science* 257:1933–36.

Donoghue, M., J. Doyle, J. Gauthier, A. Kluge, and T. Rowe. 1989. The importance of fossils in phylogeny reconstruction. *Annual Review of Ecology and Systematics* 20:431–60.

Gatsey, J., C. Hayashi, M.A. Cronin, and P. Arctander. 1996. Evidence from milk casein genes that cetaceans are the close relatives of hippopotamid artiodactyls. *Molecular Biology and Evolution* 13:954–63.

Gaudin, T.J., J.R. Wible, J.A. Hopson, and W.D. Turnbull. 1996. Reexamination of the morphological evidence for the cohort Epitheria (Mammalia, Eutheria). *Journal of Mammalian Evolution* 3 (1):31–79.

Gingerich, P.D., B.H. Smith, and E.L. Simons. 1990. Hind limbs of Eocene *Basilosaurus*: Evidence of feet in whales. *Science* 249:154–57.

Golenberg, E.M., D.E. Giannasi, M.T. Clegg, C.J. Smiley, M. Durbin, D. Henderson, and G. Zurawski. 1990. Chloroplast DNA sequence from a Miocene Magnolia species. *Nature* 344:656–58.

Goodman, M., and G.W. Moore. 1971. Immunodiffusion in the systematics of primates. Part 1, The Catarrhini. *Systematic Zoology* 20:19–62.

Goodman, M., A.E. Romero-Herrera, H. Dene, J. Czelusniak, and R.E. Tashian. 1982. Amino acid sequence evidence on the phylogeny of primates and other eutherians. *In* M. Goodman (ed.), *Macromolecular Sequences in Systematic and Evolutionary Biology*. New York: Plenum.

Graur, D., W.A. Hide, and W.-H. Li. 1991. Is the guinea-pig a rodent? *Nature* 351:649–52.

Graur, D., and D.G. Higgins. 1994. Molecular evidence for the inclusion of cetaceans within the order Artiodactyla. *Molecular Biology and Evolution* 11:357–64.

Gregory, W.K. 1910. *The Orders of Mammals*. Bulletin of the American Museum of Natural History, 27. New York: American Museum of Natural History.

Hedges, S.B., P.H. Parker, C.G. Sibley, and S. Kumar. 1996. Continental breakup and the ordinal diversification of birds and mammals. *Nature* 381:226–29.

Honeycutt, R.L., and R.M. Adkins. 1993. Higher level systematics of eutherian mammals: An assessment of molecular characters and phylogenetic hypotheses. *Annual Review of Ecology and Systematics* 24:279–305.

Irwin, D.M., T.D. Kocher, and A.C. Wilson. 1991. Evolution of the cytochrome b gene of mammals. *Journal of Molecular Evolution* 32:128–44.

Janis, C.M. 1993. Tertiary mammal evolution in the context of changing climates, vegetation, and tectonic events. *Annual Review of Ecology and Systematics* 24:467–500.

Janke, A., X. Xu, and U. Arnason. 1997. The complete mitochondrial genome of the wallaroo *(Macropus robustus)* and the phylogenetic relationships among Monotremata, Marsupialia, and Eutheria. *Proceedings of the National Academy of Sciences USA* 94:1276–81.

Legendre, S. 1986. Analysis of mammalian communities from the Late Eocene and Oligocene of southern France. *Palaeovertebrata* 16:191–212.

Luckett, W.P., and J.-L. Hartenberger. 1985. Evolutionary relationships among rodents: Comments and conclusions. *In* W.P. Luckett and J.-L. Hartenberger (eds.), *Evolutionary Relationships among Rodents: A Multidisciplinary Analysis*. New York: Plenum.

———. 1993. Monophyly or polyphyly of the order Rodentia: A possible conflict between morphological and molecular interpretations. *Journal of Mammalian Evolution* 1:127–47.

Marshall, L.G., and R.L. Cifelli. 1990. Analysis of changing diversity patterns in Cenozoic land mammal age faunas, South America. *Palaeovertebrata* 19:169–210.

McKenna, M.C. 1975. Toward a phylogenetic classification of the Mammalia. *In* W.P. Luckett and F.S. Szalay (eds.), *Phylogeny of the Primates*. New York: Plenum; London, 1976.

———. 1987. Molecular and morphological analysis of high-level mammalian interrelationships. *In* C. Patterson (ed.), *Molecules and Morphology in Evolution: Conflict or Compromise?* Cambridge and New York: Cambridge University Press.

———. 1992. The alpha crystallin A chain of the eye lens and mammalian phylogeny. *Annales Zoologici Fennici* 28:349–60.

McKenna, M.C., and S.K. Bell. 1997. *Classification of Mammals above the Species Level*. New York: Columbia University Press.

Mindell, D.P., C.W. Dick, and R.J. Baker. 1991. Phylogenetic relationships among megabats, microbats, and primates. *Proceedings of the National Academy of Sciences* 88:10322–26.

Miyamoto, M.M. 1996. A congruence study of molecular and morphological data for eutherian mammals. *Molecular Phylogenetics and Evolution* 6 (3):373–90.

Miyamoto, M.M., and M. Goodman. 1986. Biomolecular systematics of eutherian mammals: Phylogenetic patterns and classification. *Systematic Zoology* 35:230–40.

Norell, M.A., and M.J. Novacek. 1992. The fossil record and evolution: Comparing cladistic and paleontologic evidence for vertebrate history. *Science* 255:1690–93.

Novacek, M.J. 1980. Cranioskeletal features in tupaiids and selected Eutheria as phylogenetic evidence. *In* W.P. Luckett (ed.), *Comparative Biology and Evolutionary Relationships of Tree Shrews*. New York: Plenum.

———. 1990. Morphology, paleontology, and the higher clades of mammals. *In* H.H. Genoways (ed.), *Current Mammalogy*. Vol. 2. New York: Plenum.

———. 1992a. Mammalian phylogeny: Shaking the tree. *Nature* 356:121–25.

———. 1992b. Fossils as critical data for phylogeny. *In* M.J. Novacek and Q.D. Wheeler (eds.), *Extinction and Phylogeny*. New York: Columbia University Press.

———. 1992c. Fossils, topologies, missing data, and the higher level phylogeny of eutherian mammals. *Systematic Biology* 41:58–73.

———. 1994. Morphological and molecular inroads to phylogeny. *In* L. Grande and O. Rieppel (eds.), *Interpreting the Hierarchy of Nature: From Systematic Patterns to Evolutionary Process Theories*. San Diego, California: Academic Press.

Novacek, M.J., G. Rougier, J.R. Wible, D. Dashzeveg, M.C. McKenna, and I. Horovitz. 1997. Epipubic bones in eutherian mammals from the Late Cretaceous of Mongolia. *Nature* 389:483–85.

Novacek, M.J., and A.R. Wyss. 1986. Higher-level relationships of the Recent eutherian orders: Morphological evidence. *Cladistics* 2:257–87.

Novacek, M.J., A.R. Wyss, and M.C. McKenna. 1988. The major groups of eutherian mammals. *In* M.J. Benton (ed.), *The Phylogeny and Classification of the Tetrapods*. Vol. 2, *Mammals*. Systematics Association, Special Volume 35/B. Oxford: Clarendon; New York: Oxford University Press.

Pettigrew, J.D. 1986. Flying primates? Megabats have the advanced pathway from eye to midbrain. *Science* 231:1304–6.

———. 1991a. Wings or brain? Convergent evolution in the origins of bats. *Systematic Zoology* 40:199–216.

———. 1991b. A fruitful, wrong hypothesis? Response to Baker, Novacek, and Simmons. *Systematic Zoology* 40:231–39.

Pettigrew, J.D., B.G.M. Jamieson, S.K. Robson, L.S. Hall, K.I. McAnally, and H.M. Cooper. 1989. Phylogenetic relations between microbats, megabats and primates (Mammalia, Chiroptera, and Primates). *Philosophical Transactions of the Royal Society; B, Biological Sciences* 325:489–59.

Prothero, D.R., E.M. Manning, and M. Fischer. 1988. The phylogeny of ungulates. *In* M.J. Benton (ed.), *The Phylogeny and Classification of the Tetrapods*. Vol. 2, *Mammals*. Systematics Association, Special Volume 35/B. Oxford: Clarendon; New York: Oxford University Press.

Rose, K.D. 1984. Evolution and radiation of mammals in the Eocene, and the diversification of modern orders. *In* P.D. Gingerich and C.E. Badgley (eds.), *Mammals, Notes for a Short Course*. University of Tennessee Department of Geology, Studies in Geology, vol. 8. Knoxville: University of Tennessee Press.

Rose, K.D., and R.J. Emry. 1993. Relationships of Xenarthra, Pholidota, and Fossil "Edentates": The morphological evidence. *In* F.S. Szalay, M.J. Novacek, and M.C. McKenna (eds.), *Mammal Phylogeny*. Vol. 2, *Placentals*. New York and London: Springer-Verlag.

Sarich, W.M. 1969. Pinniped origins and the rate of evolution of carnivore albumins. *Systematic Zoology* 18:286–95.

Shimamura, M., H. Yasue, K. Ohshima, H. Abe, H. Kato, T. Kishiro, M. Goto, I. Munechika, and N. Okada. 1997. Molecular evidence from retroposons that whales form a clade with even-toed ungulates. *Nature* 388:666–70.

Shoshani, J. 1993. Hyracoidea-Tethytheria affinity based on myological data. *In* F.S. Szalay, M.J. Novacek, and M.C. McKenna (eds.), *Mammal Phylogeny*. Vol. 2, *Placentals*. New York and London: Springer-Verlag.

Simmons, N.B. 1995. Bat relationships and the origin of flight. *Symposium of the Zoological Society of London* 67:27–43.

Simmons, N.B., M.J. Novacek, and R.J. Baker. 1991. Approaches, methods, and the future of the chiropteran monophyly controversy: A reply to J.D. Pettigrew. *Systematic Zoology* 40:239–43.

Simpson, G.G. 1945. *The Principles of Classification and a Classification of Mammals*. Bulletin of the American Museum of Natural History, 85. New York: American Museum of Natural History.

Springer, M.S., G.C. Cleven, O. Madsen, W.W. De Jong, V.G. Waddell, H.M. Amrine, and M.J. Stanhope. 1997. Endemic African mammals shake the phylogenetic tree. *Nature* 388:61–64.

Springer, M.A., and J.A.W. Kirsch. 1993. A molecular perspective on the phylogeny of placental mammals based on mitochondrial 12S rDNA sequences, with special reference to the problem of Paenungulata. *Journal of Mammalian Evolution* 1:149–66.

Stanhope, M.J., J. Czelusniak, J.-S. Si, J. Nickerson, and M. Goodman. 1992. A molecular perspective on mammalian evolution from the gene encoding interphotoreceptor retinoid binding protein, with convincing evidence of bat monophyly. *Molecular Phylogenetics and Evolution* 1 (2):148–60.

Stucky, R.K. 1990. Evolution of land mammal diversity in North America during the Cenozoic. *In* H.H. Genoways (ed.), *Current Mammalogy*. Vol. 2. New York: Plenum Press.

Szalay, F.S. 1977. Phylogenetic relationships and a classification of the eutherian Mammalia. *In* M.K. Hecht, P.C. Goody, and B.M. Hecht (eds.), *Major Patterns in Vertebrate Evolution*. New York: Plenum.

Szalay, F.S., M.J. Novacek, and M.C. McKenna (eds.). 1993. *Mammal Phylogeny*. Vol. 1, *Mesozoic Differentiation, Multituberculates, Monotremes, Early Therians, and Marsupials*. Vol. 2, *Placentals*. New York and London: Springer-Verlag.

Thewissen, J.G.M. 1994. Phylogenetic aspects of cetacean origins: A morphological perspective. *Journal of Mammalian Evolution* 2:157–84.

Wible, J.R., and M.J. Novacek. 1988. Cranial evidence for the monophyletic origin of bats. *American Museum Novitates* 2911:1–9.

Further Reading

Gregory, W.K. 1910. *The Orders of Mammals*. Bulletin of the American Museum of Natural History, 27. New York: American Museum of Natural History.

Honeycutt, R.L., and R.M. Adkins. 1993. Higher level systematics of eutherian mammals: An assessment of molecular characters and phylogenetic hypotheses. *Annual Review of Ecology and Systematics* 24:279–85.

Janis, C.M. 1993. Tertiary mammal evolution in the context of changing climates, vegetation, and tectonic events. *Annual Review of Ecology and Systematics* 24:467–500.

McKenna, M.C., and S.K. Bell. 1997. *Classification of Mammals above the Species Level*. New York: Columbia University Press.

Miyamoto, M.M. 1996. A congruence study of molecular and morphological data for eutherian mammals. *Molecular Phylogenetics and Evolution* 6 (3):373–90.

Norell, M.A., and M.J. Novacek. 1992. The fossil record and evolution: Comparing cladistic and paleontologic evidence for vertebrate history. *Science* 255:1690–93.

Novacek, M.J. 1992. Mammalian phylogeny: Shaking the tree. *Nature* 356:121–25.

Simpson, G.G. 1945. *The Principles of Classification and a Classification of Mammals*. Bulletin of the American Museum of Natural History, 85. New York: American Museum of Natural History.

Stucky, R.K. 1990. Evolution of land mammal diversity in North America during the Cenozoic. *In* H.H. Genoways (ed.), *Current Mammalogy*. Vol. 2. New York: Plenum Press.

Szalay, F.S., M.J. Novacek, and M.C. McKenna (eds.). 1993. *Mammal Phylogeny*. Vol. 1, *Mesozoic Differentiation, Multituberculates, Monotremes, Early Therians, and Marsupials*. Vol. 2, *Placentals*. New York and London: Springer-Verlag.

PLACENTALS: ENDEMIC SOUTH AMERICAN UNGULATES

For much of the Cenozoic, South America was an island. Originally, it was populated in the Late Cretaceous or Early Paleocene by only a few orders of mammals: marsupials, edentates, and several ungulate (hoofed mammals) groups (Simpson 1980; Marshall and de Muizon 1988). It should be noted that the phylogenetic relationships of these groups are unclear (Cifelli 1985, 1993). The term "ungulate" as used here does not imply that the ungulate groups endemic to South America and modern Ungulata share a most recent common ancestor or even form a single clade (unified group) themselves. In the absence of other, more familiar, orders of mammals—such as artiodactyls, perissodactyls, proboscideans, and rodents—the groups that did live there diversified into an amazing array of small and large-bodied forms (Cifelli 1985; Marshall and

Cifelli 1989). Even after the arrival of caviomorph rodents (guinea pigs and relatives) and platyrrhine primates (those with a wide flat space between the nostrils), which arrived by crossing the ocean on rafts of debris sometime in the Late Eocene or Early Oligocene (MacFadden et al. 1985; Wyss et al. 1993, 1994), these "ancient inhabitants" (Patterson and Pascual 1968)—or "Stratum 1" taxa (Simpson 1940, 1980)—were the dominant members of South American mammal communities up until the Great American Interchange of the Late Pliocene (Marshall and Cifelli 1989; Webb 1991). While some of these "ancient inhabitants" converged (evolved similarly) remarkably in form with mammals of other continents (e.g., the horselike litoptern, *Thoatherium*), others were unique in their morphology (e.g., the unusual astrapotheres). And

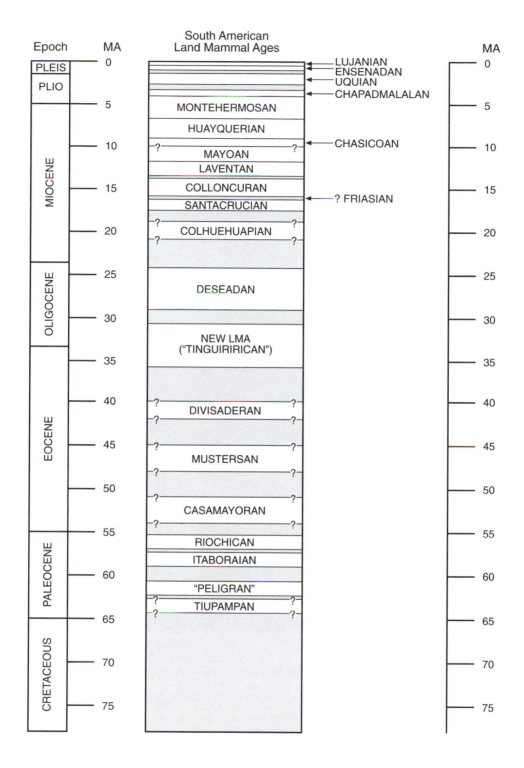

Figure 1. Geochronology of South American Land Mammal Ages (SALMAs) Symbols: *?*, boundaries that are poorly controlled by radio-isotopic dates. Illustration by Catherine P. Sexton, after Flynn and Swisher (1995).

although both marsupials and edentates (e.g., sloths, armadillos) survive to this day, all endemic South American ungulates had become extinct by the end of the Pleistocene.

The extinct ungulates can be divided into at least five orders (Cifelli 1993): Astrapotheria (including trigonostylopids), Pyrotheria, Xenungulata, Litopterna, and Notoungulata. The notoungulates alone encompass more than 140 genera of exclusively South American fossil mammals. Before entering into a discussion of these South American ungulates, however, a brief digression into the concept of "Land Mammal Ages" is necessary.

South American Land Mammal Ages (SALMAs)

Rock strata (and the fossils contained within them) can be dated in one of two ways: either absolutely (i.e., a given layer of rock is 25 million years old), or relatively (i.e., a given layer was deposited after layer X but before layer Y). Since it is not always possible to date rocks absolutely using radiometric dating techniques, the age of a fossil assemblage is described more often in a relative sense. This relative age can be based either on the rocks containing the fossils or on the taxonomic affinities (evolutionary ties between groups; singular, taxon) of the fossils themselves. In the former case, the fossil assemblage is assigned to a chronologic unit based upon geology (geochronology), such as the Late Oligocene Epoch. In the latter case, the fossil assemblage is assigned to a chronological unit based upon biology (biochronology), such as the Deseadan Land Mammal Age.

As one can imagine, correlating geochronologic units with biochronologic units can be extremely difficult, as can be placing either one of these within the context of an absolute time scale. For this reason, mammalian paleontologists often operate within a framework of biochronologic units called Land Mammal Ages. These units usually represent an absolute time that ranges from less than a million years to more than five million years in duration. Each Land Mammal Age is defined by a unique combination of fossil mammals (or a few "index taxa") that lived in a specific area over a certain span of time. Since land mammals have a limited geographic range, it is necessary to define a different sequence of Land Mammal Ages for each continent (i.e., North America and Europe both have their own distinct sequences).

In South America, the Cenozoic fossil record has been divided into approximately 20 South American Land Mammal Ages (Figure 1), or SALMAs (Flynn and Swisher 1995). Traditionally most of these Land Mammal Ages have been based on fossil localities in an area of southern South America known as Patagonia (Simpson 1948; Patterson and Pascual 1968; Madden 1997). However, the large latitudinal range of South America (65 degrees of latitude, about twice that spanned by North America) and the large proportion of land located in the equatorial tropics (about 70 percent of the continent's area) have made it difficult to integrate fossil localities from northern South America into the traditional SALMA sequence. This had been compounded by a lack of radiometric or paleomagnetic dates for most faunas and the presence of significant temporal gaps in the fossil record. Recent advances in radiometric dating techniques (namely, argon isotope dating via lasers) and the discovery of important new Cenozoic fossil localities (especially the "Tinguiririca Fauna" of Chile) have improved our understanding of the temporal relationships among SALMAs greatly (Novacek et al. 1989; MacFadden et al. 1985; Wyss et al. 1990, 1992, 1994; Flynn and Swisher 1995). Figure 1 presents the most recent synthesis of these findings and is a useful reference when discussing South American fossil taxa.

Astrapotheria (Including Trigonostylopidae)

The name *Astrapotherium*, meaning "lightning beast," was coined in reference to the North American brontotheres ("thunder beasts"), another group of extinct rhinolike mammals (Cifelli 1985). Astrapotheres are found in deposits Paleocene (Riochican) to Mid-

dle Miocene (Friasian) in age. The later forms, such as *Astrapotherium*, were quite large, graviportal animals (Cifelli 1983b) that superficially resembled modern-day tapirs or rhinos (Figure 2). (Graviportal animals are large and heavy; their legs are constructed like pillars, e.g., elephants.) Early, less derived (specialized) forms were, until recently, placed in their own order, the Trigonostylopoidea (Simpson 1933, 1967). More recent studies (Carbajal et al. 1977; Cifelli 1983b; Soria and Powell 1982; Soria 1982) have found both cranial (skull skeleton) and postcranial (body below the head) characters that suggest these groups share a common ancestor that is not shared with other major South American groups. Cifelli's (1993) phylogenetic (evolutionary history) analysis of astrapotheres supports a close relationship between these two groups, and he recognizes a single order, Astrapotheria, with two families: a monophyletic (groups with a single common ancestor) Astrapotheriidae and a paraphyletic (some, but not all, descendants of a single ancestor included in the group) Trigonostylopidae.

The order of Astrapotheria attained its maximum diversity during the Early Miocene Colhuehuapian and Santacrucian SALMAs (Marshall and Cifelli 1989; Johnson and Madden 1997) and perhaps is characterized best by the Santacrucian genus *Astrapotherium* (Figure 3) (see also Scott 1928, 1937). The skull of *Astrapotherium*, which is about 60 centimeters in length, is high and domed owing to the presence of air sinuses in an inflated nasal region. The nasal bones are retracted toward the rear of the skull, nearly to the orbits (eye sockets), indicating that a fleshy, muscular proboscis (trunk) was likely present in life. Upper incisors are lacking, but the lower incisors are procumbent (pointed forward) and are located on a lower jaw that itself protrudes past the anterior-most (frontmost) extent of the upper jaw (maxilla). It is possible that the maxilla supported a tough pad on the upper lip against which the lower incisors pressed when cropping vegetation (Savage and Long 1986). Such a pad is present in living artiodactyls.

Both upper and lower canines are enlarged as tusks; the upper canines are larger than the lower and occlude (meet) just behind them, an arrangement that provides a self-sharpening mechanism. It has been suggested that the lower tusks were used to root in the soil (Patterson and Pascual 1968; Simpson 1980). B. Patterson and R. Pascual (1968) observe that grooves often are worn into the front edges of these tusks by plants being yanked out of the ground. Recent studies of the upper tusk enamel of *Parastrapotherium* indicate that these teeth encountered significant lateral (side to side) forces (Rensberger and Pfretzchner 1992), although scholars do not know whether these forces were caused by foraging or some other activity (i.e., aggressive encounters).

The premolars are mostly reduced or lost, creating a diastema (gap) between the cheek teeth and the incisors (or the tip of the maxilla in the case of the upper teeth). The large molars are designed for processing high volumes of vegetation and show some convergent (independently evolved) similarities with the teeth of notoungulates (Cifelli 1985).

Pyrotheria and Xenungulata

The pyrotheres were never as diverse nor did they cover as great a span of time as the astrapotheres; they are known only from the

Figure 2. Reconstruction of *Astrapotherium* (Astrapotheria). Santacrucian. From Savage and Long (1986), courtesy of The Natural History Museum, London.

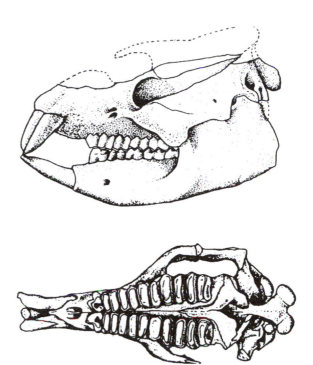

Figure 4. Skull of *Pyrotherium* in lateral and palatal view (Pyrotheria). Deseadan. After Loomis (1914).

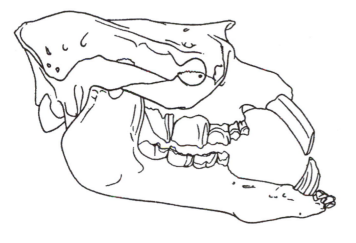

Figure 3. Skull of *Astrapotherium magnum* (Astrapotheria). Santacrucian. From Simpson (1933).

Casamayoran through Deseadan, with a maximum diversity of two contemporaneous genera (Marshall and Cifelli 1989). Currently, only one of these genera, *Pyrotherium,* is well known (Cifelli 1993). Fragmentary remains of *Pyrotherium* are characteristic of Deseadan faunas, however, and early South American paleontologists called strata of that age the "*Pyrotherium* Beds" (Simpson 1948, 1980). The name *Pyrotherium* ("fire beast"), in fact, is in reference to the Deseadan volcanic ash beds in which it is found (Savage and Long 1986).

The first complete skull of *Pyrotherium* was discovered by F.B. Loomis of Amherst College during his 1911–12 expedition (Loomis 1914). Some early scholars (e.g., Ameghino, Loomis) allied pyrotheres with the Proboscidea based on their dentition (tooth structure and arrangement) including incisor tusks and bilophodont cheek teeth (teeth with two transverse ridges). How-

ever, later work by Patterson (1977) confirmed the conclusions of A. Gaudry (1909), that these characteristics of pyrotheres are merely convergent.

About the size of a small elephant, *Pyrotherium* had retracted nasal bones and, like Astrapotherium, probably possessed a proboscis (Figure 4). There are two pairs of upper incisor tusks and a single pair of lower tusks. The top tusks are angled down roughly 45 degrees from the level of the toothrow, while the lower tusks are angled up at about the same degree from the lower toothrow, allowing the tusks to meet at their tips. A diastema separates the incisors from the battery of bilophodont cheek teeth.

Considerable uncertainty surrounds the relationship between the pyrotheres and another endemic South American group, the xenungulates ("strange ungulates"). An even less diverse group than the pyrotheres, the Xenungulata are found only in Paleocene (Riochican) faunas and include only two genera. While one of these genera, *Carodnia,* is reasonably well known, the other, *Etayoa,* is represented only by a single mandibular fragment (Villarroel 1987). Although the presence of bilophodont cheek teeth in *Carodnia* suggests a relationship between pyrotheres and xenungulates, the teeth of the more primitive (more ancient) *Etayoa* instead suggest the groups may be related more closely to the astrapotheres (Cifelli 1993).

Litopterna (and South American "Condylarths")

Next to the notoungulates, the litopterns were the most successful (in terms of diversity and longevity) of the endemic South

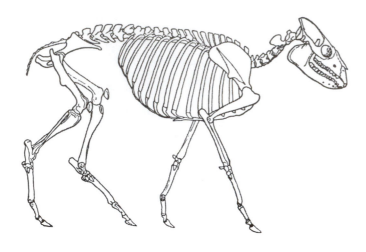

Figure 5. Skeleton of *Thoatherium* (Litopterna: Proterotheriidae). Santacrucian. From Scott (1910).

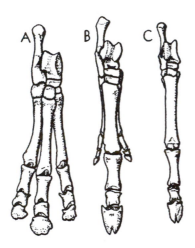

Figure 6. Hind feet of litopterns. *A*, Macrauchenia; *G*, Diadiaphorus; *C*, Thoatherium. After Scott (1910).

American ungulates. The earliest litopterns were evident in the South American Paleocene (Itaboraian), and the latest forms persisted until the close of the Pleistocene (Marshall and Cifelli 1989).

Often discussed in conjunction with litopterns are two families of small South American "condylarths": the Didolodontidae and the Sparnotheriodontidae (Cifelli 1983a, 1993). (The order Condylartha is a conglomeration of generally primitive ungulate or ungulate-like mammals; the taxon has little phylogenetic validity because its members are probably unrelated. Instead, they generally represent primitive members of other mammalian orders. For a discussion see Prothero et al. 1988; Prothero 1994.) According to R.L. Cifelli's (1993) analysis of litoptern relationships, these two groups of primitive ungulates together constitute a sister group to the order Litopterna. As would be expected of early

ungulates, the teeth of these animals are fairly generalized and bunodont (i.e., possessing low, blunt cusps). Thus, phylogenetic studies of these taxa have relied on characters of the ankle and postcrania, where available, to help sort out relationships (Cifelli 1983a, 1983b, 1993). They both are encountered most frequently in Riochican and Casamayoran faunas, though didolodontids are encountered last during the Friasian (Cifelli 1985).

The litopterns themselves are grouped into four families: Protolipternidae, Adianthidae, Prototheriidae, and Macraucheniidae (Cifelli 1983a). The earliest of these groups, the small Protolipternidae, demonstrate essentially unspecialized teeth but possess specializations in body structure that suggest they were saltators (jumpers or leapers) (Cifelli 1983b, 1985). They are found only in Riochican and Casamayoran faunas.

The remaining three families constitute a monophyletic group united by both dental and postcranial (ankle) characters (Cifelli 1993). The least well known of these groups is the Adianthidae, the pygmy litopterns, a family reviewed by Cifelli and M.F. Soria (1983). Adianthids are found in localities of Casamayoran through Friasian age, but they are uncommon, represented by isolated dental and jaw fragments. Cifelli (1991) recently described the most complete specimen of this family, *Adianthus godoyi* from the Friasian of Chile; the morphology of the muzzle and skull suggests pygmy litopterns were low-level selective feeders.

The family Prototheriidae are generally small- to medium-sized litopterns (Figure 5) that demonstrate horselike postcranial specializations. In the foot, the digits on either side of the middle digit often are reduced, creating a "mesaxonic" foot. In the most well publicized of the prototheriids, *Thoatherium* (from the Santacrucian), the lateral digits are reduced even more than the reduction in the modern horse (Figure 6). Representatives of this family are found in Riochican through Chapadmalalan faunas, reaching their peak diversity in the Santacrucian (Scott 1910). Unlike horses in the Northern Hemisphere and notoungulates in the Southern Hemisphere, proterotheriids never evolved hypsodont (high-crowned) cheek teeth (Patterson and Pascual 1968). Since hypsodonty generally is regarded as a necessary adaptation for feeding on tough grasses (Janis 1995; MacFadden and Shockey 1997), proterotheriids likely were feeding on other food, such as less abrasive leaves and buds.

Macraucheniids first appear in the Mustersan, but do not attain maximum diversity until the end of the Miocene (Huayquerian and later faunas). They are often characterized as camel-like in appearance due to the presence of an extended neck that is unique among endemic South American ungulates. Macraucheniids are the largest of the Litopterna and probably approached the size of the larger true camels in life (Patterson and Pascual 1968). A distinguishing feature of macraucheniids among litopterns is the presence of a proboscis. As in astrapotheres and pyrotheres this is indicated by the progressive reduction of the nasal bones in forms such as the Pleistocene *Macrauchenia* (Figure 7). In their study of Pleistocene herbivores from Tarija, Bolivia, MacFadden and B.J. Shockey (1997) suggest that *Macrauchenia patachonica* was a mixed feeder, eating both grasses and less abrasive leaves and buds.

literally the "southern ungulates." Though it is not possible to estimate their specific diversity (the number of valid species, inadvertently exaggerated by early scholars, still is being sorted out), a reasonable estimate of their generic diversity includes nearly 140 genera in 13 families (Figure 8). Members of this group lived in South America throughout the Cenozoic, but only a single genus, *Toxodon,* ever emigrated from South America. It spread into tropical Central America during the Pleistocene, after the Panamanian land bridge formed (Webb 1991). (Prior to this time, the two continents were separated by ocean.)

Notoungulates are united by characters of their teeth, including a structure on the upper molar called a "crochet" (Figure 9) (Patterson 1934c; Simpson 1948, 1967, 1980) and by characters of the ear region (Patterson 1932, 1934a, 1936). Cifelli's analysis of notoungulate relationships (1993) suggests that notoungulates can be divided into two main groups, toxodonts and typotheres (plus two older notoungulate families) (Figure 10). Toxodontia includes mostly large, rhino- or horselike animals, while Typotheria includes animals that are mostly rodent- or rabbitlike in overall form. In both of these groups, later forms evolved simplified, ever-growing "hypselodont" cheek teeth (Figure 11), the only ungulates besides *Elasmotherium* (Rhinocerotidae) to do so (Janis and Fortelius 1988).

Traditionally, a Northern Hemisphere group of Paleogene mammals known as Arctostylopids were included in the Notoungulata (Matthew 1915), but it now appears that the two groups evolved similar tooth structures independently (Cifelli 1983a; Cifelli et al. 1989). Thus with the exception of *Toxodon,* the notoungulate radiation was an exclusively South American phenomenon.

Primitive Groups (Henricosborniidae, Notostylopidae)
The primitive notoungulate families Henricosborniidae and Notostylopidae generally are restricted to Early Tertiary faunas of South America (perhaps Tiupampan through Mustersan SALMAs). *Acamana,* an enigmatic fragmentary fossil from the Divisadero Largo Formation (Simpson et al. 1952), and a similar form from the Deseadan may represent henricosborniids; if so, this find extends their range into the Oligocene (Cifelli 1985). Additionally, the recently discovered Tinguiririca fauna of Chile (Late Eocene/Early Oligocene) contains a notostylopid, which also considerably extends that family's range (Wyss et al. 1990, 1994).

Henricosborniids are small animals with generalized tooth patterns; their postcranial characteristics are unknown (Cifelli 1993). Notostylopids, however, are better known, and skulls have been found, in addition to postcranial material. *Notostylops* itself is especially common in Casamayoran strata—early paleontologists called these layers "*Notostylops* beds." As occurred in some later typotheres, notostylopids evolved somewhat rodentlike teeth. The first pair of incisors are enlarged, the second and third are very reduced, and there is a diastema (space) between the third incisor and the cheek teeth (Figure 12). The lower incisors are not recurved (curved back toward the throat), as they are in rodents, but are more procumbent (forward-angled), similar to the lower incisors of hyraxes. G.G. Simpson (1980) describes these incisors as being designed for "nipping," instead of gnawing.

Figure 7. Reconstruction of Macrauchenia (Litopterna: Macraucheniidae). Lujanian. From Savage and Long (1986), courtesy of The Natural History Museum, London.

Notoungulata
By far the most taxonomically diverse and numerically dominant order of endemic South American ungulates is the Notoungulata,

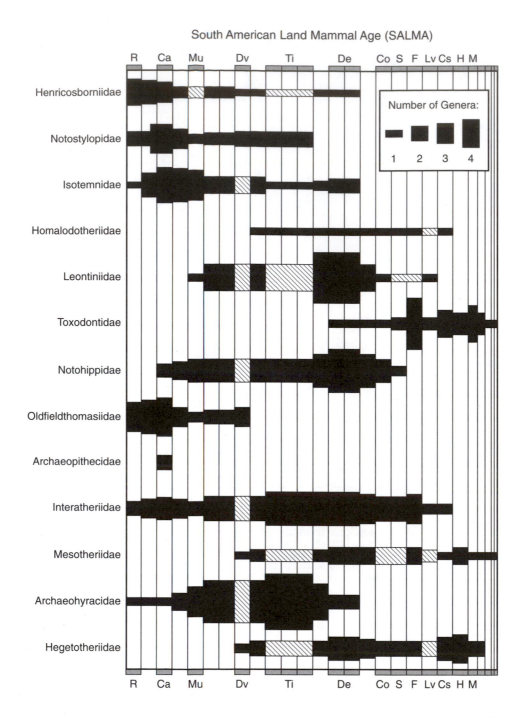

Figure 8. Notoungulate generic diversity through time. Each column represents approximately 2.5 million years (narrower columns represent less time). Width of spindle reflects generic diversity. Solid bars represent actual generic diversity (beneath SALMAs) or predicted generic diversity (beneath hiatuses in the fossil record). Predicted generic diversity is calculated as the average of the diversities of the next younger and next older SALMA in which the family is recorded. Hatched bars represent predicted generic diversity for a family that existed during a SALMA but that is not represented in its fossil record. SALMAs from Flynn and Swisher (1995). Data was compiled from Savage and Russel (1983); Madden (1990); Cifelli (1993); Wyss et al. (1994); Kay et al. (1997); Shockey (1997); and personal observations. Key: R, Riochican; Ca, Casamayoran; Mu, Mustersan; Dv, Divisaderan; Ti, "Tinguiririan"; De, Deseadan; Co, Colhuehuapian; S, Santacrucian; F, Friasian; Lv, Laventan; Cs, Chasicoan; H, Huayquerian; M, Montehermosan. Final four (unlabeled) columns represent Chapadmalalan, Uquian, Ensenadan, and Lujanian SALMAs, respectively. Illustration by Catherine P. Sexton.

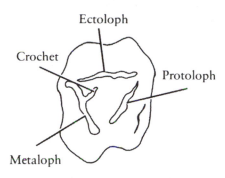

Figure 9. Diagram of notoungulate upper right molar. *To the right,* side facing the front of the mouth; *to the top,* side facing the lips. After Simpson (1980), courtesy of the publisher, Yale University Press, copyright © 1980 by Yale University Press.

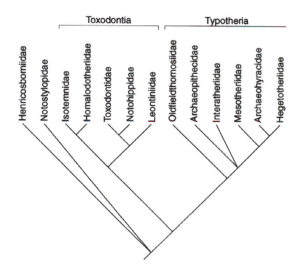

Figure 10. Cladogram of phylogenetic relationships among notoungulate families. The suborders Typotheria (six families) and Toxodontia (five families) constitute the majority of notoungulate diversity. After Cifelli (1993).

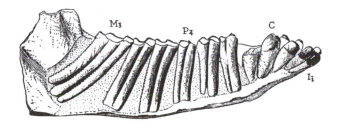

Figure 11. Lateral view of jaw of *Miochochilius* (Typotheria: Interatheriidae) with bone of jawbone pared away. Demonstrates rootless (ever-growing) cheek teeth. From Stirton (1953).

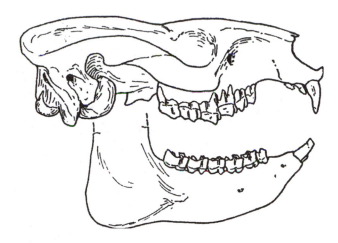

Figure 12. Skull and jaws of *Notostylops murinus* (Notoungulata: Notostylopidae). Casamayoran. From Simpson (1948).

Typotheria

Members of the suborder Typotheria (with the exception of some mesotheriids) were generally small notoungulates about the size of rabbits, large rodents, or small deer. Later forms converged on (evolved similarly to) rodents and rabbits in many respects (e.g., overall configuration of dental arcade, or arrangement, small size, hypselodonty, architecture of chewing muscles, postcranial design) but continued to thrive, even after the arrival of rodents in South America in the Late Eocene. If these animals were filling niches occupied by rodents on other continents, typotheres were well-adapted enough to seemingly be unaffected by the increased competition. Six families are included in the Typotheria (Cifelli 1993): Oldfieldthomasiidae, Archaeopithecidae, Interatheriidae, Mesotheriidae, Archaeohyracidae, and Hegetotheriidae. Among other traits, these taxa tend to share a similar "face" pattern of enamel islands in the upper molars and lower molars divided by a deep groove on the outside of the teeth (Cifelli 1993).

Oldfieldthomasiidae, like henricosborniids and notostylopids, are most common in Paleocene and Eocene faunas (Simpson 1967), although representatives are found also in the Divisadero Largo fauna (Simpson et al. 1952). Some excellent fossils of *Oldfieldthomasia* have been found leading to a better understanding of typothere anatomy. Simpson (1936) described in detail the cranial anatomy of *Oldfieldthomasia* using a set of 55 ordered cross sections, each four millimeters thick, cut parallel to the long axis of the skull. In most respects, oldfieldthomasiids are a generalized typothere form and are too primitive to assign to other, better-defined families (Cifelli 1985).

The family Archaeopithecidae is represented only by two uncommon Casamayoran genera. The name *Archaeopithecus* ("ancient ape") perhaps alludes to the very superficial resemblance of these animals' skulls to those of some fossil primates. As Simpson (1984) points out, Florentino Ameghino (pioneering South American paleontologist who described more South American taxa than any other researcher) believed all groups of modern mammals originated from South American groups. These beliefs

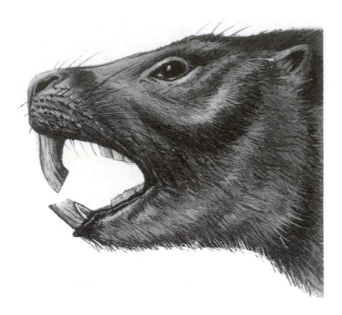

Figure 13. Reconstruction of Mesotherium (Typotheria: Mesotheriidae). Ensenadan. From Savage and Long (1986), courtesy of The Natural History Museum, London.

often were reflected in the names of the taxa he described, such as *Archaeopithecus* (see above), *Notohippus* ("southern horse"), and *Archaeohyrax* ("ancient hyrax").

Mesotheriids are the largest members of the Typotheria, with later forms the size of large sheep. Although never a very diverse group (no more than two genera are contemporaneous), mesotheres persisted until the end of the Pleistocene. Like some other typotheres, mesotheres have greatly enlarged first incisors that are implanted obliquely and meet at their tips; these teeth are separated from their ever-growing cheek teeth by a large diastema (Figure 13). The group Typotheria originally was named after a

mesothere genus, *Typotherium*, but this name later was found to be invalid (Simpson 1940). The genus is known now as *Mesotherium*, after which the family is named.

The Interatheriidae are perhaps the most successful group of notoungulates; they are the longest-ranging of all notoungulate families (Cifelli 1985) and show a diversity of approximately 20 genera, some of which still are being described. They range in time from the Riochican through the Chasicoan; the more primitive "notopitheciine" interatheriids exist in Paleogene faunas and the more advanced interatheriine interatheriids exist in Oligocene and later faunas (Figure 14). The earliest members of this family possess relatively low-crowned teeth, but later forms possess hypsodont and hypselodont dentitions. Additionally, later forms show extreme simplification of their tooth crowns (Figure 15). Some reduce the lateral digits of the feet, creating a paraxonic foot (one that carries weight on the third and fourth digits), similar to that seen in modern artiodactyls, such as pigs, deer, and cattle (Figure 16). Despite these derived features, many interatheres still retain the primitive feature of a complete dentition (Figure 17).

Archaeohyracids constitute one of the least well-known groups of notoungulates; currently only two complete skulls are known. They are encountered first in the Casamayoran and no longer seen encountered after the Deseadan. Until recently, the group's known diversity consisted of only five or six genera. In the Tinguiririan Fauna of Chile (Wyss et al. 1994), however, archaeohyracids are the most abundant and diverse group of mammals, representing between five and nine new taxa (Wyss et al. 1994). The Tinguiririan archaeohyracids include a wide variety of sizes and craniodental adaptations ranging from brachydonty (low-crowned teeth) to extreme hypsodonty, slightly enlarged to extremely enlarged front teeth, and presence to absence of spaces between tooth groups. A thorough description of these new taxa will improve significantly our understanding of archaeohyracid (and typothere) evolution. It also will help improve our understanding of the evolution of adaptations for herbivores (plant-

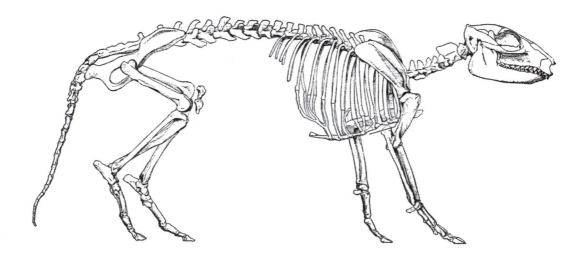

Figure 14. Skeleton of *Miochochilius* (Typotheria: Interatheriidae). Laventan. From Stirton (1953).

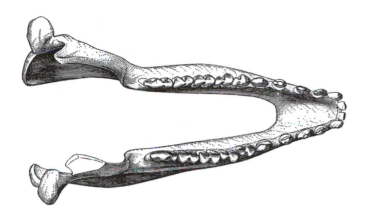

Figure 15. Lower jaws of *Miochochilius* (Typotheria: Interatheriidae), occlusal view. Demonstrates the simplification of the cheek teeth seen in later typotheres. From Stirton (1953).

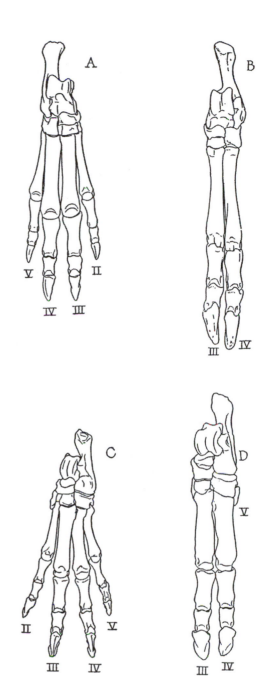

Figure 16. Hind feet of ungulates. A, Oreodont, *Merycoidodon* (Artiodactyla: Merycoidodontidae); B, Peccary, *Tayassu* (Artiodactyla: Tayssuidae); C, Typothere, *Protypotherium* (Notoungulata: Interatheriidae); D, Typothere, *Miocochilius* (Notoungulata: Interatheriidae). From Stirton (1953).

based diet), since archaeohyracids are the earliest hypsodont mammals (Patterson and Pascual 1968).

The hegetotheriids span almost as much time as the interatheriids. They first appear in Mustersan faunas (although they are not numerous then) and survive into the Pliocene. Like interatheres, hegetotheres demonstrate enlargement of the first incisor and greatly simplified cheek teeth, but members of this group tend to exhibit this trend to an even greater extent (Figure 18). The later forms (Figure 19) show remarkable convergence with modern rabbits, both in their cranial and postcranial adaptations (Cifelli 1985).

Toxodontia

The suborder Toxodontia includes the large notoungulates, most likened to rhinos (both large and small) or horses in their overall form. The five families included in this suborder are united by certain characters of the upper and lower teeth (Madden 1990). These families are Isotemnidae, Homalodotheriidae, Leontiniidae, Notohippidae, and Toxodontidae.

The toxodont family Isotemnidae is similar to the typothere family Oldfieldthomasiidae in that it includes primitive members whose relationships are not well known (Cifelli 1993). Isotemnids are found in Riochican through Deseadan faunas but are most diverse in the Casamayoran and Mustersan. The most well-known member of the order is *Thomashuxleya*, described in detail by Simpson (1967). Enough material of this taxon exists to reconstruct the entire skeleton (Figure 20). The resulting animal is about the size of a large dog but with more robust ("hefty") proportions and a larger head. In the Eocene, these animals were likely the largest of the notoungulates and one of the largest herbivores (Madden 1990).

Homalodotheriids, of which there are only a handful of genera, are unusual animals, even by notoungulate standards (Figure 21). Thanks to a fairly complete skeleton discovered by the First Marshall Field Paleontological Expedition to Argentina and Bolivia in 1923 (Scott 1930; Riggs 1937), both the cranial and postcranial anatomy of these animals are known. They are similar

to Northern Hemisphere chalicotheres (extinct forest browsers) and some other fossil groups, in that the ungules (tips of the toes), which normally are hooflike in structure, are modified into claws (Patterson and Pascual 1968). The skull is short and has a complete, generalized set of teeth that lack any diastemata. The earliest members of this family appear during then Tinguiririran (Wyss et al. 1994), and the latest members persist through the Chasicoan.

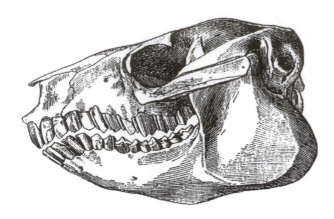

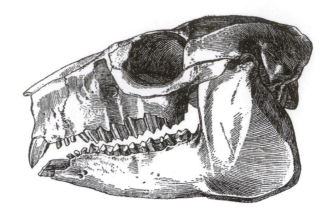

Figure 17. Skull of Protypotherium (Typotheria: Interatheriidae). Santacrucian. From Sinclair (1909).

Figure 18. Skull of *Hegetotherium* (Santacrucian; Typotheria: Hegetotheriidae). Santacrucian. From Sinclair (1909).

Leontiniids are a group of large toxodonts that exhibited their greatest diversity in the Deseadan (Figure 22). Two genera survived into the Neogene: *Colpodon* (Ameghino's index taxon for Colhuehuapian strata) and *Huilatherium,* a recently described form from La Venta fauna (Villarroel and Danis 1997). Both cranial and postcranial remains exist for leontiniids. In the skull, the incisors are reduced in most taxa and the teeth are large but fairly low-crowned. According to R.H. Madden (1990), these animals probably were feeding on soft vegetation ("browse") and possibly fruit. The postcrania are generalized (i.e., no cursorial or other specializations are immediately evident).

The Notohippidae, as their name indicates, superficially resemble horses in the overall shape of their rostrum (snout), the enlargement of the incisors for cropping vegetation and the complicated enamel crowns of their cheek teeth (Figure 23). Recently,

a number of new notoungulates have been discovered and/or described. These finds have increased significantly the group's stratigraphic range and diversity (Bond and López 1993; Wyss et al. 1994; Shockey 1997). The earliest notohippids now appear to exist in the Casamayoran (Bond and López 1993), while the youngest notohippid, *Notohippus* (after which the family is named) occurs in the Santacrucian. They are most diverse in the Deseadan, represented by six distinct genera. And though some notohippids have reduced side digits on their feet, the postcrania of other notohippids are adapted much less for running. As reconstructed by B.J. Shockey (1997), *Eurygenium,* a Deseadan notohippid, was designed more for strength than speed, and its forelimb had significant mobility (Figure 24).

Toxodontids arguably were the most successful group of the Toxodontia (Figure 25). Ranging in time from the Oligocene to the

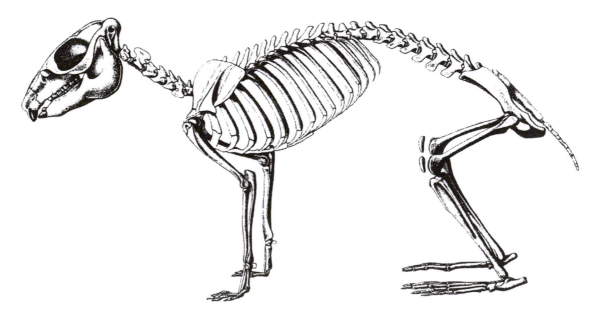

Figure 19. Skeleton of *Pachyrukhos* (Typotheria: Hegetotheriidae). Santacrucian. From Sinclair (1909).

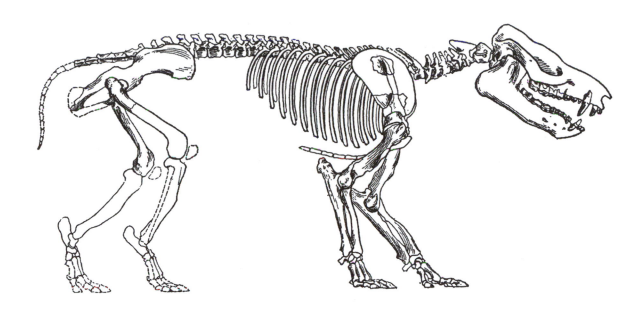

Figure 20. Skeleton of *Thomashuxleya* (Toxodontia: Isotemnidae). Casamayoran. From Simpson (1967).

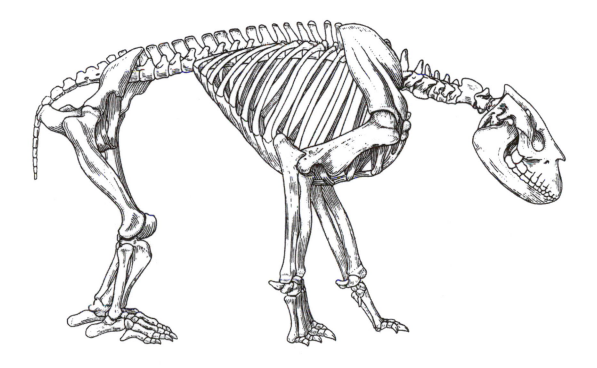

Figure 21. Skeleton of *Homalodotherium* (Toxodontia: Homalodotheriidae). Santacrucian. From Riggs (1937), courtesy of The Field Museum, Chicago.

end of the Pleistocene, they were the only notoungulates to emigrate out of South America (Webb 1991). The diversity of the group equals that of the Interatheriidae, with approximately 20 described genera, but this relatively rapid radiation (diversification and geo- graphic spread) has made it difficult to sort out the evolutionary relationships of the family (Cifelli 1993). Generally large, they were the only members of the Notoungulata to develop dermal horns similar to those seen in rhinos (Patterson and Pascual 1968). They

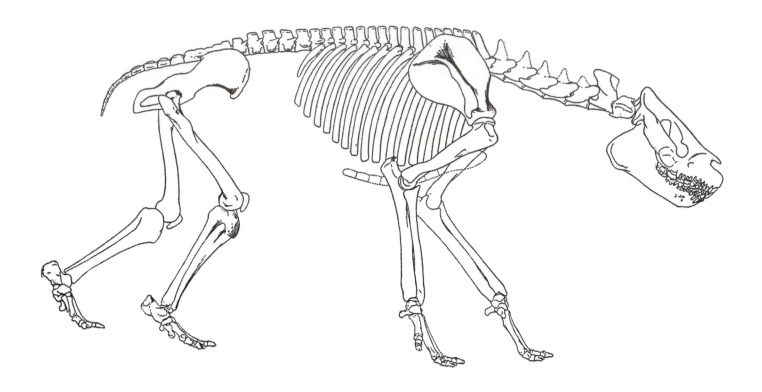

Figure 22. Skeleton of *Scarritta* (Toxodontia: Leontiniidae). Deseadan. From Chaffee (1952).

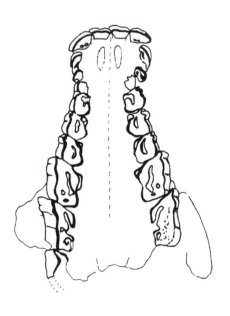

Figure 23. Palate of *Pascualihippus* (Toxodontia: Notohippidae). Deseadan. From Shockey (1997).

are distinguished from other notoungulates by their ever-growing tusks and cheek teeth and specialized incisors (Madden 1997).

Research

The endemic ungulate fauna of South America is an amazing example of how a single group of animals in isolation (the notoungulates) can diversify to fill niches occupied today by four orders of mammals: artiodactyls, perissodactyls, rodents, and lagomorphs (e.g., rabbits). Similarly, the astrapotheres and pyrotheres independently evolved forms and lifestyles similar to today's proboscideans (trunked animals, such as elephants), rhinos, and hippos. Much of the work of early paleontologists primarily dealt with trying to describe these diverse taxa and sort them into groups that share similar characteristics. Due to a number of challenges associated with South American paleontology—the relatively small number of paleontologists working on South American mammals, difficulties in correlating faunas from different areas of South America, totally unique mammals that evolved rapidly in the Early Cenozoic, and significant gaps in the fossil land mammal record—we are beginning just now to understand the large-scale patterns in South American mammal evolution.

Only in the past 10 years or so have researchers begun to apply cladistic methodologies (ranking organisms on basis of common ancestry) to groups of South American ungulates in an attempt to sort out the evolutionary relationships, both within

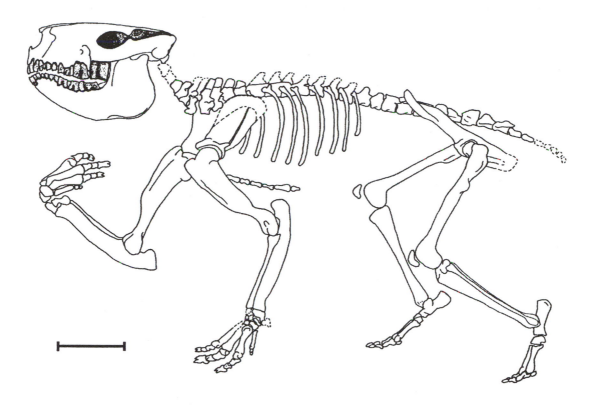

Figure 24. Skeleton reconstruction of *Eurygenium* (Toxodontia: Notohippidae). Deseadan. From Shockey (1997).

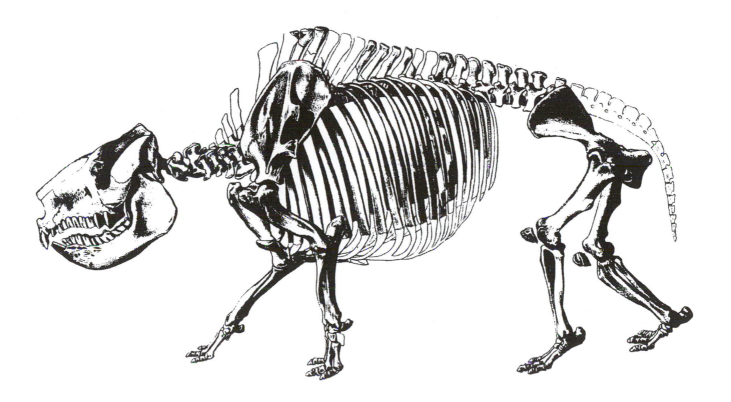

Figure 25. Skeleton of *Nesodon* (Toxodontia: Toxosontidae). Santacrucian. From Scott (1912).

and between groups (Madden 1990; Bond and López 1993; Cifelli 1993; Hitz 1994, 1995, 1997; Shockey 1997; various articles in Kay et al. 1997). Many other cladistic studies are currently under way. Until we have an accurate idea of how these animals are related to each other, we cannot move on to questions about why they evolved the way they did or how their evolutionary histories influenced their roles in evolving paleocommunities.

Additionally, only recently have other researchers, using a variety of techniques, undertaken detailed studies to figure out such aspects of life history as diet, locomotion, and social behavior, in an attempt to reconstruct a clearer picture of South American ecosystems and communities (Rensberger and Pfretzchner 1992; MacFadden et al. 1985; MacFadden and Shockey 1997; Croft 1997; Shockey 1997). In their study of Pleistocene mammal fauna from Bolivia, MacFadden and Shockey (1997) used both carbon isotope ratios and various morphometric (measurements of structures) characters to infer feeding ecology in a variety of South American mammals. The toxodont *Toxodon* was inferred to have been a grazer (feeding predominantly on abrasive grasses), while the macraucheniid *Macrauchenia* was inferred to have been a mixed feeder (feeding partly on grasses, partly on softer leaves of herbaceous and woody plants). Currently, it is not possible to determine the ecology of these ungulates more specifically, but with more scientists focusing on similar sorts of studies, the next 10 years will certainly bring significant advances in our understanding of how these animals lived.

Finally, the recent discovery of new fossil localities and the restudy of several previously known fossil localities have begun to fill in some of the significant gaps in the record of South American fossil land mammals (MacFadden et al. 1985; Marshall and De Muizon 1988; Wyss et al. 1990, 1992, 1993, 1994; Bond et al. 1996; Kay et al. 1997). As is always true in paleontology, filling in gaps in the fossil record with more fossils from more localities will increase the accuracy of interpretations of evolutionary relationships and of the evolution of South American mammal communities.

DARIN A. CROFT

Works Cited

Bond, M., and G. López. 1993. El primer Notohippidae (Mammalia, Notoungulata) de la Formación Lumbrera (Grupo Salta) del Notoeste Argentina. Consideraciones sobre la sistematica de la Familia Notohippidae. *Ameghiniana* 30:59–68.

Bond, M., G. López, and M. Reguero. 1996. "Astroponoteén plus supérieure" of Ameghino: Another interval in the Paleogene record of South America. *Journal of Vertebrate Paleontology*, supplement to no. 3, 16:23A.

Carabajal, E., R. Pascual, R. Pinedo, J.A. Salfity, and M.G. Vucetich. 1977. Un nuevo mamifero de la Formación Lumbrera (Grupo Salta) de la comarca de Carahuasi (Salta, Argentina). Edad y correlaciones. *Publicaciones del Museo Municipal de Ciencias Naturales de Mar del Plata "Lorenzo Scaglia"* 2 (7):148–63.

Carroll, R.L. 1988. *Vertebrate Paleontology and Evolution*. New York: Freeman.

Chaffee, R.G. 1952. The Deseadan vertebrate fauna of the Scarrit Pocket, Patagonia. *Bulletin of the American Museum of Natural History* 98:509–62.

Cifelli, R.L. 1983a. The origin and affinities of the South American Condylartha and early Tertiary Litopterna (Mammalia). *American Museum Novitates* 2772:1–49.

———. 1983b. Eutherian tarsals from the Late Paleocene of Brazil. *American Museum Novitates* 2761:1–31.

———. 1985. South American ungulate evolution and extinction. *In* F.G. Stehli and S.D. Webb (eds.), *The Great American Biotic Interchange*. New York: Plenum.

———. 1991. A new adianthid Litoptern (Mammalia) from the Miocene of Chile. *Rivista Chilena de Historia Natural* 64:119–25.

———. 1993. The phylogeny of the native South American ungulates. *In* F.S. Szalay, M.J. Novacek, and M.C. McKenna (eds.), *Mammal Phylogeny: Placentals*. New York and London: Springer-Verlag.

Cifelli, R.L., C.R. Schaff, and M.C. McKenna. 1989. The relationships of the Arctostylopidae (Mammalia): New data and interpretation. *Bulletin of the Museum of Comparative Zoology* 151 (1):1–44.

Cifelli, R.L., and M.F. Soria. 1983. Systematics of the Adianthidae (Litopterna, Mammalia). *American Museum Novitates* 2771:1–25.

Croft, D.A. 1997. The correlation between diet and morphology: Multivariate analyses of craniodental variables in glires and ungulates. *Journal of Vertebrate Paleontology*, supplement to no. 3, 17:40A.

Flynn, J.J., and C.C. Swisher III. 1995. Cenozoic South American land mammal ages: Correlation to global geochronologies. *In* W.A. Berggren, D.V. Kent, M.-P. Aubry, and J. Hardenbol (eds.), *Geochronology, Time Scales, and Global Stratigraphic Correlation* Society for Sedimentary Geology, Special Publication, 54.

Gaudry, A. 1909. Fossiles de Patagonie: le *Pyrotherium*. *Annales Paléontologie* 4:1–28.

Hitz, R. 1994. Systematics of the Late Oligocene/Early Miocene Salla (Bolivia) interatheres. *Journal of Vertebrate Paleontology*, supplement to no. 3, 14:29A.

———. 1995. Typothere (Notoungulata) phylogeny and proposed taxonomic revisions. *Journal of Vertebrate Paleontology*, supplement to no. 3, 15:34A.

———. 1997. Contributions to South American mammalian paleontology: New interatheres (notoungulata) from Chile and Bolivia, Typothere (Notoungulata) phylogeny, and Paleosols from the Late Oligocene Salla Beds. Ph.D. diss. University of California, Santa Barbara.

Janis, C.M. 1995. Correlations between craniodental morphology and feeding behavior in ungulates: Reciprocal illumination between living and fossil taxa. *In* J.J. Thomason (ed.), *Functional Morphology in Vertebrate Paleontology*. Cambridge and New York: Cambridge University Press.

Janis, C.M., and M. Fortelius. 1988. On the means whereby mammals achieve increased functional durability of their dentitions, with special reference to limiting factors. *Biological Reviews* 63:197–230.

Johnson, S.C., and R.H. Madden. 1997. Uruguaytheriine Astrapotheres of tropical South America. *In* R.F. Kay, R.H. Madden, R.L. Cifelli, and J.J. Flynn (eds.), *Vertebrate Paleontology in the Neotropics: The Miocene Fauna of La Venta, Colombia*. Washington, D.C., and London: Smithsonian Institution Press.

Kay, R.F., R.H. Madden, R.L. Cifelli, and J.J. Flynn (eds.). 1997. *Vertebrate Paleontology in the Neotropics: The Miocene Fauna of La Venta, Colombia*. Washington, D.C., and London: Smithsonian Institution Press.

Loomis, F.B. 1914. *The Deseado Formation of Patagonia*. Concord, New Hampshire: Runford.

MacFadden, B.J., K.E. Campbell Jr., R.L. Cifelli, O. Siles, N.M. Johnson, C.W. Naeser, and P.K. Zeitler. 1985. Magnetic polarity stratigraphy and mammalian fauna of the Deseadan (Late Oligocene–Early Miocene) Salla Beds of northern Bolivia. *Journal of Geology* 93 (3):223–50.

MacFadden, B.J., and B.J. Shockey. 1997. Ancient feeding ecology and niche differentiation of Pleistocene mammalian herbivores from Tarija, Bolivia: Morphological and isotope evidence. *Paleobiology* 23 (1):77–100.

Madden, R.H. 1990. Miocene Toxodontidae (Notoungulata, Mammalia) from Colombia, Ecuador and Chile. Ph.D. dissertation, Duke University.

———. 1997. A new toxodontid notoungulate. *In* R.F. Kay, R.H. Madden, R.L. Cifelli, and J.J. Flynn (eds.), *Vertebrate Paleontology in the Neotropics: The Miocene Fauna of La Venta, Colombia.* Washington, D.C., and London: Smithsonian Institution Press.

Marshall, L.G., and R.L. Cifelli. 1989. Analysis of changing diversity patterns in Cenozoic land mammal age faunas, South America. *Palaeovertebrata* 19 (4):169–210.

Marshall, L.G., and C. De Muizon. 1988. The dawn of the age of mammals in South America. *National Geographic Research* 4 (1):23–55.

Matthew, W.D. 1915. A revision of the lower Eocene Wasatch and Wind River faunas. Part 4. Entelonychia, Primates, Insectivora (part). *Bulletin of the American Museum of Natural History* 34:429–83.

Novacek, M.J., A. Wyss, D. Frasinetti, P. Salinas. 1989. A new ?Eocene mammal fauna from the Andean Main Range. *Journal of Vertebrate Paleontology,* supplement to no. 3, 9:34A.

Patterson, B. 1932. The auditory region of the Toxodontia. *Fieldiana: Geological Series, Field Museum of Natural History* 6 (1):5–27.

———. 1934a. The region of an Upper Pliocene Typotherid. *Fieldiana: Geological Series, Field Museum of Natural History* 6 (5):83–89.

———. 1934b. Cranial characters of *Homalodotherium. Fieldiana: Geological Series, Field Museum of Natural History* 6 (7):113–17.

———. 1934c. Upper premolar-molar structure in the Notoungulata with notes on taxonomy. *Fieldiana: Geological Series, Field Museum of Natural History* 6 (6):91–111.

———. 1936. The internal structure of the ear in some notoungulates. *Fieldiana Geological Series, Field Museum of Natural History* 6 (15):199–227.

———. 1977. A primitive pyrothere (Mammalia, Notoungulata) from the early Tertiary of northwestern Venezuela. *Fieldiana: Geology* 33:397–422.

Patterson, B., and R. Pascual. 1968. The fossil mammal fauna of South America. *Quarterly Review of Biology* 43 (4):409–51.

Prothero, D.R. 1994. Mammal evolution. *In* D.R. Prothero and R.M. Schoch (eds.), *Major Features of Vertebrate Evolution.* The Paleontological Society, Short Courses in Paleontology, no 7. Knoxville, Tennessee: Paleontological Society.

Prothero, D.R., E.M. Manning, and M. Fischer. 1988. The phylogeny of the ungulates. *In* M.J. Benton (ed.), *The Phylogeny and Classification of the Tetrapods.* Systematics Association Special Volume, 335A–35B. 2 vols., Oxford: Clarendon; New York: Oxford University Press.

Rensberger, J.M., and H.U. Pfretzshner. 1992. Enamel structure in astrapotheres and its functional implications. *Scanning Microscopy* 6:495–510.

Riggs, E.S. 1937. Mounted skeleton of Homalodotherium. *Fieldiana: Geological Series, Field Museum of Natural History* 6 (17):233–43.

Romer, A.S. 1966. *Vertebrate Paleontology.* 3rd. ed., Chicago: University of Chicago Press.

Savage, D.E., and D.E. Russel. 1983. *Mammalian Paleofaunas of the World.* Reading, Massachusetts: Addison-Wesley.

Savage, R.J.G., and M.R. Long. 1986. *Mammal Evolution.* London: British Museum of Natural History; New York: Facts on File.

Scott, W.B. 1910. Mammalia of the Santa Cruz beds. Part 1, Litopterna. *Reports of the Princeton University Expeditions to Patagonia (1896–1899)* 7:1–156.

———. 1912. Mammal of the Santa Cruz beds: Part 2: Toxodonta. *Reports of the Princeton University Expeditions to Patagonia (1896–1899)* 6:111–238.

———. 1928. Mammalia of the Santa Cruz beds. Part 4: Astrapotheria. *Reports of the Princeton University Expeditions to Patagonia (1896–1899)* 6:301–42.

———. 1930. A partial skeleton of *Homalodotherium* from the Santa Cruz beds of Patagonia. *Memoirs of the Field Museum of Natural History* 50 (1):1–39.

———. 1937. The Astrapotheria. *Proceedings of the American Philosophical Society* 77:309–93.

Shockey, B.J. 1997. Two new notoungulates (Family Notohippidae) from the Salla Beds of Bolivia (Deseadan: Late Oligocene): Systematics and functional morphology. *Journal of Vertebrate Paleontology* 17 (3):584–99.

Simpson, G.G. 1933. Structure and affinities of *Trigonostylops. American Museum Novitates* 608:1–28.

———. 1936. Structure of a primitive Notoungulate cranium. *American Museum Novitates* 824:1–31.

———. 1940. The names of *Mesotherium* and *Typotherium. American Journal of Science* 238:518–21.

———. 1948. The beginning of the age of mammals in South America. Part 1. *Bulletin of the American Museum of Natural History* 91:1–232.

———. 1967. The beginning of the age of mammals in South America. Part 2. *Bulletin of the American Museum of Natural History* 137:1–260.

———. 1980. *Splendid Isolation, the Curious History of South American Mammals.* New Haven, Connecticut: Yale University Press.

———. 1984. *Discoverers of the Lost World.* New Haven, Connecticut: Yale University Press.

Simpson, G.G., J.L. Minoprio, and B. Patterson. 1952. The mammalian fauna of the Divisadero Largo Formation, Mendoza, Argentina. *Bulletin of the Museum of Comparative Zoology* 127:239–93.

Sinclair, W.J. 1909. Mammalia of the Santa Cruz beds. Part 1, Typotheria. *Reports of the Princeton University Expeditions to Patagonia, 1896–1899* 6:1–110.

Soria, M.F. 1982. *Tetragonostylops apthomasi* (Price y Paula Couto, 1950): Su asignacón a Astrapotheriidae (Mammalia; Astrapotheria). *Ameghiniana* 19:234–38.

Soria, M.F., and J. Powell. 1982. Un primitivo Astrapotheria (Mammalia) y la edad de la Formación Río Loro, Provincia de Tucumán, Républica Argentina. *Ameghiniana* 18:155–68.

Stirton, R.A. 1953. A new genus of interatheres from the Miocene of Colombia. *University of California Publications in Geological Sciences* 29 (6):265–348.

Villarroel, C. 1987. Características y afinidades de *Etaoya* n. gen., tipo de una nueva familia de Xenungulata (Mammalia) del Paleoceno medio (?) de Colombia. *Communiciónes Paleontológicas del Museo de Historia Natural, Montevideo* 1:241–53.

Villarroel, C., and J.C. Danis. 1997. A new leontiniid notoungulate. *In* R.F. Kay, R.H. Madden, R.L. Cifelli, and J.J. Flynn (eds.), *Vertebrate Paleontology in the Neotropics: The Miocene Fauna of La Venta, Colombia.* Washington, D.C., and London: Smithsonian Institution Press.

Webb, S.D. 1991. Ecogeography and the Great American Interchange. *Paleobiology* 17 (3):266–80.

Wyss, A.R., J.J. Flynn, M.A. Norell, C.C. Swisher III, M.J. Novacek, M.C. McKenna, and R. Charrier. 1993. South America's earliest rodent and recognition of a new interval of mammalian evolution. *Nature* 365:434–37.

———. 1994. Paleogene mammals from the Andes of central Chile: A preliminary taxonomic, biostratigraphic, and geochronologic assessment. *American Museum Novitates* 3098:1–31.

Wyss, A.R., M.A. Norell, J.J. Flynn, M.J. Novacek, R. Charrier, M.C. McKenna, C.C. Swisher III, D. Frasinetti, and M. Jin. 1990. A new early Tertiary mammal fauna from central Chile: Implications for Andean stratigraphy and tectonics. *Journal of Vertebrate Paleontology* 10 (4):518–22.

Wyss, A.R., M.A. Norell, M.J. Novacek, and J.J. Flynn. 1992. New ?early Tertiary localities from the Chilean Andes. *Journal of Vertebrate Paleontologys,* Supplement to No. 3, 12:61A.

Further Reading

Cifelli, R.L. 1985. South American ungulate evolution and extinction. *In* F.G. Stehli and S.D. Webb (eds.), *The Great American Biotic Interchange.* New York: Plenum.

———. 1993. The phylogeny of the native South American ungulates. *In* F.S. Szalay, M.J. Novacek, and M.C. McKenna (eds.), *Mammal Phylogeny: Placentals.* New York and London: Springer-Verlag.

Flynn, J.J., and C.C. Swisher III. 1995. Cenozoic South American land mammal ages: Correlation to global geochronologies. *In* W.A. Berggren, D.V. Kent, M.-P. Aubry, and J. Hardenbol (eds.), *Geochronology, Time Scales, and Global Stratigraphic Correlation.* Society for Sedimentary Geology, Special Publication, 54.

Hatcher, J.B. 1903. *Bone Hunters in Patagonia: Princeton University Expeditions to Patagonia, 1896–1899.* Princeton, New Jersey: Princeton University Press.

Kay, R.F., R.H. Madden, R.L. Cifelli, and J.J. Flynn (eds.), *Vertebrate Paleontology in the Neotropics: The Miocene Fauna of La Venta, Colombia.* Washington, D.C., and London: Smithsonian Institution Press.

MacFadden, B.J., and B.J. Shockey. 1997. Ancient feeding ecology and niche differentiation of Pleistocene mammalian herbivores from Tarija, Bolivia: Morphological and isotope evidence. *Paleobiology* 23 (1):77–100.

Marshall, L.G., and R.L. Cifelli. 1989. Analysis of changing diversity patterns in Cenozoic land mammal age faunas, South America. *Palaeovertebrata* 19 (4):169–210.

Marshall, L.G., and C. De Muizon. 1988. The dawn of the age of mammals in South America. *National Geographic Research* 4 (1):23–55.

Patterson, B., and R. Pascual. 1972. The fossil mammal fauna of South America. *In* A. Keast, F.C. Erk, and B. Glass (eds.), *Evolution, Mammals, and Southern Continents.* Albany: State University of New York Press.

Savage, R.J.G., and M.R. Long. 1986. *Mammal Evolution.* London: British Museum of Natural History; New York: Facts on File.

Simpson, G.G. 1934. *Attending Marvels: A Patagonian Journal.* New York: Macmillan.

———. 1980. *Splendid Isolation, the Curious History of South American Mammals.* New Haven, Connecticut: Yale University Press.

———. 1984. *Discoverers of the Lost World.* New Haven, Connecticut: Yale University Press.

Webb, S.D. A history of savanna vertebrates in the New World. Part 2, South America and the Great Interchange. *Annual Reviews of Ecology and Systematics* 9:393–426.

Wyss, A.R., J.J. Flynn, M.A. Norell, C.C. Swisher III, M.J. Novacek, M.C. McKenna, and R. Charrier. 1994. Paleogene mammals from the Andes of central Chile: A preliminary taxonomic, biostratigraphic, and geochronologic assessment. *American Museum Novitates* 3098:1–31.

PLACENTALS: MINOR PLACENTAL ORDERS OF LARGE BODY SIZE

Dinocerata

Dinocerata ("uintatheres") is an order of primitive ungulates whose fossils can be found in North America and Asia. Uintatheres initially appeared near the end of the Paleocene, were common in the Eocene, and became extinct around the Late Eocene. They were large, hoofed herbivores, ranging from pig-sized (*Prodinoceras*), in the Late Paleocene, to rhino-sized (*Eobasileus*), in the Eocene, the giant of its day. The best-known, most typical forms are the large North American genera (groups; singular, genus) *Uintatherium, Eobasileus,* and *Tetheopsis,* all having ponderous bodies, short limbs, and heavy feet (Figure 1). Especially notable in these advanced forms are three pairs of bony swellings on top of the skull, one over the nostrils, another over the upper jaws, and a third over the forehead. The males were armed with powerful sabrelike canines. The upper incisors were usually absent, the lower ones small.

O.C. Marsh (1871) described the first uintathere remains, found in the Eocene rock strata of the Bridger Basin, Wyoming, under the name *Titanotherium? anceps* but assigned it to bron-tothere, another order of large extinct mammals. In 1873 Marsh acknowledged that these animals represented a distinct group and created the name "Dinocerata" (replacing "Dinocerea," his initial name for them) (1873a), publishing a monograph on the group in 1885. J. Leidy (1872) and E.D. Cope (1872) also published several papers on Eocene uintatheres from both Bridger and Washakie basins of Wyoming. Later, Cope (1884) united Pantodonta and Dinocerata into his order Amblypoda, suggesting that the upper molar of uintatheres evolved from *Coryphodon*-type pantodonts.

In 1898, H.F. Osborn accepted and expanded Cope's views on this mode of development. However, in 1923 H.E. Wood reinterpreted the similarities of the molar cusps (points on the grinding surface) and suggested that uintathere and *coryphodon*-like pantodonts developed at the same time and along similar lines but are unrelated. The work of G.G. Simpson (1937a and 1937b) and B. Patterson (1939) effectively undermined the concept of the Amblypoda. However, Simpson (1945) later included the Dinocerata with the Pantodonta, Pyrotheria, Proboscidea, Embritho-

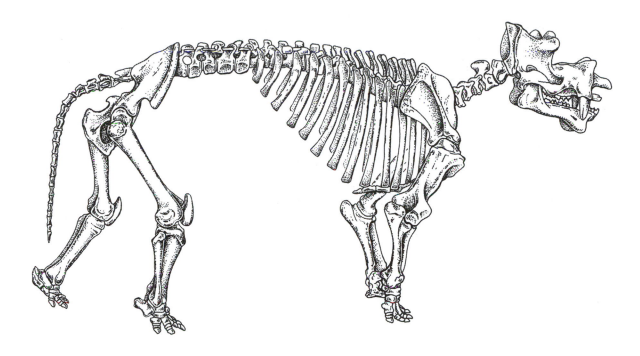

Figure 1. *Dinoceras,* a uintathere. From VERTEBRATE PALEONTOLOGY AND EVOLUTION by Robert L. Carroll, ©1988 by W.W. Freeman and Company, Used with permission, after Gregory (1957).

poda, Hyracoidea, and Sirenia. In 1961 W.H. Wheeling made a comprehensive review of dinoceratans. It was his position that no known uintathere could be derived from known pantodonts. Instead, he argued that the similarity of feet and dentition could be attributed to a common, more primitive ancestor. On the basis of molar morphology, Wheeler went on to suggest that the South American Xenungulata may be closely related to the Dinocerata. A.S. Romer (1966) included the Pantodonta, Dinocerata, Xenungulata, and Pyrotheria as suborders of the order Amblypoda. M.C. McKenna (1975) suggested that the Dinocerata might have an arctocyonid ancestry and allied them with the orders Arctocyonia, Tillodontia, Tubulidentata, Embrithopoda, and Artiodactyla.

The first Paleocene uintatheres, *Prodinoceras,* were found in 1929 in both Mongolia (Matthew et al. 1929) and Wyoming (Simpson 1929). A number of Paleocene uintatheres later were discovered in China (Chow 1960; Chow and Tung 1962; Tong 1978, 1979, 1982), which greatly increased our understanding of these creatures and their origin. Y.S. Tong (1978) proposed that they might have originated in Asia.

In 1985 R.M. Schoch and S.G. Lucas revised all known uintathere materials. They grouped them into two families. The first was Prodinoceratidae, a primitive group considered to be a sister taxon of all other dinoceratans and that consisted of the single genus *Prodinoceras.* The second was Uintatheriidae, a more advanced group that consisted of five smaller genera, *Gobiatherium, Bathyopsis, Uintatherium, Tethyopsis,* and *Eobasileus.* Schoch and Lucas suggested that "the common ancestor of uintatheres and xenungulates arose in Asia from an 'anagalid' (*Pseudictops*-like) ancestry. This group achieved a trans-Pacific distribution and gave rise to uintatheres in Asia and North America."

Tillodontia

Tillodontia is an extinct mammalian order, appearing first in the early Paleocene and becoming extinct at the end of the Eocene. In Asia they are found from the Early Paleocene to the Late Eocene, in North America from the Late Paleocene to Middle Eocene, and in Europe from the Early Eocene. The Paleocene and Early Eocene animals, such as *Esthonyx,* were widespread and were small to moderately large creatures. The advanced form, such as *Trogosus,* was as large as a big bear, stout, compact, and muscular. *Trogosus* had five clawed toes on each foot and walked on the soles of its feet (plantigrade). The skull was low, the snout slim, the braincase small. The second incisors were greatly enlarged, to become rootless, constantly growing tusks, as in rodents; the other incisors and canines were lost (Figure 2). A noticeable groove in the front surface of these teeth suggests that tillodonts probably used them to uproot vegetation or to strip leaves from stems. Lower molars particularly show a tendency toward high crown (hypsodonty) and are usually very heavily worn. This indicates ground feeding and ingestion of a considerable amount of soil (Gingerich and Gunnell 1979). Tillodonts may have been somewhat piglike in their feeding habits, with a herbivorous or omnivorous diet. They lived in highly variable climatic conditions—cool, moist winters, and relatively long, warm summers. There was wide variation in moisture, with repeated droughts (Gazin 1953).

The first tillodont was described by Leidy (1868) and named *Anchippodus riparius.* The early investigations of the tillodont include the independent research on the Bridger Basin materials by Leidy (1871) and Marsh (1871, 1873b) and Cope's work (1874) on the Wasatch fauna. Cope considered tillodonts closely allied with taeniodonts and included Creodonta, Masod-

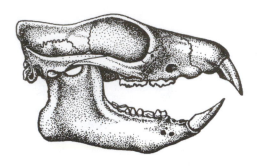

Figure 2. *Trogosus,* a Middle Eocene tillodont. Skull size is about 33 centimeters long. From Romer (1966), after Marsh (1871); used by permission of the publisher, The University of Chicago Press, copyright © 1933, 1945, 1966 by The University of Chicago.

onta, Insectivora, Tillodonta, and Taeniodonta in his order Bunotheria (1876). In 1897 J.L. Wortman first made order out of the confusion between tillodonts and taeniodonts and laid the foundation for the orders as now recognized.

W. Granger (1918) reported a nearly perfect tillodont skull and jaws from the Huerfano beds of Colorado. T. de Chardin (1922) revised tillodont materials from the Lower Eocene of France. C.C. Young (1937) reported the first tillodont discovery from Asia. Studies also include those by L.S. Russell (1935), Simpson (1937a and 1937b), and W.J. Sinclair and Granger (1912).

In 1953 C.L. Gazin examined nearly all the known materials and published a comprehensive review. He first called attention to the relationship of tillodonts and pantodonts, a relationship that is currently accepted by many researchers (Gingerich and Gunnell 1979; Zhou and Wang 1979; Stucky and Krishtalka 1983). S.Y. Ting and J.J. Zheng (1989) found a Late Paleocene tillodont with enlarged second incisors, *Interogale datangensis,* the most primitive example known, and suggested that these animals may have evolved from Asian endemic "anagalid" forms. R.K. Stucky and L. Krishtalka (1983) included all tillodonts, *Lofochaius, Meiostylodon, Esthonyx, Pleisiesthonyx, Basalina, Megalesthonyx, Adapidium, Trogosus, Kuanchuannius,* and *Tillodon,* in a single family Esthonychidae. Schoch (1986) suggested that the tillodonts may have been out-competed by taeniodont and contemporaneous piglike artiodactyls, such as achaenodonts.

Embrithopoda

Embrithopoda is an extinct order of mammals, known only from a single genus, *Arsinoitherium,* found in the Lower Oligocene of Egypt (Andrews 1906) (Figure 3). It is one of several "orphan" orders in the Early Tertiary, groups with uncertain ancestry and without known descendants. Arsinutherium was large, about rhinoceros-sized, and may have been a marsh dweller or amphibious in habit. Its limbs were graviportal (thick and adapted to support great weight), with long, massive humerus and femur, short lower segments, and a broad, spreading, five-toed foot. The most striking feature of the animal was a huge pair of bony horns on the nasal bones, together with small ones on the frontals, above the

skull, much as in rhinoceroses. The teeth form a nearly uniform series, without the enlarged incisors and conspicuous canines usually seen in other ungulates. The molars were hypsodont (high-crowned). S. Sen and E. Heintz (1979) described new materials assigned to the Arsinoitheriidae from north central Turkey and Romania; however, the specimens are smaller than the Egyptian group, with more primitive dental morphology and without horns. McKenna and E. Manning (1977) suggested that *Phenacolophus* from the Upper Paleocene or Lower Eocene of Asia might be related to the ancestry of *Arsinoitherium.*

Desmostylia

The Desmostylia are an order of marine, aquatic mammalian herbivores (plant-eaters) related to the earliest elephant ancestors, found in North America and Asia at the margins of the north Pacific. This group ranges in age from the Oligocene to the Pliocene. Desmostylia have unreduced front and hind limbs, with hands and feet modified as paddles, and elongate upper and lower jaws that have prominent incisors and canines followed by a long diastema (gap between teeth) (Carroll 1988) (Figure 4). Earlier scholars included O.P. Hay (1924) and V.L. VanderHoof (1937). The order was named by R.H. Reinhardt in 1953, and T. Shikama (1966), among others, described Japanese desmostylians.

D.P. Domning and colleagues (1986) considered both the Proboscidea and Desmostylia to be related to the Asian Paleocene genus *Minchenella.* They concluded that the animals fed on marine algae, with the earliest members of the group beginning the trend by feeding on plants in intertidal zones. Domning and colleagues (1986) suggested that the size, body shape, and dental morphology of Desmostylia indicate that they could function in the water as well as hippopotami, feeding by using their procumbent incisors and canines to scoop up masses of vegetation or scrape them off the bottom. The Oligocene desmostylid *Behemotops emlongi* from Oregon shows wear on the lower surface of its tusk (Domning et al. 1986), a wear pattern that is consistent with this lifestyle.

Pantodonta

The Pantodonta are pig- to hippo-sized terrestrial herbivores of the Paleocene and Eocene of North America, Europe, and Asia. The last ones died out in Asia (Carroll 1988). This group represents the first large radiation (diversity and geographic spread) of big terrestrial herbivores. S.G. Lucas (1998) recognized 12 groups of pantodonts and postulated that they originated in Asia from a didelphodontine-like ancestor in the Paleocene, followed by a spread into North and South America (Marshall and Muizon 1988). Pantodonts may have given rise to the tillodonts (Chow and Wang 1979).

E.L. Simons (1960) revised the Paleocene Pantodonta, and Lucas and colleagues (1998) have reviewed the order. Lucas (1982) discussed pantodont relationships and removed a variety of animals that others had included in the group. Over the last 20 years, he has worked on the Paleocene-Eocene genus *Coryphodon,* producing a variety of publications. In 1989 he used *Coryphodon* of North America, Europe, and Asia to examine the placement of the Pale-

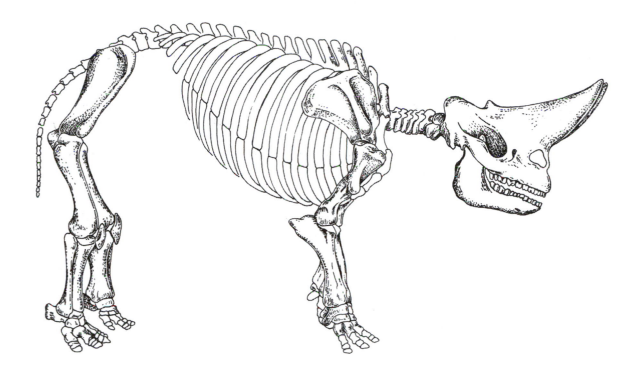

Figure 3. *Arsinoitherium,* an embritopod. Dates from the Oligocene of Egypt. From VERTEBRATE PALEONTOLOGY AND EVOLUTION by Robert L. Carroll, ©1988 by W.W. Freeman and Company, Used with permission, after Andrews (1906).

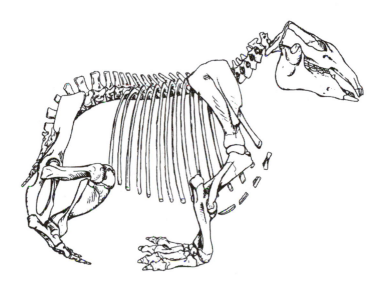

Figure 4. *Paleoparadoxia,* a desmostylian, about 2.3 meters long. From Romer (1966); used by permission of the publisher, The University of Chicago Press, copyright © 1933, 1945, 1966 by The University of Chicago.

ocene-Eocene boundary. He also reviewed studies of the fossil evidence of injuries and disease suffered by *Coryphodon,* including an injury consistent with puncture of the skull by a canine of another *Coryphodon* (Lucas 1987). Contributions from older workers are numerous (Osborn 1898; Matthew 1937; Patterson 1934; Simpson 1929); each of these researchers wrote several additional papers that included material on pantodonts. Cope (1884) placed pantodonts and uintatheres in his now-abandoned Order Amblypoda.

The least derived (specialized) pantodonts are the Asian and South American pantolambdodontids, such as the Asian *Archaeolambda,* small, gracile herbivores that may have been arboreal (living in trees) (Lucas 1998). Chinese forms included one that was gracile, antelope-like, and had a proboscis (short trunk) similar to that of a tapir (Ting et al. 1987). The North American Paleocene genus *Titanoides* (Figure 5) was a large terrestrial herbivore with clawed feet and saberlike canines; *Pantolambda* and *Caeno-*

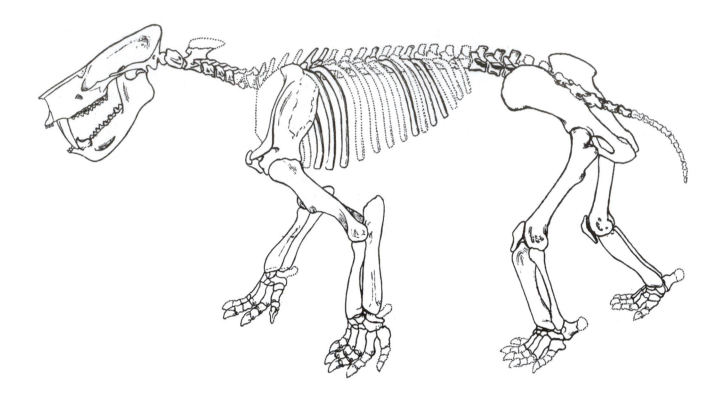

Figure 5. *Titanoides,* a pony-sized pantodont. Modified from Simons (1960).

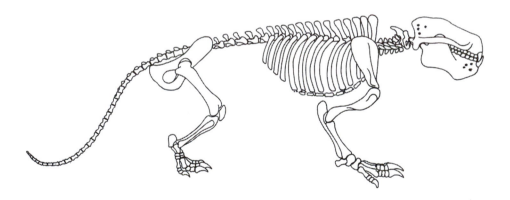

Figure 6. *Stylinodon,* a taeniodont. From Schoch (1986), courtesy of Robert M. Schoch, College of General Studies, Boston University.

lambda were terrestrial quadrupedal (four-footed) browsers; and the larger, slothlike *Barylambda* may have been capable of bipedal (two-footed) browsing (Lucas 1998). The largest, most widely distributed, and most diverse genus of pantodont was *Coryphodon,* from the Late Paleocene-Early Eocene. It had a broad arch of large canines and incisors like a hippo. Lucas (1998) considered it a browser with a lifestyle similar to today's pygmy hippo. *Coryphodon* spread to Europe and Asia rapidly near the Paleocene–Eocene boundary and underwent a small radiation in Asia, producing animals such as *Asiocoryphodon* and *Eudinoceras,* before the

lineage's eventual extinction (and the end of the pantodonts) in the Middle Eocene.

Taeniodonta

Taeniodonts are an extinct order of primitive eutherians known from the Early Paleocene to Middle Eocene of western North America. In a comprehensive revision of the order, Schoch (1986) recognized nine genera belonging to two families: the small- to medium-sized, generalized, omnivorous conoryctids; and the medium to large upland-dwelling eaters of roots and tubers, the stylinodontids. (See Lucas et al. 1998 for a summary of information on the order.) The least derived taeniodont *Onychodectes* is roughly the size of an opossum and has its generalized skeleton (Carroll 1988; Lucas et al. in press). The main early scholars in the field were Wortman (1897), W.D. Matthew (1937), and Patterson (1949). Lucas and T.E. Williamson (1993) described a new genus of Early Paleocene taeniodont and revised the group's phylogeny (evolutionary history), placing the new genus *Schochia* as more derived than previously described conoryctids and less derived than the stylinodontids.

Taeniodonts had long, heavy tails, plantigrade clawed feet with five digits, and a tendency toward high-crowned teeth. The teeth of the bear-sized Early Eocene taeniodont *Stylinodon* were rootless and grew continuously, the cheek teeth rapidly wearing to dentine cylinders with a thin enamel rim (Carroll 1988). Greatly enlarged canines formed chisel-like cutting and crushing surfaces. *Stylinodon* may have used its strong, clawed forelimbs to dig up tough, abrasive food like roots and tubers. Schoch (1986) compared the taeniodonts to the modern aardvark, considering them solitary animals with restricted ranges, possibly returning to their burrows for shelter. He also suggested that in the Eocene, competition with more modern mammals (such as artiodactyls) forced later stylinodonts into great and greater specialization and finally to extinction. Schoch rejected animals from outside of North America, which others had placed in the Taeniodonta, and rejected tillodont or edentate ties to the group, tentatively deriving it from leptictimorphs, as did Lucas (1998).

The stylinodonts (Figure 6) are one of the first groups of eutherians to attain large size and hypsodont (high-crowned) teeth (Schoch 1986). Taeniodonts reached their maximum diversity in the Early Paleocene but were never common members of paleofaunas. Schoch (1986) suggested that they are rare in the fossil record because they inhabited upland areas and had food sources that partially freed them from the need to stay close to water. A dry ecosystem would allow for much less fossil formation. The stylinodonts may have derived much of the moisture they needed from roots and tubers, and the conoryctids probably also derived moisture from their prey and from plant material.

SUYIN TING AND JUDITH A. SCHIEBOUT

See also Proboscideans; Sirenians; Ungulates, Archaic

Works Cited

Andrews, C.W. 1906. A descriptive catalogue of the Tertiary Vertebrata of the Fayum, Egypt. London: British Museum (Natural History).

Carroll, R.L. 1988. *Vertebrate Paleontology and Evolution.* New York: Freeman.

Chow, M.C. 1960. *Prodinoceras* and a summary of mammalian fossils of Sinkiang. *Vertebrata PalAsiatica* 4:99–102.

Chow, M.C., and Y.S. Tung. 1962. Notes on some new uintathere materials of China. *Vertebrata PalAsiatica* 6:368–74.

Chow, M.C., and B. Wang. 1979. Relationship between the pantodonts and tillodonts and classification of the order Pantodonta. *Vertebrata PalAsiatica* 17:37–48.

Cope, E.D. 1872. *Notice of Proboscidians from the Eocene of Southern Wyoming.* Proceedings of the American Philosophical Society, 12. Philadelphia: American Philosophical Association.

———. 1874. Report upon vertebrate fossils discovered in New Mexico, with description of new species. *Annual Report of the Chief Engineers, U.S. Army,* Appendix FF:589–606, Separatum, 1–18.

———. 1876. Report upon the extinct Vertebrata obtained in New Mexico by parties of the expedition of 1874. *U.S. Geographical Survey, West of the 100th Meridian.* Vol. 4, *Paleontology,* part 2. Washington, D.C.: U.S. Government Printing Office.

———. 1884. The Amblypoda. *American Naturalist* 18:1110–21, 1192–1202.

de Chardin, Teilhard. 1922. Les mammifères de l'éocène inférieur français et leurs gisements. *Annales de Paléontologie* 11:9–116.

Domning, D.P., C.E. Ray, and M.C. McKenna. 1986. *Two New Oligocene Desmostylians and a Discussion of Tethytherian Systematics.* Smithsonian Contributions to Paleobiology, 59. Washington, D.C.: Smithsonian Institution Press.

Gazin, C.L. 1953. *The Tillodontia: An Early Tertiary Order of Mammals.* Smithsonian Miscellaneous Collections, 121(10). Washington, D.C.: Smithsonian Institution Press.

Gingerich, P.D., and G.F. Gunnell. 1979. *Systematics and Evolution of the Genus* Esthonyx *(Mammalia, Tillodontia) in the Early Eocene of North America.* Contributions from the Museum of Paleontology, 25(7). Ann Arbor: Museum of Paleontology, University of Michigan.

Granger, W. 1918. *New Tillodont Skull from the Huerfano Basin, Colorado (Abstract).* Bulletin of the Geological Society of America, 29. Boulder, Colorado: Geological Society of America.

Gregory, W.K. 1957. *Evolution Emerging.* 2 vols. New York: Macmillan.

Hay, O.P. 1924. Notes on the osteology and dentition of the genera *Desmostylus* and *Cornwallius. Proceedings of the United States National Museum* 65 (8):1–8.

Leidy, J. 1868. Notice of some remains of extinct pachyderms. *Proceedings of the Academy of Natural Sciences of Philadelphia* 20:230–33.

———. 1871. Remarks on fossil vertebrates from Wyoming. *Proceedings of the Academy of Natural Sciences of Philadelphia* 23:228–29.

———. 1872. On some new species of Mammalia from Wyoming. *Proceedings of the Academy of Natural Sciences of Philadelphia* 1872:167–69.

Lucas, S.G. 1982. The phylogeny and composition of the order Pantodonta (Mammalia: Eutheria). *Third North American Paleontological Convention Proceedings* 2:337–42.

———. 1987. Paleopathology of early Cenozoic *Coryphodon* (Mammalia: Pantodonta). *Journal of Vertebrate Paleontology* 7 (2):145–54.

———. 1989. Fossil mammals and Paleocene-Eocene boundary in Europe, North America, and Asia. *28th International Geological Congress (Washington, D.C.) Abstracts* 2:335.

———. 1998. Pantodonta. *In* C.M. Janis, K.M. Kathleen, and L.L. Jacobs (eds.), *Evolution of Tertiary Mammals of North America.* Cambridge and New York: Cambridge University Press.

Lucas, S.G., R.M. Schoch, and T.E. Williamson. 1998. Taeniodonta. *In* C.M. Janis, K.M. Kathleen, and L.L. Jacobs (eds.), *Evolution of Tertiary Mammals of North America.* Cambridge and New York: Cambridge University Press.

Lucas, S.G., and T.E. Williamson. 1993. A new taeniodont from the Paleocene of the San Juan Basin, New Mexico. *Journal of Mammalogy* 74 (1):175–79.

Marsh, O.C. 1871. Notice of some new fossil mammals from the Tertiary formation. *American Journal of Science and Arts,* ser. 3, 2:35–44.

Marsh, O.C. 1873a. Notice of new Tertiary mammals (continued). *American Journal of Science and Arts* 5:485–88.

———. 1873b. On the gigantic fossil mammals of the order Dinocerata. *American Journal of Science* ser. 3, 5:117–22.

———. 1875. New order of Eocene mammals. *American Journal of Science* 9:221.

———. 1885. *Dinocerata, a Monograph of an Extinct Order of Gigantic Mammals.* U.S. Geological Survey Monographs, 10. Washington, D.C.: U.S. Government Printing Office.

Marshall, L., and C. de Muizon. 1988. The dawn of the Age of Mammals in South America. *National Geographic Research* 4:23–55.

Matthew, W.D. 1937. *Paleocene Faunas of the San Juan Basin, New Mexico.* Transactions of the American Philosophical Society, new ser., 30. Philadelphia: American Philosophical Society.

Matthew, W.D., W. Granger, and G.G. Simpson. 1929. Additions to the fauna of the Gashato Formation of Mongolia. *American Museum Novitates* 376:1–12.

McKenna, M.C. 1975. Toward a phylogenetic classification of the Mammalia. *In* W.P. Luckett and F.S. Szalay (eds.), *Phylogeny of the Primates.* New York: Plenum; London: Plenum, 1976.

McKenna, C.M., and E. Manning. 1977. Affinities and palaeobiogeographic significance of the Mongolian Paleocene genus *Phenacolophus. Gebios* 1:61–85.

Osborn, H.F. 1898. Evolution of the Amblypoda. Part 1, Taligrada and Pantodonta. *Bulletin of the American Museum of Natural History* 10:169–218.

Patterson, B. 1934. A contribution to the osteology of Titanoides and the relationships of the Amblypoda. *Proceedings of the American Philosophical Society* 73:71–101.

———. 1939. New Pantodonta and Dinocerata from the upper Paleocene of western Colorado. *Geological Series, Field Museum of Natural History, Fieldiana Geology* 6 (24):351–84.

———. 1949. Rates of evolution in taeniodonts. *In* G. Jepsen, G.G. Simpson, and E. Mayr (eds.), *Genetics, Paleontology and Evolution.* Princeton, New Jersey: Princeton University Press.

Reinhardt, R.H. 1953. Diagnosis of the new mammalian order Desmostylia. *Journal of Geology* 61 (2):187.

Romer, A.S. 1966. *Vertebrate Paleontology.* 3rd. ed., Chicago: University of Chicago Press.

Russell, L.S. 1935. A middle Eocene mammal from British Columbia. *American Journal of Science* 29:54–55.

Schoch, R.M. 1986. *Systematics, Functional Morphology, and Macroevolution of the Extinct Mammalian Order Taeniodonta.* Peabody Museum of Natural History Bulletin, 42. New Haven, Connecticut: Peabody Museum of Natural History, Yale University.

Schoch, R.M., and S.G. Lucas. 1985. The phylogeny and classification of the Dinocerata (Mammalia, Eutheria). *Bulletin of the Geological Institutions of the University of Uppsala,* new ser., 11:1–50.

Sen, S., and E. Heintz. 1979. *Palaeoamasia kansui* Ozansoy 1966, embrithopode (Mammalia) de l'Éocène d'Anatolie. *Annales de Paléontologie (Vertébrés)* 65:73–91.

Shikama, T. 1966. *Postcranial Skeletons of Japanese Demostylia.* Palaeontological Society of Japan Special Papers, 12. Tokyo: Palaeontological Society of Japan.

Simons, E.L. 1960. *The Paleocene Pantodonta.* Transactions of the American Philosophical Society, new ser., 50. Philadelphia: American Philosophical Society.

Simpson, G.G. 1929. *A New Paleocene Uintathere and Molar Evolution in the Amblypoda.* American Museum of Natural History Novitates, 387. New York: American Museum of Natural History.

———. 1937a. *The Fort Union of the Crazy Mountain Field and Its Mammalian Fauna.* U.S. National Museum Bulletin. Washington, D.C.: U.S. Government Printing Office.

———. 1937b. *Notes on the Clark Fork, Upper Paleocene Fauna.* American Museum of Natural History Novitates, 954. New York: American Museum of Natural History.

———. 1945. *The Principles of Classification and a Classification of Mammals.* Bulletin of the American Museum of Natural History. New York: American Museum of Natural History.

Sinclair, W.J., and W. Granger. 1912. Notes on the Tertiary deposits of the Bighorn Basin. *Bulletin of the American Museum of Natural History* 31 (5):57–67.

Stucky, R.K., and L. Krishtalka. 1983. Revision of the Wind River faunas, early Eocene of central Wyoming. Part 4, Tillodontia. *Annals of Carnegie Museum* 52:375–91.

Ting, S., J.A. Schiebout, and M.C. Chow. 1987. A skull of *Pantolambdodon,* North China (Mammalia, Pantodonta) from Ningxia. *Journal of Vertebrate Paleontology* 7:155–61.

Ting, S.Y., and J.J. Zheng. 1989. The affinities of *Interogale* and *Anchilestes* and the origin of Tillodontia. *Vertebrata PalAsiatica* 27 (2):77–86.

Tong, Y.S. 1978. Late Paleocene mammals of the Turfan basin, Sinkiang. *Memoirs of the Institute of Vertebrate Paleontology and Paleoanthropology, Academia Sinica* 13:82–101.

———. 1979. Fossils of early Eocene Dinocerata from the Chijiang basin. *In Mesozoic and Cenozoic Redbeds in Southern China.* Beijing: Science Press.

———. 1982. Chinese uintathere and the evolution of the Dinocerata. *Journal of Paleontology* 56 (2, suppl.):2, 28.

VanderHoof, V.L. 1937. A study of the Miocene sirenian *Desmostylus. University of California Publications, Bulletin of the Department of Geological Sciences* 24 (8):169–262.

Wheeler, W.H. 1961. *Revision of the Uintathere.* Peabody Museum of Natural History, Yale University Bulletin 14, New Haven, Connecticut: Peabody Museum of Natural History, Yale University.

Wood, H.E. 1923. The problem of *Uintatherium* molars. *Bulletin of the American Museum of Natural History* 48:599–604.

Wortman, J.L. 1897. The Ganodonta and their relationship to the Edentata. *Bulletin of the American Museum of Natural History* 9:59–110.

Young, C.C. 1937. An early Tertiary vertebrate fauna from Yuanchu. *Bulletin of the Geological Survey of China* 17 (3–4):413–38.

Zhou, M.Z., and B.Y. Wang. 1979. Relationships between the pantodonts and tillodonts and classification of the Order Pantodonta. *Vertebrata PalAsiatica* 17:37–48.

Further Reading

Carroll, R.L. 1988. *Vertebrate Paleontology and Evolution.* New York: Freeman.

Domning, D.P., C.E. Ray, and M.C. McKenna. 1986. *Two New Oligocene Desmostylians and a Discussion of Tethytherian Systematics.* Smithsonian Contributions to Paleobiology, 59. Washington, D.C.: Smithsonian Institution Press.

Janis, C.M., K.M. Kathleen, and L.L. Jacobs (eds.). 1998. *Evolution of Tertiary Mammals of North America.* Cambridge and New York: Cambridge University Press.

Schoch, R.M. 1986. *Systematics, Functional Morphology, and Macroevolution of the Extinct Mammalian Order Taeniodonta.* Peabody Museum of Natural History Bulletin, 42. New Haven, Connecticut: Peabody Museum of Natural History, Yale University.

Simons, E.L. 1960. *The Paleocene Pantodonta.* Transactions of the American Philosophical Society, new ser., 50. Philadelphia: American Philosophical Society.

PLACENTALS: MINOR PLACENTAL ORDERS OF SMALL BODY SIZE

There are several extinct groups of small-bodied, placental mammals that are understood poorly in terms of their evolutionary relationships and ecology. These animals, including the Anagalidae, Apatemyidae, Mixodectidae, Palaeoryctidae, Pantolestidae, and Ptolemaiidae, have little in common except for the facts that (1) no one is entirely sure how they relate to living (present-day) or better-known fossil groups and (2) they are represented primarily by skulls, jaws, and teeth from Tertiary deposits from North America, Eurasia, and (in some cases) Africa. This entry summarizes available information on these relatively obscure mammalian groups. Certain Cretaceous mammals (e.g., zalambdalestids) that may be relevant to one or more of the above taxa (groups; singular, taxon) are discussed elsewhere in this encyclopedia.

During the first half of the twentieth century, the fossil record of the Anagalidae from central Asia was believed to represent an early radiation of the living Scandentia (tree shrews). Several anagalid genera (groups of species; singular, genus) have been described from Paleocene to Oligocene sediments in China and Mongolia. The best specimens are of the Oligocene genus *Anagale* (Figure 1) and include relatively complete skulls, jaws, and postcranial (body skeleton) elements. The teeth of many of these specimens are heavily worn. This fact, in tandem with the large claws on its hands and spatulate (spoon-shaped) toes on its hind limb, has suggested to some scientists that *Anagale* was partially fossorial (i.e., a "digger"), or at least foraged in the subsurface, chewing appreciable amounts of grit-covered food.

Few scientists currently believe that anagalids are closely related to scandentians (e.g., McKenna 1963). Some believe that anagalids are related to a group of mammals including living macroscelidians (elephant shrews), lagomorphs (rabbits and pikas), and rodents. Morphological (structural) characters in support of this relationship include the shape of the lower incisors, the presence of molarlike premolars, large orbits (eye sockets) with a slight postorbital bar (which completes a bony ring around the eyeball), and ankle morphology. None of these characters are unique among mammals, however, so this arrangement is not necessarily definitive. Recent work based on mitochondrial and nuclear DNA sequences suggests that elephant shrews are not related to lagomorphs or rodents but to other African mammals, such as tubulidentates (aardvarks) and chrysochlorids (golden moles) (see Springer et al. 1997). As is the case for anagalids, the evolutionary relationships of elephant shrews have been very difficult to infer with confidence. This group is known exclusively from Africa and has a relatively long fossil history there, dating to the Late Eocene. Unfortunately, the molecular evidence referred to above supporting relationships among several African groups is unavailable for anagalids—and all other typically fossilized animals. Thus, the potential impact of extinct taxa on a possible mammalian "African clade" (unified group) cannot be taken into account using molecular evidence alone.

Apatemyids are known from the Paleocene through Oligocene of North America, and Paleocene to Eocene of Europe. With important exceptions, the group is known almost exclusively from jaws and teeth; exceptions are a single skull from the Late Oligocene of South Dakota *(Sinclairella)* and a few skeletons from the Middle Eocene of Germany *(Heterohyus)* (see Figure 2). These animals have elongate, enlarged upper and lower incisors and a reduced number of cheek teeth (only four in Eocene taxa such as *Apatemys*). The German *Heterohyus* specimens possess very elongate digits, akin to those of the living primate *Daubentonia* and the marsupial *Dactylopsila*. Like these animals, *Heterohyus* may have been a wood-boring insectivore (exposing grubs with its teeth and extracting them with wirelike fingers), occupying a niche similar to that of a woodpecker. Despite some well-preserved specimens, the Apatemyidae—although clearly a distinctive group of animals—has no clear relative among living mammals. Over the years they have been allied loosely with nearly a dozen different orders—both living and extinct. One possible arrangement, outlined by M.C. McKenna and S.K. Bell (1997), places apatemyids and a few other taxa near a group of mammals that includes the Carnivora.

The Mixodectidae is probably as enigmatic a group of mammals as one will encounter in the pages of this encyclopedia. Mixodectids are represented only by jaws, teeth, and a few skull fragments from Early Paleocene exposures in New Mexico, Wyoming, and Montana. F.S. Szalay (1969) regarded a single taxon from the Late Paleocene of France, *Remiculus,* as a mixodectid, but McKenna and Bell (1997) treated it as a nyctitheriid insectivoran. In any event, mixodectids—like apatemyids and many other mammals—possess enlarged lower incisors. Their cheek teeth are somewhat more primitive, retaining four lower premolars (in addition to the standard complement of three molars) in some taxa, as well as a prominent hypocone (an added cusp at the rear of the tooth, on the side nearest the tongue) on their upper molars. Again, this group's affinities are unclear; however, they consistently have been associated with the Tertiary Plagiomenidae, a group long thought to be related to the living Dermoptera (flying lemurs) of southeast Asia.

A few well-preserved specimens from the Paleocene and Early Eocene of western North America are known from the poorly defined family Palaeoryctidae. A single skull of *Palaeoryctes* (Figure 3) from the Paleocene of New Mexico was described by American Museum paleontologist W.D. Matthew in 1913 (at which time the "Paleocene" was not recognized as a geological epoch). More recently, palaeoryctids (e.g., *Eoryctes*) have been recovered from the basal Eocene of Wyoming. These animals possess wide, short upper molars with front and rear cusps that are close together. The lower molars have short, teardrop-shaped talonids (rear basin). Like many modern insectivorans, palaeoryctids lack zygomatic arches (cheekarches) and have an incompletely

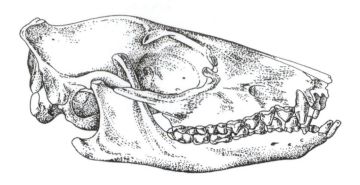

Figure 1. *Anagale gobiensis* from the Oligocene of Mongolia. From Simpson (1931), courtesy of the American Museum of Natural History.

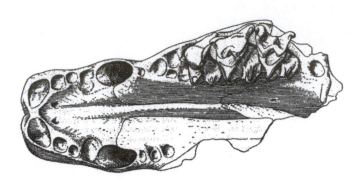

Figure 3. *Micropternodus borealis* from the Late Eocene of Montana. From Russell (1960), reproduced by permission of the Palaeontological Association.

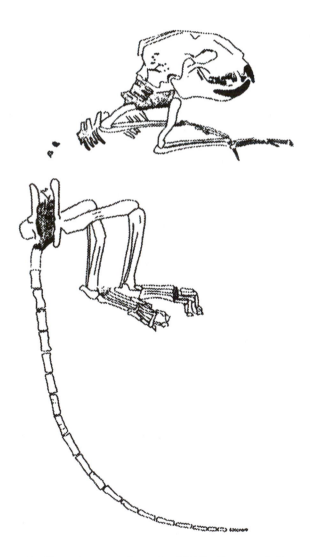

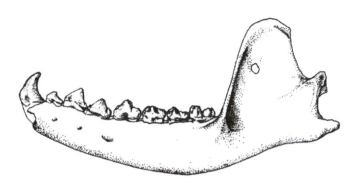

Figure 4. *Palaeoryctes puercensis* from the Late Eocene of New Mexico. From Matthew (1913), courtesy of the American Museum of Natural History.

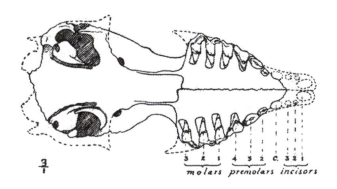

molars premolars incisors

Figure 5. *Celopatrodon ayeshae* from the Early Oligocene of Egypt. From Bown and Simons (1987).

Figure 2. *Heterohyus sp.* from the Middle Eocene of Germany. From Koenigswald and Schierning (1987), reprinted from *Nature* copyright © 1987, Macmillan Magazine, Ltd.

fused roof over the middle ear. The postcranial (body) skeleton of these taxa is virtually unknown. Very fragmentary material of possible palaeoryctids has been found in the Late Cretaceous of Spain and near the Paleocene-Eocene boundary in Africa.

The Micropternodontinae is another group known primarily from jaws and teeth; these animals may be related to palaeoryctids. In this group are numerous specimens from Paleocene exposures in central Asia (e.g., *Prosarcodon*), and the Late Eocene of Montana (e.g., *Micropternodus*) (see Figure 4). Like *Palaeoryctes,* these taxa possess lower molars with tall trigonids (front basin) and short talonids (heel of the tooth). Based on characters they share with palaeoryctids, both of these groups have consistently been associated with lipotyphlan insectivorans (particularly shrews, Caribbean shrews, tenrecs, and golden moles) and may actually represent lipotyphlans themselves.

Otters (in the carnivoran subfamily Lutrinae) did not constitute a significant element of the world's mammalian fauna until the Miocene. However, fossils that superficially resemble otters have been recovered in Paleocene through Oligocene exposures of North America and Europe; these animals have been classified in the family Pantolestidae. Less extensive records of pantolestids have been reported from Tertiary exposures in Africa and Asia. The upper molars of most pantolestids are blunt and rectangular, possibly adapted for crushing mollusks. The best-known pantolestid is probably *Buxolestes,* represented by articulated skeletal material from the Middle Eocene of Germany. This animal possesses a broad skull, as do otters, and remains of fish have been found inside one specimen's ribcage, presumably that individual's last meal.

An African group best known from the Eocene-Oligocene boundary in Egypt, the Ptolemaiidae, has been argued to be related closely to pantolestids. No ptolemaiid cranial or postcranial material is known, but the dentition of *Cleopatrodon* (Figure 5) (see Bown and Simons 1987) is reminiscent of pantolestids, as is its jaw joint. Again, however, such resemblances are not unique among mammals.

Much of the uncertainty regarding the affinities and ecology of extinct taxa is an understandable result of the paucity of their fossil record. It is simply difficult to say much about an extinct animal when all one has to work with are a few incomplete skulls, jaws, and teeth. This is not entirely the case for all of these taxa. Some are represented by relatively well-preserved skeletons (e.g., Figure 2). Nevertheless, mammals have a complex history; it is certainly possible that scientists never will understand completely the origins and interrelationships of a few of them.

ROBERT ASHER

See also Insectivorans; Placentals: Minor Placental Orders of Large Body Size

Works Cited

Bown, T.M., and E.L. Simons. 1987. New Oligocene Ptolemaiidae (Mammalia: ?Pantolesta) from the Jebel Qatrani Formation, Fayum Depression, Egypt. *Journal of Vertebrate Paleontology* 7:311–24.
Koenigswald, W. von, and H.-P. Schierning. 1987. The ecological niche of an extinct group of mammals, the early Tertiary apatemyids. *Nature* 326:595–97.
Matthew, W.D. 1913. A zalambdodont insectivore from the basal Eocene. *Bulletin of the American Museum of Natural History* 25 (5):307–14.
McKenna, M.C. 1963. New evidence against tupaioid affinities of the mammalian family Anagalidae. *American Museum Novitates* 2158:1–16.
McKenna, M.C., and S.K. Bell. 1997. *Classification of Mammals above the Species Level.* New York: Columbia University Press.
Russell, D.A. 1960. A review of the Oligocene insectivore *Micropternodus borealis. Journal of Paleontology* 34:940–49.
Simpson, G.G. 1931. A New insectivore from the Oligocene, Ulan Gochu Horizon, of Mongolia. *American Museum Novitates,* 505:1–22.
Springer, M.S., G.C. Cleven, O. Madsen, W.W. de Jong, V.G. Waddell, H.M. Amrine, and M.J. Stanhope. 1997. Endemic African mammals shake the phylogenetic tree. *Nature* 388:61–64.
Szalay, F.S. 1969. Mixodectidae, Microsyopidae, and the insectivore-primate transition. *Bulletin of the American Museum of Natural History* 140:195–330.

Further Reading

Carroll, R.L. 1988. *Vertebrate Paleontology and Evolution.* New York: Freeman.
Koenigswald, W. von, and H.-P. Schierning. 1987. The ecological niche of an extinct group of mammals, the early Tertiary apatemyids. *Nature* 326:595–97.
Springer, M.S., G.C. Cleven, O. Madsen, W.W. de Jong, V.G. Waddell, H.M. Amrine, and M.J. Stanhope. 1997. Endemic African mammals shake the phylogenetic tree. *Nature* 388:61–64.

PLACODERMS

Placoderms are an extinct class of armored jawed fishes that lived from the Silurian through the end of the Devonian Period. Their name, meaning "plated skin," alludes to their external covering of overlapping bony plates. Some of the earliest discoveries of placoderms were made in the Old Red Sandstones of Scotland and Europe. In the nineteenth century most scholars regarded them as allied to the modern ray-finned fishes. Only in the early twentieth century were they recognized as a distinct class of fishes. Today, scholars divide placoderms into some 200 known genera; these are arranged into seven major orders, the largest of which is the Arthrodira, meaning "jointed necks." This order comprises more than 60 percent of all known species.

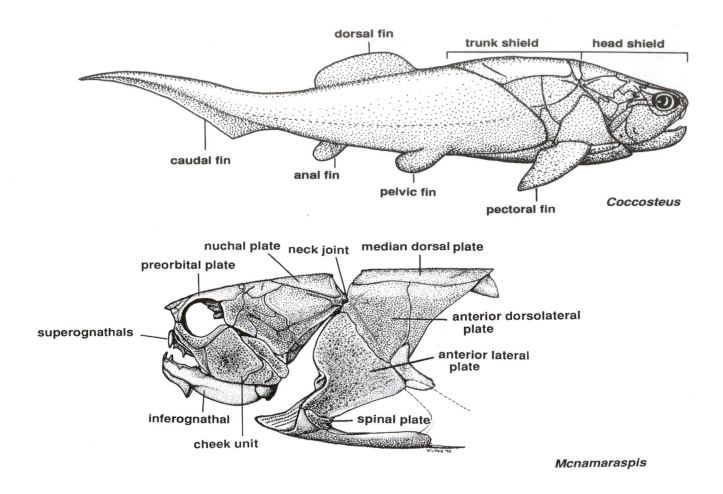

Figure 1. Basic structure of a placoderm. Above, reconstruction of the arthrodire *Coccosteus,* showing main features. Below, dermal armor of the arthrodire *Mcnamaraspis,* showing some of the major anatomical features.

Each of the seven major orders of placoderms is characterized by its pattern of bony plate shapes and sensory-line canal grooves. Each armored plate can be identified by its combination of shape, overlap areas for neighboring plates, the presence or absence of sensory-line canals, and external surface texture (the "dermal ornament"). Primitive placoderms have an ornament of simple wartlike tubercles (small knobs); advanced placoderms may develop linear or complex network patterns.

Placoderms are characterized by their overlapping series of bony plates, which form a protective cover around the head ("head shield") and the anterior (front) region of the body ("trunk shield"). In most placoderms, these shields articulate (are jointed together) by bony knobs and grooves, although in primitive forms there may be a sliding neck joint. The names of placoderm plates generally come from their position: e.g., the anterior median dorsal plate lies in the midline and occupies the front edge at the very top of the trunk armor; the "nuchal plate" covers the neck; the "suborbital" is below the eye (Figure 1).

The braincase of placoderms was well ossified (i.e., largely composed of bone), with layers of laminar perichondral bone, but in later groups it may be formed entirely of cartilage. The jaws are

simple bone rods that may have pointed, toothlike structures for gripping prey or areas with thickened tubercles or crushing toothplates. The jaw joint is simple. The lower jaws articulate against a knoblike quadrate bone mostly fused to the cheek plates. The eyes are surrounded by a sclerotic ring of three to five bones and are connected to the braincase by an eyestalk.

The placoderm body is generally torpedo-like, although some are flattened. There is only one dorsal fin, despite many erroneous early reconstructions showing two. The paired dorsal and pelvic fins have a sharklike shape and internal structure, and there is often a single anal fin. In primitive placoderms, the body is covered with thick bony platelets, each of which has similar ornamentation. In advanced placoderm lineages, the scale cover is lost.

The Stensioellida (e.g., *Stensioella*) and Pseudopetalichthyida (e.g., *Pseudopetalichthys*) are primitive orders of flattened placoderms with little bony armor. Their broad pectoral fins are reminiscent of rays, and their bodies have many small ornamented denticles (small, toothlike structures) set in the skin. Members of these groups are regarded as the most primitive of all placoderms, since they lack a number of bones found in all other groups. Both date from the Early Devonian black shales (Hunsrückschiefer) of the German Rhineland.

The Rhenanida is another group of flattened placoderms with broad pectoral fins. The skull may have many small bones, the trunk shield is short, and the tail is covered by small bony platelets. The group is known only from the marine Early Devonian of Europe and North America. Rhenanids are seen by many as being related to another group, the Acanthothoraci. Acanthothoracids are characterized by heavily ossified armor with elaborate surface ornamentation, as well as their skull pattern and short trunk shield. *Brindabellaspis* from Australia shows exquisite details of the braincase and pathways of cranial nerves and vessels (Young 1980).

The Ptyctodontida were a group of placoderms with strong crushing tooth plates and long whiplike tails. They resembled the living chimaerid fishes. They had very short trunk shields and reduced head bone cover, possibly adapted for feeding along the sea bottom on hard-shelled organisms. Members of this group are the only placoderms to show clear sexual dimorphism (physical differences between males and females): males have dermal bone-covered clasping organs. Superbly preserved ptyctodontid fossils come from the Late Devonian reef deposits at Gogo, Western Australia. Specimens of *Ctenurella gladbachensis* from similar-age rocks in Germany include whole bodies, clearly showing the outline of the fish. The Gogo ptyctodontids show a body covered by fine overlapping scales; other specimens lack this scale cover. Ptyctodontid fossils are also well known from Middle and Late Devonian deposits in Europe, North America, and Russia. Many are represented solely by their characteristic tooth plates. Such isolated fossils from North America indicate that the largest species of ptyctodontids had tooth plates about 15 to 20 centimeters long, suggesting a total fish length of approximately 2.5 meters (Denison 1978).

The Petalichthyida were placoderms with widely splayed pectoral fins and dermal bones ornamented with characteristic linear rows of little tubercles. The bones contain thick tubes that carry sensory-line nerves. The tubes are distinctly visible on the internal surface of the skull bones. Petalichthyids were probably bottom-dwelling fishes. Their remains are found in Europe, North and South America, Asia, and Australia. Reaching their peak of diversity in the Early Devonian, few species are found by Late Devonian. Unusual petalichthyid-like fishes called "quasipetalichthyids" are found in China, indicating that a minor local radiation of the group took place on the isolated South China continent. Well-preserved petalichthyid skulls also come from the Early Devonian limestones of New South Wales, Australia. Possibly the best specimens, preserved as whole fishes, come from the Early Devonian black shales of Germany (e.g., *Lunaspis*). Curiously, mouthparts of petalichthyids are never preserved, so the diet of this group is unknown.

Phyllolepids are distinguished by their flat armor, made up of a single large plate on both the top of the head and the trunk. The large plates are rimmed by a regular series of smaller plates. Plates are characteristically ornamented with fine radiating ridges and tubercles. *Phyllolepis* is known from the Late Devonian (Famennian stage) of Europe and North America, whereas the Australian phyllolepids *Austrophyllolepis* and *Placolepis* are found

in older rocks (Givetian-Frasnian) and appear to be more primitive. *Austrophyllolepis,* from southeastern Australia, shows the outline of the whole fish, along with impressions of the jaws, pelvic girdles, parasphenoid bone, and parts of the cheek. Phyllolepids may have hidden on a muddy lake bed waiting for unsuspecting prey to swim overhead. Then, using their unusually long tail to thrust upward, they could have caught their prey with their gripping jaws. Phyllolepids were probably blind, as they lacked sclerotic bones encircling the eyes, nor are there orbited notches in the head shield that would indicate the presence of eyes. Phyllolepids are now regarded as primitive arthrodires, possibly related to unusual forms like *Wuttagoonaspis* (Long 1984).

The Arthrodira have two pairs of upper jaw tooth plates (called superognathals). The skull has a regular pattern of bones, featuring eyes located to the sides of the head, and a separate cheek unit that was hinged along the side of the skull roof. The head and trunk shields are joined by a ball-and-socket type joint in all advanced arthrodires; as in primitive groups (e.g., actinolepidoids), there is a sliding neck joint. Arthrodires had sharklike bodies with a single dorsal fin; broad, fleshy, paired pectoral and pelvic fins; and an anal fin. The tail in primitive forms is covered with scales but is naked in advanced forms. Arthrodires are divided into primitive groups, which have long trunk shields with large spinal plates, and advanced groups, which have a shortened trunk shield with reduced spinals. Some advanced arthrodires have pectoral fins that are not fully enclosed by the trunk shield due to the absence of an encircling spinal plate (e.g., aspinothoracids).

The most primitive arthrodires were the long-shielded actinolepids, which flourished in the Early Devonian shallow seas and rivers, especially in Euramerica. These fish had a sliding neck joint; the head shield sat on a flat platform of bone that was present on the trunk shield. The phlyctaeniid arthrodires were the first arthrodires to evolve a primitive ball-and-socket neck joint. This innovation gave the head a greater vertical range of movement and permitted a wider gape. Some phlyctaenids have very widely splayed spinal plates and appear very streamlined. Their jaws had many small teeth and were probably used to grip soft-bodied prey. The unusual Australian arthrodire *Wuttagoonaspis* has a long skull with small distinct eye holes and a bizarre pattern of skull roof plates, quite unlike any other arthrodire. The bones have a highly distinctive ornament, somewhat akin to the radiating pattern seen in phyllolepids.

The Late Devonian Gogo fauna of western Australia includes more then 20 different arthrodires. These include the camuropiscid and incisoscutid arthrodires, small forms that flourished on the ancient Gogo reefs and were characterized by elongated armors, large eyes, and crushing tooth plates. *Rolfosteus* and *Tubonasus* evolved tubular snouts. These fishes may have been active top-water predators. *Incisoscutum* had a split in the trunk shield to free the pectoral fin. The most diverse group of arthrodires from Gogo are the plourdosteids. (The group is named after *Plourdosteus,* from the Late Devonian of Canada and Russia.) Many different plourdosteids occur at Gogo, each distinguished by a unique pattern of skull roof bones or dentition (e.g., *Harrytoombsia, Mcnamaraspis*). The lower jaws feature several well-developed cusps and toothed areas, with numerous teeth along the midline where jaws meet. The plourdosteids were predatory little fishes, ranging in size from about 30 to 50 centimeters. The broad, robust shape of their armor suggests that they hunted near the sea floor or within the cavities of the ancient reefs.

The giant dinichthyid arthrodires are known from huge skulls and bony plates excavated from the Cleveland Shales of Ohio and New York and from limestones in the Sahara Desert of Morocco. The largest of these had skull roofs more than a meter long, suggesting total lengths of six to eight meters. *Dunkleosteus* and *Gorgonichthys* had keen, sharp, pointed cusps on the lower and upper jaw tooth plates. Studies of the giant placoderms from the Cleveland Shale suggest that they may have preyed on other arthrodires or been carrion feeders. On the other hand, *Titanichthys,* from Morocco, was about seven meters long and had weak jaws that lacked sharp cusps, structures that suggest it may have been a filter feeder.

The antiarchs were placoderms mostly about 20 to 30 centimeters long, characterized by pectoral fins that are enclosed by bone ("pectoral appendages"). Most had segmented arms, although *Remigolepis* had short oarlike props. The head shield bore a single central opening for the eyes, nostrils, and pineal (third) eye. Compared to other placoderms, the trunk shield was very long and had two median dorsal plates. The group first appeared in the Silurian and was widespread by the Middle Devonian. The most primitive antiarchs (yunnanolepidoids) are found in Late Silurian–Lower Devonian rocks of Yunnan, China. These fish have a short, proplike pectoral fin that has not developed the ball-and-socket shoulder articulation of later antiarchs. Some more advanced forms have an incipient pectoral joint (e.g., *Procondylepis*). The head structure of sinolepidoids resemble the more primitive yunnanolepidoids but have reduced trunk shields and long, segmented pectoral appendages. Most come from China or Vietnam, although *Grenfellaspis,* from New South Wales, Australia, provided strong evidence that the Chinese and Australian terranes (crustal blocs) were physically near each other during the Late Devonian (Ritchie et al. 1992).

The most successful antiarchs were the bothriolepidoids and the asterolepidoids, which flourished in the Middle and Late Devonian. Asterolepidoids had long trunk shields with small heads and robust, short, segmented pectoral appendages. *Asterolepis* (Figure 2) is well known from Europe, Greenland, and North America, and *Remigolepis* from Greenland, China, and Australia. *Remigolepis* has a short, stout pectoral appendage that lacks a joint. The asterolepids first appeared in marine environments and soon after invaded freshwater river and lake systems.

The most widely dispersed and highly diverse placoderm of all time was undoubtedly *Bothriolepis,* a little antiarch having long, segmented arms, and known from more than 100 species found in the Middle-Late Devonian rocks worldwide, including Antarctica (Young 1988). Serially sectioned specimens of *Bothriolepis* show that inside the armor the fish had paired lunglike organs and a spiral intestine, preserved full of organic sediment. *Bothriolepis* was probably a mud-grubber that ingested organic-rich mud for its food. Also, it may have used its long pectoral appendages to push itself deeper into the mud for feeding. *Bothriolepis* is known mostly from freshwater deposits, as well as rarer marine sites. It dispersed around the Devonian world via shallow seaways, from which it could invade river systems.

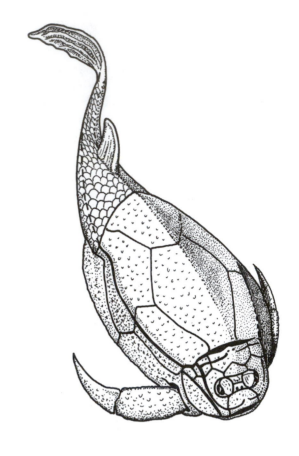

Asterolepis

Figure 2. The antiarch, *Asterolepis,* a common Old Red sandstone placoderm in Europe, Russia, and North America.

The relationship of placoderms within the gnathostomes (jawed fishes) have long been debated without reaching any general consensus. Many early scholars regarded some placoderms (e.g., phyllolepids) as jawless fishes. After first recognizing placoderms as a distinct class of fishes in the 1920s, different scholars then debated whether the group was more closely related to the chondrichthyans (e.g., sharks), or to the extinct acanthodian fishes. In the 1980s, some scholars argued for a close affinity between placoderms and osteichthyan fishes (group that includes today's bony fishes), based primarily on the extensive development of bone in the dermal skeleton of both groups. Young (1986) has summarized the data relevant to placoderm relationships. One characteristic that unites placoderms and chondrichthyans is the clasping organs in males for internal fertilization (although these are preserved in only one group of placoderms, the ptyctodontids). Placoderms and chondrichthyans share other characters. An eye-stalk connects the eyeball to the braincase. The structure of the pectoral and pelvic fins are similar, as is the shape of the braincases. Small rings of cartilage around the nasal area (annular cartilages) also support the close affinity of the two groups. The general shape of the bodies in predatory placoderms, like in *Coccosteus,* is also reminiscent of sharks and suggests that the absence of a swim-bladder was a primitive feature in the two groups.

Interrelationships among placoderms are also not clear. However, a view widely held by placoderm specialists is that the ptyctodontids, rhenanids, and acanthothoracids are probably the most primitive placoderm groups, whereas the antiarchs, arthrodires, and phyllolepids are considered the most advanced orders. Goujet and Young (1995) provide a useful summary of this topic.

Placoderm fossils are useful biostratigraphic markers because even partial plates are often identifiable down to the species level. As a result, placoderms have proven useful in correlating stratigraphic sequences around the world, especially those that were laid down in fresh water. Their remains also have been helpful in reconstructing ancient continental alignments (paleogeography) (Long 1993).

E. Stensiö (1969) wrote the first major works on the anatomical structure of placoderms; in recent years, they have been followed up by numerous publications on the superb, three-dimensional preserved placoderms from the Gogo Formation in western Australia and the Taemas district of southeastern Australia (e.g., Young 1980). Good overall summaries on placoderm morphology and their biostratigraphic uses can be found in Stensiö (1969), Denison (1978), Long (1993, 1995), and Janvier (1996).

JOHN A. LONG

See also Pharyngeal Arches and Derivatives

Works Cited

Denison, R.H. 1978. Placodermi. *In* H.-P. Schultze (ed.), *Handbook of Paleoichthyology.* Vol. 2, Stuttgart and New York: Gustav Fischer.

Goujet, D., and G.C. Young. 1995. Interrelationships of placoderms revisited. *Géobios (memoire speciál)* 19:89–96.

Janvier, P. 1996. *Early Vertebrates.* Oxford: Clarendon; New York: Oxford University Press.

Long, J.A. 1984. New phyllolepids from Victoria and ther relationships of the group. *Proceedings of the Linnean Society of New South Wales* 107:263–308.

———. (ed.). 1993. *Palaeozoic Vertebrate Biostratigraphy and Biogeography.* London: Belhaven; Baltimore, Maryland: Johns Hopkins University Press, 1994.

———. 1995. *The Rise of Fishes: 500-Million-Years of Evolution.* Baltimore, Maryland: Johns Hopkins University Press.

Ritchie, A., S.-T. Wang, G.C. Young, and G.-R. Zhang. 1992. The Sinolepidae, a family of antiarchs (placoderm fishes) from the Devonian of South China and eastern Australia. *Records of the Australian Museum* 44 (3):319–70.

Stensiö, E.A. 1969. Elasmobranchiomorphi Placodermata Arthrodires. *In* J.P. Piveteau (ed.), *Traité de Paléontologie.* Paris: Masson.

Young, G.C. 1980. A new Early Devonian placoderm from New South Wales, Australia, with a discussion of placoderm phylogeny. *Palaeontographica* 167A:10–76.

———. 1986. The relationships of placoderm fishes. *Zoological Journal of the Linnean Society* 88 (1):1–57.

———. 1988. Antiarchs (placoderm fishes) from the Devonian Aztec Siltstone, southern Victoria Land, Antarctica. *Palaeontographica* 202A:1–125.

PLACODONTS

The Placodontia were a group of predominantly bottom-dwelling, mollusc-eating marine reptiles of the Middle to uppermost Triassic (approximately 220 to 195 million years ago). They range in size up to approximately 1.5 meters in length. Their geographic range was restricted to the Tethys sea (forerunner of today's Mediterranean) and adjacent waters of circum-Mediterranean countries. Isolated examples of their large, flat, crushing teeth were originally attributed to pycnodont fishes (a type of primitive ray-finned fish). Owen (1858) correctly recognized their reptilian nature and grouped placodonts with plesiosaurs and their relatives within the Sauropterygia (Owen 1860). After some dissent (Kuhn-Schnyder 1980, 1989; Mazin 1982; Pinna 1989), this view has come full circle, and recent studies accept the Placodontia as sauropterygians (Rieppel 1995, 1997; Storrs 1991, 1993). Landmark studies of the group were conducted in the nineteenth century by von Meyer (1863) and in the early part of this century by Drevermann (1922, 1928, 1933), followed by other important studies by Peyer (1931, 1935), von Huene (1933, 1936), and Kuhn-Schnyder (1942, 1965).

The majority of placodont remains come from the Middle Triassic limestones of the Muschelkalk epicontinental seaway of Germany and from restricted basin black shales of Switzerland and northern Italy (Pinna 1990). Rarer or generally less well preserved remains are known from other Triassic units in Germany, Austria, France, Netherlands, Hungary, Poland, Rumania, Spain, Turkey, Tunisia, Egypt, and Israel (Pinna 1990; Pinna and Mazin 1993). The Upper Triassic tempestite bone beds of southwest England have produced rare dermal scutes (individual bony armor plates) that may also belong to placodonts (Storrs 1994). The sedimentology of these fossiliferous rocks and the unusual morphology of the group indicate that placodonts inhabited coastal and shallow sea environments. Like all sauropterygians, the placodonts were secondarily aquatic reptiles—they returned to the marine environment after evolving from terrestrial ancestors. The ancestral placodonts are now widely considered to have evolved from diapsid ancestors (diapsids are one of the major groups of amniotes or "reptiles") (Rieppel 1995; Storrs 1991; Sues 1987).

H.-D. Sues (1987) first recognized the diapsid affinities of placodonts but did not suggest a precise position for the group within the Neodiapsida. Zanon (1989) considered a sister-group relationship of Placodontia and Sauropterygia, and phylogenetic analysis by Storrs (1991, 1993) indicated that placodonts may occupy a position within Sauropterygia between the rather primitive (plesiomorphic) Pachypleurosauria and more advanced stem group "nothosaurs." The most recent studies (Rieppel 1994,

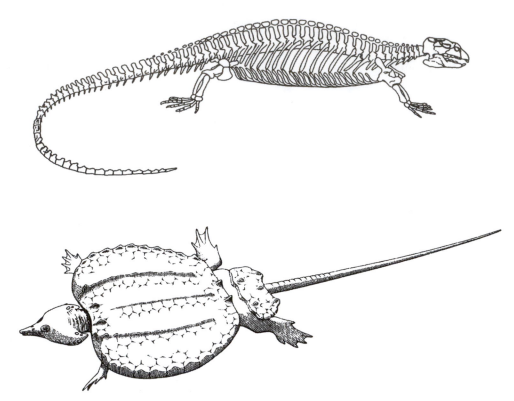

Figure 1. Two placodonts. *Top, Placodus gigas,* skeletal reconstruction; *bottom, Psephoderma alpinum,* life reconstruction. *Top,* from Peyer (1950); *bottom,* from Pinna and Nosotti (1989), copyright © 1989 by Società Italiana de Scienze Naturali, reprinted with permission.

1995) conclude that placodonts are the basal sister group to all other sauropterygians. They share with pachypleurosaurs, "nothosaurs," and plesiosaurs the following derived conditions: (1) a euryapsid skull condition, in which there is a single large opening (upper temporal fenestra) in the upper rear part of the skull; (2) loss of the lachrymal bone (a facial bone that lies just in front of the orbit, or eye opening); (3) a fixed articulation of the palate with skull base; (4) a reversed relationship of dermal (membrane-derived) and endochondral (cartilage-derived) bones in the shoulder girdle; (5) characteristic holes in the shoulder girdle (pectoral fenestration); and (6) an angulated humerus (proximal forelimb bone), among other features.

Placodontia is generally separated into two subdivisions, the nonarmored (and presumably more primitive) Placodontoidea, and the armored Cyamodontoidea (Nosotti and Pinna 1993, 1996; Rieppel 1995; Rieppel and Zanon 1997). The former includes *Placodus* and *Paraplacodus;* the latter *Cyamodus, Protenodontosaurus, Placochelys, Psephoderma,* and *Henodus.* Two or three other problematic genera may also belong. All placodonts are characterized by durophagous, crushing teeth on the palate; a broad body; elongate tail; reduced neck; and some degree of limb-dominated propulsion. Some cyamodontoids have a particularly broad, flat, superficially turtlelike, rigid carapace (shell) composed of numerous articulating bony plates, and, on occasion, a variety of osteoderms (bony dermal plates) fused to the back of the skull (Pinna and Nosotti 1989).

The skull of placodonts is stout and rigid, with a broad cheek region or temporal arch below the single upper temporal fenestra typical of sauropterygians (Drevermann 1928; Nosotti and Pinna 1993, 1996; Rieppel 1995; Sues 1987). The broad cheek is no doubt a response to increased chewing stresses related to a diet of molluscs. Such a diet is obvious from the anvil-like teeth on the palate and normally also on the maxilla (main upper jawbone) and dentary (main lower jawbone). Some seemingly advanced forms, such as *Henodus,* show a tendency to reduce the number of teeth. At the very front of the upper and lower jaws, placodontoids possess procumbent (forward-projecting), peglike incisors that were perhaps used to lever molluscs from rocks or to root about in bottom muds. Huene (1933) noted an apparent correlation of *Placodus* teeth with brachiopod accumulations *(Terebratula),* which may support the idea that placodonts browsed along the bottom. Foramina (small holes) on the snout possibly housed sensory nerves that gave the animal a heightened tactile sense useful in exploring muddy substrates. The broad, high skull and high coronoid process projecting upward from the lower jaw indicate the presence of large jaw-closing muscles and a powerful bite.

As currently comprised, cyamodontoids exhibit two basic body types. Most genera have an elongate and very narrow snout, toothless at the front, which scholars believe helped the animal extract endobionts (burrowing invertebrates) from soft substrates, (Mazin and Pinna 1993). *Henodus* is unique. It possesses a very broad, flat-ended muzzle and only remnant teeth in the back of the mouth (Huene 1936). Its behavior is less clear, but scholars hypothesize that it included bottom-walking and mud-grubbing for relatively soft invertebrates (Mazin and Pinna 1993). Found in the Carnian Gipskeuper of southern Germany, *Henodus* seems to have been less fully marine than its cousins, for the Gipskeuper was a brackish lagoon deposit related to the Keuper regression (a time of dropping sea levels). The broad, armored carapace of all cyamodontoids suggests that they may have protected themselves from potential predators by holding themselves close to the bottom (Pinna and Nosotti 1989). The heavy bony plates may have supplemented the dense skeleton of cyamodontoids to produce negative buoyancy.

Paleogeographic study suggests that placodonts originated along the northern Tethyan coast and soon diverged to form the placodontoid and cyamondontoid lineages (Rieppel 1995). They may have entered the Germanic Basin through an eastern seaway gate, and thereafter became well established in the Muschelkalk sea. The extinction of the Placodontia at the end of the Triassic may have concluded a period of decline caused by the general withdrawal of the Triassic sea from Europe during the Keuper regression. The extinction can most probably be correlated with overall environmental factors linked to the breakup of Tethys and the disappearance of the shallow marginal platform environments to which placodonts were adapted (Pinna and Mazin 1993).

GLENN W. STORRS

See also Aquatic Locomotion; Aquatic Reptiles

Works Cited

Agassiz, L. 1833–45. *Recherches sur les poissons fossiles.* Vol. 2, Neufchatel: Petitpierre.

Drevermann, F. 1922. Das Skelett der Placodontier. *Paläontologische Zeitschrift* 4:98–104.

———. 1928. Die Placodontier. 1, Schädel und Unterkiefer von *Cyamodus. Abhandlungen der senckenbergischen naturforschenden Gesellschaft* 38:291–309.

———. 1933. Die Placodontier. 3, Das Skelett von *Placodus gigas* Agassiz im Senckenberg-Museum. *Abhandlungen der senckenbergischen naturforschenden Gesellschaft* 38:319–64.

Huene, F.v. 1933. Die Placodontier. 3. Zur Lebensweise und Verwandschaft von *Placodus. Abhandlungen der senckenbergischen naturforschenden Gesellschaft* 4:365–82.

———. 1936. *Henodus chelypos,* ein neuer Placodontier. *Palaeontographica,* A, 84:99–148.

Kuhn-Schnyder, E. 1942. Über einen weiteren Fund von *Paraplacodus broilii* Peyer aus der Trias des Monte San Giorgio. *Eclogae Geologicae Helvetiae* 35:174–83.

———. 1965. Der Typus-Schädel von *Cyamodus rostratus* (Münster 1839). *Senckenbergiana Lethaea* 46a:257–89.

———. 1980. Observations on temporal openings of reptilian skulls and the classification of reptiles. *In* L.L. Jacobs (ed.), *Aspects of Vertebrate History.* Flagstaff: Museum of Northern Arizona Press.

———. 1989. The relationships of the Placodontia. *Neues Jahrbuch für Geologie und Paläontologie, Monatshefte* 1989:17–22.

Mazin, J.-M. 1982. Affinités et phylogénie des Ichthyopterygia. *Géobios Mémoire Spécial* 6:85–98.

Mazin, J.-M., and G. Pinna. 1993. Palaeoecology of the armoured placodonts. *Paleontologia Lombarda* 2:83–91.

Meyer, H.v. 1863. Die Placodonten, eine Familie von Sauriern der Trias. *Palaeontographica* 11:175–221.

Münster, G. 1830. *Über einige ausgezeichnete fossile Fischzähne aus dem Muschelkalk bei Bayreuth.* Bayreuth: Birner.

Nosotti, S., and G. Pinna 1993. New data on placodont skull anatomy. *Paleontologia Lombarda* 2:109–14.

———. 1996. Osteology of the skull of *Cyamodus kuhnschnyderi* Nosotti and Pinna 1993 (Reptilia, Placodontia). *Paleontologia Lombarda* 6:1–42.

Owen, R. 1858. Description of the skull and teeth of *Placodus laticeps* Owen, with indications of other new species of *Placodus,* and evidence of the saurian nature of that genus. *Philosophical Transactions of the Royal Society of London* 148:169–84.

———. 1860. *Palaeontology; or, A Systematic Summary of Extinct Animals and Their Geological Relations.* New York: Arno, 1980.

Peyer, B. 1931. *Paraplacodus broilii* nov. gen. nov. sp., ein neuer Placodontier aus der Tessiner Trias. Vorläufige Mitteilung. *Zentralblatt für Mineralogie, Geologie und Paläontologie,* B, 1931:570–73.

———. 1935. Die Triasfauna der Tessiner Kalkalpen. Weitere: Weitere Placodontierfunde. *Abhandlungen der Schweizerischen Paläontologischen Gesellschaft* 55:1–26.

———. 1950. *Geschichte der Tierwelt.* Zürich: Büchergilde Gutenberg.

Pinna, G. 1989. Sulla regione temporo-jugale dei rettili placodonti e sulla relazioni fra placodonti e ittioterigi. *Atti della Società Italiana di Scienze Naturali e del Museo Civico di Storia Naturale di Milano* 130:149–58.

———. 1990. Notes on stratigraphy and geographical distribution of placodonts. *Atti della Società Italiana di Scienze Naturali e del Museo Civico di Storia Naturale di Milano* 131 (7):145–56.

Pinna, G., and J.-M. Mazin. 1993. Stratigraphy and paleobiogeography of the Placodontia. *Paleontologia Lombarda* 2:125–30.

Pinna, G., and S. Nosotti. 1989. Anatomia, morfologia funzionale e paleoecologia del rettile placodonte *Psephoderma alpinum* Meyer, 1858. *Memorie della Società Italiana di Scienze Naturali e del Museo Civico di Storia Naturale di Milano* 25:15–50.

Rieppel, O. 1994. Osteology of *Simosaurus gaillardoti* and the relationships of stem-group Sauropterygia. *Fieldiana, Geology,* new ser., 28:1–85.

———. 1995. The genus *Placodus:* Systematics, morphology, paleobiogeography, and paleobiology. *Fieldiana, Geology,* new ser., 31:1–44.

———. 1997. Sauropterygia: Introduction. *In* J.M. Callaway and E.L. Nicholls (eds.), *Ancient Marine Reptiles.* San Diego, California: Academic Press.

Rieppel, O., and R. Zanon. 1997. The interrelationships of Placodontia. *Historical Biology* 12:211–27.

Storrs, G.W. 1991. *Anatomy and Relationships of Corosaurus alcovensis (Diapsida: Sauropterygia) and the Triassic Alcova Limestone of Wyoming.* Bulletin of the Peabody Museum of Natural History. New Haven, Connecticut: Peabody Museum of Natural History.

———. 1993. The systematic position of *Silvestrosaurus* and a classification of Triassic sauropterygians (Neodiapsida). *Paläontologische Zeitschrift* 67:177–91.

———. 1994. Fossil vertebrate faunas of the British Rhaetian (latest Triassic). *Zoological Journal of the Linnean Society* 112:217–59.

Sues, H.-D. 1987. On the skull of *Placodus gigas* and the relationships of the Placodontia. *Journal of Vertebrate Paleontology* 7:138–44.

Zanon, R. 1989. *Paraplacodu* and the diapsid origin of Placodontia. *Journal of Vertebrate Paleontology* 9:47A.

Further Reading

Benton, M.J. 1990. *The Reign of the Reptiles.* New York: Crescent.

———. 1993. Four feet on the ground. *In* S.J. Gould (ed.), *The Book of Life.* New York: Norton; London: Ebury Hutchison.

Mazin, J.-M., and G. Pinna. 1993. Palaeoecology of the armoured placodonts. *Paleontologia Lombarda* 2:83–91.

Nosotti, S., and G. Pinna. 1996. Osteology of the skull of *Cyamodus kuhnschnyderi* Nosotti and Pinna 1993 (Reptilia, Placodontia).

Paleontologia Lombarda 6:1–42.

Rieppel, O. 1995. The genus *Placodus*: Systematics, morphology, paleobiogeography, and paleobiology. *Fieldiana, Geology,* new ser., 31:1–44.

Storrs, G.W. 1993. Function and phylogeny in sauropterygian (Diapsida) evolution. *American Journal of Science* 293A:63–90.

Sues, H.-D. 1987. On the skull of *Placodus gigas* and the relationships of the Placodontia. *Journal of Vertebrate Paleontology* 7:138–44.

PLANTS: OVERVIEW

The enigma of exactly when plant life made the transition from the aquatic to terrestrial realm continues to be one of the most sought-after benchmarks in paleobotanical research. Although there appears to be several lines of evidence indicating that bacteria, algae, and lichens formed an extensive vegetational mosaic around 3.5 billion years ago and that endolithy (living within rocks or penetrating deeply into rocks) and the formation of cryptogamic crusts (crusts formed by bacteria, algae, and lichens) represent some of the most ancient modes of life on Earth, the vascular plants or tracheophytes are notably absent from the terrestrial and aquatic realms until the early part of the Phanerozoic. The process of terrestrialization appears to be linked, in part, with the amount of ozone present in the atmosphere. Once ozone reached levels that reduced the amount of harmful ultraviolet radiation reaching the planet's surface, sometime during the Late Pro-terozoic/Early Phanerozoic, terrestrialization proceeded quickly. Also required were a major reorganization from a haplobiontic to a diplobiontic life cycle (i.e., from a life cycle with a single multicellular stage to one with two multicellular stages) and evolution of a number of structural and functional modifications that allowed early land plants to adapt to a desiccating environment.

That the land plants evolved from the Chlorophyta or a green-algal ancestor is accepted commonly among botanists (Kendrick and Crane 1997a). Within the Chlorophyta, the Charophyceae (Charales and Coleochaetales) appear to be more closely related to the bryophytes (mosses, liverworts, and hornworts) and vascular plants than to other representatives of the green algae (Graham 1993; Kendrick and Crane 1997a; Kendrick and Crane 1997b). Ultrastructural and biochemical features shared between the land plants and the Charales and Coleochaetales include the presence of two types of chlorophyll, a and b: storage of the starch α-1,4 glucan in the chloroplast; persistent spindle; complex flagellar base; presence of glycolate oxidase; and cellulose in the cell walls.

The transition from a charophycean ancestor to that of an early land plant required a number of new innovations. Among these was the advent of a new life cycle. The Charophyceae possess a haplobiontic life cycle in which the zygote undergoes meiotic division, forming haploid zoospores that then germinate and develop into haploid multicellular gametophytes. In turn, the gametophytes produce egg and sperm that, under favorable con-

ditions, fuse to form a diploid zygote. Here the gametophyte phase dominates the life cycle and the sporophyte phase is represented only by the zygote (Figure 1). In sharp contrast, the life cycle of the land plants is characterized by two multicellular generations, with the diploid sporophyte dominating the life cycle (Figure 2). Although two hypotheses have been proposed for the evolution of the diplobiontic life cycle, it must be remembered that the fossil record provides no direct evidence to support either hypothesis.

The "homologous" or "transformation" theory, first proposed by Pringsheim (1878), was based on the idea that the green-algal ancestor of the land plants possessed morphologically identical (isomorphic) multicellular sporophyte and gametophyte generations (Figure 3). This hypothesis was supported by observations of some present-day members of the algal groups (Rhodophyta, Chlorophyta, and Phaeophyta), which exhibit two alternating free-living isomorphic forms. Here the gametophyte and sporophyte generations differ only in the number of chromosome in the cells: the gametophytes are haploid and produce gametes, while the sporophytes are diploid and produced spores. Proponents of this hypothesis believe sporophyte complexity increased, ultimately becoming the dominant phase of the life cycle. This hypothesis implies that the vascular plants evolved from the Chlorophyta and that the earliest plants should have free-living isomorphic gametophyte and sporophyte phases.

Recent investigations on the anatomically preserved gametophytes from the Early Devonian Rhynie chert locality in Scotland appear to support the homologous theory to some degree (Remy et al. 1993; Kenrick 1994). Specimens of *Langiophyton mackiei, Lyonophyton rhyniensis,* and *Kidstonophyton discoides* possess aerial axes that terminate in a bowl-shaped structure, called the "gametangiophore," which bears male or female structures (Figures 4, 5B). Although plants in this group were producing separate male and female reproductive structures, it is not known if these gametophytes were uni- or bisexual. The antheridia (sperm-producing organ) and archegonia (egg-producing organ) of these fossils closely resemble those of the living bryophytes (e.g., mosses) more than those of the tracheophytes (e.g., ferns and seed plants), but the antheridia of *L. rhyniensis* are more complex than that seen in any bryophyte or tracheophyte. The archegonia resemble those of modern liverworts. Though it is not yet possible to determine whether these gametophytes are related more closely to the bryo-

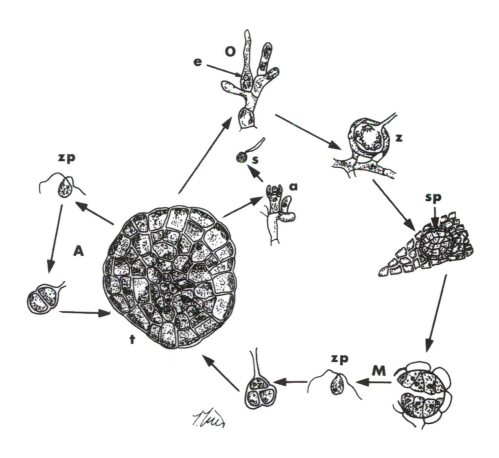

Figure 1. Life cycle of the freshwater green alga, *Coleochaete scutata* Brébisson. The thallus forms a pseudoparenchymatous haploid disc. Sexual reproduction is oogamous (only one flagellate sperm fuses with a non-flagellate egg cell), with each antheridium producing a flagellate spermatozoid. Each flask-shaped oogonium produces one egg. The spermatozoid swims into the oogonium, fertilizing the egg, and forming a diploid zygote. The zygote is retained on the gametophyte and ultimately becomes enveloped by another layer of cells. The zygote, oogonium, and extra layer of cells, now referred to as a "spermocarp," remain dormant through winter. In the spring, the zygote divides meiotically, producing 8–32 biflagellate zoospores that develop into new thalli. These algae are also able to reproduce asexually *(A)*, through production of biflagellate zoospores *(zp)* that develop into new thalli. Key: *t*, thallus; *a*, antheridium; *s*, flagellate spermatozoid; *o*, oogonium; *e*, egg; *z*, diploid zygote; *sp*, spermocarp, which consists of the zygote, oogonium, and an extra layer of cells; *M*, meiotic division; *zp*, zoospores; *A*, asexual reproduction; *zp*, zoospores, which develop into new thalli. Redrawn by Tania Treis from Lee (1989).

phytes or tracheophytes, the Rhynie chert flora provides the first clear evidence for alternation of isomorphic generations and a diplobiontic life cycle (Figure 5). Further discussion and details on this topic are provided by W. Remy and colleagues (1993) and P. Kenrick (1994).

Alternatively, proponents of the "antithetic" or "interpolation theory" believe that a green-algal ancestor of land plants had a haplobiontic life cycle that was dominated by the gametophyte. A delay in zygotic meiosis allowed the zygote to evolve into a multicellular sporophyte (Figure 6). L. Celakovsky (1874) first proposed this hypothesis, suggesting that the unicellular zygote gradually became a self-sufficient, photosynthesizing, multicellular sporophyte from its parasitic existence on a multicellular gametophyte. The living *Coleochaete*, a freshwater green algae, possesses such a life cycle (Figure 1), and examining the life cycle of a typical bryophyte indicates a similar but slightly more

advanced stage than that seen in *Coleochaete* (Figure 7). According to F.O. Bower (1935), the similarities between the *Coleochaete* and bryophyte life cycles provide sufficient evidence to explain the evolution of the vascular plants from a bryophyte ancestor. Recent systematic analyses (studies of evolutionary relationships) strongly support the antithetic hypothesis for origin of the diplobiontic life cycle from an ancestral charophycean haplobiontic life cycle (Mishler and Churchill 1985; Graham 1985, 1993; Graham et al. 1991).

Exactly when the vascular plants first evolved continues to be contentious. Reports of vascular plant remains from the Ordovician and Early Silurian are numerous (Pratt et al. 1978; Cai et al. 1996; Strother et al. 1996), but taken singly or collectively these remains do not demonstrate unequivocally the existence of land plants. Nevertheless, the microfossil record does provide evidence of highly resistant spore tetrads, cuticle (protec-

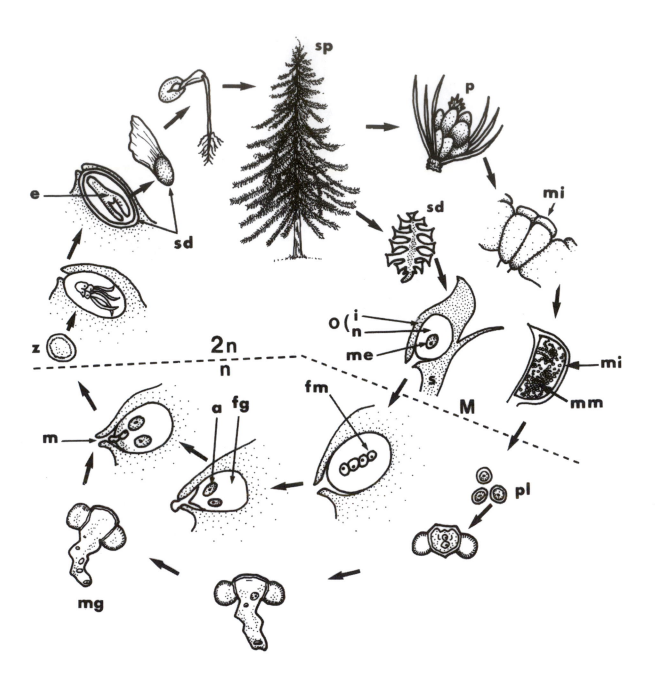

Figure 2. Life cycle of a typical conifer. The mature multicellular sporophyte produces pollen and seed-bearing cones. The pollen cones are composed of modified leaves called microsporophylls, upon which microsporangia are borne on the lower surface of the microsporophyll. Within each microsporangium, microspore mother cells undergo meiosis producing microspores called pollen grains that will develop into the male gametophytes. The seed cones consist of helically arranged ovuliferous scales; the upper surface of each scale bears ovules, or megasporangia (ovules consist of an integument and nucellus). Within the nucellus, the megasporocyte undergoes meiosis to produce four haploid megaspores. Of these, three degenerate and the remaining one, a functional megaspore, develops into the female gametophyte. Within the female gametophyte archegonia develop at the mycropylar end. Each archegonium produces an egg that will be retained in the female gametophyte even after fertilization has occurred. The male gametophyte gains access to the ovule through the micropyle and grows toward the archegonium. Sperm released from the male gametophyte unites with the egg, forming a diploid zygote. The zygote develops into an embryo, and at maturity the seed is released from the ovuliferous scale. Under favorable conditions the embryo resumes growth and develops into a young seedling that will ultimately grow into a mature plant. Key: *sp*, mature multicellular sporophyte; *p*, pollen; *sd*, seed-bearing cones; *mi*, microsporangium; *mm*, microspore mother cells; *M*, meiosis; *pl*, microspores (pollen grains); *mg*, male gametophytes; *s*, ovuliferous scales; ovules, which consist of an *i*, integument (part of ovule); *n*, nucellus (part of ovule); *me*, megasporocyte; *M*, meiosis, which produces four haploid megaspores; *fm*, functional megaspore; *fg*, female gametophyte; *a*, archegonium; *m*, micropyle; *z*, diploid zygote; *e*, embryo; *sd*, seed. Redrawn by Narda Quigley from Taylor and Taylor 1993.

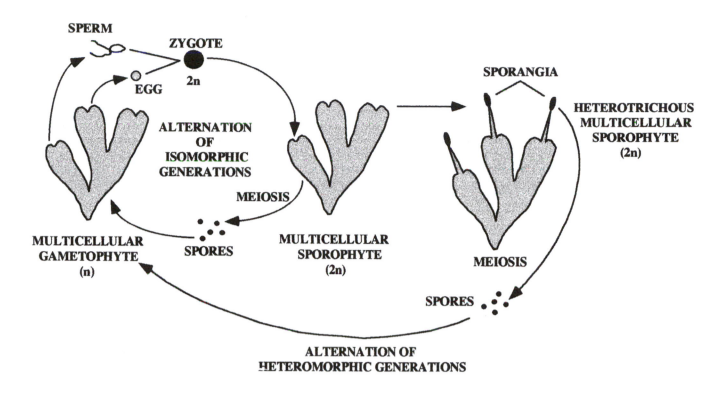

Figure 3. Origin of alternation of generations based on the homologous or transformation theory. This theory is based on the premise that the sporophyte in a green alga possessing alternation of isomorphic generations became structurally and physiologically more complex and ultimately dominated the life cycle, while the gametophyte became reduced. Modified from Taylor and Taylor (1993).

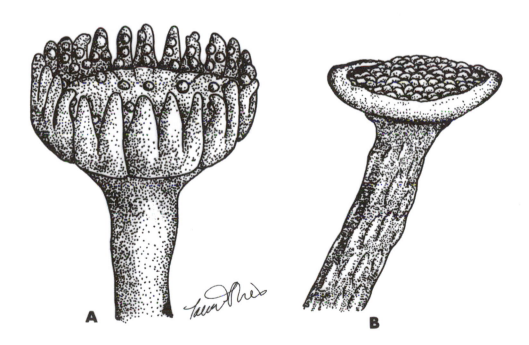

Figure 4. Male gametophytes from the Lower Devonian Rhynie chert of Scotland. *A*, a gametangiophore of *Lyonophyton rhyniensis*; *B*, a gametangiophore of *Kidstonophyton discoides*. Redrawn by Tania Treis from Remy et al. (1993).

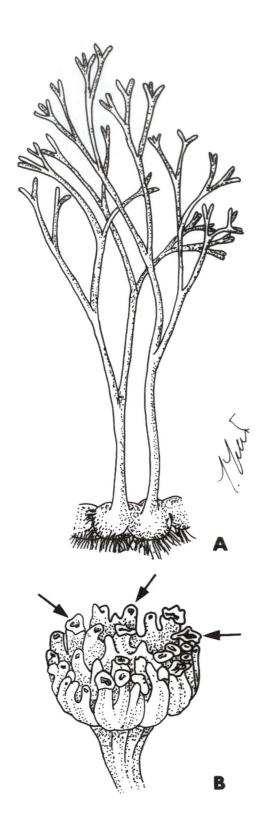

Figure 5. Proposed sporophyte-gametophyte combination. *A,* a reconstruction of the habit of the sporophyte *Horneophyton lignieri* (Kidston & Lang) Barghoorn. *B,* the putative archegoniate gametophyte of *Horneophyton,* called *Langiophyton mackiei,* showing a terminal gametangiophore. Symbol: *arrow,* archegonia. Redrawn by Tania Treis from Kenrick and Crane (1997a).

tive coating), and water-conducting cells (Gray 1993), all organs and tissues that are not found in algae. These fossils date from the plant-based Eoembryophytic (476–432 million years) epoch. That the spores are decay-resistant implies that the organism that produced them had evolved the biochemical pathways needed to synthesize and incorporate sporopollenin into their spore walls early in their evolutionary history. Moreover, the spores are arranged in a tetrahedral fashion, a pretty clear indication that these are haploid meiotic products. Although unequivocal plant megafossil remains are lacking for the Eoembryophytic, these organs and tissues are all diagnostic features of the vascular plants.

The appearance of *Cooksonia* (Figure 8) and *Baragwanathia,* the first unequivocal evidence of land plants during the Eotracheophytic (432–402 million years), from the Silurian of Europe, Australia, Bolivia, and China represents one of the most significant innovations in the evolutison and biodiversification of terrestrial land plants from a green-algal ancestor. Although the Eotracheophytic plant megafossil record is relatively sparse compared to that of the Eutracheophytic (402–256 million years), it documents a dramatic and rapid increase in land-plant diversity, abundance, and complexity from the Silurian into the Early Devonian.

The transition from the aquatic to terrestrial realm coincides with a number of key structural, physiological, and biochemical changes. These include a water-absorbing system, an anchoring system, a vascular system to transport water and nutrients, a structural support system, cuticle to prevent water loss, and stomata (pores) to facilitate gas exchange. The reproductive system incorporated desiccation-resistant propagules (e.g., spores) that would facilitate dispersal and ensure survival in a nonaqueous environment. While there is no way of knowing the order in which these features were incorporated into the early plants, the exquisitely preserved fossil plants from the Early Devonian Rhynie chert indicate that all were part of the land-plant bauplan (design) at least 400 million years ago.

Also of considerable importance is a hypothesis put forward by K.A. Pirozynski and D.W. Malloch (1975). These authors proposed that the terrestrial colonization and evolution of land plants

Figure 7. (on page 927 bottom) Life cycle of a typical moss. Spores germination results in the production of a simple protonema, which develops into a gametophyte. Sperm-producing antheridia and egg-producing archegonia are borne on the gametophytes. At maturity flagellated sperm released from the antheridia swim into each archegonium, fertilizing the eggs, and forming a diploid zygote. The zygote, which is retained on the gametophyte develops into a conspicuous sporophyte. The sporophyte is borne near the apex of the gametophyte and completely dependent on the gametophyte for nutrition. Each sporophyte produces a terminal sporangium, within which spore-mother cells undergo meiosis, producing haploid spores that are released when mature. Key: *s,* spore; *p,* protonema; *g,* gametophyte; *a,* sperm-producing antheridia; *ar,* egg-producing archegonia; *fs,* flagellated sperm; *e,* eggs; *z,* diploid zygote; *sp,* sporophyte; *ts,* terminal sporangium. Redrawn by Tania Treis from Taylor and Taylor (1993).

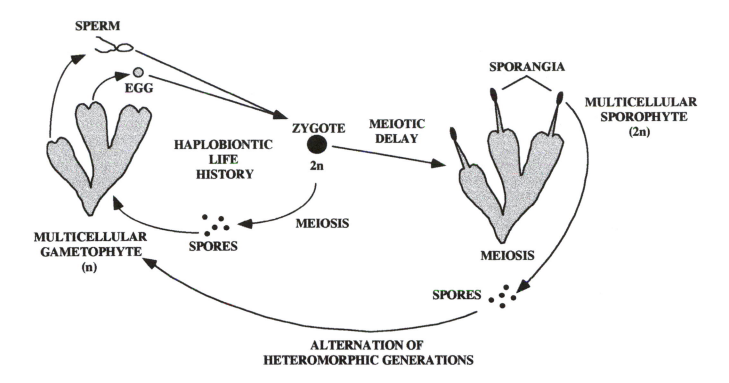

Figure 6. Origin of alternation of generations based on the antithetic or interpolation theory. This theory is based on the premise that a green alga possessing a haplobiontic life cycle with a dominant multicellular gametophyte allowed the sporophyte to evolve later due to a delay in zygotic meiosis. The unicellular zygote, which initially was parasitic on the gametophyte, ultimately evolved into a complex multicellular sporophyte. Modified from Taylor and Taylor (1993).

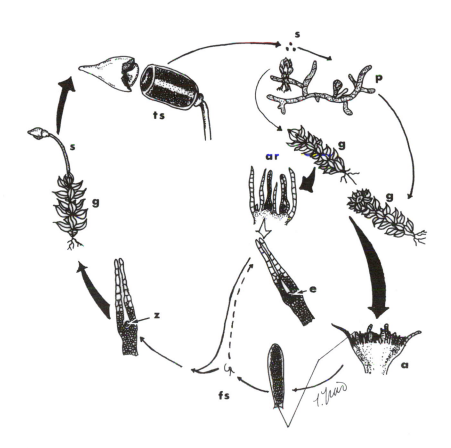

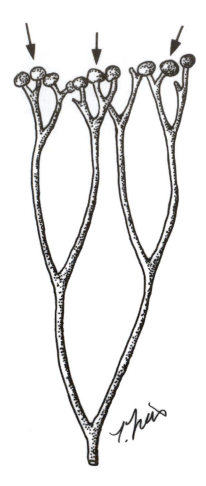

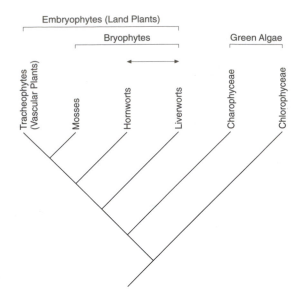

Figure 9. Cladistic relationships showing the monophyly of the land plants (embryophytes), with the Charales or Coleochaetales (Charophyceae), the sister group to the embryophytes. Note the basal position of the liverworts, with the mosses or hornworts occurring as the sister group to the vascular plants. Redrawn from Kenrick and Crane (1997a).

Figure 8. A reconstruction of a Lower Devonian plant, *Cooksonia caledonica*. These plants were simple, dichotomously branched, and leafless; they bore terminal kidney-shaped sporangia. Symbol: *arrows,* sporangia. Redrawn by Tania Treis from Stewart and Rothwell (1993).

may not have been possible without the establishment of a mutualistic relationship between an ancestor of the Coleochaetaceae-Charales lineage and an aquatic oomyceteous fungus. Recent studies by Remy and colleagues (1994) and T.N. Taylor and colleagues (1995) provide incontestable evidence for such endomycorrhizal symbioses in the Rhynie Chert paleoflora, demonstrating the antiquity of plant-fungal symbioses. In such partnerships plants benefit because the fungus increased the amount of phosphorus and nutrient that the plant could take up from the soil, whereas the fungus was afforded protection and provided with a source of carbon. There is little doubt that the evolution and establishment of mutualistic symbioses (those that benefit both parties) was of great significance for land-plant evolution, for it allowed the early land plants to occupy and prosper in what would have been a nutrient-deficient environment.

The monophyly of the land plants (embryophytes) is supported strongly by cladistic studies based on morphological and molecular characters, with the Charales or Coleochaetales (or a group containing both) being the sister group (the most closely related group) to the embryophytes (Figure 9) (Kenrick and Crane 1997a, 1997b). Although basal relationships among the embryophytes are far from being fully resolved, the best supported hypothesis indicates that the liverworts are basal, with the mosses or hornworts occurring as the sister group to the vascular plants. This theory implies that sister groups should appear in the fossil record at about the same time, but the bryophytes appear considerably later in the fossil record than do the vascular plants. As noted by Kenrick and P.R. Crane (1997a), the late appearance of the bryophytes is inconsistent with their predicted basal position and with Mid-Ordovician appearance of fossil plant-like remains that indicate a bryophyte-level land flora. This discrepancy however, may be due to factors that include collecting bias, lack of preservational potential, and inability of paleobotanists to recognize bryophyte fossils (Krassilov and Schuster 1984). Nevertheless, this gap in the plant fossil record clearly illustrates future avenues of research and the dire need for well-documented and exquisitely preserved embryophyte remains.

BEN A. LePAGE

See also Algae; Angiosperms; Bryophytes; Club Mosses and Their Relatives; Coniferophytes; Cycads; Defensive Structures:

Plants; Ferns and Their Relatives; Forests, Fossil; Fungi; Ginkgos; Gnetophytes; Gymnosperms; Horsetails and Their Relatives; Palynology; Plants: Adaptive Strategies; Plants: Mechanical Plant Design; Plants: Vegetative Features; Problematic Plants; Progymnosperms; Reproductive Strategies: Plants; Seed Ferns; Vascular Plants, Earliest

Works Cited

Bower, F.O. 1935. *Primitive Land Plants*. London: Macmillan.

Cai, S., S. Ouyang, Y. Wang, Z. Fang, J. Rong, L. Geng, and X. Li. 1996. An Early Silurian vascular plant. *Nature* 379:592.

Celakovsky, L. 1874. Über die verschiedenen Formen und die Bedeutung des Generationswechsels der Pflanzen. *Sitzungberichte der K. Böhmischen Gesellschaft der Wissenschaften*. N.p.

Graham, L.E. 1985. The origin of the life cycle of land plants. *American Scientist* 73:178–86.

———. 1993. *Origin of Land Plants*. New York: Wiley.

Graham, L.E., C.F. Delwiche, and B.D. Mischler. 1991. Phylogenetic connections between the "Green Algae" and the "Bryophytes." *Advanced in Bryology* 4:213–44.

Gray, J. 1993. Major Paleozoic land plant evolutionary bio-events. *Palaeogeography, Palaeoclimatology, Palaeoecology* 104:153–69.

Kenrick, P. 1994. Alternation of generations in land plants: New phylogenetic and palaeobotanical information. *Biological Reviews* 69:293–330.

Kenrick, P., and P.R. Crane. 1997a. *The Origin and Early Diversification of Land Plants: A Cladistic Study*. Washington, D.C.: Smithsonian Institution Press.

———. 1997b. The origin and early evolution of plants on land. *Nature* 389:33–39.

Krassilov, V.A., and R.M. Schuster. 1984. Paleozoic and Mesozoic fossils. *In* R.M. Schuster (ed.), *New Manual of Bryology*, vol. 2. Miyazaki: Hattori Botanical Laboratory, Nichinan.

Lee, R.E. 1989. *Phycology*. 2nd ed., Cambridge and New York: Cambridge University Press.

Mishler, B.D., and S.P. Churchill. 1985. Transition to a land flora: Phylogenetic relationships of the green algae and bryophytes. *Cladistics* 1:305–28.

Pirozynski, K.A., and D.W. Malloch. 1975. The origin of land plants: A matter of mycotropism. *BioSystems* 6:153–64.

Pratt, L.M., T.L. Phillips, and J.M. Dennison. 1978. Evidence of non-vascular land plants from the Early Silurian (Llandoverian) of Virginia, U.S.A. *Review of Palaeobotany and Palynology* 25:121–49.

Pringsheim, N. 1878. Über die Sprossung der Moosfrüchte. *Jahrbuch für Wissenschaftliche Botanik* 11:1–46.

Remy, W., P.G. Gensel, and H. Hass. 1993. The gametophyte generation of some Early Devonian plants. *International Journal of Plant Sciences* 154:35–58.

Remy, W., T.N. Taylor, H. Hass, and H. Kerp. 1994. 400 million-year-old vesicular arbuscular mycorrhizae (VAM). *Proceedings of the National Academy of Sciences, USA* 91:11841–43.

Stewart, W.N., and G.W. Rothwell. 1993. *Paleobotany and the Evolution of Plants*. 2nd ed., Cambridge and New York: Cambridge University Press.

Strother, P.K., S. Al-Hajri, and A. Traverse. 1996. New evidence for land plants from the lower Middle Ordovician of Saudi Arabia. *Geology* 24:55–58.

Taylor, T.N., W. Remy, H. Hass, and H. Kerp. 1995. Fossil arbuscular mycorrhizae from the Early Devonian. *Mycologia* 87:560–73.

Taylor, T.N., and E.L. Taylor. 1993. *The Biology and Evolution of Fossil Plants*. Englewood Cliffs, New Jersey: Prentice-Hall.

Further Reading

Edwards, D.E. 1997. Charting diversity in early land plants: Some challenges for the next millennium. *In* K. Iwatsuki and P.R. Raven (eds.), *Evolution and Diversification of Land Plants*. New York: Springer.

Graham, L.E. 1993. *Origin of Land Plants*. New York: Wiley.

Kenrick, P., and P.R. Crane. 1997. *The Origin and Early Diversification of Land Plants: A Cladistic Study*. Washington, D.C.: Smithsonian Institution Press.

Stewart, W.N., and G.W. Rothwell. 1983. *Paleobotany and the Evolution of Plants*. Cambridge and New York: Cambridge University Press; 2nd ed., 1993.

Taylor, T.N., and E.L. Taylor. 1993. *The Biology and Evolution of Fossil Plants*. Englewood Cliffs, New Jersey: Prentice-Hall.

PLANTS: MECHANICAL PLANT DESIGN

As plants evolved onto land and radiated (diversified and spread geographically) into different habitats, they had to adapt to a new environment that differed from that of their aquatic ancestors in many fundamental ways (Graham 1993). For instance, unlike their aquatic predecessors, whose plant bodies were constantly replenished and buoyed by water, the first land plants had to cope with the dehydrating effect of moving air and the mechanical effects of gravity and wind pressure (Niklas 1992). Plants were enabled to conserve water on land through the evolutionary innovation of a "cuticle," a layer of hydrocarbons and other chemicals that coats the exposed surfaces of aerial plant organs such as stems and leaves (Raven 1985). The cuticle is impermeable to water molecules, so water cannot pass through it from moist tissues and out into the drier atmosphere. In watery environments, the cuticle is a liability because it prevents water from diffusing into cells, movement that is essential for physiological processes. (In diffusion, substances move in and out of cells via the random, natural movement of all molecules.) As a result, the cuticle is absent or highly reduced on the surfaces of land plant roots, which absorb water from the environment. The cuticle is also not produced on the gametophyte generation (generation in which sexual organs are present) of many nonvascular land plants (mosses, liverworts, and hornworts). These plants can suspend physiological activity when water is limited. But, the sporophyte generations (the spore-bearing generations) of all land-dwelling vascular plants do produce a cuticle.

In addition to preventing the diffusion of water molecules, the cuticle is also impermeable to oxygen and carbon dioxide molecules, essential materials to photosynthesis and respiration (Kolattukudy 1981; Raven 1985). Accordingly, small holes perforate the cuticle to permit the exchange of gases between the moist surfaces inside the plant body and the drier atmosphere outside it. In the case of some bryophytes and all vascular plants, these perforations are called stomata (singular, stoma). Each stoma is flanked by two kidney-bean-shaped guard cells, which can expand or contract, depending on the availability of water to plant tissues. On either side of a stoma is a guard cell. When water is available in plant tissues, the guard cells swell and open, permitting gas diffusion. When water is not available, the guard cells shrink, closing the stoma to prevent excessive tissue dehydration.

Another important adaptation to plant life on land was the formation of specialized cells to conduct water and to transport nutrients dissolved in living cytoplasm. All but the very smallest land plants require these cells because water and metabolites diffuse from one cell to the next too slowly to keep pace with the metabolic demands of living cells elevated above ground, far from the source of water and minerals. The most efficient mechanical design for cells specialized for bulk flow is cylindrical, which permits rapid flow preferentially in one direction (Zimmermann 1983). In the case of a water-conducting cell, the best structure is a dead cell wall (in which there are no living materials or structures) so that the flow of water is unobstructed. Hydroids, which are the water-conducting cells found in some bryophytes, are dead, hollow cells whose longitudinal sides parallel the lengths of stem- and leaflike organs. Tracheids and vessel members, which are the water-conducting cells in vascular plants, are similarly shaped and oriented in stems, leaves, and roots. In nutrient-transporting cells, the living cytoplasm is retained because it is necessary for active metabolic transport (transport of substances that requires energy from the cell and specialized cell structures). Leptoids in some bryophytes and living phloem cells in vascular plants transport nutrients.

Land plants also had to cope with the mechanical forces of gravity and wind pressure (Niklas 1992; Vogel 1996). Almost all living plant tissues are composed primarily of water. Thus, aquatic plants are essentially neutrally buoyant—they neither sink nor rise in the water column, which means they do not experience the force of gravity that compresses the tissues of moderate- to larger-sized terrestrial plants. For very small and short land plants, like modern-day mosses, gravity is essentially negligible, so aerial plant organs can be mechanically supported by thin-walled, living tissues (parenchyma cells), such as tissues that constitute the flesh of an apple. Each parenchyma cell mechanically operates as a "hydrostatic device." Much like the air in an auto-

mobile tire, the watery cytoplasm exerts pressure—"hydrostatic pressure"—on the thin walls of each parenchyma cell, stretching and stiffening them. Within the cell wall, hydrostatic pressure creates tension in numerous microscopic strands ("microfibrils") of cellulose. This tension enables the cell to resist the pull of gravity because, given its density, cellulose under tension is one of the strongest materials known. However, owing to their chemical structure, compressed cellulose microfibrils are exceptionally weak, and gravity is a compressive force. Therefore, as parenchyma cells dehydrate (lose water), their cell walls provide less and less resistance to gravity. To be effective as a stiffening agent in stems or leaves, parenchyma or similar plant tissues must be fully hydrated. When deprived of water, organs composed predominantly of hydrostatic tissues wilt—that is, they shrink and mechanically collapse under their own weight.

One way to increase the strength of even thin-walled, living plant cells is to stiffen them with a bulking agent that resists compression. Lignin, a biological compound with a complex molecular structure, is such an agent. This essentially amorphous (shapeless) substance is synthesized by the cell's living cytoplasm, then is transported and sequestered in cell walls, where it stiffens and strengthens walls by providing mechanical support to other cell wall constituents. The capacity to synthesize lignin or ligninlike substances is found in some algae and some nonvascular land plants, as well as all vascular plants. These chemicals defend against microbial attack and provide living cytoplasm some protection against the effects of intense solar radiation (Graham 1993). In addition, these chemicals may provide a biochemical method to detoxify cells of excess, potentially harmful primary waste products that, unless polymerized and sequestered, would accumulate and eventually kill cells. Regardless of why lignin and ligninlike substances are synthesized, it is clear that they provided the cell walls of early vascular land plants with some mechanical support.

The branched, stemlike structures of some very ancient land plants (e.g., *Cooksonia*, *Steganotheca*, *Rhynia*) contained lignified cell walls (Stewart and Rothwell 1993; Taylor and Taylor 1993). The organs of these plants also were composed almost exclusively of parenchyma-like tissues and thus relied on hydrostatics for mechanical support. The evolution of larger and taller land plants required stiffer and stronger tissues for mechanical support. For many plant tissues, there is a correlation between cell wall thickness and tissue stiffness and strength (Niklas 1992). For example, parenchyma, which has very thin-walled cells, is the least stiff and strong plant tissue known, whereas wood, which is composed of many different kinds of thick-walled (typically dead) cells, is the stiffest and strongest of all plant tissues. It comes as no surprise, therefore, that the vertical stems of the tallest and largest terrestrial plant species are composed almost exclusively of wood. Nevertheless, other plant tissues are nearly as stiff and strong as wood, and they, too, have been used to construct stems nearly equivalent in size and height to the most massive and tallest composed of wood. For example, collenchyma, which consists of living cells with thicker cell walls than parenchyma, is stiffer and stronger than most types of parenchyma. Similarly, sclerenchyma, a tissue composed of cells with comparatively thick, often lignified walls, can be as strong and stiff as many kinds of wood.

A review of the plant fossil record indicates that the appearance of taller and more profusely branched plants bearing many leaves took place at the same time that stiffer and stronger tissues evolved (Stewart and Rothwell 1993; Taylor and Taylor 1993). As noted, like their aquatic ancestors, the earliest land plant remains from the late Silurian were composed almost exclusively of parenchyma (Graham 1993). These plants were comparatively short, measuring approximately a few centimeters in height (e.g., *Cooksonia*). By early Devonian times, many land plants evolved the ability to produce limited numbers of specialized water-conducting cells, which tend to have thicker and, therefore, stiffer cell walls. These vascular plants were taller than their antecedents, measuring on the order of a meter in height (e.g., *Psilophyton*). By the end of the Devonian period, the ability to produce sclerenchyma (and later wood) permitted the construction of very tall stems, rivaling the height of today's tallest living plant species (e.g., *Archaeopteris* and *Lepidodendron*).

The locations of different kinds of tissues in vertical stems and leaves is as important as the stiffness and strength of those tissues. Engineering theory indicates that invariably one can maximize the height of a vertical column composed of different materials by placing the stiffest and strongest material (tissue) at or very near the surface of the column (Niklas 1992; Wainwright et al. 1976). This is because the mechanical forces that result from bending are the most intense at the surface of vertical or cantilevered beams or columns. This mechanical principle is evident when scholars examine the anatomies of fossil and living land plants. In general, most plant species deploy their stiffest and strongest tissue very near the perimeter of cross sections through their leaves and stems. Among modern-day plants, strands or layers of lignified sclerenchyma are typically located below the epidermis ("skin") of stems and leaves that lack the capacity to produce wood. In many plant species, vascular fibers associated with primary xylem and phloem, which also contain thickened lignified cell walls, also tend to develop near the surface of the stems and leaves. In each case, these tissues are located where mechanical forces are most intense; thus, each tissue serves as the principal stiffening agent in elevated plant organs. Because these organs must support their own weight against the force of gravity, as well as the mechanical forces of wind pressure, and because their anatomies comply with good engineering practice, it is reasonable to suppose that natural selection has molded the internal structure of land plants.

Naturally, plants must perform many biological functions to survive and grow. In addition to conferring mechanical stability, cells in the vertical stems of the earliest land plants carried out photosynthesis. These stems' dual function presented an evolutionary challenge, because the best location for photosynthetic tissues is also the best location for mechanical tissues—at or near the surface of stems and leaves. Here, the intensity of light, the concentrations of oxygen and carbon dioxide, and magnitudes of mechanical forces are highest. Fortunately, for small and short land plants, hydrostatic living photosynthetic tissue also can provide ample mechanical support. However, taller and larger plants require mechanical tissues with thick cell walls, which are poorly adapted for photosynthesis. Since two tissues cannot occupy the same location at the same time, a compromise solution is to place stiff, strong tissues near the surfaces at the base of vertical stems and to locate living photosynthetic tissues near the surfaces at the top of those stems. This solution is seen in modern-day plant species like *Psilotum nudum*, which superficially has the general appearance of fossil plants like *Rhynia* (Steward and Rothwell 1993; Taylor and Taylor 1993). An alternative compromise is to alternate longitudinal strips of mechanical and photosynthetic tissues along the length of stems. This anatomy is found in many modern species of grasses.

Wood is formed by a tissue called vascular cambium in stems. This important evolutionary innovation permitted the growth of massive and exceptionally tall plant species. Vascular cambium produces wood toward the inside of stems and roots, and then grows outward, expanding in diameter as layers of wood accumulate from year to year. As a result, the oldest layers are found toward the inside of stems, while the youngest layer of wood is pressed against the inner surface of the cylindrical cambium that runs vertically along the length of stems. Vascular cambium also sequentially produces layers of secondary phloem, so that the youngest phloem cells are next to the outer surface of the cambium layer and pushing older phloem cells progressively farther away from the vascular cambium. Still other layers of cells are produced by tissue called cork cambium, which lies near the surface of woody stems. Together, the vascular cambium and the cork cambium produce tapered trunks and branches that are thicker at their base and progressively thinner toward their growing tips. This pattern of growth and development allows the living layers of cells that cover the structure like a sleeve to have access to oxygen and carbon dioxide (through the outer bark of stems) and provides inner dead layers of cells (wood) that mechanically support organs and the conduits for water transport. Engineering theory shows that a tapered vertical column is exceptionally stiff and strong because its mass is distributed in such a way that most of the weight is at the base. A tapered column is also difficult to blow over because it is bottom heavy. Even in the absence of an anchoring root system (which is essential for water and mineral absorption), simple friction at the base of a tall and massive tree trunk is normally sufficient to prevent windthrow (uprooting and overthrow due to wind), although this can happen under exceptionally high winds.

Naturally, all structures, whether biological or engineered, will mechanically fail when they experience exceptional loads. Old and tall tress will turn over in severe storms (Vogel 1996). But land plants have evolved numerous ways to reduce such events. The leaves and young twigs of tree species bend and curve to reduce their presented surface areas in the face of oncoming wind. These "deformations" reduce the drag forces on tree trunks, decreasing the likelihood of mechanical failure. Extensive root crowns provide a horizontal "platform," which increases the leverage force required to turn over massive and tapered trunks. These mechanical adaptations to reduce the likelihood of windthrow are evident by Devonian and Carboniferous times. The progymnosperm *Archaeopteris* and the arborescent lepidodendrids like *Lepidodendron* had tapered and massive trunks with flexible leaves and young branches anchored to the ground by large, horizontal root crowns (Stewart and Rothwell 1993; Taylor and Taylor 1993).

There are many ways to build a tree, however. Numerous fossil and living plants have evolved ways to construct tall stems, even if they cannot produce wood (Niklas 1997). For example, many fossil ferns employed an external mantle of stiff and strong adventitious roots (roots that grow from "unusual" locations, such as trunks or branches) or intertwining stems for mechanical support (e.g., *Psaronius* and *Tempskya*). These mantles possessed lignified sclerenchyma cells and were located at the surface of vertical stems, where bending mechanical forces are intense. Some of the "tree" ferns could grow as much as 15 to 20 meters tall without the benefit of woody stems. Likewise, modern-day palm species can grow to equivalent heights without woody stems. Instead, their stems have numerous primary vascular bundles running through their length. Most of these bundles, which have lignified thick-walled cells, tend to be concentrated toward the perimeter of cross sections through stems, maximizing the overall strength and stiffness of palm "tree" species.

Numerous other examples of mechanical "designs" seen in independent lineages attest to the fact that plant life has coped with life on land in ways that beautifully comply with engineering theory and practice. Many of these designs converge on the same engineering principle—the deployment of the stiffest available tissue at or near the surface of vertical stems. In biology, convergent evolution (independent evolution in unrelated groups) provides some of the best evidence for adaptation through natural selection. The mechanical designs of land plants provide some of the best evidence that the size, shape, and internal structure of plants are exceptionally well adapted (Niklas 1997).

KARL J. NIKLAS

See also Defensive Structures: Plants; Forests, Fossil; Plants: Adaptive Strategies; Plants: Vegetative Features; *particular taxa discussed in this essay*

Works Cited

Graham, L.E. 1993. *Origin of Land Plants.* New York: Wiley.
Kolattukudy, P.E. 1981. Structure, biosynthesis, and biodegradation of cutin and suberin. *Annual Review of Plant Physiology* 32:539–67.
Niklas, K.J. 1992. *Plant Biomechanics: An Engineering Approach to Plant Form and Function.* Chicago: University of Chicago Press.
———. 1997. *The Evolutionary Biology of Plants.* Chicago: University of Chicago Press.
Raven, J.A. 1985. Comparative physiology of plant and arthropod land adaptation. *Philosophical Transactions of the Royal Society of London,* ser. B, 309:273–388.
Stewart, W.N., and G.W. Rothwell. 1993. *Paleobotany and the Evolution of Plants.* 2nd ed., Cambridge and New York: Cambridge University Press.
Taylor, T.N., and E.L. Taylor. 1993. *The Biology and Evolution of Fossil Plants.* Englewood Cliffs, New Jersey: Prentice-Hall.
Vogel, S. 1996. Blowing in the wind: Storm-resistant features in the design of trees. *Journal of Arborculture* 22:92–98.
Wainwright, S.A., W.D. Biggs, J.D. Currey, and J.M. Gosline. 1976. *Mechanical Design in Organisms.* New York: Wiley; London: Edward Arnold.
Zimmermann, M.H. 1983. *Xylem Structure and the Ascent of Sap.* New York: Springer-Verlag.

Further Reading

King, J. 1997. *Reaching for the Sun: How Plants Work.* Cambridge and New York: Cambridge University Press.
Niklas, K.J. 1992. *Plant Biomechanics: An Engineering Approach to Plant Form and Function.* Chicago: University of Chicago Press.
———. 1996. How to build a tree. *Natural History* 105 (2):48–52.
———. 1997. *The Evolutionary Biology of Plants.* Chicago: University of Chicago Press.

PLANTS: VEGETATIVE FEATURES

The advent of plants on the continents was one of the major steps in the history of plant life (Kenrick and Crane 1997). Ancestors of our modern trees, shrubs, and herbaceous plants colonized land during the Late Ordovician, about 450 million years ago. When plants emerged from their aquatic habitat, they faced an environment that was hostile, gaseous, and desiccating (able to dry something out completely). The complex multicellular body of a land plant is a result of evolutionary specialization under these fundamentally new growth conditions. These conditions have led to the establishment of morphological (structural) and physiological differences between various parts of the plant and the development of organs.

The fossil record of spores suggests that the earliest colonizers were the bryophytes. Botanists commonly believe that this group evolved from multicellular ancestral freshwater green algae (Charophyceae). Bryophytes comprise the simplest land plants such as the liverworts (Hepaticophyta), hornworts (Anthocero-topsida), and mosses (Bryopsida). Basically, they all differ from the "higher land plants" by the absence of a true vascular tissue (tissue that functions much like blood vessels in animals) and a waxy layer (cuticle) on the aerial (above-ground) systems, which prevents the latter from desiccating. Bryophytes also show a primitive life cycle involving a distinct alternation of sexual and asexual generation, termed the gametophyte and the sporophyte, respectively. The gametophyte (the generation that produces gametes) consists of aerial shoots with leafy structures and is anchored in the substrate, or surface upon which it grows, by hairlike processes (rhizoids) that absorb water and nutrients. By contrast, the sporophyte (spore-producing generation) is a stalked capsule that lacks "leaves" and is supported by the gametophyte. The latter is strongly dependent on water for its production. Thus mosses occur characteristically on places that experience moist conditions, at least periodically. In spite of several equivocal records in the Early Devonian, the first true representatives of bryophytes are

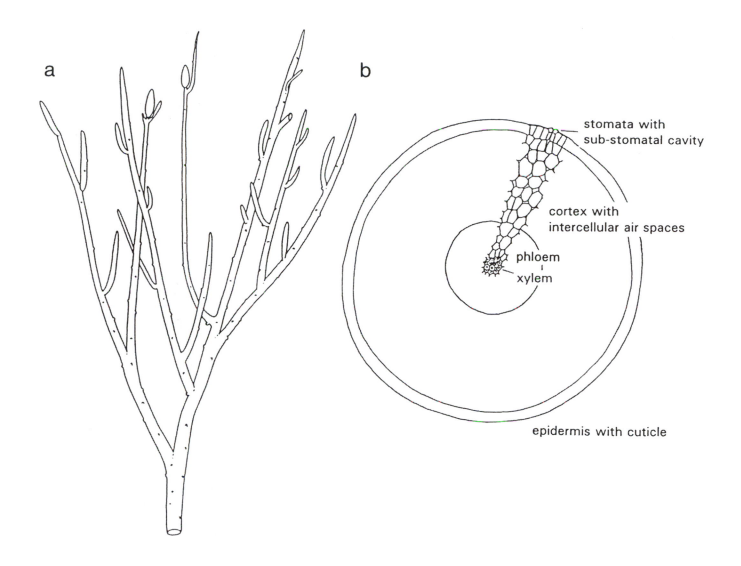

Figure 1. *Rhynia gwynne-vaughanii. A,* reconstruction of the fertile shoot; *B,* transverse section through a stem. From Edwards (1980), with kind permission of Elsevier Science - NL, Sara Burgerhartstraat 25, 1055 KV Amsterdam, The Netherlands.

known with certainty only since the Carboniferous (Oostendorp 1987).

All higher land plants have distinct vegetative organs (those that are not involved in reproduction) made of specialized tissues, such as aerial shoots with stems and leaves and underground anchoring roots. Although these tissues may vary considerably in form, they fulfill the common functions of support, defense, transport, storage, photosynthesis, and nutrient and water acquisition, as well as anchorage.

Stems and Branches
As the plant life on land becomes more differentiated, higher land plants develop a sophisticated fluid-conducting system. Water and nutrients are carried from the substrate to the apical part of the plant through vascular tissue called xylem, whereas photosynthetic products are transported through vascular tissue

called phloem. The xylem also provides support by incorporating the biopolymer lignin in the cell walls. In the fossil record the earliest vascular plants, the Rhyniopsida, occur in the Middle Silurian, some 420 million years ago. These are small plants, only a few centimeters high, consisting of dichotomously (two-part) branched, delicate axes without any appendages, terminated by sporangia (spore-producing organs) (Figure 1A). The Rhyniopsids, such as *Cooksonia* and *Rhynia,* possessed a vascular system consisting of a protostele, which consisted of a centrally placed xylem strand of tracheids that had broad, annular thickenings, surrounded by a thin-walled, phloemlike region and a thick cortex (Figure 1B). However, among the Rhynopsida there also exists an intermediate form between vascular land plants and mosses, *Aglaophyton (Rhynia) major.* Its central conducting strand fails to show tracheids but consists of cells that appear to be similar to water-conducting cells found in mosses (Edwards 1980). This is the basic structure from which all other vascular systems

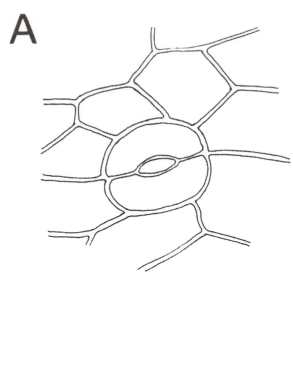

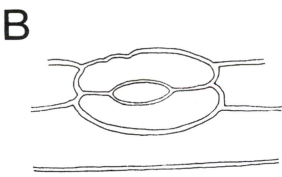

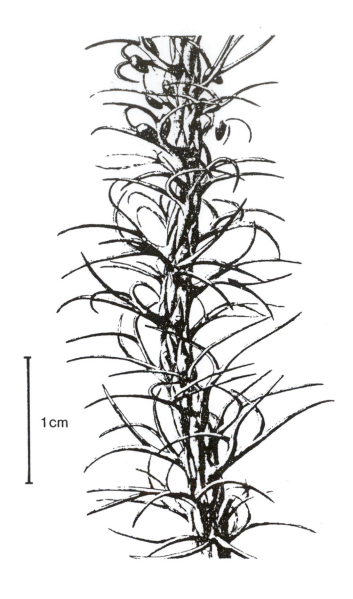

Figure 2. *A*, stoma of *Aglaophyton (Rhynia) major*. *B*, stoma of *Rhynia gwynne-vaughanii*.

Figure 3. Reconstruction of the fertile shoot of *Protolepidodendron (Estinnophyton) wahnbachense*. From Schweitzer (1987), reprinted with permission.

in plants can be derived. Subsequently, vascular systems with even more complex arrangements evolved by formation of "pith" in the central xylem body, resulting in a tubelike structure (the siphonostele typified by horsetails and Carboniferous giant club mosses, the Lepidodendrales). Another new structure is the eustele, consisting of pith and five surrounding strands of vascular tissue, from which the leaf traces (structures that give rise to leaves) originate. The latter is typical for all seed plants.

During the Devonian, vegetation became denser, and competition for light became more important, giving rise to higher, eventually treelike plants (Chaloner and Sheerin 1979). These plants formed "secondary tissue," tissue required to achieve the girth necessary for growing upward. The most important part of this secondary tissue, which gives strength to the stem, is the "secondary wood." Next to that, secondary phloem and cortex are formed. In the Lep-

idodendrales, the cortex constitutes the main body of the stem. In all other arborescent plants, thickening of the stem is achieved by the formation of lignified secondary vascular tissue.

In answer to their desiccating environment, all vascular plants—and probably also the intermediate forms between vascular plants and mosses—developed a waxy layer (cuticle) on aerial branch systems in order to conserve water. (This layer cuts down on the amount of water that evaporates through the epidermis of the stems and leaves.) In addition, land plants were forced to generate stomata (microscopic openings) in their epidermis and cuticle, to control the rate of gas exchange with the ambient atmosphere, mainly CO_2 diffusion into the plant and water and O_2 out of the plant. The stomatal complex has a closing mechanism that consists of a pair of cells called guard cells, which surround a tiny pore above a chamber in the cortex. The regulation of this stomatal opening reflects a compromise between carbon gain and water loss. The first indisputable record of cuticles with stomatal complexes is known from the Rhyniopsida (Figure 2). In these early land plants, stomata were distributed sparsely over the whole surface of the aerial branch, indicating that photosynthesis took place in their entire stem. With successive specialization of plant organs, photosynthetic active tissue and stomata became concentrated in the leaves.

Leaves

A leaf is a lateral outgrowth of the stem, mostly flattened and with a layering of materials between its top and bottom surfaces. To maximize the capture of light and an adequate supply of CO_2 for the assimilating tissue, leaf laminae (blades) usually tend to be thin and broad. Their arrangement in the plant body serves the same aim. Leaves are conventionally classified into microphylls and macrophylls.

Microphylls typically have only one (eventually bifurcated, or split into two equal parts) vein and are developed from a lateral (side) branch, which became restricted in growth and was reduced to a plane structure due to webbing (Figure 3). This kind of leaf is found in *Lycopodium, Selaginella, Isoetes, Psilotum,* and horsetails. Such outgrowths of the stem provided plants with a larger area for gas exchange and light acquisition and a greater space for photosynthetic activity. This morphological invention may have improved the plants' physiological performance and made them more competitive than their neighboring rival species.

Characteristically, the macrophyll has a pinnate (feather) shape, with a primary vein that supports lateral veins. This type of leaf is typical of the ferns (Pteropsida), and is regarded as having evolved from a branch with microphyll leaves that became limited in growth and developed a leaflike form. A comparable type of leaf developed in the ancestors of the seed plants.

Leaf Dimorphism

The diversity of leaf morphology and anatomy in broad-leaved trees is a well-known botanical phenomenon. Contrasting microhabitats (small habitats) determined by the position in the tree yield distinct environmental leaf morphotypes (specialized shapes to meet certain functions) such as sun and shade leaves. Basically, sun leaves tend to be thicker and smaller. They also have a higher density of stomata, which increases their capacity to assimilate CO_2 as well as rates of transpiration (water loss) for cooling. Gross features such as leaf area, degree of lobing, and density of veins, as well as leaf surface characters (e.g., epidermal cell density, stomatal density), and in some cases even the properties of the mesophyll (central cell layers in the leaf), are very useful characters for distinguishing sun and shade morphotypes in fossil angiosperm leaf assemblages (Kürschner 1997).

Kranz Anatomy

Only some 7 million years ago, in the Late Miocene, a novel anatomical feature appears in the fossil record. Well-preserved grass

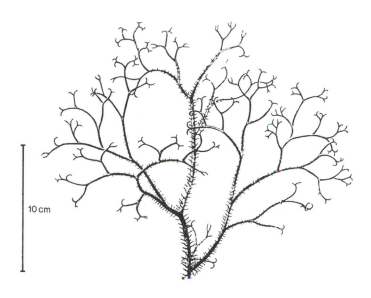

Figure 4. Reconstruction of the areal shoot from *Psilophyton burnotense*. From Schweitzer (1987), reprinted with permission.

10 cm

leaf fragments, which have been assigned to the subfamily Chloridoideae, show features such as pronounced bundle sheath cells (fibers) with thick cell wall layers (Thomasson et al. 1986). The presence of this so-called Kranz anatomy in the leaves is anatomical evidence of a specialized form of photosynthesis called C_4 metabolism. The C_4 pathway is a modification of the more common C_3 pathway. Here, the initial CO_2 acquisition is separated from the final step, carbohydrate synthesis. Briefly, the C_4 pathway is a two-step system, in which atmospheric CO_2 initially is fixed in the leaf's mesophyll cells, then transported to the bundle sheath cells, where the CO_2 is released. In C_4 photosynthesis, photorespiration (inhibition of carbon fixation by the presence of oxygen) of plants becomes negligible, and water-use efficiency is improved. Therefore, environments characterized by low atmospheric CO_2 concentrations as well as aridity and high temperatures favor plants with a C_4 over plants with the more common C_3 photosynthetic metabolism (Ehleringer et al. 1991; Ehleringer and Cerling 1995). Paleobotanists can estimate levels of atmospheric CO_2 in the geological past from stomata counts on fossil leaves, since the frequency of stomata appears to be inversely related to atmospheric CO_2 concentration (Woodward 1987). Results from analysis of extant (present-day) and fossil angiosperm leaves suggest that paleoatmospheric CO_2 levels were periodically reduced to values below 300 parts per million during the Late Miocene, a situation in which C_4 plants were more competitive than C_3 plants (Van der Burgh et al. 1993; Kürschner et al. 1996). Evidence from the carbon isotopic composition of carbonates and organic matter in the soil reveal a rapid proliferation of plants with the C_4 pathway on a global scale during that period (Cerling et al. 1993). This proliferation has led to their superior position in the present-day tropical and temperate grasslands.

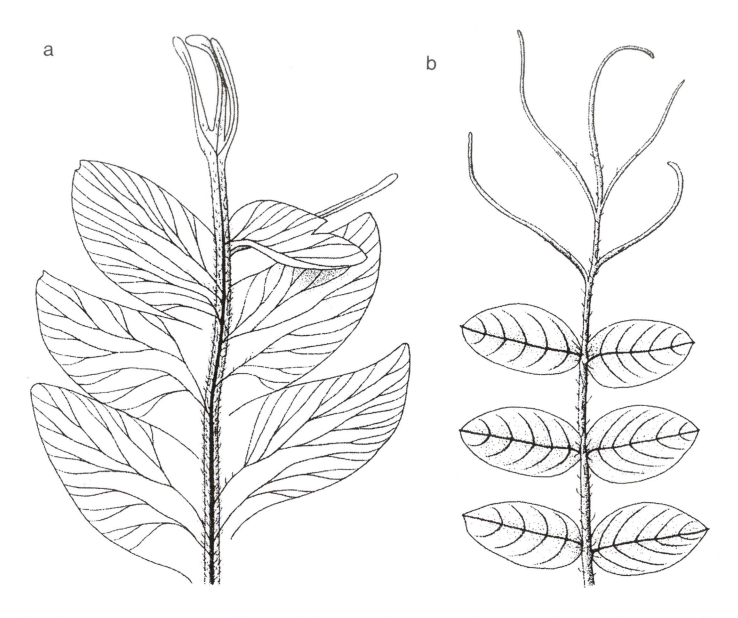

Figure 5. *Left, A,* reconstruction of a modified pinna (leaf) terminal with immature tendrils *Lescuropteris genuina*; *B,* comparison with a modified leaf apex of a modern climber *Vicia sepium*. From Krings and Kerp (1997), reprinted by permission of the publisher, Academic Press Limited, London.

Spines

Spines are a very ancient vegetative feature of the epidermal tissue, found very early among the Rhyniopsida, for example *Psilophyton princeps* and *P. burnotense* (Figure 4). Spines may have evolved as a structure to help spore-gathering arthropods (insects) to climb stems and reach the sporangia; such a system would improve the dispersal of the spores (Smart 1971). On the other hand, spines can be interpreted as defense structures to protect the plants against herbivorous invertebrates (Chaloner 1970).

Holdfasts

Climbing plants can be defined as plants rooted in the ground, with aerial parts supported by other plants. Some climbing plants flourish only when they reach the sunlight in the upper canopy (the top layer of branches and leaves); others are adapted to the shady understory (layers lower down). Despite their variety in habit and habitat almost all climbers bear specialized climbing organs such as hooks, tendrils, or, in some cases, even spines. In the fossil record, climbers are numerous in Carboniferous sediments and evolved in several taxa. For example, *Sphenophyllum* and *Lescuropteris genuina* had a climbing habit, evident from spines, terminal hooks, and tendrils for attachment to the substrate or host plant (Batenburg 1981; Krings and Kerp 1997) (Figure 5).

Roots

At the very beginning, the earliest land plants, such as *Rhynia*, pos-

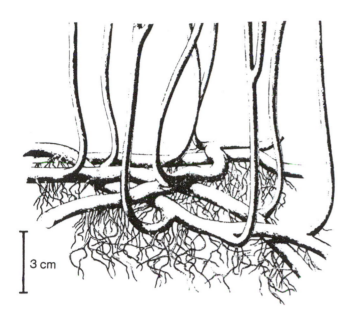

Figure 6. Reconstruction of the basal shoot of *Stockmansella (Taeniocrada) langii*, with roots. From Schweitzer (1987), reprinted with permission.

sessed only a relatively simple water-absorbing/anchorage system, typically consisting of underground stems (rhizomes) with extensions of epidermal cells (rhizoids). Roots had evolved already in Lower Devonian plants (Figure 6) and show complex, branched root structures (*Drepanophycus, Stockmansella,* in Schweitzer 1980a, 1980b). Very early in the history of land plants, a symbiosis (mutual interdependence) developed between these plants and fungi, resulting in primitive mycorrhiza (fungal filament) structures (Remy et al. 1994). Mycorrhizae enabled plants to dissolve rocks in order to obtain important minerals. All plants bear roots with principally the same design, which differs slightly from that of the stems: xylem and phloem are not organized in two concentric tubes, with phloem in the outer tube, but occur side-by-side in one tubelike structure. Secondary growth normally changes this arrangement. The tip of all roots also bears a caplike structure (calyptra) for protection as the root penetrates the substrate. Because roots are able to thicken, they are also a major factor in breaking down the physical structure of mineral rock. Consequently, the evolution of roots is thought to have been an important factor in the reduction in the amount of carbon dioxide in the atmosphere during the Devonian and Carboniferous periods, through enhanced weathering caused by mechanical disruption and soil acidification (Berner 1992; Mora et al. 1996). On the other hand, roots also are able to keep the weathered rock (soil) in place, and in this way plants greatly reduce the abrasion of the Earth.

WOLFRAM MICHAEL KÜRSCHNER AND JOHAN VAN DER BURGH

Works Cited

Batenburg, L.H. 1981. Vegetative anatomy and ecology of *Sphenophyllum zwickaviense, S. emarginatum,* and other "compression species" of *Sphenophyllum. Review of Palaeobotany and Palynology* 32:275–313.

Berner, R.A. 1992. Weathering, plants and the long-term carbon cycle. *Geochimica et Cosmochimica Acta* 56:3225–231.

Cerling, T.E., Y. Wang, and J. Quade. 1993. Expansion of C_4 ecosystems as an indicator of global ecological change in the Late Miocene. *Nature* 361:344–45.

Chaloner, W.G. 1970. The rise of the first land plants. *Biological Reviews of the Cambridge Philosophical Society* 45:353–77.

Chaloner, W.G., and A. Sheerin. 1979. Devonian macrofloras. *In* M.R. House, C.T. Scrutton, and M.G. Basset (eds.). The Devonian System. *Special Papers in Palaeontology* 23:145–61.

Edwards, D.S. 1980. Evidence for the sporophytic status of the Lower Devonian plant *Rhynia gwynne-vaughanii* Kidston and Lang. *Review of Palaeobotany and Palynology* 29:177–88.

———. 1986. *Aglaophyton major,* a non-vascular land-plant from the Devonian Rhynie Chert. *Botanical Journal of the Linnean Society* 93:173–204.

Ehleringer, J.R., and T.E. Cerling. 1995. Atmospheric CO_2 and the ratio of intercellular to ambient CO_2 concentrations in plants. *Tree Physiology* 15:105–11.

Ehleringer, J.R., R.F. Sage, L.B. Flanagan, and R.W. Pearcy. 1991. Climate change and the evolution of photosynthesis. *Trends in Ecology and Evolution* 6:95–99.

Kenrick, P., and P.R. Crane. 1997. The origin and early evolution of plants on land. *Nature* 389:33–39.

Krings, M., and H. Kerp. 1997. Cuticles of *Lescuropteris genuina* from the Stephanian (Upper Carboniferous) of Central France: Evidence for a climbing growth habit. *Botanical Journal of the Linnean Society* 123:73–89.

Kürschner, W.M. 1997. The anatomical diversity of recent and fossil leaves of the Durmast oak (*Quercus petraea,* Lieblein/*Q. pseudocastanea,* Goeppert)—Implications for their use as biosensors of palaeoatmospheric CO_2 concentrations. *Review of Palaeobotany and Palynology* 96:1–30.

Kürschner, W.M., J. Van der Burgh, H. Visscher, and D.L. Dilcher. 1996. Oak leaves as biosensors of late Neogene and early Pleistocene palaeoatmospheric CO_2 levels. *Marine Micropaleontology* 27:299–312.

Mora, C.I., S.G. Driese, and L.A. Colarusso. 1996. Middle to late Palaeozoic atmospheric CO_2 concentrations from soil carbonate and organic matter. *Science* 271:1105–7.

Oostendorp, C. 1987. The Bryophytes of the Palaeozoic and the Mesozoic. *Bryophytorum Bibliotheca* 34. Berlin: Cramer.

Remy, W., T.N. Taylor, H. Hass, and H. Kerp. 1994. Four hundred-million-year-old vesicular arbuscular mycorrhizae. *Proceedings of the National Academy of Sciences USA* 91:11841–43.

Schweitzer, H.J. 1980a. Die Gattungen *Taeniocrada* White und *Sciadophyton* Steinmann im Unterdevon des Rheinlandes. *Bonner paläobotanische Mitteilungen* 5:1–38.

———. 1980b. Über *Drepanophycus spinaeformis* Göppert. *Bonner paläobotanische Mitteilungen* 7:1–29.

———. 1987. Introduction to the plant bearing beds and the flora of the Lower Devonian of the Rhineland. *Bonner paläobotanische Mitteilungen* 13:1–94.

Smart, J. 1971. Palaeoecological factors affecting the original winged insects. *Proceedings of the XIIIth Entymological Congress, Moscow 1968.* Moscow: n.p.

Thomas, B.A., and R.A. Spicer. 1986. *The Evolution and Palaeobiology of Land Plants.* Portland, Oregon: Discorides; London: Croom Helm.

Thomasson, J.R., M.E. Nelson, and R.J. Zakrzewski. 1986. A fossil grass (Gramineae: Chloridoideae) from the Miocene with Kranz anatomy. *Science* 233:876–78.

Van der Burgh, J., H. Visscher, D.L. Dilcher, and W.M. Kürschner. 1993. Paleoatmospheric signatures in Neogene fossil leaves. *Science* 260:1788–90.

Woodward, F.I. 1987. Stomatal numbers are sensitive to increases in CO_2 concentration from preindustrial levels. *Nature* 327:617–18.

Further Reading

Gifford, E.M., and A.S. Foster. 1959. *Comparative Morphology of Vascular Plants.* San Francisco: Freeman; 3rd ed., *Morphology and Evolution of Vascular Plants,* New York: Freeman, 1989.

Kenrick, P., and P.R. Crane. 1997. *The Origin and Early Diversification of Land Plants: A Cladistic Study.* Washington: Smithsonian Institution Press.

———. 1997. The origin and early evolution of plants on land. *Nature* 389:33–39.

Stewart, W.N., and G.W. Rothwell. 1983. *Paleobotany and the Evolution of Plants.* Cambridge and New York: Cambridge University Press; 2nd ed., 1993.

Taylor, T.N., and E.L. Taylor. 1993. *The Biology and Evolution of Fossil Plants.* Englewood Cliffs, New Jersey: Prentice-Hall.

Thomas, B.A., and R.A. Spicer. 1986. *The Evolution and Palaeobiology of Land Plants.* Portland, Oregon: Dioscorides; London: Croom Helm.

PLANTS: ADAPTIVE STRATEGIES

A successful and healthy plant has plenty of all the basic requirements for growth: water, sunlight, warmth, nutrients, space, oxygen, and carbon dioxide. If these needs were met in all habitats for all plants, we probably would see little variation from plant to plant. However, the Earth is covered with plants like cacti, water lilies, pines, orchids, and vines. This variation speaks clearly about a history of devising a variety of methods to meet the basic requirements for growth. Consider an environment in which plants are rare, such as a rock outcrop, devoid of plants. What is lacking? Water may be limited; space and nutrients also are likely to be limited. If there are a few plants on an outcrop, notice that they are clinging to tiny ledges where a root penetrates rock layers or grows into the few grains of loose sediment. Similarly, few if any plants grow in caves. The lack of sunlight completely limits their ability to photosynthesize. These are extreme cases. In most natural systems the requirements for healthy growth vary along a continuum. Plants living along the continuum must be able to make do with the availability of such factors as sunlight, nutrients, and water at that particular spot. The presence of these many resource gradients has allowed the range of forms we see in the plant kingdom to survive.

Plants are sessile—once they have germinated, they cannot move to a new habitat or even down to the stream bank. Therefore, plants able to live and reproduce successfully in suboptimal conditions leave more offspring than those that require perfect conditions. By examining deficits or superabundances in each of the necessary plant resources, we can focus on the strategies that have allowed some plants to succeed where other plants failed. You will see that three basic classes of response are present in most plant adaptive strategies to abiotic stress (extremes of inorganic factors): completely avoid the stress, use other plants or organisms to help ameliorate the stress, or modify their own morphology or physiology to accommodate the stress.

Sunlight

Too little sunlight is a more substantial problem for most plants than too much. Under the shade of a dense forest, few plants sur- vive. Some seeds fail to germinate if they do not receive a particular wavelength of light. Even if seeds do germinate, the options for most plants are few in low light. Slow growth leads to slower reproduction than plants causing the shade. Soon plants receive too little energy to sustain their own growth, much less the growth of reproductive organs.

One strategy for success in a shady environment is to grow out of it rapidly. Climbing plants do this by investing little energy in woody structures like trunks, which serve primarily for support, and more energy in elongating stems and rapidly expanding leaves. They reach the canopy of the forest by using other plants for support on their way. Once in the canopy they invest heavily in flowers, fruits, and seeds. Another means to escape a shady habitat is to germinate seeds up in the limbs of tall shading trees. "Epiphytes" (literally, on-the-plant), like *Philodendron* and bromelids, may send roots into the litter that accumulates in the crotches of the host tree or all the way down to the forest floor. In either case, they invest almost nothing in structural stems to reach the canopy. Strangling figs, whose seeds germinate on high tree branches, bear fruits palatable to birds. They eat the fruits and defecate the seeds in the tree tops, thus facilitating the epiphyte's strategy. Mosses and liverworts often survive in tropical forests by living on top of vascular plants. Some even specialize on living on the upper surface of leaves; these are "epiphylls." Finally, other plants are adapted to low light conditions by having a large leaf surface area. The large leaves are retained on the plant for periods longer than a year so that the cost of creating the leaf is amortized over several years of growth.

What about too much sunlight? In deserts, sunlight may be excessive, in combination with high temperatures. Because enzymes essential to metabolism are effective over a limited range of temperatures, it is advantageous for organisms living in a desert habitat to reflect the sun's rays rather than absorb them. Desert plants, such as *Yucca* and jojoba *(Simmondsia),* orient their leaves and stems parallel to the sun's rays. This diminishes the angle of incidence of the sunlight, thus decreasing the heat load on the plant. Desert plants often have a grey-green appearance caused by a deposit of opaque waxes or a fine layer of hairs, both of which reflect the sunlight from the plant and thus decrease the heat load.

Warmth

Within limits, plants adjust to daily temperature fluctuations. In the temperate zone, diurnal (day-night) temperatures can fluctuate as much as 25–30 degrees centigrade in some seasons. Daily fluctuations, above 0 degrees and below approximately 40 degrees centigrade are tolerated by many plants. However, fluctuations that include temperatures above or below this range require some modifications to the typical morphology (shape and structure) and physiology of a plant.

The most obvious means to avoid excessive temperatures (either high or low) is simply to abscise (drop off) water-filled tissues (leaves and small stems) when adverse temperatures start, and regrow the organs again when more moderate temperatures resume. Under very high temperatures some metabolic processes, especially photosynthesis, are limited. Some plants utilize alternative carbon assimilation pathways called C_4 and CAM, both of which are more effective under higher temperatures than is the more common C_3 photosynthetic pathway. These alternative pathways are found in plants that live under high temperatures. In addition, high temperatures have severe negative effects on the stability of plant cell membranes; some plants have circumvented this problem by changing the degree of saturation in the fatty acids of the membranes.

Under freezing temperatures, any water-filled tissue is at risk. The strategy used by temperate-zone hardwood trees is to reduce metabolic activity. This alteration limits the production of sensitive tissues. These trees also drop leaves and small stems as the period of cold temperatures approaches. This is characteristic of elms, maples, beeches, hickories, and poplars. Desert plants have a very different strategy. Because they may encounter freezing temperatures in many deserts almost any night of the year, it would not be advantageous to discard photosynthetic tissues for long periods. Instead, plants in the desert often bear no leaves; their photosynthesizing cells are found in their stems. This, however, does not solve the problem of freezing in water-filled tissues. In the cells of many plants that regularly withstand freezing temperatures, there is a higher concentration of solutes in their cells; these substances depress the freezing point. Such an adaptation is not found in tropical plants, which virtually never encounter freezing temperatures.

Nutrients

A wide array of inorganic nutrients are essential to plant growth. Plants exhibit stunted or sickly growth if essential minerals are lacking. However most plants use very, very minor amounts of the essential minerals. Thus, nutrient deficiencies usually are limited to the nutrients plants use in larger amounts (macronutrients), like nitrogen, phosphorus, potassium, sulfur, calcium, magnesium, and iron.

One might expect that tropical rain forests are wonderful places for plant growth: it certainly looks like it in all the nature films. However nutrients are in high demand in most tropical rain forests because water rapidly leaches (washes) the soil. To address this condition, tropical rain forest trees often have shallow roots, which can capture the nutrients released from decomposing plant litter close to the soil surface. The larger of these roots provide stability by taking the form of large buttresses, for which rain forests are renown. In temperate rain forests of the Pacific Northwest and cloud forests of Costa Rica, on the other hand, trees produce roots from stems high in their own canopies. There the roots recycle the nutrients from trapped plant litter decomposing in the high branches (Nadkarni 1985).

Probably the most important plant adaptation is the symbioses (partnership) that many plant roots form with fungi. This association is called "mycorrhizae." These associations benefit a plant because they increase the plant's ability to absorb nutrients and water via the increased surface area of the fungus. The associations benefit the fungus through photosynthetic products created by the plant. Some of the more bizarre adaptations that facilitate increased nutrient acquisition are seen in carnivorous plants. These plants actively trap and digest insects, circumventing at least some of the requirement for taking up nutrients from the soil. A complete dependence on other organisms for nutrients is seen in parasitic plants like mistletoes and dodders, who gain nutrients directly from the phloem (nutrient-transporting system) of their host plants. Such parasites require no other nutrient resources.

Space

Physical space required by plants is intimately related to the most limited resource over which plants in a particular environment might compete. Theoretically, as long as there were sufficient light, nutrients, and water, plants could (and do) live in very small spaces. However, nutrients, water, and sunlight diminish in quantity when many plants are crowded together; therefore, plants compete to occupy the largest possible space. In areas where nutrients or water are limiting, plant communities have an open appearance with large spaces between plants. A desert environment illustrates this very well. In areas where sunlight is limiting, like the understory (lower level) of a tropical forest, the vertical space is packed densely with plants, each one intercepting light missed by those perched above them. Stacking has fostered adaptations that facilitate growth attached to a vertical substrate. For example, vines produce a variety of tendrils, suction holdfasts, and twining mechanisms that allow them to exploit vertical surfaces.

Water

Water stress is probably one of the most common stresses encountered by plants. Many plants can survive short periods of water stress with almost no negative effects: they wilt during midday heat but revive shortly after temperatures fall. All vascular land plants have stomata: a pair of guard cells that surround a pore that can be opened and closed, depending on the water conditions of the surrounding cells. The degree of water stress that can be tolerated before the guard cells close varies widely among different plant species. Regulation of stomata is one of the simplest and most widespread adaptive strategies in the plant kingdom. For example, stomata may be sunken in cavities on the lower leaf surface. Plants with this adaptation lose water vapor slowly in comparison to a plant with stomata on the flat upper surface of a leaf.

In cases of recurrent, severe drought, plants either avoid the dry seasons, or cope with dryness with specific adaptations that involve more than just opening and closing their stomata. Plants that avoid dry periods produce leaves only when sufficient water is available. The ocotillo *(Foqueria)* and palo verde *(Cercidium)* of the southwestern deserts of the United States leaf out rapidly in response to spring rains, then lose their leaves soon after they have flushed. Their period of photosynthesis using leaves is very short, so regulation of stomata is almost unnecessary—the entire leaf soon is discarded. For the majority of the growing season, photosynthesis is carried out by young branches. Other desert plants fold their leaves in the heat of the day, so that little sunlight reaches them. This strategy also conserves water by exposing less surface area to the hot, dry atmosphere.

In contrast, annual plants avoid periods of late summer drought by compressing the entire life cycle so that the plant goes from seed to seed before drought appears. During the dry season, plants that cope with dryness continue most metabolic processes at a normal rate. They achieve this by changing the osmotic relationships (ratio of water to solutes) in their cells. This strategy may limit some but not all metabolic processes or may change the elastic quality of tissues, such that they can lose water but not lose structural support during water stress. In addition, decreasing the size of the pores between water conducting elements can avoid the dangerous condition of producing air bubbles, or embolisms, in water conducting tissues.

Finally, some plants maintain high water potentials during drought periods by modifying their growth form. Plants with extremely deep roots persist in dry areas ("phreatophytes") and even bring water closer to the surface for other, nontolerant plant species. The gymnosperm *Welwitschia* grows only in the deserts of tropical Africa and is cultivated most successfully by using long drain pipes for the roots that simulate the distance over which the roots penetrate the earth in search of water. Both the saguaro *(Carnegiea)* and the boojum *(Idria)* can store enormous amounts of water that last through times of drought. The saguaro has a pleated trunk that expands as the volume of stored water increases and closes as water is used, exposing less surface area to the dry environment. Some plants absorb water from the air, especially from fog, and survive in foggy but rain-free deserts, like the Atacama desert of Peru, where *Tillandsia* flourishes. Hemiparasites, like mistletoe, use water from their hosts, thus surviving during periods of drought—and presumably making survival even more difficult for their host. A purely mechanical adaptation to water loss includes the production of spines and unpalatable constituents of epidermal cells. Such adaptations deter animals seeking water from taking a bite.

ROBYN J. BURNHAM

See also Defensive Structures: Plants; Plants: Mechanical Plant Design; Plants: Vegetative Features; Reproductive Strategies: Plants

Work Cited

Nadkarni, N.M. 1985. Roots that go out on a limb. *Natural History* 94 (2):43–49.

Further Reading

Fowden, L., T. Mansfield, and J. Stoddart. 1993. *Plant Adaptation to Environmental Stress.* London and New York: Chapman and Hall.

Mauseth, J.D. 1991. *Botany: An Introduction to Plant Biology.* Philadelphia: Saunders College; 2nd ed., 1995.

Nadkarni, N.M. 1985. Roots that go out on a limb. *Natural History* 94 (2):43–49.

Nilsen, E.T., and D.M. Orcutt. 1996. *The Physiology of Plants under Stress: Abiotic Factors.* New York: Wiley.

Sakai, A., and W. Larcher. 1987. *Frost Survival of Plants: Responses and Adaptation to Freezing Stress.* Berlin and New York: Springer-Verlag.

Talalaj, S., D. Talalaj, and J. Talalaj. 1991. *The Strangest Plants in the World.* Melbourne: Hill of Content.

PLATE TECTONICS AND CONTINENTAL DRIFT

The idea that the continents are not fixed in place, but capable of shifting around the Earth's surface, is an old one. As soon as decent maps of the world became available, several scholars noticed that the Atlantic coasts of Africa and South America were a good match, suggesting that these two continents once fit together. But it was not until the twentieth century that the idea of continental drift went from a wild notion to the prevailing orthodoxy among geologists.

In 1915 the German meteorologist Alfred Wegener published the first detailed work to argue that continents had moved over time. His ideas were ridiculed by geologists; no one could imagine the continents plowing through the oceanic crust without leaving huge crumpled mountains built from the ocean floor in front of them. However, some Southern Hemisphere geologists (especially in South Africa) were advocates of continental drift. They pointed to the peculiar distribution of distinctive Permo-Triassic plants (such as the seed fern *Glossopteris*) and animals (the aquatic reptile *Mesosaurus,* the synapsids *Lystrosaurus* and *Cynognathus*) as evidence for the former existence of a southern continent called Gondwanaland, consisting of Africa, South America, India, Australia, Antarctica, and Madagascar. They also pointed to three distinct Late Paleozoic floral provinces: a southern flora, dominated by *Glossopteris,* found on most of the Gondwana continents, which were at temperate and polar latitudes; a northern flora found in the great coal swamps of the late Carboniferous, which was dominated by lycopsids (scale trees and club mosses) and located in the ancient tropics; and a third, distinctive Asiatic floral province. These provinces are oddly scattered on a modern map of the world, but if they were placed in their late Paleozoic continental positions, all the Gondwana fragments (Africa, South America, India, Australia, and Antarctica) would come together, as would the northern continents, to form a supercontinent known as Laurasia (North America plus western Eurasia). In the Pennsylvanian, the fragments of Asia had not yet collided with Siberia, but in the Permian this collision formed a single global continent called Pangaea.

The continental drift hypothesis was scorned by Northern Hemisphere geologists until the late 1950s and 1960s, when new evidence emerged from the seafloor and from geophysics. Ancient magnetic directions recorded in rocks around the world showed their continents had moved long distances with respect to the Earth's magnetic poles. Oceanographic surveys showed that there was an immense range of mountains (the longest and highest in the world) that ran down the middle of the Atlantic, and that there were also ranges in the middle of the Pacific and Indian oceans. These midocean ridges turned out to be the be sites where the Earth's crust pulls apart in a process called seafloor spreading. In addition, at the edges of some continents, there were long chains of volcanoes and regions of high seismic activity, such as the "ring of fire" around the Pacific. Geophysical data showed that in these regions one continent is plunging underneath another in a process called subduction. The friction between the overriding and downgoing slabs produces earthquakes, and the melting of the downgoing slab as it plunges into the hot mantle produces the chain of volcanoes above each subduction zone.

By the mid-1960s geology had undergone a scientific revolution in its understanding of the Earth, known as plate tectonics. The Earth's crust is broken up into more than 20 distinct tectonic plates that move around and slide over the mantle and pull away or collide with one another as they do so. Where they separate, new oceanic crust is formed by seafloor spreading; where they collide, crust is consumed in subduction zones. In a few places, the plates are neither spreading nor colliding, but sliding past one another in what are known as transform faults. These great fault zones, such as the San Andreas Fault of California, generate enormous friction and huge earthquakes as two plates grind past one another.

In the 30 years since the plate tectonic revolution, many scientists have reconstructed detailed maps showing the ancient distribution of continents (e.g., Bambach et al. 1980; Scotese and Golonka 1992). For the last 200 million years, the present continents have been moving apart as they split away from the global supercontinent of Pangea. In the late Triassic and Jurassic, North America separated from Pangea, causing the opening of the North Atlantic. In the Cretaceous, South America and Africa split open along the South Atlantic, and both separated from Antarctica-Australia. Also in the Cretaceous, India broke away from the southern continents and raced across the Indian Ocean, plowing into southern Asia in the Early Eocene to form the Himalayas.

Australia did not separate from Antarctica until the Late Eocene, and it is now beginning to collide with Asia. Since the Cretaceous, a great tropical Tethyan seaway ran from the Mediterranean to Indonesia. It was fragmented when India collided with Asia, and Africa began its collision with Eurasia to form the Alps and the collision zone between the Arabian Peninsula and Iran.

Prior to the Permian supercontinent, a number of different plate configurations were found in the Paleozoic. The Gondwanaland supercontinent has existed for at least 800 million years. However, the northern continents jostled around in a variety of configurations during the Paleozoic. For example, North America was located in the tropics and rotated by 90 degrees during the Cambrian. By the Devonian, North America had collided with Europe to form the Caledonian-Acadian mountains. In the Pennsylvanian, southern North America began to collide with the African and South America portions of Gondwanaland, causing the Appalachian mountain belt. In the Permian, Siberia collided with Europe, crumpling up the Ural Mountains between them.

Prior to the Paleozoic, the positions of the continents are more controversial, since the evidence is difficult to interpret. Most geologists agree that about 700 million years ago there was another supercontinent, known as Rodinia, which placed western North America adjacent to Antarctica and placed fragments of Africa and South America adjacent to eastern North America and Europe; Siberia abutted Greenland. However, there are many other interpretations of how these Late Proterozoic continents were assembled, and so far no reconstruction is supported by all the evidence. Plate reconstructions prior to 700 million years ago are much more speculative, since the evidence is so poor.

The motions of continents are important not only in explaining past geographic puzzles, but they also had climatic and oceanographic effects that were equally important. For example, the circum-Antarctic current currently circulates around Antarctica in a clockwise fashion, locking the cold air and water in around the South Pole. Consequently, there is little mixing of tropical and temperate water with the cold Antarctic waters, enhancing not only the refrigeration of the South Pole but also the extremes between poles and equator. But in the Eocene, Antarctica was still connected to both South America and Australia, and there was no connection of the South Atlantic, South Pacific, and Indian Oceans. Instead, each of these oceans was much warmer and milder because tropical and temperate waters mixed with those of the polar regions. When Australia broke away in the Late Eocene and South America in the Late Oligocene, the circum-Antarctic current formed, and the Antarctic has been refrigerated ever since. This current is ultimately responsible for the global cooling that has occurred in the last 50 million years.

Plate Tectonics and Paleobiogeography

Once the mobility of continents was appreciated, many biogeographic puzzles finally were solved. Paleontologists long had been mystified by the fact that Cambrian trilobite provinces did not follow the present-day distribution of continents. The European faunal province, characterized by the trilobite *Paradoxides,* was found not only in Europe but also in the southeastern United

States, Boston, Rhode Island, Nova Scotia, and eastern New-foundland. Most of North America was one distinct American province, the *Ogygopsis* fauna, but so was Scotland and western Newfoundland. Paleontologists tried to explain this odd pattern by suggesting differences in water depths or land barriers, but nothing made sense. Only after plate tectonics came along did an explanation present itself. Apparently the southeastern United States, eastern New England, Nova Scotia, and eastern New-foundland were on the European side of the Proto-Atlantic Ocean during the Cambrian, while Scotland was on the North American side. The Proto-Atlantic then closed in the Late Paleozoic, forming the supercontinent of Laurasia. When the present-day Atlantic was formed by splitting up this supercontinent in the Triassic and Jurassic, it did not follow the line of closure of the old ocean, but split open along a new line, and it left parts of ancient Africa (the southeastern United States) and ancient Europe (New England, Nova Scotia, and eastern Newfoundland) attached to present-day North America and parts of ancient North America (Scotland) attached to Europe.

Paleobiogeographic evidence not only suggested that continents had drifted apart, but even opened the door to our understanding of how continents are put together. Decades ago, paleontologists found Permian fusulinid foraminifera (single-celled organisms) in the central British Columbia Rockies that had affinities with the Tethyan seaway that once stretched from the Straits of Gibraltar to Indonesia. How did these peculiar Permian foraminifera get there? Was there an arm of the warm tropical Tethys that reached up to British Columbia? Or were they part of a moving continental fragment that used to be in the Tethys but crossed the Pacific and became sutured to British Columbia? Although the latter idea seems outrageous at first, as more and more evidence accumulated, it became the best explanation. It turns out that the western Cordillera of North America is made up of numerous exotic terranes that have rafted from across the Pacific and collided with North America at various times during the Mesozoic and Cenozoic. Several of these terranes not only have peculiar Tethyan faunas, but the temperature preferences of their fossils suggest that in the Permian the Cache Creek terrane was part of the tropical Tethys, the Alexander terrane was at subtropical to warm-temperate latitudes, and Wrangellia came from the cool southern latitudes. Today, Wrangellia is the bedrock for southeastern Alaska and Vancouver Island, and the Cache Creek and Alexander terranes are located deep in the British Columbia Rockies—quite a distance for that much land to travel in about 250 million years. In addition to fusulinids, the Triassic ammonoids show the previous position of these terranes, and the Jurassic ammonites have been used as evidence of dramatic northward movement of many of these terranes (for a review of these data, see Hallam 1986).

Most of the concepts of biogeography were developed under the assumption that the continents were fixed. When plate tectonics came along, it was possible for organisms (or their fossils) to get from point A to point B without doing the walking themselves. M.C. McKenna (1973, 1983) suggested several other possible mechanisms where the plates do most of the traveling. If a landmass were to rift away from one area, travel across the ocean, and then collide into another, it could transport its inhabitants to a new land. McKenna (1973) called this a Noah's Ark since it bears similarities to the transport of animals by the biblical boat. Although it is hard to document examples of Noah's Ark transport in the fossil record, several authors have suggested that the transport of India from Gondwanaland to the southern part of Asia may be such a case. India drifted away from Gondwanaland in the Cretaceous and may have had its own endemic archaic mammals. India began its collision with Asia, forming the Himalayas, in the Early Eocene. This is when several advanced groups of mammals (both even-toed artiodactyls and odd-toed perissodactyls, as well as advanced primates) suddenly appeared in Asia and around the world. If those groups had evolved in isolation in India and then spread during the Early Eocene after India docked, it would explain why we do not see them, or their ancestors, anywhere in the world during the Early Paleocene. Unfortunately, we do not yet have much of a fossil record for the Cretaceous or Paleocene in India to test this hypothesis.

But the organisms do not even have to be alive for the plates to move them around. They can just as easily be incorporated as fossils in the rocks, and then be found in another area when continents collide. McKenna (1973) called these beached Viking funeral ships, in reference to the way the Vikings used to send their dead warriors to Valhalla on their longboats, filled with their weapons and wealth and then set ablaze. The Cambrian European trilobites in North America and American trilobites in Scotland mentioned previously are examples of this phenomenon, as are the Tethyan fusulinids now found in British Columbia.

It is even possible that the geographic range of the organisms is older than the land they are living on. McKenna (1983) suggested two mechanisms that could produce this interesting paradox. Midocean ridge islands, such as Iceland, are continually changing as their spreading ridge drifts apart and sinks down into the ocean. The oldest rocks in Iceland are only 13 million years old, yet it is likely that there has been an island in Iceland's position since the North Atlantic first opened in the Jurassic. If so, then an organism could stay on the island for millions of years while the island slowly spread apart and sank away underneath it, analogous to staying in one place by walking up the down escalator (or escalator counterflow in McKenna's terminology).

A similar mechanism might be called escalator hopscotch. The Hawaiian Islands, for example, are part of a long chain of seamounts that extend to the submerged Emperor Seamount chain in the western Pacific. Each Hawaiian island erupted and formed as it sat over the mid-Pacific mantle hotspot, then sank away as its plate moved away from the hotspot. The hotspot is currently under the big island of Hawaii (producing the active Kilauea Volcano), and the rest of the extinct volcanoes of the other Hawaiian Islands are progressively older as you move northwest along the chain. Thus, an organism could hopscotch from a dead, sinking island that is about to become a submerged seamount to an active volcanic island, and the faunas of such an island chain could be older than the islands themselves. So far, no clear-cut cases of either of these mechanisms have been documented, but they are clearly plausible.

DONALD R. PROTHERO

See also Faunal and Floral Provinces; Paleobiogeography; Paleoecology; Seas, Ancient; Seismic and Surface Activity

Works Cited

Bambach, R.K., C.R. Scotese, and A.M. Ziegler. 1980. Before Pangea: Geographies of the Paleozoic world. *American Scientist* 68:26–38.

Hallam, A. 1986. Evidence of displaced terranes from Permian to Jurassic faunas around the Pacific margins. *Journal of the Geological Society of London* 143:209–16.

McKenna, M.C. 1973. Sweepstakes, filters, corridors, Noah's arks, and beached Viking funeral ships in paleogeography. *In* D.H. Tarling and S.K. Runcorn (eds.), *Implications of Continental Drift to the Earth Sciences*. London and New York: Academic Press.

———. 1983. Holarctic land mass rearrangement, cosmic events, and Cenozoic terrestrial organisms. *Annals of the Missouri Botanical Garden* 70:459–89.

Scotese, C., and J. Golonka. 1992. *Paleogeographic Atlas*. Arlington: Department of Geology, University of Texas.

Further Reading

Bambach, R.K., C.R. Scotese, and A.M. Ziegler. 1980. Before Pangea: Geographies of the Paleozoic world. *American Scientist* 68:26–38.

Condie, K.C. 1976. *Plate Tectonics and Crustal Evolution*. New York: Pergamon; 4th ed., Oxford and Boston: Butterworth Heineman.

Cox, A., and R.B. Hart. 1986. *Plate Tectonics: How It Works*. Palo Alto, California: Blackwell.

Gray, J., and A.J. Boucot. 1979. *Historical Biogeography: Plate Tectonics and the Changing Environment*. Corvallis: Oregon State University Press.

Hallam, A. 1973a. *Atlas of Paleobiogeography*. Amsterdam and New York: Elsevier.

———. 1973b. *A Revolution in the Earth Sciences: From Continental Drift to Plate Tectonics*. Oxford: Clarendon Press.

———. 1986. Evidence of displaced terranes from Permian to Jurassic faunas around the Pacific margins. *Journal of the Geological Society of London* 143:209–16.

Hughes, N.F. (ed.). 1973. *Organisms and Continents through Time*. Palaeontological Association Special Papers in Palaeontology, 12. London: Palaeontological Association.

McKenna, M.C. 1973. Sweepstakes, filters, corridors, Noah's arks, and beached Viking funeral ships in paleogeography. *In* D.H. Tarling and S.K. Runcorn (eds.), *Implications of Continental Drift to the Earth Sciences*. London and New York: Academic Press.

———. 1983. Holarctic land mass rearrangement, cosmic events, and Cenozoic terrestrial organisms. *Annals of the Missouri Botanical Garden* 70:459–89.

Scotese, C., and J. Golonka. 1992. *Paleogeographic Atlas*. Arlington: Department of Geology, University of Texas.

Wegener, A. 1924. *The Origin of Continents and Oceans*. London: Methuen; New York: Dover, 1966; as *Die Entstehung der Kontinente und Ozeane*, Braunschweig: Vieweg, 1915.

Wyllie, P. 1976. *The Way the Earth Works*. New York: Wiley.

PNEUMATIC SPACES

The presence of "pneumatic bones" (bones that include hollow air spaces) in dinosaurs was first noted by Richard Owen (1842) in the theropod *Altispinax (Megalosaurus)*. He noted that the large cavities ("fossae") in the vertebrae of the back were similar to those occupied by extensions of the lungs in extant (present-day) birds. The pneumatic nature of the vertebrae of theropod and sauropod dinosaurs was accepted generally until the early 1900s, when it fell out of favor, apparently due to the influence of Henry Fairfield Osborn. During the next nine decades of the twentieth century, only Janensch (1947) conducted a study of pneumatic spaces in dinosaur bones. The pneumatic nature of bones in pterosaurs (flying reptiles), however, has been accepted almost since the group was recognized, and the interpretation has not been challenged. Recent research (Britt 1993) revived the pneumatic interpretation of the fossae and foramina, often termed "pleurocoels" in saurischian dinosaur vertebrae.

Within the Dinosauria, postcranial pneumatic bones are present only in the Saurischia (theropods, prosauropods, and sauropods), they are absent in Ornithischia. In the Sauropodomorpha (prosauropods and sauropods), in non-avian theropods, and even in the oldest bird, *Archaeopteryx,* postcranial pneumaticity is limited to the vertebrae, usually the cervical (neck) and dorsal (back) vertebrae and some ribs. This contrasts sharply with the condition in the flying archosauromorphs, pterosaurs, and extant birds.

Here, an array of nonaxial postcranial bones (limb bones), are often pneumatized. Evidence that the vertebrae of pterosaurs and saurischian dinosaurs were pneumatic is based on large fossae, foramina (smaller openings), and remodelling textures preserved on and in the vertebrae—structures that closely match pneumatic features on living bird vertebrae. Typical external pneumatic features of coelurosaurian theropod vertebrae are shown in Figure 1 and internal structures in Figure 2.

To understand the pneumatic bones of extinct archosauromorphs it is important to have a basic understanding of pneumatic bones in extant birds—the only living animal with pneumatic postcranial bones. In birds, postcranial bones are filled with air (pneumatized) by air sacs (balloonlike structures) of the lungs. Simply put, bird lungs are composed of distinct components that provide for gas exchange and for pumping air. The core of the lung (paleopulmo or *pulmo arcuiformis*) is small and compact, compared to nonavian lungs, and is composed of numerous, subparallel tubes (parabronchi). Gas exchange—the uptake of oxygen and throwing off carbon dioxide—takes place in the lung core. The major air sacs, located mainly before and behind the exchange portion of the lung, act as passive bellows that control air flow. Gas exchange does not occur within the air sacs. Air sac volume is controlled by rib and sternum movement. Essentially, the air only flows forward through the core of the lung. In fact, air flows forward during both inhala-

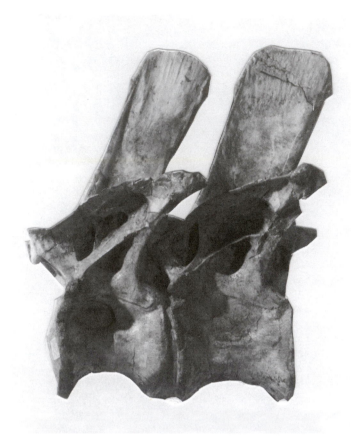

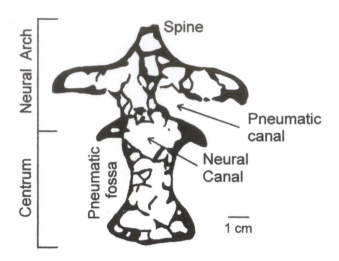

Figure 2. Transverse (crosswise) section of a therizinosaur (segnosaur) cervical vertebra, based on a CT scan, showing extreme pneumatization typical of tetanuran theropods. Bone is black. In life, with the exception of the neural canal (the space through which the spinal cord passes), all spaces within the vertebra were air-filled. Not all trabeculae are preserved.

Figure 1. Dorsal vertebrae 4 and 5 of the Chinese theropod. *Sinraptor dongi*, left lateral view. In life, all of the visible fossae (dark recesses) were occupied by nonrespiratory, pneumatic extensions of the lungs. A pneumatic fossa is present on the centrum of dorsal 4 but absent on dorsal 5. From Currie and Zhao (1993).

tion and exhalation via coordinated changes in pressure in the cranial (skull) and caudal (tail) air sacs. No other extant vertebrate has such an efficient and derived lung. By comparison, lungs of mammals are composed of blind sacs, many times larger than the parabronchi. The degree of postcranial pneumatization in modern birds varies from group to group. The pigeon is typical of most birds in that the cervical (neck), dorsal, and sacral (lower back) vertebrae as well as the ribs, sternum, humerus (upper arm bone), and femur (thigh bone) are pneumatic. Pneumatization of postcranial bones occurs well after the bird hatches, when branches of the air sacs invade and gradually replace most of the marrow and fatty tissues within affected bones.

It frequently is stated that pneumatization of avian bones was an adaptation to flight because the replacement of marrow by air reduces the overall mass of a bone. The highly corroborated theory that birds descended from theropod dinosaurs, which also have pneumatic bones, however, argues against the flight hypothe-

sis. Birds inherited postcranial pneumatic bones from their theropod ancestors. Therefore the pneumatic condition is preadaption—a condition that arose before it became an advantage to a certain function, in this case, flight. The re-recognition of the pneumatic nature of saurischian vertebrae provides further evidence of the close relationship between dinosaurs, especially theropods, and birds. The presence of pneumatized postcranial bones, indicating air sacs with extensions, in saurischians theropods indicates theropods had lungs approaching the avian condition.

BROOKS B. BRITT

See also Birds; Pterosaurs; Theropods

Works Cited

Britt, B.B. 1993. Pneumatic Postcranial Bones in Dinosaurs and Other Archosaurs. Ph.D. diss., University of Calgary.

Currie, P.J., and X. Zhao. 1993. A new carnosaur (Dinosauria, Theropoda) from the Jurassic of Xinjiang, People's Republic of China. *Canadian Journal of Earth Sciences* 30 (10–11):2037–81.

Janensch, W. 1947. Pneumatizitat bei Wirbeln von Sauropoden und anderen Sauriern. *Palaeontographica* (7) 3:1–25.

Owen, R. 1842. Report on British fossil reptiles, part II. *British Association for the Advancement of Science* 11:60–204.

POPULATION DYNAMICS

A population is a group of individuals belonging to the same species. Population dynamics is the description, often in mathematical terms, of how population abundance changes through time. Two key parameters often used to describe these changes are (1) intrinsic rate of increase, often symbolized by r, and (2) carrying capacity, often symbolized by K. Intrinsic rate of increase refers to the ability of the population to grow under optimal environmental conditions. A pair of mice, for example, can produce many hundreds of offspring in just a few years, whereas a pair of elephants would take centuries to produce the same number of offspring. Mice thus have a much higher intrinsic rate of increase than elephants. Factors that promote such high rates of increase include short generation times and large litters.

Carrying capacity refers to the maximum population size that the environment can sustain for long periods. A few acres of land can sustain many mice, for example, but very few (if any) elephants for long periods. Carrying capacity is determined by the combination of physical and biological limitations. Physical limitations include available space and water supply. Biological limitations include the presence of natural enemies and competitors.

Population dynamics generally occur so rapidly that the details are not preserved in the fossil record. The fossil record rarely contains data on events that occur on time spans of weeks to decades because fossil deposition is not constant over such small time scales. On the other hand, it is possible to observe changes in population dynamics over very long periods of time in the fossil record. The process of time-averaging occurs when short-term ecological events are "averaged" or intermixed in the fossil record. Detailed studies of time-averaged fossil abundance indicate that most species were apparently consistently rare or consistently common throughout their entire geological ranges, often for many millions of years (Brett and Baird 1995; McKinney et al. 1997).

Such data indicate that populations tend to be surprisingly stable over very long periods of time. Comparison with living populations implies that this occurs because organisms are well adapted to their environment. Furthermore, whenever the environment changes, populations will migrate in order to stay within their optimal living conditions. This stability also implies that population levels tend to remain near their environmental carrying capacities for very long periods of time, as predicted by theoretical population dynamic models.

The fossil record also contains important information about the geographic distribution of populations. Living species are rarely randomly distributed geographically. Rather, their populations tend to be clumped, with areas of high abundance that taper off in different directions (Maurer 1994). This same spatial pattern has been found when paleontologists have sampled fossil abundance of a species in laterally adjacent rocks of similar age (Miller 1988). A related finding is that, in living organisms, rare species tend to have greater geographic population variability, being less evenly distributed across the landscape (Maurer 1994, Gaston 1994). This seems to be true in fossils as well (McKinney et al. 1997).

Such geographic variability reflects the spatially dynamic nature of populations. In many species, local populations will frequently become extinct. The species persists only because those local populations are quickly replaced by recolonization from nearby populations. This constant process of local extinction and recolonization is called metapopulation dynamics and is a rapidly growing area of study in ecology (Hanski and Gilpin 1997). While it is not possible to directly study metapopulation dynamics in fossils, it is possible to see many of its long-term consequences for paleoecology and evolution (McKinney and Allmon 1995).

Biological communities are composed of particular assemblages of populations. Similarly, fossil communities are composed of recurring fossil assemblages in which relative species abundances remain generally constant through long periods of time (Brett and Baird 1995). Communities often are named after the most dominant (common) species within them. An example would be a brachiopod community, or more specifically, a *Pentamerus* community of the Paleozoic era. That fossil communities tend to recur with generally constant species abundances conforms to the inferences about population stability through long geological time spans. The fact that populations of the same associated species are found in constant coexistence may indicate that the species were interdependent on each other. Alternatively, it may indicate that the species were all adapted to the same physical environment, and that they simply coexisted because they occupied similar habitats and the populations had little or no direct interaction.

MICHAEL L. MCKINNEY

See also Biomass and Productivity Estimates; Coevolutionary Relationships; Faunal and Floral Provinces; Faunal Change and Turnover; Mortality and Survivorship; Paleobiogeography; Paleoecology; Predation; Trace Fossils; Trophic Groups and Levels; Vent and Seep Faunas

Works Cited

Brett, C.E., and G.C. Baird. 1995. Coordinated stasis and evolutionary ecology of Silurian to Middle Devonian faunas in the Appalachian Basin. *In* D.H. Erwin and R.L. Anstey (eds.), *New Approaches to Speciation in the Fossil Record*. New York: Columbia University Press.

Gaston, K.J. 1994. *Rarity*. London and New York: Chapman and Hall.

Hanski, I., and M. Gilpin (eds.). 1997. *Metapopulation Biology*. San Diego, California: Academic Press.

Maurer, B.A. 1994. *Geographical Population Analysis*. Oxford and Boston: Blackwell Scientific.

McKinney, M.L., J.L. Lockwood, and D.R. Frederick. 1997. Does ecosystem and evolutionary stability include rare species? *Palaeogeography, Palaeoclimatology, Palaeoecology* 127:191–207.

McKinney, M.L., and W.D. Allmon. 1995. Metapopulations and disturbance: From patch dynamics to biodiversity dynamics. *In* D.H. Erwin and R.L. Anstey (eds.), *New Approaches to Speciation in the Fossil Record*. New York: Columbia University Press.

Miller, A.I. 1988. Spatial resolution in subfossil molluscan remains: Implications for paleobiological analyses. *Paleobiology* 14:91–103.

Further Reading

Brown, J.H. 1995. *Macroecology.* Chicago: University of Chicago Press.

Gaston, K.J. 1994. *Rarity.* London and New York: Chapman and Hall.

Hanski, I., and M. Gilpin (eds.). 1997. *Metapopulation Biology.* San Diego, California: Academic Press.

POSITIONAL SENSE

See Hearing and Positional Sense

PREDATION

Predation has been a fundamental force in evolution and ecology throughout the Phanerozoic. All animals must capture food in order to survive and reproduce. In turn, all animals themselves must avoid being eaten by others. The effects of predation are apparent in several important ways: in the morphological and behavioral adaptations of organisms, in the geographic and ecologic distribution of populations, and in the diversity and structure of biological communities.

Observing Predation in the Fossil Record

Some modes of predation are much more apparent in the fossil record than others. In general, we can draw inferences about the predatory habits of animals by looking at the morphology (shape and structure) of the predators, in particular their appendages and mouthparts (which are typically heavily skeletonized and, therefore, likely candidates for fossilization), and their sense organs. Or, we can look at the remains of the victims of predation. Hard parts, themselves frequently adaptations against predation, also happen to facilitate the study of predation. Thus, we find that the study of predation in the fossil record, as with many other aspects of paleontology, is biased in favor of those groups with preservable hard parts. In particular, predation on bivalve and gastropod molluscs is well studied. Their fossilized shells provide the evidence.

Predators such as crabs, stomatopods (shrimplike crustaceans), and muricid and naticid gastropods leave characteristic injuries on bivalve and gastropod prey. Some of the time, potential victims manage to survive these attacks and repair their shells, thereby leaving an interesting and informative record of predator–prey interaction.

The History of Predation

The importance of predator–prey interactions as a primary driving force for evolutionary change has been described in a series of books and papers by G.J. Vermeij (1977, 1987). In the extended arms race of "escalation," predators become more efficient at gaining prey, leading in turn to the evolution of stronger defense mechanisms in prey lineages. Indeed, the Phanerozoic fossil record does show striking increases in the abundance of predators and in the variety and complexity of antipredatory defenses.

The Ediacaran fauna, present worldwide in the Late Proterozoic (590 to 550 million years ago), is characterized by relatively large (up to 45 centimeters), soft-bodied organisms. The apparently unprotected nature of these organisms indicates that predation was not yet a major factor in animal evolution. Early in the Cambrian period, however, we see the evolution of a variety of animals with preservable hardparts: tiny tubes, cones, and shelly bits of various shapes and chemical compositions, many of which were made by unknown organisms. Some have argued that this rapid evolution of skeletonized invertebrate life was, in fact, caused by the evolution of predators (Stanley 1973), whereas others have emphasized changes in the physical-chemical nature of the environment. Although the predators themselves are not preserved, the presence of small boreholes in some specimens, probably caused by some predators, and the apparently interlocking nature of some skeletal elements to form a kind of external armor argue for an important role for predation in the evolution of Early Cambrian life.

By the time that the deposits of the Middle Cambrian Burgess Shale were laid down, a variety of predators had evolved, including the largest known Cambrian animal *Anomalocaris*. This bizarre and spectacular predator was up to half a meter long, with a pair of appendages for catching prey, and a circular jaw for crushing them. The Middle Paleozoic witnessed the first large-scale diversification of predatory animals (Signor and Brett 1984). Foremost among these were the jawed fishes, which arose in the Late Silurian and diversified dramatically in the Devonian. Placoderms were the dominant fishes of the Devonian and include the most powerful predators of this period. Most placoderms were heavily armored on the head and forward trunk and therefore were not particularly maneuverable. Some Late Devonian forms exceeded 10 meters in length. Placoderms exhibit a variety of tooth types, including large crushing teeth, probably for eating molluscs and arthropods. Sharks and ray-finned fishes also evolved in the Devonian: The latter group eventually came to dominate both freshwater and marine habitats in the Mesozoic and Cenozoic.

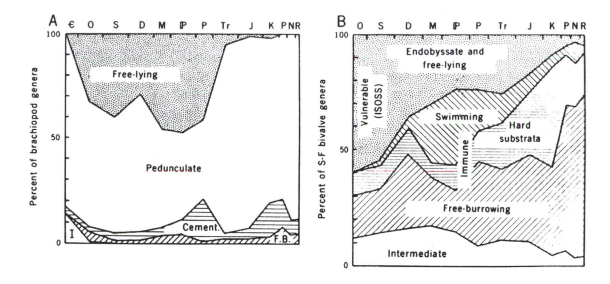

Figure 1. Percentage of brachiopods (A) and bivalves (B) in major adaptive zones throughout the Phanerozoic. Note the overall decline in free-lying forms. Reprinted with permission from Thayer (1979). Copyright © 1979 American Association for the Advancement of Science.

Two important groups of predatory invertebrates also diversified in the Middle Paleozoic. Eurypterids, relatives of scorpions and horseshoe crabs, are somewhat rare in the fossil record but are nonetheless spectacular. Most eurypterids were less than 20 centimeters long, although several forms were huge. The largest arthropod known is a Devonian eurypterid nearly two meters long. Ammonoid cephalopods first appear in the Devonian, although they may not have evolved shell-crushing abilities until the Triassic, when the first calcified jaws are found.

An even greater variety of predatory organisms arose, or developed shell-crushing habits, during the Mesozoic, including teleost fishes, sharks, rays, birds, lobsters, crabs, stomatopods, and gastropods (e.g., clams, snails). Naturally, the evolution of so many predators is apparent in the morphology and patterns of abundance of a great many prey groups as well. For example, Vermeij (1977, 1987) described trends in gastropod morphology that reflect increased sturdiness of the shell (reduced umbilicus; decrease in planispiral and open-coiled shells) or increased protection of the animal inside (via external spines or reduced apertural size); (see also Stanley 1977; Signor and Brett 1984).

These Late Mesozoic changes in predator and prey habits and abundance, which Vermeij calls the Mesozoic marine revolution, resulted in a profound restructuring of benthic (bottom-dwelling) communities. Paleozoic communities are characterized by brachiopods and stalked crinoids that lived on the seafloor or partially buried in soft sediment. Throughout much of the Mesozoic, bivalves lived in abundance on top of the sediment surface. By the late Cretaceous these lifestyles were no longer tenable. The increasing abundance of predators in the Mesozoic resulted in selection for lineages that could respire and feed while buried within the sediment (infaunal) (Figure 1). Consequently, the fossil record reflects a great diversification of infaunal organisms, particularly gastropods, bivalves, and echinoids, in the Jurassic and Cretaceous.

Overall, abundant evidence points to an increased role for predation over the Phanerozoic. The increases are not gradually accumulating, however, but are concentrated in particular intervals of time, notably the Early Cambrian, Middle Paleozoic, and Mid-Late Mesozoic.

DANA H. GEARY

See also Defensive Structures; Diet; Exoskeletal Design; Ornamentation; Skeletized Organisms and the Evolution of Skeletized Tissues; Teeth

Works Cited

Signor, P.W., and C.E. Brett. 1984. The Mid-Paleozoic precursor to the Mesozoic marine revolution. *Paleobiology* 10:229–45.

Stanley, S.M. 1973. An ecological theory for the sudden origin of multicellular life in the late Precambrian. *Proceedings of the National Academy of Sciences USA* 70:1486–89.

———. 1977. Trends, rates, and patterns of evolution in the Bivalvia. *In* A. Hallam (ed.), *Patterns of Evolution as Illustrated by the Fossil Record*. Amsterdam and New York: Elsevier.

Thayer, J. 1979. Biological bulldozers and the evolution of marine benthic communities. *Science* 203:458–61.

Vermeij, G.J. 1977. The Mesozoic marine revolution: Evidence from snails, predators, and grazers. *Paleobiology* 3:245–58.

———. 1987. *Evolution and Escalation*. Princeton, New Jersey: Princeton University Press.

Further Reading

Hallam, A. (ed.). 1977. *Patterns of Evolution as Illustrated by the Fossil Record*. Amsterdam and New York: Elsevier.

Vermeij, G.J. 1987. *Evolution and Escalation*. Princeton, New Jersey: Princeton University Press.

PREPARATION TECHNIQUES

The preparation of fossils is almost as complex and varied as the organisms themselves. Each fossil is unique in itself, is preserved uniquely, and is encased in matrix that can vary from inch to inch in its makeup. (Matrix is simply the rock and dirt around and within a fossil.) Because of these factors, there is no set course describing how to prepare fossils (the final removal of matrix from the fossil). As one textbook says, the person who prepares fossils "must be part chemist, part anatomist and part artist, added to which he [or she] must be capable of working in a variety of materials ranging from all forms of plastic to mild steel. He [or she] is a living contradiction of the old adage, for he [or she] must be a jack of all trades in order to be the master of his [or her] own" (Rixon 1976). The most important factor preparators must realize is their own limitations. Not doing so may result in damage to the fossil but, even more so, to the preparator.

Microfossils, plants, and vertebrate fossils each require their own methods of final extraction from their sedimentary tomb. Microfossils (fossils of smaller organisms such as shells) usually are extracted in the field in bulk samples from the rock. Using acids, the bulk material is softened through soaking in a well-ventilated, secure portion of the lab. These acids (often acetic or formic) break down the matrix, separating the fossil organisms. Eventually, however, the acids will attack the fossils themselves so after a period of time, the materials are put into a neutralizing bath, which breaks down the acids. This process is often repeated one or more times until sufficient matrix is removed. Once softening has taken place, the fossils can be picked over, using a microscope.

Slightly larger plants require a different methodology because the carbonized remains often are susceptible to disfigurement or damage by an improper touch alone. Preparation using small, fine dental tools will remove much of the matrix, as the plant often acts as a separator between layers of sediment. Securing the fossil then requires a light spray of adhesives.

Vertebrate fossils are probably the most difficult and expensive to prepare, primarily due to their size. Work on one of these specimens, say a dinosaur, requires a large lab with secure floors and good ventilation (to remove dust). The tools needed vary depending on how solid the bone is and how resistant the matrix is. Examples of tools used include pencil-sized pneumatic jackhammers (generally called air scribes) and sand blasters, along with dental tools and scalpels. Each is used to pick the rock away from the fossil. The general philosophy is to follow along the known surface of the bone into the rock, inch by inch. This is a safer procedure than working through the rock until reaching the bone. The fossil, in all its contorted shape, dictates the pace and level of preparation.

As the bone is exposed, glues are applied, saturating the bone. This is done to restrict the amount of further breakage. A thicker concentration of glue is used to actually cement pieces together. These glues have changed over the years, but today most laboratories use synthetic adhesives that can be diluted to desired mixtures in aromatic solvents. For example, Acryloid B-72 is a common adhesive that is dissolved in acetone.

Sometimes acids are used to prepare vertebrate fossils, when the matrix is calcium-carbonate based, and the fossil is too delicate for either pneumatic or manual tools. Often this technique is done on fossils from marine deposits.

One of the most important things to remember in preparation is always to label the specimen with a catalog number or, at least, the specimen's origin. It is not uncommon for a fossil preparator to work on more than one project at a time (these projects take weeks, months, or even years to complete) and without this information, the specimen becomes almost useless. Another important feature of preparation is that many of the chemicals are toxic and/or flammable. Consultation with occupational health and safety groups is advised strongly. Once the preparation is done, the detailed interpretation can begin. It is important to note that the quality of the interpretation often depends on the quality of preparation.

Within the last 30 years, the knowledge of various preparation techniques has increased tremendously. The major published works include *Handbook of Paleontological Techniques* (Kummel and Raup 1965), an edited book with over 80 subsections, ranging from the major groups of fossils recovered, collecting, preparation, photography, and chemical-preparation techniques. Another major work, Rixon's *Fossil Animal Remains* (1976), pertains only to that type of fossil. More recently, Leiggi and May co-edited the first volume of *Vertebrate Paleontological Techniques* (1994), upgrading the new discoveries in fossil extraction, preparation, and data recording. In these three publications, there are enough references, supplier lists, and contacts, to familiarize anyone with the task of preparation.

The actual handling of fossil remains has become of such importance that some groups, such as the Society of Vertebrate Paleontology, have specific sessions on preparation techniques at their annual conference. Whatever the method or fossil, the quality of fossil preparation will depend not only on one's skills, but on one's experience. Generally, the more fossils an individual previously has prepared, the better each new preparation will be.

TIM T. TOKARYK

See also Field Techniques; Paleontology: Overview

Works Cited and Further Reading

Kummel, B., and D. Raup (eds.). 1965. *Handbook of Paleontological Techniques*. San Francisco: Freeman.

Leiggi, P., and P. May (eds.). 1994. *Vertebrate Paleontological Techniques*. Vol. 1., Cambridge and New York: Cambridge University Press.

Rixon, A.E. 1976. *Fossil Animal Remains, Their Preparation and Conservation*. London and Atlantic Highlands, New Jersey: Athlone Press of the University of London.

PRIMATES

Primates is the order of mammals to which humans belong, together with the greater and lesser apes, the Old and New World monkeys, the tarsiers, the bushbabies, the lemurs, and various extinct groups. The relationships of the primates among the mammals have long been debated, but today Primates is most often considered to group with the orders Scandentia (tree shrews), Dermoptera (colugos or flying lemurs), and Chiroptera (bats) to form the larger grouping Archonta. Apart from the ubiquitous *Homo sapiens* (and to a lesser extent various types of macaques) all extant (modern-day) primates are tropical or subtropical, and the vast majority of species are confined to forested or wooded environments.

Definition and Classification of Primates

Arriving at a morphological definition of the order Primates always has posed a problem since it is, of course, phylogeny (evolutionary history) rather than morphology (form) that ultimately gives the group its unity. Nonetheless, if we disregard the "archaic" forms of the Paleocene, we can follow W.E. Le Gros Clark in characterizing Primates in terms of a number of "progressive trends" that marked the order's evolution. All these trends indicate the ways in which the order has diverged from other major mammalian lineages. These trends include decreased importance of olfaction (the sense of smell) and increased importance of stereoscopic vision; enhanced grasping and manipulative capacities, associated with the replacement of claws by nails that back sensitive pads on all or nearly all digits; and a tendency toward enlargement of the "higher" centers of the brain, notably the association areas of the neocortex.

Classification of the 200-odd species of primates is currently in flux and probably always will be. Partly, this is because classifications are inevitably a matter of taste, but there are also some major uncertainties about relationships within the order. The principal uncertainty concerns the tarsiers (*Tarsius*), which have been grouped with both the "lower" primates (the lemurs, bushbabies, and lorises) and the "higher" primates (the Old and New World monkeys, apes, and humans). Scholars who adhere to the former scheme classify the living primates into two suborders: Prosimii (lemurs and relatives, plus tarsiers) and Anthropoidea (the rest). Scholars who classify the tarsiers along with the higher primates also produce two divisions: Strepsirhini (lemurs, bushbabies and lorises) and Haplorhini (tarsiers and the rest). Table 1 details these relationships.

The question is far from being resolved, but majority opinion probably rests with the second option, which we follow in the classification presented here. It is consistent with the family-level phylogeny of the primates presented in Figure 1. Because of the ongoing, active debate, we stress that this cladogram is provisional.

The Living and Subfossil "Lower" Primates

The Strepsirhini are often known as lower primates because they more closely resemble the earliest "primates of modern aspect" than

do the haplorhines. In general, strepsirhinines have smaller brain-to-body weight ratios than higher primates, and more poorly developed diurnal (daytime) vision—they lack postorbital closure (a true eye socket) and have limited color vision at best. They also retain more elaborate olfactory equipment that includes a tethered upper lip (one with limited movement), and a moist rhinarium ("wet nose") that communicates with a relatively well developed vomero-nasal organ (that is used to detect pheromones). This emphasis on the sense of smell is reflected in the ways in which strepsirhines communicate, which involves a great deal of scent marking though urine, feces, and exudations produced by specialized glands. Strepsirhines have abducted (well-separated) first digits and strong grasping capabilities, but compared to the higher primates, their ability to grasp with their hands is imprecise.

Strepsirhini is a diverse group, with five extant families in Madagascar and two in Africa/Asia. All strepsirhines are united by the possession of a "toilet claw" on the second pedal (foot) digit and a "tooth comb" in the lower jaw, consisting of slender, totally procumbent (horizontally projecting) front teeth. Body sizes range from about 30 to 60 grams in the tiny mouse lemurs (Microcelous) to about seven kilograms in the largest sifakas (Propithecus) and the babakoto (Indri). Until very recently (within the last one thousand years), Madagascar harbored a much wider diversity of lemurs. The larger-bodied forms apparently succumbed rapidly to the activities of late-arriving human beings. These extinct "subfossil" forms are known mostly from Holocene cave and marsh deposits throughout the island. All these forms are effectively members of the modern

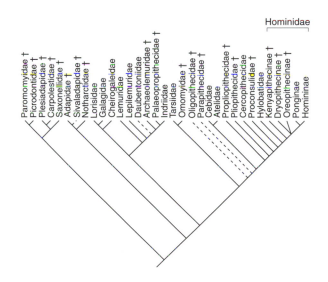

Figure 1. Consensus cladogram of primate families, with subfamilies of Hominidae. Symbols: †, extinct group; ...., probable placement of questioned taxa.

lemur fauna, so they are most appropriately considered in this section, along with their surviving relatives.

Perhaps the most remarkable of the extinct strepsirhines of Madagascar are the "sloth lemurs," family Palaeopropithecidae (Figure 2). The three smaller genera of this family show increasing suspensory adaptation with body weight (estimated to range from about 10 to 60 kilograms). Throughout the skeleton of the largest group, *Palaeopropethecus*, the joints were built for mobility rather than for stability and strength, except in the long, hooklike hands, where the tongue-in-groove phalangeal joints limited movement to a single plane and maximized power grasping. However, with an estimated weight of up to 200 kilograms, *Archaeoindris*, the largest palaeopropethecid of all, was clearly too large to have led an arboreal existence. Members of the genus almost certainly filled in Madagascar a similar niche to that occupied in the southwestern United States by the Pleistocene giant ground sloths.

Equally unusual were the species of *Megaladapis*, giant relatives (40 to 80 kilograms) of today's *Lepilemur*. Its extraordinarily long hands and feet, adapted for very strong grasping, testify that *Megaladapis* was arboreal (lived in trees), but its very short fore and hind limbs and high body weight suggest a certain lack of agility—leaping ability in particular—in this vertical clinger. This may explain its unusual skull morphology. The skull is peculiarly elongate. The foramen magnum (opening in the skull for the spinal cord) points backward, and the face is tilted up on the cranial base. These adaptations would have converted the head into a long extension of the neck, maximizing the radius within which the *Megaladapis* could crop leaves from a single sitting position. This method of eating may be reflected in the replacement of the upper incisors with a horny pad and perhaps also by the presence of a mobile snout, suggested by the heavily vascularized bone (bone with an unusually large supply of blood vessels) that overhangs the nasal aperture.

Less committed to an arboreal lifestyle were the archaeolemurids. These short-limbed, powerfully built quadrupeds had short extremities that indicate a more terrestrial way of life. These medium-bodied primates (about 15 to 25 kilograms) probably were most similar in appearance to today's baboons. One genus, *Hadropithecus*, is reminiscent of the "manual grazing" geladas in its short face, reduced front teeth, and the expansion of its cheek teeth into a formidable grinding battery.

The surviving strepsirhines of the African and Asian continents are all classified as lorisoids, with two distinctive families: Lorisidae, the slow-climbing lorises and pottos, and Galagidae, the vertical clinging and leaping bushbabies. Also included is the endemic (insular) Malagasy family Cheirogaleidae, the dwarf and mouse lemurs. All lorisoids are small-bodied (under one kilogram) and nocturnal. Although social, they are relatively nongregarious, relying heavily on scent-marking for communication between individuals.

More diverse than the lorisoids are the exclusively Malagasy lemuroids. The families Lepilemuridae (weasel lemurs) and Daubentoniidae (the aye-aye) are exclusively nocturnal, but two of the three genera are diurnal, and most of the lemuroids are cathemeral (active on a 24-hour basis). Social organization varies widely among the diurnal and cathemeral forms. Groups range from bonded pairs with immature offspring, through small, male-only

and female-only groups, to large heterosexual groups of 30 or more. A few lemur species are specialized folivores (leaf eaters), and insects form a significant proportion of the diet of most of the dwarf and mouse lemurs. However, most lemur diets vary according to season and location. In general, the diurnal strepsirhines seem to be as opportunistic in the exploitation of their environments as are their "higher" primate relatives—they will eat whatever type of food is at hand.

Although tarsier-like primates were rather diverse during the Eocene, they are now restricted to four or five species of a single genus, and are found only on islands in the Philippines and Indonesia. These tiny, basically nocturnal animals live in bonded pairs and eat mainly animal protein (insects and small vertebrates). They are characterized by relatively huge eyes and eyesockets that almost fully surround the rear of the eyeball; a dry nose with a mobile upper lip; and elongate tarsal bones (ankle and rear foot bones) (hence their name) that permit them to leap large distances, often pouncing on prey. The dry nose, along with derived features of their placenta, link tarsiers to the anthropods, while the lack of a tooth comb and toilet claw separates them from the strepsirhines. Thus, they are here formally classified within the Haplorhini. Despite this classification, tarsiers, along with their extinct omomyid relatives, are best discussed with the "lower" primates as they still retain many primitive features.

The Living "Higher" Primates

Today, the major subdivision of the Haplorhini, the Anthropoidea, includes three extant superfamilies: Ateloidea (the South American—or New World—monkeys of the infraorder Platyrrhini); Cercopithecoidea (Old World monkeys); and Hominoidea (humans and apes). The latter two major taxa are combined to form an even larger group, the Catarrhini. It is important to note that the two "monkey" superfamilies are *not* each other's closest relatives—"monkey" is basically a grade-level grouping of anthropoids that are held together simply by their retention of primitive anthropoid features. Living "monkeys" are not a monophyletic group, i.e., one in which all members share a direct common ancestor.

The New World primates are in many ways the most diverse haplorhine (or even primate) clade. The smallest-bodied forms (usually under one kilogram) are the Callitrichinae (marmosets and tamarins), which live in groups of one or two pairs with offspring, often inhabiting vine tangles and low bushes. These small animals eat insects, fruit, and tree gums, and the males participate fully in infant care. Their morphology includes superficially "primitive" clawed digits and triangular upper molars. However, these features probably are evolutionary reversals rather than retained ancestral conditions.

Like callitrichines, the Cebinae (capuchin and squirrel monkeys) have a lightly built masticatory (chewing) apparatus, a mainly insectivorous diet, and a tendency to reduce the third molar (which is fully lost in marmosets). Although grouping these two subfamilies together into the family Cebidae is a relatively recent hypothesis (Rosenberger 1992) and is often questioned by other morphologists, recent molecular systematic research has, for the most part, supported it strongly.

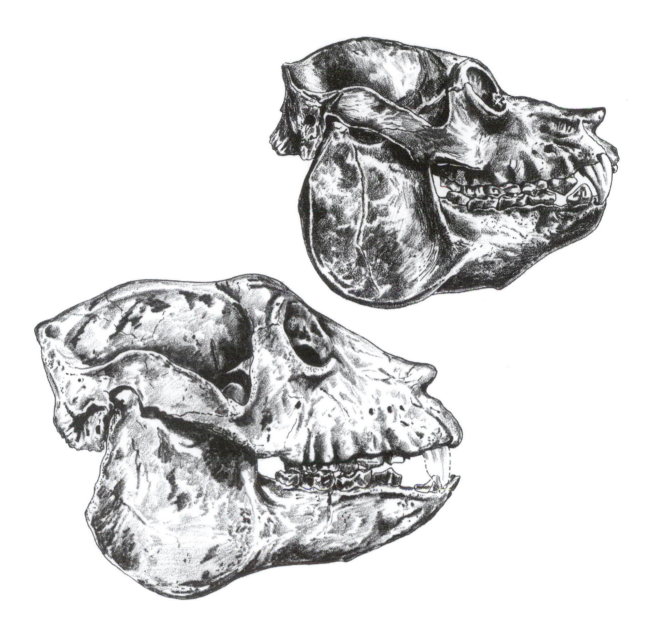

Figure 2. Side view of skulls of *(above)* *Palaeopropithecus maximus* and *(below)* *Archaeoindris fontoynonti* (family Palaeopropithecidae). Illustration by Nicholas Amorosi.

Rosenberger's second platyrrhine family, Atelidae, is less readily characterized morphologically but is also supported by genetic studies. The large-bodied, often acrobatic Atelidae (howler and spider monkeys) have derived prehensile (grasping) tails; their robust masticatory system is suited for diets that mix fruit and leaves. Another subfamily, Pitheciinae, is more diverse, and includes the saki-uakari group *Callicebus,* and perhaps the nocturnal (or cathemeral) *Aotus.* Molecular studies often link the latter genus with cebids, but its apparently conservative features may be "confusing" this result. Pitheciines generally eat hard fruits and seeds. They have relatively robust jaws, a feature shared with atelines.

The catarrhine Old World monkeys have the most species of any primate family. Their characteristic bilophodont molars (which have two cross-ridges) and perhaps their terrestrial locomotion may be "key characters" at the root of their success. Members are widespread in Africa and eastern Asia today, while extinct relatives inhabited the circum-Mediterranean region as well. Cercopithecoids belonging to the subfamily Cercopithecinae (macaques, baboons, and their relatives) monkeys are characterized by cheek pouches for temporary food storage and relatively bunodont (low-crowned) molars. They have eclectic diets centering on fruits. The smaller-bodied guenons and mangabeys of Africa typically live in "harems" dominated by a single male, while the social organization of Asian macaques and the larger-bodied African baboons includes both large heterosexual troops of 30 to 100 individuals and one-male units that often merge into large herds of up to 500 individuals. Cercopithecoids belonging to the subfamily Colobinae (langurs and their relatives) have sharper-cusped molars with higher relief and complex sacculated (multi-chambered) stomachs. This digestive system supports foregut fermentation to break down plant cellulose, allowing a diet of both young and mature leaves. Colobine social structure also features one-male groups (often with infanticide seen during takeover by a new male), but heterosexual groups of 30 or more and even rare pair-bonded units are found in these primarily arboreal monkeys.

The Hominoidea (apes and humans) includes only five living genera, but because one of these is *Homo,* interest in their morphology and behavior has produced an immense literature. The gibbons *(Hylobates)* are usually placed in a monotypic family (i.e., only with one genus) characterized by elongate limbs and a brachiating (arm-swinging) mode of locomotion. Gibbons also have relatively conservative skulls and teeth, pair-bonded social organization, and a diet of fruit or leaves. The great apes were previously classified together in the family Pongidae, but molecular systematic studies in particular have demonstrated that the orangutan is the sister group to African apes plus humans (the Homininae). The physical characteristics of chimpanzees are most similar to gorillas, but genetic analyses place chimps closer to humans. For such a small taxonomic unit, these four genera present a great diversity of locomotor, dietary, and social patterns (even if one does not consider modern human technology).

Primate Origins and Early Evolution

The origins of the primate order are poorly documented but almost certainly extend back into the Late Cretaceous. Most of the primate fossils of the Paleocene radiation (approximately 65 to 55 million years ago) come from the northern continents, notably Europe and the western United States, but it is likely that Africa, about which very little is known before the Late Eocene, was also an early center of primate evolution. Indeed, Africa may harbor the link between the earliest primates and the later primate radiations. There has been some debate over whether the Paleocene forms (the Plesiadapiformes) properly belong in Primates. This is because these animals are both adaptively different from undoubted primates and lack any known direct links to them. Nonetheless, an exclusive shared ancestry of the Plesiadapiformes and the Primates, possibly in the late Cretaceous, is indicated quite strongly by their cheek teeth and postcranial skeletons and by aspects of the morphology of the bony ear (Figure 3).

The best-known plesiadapiform group is *Plesiadapis* (Figure 3a), found in Late Paleocene through earliest Eocene sites in both Europe and North America. Like its relatives, this animal was small-brained (compared to later primates, although not to its nonprimate mammalian contemporaries), lacked the postorbital bar that defines the outer edge of the orbit (eye opening) in all living primates, had an elongate face with enlarged and complex front teeth, and retained clawed extremities. Heavily built though they were, there is no doubt that species of *Plesiadapis* (some 15 have been recognized) were arboreal. Dental evidence suggests that *Plesiadapis* was fully herbivorous. Indeed, although the diets of the plesiadapiforms were evidently quite varied, they show a strong

tendency toward lowered molar cusp relief, which suggests that there was a shift away from insect-based diets and toward diets based on plants at a very early stage of primate evolution. Abundant throughout the Paleocene, the plesiadapiforms declined as primates of modern aspect began to diversify. None survived the end of the Middle Eocene.

Evolution of the "Lower" Primates

The Eocene epoch (approximately 55 to 34 million years ago) witnessed a dramatic radiation of primates of modern aspect (semi-order Euprimates). These forms, which first arose toward the end of the Paleocene, are most abundantly known from fossils in Europe and North America. Scholars agree that these early primates, the first to resemble (in a general way) today's primates, fall into two major groups. The details of their classification are still matters of debate. One group has traditionally been aligned with Madagascar's lemurs and is assigned here to the infraorder Adapiformes of the suborder Strepsirhini. The other group's affinities have seemed to lie with the tarsiers, and accordingly the diverse Eocene superfamily Omomyoidea is classified along with the enigmatic and poorly known middle Eocene Chinese fossil *Eosimias* (Eosimiidae) in the hyporder Tarsiiformes of the suborder Haplorhini. However, it is becoming clear that this simple division obscures a more complex situation, and any classification of the Eocene primates currently remains highly tentative.

The adapiform primates lack the tooth combs and toilet claws of the strepsirhines but in many other respects are similar to Madagascar's lemurs, at least functionally. Similarly, the omomyoids possessed a recognizably modern level of organization. Eocene primates were undoubtedly arboreal, with grasping hands and feet that functioned much like those of strepsirhines. The first toe and thumb were opposed to the remaining digits, and sensitive digital pads were backed by flat nails. Braincases were relatively large and faces reduced, presumably in concordance with a decreased importance of olfaction compared to the archaic primates of the Eocene. A postorbital bar was present and, in some of the larger-eyed omomyoids, there was a certain degree of postorbital closure (i.e., a partial eye socket). This converges on the condition seen in haptorhines. The eyes were relatively forward-facing, which enhanced overlap of the visual fields and thus improved stereoscopic vision. Only a few Eocene primates had teeth that resemble those of modern strepsirhines, and it is hard to demonstrate that any known fossils of the Eocene radiations from the northern continents are the direct ancestor of any species today.

The modern groups of lower primates have sparse fossil records indeed. In the latest Eocene deposits of Egypt's Fayum, there are fossils assigned to the genus *Plesiopethecus,* whose jaws carried an enlarged daggerlike incisor. This animal has been provisionally classified as a lorisiform strepsirhine. By the Miocene epoch (approximately 24 million years ago), lorisids are more fully documented in East Africa by *Mioeuoticus* and in Pakistan by *Nycticeboides* and perhaps by *Indraloris.* The documented evolutionary history of the galagids is shorter yet, extending back to the Late Pliocene (approximately 5 million years ago) in East Africa, and only very dubiously beyond that to Miocene East African forms such as *Progalago* and *Komba*. In Madagascar the lemuriforms and the lorisiform cheirogaleids are bereft of any ancient fossil record at all, although there is a diverse late Pleistocene assemblage, along with its surviving extant members.

Early Evolution of the "Higher" Primates

The origin of the Anthropoidea has been controversial for well over a century. As more and more early primate fossils are recovered, new hypotheses of relationships to living monkeys and apes multiply. Despite earlier suggestions that platyrrhines and catarrhines might have evolved independently to "higher" primate status, modern scholars almost universally accept the idea that anthropoid primates have a single, common ancestor, probably among the tarsiiforms, typified by the Omomyidae.

In recent years, scientists have proposed a number of specific candidates for the role of earliest anthropoid. *Altiatlasius,* from the Late Paleocene of Morocco is, at best, an omomyid relative. It may, in fact, be a basal euprimate. *Eosimias,* from the Middle Eocene of China, is probably a true tarsioid, closer to the living genus than are the known omomyids. Its primitive features throw some light on the morphology of early haplorhines. A variety of other Eocene genera from Asia (including *Pondaungia* from Burma, *Siamopithecus* from Thailand, and *Hoanghonius* from China) and Africa (such as *Djebelemur* from Morocco) probably represent distinctive adapiforms unrelated to anthropoid origins. The oldest plausible anthropoid now appears to be *Algeripithecus* from the Middle Eocene (approximately 45 million years ago) of Glib Zegdou, Algeria. The few isolated molars that are known from this form are similar to those of the well-known parapithecids from the younger Egyptian Fayum sequence.

The oldest Fayum horizon, known as Quarry L-41, is latest Eocene in age. It produced the most archaic of all anthropoids, *Catopithecus,* represented by several damaged skulls and lower jaws. These present a mosaic of conservative (primitive) and derived (advanced) features. It is more primitive than later anthropoids in its dental morphology and in possessing an unfused joint between the left and right halves of the lower jaw. It aligns with later anthropoids in the loss of the interfrontal (metopic suture) of the forehead and the possession of a ringlike ectotympanic (bone that holds the eardrum) affixed to the margins of the bony middle ear opening.

In their molar morphology, *Catopithecus* and its younger relative *Oligopithecus* are significantly more primitive than *Algeripithecus.* This suggests that these Egyptian forms (collectively called oligopethecids) are little changed from basal anthropoids that lived prior to 45 million years ago. In their time, the oligopithecids were therefore "living fossils."

Oligopithecids have only two premolars, an advanced feature seen in catarrhines. This trait has prompted some workers to link them with the later propliopethecids. However, other aspects of their morphology argue against such an association.

Although present in L-41, the Fayum parapithecids are more common in the upper levels of the sequence, especially at about 33 million years ago, where *Apidium* (Figure 3e) is the most abundant small mammal. These three-premolared genera are characterized by a tendency to develop an increased number of bunodont (low, blunt) molar cusps as well as the unique presence of a central conulr (small cusp) on the upper premolars. *Apidium* has canine teeth that clearly show sexual dimorphism (males and females are physically distinct). By contrast, *Catopethecus* shows only a hint of sexual dimorphism. *Apidium* is clearly anthropoid in its fused frontal bones, fused mandibular symphysis (intermandibular joint), and possession of a fully closed orbit (eye socket). Its locomotor morphology is specialized, as it was clearly adapted to arboreal running and leaping. *Parapithecus (Simonsius),* a somewhat larger parapithecid, had lost both lower incisors, so that the two lower canines met at the symphysis (midline) of the lower jaw. Parapithecids were once thought ancestral to Old World monkeys (or at least early catarrhines), but both dental and skeletal features place them as unrelated early anthropoids, as is also true of the more conservative oligopithecids. The rare, three-premolared *Proteopithecus* from L-41 might somehow link these two families or be distantly related to the platyrrhines.

The third major group of Fayum anthropoids, on the other hand, appears to sit at or near the origin of the Catarrhini. *Propliopithecus* (including the species formerly called *Aegyptopithecus*) (Figure 3f) is known by several species from the upper Fayum horizons. Fossils of the skull and face share the derived anthropoid features noted for *Apidium,* including the conservative annular (ringlike) ectotympanic bone and a relatively small brain size. The molars are morphologically close to those of Miocene noncercopithecid catarrhines, the two premolars lack a central cuspule, and the incisors and canines are robust. Scattered postcranial remains have catarrhine-like features and indicate moderately acrobatic branch-running locomotion.

Diversification of the Modern Anthropoids

The Miocene epoch witnessed the rise of both platyrrhines and catarrhines in the southern continents. The source of the New World monkeys is still a matter of some disagreement. Once scholars realized that in the Eocene the South Atlantic was significantly narrower than today, some suggested that early African anthropoids somehow crossed to South America on rafts of floating vegetation and, once there, proliferated into platyrrhines. But no known Eocene primate is a potentially reasonable "structural ancestor" for the New World monkeys, except possibly the recently discovered Fayum *Proteopithecus.* The alternative proposal is that a North American omomyoid managed to cross the water gap across what is now Central America (perhaps via the emerging Caribbean islands). This theory implies that protoanthropoid omomyoids inhabited both eastern Asia and western North America in the Early Eocene. If one assumes omomyoid ancestry for the Anthropoidea, then this theory requires the common ancestor of platyrrhines and catarrhines to be very old, much older than the common ancestor required by an Afro-South American dispersal. The latter probably involved traveling a longer distance, but the currents were more favorable, and newly emerged islands in the mid-Atlantic may have served as stop overs. In either case, the most ancient known platyrrhine *Branisella* (which may subsume

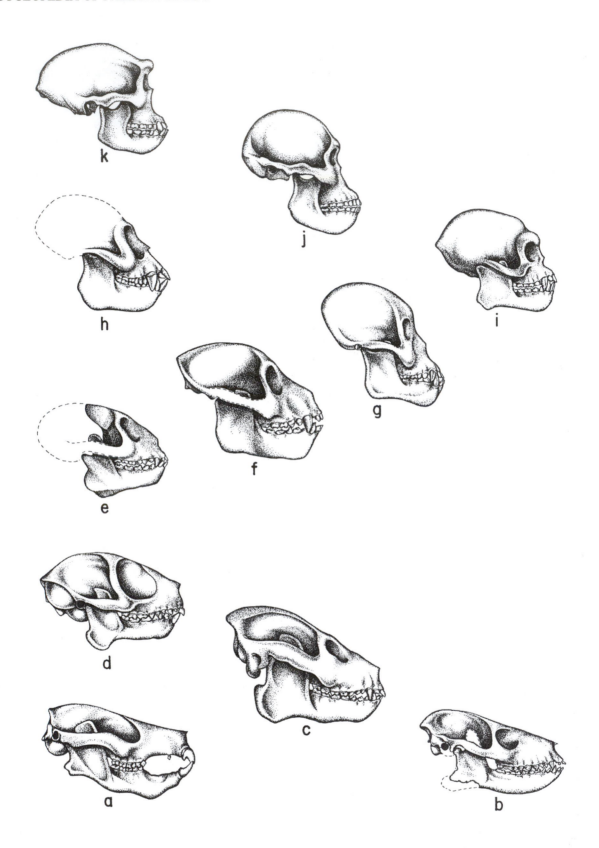

Figure 3. Side view of various extinct primates. *a, Plesiadapis tricuspidens* (a plesiadapiform); *b, Notharctus tenebrosus* (an adapid); *c, Leptadapis magnus* (an adapid); *d, Necrolemur antiquus* (an omomyid); *e, Apidium phiomense* (a parapithecid); *f, Propliopithecus (Aegyptopithecus) zeuxis* (an anthropoid); *g, Proconsul heseloni* (a hominid); *h, Cebupithecia sarmientoi* (a platyrrhine); *i, Pliopithecus vindobonensis* (a catarrhine); *j, Australopithecus africanus* (a hominid); *k, Homo erectus.* Not to scale. Illustration by Don McGranaghan.

the coeval genus *Szalatavus*), has been recovered only from the late Oligocene of Salla (Bolivia), approximately 27 million years ago, leaving a long time gap between it and any postulated ancestral form. That ancestor would have to be between 50 and 35 million years old, depending on which theory of dispersal is utilized. *Branisella* has been tentatively linked to one of the two platyrrhine families, Cebidae, in part because of apparent third molar reduction. This pattern of deep ancestral roots is characteristic of platyrrhines; catarrhines, on the other hand, evolve in a succession of bushlike radiations.

As recently as the late 1970s, almost all known platyrrhine fossils could be held in one's cupped hands. Intensive collecting in Argentina and Venezuela, as well as research in Chile, Bolivia, Brazil, and the Caribbean, has increased exponentially the number of fossils and taxa available for study. The new abundance has led, in turn, to a variety of conflicting hypotheses about their relationships. At least six genera are known from the Early Miocene (approximately 20 to 17 million years ago) of southern Argentina and Chile. Three of these are relatively generalized pithecines. Another is *Tremacebus,* a platyrrhine that seems to show the beginning of orbital enlargement that reaches its zenith in the living nocturnal/cathemeral *Aotus.* Two cebines round out the tally of genera. One of these, *Dolichocebus,* has a hole connecting right and left orbits (interorbital fenestra), a feature that is otherwise only found in squirrel monkeys *(Saimiri).* An even higher concentration of taxa has been recovered from the 13-million-year-old La Venta fauna of Colombia. Among over half a dozen genera are a pitheciine close to the modern saki-uakaris, a howler-like ateline, two possible callitrichines, and species that have been tentatively included in two modern genera, *Aotus* and *Saimiri.* The Late Pleistocene caves of eastern Brazil have recently yielded partial skeletons of two atelines significantly larger than their large-bodied living relatives, while specimens from Cuba, Hispaniola, and Jamaica testify that a diverse monkey fauna lived in the Caribbean several thousand years ago or less. Although most scholars recognize distinctive atelines, pitheciines, and cebines in this assemblage, others have suggested that they all represent a unique, perhaps ancient lineage that is separate from those known today and that entered the Caribbean during the Miocene.

By contrast, few Miocene catarrhines can be linked to modern subfamilies, much less to living genera. At least four separate groups of catarrhines are known in the Early to Middle Miocene. The most archaic or conservative of these is, paradoxically, the last to appear. This "extinct living fossil" clade is the Pliopithecidae. Pliopithecids are reasonably common in Europe and China from 19 to 9 million years ago, and a few specimens are known from Pakistan and Thailand. Their teeth and postcranial skeleton resemble those of the Oligocene propliopehtecids, with wide upper molars and molar cusps that are generally arranged along the margin of each tooth. The face is short and broad, superficially resembling those of gibbons (Hylobatidae). With gibbons pliopethecids also share relatively long, gracile limbs. As a result they once were considered hylobatid ancestors. However, pliopethecids do not have any derived features that would unite them with hylobatids or any other group of hominoids. Instead, they retain many primitive catarrhine features in their postcranial skeleton and in their skull

such as the presence of an only partly tubular ectotympanic. Cladistic analysis of their character states places pliopithecids just above the propliopithecids in the comblike cladogram of catarrhine taxa.

Somewhat more modern in their dentition (with more fully squared upper molars) and postcranial skeleton are several genera found in the Early and Middle Miocene of eastern Africa. *Dendropithecus* is perhaps the best known of these taxa, which do not form a monophyletic (exclusive) group but instead can be arranged as an ascending ladder of increasingly more advanced catarrhine lineages lying below the node that marks the split between the cercopithecoids and the hominoids.

Although many researchers previously held that Old World monkeys were generally more "primitive" than apes, the prevailing view today is that cercopithecids are *more* derived than hominoids, not only dentally but also in their increased commitment to terrestrial locomotion. The oldest known members of the group are represented by fragmentary jaws and teeth from northern and eastern Africa, dated between 19 and 16 million years old. From the site of Maboko Island, in Kenya's Lake Victoria, however, deposits dated between 15 and 14 million years old have produced hundreds of teeth in numerous jaws, many postcranial elements, and most recently, a nearly complete cranium of *Victoriapithecus.* Detailed analyses have shown that this primate has the bilophodont molars of modern cercopethecids, but that it also retains a small hypoconulid at the back of the first two lower molars, a cusp that is lost in all species after the Middle Miocene. Moreover, the cranium reveals an unexpected mosaic of character states: a long snout with elongate, narrow nasal bones and only moderately wide space between the eyes, rather like the cercopithecines, which were often thought more derived than the short-faced colobines. The postcranial skeleton of *Victoriapithecus* shows most of the adaptations associated with moderately terrestrial locomotion, which characterizes later cercopithecids and supports the idea that this was a basic feature of the group's origin. The diet of *Victoriapithecus* probably consisted mainly of fruit and possibly some seeds, rather than the leafy diet of colobines, whose teeth and guts are especially adapted to this monotonous fare.

Their specialized folivorous diet may have allowed colobines to spread more widely than the cercopithecines in the Late Miocene. The small *Microcolobus* is represented by a few fossils from Kenya that date to 10 million years ago. At about the same time *Mesopithecus* appears in Europe. The title of "oldest colobine" probably goes to the latter, depending upon the exact age assigned to an isolated tooth from the German site of Wissberg. The tooth's age is generally thought to be approximately 11 million years, but scholars cannot rule out the possibility that the assemblage contains fauna from a number of time periods. In many ways, *Mesopithecus* is comparable to the living hanuman langur *Semnopithecus,* with moderate terrestrial adaptations in the limbs. Dozens to hundreds of individuals are known from the Balkans, especially at Pikermi (Greece), now estimated at approximately 8.5 million years ago; the species also extended into Afghanistan. Teeth of similar size have been recovered from a 7-million-year-old site in Pakistan that lies on the other side of an important faunal barrier that existed at this time between Europe and Asia. A single *Mesopithecus*-like tooth has been recorded from a 5.5-million-year-old site in

China. Other colobine species are known in the later Late Miocene in North Africa, and the earliest cercopithecines show up there also. These are mostly represented by isolated teeth of the dentally more conservative tribe Papionini and are attributed to *Macaca,* in part because of their presence north of the Sahara. This genus apparently entered Eurasia at the very end of the Miocene, since a few teeth found in both Spain and China date from approximately 5.5 million years ago.

The Pliocene saw a strong increase in the variety of cercopithecids and their adaptive patterns. In Africa, large colobines are known across the eastern region but are rarer in the south. *Cercopithecoides* was apparently highly terrestrial, and its diet may have included a fair amount of grit, which caused heavy tooth wear (unlike ceropithecines, colobines generally do not have thick enamel to protect against such wear). The mainly arboreal *Paracolobus* (Figure 4c) may have been the largest colobine ever—up to 50 kilograms for big males. Other species, represented only by teeth, were closer to the size of living African colobines—approximately 10 kilograms for males. Papionin cercopithecines, on the other hand, may have been more diverse in South Africa, where the cave sites yielding australopiths also produce species of *Parapapio, Papio,* and *Theropithecus* (Figure 4a). Only the latter genus is common in eastern Africa, where two lineages appear to have diverged from *Papio* before 4 million years ago and from each other by 3.5 million years ago. One lineage shows an intriguingly steady increase in size through the Pliocene and well into the Middle Pleistocene, before becoming extinct. Teeth of cercopithecines appear rarely during the Pliocene and Pleistocene, indicating little more than that the group was present, probably in forests, from which there are few samples.

In Eurasia, *Mesopithecus* continued in Europe, as did a possible descendant, the larger and more terrestrial *Dolichopithecus* (Figure 4d). A few similar specimens from Mongolia and Siberia recently have been named *Parapresbytis,* but this may well be a northeastern subgenus of *Dolichopithecus.* This genus thrived in the moist forests of the southern European Early Pliocene, but by about 2.5 million years ago colobines disappeared from Europe and northern Asia. Macaques also spread widely across the continent early in the Pliocene, and several varieties in Europe may be relatives of today's living North African species. Asian forms are generally poorly known. Large terrestrial papionins occur late in the Pliocene and into the Early Pleistocene in southern Europe and Tajikistan, where they are known as *Paradolichopithecus* (Figure 4b), and in the Indian Siwaliks and China, where they are termed *Procynocephalus.* Facial differences separate these taxa, but it is possible that only one genus is actually represented; it is not certain if these populations were independent macaque derivatives or shared a unique ancestry. The Romanian population of *Paradolichopithecus* is well sampled, with males weighing up to 35 kilograms and females perhaps 20. Nonetheless, there is surprisingly low dimorphism (difference between males and females) in the cranium itself.

The Pleistocene saw the spread of modern genera of cercopithecids, after a wave of Late Pliocene extinction. Baboons and mangabeys replaced the large colobines and eventually *Theropithecus* (except for the relict population found today in the high mountains of Ethiopia), but not before some populations of the latter reached body weights of 60 to 90 kilograms. Rare specimens even document *Theropithecus* in Spain and India. A Chinese population of the large "golden monkey," *Pygathrix (Rhinopithecus),* also seems to have reached a size nearly twice that of living varieties.

Apes and Human Ancestors

For many decades, it has been dogma that the earliest generally accepted hominoid, *Proconsul* (Figure 3g), first appeared in the Miocene (approximately 22 to 15 million years ago) of eastern Africa. But in the early 1990s, Middle Miocene deposits at Lothidok (Kenya), southwest of Lake Turkana, were reassessed and found to date approximately to 26 million years ago. That pushes back the appearance of these hominoids into the Late Oligocene. Jaw fragments named *Kamoyapithecus* from this site appear to be similar to those of *Proconsul* species and can be included in the Proconsulidae. Proconsulids present a number of derived hominoid features. The skull is large and houses a somewhat expanded brain. Joint stability is enhanced by the development of a round humeral (upper arm bone) head and other postcranial modifications. The tail is absent. The upper molar teeth are broad and the molar cusp pattern is recognizably hominoid. Premolars are less heteromorphic than in more primitive catarrhines; in other words the first premolar is rather similar to the second. Proconsulids do not seem to have had much capacity for suspensory postures—they had no special adaptations for hanging below a branch. Therefore, it is postulated that they gathered fruit from a position above the branch.

The gibbon family Hylobatidae is represented in the fossil record only by later Pleistocene dental remains from China and southeast Asia. In fact, recognizing early fossil gibbons is a major problem in the study of hominoid evolution. Since their crania and teeth are relatively conservative, scholars rely on the limb bones to assess affiliation. These bones combine basal hominoid similarities (they are, however, more derived than those of proconsulids) with the elongation associated with brachiation (arm-swinging). Unfortunately, limb bones are rarely preserved. Thus, later Miocene proto-hylobatids may already have been recovered, but no derived features that could potentially link them to the modern genus have as yet been identified. Previous claims that propliopithecids, pliopithecids, or *Dendropithecus*-like forms were gibbon ancestors have been rejected because these groups have no derived features that would link them with gibbons or even hominoids.

The remaining members of Hominoidea can all be included in the family Hominidae, redefined from its earlier arrangement that included only the human lineage. The earliest hominids, the Kenyapithecinae, occur mainly in eastern Africa, but also pop up in Turkey, central Europe, and perhaps Namibia, between approximately 20 and 14 million years ago. These taxa share with later hominids relatively large upper premolars, a premaxilla (bone that holds the upper incisors) that is reoriented relative to the palate, and a somewhat more stable elbow joint. The vertebrae of the newly recognized *Morotopithecus,* dated at 20 million years old, also indicate an apelike posture, although it is not clear that this genus is truly distinct from the slightly younger *Afropithecus.* *Griphopithecus* appears to have been the first hominoid to exit

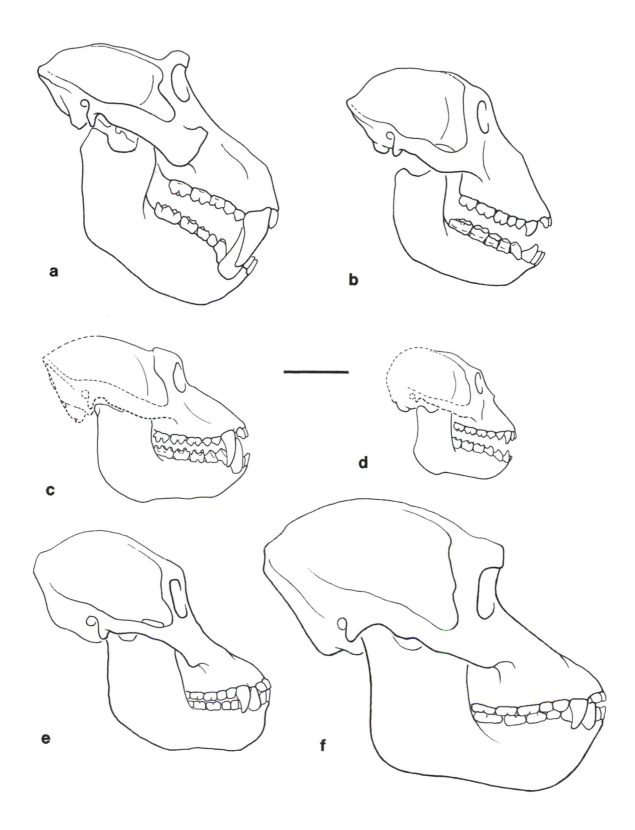

Figure 4. Side view of skulls of selected extinct catarrhines. *a, Theropithecus brumpti; b, Paradolichopithecus arvennensis; c, Paracolobus chemeroni; d, Dolichopithecus ruscinensis; e, Sivapithecus indicus; f, Graecopithecus freybergi.* Top row: cercopithecines; middle row: colobines; bottom row: hominids. All specimens are male except *b* and *d*. Scale: bar = 5 centimeters. Illustration by Lorraine Meeker (after Biruta Akerbergs).

Africa, dispersing from Africa through Turkey (approximately 16 to 15 million years ago) and into central Europe (approximately 16 to 14 million years ago), soon after the Afro-Arabian and Eurasian tectonic plates came into contact. Few African hominid fossils are known in the interval between 14 and 5 million years ago, during which time Eurasian taxa are better represented.

European genera such as *Dryopithecus* (approximately 14 to 10 million years ago) and the dentally unique *Oreopithecus* (approximately 8 million years ago) represent forms close to the common ancestor of the two modern hominoid subfamilies. All share further postcranial similarities with both modern groups, but no derived features characteristic of one in particular. Some scholars have suggested that *Graecopithecus* (approximately 9 to 8 million years old) displays a few specialized facial features that link it to the Homininae, but this placement is in dispute. A single maxilla (upper jaw) of similar age from the Samburu Hills of Kenya might be an African equivalent.

A more definite clade can be recognized within the Ponginae. Living orangutans *(Pongo)* have an extensive series of derived features in the face and skull: an up-tilted face with protruding incisor jaw regions set below tall, narrow, and close-set orbits and weakly projecting brows. Seen from the side, the center of the face is strongly concave, and the cheek region is expanded to the side. These features are seen in nearly modern form in *Sivapithecus* (Figure 4e), known from the Indo-Pakistani Siwalik Hills, between 12 and 8 million years ago. (Specimens previously termed *Ramapithecus* and thought to be direct human ancestors are now agreed to be female *Sivapithecus*.) A well-preserved face from 11-million-year-old Turkish deposits known as *Ankarapithecus* may represent an earlier stage in this lineage (perhaps an intermediate between *Dryopithecus* and *Sivapithecus*), despite its younger age—another "extinct living fossil."

Other potential pongines include several Chinese taxa. *Lufengpithecus* was probably a conservative dryopithecine (dating 9 to 7 million years ago). Another candidate is found in as yet incompletely published material of Mio-Pliocene Age from southwest China. Still another is the Pleistocene *Gigantopithecus*, perhaps the largest of all primates. None of these genera have the diagnostic molar wrinkling seen in living or Pleistocene fossil orangutans, and their precise relationships are uncertain.

No fossil record exists for the African great apes, *Gorilla* and *Pan*. Molecular systematic studies suggest that the human clade (hominins) had split off from proto-chimpanzees by 6 million years ago, although some researchers have argued for a significantly more recent age for this split, unreasonably implying a bipedal ancestry for *Pan*. Other than fragmentary teeth, the first probable hominin (dating approximately 4.4 million years ago) is Ethiopian *Ardipithecus*, represented by teeth with a mosaic of human-like and apelike features, a relatively forward placement of the foramen magnum (implying upright posture) and a partial skeleton whose locomotor adaptations have not yet been described.

Species of *Australopithecus* range between 4.2 and 2.3 million years old in South Africa, in Chad, and in the Rift Valley, from Tanzania through Ethiopia. These specimens preserve far more morphological detail, including crania with capacities of 400 to 500 milliliters but jaw muscles small enough that they do not require strong bony ridges for attachment sites. The teeth of these specimens include moderately large incisors, relatively small and partly incisivized (spatulate) canines, thick-enameled molars, and a broadly "humanlike" dental arch. The specimens also have a skeleton clearly adapted to upright bipedalism (supported by footprint trails), although different in detail from modern humans, with relatively short legs. Their body weight has been estimated at approximately 30 kilograms for females, up to 60 kilograms for males. Although the brain had not yet expanded to the degree seen in *Homo,* it was larger than that found in living chimpanzees of comparable size. These forms probably had an omnivorous diet, including fruits, seeds, and perhaps scavenged animal protein. There is no evidence for tool making.

The so-called robust australopiths, often placed in the genus *Paranthropus,* were generally younger (approximately 2.6 to 1.3 million years) and exhibited more specialized facial and skull anatomy. The teeth behind the canines were greatly enlarged and adapted to crushing and grinding hard food items, and (except in the earliest forms) the canines and incisors were strongly reduced. "Sagittal" (midline on top of the skull) and "nuchal" (for neck muscles at the back of the skull) crests were present to serve as attachments for the large muscles that covered the skull, and the brain was only slightly larger than that of *Australopithecus.* The postcranial skeleton is poorly known, but structure and body size were probably not much different from the earlier genus. Although some have suggested that *Paranthropus* could have made tools, there is no clear evidence of this.

Instead, the earliest tool-makers probably were species included in the living genus *Homo* (Figure 4k), first identified in deposits 2.4 to 2.2 million years old in Malawi, Kenya, and Ethiopia, soon after the oldest stone tools appeared. The exact number and interrelationships of *Homo* species is a subject of much debate, but it seems clear that early populations evolved in Africa and dispersed to eastern Eurasia between 2 and 1.5 million years ago. Continental Europe may not have been colonized until about 1 million years ago. Two major clades (each comprised of several species or subspecies) dominated the Middle Pleistocene of the western Old World. One in Europe led eventually to the Neanderthals of the last few hundred thousand years; the other, in Africa, evolved more circuitously into anatomically modern humans, some of whom dispersed via southwestern Asia to colonize the rest of the globe approximately 100,000 years ago.

IAN TATTERSALL AND ERIC DELSON

See also Hominids

Work Cited

Rosenberger, A.L. 1992. Evolution of feeding niches in New World monkeys. *American Journal of Physical Anthropology* 88:525–62.

Further Reading

Fleagle, J.G. 1988. *Primate Adaptation and Evolution.* San Diego, California: Academic Press.

Kay, R.F., C. Ross, and B.A. Williams. 1996. Anthropoid origins. *Science* 275:789–804.

Mittermeier, R.A., I. Tattersall, W.R. Konstant, D.M. Meyers, and R.B. Mast. 1994. *Lemurs of Madagascar.* Washington, D.C.: Conservation International.

Szalay, F.S., and E. Delson. 1979. *Evolutionary History of the Primates.* New York: Academic.

Tattersall, I. 1995. *The Fossil Trail: How We Know What We Think We Know about Human Evolution.* New York: Oxford University Press.

———. 1997. Out of Africa . . . again . . . and again. *Scientific American* 276 (4):46–53.

Tattersall, I., E. Delson, J.A. Van Couvering, and A.S. Brooks (eds.). 1988. *Encyclopedia of Human Evolution and Prehistory.* Chicago: St. James; 2nd ed., New York: Garland, 1997.

PROBLEMATIC ANIMALS: OVERVIEW

Problematic fossils are those that cannot be placed into taxonomic categories that reveal their relationship to other living organisms. In other words, "problematica," as they are sometimes called, are the unidentified objects of paleontology and biology.

The identification of any organism, living or fossil, involves two steps. The first step is giving the specimen in question a name. Sometimes the name used is common and local to a given language or region, such as the name "rainbow trout" as it is used in the United States. For international purposes of species recognition, an official binomial (two-part name) such as *Salmo gairdnerii* is used for this fish. This name consists of a genus (group; plural, genera) name *(Salmo)* paired with a "trivial" (specific) name that always must be used in combination with the genus or its abbreviation (i.e., *S. gairdnerii*).

The identification of species and even genera is not guaranteed for any given specimen. Sometimes insufficient information is available for the diagnosis; lack of information is a particular problem for classifying incomplete fossils. At other times, one may be dealing with a species or even genus that has not been given a scientific name.

A contemporary goal of binomial classification is to reflect the genealogical relationships between various forms of life. For example, all members of a given genus, family, or class are supposed to be related more closely to one another than they are to members of other genera, families, or classes, respectively. In practice, the information available may not allow a completely accurate rendering of genealogical relationships when new taxa are named. This is not a serious problem, however, for the process of naming and identifying forms is iterative and potentially self-correcting. If subsequent information shows that a new species was improperly placed in a given genus, then its genus placement can be amended in later work. Thus, all taxonomic assignments have a provisional aspect.

Problematic specimens are those forms that cannot be placed in recognizable, usually higher taxonomic categories. For a typical fossil shell or bone, it is fairly easy to determine its main taxonomic category (such as Molluska, Brachiopoda, Arthropoda, Chordata). But in a few cases the larger category to which a particular organism belongs is by no means obvious.

The reasons for organisms being problematic are numerous and can involve a variety of factors. Such organisms may be members of a relatively short-lived higher taxon. Then there will be no living representatives, rendering comparison with familiar, living species difficult or impossible. An organism may have unusual behaviors or life habits that have, over the course of evolutionary time, led to such profound modifications in its body architecture that it can no longer be recognized as belonging to a higher taxon from which it descended. An organism may have poor preservation potential—for instance, it may be soft-bodied or occupy a habitat with limited opportunities for fossilization—thus little or no fossil record exists to help relate it to other forms.

Problematica are often participants in what evolutionists call *adaptive radiations,* a relatively brief interval of rapid evolutionary change and proliferation of species. Such radiations often are associated with unusual, even bizarre morphologies. These "oddballs" have been termed "experiments," although calling problematic forms "experimental" involves judgment of their supposed competitive inferiority. Forces of chance and contingency might just as easily explain why any given taxon failed to flourish over the long term (Conway Morris 1991; Gould 1989). This judgmental tendency has also been identified by paleontologists who note that "failures are not phyla"; in other words, recognition of major groups is skewed in favor of those that have been most successful over time (Glaessner 1984).

The importance of problematica resides in what they can tell us about the evolutionary process and about the potentials and limits to evolutionary change. They are thus some of the most important test cases for researchers scrutinizing contemporary evolutionary theories. Furthermore, problematic forms give the paleontologist clues to the nature of ancient environmental settings. If one accepts the premise that the structural characteristics of any organism result at least in part from, or are a function of, the environment in which the organism lives or lived, then the morphology of unusual forms may tell us about the type of environment in which the organism existed. The Ediacaran biota is providing paleontologists with crucial information of this sort (McMenamin 1997).

Since problematic fossils provide key data and insights into the nature of past environments and even the evolutionary process itself, interest in such forms has risen dramatically in recent years. Previously shunned by paleontologists because of their confused pedigree, problematica are now a "hot topic," and many researchers now seek out problematic forms, particularly in the Burgess Shale of western Canada (Cambrian) and in the Nama Group sediments of Namibia (Late Precambrian).

Problematic forms are not randomly distributed through geological time. Most of the Precambrian is devoid of such fossils. The fossil record of this great interval is dominated by bacteria (especially cyanobacteria) quite similar (at least in terms of external morphology apparent in the fossils) to extant forms. The interval between the Late Precambrian and the end of the Paleozoic may be considered the heyday of problematica. The majority of all problematic forms appear during this time. After the end of the Paleozoic, the number of problematic forms drops considerably, owing to the fact that many rare and unusual groups are lost to the mass extinctions of the Paleozoic. Many of the survivors of the Mesozoic and later periods have living representatives and are thus not considered problematic. A major focus of contemporary paleontological research, one that has met with some success in recent years, has been the attempt to remove Late Precambrian-Paleozoic fossils from the ranks of the problematica and place them, after detailed study of their anatomy, into recognized taxa. Nevertheless, problematica will always be with us, and they will continue to pose some of the most difficult and interesting problems in paleontology.

MARK A.S. McMENAMIN

See also Ediacaran Biota; Microbial Fossils, Precambrian; Problematic Animals: Phanerozoic Problematica; Problematic Animals: Poorly Characterized Problematica; Skeletized Microorganisms

Works Cited

Conway Morris, S. 1991. Problematical taxa: A problem for biology or biologist? *In* A.M Simonetta and S. Conway Morris (eds.), *The Early Evolution of Metazoa and the Significance of Problematical Taxa.* Cambridge and New York: Cambridge University Press.

Glaessner, M.F. 1984. *The Dawn of Animal Life: A Biohistorical Study.* Cambridge and New York: Cambridge University Press.

Gould, S.J. 1989. *Wonderful Life: The Burgess Shale and the Nature of History.* New York: Norton; London: Hutchinson, 1990.

McMenamin, M.A.S. 1997. *The Garden of Ediacara.* New York: Columbia University Press.

PROBLEMATIC ANIMALS: PHANEROZOIC PROBLEMATICA

Most problematica are found in the Early Phanerozoic. The evolutionary relationships between these forms and extant phyla is unclear, which is why they are called problematica.

Problematica appear not to be distributed within any particular region of the globe. Actually, the distribution of problematica as a whole (and several of the problematic groups in particular) is quite cosmopolitan. For a variety of groups, there are showcase localities, such as the Burgess Shale of British Columbia, first discovered by Charles Walcott. The famous Phyllopod bed quarry is now treated as a pilgrimage site, even though the rock units bearing typical Burgess Shale fossils extend far beyond its confines. Other deposits, such as the shale nodules of Mazon Creek, Illinois, represent localized conditions of unique preservation particularly favorable to the fossilization of problematica.

Following is a brief description of problematica known from entire body fossils or intact cuticle (tough outer "coat"), as opposed to isolated sclerites or other skeletal elements.

Amiskwia

This attractive but entirely soft-bodied animal (Figure 1) is known from impressions in the Burgess Shale. They show lateral and posterior fins (the latter resembling paddles), an intestine, tentacle-like structure in the vicinity of the head, a brain (cephalic nerve ganglion), and an associated nerve chord. S. Conway Morris (Briggs and Conway Morris 1986) concluded that *Amiskwia* was neither an arrow worm (chaeotgnath) nor a nemertean; thus, the systematic position of this creature is unknown. The curved tentacle-like structures and lateral fins, however, give *Amiskwia* a (possibly superficial) similarity to the anomalocarids, which will be discussed in the next section.

Anomalocarids

Anomalocarids (Figures 2, 3) are one of the most important of the Cambrian problematica. Anomalocarids appear to have been the world's first large top predators, attaining lengths of up to two meters. Two genera are recognized, *Anomalocaris* and *Laggania,* both of which are quite similar in general body form (Collins 1996). The elongate body has imbricate (overlapping) lobes on either side and a tail with six (three on each side) stiff fins that project upward from the posterior end of the animal. The lateral lobes were flexible and apparently allowed the animal to swim by undulation. The animal's head bears two large eyes, a pineappling-ring shaped mouth lined with shark-tooth-shaped teeth, and a pair of segmented anterior appendages. Apparently, these appendages served to draw food into the circular mouth.

The history of discovery of anomalocarids has generated a great deal of interest and exemplifies, as put by Desmond Collins (1996), "the great difficulty of visualizing and classifying, from fossil remains, the many Cambrian animals with no apparent living descendants." Anomalcarids proved to be a difficult case in this regard because these large animals tended to break apart after death. Scholars first described isolated anterior appendages (Figure 3), and mistakenly assumed the structures were the abdomen of a small shrimplike creature, missing only its head. Later, the isolated mouth was described as the jellyfish *Peytoia nathorsti.* Only when very complete specimens from the Burgess Shale were recognized and described were all the pieces put back together to give us our current picture of this voracious predator. Anomalocarids have been blamed for scars seen on fossilized carapaces of Cambrian trilobites and this accusation seems fully justified. Because of the recent discovery of anomalocarid appendages in Cambrian sediments of Australia, we now know that anomalocarids ranged worldwide.

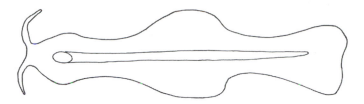

Figure 1. *Amiskwia,* a soft-bodied animal from the Middle Cambrian Burgess Shale (Canada). Length, 22 millimeters.

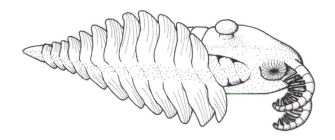

Figure 2. *Anomalocaris,* a large marine Cambrian predator. Length of animal, 1.5 meters.

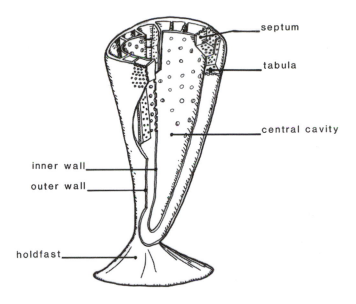

Figure 4. Cambrian regular archaeocyath, showing the inner and outer walls with vertical partitions (septa; singular, septum) and horizontal partitions (tabulae; singula,r tabula). Height, two centimeters. From McMenamin and McMenamin (1990).

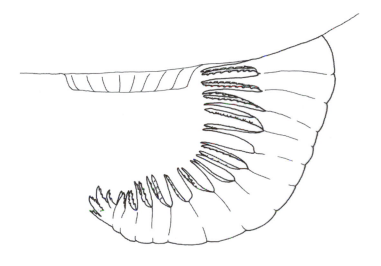

Figure 3. Detail of anomalocarid mouthparts, showing side view of circular mouth and one adjacent grasping appendage.

The affinities of anomalocarids has been a subject of considerable debate. Some paleontologists emphasize the similarities between anomalocarids and arthropods, such as the presence of jointed appendages, even though the anomalocarids have only a single pair (the anterior graspers) (Figure 3). Other paleontologists emphasize the oddity of the overall anomalocarid body plan and argue that the group ought to be placed in its own phylum. This latter view seems preferable, considering that anomalocarids bear a collection of traits that can be compared to a variety of animal phyla. For example, the anterior appendages are most comparable to features seen in arthropods, but the circular mouth seems as if it could have been derived from the mouth of a flatworm (Figure 3).

Archeocyaths

Archeocyaths (also called archeocyathids or archeocyathans) (Figure 4) are an exclusively Cambrian group, best known from the Early Cambrian. At that time, they filled the shallow marine habitats of Earth with an impressive array of different genera and species. The group dwindled rapidly after its early successes. All forms have calcareous (calcium-based), spongelike skeletons, but rather than being formed of spicules (spiked structures that provide support internally), as is the case in true sponges, Archeocyaths have cup-shaped skeletons composed of calcium carbonate (Boardman et al. 1987).

The archeocyath skeleton usually consists of porous outer and inner walls connected by radially arranged and similarly porous septa (partitions). In regular archeocyaths (e.g., *Robustocyathus,* which looks like a wagon wheel in cross section) the septa are more or less planar, while in irregular archeocyaths (such as *Markocyathus*), the septa are modified to form wavy and highly complex plates and subradial partitions called "taenae" (Debrenne and Zhuravlev 1992). The high porosity of both regular and irregular archeocyaths strongly suggests that these creatures were filter feeders, gleaning their nutrition from waters that flowed passively through the archeocyath's lacelike skeleton. Many archeocyath specimens show strange outgrowths of the skeleton; they may be responses to injury or perhaps a defense against other organisms, including competing archeocyaths, that settled too closely nearby.

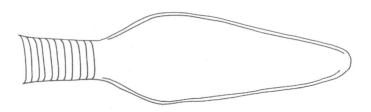

Figure 5. *Banffia*, a wormlike impression from the Middle Cambrian Burgess Shale (Canada). Length, 57 millimeters.

Current opinion seems to favor placing the archeocyaths with the sponges. A strong case can be made, however, that the resemblance between the archeocyath body plan and the sponges is superficial. Archeocyaths may have developed a spongelike body form and lifestyle independently from the sponges, in which case archeocyaths could indeed merit their own phylum.

Banffia

This wormlike creature (Figure 5), known from numerous specimens in the Burgess Shale's Phyllopod bed, consists of a slightly swollen posterior end and an annulated (formed by a series of rings), tubular anterior end separated by a constriction. The entire creature can reach eight centimeters in length. Although *Banffia* clearly seems to be some type of animal, there is no convincing evidence to link it to any of the known animal phyla (Briggs and Conway Morris 1986).

Chancelloriids

Chancelloriids are presumably metazoans with scleritomes composed of multielement, hollow aragonite spicules (Figure 6A). Based on complete, intact scleritome specimens of *Chancelloria* from the Burgess Shale, the creature appears to have been completely surrounded by its spicular coat (Figure 6B), leaving paleontologists guessing as to its mode of locomotion. If it used a molluscan-style foot, that would imply that at least part of the body was not covered in the spicules of the scleritome. Perhaps chancelloriids were immobile filter feeders and relied on their spiny exoskeletons (individual elements of which somewhat resemble sponge spicules) for protection (McMenamin and McMenamin 1990).

Conularids

Conularids (also referred to as conulariids) (Figure 7) are one of the classical problematica of paleontology—their affinities have been debated for over 170 years (Simonetta and Conway Morris 1991). Although there may be some Cambrian examples, the geologic range of confirmed conularids is from Early Ordovician to Late Triassic. They have been considered alternately to be members of Phylum Cnidaria, members of the Ediacaran biota, and members of an independent, extinct phylum.

Conularids consist of four-sided pyramidal/conical exoskeletons that show bilateral symmetry and are composed of apatite (cal-

cium phosphate). Adult conularids were attached to the substrate by an elongate, flexible stalk. In some species the exoskeleton itself was flexible and was stiffened by rods (transverse thickenings). Faces of the exoskeletal pyramid are separated by longitudinal invaginations at each of the four corners. Some researchers have interpreted diffuse structures on the inside of the conularid skeleton as internal organs of a coelomate—a metazoan with a true body cavity, or coelom. Others disagree, and have proposed that these structures might represent commensal or symbiotic organisms. Absence of tentacles in the best preserved conularids has weakened the argument that these fossils are cnidarians (e.g., jellyfishes). Conularids thus remain an important paleontological enigma.

Dinomischus

The name of this organism is derived from two Greek terms, one for goblet *(dinos)* and the second for stem or stalk *(mischos)*. Indeed, this creature does resemble a goblet (the calyx) on a tall thin stalk that has a swollen tip to create a holdfast (rootlike structure that anchors the animal) (Figure 8). *Dinomischus* was first discovered in the Burgess Shale, but even there it is extremely rare. The lip of the calyx is ringed with armlike structures, and a U-shaped structure seen inside the calyx has been interpreted as a gut. The gut appears to have been connected to the inner walls of the calyx by suspensory fibers. Some researchers have suggested a relationship between *Dinomischus* and stalked lophophorates such as brachiopods. Others have proposed affinities with stalked echinoderms such as crinoids. These suggestions are questionable given the absence of both a lophophore (coiled feeding arm bearing tentacles) and a calcite skeleton (Briggs and Conway Morris 1986). The genus may be unique enough to require classification in a new phylum.

In Chengjiang, China, scholars have discovered new specimens of *Dinomischus* with a peculiar tubular structure that apparently extends upward from the calyx. It has been speculated that this structure is an anal tube, but this interpretation remains controversial (Simonetta and Conway Morris 1991).

Eldonia

First described from the Burgess Shale by Charles Walcott, *Eldonia* (Figure 9) is a soft-bodied form with an imperfect radial symmetry. The perimeter of the specimen consists of radial partitions, and the center of the specimen contains a coiled structure that some paleontologists interpret as a gut. Presumed tentacles have been observed on one end of the gut, but their identification as such is far from secure. *Eldonia* has been interpreted as a probable holothurian echinoderm (sea cucumber), but Early Cambrian specimens from Chengjiang have led recent authors to a more cautious assessment of its phylogenetic relationships. A possible relationship to the cnidarian medusae has been suggested (Junyun et al. 1995).

Halkieriids

Halkieriids, long known exclusively from isolated sclerites such as the specimens of the genus *Halkieria*, became known in complete form with the discovery in 1989 of specimens of the complete halk-

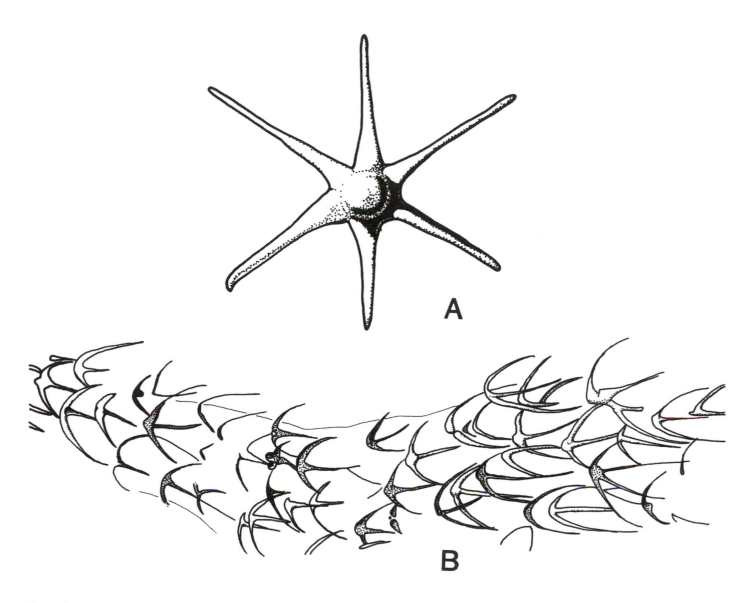

Figure 6. *Chancelloria. A,* a single chancelloriid sclerite; width, from spine tip to spine tip, approximately six millimeters; *B,* a sclerite map of a nearly complete *Chancelloria* scleritome from the Burgess Shale (Canada). Key: *anchor-shaped object,* a flattened sclerite. Length of scleritome, 27 millimeters. From McMenamin and McMenamin (1990).

ieriid scleritome (Figure 10), from Lower Cambrian strata of northern Greenland (Conway Morris and Peel 1990). This was an astonishing find, a "Rosetta Stone," that revealed the halkieriid scleritome to be composed of at least five different types of sclerites, all arrayed across the dorsal (back) surface of the animal. Short triangular sclerites run down the animal's dorsal midline. These are flanked by alternating rows of short blade-shaped and scimitar-shaped sclerites. Most unusual, however, are the large circular shells, complete with concentric growth lines, present at the anterior and posterior ends of the animal. One specimen appears to show the impression of a sinuously curving gut beneath the coat of sclerites.

The anterior and posterior shells, which look like isolated univalves (half shells) from a brachiopod, have generated considerable interest and speculation. Did they function as opercula (lids) at opposite ends of a U-shaped burrow? If so, why did the animal

need all of the other sclerites? What relationship, if any, do these anterior and posterior shells have to the shells of bivalved brachiopods and molluscs? Could a brachiopod or a clam represent a descendant of a halkieriid in which all of the smaller sclerites had been lost through evolution, as the number of skeletal parts were reduced over time? These questions remain unresolved; nonetheless, it is clear that the Greenland halkieriid specimens will play an important role in future clarifications of the relationships between skeletonized invertebrate phyla.

Hyoliths

Hyoliths are exclusively Paleozoic fossils that are represented by at least 40 genera and that occur at sites throughout the world. Hyoliths have a more or less conical shell with a ventral (belly-

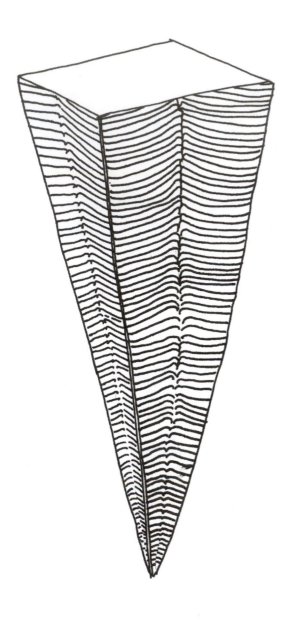

Figure 7. A Paleozoic conulariid. Length, three centimeters.

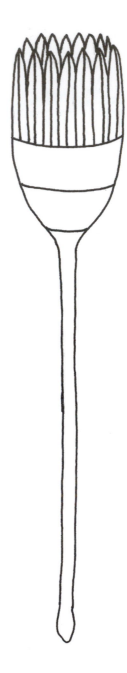

Figure 8. *Dinomischus*, a stalked form from the Cambrian of China and Canada. Height, seven centimeters.

side) lip; the shell opening is capped by an operculum. Two appendages, called "helens," extend posteriorly from the space between the operculum and the shell aperture (Figures 11, 12).

Hyoliths have attracted a considerable amount of attention. A large number of well-preserved fossils show muscle scars (impressions at sites of muscle attachment) on the interior of the main shell and scars of the retractor muscles of the operculum. Furthermore, *Gompholites,* an Ordovician orthothecid hyolith, has been discovered with its sinusoidal gut filled with sediments, which has led researchers to propose a number of reconstructions of the morphology of hyolith soft parts.

In spite of this rich database of information, the systematic position of hyoliths is still uncertain. They have been considered as a class of molluscs, an unusual type of monoplacophoran (another mollusc), and as a distinct phylum sharing a common ancestry with the Mollusca. Under the last interpretation compar-

isons have also been made to the morphology of sipunculoid worms (Boardman et al. 1987).

Libodiscus

This enigmatic creature (Figure 13) is from the Devonian to Carboniferous Exshaw Formation of Alberta, Canada. *Libodiscus* consists of a flasklike body bearing transverse markings that stand out in clear relief. The body has a flange (surrounding lip) of flattened plates. At the narrow end of the flask, a pair of arms connect the neck of the flask to a broad, flat, concentrically grooved structure that covers the flask like an umbrella.

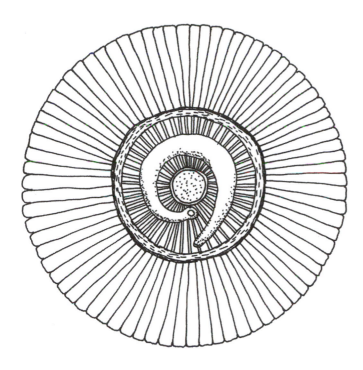

Figure 9. *Eldonia,* a soft bodied problematicum from the Middle Cambrian Burgess Shale (Canada). Diameter, five centimeters.

Comparisons of *Libodiscus ascitus* with plants and metazoans have been dismissed, but the umbrella structure has similarities (possibly superficial) with the chambered flotation structures of hydrozoan cnidarians (Conway Morris et al. 1991). It is also possible that *Libodiscus* represents a gigantic chitinozoan, which is itself a problematic group.

Nectocaris

The species *Nectocaris pteryx,* known for many years from a single specimen in the Burgess Shale, is a slender, tapering creature with a laterally compressed, segmented body and a head enclosed by two oval shieldlike structures (Figure 14). A pair of large eyes and several sets of appendages are visible on the head. Fins, supported by fine rays, run along the dorsal and ventral sides of the animal. Conway Morris has suggested that *Nectocaris* was a swimming predator that had appendages and eyes to aid it in capturing prey. Several other investigators have suggested that *Nectocaris* might be a fossil chordate. However, in the absence of other chordate characters, such as gill slits and a notochord, it may be that the genus is best assigned to its own phylum (Briggs and Conway Morris 1986).

Odontogriphus

This genus, whose name means toothed riddle, has a flattened elongate body with annulations or segments (Figure 15) and what appears to be a straight gut. At the anterior, or head, end of the organism are circular or horseshoe-shaped structures. The

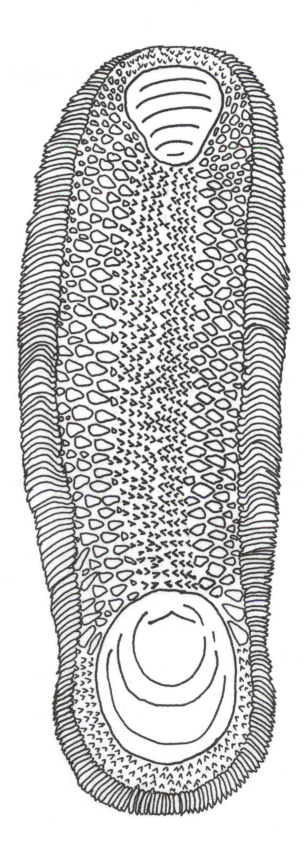

Figure 10. A complete specimen of *Halkieria* from the Lower Cambrian, Greenland. Length, 55 millimeters.

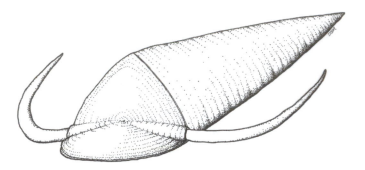

Figure 11. A Cambrian hyolith, showing operculum and helens in place. Length of hyolith shell, one centimeter.

Figure 12. Internal mold of a hyolith from Lower Cambrian strata, Sonora, Mexico. Length of specimen, two millimeters. Source: Puerto Blanco Formation, unit 2, Cerro Rajón area, sample 5.5+ of 12/17/82, specimen IGM 3614(25).

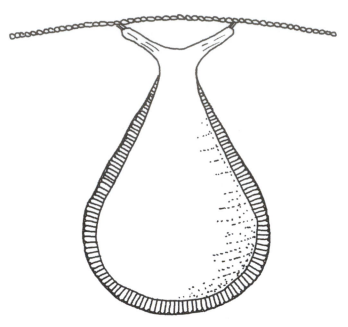

Figure 13. *Libodiscus,* an enigmatic creature from the Devonian to Carboniferous Exshaw Formation of Alberta (Canada). Greatest dimension, 15 millimeters.

Figure 14. *Nectocaris pteryx,* a swimming predator from the Burgess Shale (Canada). Length, 17 millimeters.

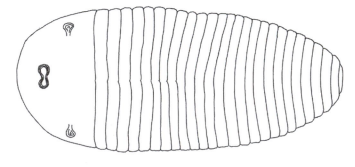

Figure 15. *Odontogriphus,* a flattened form from the Burgess Shale (Canada). Length, five centimeters.

centermost of these have been interpreted by Conway Morris (Briggs and Conway Morris 1986) as a lophophore-like feeding apparatus, and the lateral ones as palps (fleshy flaps). Small toothlike structures are present within the feeding apparatus. The putative lophophore (less than five millimeters across) would appear to be too small to sustain a six- to eight-centimeter long animal, but perhaps in life the organ was able to expand somewhat. The same might be true of the palps, which are situated quite far from what may be the creature's mouth. Whether or not *Odontogriphus* was indeed able to swim by undulating its flattened body, as suggested by Conway Morris (Briggs and Conway Morris 1986), is not known.

Oesia

This enigmatic Cambrian form, another fossil from the Burgess Shale, lacks a skeleton and consists of a subspherical or elliptical bag at the anterior end attached to an elongate trunk (Figure 16).

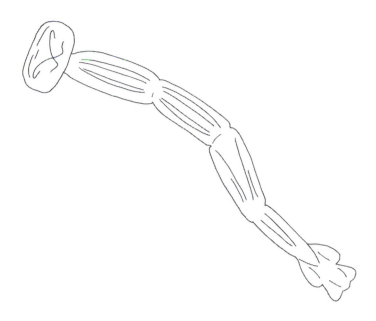

Figure 16. *Oesia,* an enigmatic Cambrian form from the Burgess Shale (Canada). *Oesia* lacks a skeleton and consists of a subspherical or elliptical bag at the anterior end; the bag is attached to an elongate trunk. Total length, eight centimeters.

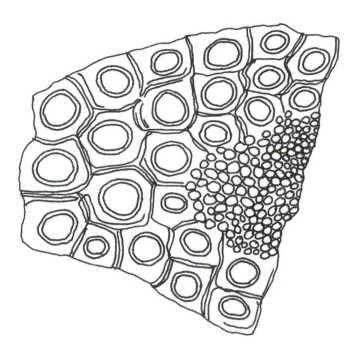

Figure 18. An example of phosphatized palaeoscolecid cuticle from Lower Cambrian strata. Width of fragment, 0.19 millimeters.

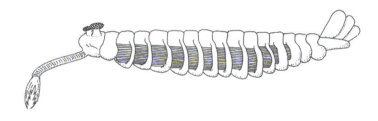

Figure 17. *Opabinia,* a segmented Cambrian form from the Burgess Shale (Canada). Length, six centimeters.

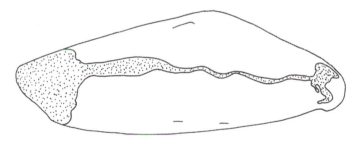

Figure 19. *Pollingeria,* a problematical Cambrian form from the Burgess Shale (Canada). Length, six millimeters.

From 1920 to 1934, H. Lohmann argued that *Oesia disjuncta* was a member of a family of sea squirts called the Larvacea or Appendicularia (Briggs and Conway Morris 1986). These remarkable sea squirts retain juvenile habits throughout their lifetimes (an evolutionary phenomenon called neoteny) so that adults never settle down to attach to the substrate as do most sea squirts. Some years ago, Walter Garstang suggested that vertebrates first evolved from larval sea squirts that had retained the juvenile swimming habit throughout life, although this hypothesis has been disputed in recent years. If *Oesia* does indeed represent this ancestor tunicate (recent studies have neither confirmed nor rejected the idea), the genus will have tremendous importance for studies of early chordate evolution.

Opabinia

This segmented Cambrian form from the Burgess Shale has been the focus of much paleontological scrutiny, with some scientists arguing vociferously for its uniqueness and others strongly advocating its similarities to extant phyla, particularly Phylum Arthropoda. *Opabinia* lacks jointed appendages, which led H. Whittington and other paleontologists (Briggs and Conway Morris 1986) to remove it from the arthropod phylum. The animal does, however, have a row of imbricate lobes on both sides of its body (Figure 17). Perspectives published more recently tend to view *Opabinia* as an aberrant arthropod. Its front end is unorthodox, to say the least, consisting of five eyes on stalks and a flexible, tubular, snorkel-like structure with spines on its end, presumably used to seize prey organisms and carry them into the mouth. As in trilobites, the mouth was directed backward.

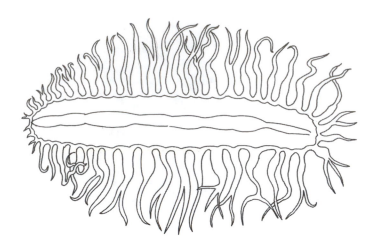

Figure 20. *Portalia,* a tubular soft-bodied fossil covered with bifurcating tentacle-like projections known from the Middle Cambrian Burgess Shale (Canada). Length, nine centimeters.

Palaeoscolecida

These Paleozoic wormlike organisms are known from both compressed carbonaceous films and from beautifully preserved examples of phosphatized cuticle (Figure 18). These cuticular fragments are covered by nipplelike mounds packed together in a hexagonal pattern. Scattered among the nipples are larger annulated spikelike projections.

Comparisons have been made between compressed specimens of the paleoscolecida from Chengjiang, China, and nematomorphs (members of a wormlike phylum probably related to nematode worms), but it would be premature at this point to definitively assign paleoscolecids to this group. The possibility has been raised that the phosphatized cuticular fragments may not belong to a wormlike creature at all (Zhang and Pratt 1996).

Pollingeria

It is not clear whether this fossil, which is shaped like an elongate chip of wood, represents an entire organism or merely represents a fragment of a dispersed scleritome (Briggs and Conway Morris 1986). Known from the Cambrian of western Canada, *Pollingeria* has meandering patterns visible in or on it (Figure 19). These meanders resemble gut traces but occur so irregularly that scholars have no confidence in claims that the traces do indeed represent a preserved alimentary tract. The taxonomic placement of *Pollingeria* is unknown, primarily owing to uncertainties as to the nature of the fossil itself.

Portalia

Portalia, found in the Middle Cambrian Burgess Shale, is a tubular, soft-bodied fossil covered with bifurcating (forked) tentacle-like projections (Figure 20). A medial structure possibly representing a fossil gut is visible (Briggs and Conway Morris 1986). The nature of the surface projections is unknown, but they have led to

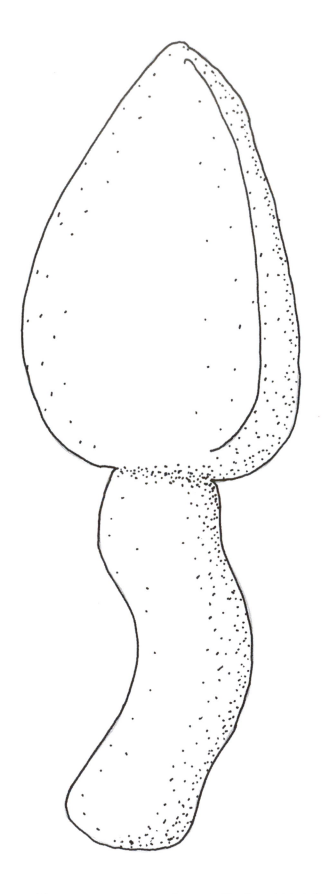

Figure 21. *Priscansermarinus,* a barnacle-like form known from the Cambrian Burgess Shale (Canada). Length, 33 millimeters.

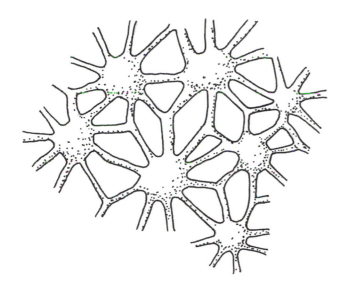

Figure 22. Sketch showing the star-shaped elements, or "nesasters," that compose the wall of a Cambrian radiocyath. Width of view, four millimeters.

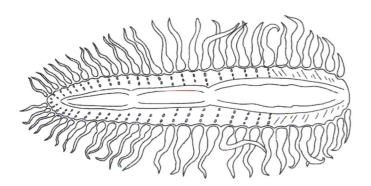

Figure 23. *Redoubtia polypodia,* a bilaterally symmetric form with numerous flimsy appendage-like structures attached to its flanks. From the Middle Cambrian Burgess Shale (Canada). Length, seven centimeters.

comparisons between *Portalia* and modern sea cucumbers (a type of echinoderm). Some of the latter can walk on the seafloor by means of similar projections. However, the way that *Portalia's* tentacles are deployed suggests that they were bunched into annular rings or nodes. If so, this could weaken the sea cucumber interpretation of this form and support interpretation of it as a segmented animal. It may even be an alga, given certain similarities between *Portalia* and the Cambrian algal genera *Margaretia* and *Yuknessia.* The only known specimen of *Portalia* is rather poorly preserved, so further analysis must await the discovery of better specimens.

Priscansermarinus

Priscansermarinus, known from a single slab of Burgess Shale containing over 60 specimens, was described in 1981 as a Cambrian gooseneck barnacle (Collins and Rudkin 1981). This interpreta-

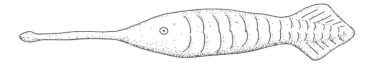

Figure 24. *Tullimonstrum,* an enigmatic animal, is known only from Carboniferous ironstone nodules in three areas in central Illinois. Length, 15 centimeters.

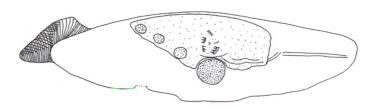

Figure 25. *Typhloesus,* a bizarre, submarine-shaped Carboniferous conodont predator from the Bear Gulch Limestone (Montana). Length, 44 millimeters.

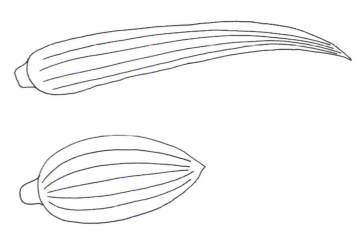

Figure 26. Elongate *(top)* and broad *(bottom)* ribbed scales of Cambrian scaly animal *Wiwaxia.* Length of long sclerite, 12 millimeters.

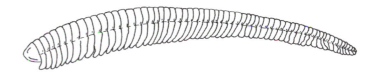

Figure 27. *Worthenella,* from the Middle Cambrian Burgess Shale, British Columbia (Canada). Length, five centimeters.

tion has been disputed, with critics complaining that no features that unquestionably belong to barnacles are visible on the fossils (Briggs and Conway Morris 1986). The animal is shaped very much like a newly emergent mushroom with a narrow "cap" and a broad flexible stalk. The thick stalk terminates in a disc, possibly used for attachment, although no specimens are known to have in fact been attached to anything. The cap appears to consist of a possibly bivalve carapace that obscures any features within the body of the creature.

It is possible that *Priscansermarinus* developed a barnacle-like shape, consisting of a body attached to a short stalk (Figure 21), by means of convergent evolution. If so, the animal could belong to any of a number of different phyla (particularly brachiopods, which have bivalved shells and can have a stalk, called the pedicle) or even to a phylum of its own. Further clarification of this problem awaits additional fossil material. A discovery of specimens attached to their substrate (if indeed this is what *Priscansermarinus* did in life) would be particularly useful for further analysis of this unusual creature.

Radiocyaths

Radiocyaths are exclusively Cambrian, spongelike fossils known from Australia, Siberia, Mongolia, Canada, and Antarctica. Their skeletons, which have two walls, may be conical, pyriform, or spherical (Zhuravlev 1986). The walls are composed of star-shaped elements called "nesasters" (Figure 22). The rays of each nesaster all are along the same plane, making each single nesaster superficially resemble a chancelloriid sclerite. The rays of the nesasters fuse to form the walls of the radiocyath. The nesaster rays of early radiocyaths (such as the earliest known genus, *Gonamispongia*) are long in comparison to the nesasters of later radiocyaths, which tend to be shorter and broader.

Since they lack spicules, radiocyaths cannot be classified with the sponges, and the nesaster wall structure argues against classifying radiocyaths with the archeocyaths. Based on similarities with protoctistan fossils called receptaculitids, Zhuravlev has argued for placing the radiocyaths in the Protoctista, thus removing them from kingdom Animalia. This is not an unreasonable proposal and serves to highlight the uncertainties encountered in attempts to classify these fossil organisms.

Redoubtia

Redoubtia polypodia, from the Middle Cambrian Burgess Shale, is a bilaterally symmetric form with numerous flimsy appendage-like structures attached to its flanks (Figure 23). The trunk of the creature tapers in the direction of its posterior, and the trace of what may be a very broad gut is visible. As with *Portalia,* *Redoubtia* has been compared to sea cucumbers and annelid worms, but neither interpretation has been viewed as convincing by most paleontologists (Briggs and Conway Morris 1986). The "appendages" of *Redoubtia* do not seem to be stiff enough to have been of much use for locomotion, unless, like the tube feet of sea cucumbers, they were kept rigid by hydrostatic pressure during life. This mechanism might accord with the sea cucumber inter-

pretation. It may be possible to make comparisons between *Portalia, Redoubtia,* and nudibranch molluscs such as *Glaucus,* although morphological similarities in these cases could easily be due to convergent evolution.

Tullimonstrum

This enigmatic animal is known only from Carboniferous ironstone nodules in three areas of central Illinois. It was first discovered in the Mazon Creek region in 1958 by Francis Tully and was named in 1966 by Eugene Richardson, who called it *Tullimonstrum gregarium,* or "Tully's abundant monster." This entirely soft-bodied creature is preserved as a flattened outline; there are some expressions of the internal morphology of the body. The body was flexible and apparently segmented (Figure 24). It bore dorsoventrally oriented (vertical) posterior fins that were slightly asymetrical. The head end of the creature bore two eyelike structures connected across the head region of the animal by a rigid transverse bar. The anterior end of the animal extended into a proboscis that terminated in a mouthlike structure. In the fossil specimens the proboscis is often found folded back across the rest of the body.

Tullimonstrum has defied all attempts at proper classification. Comparisons have been made to pelagic gastropods and other molluscs, echiurans, sipunculans, nemerteans, conodont animals, and polychaete annelids. For the time being, it is perhaps best to place this paleontological enigma in a phylum of its own (Simonetta and Conway Morris 1991).

Typhloesus

This bizarre, submarine-shaped Carboniferous fossil, best known from the Bear Gulch Limestone, Montana, was once thought to be the true bearer of the conodont "apparatus." Now, *Typhloesus* is known to have been a predator with a voracious appetite for conodonts. The conodont elements associated with *Typhloesus wellsi* are found within its gut (Purnell 1993). The remains of as many as eight conodonts have been found within *Typhloesus.*

Within its cigar-shaped body, *Typhloesus* has an elliptical-to-inverted subtriangular dark region; the lower part of this structure contains the conodont elements (Figure 25). At the apex on the bottom of the inverted triangle is a flattened, dark-colored, circular structure. This morphology compares to no known animal, extant or extinct, and thus *Typhloesus* is (unlike its conodont prey) truly problematical. Based on similarities in shape, the problematic *Pollingeria* from the Cambrian Burgess Shale is a possible relative/ancestor for *Typhloesus.*

Wiwaxiids

The species *Wiwaxia corrugata* is represented by the fossil of an animal covered in broad or elongate ribbed scales (Briggs and Conway Morris 1986; Whittington 1985) (Figure 26). The scales were unmineralized—they were instead composed of an organic material. The scales have obscured most of the internal anatomy of *Wiwaxia;* nonetheless, a few features may be seen. A feeding apparatus with small denticles is present and has been compared to the scraping organ (radula) in molluscs. The comparison is not certain, and a mouth region with small teeth could belong to any of a number of animal phyla. The trace of a gut is visible. One wiwaxiid specimen was apparently in the process of shedding its sclerites when it was buried.

Wiwaxiids have been compared to polychaete worms, turbellarian flatworms, and primitive molluscs, because many species of these three types of animals are covered by scales. Such a coating might be thought of as a nonmineralized scleritome. The true affinities of wiwaxiids are not yet known, but seeing as they bear features in common with several well-known animal phyla, it would not be unexpected if wiwaxiids eventually find a home in a known phylum.

Worthenella

Worthenella, known from only a single example in the Burgess Shale, at first glance resembles a fossil millipede (Figure 27). But where a millipede has jointed legs, *Worthenella* displays flattened, somewhat wavy appendages of an obscure nature. The body apparently is divided into numerous segments, and, together with the weakly differentiated appendages, such segmentation might indicate that *Worthenella* belongs with the other lobopod (lobe foot) animals such as the velvet worms (onychophorans) and water bears (tardigrades). Another possibility is that *Worthenella* actually represents an isolated appendage; that is, what appears to be an individual animal may in fact be part of a larger animal, analogous to the anterior appendages in anomalocarids. A clearer understanding of this organism will have to await discovery of additional material (Briggs and Conway Morris 1986).

MARK A.S. MCMENAMIN

See also Ediacaran Biota; Metazoan Phyla, Minor; Problematic Animals: Overview; Problematic Animals: Poorly Characterized Problematica; Reefs and Reef-Building Organisms; Skeletized Microorganisms

Works Cited

Boardman, R.S., A.H. Cheetham, and A.J. Rowell. 1987. *Fossil Invertebrates.* Palo Alto, California: Blackwell Scientific.

Briggs, D.E.G., and S. Conway Morris. 1986. Problematica from the Middle Cambrian Burgess Shale of British Columbia. *In* A. Hoffman and M.H. Nitecki (eds.), *Problematic Fossil Taxa.* Oxford: Clarendon; New York: Oxford University Press.

Chen Junyun, Zhu Maoyan, and Zhou Guiqing. 1995. The Early Cambrian medusiform metazoan *Eldonia* from the Chengjiang Lagerstaette. *Acta Palaeontologica Polonica* 40:213–44.

Collins, D. 1996. The "evolution" of *Anomalocaris* and its classification in the arthropod Class Dinocarida (nov.) and Order Radiodonta (nov.). *Journal of Paleontology* 70:280–93.

Collins, D., and D.M. Rudkin. 1981. *Priscansermarinus barnetti,* a probable lepadomorph barnacle from the Middle Cambrian Burgess Shale of British Columbia. *Journal of Paleontology* 55:1006–15.

Conway Morris, S., and J.S. Peel. 1990. Articulated halkieriids from the Lower Cambrian of north Greenland and their role in early protosome evolution. *Nature* 345:802–5.

Conway Morris, S., L.E. Savoy, and A.G. Harris. 1991. An enigmatic organism from the "Exshaw" Formation (Devonian-Carboniferous), Alberta, Canada. *Lethaia* 24:139–52.

Debrenne, F., and A. Zhuravlev. 1992. *Irregular Archaeocyaths.* Paris: CNRS.

McMenamin, M.A.S., and D.L.S. McMenamin. 1990. *The Emergence of Animals: The Cambrian Breakthrough.* New York: Columbia University Press.

Purnell, M.A. 1993. The *Kladognathus* apparatus (Conodonta, Carboniferous): Homologies with Ozarkodinids, and the Prioniodinid Baüplan. *Journal of Paleontology* 67:875–82.

Simonetta, A.M., and S. Conway Morris (eds.). 1991. *The Early Evolution of Metazoa and the Significance of Problematic Taxa.* Cambridge and New York: Cambridge University Press.

Whittington, H.B. 1985. *The Burgess Shale.* New Haven, Connecticut: Yale University Press.

Xi-Guang Zhang, and B.R. Pratt. 1996. Early Cambrian palaeoscolecid cuticles from Shaanxi, China. *Journal of Paleontology* 70:275–79.

Zhuravlev, A. Yu. 1986. Radiocyathids. *In* A. Hoffman and M.H. Nitecki (eds.), *Problematic Fossil Taxa.* Oxford: Clarendon; New York: Oxford University Press.

Further Reading

Hoffman, A., and M.H. Nitecki (eds.). 1986. *Problematic Fossil Taxa.* Oxford: Clarendon; New York: Oxford University Press.

Simonetta, A.M., and S. Conway Morris (eds.). 1991. *The Early Evolution of Metazoa and the Significance of Problematic Taxa.* Cambridge and New York: Cambridge University Press.

PROBLEMATIC ANIMALS: POORLY CHARACTERIZED PROBLEMATICA

This article concerns problematic organisms represented by incomplete skeletons, such as tubular and conical fossils called small shelly fossils, and scattered skeletal elements, such as isolated sclerites (the fundamental elements of the exoskeleton). The following are descriptions of the main types of these problematica.

Anabaritids

Anabaritids were Lower Cambrian (Tommotian and Atdabanian stages) tube-dwelling creatures that occur in some of the earliest Cambrian strata. Anabaritids are found in most parts of the world (Australia, China, Baltica, Siberia), in places where limestones of appropriate age have been deposited.

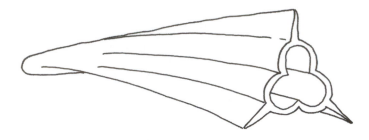

Figure 1. *Anabarites,* a basal Cambrian tubular shelly fossil. Note the triradial nature of the tube and the radial flanges projecting from the tube surface. Length of tube, five millimeters.

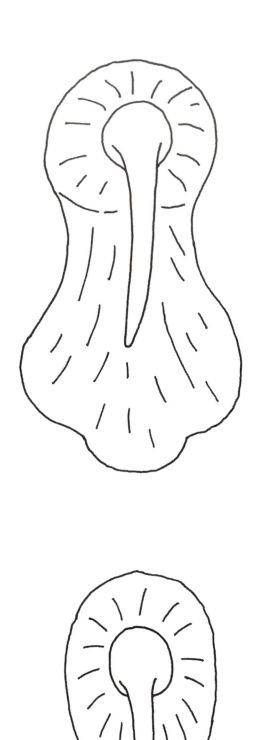

Figure 2. *Ardrossania paveyi,* a Cambrian planispirally coiled tubular shell that superficially resembles a snail. Diameter, 0.55 millimeters.

Anabaritids formed a relatively straight tubular shell of aragonite; the shell was apparently a dwelling tube (Figure 1), as opposed to part of a scleritome (multielement external skeleton). The shell apparently had a bilayer structure, consisting of an inner lamella with a chevron-shaped ultrastructure and an outer layer consisting of striae at right angles to the axis of growth (Conway Morris and Menge 1989). The mature shell is distinctive for its tri-radially symmetric (trisulcate) form.

During ontogeny (growth and development) the shape of the tubular shell changed from cylindrical in cross section to clover-leafed in cross section. The furrows between anabaritid lobes generally are parallel to the growth axis of the shell, although some anabaritids twist in a helical fashion as they grow. In a few cases, vanes, or "wings," projected from the outer part of each of the three lobes, an arrangement which may have stabilized the shell and kept it from rolling. Other anabaritids may show short longitudinal ridges or welts on the outside of the tubular shell,

Figure 3. Sclerites of *Cambroclavus,* an Early Cambrian spiny animal. *Top:* a sclerite with a shield-shaped base, belonging to the cambroclavid morph; *bottom,* a sclerite with a boss-shaped base, belonging to the zhijinitid morph. Length of the cambroclavid morph sclerite, 0.63 millimeters.

adjacent to and parallel to the furrows. Along the axis of the shell may be a somewhat regular series of swellings and depressions, as if the aperture of the anabaritid shell expanded and contracted in a rhythmic fashion throughout the life of the animal. The anabaritid shell may have had an operculum, a lid that served to close off the opening of the tube.

Various species of the genus *Anabarites* have been identified as cases of parallel evolution. Through an evolutionary process known as iterative evolution, these species independently developed sixfold radial symmetry in the cross section of the tubular shell. This "hexasulcate condition" apparently evolved from the trisulcate anabaritid state, and occurred independently in at least two anabaritid lineages (trisulcate *Anabarites trymatus* evolved into the hexasulcate *Anabarites sexalox; Anabarites hexasulcatus* is descended from a trisulcate ancestor). These evolutionary transitions have been identified as examples (Conway Morris and Menge 1989; Bengtson et al. 1990) of heterochronic acceleration, also called "peramorphosis." Peramorphosis is an evolutionary pattern in which the rate of development increases, leading to a transition over time from a less developed species (trisulcate) to a more developed species (hexasulcate). The more developed species passes through the earlier (trisulcate) stage during its ontogeny. The functional significance of the hexasulcate form is unknown.

Ardrossaniids

This Early Cambrian problematicum, known only from the single Australian species *Ardrossania paveyi,* is represented by coiled tubular shells that superficially resemble snails (Figure 2). The shell's ultrastructure, however, is decidedly not typical of gastropods, consisting of inner and outer shell wall layers separated by vertical walls (Bengtson et al. 1990). A shallow groove also may be present on the periphery of the last whorl, a feature somewhat similar to a single furrow on the surface of an anabaritid.

Cambroclaves

Cambroclaves are known only as disarticulated sclerites from the Lower Cambrian of Australia, China, and Kazakhstan (Bengtson et al. 1990). The sclerites bear a single, prominent, hook-shaped spine, which gives them a distinctive shape, rather like a door-mounted coat hook (Figure 3). The spine projects outward from a base that is either shaped like a boss (knob) or shield. Sclerites with the boss-shaped base belong to the "zhijinitid morph"; those with a shield-shaped base belong to the "cambroclavid morph." The sclerites of the living animal are presumed to have been calcareous in composition, although most known fossils have been phosphatized. The surfaces of sclerites have radiating striae, which result from a crystalline biomineralization fabric.

Although a complete cambroclave scleritome has not been found yet, pairs of articulated sclerites have been recovered after acid dissolution of cambroclave-bearing limestones. These pairs indicate that the cambroclave scleritome consisted of imbricated (overlapping) sclerites set in rows on the animal's back like roofing tiles, with spines projecting outward. The array of spines would have constituted a formidable deterrent to predators of the time.

Figure 4. Paleozoic chitinozoan showing perforate appendages extending from the base of the test. Length of test, 0.18 millimeters.

Chitinozoans

Chitinozoans are a group of tiny (up to two millimeters in length) organisms, known from marine sediments of Ordovician to Devonian age (Haq and Boersma 1978). The organic-walled test (external protective body covering) of a chitinozoan is bottle-shaped. The broad end is closed; the narrow end extends into a neck, which opens to form an aperture. The aperture is closed by a thin operculum.

The base of the chitinozoan test is flattened. In the center of the base is a pore; this pore is surrounded by concentric circular ribs to form a bulls-eye pattern. The chamber (i.e., the part below the neck) of the chitinozoan may have a variety of types of ornamentation on its surface (Figure 4), including planar flanges (carinae), branching or perforated spines, and rows of spines that are connected at their tips by longitudinal bars. An evolutionary series has been identified in chitinozoans in which the test chamber ornamentation evolves from tufts of linked spines (*Conochitina robusta*) to longitudinal rows of spines linked at their tops by longitudinal bars (*Conochitina crickmayi spinetum*) to nonper-

Figure 5. The cloudinid *Sinotubulites* from the Late Precambrian La Ciénega Formation of Sonora (Mexico). Length of shell, approximately 1.2 centimeters. From McMenamin and McMenamin (1990).

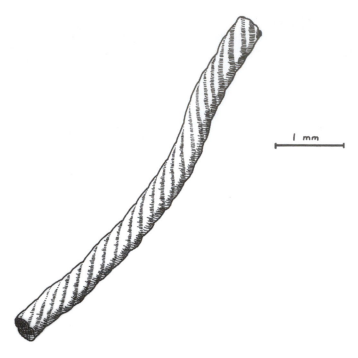

Figure 6. The coleolid *Coleoloides* showing its distinctive spiral ornament. These calcitic Cambrian tubes are often found in clusters. Length of tube, 6.5 millimeters.

forate flanges or carinae *(Conochitina crickmayi normalis)*. The tests of chitinozoans may be joined together to form chains; such linear chains are known in most of the common chitinozoan genera. The chains can be very long in some species. The chain on one species is whorled and packed into a compact mass called the cocoon.

The affinities of chitinozoans are not well understood, although it seems likely that they represent the fossils either of an animal or of a protist (single-celled "animal").

Cloudinids

Cloudinids are the earliest shelly fossils known in the fossil record. They are found in Late Precambrian marine sediments all over the globe. Undoubted cloudinid specimens are not found in rock strata above the Precambrian-Cambrian boundary. In Namibia and Mexico cloudinids co-occur with members of the Ediacaran biota. Three cloudinid genera are recognized: *Wyattia*, *Cloudina*, and *Sinotubulites*.

The cloudinid shell, originally calcareous in composition, consists of extremely thin layers of shell material (Figure 5). Each layer forms a cup-shaped surface with a rounded bottom part. Successive skeletal layers are nested in a cup-in-cup arrangement. The margin of the latest layer, at the aperture of the shell, flares out quite broadly as if to support a layer of tissue. (Some hypothesize that this tissue was photosynthetic.) The flared margin of this and previous shell layers, however, is quite fragile and is usually broken off in fossil specimens. Such breakage gives the surface of a cloudinid specimen a pseudoannulation—structures that appear to be growth rings actually are the broken margins of the outwardly directed parts of the shell layers.

Cloudinid fossils can be locally quite abundant, forming shell hash deposits of thicknesses of a meter or more, as in the Schwartzrand Limestone of Namibia and in the La Ciénega For-

mation dolostones of Mexico (McMenamin 1998). Reports of cloudinids with bore holes caused by predators are controversial.

Coleolids

Coleolids are an Early Cambrian small shelly fossil group with very long shells up to a centimeter or more in length. Shell shape varies from cylindrical to weakly tapering. The shells may be straight to strongly curved and may bear longitudinal, annular, or an attractive spiral ornament, as for instance in the genus *Coleoloides* (Figure 6). In Lower Cambrian limestones of southeastern Newfoundland, the tubular shells of this genus are found clustered together, the fossils oriented vertically, presumably in their original positions. These Newfoundland specimens are curious to behold, and numerous horizons in the limestone display thousands of these fossils clustered together, resembling straws (about a millimeter in diameter and up to several centimeters long) stuck in the mud (McMenamin and McMenamin 1990).

Cornulitids

Cornulitids are small, conical, tubular fossils (Figure 7) of an animal that cemented its shell to a hard substrate. Often the substrates are the surfaces of other shells such as brachiopods and trilobites. Extending from the Ordovician to the Pennsylvanian (Lescinsky 1997), cornulitids are widely distributed throughout the world. The cone of the cornulitid shell may show fine growth lines or coarser annulations.

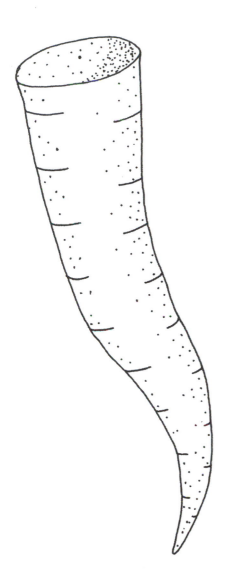

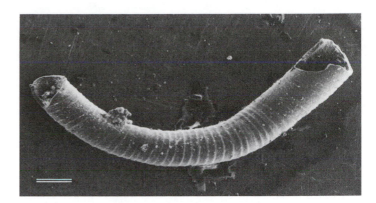

Figure 9. The hyolithelminth *Hyolithellus,* a Cambrian phosphatic tubular fossil from Sonora (Mexico). Scale bar = 0.2 millimeters. From McMenamin and McMenamin (1990).

The affinities of cornulitids are unknown, although some authors have placed them with the annelids (segmented worms) or with the molluscs. Cornulitids play an important role in paleoecological studies, for the preferred orientations of the cornulitid apertures can give clues to the life orientation of the host shell. For example, the distribution of *Cornulites* epibionts on the Devonian brachiopod *Mucrospirifer* shows that none of the cornulitid tubes cross the brachiopod's commissure. This arrangement indicates that the brachiopod was alive at the time of cornulitid infestation of its shell surface.

Hadimopanellids

Hadimopanella is a phosphatic sclerite up to about a half millimeter in diameter (Figure 8), and is best know from deposits on the Siberian Platform. These sclerites take the form of smooth to somewhat oblong discs. One side of the disc is smooth and convex, whereas the other tapers upward to a flattened crest covered with small nodes, giving the sclerite the appearance of a castle surrounded by a glacis. Clearly, the sclerites were part of a multielement scleritome (skeleton formed of sclerites), and the smooth and slightly convex side of each sclerite was attached to the animal's soft tissues. Each sclerite has a porous core, surrounded by denser phosphatic material that resembles the dentine in vertebrate teeth. Indeed, S. Bengtson (1977) suggested that there might be affinities between hadimopanelids and members of the phylum Chordata, and this suggestion seems plausible (note that *Lenargyrion* is a junior synonym of *Hadimopanella*).

It has been suggested that the sclerites of hadimopanellids (plus the sclerites belonging to the genera *Kaimenella, Milaculum,* and *Utahphospha*) are the remains of palaeoscolecidan worms (Hinz et al. 1990).

Hyolithelminths

Hyolithelminths are elongate, phosphatic, tubular fossils (Figure 9) known from Lower Paleozoic strata throughout the world. The tubes are thought to have lacked any type of skeletonized

Figure 7. The small conical tubular fossil of the cornulitid *Cornulites,* a Paleozoic animal that cemented its shell to a hard substrate. Length of shell, five millimeters.

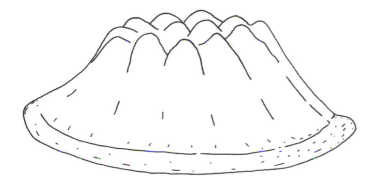

Figure 8. The hadimopanellid *Hadimopanella,* a phosphatic sclerite from strata of the Lower Cambrian. Diameter of sclerite, 0.14 millimeters.

operculum. The two main genera of hyolithelminths are *Hyolithellus* and *Torellella*. *Hyolithellus* is distinguished by its circular shape in cross section and *Torellella* by its oval or flattened shape in cross section.

The affinities of hyolithelminths are unknown, and the best chance of establishing their affinities (if any) with other shelly animals will lie in studies of the ultrastructure of the shell (Bengtson et al. 1990). Preliminary studies reveal that the tube wall consists of two layers, an inner layer with fine (less than 0.5 micron thick) laminations, and an outer layer with chevron-shaped lamellae that may be similar to those formed by the collar gland of serpulid polychaete annelid worms.

Mobergella

Mobergella is a cap-shaped fossil (Figure 10) of wide geographic distribution but, as is true of many Lower Cambrian shelly problematica, narrow temporal range. *Mobergella* is known only from the Tommotian to upper Atdabanian Stages of the Lower Cambrian. The genus *Discinella* is closely related.

Mobergella is a broad hat-shaped operculum or low shell with a distinctive set of radiating, internal muscle scars (Bengtson et al. 1990). The shell is built up of superimposed lamellae of phosphatic shell material. The lamellae were added in incremental fashion to the shell's concave (inner) surface. The radiating muscle scars show a finely punctate (pitted) pattern. The phosphatic shell lamellae show a nacreous (mother-of-pearl) luster in well-preserved specimens, and there may be a carbonaceous film between the layers of laminae.

Mobergella shells resemble the shells of monoplacophoran molluscs because of the presence of multiple, radiating muscle scars. The extremely low profile of *Mobergella*, however, would provide little room for the mollusc's large body. Thus, it has been suggested that *Mobergella* was the operculum that fitted to the end of a tube that housed a wormlike animal. To the consternation of researchers, however, the hypothesized *Mobergella* dwelling tube has never been located. If it existed, this tube must have been difficult to fossilize. Perhaps it was composed of particles of sediment, as was the case for the Lower Cambrian tubular fossil *Onuphionella*. Its tube was composed of oriented mica-flakes (Signor and McMenamin 1988). Specimens of *Mobergella* showing predatorial damage have been recognized (Bengtson 1968).

Paiutiids

Paiutiids are tubular, cylindrical, phosphatic (Bengtson 1994) shells known from Lower Cambrian (Atdabanian to Botoman stages) of the United States and Mexico (McMenamin et al. 1994). The shells are distinguished by internal, longitudinal septa. The septa may be continuous and bladelike, discontinuous, or even cusped (Figure 11) along the septal plane. The number of septa varies from one to seven. Based on resemblances to septate corals, M.C. Tynan (1983) placed *Paiutitubulites* in the phylum Cnidaria, but this assignment may be questioned (Bengtson 1994). It is possible that paiutiids require their own separate phylum.

Figure 10. *Mobergella*, a cap-shaped phosphatic fossil from the Lower Cambrian. Greatest diameter of shell, two millimeters.

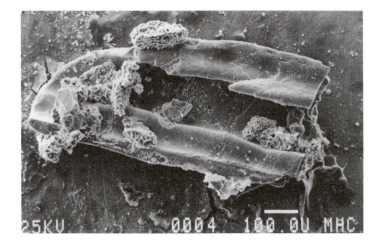

Figure 11. Interior view of the paiutiid *Paiutitubulites* showing longitudinal septa. Upper septum has a cusp, which here points to the left. Scale: *bar*, 0.1 millimeters. From Unit 3 of the Cambrian Puerto Blanco Formation, Cerro Clemente, Sonora, Mexico, sample 1 of 12/15/82; IGM 3614[41].

Protohertzina

Protohertzina is a small, slender, spine-shaped, phosphatic shelly fossil (Figure 12) known from strata just above and just below the base of the Cambrian. It is geographically widespread, occurring

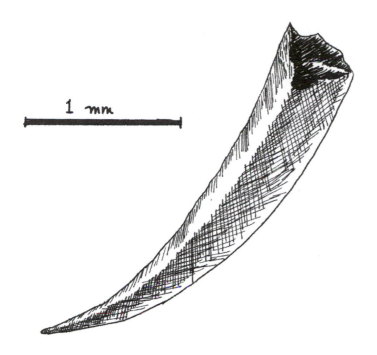

Figure 12. *Protohertzina*, a small, slender, spine-shaped, phosphatic shelly fossil known from the just above and just below the base of the Cambrian. Scale: *bar,* one millimeter. Length of spine, 2.2 millimeters.

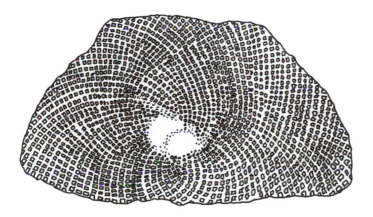

Figure 13. A Paleozoic receptaculitid fossil, showing the distinctive spiraling pattern of individual calcareous units called "meroms." Width of specimen, four centimeters.

on the Siberian Platform (where it was first described), Iran, Canada, Australia, Mongolia, Kazakhstan, and India.

The protohertzinids are informally placed in a group of fossils called the protoconodonts (a group that also includes the cat-claw–shaped genus *Mongolodus*) because in composition, size, and presumably function, they resemble true conodonts. *Protohertzina* is distinguished by its roughly triangular cross section. It compares closely in morphology and ultrastructure to the chitinous grasping

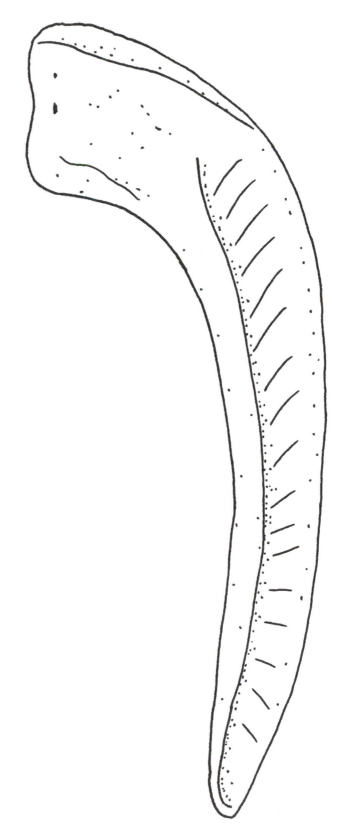

Figure 14. A siphogonuchitid sclerite, belonging to the genus *Siphogonuchites*, from Lower Cambrian strata. Length of sclerite, 1.7 millimeters.

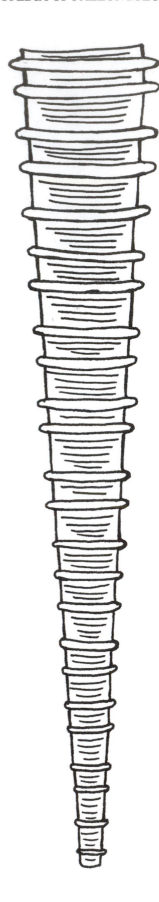

Figure 15. A Paleozoic specimen of *Tentaculites* from eastern North America. Length of tubular shell, 14 millimeters.

Figure 16. A sclerite of the tommotiid *Lapworthella* from Lower Cambrian strata of Sonora (Mexico). Greatest dimension of sclerite, 1.6 millimeters. From McMenamin and McMenamin (1990).

spines of chaetognaths (arrowworms), so a relationship has been proposed between the chaetognaths and the protoconodonts (Bengtson et al. 1990; McMenamin and McMenamin 1990). *Protohertzina* has the distinction of being the earliest fossil that can be confidently attributed to a predatory animal (Bengtson et al. 1990; McMenamin and McMenamin 1990).

Receptaculitids

Once thought to be corals (hence, their popular name "sunflower corals") or even sponges, receptaculitids subsequently were regarded as a type of calcareous green algae. But the green algal link has been questioned by some paleontologists (Beadle 1988), so the receptaculitids remain problematical, although they may represent fossils of some type of photosynthetic protist.

Receptaculitid fossils are striking, showing a distinctive spiraling pattern of individual calcareous units called "meroms" (Figure 13). The fossils occur in a wide variety of marine environments, ranging from tropical reefs (where their sturdy skeletons could stand up to beating waves) to cooler water in high latitudes. The animals are worldwide in distribution and lived from the Ordovician to the Devonian.

Siphogonuchitids

Siphogonuchitids are isolated sclerites known primarily from Lower Cambrian (Tommotian to Botomian stages) strata of China (represented by genus *Siphogonuchites*) and other parts of the world.

The sclerites are claw-shaped, usually with two shallow grooves along either side (Figure 14).

The scaly shells of *Maikhanella* are now thought to be composed of tiny, fused siphogonuchitid sclerites. This arrangement, and the anterior and posterior shells of the complete Greenland scleritomes of *Halkieria*, are taken as evidence that the shells of molluscs are derived from the evolutionary fusion of individual sclerites. Furthermore, siphogonuchitids (including *Maikhanella*) and the halkieriids are felt to by phylogenetically close to, or perhaps even ancestral to, the molluscs (Bengtson 1994).

Tentaculitoidea

Tentaculitids are a group of problematic conical shelly fossils known from the middle part of the Paleozoic (Silurian and Devonian) throughout many parts of the world; the animals are well represented by specimens in eastern North America (Figure 15). They have been compared to annelid worms and molluscs, but neither of these phyla can easily accommodate the Class Tentaculitoidea.

The calcareous shell of *Tentaculites* is narrow and conical, and it reaches up to four centimeters in length (Lindemann and Melycher 1997). Prominent rings are present along the length of the cone. Septa may be present at the proximal part of the cone.

Where they occur, fossil tentaculitids may be locally abundant, and bedding plane surfaces in both limestones and sandstones may be littered with their remains.

Tommotiids

Tommotiids, known from a number of primarily Lower Cambrian genera (*Camenella, Eccentrotheca, Kelanella, Kennardia, Kulparina, Lapworthella, Patermitra, Sunnaginia,* and *Tommotia*), are characterized by a multielement skeleton or scleritome composed of cone, horn, or pyramid-shaped sclerites (as, for instance, in the genus *Lapworthella;* Figure 16). Sclerites are of highly irregular shape in the species *Eccentrotheca guano*. The sclerites are composed of calcium phosphate (hydroxyapatite) and grew by adding new shell material to the inside of the cone, a process known as "basal internal secretion" (Bengtson et al. 1990). Under high magnification fractured edges of sclerites show the internal layering that indicates this mode of growth.

Plausible reconstructions have been proposed for lapworthellids (McMenamin and McMenamin 1990), although, unlike the situation with the halkieriids, no complete or intact lapworthellid scleritomes have been discovered.

MARK A.S. McMENAMIN

See also Problematic Animals: Overview; Problematic Animals: Phanerozoic Problematica; Skeletized Microorganisms

Works Cited

Beadle, S.C. 1988. Dasyclads, cyclocrinitids and receptaculitids: Comparative morphology and paleoecology. *Lethaia* 21:1–12.

Bengtson, S. 1968. The problematic genus *Mobergella* from the Lower Cambrian of the Baltic area. *Lethaia* 1:325–51.

———. 1977. Early Cambrian button-shaped phosphatic microfossils from the Siberian Platform. *Palaeontology* 20:751–62.

——— (ed.). 1994. *Early Life on Earth.* New York: Columbia University Press.

Bengtson, S., S. Conway Morris, B.J. Cooper, P.A. Jell, and B.N. Runnegar. 1990. *Early Cambrian Fossils from South Australia.* Memoir of the Association of Australasian Palaeontologists, 9. Brisbane: Association of Australasian Palaeontologists.

Conway Morris, S., and Chen Menge. 1989. Lower Cambrian anabaritids from south China. *Geological Magazine* 126:615–32.

Haq, B.U., and A. Boersma. 1978. *Introduction to Marine Micropaleontology.* Amsterdam and New York: Elsevier.

Hinz, I.C.U., P. Kraft, M. Mergl, and K.J. Mueller. 1990. The problematic *Hadimopanella, Kaimenella, Milaculum* and *Utahphospha* identified as sclerites of Palaeoscolecida. *Lethaia* 23:217–21.

Lescinsky, H.L. 1997. Epibiont communities: Recruitment and competition on North American Carboniferous brachiopods. *Journal of Paleontology* 71:34–53.

Lindemann, R.H., and D.A. Melycher. 1997. *Tentaculites* (Tentaculitoidea) from the Manlius Limestone (Lower Devonian) at Schoharie, New York. *Journal of Paleontology* 71:360–68.

McMenamin, M.A.S. 1998. *The Garden of Ediacara.* New York: Columbia University Press.

McMenamin, M.A.S., and D.L.S. McMenamin. 1990. *The Emergence of Animals: The Cambrian Breakthrough.* New York: Columbia University Press.

McMenamin, M.A.S., S.L. Pittenger, M.R. Carson, and E.M. Larrabee. 1994. Upper Precambrian-Cambrian faunal sequence, Sonora, Mexico and Lower Cambrian Fossils from New Jersey, United States. *New York State Museum Bulletin* 481:213–27.

Signor, P.W., and M.A.S. McMenamin. 1988. The Early Cambrian worm tube *Onuphionella* from California and Nevada. *Journal of Paleontology* 62:233–40.

Tynan, M.C. 1983. Coral-like microfossils from the Lower Cambrian of California. *Journal of Paleontology* 57:1188–211.

Further Reading

Beadle, S.C. (ed.). 1994. *Early Life on Earth.* New York: Columbia University Press.

McMenamin, M.A.S. 1998. *The Garden of Ediacara.* New York: Columbia University Press.

McMenamin, M.A.S., and D.L.S. McMenamin. 1990. *The Emergence of Animals: The Cambrian Breakthrough.* New York: Columbia University Press.

PROBLEMATIC PLANTS

Much knowlege of the plant fossil record consists of detailed information concerning fossil fragments that may occur abundantly but not in sufficiently complete form to fit the pieces together into a whole plant with confidence. Seeds and fruits are naturally dispersed, leaf fall may be the result of a cold or dry dormant season, and branch and twig material is often deposited as a result of storm damage. It is a rare discovery indeed when scholars find leaves and reproductive structures that were fossilized while still organically attached to the parent plant. Many of our whole plant concepts are the result of repeatedly finding separate plant parts preserved together in the same locality. With this in mind, almost all plant fossils can be regarded as problematic to some extent.

Two characteristics of plant fossils exacerbate the problem of fragmentary evidence. First, leaves, spore-producing organs, cones, or fruits grow individually, on various regions of the branch system. Unlike dinosaur bones, plant parts are not required to fit together into a mechanically functional whole. While a few characteristically shaped bones can be used to reconstruct a whole animal, many widely known fossil plant parts come from wholly unknown plants. Second, different plant parts are preferentially preserved under different conditions. Stems having thick-walled transporting cells or woody trunks are often preserved in beautiful three-dimensional detail, because during fossilization the cellular walls are replaced or impregnated with minerals such as calcium carbonate, silica, or phosphates. However, this preservational environment does not preserve leaf material well. Leaves and large complex frond systems are best preserved as two-dimensional compressions in fine-grained shales and mudstones that result from episodic floods. The tendency for different plant parts to be preserved selectively under different conditions also contributes to a plant fossil record of largely unassociated parts.

Prototaxites

Prototaxites is a genus represented by large treelike trunks that are found in Devonian deposits in southern Ontario, Ohio, and central New York state. These fossils were first interpreted as the trunks of large conifer trees. However, no roots, leaves, or lateral branches were found. When these fossils, which may be as much as 90 centimeters in diameter, were sectioned with a rock saw and examined microscopically, it was found that the material did not have a cellular structure characteristic of wood at all. Instead, researchers found that the internal structure consisted of large tubes imbedded in a felt-like mass of denser small tubes. Workers then suggested that these fossils may represent a brown alga and that the large tubes may be comparable to the stipe (supporting stalk) of giant kelps. To test this interpretation, Niklas (1976) used mass spectrometry to identify biochemicals unique to the various algal groups or terrestrial plants. However, when applied to very old fossils, the validity of this analytical tool has come under question. An additional problem in this interpretation is that the cells in brown algae do not involve rigid cell walls. If these trunklike organisms were in fact terrestrial, standing upright like a grove of short telephone poles, then one needs to explain their rigidity. An alternative explanation is that the loglike masses were never erect—they lived horizontally. If this were the case, however, we would expect the "logs" to be less radially symmetric than they are. Instead, the side resting on the ground would be flattened. The shape of most specimens refutes this interpretation.

Closer examination of the cellular detail indicates that the large tubes are septate (divided by cell walls), and that a distinctive pore occurs in each cross-wall (Schmid 1976). This suggests the cell structure of recent fungi. The tubes may represent hyphae (tubular filaments). The size differences may be interpreted as two or more species of fungi growing in a symbiotic relationship. The most recent interpretation by F. Hueber theorizes that the structure had the rigidity of a recent bracket fungus. Fungi, however, are heterotrophic. They must derive their nutrients from a living host or dead organic material. There is no evidence for this lifestyle in *Prototaxites*. The common shelf fungus is a member of the Basidiomycota, a group of fungi that have distinctive spore-bearing structures (basidia), and a distinctive cell structure having clamp connections. Neither structure has yet been identified in *Prototaxites*, despite the sectioning and microscopic examination of large numbers of specimens.

Protosalvinia

Protosalvinia is another Devonian fossil group of unknown affinity. The group is represented by specimens up to two centimeters in length having a flattened thallus with widely forked disk-shaped tips, somewhat resembling a liverwort. Specimens are consistently recovered from black shales, which indicates an off-shore marine environment and which signals they may be marine. Their outward shape resembles a reduced form of a brown alga such as *Fucus* (rockweeds). However, other evidence indicates a relationship to land plants. The surface texture and coherence suggests the presence of cutin, the waxy epidermal covering of land plants that retards water loss. On the surface of some specimens are small cups that bear spores arranged in tetrads. Ultrastructural analysis of the spores provides evidence for a resistant wall, further supporting the hypothesis that these were early land plants (Taylor and Taylor 1987). J. Gray and A.J. Boucot (1979) interpret *Protosalvinia* as a transitional form between an advanced alga and a true land plant such as a primitive bryophyte. Several species have been named based primarily on size differences. However, subsequent studies have interpreted these "species" as different ontogenetic (growth) stages of the same organisms (Niklas and Phillips 1979).

Cladoxylales

The Cladoxylales are a predominantly Devonian group represented by permineralized axes (stems, singular axis) and petiole bases of small size. The most completely known genus is *Pseudosporochnus* (Stein and Hueber 1989), which may have been a short, treelike plant a few meters tall. Like many Devonian plants, this group did not have true leafy foliage. Instead, the photosynthetic units were finely branched appendages resembling naked leaf veins without the interwebbing of a lamina (the flattened part of a leaf). Frondlike lateral branches emerge from the trunk as an apical (growing from the tip) crown, divide into two several times, then terminate in fine photosynthetic branches. In fertile fronds, sporangia (spore-producing structures) are borne at the tips of these branches. The group's most interesting feature, however, is the unusual arrangement of vascular (water-conducting) tissue in the stems. Radiating outward from the center of the stem are U or V-shaped plates of xylem, forming interwoven, dividing ribs of supporting tissue. Nests of thick-walled sclerenchyma cells form a distinctive texture in the cortex (outer stem), assumably supplying additional support. At the tips of each xylem rib is an island of thin-walled parenchyma cells and associated protoxylem (embryonic xylem) that is called a "peripheral loop." This character and the superficially frondlike appearance of the photosynthetic units has led scholars to interpret this group as ancestral to ferns. Other scholars have linked this group to several other early plant groups.

Understanding the Cladoxylales becomes less problematic if we view it as an isolated evolutionary lineage that left no modern descendants. Individual plants probably grew in a sufficiently dense community that competition for light became a critical factor. The dense, ropelike or cable structure of the primary xylem was one way to provide sufficient strength for a plant of treelike stature. Members of the Cladoxylales are best represented as an evolutionary experiment that provided much diversity at the time, but was subsequently replaced by more successful evolutionary innovations in trunk structure.

Calamopityaceae

The Calamopityaceae are another early plant group represented primarily by highly fragmentary but beautifully preserved permineralized axes. Occurrences are found in rock strata of the Lower Carboniferous. Abundant specimens have been recovered from the New Albany Shale of Kentucky, in the United States, the Calciferous Sandstone Series of Great Britain, the Saalfeld of Germany, and the Montagne Noire region of France. The group often is described as gymnosperms, based on the presence of secondary xylem, cortical sclerenchyma (sparganum), and leaf stalks that fork at their bases, but no attached reproductive structures have ever been found. The group is of interest because the spatial arrangement of the primary xylem (stele) of the various genera forms a structural transition series from the three-part protostele of *Stenomyelon,* through intermediate forms of mixed protosteles having various amounts of pith, to the eustele of *Calamopitys* (Galtier and Meyer-Berthaud 1989) that is similar in appearance to the eustele shared by recent conifers and dicot angiosperms (Namboodiri and Beck 1968). Because the Calamopityaceae are phylogenetically isolated from more probable conifer ancestors, the evolutionary development of this anatomy is probably the result of independent changes, not relatedness.

Rhacophytaceae

The Rhacophytaceae are a family of predominantly Devonian free-sporing plants that lacked true flat-bladed leaves but instead had tufts of finely divided photosynthetic branches typical of many Devonian land plants, such as the Cladoxylales. Several genera and species assignable to the Rhacophytaceae have been described from Belgium, Germany, Spitzbergen, Ellsmere Island, China, and West Virginia. *Rhacophyton* is represented by plants consisting of a slender upright axis, up to one meter in height, with spirally arranged lateral axes (side stems) organized somewhat like a fern frond. This structure has led many scholars to regard the Rhacophytaceae as a group ancestral to ferns. However, unlike recent fronds, in which the leaflets are biseriate (arranged in two ranks so as to be bilaterally symmetric), portions of the fronds of *Rhacophyton* are quadriseriate (leaflets are attached at right angles to each other to form a cylindrically symmetric unit). Clusters of small, torpedo-shaped sporangia with curving pointed tips were borne on densely branched structures, forming "puffs" attached to the main axis just below the point where the lateral axes were attached.

The internal anatomy of *Rhacophyton zygopteroides* from Belgium is well known (Leclercq 1951). Unlike recent ferns, the main axis and petiole bases have small amounts of secondary xylem (wood), leading other scholars to suggest an affinity with the progymnosperms (Andrews and Phillips 1968). The primary xylem of the main axis forms a star-shaped core. The vascular traces of the lateral axes are shaped like a bar with thickened ends extending outward into a "dog-bone" (clepsydroid) shape. The leaflet traces are cast off the expanded ends of the clepsydroid, resulting in peripheral loops (islands of thin-walled cells), a diagnostic character of the group that has led some scholars to hypothesize a possible relationship with the Cladoxylales.

A similar genus, *Chlidanophyton dublinensis,* from the Price Formation of southwestern Virginia and the Pocono Formation of West Virginia is Mississippian in age (Gensel 1973). This indicates that a relictual diversity of one or a few derived forms of this otherwise primitive group may have persisted over a long period of time, much like the taxa of today that we refer to as "living fossils." In this genus, the photosynthetic branches are longer, and the ellipsoid sporangia are borne on delicate recurved (curved backward) branches attached at intervals along the length of the fertile branch systems. Despite the collection and examination of large numbers of fossils, scholars have recovered no specimens of *Chlidanophyton* that clearly preserve internal structure. It is, therefore, impossible to determine if this genus shared the clepsydroid anatomy that characterizes the Rhacophytaceae. The Rhacophytaceae may best be regarded as a group that shared primitive characteristics with several major plant groups.

"Pteridosperm" Foliage

Large amounts of fernlike foliage have been described from compression fossils occurring in rock strata from the Carboniferous Age. (Compression fossils are flattened remains found in fine-grained sediments deposited in oxygen-free environments, free of organisms that might otherwise decompose the remains.) These plants made up the extensive coal-producing swamps of that period. A fortuitous discovery of seeds borne in small leafy cupules and having distinctive epidermal hairs (comparable to those found on associated fernlike foliage) indicated that this foliage type was actually borne on seed plants. So, scholars adopted the term "Pteridosperm," or seed fern (Oliver and Scott 1904). We now know that these plants of fernlike foliage predate true ferns. Thousands of fossil taxa having fernlike fronds in which many leaflets extend from either side of a long, stemlike structure (a rachis) have been loosely grouped together as "pteridospermic," without evidence of their reproductive biology. We now recognize that this seemingly complex frond organization is actually the primitive state for photosynthetic structures of several different early major plant groups, including possibly some progymnosperms, early seed plants ("pteridosperms"), and the younger true ferns. We also have come to accept that two-dimensional frondlike appearance may be the result of the fossilization process itself, in which a three-dimensional branch system is compressed and flattened, distorting the organism's true appearance.

Triphyllopteris-Genselia and the Concept of Form Genera

The fragmentary nature of the plant fossil record has led to the practice of using a tentative and highly artificial taxonomy called "form genera." Assigned to these form genera are plant fossils that are often not uniquely diagnosed or assignable to higher order taxa, in the expectation that eventually more complete evidence will be unearthed. This practice became applied especially heavily in biostratigraphy. Fossils representing plant remains are often recognizable in rock cores drilled in the process of coal exploration. Leaf forms that indicate strata of a certain age are called "index fossils." Historically, specimens were assigned to broadly defined "index form genera" for the purpose of age determination, without any evidence that they shared a common whole plant form, internal structure, or reproductive biology. This practice has made it difficult to interpret fossil plant lists published in the early literature. Also hindered were recent attempts to infer community structure or to compare global diversity over time, because form genera do not represent true taxonomic entities with discrete population sizes, time spans, and geographic ranges.

This problem became especially evident with the form genus *Triphyllopteris*, a valuable index fossil for the Visean (Lower Carboniferous). The genus was first described by Schimper in 1859, based on many fragmentary specimens collected from the Vosges Mountains of France. The plant is represented by foliage that bears leaflets of highly variable sizes and shapes, ranging from simple up to five-lobed and linear to rhomboidal (Figure 1A). Schimper's official species description did not clearly distinguish between the range of variation among specimens and the range of variation on a single frond. The original specimens were lost in a fire, so they were unavailable for further comparative study. The generic assignment became a taxonomic dumping ground for foliage having leaflets of loosely tri-lobed shapes. For the purpose of age determination, many equivocal assignments were made to this broadly conceived form genus.

This situation did not change until recently. In the 1930s, W. Gothan had distributed a suite of specimens assigned to the type species *Triphyllopteris collombiana* to separately housed collections. Later, the materials were reconsolidated in Berlin into one collection, and only then could an accurate idea of the overall frond shape and spatial distribution of the different leaflet shapes become possible (Knaus 1994). It also became clear that the many specimens from North America assigned to the same genus by D. White and C. Read represented foliage of a completely different plant. For example, the European *Triphyllopteris* is represented by a large spade-shaped frond. The rachis is stout at the base and tapers toward the tip. The parent plant may have superficially resembled a cycad or a palmetto. However, the North American species are represented by elongate linear fronds or branchlets with a fine rachis of fairly constant width. Curiously, the end of the petiole exhibits a clean separation layer indicating that these photosynthetic units were abscised (died and fell away) from a long-lived and possibly woody parent plant. In 1994, M.J. Knaus revised the North American species to the genus *Genselia*.

Historically, like much Lower Carboniferous foliage of loosely frondlike organization, *Triphyllopteris* and *Genselia* species were called "pteridospermic," without any evidence of attached seed-bearing structures. A characteristic of the fronds of true seed-bearing plants is a forking at the base of the frond into two asymmetric halves (see *Neuropteris*). This character is now known to be absent in *Genselia* and most probably also in *Triphyllopteris*. It is possible that plants of these species represent leafy forms of progymnosperms (free-sporing plants) that persisted into the Carboniferous, or, alternatively, a poorly known and now fully extinct group of early seed plants. While phylogenetic relationships are still a mystery, the discovery of more complete specimens provides a clearer picture of frond architecture and the scope of variation among related species.

Sanmiguelia

Although flowering plants now represent by far the greatest diversity of recent plants, fruits and flowers were a relatively late evolutionary innovation. Unlike animals, in which recent phyla had evolved by the Cambrian period (approximately 530 million years ago), flowering plants did not diversify until well into the Cretaceous period (approximately 120 million years ago). Until recent discoveries provided new information on angiosperm origins, flowering plants appeared to have burst upon the fossil record in the early Late Cretaceous with no solid candidates for their ancestral group. Charles Darwin described the origin of angiosperms as "an abominable mystery." Recent work involving the molecular systematics and estimated divergence times of major plant groups implies an earlier origin for angiosperms. Transitional angiosperms may have evolved in upland areas, where fossilization was rarer, and thereby remained hidden from the fossil record for millions of years. This hypothesis has kindled much interest in problematic fossil plants of the Triassic as possible ancestors to flowering plants.

One of these discoveries was that of the plant *Sanmiguelia lewisii* from the Late Triassic of Colorado and western Texas. The plant has large plicate (folded like a fan) elongate leaves with parallel veins that taper to a point. When first described by R.W. Brown (1956), an affinity with palms was suggested. More com-

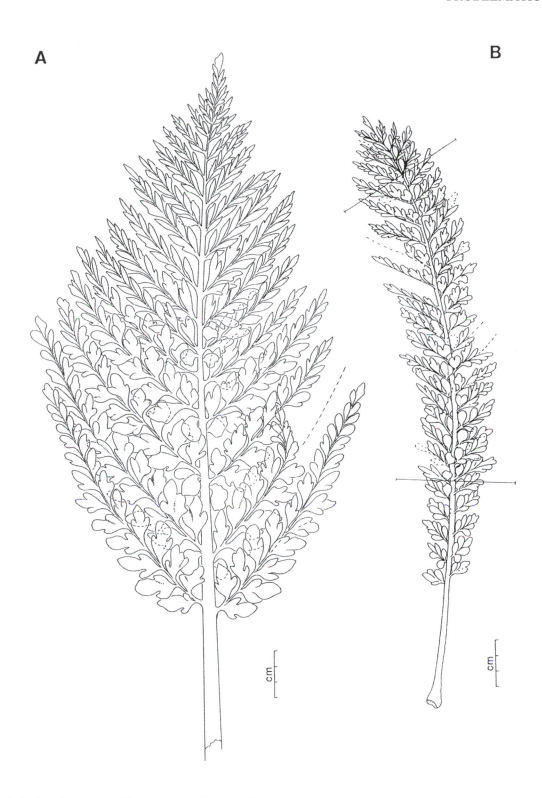

A

B

Figure 1. Two whole frond reconstructions representing specimens originally assigned to the same form genus *Triphyllopteris* and illustrating how very different species came to be assigned to the same loosely defined genus based on fragmentary specimens before a fuller understanding of the whole plant was realized. *A, Triphyllopteris collombiana* based on four fossil fragments collected by W. Gothan from Kossberg bei Plauen, Germany. Note that leaflets in the basal frond region are large and tri-lobed, but leaflets in the apical region are small and linear. The true length of the petiole base is unknown. *B, Genselia rarinervis* based on three fossil fragments from the Price Formation of southwestern Virginia in the United States. Comparable specimens were originally assigned to *Triphyllopteris* by C. Read. Note the difference in frond shape, rachis width, leaflet size, and overall degree of lobing. Specimens of *Genselia* exhibit a separation layer at the tip of the elongate petiole indicative of regular leaf abscission. From Knaus (1995); used by permission of the publisher, The University of Chicago Press, copyright © 1995 by The University of Chicago.

plete evidence, including pollen and ovule-bearing (seed-producing) structures, has led B. Cornet (1989) to the hypothesis that this plant represents an early angiosperm. If correct, this theory extends the first occurrence of flowering plants back into the Triassic by an additional 75 million years. One of the problems in interpreting early fossils as flowers is the difficulty in distinguishing carpels (the structure that encloses angiosperm seeds and defines the group) from compressed bracts (modified, leaf-like structures), and the seed-bearing "flower" spikes of *Sanmiguelia* include numerous associated bracts. Cornet's interpretation of *Sanmiguelia* as a true flowering plant has since been discredited.

Another major defining characteristic of flowering plants is double fertilization. In one fertilization, one sperm and egg unite; in the other, a sperm and two polar nuclei join to form the primary endosperm, a food source for the developing plant. Recent work by W.E. Friedman and J.S. Carmichael (1996) documents double fertilization in recent members of the Gnetales, reviving the hypothesis that this small group of unusual gymnosperms represents highly specialized relics of a more diverse group of plants that gave rise to angiosperms. An impediment to this hypothesis is that, despite extensive fossil specimens of pollen, well-substantiated megafossils of the Gnetales are essentially unrepresented in the fossil record (with the exception of *Drewria potomacensis*) (Crane and Upchurch 1987) from the Cretaceous of Virginia and perhaps the Triassic genera *Dechellyia* and *Piroconites* (Crane 1996). Perhaps *Sanmiguelia* similarly represent a previously unrecognized early diversification of the Gnetales. The large plicate leaves of *Sanmiguelia* resemble those of *Welwitschia*, an unusual gnetophyte endemic to the desert coasts of Namibia, but have more normally placed meristems (areas that produce undifferentiated cells).

MARGARET JANE KNAUS

Works Cited

Andrews, H.N., and T.L. Phillips. 1968. *Rhacophyton* from the Upper Devonian of West Virginia. *Botanical Journal of the Linnean Society* 61:37–64.

Brown, R.W. 1956. Palmlike plants from the Dolores Formation (Triassic) of southwestern Colorado. *U.S. Geological Society Professional Paper* 274:205–9.

Cornet, B. 1989. The reproductive morphology and biology of *Sanmiguelia lewisii*, and its bearing on angiosperm evolution in the Late Triassic. *Evolutionary Trends in Plants* 3:25–51.

Crane, P.R. 1996. The fossil history of the Gnetales. *In* W.E. Friedman (ed.), *Biology and Evolution of the Gnetales, International Journal of Plant Sciences* 157 (6 suppl.):S50–S57.

Crane, P.R., and G.R. Upchurch Jr. 1987. *Drewria potomacensis* gen. et sp. nov., an Early Cretaceous member of Gnetales from the Potomac group of Virginia. *American Journal of Botany* 74:1722–36.

Friedman, W.E., and J.S. Carmichael. 1996. Double fertilization in Gnetales: Implications for understanding reproductive diversification among seed plants. *In* W.E. Friedman (ed.), *Biology and Evolution of the Gnetales, International Journal of Plant Sciences* 157 (6 suppl.):S77–S94.

Galtier, J., and B. Meyer-Berthaud. 1989. Studies of the Early Carboniferous pteridosperm *Calamopitys*: A redescription of the type material from Saalfeld (GDR). *Palaeontographica* 213B:1–36.

Gensel, P.G. 1973. A new plant from the Lower Mississippian of Southwestern Virginia. *Palaeontographica* 142B:137–53.

Gray, J., and A.J. Boucot. 1979. The Devonian land plant *Protosalvinia*. *Lethaia* 12:57–63.

Knaus, M.J. 1994. *Triphyllopteris collombiana*: A clarification of the generic concept based on rediscovered specimens from Kossberg bei Plauen, Germany, and a reassignment of the North American species of *Triphyllopteris* to *Genselia* gen. nov. *International Journal of Plant Sciences* 155:97–116.

———. 1995. The species of the Early Carboniferous fossil plant genus *Genselia*. *International Journal of Plant Sciences* 156:61–92.

Leclercq, S. 1951. Étude morphologique et anatomique d'une fougère du Dévonien supérieur, le *Rhacophyton zygopteroides* nov. sp. *Annales de la Société Géologique de Belgique* 40 (9):1–62.

Namboodiri, K.K., and C.B. Beck. 1968. A comparative study of the primary vascular systems of conifers. 3. Stelar evolution in gymnosperms. *American Journal of Botany* 55:464–72.

Niklas, K.J. 1976. Chemotaxonomy of *Prototaxites* and evidence for possible terrestrial adaptations. *Review of Palaeobotany and Palynology* 22:1–17.

Niklas, K.J., and T.L. Phillips. 1979. Morphology of *Protosalvinia* from the Upper Devonian of Ohio and Kentucky. *American Journal of Botany* 63:9–29.

Oliver, F.W., and D.H. Scott. 1904. On the structure of the Palaeozoic seed *Lagenostoma lomaxi*, with a statement of the evidence upon which it is referred to *Lyginodendron*. *Philosophical Transactions of the Royal Society, London* 197B:193–247.

Schmid, R. 1976. Septal pores in *Prototaxites*, an enigmatic Devonian plant. *Science* 191:287–88.

Stein W.E., and F.M. Hueber. 1989. The anatomy of *Pseudosporochnus*: *P. hueberi* from the Devonian of New York. *Review of Palaeobotany and Palynology* 60:311–59.

Taylor, W.A., and T.N. Taylor. 1987. Spore wall ultrastructure of *Protosalvinia*. *American Journal of Botany* 74:437–43.

PROBOSCIDEANS

The proboscideans, whose only surviving members are the Asian and African elephants, represent what was once one of the most spectacular and successful groups in the evolutionary history of the mammals. They exhibited a huge diversity of forms, ranging from pig-sized, semiaquatic animals such as *Moeritherium* to the majestic Pleistocene mammoths. Successfully reaching all of the continents except for Australia and Antarctica, the proboscideans have been, at least over the last 20 million years,

Figure 1. Reconstruction and skull of the primitive proboscidean *Moeritherium* (North Africa, Late Eocene–Early Oligocene). Reconstruction from Fenton and Fenton (1989); skull from Romer (1966), used by permission of the publisher, The University of Chicago Press, copyright © 1933, 1945, 1966 by The University of Chicago.

the largest of all land mammals. This once-great radiation (diversity and geographic dispersal) has now been reduced to a mere splinter of its former self, and today even this splinter is threatened with extinction.

If asked to list the proboscideans' distinguishing features, undoubtedly most people would include the presence of a trunk, more formally referred to as a "proboscis." Indeed, this proboscis is the basis for the group's formal name. Other features that typically distinguish proboscideans from other living mammals include (1) tusks—specifically, enlarged second upper incisors; (2) the absence of canines; (3) serial tooth replacement—a curious cheek tooth replacement pattern in which premolars (both milk and permanent) and molars are replaced from back to front far into adulthood, ending when the third molar has erupted and the second molar has been cast out; and (4) thick (graviportal) limb bones—an adaptation for supporting great weight that is found in many very large mammals and in dinosaurs. However, these features are typical of living elephants and were not present in the oldest members of this group. Rather unglamorously, the most primitive proboscideans are linked to their later, more advanced cousins by shared unique features of the ankle and shoulder (Shoshani et al. 1996).

The proboscideans first arose near the end of the Paleocene epoch from primitive hooved mammals (condylarths) either in North Africa or southwest Asia. At this time (approximately 58 million years ago), this land mass lay on the shores of an ocean called the Tethys, whose modern remnant is the Mediterranean Sea. Other mammal groups considered closely related to the proboscideans, such as the sirenians (manatees and dugongs) seem to have arisen first in the same region, although they do not appear in the fossil record until later. Because of this affinity with the Tethys Ocean, proboscideans and these other mammal groups are usually placed into a larger group called the tethytheres (literally translated from Greek, "beasts of the Tethys") (Fischer 1996).

The best known of the early proboscideans is an odd-looking animal called *Moeritherium* (named after Lake Moeris in Egypt). Around the beginning of the twentieth century, *Moeritherium* was discovered in Late Eocene and Early Oligocene sediments in North Africa. In many respects, this animal is a rather unlikely-looking proboscidean (Figure 1). It possessed an upper canine and completely lacked a proboscis, a characteristic indicated by the location of its nasal bones low and far forward on the face. (The large muscles necessary for a proboscis require considerable room, and to provide it the bones of the nasal region generally are pushed up and backward.)

Moeritherium did possess one clearly advanced feature—tusks—although it still retained smaller incisors as well. While not a small animal (it was around the size of a pig), *Moeritherium* was definitely not a giant, and its body was elongate and low to the ground, resembling a small tapir more than a modern elephant. The sediments in which *Moeritherium* is found indicate that it lived in a marshy habitat, and it is commonly believed to have been semiaquatic (Shoshani et al. 1996).

Figure 2. Reconstruction and skull of *Paleomastodon* (North Africa, Late Oligocene). Reconstruction from Fenton and Fenton (1989); skull from Romer (1966), used by permission of the publisher, The University of Chicago Press, copyright © 1933, 1945, 1966 by The University of Chicago.

The oldest known proboscidean that shows a number of advanced proboscidean features is *Paleomastodon. Paleomastodon* was discovered around the same time and in the same region as *Moeritherium,* although in younger Middle or Late Oligocene sediments. *Paleomastodon* was considerably more advanced than *Moeritherium.* It had lost its upper canine, lost all of its incisors except for the second (which formed tusks, both upper and lower), and retracted its nasal bones modestly, presumably to accommodate a small proboscis (Figure 2). *Paleomastodon* was considerably larger than *Moeritherium,* approximately two meters high at the shoulder, with distinctly graviportal limbs and an overall body form that was clearly elephant-like. However, *Paleomastodon* did not have serial tooth replacement (Romer 1966).

In Africa, sometime during the Late Oligocene or perhaps earliest Miocene (about 24 million years ago), *Paleomastodon* (or more likely some of its close relatives) gave rise to two major lineages of proboscideans: the true mastodonts, which are more properly called "mammutids," and the gomphotheres, sometimes improperly called "mastodonts." All the advanced proboscidean features discussed earlier were present in both of these lineages, including serial cheek tooth replacement (Tassy 1996). Because members of both groups clearly resembled elephants in the most obvious respects (indeed, modern elephants themselves are part of this radiation), these two lineages together are referred to as the "elephantoids." When the elephantoids first arose, Africa was still an island continent, separated from Eurasia by the Tethys Seaway.

(By that point, this body of water was no longer large enough to justify calling it an ocean.) Thus, at first the elephantoids were restricted to Africa. However, approximately 20 to 18 million years ago, during the Early Miocene, Africa collided with Eurasia, and the elephantoids exploited the newly formed land bridge in what is now the Middle East to wander into Eurasia. Ultimately, crossing a landbridge over what is now the Bering Strait, they reached the Americas from Asia (Lambert 1996).

At this point, it is important to talk about the structure of proboscidean cheek teeth, since changing tooth structure is a crucial aspect of the evolution of the elephantoids (Figures 3 and 4). The cheek teeth are used to grind food. The crowns of all proboscidean cheek teeth initially consist of isolated, tapered pillars of enamel called "cones." When these cones are ground down by chewing, however, the cones become rings that merge sideways with their neighbors to form ridges of enamel called "lophs." The cheek teeth of pre-elephantoid proboscideans essentially consisted of two simple lophs, one in the front and one in the back. However, in primitive elephantoids the structure of the cones is complicated by the addition of extra ridges called "conules," which, when worn, give the enamel rings a three-leafed clover look called a "trefoil" (literally translated "three-leaved"). The number of lophs also is increased to three or more. Some mammoths have more than 20 (Tobien 1996).

The most conservative of these two elephantoid lineages was the mammutids, or true mastodonts, which have been known to

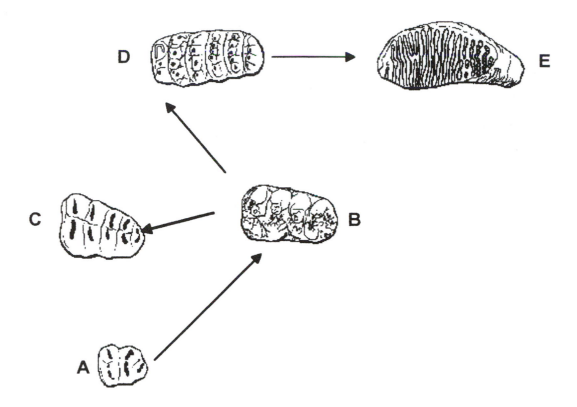

Figure 3. Trends in the evolution of proboscidean cheek teeth. *A, Moeritherium,* demonstrating the primitive proboscidean condition; *B,* generic elephantoid tooth, demonstrating the primitive condition (e.g. *Zygolophodon, Gomphotherium*); *C, Mammut,* demonstrating the advanced mammutid condition; *D, Stegotetrabelodon,* demonstrating the primitive elephant condition; *E, Mammuthus,* demonstrating the advanced elephant condition. After Colbert (1980).

science since at least late in the eighteenth century. The earliest members of the group, such as *Eozygolophodon* and *Zygolophodon,* possessed such primitive elephantoid features as simple trefoils on the cheek teeth and both upper and lower tusks. Around 20 to 18 million years ago, the genus *Zygolophodon* moved out of Africa and into Eurasia. This genus never became particularly abundant or evolved into any new forms in the Eastern Hemisphere, however, and the mammutids vanished from the region well before the end of the Miocene. Around 16 million years ago *Zygolophodon* crossed the Bering land bridge to reach North America, where it was much more successful than in the Old World.

Zygolophodon (in North America sometimes called *Miomastodon*) became widespread across the continent by the Middle Miocene (around 15 million years ago) and became extinct around 12 million years ago. However, by that time it had given rise to the new genus *Mammut,* which is sometimes informally called the American mastodon. Early *Mammut* (sometimes called *Pliomastodon*) did not look dramatically different from *Zygolophodon.* Primarily, *Mammut* lacked trefoils from its cheek teeth and had reduced lower tusks. By the Pliocene these lophs were reduced to simple enamel ridges, and the lower tusks had been completely lost (Figures 3 and 5). *Mammut* became abundant during the Pleistocene; it has been found in many fossil sites all over North America. At the end of the Pleistocene, it vanished (Tobien 1996).

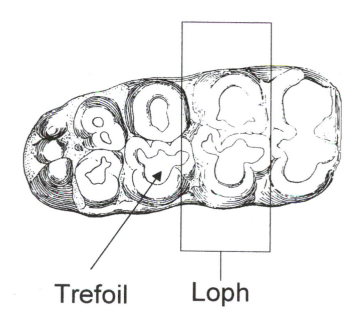

Trefoil   Loph

Figure 4. Primitive elephantoid cheek tooth (*Gomphotherium* third molar).

Figure 5. Reconstruction of Pleistocene *Mammut* (North America). From Fenton and Fenton (1989).

Owing to the discovery of numerous excellent fossils, quite a bit is known about the biology of Pleistocene *Mammut*. Specimens show that it stood about three meters tall and was covered with shaggy fur. Stomach contents found associated with some spectacular specimens consist of some grass but mainly of browse. Browsers feed on shoots, twigs, and leaves of trees. Here the browse included conifer leaves, twigs, and even cones. Although widespread across North America, Pleistocene *Mammut* fossils are most common around the Great Lakes and the northern Pacific and Atlantic coastal regions, suggesting that this animal favored cool, moist climates (Kurtén and Anderson 1980).

The other elephantoid lineage—the gomphotheres—was much more successful than the mammutids, both in terms of the diversity of forms it gave rise to and in sheer numbers of individuals. Encompassing the Asian and African elephants, the gomphotheres is the only proboscidean lineage that still survives.

The earliest known gomphothere, and the presumed ancestor of the entire gomphothere radiation, is *Gomphotherium*. First scientifically described during the early nineteenth century, *Gomphotherium* was a very conservative elephantoid—that is, it had not evolved a great deal from the pattern in *Zygolophodon* (Figure 6). Like *Zygolophodon*, *Gomphotherium* had simple trefoils on its cheek teeth and well-developed upper and lower tusks. Also like *Zygolophodon*, *Gomphotherium* first arose in Africa during the Early Miocene (around 20 to 18 million years ago), quickly entering Eurasia through the newly formed Middle East and reaching North America around 15 million years ago. *Gomphotherium* survived only a relatively short time in the Eastern Hemisphere, becoming extinct during the Middle Miocene. However, in North America it flourished, becoming an important part of fossil faunas all over the continent and surviving at least into the earliest Pliocene, around 5 million years ago (Lambert 1996).

Gomphotherium (and, in general, typical gomphotheres that evolved from it) mostly ate browse, although it probably ate significant quantities of grass from time to time as well. In many respects it probably lived much like modern African elephants, using its upper and at times lower tusks to peel bark from tree trunks and its proboscis to break off tree branches and leaves. When opportunity arose, it probably ate considerable amounts of

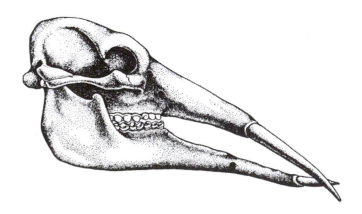

Figure 6. Primitive elephantoid condition in *Gomphotherium* skull (Miocene–earliest Pliocene, Africa, Eurasia, and North America). From Romer (1966), used by permission of the publisher, The University of Chicago Press, copyright © 1933, 1945, 1966 by The University of Chicago.

Figure 7. Reconstruction and lower jaw of the shovel-tusked *Amebelodon* (Middle Miocene–earliest Pliocene, Africa, Asia, and North America). *Amebelodon* portrayed slicing bark from a tree trunk with its lower tusks. Reconstruction from Lambert (1992); jaw from Romer (1966), used by permission of the publisher, The University of Chicago Press, copyright © 1933, 1945, 1966 by The University of Chicago.

fruit as well. Unlike the mammutids, which were also browsers, *Gomphotherium* seems to have preferred savanna habitat (an open mixture of trees and grass) over forest. In this way, too, it probably lived very much like today's African elephants (Webb et al. 1995).

While the form of *Zygolophodon* and most mammutids evolved very little over time, the descendants of *Gomphotherium* experimented with a wide variety of forms in both the Eastern and Western Hemispheres. Only a small fraction can be discussed here. Some gomphotheres were only relatively minor variations of the *Gomphotherium* theme. For example *Rhynchotherium,* known from the Late Miocene and Pliocene of North and Central America, is distinguished mainly by lower tusks that jut downward at an angle rather than straight forward. Other groups exhibited greater changes.

During the Pliocene a descendant of *Rhynchotherium, Cuvieronius,* lost its lower tusks. *Cuvieronius* became widespread across southern North America and extended into Central America. Between 2 and 1 million years ago it crossed the newly formed Panamanian land bridge to reach South America, where it was very successful and was briefly hunted (and possibly exterminated) by Paleoindians. *Cuvieronius* vanished at the end of the Pleistocene, about 1 million years ago (Lambert 1996; Dudley 1996).

One of the most spectacular *Gomphotherium* offshoots was the shovel-tusked gomphotheres. As suggested by their name, these animals had broad and flat lower tusks reminiscent of shovels. The two best known shovel-tusker groups are *Platybelodon* (Early to Late Miocene) and *Amebelodon* (Middle Miocene to Early Pliocene),

found throughout the Old World and North America. Both are traditionally portrayed as scooping water plants such as lily pads with their lower tusks. *Amebelodon* is believed also to have used its lower tusks to strip bark from trees like a paring knife (Figure 7), while *Platybelodon* apparently only used its broad tusks (which, unlike those of *Amebelodon,* had sharp edges) in conjunction with its proboscis to cut vegetation in a fashion like a hand sickle (Figure 8).

During the Miocene a number of Eastern Hemisphere gomphothere lineages became very progressive in increasing the complexity of their cheek teeth, adding lophs and reducing or eliminating their lower tusks. These changes are probably related to increasing quantities of grass in the diet (grass is much more abrasive and much tougher to shred than ordinary broad leaves). During the Late Miocene one lineage in Africa gave rise to *Stegotetrabelodon,* generally considered to have been the first true elephant. Typical of gomphotheres and unlike later elephants, *Stegotetrabelodon* retained small lower tusks. However, its cheek teeth were very different from typical gomphotheres: multiple lophs (in elephants, usually called plates) were added—as many as 11—and the cones in each plate were smaller and more numerous (Figure 3). When worn down, these plates formed thinner, sharper ridges than the lophs of more primitive gomphotheres. *Stegotetrabelodon* was probably a grazing specialist. This preference for a diet of grass is a trend that characterizes the elephants as a whole. (Surprisingly, living elephants violate this trend, preferring browse.) In later elephants, the plates of the cheek teeth became even thinner and greater in number (Todd and Roth 1996) (Figure 3).

Figure 8. Reconstruction and lower jaw of the shovel-tusked *Platybelodon* (Early-Late Miocene, Africa, Asia, and North America). *Platybelodon* portrayed slicing a piece of vegetation with its proboscis and lower tusks. Reconstruction from Lambert (1992); jaw from Romer (1966), used by permission of the publisher, The University of Chicago Press, copyright © 1933, 1945, 1966 by The University of Chicago.

Figure 9. Reconstruction of the wooly mammoth *Mammuthus primigenius* (Late Pleistocene, tundra regions of Europe, Asia, and North America). From Fenton and Fenton (1989).

Three elephant groups arose in Africa during the Pliocene: *Loxodonta,* which includes the living African elephant; *Elephas,* which includes the living Asian elephant; and *Mammuthus,* which includes all of the mammoths. *Loxodonta* never left Africa, where it remains today. *Elephas* and *Mammuthus,* however, both moved into Europe and Asia during the Pliocene, and at the end of the Pliocene or Early Pleistocene (about 1.5 million years ago), *Mammuthus* reached North America (Todd and Roth 1996; Kurtén and Anderson 1980).

The mammoth may have had religious significance to paleolithic humans in Europe since they were common subjects in cave paintings, and mammoth remains have played a major role in human mythology. Mammoth bones dug up or found exposed on the surface almost certainly contributed to legends of giants, while mammoth skulls, with their large nasal regions that resemble a single central eye socket, probably were the basis for the myth of the cyclops.

The mammoth best known to science is *Mammuthus primigenius,* more commonly referred to as the wooly mammoth (Figure 9). It inhabited glacial tundra throughout Europe, Asia, and North America during the Late Pleistocene. A considerable number of wooly mammoths have been found essentially freeze-dried in old glacial ice in Siberia and Alaska. This form of preservation has allowed the scientific study of the animal's soft body parts and even of intact cells with DNA (Shoshani 1992). True to its name, the wooly mammoth was covered with a thick coat of coarse hair. Like living elephants, it was a social animal, with herds probably consisting mainly of females and immature males. The diet mostly consisted of short grasses and grasslike plants such as sedges (Haynes 1991). Mammoths other than woolies lived in warmer regions throughout the Eastern Hemisphere and North America. These animals probably ate a mixture of grass and browse.

Elephants suffered greatly from the great mammal extinctions at the end of the Pleistocene. Mammoths vanished worldwide except for a small relic population of dwarfs that held on a few thousand years into the Recent on a small island off Siberia. *Elephas* disappeared from Africa and Europe. As in the cases of the mammutids and gomphotheres, the causes of these extinctions are not well understood; however, circumstantial evidence suggests human hunting played a role (Fischer 1996). It is to be hoped that this tragedy will not be repeated, and that humans in our times will not eradicate the last of proboscideans from the face of the earth.

W. DAVID LAMBERT

Works Cited

Colbert, E. 1980. *Evolution of the Vertebrates.* New York: Wiley.

Dudley, J. 1996. Mammoths, gomphotheres, and the Great American Faunal Interchange. *In* J. Shoshani and P. Tassy (eds.), *The Proboscidea: Evolution and Paleoecology of Elephants and Their Relatives.* Oxford and New York: Oxford University Press.

Fenton, C.L., and M.A. Fenton. 1989. *The Fossil Book.* 2nd ed., New York: Doubleday.

Fischer, M. 1996. On the position of Proboscidea in the phylogenetic system of Eutheria: A systematic review. *In* J. Shoshani and P. Tassy (eds.), *The Proboscidea: Evolution and Paleoecology of Elephants and Their Relatives.* Oxford and New York: Oxford University Press.

Haynes, G. 1991. *Mammoths, Mastodons, and Elephants: Biology, Behavior, and the Fossil Record.* Cambridge and New York: Cambridge University Press.

Kurtén, B., and E. Anderson. 1980. *Pleistocene Mammals of North America.* New York: Columbia University Press.

Lambert, W. D. 1992. The feeding habits of the shovel-tusked gomphotheres: Evidence from tusk wear patterns. *Paleobiology* 18(2):132–47.

——. 1996. The biogeography of the gomphotheriid proboscideans of North America. *In* J. Shoshani and P. Tassy (eds.), *The Proboscidea: Evolution and Paleoecology of Elephants and Their Relatives.* New York and Oxford: Oxford University Press.

Romer, A.S. 1966. *Vertebrate Paleontology.* 3rd ed., Chicago: University of Chicago Press.

Shoshani, J. 1992. *Elephants: Majestic Creatures of the Wild.* Emmaus, Pennsylvania: Rodale.

Shoshani, J., R.M. West, N. Court, R.J.G. Savage, and J. Harris. 1996. The earliest proboscideans: General plan, taxonomy, and paleoecology. *In* J. Shoshani and P. Tassy (eds.), *The Proboscidea: Evolution and Paleoecology of Elephants and Their Relatives.* Oxford and New York: Oxford University Press.

Tassy, P. 1996. Who is who among the Proboscidea? *In* J. Shoshani and P. Tassy (eds.), *The Proboscidea: Evolution and Paleoecology of Elephants and Their Relatives.* Oxford and New York: Oxford University Press.

Tobien, H. 1996. Evolution of zygodons with emphasis on dentition. *In* J. Shoshani and P. Tassy (eds.), *The Proboscidea: Evolution and Paleoecology of Elephants and Their Relatives.* Oxford and New York: Oxford University Press.

Todd, N.E., and L. Roth. 1996. Origin and radiation of the Elephantidae. *In* J. Shoshani and P. Tassy (eds.), *The Proboscidea: Evolution and Paleoecology of Elephants and Their Relatives.* Oxford and New York: Oxford University Press.

Webb, S.D., R.C. Hulbert, and W.D. Lambert. 1995. Climatic implications of large herbivore distributions in the Miocene of North America. *In* E.S. Vrba, G.H. Denton, T.C. Partridge, and L.H. Burckle (eds.), *Paleoclimate and Evolution with Emphasis on Human Origins.* New Haven, Connecticut: Yale University Press.

Further Reading

Coppens, Y., V.J. Maglio, C.T. Madden, and M. Beden. 1978. Proboscidea. *In* V.J. Maglio and H.B.S. Cooke (eds.), *Evolution of African Mammals.* Cambridge, Massachusetts: Harvard University Press.

Lambert, W.D. 1992. The feeding habits of the shovel-tusked gomphotheres: Evidence from tusk wear patterns. *Paleobiology* 18, 132–47.

Osborn, H.F. 1936. *Proboscidea.* New York: American Museum.

Owen-Smith, N. 1988. *Megaherbivores.* Cambridge: Cambridge University Press.

Simpson, G.G. 1980. *Splendid Isolation.* New Haven, Connecticut: Yale University Press.

Tassy, P., and J. Shoshani. 1988. The Tethytheria and their relatives. *In* M.J. Benton (ed.), *The Phylogeny and Classification of the Tetrapods.* Vol. 2, Oxford: Clarendon Press; New York: Oxford University Press.

PRODUCTIVITY ESTIMATES

See Biomass and Productivity Estimates

PROGYMNOSPERMS

Progymnosperms are Middle Devonian to Early Carboniferous plants that were the Earth's first woody trees and that formed its first forested landscapes. Progymnosperms have vegetative and reproductive features found in gymnosperms (cone-bearing trees) but freely shed their spores into the air from sporangia (spore-producing structures), more like ferns. (Gymnosperms, on the other hand, retain and nourish the large female spores, called "megaspores," in ovules that become seeds when fertilized.) This unique set of characters and the times of their occurrences—just before and contemporaneous with the first gymnosperms of the Late Devonian—led Charles Beck (1960a, 1960b, 1962, 1966, 1976) to propose the Progymnospermopsida as a new group of extinct plants that were possibly ancestral to gymnosperm seed plants. Beck's proposal was stimulated by his 1960 discovery that fernlike, reproductive branches of *Archaeopteris* were attached to woody, conifer-like trunks called *Callixylon*. (Because plant parts such as leaves and stems are often separated, they are given their own names [form genera]. In that way, botanists can discuss them without having to wait until an intact fossil is found.) Beck was also influenced by his earlier (1957) study of Late Devonian *Tetraxylopteris*, a free-sporing plant with anatomy reminiscent of Carboniferous seed ferns.

Three kinds of progymnosperms are now well known. The oldest are the Middle to Late Devonian (370 to 350 million years ago) Aneurophytales (for *Aneurophyton, Rellimia, Tetraxylopteris, Triloboxylon, Proteokalon,* and a few lesser known taxa); they resemble seed ferns (extinct gymnosperms with fernlike leaves) and have frondlike lateral branches. The next kind, mostly from Late Devonian (360 to 345 million years ago), is Archaeopteridales (for *Archaeopteris* and its anatomically preserved trunks, branches, and roots—called *Callixylon*—and for late Middle Devonian *Svalbardia,* as well as a few lesser known fossils). Members of this group have conifer-like (e.g., pine or spruce) construction; lateral branches bear simple forked or entire leaves. The final, and youngest group, is Early Carboniferous (345 to 330 million years ago) Protopityales (for *Protopitys*), which have aneurophyte-like fertile organs and large woody trunks with a two-sided, alternating, branching pattern. Other Mid- to Late Devonian and Carboniferous plants (such as *Stenokoleos, Noeggerathia,* and *Cecropsis*) might prove to be fourth or fifth kinds of progymnosperms (Matten 1992; Matten and Banks 1969; Rothwell and Erwin 1987; Rothwell and Scheckler 1988; Stubblefield and Rothwell 1989) or may be derived (modified) continuations of older lineages. This may be the case with *Noeggerathia,* the fertile parts of which resemble *Archaeopteris* (Beck 1981), when more is known about it.

Members of Aneurophytales have uniform characters that support their status as a natural group (i.e., one whose members share a common ancestor). All have three-dimensional, highly regular, alternate or opposite branch systems built upon an unequal forking of branch tips. These declined in growth capacity as the branches became smaller, eventually ceasing. Only the smallest, last order of twigs bore the forked, leaflike final segments that fully stopped growing (Beck 1957; Beck and Wight 1988; Scheckler 1975, 1976; Scheckler and Banks 1971a, 1971b; Serlin and Banks 1978). Major branches of *Aneurophyton* and *Rellimia* (Schweitzer and Matten 1982), however, can end in forks, but these are much larger than the forked leaflike segments of the small twigs. Growth models of other aneurophytes (Scheckler 1976) also predict forked branch endings for the younger members, such as *Tetraxylopteris* and *Triloboxylon*. Fertile organs replace various sizes of vegetative branches (those that carry no reproductive structures) and differ from them by forking once or twice before bearing clusters of small spore-containing sacks (sporangia) toward the top side. Sporangia have a pointed tip and are partially split along the middle of facing sides of pairs to release the spores (Bonamo and Banks 1967; Leclercq and Bonamo 1971, 1973; Scheckler 1982, 1986d). Only one type of spore ("homospory") is produced by each species, which scholars interpret as indicating fernlike reproduction. Spores of *Rellimia* and *Tetraxylopteris (Rhabdosporites langii),* however, resemble some gymnosperm pollen (Taylor and Scheckler 1996). This suggests that there may be two kinds of spores ("heterospory"), with the large, female spores (megaspores) as yet unknown. Branch anatomy follows morphology and has three- or four-ribbed, solid xylem (water-carrying) strands (protosteles) that matured from the inside (mesarch), while the final leaflike segments are supplied by round xylem strands. Secondary tissues and cortex are constructed like those of seed ferns.

Members of Archaeopteridales also have uniform characters that support their status as a natural group. Overall, these are larger trees, with some *Archaeopteris* known to have trunks 10 to 30 meters high with large, buttresslike, and deeply penetrating root systems (Algeo and Scheckler 1998; Arnold 1931; Beck and Wight 1988; Snigirevskaya 1984, 1988, 1995). Branching by unequal forking of branch tips (with progressive decline of growth capacity) is even more regular. Except for leaves, no part of the shoot system is forked. Although crown shape is unknown, trunks and major branches bore short-lived (growing for just one season) branching systems called *Archaeopteris* or *Svalbardia* (Beck 1962, 1971; Scheckler 1978). They were shed as units of two orders (major and minor) of leafy branch. The base of major branches had swollen basal detachment/abscission points, with a pair of large basal leaves that partly wrapped around the bottom and bore minor branches and flattened leaves (finely divided in *Svalbardia,* but whole in most *Archaeopteris* species). These were arranged in an alternate spiral-to-opposite pattern (Nathorst 1902; Hoeg

1942; Beck 1962, 1971; Scheckler 1978). Minor branches bore only leaves or forked fertile leaves (sporophylls) in loose (*Svalbardia*) or compact (*Archaeopteris*) "cones" (Hoeg 1942; Beck 1971; Phillips et al. 1972; Scheckler 1978, 1986c; Beck and Wight 1988). Forked sporophylls bore pairs of sporangia on their tops. Sporangia were split along the facing side of pairs, but unlike those of aneurophytes, also split over the apex and part way down the other side so that they gape fully open and readily disperse the spores (Andrews et al. 1965; Carluccio et al. 1966; Phillips et al. 1972; Hill and Scheckler 1996).

Spores of two sizes (small ones are *Apiculatiasporites, Cyclogranisporites, Aneurospora greggsii,* or *Geminospora;* large ones are *Contagisporites* or *Biharisporites*) occur in *Svalbardia* and *Archaeopteris* (Hill and Scheckler 1996) and suggest heterosporous reproduction by large female and small male spores (Phillips et al. 1972; Beck and Wight 1988). Spores have internal (endosporic) cell divisions in *Archaeopteris archetypus* (similar to *A. obtusa*); they produce large and small multicellular haploid plantlets (mega- and microgametophytes) prior to spore dispersal, confirming a key attribute of *biological* heterospory for this group (Snigirevskaya 1988; Scheckler et al. 1997). Trunk anatomy is conifer-like, with a large pith inside the many-stranded primary xylem (eustele), the strands of which mature from the inside (mesarch), that is all surrounded by dense wood. Branches vary from three-, four-, or five-ribbed, solid xylem cores (protosteles) to multiribbed eusteles, depending on the order and position of branch (Carluccio et al. 1966; Beck 1971; Scheckler 1978; Beck and Wight 1988; Kenrick and Fairon-Demaret 1991).

Protopityales, with just *Protopitys,* is less known. It also has uniform trunk and branch construction, which supplies the two rows of leaves and fertile organs. Fused traces arise from each of the paired mesarch bundles at one edge of its elliptical, four-stranded eustele. Fertile organs and sporangia are similar to those of the aneurophyte *Tetraxylopteris* (Walton 1957; Smith 1962; Bonamo and Banks 1967; Scheckler 1986d), but *Protopitys* has widely varying sizes of spores (anisospory) within its sporangia.

Progymnosperms share many vegetative characters with older plants like *Psilophyton* and *Pertica* (trimerophytes), which also have unequally forked branching from main axes and forked branch tips or final leaflike segments in more terminal parts, as well as mesarch primary xylem with lobes or ridges at points of branch departure. Progymnosperms share other characters found only in younger gymnosperms. Characters unique to progymnosperms and gymnosperms include (1) a two-sided (bifacial) vascular cambium that makes secondary xylem (wood) internally and secondary phloem (inner bark) externally; (2) adventitious (side) shoots (*Archaeopteris*) and roots from older woody trunks, plus main roots; (3) roots with lateral rootlets that are produced from the inside (endogenous); (4) outer cortex with fiber bundles and periderm (cork) in older axes; and (5) either determinate, leaflike, lateral branches (some Aneurophytales) or compound leaves (Protopityales) and forked, *Sphenopteris*-like ultimate appendages (some Aneurophytales) or dichotomously veined, simple conifer-like leaves (most *Archaeopteris*) (Algeo and Scheckler 1998; Arnold 1930a, 1930b; Beck 1953; Phillips et al. 1972; Scheckler 1975, 1976, 1978; Scheckler and Banks 1971a, 1971b, 1974; Stein and Beck 1983; Trivett 1993).

Similarly, progymnosperms share many reproductive characters with older trimerophytes. Both have clusters of paired elongate sporangia that split longitudinally. Other reproductive features are found only in younger gymnosperms. These include the cell patterns of sporangial epidermis, which causes these cells to shrink when drying out (cohesion epidermis of *Tetraxylopteris, Archaeopteris,* and *Protopitys*), incomplete sporangial splitting (*Tetraxylopteris* and other Aneurophytales), and an elongate, tubular sporangial apex filled with thin-walled cells (*Tetraxylopteris* and *Protopitys*). These structures compare with the seed sporangium (nucelus) epidermis and pollen-capturing sporangial tip (lagenostome) of early gymnosperms (e.g., *Elkinsia*), as well as "winged" spores (pseudosaccate) with layered, but porous spore coats (lamellate/aveolate sporoderm) of *Tetraxylopteris.* (These compare with some gymnosperm pollen.) Progymnosperms are characterized by heterospory, with multicellular megagametophytes produced by internal, inward-directed cell divisions (*Archaeopteris archetypus*). This resembles the unique inward-growing cellularization of gymnosperm megagametophytes (alveolarization) (Walton 1957; Scheckler 1982, 1986d; Rothwell and Scheckler 1988; Rothwell et al. 1989; Taylor and Scheckler 1996; Snigirevskaya 1988; Scheckler et al. 1997).

Concluding that progymnosperms are the ancestors of gymnosperms is logical given these numerous and unique shared features. Current debates (Beck and Wight 1988) focus on whether gymnosperms arose just once or several times and from which one (or more) progymnosperm group(s) they evolved. For instance, Beck's Hypothesis states that seed ferns arose from aneurophytes, and conifers arose from archaeopterids. Meyen's Hypothesis posits that seed ferns and conifers arose independently from archaeopterids. Rothwell's Hypothesis says that all gymnosperms arose from aneurophytes. Finally, Doyle and Donoghue's Hypothesis states that all gymnosperms arose from an as yet unknown sister group of progymnosperms. Such questions will be resolved when missing data are provided for progymnosperms, early gymnosperms, and other similar plants.

Ecologically, progymnosperms were major components of early terrestrial communities. Middle Devonian landscapes were quickly dominated by aneurophytes, along with cladoxylalean and iridopterid ferns and herbaceous as well as early tree lycopods (extinct club mosses). These shrubby progymnosperms were well adapted to levees and other seasonally dry habitats but were replaced abruptly by *Archaeopteris* in the Late Devonian, which became dominant worldwide at this time (Beerbower et al. 1992; Scheckler 1986a, 1986b). *Archaeopteris* forests, however, lacked diversity (the genus may consist of just five, six, or seven species, and many large forest biomes had only one to three species at a time). But they were well adapted to seasonally dry as well as wetter portions of floodplains. *Archaeopteris* produced the world's first extensive horizontally and vertically stratified forests that ranged from equatorial to boreal paleolatitudes until the beginning of the Carboniferous. Dense forests, thick leafy canopies, shaded and litter-strewn understories, and woody fuel buildup all contributed to a rapid and vast expansion of terrestrial primary production in the Late Devonian.

The vigorous and deep root systems of progymnosperms, especially those of *Archaeopteris,* which penetrated up to one meter or more of soil, also permanently changed the ancient world by creating a stable interface between root structures and the soil. This zone was characterized by intense chemical weathering of its mineral components. Among the consequences were a rapid colonization and stabilization of coastal and upland flood plains that permanently expanded Earth's vegetated zones. There also was an equally rapid drawdown of atmospheric CO_2 levels in the Late Devonian to near modern levels; this led to global cooling as soil carbonates and new types of silicate clays were formed and plant biomass was buried. The discharge of nutrients from land increased as the depth and aerial extent of chemical weathering of soils expanded; this led to nutrient saturation of many nearshore marine habitats. Coinciding with these events, there were a series of Late Devonian marine geochemical perturbations and invertebrate extinctions (Algeo et al. 1995; Algeo and Scheckler 1998).

Extinction of *Archaeopteris* at the end of the Devonian temporarily ended these forested biomes and profoundly altered Earth's landscapes. Shrubby gymnosperms which had been only minor components of Late Devonian primary successional and disturbed habitats rapidly expanded on dry floodplains; shaded forests did not reappear until late in the Early Carboniferous with the advent of large gymnosperm (e.g., *Pitus*) and progymnosperm (i.e., *Protopitys*) trees (Scheckler 1986a, 1986b; Rothwell and Scheckler 1988; Beerbower et al. 1992). Little is known about the ecology of *Protopitys*, except that it was a minor forest component of landscapes created by volcanic activity and characterized by seasonal rainfall and fire climax habitats (Rex 1986; Rex and Scott 1987; Scott et al. 1984; Scott and Rex 1987; Beerbower et al. 1992).

STEPHEN E. SCHECKLER

See also Gymnosperms

Works Cited

Algeo, T.J., R.A. Berner, J.B. Maynard, and S.E. Scheckler. 1995. Late Devonian oceanic anoxic events and biotic crises: "Rooted" in the evolution of vascular land plants? *GSA Today* 5 (3):45, 64–66.

Algeo, T.J., and S.E. Scheckler. 1998. Terrestrial-marine teleconnections in the Devonian: Links between the evolution of land plants, weathering processes, and marine anoxic events. *Philosophical Transactions B: Biological Sciences* 353:1–18.

Andrews, H.N., T.L. Phillips, and N.W. Radforth. 1965. Paleobotanical studies in arctic Canada. Part 1, *Archaeopteris* from Ellesmere Island. *Canadian Journal of Botany* 43:545–56.

Arnold, C.A. 1930a. Bark structure of *Callixylon*. *Botanical Gazette* 90:427–31.

———. 1930b. The genus *Callixylon* from the Upper Devonian of central and western New York. *Papers of the Michigan Academy of Sciences, Arts and Letters* 11:1–50.

———. 1931. On *Callixylon newberryi* (Dawson) Elkins et Wieland. *Contributions from the Museum of Paleontology, University of Michigan* 3 (12):207–32.

Beck, C.B. 1953. A new root species of *Callixylon*. *American Journal of Botany* 40:226–33.

———. 1957. *Tetraxylopteris schmidtii* gen. et. sp. nov., a probable pteridosperm precursor from the Devonian of New York. *American Journal of Botany* 44:350–67.

———. 1960a. Connection between *Archaeopteris* and *Callixylon*. *Science* 131:1524–25.

———. 1960b. The identity of *Archaeopteris* and *Callixylon*. *Brittonia* 12:351–68.

———. 1962. Reconstructions of *Archaeopteris* and further consideration of its phylogenetic position. *American Journal of Botany* 49:373–82.

———. 1966. On the origin of gymnosperms. *Taxon* 15:337–39.

———. 1971. On the anatomy and morphology of lateral branch systems of *Archaeopteris*. *American Journal of Botany* 58:758–84.

———. 1976. Current status of the Progymnospermopsida. *Review of Palaeobotany and Palynology* 21:5–23.

———. 1981. *Archaeopteris* and its role in vascular plant evolution. *In* K.J. Niklas (ed.), *Paleobotany, Paleoecology, and Evolution*. Vol. 1. New York: Praeger.

Beck, C.B., and D.C. Wight. 1988. Progymnosperms. *In* C.B. Beck (ed.), *Origin and Evolution of Gymnosperms*. New York: Columbia University Press.

Beerbower, R., J.A. Boy, W.A. DiMichele, R.A. Gastaldo, R. Hook, N. Hotton III, T.L. Phillips, S.E. Scheckler, and W.A. Shear. 1992. *Paleozoic Terrestrial Ecosystem. In* A.K. Behrensmeyer, J.D. Damuth, W.A. DiMichele, R. Potts, H.-D. Sues, and S.L. Wing (eds.), *Terrestrial Ecosystems through Time*. Chicago: University of Chicago Press.

Bonamo, P.M., and H.P. Banks. 1967. *Tetraxylopteris schmidtii*: Its fertile parts and its relationships within the Aneurophytales. *American Journal of Botany* 54:755–68.

Carluccio, L.M., F.M. Hueber, and H.P. Banks. 1966. *Archaeopteris macilenta*, anatomy and morphology of its frond. *American Journal of Botany* 53:719–30.

Hill, S.A., and S.E. Scheckler. 1996. Reproductive architecture of archaeopterid progymnosperms. *Fifth International Organisation of Paleobotany Congress*. Santa Barbara, California: International Organization of Paleobotany.

Hoeg, O.A. 1942. The Downtonian and Devonian Flora of Spitsbergen. *Norges Svalbard og Ishavs-Unders Ækelser, Skrifter* 83:1–228.

Kenrick, P., and M. Fairon-Demaret. 1991. *Archaeopteris roemeriana* (Göppert) *sensu* Stockmans 1948 from the Upper Famennian of Belgium: Anatomy and leaf polymorphism. *Bulletin de l'Institute Royal des Sciences Naturelles de Belgique, Sciences de la Terre* 61:179–95.

Leclercq, S., and P.M. Bonamo. 1971. A study of the fructification of *Milleria (Protopteridium) thomsonii* Lang from the Middle Devonian of Belgium. *Palaeontographica*, ser. B, 136:83–114.

———. 1973. *Rellimia thomsonii*, a new name for *Milleria (Protopteridium) thomsonii* Lang 1926 Emend. Leclercq and Bonamo 1971. *Taxon* 22:435–37.

Matten, L.C. 1992. Studies on Devonian plants from New York State: *Stenokoleos holmesii* n. sp. from the Cairo Flora (Givetian) with an alternative model for lyginopterid seed fern evolution. *Courier Forschungs-Institut Senckenberg* 147:75–85.

Matten, L.C., and H.P. Banks. 1969. *Stenokoleos bifidus* sp. n. in the Upper Devonian of New York State. *American Journal of Botany* 56:880–91.

Nathorst, A.G. 1902. Zur Oberdevonischen Flora der Bären-Insel. Kongl. *Svenska Vetenskaps-Akademiens Handlingar* 36:1–60.

Phillips, T.L., H.N. Andrews, and P.G. Gensel. 1972. Two heterosporous species of *Archaeopteris* from the Upper Devonian of West Virginia. *Palaeontographica*, ser. B, 139:47–71.

Rex, G.M. 1986. The preservation and palaeoecology of the Lower Carboniferous silicified plant deposits at Esnost, near Autun, France. *Géobios* 19:773–800.

Rex, G.M., and A.C. Scott. 1987. The sedimentology, paleoecology, and preservation of the Lower Carboniferous plant deposits at Pettycur, Fife, Scotland. *Geological Magazine* 124:43–66.

Rothwell, G.W., and D.M. Erwin. 1987. Origin of seed plants: An aneurophyte/seed-fern link elaborated. *American Journal of Botany* 74 (6):970–73.

Rothwell, G.W., and S.E. Scheckler. 1988. Biology of ancestral gymnosperms. *In* C.B. Beck (ed.), *Origin and Evolution of Gymnosperms.* New York: Columbia University Press.

Rothwell, G.W., S.E. Scheckler, and W.H. Gillespie. 1989. *Elkinsia* gen. nov., a Late Devonian gymnosperm with cupulate ovules. *Botanical Gazette* 150:170–89.

Scheckler, S.E. 1975. A fertile axis of *Triloboxylon ashlandicum,* a progymnosperm from the Upper Devonian of New York. *American Journal of Botany* 62 (9):923–34.

———. 1976. Ontogeny of progymnosperms. Part 1, Shoots of Upper Devonian Aneurophytales. *Canadian Journal of Botany* 54 (3–4):202–19.

———. 1978. Ontogeny of progymnosperms. Part 2, Shoots of Upper Devonian Archaeopteridales. *Canadian Journal of Botany* 56 (24):3136–70.

———. 1982. Anatomy of the fertile parts of *Tetraxylopteris schmidtii* (Progymnospermopsida). *Botanical Society of America. Miscellaneous Publications* 162:64.

———. 1986a. Geology, floristics, and paleoecology of Late Devonian coal swamps from App lachian Laurentia (U.S.A). Special Volume "Aachen 1986." *Annales de la Société Géologique de Belgique (Liège)* 109:209–22.

———. 1986b. Floras of the Devonian-Mississippian transition. *In* T.W. Broadhead (ed.), *Land Plants: Notes for a Short Course,* organized by R.A. Gastaldo. Studies in Geology 15. Nashville: University of Tennessee, Department of Geological Sciences.

———. 1986c. Ancestral character states of Archaeopteridales (Progymnospermopsida). *American Journal of Botany* 73 (5):704–5.

———. 1986d. Evidence for the relationship between Protopityales and Aneurophytales (Progymnospermopsida). *American Journal of Botany* 73 (5):705–6.

Scheckler, S.E., and H.P. Banks. 1971a. Anatomy and relationships of some Devonian progymnosperms from New York. *American Journal of Botany* 58 (8):737–51.

———. 1971b. *Proteokalon* a new genus of progymnosperms from the Devonian of New York State and its bearing on phylogenetic trends in the group. *American Journal of Botany* 58 (9):874–84.

———. 1974. Periderm in some Devonian Plants. *In* Y.S. Murty, B.M. Johri, N.Y. Mohan Ram, and T.M. Varghese (eds.), *Advances in Plant Morphology.* Meerut: Meerut City (Sarita Prakasham) University Press.

Scheckler, S.E., N.S. Snigirevskaya, and S.A. Hill. 1997. Endosporic gametophytes of the heterosporous Late Devonian (Famennian) progymnosperm *Archaeopteris archetypus* (=*A. obtusa*). *American Journal of Botany* 84 (6):141.

Schweitzer, H.-J., and L.C. Matten. 1982. *Aneurophyton germanicum* and *Protopteridium thomsonii* from the Middle Devonian of Germany. *Palaeontographica,* ser. B, 184:65–106.

Scott, A.C., J. Galtier, and G. Clayton. 1984. Distribution of anatomically preserved floras in the Lower Carboniferous of Western Europe. *Transactions of the Royal Society of Edinburgh, Earth Sciences* 75:311–40.

Scott, A.C., and G.M. Rex. 1987. The accumulation and preservation of Dinantian plants from Scotland and its borders. *In* J. Miller, A.E. Adams, and V.P. Wright (eds.), *European Dinantian Environments.* Geological Society Journal Special Issue 12. Chichester and New York: Wiley.

Serlin, B., and H.P. Banks. 1978. Morphology and anatomy of *Aneurophyton,* a progymnosperm from the Late Devonian of New York. *Paleontographica Americana* 8:343–59.

Smith, D.L. 1962. Three fructifications from the Scottish Lower Carboniferous. *Palaeontology* 5:225–37.

Snigirevskaya, N.S. 1984. Root system of archaeopterids from the Upper Devonian of Donets Basin. *In Annual Report of the All-Union Paleontology Society,* 27. Leningrad: Akademy of Sciences, SSSR. [in Russian.]

———. 1988. The Late Devonian: The time of the appearance of forests as the natural phenomenon. *In Contributors' Papers: The Formation and Evolution of the Continental Biotas, L.* 31st Session of the All-Union Palaeontological Society. Akademy of Sciences, SSSR. [in Russian.]

———. 1995. Archaeopterids and their role in the land plant cover evolution. *Botanicheski Zhournal* 80 (1):70–75.

Stein Jr., W.E., and C.B. Beck. 1983. *Triloboxylon arnoldii* from the Middle Devonian of western New York. *Contributions from the Museum of Paleontology, University of Michigan* 26:257–88.

Stubblefield, S.P., and G.W. Rothwell. 1989. *Cecropsis luculentum* gen. et sp. nov.; Evidence for heterosporous progymnosperms in the Upper Pennsylvanian of North America. *American Journal of Botany* 76:1415–28.

Taylor, T.N., and S.E. Scheckler. 1996. Devonian spore ultrastructure: *Rhabdosporites.* Maurice Streel Commemorative Volume. *Review of Palaeobotany and Palynology* 93:147–58.

Trivett, M.L. 1993. An architectural analysis of *Archaeopteris,* a fossil tree with pseudomonopodial and opportunistic adventitious growth. *Botanical Journal of the Linnean Society* 111:301–29.

Walton, J. 1957. On *Protopitys* (Göppert): With a description of a fertile specimen *"Protopitys scotica"* sp. nov., from the Calciferous Sandstone Series of Dunbartonshire. *Transactions of the Royal Society of Edinburgh* 63 (2):333–40.

Further Reading

Beck, C.B. (ed.). 1988. *Origin and Evolution of Gymnosperms.* New York: Columbia University Press.

Stewart, W.N. 1983. *Paleobotany and the Evolution of Plants.* Cambridge and New York: Cambridge University Press; 2nd ed., with G.W. Rothwell, 1993.

Taylor, T.N., and E.L. Taylor. 1993. *The Biology and Evolution of Fossil Plants.* Englewood Cliffs, New Jersey: Prentice-Hall.

PROTISTS

See Skeletized Microoganisms: Protozoan and Chitozoans

PTERIDOPHYTES

See Ferns and Their Relatives

PTEROSAURS

The Pterosauria, the flying reptiles of the Mesozoic Era, were the first radiation (diversification and geographic spread) of vertebrates that developed active, powered flight. Pterosaurs form a clearly defined clade (group with a common ancestor) within the Archosauromorpha that first appeared in the fossil record in the Upper Triassic. They diversified and flourished for the next 165 million years, until the end of the Mesozoic, apparently becoming extinct in the major extinction at the end of the Cretaceous.

Shape and Structure

Rhamphorhynchus, found in the Upper Jurassic Solnhofen Limestone of southern Germany, is probably the best-known early pterosaur (Figure 1). It was a middle-sized pterosaur with a wingspan of up to 1.8 meters. It had a relatively large skull, a neck with eight large cervical vertebrae-bearing ribs, a short trunk with 15 dorsal (central back) and three or four sacral (lower back) vertebrae, and a long slender tail stiffened by overlapping bony rods. The pectoral girdle (the system that includes the scapulae, clavicles, sternum, and other bones) consisted of an elongate scapula (shoulder blade) extending back over the chest skeleton and an elongate coracoid (structure extending from the scapula) that articulated with a large bony sternum. The sternum was fused with associated clavicle bones. The bones of the forelimb were large and long. The humerus had a very large bony crest that served as the attachment site for powerful flight muscles. The two rows of wrist bones were fused, limiting the movement of the wrist. A pteroid bone, unique to pterosaurs, extended inward toward the body from the wrist. On the hand, the first three fingers were of normal size and bore large claws; the fourth finger was very elongate, having four bones but no claw. The pelvic girdle consisted of an elongate ilium (upper pelvic bone, along the spine) and a short, deep, bony plate toward the belly, formed of the lower two pelvic bones, the pubis and ischium. The hip joint permitted the hind limb to be brought under the body for walking and directed laterally to the side in the plane of the wing in flight. The hind limb was elongate, and the fibula was very reduced so that it did not reach to the ankle. The first four metatarsals (foot bones) were long and slender, terminating in toes of about equal length; the fifth metatarsal was short, terminating with a toe having only two very elongate phalanges and lacking a claw.

The wings of *Rhamphorhynchus* consisted of a wing membrane (patagium) of stretchable skin spread between the fore- and hind limbs and the tail. The patagium can be divided into three sections: the triangular propatagium, in front of the humerus (upper arm) and ulna (a bone in the forearm), the brachiopatagium, between the fore- and hind limbs; and the uropatagium, between the hind limb and the tail. The brachiopatagium was reinforced along the side by the fine filaments called "actinofibrils," which were 0.05 millimeters in diameter and spaced to 8 per millimeter (Wellnhofer 1975; Padian and Rayner 1993). The limbs controlled the patagium, the pteroid bone in particular controlled the propatagium, and the elongate fifth toe helped control the uropatagium.

The earliest known pterosaur is *Preondactylus* from the Forni Dolomite of the Upper Triassic (Norian) of northern Italy. *Preondactylus* was quite small, with a wingspan of about 46 centimeters, and it seems to be the most primitive pterosaur known because its femur and tibia were relatively longer than its humerus and ulna, respectively, and the wing was relatively short (Wild 1984b). This suggests that *Preondactylus* was not as good a flier as later pterosaurs. However, *Preondactylus* exhibits the basic body plan typical of pterosaurs, and no nonflying ancestors or intermediates are known. Fossils of two other pterosaurs, *Eudimorphodon* and *Peteinosaurus,* have been found in the Zorzino Limestone of northern Italy, only slightly later than *Preondactylus.* These animals were also small, with wingspans of about 60 centimeters to 1 meter (Wild 1978). *Preondactylus, Eudimorphodon,* and *Peteinosaurus* were sufficiently different from one another that they have been placed in separate families. The very first pterosaur must have appeared some time earlier.

Over the next 50 million years, the pterosaurs evolved and diversified but retained the basic long-tailed body plan found in *Rhamphorhynchus.* These long-tailed pterosaurs were grouped together in the more comprehensive group Rhamphorhynchoidea (Plieninger 1901, Wellnhofer 1978); however, the group is paraphyletic, that is, it consists of groups that are, at best, distantly related. Most "rhamphorhynchoids" were rather similar and seem to have eaten fish, but *Anurognathus,* from the Upper Jurassic of Germany, and *Batrachognathus,* from Kazakhstan, had short, low skulls with very wide mouths, well suited for feeding on flying insects.

In the Late Jurassic, pterosaurs underwent a major reorganization of body plan, as a derived (specialized) group, the Pterodactyloidea, appeared and eventually replaced the rham-

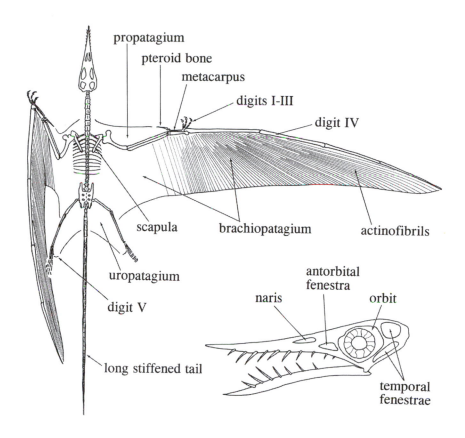

Figure 1. Skeletal reconstruction of *Rhamphorhynchus muensteri*. *Left*, dorsal view, with outlines of the wing membranes; right wing is spread as in flight, left wing partially folded; *right*, skull in left lateral view. In the outer part of the wing, the radiating pattern of lines represents the actinofibrils that stiffened the wing membrane; in actuality, the actinofibrils were much finer and more numerous than shown here. After Wellnhofer (modified), 1978, 1981b.

phorhynchoids. In Pterodactyloids, typified by *Pterodactylus,* separate openings for the nose and below the eye have joined. There are seven cervical and 14 dorsal vertebrae, a short tail, an elongate metacarpus (bone in the forearm), and a short fifth toe on its foot (Figure 2). Specimens of the genus *Pterodactylus* from the Solnhofen Limestone of southern Germany, in which impressions of soft tissues are preserved, show that the brachiopatagium did not attach as far down the hind limb as in rhamphorhynchoids and that the uropatagium was smaller. Except for the alterations in the skull and vertebrae, these changes seem to be related to the evolution of wings with higher aspect ratios (the relationship between the span, or distance from wing tip to wing tip, and chord, or distance from the front edge of the wing to the back). The changes also would decrease flight stability, which suggests that the pterodactyloids had more refined flight control and so were better flyers than rhamphorhynchoids.

In the Early Cretaceous, another major modification of body plan produced an even more derived group of pterodactyloids, the Dsungaripteroidea, which replaced the earlier pterodactyloids. Dsungaripteroids had accessory articulations (connections) between the cervical vertebrae, which strengthened the neck: the vertebrae of the upper back and their dorsal ribs were fused to form a single rigid structure termed a "notarium." Also,

the scapula, instead of extending rearward over the ribcage, was rotated inward so that it articulated with the notarium, forming a stiff and robust pectoral girdle-trunk complex (Figure 3). Vertebrae farther along the back, those of the lower back, and those at the beginning of the tail all join to form a synsacrum. It has been suggested that the Dsungaripteroidea may not be closely related, that various lines of pterodactyloids independently evolved these vertebral modifications and advanced pectoral girdles (Unwin 1995); however, recent phylogenetic (genetic history) analyses support the monophyly (unified line of descent) of the group and a single origination of the advanced pectoral girdle (Bennett 1989, 1994; Kellner 1996). Dsungaripteroids were generally much larger than the early pterodactyloids of the Jurassic. It is likdly that the vertebral modifications and advanced pectoral girdles permitted such great size (wingspans up to 6 meters in *Pteranodon* and 11 meters in *Quetzalcoatlus*) (Lawson 1975; Langston 1981).

The skeleton of dsungaripteroids also exhibited extensive pneumatization—that is, air spaces existed within the bones, and special structures tied those spaces to the respiratory system. Some of this had been seen in earlier pterosaurs, but pneumatization was greatly increased in dsungaripteroids. In *Pteranodon* all vertebrae in front of the sacrum, some ribs, the shoulder blade-coracoid complex, the sternum, and the entire forelimb (including the

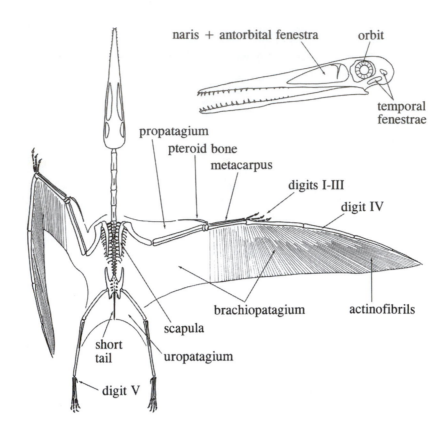

Figure 2. Skeletal reconstruction of *Pterodactylus kochi. Left,* dorsal view with outlines of the wing membranes; right wing spread as in flight, left wing partially folded; *right,* skull, left lateral view. After Wellnhofer (modified), 1978, 1991b.

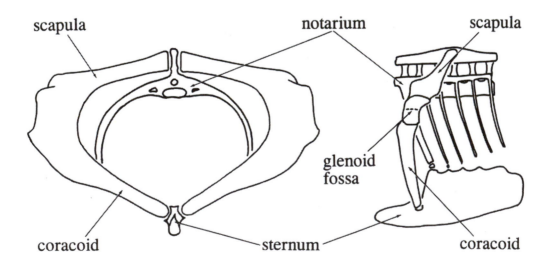

Figure 3. Notarium and pectoral girdle of *Pteranodon. Left,* anterior view; *right,* left lateral view. The dorsal vertebrae and their ribs are fused to form a single structure called the notarium; also the scapula is rotated so that its end is braced against the notarium and articulates with it. Compare with the scapula in *Rhamphorhynchus* and *Pterodactylus* (Figures 1 and 2).

claws on the three small fingers) were pneumatic (Bennett). Pneumatization of limb bones allowed air to take the place of marrow, lightening the bone. It also allowed the diameter of the bones to be increased, increasing the volume of the bone cavity without increasing the bone's weight, which an increased volume of marrow would do. At the same time the thickness of the wall of the bone decreased. Such large-diameter, thin-walled bones are stronger than small-diameter, thick-walled bones of the same weight.

It is possible to divide pterosaur evolution into three major pulses of innovation in morphology (shape and structure), each producing major reorganizations of body plan and each separated by periods of comparative morphological stasis and major radiations. First, there was the evolution of wings and powered flight from nonflying ancestors, producing the basic pterosaurian body plan. Second, there was the evolution of higher aspect ratio wings with more advanced flight control, producing the pterodactyloid body plan. Third, there were the vertebral modifications, including the evolution of the notarium and the inward rotation of the scapula to form a stiff pectoral girdle-trunk complex, which produced the dsungaripteroid body plan.

The taxonomic and morphological diversity of pterosaurs seem to have increased steadily throughout most of the Mesozoic. We know of only five species in three genera (larger groupings, singular genus) from the Triassic, but in the Jurassic there are 22 species of rhamphorhynchoid in 14 genera and 14 species of pterodactyloid in 8 genera, and in the Cretaceous there are 42 species in 21 genera. However, the number of genera seems to have decreased in the Late Cretaceous. It is possible that this apparent decrease actually reflects the fact that, so far, the fossils have not been found. If the decrease is real, it may have been because pterosaurs kept getting bigger; in any ecosystem there are fewer big birds than small, and the same would probably have been true of pterosaurs. Or, the decrease in diversity may have been due to competition with birds.

The evolutionary relationship of the Pterosauria to other reptiles is controversial. It has been generally accepted that pterosaurs and archosauriforms (the group including birds and crocodiles) (the Archosauria of Romer 1956 and Carroll 1988) because they had an antorbital fenestra (opening in front of the eye socket) (Wellnhofer 1978). Despite that, R. Wild (1978, 1983) argued that pterosaurs were not archosauriforms, but shared a number of features with "eosuchians" (distant relatives of snakes and lizards) and were most closely related to prolacertiforms (typically, long-necked, superficially lizardlike creatures). According to this interpretation, the antorbital fenestra of pterosaurs was convergent (independently evolved) with that of archosauriforms. Subsequently, a series of cladistic analyses, which rank organisms on the basis of splitting evolution or common ancestry, placed pterosaurs as the major sister group (a group most closely related to another) of the Dinosauria, in a group called the Ornithodira (Padian 1984; Gauthier 1986; Benton 1990; Sereno 1991). This relationship was based on the similarity of a suite of hind limb features in pterosaurs and dinosaurs. Recently, an alternative cladistic analysis suggested that pterosaurs were basal (primitive and/or early) archosauriforms (Bennett 1996b). According to this view, the similarity of the hind limb features of pterosaurs to those of dinosaurs is entirely convergent and is not related to bipedal locomotion.

The origin of flight in pterosaurs has also been controversial. F. von Huene (1914) suggested that pterosaurs had many features that indicated an arboreal (tree-dwelling) climbing and leaping lifestyle: the light body, hooked manual claws suited for climbing, long hind limb suited for leaping, plantigrade feet (flat feet, in which the heel rests on the ground), and the long flexible tail. Thus, it was suggested that pterosaurs descended from an arboreal leaping animal and evolved flight by leaping and gliding from trees. Wild argued for an arboreal parachuting origin of flight (1978, 1983, 1984a). He argued that a patagium would only evolve in a climbing or arboreal animal, not in a terrestrial animal (one confined to the ground), and noted that the presence of large claws indicated pronounced climbing ability in pterosaurs and their immediate ancestors. He also argued that the ancestor of pterosaurs was a small arboreal insectivorous animal with a lizardlike body and limbs of moderate length. Such an animal could drop or jump from branches to escape predators or pursue prey and, because of its small size, could parachute to the ground without injury. A patagium evolved, increasing body surface area, decreasing the rate of descent, and leading to gliding. Subsequently, the patagium and the inherited large fourth digit were further enlarged as gliding ability increased and flapping flight evolved.

An alternative theory of the origin of pterosaur flight presented by K. Padian (1938b, 1984, 1985) was essentially an adaptation of the cursorial (running) theory of the origin of bird flight (Ostrom 1974, 1979, 1985). Padian (1983a, 1983b) argued that pterosaurs could not use the forelimbs in normal quadrupedal (four-footed) walking and that the pelvic girdle and hind limb exhibited many features indicative of rapid running. He argued that pterosaurs were obligate bipeds (could only walk on two feet), and that the ancestor of pterosaurs ran along the ground until they reached a certain speed, then jumped into the air to catch insects or escape predators. Once in the air, the animal would swing its forelimbs to prolong and control the jump, much as human athletes swing their arms for control when performing the long jump. This forelimb swinging was the precursor of wing flapping. Subsequently, a patagium evolved, increasing the aerodynamic effect of the forelimb swinging. Therefore, selection for longer and higher jumps led directly to flapping flight, without passing through a gliding stage.

Recently, studies of the functional morphology of the limbs have shown that pterosaurs were capable of erect quadrupedal walking, and suggest that owing to the presence of arboreal features, pterosaurs were well suited to an arboreal climbing and leaping lifestyle (Bennett 1997a, 1997b). This conclusion agrees with Huene's arboreal leaping theory of the origin of flight. The main difference between the arboreal parachuting theory and the leaping theory is that the parachuting theory posits that flight developed from passive falling to the ground, while the arboreal leaping theory posits that flight developed as an extension of active aerial locomotion in the treetops, leaping from branch to branch or tree to tree. Despite these differences, there is now a consensus that pterosaurs evolved flight from arboreal ancestors.

All pterosaurs seem to have been capable of active flapping flight. Padian (1983b) noted many structural similarities between the wings of pterosaurs, birds, and bats, and suggested that pterosaurs were capable of flapping their wings in the same figure-eight motion used by birds and bats. However, unlike birds, the hind limb was involved in the wing and must have flapped up and down in synchrony with the forelimb. Various authors have attempted to reconstruct the flight performance of pterosaurs (Kripp 1943; Holst 1957; Bramwell and Whitfield 1974; Heptonstall 1971), but there is considerable uncertainty as to the wing area and weight of pterosaurs. Larger pterosaurs, such as *Pteranodon,* were too large and heavy to flap continuously but were well suited to soaring flight (Brower 1983).

The terrestrial locomotion of pterosaurs has been controversial. H.G. Seeley (1901) reconstructed pterosaurs in various quadrupedal and bipedal poses, always with erect hind limb posture and a digitigrade (walking on the toes) hind foot. However, other scholars reconstructed pterosaurs as walking with an ungainly, sprawling gait or as crawling on their bellies, based in part on some perceived similarity to bats. Subsequently, Padian (1983a, 1983b) noted that the structure of pterosaur hind limb was similar to that of bipedal dinosaurs. Arguing that the forelimbs of pterosaurs could not be used in normal quadrupedal walking, Padian concluded pterosaurs must have been digitigrade bipeds, much like birds. Other workers argued against bipedality and erect hind limb posture (Wellnhofer 1988, 1991a; Unwin 1988; Unwin and Bakhurina 1994). Much of the controversy surrounded the hip joint. Padian (1983b) argued that the hip joint restricted hind limb movement to swinging forward and backward, parallel to the midline plane of the body, whereas other workers argued that the hip directed the hind limb to the side, preventing it from moving forward and backward. Recently, an intermediate view has emerged, in which pterosaurs are reconstructed as quadrupedal but having a more or less erect limb posture (Bennett 1997a) (Figure 4). This interpretation is in full agreement with pterosaur trackway evidence (Stokes 1957; Lockley et al. 1995; Mazin et al. 1995). These trackways from the western United States and France show that the pterosaurs walked quadrupedally with a plantigrade foot.

It is generally accepted that the earliest pterosaurs were insectivorous. *Eudimorphodon* had teeth with one, three, or five points (cusps), which were well suited for catching and eating insects. *Preondactylus* and *Peteinosaurus* both had simple cone-shaped teeth, which also were suited to catching insects and/or fishes. In addition, the Upper Jurassic rhamphorhynchoids *Anurognathus* and *Batrachognathus* probably fed on flying insects. However, most pterosaurs seem to have fed on fishes. Many genera (e.g., *Rhamphorhynchus, Pterodactylus, Anhanguera*) had widely spaced, long, sharply pointed teeth well suited to capturing and holding fishes. Likewise the slender, pointed, toothless jaws of *Pteranodon* and *Nyctosaurus* are well suited to catching fishes. In addition, the stomach contents of *Rhamphorhynchus, Pteranodon,* and *Nyctosaurus* have included the remains of fishes. One family of pterodactyloids, the Ctenochasmatidae, evolved long jaws with many closely spaced, long, slender teeth that formed a basket or sieve suited to catching small aquatic prey. *Pterodaustro* had hundreds of long teeth in its lower jaw, which permitted it to sieve tiny organisms out of the water, much like the flamingos. *Dsungaripterus* had peglike teeth, which it probably used to feed on hard-bodied invertebrates such as bivalves, and *Tapejara* had short, deep, toothless jaws, which it may have used to feed on fruits (Wellnhofer and Kellner 1991).

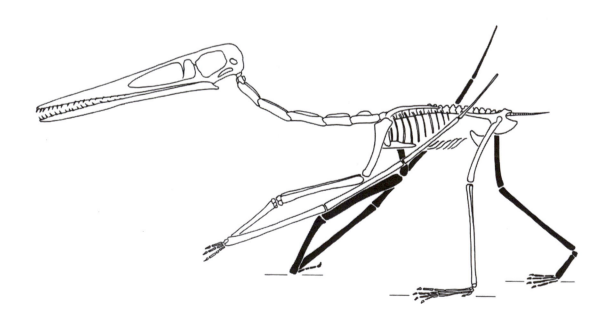

Figure 4. Reconstruction of *Pterodactylus* in erect quadrupedal locomotion based on *Pteraichnus* trackways. The left forelimb is moving forward above the ground. The right fore- and hind limbs are blackened and the straight lines by the right hand and the hind feet indicate that they are touching the ground, while the left forelimb is moving forward above the ground.

Some scholars have suggested that pterosaurs probably caught their fish while flying low over the water. This interpretation reflects the notion that pterosaurs would not be able to swing well or might have had difficulty taking off from the water. For example, *Rhamphorhynchus* has been reconstructed as fishing like the Black Skimmer *(Rhynchops),* which flies over the surface of the water with its lower jaw cutting through the water in search of fishes. Also, some dsungaripteroids have been reconstructed as dipping their jaws into the water to catch fish swimming just at the water's surface (Wellnhofer 1991b). However, specimens of *Pterodactylus* have been found with traces of webbing between the toes of the hind foot, suggesting that they could swim well, and there is no reason to think pterosaurs would have difficulty taking off from the water. Therefore, pterosaurs may have fished while swimming at the water surface or dived into the water from low altitudes after fishes, much as some birds do.

There is some controversy regarding the metabolic rate and activity levels of pterosaurs. Seeley (1901) suggested that pterosaurs probably were endothermic (warm-blooded) because they were active flyers and had pneumatic bones like birds. It was thought that only an endothermic animal would be able to sustain the energy needed for active flapping flight; however, there is little or no evidence to support that suggestion. Seeley suggested that pterosaurs might have been covered with an insulating fur. A number of authors have noted small dots on preserved wing membranes, which they interpreted as short hairs, but there is no evidence of longer insulating hairs on the body. When specimens of the rhamphorhynchoid *Sordes* were found with what appeared to be a dense covering of long hairs on the body (Sharov 1971), the idea of furry pterosaurs became entrenched in the popular literature. However, recent studies have shown that what were taken as hairs were actually some sort of structural fiber within the wing membrane (Unwin and Bakhurina 1994). Thus, at present there is no evidence of a hairlike body covering in pterosaurs.

Little work has been done on the pattern or rate of growth in pterosaurs. A recent study of *Rhamphorhynchus* from the Solnhofen Limestone suggested that it grew at about the same rate as the present-day *Alligator* and would take at least three years to reach an adult wingspan of 1.5 to 1.8 meters (Bennett 1995). This growth rate would be consistent with an ectothermic (cold-blooded) metabolism. Pterodactyloid pterosaurs from the Solnhofen Limestone seem to have similar growth rates (Bennett 1996a). Another study suggested that the growth pattern of the dsungaripteroid *Pteranodon* was quite different (Bennett 1993). The youngest individuals of *Pteranodon* found in the Niobrara Formation were nearly fully grown and exhibited a bone histology indicative of relatively rapid growth, whereas adults had stopped growing and their bone histology indicates very slow to no growth. This suggests that the young of *Pteranodon* grew rapidly to adult size before flying out to sea, and until then they probably would have required parental feeding.

There is little evidence of sexual dimorphism (physical differences between males and females) in rhamphorhynchoid pterosaurs, although it has been suggested that skull size in this group was slightly dimorphic (Wellnhofer 1975; Bennett 1995). However, in the dsungaripteroid, *Pteranodon,* there is evidence of marked sexual dimorphism. *Pteranodon* males had a large body (50 percent larger than that of females) and large cranial crest, whereas females had a small cranial crest, and their pelvis was deeper, with a relatively larger pelvic canal, than that of males (Bennett 1992). Females probably had a large pelvic canal to permit the passage of relatively large eggs, and males probably used their large cranial crest to intimidate other males or as a display to attract females. It is possible that other dsungaripteroids were also dimorphic in body and crest size, but so far the evidence is inconclusive.

Marked sexual dimorphism provides one explanation for the function of the cranial crest in *Pteranodon,* as an intraspecific (between individuals of the same species) display structure, but other explanations have been offered. Crests also have been interpreted as rudders (Kripp 1943; Heptonstall 1971; Stein 1975) and, in the case of *Pteranodon,* as an aerodynamic counterbalance for the large head (Bramwell and Whitfield 1974). Although these explanations may be plausible, they cannot explain the marked dimorphism of crest size in this group.

The first pterosaur ever found was a complete skeleton of what is now known as *Pterodactylus antiquus,* discovered in the Upper Jurassic Solnhofen Limestones near Eichstätt, Bavaria, Germany. When C.A. Collini first described it in 1784, he did not recognize it as a flying animal or as a reptile; he thought it was an unknown sea creature. Other early workers interpreted it as an aberrant bat. It fell to Georges Cuvier (1801) to properly interpret it as a reptile that flew, calling it a *Pterodactyle.* Subsequently, many other specimens of pterosaurs were discovered in the Solnhofen limestones, and later in the Lower Jurassic Posidonia shales of Holzmaden, Germany. Various scholars studied the Solnhofen and Holzmaden pterosaurs, which included both rhamphorhynchoids and pterodactyloids. Most contributions were purely descriptive but F. Plieninger's classification of the Pterosauria introduced the suborders Rhamphorhynchoidea and Pterodactyloidea (1901). The framework of Plieninger's classification is still used today (e.g., Wellnhofer 1978, 1991b).

Elsewhere in Europe, in 1851, pterosaur bones were found in the Early Cretaceous Cambridge Greensand of England. The Greensand subsequently produced a major collection of dsungaripteroids in the form of fragmentary materials that appear to represent a lag deposit. Lag deposits are made up of those coarser materials that are left after wind or water erosion carry away the finer and lighter materials. In the case of the pterosaur fossils in the Cambridge Greensand, lighter bones and fragments have been carried away leaving heavy bones, broken articular ends of bones, and so forth. Thus the sample of bones is incomplete and biased. Some of this material was described by Sir Richard Owen, but Seeley (1870, 1901) was the major interpreter of the Greensand pterosaurs. He described much of the material but, more importantly, argued forcefully that pterosaurs were large-brained, warm-blooded, active flyers that differed from the popular image of cold-blooded reptiles to as great a degree as do modern birds and mammals.

The next significant set of discoveries of pterosaurs took place in the 1870s in the Late Cretaceous Niobrara Formation of the western interior of today's western Kansas in North America. The Niobrara has produced vast numbers of a single genus of dsungaripteroid, *Pteranodon,* plus small numbers of a second genus, *Nyctosaurus,* which were described by O.C. Marsh, S.W. Williston, and F. Plieninger. Subsequently, G.F. Eaton (1910) produced a monograph describing *Pteranodon.* It was his description and interpretation that provided much of the basis for the popular image of large pterosaurs.

After Eaton's monograph, little work was done on pterosaurs until C.C. Young and P. Wellnhofer began their studies in the 1960s. Young (1964) described the dsungaripteroid, *Dsungaripterus,* from Sinkiang, China, and presented a classification that included the Dsungaripteroidea. He viewed the group as essentially comprising a number of large pterodactyloids with cranial crests and notaria. Wellnhofer (1970, 1975) redescribed and revised the taxonomy of much of the German material and since then has continued to study other pterosaurs.

As this review of the history of pterosaur finds makes clear, pterosaurs seem to have achieved a worldwide distribution. Their fossils, although generally rare, have been found on all continents, including Antarctica, and on Greenland, Australia, and New Zealand. All Triassic pterosaurs are known from northern Italy. This may indicate that pterosaurs originated in Europe, but also it could be merely that there are not good exposures of Triassic rocks elsewhere. In the Lower Jurassic, pterosaurs are found in Europe, North America, India, and Antarctica, and by the upper Jurassic they essentially had a worldwide distribution.

In general, pterosaur bones were lightly constructed and quite fragile. Therefore, they are preserved rarely and the fossil record of pterosaurs is quite patchy. Although pterosaurs are found on all continents, only a few localities have produced the majority of pterosaur specimens: the Posidonia Shale and Solnhofen Limestone of southern Germany, the Cambridge Greensand of England, the Santana Formation of Brazil, and the Niobrara Formation of western Kansas.

The bituminous Posidonia Shale of Holzmaden, Germany, is an important locality that has produced beautifully articulated skeletons of two Lower Jurassic genera, *Campylognathoides* and *Dorygnathus.* In addition to the pterosaurs, the fauna of the Posidonia Shale included abundant invertebrates, such as belemnites and crinoids of the Mesozoic, sharks and bony fishes, ichthyosaurs, and plesiosaurs (large marine reptiles), and marine crocodiles.

The first and perhaps most important site where pterosaurs were found were quarries in the Upper Jurassic Solnhofen Limestone, which was laid down in shallow nearshore lagoons. Since the 1700s, nearly 200 specimens of both rhamphorhynchoid and pterodactyloid pterosaurs have been collected. The specimens are excellently preserved in a fine lithographic limestone, often as fully articulated (complete and intact) skeletons and often with impression of soft parts, such as the wing membranes and webbing between the toes (Wellnhofer 1970, 1975). The fauna of the Solnhofen Limestone includes varied invertebrates, sharks and bony fishes, small crocodilians, ichthyosaurs, and the bird *Archaeopteryx.* Stomach contents in some pterosaurs (e.g., *Rhamphorhynchus*) show that they fed on fishes, but the long jaws with numerous long slender teeth of *Gnathosaurus* and *Ctenochasma* suggest that they were sieving very small fishes and invertebrates out of the water.

The Cambridge Greensand is a deposit of Early Cretaceous sands and muds near Cambridge, England. It contains nodules of phosphate of lime that were mined in the mid-1880s for fertilizer. Many of the nodules contain fossils, and over 2,000 pterosaurs were found. Most of the fossils are in the form of fragments of wing bones, jaws, and vertebrae. Since there were no complete long bones, it is difficult to identify and reconstruct the animals.

Early Cretaceous pterosaur fossils also have been found in the Santana Formation of northeastern Brazil, which was a nearshore marine deposit. The pterosaurs occur in limestone concretions (deposits that cemented together), which formed around the bones soon after they were buried in mud. The concretion protected the bone from being crushed by the weight of accumulating sediments. In some cases, this process also preserved soft parts of the body. The limestone concretions can be dissolved away with acid to free the perfectly preserved bones. The Santana Formation is especially interesting because fossils of many sorts of pterosaurs have been found there, some of which are very similar to the pterosaurs from the Cambridge Greensand. In addition to the pterosaurs, the fauna of the Santana Formation included abundant bony fishes and turtles, crocodilians, dinosaurs, and birds. Most of pterosaurs seem to have been piscivorous (fish-eating).

The Niobrara Formation of western Kansas has produced nearly 1,200 specimens of the dsungaripteroid *Pteranodon* and a small number of a smaller pterosaur, *Nyctosaurus.* These specimens are generally incomplete and crushed flat, but they do preserve very fine details of skeletal anatomy. The Niobrara pterosaurs were buried in a fine chalk laid down some 200 kilometers from the near shore of the Western Interior Seaway, over which the animals must have been flying. *Pteranodon* is so abundant that it must have been a common resident of the area. The fauna of the Niobrara Formation also includes sharks and bony fishes, large marine reptiles (mosasaurs and plesiosaurs), turtles, small flying birds, and flightless diving birds. Stomach contents containing vertebrae and other bones indicate that *Pteranodon* and *Nyctosaurus* were feeding on bony fishes.

S. CHRISTOPHER BENNETT

See also Aerial Locomotion

Works Cited

Bennett, S.C. 1989. A pteranodontid pterosaur from the Early Cretaceous of Peru, with comments on the relationships of Cretaceous pterosaurs. *Journal of Paleontology* 63:669–77.

———. 1992. Sexual dimorphism of *Pteranodon* and other pterosaurs, with comments on cranial crests. *Journal of Vertebrate Paleontology* 12:422–34.

———. 1993. The ontogeny of *Pteranodon* and other pterosaurs. *Paleobiology* 19:92–106.

———. 1994. *Taxonomy and Systematics of the Late Cretaceous Pterosaur* Pteranondon *(Pterosauria, Pterodactyloidea).* Occasional Papers of the Museum of Natural History, University of Kansas, 169. Lawrence: University of Kansas.

———. 1995. A statistical study of *Rhamphorhynchus* from the Solnhofen Limestone of Germany: Year-classes of a single large species. *Journal of Paleontology* 69:569–80.

———. 1996a. Year-classes of pterosaurs from the Solnhofen Limestone of Germany: Taxonomic and systematic implications. *Journal of Vertebrate Paleontology* 16:432–44.

———. 1996b. The phylogenetic position of the Pterosauria within the Archosauromorpha. *Zoological Journal of the Linnean Society* 118:261–309.

———. 1997a. Terrestrial locomotion of pterosaurs: A reconstruction based on *Pteraichnus* trackways. *Journal of Vertebrate Paleontology* 17:104–13.

———. 1997b. The arboreal leaping theory of the origin of pterosaur flight. *Historical Biology* 12:265–90.

Benton, M. 1990. Origin and interrelationships of dinosaurs. *In* D.B. Weishample, P. Dodson, and H. Osmolska (eds.), *The Dinosauria.* Berkeley: University of California Press.

Bramwell, C.D., and G.R. Whitfield. 1974. Biomechanics of *Pteranodon.* *Philosophical Transactions of the Royal Society, B,* 267:503–81.

Brower, J.C. 1983. The aerodynamics of *Pteranodon* and *Nyctosaurus,* two large pterosaurs from the Upper Cretaceous of Kansas. *Journal of Vertebrate Paleontology* 3:84–124.

Carroll, R.L. 1988. *Vertebrate Paleontology and Evolution.* New York: Freeman.

Collini, C.A. 1784. Sur quelques Zoolithes du Cabinet d'Histoire naturelle de S.A.S.E. Palatine et de Bavière, à Mannheim. *Acta Academiiae Theodoro-Palatinae Mannheim* 5 (pars physica):58–103.

Cuvier, G. 1801. Reptile volant. Extrait d'un ouvrage sur les espèces de quadrupèdes dont on a trouvé les ossemens dans l'intérieur de la terre. *Journal de Physique, de Chimie et d'Histoire Naturelle et des Arts* 52:253–67.

Eaton, G.F. 1910. Osteology of *Pteranodon. Memoirs of the Connecticut Academy of Arts and Sciences* 2:1–38.

Gauthier, J.A. 1986. Saurischian monophyly and the origin of birds. *In* K. Padian (ed.), *The Origin of Birds and the Evolution of Flight.* Memoir, California Academy of Science, 8. San Francisco: California Academy of Sciences.

Heptonstall, W.B. 1971. An analysis of the flight of the Cretaceous pterodactyl *Pteranodon ingens. Scottish Journal of Geology* 7:61–78.

Holst, E. von. 1957. Der Saurierflug. *Paläontologische Zeitschrift* 31:15–22.

Heune, F. von. 1914. Beiträge zur Geschichte der Archosaurier. *Geologische und Paläontologische Abhandlungen,* N.F., 13:1–53.

Kellner, A.W.A. 1996. Pterosaur phylogeny. *Journal of Vertebrate Paleontology* 16:45A.

Kripp, D. von. 1943. Ein Lebensbild von *Pteranodon ingens* auf flugtechnischer Grundlage. *Nova Acta Leopoldina,* N.F., 12(83):16–32.

Langston Jr., W. 1981. Pterosaurs. *Scientific American* 244:122–36.

Lawson, D.A. 1975. Pterosaur from the latest Cretaceous of West Texas: Discovery of the largest flying creature. *Science* 187:947–48.

Lockley, M.G., T.J. Logue, J.J. Mortalla, A.P. Hunt, R.J. Schultz, and J.W. Robinson. 1995. The fossil trackway *Pteraichnus* is pterosaurian, not crocodilian: Implications for the global distribution of pterosaur tracks. *Ichnos* 4:7–20.

Mazin, J.-M., P. Hantzpergue, G. Lafaurie, and P. Vignaud. 1995. Des pistes de ptérosaures dans le Tithonien de Crayssac (Quercy, France). *Comptes Rendus de l'Académie des Sciences,* série 2a, 321:417–24.

Ostrom, J.H. 1974. *Archaeopteryx* and the origin of flight. *Quarterly Review of Biology* 49:27–47.

———. 1979. Bird flight: How did it begin? *American Scientist* 67:46–56.

———. 1985. The cursorial origin of avian flight. *In* M.K. Hecht, J.H. Ostrom, G. Viohl, and P. Wellnhofer (eds.), *The Beginnings of Birds: Proceedings of the International Archaeopteryx Conference, Eichstätt 1984.* Eichstätt: Freunde des Jura-Museums Eichstätt.

Padian, K. 1983a. A functional analysis of flying and walking in pterosaurs. *Paleobiology* 9:218–39.

———. 1983b. Osteology and functional morphology of *Dimorphodon macronyx* (Buckland) (Pterosauria: Rhamphorhynchoidea) based on new material in the Yale Peabody Museum. *Postilla* 189:1–44.

———. 1984. The origin of pterosaurs. *In* W.-E. Reif and F. Westphal (eds.), *Third Symposium of Mesozoic Terrestrial Ecosystems.* Tübingen: Attempto Verlag.

———. 1985. The origins and aerodynamics of flight in extinct vertebrates. *Palaeontology* 28:413–33.

Padian, K., and J.M.V. Rayner. 1993. The wings of pterosaurs. *American Journal of Science* 293-A:91–166.

Plieninger, F. 1901. Beiträge zur Kenntnis der Flugsaurier. *Palaeontographica* 48:65–90.

Romer, A.S. 1956. *Osteology of the Reptiles.* Chicago: University of Chicago Press.

Seely, H.G. 1870. *The Ornithosauria: An Elementary Study of the Bones of Pterodactyles.* Cambridge: Deighton, Bell.

———. 1901. *Dragons of the Air: An Account of Extinct Flying Reptiles.* London: Methuen; New York: Appleton.

Sereno, P.C. 1991. Basal archosaurs: Phylogenetic relationships and functional implications. *Society of Vertebrate Paleontology Memoir 2, Journal of Vertebrate Paleontology* 11(Supplement to No. 4): 1–153.

Sharov, A.G. 1971. New flying reptiles from the Mesozoic of Kazakhstan and Kirgizia. *Akademia Nauk, Paleontological Institute, Trudy* 130:104–13.

Stein, R.S. 1975. Dynamic analysis of *Pteranodon ingens:* A reptilian adaptation to flight. *Journal of Paleontology* 49:534–48.

Stokes, W.L. 1957. Pterodactyl tracks from the Morrison Formation. *Journal of Paleontology* 31:952–54.

Unwin, D.M. 1988. New remains of the pterosaur *Dimorphodon* (Pterosauria: Rhamphorhynchoidea) and the terrestrial locomotion of early pterosaurs. *Modern Geology* 13:57–68.

———. 1995. Preliminary results of a phylogenetic analysis of the Pterosauria (Diapsida: Archosauria). *In* A. Sun and Y. Wang (eds.), *Sixth Symposium on Mesozoic Terrestrial Ecosystems and Biota, Short Papers.* Beijing: China Ocean.

Unwin, D.M., and N.N. Bakhurina. 1994. *Sordes pilosus* and the nature of the pterosaur flight apparatus. *Nature* 371:62–64.

Wellnhofer, P. 1970. *Die Pterodactyloidea (Pterosauria) der Oberjura-Plattenkalke Süddeutschlands.* Bayerische Akademie der Wissenschaften, Mathematisch-Wissenschaftliche Klasse, Abhandlungen, 141. Munich: Verlag der Bayerischen Akademie der Wissenschaften.

———. 1975. Die Rhamphorhynchoidea (Pterosauria) der Oberjura-Plattenkalke Süddeutschlands. *Palaeontographica, A,* 148:1–33; 148:132–86; 149:1–30.

———. 1978. *Pterosauria.* Handbuch der Paläoherptologie, Teil 19. Stuttgart and New York: Fischer Verlag.

———. 1988. Terrestrial locomotion in pterosaurs. *Historical Biology* 1:3–16.

———. 1991a. Weitere Pterosaurierfunde aus der Santana-Formation (Apt) der Chapada do Araripe, Brasilien. *Palaeontographica* 215:43–101.

———. 1991b. *The Illustrated Encyclopedia of Pterosaurs.* London: Salamander; New York: Crescent.

Wellnhofer, P., and A.W.A. Kellner. 1991. The skull of *Tapejara wellnhoferi* Kellner (Reptilia, Pterosauria) from the Lower Cretaceous Santana Formation of the Araripe Basin, northeastern Brazil. *Mitteilung der Bayerischen Staatssammlung für Paläontologie und historische Geologie* 31:89–106.

Wild, R. 1978. Die Flugsaurier (Reptilia, Pterosauria) aus der Oberen Trias von Cene bei Bergamo, Italien. *Bolletino della Società Paleontologica Italiana* 17:176–256.

——. 1983. Über den Ursprung der Flugsaurier. *In* Weltenberger Akademie (ed.), *Erwin Rutte-Festschrift*. Weltenburg: Kelheim.

——. 1984a. Flugsaurier aus der Obertrias von Italien. *Naturwissenschaften* 71:1–11.

——. 1984b. A new pterosaur (Reptilia, Pterosauria) from the Upper Triassic (Norian) of Friuli, Italy. *Gortania. Atti del Museo Friulano di Storia Naturale* 5:45–62.

Young, C.C. 1964. On a new pterosaurian from Sinkiang, China. *Vertebrata PalAsiatica* 8:221–55.

Further Reading

Currie, P.J. 1991. *The Flying Dinosaurs: The Illustrated Guide to the Evolution of Flight*. Red Deer, Alberta: Red Deer College Press.

Langston Jr., W. 1981. Pterosaurs. *Scientific American* 244:122–36.

Padian, K. 1985. The origins and aerodynamics of flight in extinct vertebrates. *Palaeontology* 28:413–33.

Seely, H.G. 1901. *Dragons of the Air: An Account of Extinct Flying Reptiles*. London: Methuen.

R

RADIOLOGICAL IMAGING AND ASSOCIATED TECHNIQUES

Almost immediately after the discovery of X-rays in 1895, radiography first was used to assess both vertebrate and invertebrate fossils (Brühl 1896). Ever since, it has become a standard investigative method to visualize the internal morphology of fossils. A more recent breakthrough in radiological technique in paleontology has been the development of high-resolution computed tomography (CT) and associated sophisticated computer graphics applications.

Conventional Radiography

In conventional radiography an object is placed between an X-ray source and X-ray sensitive film, and the image of the object thus formed represents the distribution and degree of X-ray penetration through the object. A consequence is that all structures in the path of the X-rays appear superimposed in the image and cannot be distinguished from each other (Figure 1). Radiographs therefore provide only limited information of more complex three-dimensional objects. Moreover, in the case of fossils any morphological information is blocked by the presence of sedimentary matrix (e.g., encasing rock) of a higher density (X-ray opacity) than the fossil itself. Within these limitations, conventional radiography can provide useful qualitative and quantitative information when applied to fossil morphology with relatively simple shapes, such as invertebrate specimens (Morris 1985), pneumatic (air) spaces and dentition (teeth) of vertebrate crania (Skinner and Sperber 1982), and postcranial bones (Runestad et al. 1993), and to specimens that are compressed into one plane in the process of fossilization, as is frequently seen with vertebrate skeletons. Compared with CT, conventional radiography will tend to have a higher spatial resolution (i.e., can distinguish adjacent small features better) and is cheaper and easier to use.

Computed Tomography (CT)

In medical CT scanners, the scanner used most frequently to study fossils, an X-ray source and a line of detectors circle the object and measure its density in a great number of directions. By repositioning the table with the object, the plane in which measurements are taken can be changed. Digital cross-sectional images, which map the different densities in the slice, are calculated from the measurements and are shown on a computer monitor using a gray scale. Frequently, prints on film (hard copies) are made of such CT scans, but it is important to emphasize that for most scientific purposes the actual digital image data should be archived and studied.

CT has become the prime nondestructive method for investigating the internal morphology of vertebrate fossils. It overcomes the problems of the superimposition of structures encountered with conventional radiography because it produces cross-sectional images, and it can detect small density differences between fossilized bone and attached matrix (Figure 2). Common applications include imaging the paranasal sinuses, the middle and inner ear, the brain cavity, the structure of the cranial vault, the dentition, cortical bone geometry of long bones and the mandible, as well as any structure or surface of a fossil hidden by matrix. Provided a number of inherent limitations of the CT technique are taken into account, accurate linear, angular, and areal measurements can be taken from CT scans (Spoor et al. 1993). The main problems encountered when scanning highly mineralized or matrix-filled fossils with regular medical CT scanners is that their density may be outside the normal range used for patients, or the capacity of the X-ray tube may be insufficient, which in both cases results in reduced image quality (Zonneveld and Wind 1985; Zonneveld et al. 1989; Spoor and Zonneveld 1984).

Apart from medical CT scanners with a minimum scan slice thickness of one millimeter, and a spatial resolution of around one-half millimeter, dedicated industrial and research micro-CT scanners have been developed, which can provide much higher spatial resolutions and are ideal for small and highly mineralized fossils (Rowe et al. 1993). It is worth mentioning that magnetic resonance imaging (MRI) is generally not useful in paleontology because, unlike soft tissue, fossil bone does not emit an appropriate signal.

Three-Dimensional Reconstruction

Using sophisticated computer graphics techniques, a series of contiguous CT scans can be stacked to provide a three-dimensional reconstruction of the scanned object. Even for those who are expe-

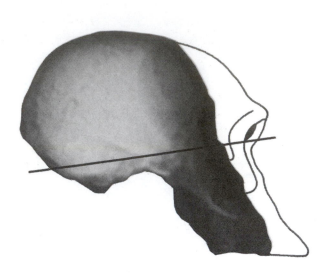

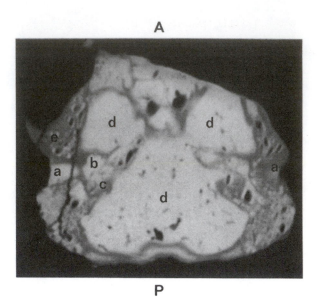

Figure 1. Lateral radiograph of the *Australopithecus africanus* cranium MLD 37/38 from Makapansgat, South Africa, shown with a reconstructed face and a black line indicating the scan plane of the transverse CT scan in Figure 2. Courtesy of F. Zonneveld.

Figure 2. Transverse (horizontal) CT scan in the plane indicated in Figure 1. *A*, anterior; *P*, posterior; *a*, external auditory meatus; *b*, middle ear; *c*, inner ear; *d*, matrix-filled cranial cavity; *e*, pneumatized roof of the zygomatic arc. Notice that the sedimentary matrix has a higher density (has a lighter gray value) than the fossil bone. Courtesy of F. Zonneveld.

rienced with interpreting the cross-sectional shapes shown in individual scans, such reconstructions provide a better and more realistic impression of the overall morphology. The three-dimensional effect is enhanced by shading the surface by means of one or more virtual light sources, and by generating stereo pairs of images and animation sequences simulating movement. A particularly appealing method of presenting CT-based three-dimensional reconstructions is through stereolithography, which provides life-sized or enlarged plastic models that can be handled manually (Zollikofer et al. 1995).

Three-dimensional reconstruction offers an advanced way of visualizing internal morphology by selectively reconstructing or translucently imaging parts of the fossil, as first was demonstrated by Conroy and Vannier (1984) for an Oligocene ungulate cranium. Also, fragile fossils that are still largely embedded in the surrounding matrix can thus be visualized as an important aid in the subsequent preparation process. A second category of applications is the reconstruction of fossils by complementing missing parts through mirror imaging (Zollikofer et al. 1995), with the possibility of combining fossils of more than one individual, which requires the additional step of scaling to obtain matching sizes (Kalvin et al. 1995). The bones of a crushed fossil can be "electronically dissected" and reassembled, and deformations can be corrected. Apart from allowing conventional quantitative analyses, recording dimensions, angles, surfaces, or volumes (Hildebolt et al. 1990), the surface descriptions extracted from three-dimensional reconstructions provide the input for advanced multivariate shape-analysis methods commonly known as geometric morphometrics (Marcus et al. 1996). Finally, CT-based three-

dimensional images can be used to make biomechanical models of fossil bones and their joints, to study locomotion and mastication in extinct species.

FRED SPOOR

See also Computer Applications in Paleontology

Works Cited

Brühl. 1896. Über Verwendung von röntgenschen X-Strahlen zu paläontologisch-diagnostischen Zwecken. *Archiv für Anatomie und Physiologie* 547–50.

Conroy, G.C., and M.W. Vannier. 1984. Noninvasive three-dimensional computed imaging of matrix-filled fossil skulls by high-resolution computed tomography. *Science* 226:456–58.

Hildebolt, C.F., M.W. Vannier, and R.H. Knapp. 1990. Validation study of skull three-dimensional computerized tomography measurements. *American Journal of Physical Anthropology* 82:283–94.

Kalvin, A.D., D. Dean, and J.-J. Hublin. 1995. Reconstruction of human fossils. *IEEE Computer Graphics and Applications* 15, January:12–15.

Marcus, L.F., M. Corti, A. Loy, G.J.P. Naylor, and D.E. Slice (eds.). 1996. *Advances in Morphometrics*. New York: Plenum.

Morris, S.C. 1985. Fossil radiography. *Nature* 318:14–15.

Rowe, T., W. Carlson, and W. Bottorff. 1993. *Thrinaxodon, Digital Atlas of the Skull* (CD-Rom). Austin: University of Texas Press.

Runestad, J.A., C.B. Ruff, J.C. Nieh, R.W. Thorington, and M.F. Teaford. 1993. Radiographic estimation of long bone cross-sectional geometric properties. *American Journal of Physical Anthropology* 90:207–13.

Skinner, M.F., and G.H. Sperber. 1982. *Atlas of Radiography of Early Man.* New York: Liss.

Spoor, F., and F.W. Zonneveld. 1984. The bony labyrinth in Homo erectus: A preliminary report. *Courier Forschungsinstitut Senckenberg* 171:251–56.

———. 1998. CT-based 3-D imaging of hominid fossils, with notes on internal features of the Broken Hill 1 and SK 47 crania. *In* T. Koppe, H. Nagai, and K.W. Alt (eds.), *The Paranasal Sinuses of Higher Primates: Development, Function and Evolution.* Berlin: Quintessenz.

Spoor, C.F., F.W. Zonneveld, and G.A. Macho. 1993. Linear measurements of cortical bone and dental enamel by computed tomography: Applications and problems. *American Journal of Physical Anthropology* 91:469–84.

Vannier, M.W., G.C. Conroy, J.L. Marsh, and R.H. Knapp. 1985. Three-dimensional cranial surface reconstructions using high-resolution computed tomography. *American Journal of Physical Anthropology* 67:299–311.

Zonneveld, F.W., C.F. Spoor, and J. Wind. 1989. The use of computed tomography in the study of the internal morphology of hominid fossils. *Medicamundi* 34:117–28.

Zonneveld, F.W., and J. Wind. 1985. High-resolution computed tomography of fossil hominid skulls: A new method and some results. *In* P.V. Tobias (ed.), *Hominid Evolution: Past, Present and Future.* New York: Liss.

Zollikofer, C.P.E., M.S. Ponce de Leon, R.D. Martin, and P. Stucki. 1995. Neanderthal computer skulls. *Nature* 375:283–85.

REEFS AND REEF-BUILDING ORGANISMS

Reefs are biologically constructed features raised significantly above the surrounding seafloor as mounds, barriers, or platforms. Most are formed in shallow tropical marine environments by organisms that secrete calcium carbonate (limestone, $CaCO_3$) to construct internal, external, or basal skeletons. In the process, they commonly form a framework, or a pile of skeletal debris, to which others attach. Equatorial coral reef complexes, like the over-1,200-kilometer-long Great Barrier Reef that lines the eastern shelf of Australia, are today's best and most striking examples, but these are not necessarily typical of those in the past.

Reefs are ocean metropolises composed of myriads of organisms that form a complex, interacting, usually highly diverse, primarily biologically controlled community, much like the tropical rainforest on land. Yet, reef-building organisms are normally very small, and their soft tissues at best form only a millimeter-thin veneer on top of and around their skeletons. Reefs represent the primary storehouse of carbon on planet Earth. Over the long term, more carbon is stored in reefs than in all other ecosystems combined.

So how do reef organisms lock up so much carbon? They do it by extracting soluble calcium bicarbonate from seawater and using it to build their skeletons. In contrast, rainforests lock up carbon dioxide from the atmosphere and use it to produce cellulose. The primary reef-builders of today, the stony corals, secrete calcium carbonate with the help of symbiotic, photosynthetic algae called "zooxanthellae" (these occur in millions per square centimeter and give the corals their vivid colors). Under sunlight, the algae capture carbon dioxide and release oxygen, which accelerates the precipitation of calcium carbonate in the coral skeleton. In return, the coral acts as a host to the algae, providing the nutrients they require for growth. This cooperative process restricts the most vigorous reef growth to shallow, clear waters that receive ample sunlight, and, the fact that calcium carbonate is precipitated much more easily in warm water, confines most reefs to the tropical eastern continental coastlines (Figure 1). There, warm, westwardly flowing currents spill over the continental shelves or envelop oceanic islands and spread the coral lar-

vae. Reefs are favored by tropical sea temperatures between about 24 and 34 degrees centigrade (such areas cover only, at best, about 1.5 million square kilometers today). At times of global cooling events, reefs shrink to lower latitudes. These tropical belts also are known for their strong cyclone and hurricane systems. The reef community appears to be well adapted to such weather; rapid recovery normally takes less than a century. Since western coastlines are influenced by cold polar currents, reefs are very rare there.

Most reef-building organisms cannot tolerate fresh water. Nor can they thrive in muddy or silty runoff from rivers, which clogs their systems. This prevents reefs from forming around rivermouths or deltas (the same conditions, however, encourage the growth of mangroves, which flourish in such coastal areas). In addition, certain nutrients, especially phosphates, inhibit the precipitation of calcium carbonate in reefs, so pollution and cold, phosphate-rich upwellings are often fatal. Only a few reef-builders can survive periodic emersion in the intertidal zone: this means that reefs terminate at the low tide level. Such a reaction forms an excellent marker for global sea level change. This means that coral reefs formed in shallow tropical waters can be remarkable indicators for the "health" of the planet and for global climate change.

Reefs built up during the last half billion years were dominated primarily by skeletal invertebrates—the cnidarians (corals), poriferans (sponges), shelly animals such as brachiopods or molluscs, and echinoderms—but carbonate-secreting red and green algae, and microbial organisms (calcimicrobes, sometimes labelled as nanofossils) also played a critical encrusting and modifying role—sporadically even a prevailing one—in the fossil record. Reef organisms play a variety of roles. Some are constructors, whose skeletons pile up to build the main reef body. Others are recyclers, which bore into hard reef rock or burrow into its soft sediment for food or shelter. Still others, like the mobile fishes, arthropods, snails, or cephalopods, play more transitory roles, using the reef biota as food resource and reef crevices as hiding places from predators or storms. All may add their skeletons to the reef sedimentary edifice: reefs can grow rapidly into the surf zone, usually more

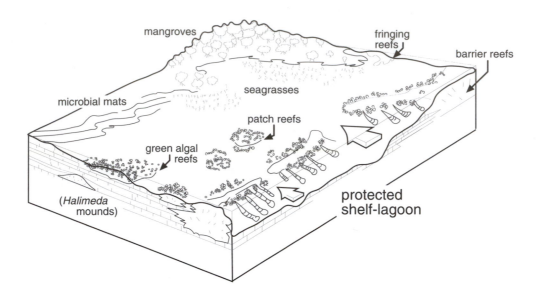

Figure 1. Reefs on tropical carbonate shelves: idealized diagram of reef development under optimum equatorial climates. Stress is confined to local factors such as siliciclastic sediment input, salinity, nutrient oversupply, and availability of hard substrates. Illustration by Catherine P. Sexton, after Copper (1994).

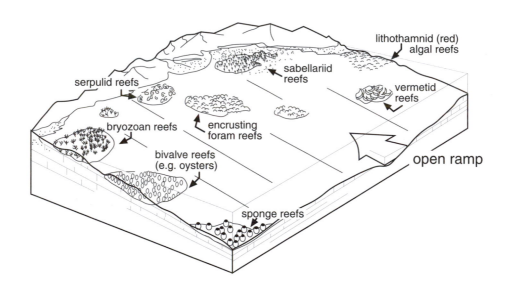

Figure 2. Reefs on cold-water carbonate ramps: idealized block diagram of reef potential in a stressed marginal environment, such as cold-water or deeper-water regimes. Reefs in cooler-water high latitudes feature groups that are temperature tolerant (e.g., lithothamniid red algae, bryozoans, small forams, siliceous sponges, mussel-oyster associations, vermetids, and tube-constructing sabellariid polychaetes). Illustration by Catherine P. Sexton, after Copper (1994).

rapidly than sea level rise, and spread out from the edges by exporting their aprons of sediments.

As many as 60 to 80 different phyla participate in the modern reef community, which makes it, on the large scale, more diverse than tropical rainforests, which have fewer than 30 phyla (dominated structurally by the vascular plants and in terms of species by the insects). Today, the most diverse reef communities are those of the Indonesian and Philippine Archipelagoes which are the home of more than 800 stony corals, compared with the Bar-

rier Reef's 500 species. The total number of organisms involved in reef development today is unknown, since many are still undescribed or poorly known. Reefs also may occur under more stressed conditions, such as cooler or deeper waters, higher latitudes, under abnormal ocean salinities, and higher rates of sedimentation (Figure 2). However, such reefs have a highly restricted, low-diversity biota of specialized sponges, bryozoans, molluscs, worms, or microbial elements. Also, such reefs are usually much smaller, involving low rates of calcium carbonate production.

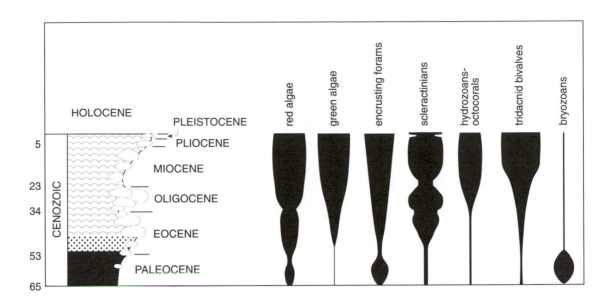

Figure 3. Distribution and abundance of the main reef-building groups of the Cainozoic (Paleocene-Holocene). Coral diversity and reef development appears to have suffered minor declines in the Late Eocene, Late Oligocene, and Pleistocene, but this is not yet adequately documented. During Oligocene time coral reefs appear to have been more widespread geographically (e.g., in the Mediterranean where they are absent today) and had greater latitudinal ranges than in the Holocene (Frost 1981). Holocene reefs appear to have recovered rapidly from glacial lowstands in sea level, but diversity losses are not known. Illustration by Catherine P. Sexton, after Copper (1989).

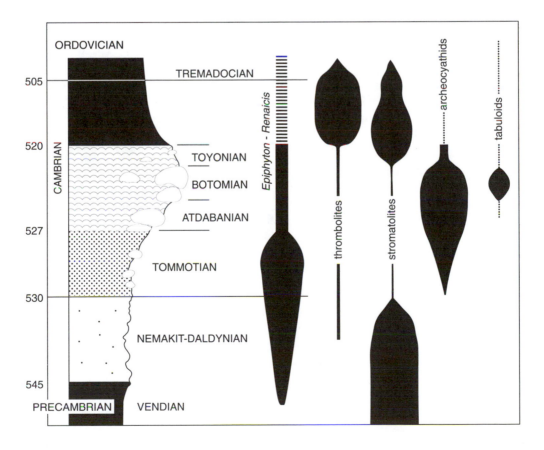

Figure 4. Distribution and approximate abundance of the main reef-building and inhabiting fauna and flora of the early Paleozoic (Tommotian-Tremadocian). Illustration by Catherine P. Sexton, after Copper (1989).

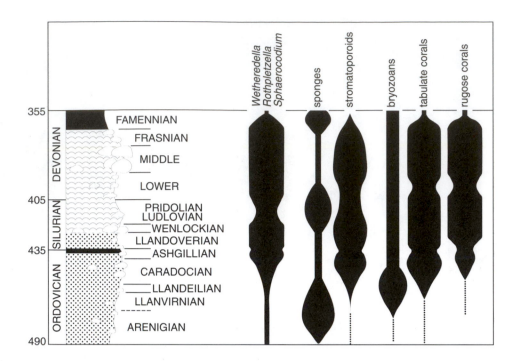

Figure 5. Distribution and approximate abundance of the main reef-building groups of the Mid-Paleozoic (Arenigian-Famennian). Illustration by Catherine P. Sexton, after Copper (1989).

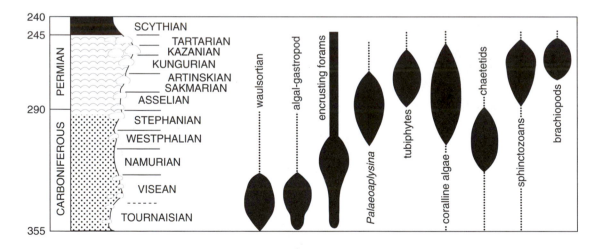

Figure 6. Distribution and approximate abundance of the main reef-building of the late Paleozoic. Illustration by Catherine P. Sexton, after West (1988).

Prior to the Cambrian evolution of eucaryotic organisms capable of secreting a hard skeleton (about 544 million years ago), reefs were built by the calcium carbonate precipitation and mediation activities of a range of encrusting and mat-building microbes (Figure 3). Especially important were some of the photosynthetic bacteria (the cyanobacterians, or "blue-greens"), which built structures commonly referred to as "stromatolites." Most cyanobacteria found in stromatolites were capable of binding, trapping, and to

some extent cementing minerals like calcium sufficiently to produce reefs elevated above the surrounding seafloor. In latest Precambrian time, some stromatolite-mound builders acquired the capacity to precipitate calcium carbonate within or around their tissues (e.g., the cyanobacteria, red algae, and possibly green algae). But the diversity of the Precambrian stromatolites declined in the last 100 million years or so of the Precambrian era. At the same time, the first soft-bodied animals appeared (Figure 4). Scholars have found

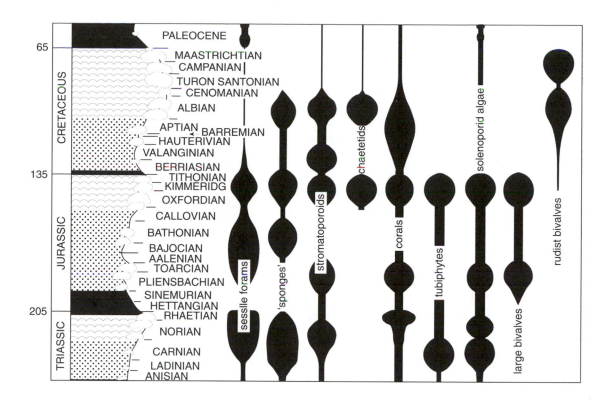

Figure 7. Distribution and approximate abundance of the main reef-building groups of the Mesozoic. Illustration by Catherine P. Sexton, after Stanley (1988).

the first recognizable "trace fossils" produced by animals in the form of trails made by organisms capable of plowing through organic-rich sediment or possibly digesting soft microbial mats. Nevertheless, the first stage of the Cambrian period (now called the Nemakit-Daldynian) is marked by only a few calcimicrobial reefs, since the first metazoans did not begin to build reefs until the arrival of archeocyath sponges in the Tommotian period. They were the first skeletal animals active in reef construction, producing very porous, cuplike, leafy, platy, or branching skeletons of granular calcite. Usually, archeocyath reefs were encrusted by dense communities of lime-precipitating microbes, some on the surface and many also in reef cavities. Some sponge reefs formed complexes many meters thick and kilometers long. They marked an explosive, worldwide development, since such early reefs are found on all modern continents. Other organisms also began to bore into, or live around or within the reefs (echinoderms, brachiopods, molluscans). Curiously, although some coral-like organisms built skeletons, they appear to have played only a trivial role in reefs at this time.

At the same time (the Early Cambrian), tube worms, which constructed mounds by sticking sand grains together, and which lacked the ability to secrete a lime skeleton, appeared widely in the fossil record. These animals built reeflike mounds or layers of cemented sand grains called "pipe-rock," or *Skolithos*. (A similar process can be seen in modern-day sabellariid worm reefs found on the temperate to tropical seashore; these worms are incapable of burrowing or boring.) This first global metazoan reef ecosystem collapsed

after 10 million years, a failed first experiment. The failure led to the first mass extinction of the invertebrate reef ecosystem (archeocyaths never returned), with the causes variously attributed to changes in upwellings of cold, nutrient-rich waters, megaburps of anoxia (oxygen starvation) from the ocean depths, or a global drop in sea level, which left the reef platforms open to erosion and exposure.

This first mass extinction of reef organisms was followed by an unusual, 50-million-year long recovery period. Tropical reefs were dominated by calcimicrobes, with lithistid sponges playing only a minor role, even though wide limestone platforms and interior sea lanes were widespread, and global climates were relatively warm. The reef ecosystem began to recover in the Middle Ordovician (about 475 million years ago), a time in which corals, lime-secreting sponges, red and green algae, and a host of skeleton-secreting organisms such as brachiopods, molluscs, and echinoderms began to diversify (Figure 5). By the Late Ordovician, most of the common reef elements were in place, characterizing what many have called the mid-Paleozoic shallow-water reef community. It included the tabulate and rugose corals, stromatoporoid sponges, and bryozoans, which secreted a basal skeleton. Both large- and microscopic-scale boring into reefs was common. During the Late Ordovician mass extinction, when there also were a set of glacial episodes in North Africa, reef building went through a relatively short interruption. On the whole, however, even though some elements were lost, the structure of the reef community was not affected greatly. By the Silurian and Devonian, at a time when global temperatures were on average 8 to 10 degrees centigrade warmer than today's and the world enjoyed "hothouse" climates, reefs expanded enormously into the higher latitudes (as high as 40° to 50°). Reef complexes extended for several thousand kilometers along continental shelves and inland seas, and reef diversity and complexity appears to have been even greater than today's. At this time, corals reached maximum diversity, featuring high rates of annual growth comparable to modern corals. Giant colony sizes exceeded several meters.

This mid-Paleozoic expansion lasted about 100 million years, coming to an end in the Late Devonian mass extinction, probably the second-most severe extinction affecting the reef ecosystem (only the one at the end of the Permian was more dramatic) (Figure 6). The Late Paleozoic, defined by the Carboniferous and Permian periods, marked a shift into global "icehouse" conditions initiated in the Late Devonian, with much lower levels of carbon dioxide in the atmosphere, higher oxygen, and the rise of rainforests and vascular plants on land. Coral reefs were almost universally absent, and the reef-building stromatoporoid sponges had vanished. Reefs reverted to microbial "mounds," featuring a range of bryozoans, sponges, some specialized reef-associated brachiopods, molluscans, and echinoderms. Such components were typical of stress-related reefs of the earlier Paleozoic, reefs that occurred in cooler, deeper, or sediment-laden waters. By the Late Permian, reefs featured a range of organisms, especially sponges, brachiopods, low-diversity rugose and tabulate corals, molluscs, and enigmatic tube builders, as well as red and green algae and calcimicrobial constructors. Two sharp extinction episodes at the end of the Permian brought this system to a close, wiping out the remaining corals. No reefs are known from the first stage in the succeeding Mesozoic (the Scythian), a worldwide barren oceanic benthic system featuring a "dead zone" marked only by some stromatolites.

The Triassic saw the rise of the "modern" reef ecosystem, which has continued for more than 230 million years to the present day, with some interruptions only at the end of the Triassic and Cretaceous (Figure 7). By Late Triassic time, the scleractinian corals were in place, playing lead roles in reef construction alongside a range of sponges (including the stromatoporoids, which reappeared), large bivalves, gastropods, echinoderms, red and green algae, and calcimicrobial encrusters. In the tropical Tethys ocean of the Late Jurassic and Cretaceous, giant rudist bivalves played a major reef role, suppressing the corals, but these bivalves became extinct globally sometime before the last dinosaurs van-

ished. The Cenozoic shifted the Earth into an "icehouse" mode, with oscillating climates that became most severe in the Pleistocene. The Ice Ages reduced the Caribbean reef province to lower-diversity, older, long-lived taxa, but the Indo-Pacific reefs continued to flourish.

PAUL COPPER

See also Algae; Anthozoans; Brachiopods; Bryozoans; Echinoderms; Metazoan Phyla, Minor; Problematic Animals; Skeletized Microorganisms; Sponges and Sponge-like Organisms

Works Cited

Copper, P. 1989. Enigmas in Phanerozoic reef development. *Memoirs of the Association of Australian Paleontologists* 8:371–85.

———. 1994. Reefs under stress: The fossil record. *Courier Forschungsinstitut Senckenberg* 172:87–94.

Frost, S.H. 1981. Oligocene reef coral biofacies of the Vicentin, northeast Italy. *Special Publications, Society of Economic Paleontologists and Minerologists, Tulsa* 30:483–539.

Stanley, G.D. 1988. The history of Early Mesozoic reef communities. A three-step process. *Palaios* 3:170–83.

West, R.R. 1988. Temporal changes in Carboniferous reef mound communities. *Palaios* 3:152–69.

Further Reading

Geldsetzer, H.H.J., N.P. James, and G.E. Tebbutt. 1988. *Reefs: Canada and Adjacent Areas*. Memoirs of the Canadian Society of Petroleum Geologists, 13. Calgary: Canadian Society of Petroleum Geologists.

Fagerstrom, J.A. 1987. *The Evolution of Reef Communities*. New York: Wiley Interscience.

Lessios, H.A., and I.G. MacIntyre (eds.). 1996. *Proceedings of the 8th International Coral Reef Symposium, Panama*. Panama City: Universidad de Panama.

Perejon, A., and J. Comas-Rengifo (eds.). 1997. *Proceedings of the 7th International Symposium on Fossil Cnidaria and Porifera*. 2 vols. Salamanca: Real Sociedad Española de Historia Natural.

Scholle, P.A., D.G. Bebout, and C.H. Moore. 1983. *Carbonate Depositional Environments*. American Association of Petroleum Geologists, Memoir 33. Tulsa, Oklahoma: American Association of Petroleum Geologists.

REPRODUCTIVE STRATEGIES: PLANTS

Asexual Reproduction

Plants may reproduce sexually or asexually (the latter literally, without sex; also called vegetative propagation or vegetative reproduction). In some plants both modes of reproduction occur, while in others only one or the other takes place. In asexual reproduction only mitotic cell divisions occur, therefore the resulting offspring

is genetically identical with the single parent plant, it is a clone of the parent. Asexual reproduction may take many forms. Perhaps the best known mode is found in the cultivated strawberry plant that grows runners or stolons. These are slender stems that grow along the soil surface. At every second node of the runner, adventitious roots may form and then a new shoot develops, which continues to grow a runner. The internode between the new plants disintegrates or is cut by the gardener, and the new plants are separated from the parent plant and are on their own. In many grasses, horizontal underground stems, the rhizomes, grow out from the parent plant and give rise to new plants in an analogous way to that of the runners. Each node of the rhizome can produce a new plant and hence form a dense lawn. Such lawns may be highly desirable, but rhizomes are also produced by weeds that may produce undesirable, difficult to control, noxious infestations. Other modified, underground stems, such as tuber (potato), corm (glads, Gladiolus), bulb (tulip, onion) are also vegetative reproductive organs that are equipped with storage products for the new plant. Rooting of stem cuttings is a generally practiced form of asexual reproduction for many cultivated plants.

Roots often produce adventitious stems, suckers, that produce new plants. Whole colonies of raspberries, blackberries, apples, cherries, or quaking aspen may be formed from suckers that originate from a single parent plant. Taproots that are not entirely pulled out from the soil, as may happen in weeding dandelions, give rise to a new plant. More useful suckers are the seedless banana plants that are propagated entirely from adventitious shoots.

In addition to stems and roots, leaves can also be involved in asexual reproduction, although this occurs less often. The most familiar example is the appropriately called "mother-of-thousands" plant, *Kalanchoe daigremontiana,* a common house plant. In mature plants, along the margin of the fleshy leaves, numerous miniature plantlets develop, complete with roots and a shoot. When they drop onto the soil, new Kalanchoe plants start to grow. Begonia leaves may be rooted by cutting the midrib of a leaf and placing it on moist soil. Roots will develop at the cut followed by the formation of a shoot.

Even seeds may be produced asexually, in a process called apomixis. A completely normal seed is formed, but the embryo arises not from the fertilized egg but from a vegetative cell in the embryo sac of a flowering plant. Provided they come from desirable stock, such seeds can be very valuable because they are clones of the parent and therefore produce genetically identical offspring. Kentucky bluegrass varieties are perhaps the most familiar example. Some citrus species and some sorghum varieties also belong in this category, as well as many hawthorn species and the dandelions.

Plants that reproduce without seeds (mosses and liverworts, as well as ferns and their allies) often have special vegetative reproductive structures, such as bulbils or gemmae, or as in the walking fern, the leaf tips that may form roots and then a new shoot. In algae, asexual reproduction occurs through mitospores, spores that arise from mitotic cell division.

Asexual reproduction gives rise to offspring, often faster than sexual reproduction, and the progeny is an exact genetic replicate, suited to its environment. Asexual reproduction can have advantages in crop plants for which humans prepare a specific and uniform environment in which these plants will thrive.

If one accepts that meiosis and the fusion of gametes are integral to sexual reproduction, then meiospores, spores that result from meiosis, must not be considered "asexual" spores because they give rise to the gamete-producing plants or structures. The spore mother cell in the sporophyte produces meiospores that then divide by mitosis to form, for instance, the male gametophyte, the pollen grains in seed plants. It is the haploid pollen grain that forms the sperms, the male gametes. Without the meiospore-producing sporophyte and the gamete-producing gametophyte sexual reproduction could not occur in plants. This is discussed in greater detail in the next section.

Sexual Reproduction: Life History and Alternation of Generations

There is no reasonable explanation for the evolution and retention of the sexual process as a general feature of eukaryotes (organisms composed of cells with nuclei and organelles). The generally accepted hypothesis—that sex increases adaptation to a changing environment—has been challenged by results with budding yeast, *Saccharomyces cerevisiae,* showing that vegetatively reproducing populations (e.g., reproduction via budding) have increased mean fitness in environments that require new adaptations. The most recent hypothesis states that purging deleterious mutations may be the main function of sex (Zeyl and Bell 1997).

Sexual reproduction in plants can be traced back to algal precursors in which the gametophyte stage of development produces flagellated gametes that unite to form a diploid zygote—a single cell that has two sets of chromosomes, one set from each gamete. The timing and location of meiosis is critical for the life cycle of the organism. (1) Meiosis may take place with the zygotic division, resulting in haploid organisms in which any cell may function as gamete. The zygote is the only diploid cell in these organisms (many algae) with a monobiontic life history (Figure 1A). (2) Meiosis may be delayed until after the zygote has undergone mitoses and forms a diploid organism, the sporophyte. Meiospores (spores produced through meiosis) are formed on the sporophyte. They germinate and form the haploid gametophyte thus completing the life cycle of a dibiontic organism with the mitotic production of gametes (some algae, all plants) (Figure 1B).

The sequence of a gametophyte followed by a sporophyte constitutes the alternation of generations (AG). Gametophyte and sporophyte may be of equal size and morphology (isomorphic AG), which occurs only in algae. Gametophyte and sporophyte of different size and morphology (heteromorphic AG) are present in all cryptogams (plants without seeds), including some algae, and in all seed plants. The dibiontic life cycle has been conserved throughout the evolution of plants. It is still evident in modern angiosperms (flowering plants), albeit with a greatly reduced gametophytic phase: seven cells (eight nuclei) in the female gametophyte and three cells in the male gametophyte. The large, multicellular sporophyte is the paradigm of a plant. Beginning with the vascular cryptogams, the sporophyte evolved to become the dominant phase of the life cycle, and the gametophyte became reduced in size and life span. A separate organism in most algae and in the vascular cryptogams, the gametophyte is retained as a part of the sporophyte of the seed plants, depending on it for nutrition; it is the ephemeral generation. In the mosses and liverworts, however, the gametophyte is the persistent generation, and the smaller sporophyte with the spore capsule depends on the gametophyte for structural support and nutrition.

The Dependence on Liquid Water in the Sexual Reproduction of Cryptogams and Some Seed Plants

Presumably, sexual reproduction evolved in a watery environment through which gametes with flagella (long slender structures that propel the cell with a whiplike motion) swam to locate gametes of the opposite mating type. One gametic type, which increased in size and became sessile (fixed in place), is called the female gamete. The smaller, mobile gamete, the male gamete (sperm or spermatozoid) retained the flagella. The male gamete must swim to reach the female gamete. As a retention of an algal trait, the flagella are found on the male gametes of the early land plants, liverworts (Hepaticophyta), hornworts (Anthocerotophyta), mosses (Bryophyta), clubmosses (*Lycopodium, Selaginella,* and other Lycophyta), horsetails (*Equisetum,* Sphenophyta), and ferns (Pteridophyta). These taxa (groups; singular, taxon) depend, therefore, on liquid water for their sperm to swim into the neck canal cells of the archegonium (female sex organ) to reach the egg cell, the female gamete. As a separate organism, gametophytes grow close to the ground where water for the sperm would be available.

Some seed plants still depend on flagellated sperm for reproduction, showing their link to cryptogams and precursor algae. It also demonstrates the conservative nature of the sexual process. In cycads (Cycadophyta) a relatively short pollen tube (2 to 4 millimeters) digests its way through the tissue of the megasporangium and discharges its two sperm into the archegonial chamber. The sperm, the largest in the plant kingdom—*Zamia chigua* sperm are approximately 0.4 millimeters long and equipped with approximately 70,000 spirally arranged flagella—swim in the fluid derived from the burrowing activity of the pollen tube to the egg cell. The journey is aided by protrusions from the egg cell, which draw the sperm into the egg cytoplasm. In contrast to cryptogams, where the liquid comes from external sources—a dew or rain drop may suffice—in these seed plants the required liquid medium is derived from the sporophyte by the disintegration of megasporangial cells. Since availability of water is not reliable in nature, these taxa, which flourished in the Mesozoic, some 200 to 250 million years after plants first invaded land, recreate a bit of the "primordial sea" for the union of their gametes. Plants did not gain independence from liquid water for sexual reproduction until the evolution of syphonogamy in conifers, a process in which the pollen tube delivers sperm directly to the egg cell.

Wind Dispersal of Spores

While water was crucial for sexual union of flagellate gametes, wind-dispersed "meiospores," which germinate, develop into a multicellular male gametophyte, and produce gametes, inherited the earth. Lightweight spores of the vascular cryptogams ride the air currents and may be disseminated far from the parent plant to invade new territory.

Pollination Strategies

Wind and Water Pollination

Pollen grains of seed plants and flowering plants are evolved from meiospores and contain an immature or mature male gameto-phyte, which in angiosperms consists of only three cells. Some pollen is especially equipped for wind dissemination, such as the characteristically winged pollen of pines (Coniferophyta). However, the pollen of many species lack wings, including the early seed plants and the last plants to evolve, the angiosperms. These plants, such as the grasses, sedges, oaks, birches, and cottonwoods, depend on air currents for pollen transport. Because most pollen can travel only relatively short distances (less than 100 meters), wind-pollinated plants usually form dense stands and produce massive amounts of pollen. The large areas of grasslands (savanna, prairie) and conifer and birch forests of the northern temperate zone attest to how well wind pollination works.

Water plants, such as *Vallisneria,* have solved the pollination problem in a most ingenious way. The plant produces male and female flowers. Numerous male flowers with two stamens are released, float on the water like small boats, and carry the pollen to the female flowers, which float on the water surface with their stigmas outward.

Pollination by Animals

Animals that transfer pollen precisely from plant to plant, even those widely separated, clearly serve an important function in the sexual reproduction of many angiosperms and in some gymnosperms. The coevolution (evolution of two species where each affects the other's evolutionary changes) of plants and pollen carriers, mostly insects, but also other arthropods (e.g., spiders), some birds and a few mammals, has played a major role in the rapid diversification and geographic spread of the angiosperms. This led to these plants' evolutionary success. As a result of plant-animal interaction, an increased specialization of flowers and of their pollinators has become established.

Animal Pollination in Flowering Plants

In angiosperms, unique features of flowers and fruits are the basis for the evolutionary success of their sexual reproduction. The interactions between animals and flowers allow immobile plants to transfer their gametes over long distances and thereby avoid inbreeding. The precision of pollen transfer depends on coordinated development and activity of plants and animals. Key elements are the biochemical, structural, and ecological characteristics of the flowers, features that attract pollen vectors (pollinators) at the appropriate time of day and season.

Bees—some 20,000 species—are the archetypical pollinators and play a dominant role in angiosperm reproduction. The colored petals of flowers, especially those containing carotenoids (pigments) that reflect both visible and ultraviolet light resulting in "bee's purple," are highly visible and attractive to bees. Characteristic stripes and dots, not unlike landing aids on airport runways, direct insects to "landing sites" and nectaries. Nectar is the main reason for a bee to visit flowers, because nectar constitutes one of the bee's major food resources. Pollen, high in proteins, is also foraged for and gathered as a food resource by some pollinators. All vectors, however, transport pollen to other flowers of the same species, which is the main objective for the plants but only incidental to the vectors.

A

Monobiontic Life History

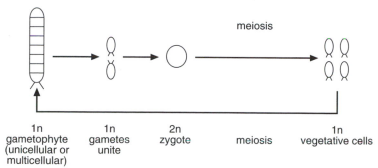

B

Dibiontic Life History

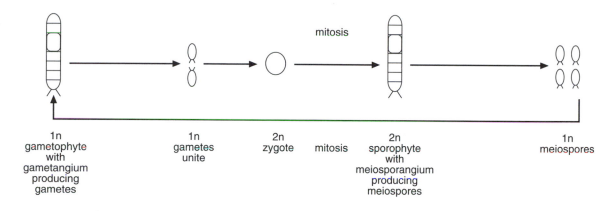

Figure 1. Monobiontic and dibiontic life histories. *A,* Monobiontic life history. The haploid (1n) generation may be either unicellular, or, as shown, multicellular. In a unicellular gametophyte the entire cell is changed into a gametangium. In a multicellular gametophyte a specific cell(s) is changed into a gametangium. Gametes are formed by mitosis. Haploid gametes unite to form a diploid (2n) zygote that divides by meiosis. The resulting haploid cells form new gametophytes. Note: in contrast to the monobiontic haploid life history shown here, which occurs in most algae, in the monobiontic diploid life history characteristic of mammals and some algae (diatoms), all cells except the gametes are diploid. The gametes in the monobiontic diploid life history are, therefore, produced as a result of meiosis. *B,* Dibiontic life history. The haploid (1n) gametophyte differentiates a specific cell(s) as gametangium that forms gametes by mitosis. Gametes unite to form a diploid (2n) zygote that divides by mitosis to form a diploid (2n) multicellular sporophyte. In the sporophyte, specific cell(s) are differentiated into a meiosporangium that produces meiospores as a result of meiosis. The haploid (1n) meiospores divide by mitosis and form the haploid gametophyte. Shown in the figure is an isomorphic alternation of generations in which gametophyte and sporophyte are of equal size and morphology. A heteromorphic alternation of generations—gametophyte and sporophyte of different size and morphology—is characteristic for some algae and all plants. Excepting the mosses, the large, multicellular sporophyte represents "plants." Illustration by Catherine P. Sexton.

Some flowers have special mechanisms that assure that the pollen on visiting animals comes into contact with the stigma, which houses the female reproductive structures (Bernhardt 1996). Anthers, which bear pollen, and styles, which connect the stigma and ovary, are so positioned that they touch the animal in search for nectar, the reward offered for visiting the plant. Some plants (e.g., *Kalmia latifolia,* or mountain laurel, and *Sparmannia*) are sensitive to touch. Upon contact with insects, the stamens are "fired," dusting the visitors with pollen. In *Mimulus*

cardinalis, the stigma lobes fold rapidly when touched, trapping pollen.

Many flowers are highly scented, especially in night-blooming plants, and the odor serves to attract and direct nocturnal animals, such as moths, bats, and certain marsupials. In contrast to the highly colored flowers that attract bees and butterflies in daylight, night-blooming flowers are often white, since color is not visible in the dark. Flowers adapted for bat-pollination often are suspended from long stalks, open at dusk, and have a mouselike smell.

Beetles forage mostly for pollen, since their mouth parts are usually unsuitable for sucking nectar. They visit flowers that lack nectaries, and are often dull in color but are strongly scented.

Pure bright red flowers are almost invisible to bees but highly conspicuous and attractive to hummingbirds. These flowers are specialized for hummingbird-pollination—they have a deep floral tube and copious amounts of nectar. A visit to a single one of such flowers would satisfy an insect's food requirement; therefore, it would not need to visit another flower, which means cross pollination would not occur. That is genetically undesirable. Therefore, the nectaries in "hummingbird flowers" are located at the end of the long corolla tube, out of reach for most insects. Since the sense of smell is not well-developed in hummingbirds, the flowers they pollinate are usually not scented.

Reproduction is so important that plants have evolved deceptive practices to entice pollinators. *Stapeli nobilis,* the carrion plant, looks and smells like rotten flesh. Some fleshflies even lay eggs into the Stapelia flowers, even though the larvae will not find sufficient food there. *Aristolochia* has large mottled flowers that mimic gregarious flies, thereby attracting others. The *Arum* (skunk cabbage) inflorescence (cluster of flowers) forms a temporary fly trap. The temperature in the structure rises above that of the surrounding air. This increases the emission of scent. The imprisoned flies crawl over the stigmas, pollinating them. The next day, the anthers open, and the flies, having picked up new pollen, are released from confinement and fly to the next *Arum* flower.

The prize for deception goes to certain orchids that drug the pollinating insect with narcotic fragrances. As soon as pollination is accomplished, the scent abruptly ceases, and the insect recovers and escapes. In the bucket orchid, the bucket-shaped lip is filled with a watery secretion. The pollinating insect falls into the fluid, escapes through a trap door that ensures transfer of pollen to the stigma. The most bizarre pollination mechanism, however, occurs in certain North African, Australian, and European orchids. The petals of *Ophrys tenthredinifera* are formed and colored to resemble a female wasp. Male wasps, emerging from their pupae earlier than the females, are lured to the orchid flower, some of which even emit the insect-specific pheromone, and try to copulate with the flowers. All the males accomplish is the spreading of orchid pollen.

The majority of flowering plants are hermaphrodites—both stamens and pistils develop within the same flower. Plants employ several methods to prevent self-pollination (selfing), in which a plant's own sperm joins with the plant's own eggs. In some plants the physical structures of the pistil and the stamen prevent fertilization. In other plants, stamens and pistils mature at different times. Animal pollination helps assure cross-pollination (outcrossing). Within a self-incompatible plant, pollen is prevented from transferring its gametes to the egg cell. On the other hand, while outcrossing is advantageous, many plant species are self-pollinators. Not needing to attract animals, often these plants have small, inconspicuous, nonscented flowers. In some plants the flowers do not open for pollination. Selfing species avoid the cost of advertising that species with showy floral displays incur. Therefore selfing can be advantageous, especially in species well adapted to their habitats. Also, selfing produces more genetically uniform progeny than outcrossing. Many important crop plants, for which growers carefully create a uniform habitat, are self-pollinating. Unfortunately, so are the weeds that accompany the crops and compete with them.

Strong selective pressure for sexual reproduction in angiosperms has led to the evolution of floral and fruit displays unparalleled in nature. Measured by success, producing elaborate floral structures and showy, nutrient-rich fruits is well worth the biological costs. The advantage of attracting vectors by floral displays is so high that other organisms (e.g., fungi) have usurped it. The smut fungus *Microbotryum violaceum (Ustilago violacea)* completes its life cycle in the anthers of its host plants. Insects visiting the flowers unknowingly transfer fungal spores from diseased plants to healthy hosts, thereby disseminating disease instead of the plant's gametes (Ruddat et al. 1991). The pollen vector is misappropriated as an agent for spreading a venereal disease. Similarly, the rust fungus *Puccinia monoica* inhibits flowering in its host species of *Arabis* by drastically modifying the upper vegetative leaves into a showy yellow structure that mimics the flowers of unrelated species. With their color, smell, and nectar, these pseudoflowers attract insects that transfer the nonmotile fungal gametes to other host plants (Roy 1993).

Fruit and Seed Dispersal Strategies

The evolution of fruits, as spectacular as those of flowers, is integral to the reproductive strategies of flowering plants. Wind, water, and animals, including humans, participate in the dissemination of fruits and seeds. Several examples will demonstrate the diversity of techniques.

Environmental elements are common dispersal methods. Orchid seeds lack a fully developed embryo, so the seeds are tiny and light and can be carried by air currents for miles. Other plants' seeds are enveloped in fruits that form a plume or pappus (e.g., dandelion or thistle) and are wind-dispersed. Outer coverings of woolly hairs (cottonwood, willow) or the formation of wings (elm, ash, or maple) all are adaptations for wind dispersal. Water also serves as an effective agent for dispersal. Coconuts, equipped with a buoyant fibrous covering, can drift over long distances in the ocean. Water dispersal of fruits from plants that grow on or near beaches is one important way that plants colonize islands.

Physical features also aid dispersal. Fleshy fruits, often shiny and brightly colored, highly attractive to animals, provide them with nutrition. The seeds within the fruit pass undigested through the gut and are dropped with the feces. Because of special adaptations, passage through the alimentary canal does not damage the seed; on the contrary, it aids germination. Birds disseminate seeds in this manner, miles away from their feeding place. Other fruits, such as acorns, are collected and buried by squirrels. Since they do not dig up all of their cache, the seeds germinate and grow. Other fruits are equipped with hooks, hairs, or sticky layers that attach them to fur or feathers to be carried away from the parent plant.

The selective pressure for seed dispersal is so strong that some plants literally shoot their seeds away. *Impatiens pallida* (touch-me-not), *Ecballium elaterium* (shooting cucumber), and *Hamamelis virginiana* (witch hazel) explosively disperse their seeds over considerable distances to allow the offspring to invade new places.

Most seeds are disseminated in their dormant or quiescent state, prior to germination. Mangrove seeds, however, follow a very unusual pattern. They must germinate on the parent tree for successful dissemination. As the new plants develop, they produce a primary root that is about 30 centimeters long. When the new plant is released from the parent plant, the primary root plunges arrowlike into the mudflat. Seedlings that fail to be anchored securely by their root will be carried to their death in the ocean.

Humans are perhaps the most active seed dispersal agents, planting millions of acres each year and cultivating the seedlings to produce mature, reproducing plants. Many cultivated species (e.g., maize) are completely dependent on man for propagation and would not survive in the wild.

Lacking the advantage of mobility and courtship behavior, plants nevertheless can exercise mate choice through animal pollen vectors and self-incompatibility, as well as being able to invade territories far removed from the place of their origin by a large variety of seed dispersal mechanisms.

MANFRED RUDDAT

Works Cited

Bernhardt, P. 1996. Anther adaptations in animal pollination. *In* W.G. D'Arcy and R.C. Keating (eds.), *The Anther: Form, Function, and Phylogeny.* Cambridge and New York: Cambridge University Press.

Roy, B.A. 1993. Floral mimicry by a plant pathogen. *Nature* 362:56–58.

Ruddat, M., J. Kokontis, L. Birch, E.D. Garber, K.S. Chiang, J. Campanella, and H. Dai. 1991. Interactions of *Microbotryum violaceum (Ustilago violacea)* with its host plant Silene alba. *Plant Science* 80:157–65.

Zeyl, C., and G. Bell. 1997. The advantage of sex in evolving yeast populations. *Nature* 388:465–68.

Further Reading:

Asker, Sven E. and Lenn Jerling. 1992. *Apomixis in Plants.* Boca Raton, Florida: CRC Press.

Doust, Jon L. and Lesley L. Doust. 1988. *Plant Reproductive Ecology: Patterns and Strategies.* Oxford: Oxford University Press.

Farley, John. 1982. *Gametes and Spores.* Baltimore: Johns Hopkins University Press.

Fenner, Michael. 1985. *Seed Ecology.* New York: Chapman and Hall.

Jackson, Jeremy B.C., Leo W. Buss, and Robert E. Cook. 1985. *Population Biology and Evolution of Clonal Organisms.* New Haven, Conn.: Yale University Press.

Richards, A.J. 1986. *Plant Breeding Systems.* London: Allen and Unwin.

REPRODUCTIVE STRATEGIES: VERTEBRATES

The reproductive physiology of extinct vertebrates can be inferred either from the fossil record or, more consistently, from deductions based on the physiology of extant (modern-day) vertebrates. It is possible to infer evolutionary trends in reproductive physiology, ranging from the ancestral pattern of external fertilization typical of the earliest vertebrates, to more derived (evolved) behaviors and conditions (e.g., internal fertilization, live birth, or altricially, which is the birth of offspring that are helpless and require much parental care).

External fertilization of the egg is typical of living agnathan (jawless) vertebrates and most of the primitive gnathostome (jawed) vertebrate groups, including the bony fishes and amphibians. During the breeding season, today's agnathans, which include hagfish and lampreys, shed eggs and sperm from the gonads directly into the coelom, or body cavity, where they combine to form gametes. Gametes then exit the body via a series of genital pores at the rear of the body. After fertilization takes place, no further parental care is provided. In this pattern called "oviparous," the eggs are fertilized and development takes place outside the body. This method was probably present in the earliest Paleozoic vertebrates, the jawless ostracoderms.

Internal Fertilization and the Evolution of Viviparity

In all jawed vertebrates the primitive open reproductive system is replaced by a series of tubes or ducts that direct the flow of eggs and sperm outside the body. Male gnathostomes possess an entirely closed system that leads from the testes directly to the major sperm-carrying duct (vas or ductus deferens); in females, eggs are still shed from the ovaries into the coelom. However, the female system is functionally closed, since the eggs are nearly always directed immediately into the funnel-like opening of the reproductive tract.

Internal fertilization is practiced by some bony fish and amphibians, all extant cartilaginous fishes (sharks, rays, and chimaeras), and all amniote vertebrates (those that lay shelled eggs or whose ancestors did). Fertilization in these groups is accomplished by introduction of sperm into the female reproductive tract by means of an "intromittent organ," such as the claspers of male sharks, the "tail" of the frog *Ascaphus,* the hemipenes of lizards and snakes, and the mammalian penis. The earliest physical evidence of internal fertilization comes from well-preserved Paleozoic fossils of sharks and placoderms (Long 1995). Fossils from both of these taxa show evidence of intromittent organs similar to the claspers of living sharks.

Internal fertilization allowed vertebrates to separate the act of mating from egg-laying. Delaying the deposition of eggs allowed females to search for a protected environment in which to incubate the fertilized eggs. Extended retention of fertilized eggs, accompanied by embryo development within the female reproductive tract, is generally agreed to have been the necessary intermediate step leading to the evolution of live birth. Moreover, internal fertilization enabled sperm storage and delayed fertilization in some groups, thus permitting the female to wait for optimal environmental conditions before laying eggs.

Live birth (including ovoviviparity and viviparity) has evolved numerous times in all vertebrate classes that practice internal fertilization, with the notable exception of turtles, crocodiles, birds, and presumably the dinosaurs (Shine 1989). In ovoviviparity the fertilized egg is retained within the female's reproductive tract until birth; development is supported by a yolk supply adequate to fulfill the embryo's nutritional requirements. A likely selective advantage of ovoviviparity was that the mother was able to regulate behaviorally and/or physiologically the embryo's physical environment, increasing survivorship of offspring and reproductive success. The young of live-bearing vertebrates are generally larger, fewer, and are born at an advanced stage relative to those of most oviparous species, a factor possibly further increasing juvenile survivorship. The evolution of ovoviviparity was undoubtedly a crucial intermediate step in the evolution of true viviparity.

True viviparity, involving a placenta, an organ that enabled a vascular exchange between the mother and developing fetus, has evolved independently in several vertebrate taxa, including some sharks, squamate reptiles, and all placental (eutherian) mammals. In the squamates, placentation has evolved multiple times in several families of snakes and at least one lizard family (Goin et al. 1978). The evolution of homeothermy (the ability to internally regulate body temperature) within Late Permian therapsids (mammal-like reptiles that were probably oviparous, as are modern monotreme mammals) and glandular secretions of a nutritious "milk" by the mother are thought to have been two "preadaptations" that led to the evolution of mammalian viviparity (Packard et al. 1989). Marsupials appear to represent an intermediate stage: All are live bearing, but placentation is limited, and young are born in an embryonic state, then develop in a pouch supported by the marsupial (epipubic) bones.

Parental Care and the Evolution of Altriciality

Neonates (the newborn) of both egg-laying and viviparous vertebrates exhibit a continuum of developmental maturity, ranging from highly "precocial" (mobile and relatively independent of parental care) to highly "altricial" (developmentally immature and entirely dependent on parental care). Precociality, with varied degrees of parental care, is typical of lower vertebrates and is the primitive condition. The evolution of extended parental care among precocial taxa appears to have been the primary prerequisite for the evolution of altriciality. Altriciality among living vertebrates is limited to birds and mammals.

Among living birds, neonatal development ranges from super-precocial (Australasian mound builders and the black duck) to highly altricial (all song birds), with a range of intermediate states. Precociality is common among more primitive avian orders. Most altricial birds are relatively small and therefore must produce eggs with relatively little yolk. Additionally, while inaide

the mother, smaller eggs place fewer constraints on flight in small birds. However, reduced yolk supply dictates that young must hatch in a relatively premature and helpless condition. Consequently, altricial birds generally nest in protected environments, such as cavities or trees, which protect the helpless hatchlings from predators. Post-hatching growth is rapid compared to precocial birds.

Dinosaurs have a close evolutionary relationship to birds, and it has been suggested on the basis of skeletal information that at least some dinosaurs may have exhibited birdlike altricial behavior, with nest-bound neonates that were developmentally immature. However, recent analysis of known embryonic dinosaur skeletons indicates that the degree of ossification (bone-formation) of the pelvic bones was identical to that of extant precocial reptiles and birds, implying that these neonate dinosaurs were most likely precocial (Geist and Jones 1996). This conclusion is based upon the fact that mobility at hatching requires a rigid site of attachment for hindlimb muscles. This is provided by the well-ossified pelvic girdles typical of precocial birds and reptiles. Therefore, it seems likely that avian altriciality is a derived condition that probably evolved during the Tertiary adaptive radiation of birds.

Developmental status of neonatal mammals, like birds, ranges from precocial to altricial. Fully altricial neonate mammals (i.e., tree-shrews, numerous rodents, and insectivores) are developmentally immature at birth but grow and reach sexual maturity rapidly. Mammalian altriciality seems to have evolved as a strategy to increase fecundity among populations subject to high predation pressures and/or limited seasonal availability of resources (Vaughn 1986).

NICHOLAS R. GEIST

See also Egg, Amniote; Paleoethology; for discussion of reproduction in invertebrates, see particular invertebrate taxa

Works Cited

Geist, N.R., and T.D. Jones. 1996. Juvenile skeletal structure and the reproductive habits of dinosaurs. *Science* 272:712–14.

Goin, C.J., O.B. Goin, and G.R. Zug. 1978. *Introduction to Herpetology.* New York: Freeman.

Long, J.A. 1995. *The Rise of Fishes.* Baltimore, Maryland: Johns Hopkins University Press.

Packard, G.C., R.P. Elinson, J. Gavaud, L.J. Guillette Jr., J. Lombardi, J. Schindler, R. Shine, H.C. Tyndale-Biscoe, M.H. Wake, F.D.J. Xavier, and Z. Yaron. 1989. Group report: How are reproductive systems integrated and how has viviparity evolved? *In* D.B. Wake and G. Roth (eds.), *Complex Organismal Functions: Integration and Evolution in Vertebrates.* New York and Chichester: Wiley.

Shine, R. 1989. Ecological influences on the evolution of vertebrate viviparity. *In* D.B. Wake and G. Roth (eds.), *Complex Organismal Functions: Integration and Evolution in Vertebrates.* New York and Chichester: Wiley.

Vaughan, T.A. 1986. *Mammalogy.* 3rd ed., Philadelphia: Saunders.

RESPIRATION

All animals convert food molecules into the energy required for physical activity, through a metabolic process called "cellular respiration." This process requires oxygen, which vertebrates acquire in a variety of means that involves structures such as gills and lungs. The more active an organism is, the more energy is required, and thus the more oxygen is required. The need for an adequate oxygen supply has been one of the evolutionary pressures on all living things. The evolution of vertebrates reflects a trend toward increasingly active lifestyles that required high metabolic rates and correspondingly high demands for oxygen uptake.

The ancestors of vertebrates are thought to have been small aquatic creatures that absorbed oxygen directly from the surrounding water through their skin surface (similar to amphioxus, an extant (present-day) member of the group Cephalochordata). The earliest vertebrates were jawless fishes (agnatha) that had internal gills; these structures increased the surface area available for gas exchange (the absorption of oxygen from water and disposal of carbon dioxide, a "waste product" of metabolism). A muscular branchial basket pumped a constant flow of fresh water over the gills. Agnathans expel water from the pharynx through muscle contraction, but they take in water by elastic recoil of the branchial basket. In the evolution of the jawed fishes (Gnathostomata), the gill pump became more effective. Inspiratory muscles evolved to expand the pharynx, the expiratory muscles were expanded and strengthened, and jaw adductor muscles were added to close and seal the mouth during forceful expiration. These adductor muscles attached to the frontmost (anterior) branchial arch (mandibular arch), and in response, this arch became larger and more robust. The enlarged mandibular arch with strong adductor muscles was then co-opted for feeding; the arch moved forward and became the jaws of gnathostome fishes (Mallatt 1996). The oral cavity now drove respiration.

In early bony fishes a single, bony element evolved that covered the gill cavity (the operculum), which contributed an "opercular pump" to the oral cavity–based "buccal pump" already present in gnathostomes. In addition, the larval forms of early bony fishes had external gills; such gills are present today in the larvae of polypterid fishes, lungfishes, and some amphibians.

Lungs and the ability to breathe air also evolved early in the history of vertebrates (Liem 1988; Packard 1974). Soft tissues such as lungs rarely fossilize; thus, we must rely on the distribution of lungs in extant vertebrates to infer when lungs evolved (although there is one contested report of fossil lungs in a placoderm fish, *Bothriolepis*) (Denison 1941). Lungs are present in extant, archaic ray-finned fishes (Actinopterygii), lungfishes (Dipnoi), and tetrapods, indicating that lungs were present in the common ancestor of bony fishes (Osteichthyes) approximately 420 million years ago (Figure 1). This pattern indicates that lungs evolved first in aquatic animals that also had gills and could obtain oxygen from water. Lungs potentially served three simultaneous functions in early bony fishes. First, the ability to utilize atmospheric oxygen may have allowed them to invade new environments, such as tropical swamps, in which the water was warm and stagnant and thus contained little oxygen. Second, the presence of air-filled lungs would have increased buoyancy, improving the swimming ability of heavily armored fishes, such as the paleoniscoids. Third, the presence of lungs may have increased the oxygen available to the heart, thus allowing increased activity levels in early fishes (Farmer 1997).

Along with lungs, early bony fishes must also have evolved a mechanism for pumping air into their lungs. Studies of extant, air-breathing fishes indicate that they probably used a pulse pump (mouth pump) for lung ventilation. In pulse pump ventilation, the animal takes a bubble of fresh air into its mouth cavity, then compresses the mouth cavity to pump the air into the lungs. The pulse pump is thought to have evolved from buccal pumps originally used for gill ventilation and suction feeding (McMahon 1969; Brainerd 1994a).

It is clear that lungs are ancient structures (Figure 1); thus both the Actinopterygii (ray-finned fishes) and the Sarcopterygii (lobe-finned fishes and tetrapods) inherited lungs from their ancestors. Within the actinopterygians, the paired lungs evolved into a single, gas-filled sac that functions to regulate buoyancy and is called a "swim bladder." In advanced teleost fishes (e.g., perch and sunfishes), the swim bladder has lost all connection with outside air; instead, the bladder is filled with gasses from the blood. Within the Sarcopterygii, the coelocanth *Latimeria* has a single, fat-filled bladder, the Australian lungfish *Neoceratodus* has a single lung, and the South American and African lungfishes *Lepidosiren* and *Protopterus* have paired lungs.

All tetrapods (terrestrial vertebrates that move on legs) have paired, ventrally located lungs and internal nostrils (choanae), which provide a direct passage for air from the environment to the lungs. It is controversial whether any of the lobe-finned fishes that gave rise to tetrapods had true choanae. Lungfishes have choanae that may or may not be homologous (derived from a common ancestor) with those of tetrapods, and modern lungfishes breathe through their mouths rather than through the choanae. The fossil fishes most closely related to tetrapods, *Eusthenopteron* and *Panderichthys*, show holes in the bony palate that may have been choanae, but these could have been covered with soft tissue (Rosen et al. 1981; Schultze 1987).

Two additional controversies remain in relation to the respiratory strategy of early tetrapods: (1) Were they primarily aquatic or terrestrial, and (2) did they use a pulse pump or an aspiration pump to ventilate their lungs? Recently published material indicates that the earliest known tetrapod, *Acanthostega*, was primarily aquatic (Coates and Clack 1991). This large tetrapod had flipper-like limbs with eight digits on the forelimb, a tail fin, and internal gills. Other scholars, however, have suggested that terrestriality evolved early in the tetrapod line, as evidenced by the absence of gills in *Tulerpeton* and *Icthyostega* (Janis and Farmer 1999).

A second controversy centers around the breathing mechanism of early tetrapods. All extant, air-breathing fishes use a pulse

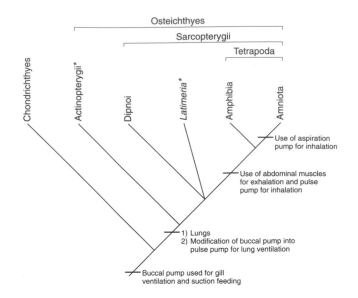

Figure 1. Phylogeny (evolutionary history) of extant gnathostome vertebrates with respiratory characters mapped onto the phylogeny. Note that lungs are present in basal actinopterygians (such as *Polypterus, Amia,* and *Lepisosteus*), lungfishes (Dipnoi), and tetrapods, indicating that lungs are primitive for Osteichthyes. Purely from paleontological evidence, it is often impossible to infer the presence or absence of soft tissues, such as lungs, and physiological characters, such as lung ventilation mechanisms. Thus, the distribution of characters in extant animals is often used to infer the presence or absence of these features in extinct animals. *Advanced actinopterygians have a gas-filled swim bladder that is derived from primitive lungs; the living coelacanth, *Latimera,* has a fat-filled swim bladder.

pump (described above). All extant amniotes (reptiles, birds, and mammals) use a "costal aspiration pump." Abdominal muscles contract to force air out of the lungs; then ribs and intercostal musculature act to expand the chest cavity and aspirate air into the lungs. Modern amphibians (Lissamphibia) use an intermediate system: they use abdominal musculature for exhalation, as in amniotes, but they use a pulse pump for inhalation, as in air-breathing fishes (Figure 1) (Brainerd et al. 1993).

It is unclear whether the earliest tetrapods ventilated their lungs in the same manner as modern amphibians. Early tetrapods were very different from lissamphibians. Some were large (some over one meter long) and heavily armored; a few had well-developed ribs. Lissamphibians may have evolved from these creatures through a process known as "paedomorphosis," in which larval and juvenile characteristics are retained into adulthood. This process would explain why modern amphibians are relatively small, smooth-skinned, and have short, peglike ribs.

Some scholars have proposed that the large, armored, early tetrapods must have been aspiration breathers (Gans 1970). In this argument, Gans assumes that since these animals were prima-

rily terrestrial, they would have had to eliminate all of their carbon dioxide (CO_2) through their lungs. He then argues that this situation would have required a high rate of lung ventilation, which could only have been accomplished with an efficient aspiration pump. But other scholars disagree. It is unclear whether the early tetrapods were primarily terrestrial, and it is possible that they could have excreted much of their CO_2 across moist skin and gill surfaces (Packard 1976; Romer 1972).

It is also possible that aspiration in early tetrapods was assisted by the stiffness of their ventral (belly) armor. An extant air-breathing fish, *Polypterus,* has been shown to use "recoil aspiration" to assist lung inflation (Brainerd 1994b; Brainerd et al. 1989). In these fishes, exhalation deforms the jacket of scales on the belly; then elastic recoil expands the body and aspirates air down into the lungs. Early tetrapods had similar ventral scales, known as "gastralia," and may have used recoil aspiration to assist lung ventilation.

Although early tetrapods may have used recoil aspiration to assist lung ventilation, the bulk of paleontological evidence indicates that they probably did not use costal aspiration as their primary lung ventilation mechanism. A few species, such as *Icthyostega,* had long ribs that enclosed the thorax (chest), but most species, such as *Cacops,* had relatively short ribs that enclosed only the dorsal half of the thorax. Furthermore, virtually all extinct amphibians had broad, flat heads that would have provided a large volume for pulse pumping. Only in the evolution of amniotes (tetrapods that lay shelled eggs), which were aspiration breathers, do we see the elaboration of elongate and laterally flattened head shapes, suggesting that this broad, flat head was required for pulse pumping.

Early amniotes were almost certainly aspiration breathers, given that aspiration is used by all extant amniotes (Figure 1), but they probably had relatively low stamina for sustained locomotion. These animals had a sprawling gait, similar to many modern lizards, and their locomotion included a lot of lateral (side-to-side) bending of the body. The ribs and intercostal muscles were required both for lateral bending and for breathing; therefore, the early amniotes were probably unable to run and breathe at the same time (Carrier 1987).

Birds and mammals have solved this problem, enabling them to have much greater sustained locomotion and energy expenditure. The keys lie in mammalian upright posture, which reduces lateral bending, and an energetically efficient aspiration pump, which consists of elastic lungs and a diaphragm muscle (Perry 1989). Birds evolved a rigid lung and flexible air sacs, which produce a unidirectional flow of air over the gas exchange surface, thus extracting more oxygen from air (Bretz and Schmidt-Nielsen 1972). In both birds and mammals, locomotion and respiration are not completely decoupled; rather, these animals have developed systems in which locomotor movements actually assist the ventilation of the lungs (Bramble and Carrier 1983; Boggs et al. 1997).

Birds and mammals possess large nasal cavities containing thin, scroll-like bones or cartilages known as "respiratory turbinates" (Hillenius 1994). Respiratory turbinates help conserve body heat and water by warming and humidifying air during inhalation, then cooling and recovering water vapor from exhaled air.

Respiratory turbinates evolved independently in birds and mammals, and their roles in heat and water conservation are thought to be essential for endothermic (warm-blooded) animals with high rates of lung ventilation. Theropod and ornithischian dinosaurs appear to have lacked respiratory turbinates, a characteristic pointed to as evidence that they had relatively low metabolic rates (Ruben et al. 1996).

It is unclear what types of lungs and ventilatory mechanisms the dinosaurs may have possessed. Some scholars have proposed that some dinosaurs may have had air sacs and birdlike lungs. Birds have air spaces (pneumatopores) in their vertebrae and long bones, and pneumatopores have been found in the vertebrae of some dinosaurs. These could, however, be attachment sites for a lizardlike lung. This arrangement is seen in monitor lizards, where the lung is firmly attached to the body wall. Other scholars have proposed that some dinosaurs may have used a hepatic-piston ventilation mechanism, as is seen in extant crocodilians. Here, a dome-shaped liver is pulled back by muscles, thus functioning in a similar manner to the mammalian diaphragm (Ruben et al. 1997).

ELIZABETH L. BRAINERD

See also Odor and Pheromone Receptors; Paleoethology; Pharyngeal Arches and Derivatives; Sarcopterygians; Sensory Capsules; Tetrapods: Overview; Terrestrialization of Animals; Thermoregulation

Works Cited

Boggs, D.F., F.A. Jenkins, and K.P. Dial. 1997. The effects of the wingbeat cycle on respiration in black-billed magpies (*Pica pica*). *Journal of Experimental Biology* 200:1403–12.

Brainerd, E.L. 1994a. The evolution of lung-gill bimodal breathing and the homology of vertebrate respiratory pumps. *American Zoologist* 34:289–99.

———. 1994b. Mechanical design of polypterid fish integument for energy storage during recoil aspiration. *Journal of Zoology, London* 232:7–19.

Brainerd, E.L., J.S. Ditelberg, and D.M. Bramble. 1993. Lung ventilation in salamanders and the evolution of vertebrate air-breathing mechanisms. *Biological Journal of the Linnean Society* 49:163–83.

Brainerd, E.L., K.F. Liem, and C.T. Samper. 1989. Air ventilation by recoil aspiration in polypterid fishes. *Science* 246:1593–95.

Bramble, D.M., and D.R. Carrier. 1983. Running and breathing in mammals. *Science* 219:251–56.

Bretz, W.L., and K. Schmidt-Nielsen. 1972. Movement of gas in the respiratory system of a duck. *Journal of Experimental Biology* 56:57–65.

Carrier, D.R. 1987. The evolution of locomotor stamina in tetrapods: Circumventing a mechanical constraint. *Paleobiology* 13 (3):325–41.

Coates, M.I., and J.A. Clack. 1991. Fish-like gills and breathing in the earliest known tetrapod. *Nature* 352:234–36.

Farmer, C. 1997. Did lungs and the intracardiac shunt evolve to oxygenate the heart in vertebrates? *Paleobiology* 23 (3):358–72.

Gans, C. 1970. Strategy and sequence in the evolution of the external gas exchangers of ectothermal vertebrates. *Forma et Functio* 3:61–104.

Hillenius, W.J. 1994. Turbinates in therapsids: Evidence for late Permian origins of mammalian endothermy. *Evolution* 48:207–29.

Janis, C.M., and C. Farmer. 1999. Proposed habitats of early tetrapods: Gills, kidneys, water-land transition. *Zoological Journal of the Linnean Society* 126 (1):117.

Liem, K.F. 1988. Form and function of lungs: The evolution of air breathing mechanisms. *American Zoologist* 28:739–59.

Mallatt, J. 1996. Ventilation and the origin of jawed vertebrates. *Zoological Journal of the Linnean Society* 117:329–404.

McMahon, B.R. 1969. A functional analysis of aquatic and aerial respiratory movements of an African lungfish, *Protopterus aethiopicus* with reference to the evolution of the lung-ventilation mechanism in vertebrates. *Journal of Experimental Biology* 51:407–30.

Packard, G.C. 1974. The evolution of air-breathing in Paleozoic gnathostome fishes. *Evolution* 28:320–25.

———. 1976. Devonian amphibians: Did they excrete carbon dioxide via skin, gills, or lungs? *Evolution* 30:270–80.

Perry, S.F. 1989. Mainstreams in the evolution of vertebrate respiratory structures. *In* A.S. King and J. McLelland (eds.), *Form and Function in Birds*. Vol. 4, London and New York: Academic Press.

Romer, A.S. 1972. Skin breathing—primary or secondary? *Respiration Physiology* 14:183–92.

Rosen, D.E., P.L. Forey, B.G. Gardiner, and C. Patterson. 1981. Lungfishes, tetrapods, paleontology and plesiomorphy. *Bulletin of the American Museum of Natural History* 167:159–276.

Ruben, J.A., W.J. Hillenius, N.R. Geist, A. Leitch, T.D. Jones, P.J. Currie, J.R. Horner, and G. Espe. 1996. The metabolic status of some Late Cretaceous dinosaurs. *Science* 273:1204–7.

Ruben, J.A., T.D. Jones, N.R. Geist, and W.J. Hillenius. 1997. Lung structure in theropod dinosaurs and early birds. *Science* 278:1267–70

Schultze, H-P. 1987. Dipnoans as sarcopterygians. *In* W.E. Bemis, W.W. Burggren, and N.E. Kemp (eds.), *The Biology and Evolution of Lungfishes*. New York: Liss.

Further Reading

Carrier, D.R. 1987. The evolution of locomotor stamina in tetrapods: Circumventing a mechanical constraint. *Paleobiology* 13 (3):325–41.

Gans, C. 1970. Strategy and sequence in the evolution of the external gas exchangers of ectothermal vertebrates. *Forma et Functio* 3:61–104.

Graham, J.B. 1997. *Air-Breathing Fishes: Evolution, Diversity, and Adaptation*. San Diego, California: Academic Press.

Liem, K.F. 1988. Form and function of lungs: The evolution of air breathing mechanisms. *American Zoologist* 28:739–59.

Ruben, J.A., T.D. Jones, N.R. Geist, and W.J. Hillenius. 1997. Lung structure in theropod dinosaurs and early birds. *Science*.

RODENTS

See Glires

ROMER, ALFRED SHERWOOD

American, 1894–1973

As a young boy, Alfred Sherwood Romer visited the New York Zoo and the American Museum of Natural History in New York City. As an undergraduate at Amherst, he initially was interested in history, but a course on evolution taught by F.B. Loomis, combined with his childhood interests, redirected his interest to vertebrates. After military service in France during World War I, Romer pursued graduate work in comparative anatomy and vertebrate paleontology under the supervision of W.K. Gregory at Columbia University. In only two years he completed a doctoral thesis on the comparative anatomy and evolution of the limb musculature in primitive tetrapods, which remains the classic work on this subject to the present day. Romer subsequently followed this project with detailed reconstructions of the musculature of the pelvis and hind limb in dinosaurs as well as several studies on the development of limb muscles in extant reptiles.

After a two-year stint as a lecturer at the Bellevue Medical School of New York University, Romer accepted an appointment as associate professor of vertebrate paleontology at the University of Chicago. The rich collections of vertebrates from the Permo-Carboniferous red beds of Texas at the Walker Museum (now housed in Chicago's Field Museum) caught his interest, and Romer developed a life-long program of research and (starting in 1926) fieldwork aimed at the recovery of additional fossils and the establishment of a stratigraphic framework for the faunal succession.

Early during his teaching career at Chicago, Romer prepared for use in class a typescript that was to become his famous textbook, *Vertebrate Paleontology*. First published in 1933, this work went through three editions and remained the authoritative text on the subject for five decades. In 1933 Romer also published the first edition of *Man and the Vertebrates,* which represented an expanded version of a chapter for an undergraduate textbook entitled *The Nature of the World and Man*, which was edited by H.H. Newman and appeared in 1926. A substantially modified version of Romer's book, *The Vertebrate Story* (1959), became a best-selling popular account of the evolution of the vertebrates.

In 1934 Romer accepted a joint appointment as professor of zoology at Harvard University and curator of vertebrate paleontology at the Museum of Comparative Zoology at Harvard. He rapidly built up the museum's small collections of fossil vertebrates through his fieldwork in Texas, and, as director of the museum (1946–61), greatly increased its endowment and established its reputation as one of the world's foremost centers for systematic zoology.

Romer's research on Permo-Carboniferous vertebrates from Texas and adjacent regions resulted in many papers as well as two classic monographs, *Review of the Pelycosauria* (with L.I. Price, 1940) and *Review of the Labyrinthodontia* (1947).

In 1956, Romer published his *magnum opus* entitled *Osteology of the Reptiles,* an encyclopedic, richly illustrated survey of the skeleton of reptiles (sauropsids) and nonmammalian synapsids (mammal-like reptiles), combined with a classification of all known extant and extinct taxa referable to these two groups.

Although now outdated in many respects, it is still the single authoritative source on these subjects. Romer also wrote a widely used textbook on comparative anatomy of the vertebrates, *The Vertebrate Body,* which first appeared in 1949. It went through five editions and was translated into many foreign languages.

In 1958 and in 1964–65, Romer organized and led several expeditions to collect Triassic vertebrates from the Chañares and Ischigualasto formations in northwestern Argentina. The great success of his fieldwork led to renewed general interest in Early Mesozoic tetrapod assemblages from South America. Romer's last completed research project was a series of descriptions of many new taxa of archosaurian reptiles and cynodont therapsids from the Middle Triassic Chañares Formation.

Romer was a skilled writer renowned for the clarity of his prose. His books have exerted a profound influence on several generations of students in vertebrate paleontology and comparative anatomy, especially in North America. During his long career, Romer published systematic and descriptive-anatomical papers on representatives of most major groups of vertebrates except birds. However, his most enduring contributions are the studies on Late Paleozoic tetrapods, primarily from Texas and adjoining regions, and Triassic reptiles and therapsids from Argentina. His monograph *Review of the Pelycosauria,* which was beautifully illustrated by L.I. Price, ranks as one of the classic works of vertebrate paleontology. Romer wrote extensively on anatomical and paleobiological aspects of the major transitions during the evolutionary history of vertebrates. He advocated a freshwater rather than marine origin of vertebrates; most workers then and now consider nearshore marine settings the ancestral habitat for vertebrates. Romer interpreted the origin of tetrapod limbs not as an adaptation for moving from an aquatic to terrestrial mode of life, but rather as a means that would have permitted prototetrapods to migrate to other bodies of water when the original ponds dried up during seasonal dry spells. More recent discoveries, however, indicate that limbs already had developed in persistently aquatic stem tetrapods.

HANS-DIETER SUES

Biography

Born in White Plains, New York, 28 December 1894. Received A.B., Amherst College, 1917; Ph.D., Columbia University, 1921. Lecturer, Bellevue Medical School, New York University, 1921–23; associate professor of vertebrate paleontology, University of Chicago, 1923–34; professor of zoology, Harvard University, 1934–61; curator of vertebrate paleontology (1934–1961) and director (1946–61), Museum of Comparative Zoology, Harvard University. Elected president, Society of Vertebrate Paleontology, 1940; member, National Academy of Sciences, 1944; president, American Society of Zoologists, 1951; president, Society for Systematic Zoology, 1952; president, Society for the Study of Evolution, 1953; received Thompson Medal (1956) and Elliot Medal (1960), National Academy of Sciences; received Penrose

Medal of the Geological Society of America, 1962; president, Twenty-Fourth International Zoological Congress, Washington, D.C., 1963; president, American Association for the Advancement of Science, 1966; received Paleontological Society Medal, 1967; elected foreign member, Royal Society, London, 1969; received Linnean Medal of the Linnean Society of London, 1972; received Wollaston Medal of the Geological Society of London, 1973; received honorary degrees from Harvard, Amherst, Dartmouth, Buffalo, and Lehigh. Wrote several influential books on vertebrate paleontology and comparative anatomy of vertebrates; made important contributions to anatomy and phylogeny of Late Paleozoic and Triassic vertebrates. Died in Cambridge, Massachusetts, 5 November 1973.

Major Publications

1933a. *Vertebrate Paleontology.* Chicago: University of Chicago Press; 3rd ed., 1966.

1933b. *Man and the Vertebrates.* Chicago: University of Chicago Press; 4th ed. as *The Vertebrate Story,* 1959.

1940. With L.I. Price. *Review of the Pelycosauria.* Geological Society of America Special Paper 28. Boulder, Colorado: Geological Society of America; Lawrence: University of Kansas.

1947. *Review of the Labyrinthodontia.* Bulletin of the Museum of Comparative Zoology, Harvard University 99 (1). Cambridge, Massachusetts: Harvard University Press.

1949. *The Vertebrate Body.* Philadelphia; Saunders; 6th ed., with T.S. Parsons, 1986.

1956. *Osteology of the Reptiles.* Chicago: University of Chicago Press; London: University of Chicago Press, 1968.

1968a. *Notes and Comments on Vertebrate Paleontology.* Chicago: University of Chicago Press.

1968b. *The Processions of Life.* New York: World; London: Weidenfeld and Nicolson.

Further Reading

Colbert, E.H. 1982. Alfred Sherwood Romer: December 28, 1894– November 5, 1973. *National Academy of Sciences, Biographical Memoirs* 53:264–94.

Thimann, K.V., and E.C. Olson. 1976. Alfred Sherwood Romer (1894– 1973). *Year Book of the American Philosophical Society* 1975:148–57.

Westoll, T.S., and F.R. Parrington. 1975. Alfred Sherwood Romer 1894– 1973. *Biographical Memoirs of Fellows of the Royal Society* 21:497–516.

RUSSIA AND THE FORMER SOVIET UNION

The history of paleontological research in Russia is many-faceted, for several reasons. First, the country is huge, and its complex paleogeography encompasses several geological epochs, each with unique climates and shifting ratios of land and sea. Second, the lithological structure of the formations is complex, as is the variety of species that they contain. And finally, Russian paleontology has a rich conceptual base, with many important individuals, research that moves in many different directions, and various schools of thought.

Russian paleontology begins with Tsar Peter the Great, who established in 1718 the "Kunstcamsmera," an organization dedicated to promoting conservation of the country's valuable fossils. One hundred years later, the Mineralogical Society was founded in St. Petersburg, bringing together outstanding geologists and paleontologists. New fossil finds resulted mainly from geological research in the Ordovician and Silurian of the region called the "Silurian platform." This land formation extends from the southern coast of Lake Ladoga, through St. Petersburg, and on to northern Estonia (Gekker 1987).

In 1816 a young geologist named Thomas Horner Fox Strangways arrived in St. Petersburg to work for the British embassy. He conducted the earliest geological investigations of the Silurian platform. Between 1821 and 1824 Strangways published sketches "on the geology of the European part" of Russia, in the *Transactions of the Geological Society of London* (1821). Accompanying his work was a small-scale map of the region. However, some of Strangways' estimates of the strata's geological age—estimates based upon the petrographic data—were inaccurate and resulted in gross blunders (Murchison 1841). The problem was that very little was known about fossils at that time; sufficient data became available only some 30 to 60 years later, when the founding fathers of Russian paleontology began publishing their findings.

The Beginnings of Paleontological Research

The study of Ordovician fossils on the Silurian Platform received valuable contributions from many brilliant Russian scientists, all of whom were well educated in the universities of western Europe. Perhaps the brightest of these was C.H. Pander, whom Charles Darwin later recognized as one of his predecessors. Pander attended universities at Tartu, Berlin, and Gottingen, then in 1819 returned to Russia. He began to systematically collect and study fossils found in the vicinity of St. Petersburg and the Baltic area. At his own expense, Pander published his magnificent monograph on the *Geognosie of Russia* (1830), with 30 plates of drawings of Ordovician fossils, mainly brachiopods.

As head of the Geological Committee for 40 years, Pander organized research on the Silurian Platform and also on the Devonian and Carboniferous periods in the Moscow and Novgorod regions. The work culminated in the 1850s and 1860s with the publication of three monographs on agnathans (jawless fishes) and fishes (Pander 1856) and one on conodonts of the Baltic. Conodonts are small, toothlike fossils that belong to a group of extinct chordates. The hard parts of these animals serve as important index fossils because they are distinctive at the generic level and each type occurs within a restricted time interval. They have thus been used to correlate Paleozoic strata all over the world.

Pander was the first scholar to study conodonts with a microscope, and he described these fossils as "small fish teeth." He so loved these fossils that he ordered his tailor to make him a coat with special pockets—this allowed him to carry his finds with him and examine them many times in a day. In his honor, in 1967 the Pander Society was founded at Columbia University. Its membership includes conodont researchers from all over the world.

At about the same time, A.F. Volborth (1800–76) a graduate from Tubingen University in Germany, began his work on trilobites and echinoderms (Volborth 1847). Volborth's work is characterized by the precision of a surgeon—his other occupation. He assembled a huge collection of some thousands of trilobites, including the small endemic (unique to a certain area) genus called *Crotaburus*. The collection is preserved in the Mineralogical Museum of St. Petersburg.

After graduating from Berlin University, C.E. Eichwald devoted a large part of his life to teaching in Russian universities. An ideological opponent of Volborth, Eichwald wrote two large monographs, *Paleontology of Russia* (four volumes; 1840–48) and *Lethaea Rossica* (5 volumes; 1852–68). These publications included atlases with numerous drawings of fossils. However, the work drew sharp criticism from the Volborth-Schmidt party because of several discrepancies they contained.

Another outstanding figure in Russian paleontology was S.S. Kutorga (1805–61). Kutorga was a consummate lecturer and an evolutionist. He studied and described trilobites and brachiopods from the Ordovician and published a detailed geological map of the St. Petersburg province. He was also a director of the Mineralogical Society and editor of the *Verhandlungen der Russisch-Kaiserlichen Mineralogischen Gesellschaft zu St. Petersburg.*

F.B. Schmidt (1832–1908) belonged to a later generation of St. Petersburg paleontologists. As one of Pander's disciples, Schmidt studied trilobites, brachiopods, and echinoderms from the Ordovician and echinoderms of the Baltic area. Originally educated as a botanist, Schmidt described about 250 species of trilobites, 120 of which were new. In 1868 he led an expedition to the Yenisey River in eastern Siberia to study the remains of wooly mammoth. The diverse results of this expedition (Schmidt 1872) brought him wide popularity and the title of Academician of the Russian Academy of Sciences. Colleagues called him "Mammoth-Schmidt" because of his bearded, stout appearance. A splendid bronze sculpture of a mammoth, a gift to him from his colleagues, now is exhibited in the Museum of Paleontology in Moscow.

Interesting Mistake of a Past Century

Fossils from the Ordovician deposits of the St. Petersburg region arouse great interest all over the world. Limestone and marl are exposed on the coast of the Baltic Sea and Lake Ladoga. Since the beginning of the nineteenth century, different fossils have been collected systematically, including various trilobites, bryozoans, large orthocone (straight-shelled) cephalopods, and many brachiopods. The Lower Ordovician fauna marks the transformation of the so-called Paleozoic Evolutionary Fauna, which features the first appearance of many Recent classes. For example, all five extant classes of echinoderms appeared during the Ordovician: crinoids (sea lilies); echinoids (sea urchins); asteroids (starfishes); ophiuroids (brittle stars); and holothurians (sea cucumbers). Ancient representatives of each of these classes occur in the Baltic Ordovician Paleobasin.

However, reconstructing the appearance of the extinct animals from their skeletal parts is not always easy, for ancient forms may differ greatly from Recent ones. Scientists often have misinterpreted these skeletons. For instance, in the early 1900s, the eminent German paleontologist O. Jaekel (1909) made wide use of Russian echinoderm collections and tried to reconstruct their appearance. In most cases, Jaekel was correct, but not always. Once, while working with limestone slabs that held parts of several echinoderms, Jaekel assembled the parts to form a complete animal. The resulting (fantastic-looking) creature had barrel-like cysts on the lower part of the biserial stem, and plane appendages containing gonads attached to the middle of the stem. The top of the stem was crowned by a big cuplike formation of large plates, which carried the major soft parts.

Many years later, Russian paleontologist R.F. Gekker reinvestigated the same Ordovician deposits and fossils and concluded that Jaekel had united in one animal the skeletal parts of echinoderms from *four* different classes. Gekker's work was confirmed later. The cysts in the lower part of the stem in Jaekel's animal were the thecae (enveloping body sheaths) of the eocrinoid *Bockia*. The plane appendages of the stem represented two eocrinoid genera, *Rhipidocystis* and *Neorhipidocystis*. The stem itself was a tail of a solute called *Heckericystis*. (Solutes were animals that primarily lacked radial symmetry; their structure combines features of the echinoderms and the chordates.)

Finally, the cuplike formation at the top of the stem was shown to be the test (central skeletal housing) of the echinoderm *Volchovia*. *Volchovia* is the earliest representative of a class of free-living echinoderms called the ophiocistioids. (The ophiocistioid test is composed of large thin plates, through which extend ambulacral, or tube feet, used in locomotion.) The reconstructed body of Jaekel's animal was thus a remarkable combination of the skeletal parts of five different genera of echinoderms, later assigned to four different families from three different classes and two phyla (Rozhnov 1989).

Paleogeographical Research

During the latter part of the nineteenth century, interest began in exploring the geology and biotas of the Cenozoic midland basins of southern Russia. N.I. Andrussov (1861–1924), Academician of the St. Petersburg and Ukrainian Academies of Science was its greatest exponent.

In the first half of the Cenozoic era (Paleogene period), large areas, ranging from central Europe to Middle Asia, were covered by inland seas. (The level of salinity approximated that of normal ocean water.) Wide channels connected these basins with the Tethys Ocean (the precursor of today's Mediterranean Sea) and with the seas of northern Europe. Later, in the Neogene and Quaternary periods, a peculiar basin called the "Paratethys" appeared (today its remnants are the Black, Azov, Caspian, and Aral Seas) (Figure 1).

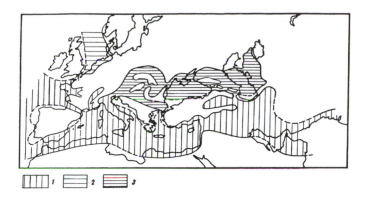

Figure 1. Paleogeographic scheme of Paratethys and neighboring basins in the Early-Middle Miocene (Tarkhanian-Tshokrakian): *1*, Tethys, or Mediterranean Sea; *2*, Northern European boreal basin; *3*, Paratethys. From Trudy Paleontologocheskogo Instituta (1986).

The Paratethys was not connected with northern seas, and the degree to which it was connected to the Tethys was very changeable. As a result, the level of salinity in the basins fluctuated from normal marine to approximately freshwater. When the salinity level fell, marine biotas perished almost completely. Only a few eurybiont forms continued to exist, and these gave rise to specific endemic assemblages. When the connections between the Mediterranean Sea and the Paratethys widened, the salinity level increased, and marine emigrants returned to the Paratethys. Such fluctuating environmental conditions and their resultant biotas formed a very exact and detailed stratigraphy. Andrussov and his followers established in Paratethys a series of horizons that later acquired the status of regional stages. Scholars have tried to correlate these stages with Mediterranean stratigraphic units, and data is still being accumulated.

Over time, the investigation of the fossils themselves have became more and more profound. Scholars have detailed the relationships between many invertebrates and vertebrates and worked out general laws for the development of biotas in unstable, semi-enclosed basins. The research in the Paratethys exploration provides scholars with an excellent model for studying basins of other regions and other geological epochs.

Ammonites and Evolutionary Ideas

Many stratigraphical schemes for the Paleozoic and Mesozoic are based on ammonites. These shelled animals belonged to the subclass of cephalopods and were long known as "Ammon's horns." Some ammonites, such as the Triassic *Doricranites* and the Jurassic *Virgatites,* are Russian endemics with a restricted spatial distribution.

The birth of Darwinism in the middle of nineteenth century had many effects on the development of ammonitology (study of ammonites). The idea of recapitulation became quite popular. According to this theory, as an organism develops it passes through the adult stages of its ancestors. This idea is encapsulated in the catch phrase "outogeny recapitulates phylogeny."

Between the 1860s and 1890s the American A. Hyatt (1838–1902) used this theory to reconstruct the phylogeny of Jurassic ammonites. As a result, he established that over the history of this group, the ancestral features repeated in the ontogeny of descendants shifted to an earlier and earlier stage of development, became condensed, and ultimately disappeared from the process. Hyatt named this phenomenon "the law of acceleration."

Soon afterwards, Academician A.P. Karpinsky (1847–1936), who was studying shell suture lines of Permian medlicottiids, showed that in their ontogeny the medlicottids express features seen in their ancestors, the Carboniferous pronorotids. While studying another type of ammonite, the kosmoceratids (Jurassic), Academician A.P. Pavlov (1854–1929) established some alterations in their development. New features that initially appear in early ontogenetic stages of their ancestors, postpone their onset in the kosmoceratids so that they appear late in ontogeny and persist into maturity.

The German scientist O.H. Schindewolf (1921) observed similar ontogenetic changes in other Jurassic ammonites. He named this process "proterogenesis"; the term has since been changed to "progenesis." About the same time, D.L. Sobolev established progenesis in Devonian ammonites, explaining that the phenomenon was governed, not by the environment, but by independent, internal laws of development. Darwinists reacted negatively to Sobolev's ideas, but his theories have indirectly affected recent views on the evolution of many fossil groups.

In Moscow, the ontogenetic approach to ammonite study was developed further by Professor V.E. Ruzhentsev (1899–1976) and his numerous followers. These researchers established a variety of ontogenetic changes in the shells and suture lines of ammonites (Ruzhentsev and Orlov 1960). At the same time, the work showed that the evolution of such changes usually involved the occurrence of new features at late ontogenetic stages, which then, over time, were displaced to earlier and earlier stages.

Development of Paleoecology

Research in paleoecology began in the middle of the nineteenth century. Its first practitioner was C. Rouillier (1814–58), the first paleontology professor at Moscow University. In his lectures Rouillier developed the ideas of French transformists E. Geoffroy Saint-Hilaire and G. Buffon. Rouillier's research concentrated on Jurassic brachiopods of central Russia, associating their morphological variability with environment. Later, such research was called "autecological." Rouillier's main purpose was to reveal the way that peculiarities in an organism's ecology were reflected in the morphology of separate groups.

W.O. Kovalevsky (1840–83) and N.N. Jakovlev (1870–1966) successfully developed autecology. Kovalevsky mainly studied adaptations in vertebrates, particularly within the evolution of horses; Jakovlev investigated marine invertebrates, focusing on functional morphology (the association between form and function). Kovalevsky is considered the father of evolutionary paleontology in Russia. A Darwinist, he theorized that all ungulates (hoofed mammals) descended from a common ancestor (monophyly) and diversified through the process of natural selection (1873). Later, H.F. Osborn (1902) introduced the term "adaptive radiation" to described this process. M.V. Pavlova (1854–1938) continued to investigate the origin of equids. She was the first to introduce the idea that the Old World horses—namely the Palaeotheriidae—whose oldest representatives were found in the Caucasus, evolved independently from other branches (Pavlova 1929).

Other academicians also contributed a great deal to the development of autecology and evolutionary paleontology, primarily P.P. Sushkin (1868–1928), A.A. Borissiak (1872–1936), and I.A. Orlov (1893–1966). Sushkin's works on Permian labyrinthodonts (primitive tetrapods) and amniotes (1922–36) contain detailed descriptions of skull structures and interpretations that illustrated how a particular structure was interrelated with the animals' ethology (behavior), habitat, and phylogeny (Sushkin 1926). Sushkin was one of the first scientists who amended L. Dollo's law about the irreversibility of evolution. For instance, using the example of the penguin flipper, Sushkin showed that it was possible for primitive features of the archaic birds to reappear as the result of accelerated ontogenetic development in their decendants.

A.A. Borissiak founded the Museum of Paleontology and was the first director of the Institute of Paleontology in Moscow (1936–44). His work concentrated on the adaptive radiation of various groups of animals, especially of fossil ungulates and proboscideans (elephants and related forms). Borissiak also wrote a two-volume textbook on paleontology (1905, 1906) and one on historical geology, on which he worked with several other editors.

In 1945, Orlov became the director of the Institute of Paleontology (1945–66) and the head of Moscow University's Paleontology Department. He contributed considerably to establishing the new Museum of Paleontology in Moscow (1972), the construction of which was not completed until after his death. (The museum did not begin operations until 1987, when Academician L.P. Tatarinov was director of the Paleontology Institute.) Orlov was one of the greatest experts in the field of vertebrate paleontology. He contributed much to the research and reconstruction of the mammalian brain, in particular that of a giant marten, *Perunium* (1941, 1947). Orlov considered disproportions in the development of this animal's brain as one of the reasons that they became extinct when great changes in habitats occurred in the Middle and Late Pleistocene.

Another important phase in the development of paleoecology was embarked upon when researchers turned their attention to entire communities of organisms. This type of research began with Andrussov's investigations of Paratethys, and it expanded through the work of Gekker (1900–91).

Gekker established a school for paleoecologists in the Institute of Paleontology of Moscow and, together with his colleagues and followers, introduced complex methods for researching geological formations in different regions of the former Soviet Union. These included the Devonian and Carboniferous periods of the eastern European Platform, the Jurassic of Karatau (Kazakhstan), and the Paleogene of Fergana (Uzbekistan) (Gekker et al. 1962; Ivanova 1958). Gekker wrote a number of theoretical and methodological works in paleoecology, the most important of which is his *Introduction to Paleoecology* (1957), which has been translated into French, English, Polish, Chinese, and Japanese. Gekker's followers have continued his work on fossil echinoderms at the Institute of Paleontology of Moscow.

Paleoichthyological Research

The first information about Russia's Paleozoic ichthyofauna (ancient fishes) appeared in the 1830s and was explored mainly in the works of Pander, Eichwald, I. Rohon, and I. Trautschold. At the beginning of this century, there was sporadic accumulation of data on some fish groups. One of the most fruitful was I. Lopatin's expedition to western Siberia (Minusa), where he recovered limestone containing whole skeletons of Permian paleoniscids, members of the actinopterygians (ray-finned bony fishes). Of special interest is an 1889 monograph written by A.P. Karpinsky, in which he reconstructed the tooth spiral in an unusual group of bradiodonts (a group of chondrichthyans) from Carboniferous and Permian deposits.

In the middle of the twentieth century, paleoichthyological research was conducted mostly by the Geological Committee, in an attempt to solve stratigraphic problems. In the 1930s work had begun on *The Atlas of the Leading Forms of Fossils in Faunas of the USSR*, but it was interrupted by war (Chabakov 1934–41). The volume, devoted to the Devonian, finally appeared in 1947. In 1940, L.S. Berg's fundamental book, *The System of Fishlike Animals and Fishes, Living and Fossil* (1955), appeared, as did some of his papers on actinopterygians from Upper Paleozoic and Lower Mesozoic of Russia. These works have played an important role in the development of ichthyology and paleoichthyology.

In the early 1950s D.V. Obruchev created a laboratory for fish paleontology at the Institute of Paleontology, Academy of Science in Moscow. This lab was the basis of the well-known "Obruchev school" and has produced cutting edge research in different regions of Russia. In the northwest areas of Russia and the Baltic countries, investigations centered on the territory of the main Devonian Field and Silurian Platform. In eastern Siberia, scholars researched the Devonian to Carboniferous deposits, while in east Kazakhstan, studies concentrated on the Permo-Carboniferous. In Uzbekistan the focus was the Triassic; in the Caucasus, the Cainozoic; and in Russia and other regions, the central Devonian Field.

Between the 1960s and the 1990s, many of Obruchev's pupils and younger colleagues proposed and defended theses concerning various groups of fossil fishes. These studies included the jawless psammosteids (E. Mark-Kurik, Estonia), antiarchs (V. Karatajute-Talimaa of Lithuania and L. Larskaya of Latvia), thelodonts (V. Karatajute-Talimaa), palaeoniscoids (A. Kazanceva), actinopterygians (V. Jakovlev and E. Sichevskaya), heterostraceans (L. Novitskaya), osteostracans (O. Afanasjeva), and dipnoans (N. Krupina). All of these researchers were associated with the Institute of Paleontology of Moscow.

In 1964, Obruchev edited the book *Agnathans and Fishes of the Bases of Paleontology*. The work contained diagnoses (detailed descriptions) of all of genera of fossil fish then known; it also contained discussions of the morphology, phylogeny, ecology, and biostratigraphy of the groups. This publication was significant, and in 1968 the text was translated into English.

Fish remains from Russia's territory are mostly incomplete, though there are some perfectly preserved fossils, such as heterostracans, crossopterygians, and paleoniscids. The large number and diversity of these fossils allows scholars to reconstruct the morphology and evolution of some groups that have no analogs in the Recent ichthyofauna. For example, researchers have used the imprints of soft tissue preserved on the internal surface of the skulls of heterostracians, which lived approximately 350 to 400 million years ago, to reconstruct the skulls' interior contents. Such reconstructions led to the hypothesis that the brain of these animals was similar to sharks.

Paleontologists have also successfully used the remains of agnathans and jawed fishes to make regional and interregional correlations between the deposits of different geological ages: from the Silurian up to the Pleistocene. Some endemic taxa have generated considerable interest. Among these are an assemblage of heterostracans from the Lower Devonian of Siberia (Novitskaya 1971) and a group of crossopterygians from the Carboniferous of Yakutia (Vorobyeva 1977).

One of the most interesting finds occurred in the 1970s in the Lode locality, near Riga, in Latvia. On the site of a factory that manufactured drainage pipes, scholars discovered whole skeletons of antiarchs (a type of placoderm) and crossopterygians from the Upper Devonian lying close together. The numerous skeletons of these fishes were concentrated in a layer of clay that was two meters deep. The state of preservation of these fishes and their association with ancient ferns support the view that these fishes perished in a shallow lagoon.

There is special interest in the occurrence of *Panderichthys rhombolepis* in deposits of the same age in West Miguasha, in Canada. This genus is recognized as the sister group (the closest related group) to tetrapods (Vorobyeva and Schultze 1991). *Panderichthys rhombolepis*, a fish with a crocodile-like head, was probably an ambush predator and could move across firm ground using its flipperlike paired fins. The morphology of the skull and brain of *Panderichthys* shares some features in common with the oldest tetrapods from the Devonian of East Greenland, in particular with *Ichthyostega.* However, unlike *Ichthyostega,* which possessed seven or eight fingers, the pectoral fin of *Panderichthys* ended in an undivided plate (Vorobyeva and Hinchliffe 1996).

In 1982, near the village of Andreevka, near Tula, a deposit from the Upper Devonian was initially opened because of ostracod finds (ostracods are a type of shelled crustacean). The fish fauna here is close to the fauna found in eastern Greenland, and includes *Ichthyostega.* In addition to various fish groups (crossopterygians, dipnoans, elasmobranchs), scientists also found the six-digit tetrapod, *Tulerpeton curtum.* This species is the oldest reptiliomorph tetrapod (Lebedev and Coates 1995) and retains many ancestral fish-like characters, such as scales on the body and limbs and a connection between skull and pectoral girdle. This find confirms the hypothesis (Vorobyeva 1992), that for a long time (probably up to the Permian) the evolution of Paleozoic tetrapods was connected to water, so many retained fishlike features.

Permian and Triassic Tetrapods

The Permian period is associated with an increase in tetrapod diversity. At the beginning of the period, the climate in the Northern Hemisphere was arid and hot, which accelerated the replacement of basal tetrapods by amniotes (tetrapods that lay shelled eggs), which became the dominant terrestrial group.

The Permian deposits of eastern Europe stretch like a wide belt across Russia. Moving from east to west, this belt extends from the meridian, where one finds Moscow to the western slope of the Urals; looking from north to south, it stretches from the coast of the Arctic Ocean to the Caspian Sea. Altogether the deposit covers an area of more than a million square kilometers. At the onset of the Permian, this territory was occupied by the small East European Sea and the gulf of the European-Siberian Boreal Ocean, which was bordered on the east by the Paleoural mountains. Only in the northeastern region, in the area of the Pechora depression, did one find a marshy plain that was inhabited by aquatic and semiaquatic tetrapods belonging to the same families as in North America and western Europe. During the Permian, geographic and environmental changes brought about alterations in the faunal assemblages.

The Upper Permian strata of Russia are associated with deposits of many useful minerals (e.g., copper ores, potassium salts, titanium, coal, oil, and gas). Hence, the first finds of the tetrapods bones were associated with the extraction of these valuable minerals. For instance, the bones of various tetrapods were found in the copper sandstones of the Urals. In the past century, Kutorga, Eichwald, Trautschold, and Rjabinin published the first descriptions of these rare fossils, which totalled 17 species.

Another important event in Permian tetrapod research was the discovery of the Northern Dvina assemblage. The expedition to the Northern Dvina (Figure 2) was organized by a St. Petersburg University professor, A.P. Amalitsky (1860–1917). Amalitsky found anthrocosid bivalves in the "silent" Permian deposits of Russia. These were similar to ones found in the Karroo Formation of Late Permian age in South Africa. Since scholars had collected many skeletons of different tetrapod groups in the Karroo basin, Amalitsky presumed that he should be able to find similar animals in Russia. His prediction was confirmed in the 1890s, when researchers working near the town of Kotelnish, discovered a deposit rich in tetrapods, including 12 new forms of amphibians and reptiles ranging in size from small to very large.

At present, these fossils are housed in the famous Northern Dvina Gallery of the Museum of Paleontology in Moscow. Among them, the most common was the two to three meter-long skeletons of pareiasaur *Scutosaurus,* a huge plant-eating thick-cheeked primitive anapsid (early reptile). These had been the prey of the carnivorous therapsids. Alongside large carnivorous therapsids, paleontologists discovered the remains of the small cynodont *Dvinia.* Cynodonts are the group of therapsids from which mammals arose. Another group of therapsids represented in the *Dvinia* assemblage are the dicynodonts—squat herbivores with largely toothless jaws tipped with a turtlelike beak. One dicynodont species from this assemblage had a stout nasal horn.

The next stage in studying Late Permian therapods began in the middle of the 1930s and was marked by investigations by Orlov, I.A. Efremov, A.P. Gortman, A.P. Bystrov, B.P. Vyushkov, E.D. Konzhukova, and P.K. Tchudinov. These scholars carried out excavations at a number of large sites, including those at Isheevo, Kamennyi Ovrag (in the middle of the Volga, near the town of Tetyushi, Tartar Republic), and Ocher. Excavations at the rich Late Permian locality of Isheevo began in 1930, at first under the

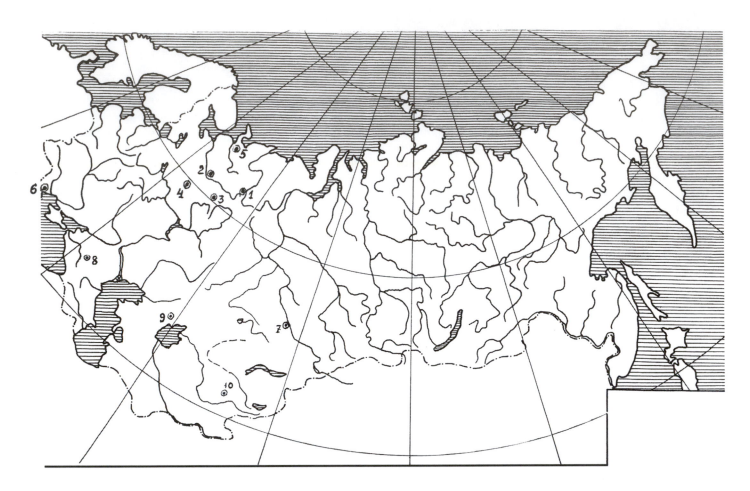

Figure 2. Some localities of the Permian-Triassic and Tertiary-Quaternary age on the territory of the former USSR. *1*, Ocher; *2*, North Dvina, Kotelnich; *3*, Isheevo; *4*, Vjazniki; *5*, Mezen; *6*, Odessa; *7*, Pavlodar; *8*, Belomechetskaya; *9*, Chelkar-Teniz; *10*, Fergana Valley (Madegen).

leadership of Leningrad geologists, and then by an expedition headed by Efremov and Orlov and sponsored by the Institute of Paleontology (Moscow). These excavations provided numerous collections of carnivorous reptiles, including therapsids. Outstanding among the latter were the primitive titanosuchids, which retained many features of earlier relatives from the Lower Permian red bed deposits in North America.

Titanophoneus patens, or "titanic murderer" (Efremov 1954), was investigated the most completely. This animal reached the length of three meters and had a bulldoglike snout and flipperlike limbs, both of which are evidence for an amphibious lifestyle and a diet of fish. However, *T. patens* could also hunt its herbivorous "relatives" (e.g., the ulemosaur, *Ulemosaurus svilagensis*, closely related to the South African herbivorous dinocephalian *Moschops*). Other titanosuchid relatives also were found at Isheevo: a larger carnivore, *Doliosauriscus*, "king of animals," and its smaller relative *Syodon efremovi* (Orlov 1958), which was about 1.5 meters long and probably hunted for small terrestrial animals.

Discovery of the dinocephalian *Venukovia invisa* (Efremov 1940) is of particular interest. This animal is an endemic form,

which confirms that dinocephalians originated from titanosuchids. Pockets of therocephalians, dog-headed carnivorous reptiles known from the Triassic of South Africa, also were found. Another discovery was *Lanthanosuchus gualeni*, an animal that combines the features of ancient amphibians and reptiles. Along with the Upper Permian *Kotlassia* (Northern Dvina) and *Seymouria* from the Lower Permian (North America), *L. gualeni* was classified in a separate subclass Batrachosauria (Efremov 1946b). In the Isheevo region, the bones of fish-eating labyrinthodonts *(Tryphosuchus)* and numerous bones of sharks testify to how close the area was to the sea.

Following investigations of numerous vertebrate localities, Efremov created a new field of paleontology, "taphonomy," the study of the laws of fossilization. By studying the fossilization process, scholars now can determine much about particular fossils. As Efremov studied fossil preservation in Isheevo, he made two conclusions: (1) the structure of bone beds and distribution of skeletons indicated that animals lived near the places where they died, and (2) that this burial place was similar to that of large alligators in North America. There, the animals died during the floods in the lower reaches of the Mississippi; then, the water abated quickly, leaving standing water in shallow canals. The animals died quickly, then were left undisturbed.

By the end of the 1930s, Efremov had already devised the first sequence of tetrapod faunal replacement. He distinguished the Early Permian, Lower and Upper Dinocephalian, transitional, and Northern-Dvinan stages (zones) as main stratigraphical divisions. Later, he and his disciple, Vyushkov (Efremov and Vyushkov 1955) began to hypothesize that these zones reflected the ecological differentiation of tetrapod assemblages. In his paper *The Terrestrial Vertebrate Fauna in the Permian Copper Sandstones of the Western Fore-Urals* (1954), Efremov reviewed the scattered descriptions of Permian tetrapods over 100 years, and added 59 new species to the 29 already-known species.

Essential to the subsequent development of this scheme was the unique fauna of eutheriodonts and deinocephalians, found near the town of Ocher, Perm area (Tchudinov, one of Efremov's disciples, performed excavations there in the 1960s). This complex, which is older than the Isheevo, is noted for its titanosuchids, which are characterized by features retained from their ancestors, the pelycosaurs. *Estemmenosuchus mirabilis*, the "crowned saurian," is endemic among them. This animal was up to four meters long and exhibited a number of strange protuberances on the skull. These structures probably were secondary sexual characters that developed upon sexual maturity and provided protection for males during battles. Estemmenosuchus may have looked similar to the South African Anteosauridae, probably as a result of convergence. Ocher's reptiles are diverse in morphology and way of life. Moreover, a number of labyrinthodonts, ganoid fishes and sharks, as well as anthracosid bivalves, were found here.

New research on Permian deposits has transformed Efremov's system into a circuit with three basic complexes: Ocher, Isheevo, and Northern-Dvina assemblages. The first corresponds approximately to the upper parts of the Pelycosaur Fauna from North America; the two others correspond to the *Tapinocephalus* Zone of South Africa. By the early 1970s Efremov and his followers had established the fundamental basis for morphological, taxonomic, faunal, and biostratigraphic investigations of Permian-Triassic amphibians and reptiles in eastern Europe.

The development of this system was associated with the studies conducted by many well-known Russian paleontologists from the Institute of Paleontology (Moscow) and Saratov University. For example, Academician L.P. Tatarinov (1976) developed the conception of mammal origin through mammalization of higher therapsids. M.A. Shishkin (1973) investigated the evolution of brachyopid labyrinthodonts and the role of neoteny in amphibian evolution. M.F. Ivakhnenko (1979) studied the evolution of the Parareptilia.

In recent years a number of new tetrapod assemblages from the Permian and Triassic were discovered. A.G. Sennikov (1995) performed paleoclimatic reconstructions for the Permian-Triassic Assemblages. Scholars now pay special attention to the thecodonts, a group of extinct reptiles diagnosed on the basis of the tooth structure by Richard Owen in the last century. Fossils of these animals have been found on all continents and, hence, are successfully used as index fossils. In particular, discovery of a crocodile-like rauisuchid on the River Vetluga (Sennikov 1990) settled a long-term dispute concerning the age of the variegated strata in the north European part of Russia in favor of the Triassic. The first reliable thecodont, *Archosaurus rossicus* (Tatarinov 1960), is known from the Permian, Upper Tatarian Substage. It was a large carnivore from the thecodont-dicynodont community known as the Vyazniki Assemblage, which probably was of the same age as the *Daptocephalus* Zone of South America.

In the European Triassic of Russia, scholars can distinguish four main stages of evolution of the tetrapod fauna: Vetlugian and Yarenian of Early Triassic, as well as Donguzian and Bukobaian of the Middle Triassic. The first stage is comparable to the *Lystrosaurus* Zone of South Africa and is characterized by small procolophids (such as *Tichninskia*); numerous specimens of an advanced proterosuchid called *Chasmatosuchus;* a number of species belonging to the rauisuchid genus *Tsylmosuchus;* and the rise of the lizard's ancestors, the Prolacertilia. This assemblage is present in Russia's northern regions (Moscow, Mezen, Pechora syneclise, and northern Urals) and its southern ones (southern Fore-Urals). The Yaren Assemblage is characterized by carnivorous trilophosaurs and large specialized rauisuchids.

The strata of the Donguz and Bukobai groups have been found only in the southern Fore-Urals. The Donguz ages are characterized by large specialized erythrosuchids and by small carnivorous rauisuchids. The age of Donguz Group is comparable with the Mencopy Formation of North America.

Marine Reptiles, Flying Reptiles, and Birds

As early as the middle of the last century, K.F. Rulie and G.F. Fischer mentioned finds of marine reptiles in the Jurassic of the Moscow area. From time to time, the workers in shale mines along the banks of the Volga found fossils of large reptiles, along with the fish bones, molluscs, and other invertebrates. Two complete skeletons of Jurassic ichthyosaurians (fishlike dinosaurs) were found in a mine in the Saratov area. In the Jurassic of the Volga district, fossils of plesiosaurs and huge pliosaurs (up to eight meters long) were found. On the other hand, crocodiles and turtles, both characteristic of the Jurassic of other countries, were not found in the Jurassic of the Volga region.

In the Early Mesozoic era (Triassic), small reptiles that moved mainly on their hind legs appeared among thecodonts. Their descendants gave rise to dinosaurs, flying reptiles (pterosaurs), and birds. However, dinosaurs are scarce in Russia. Those finds that have been described by Russian scientists originate mainly from Kazakhstan and Mongolia, as a result of long-term work of the Soviet-Mongolian Expedition. This expedition was organized by the Institute of Paleontology of the Russian Academy of Sciences in 1946 and was headed initially by Efremov. Efremov described the first three years of the fieldwork on the Mesozoic strata of the waterless Gobi Desert in his book *The Winds Route* (1957, 1962). Their experiences were also recounted by his disciple, A.K. Rozhdestvensky, *In the Footsteps of the Dinosaurs in the Gobi Desert* (1969). This expedition's work has continued to the present, with only a few gaps in activity. Russian and Mongolian researchers have published papers describing their findings, and the fossil skeletons of vertebrates living in Mongolia during the Cretaceous and Paleogene are displayed in the exhibits of the Museum of Paleontology in Moscow.

In the 1960s, the Expedition of the Institute of Paleontology, sponsored by the Russian Academy of Sciences, found strange fossils of flying reptiles not far from the city of Leninabad (Uzbekistan). The fossils are located in Triassic strata laid down by an ancient river, which flowed in the Fergana Valley (Madegen locality). One of these animals, *Longisquama,* had a gliding apparatus composed of parallel arrays of elongated scales that extended laterally from the middle of its back. The other animal, named *Sharovipteryx* after its discoverer, was equally bizarre. Its primary gliding membrane stretched between its hindlimbs and tail (Sharov 1971).

In the same years, scholars investigating Jurassic lake deposits of the Karatau Ridge (Kazakhstan) found some fossil pterosaurs (rhamphorhynchoids) preserved with their fur intact. One of these pterosaurs was named *Sordes pilosus* ("hairy hobgoblin"); apparently, it fed on insects and fishes, since the bones of the latter were found along with gastroliths (gizzard stones) from its stomach.

Fossil birds are rare in Russia, although deposits yielding enantiornithines exist in Uzbekistan and remains of the aquatic hesperornithines have been found in Central Russia and Kazakhstan. These toothed birds have been described by Kurochkin (1968) and Nessov (1992), among others. Representatives of many groups of modern neognathous birds are known from Ukrainian Neogene and Pleistocene deposits and were described by P.V. Serebrovsky and A.Y. Tugarinov (the founders of ornithology in Russia) and later by M.A. Voinstvensky and A.S. Umanskaya, between 1950 and 1989.

Important avian fossils of Cretaceous age have been found in Mongolia and the Baikal region. The Mongolian form *Ambiortus* is considered by Kurochkin (1996) to be the earliest neornithine (modern bird).

The Cenozoic Mammals and Others
The Late Pliocene Fauna of the Black Sea Region
The city of Odessa is situated high on the coast of the Black Sea, on limestone that can be as thick as 12 meters. This limestone was used for constructing buildings, especially from 1795, when Odessa was founded. Many long years of limestone extraction produced a complex network of passageways and cavities, forming the well-known Odessa catacombs. It was here that a pliocene fauna, represented mainly by fossil mammals, was found.

The most outstanding animals found in the catacombs were mastodons, which in the Late Pliocene were widespread throughout southern Europe, including the regions around Russia's Black and Azov seas. Also found were approximately 400 camels *(Paracamelus alexejevi),* presumed ancestors of the present-day wild Bacterian camel, which often is domesticated in central Asia. *Paracamelus* skeletons are displayed in the Ukrainian Academy of Sciences (Kiev) and in the Museum of Paleontology of the Odessa State University. The catacombs contained skeletons of many other mammals, such as antelopes, deer, various rodents, saber-toothed tigers, lynx, hyenas, bears, foxes, polecats, badgers, and

hedgehogs. Scholars also discovered fossils of birds (e.g., ostriches, partridges, eagles, and falcons), fishes (zanders and pike), and amphibians. The wide variety of fossils testifies to the richness of the Odessa karst and to the productivity of the area's steppe and mixed forest-steppe ecology.

The Hipparion Fauna
The Irtysh River forms a natural dividing line through the Tertiary and Quaternary strata of western Siberia. Near the town Pavlodar, on the right bank of the Irtysh, stretches an extensive outcrop of ocher sands and reddish clay. Starting with the 1930s, paleontologists of the Academy of Sciences from Moscow and Kazakhstan performed excavations here. They found a cemetery with a characteristic Pikermian Fauna (named after the village of Pikermi, Athens) and the Hipparion Fauna (in which fossils of a three-toed horse called *Hipparion* prevail). In the Pavlodar region, the bone bed is 10 to 12 meters thick. Surprisingly, although scholars have found hundreds of ungulate specimens (horses, rhinoceroses, giraffes, and proboscideans), they have found only a few carnivores. On the other hand, the dig did produce a rather large collection of small vertebrates such as rodents, amphibians, and birds (Orlov 1989).

The largest animals in the Pavlodar area were proboscideans (mastodons and deinotheries). The rhinoceroses are represented by a hornless genus, *Chilotherium;* this animal is widespread in the Miocene-Pliocene in North America, Asia (particularly in China), and eastern Europe. This short-legged, hippopotamus-like rhinoceros possessed forward-protruding lower incisors, which probably were used as a weapon and as a tool for digging up plant roots for food.

In 1929 and 1930 the finds of one hipparion species *(Hipparion elegans)* included more than 15,000 specimens. Judging from the limb and tooth structure, as examined by V.I. Gromova and K.K. Flerov, this animal spent the majority of its life on soft, marshy ground of steppes and bogs, feeding on soft herbaceous plants. The other rare species found in this region was *Hipparion longipes,* which is distinguished by long and thin legs.

The giraffes from the Pavlodar Fauna were primitive, distinguished by a moderately elongate neck and slightly lengthened legs. Resembling the present-day okapi, found in the forests of central Africa, these early giraffes were divided into two genera, *Samotherium* (also known from Iran) and *Paleotragus* (also known from China).

Rather numerous fossil deer of the genus *Cervavitus* were widely represented in the Hipparion Fauna from Moldova to China. An antelope, *Tragocerus amaltens,* known from the Neogene of Greece and Asia Minor, also was discovered. However, the fact that no monkeys were found in these areas probably is attributable to its northern location.

A large saber-toothed tiger, *Machaeroides,* was characterized by archaic features. In addition, scholars found several smaller cats that were approximately lynx-sized. Among still other carnivores, *Ictitherium* represents a transition between viverrids (e.g., civets, genets, mongooses) and hyenas. It also ranged through western and southeastern Europe and became extinct in the Pliocene. The discovery of *Semantor,* representative of a new family of pinnipeds (e.g., seals, sea lions, walruses) (Orlov 1933), is interesting. Apparently *Semantor* was an intermediate form, between otterlike martens and seals; this find confirmed the assumption of a probable origin of seals from martens.

In general, the Pavlodar locality contains animal species widespread in Europe and western Asia (e.g., hyena, *Ictitherium,* and gazelle), East Asia (e.g., badger and parataxidea), and western Siberia (e.g., *Machaeroides* and *Semantor*) at the end of the Miocene and Lower Pliocene. *Perunium ursogulo,* a giant marten found near Moldova, is of special interest. Scholars discovered an excellent fossilized skull for this member of the Hipparion Fauna, a skull that indicated the animal had a bearlike brain.

Gromova (1952) presumed that *Hipparion* appeared in North America and entered the Old World by way of routes through northern lands with wet landscapes similar to those of western Siberia. According to modern data, *Hipparion* spread into Eurasia about 12 million years ago, and then migrated south, to Africa. Orlov's hypothesis (1968) that central Asia was the center for the Hipparion Fauna has been confirmed in the subsequent research of other Russian paleontologists (Dmitrieva 1977; Zhegallo 1978; Godina 1979). From central Asia, the Hipparion Fauna spread to the south of Europe, the greater part of Africa, central Asia, part of southern Asia, and eventually the Indochinese peninsula.

The Anchitherium *Fauna*

In 1926 in the talus (rocky slope) of the right bank of the River Kuban, near the Station Belomechetskaya, several mastodon teeth and miscellaneous bone fragments were found. In 1927 geologists from Leningrad performed excavations in the area and discovered a complex of terrestrial mammals (e.g., ungulates, carnivores) of the Middle Miocene. The assemblage was named the *Anchitherium* Fauna, since its characteristic representative was *Anchitherium,* a three-toed horse with low (brachyodont) molars. As early as 1894, M.V. Pavlova (Moscow University), the greatest expert in ungulate vertebrates, had predicted that *Anchitherium* Fauna would be discovered in the territory of Russia.

Later, the Institute of Paleontology of the Academy of Moscow and the Institute of Paleobiology of the Georgian Academy of Sciences carried out excavations in this region. The largest forms were proboscideans and, among them, *Platybelodon danovi.* Borissiak (1928) described this animal as a descendant of the ancient Paleogene mastodon *Phiomia,* known from the Oligocene of Africa. The front end of the *Platybelodon*'s lower jaw was shaped like a spoon; the upper tusks were weakly developed upper tusks, and the upper lip was rather short. A proper trunk was probably not present. Presumably, *Platybelodon* had an amphibious way of life, feeding on aquatic plants. A rhinoceros, *Dicerorhinus caucasicus* (the same genus as the living Sumatran rhinoceros), as well as two species of horses also occur in the Belomechetskaya.

In addition to *Anchitherium,* which spread into western Europe, a new genus, *Paranchitherium,* was found here. This animal was an analog of (species similar to) *Parahippus* from the Miocene of North America and, in some characters, resembled the North American *Merychippus.* Thus, *Paranchitherium* was a probable ancestor of *Hipparion.* In due time, Kovalevsky (1873) used *Anchitherium* as the basis of his classic study of horse evolution. Based on the fact that *Anchitherium* and *Paranchitherium* were endemic to the Old World, Borissiak (1937, 1945) hypothesized that horses probably evolved independently in the New and Old World.

The diverse artiodactyls of the Belorechenskaya Fauna are represented by a number of species: a huge long-snouted pig, *Cubanochoerus robustus;* some primitive deer (in particular, *Paradicrocerus flerovi,* which is characterized by short forklike horns); and an antelope, *Hypsodontus miocenicus,* characterized by very high molars. All provide evidence for the early radiation of the Bovidae (Sokolov 1949).

The Indricotherium *Fauna*

In 1913, in the Aktyubinsk district of Kazakhstan, near Lake Chelkar-Teniz (today, this is a salt basin), a student found the bones of a huge hornless rhinoceros, described as *Indricotherium transuralicum* (Pavlova 1922) in honor of the fantastic "Indrik-animal." Somewhat later, a mammalian fauna of Middle Miocene age containing perrisodactyls (odd-toed ungulates), suids (pigs), reminant (cud-chewing) artiodactyls, and rodents was discovered in this place and named the *Indricotherium* Fauna.

Borissiak conducted a detailed investigation of *Indricotherium* (1923). Based on the functional morphological analysis of isolated bones, he reconstructed the muscular system and appearance of this animal, the largest terrestrial mammal. Today one can view an *Indricotherium* skeleton three meters tall at the Museum of Paleontology in Moscow. Notwithstanding its giant size, *Indricotherium* displays many archaic features in common with horses and tapirs. It possessed slender legs of the single blade pattern (the side toes were weakened and directed toward the rear, so that a single toe bears most of the animal's weight, something also seen in horses). Its molars were simple, lacking the plicae (foldings) typical of teeth found in later rhinoceroses, and obviously were adapted for feeding on leaves and young shoots. Rhinoceroses of this family were also found on the coast of the Aral Sea, in Transcaucasia, China, and Mongolia. In Mongolia they were first described by C.F. Cooper (1913) as the genus *Baluchitherium.* Another rhinoceros from Chelkar-Teniz was *Allocerops turganicum* (Borissiak 1915; Belyaeva 1954). It resembled a small horse and possessed slightly plicate teeth. Probably, in that period, both groups of rhinoceroses lived together in the forests and groves.

A third rhinoceros, *Chyracodon (Parachyracodon),* was represented by two species. It possessed plicate molars, which were adapted for feeding on herbaceous vegetation. This running rhinoceros was found in Mongolia, in the Oligocene of central Asia, and in the Paleogene of North America. However, some scholars question whether this group originated in Asia (Belyaeva 1952, 1954).

In addition to rhinoceroses, a peculiar perissodactyl, the chalicothere *Schizotherium,* also was part of *Indricotherium* Fauna. Its hooked toes bore stout claws instead of hoofs. Chalicotheres were widespread in the Paleogene and Neogene of Europe, Asia (their probable native land), and in North America. Additionally, the fossils of the Tapiroidea and Suiformes, the latter represented by the very large *Entelodon major* (closely related to *Archeotherium* from the Oligocene of North America) were found in Chelkar-Teniz. Also found were fossils of ancient cervids (deer), including miniature *Lophiomeryx turgaicus* (Flerov 1938), a rabbit-sized animal that resembled a deerlike tragulid *(Hyemoschus)* from forest bogs of west Africa. One of the most interesting carnivorous mammals from Chelkar-Teniz is a late-surviving creodont, *Tshelkaria*. Unrelated to modern carnivorans, creodonts may have arisen from the Insectivora (shrews, moles) (Gromova 1960). According to K.K. Flerov (1961), the animals from the Middle Oligocene of Kazakhstan were divided into two communities, each of which corresponded to a different landscape. One lived in humid forests, and the other lived in dry savanna steppes.

New Directions in Paleontology

Precambrian Paleontology

In the Precambrian rocks, Russian paleontologists have made dramatic strides in the study of Archean and Proterozoic life; the period that first gave rise to living things on Earth. In the early 1930s V.P. Maslov, P.V. Krasnopeeva, and A.G. Vologdin initiated a biogeographic study of Precambrian organic-walled microfossils (e.g. acritarchs). They also hoped to use stromatolites (lithified hummocks of sediment of trapped by cyanobacteria) for age correlations in Precambrian deposits.

In the late 1940s S.N. Naumova carried on these studies; later work was done by B.V. Timofeev, N.A. Volkova, and others. The pioneering studies in this field used techniques normally used in palynology (the study of living and fossil pollen and spores). These included breaking up the rocks that included the microfossils, then dissolving the rock with strong acids. This treatment creates a slurry and releases the microfossils, which then can be separated by filtering or straining. Taken together, such investigations revealed a previously obscure world of diverse and abundant microorganisms of Precambrian Earth.

Essential progress in the study of stromatolites was achieved in the 1950s when about 20 specialists at the geological institutes and surveys of Moscow, Yakutsk, Novosibirsk, and other cities collected an enormous amount of data from the great expanse of the Urals and Siberia. By the early 1960s, a Late Proterozoic stromatolite stratigraphy, with a time resolution of 100 to 300 million years, was established, a major breakthrough in Precambrian stratigraphy. Traditional binomial Latin names were given to stromatolites, in spite of the uncertain nature of the organisms that created them. A few scholars developed classifications based on the gross morphology and microstructures of the microscopic layering of stromatolites. Recent interest in stromatolites is related to the fact that these biogenic sedimentary structures span over three billion years of Earth's history.

Scholars obtained considerable paleobiological information during the study of the Upper Precambrian rocks of the Vendian System, which immediately preceded the Cambrian. Identified in the 1950s by B.S. Sokolov as a special geological system and period, the Vendian has been fully defined only recently. Sokolov, B.M. Keller, M.A. Fedonkin, and others have made major contributions to the study of Vendian fossils. Major discoveries of world class fossil localities—in the White Sea region, the Olenek Uplift, the Urals and

other parts of Russia—have yielded thousands of body fossils and trace fossils (Sokolov and Fedonkin 1990). A number of new high-rank taxa (classes and phyla) were recognized. This body of work has revealed a whole new period in early animal evolution.

Bacterial Paleontology

Bacterial paleontology is connected closely with the Precambrian era. This direction in paleontological research emerged in the early 1960s in the United States, when the remains of cyanobacteria were recovered from chert deposits. In recent years Russian scholars discovered fossilized bacteria in many types of rocks, including phosphorites, carbonates, and shales with high carbon content (Rozanov and Zhegallo 1989; Zhmur et al. 1995). In many cases, these cyanobacteria are well preserved, which may be explained by the extremely short time (a few hours) in which fossilization (e.g., phosphatization and silification) occurred. This was proved experimentally in living cyanobacteria (Gerasimenko et al. 1996).

Data obtained from bacterial paleontology are very important. For instance, black shales once were considered to be deep-water sediments. Then scholars discovered cyanobacterial mats (sheets) in black shales. Such organisms grow only in the photic zone (the sunlit, uppermost layer of the water column). Therefore, the shales must have been built up in shallower waters. Many Precambrian rocks contain remains of the cyanobacterial mats. This indicates that oil and gas probably formed much more frequently and abundantly in the Precambrian than it was previously thought.

The Earliest Skeletonized Fossils

In the early 1960s Russian scientists discovered that many animals acquired the ability to form a skeleton at the boundary between the Precambrian and the Cambrian (Rozanov 1984). This discovery opened a new topic for paleontologists—the study of the earliest skeletonized organisms (Rozanov and Missarzhevsky 1966). In the earliest Cambrian strata, numerous, very small, and usually phosphatic skeletons (shells) and isolated sclerites were discovered. Based on these fossils, scholars established the Tommotian Stage in Siberia. The Tommotian fauna contains many organisms of high taxonomic rank, further evidence that they evolved rapidly. At present, scientists of many countries are studying these earliest skeletonized organisms, known as "small shelly fossils."

EMILIA I. VOROBYEVA

See also Europe: Eastern Europe

Works Cited

Belyaeva, E.I. 1952. Primitivyne nosorogoobraznye Mongolii [Primitive rhinoceroses from Mongolia]. *Trudy Paleontologocheskogo Instituta [Trudy Paleontological Institute]; Akademii Nauk SSSR* 41:120–42.
———. 1954. Novye materialy po tietichinym nosorogoobraznym Kazakhstana [New materials on Tertiary rhinoceroses from Kazakhstan]. *Trudy Paleontologocheskogo Instituta [Trudy Paleontological Institute]; Akademii Nauk SSSR* 47:24–54.

Berg, L.S. 1955. Sistema ryboobraznykh i ryb, nyne zhivushchikh i iskopaemykh [The system of fishlike animals and fishes, recent and fossil]. *Trudy Paleontologocheskogo Instituta [Trudy Paleontological Institute]; Akademii Nauk SSSR* 20:1–286.

Borissiak, A.A. 1905–6. *Course of Palaeontology*. Vol. 2, *Vertebrates*. 2 vols. Moscow: Sabashnikov. [in Russian]

———. 1915. On remains of Epiceratherium turganicum. n.sp. *Izvestia Russ. Akad. Nauk* 6 (8):781–87.

———. 1923. On the genera Indricotherium nov. gen. (fam. Rhinocerotidae). *Zapisky Russian Akad. Nauk, physic.-mathem. Dept.*, 8th ser, 35 (6):1–128.

———. 1928. On Platybelodon danovi gen. et sp. nov.: New mastodont from choraksky deposits of Kubanskoy district. *Ezhegodnik of Russ. Palaeont. Soc.* 7:105–20.

———. 1937. On *Parachitherium Karpinskii* gen. et spec. nov.: New representatives of Equidae from Middle Miocene of Kaukasus. *Izvestia Akademii Nauk SSSR, Math.-Natur.* 789–93.

———. 1945. On the remains of representatives of fam. Equidae from Middle Miocene of the North Caucasus. *Trudy Paleontologocheskogo Instituta [Trudy Paleontological Institute]; Akademii Nauk SSSR* 20 (5):1–73.

Chabakov, A.V. 1934–41. *Atlas of Main Fossil Forms of USSR*. Vols. 4 and 5, *Carboniferous Pices*. N.p.

Cooper, C.F. 1913. *Thaumastotherium osborni:* A new genus of perissodactyls from the Upper Oligocene deposits of the Bugti Hills of Balauchistan. *Annual Magazine of Natural History*, ser. 8, 12 (67):376–504.

Dmitrieva, E.L. 1977. Antilopy neogena Mongolii i sopredelnkh territorii [Antelope from the Neogene of Mongolia and adjacent territories]. *Trudy Paleontologocheskogo Instituta [Trudy Paleontological Institute]; Akademii Nauk SSSR Trudy Sovmestnaia sovetsko-mongolskaia paleontologicheskaia* 6:5–116. Moscow: Nauka.

Efremov, I.A. 1940. Kurze Übersicht über die Formen der Perm- und der Triass-Tetrapoden-Fauna der USSR. *Aentralbl. fur Mineralogy ets (Zentr. Miner. Abt. B.)* 12:372–83.

———. 1946a. Almaznaia truba; Rasskazy. *Biblioteka Ogonek* 43:1–47.

———. 1946b. On the subclass Batrachosauria as a group between Amphibia and Reptilia. *Izvestia Akademii Nauk SSSR Seriya Biologicheskaya* 6:615–38.

———. 1954. Fauna nazemnykh pozvonochnykh v permskikh medistykh peschanikakh Zapadnogo priuralia. [The terrestrial vertebrate fauna in the Permian Cooper Sandstones of the Western Fore Urals]. *Trudy Paleontologocheskogo Instituta [Trudy Paleontological Institute]; Akademii Nauk SSSR* 54:1–416.

———. 1962. *The Wind's Route*. 2nd. ed., Moscow: State Publications in Haus for Georgia Books. [in Russian]

Efremov, I.A., and V.P. Vyushkov. 1955. List of the localities of Permian and Triassic tetrapods on the territory of the USSR. *Trudy Paleontologocheskogo Instituta [Trudy Paleontological Institute]; Akademii Nauk SSSR* 46:1–185. [in Russian]

Eichwald, C.E. 1840–48. *Die Urwelt Russlands, durch Abbildungen erläutert. [Paleontology of Russia]*. 4 vols., St. Petersburg: Druckerei des journal de Staint-Petersburg.

———. 1852–68. *Lethaea rossica: Ou paleontologie de la Russie decrite et figuree*. 3 vols. Stuttgart: Schweizerbart.

Flerov, K.K. 1938. Remains of Ungulata from Bet-pak-dala. *Doklady Akademii Nauk SSSR* 21:94–96.

———. 1961. The biological and paleozoogeographical characteristic of Indricotherium Fauna. *Palaeontological Journal* 1:12–22. [in Russian]

Gekker, R.F. 1957. *Introduction to Paleoecology*. Moscow: Gos nauchno tekhn.

———. 1987. *Na Siluriiskom plato [On the Silurian Plateau]*. Ocherki po istorii geologicheskikh znaii 24. Moscow: Publications Akademii Nauk SSSR.

Gekker, R.F., A.I. Osipova, and T.N. Belskaya. 1962. *Fergeamskii Aliv paleogenovogo moriia Srednei Azii [Fergana Gulf of the Palaeogene Sea in Middle Asia]*. Moscow: Publications Akademii Nauk SSSR.

Gerasimenko, L.M., I.V. Goncharova, E.A. Zhegallo, G.A. Zavarzin, L.V. Zaizeva, V.K. Orleansky, A.Y. Rozanov, and G.T. Ushatinskaya. 1996. Process of mineralization (phosphatization) of cyanobacteria. *Litology a. Mineral Resources* 2:208–14. [in Russian]

Godina, A.J. 1979. Istoricheskoe razvitie zhiraf rod Palaeotragus [Evolution of giraffes (Genera Palaeotrgus)]. *Trudy Paleontologocheskogo Instituta [Trudy Paleontological Institute]; Akademii Nauk SSSR* 117:3–114.

Gromova, V.I. 1952. Gaippariony: Po materialam Taraklii, Pavlodara, i drugim [Hipparion from Taraklia, Paqvlodar and other places]. *Trudy Paleontologocheskogo Instituta [Trudy Paleontological Institute]; Akademii Nauk SSSR* 36:1–478.

———. 1960. On a new family (Tshelkariidae) of primitive Creodonta from the Oligocene of Asia. *Trudy Paleontologocheskogo Instituta [Trudy Paleontological Institute]; Akademii Nauk SSSR* 5 (77):41–78.

Ivankhnenko, M.F. 1979. Permian and Triassic procolophones of Russian Platform. *Trudy Paleontologocheskogo Instituta [Trudy Paleontological Institute]; Akademii Nauk SSSR* 164:1–80. [in Russian]

Ivanova, E.I. 1958. Faunistic evolution in connection with environments. *In* Faunistic evolution of Middle and Upper Carboniferous sea in West Part of Moscow region. *Trudy Paleontologocheskogo Instituta [Trudy Paleontological Institute]; Akademii Nauk SSSR* 69:1–351.

Jaekel, O. 1909. Ueber Carpoideen, eine neue Klasse von Pelmatozoen. *Zeitschrift Deutschen Geol. Ges.* 52 (4):661–77.

Karpinsky, A.P. 1889. Über die Ammoneen der Artinsk-Stufe und einige mit denselben verwandten carbonischen Foramen. *Mémoires de l'Académie Impériale des Sciences de St. Pétersbourg*, ser. 7, 37 (2):1–104.

Kovalevsky, W. 1873. Sur l'Anchiterium aurelianense Cuv. et sur l'histoire paléontologique des chevaux. *Mémoires de l'Académie Impériale des Sciences de St. Pétersbourg* 20 (5):1–73.

Kurochkin, E.N. 1969. Principal problems of the study of fossil birds. *In* C.P. Poznaniw (ed.), *Reviews of Science, Vertebrate Zoology: Problems of Ornithology*. Moscow: VINITI.

———. 1996. Synopsis of Mesozoic birds and early evolution of class Aves. *Archaeopteryx* 13:47–66.

Lebedev, O.A., and M.I. Coates. 1995. The postcranial skeleton of the Devonian tetrapod Tulerpeton curtum Lebedev. *Zoological Journal of the Linnean Society of London* 114:307–48.

Murchison, R.I. 1841. Tours in the Russian provinces. *Quarterly Review* 67:344–75.

Nessov, L.A. 1992. Record of the localities of Mesozoic and Paleogene with avian remains in the USSR, and the description of new findings. *Russian Ornithological Journal* 1:7–50.

Novitskaya, L.I. 1971. Les amphiaspides (Heterostraci) du Dévonien de la Sibérie. *In Cahiers de Paléontologie*. Paris: Editions du Centre National de la recherche scientifique.

Obruchev, D.V. (ed.). 1964. *Agnathans and Fishes, Oxnovy of Palaeontology*. Moscow: Nauka [in Russian]; Tel Aviv, 1968 [in English].

Orlov, I.A. 1933. Semantor macrurus (ordo Pinnipedia, fam. Semantoridae fam.nov.) aus den Neogen-Ablagerungen West-Sibirien. *Trudy Paleontologocheskogo Instituta [Trudy Paleontological Institute]; Akademii Nauk SSSR* 2:165–268.

———. 1941. Tretichnye mlekopitaiushchie i mestonakhozhdeniia ikh ostatkov [Tertiary mammals and the localities of their remains]. *Trudy Paleontologocheskogo Instituta [Trudy Paleontological Institute]; Akademii Nauk SSSR* 8 (3):1–102.

———. 1947. Peruniinae: A new subfamily of martens from Neogene of Euroasia. *Trudy Paleontologocheskogo Instituta [Trudy Paleontological Institute]; Akademii Nauk SSSR* 10 (3):1–56. [in Russian]

———. 1958. Khishchnye deinotsefaly fauny isheeva (Titanozukhi) [The coniferous dinocephalians of the Isheevo fauna (Titanosuchia)]. *Trudy Paleontologocheskogo Instituta [Trudy Paleontological Institute]; Akademii Nauk SSSR* 72:1–112.

———. 1968. *V mire drevnikh zhivotnykh [In the World of Ancient Animals]. Ocherky on the Palaeontology of Vertebrates.* 2nd ed., Moscow: Nauka; 3rd ed., *The World of Early Animals,* 1989. [in Russian]

Osborn, H.F. 1902. Homoplasy as a law of latent or potential homology. *American Naturalist* 36:259–71.

Pander, C.H. 1830. *Beiträge zur Geognosie des Russischen Reiches.* St. Petersburg: Gedruckt bei K. Kray.

———. 1856. *Monographie der fossilen Fische des Silurischen Systems des Russisch-Baltischen Gouvernements.* St. Petersburg: Buchdr. Der K. Akademie der Wissenschaften.

Pavlov, A.P. 1901. Le Crétacé inférieur de la Russie et sa faune. *Nouv. Mém. Soc. Impér. natur. Moscou* 16 (3):1–87.

Pavlova, M.V. 1922. Indricoterium transoralicum m.sp. provenant du district de Tourgay. *Bulletin of the Society of Nature of Moscow* 31:95–116.

———. 1929. *Palaeozoology.* Vol. 2, *Vertebrates.* Moscow: n.p.

Rozanov, A.I. 1984. The Precambrian-Cambrian Boundary in Siberia. *Episodes* 7 (1):20–24.

Rozanov, A.I., and V.V. Missarzhevsky. 1966. Biostratigraphy and fauna of the lower Cambrian. *Transactions of the Beolarus Institute of the Academy of Sciences of the USSR,* 1.

Rozanov, A.I., and E.A. Zhegallo. 1989. To the problem of old phosphorites genesis in Asia. *Lithology and Mineral Resources* 3:67–82. [in Russian]

Rozhdestvensky, A.K. 1969. *In the Footsteps of the Dinosaurs in the Gobi Desert.* 3rd. ed., Moscow: Nauka.

Rozhnov, S. 1989. New data about rhipidocystids (Eocrinoicdea). *In* D. Kaljo (ed.), *Fossil and Recent Echinoderm Researches.* Tallinn: Akademiia nauk Estonskoi SSR.

Ruzhentsev, V.E., and I.A. Orlov. 1960. Printsippy sistematiki, sistema i filogeniia paleozoiskikh ammonoidea [Principles of systematics, system and phylogeny of Paleozoic ammonoidea]. *Trudy Paleontologocheskogo Instituta [Trudy Paleontological Institute]; Akademii Nauk SSSR* 83:1–331.

Schindewolf, O.H. 1921. Versuch einer Paläogeographie des europaischen Oberdevonmeeres. *Gesellschaft* 73 (3):137–223.

———. 1925. Entwurf einer Systematik der Perisphincten. *Neus Jahrb. Miner. Geolol. Paläontol., Abt. B.* 52:309–43.

Schmidt, F. 1872. *Wissenschaftliche Resultate zur Aufsuchung eines angekundtigten Mammuth cadavers von Kaiserlichen Akademie der Wissenschaften an den Unteren Jenissei ausgesandten Expedition.* Mémoires de l'Académie Impériale des Sciences de St. Pétersbourg, Ser. 7, 18, N1. St. Pétersburg: Académie Impériale des Sciences de St. Pétersbourg.

Sennikov, A.G. 1990. New data on rauisuchiids. *Palaeontological Journal* 24 (3):3–16. [in Russian]

———. 1995. Rannie tekodonty vostochnoi Evropy [Early Thecodonts of Eastern Europe]. *Trudy Paleontologocheskogo Instituta [Trudy Paleontological Institute]; Akademii Nauk SSSR* 263:1–138.

Sharov, A.G. 1971. New Fliegende Reptilien aus dem Mesozoikum von Kasakhstan und Kirfisien. *Trudy Paleontologocheskogo Instituta [Trudy Paleontological Institute]; Akademii Nauk SSSR* 130:104–113.

Shishkin, M.A. 1973. Morfologiia drevnikh zemnovodnykh i problemy evoliutsii nizshikh tetrapod. [Morphology of the early amphibians and problems of evolution of lower tetrapods. *Trudy Paleontologocheskogo Instituta [Trudy Paleontological Institute]; Akademi Nauk SSSR* 137:1–260.

Sokolov, B.S., and M.A. Fedonkin (eds.). 1990. *Vendian System Paleontology.* Vol. 2, *Regional Geology.* Berlin and New York: Springer-Verlag; as *Vendskaia sistema,* vol. 2, Moscow: Nauka.

Sokolov, I.I. 1949. Ob ostatkakh polorogikh (Bovidae, mammalia) iz srednego miotsena severnogo Kavkaza [On remains of Bovidae (Mammalia) from Middle Miocene of Caucasus]. *Doklady Akademii Nauk SSSR,* new ser., 67 (6):1101–4.

Strangways, W.T.H.F. 1821. Geological sketch of the environs of St. Petersburg. *Transactions of the Geological Society of London* 5:392–458.

Sushkin, P.P. 1926. Notes on the prejurassic Tetrapoda from Russia. *Paleonto. Hungarica* 1:323–44.

Tatarinov, L.P. 1960. The opening of pseudosuchians from Upper Permian of USSR. *Palaeontological Journal* 4:74–80. [in Russian]

———. 1976. *Morfologicheskaia evolintsiia teriodontov i obshchie voprosy filogenetiki [Morphological Evolution of the Theriodonts and General Problems of Phylogenetics].* Moscow: Nauka.

Trudy Paleontologocheskogo Instituta. 1986. *History of Neogene Molusk of Paratethys.* Moscow: Nauka.

Volborth, A. 1847. Über einige russische Trilobiten. *Verhandlung der Russisch Mineral. Gesellschaft St. Petersburg, Jahrbuch* 16:3.

Vorobyeva, E.I. 1977. Morphology and nature of evolution of crossopterygian fishes. *Trudy Paleontologocheskogo Instituta [Trudy Paleontological Institute]; Akademii Nauk SSSR* 163:1–239.

———. 1992. *Problem of Tetrapod Origin.* Moscow: Nauka. [in Russian]

Vorobyeva, E.I., and R. Hinchliffe. 1996. From fins to limbs: Developmental perspectives on paleontological and morphological evidence. *In* M. Hecht, R.J. MacIntyre, and M.T. Clegg (eds.), *Evolutionary Biology.* London and New York: Plenum.

Vorobyeva, E.I., and H.-P. Schultze. 1991. Description and systematics of Panderichthyid fishes with comments on their relationship to tetrapods. *In* H.-P. Schultze and L. Trueb (eds.), *Origins of the Higher Groups of Tetrapods.* Ithaca, New York: Cornell University Press.

Zhegallo, V.I. 1978. Gippariony Tsentralnoi Azii [Hypparion fauna of the Central Asia]. *Trudy Sovmestnaia sovetsko-mongolskaia paleontologicheskaia ekspeditsiia; Akademii Nauk SSSR* 7:1–156.

Zhmur, S.I., M.B. Bursin, and V.M. Gorlenko. 1995. Cyanobacteria and formation of carbon rocks in Later Precambrian. *Litology a. Mineral Resources* 2:206–14. [in Russian]

Further Reading

Andrussov, N.I. 1896. Die südrussischen Neogenablagerungen. Teil 1. Alteres Miocan. *Zapiiski St. Petersberg Mineralogical Society* 34:194–245.

Gekker, R.F. 1940. Lower Silurian and Devonian echinoderms. Carpoidea, Eocrinoidea and Ophiocistia of Lower Silurian of Leningrad district and Estland. *Trudy Paleontologocheskogo Instituta [Trudy Paleontological Institute]; Akademii Nauk SSSR* 9 (4):5–82. [in Russian]

Jakovlev, V. 1916. Triassic fauna of vertebrates from gaycolor deposits in Vologodskaya and Kostromskaya provences. *Vestnik of Geology* 2 (4):157–65. [in Russian]

Karpinsky, A.P. 1889. *Über die Ammoneen der Artinsk-Stufe und einige mit denselben verwandten carbonischen Formen.* Mémoires de l'Académie Impériale des Sciences de St. Pétersbourg, ser. 7, 37 (2):1–104.

Kovalevsky, W. 1874. Monographie der Gattung Anthracotherium Cuv. und Versuch einer natürlichen Klassification der fossilen Huftiere. *Palaeontographica* 22 (5):131–346.

Pander, C.H. 1830. *Beiträge zur Geognosie des Russischen Reiches.* St. Petersburg: Gedruckt bei K. Kray.

Serebrovsky, P.V. 1948. Birds of the Binagada asphalt deposits. *Proc. Natur. Hist. Mus. Azerbajdzan Akademii Nauk SSSR* 1–2:21–68. [in Russian]

Tugarinov, A.Y. 1940. New data on Tertiary ornithofauna of the USSR. *Trans Akademii. Nauk SSSR* 26 (2):307–9. [in Russian]

Umanskaya, A.S. 1981. Miocene birds of western Cis-Black Sea of the Ukraina. Part 2, *Vestnik of Zoology* 3:17–21.

Voistvensky, M.A. 1960. Steppe birds of the European part of the USSR. Kiev: Publishing House of Ukrain Akademii Nauk. [in Russian]

S

SARCOPTERYGIANS

The Sarcopterygii (lobe-finned fishes) and the Actinopterygii (ray-finned fishes) are the two groups that make up the osteichthyans (bony fishes). Sarcopterygians were distributed worldwide from the Devonian to the Cretaceous; in the Cenozoic, they are restricted to the Southern Hemisphere. The sarcopterygians are divided into eight subcategories (Figure 1): the Dipnoi (lungfishes), Actinistia (coelacanths), Onychodontida, Porolepiformes, Rhizodontida, Osteolepiformes, Elpistostegalia (panderichthyids), and Tetrapoda (limbed vertebrates).

Distinctions between the various groups are based in part upon differences in the structure of the skull and of the pectoral fin, which is found below and behind the shoulder girdle. At present, the interrelationships between the eight groups are disputed strongly (Schultze 1994), but most (Schultze 1987; Panchen and Smithson 1987; Cloutier and Ahlberg 1996) agree with the interrelationships of the tetrapods and their three closest relatives, called the Choanata. Within it, the Elpistostegalia is the sister group (the closest relative) of the Tetrapoda; the two combine to form a larger group that is the sister group to the Osteolepiformes, and the Rhizodontida is the sister group of all three. The name Choanata (node 4 in Figure 1) comes from the fact that all members of the group have a "choana," an internal nasal opening that is connected with one external opening. The Choanata also share another characteristic: All possess the "tetrapod articulation," or joint morphology, of the pectoral fin. The proximal end (the one closest to the body) of the humerus (upper arm bone) is shaped like a ball to form a joint with a socket called the glenoid fossa of the shoulder girdle (Figure 6).

Porolepiformes is the sister group of the Choanata. Usually Porolepiformes and Choanata are combined as Rhipidistia (Schultze 1987; Panchen and Smithson 1987); they possess (node 3 in Figure 1) plicidentine (a specialized type of dentine); tusks on vomers (bones near the front of the roof of the mouth); two tectals (bones near the external nasal opening[s]); four infradentaries (bones called splenial, postsplenial, angular, and surangular) that lie below the dentary (the lower jawbone on which marginal teeth are found); narrow submandibulars (bones that border the lower jaw) between lower jaw and gular plates (the bones that form the floor of the mouth); extratemporal (an additional bone on the lateral margin of the skull roof toward the rear); and trifurcation (basal division into three parts) of the pectoral fin skeleton.

The placement of the Dipnoi, Actinistia, and Onychodontida is in dispute. R. Cloutier and P.E. Ahlberg (1996) follow A.L. Panchen and T.R. Smithson (1987) and M.-M. Chang (1991), by setting the Dipnoi as the sister group of the Porolepiformes within a larger category called "Rhipidistia." In contrast, H.-R. Schultze (1987) places the Dipnoi as the sister group of all other sarcopterygians, combining all sarcopterygians above lungfishes into the group Crossopterygii. The crossopterygians (node 2 in Figure 1) are characterized by an intracranial joint, a two-headed hyomandibula (upper element in the second gill arch), presence of tabular bones on the skull roof, a cheek with a squamosal bone, vertical preopercle (a bone just in front of the gill cover), and a large quadratojugal (a bone in the back of the upper jaw).

Sarcopterygians are distinct from actinopterygians, as shown by a large number of characters (node 1 in Figure 1) (Cloutier and Ahlberg 1996). The teeth, dermal bones (those of the skull and shoulder girdle) and scales possess true enamel on their surface. A broad peg is found on the dorsal margin (the "top" edge) of the rhombic (rhomboidal shaped) scales. Cosmine, found in many sarcopterygians, consists of a thick layer of dentine and a thin covering layer of enamel. It is pervaded by a "pore-canal system," which contains a complex cutaneous vascular system involved in the deposition of mineralized tissue. In the head, the premaxilla (the front bone of the upper jaw) does not reach the orbit (eye opening), the eye is surrounded by more than four sclerotic plates, the squamosal (a large bone in the cheek) is separate from preopercle, only one branchiostegal ray lies below the gill cover, the hyomandibula has two proximal articular heads, two or four infradentaries are in the lower jaw, submandibulars lie between lower jaw and gular plates and lateral line canals (mucous-filled canals with nerve endings to sense changes of water pressure) run from jugal to preoperculum (jugal canal) and in the infradentaries (mandibular canal). In contrast to actinopterygians, the mandibu-

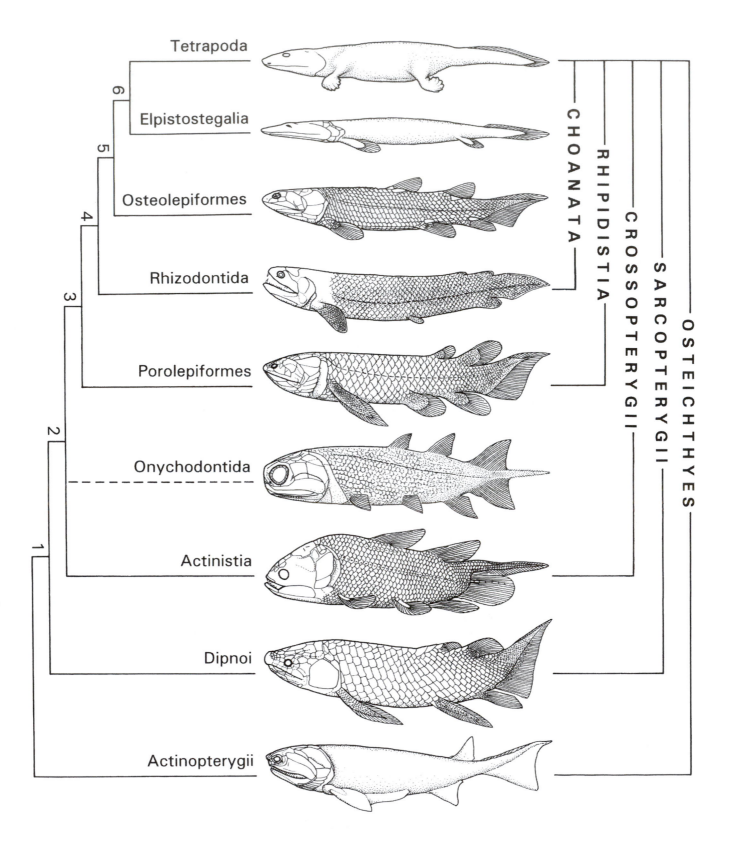

Figure 1. Interrelationships of the Sarcopterygii. Actinopterygii represented by *Cheirolepis canadensis* (after Arratia and Cloutier 1996); Dipnoi by *Uranolophus wyomingensis* (after Schultze 1992b); Actinistia by *Miguashaia bureaui* (after Schultze 1973); Onychodontida by *Strunius walteri* (after Jessen 1967); Porolepiformes by *Holoptychius jarviki* (after Cloutier 1996b); Rhizodontida by *?Strepsodus anculona-mensis* (after Andrews 1985); Osteolepiformes by *Osteolepis macrolepidotus* (after Jarvik 1948); Elpistostegalia by *Panderichthys rhombol-epis* (after Vorobyeva and Schultze 1991); Tetrapoda by *Acanthostega gunnari* (after Coates 1996). Explanation of nodes 1–6 in text.

lar canal does not enter the dentary (tooth-bearing lower jaw-bone), and the preopercular canal does not reach the tip of the preoperculum. In the pectoral fin there is only a single proximal element; the first dorsal fin (along the back) is supported by a basal plate.

Sarcopterygians are known since the Late Silurian of China. The osteichthyan *Lophosteus* from the Baltic region may belong to the group—it is of similar age, and its scales have a similar ornamentation. *Lophosteus* bones and scales are formed by bone and superimposed denticles (small teeth) but without enamel. This histology could be basal to either ganoid (primitive actinopterygian type) or cosmoid scales. Nonetheless, scholars are not yet certain about whether *Lophosteus* belongs with the sarcopterygians or actinopterygians.

Dipnoi

Lungfishes are known since the Early Devonian; today they are restricted to the southern continents (Australia: *Neoceratodus;* Africa: *Protopterus;* South America: *Lepidosiren*). No fossil lungfish with food remains in its stomach is known. Probably they fed on plants, worms, and molluscs as do Recent lungfishes. Some inferences can be made from their dentition. Tooth plates (teeth fused to plates on the surface of the pterygoid bones of the palate and of the prearticular bones of the inner side of the lower jaws) are characteristic of Recent, Cenozoic, and Mesozoic lungfishes. Paleozoic lungfishes are known to have tooth plates, dentine plates or enamel-covered teeth or tubercles (dentinal protrusions). K.S.W. Campbell and R.E. Barwick (1990) base their lungfish phylogeny (evolutionary history) on different functional systems of the jaw apparatus. They recognize two distinct lineages of lungfishes: one with denticulated jaws (those with teeth on the jawbones) and one with dental plates. The latter lineage is divided into one with dentine plates and one with tooth plates.

Lungfishes are recognized by their unique pattern of the bones that form the roof of the skull (Figure 2), especially a unique bone at the back of the skull roof (called the "B-bone"), the lack of maxillae and separate premaxillae, the presence of an upper lip that is ossified (formed by bone, as in most Devonian forms) or unossified (all post-Devonian lungfishes), lack of external nasal openings, and presence of broad submandibulars. Both nasal openings—those that draw in water (incurrent) and force water out (excurrent)—lie on the palate. The arrangement and course of lateral line canals of the lower jaw are unique to lungfishes. The upper jaw (palatoquadrate) is fused to the endocranium, the bony capsule around the brain (this jaw attachment is called autostyly). The ridges on the tooth plate, or the entire tooth plate, are reinforced by a special, permanently growing tissue called petrodentine.

It is easy to demonstrate changes on lungfish features over time, but a coherent phylogeny of the group is not forthcoming because of a high level of homoplasy—characters have evolved in similar ways (convergence) in several unrelated forms (Schultze and Marshall 1993). Upper and lower lips become unossified in Late Devonian lungfishes and in all forms in later time periods. The number of skull roof bones diminishes, either through out-

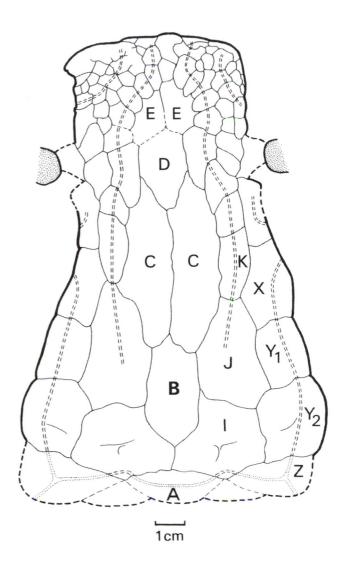

Figure 2. Skull roof of the primitive lungfish *Uranolophus wyomingensis.* A-B-C nomenclature of skull roofing bones. Redrawn after Schultze (1992a).

right loss or through fusion of adjacent bones; the protective cosmine cover found in early lungfishes is lost; bones become thinner; the shape of scales changes from rhombic in the Early Devonian, to round scales with cosmine, then to flexible round scales without cosmine; and unpaired fins fuse with the originally heterocercal (upwardly tilted) caudal (tail) fin to form an undivided diphycercal (straight, tapering) caudal fin.

Distributed worldwide in the Paleozoic and Mesozoic, and restricted to southern continents in the Cenozoic, in the Devonian Dipnoi are the most species-rich sarcopterygian group, with 80 species within 35 genera. The Uranolophidae includes primitive lungfishes with denticulated jaws; the Dipnorhynchidae includes primitive dentine-plated genera. Other Devonian genera are assigned to six families: Chirodipteridae, "Dipteridae," Fleurantiidae, Phaneropleuridae, Rhynchodipteridae, and Stomiahykidae. Over time, the number of genera decreases, to 12 in the Carboniferous and five in the Permian. These groups are set into five families: the Conchopomatidae, Ctenodontidae, Gnathorhizidae, Sagenodontidae, and Uronemidae. In the Mesozoic there is a comparable decrease, from over 10 genera and over 40 species in the Triassic to three genera in the Jurassic and Cretaceous. All Mesozoic genera are included in three families: "Ceratodontidae," Neoceratodontidae, and Lepidosirenidae. Tertiary genera and species are more common than those in the Quaternary. In the Tertiary, ceratodontids still could be found in South America and Africa.

Early Devonian lungfishes occur in coastal marine (e.g., the North American genera *Uranolophus* and *Melanognathus*) or fully marine deposits (*Ichnomylax, Dipnorhynchus,* and *Speonesydrion* in Australia and Germany, *Sorbitorhynchus* in China). Some believe that lungfishes that date from the Middle and Late Devonian (Old Red Sandstone, Scotland) are freshwater fishes; however, the same genera occur in marine deposits. Lungfishes are the most common fishes in the marine Upper Devonian deposits of Bergisch-Gladbach (western Germany). The same genera also occur in such marine deposits as those found in Koknese (Latvia). *Griphognathus* of Bergisch-Gladbach and Koknese occurs together with many other lungfishes (*Chirodipterus, Holodipterus, Gogodipterus,* and *Pillararhynchus*) in the concretions of the Gogo locality (western Australia). (In most deposits, the pressure from sediment compaction crushes the specimens—Gogo is famous for its concretions with three-dimensionally preserved fishes. When they are prepared with an acetic acid method, the results are comparable to preparations of extant fishes.) Another famous locality for Late Devonian lungfishes (*Scaumenacia, Fleurantia*) is at Miguasha (also known as Scaumenac or Escuminac Bay, Quebec). The long-snouted *Soederberghia* occurs with *Jarvikia* and *Oervigia* in red sediments of East Greenland, and *Soederberghia* also is found in reddish sediments of New South Wales (Australia). Such a widespread and various distribution only can indicate that the fish is "euryhaline"—it is able to tolerate a wide range of salinity, from salty marine to freshwater environments.

Carboniferous lungfishes (*Conchopoma, Ctenodus, Gnathorhiza, Megapleuron, Sagenodus, Tranodis*) occur in near-shore deposits (e.g., Mazon Creek, Illinois; Robinson and Hamilton, Kansas; and Greer, West Virginia) in North America, whereas scholars interpret the settings of the European Carboniferous lungfishes (*Conchopoma, Ctenodus, Megapleuron, Sagenodus*) as deposits from freshwater inland lakes. Triassic lungfishes mainly are known by tooth plates from freshwater deposits; a few are known by their skull roof. Ceratodont tooth plates are described from Jurassic and Cretaceous freshwater and marine deposits in Europe, Africa, Asia, Australia, and North and South America.

Diabolepis from the Lower Devonian of Yunnan, southern China, is the sister taxon of the Dipnoi (Chang 1995). It had dental plates with radial rows of teeth and an unpaired bone B in the posterior skull roof as seen in Dipnoi. In contrast to Dipnoi, anterior and posterior nasal openings lay close to the margin of the upper jaw outside the palate; the premaxillae form the anterior margin of the upper jaw and reach onto the palate; the palatoquadrate is not fused to the endocranium. The nasal openings and the premaxillae are "on the move onto the palate" to reach the lungfish level (i.e., in which there is no outer dental arcade [marginal tooth row], and both nasal openings are on the palate).

Actinistia

Like the Dipnoi, the Actinistia (coelacanths) are characterized by many unique features. The Actinistia are the only fishes with a special rostral organ in the snout, a deep fourth coronoid (bone on the dorsal margin of the lower jaw between dentary and prearticular), a tandem double articulation of the lower jaw, a postspiracular bone, and an additional bone, the "extracleithrum," in the shoulder girdle (Figure 3a). Like lungfishes, coelacanths lack the maxilla and have a short dentary. In contrast to lungfishes, the palatoquadrate is free and the intracranial joint is activated by a basicranial muscle, a feature unique within extant (present-day) fishes. The simple conical teeth are covered by enamel. Except for the Late Devonian *Miguashaia* and the Late Viséan *Allenypterus*, actinistians are recognized easily by their caudal fin, with equally sized lobes and unbranched lepidotrichia (fin rays) that are separated by an axial lobe of the notochord (a stiff fluid-filled tube that lies beneath the spinal column and functions as a support structure for vertebral elements) (Figure 3b). Like Dipnoi, coelacanths are an excellent example of rapidly declining rate in the evolution of shape and structure after the Devonian. Coelacanths also represent a sequential series of genera through time, of which only a few genera in the Triassic and Cretaceous can be grouped together (Cloutier 1991).

The first coelacanths occur in the Middle Devonian. These fishes were, and still are, carnivorous—two specimens (*Holophagus* and *Rhabdoderma*) have been discovered with actinopterygians in the stomach region. Only five genera with eight species are known from the Late Devonian; they are included in two families, Miguashaiidae (of which the primitive genus *Miguashaia* is a member) and Diplocercidae. Similar numbers of genera are known from the Carboniferous (six genera with 11 species) and Permian (five genera with five species); they are placed in two families, Hadronectoridae, which include genera from the Bear Gulch fauna (Montana), and "Rhabdodermatidae." In the Mesozoic, especially during the Triassic, coelacanths are rich in species (19 genera with 28 species); these are divided into three families, Laugiidae, Whiteiidae, and Coelacanthidae. Some Triassic genera are included with Jurassic and Cretaceous genera in the family Mawsoniidae, the sister taxon of all remaining Jurassic, Cretaceous, and extant genera, included in the Latimeriidae.

Actinistians are known from the Northern Hemisphere in the Late Devonian and Carboniferous, worldwide from Permian to Cretaceous, unknown through the Tertiary, and today are restricted to waters surrounding the Comoro islands. The osteological and endocranial features were well known in 1938 when *Latimeria,* the living coelacanth, was discovered by Ms. M. Courtenay-Latimer at East London, South Africa. The anatomy of *Latimeria* has been studied intensively. It exhibits sexual dimorphism (physical distinctions between males and females)—the female is longer (up to 1.8 meters) than the male (up to 1.4 meters). *Latimeria* produces the largest eggs (nine centimeters in diameter) of any bony fish, and it is ovoviviparous (eggs develop and hatch internally). Up to 30 developing young have been found in one female. The Late Jurassic *Undina* also was ovoviviparous; one adult specimen has been described with two young close to the pelvic region, in birth position. In contrast, hatchlings of

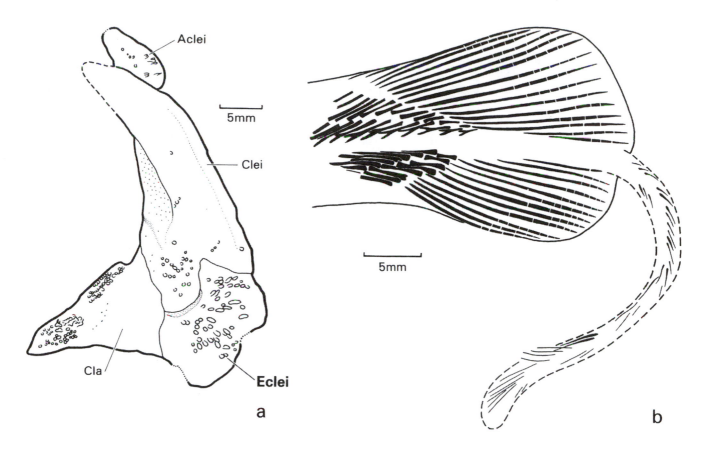

Figure 3. *a*, Shoulder girdle of the primitive coelacanth, *Miguashaia bureaui*; *b*, caudal fin of a juvenile coelacanth, *Rhabdoderma exiguum*, with extended axial notochordal lobe. Key: *aclei*, anocleithrum; *cla*, clavicle; *clei*, cleithrum; *eclei*, extracleithrum. *a*, redrawn after Cloutier (1996a); *b*, redrawn after Schultze (1972).

the small Late Carboniferous *Rhabdoderma exiguum* from Mazon Creek are abundant compared to other fishes of the locality. These newborns show all stages, from specimens with large yolk sac to those with partly and completely resorbed yolk sac. In the same locality, large eggs (3.5 centimeters in diameter) and unhatched specimens on large yolk sac (three centimeters in diameter) support the interpretation that the much smaller early coelacanths were egg-laying, as are all other sarcopterygians. These juveniles also have an elongate axial notochordal lobe (Figure 3b).

The coelacanths are mainly marine. In the Carboniferous and Mesozoic, a few forms were able to enter freshwater. All Devonian representatives are marine, including *Miguashaia*. The marine upper Viséan Plattenkalk deposits of Bear Gulch show an abundance of coelacanths. They are divided into five genera—*Polyosteorhynchus, Hadronector, Lochmocerus,* and *Caridosuctor,* all with the typical coelacanth caudal fin, and *Allenypterus* with a pointed end to the tail. They are found with palaeoniscoid actinopterygians (ray-finned fishes), chondrichthyans (cartilaginous fishes), rare acanthodians (spiny "sharks"), and one other sarcopterygian, a large rhizodont represented only by scales. Coelacanths are also common in marine and coastal North American midcontinental (*Rhabdoderma* in Mazon Creek and in Linton, Ohio; *Synaptotylus* in Garnett, Kansas) and European Upper Carboniferous deposits.

In Lower Triassic deposits of West Spitsbergen occurs another concentration of coelacanths, comparable to that in Bear Gulch. They are divided into five genera (*Axelia, Mylacanthus, Sassenia, Scleracanthus, Wimania,* with nine species) where they are found with many actinopterygians, a few elasmobranchs (primitive rays and sharks), and some amphibians. Northern Madagascar has deposits that contain three genera.

In contrast to lungfishes, coelacanths are found in the marine Middle Triassic of Europe. *Diplurus* is a common fish in the Upper Triassic and Lower Jurassic deposits of the Newark Supergroup in the eastern United States. Many species of three genera are described from Upper Jurassic deposits of the Solnhofen region (southern Germany). Coelacanths are well represented in the Lower Cretaceous of Brazil, Africa, England, and India. The latest fossil coelacanth found is also the largest: *Megalocoelacanthus* (3.5 meters in length), from the Upper Cretaceous of eastern United States.

Onychodontida

The Onychodontida are a small group of carnivorous active swimmers in the free water column (open waters below the surface and above the seafloor). Scholars know of only one family, Onychodontidae, which contains only three genera (*Grossius, Onychodus,*

Strunius). Onychodonts share characteristics with several other groups. As in actinopterygians, onychodonts possess a maxilla with a deepened region near the back (Figure 4). Onychodonts also have a whorl-like arrangement of teeth, called a parasymphysial tooth whorl, on the symphysis (front midline joint of the lower jaws). (This structure also is seen in primitive rhipidistians, such as *Youngolepis, Powichthys,* and Porolepiformes.) Onychodonts also have an intracranial joint, as seen in all crossopterygians.

Onychodonts have distinct characters. There are extremely long postparietals (bones that cover the back part of the skull roof), a premaxilla that is arched dorsally (upward) at the middle part of its oral border, and a lower jaw with an elongate infradentary. *Strunius* has a separated surangular (a bone at the back end of the lower jaw). The teeth are quite distinctive and easily recognized. They do not possess plicidentine. They fit into saclike structures like plugs in sockets; this structure forms vertical dentine folds (Schultze 1969). The enamel is striated on the lingual (tongue) side of teeth that are arched slightly toward the cheek. Each enamel ridge has ribbing in a chevron pattern. The opercular (gill cover) series is reduced. A triphycercal (three-lobed) tail with middle axial lobe is known from *Strunius.*

Onychodonts are restricted to the Devonian, though distributed worldwide. Partial specimens are known from marine Middle Devonian deposits of the United States, Spain, and Germany and from marine Upper Devonian deposits of Iran, Latvia, Germany, and West Australia. The only complete specimens are the small (8 to 12 centimeters long) *Strunius* from marine Upper Devonian deposits of Bergisch-Gladbach. In contrast, *Onychodus* species may reach several meters in length.

Porolepiformes

Porolepiforms are carnivorous sarcopterygians that are restricted to the Devonian. The Lower Devonian occurrences of complete specimens of *Porolepis* in Spitsbergen are interpreted tentatively as freshwater deposits; other Early Devonian porolepiforms occur in marine deposits of Northern Canada. The Old Red Sandstone occurrences of holoptychiids are also interpreted as freshwater deposits; nevertheless, the same genera are distributed widely and found more often in marine or coastal marine deposits (Miguasha, Baltic region, Russia, western United States).

Typically, Porolepiformes have dendrodont plicidentine, in which the first globular deposition of dentine is arranged in regular Christmas tree–like folds (Figure 5f). In addition, the group's monophyly (the descent of all groups from a single common ancestor) is supported by the presence of subsquamosals and a posterior skull roof covered by two pair of bones (a tabular and a postparietal that may include a supratemporal). The otic lateral line canal, which lies above the part of the endocranium that houses the inner ear, passes through the postparietal growth center. The median (center) extrascapular overlaps the lateral (side) extrascapulars.

Porolepiforms have two external nasal openings (a primitive feature for osteichthyans) and possibly an internal nasal opening. The symphysis carries a pair of tooth whorls; each has one main tooth row and smaller parallel tooth rows. The opercle is small, and there are few branchiostegals (platelike bones below the oper-

cle). A bone unique to porolepiforms, the preoperculosubmandibular, carries the preopercular lateral line canal from the preopercle to the lower jaw. The lobe of the pectoral fin is especially elongate and contains an archipterygium (chain of bones with lateral branching radials) with large central elements; this structure is similar to the one found in coelacanths. All porolepiforms have a heterocercal tail, broadly lobed pelvic fins, and two dorsal fins, except *Quebecius,* in which the pelvic fins have a long base.

Two families are distinguished: The Early Devonian Porolepidae (two genera) has rhombic and/or round scales and cosmine on bones and scales; the Middle-to-Late Devonian Holoptychiidae (eight genera) has flexible round scales that lack cosmine.

Two Early Devonian genera, *Youngolepis* (southern China and Vietnam) and *Powichthys* (Arctic Canada) are primitive rhipidistians whose position in sarcopterygian relationships is unclear. *Youngolepis* occurs with *Diabolepis* and two other primitive rhipidistians in the Lower Devonian Xitun Formation of Yunnan province, southern China. Sometimes, scholars place them with Dipnoi and *Diabolepis* as Dipnoiformes to bridge the gap between lungfishes and porolepiforms (Cloutier and Ahlberg 1996; Janvier 1996), at other times, with porolepiforms (Chang 1991), still other times separately (i.e., *Powichthys* with porolepiforms and *Youngolepis* at the base of the Choanata) (Panchen and Smithson 1987). Postparietals and parietals are framed by a row of smaller bones that bear the otic lateral line canal. The parasymphysial tooth whorl rests on the mentomeckelian bone (as seen in an unnamed Silurian rhipidistian from southern China) and not on the dentary (as in onychodonts and porolepiforms). The intracranial joint is fused in *Powichthys,* whereas at least a suture exists in *Youngolepis.* Structures of and around the sphenoid (middle region of the endocranium, inside the orbits) of *Youngolepis* resemble similar structures in actinopterygians. Such a mixture of features makes it difficult to place the two genera within the phylogenetic framework.

Rhizodontida

Most rhizodonts are very large fishes that may have reached seven meters in length. The only family, Rhizodontidae, includes five genera. Rhizodonts occur in coastal marine to freshwater deposits from the Late Devonian (North America) to the early Late Carboniferous (Europe, Turkey, North America, Australia, and Antarctica). Rhizodonts were the top predators wherever they occurred.

Members of the group can be characterized by robust lepidotrichia (fin rays) with an extremely long unjointed segment near the point of insertion into the skin. On the cleithrum of the shoulder girdle, there is a depressed rear flange and elaborate double (lateral and medial) overlap areas for the clavicle (Figure 6). Rhizodonts lack cosmine and have round, flexible scales with a longitudinal boss (protrusion) on the inside. The teeth have polyplocodont plicidentine. The long postparietals are bordered on each side by tabular and supratemporal bones. According to S.M. Andrews (1985), the otic lateral line canal passes through the growth center of the postparietal. The number of external nasal openings is unknown, and the existence of a choana is doubtful. The intracranial joint is formed as in other Choanata. The lower jaw carries a long symphysial fang.

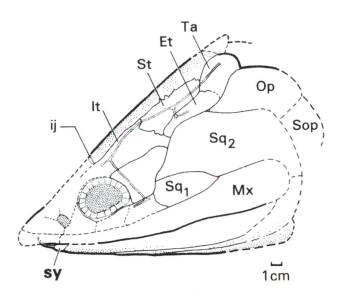

Figure 4. Skull of the onychodont, *Grossius aragonensis*. Key: *et*, extratemporal; *ij*, intracranial joint; *it*, intertemporal; *mx*, maxilla; *op*, operculum; *sop*, suboperculum; *sq₁* and *sq₂*, squamosals; *st*, supratemporal; *sy*, parasymphysial tooth spiral; *ta*, tabular. From Schultze (1973).

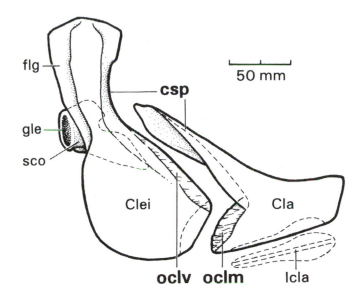

Figure 6. Shoulder girdle of the rhizodont, *Rhizodus hibberti*. Key: *cla*, clavicle; *clei*, cleithrum; *csp*, clavicular spine; *flg*, depressed posterior flange of cleithrum; *gle*, glenoid fossa; *icla*, interclavicle; *oclm*, overlap area for cleithrum; *oclv*, overlap area for clavicle; *sco*, scapulocoracoid. From Andrews (1985). Reproduced by permission of the Royal Society of Edinburgh.

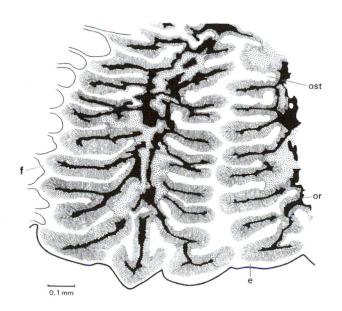

Figure 5. Dendrodont plicidentine in a coronoid fang of the porolepiform, *Porolepis* sp. Key: *e*, enamel; *f*, regular, Christmas tree–like folds of globular zone; *or*, orthodentine; *ost*, osteodentine. From Schultze (1969).

Osteolepiformes

The Osteolepiformes are a species-rich (about 60 species in 25 genera) Paleozoic sarcopterygian group that is difficult to define. Members of the group may share the characteristic of scutes (enlarged scales) on paired and unpaired fins. The bar-shaped preopercle may be another unique character. Osteolepiforms possess one external nasal opening (Figure 7), a structure comparable (homologous) to the front external nasal opening of porolepiforms, and, as Choanata, an internal nasal opening (choana).

The dermal skull bones and the body are best known from the primitive Middle Devonian Osteolepidae. The cranial anatomy of *Eusthenopteron* is better known than that of any other fish as a result of lifelong research by E. Jarvik (Jarvik 1980). A postparietal shield is formed by paired postparietals flanked by tabulars and supratemporals and followed by extrascapulars. Flanking the parietals are intertemporals and supraorbitals. The pineal opening lies between the parietals. A median unpaired postrostral flanked by nasals lies in front of the parietals. (The terminology used here is transferred from tetrapods via the Elpistostegalia, see Janvier 1966.)

A number of bones surround the orbit—lacrimal, jugal, and postorbital—and are followed by one squamosal, preopercle, and quadratojugal on each cheek, again as in tetrapods. In contrast to tetrapods and some Elpistostegalia, jugal and quadratojugal in osteolepiforms do not meet. The nasal opening is surrounded by the ventral rostral and the dorsal anterior tectal, as in early tetrapods. Premaxilla and maxilla in the upper jaw and dentary in the lower jaw carry the marginal teeth. Fangs are located on bones that lie medial (internal) to the bones that carry the marginal teeth. Fang-bearing bones include the vomer; dermopalatine and ectopterygoid in the upper jaw and on three coronoids in the lower jaw. Upper and lower fangs interlock.

Both parasphenoid and entopterygoids with small teeth cover the palate. The parasphenoid is restricted to the ventral side (underside) of the front part of the endocranium (this part houses the nasal capsule and the front part of the brain), in front of the intracranial joint. The intracranial joint lies in front of the exit for the trigeminal (fifth cranial) nerve. The posterior otico-occipital endocranium houses the labyrinth (inner ear) and the posterior brain. The unrestricted notochord extends below the otico-occipital region to the posterior end of the ethmosphenoid, the front part of the endocranium. Subcranial longitudinal muscles connect both parts of the braincase. They are covered ventrally by toothed parachordal plates.

Eusthenopteron has a complete gill cover (opercle, subopercle) and a bone-covered gular region (submandibulars between lower jaw and gulars). The palatoquadrate and gill arches also are preserved. The exoskeletal shoulder girdle is composed (from ventral to dorsal) of interclavicle, clavicle, cleithrum, anocleithrum, and supracleithrum. The posttemporal connects the girdle with the skull roof. The endoskeletal shoulder girdle (that part which is preformed in cartilage) forms one unit, which is attached to the inside of the cleithrum by three buttresses (trifurcation).

The pectoral fin is jointed (articulates) in tetrapod-like fashion with the scapulocoracoid. A proximal element (humerus) is followed by a segment that has two elements (radius and ulna). At the far end of this structure are divided elements that Jarvik interpreted as pentadactyl (five-finger) design. However, one may count more or less elements, since there occur many variations—for instance, early tetrapods have more than five digits (up to eight). The osteolepiform pelvic girdle and fin are less like those of tetrapods than are the pectoral girdle and fin. The unrestricted notochord is surrounded by bony elements comparable to those in tetrapods. This is only a glimpse at the details known of the anatomy of *Eusthenopteron*. Jarvik was able to make such detailed research and interpretation because of the excellent preservation of the material from Miguasha. Because of these general similarities, for a long time the osteolepiforms were considered to be the closest relatives of tetrapods. Nevertheless, it is difficult to find shared derived characters (synapomorphies) for Osteolepiformes, Elpistostegalia, and Tetrapoda (node 5 in Figure 1: vomer with backward directed process).

The Osteolepiformes can be divided into five families. The "Osteolepidae" are primitive osteolepiforms with bones (Figure 7) and scales covered by cosmine with tiny pores. This group has an opening called the "pineal foramen," which contained extensions of the posterior part of the midbrain that functioned as a sensory organ; the opening is found between the parietals. The group also has an extratemporal bone and an adsymphysial dental plate with fine denticles. The Middle Devonian Chinese osteolepid, *Kenichthys,* has primitive characters in common with *Youngolepis* and *Powichthys* (i.e., squamosal, quadratojugal, and preopercle fused into one bone; the infraorbital lateral line canal follows the suture between premaxilla and the adjacent part of the skull).

The Megalichthyidae are related most closely to the "Osteolepidae." Megalichthyids are characterized by a closed pineal foramen, broad vomers that barely meet at the midline, posterior nasal bones notched into the parietals, and a short broad parasphenoid. The Canowindridae possess a posteriorly broad postparietal shield; the lateral extrascapulars meet nearly in the anterior midline, and the postorbital bone does not reach the orbit. Other families include the Tristichopteridae (Eusthenopteridae) and Rhizodopsidae, which have lost cosmine and possess flexible round scales with a short

median ridge on the internal surface. Finally, the Tristichopteridae are characterized by the presence of a postspiracular bone between the opercle and lateral extrascapular.

Osteolepiforms were distributed worldwide from the Early Devonian into the Early Permian. They were predators whose place in the food chain depended on their size—small osteolepids were low in the chain, large canowindrids at the top. The Osteolepidae are the osteolepiforms of the Devonian with some Carboniferous representatives. Members of this family are common in some Middle Old Red Sandstone localities in northern Scotland and in the Orkney Islands, both of which commonly are interpreted as freshwater deposits. Nevertheless, closely related forms occur in coastal marine beds of Germany, the Baltic region, Russia, Canada, and Australia.

The Canowindridae are restricted to the Upper Devonian of Australia and Antarctica. They are part of the species-rich Aztec fish fauna of Antarctica, which include sharks. Here, as elsewhere, they should be regarded as coastal marine to freshwater fishes. Tristichopteridae are restricted to the latest Givetian and the Late Devonian worldwide. The excellently preserved *Eusthenopteron* occurs with other sarcopterygians (*Miguashaia, Scaumenacia, Fleurantia, Holoptychius, Quebecius, Elpistostege*) in the Upper Devonian (Middle Frasnian) locality of Miguasha. Earlier scholars interpreted this location as deposits in a freshwater inland rift valley; however, recent investigations have shown that presence of acritarchs (cystlike microfossils), trace fossils, geochemistry, and comparisons with other areas with similar fauna (e.g., *Eusthenopteron* is known from other marine localities in Nevada and the Baltic region) indicate a coastal marine to estuarine environment. The Megalichthyidae and Rhizodopsidae range from the Carboniferous into the Permian. They are found in marginal marine deposits such as Mazon Creek and the Texas Red Beds. They are known also from supposedly freshwater deposits of Europe and Australia.

Elpistostegalia

The Elpistostegalia (also known as Panderichthyida) are the only fishes with paired frontals (bones in front of parietals); a flattened skull with a narrow space between the orbits, which are positioned on the dorsal side of the head; a pineal opening to the posterior to the orbits; a posterior squamosal embayment ("otic notch"); marginal position (along the edges of the upper jaw) of the external nasal opening; the lack of dorsal and anal fins; and a caudal fin similar to that of early tetrapods, in which the epichordal lepidotrichia (fin rays that lie above the notochord) are longer than the hypochordal lepidotrichia (those that lie below the notochord) (node 6 in Figure 1).

Members of this group also have labyrinthodont plicidentine similar to that of *Ichthyostega* (a primitive Devonian tetrapod), and in some specimens an elongate jugal that meets the quadratojugal. (The latter feature has been used to identify incomplete specimens, such as *Ventastega,* as tetrapods.) Parietals and postparietals contact each other with a zigzag suture (i.e., without an external intracranial joint). The postparietals are shorter in Elpistostegalia than in other rhipidistians but are longer than in tetrapods. The monophyly (having one common ancestor) of the Elpistostegalia is supported by

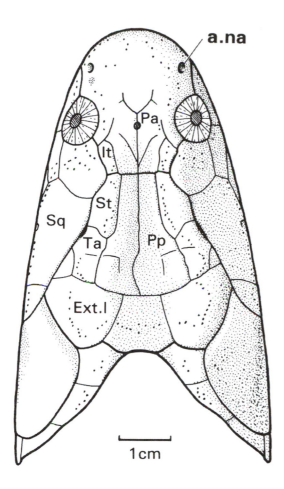

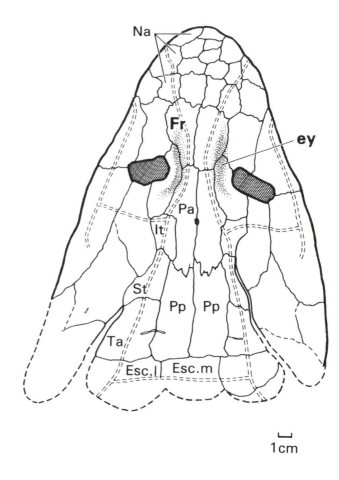

Figure 7. Skull roof of the osteolepiform, *Osteolepis macrolepidotus*. Key: *a.na*, external anterior nasal opening; *ext.l*, lateral extrascapular; *it*, intertemporal; *pa*, parietal; *pp*, postparietal; *sq*, squamosal; *st*, supratemporal; *ta*, tabular. From Jarvik (1948).

Figure 8. Skull roof of the elpistostegalian, *Panderichthys rhombolepis*. Key: *ey*, supraorbital ridge ("eyebrows"); *ext.l*, *ext.m*, lateral and median extrascapular; *fr*, frontal; *it*, intertemporal; *na*, nasals; *pa*, parietal; *pp*, postparietal; *st*, supratemporal; *ta*, tabular. Redrawn, after Vorobyeva and Schultze (1991).

ridges ("eyebrows") between the orbits (Figure 8), a large median rostral that separates the premaxillae, paired posterior postrostrals, a very large median gular, lateral recess in nasal capsule, and a prominent snout. The Elpistostegalia are large fishes (up to 1.5 meters) with relative small paired fins. The radials (bony fin supports) of the pectoral fin are, with one exception, fused to a plate in the third segment of the pectoral fin. Besides paired fins, Elpistostegalia possess a complete opercular apparatus with opercle, subopercle, one branchiostegal, submandibulars, and lateral and median gulars, as in other sarcopterygian fishes. The exoskeletal shoulder girdle is complete, with interclavicle, clavicle, cleithrum, anocleithrum, supracleithrum, and posttemporal; the structure connects to the posterior skull roof as in all other piscine sarcopterygians.

Panderichthys teeth (*Polyplocodus*) first were discovered in the middle of the last century, and complete specimens are known since 1970. Earlier, *Panderichthys* was placed within osteolepiforms. The rear section of the skull roof of *Elpistostege* was discovered in the 1930s and first assigned to tetrapods. The 1980 discovery of the front section of a skull in the same deposits of

Miguasha demonstrated closer affinities to *Panderichthys* and close resemblance to tetrapods.

The Elpistostegalia are restricted to the shallow marine environment of the late Middle and Late Devonian. They are known from eastern Canada, the Baltic region, and Russia. In a clay pit at Lode, Latvia, were found complete specimens of *Panderichthys*, together with complete specimens of the onychodont *Strunius*, the porolepiform *Laccognathus*, the osteolepiform *Latvius*, many specimens of the acanthodian *Lodeacanthus*, and the placoderm *Asterolepis*. The locality represents submarine deposits formed by a river delta. Coastal marine environments also are postulated for the occurrences of *Panderichthys* in Russia and *Elpistostege* in Miguasha. The transition from Elpistostegalia to tetrapods took place in the intertidal region.

Tetrapoda

The Late Devonian tetrapods were aquatic creatures, together with sarcopterygians. Terrestrial tetrapods appear only in the Carboniferous. Forms (*Obruchevichthys* and *Panderichthys bystrowi*) known only by jaws or parts of the head previously were placed within Elpistostegalia but now are considered tetrapods (i.e., *Elginerpeton*, *Ventalepis*, and *Metaxygnathus*) (Ahlberg 1995). However, the dactyly (digital morphology) of the extremities of these five forms has not been shown, in contrast to the latest Devonian tetrapods *Acanthostega*, *Ichthyostega*, and *Tulerpeton*, all of which had more than five digits on the hands and feet.

HANS-PETER SCHULTZE

See also Fins and Limbs, Paired; Skeleton: Dermal Postcranial Skeleton; Skull; Tetrapods; Vertebrate Hard Tissues

Works Cited

Ahlberg, P.E. 1995. *Elginerpeton pancheni* and the earliest tetrapod clade. *Nature* 373:420–25.

Andrews, S.M. 1985. Rhizodont crossopterygian fish from the Dinantian of Foulden, Berwickshire, Scotland, with a re-evaluation of this group. *Transactions of the Royal Society of Edinburgh: Earth Sciences* 76:67–95.

Arratia, G., and R. Cloutier. 1996. Reassessment of the morphology of *Cheirolepis canadensis* (Actinopterygii). *In* H.-P. Schultze and R. Cloutier (eds.), *Devonian Fishes and Plants of Miguasha, Quebec, Canada*. Munich: Pfeil.

Campbell, K.S.W., and R.E. Barwick. 1990. Paleozoic dipnoan phylogeny: Functional complexes and evolution without parsimony. *Paleobiology* 16:143–69.

Chang, M.-M. 1991. "Rhipidistians," dipnoans and tetrapods. *In* H.-P. Schultze and L. Trueb (eds.), *Origins of the Higher Groups of Tetrapods: Controversy and Consensus*. Ithaca, New York: Cornell University Press.

———. 1995. *Diabolepis* and its bearing on the relationships between porolepiforms and dipnoans. *Bulletin du Muséum National d'Histoire Naturelle* 4. série, 17, section C:235–68.

Cloutier, R. 1991. Patterns, trends, and rates of evolution within the Actinistia. *Environmental Biology of Fishes* 32:23–58.

———. 1996a. The primitive actinistian *Miguashaia bureaui* Schultze (Sarcopterygii). *In* H.-P. Schultze and R. Cloutier (eds.), *Devonian Fishes and Plants of Miguasha, Quebec, Canada*. Munich: Pfeil.

———. 1996b. Porolepiform fishes (Sarcopterygii). *In* H.-P. Schultze and R. Cloutier (eds.), *Devonian Fishes and Plants of Miguasha, Quebec, Canada*. Munich: Pfeil.

Cloutier, R., and P.E. Ahlberg. 1996. Morphology, characters, and the interrelationships of basal sarcopterygians. *In* M.L.J. Stiassny, L.R. Parenti, and G.D. Johnson (eds.), *Interrelationships of Fishes*. London and San Diego, California: Academic Press.

Coates, M.I. 1996. The Devonian tetrapod *Acanthostega gunnari* Jarvik: Postcranial anatomy, basal tetrapod interrelationships and patterns of skeletal evolution. *Transactions of the Royal Society of Edinburgh: Earth Sciences* 87:363–421.

Janvier, P. 1996. *Early Vertebrates*. Oxford Monographs on Geology and Geophysics, 33. Oxford: Oxford University Press.

Jarvik, E. 1948. On the morphology and taxonomy of the Middle Devonian osteolepid fishes of Scotland. *Kungliga svenska Vetenskaps Akademiens Handlingar* 3, 25 (1):1–301.

———. 1980. *Basic Structure and Evolution of Vertebrates*. Vol. 1. London and New York: Academic Press.

Jessen, H. 1967. Die Crossopterygier des Oberen Plattenkalkes (Devon) der Bergisch-Gladbach—Paffrather Mulde (Rheinisches Schiefergebirge) unter Berücksichtigung von amerikanischem und europäischem *Onychodus*-Material. *Arkiv för Zoologi, Stockholm* 2 (18):305–89.

Panchen, A.L., and Smithson, T.R. 1987. Character diagnosis, fossils, and the origin of tetrapods. *Biological Reviews, Cambridge Philosophical Society* 62:341–438.

Schultze, H.-P. 1969. Die Faltenzähne der rhipidistiiden Crossopterygier, der Tetrapoden und der Actinopterygier-Gattung *Lepisosteus*: Nebst einer Beschreibung der Zahnstruktur von *Onychodus* (struniiformer Crossopterygier). *Palaeontographica Italica* 65:63–137.

———. 1972. Early growth stages in coelacanth fishes. *Nature New Biology* 236:90–91.

———. 1973. Crossopterygier mit heterozerker Schwanzflosse aus dem Oberdevon Kanadas, nebst einer Beschreibung von Onychodontida-Resten aus dem Mitteldevon Spaniens und aus dem Karbon der USA. *Palaeontogrphica*, ser. A, 143:188–208.

———. 1987. Dipnoans as sarcopterygians. *Journal of Morphology*, Supplement 1:39–74.

———. 1992a. A new long-headed dipnoan (Osteichthyes, Pisces) from the Middle Devonian of Iowa, USA. *Journal of Vertebrate Paleontology* 12:42–58.

———. 1992b. Dipnoi. *In* F. Westphal (ed.), *Fossilium Catalogus*. Part 1, *Animalia*. Pars 131. Amsterdam and New York: Kugler Publications.

———. 1994. Comparison of hypotheses on the relationships of sarcopterygians. *Systematic Biology* 43:155–73.

Schultze, H.-P., and C.R. Marshall. 1993. Contrasting the use of functional complexes and isolated characters in lungfish evolution. *Memoirs of the Association of Australasian Palaeontologists* 15:211–24.

Vorobyeva, E., and H.-P. Schultze. 1991. Description and systematics of panderichthyid fishes with comments on their relationship to tetrapods. *In* H.-P. Schultze and L. Trueb (eds.), *Origins of the Higher Groups of Tetrapods: Controversy and Consensus*. Ithaca, New York: Cornell University Press.

Further Reading

Janvier, P. 1996. *Early Vertebrates*. Oxford Monographs on Geology and Geophysics, 33. Oxford: Oxford University Press.

Jarvik, E. 1980. *Basic Structure and Evolution of Vertebrates*. Vol. 1. London and New York: Academic Press.

SAURISCHIANS

Saurischia and Ornithischia represent the two great orders of dinosaurs, components of a two-part system that has remained a fundamental feature of dinosaur taxonomy (classification) for over a century. Since Dinosauria is defined as "the most recent common ancestor of Saurischia and Ornithischia plus all its descendants" (Gauthier 1986), these two orders include all dinosaur taxa (groups; singular, taxon). As a result, both groups include a diversity of forms that ranged widely in size, feeding habit, speed, body shape, social behavior, and habitat.

Saurischia has been divided into three groups—theropods, sauropods, and prosauropods—since the term was first coined by J.G. Seeley (1887). His description highlighted the "triradiate" (or "propubic") pelvis, with its forward-pointing pubis bone, as characteristic of saurischians, in contrast to the "tetraradiate" (or "opisthopubic") pelvis of ornithischians. Ironically, this feature is not diagnostic, since it is present in many other archosaurs (other archosaurs include crocodilians, pterosaurs, and aetosaurs) and lacking in some saurischians. Later studies (Huene 1909, 1923, 1929) created a more detailed saurischian taxonomy that survived in modified form for many decades (Romer 1966, 1968; Steel 1970). However, these and other authors (Charig 1972, 1979) questioned whether saurischians represented a "natural" evolutionary group (one with a single common ancestor), suggesting instead that several saurischian lineages evolved independently from different "thecodont" (basal archosauromorph) ancestors. These scholars highlighted the fact that it was difficult to find features present in saurischians but not in ornithischians or other archosaurs.

Although some workers objected to a polyphyletic Saurischia (one with many ancestors) (Bakker and Galton 1974), only recently was the group diagnosed as monophyletic by a set of unique features (Figure 1) (Gauthier 1986), which affect three major areas. Some changes affect the head region. The chewing muscles are extended onto the frontal bone, which may have increased the strength of the jaws. Contact between the nasal bone and the premaxilla bone (which supports most of the upper front teeth) is reduced or lost. And an opening (foramen) developed in the skull below the nasal opening.

The second set of distinct characteristics affect the vertebrae. Each posterior (caudal) neck vertebra elongates, which lengthens the neck. Accessory articulations develop between the vertebrae along the back. Articular processes in the anterior neck are elaborated. The third set of distinctive changes affect the structure of the arm and hand. The hand lengthens so that it takes up more than 45 percent of the total length of the arm. Metacarpals 4 and 5 in the hand shift position in relation to the wrist, enabling greater flexibility through movement from side to side. Digit 2 enlarges, producing an asymmetrical hand. Finally, the hand acquires an unusually short robust thumb, which bears a large claw.

Although no fossils of ancestral saurischians are known, the common features of primitive prosauropods, theropods, and dinosauriforms (Sereno and Arcucci 1993, 1994) indicate that archaic saurischians were probably medium-sized (a few tens of kilograms), bipedal carnivores (Sereno et al. 1993). Their unique features include forelimbs modified for grasping and manipulation, a long and presumably mobile neck, and a strengthened vertebral column, perhaps to stabilize bipedal posture. Together, they suggest that early saurischians were active predators.

Saurischia includes the groups Theropoda (including birds) and Sauropodormorpha, which consists of Sauropoda and Prosau-

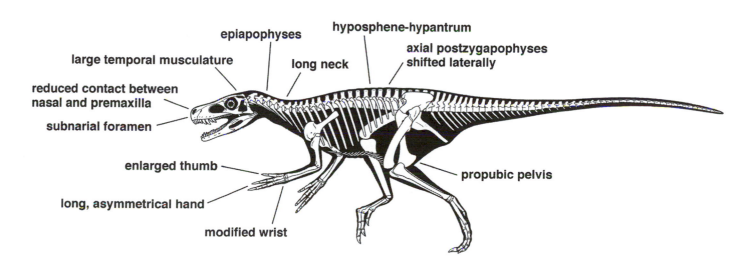

Figure 1. Diagnostic saurischian features represented by the skeleton of the theropod *Herrerasaurus*. This Middle Triassic carnivore represents the earliest known dinosaur and one of the most primitive known theropods. Modified with permission from Sereno and Novas (1992). Copyright © 1992 American Association for the Advancement of Science.

ropoda. Theropods were bipedal, almost exclusively carnivorous, and ranged from a few kilograms to several tons (Osmólska 1990). Examples would be velociraptors and tyrannosaurs. One specialized group of theropods, the birds, modified the unusual saurischian forelimb into a structure adapted for flight. Theropods are among the earliest-known dinosaurs (Rogers et al. 1993), and they survived through the Late Cretaceous (birds have survived until the present day). Prosauropods are known only from the Middle Triassic to Early Jurassic and are remarkably uniform in morphology (shape and structure), with a long neck, small head, leaf-shaped teeth, and enlarged thumb. They were the earliest large dinosaurs (hundreds of kilograms), herbivorous to omnivorous, and moved both bipedally and quadrupedally (Galton 1985, 1990). Sauropods are known from the Early Jurassic through Late Cretaceous but probably appeared somewhat earlier. They include the largest terrestrial animals known (weighing many tens of tons) and are characterized by a small head, long neck and tail, and quadrupedal, columnar posture (McIntosh 1990). Examples would be brachiosaurs and aptasaurs (once known as brontosaurs).

Saurischians include nearly 60 percent of all dinosaurs, or about 550 species—a somewhat misleading number, since many dinosaurs are based on very poor fossil material. Of these, the majority are theropods, perhaps the most diverse dinosaur group overall. Saurischian diversity increased threefold from the Late Triassic to the Late Jurassic, with a more modest increase into the Late Cretaceous. The poor Middle Jurassic fossil record obscures many early evolutionary transitions, but later aspects of evolution likely are tied to habitat diversification in the Cretaceous, when the early single landmass called Pangaea broke apart (Sereno 1997). Saurischians inhabited all continents, spanned the entire time range of dinosaurs, and are found in nearly all geographic localities, paleoenvironments, and dinosaur-bearing formations (Weishampel 1990).

Reconstructions of soft tissues in saurischians are based largely on comparative studies of crocodilians and birds (Romer 1923; Rowe 1986) and reveal a muscle arrangement intermediate between these two groups. As with other dinosaurs, the saurischian's large muscular tail was important for anchoring leg muscles (Charig 1972; Tarsitano 1983; Gatsey 1990). Some direct evidence of soft tissue structures have been preserved in theropods, including skin impressions (Bonaparte et al. 1990), possible muscle fibers (Kellner 1996), claw keratin (Norell et al. 1995), and other biomolecules (Schweitzer et al. 1997).

Recent discoveries also bolster our understanding of saurischian reproduction and growth, which also combine crocodilian and avian features. Eggs and nests, some including embryos and neonates (newborns), are known from many saurischians (Bonaparte and Vince 1979; Jain 1989; Joshi 1995; Norell et al. 1995; O'Brien 1995; Mateus et al. 1997). The paired eggs in nests of *Troodon* suggest that theropods, at least, possessed two functioning oviducts, not just one as in birds (Varricchio et al. 1997). Growth series—available for the theropods *Allosaurus* (Madsen 1976), *Tarbosaurus* (Rozhdestvensky 1965) and *Troodon,* as well as the prosauropods *Mussasaurus* (Bonaparte and Vince 1979), *Massospondylus* (Chinsamy 1991), and *Lufengosaurus* (Rozhdestvensky 1965)—indicate variable and cyclic growth

rates. Fossils of the theropod *Oviraptor* (Osborn 1924; Norell et al. 1995; Dong and Currie 1996) apparently record brooding behavior (i.e., care of young after hatching), but parental care is undocumented in other saurischians. Other aspects of behavior are more difficult to deduce, but trackways—fossilized footsteps, often found along former riverbeds—are known that appear to show herding behavior in sauropods (Bird 1985). The stride—the distance between footsteps—seems to indicate high speeds of travel in some theropods (Farlow 1981).

MATTHEW T. CARRANO

See also Sauropodomorphs; Theropods

Works Cited

Bakker, R.T., and P.M. Galton. 1974. Dinosaur monophyly and a new class of vertebrates. *Nature* 248:168–72.

Bird, R.T. 1985. *In* V.T. Schreiber (ed.), *Bones for Barnum Brown.* Fort Worth: Texas Christian University Press.

Bonaparte, J.F., F.E. Novas, and R.A. Coria. 1990. *Carnotaurus sastrei* Bonaparte, the horned, lightly built carnosaur from the Middle Cretaceous of Patagonia. *Contributions in Science, Natural History Museum of Los Angeles* 416:1–41.

Bonaparte, J.F., and M. Vince. 1979. El hallazgo del primer nido de dinosaurios triasicos (Saurischia, Prosauropoda), Triasico Superior de Patagonia, Argentina. *Ameghiniana* 16 (1–2):173–82.

Charig, A. 1972. The evolution of the archosaur pelvis and hindlimb: An explanation in functional terms. *In* K.A. Joysey and T.S. Kemp (eds.), *Studies in Vertebrate Evolution.* Edinburgh: Oliver and Boyd; New York: Winchester.

———. 1979. *A New Look at the Dinosaurs.* London: Heinemann; New York: Mayflower.

Chinsamy, A. 1991. The bone histology and possible growth strategy of the prosauropod dinosaur *Massospondylus carinatus. In* Z. Kielan-Jaworowska, N. Heintz, and H.A. Nakrem (eds.), *Fifth Symposium on Mesozoic Terrestrial Ecosystems and Biota.* Contributions from the Paleontological Museum, University of Oslo, 364. Oslo: University of Oslo.

Dong, A., and P.J. Currie. 1996. On the discovery of an oviraptorid skeleton on a nest of eggs at Bayan Mandahu, Inner Mongolia, People's Republic of China. *Canadian Journal of Earth Sciences* 33 (4):631–36.

Farlow, J.O. 1981. Estimates of dinosaur speeds from a new trackway site in Texas. *Nature* 294:747–48.

Galton, P.M. 1985. Diet of prosauropod dinosaurs from the Late Triassic and Early Jurassic. *Lethia* 18:105–23.

———. 1990. Basal Sauropodomorpha—Prosauropoda. *In* D.B. Weishampel, P. Dodson, and H. Osmólska (eds.), *The Dinosauria.* Berkeley: University of California Press.

Gatsey, S.M. 1990. Caudofemoral musculature and the evolution of theropod locomotion. *Paleobiology* 16 (2):170–86.

Gauthier, J. 1986. Saurischian monophyly and the origin of birds. *In* K. Padian (ed.), *The Origin of Birds and the Evolution of Flight.* Memoirs of the California Academy of Sciences, 8. San Francisco: California Academy of Sciences.

Huene, F. von. 1909. Skizze zu einer Systematik und Stammesgeschichte der Dinosaurier. *Centralblatt für Mineralogie, Geologie und Paläontologie* 1909:12–22.

————. 1923. Carnivorous Saurischia in Europe since the Triassic. *Bulletin of the Biological Society of America* 34:449–58.

————. 1929. Kurze Übersicht über die Saurischia und ihre natürlichen Zusammenhänge. *Paläontologische Zeitschrift* 11:269–73.

Jain, S.L. 1989. Recent dinosaur discoveries in India, including eggshells, nests and coprolites. *In* D.D. Gillette and M.G. Lockley (eds.), *Dinosaur Tracks and Traces.* Cambridge and New York: Cambridge University Press.

Joshi, A.V. 1995. New occurrence of dinosaur eggs from Lameta rocks (Maestrichtian) near Bagh, Madhya Pradesh. *Journal of the Geological Society of India* 46:439–43.

Kellner, A.W.A. 1996. Fossilized theropod soft tissue. *Nature* 379:32.

Madsen Jr., J.H. 1976. *Allosaurus fragilis:* A revised osteology. *Utah Geological and Mineral Survey Bulletin* 109:1–163.

Mateus, I., H. Mateus, M. Telles Antunes, O. Mateus, P. Taquet, V. Ribiero, and G. Manuppella. 1997. Couvée, oeufs et embryons d'un Dinosaure Théropode du Jurassique supérieur de Lourinhã (Portugal). *Comptes Rendus de l'Académie des Sciences, Paris,* ser. 2a, 325:65–70.

McIntosh, J.S. 1990. Sauropoda. *In* D.B. Weishampel, P. Dodson, and H. Osmólska (eds.), *The Dinosauria.* Berkeley: University of California Press.

Norell, M.A., J.M. Clark, L.M. Chiappe, and D. Dashzeveg. 1995. A nesting dinosaur. *Nature* 378:774–76.

O'Brien, C.O. 1995. Dinosaur embryos spark excitement, concern. *Science* 267:1760.

Osborn, H.F. 1924. Three new Theropoda, *Protoceratops* zone, central Mongolia. *American Museum Novitates* 144:1–12.

Osmólska, H. 1990. Theropoda. *In* D.B. Weishampel, P. Dodson, and H. Osmólska (eds.), *The Dinosauria.* Berkeley: University of California Press.

Rogers, R.R., C.C. Swisher III, P.C. Sereno, A.M. Monetta, C.A. Forster, and R.N. Martinez. 1993. The Ischigualasto tetrapod assemblage (Late Triassic, Argentina) and ^{40}Ar/^{39}Ar dating of dinosaur origins. *Science* 260:794–97.

Romer, A.S. 1923. The pelvic musculature of saurischian dinosaurs. *Bulletin of the American Museum of Natural History* 48 (19):605–17.

————. 1966. *Vertebrate Paleontology.* Chicago and London: University of Chicago Press.

————. 1968. *Osteology of the Reptiles.* Chicago and London: University of Chicago Press.

Rowe, T. 1986. Homology and evolution of the deep dorsal thigh musculature in birds and other Reptilia. *Journal of Morphology* 189:327–46.

Rozhdestvensky, A.K. 1965. Vosractnay ismenchivosty i nektorie voprosi sistematiki dinosavrov Asii. *Paleontologicheskiy Zhurnal* 1965 (3):95–109.

Schweitzer, M.H., C. Johnson, T.G. Zocco, T.G. Horner, and J.R. Starkey. 1997. Preservation of biomolecules in cancellous bone of *Tyrannosaurus rex. Journal of Vertebrate Paleontology* 17 (2):349–59.

Seeley, J.G. 1887. On the classification of the fossil animals commonly named Dinosauria. *Proceedings of the Royal Society of London* 43:165–71.

Sereno, P.C. 1997. The origin and evolution of dinosaurs. *Annual Reviews of Earth and Planetary Sciences* 25:435–89.

Sereno, P.C., and A.B. Arcucci. 1993. Dinosaurian precursors from the Middle Triassic of Argentina: *Lagerpeton chanarensis. Journal of Vertebrate Paleontology* 13 (4):385–99.

————. 1994. Dinosaurian precursors from the Middle Triassic of Argentina: *Marasuchus lilloensis,* gen. nov. *Journal of Vertebrate Paleontology* 14 (1):53–73.

Sereno, P.C., C.A. Forster, R.R. Rogers, and A.M. Monetta. 1993. Primitive dinosaur skeleton from Argentina and the early evolution of Dinosauria. *Nature* 361:64–66.

Sereno, P.C., and F.E. Novas. 1992. The complete skull and skeleton of an early dinosaur. *Science* 258:1137–40.

Steel, R. 1970. Saurischia. *Encyclopedia of Paleoherpetology,* vol. 14, Stuttgart and Portland: Fischer Verlag.

Tarsitano, S. 1983. Stance and gait in theropod dinosaurs. *Acta Palaeontologica Polonica* 28 (1–2):251–64.

Varricchio, D.J., F. Jackson, J.J. Borkowski, and J.R. Horner. 1997. Nest and egg clutches of the dinosaur *Troodon formosus* and the evolution of avian reproductive traits. *Nature* 385:247–50.

Weishampel, D.B. 1990. Dinosaur distribution. *In* D.B. Weishampel, P. Dodson, and H. Osmólska (eds.), *The Dinosauria.* Berkeley: University of California Press.

Further Reading

Currie, P.J., and K. Padian (eds.). 1997. *Encyclopedia of Dinosaurs.* San Diego, California: Academic Press.

Fastovsky, D.E., and D.B. Weishampel. 1996. *The Evolution and Extinction of the Dinosaurs.* Cambridge and New York: Cambridge University Press.

Norman, D.B. 1985. *The Illustrated Encyclopedia of Dinosaurs.* New York: Crescent; London: Salamander.

Weishampel, D.B., P. Dodson, and H. Osmólska (eds.). *The Dinosauria.* Berkeley: University of California Press.

SAUROPODOMORPHS

The Saurischia is one of the two orders (the other being Ornithiscia) comprising the Dinosauria. The Sauropodomorpha were Saurischian (lizard-hipped) dinosaurs. All sauropodomorphs are thought to have been herbivores, unlike the carnivorous Theropoda (the other Saurischians). The basic sauropodomorph body plan included a large claw on the pollex (the "thumb," or first digit of the front limbs), a tibia (main bone in the calf) shorter than the femur (thigh bone), 10 or more elongate cervical (neck) vertebrae, and a relatively small skull with large external nares (nasal openings). What really distinguishes sauropodomorphs from all other animals is the long neck, small head, thick legs, and long tail—and a tendency to be huge. There were two sister groups of sauropodomorphs, the Prosauropoda and the Sauropoda, and the two groups (infraorders) include some of the most familiar of all dinosaurs.

Prosauropoda

Fossil prosauropods have been found in rocks of Upper Triassic to Early Jurassic age (220 to 190 million years old). Their time span was, therefore, short compared to most other dinosaur groups. Prosauropod remains occur in Europe, Africa, China, and in North and South America, making them the first dinosaurs to have had such a wide geographic distribution. They are often the dominant terrestrial vertebrate fossils at the sites where they are found. They are also among the best-known dinosaurs, having been found as almost complete and partially articulated skeletons, although complete skulls are rare. (An articulated skeleton is preserved in such a way that the joints are maintained and the original arrangement of the skeleton is intact.)

The first prosauropods to be described—anchisaurids and plateosaurids—were named at the end of the nineteenth century by Othniel C. Marsh, but it was not until 1920 that the German paleontologist Friedrich von Huene erected the order Prosauropoda to accommodate them and their relatives.

Descriptive Morphology

Prosauropods were medium-sized dinosaurs, from 2.5 to 10 meters long. The back legs were longer than the front ones, so many paleontologists think prosauropods were able to walk or feed while balancing on their hind limbs. Their moderately elongate neck held a rather small head containing coarsely serrated, spatulate (spoon-shaped) teeth whose crowns were wider than their roots, a shape reminiscent of that of modern herbivorous lizards. Sclerotic (bony) rings composed of 18 plates surrounded the eyes of *Plateosaurus,* a condition perhaps common to other prosauropods.

As in all sauropodomorph dinosaurs, the number of bones in the different sections of the vertebral column is used as a formula for distinguishing groups. *Plateosaurus* had 10 cervical (neck) vertebrae, 15 dorsals (back), 3 sacrals (lower back), and 50 caudals (tail), and this formula (or a similar one) relates to the general body proportions of all prosauropods: long neck, medium body, and long tail. The neck vertebrae near the head were long and low, becoming gradually shorter and taller until they merged with the dorsal vertebrae between the scapulae ("shoulder blades"). The cervical ribs were of unusual shape: very slender, with a long, backward-directed process (bony extensions)—some ribs were so long that they overlapped the ribs of the next two vertebrae. Together they formed continuous bundles running below the neck vertebrae to help brace the whole structure and to keep it rigid.

The dorsal vertebrae were short and were compressed transversely (from side to side). The tall neural arches and spines had an elaborate articulation (jointing) system that helped prevent twisting of the back. The sides of the last few dorsal vertebrae were hollowed out (the hollows are called "pleurocoels"), either to provide both lightness and strength or to accommodate air sacs with a specific (but unknown) function. Prosauropods had gastralia (abdominal ribs).

The first digit of the manus ("hand") carried an inward-directed, robust claw that has been variously interpreted as being for digging, for defense, or for manipulating food when in bipedal pose. The femur was s-shaped, with no distinct "neck" section, and the foot had a reduced fifth digit.

Prosauropod Taxonomic Diversity

All prosauropod families followed the same general body plan. The main differences lay in skull shape, limb length, and overall size.

The Thecodontosauridae was perhaps the most primitive prosauropod family. These animals were small, light, and apparently bipedal. *Thecodontosaurus* itself is known from hundreds of isolated bones and incomplete skeletal fragments in Late Triassic fissure-fill deposits in western Great Britain. (Fissure-fill deposits are ancient fissures in which large numbers of fossils accumulated by various means.) *Thecodontosaurus* seems to have been about 2.5 meters long, although some fossils indicate juveniles of about 1 meter. The other Thecodontosaurid, *Azendohsaurus,* is only known from a few fragmentary remains from the Carnian of Morocco and is the earliest known prosauropod.

The Plateosauridae was the most diversified prosauropod family. *Plateosaurus* is the best-known genus of all prosauropods, with many complete specimens known from Germany, Switzerland, and France. It was up to 9 meters long. The skull was narrow, with a long snout, and the tail was long, with the "whiplash" end found on a number of sauropods. About 20 specimens of *Sellosaurus,* a close relative, have also been collected in Germany. It was about 6.5 meters long.

The South African *Euskelosaurus* was the largest plateosaurid, at 10 meters long, and is also one of the oldest known prosauropods, at 225 million years. Its skull remains unknown. Perversely, *Coloradisaurus* from South America is only known from its skull, showing it to have had a short snout. *Mussaurus* ("mouse lizard") also was discovered in South America. One well-known specimen is a very small skeleton just 25 centimeters long, presumably a hatchling. Other specimens indicate that the subadults were about 3 meters long, and it has been suggested that *Mussaurus* could be the juvenile stage of *Coloradisaurus.*

Ammosaurus was about 4 meters long. The remains of 4 incomplete skeletons of both juveniles and adults were found in Early Jurassic deposits in North America, but no skull has been discovered. *Lufengosaurus,* a close relative of *Plateosaurus* from the Early Jurassic of China, was 5 meters long. At least 30 articulated skeletons of this genus were found in one area.

The Anchisauridae consists of one genus, *Anchisaurus,* known from a nearly complete skeleton with skull and other partial remains from the Lower Jurassic of the eastern United States. This animal was about 2.5 meters long. Despite the good original material, the popular reconstruction was completed using information from *Plateosaurus,* which lived, as far as we know, only in Europe and 15 million years earlier. Anchisaurus was rather lightweight and had a long neck and body, leading some paleontologists to suggest that it was a bipedal high browser (leaf and twig eater).

The Massospondylidae, too, is represented only by one genus, the 5 meter-long *Massospondylus.* About 80 partial skeletons have been found in the Lower Jurassic of southern Africa.

The Melanorosauridae includes three Late Triassic genera: *Melanorosaurus* (7.5 meters) from South Africa, *Riojasaurus* (9 meters) from Argentina, and the very poorly known *Camelotia* (said to be 10 meters long) from England. *Yunnanosaurus* is the only member of the Yunnanosauridae, from China. Its teeth were unusual: more spatulate than in other prosauropod families and having no serrations. Finally, the Blikanosauridae is a poorly known family based on scarce remains of *Blikanosaurus* from the Late Triassic of South Africa.

Evolutionary Relationships

The Prosauropoda have long been regarded as ancestral to the Sauropoda, as their name implies, but they are now thought to have been the sister group (closest related group) of sauropods, while the true "ancestral" sauropodomorph remains unknown.

Prosauropods were a relatively diverse group, whose evolutionary history remains unresolved. For example, the most primitive, like *Thecodontosaurus,* are not the oldest, while the most derived, including *Melanosaurus,* were not the latest. In fact, from the limited fossil evidence, it seems that the different lineages of prosauropods coexisted throughout most of the 30 million years that they were the dominant herbivores. They became extinct some time in the Early Jurassic, after the demise of the last known Anchisaurids of the Newark supergroup of eastern North America.

Biology and Behavior

Fossil prosauropods are such a large element of the vertebrate faunas of the deposits in which they occur that we assume them to have been common, perhaps the dominant animals in what has been described as "prosauropod empire," the low-lying, seasonally wet and dry margins (edges) of the early Mesozoic "Gondwanaland" supercontinent. (Gondwanaland was one of two supercontinents. It consisted of today's South America, Africa, Antarctica, Australia, and India.) The first prosauropods shared this world with thecodont reptiles (the earliest dinosaurs), temnospondyl amphibians (the ancestors of frogs and salamanders), and mammal-like reptiles. The last prosauropods were associated with crocodiles, the first ornithischian dinosaurs (bird-hipped dinosaurs), theropod dinosaurs, and early mammals.

Prosauropod biomechanics and locomotion remain rather poorly known. Until the 1970s, most life reconstructions and museum mounts showed them as very upright bipeds, but now it is thought that most prosauropods only adopted bipedal posture when feeding, using four limbs, with the body balanced over the hips in a fairly horizontal position (like other saurischian dinosaurs), when resting and in locomotion. The small, light *Thecodontosaurus* may have been fully bipedal, while *Riojasaurus,* with its robust front legs and heavy 11-meter-long body, seems to have been fully quadrupedal.

No prosauropods had forelimbs long enough to bring food directly to the mouth, although some scholars have suggested that the large claw on the first digit had a role in digging. The mouth, positioned in a small head on a longish neck, was therefore the only food-gathering apparatus. Indeed, this was almost the only role for the mouth, since it is unlikely that oral food processing was important for prosauropods, for three reasons. The teeth were small, relative to the size of the animal. No prosauropods (except *Yunnanosaurus*) had tooth-to-tooth wear facets (places that indicate where upper and lower teeth rubbed together); this indicates that the teeth were used only for pulling and nipping off plant material but not for grinding it. And finally, the jaw articulation did not permit any lateral (side-to-side), grinding movement of the mandibles. The weakness of the mouth is clear when compared to ornithischian dinosaurs, which had many adaptations for processing tough plant material.

Instead, food processing in prosauropods was probably performed by gastroliths (stomach stones) in a muscular area of the gut. Although it is not known whether prosauropods had a crop or gizzard, polished stones that the process would have produced have been found associated with fossils of *Ammosaurus, Massospondylus,* and *Sellosaurus.* Prosauropods also had a wide rib cage and broad pubic bones, giving them a big gut volume, perhaps for fermentation of plant food. (Fermentation is a common method by which herbivores remove nutrients from plant cellulose.)

All the anatomical evidence supports the assumption that prosauropods were herbivorous. However, one specimen of *Ammosaurus* contained the remains of a small reptile among the gastroliths within the body cavity. A claim that this indicated omnivory (a diet of both plants and animals) has been rejected by several paleontologists, although it is true that living animals (except the most highly diet-specialized) eat a far wider range of food items than their dentition suggests. Perhaps prosauropods also varied their usual vegetarian diet from time to time.

Several fossil sites have yielded monospecific assemblages (i.e., groups of just one type of prosauropod), evidence interpreted by some scholars to mean that these dinosaurs lived in herds. The relatively large sample of prosauropod specimens in these assemblages includes animals of different ages, but no convincing case has been made yet for social organization within herds. Herding behavior, size, and the large claw on the manus may have been the main means of defense for prosauropods.

Sauropods

Probably the most popular dinosaurs, sauropods were the biggest animals that ever walked on Earth. The famous *Diplodocus* was about 27 meters long, but some incomplete specimens seem to indicate that some grew to sizes up to 40 meters, like *Seismosaurus.* Sauropods were large, quadrupedal, herbivorous dinosaurs. Their body proportions—a small head on a very elongate neck, an elephant-like body, four strong limbs, and a long tail—are very familiar.

Taphonomic (fossilization) studies of large terrestrial vertebrate carcasses help explain the rarity of complete, articulated fossil sauropod skeletons. A dead sauropod's limb bones were easily scattered after its soft tissues decayed, and the vertebrae consisted mostly of fragile bony blades and deep cavities. Skulls were small in comparison with the huge body size, made of very thin bones, and only weakly connected to the neck. It would be unusual for a force such as a river to transport a complete carcass of such large size to a propitious place for burial and preservation. Even after arrival at a suitable site, burial may have been too slow to prevent dessication (drying out), weathering, or scavenging by organisms large, small, and microscopic. For these reasons (and others, no doubt), near-complete sauropod skeletons are known for only 5 of the 90 valid genera, and only 11 genera are based on adequate skull material.

Sauropods ruled over the entire Mesozoic, from earliest Jurassic to latest Cretaceous. At one time or another, their geographical range probably encompassed all the present continents except Antarctica, as evidenced by fossil bones, as well as the sauropod trackways (fossilized footprints) now recorded from more than 190 localities around the world.

History of Discoveries, Important Sites, and Discoverers

The first mention of a sauropod fossil was in 1841, when Richard Owen described some poorly preserved remains of an animal he called *Cetiosaurus* ("whale lizard") from several localities in England. *Cetiosaurus* was one of Owen's five original "dinosauria," but he did not recognize it as a sauropod; in fact, he later referred to it as a new marine crocodile. John Phillips' description of more complete material in 1871, including at least one partial skeleton, referred Owen's type specimens (specimens that provide the first description of a group) to the genus and refined the definition of *Cetiosaurus*.

By 1877, there existed a raging rivalry between Othniel C. Marsh and Edward D. Cope to find new dinosaur sites and specimens in North America, and it was producing huge amounts of bones. The number of groups increased quickly, leading to Marsh's creation in 1878 of a new order of reptiles, the Sauropoda. In the following year, Marsh redescribed the Sauropoda as a suborder of the Dinosauria, and in 1883 he made the first complete reconstruction of a sauropod skeleton with his *"Brontosaurus."*

In the fever of competition, Marsh and Cope created numerous new taxa (groups; singular, taxon)—and taxonomic chaos. *Apatosaurus* provides a perfect example of the problems. *Apatosaurus* was first named by Marsh in 1877. In 1879 the Marsh team discovered a skeleton with no skull, naming it *Brontosaurus* the following year. For the 1883 reconstruction Marsh combined the new *Brontosaurus* material plus numerous bones, including a short-snouted skull, of *Camarasaurus*. This chimera became the famous "brontosaurus." The discovery of a well-preserved specimen of *Apatosaurus* in 1915 showed that *"Brontosaurus"* was actually an *Apatosaurus*. But it was not until 1978 that, thanks to the work of John McIntosh and David Berman, Marsh's sleight of hand was revealed, the true nature of *Apatosaurus'* skull demonstrated, and the impostor skull replaced with a correct one.

In 1893 Richard Lydekker, working on material from Argentina, described a new sauropod family, the Titanosauridae. Around 1900 the important sites of Como Bluff (Wyoming), Dinosaur National Monument (Utah), and Bone Cabin Quarry (Colorado) yielded hundreds of bones of *Diplodocus, Apatosaurus, Haplocanthosaurus,* and *Camarasaurus,* including several skulls. The early twentieth century saw German expeditions to Tendaguru (East Africa), which produced huge amounts of sauropod remains including *Brachiosaurus, Dicraeosaurus,* and *Janenschia*. Since the 1920s, joint Chinese, Swedish, and Canadian expeditions have excavated many localities in China, leading to the discovery of a large number of new genera, including *Shunosaurus, Omeisaurus, Mamenchisaurus, Tienshanosaurus, Euhelopus,* and *Datousaurus*. Recently, new discoveries in North and South America have added giants like *Seismosaurus* and *Argentinosaurus* to the list.

Evolutionary Relationships

Sauropods appeared in the Early Jurassic and flourished until the end of the Cretaceous. Their monophyly (descent from a common ancestor within the same taxon) among the Saurischia is universally acknowledged (although long necks and other common characters may have evolved more than once). The ancestry of sauropods is unknown, although their apparent diversity from the beginning of their fossil record indicates that the ancestor (inferred by some to have been a small bipedal animal) should be sought far back in the Late Triassic. It would take that much time for such diversity to evolve. As noted above, prosauropods have been regarded traditionally as the sauropods' ancestors; however, because the fifth metatarsal (footbone) is vestigial (reduced in size and nonfunctional) in prosauropods but full-sized in sauropods, this cannot be so.

Vulcanodon from Zimbabwe is the best-known early sauropod; other sauropods from the very Early Jurassic are too incomplete to indicate their relationships with later forms. The number of cervical vertebrae of these Early Jurassic sauropods is unknown, but they certainly had begun to increase—with a matching reduction in trunk vertebrae—by the Middle Jurassic. The Early and Middle Jurassic saw the radiation (diversification and geographic spread) of the Euhelopodidae in China and the occurrence of the first Cetiosauridae elsewhere. During the Late Jurassic and Early Cretaceous, the familiar families Diplodocidae, Camarasauridae, and Brachiosauridae appeared and diversified, to be completely replaced after the Middle Cretaceous by members of the Titanosauridae. Sauropod systematics (classifications) and phylogeny (evolutionary history) are plagued still by a lack of good fossils and remain unsettled.

Descriptive Morphology

Sauropods had very large bodies, relatively very small skulls, elongate necks, massive legs, and long tails. Four types of simple teeth characterize various taxa: peglike teeth in *Diplodocus,* spoonlike teeth in *Camarasaurus,* compressed conical chisel-like teeth in *Brachiosaurus,* and plain chisel-like teeth in *Titanosaurus*.

The external nares of sauropods were located high on the muzzle, or even between or behind the orbits (eye sockets). The endocranial cavity (space occupied by the brain) was small. The cervical vertebrae were elongate, and some genera had as many as 19. Cervical and dorsal vertebral centra had deep pleurocoels and the neural arches (dorsal half of vertebra) had complex internal laminae (structures supporting the various projections of the vertebra). The neural spines were bifurcated (divided into two parts) in some genera, the deepest bifurcation occurring over the shoulders. A hyposphene-hypantrum (extra vertebral articulating surface) was well developed in most sauropods (except Titanosaurids). The degree of fusion of the five sacral vertebrae varied in the different taxa and also between individuals.

Scapula and coracoid (shoulder bones) were fused in adult sauropods, and the sternal bones were paired, broad, oval plates. The femur lacked a distinct neck and the carpus and tarsus (wrist and ankle bones, respectively) were reduced to one or two bones. The forelimbs of most taxa were shorter than the hind limbs.

Taxonomic Diversity

As noted above, sauropod taxonomy and phylogeny remain unresolved. Although skulls generally provide diagnostic characters, very few sauropod skulls are preserved. More than 150 species have been named, many on the basis of exceedingly scanty remains, some on a few teeth or isolated limb bones. Fewer than 20 genera are based on reliably complete individual skeletons. Convergence (independent evolution of traits) and parallelism (similar development of characteristics) appear to have been common among sauropods, making their taxonomy (classification) even more difficult.

Marsh was the first to work on sauropod taxonomy and to propose about six different families. In 1929 Werner Janensch proposed a new classification for sauropods based on tooth morphology, separating peglike teeth and spatulate ones. His classsification lumped titanosaurids and diplodocids together because they had peglike teeth, even though they seem to have had no other characters in common. In 1990 J. McIntosh proposed six families, but more recently scholars using cladistic methods divided sauropods into nine families: Vulcanodontidae, Euhelopodidae, Cetiosauridae, Brachiosauridae, Camarasauridae, Titanosauridae, Nemegtosauridae, Dicraeosauridae, and Diplodocidae.

The Vulcanodontidae contains the most primitive sauropods. Members of this group had teeth with denticles on the edges, pubic bones like those of prosauropods, and lacked pleurocoels on the vertebrae. *Vulcanodon* from the Triassic-Jurassic boundary of Africa is preserved incompletely but had these very primitive features. The Indian Early Jurassic *Barapasaurus* is well preserved except for the skull and the feet, which remain unknown, and is referred to the Vulcanodontidae pending its redescription. *Ohmdenosaurus* from the Toarcian of Germany and *Zizhongosaurus* from the Lower Jurassic of China may have been members of the Vulcanodontidae.

The Cetiosauridae is based on *Cetiosaurus* from England. Members of this family had numerous spatulate teeth and vertebrae with simple pleurocoels and relatively primitive morphology. Apart from *Cetiosaurus*, *Amygdalodon*, and *Patagosaurus* (the last two from the Middle Jurassic of Argentina), cetiosaurids are poorly known, and new finds are needed to sort out the relationships of the family.

The Euhelopodidae includes the Chinese genera *Omeisaurus*, *Mamenchisaurus*, *Shunosaurus*, *Datousaurus*, and *Euhelopus*. Some members of this family had a bony tail club, a feature not seen in any other sauropod family. The type specimen of *Euhelopus*, discovered during one of the Chinese-Swedish expeditions and described in 1929, has a complete neck with elongate, overlapping cervical ribs like those in *Mamenchisaurus*. *Mamenchisaurus* had an enormously elongate neck of (apparently) 19 vertebrae. The neck was 11 meters long, for a total head-to-tail length of about 22 meters. The Euhelopodidae had a short, high skull with rather massive jaws. A number of convergences with the Diplodocidae, for example the use of the tail as a weapon of defense, can be found in this family.

The Brachiosauridae is based on the 23-meters-long *Brachiosaurus* discovered in Upper Jurassic deposits of Tanzania and North America. *Brachiosaurus* was one of the most massive sauropods. Its very large nares were located on the top of the skull, and its tail was shorter than in diplodocids. Traditionally, its front limbs have been reconstructed longer than the hind limbs, giving it a "giraffelike" appearance. Recent study of the neck suggests, however, that it did not attain a "swanlike" pose (Figure 1). The well-preserved juvenile material of *Lapparentosaurus* from the Middle Jurassic of Madagascar is considered a member of the Brachiosauridae, as are *Volkheimeria* from the Middle Jurassic of Argentina and *Pleurocoelus* from the Early Cretaceous of England.

The Camarasauridae includes the well-known *Camarasaurus* from the Early Jurassic of North America. This medium-sized (18 meters long) sauropod had a short, high skull. A fairly complete specimen of a juvenile *Camarasaurus* was described by C.W. Gilmore in 1936.

The Diplodocidae contains *Diplodocus*, *Apatosaurus*, *Barosaurus*, and, perhaps, *Seismosaurus*. Diplodocids had peglike teeth, low and elongate skulls, with a long and wide snout, and external nares located above and between the eye sockets, which were themselves well to the back of the skull. Like other diplodocids, *Apatosaurus* had a very elongate "whiplash" tail, but its neck was shorter and more massive than in other members of the family. The neck of *Diplodocus*, while longer than that of *Apatosaurus*, was substantially less flexible (Figure 2). Barosaurus was very similar to *Diplodocus*.

The Dicraeosauridae includes *Dicraeosaurus* from the Late Jurassic of Tanzania and *Amargasaurus* from the Early Cretaceous of Argentina. *Dicraeosaurus* was quite a small and stout sauropod 10 meters long. Its skull was low and long, with slender, peglike teeth. Both genera had very elongate, bifurcated neural spines along the neck and back.

The poorly known Nemegtosauridae contains *Nemegtosaurus* and *Quaesitosaurus* from the Late Cretaceous of Mongolia. These two genera are known only from their skulls, which are reminiscent of the Diplodocidae.

The Titanosauridae includes *Titanosaurus* itself from India and Europe, *Malawisaurus* from the Early Cretaceous of Malawi, *Alamosaurus* from the Late Cretaceous of North America, *Saltasaurus* from the Late Cretaceous of Argentina, and *Andesaurus* from the Middle Cretaceous of Argentina. The caudal vertebrae in Titanosaurids were procoelous. Often, dermal plates (bony structures that arose from the skin) are found associated with titanosaurid remains, indicating that members of this family possessed dermal armor covering their back.

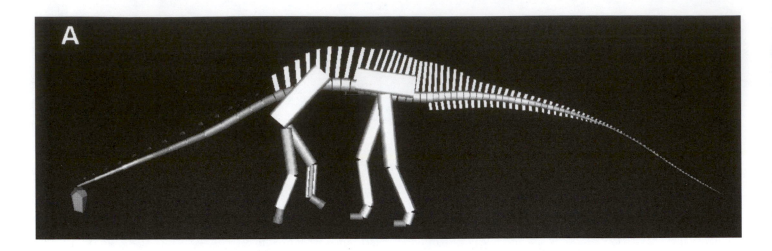

Figure 1. A reconstruction of *Brachiosaurus,* based on a reevaluation of the neck bones. Unlike the traditional "swan-neck" pose, this sauropod probably held its neck only slightly above horizontal. Three-dimensional computer reconstruction by Kent A. Stevens.

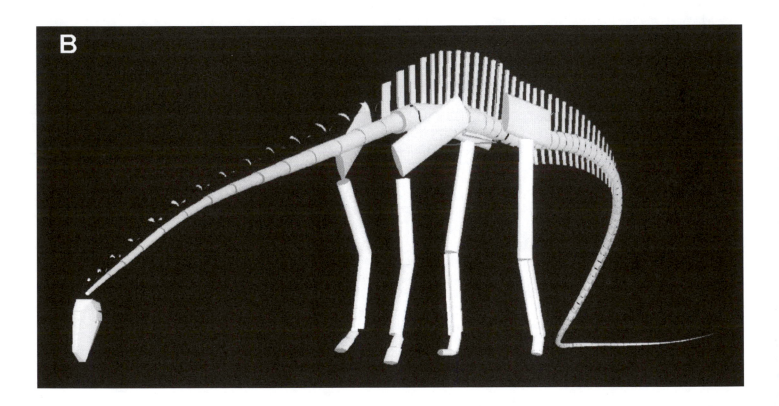

Figure 2. *Diplodocus,* despite its gracile body plan, was surprisingly incapable of raising its head much above the level of its shoulders. Three-dimensional computer reconstruction by Kent A. Stevens.

Biology and Behavior

Because of their size, and perhaps also as a result of nineteenth-century popular confusion of biological evolution with progress, sauropods were long supposed to have been too heavy to support their own weight. Because of the high position of the external nares, they were traditionally reconstructed as semisubmersible lacustrine (lake-living) animals, feeding on soft water plants and breathing at the surface by "snorkeling." We now know, from biomechanical and physiological studies, that sauropods were fully terrestrial (land-living). The position of the external nares high up on the "forehead" is only shared with elephants and tapirs (both possessors of a proboscis, or trunklike structure) among living large terrestrial herbivores. So, some paleontologists are beginning to speculate that sauropods had this unusual skull morphology to give space for the attachment of muscles controlling a trunk, or a proboscis, to help with food collecting.

At least in the Late Jurassic Morrison Formation, the fossil flora indicates that sauropods were living in lowland basins, where there were shallow lakes and swamps. The savanna-like vegetation was dominated by ferns, conifers, cycads, and gingkos. Presumably the sauropods fed on some elements of this varied flora. Ferns, which were the dominant herbaceous plant, are considered by some to have been the most likely sauropod diet.

Analysis of microwear patterns on the teeth of some sauropods provides further evidence for their diet. The wear patterns suggest that adult *Camarasaurus* ate coarser food than *Diplodocus,* although a juvenile specimen of *Camarasaurus* had microwear similar to that of *Diplodocus,* indicating a possible change of diet with age. In *Diplodocus,* the tooth wear patterns seem to show that the animals stripped foliage from plant stems between the front teeth by pulling the head back while biting. Diplodocid skulls were certainly capable of limited propalinal movements (moving the lower jaw back and forth), helping to cut vegetation and strip foliage. Diplodocids, like titanosaurids, had rather weak, peglike teeth located only in the frontmost part of the mouth. Although capable of nipping (cropping) or stripping vegetation, this dentition was not suitable for chewing. Camarasaurid skulls could perform both propalinal and side-to-side movements, indicating that they could partially process their food in the mouth by chewing.

Like some modern birds, sauropods almost certainly had gastric mills (gizzardlike structures). Some well-preserved specimens show gastroliths preserved within the rib cage. For example, two sauropod skeletons from Argentina each had six rounded stones with roughened surfaces preserved in the gut region, ranging in weight from 190 to 850 grams. Some paleontologists consider gastroliths to have been essential for food processing in sauropods because of their apparent inability to chew before swallowing. Indeed, it is possible that the gastric mill was the evolutionary development that made it possible for sauropods to dispense with grinding teeth and thus to reduce the head size and ultimately to lengthen the neck. Some food processing also may have occurred by microbial fermentation in the gut, as in some living, large, herbivorous mammals.

Sauropod physiology has been the subject of unresolved speculation since the first discoveries. Their enormously long necks have posed problems: how did they breathe or regulate blood pressure? (Clearly, these were not problems for sauropods.) A solution of the respiration problem may be found in the deep and ubiquitous (ever-present) vertebral pleurocoels, perhaps the sites of interconnected air sacs. The traditional "swan-neck" reconstructions of *Brachiosaurus* and diplodocids prompted discussions about how the resulting high blood pressure could be controlled; recent biomechanical studies (see Figures 1 and 2), however, cast doubt on such reconstructions and obviate the need for special cardiovascular apparatus.

Some sauropod fossil-bearing deposits consist of monospecific assemblages, like those from Patagonia *(Patagosaurus)* and Sichuan, China *(Shunosaurus),* showing the coexistence of adults with juveniles of different ages. These assemblages suggest that sauropods may have developed complex social behavior, with herding and parental care of juveniles. There is as yet no direct evidence for post-hatching parental care, however, as no very young sauropods have been found associated with nests and adults, as has been found for the hadrosaur *Maiasaura.* No fossil dinosaur eggs containing sauropod embryos have been found at the time of writing.

The very rich worldwide sauropod trackway record provides information about their behavior and locomotion. Further evidence of herding comes from a Texas site with the parallel tracks of 23 individuals, including juveniles. In Portugal, a group of tracks shows a small herd of juveniles apparently flanked by larger individuals walking in the same direction. The lack of tail marks in sauropod trackways indicates that the tail was held well above the ground when walking. Estimates of speed have been made based on sauropod trackways. Middle Jurassic tracks from Portugal give speeds of 3.6 to 4.7 kilometers per hour; from a set of three parallel trackways in Utah the recorded speed is in the same range (3.4 to 3.9 kilometers per hour).

Very rare fossilized skin impressions provide clues to the external appearance of sauropods. In the best example, associated with a fine specimen of *Diplodocus,* a typically "reptilian" pattern, with polygonal scales of various sizes from one to three centimeters, suggests that the traditional, but conjectural, reconstructions of sauropods with smooth, elephant-like leathery hide were wrong. Dermal spines were also associated with this *Diplodocus* specimen, leading to a new life reconstruction significantly different from all earlier interpretations. Fourteen dermal spines were identified, apparently forming a row along the dorsal median line. They may have been for visual recognition, and were perhaps another manifestation of sauropods' social behavior.

Titanosaurids had osteoderms (bones formed in the skin), as shown by platelike scutes (skin plates) associated with bones of members of this family found in Argentina, southern France, and Spain. These osteoderms were of various rounded or polygonal shapes, but their exact arrangement on the animals remains conjectural. It is possible that both osteoderms and scales on sauropods had a mechanical function (as they do in crocodilians), providing attachments for muscles that helped to brace the long neck, body, and tail.

Equally, osteoderms, dermal spines, and scales may have been part of the sauropods' defensive armor, as were, perhaps, the whiplash or bony club ends of the tails. Their large body size and herding behavior could also have been part of sauropods' repertoire of defensive adaptations.

Amargasaurus had enormously elongate, bifurcated neural spines along its neck, back, and tail. Although there was a double row of spines, it is not possible to determine whether on the living animal there were two parallel ridges or a single thick one. Presumably the spines were connected by soft tissues and skin, forming a "sail." The spines may have served as a physical defense against biting by large predators, or it may, by increasing the apparent size of the *Amargasaurus,* simply have intimidated potential attackers. The sail might also have had a function for visual recognition by other members of the species, for display, or for sexual selection. It has also been suggested that the elongate spines of *Amargasaurus,* by increasing the animal's body surface area, may have played a role in thermoregulation. (The large surface area may have provided a means for dissipating heat, similar to an elephant's ears.) The large body size of all adult sauropods provided thermal stability.

The long neck of sauropods was probably less flexible than has been suggested in the popular reconstructions, which show them with a swanlike curved neck. Anatomical and biomechanical studies show that sauropod necks were quite rigid structures that were normally held more or less horizontally. Some diplodocids, as well as the camarasaurids and the euhelopids, were particularly stiff-necked, with a very small range of possible movements. This rigidity was provided by the complex intervertebral joints and the enormously elongate, backward-directed cervical ribs, which formed a stiff bracing system for the neck. The long neck probably increased feeding efficiency, allowing the animal to sweep the head from side to side and up and down to cut a series of curved swathes through the vegetation with each step forward. Many sauropods may have been efficient low- and midheight "grazers."

Sauropods have been said to be capable of bipedalism. This position may (or possibly must) have occurred sometimes, at least for mating. Some diplodocids may have been capable of rearing up onto their hind legs to increase the vertical feeding range, but for heavier sauropods such a posture seems unlikely, in view of the construction of vertebral column and hips and the risks and energy expenditure, given their great weight.

Theropod toothmarks have been found on some sauropod bones. The different types of toothmarks (punctures, scores, pits, and furrows) and their nonrandom positions seem to indicate scavenging on sauropod carcasses. Toothmarks do not seem to give reliable evidence of direct predation on sauropods by theropods; in any case, killing bites might have occurred in soft tissues.

VALÉRIE MARTIN-ROLLAND AND JOHN MARTIN

See also Biomechanics

Works Cited
Berman, D.S., and J.S. McIntosh. 1978. Skull and relationships of the Upper Jurassic sauropod *Apatosaurus* (Reptilia, Saurischia). *Bulletin of the Carnegie Museum of Natural History* 8:1–35.

Gilmore, C.W. 1936. Osteology of *Apatosaurus* with special reference to specimens in the Carnegie Museum. *Memoir of the Carnegie Museum* 11:175–300.

Lockley, M., V.F. Santos, C. Meyes, and A. Hunt (eds.). 1994. *Aspects of Sauropod Paleobiology, GAIA.*

McIntosh, J. 1990. Sauropoda. *In* D. Weishampel, P. Dodson, and H. Osmolska (eds.), *The Dinosauria.* Berkeley: University of California Press.

Further Reading
Dodson, P. 1990. Sauropod paleoecology. *In* D. Weishampel, P. Dodson, and H. Osmolska (eds.), *The Dinosauria.* Berkeley: University of California Press.

Dong, Z. 1988. *Dinosaurs from China.* Beijing: China Ocean Press; London: British Museum (Natural History).

Galton, P. 1990. Basal Sauropodomorpha-Prosauropoda. *In* D. Weishampel, P. Dodson, and H. Osmolska (eds.), *The Dinosauria.* Berkeley: University of California Press.

Gilmore, C.W. 1925. A nearly complete articulated skeleton of *Camarasaurus,* a saurischian dinosaur from the Dinosaur National Monument, Utah. *Memoir of the Carnegie Museum* 10:347–84.

Hatcher, J.B. 1901. *Diplodocus* (Marsh): Its osteology, taxonomy and probable habits, with a restoration of the skeleton. *Memoir of the Carnegie Museum* 1:1–63.

Huene, F. von. 1932. Die fossile Reptil-Ordnung Saurischia, ihre Entwicklung und Geschichte. *Monographien zur Geologie und Paläontologie,* ser. 1, 4:1–361.

Janensch, W. 1950. Die Skelettrekonstruktion von *Brachiosaurus brancai. Paläontographica,* supplement 7, 1:95–103.

———. 1961. Die Gliedmassen und Gliedmassengürtel der Sauropoden der Tendaguru-Schichten. *Paläontographica,* supplement 7, 3:177–235.

McIntosh, J. 1990. Sauropoda. *In* D. Weishampel, P. Dodson, and H. Osmolska (eds.), *The Dinosauria.* Berkeley: University of California Press.

Osborn, H.F., and C.C. Mook. 1921. *Camarasaurus, Amphicoelias* and other sauropods of Cope. *Memoir of the American Museum of Natural History* 3:247–387.

Ostrom, J.H., and J. McIntosh. 1966. *Marsh's Dinosaurs.* New Haven: Yale University Press.

Salgado, L., and J. Bonaparte. 1991. Un nuevo sauropodo dicraeosauridae, *Amargasaurus cazaui* gen. et sp. nov., de la fromacion la amarga, neocomiano de la provincia del neuquen, argentina. *Ameghiniana* 28 (3–4):333–46.

Upchurch, P. 1995. The evolutionary history of sauropod dinosaurs. *Philosophical Transaction of the Royal Society of London,* ser. B, 349:365–90.

SAUROPSIDS

Amniotes (organisms that reproduce via a shelled egg that houses specialized membranous structures) can be divided into two large groups: synapsids and sauropsids. Synapsids include mammals and all fossil amniotes more closely related to mammals than to reptiles. Sauropsids include Testudines (turtles), diapsids (including birds), and all the fossil amniotes more closely related to them than to mammals.

Many sauropsids previously were classified as anapsids, referring to the absence of any temporal fenestrae (openings of the skull in the temple region) next to the orbits (eye sockets). These include mesosaurids, parareptiles, captorhinids, and the so-called protorothyridids. The taxon Anapsida does not have any phylogenetic (evolutionary) significance, however, being largely based on the absence of a series of derived characters. These amniotes should not be considered together because they represent several groups of distantly related taxa.

Mesosaurs are the first fully aquatic amniotes. They are known from the Permian of southern Africa and eastern South America. Their presence on both sides of the Atlantic has been used to support the theory of continental drift. Mesosaurs are highly specialized amniotes, characterized by numerous unique physical adaptations in most parts of their skeletons. The bones of the snout were very long and slender, and their unusually long teeth extended forward (near the tip of the snout), to the side (on the front half of the sides of the snout), and down and to the side (on the rear half of the sides of the snout) from the upper jaw. Taken together, the teeth seem to have formed a basket for filtering water and capturing small invertebrates. The neck was long, an adaptation found in several aquatic amniotes. The tail, which was long and compressed from side to side, probably was used for swimming. The trunk ribs are "pachyostotic"; they were very thick and heavy. They served as ballasts. The shoulder blade was very short, as in several other aquatic amniotes. Contrary to previous interpretations, there is no evidence for a lateral temporal fenestra in these forms.

The Parareptilia includes turtles and their close relatives and is classified into four main groups; millerettids, pareiasaurs, procolophonids, and turtles (Laurin and Reisz 1995). Members of this group are united by several characteristics, including an enlarged bone on the side of the head, close to the back, where it borders a bone articulating with the lower jaw. Millerettids appear at the beginning of the Upper Permian. They were small, insectivorous animals superficially similar to lizards. Several millerettids have either a lower temporal fenestra or a deep cheek emargination (outward-bending the rim, or edge, of the bone). Millerettids appear to be the first amniotes to acquire a tympanum (eardrum). It may be homologous (have evolved from a common ancestor) to the tympanum of turtles, but it is not homologous to the tympanum found in diapsids, in mammals, or in frogs and temnospondyls (froglike animals), all of which evolved this structure independently.

Pareiasaurs were large, herbivorous (plant-eating) amniotes. Found in the Upper Permian in Africa, Western Europe, Russia, and China, pareiasaurs were among the largest Paleozoic amniotes; they reached a length of three meters. The body was covered by an extensive armor of osteoderms (dermal bony scales), and the skull was massive, broad, and had strange bony processes (protuberances) in the cheek and lower jaw. They probably had a parasagittal posture—their feet were placed directly beneath the body. Their scapular blade was very high. They had a reduced number of bones in the foot, a character advantageous for an animal having a parasagittal posture. Along with turtles and procolophonids, pareiasaurs share a reduction in width of the bone in the rear of the skull, near the base, high prearticular (narrow dermal bone on the median surface of the lower jaw) and dorsally opened adductor fossa (opening for attachment of chewing muscles). The prearticular is narrow and the adductor fossa faces medially in most other amniotes. In addition, pareiasaurs had a reduced number of ankle bones.

Procolophonids were small and primitively insectivorous, as millerettids were, but late procolophonids have broad teeth from side to side, which may indicate a herbivorous diet. Procolophonids appeared in the fossil record at the very end of the Upper Permian and became extinct at the end of the Triassic. The orbit (eye socket) is expanded to the rear (posteriorly), especially in late procolophonids. The last procolophonids had strange bony processes, and their orbit was much longer posteriorly than the one found in early procolophonids.

The only surviving parareptiles are the testudines, which appear in the fossil record in the Upper Triassic, but they must have been present since the Upper Permian. This is when their probable sister groups (closest related groups), either the Procolophonidae or the Pareiasauridae, appear in the fossil record.

Captorhinids were one of the most successful groups of early amniotes (Figure 1). They appear in the fossil record in the Lower Permian and became extinct in the Upper Permian. Captorhinids are found mainly from sediments of North America, but a few individual taxa have also been recovered from North and

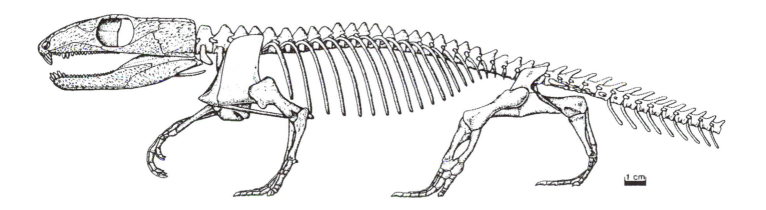

Figure 1. Skeletal reconstruction of *Captorhinus*. Scale: bar, one centimeter. From Heaton and Reisz (1980).

Central Africa, from India, and from Russia, making it the earliest known group of reptiles to have a cosmopolitan distribution. Early captorhinids were relatively small and had a single row of marginal teeth, but soon after the appearance of the group, several captorhinids developed multiple rows of teeth along the edges of the upper and lower jaws. These tooth rows are restricted to the maxilla in the upper jaw, and the dentary in the lower jaw. Some of the more derived (specialized) taxa, such as *Moradisaurus,* had up to 12 rows. The rows resulted by medial additions of teeth while the lateral teeth were not resorbed or lost. All captorhinids are characterized by relatively broad skulls, as indicated by swollen cheeks and broad temporal regions, and by distinctive sculpturing of the elements of the roof of the skull. In the derived, large captorhinids from the upper part of the Early Permian and from the Late Permian, the cheeks are expanded greatly. In all known members of the group, the front of the snout is hooked or ventrally tilted downward, giving captorhinids a distinctive look. These reptiles also have well-developed vertebrae with swollen neural arches (openings for the spinal cord), two sacrals, and a broad ribcage. The limbs were relatively short and massively built, with broad hands and feet.

The morphology of small captorhinids is known best from a vast amount of material collected from a Lower Permian fissure-fill locality near Fort Sill, Oklahoma. The overwhelming majority of the bones in these fissure fills are attributable to a single taxon, the small, multiple tooth-rowed *Captorhinus aguti* (Olson 1991). At least two other small captorhinids are present at Fort Sill, as indicated by a few disarticulated elements (Modesto 1996).

Among the large captorhinids, the most commonly found form is the single tooth-rowed *Labidosaurus.* Despite the large number of known specimens of *Labidosaurus,* collected from various localities in Texas and Oklahoma, this form has yet to be described in detail. However, a recent redescription of one of the large, multiple tooth-rowed forms, *Labidosaurikos,* coupled with a phylogenetic (evolutionary-historical) analysis of captorhinid relationships (Dilkes and Modesto 1995), has resolved some problems of captorhinid relationships and has demonstrated conclusively that the multiple tooth-rowed condition evolved independently twice in this group, first in the small, early forms and later in the late, large taxa. Captorhinids once were believed to be closely related to turtles, because they have no ectopterygoid (a bone in the palate) and no tabular (bone at the rear of the skull) and because there is a medial process on the jugal (cheekbone). Even though these characters are found also in turtles, other early amniotes share more derived characters with turtles than captorhinids, so captorhinids are no longer believed to be closely related to turtles. However, captorhinids are related to diapsids.

Protorothyridids are a group of small (100 millimeters from snout to base of tail), lizardlike sauropsids. We are not certain that they are a monophyletic group (descended from a common ancestor), because the interrelationships of members of this group have not been analyzed. Previous studies have considered them only in terms of a generalized basal amniote pattern (Carroll and Baird 1972). Consequently, in most recent phylogenetic analyses of amniote relationships, only one representative of this group has been included, and a thorough reevaluation of these forms remains to be undertaken. Protorothyridids probably are related closely to diapsids, because both groups have long and slender hands and feet (they are broad and robust in other amniotes).

The fossil record of protorothyridids is restricted to the Pennsylvanian and Early Permian of North America and Europe, and all the known taxa are represented either by a single, incomplete skeleton (the "holotype") or at most by a handful of partially preserved specimens. Although relatively rare in the fossil record, protorothyridids include some of the oldest known amniotes. The oldest protorothyridid is *Hylonomus* from the Middle Pennsylvanian (Westphalian A) of Joggins, Nova Scotia. All the specimens have been collected from the inside of hollowed-out upright *Sigillaria* stumps. Although known from several partial skeletons, all the specimens are disarticulated completely (out of anatomical position), and poorly preserved (Carroll 1964). A better known protorothyridid is *Paleothyris,* represented by three nearly complete skeletons from the Middle Pennsylvanian (Westphalian D) of Florence, Nova Scotia. Although these specimens also were collected from upright *Sigillaria* stumps, their preservation is superior to that of *Hylonomus,* allowing for a more detailed study. *Protorothyris* is a slightly larger form from the Early Permian of Texas (Clark and Carroll 1973). This form is known from a few skulls and a partial skeleton.

The meager evidence provided by the known protorothyridids gives the general impression that they resembled early captorhinids but had more slender limbs and narrow neural arches. This general impression is reinforced by the similarities between captorhinids and such taxa as *Protorothyris* and the recently described *Thuringothyris* (Boy and Martens 1991). R.L. Carroll (1988) believes that protorothyridids are ancestral to most other amniotes or that they represent the primitive morphotype of amniotes, but this is not supported by the latest phylogenetic analyses of amniotes or by simple out-group comparisons with diadectomorphs. Phylogenetic analyses indicate, instead, that protorothyridids may be the sister group of diapsids (Reisz 1997).

Early Diapsids and Lepidosaurs

Diapsids include all modern reptiles except turtles. They also include birds and several groups of extinct marine, flying, and terrestrial reptiles such as dinosaurs. The early history of this highly successful group extends into the Early Permian and the Late Pennsylvanian, represented by the early diversification of the Araeoscelidia. Three well-known members of this group are now known: *Petrolacosaurus, Araeoscelis,* and *Spinoaequalis* (de Braga and Reisz 1995) (Figure 2).

The oldest known diapsid is *Petrolacosaurus* from the Upper Pennsylvanian of Kansas (Reisz 1977). Numerous specimens have been recovered from sediments that filled in a Late Carboniferous tidal channel and preserved the most diverse amniote assemblage known for that period. *Petrolacosaurus* is the amniote found most commonly at this small site. Others represent a wide variety of endemic synapsids. This small diapsid is characterized by an exceedingly delicate skull that carries numerous, delicately built, marginal teeth. *Petrolacosaurus* is unique among Late Pennsylvanian terrestrial vertebrates in that it had an unusually elongate neck, a long, slender tail, and slender, elongate limbs. Particularly

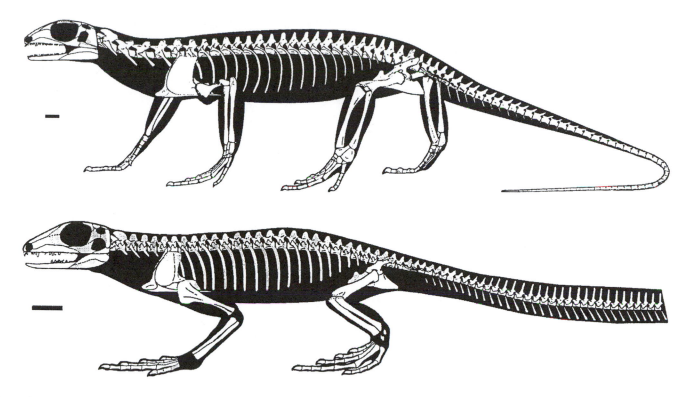

Figure 2. Skeletal reconstructions of *Petrolacosaurus* and *Spinoaequalis*. Scale: bar, one centimeter. From de Braga and Reisz (1995), reproduced by permission of the Palaeontological Association.

striking among these is the delicately constructed forelimb, with long, slender fingers. The well-preserved skeletal anatomy provides clear evidence that the oldest known diapsid was the most agile amniote of its time.

Araeoscelis, from the Lower Permian of Texas, is also a small diapsid, with a lightly built, slender skeleton, but its skull is much more massively built than that of *Petrolacosaurus,* and its marginal teeth are bulbous and transversely expanded (side-to-side). *Araeoscelis* is a particularly fascinating early diapsid because there is strong evidence to indicate that it exhibits a lower temporal fenestra that closed as it evolved (Reisz et al. 1982), possibly associated with the specialized dentition. Both *Petrolacosaurus* and its close relative *Araeoscelis* are diagnosed by several derived characters, including elongate cervical vertebrae, with mammillary processes (bony protuberances) on the neural spines. Both of these diapsids are represented by several good skeletons, but the third, a recently described araeoscelidian, *Spinoaequalis,* from the Late Pennsylvanian of Kansas, is known only from a single partial skeleton. This small reptile is only slightly younger than *Petrolacosaurus.* It lacks the elongate neck, but has elongate limbs, as seen in the other two members of this clade (related group). The appearance of *Spinoaequalis* in the fossil record, so soon after *Petrolacosaurus,* provides direct evidence for the diversification of diapsids within the Carboniferous. Of particular interest is the discovery of a number of skeletal features in *Spinoaequalis* that display evidence for aquatic specializations. Most striking among these is the presence of a dorsoventrally (vertically) expanded tail. Araeoscelidians also share the typical diapsid characters with more recent diapsids:

There are two temporal fenestrae: the upper one between postorbital, parietal, and squamosal bones and a lower one between the postorbital, squamosal, and jugal bones. There is also a suborbital fenestra between the maxilla, palatine, and ectopterygoid bones. However, these forms retain a number of features that appear in derived form in all other diapsids. Most important among these is the anterior extension of the lacrimal bone (bone in front of the eye) to the external nostril, and the presence of a relatively broad subtemporal process of the jugal.

Younginiforms are an important group of fossil diapsids from the Upper Permian and Lower Triassic of South Africa, eastern Africa and Madagascar. *Youngina* is the best-known member of this group. Younginiforms and modern diapsids form a monophyletic group called the Neodiapsida. They are united by the presence of a flange of the parietal on which the jaw musculature originated.

ROBERT R. REISZ

See also Aquatic Reptiles; Birds; Lepidosauromorphs; Parareptiles; Turtles; Sauropterygians; Synapsids

Works Cited

Boy, J.A., and T. Martens. 1991. Ein neues captorhinomorphes Reptil aus dem thüringischen Rotliegend (Unter-Perm; Ost-Deutschland). *Paläontologische Zeitschrift* 65:363–89.

Carroll, R.L. 1964. The earliest reptiles. *Zoological Journal of the Linnean Society* 45:61–83.

———. 1988. *Vertebrate Paleontology and Evolution*. New York: Freeman.

Carroll, R.L., and D. Baird. 1972. Carboniferous stem-reptiles of the Family Romeriidae. *Bulletin, Museum of Comparative Zoolology* 143:321–64.

Clark, J., and R.L. Carroll. 1973. Romeriid reptiles from the Lower Permian. *Bulletin, Museum of Comparative Zoology* 144:353–407.

de Braga, M., and R.R. Reisz. 1995. A new diapsid reptile from the uppermost Carboniferous (Stephanian) of Kansas. *Palaeontology* 38:199–212.

Dodick, J.T., and S.P. Modesto. 1995. The cranial anatomy of the captorhinid reptile *Labidosaurikos meachami* from the Lower Permian of Oklahoma. *Palaeontology* 38:687–711.

Heaton, M.J., and R.R. Reisz. 1980. A skeletal reconstruction of the Early Permian captorhinid *Eocaptorhinus laticeps* (Williston). *Journal of Paleontology* 54:136–43.

Laurin, M., and R.R. Reisz. 1995. A reevaluation of early amniote phylogeny. *Zoological Journal of the Linnean Society* 113:165–223.

Modesto, S.P. 1996. A basal captorhinid reptile from the Fort Sill fissures, Lower Permian of Oklahoma. *Oklahoma Geology Notes* 56:4–14.

Olson, E.C. 1991. An eryopoid (Amphibia: Labyrinthodontia) from the Fort Sill fissures, Lower Permian, Oklahoma. *Journal of Vertebrate Paleontology* 11:130–32.

Reisz, R.R. 1977. *Petrolacosaurus*, the oldest known diapsid reptile. *Science* 196:1091–93.

———. 1997. The origin and early evolutionary history of amniotes. *Trends in Ecology and Evolution* 12:218–22.

Reisz, R.R., M.J. Heaton, and B.R. Pynn. 1982. Vertebrate fauna of Late Pennsylvanian Rock Lake Shale near Garnett, Kansas: Pelycosauria. *Journal of Paleontology* 56:741–50.

Further Reading

Carroll, R.L. 1964. The earliest reptiles. *Zoological Journal of the Linnean Society* 45:61–83.

———. 1988. *Vertebrate Paleontology and Evolution*. New York: Freeman.

Laurin, M., and R.R. Reisz. 1995. A reevaluation of early amniote phylogeny. *Zoological Journal of the Linnean Society* 113:165–223.

Reisz, R.R. 1997. The origin and early evolutionary history of amniotes. *Trends in Ecology and Evolution* 12:218–22.

SAUROPTERYGIANS

Sauropterygians are predominantly a group of aquatic reptiles that includes the plesiosaurs, nothosaurs, and placodonts. They are characterized by a modified diapsid skull in which there is a pair of large openings atop the skull, called the supratemporal fenestrae, and a deep cheek plate of bone on the sides (Figure 1). Throughout the evolution of sauropterygians, their skeletons show specializations for aquatic life, especially for aquatic locomotion. The most significant changes include increasing the surface area for the attachment of powerful swimming muscles in the chest and pelvis and the modification of the limbs into flippers (Figure 2). Sauropterygians were a successful group, first appearing in the lower Triassic and surviving until the end of the Cretaceous, a span of 180 million years.

Claudiosaurus, from the Upper Permian of Madagascar, is the closest sister group of the Sauropterygia. It has lost the lower bar of bone behind the eyes and has closed the openings in the roof of the mouth (Carroll 1981). The result is a skull that looks remarkably like that of the primitive sauropterygian *Neusticosaurus* (compare Figures 1A, 1B). The skeleton of *Claudiosaurus* is about 70 centimeters long and is lizardlike (Figure 2A). *Claudiosaurus* does not show the skeletal adaptations for aquatic life, such as those seen in pachypleurosaurs or plesiosaurs, so it is not certain how much of its life was spent in water. In water, however, it probably swam by moving its body and tail side-to-side in sinuous motions much like a crocodile or lizard.

The most primitive sauropterygians used to be called nothosaurs. Scholars used to characterize them has having long necks and bodies, flat, platelike chest and lower pelvic bones, and thickened (pachyostotic) bones. The limbs were not modified into flippers, but otherwise nothosaurs were thought to make good antecedents to plesiosaurs. More recent cladistic work (cladistics is one technique for establishing evolutionary relationships) by G.W. Storrs (1993), however, has shown these characteristics were superficial, and that some of these primitive sauropterygians are less closely related to plesiosaurs than originally thought. They are now divided into the Pachypleurosauria and the Nothosauriformes, which includes all the non-pachypleurosaur "nothosaurs" plus the placodonts and plesiosaurs. Among the characters that make pachypleurosaurs distinct is the lack of the ectopterygoid, a distinctive bone in the skull. This bone, however, is still found in *Claudiosaurus*, non-pachypleurosaur "nothosaurs," and plesiosaurs. The presence of this bone is the primitive condition and its loss in pachypleurosaurs is considered the derived (further evolved) condition. This single derived feature is enough to eliminate pachypleurosaurs from the ancestry of plesiosaurs because once a bone is lost, it cannot re-evolve. Although the nothosauriforms still retain the ectopterygoid, they share the derived feature of an elongate supratemporal fenestra (it is small in pachypleurosaurs; compare Figure 1).

Pachypleurosaurs are only known from the Early and Middle Triassic, a span of about 15 million years. They occur mostly in central Europe, where they are represented by hundreds of individuals from Switzerland and neighboring parts of Germany and Italy. Most pachypleurosaurs are less than one meter long and have long necks of 18 or more vertebrae (Figure 2B). Their teeth are pointed (Figure 1B) and, because they are found in near-shore marine rocks, must have been piscivores, catching small fish by ambush. *Neusticosaurus* is the most common pachypleurosaur, and it is well represented by an entire growth series from embryos to adults. The other reptiles that used to be called

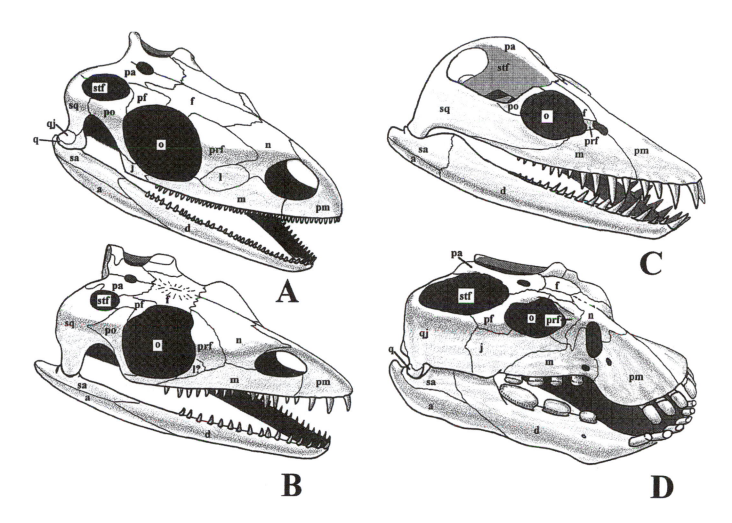

Figure 1. Skulls. *A, Claudiosaurus; B,* the pachypleurosaur *Neusticosaurus; C,* the elasmosaur *Libonectes; D,* the placodont *Placodus.* Abbreviations: *a,* angular; *d,* dentary; *f,* frontal; *j,* jugal; *l,* lachrymal; *m,* maxilla; *n,* nasal; *o,* orbit; *pa,* parietal; *pf,* postfrontal; *pm,* premaxilla; *po,* postorbital; *prf,* prefrontal; *q,* quadrate; *qj,* quadratojugal; *sa,* surangular; *sq,* squamosal; *stf,* supratemporal fenestra.

nothosaurs have not been given a group name, and it is doubtful they are all closely related evolutionarily. For now, we will call them non-pachypleurosaur "nothosaurs," or "nothosaurs" for short. "Nothosaurs" are known from Lower to Upper Triassic marine rocks of Europe, North America, Asia, and Africa. They resemble pachypleurosaurs in overall body shape, but with varying proportions of the head and neck. Some were giants up to four meters in length. As with pachypleurosaurs, the teeth are long and pointed, suggesting a diet primarily of fish. It is possible, however, that the larger forms, such as *Ceresiosaurus,* may have been more active predators, feeding on smaller "nothosaurs" as well.

The transition between the terrestrial locomotion of primitive reptiles and the very specialized aquatic locomotion in plesiosaurs is thought by R.L. Carroll (1988) and G.W. Storrs (1993) to be represented among the pachypleurosaurs and "nothosaurs." The primitive swimming style of side-to-side motions of the body and tail was probably still used by the pachypleurosaurs (Figure 3), and some "nothosaurs" that still had short limbs and underdeveloped chest, pelvic, wrist, and ankle bones. As with many aquatic

animals, including the manatee today, pachyostotic (thick, dense) bones in "nothosaurs" probably functioned as ballast, making it easier for these reptiles to remain underwater. In certain advanced "nothosaurs," notably *Nothosaurus,* swimming probably involved more of the limbs because of the much broader area for muscle attachment on the chest (coracoids, part of the scapulas, and the interclavicle) and pelvis (pubis and ischium), and by an increase in the number of finger and toe bones (hyperphalangy) into a more flipperlike appendage. These changes are further developed in plesiosaurs. Still, the small size of the limbs in advanced "nothosaurs" compared to the body length suggests that they were not powerful swimmers, making it doubtful that they were pursuit predators.

The oldest and most primitive plesiosaur is *Pistosaurus* from the Middle Triassic (approximately 238 million years ago) of Germany (Figure 2C). The skull has a long, slender snout, with the premaxillaries (paired bones forming the front of the snout) extending back to contact the frontal bones between the orbits as in some other plesiosaurs. In addition, the rear part of the palate retains an opening that is closed in pachypleurosaurs and "nothosaurs." Although it is possible for the opening to reappear (a con-

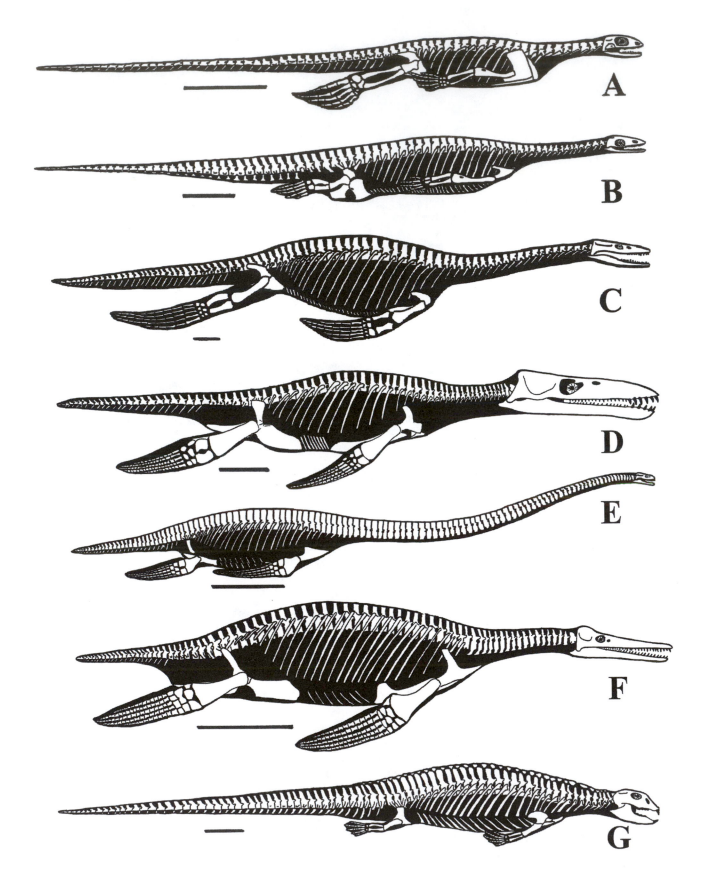

Figure 2. Skeletons. *A, Claudiosaurus; B,* the pachypleurosaur *Neusticosaurus; C,* the primitive plesiosaur *Pistosaurus; D,* the pliosaur *Liopleurodon; E,* the elasmosaur *Hydrotherosaurus; F,* the polycotylid *Dolichorhynchops; G,* the placodont *Placodus.* Heavy bars = 10 cm for *A, B, C, G;* 1 m for *D–F.* The limbs of *Pistosaurus* are not completely known and their appearance as flippers is conjectural.

Figure 3. The pachypleurosaur *Neusticosaurus* probably retained the primitive swimming mode of side-to-side motion.

dition called reversal), it seems more probable that the lack of this opening excludes any of them from ancestry of *Pistosaurus* and other plesiosaurs. The skeleton of *Pistosaurus* is incompletely known, but it is known that the bones in the chest, especially the coracoid, were greatly expanded for muscles much like those seen in later plesiosaurs. The forearm bones, the ulna and radius, are still long, reflecting the ancestral or primitive condition. *Pistosaurus* is known from offshore marine deposits, where it probably fed primarily on fish.

Plesiosaurs more advanced than *Pistosaurus* are known from the earliest Jurassic or latest Triassic. Plesiosaur evolution during the intervening 30 million years is unknown. It must have been slow because the Early Jurassic plesiosaurs still show some primitive features of *Pistosaurus*, including the elongate distal limb bones, although these are not as long (Figure 2D). Traditionally, neck length has divided these more advanced ple-

siosaurs into short-necked pliosaurs and long-necked plesiosauroids (e.g., Figures 2D, 2E). Work by Carpenter (1997) suggests that this classification is an oversimplification. Pliosaurs (Early Triassic–Early Late Cretaceous, a span of about 114 million years), characterized by *Liopleurodon* (Figure 2D), have short necks, very large heads with very large teeth clustered at the front of the mouth, and proportionally small flippers. One of these, *Kronosaurus,* from the Lower Cretaceous of the Southern Hemisphere, was a true giant, measuring 12 meters long. Plesiosaurids, on the other hand, are a more diverse group. Included within this group are the plesiosaurs of the Jurassic, which had necks of intermediate length; the Cretaceous elasmosaurs, which had very long necks (Figure 2E); and the short-necked polycotylids, which also appeared during the Cretaceous (Figure 2F). Except for the polycotylids, which evolved their large skulls independently of pliosaurs, plesiosauroids typically have small

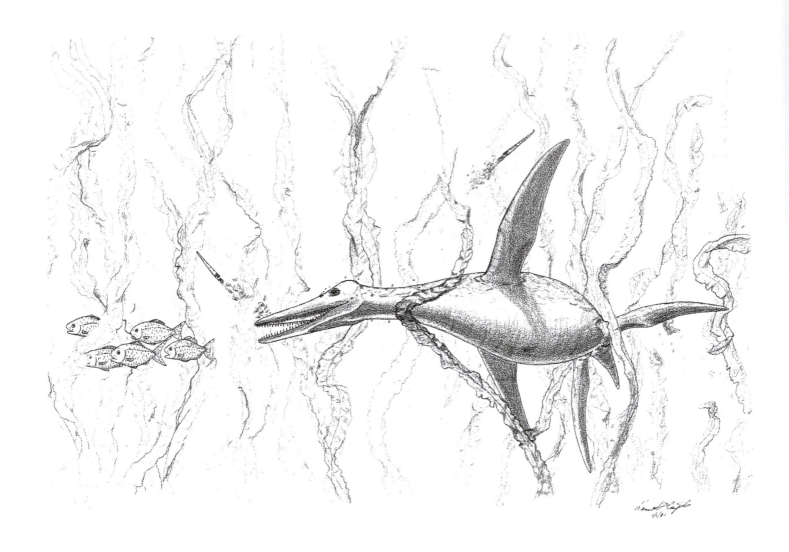

Figure 4. The polycotylid *Dolichorhynchops* as a pursuit predator.

heads relative to body size, proportionally smaller teeth, and proportionally large flippers. The closed palate of pachypleurosaurs and "nothosaurs" was acquired independently by the elasmosaurs and polycotylids, suggesting a close relationship between these two.

Throughout their evolution, plesiosaurs show a reduction in the length of the distal limb bones (ulna, radius, tibia, and fibula), resulting in short rectangular blocks in the elasmosaurs and polycotylids (compare Figure 2D with Figures 2E and 2F). In addition, the wrist and ankle bones became interlocked with each other and with the blocky distal limb bones. The result was to make the flippers rigid foils, more suitable for fast swimming. How the limbs moved in swimming has been the subject of debate. Traditionally, plesiosaurs where thought to row along, using their flippers like boat oars, but a study of plesiosaur locomotion by Robinson (1975) concluded that plesiosaurs "flew" underwater by moving their limbs like birds or sea turtles. By moving the limbs in figure eights, the limbs provided propulsion

in both the up- and downstrokes. This hypothesis, however, was challenged by S.J. Godfrey (1984), who argued that the bulk of the muscles were on the underside of the body, making the power or propulsive stroke downward and backward. This mode of swimming, employed by sea lions today, was thought to have originated among the more advanced "nothosaurs" by G.W. Storrs (1993).

J.A. Massare (1988) has examined locomotion in plesiosaurs as an indicator of hunting style. She notes that the large flippers in such short-necked forms as *Dolichorhynchops* (Figure 2F) could generate powerful strokes and were pursuit predators (Figure 4). On the other hand, long-necked plesiosaurs and elasmosaurs (Figure 2E) with smaller flippers were probably slower swimmers and may have ambushed prey from a blind spot below (Figure 5). Stomach contents are known for a few plesiosaurs, but these neither support nor refute Massare's conclusions. Small fish bones, cephalopod hooklets (possibly from squids), and dinosaur bone fragments are known for pliosaurs (Massare 1987;

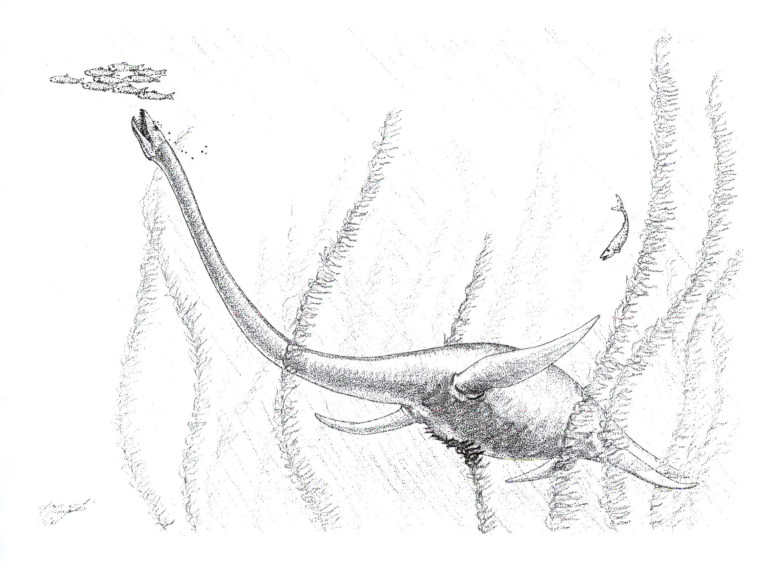

Figure 5. Ambush predation by the elasmosaur *Libonectes.*

Taylor et al. 1993). Fish bones, pterosaur bones, and ammonites have been found associated with elasmosaurs (Massare 1987). During their 173-million-year history, plesiosaurs were a very successful group, spreading throughout the world's oceans. Fossils have been found on every continent, including Antarctica, which was ice-free during the Mesozoic.

The oddest nothosauriforms are the Placodontia, which lived during the Middle to Late Triassic (about 30 million years). Geographically, they are restricted to the nearshore marine deposits of Europe, especially of Germany and Poland. Primitively, placodonts have a single row of armor along the back (Figure 2G), but more derived forms, such as *Placochelys*, have expanded this armor to encase the body in a turtlelike carapace. Most placodonts were large, over 1 meter in length, and *Placochelys* was over 2.5 meters long. Like all sauropterygians, their skulls have a single supratemporal opening and a deep cheek plate of bone (Figure 1D). However, this cheek plate is formed mostly by the quadratojugal, a bone that is small in pachypleurosaurs and

absent in "nothosaurs" and plesiosaurs. The palate is closed off in placodonts, as it is in the pachypleurosaurs and the "nothosaurs." However, the teeth are not the slender fish-eating type seen in other sauropterygians, but low, broad, crushing plates along the sides and on the roof of the mouth. Such teeth seem best suited for crushing the shells of molluscs and crustaceans. There has been some debate as to whether or not placodonts are sauropterygians, but a detailed cladistic analysis of pachypleurosaurs, "nothosaurs," plesiosaurs, and placodonts by G.W. Storrs (1991, 1993), places them as more derived than pachypleurosaurs, but less than "nothosaurs."

Sauropterygians were a highly successful group throughout the Mesozoic, a span of about 180 million years. Their extinction pattern, however, is puzzling. The first extinction, occurring at the Middle-Late Triassic boundary (208 million years ago), eliminated the pachypleurosaurs and most of the "nothosaurs" and placodonts. N. Bardet (1994) suggested that these extinctions resulted from the loss of habitat owing to a drop in sea level, which eliminated the shallow coastal waters. A second, smaller extinction event occurred at the end of the Jurassic (144 million years ago), when most of the pliosaurids and all of the plesiosaurids were eliminated. J.A. Massare (1988) believes this extinction and the subsequent low diversity of plesiosaurs throughout the Cretaceous resulted from the dominance of faster-swimming bony fishes (teleosts). She argued that the elasmosaurs and polycotylids never were able to develop adequate swimming speeds for pursuit because of anatomical constraints. The extinction of the sauropterygians at the end of the Cretaceous 65 million years ago may have been owing to the collapse of the marine food chain (Bardet 1994) associated with the asteroid impact thought to be responsible for the extinction of the dinosaurs. In their time, however, sauropterygians were a very successful group, with a longer history than that of the dinosaurs.

KENNETH CARPENTER

See also Aquatic Locomotion; Aquatic Reptiles; Placodonts

Works Cited

Bardet, N. 1994. Extinction events among Mesozoic marine reptiles. *Historical Biology* 7:313–24.

Carpenter, K. 1997. Comparative cranial anatomy of two North American Cretaceous plesiosaurs *In* J.M. Calloway and E.L. Nichols (eds.), *Ancient Marine Reptiles.* London: Academic Press.

Carroll, R.L. 1981. Plesiosaur ancestors from the Upper Permian of Madagascar. *Philosophical Transactions of the Royal Society of London* 293:315–83.

———. 1988. *Vertebrate Paleontology and Evolution.* New York: Freeman.

Godfrey, S.J. 1984. Plesiosaur subaqueous locomotion: A reappraisal. *Neues Jahrbuch für Geologie und Paläontologie, Monatshefte* 11:661–72.

Massare, J.A. 1987. Tooth morphology and prey preference of Mesozoic marine reptiles. *Journal of Vertebrate Paleontology* 7:121–37.

———. 1988. Swimming capabilities of Mesozoic marine reptiles: Implications for methods of predation. *Paleobiology* 14:187–205.

Robinson, J.A. 1975. The locomotion of plesiosaurs. *Neues Jahrbuch für Geologie und Paläontologie, Abhandlungen* 149:286–332.

Storrs, G.W. 1991. Anatomy and relationships of *Corosaurus alcovensis* (Diapsida: Sauropterygia) and the Triassic Alcova Limestone of Wyoming. *Peabody Museum of Natural History Bulletin* 44:1–151.

———. 1993. Function and phylogeny in sauropterygian (Diapsida) evolution. *American Journal of Science* 293-A:63–90.

Taylor, M.A., D.B. Norman, and A.R Cruickshank. 1993. Remains of an ornithischian dinosaur in a pliosaur from the Kimmeridgian of England. *Palaeontology* 36:357–60

SCANDENTIANS
See Tree Shrews

SCHINDEWOLF, OTTO HEINRICH

German, 1896–1971

Otto Heinrich Schindewolf is one of the most important paleontologists of the twentieth century in continental Europe. His more than 190 technical publications encompass a wide range of topics, primarily ammonoids (extinct shelled marine animals), corals, evolutionary theory, biostratigraphy (the use of fossils to date rock strata), and mass extinctions. These essays are famous because of their trenchant definitions and clear, well-written conclusions.

Schindewolf started his study of natural sciences at Göttingen University in 1914 but soon after followed his teacher Rudolf Wedekind to Marburg. There, Schindewolf wrote his dissertation on the Late Devonian and earliest Carboniferous cephalopod (marine invertebrates with multiple arms, such as octopuses and squid) limestones of the Saxothuringian Zone and their paleogeographical position, published in 1921 and 1923. From that time on, he was one of the leading biostratigraphers in central Europe. Early in his scientific career, Schindewolf focused on the systematics and biostratigraphy of Late Devonian ammonoids and soon became the world's best expert on the clymeniid ammonoids. His outstanding study of the Late Devonian Wocklumeria Stufe (1937) was a landmark in applying paleontological methods in stratigraphy.

Schindewolf's interest in fossil cephalopods expanded rapidly to different paleobiological fields. He was especially interested in the role and significance of ontogenetic development (development of an embryo) and how stages in development may reveal evolutionary history. This led to a study of the formation of sutures (joinings of shell sections) of numerous ammonoids from the Devonian up to the Cretaceous. In 1929 and 1933, Schindewolf published two monographs on genetically controlled ammonoid sutures and the ways these patterns can be used in the systematic classification of ammonoids. These essays were followed by sporadically published articles on the terminology as well as ontogenetic development of ammonoid sutures. In the 1960s, Schindewolf continued to investigate Mesozoic ammonoids, creating his monumental "Studien zur Stammesgeschichte der Ammoniten" (1961–68), one of the largest treatises ever published about this group. Considering a huge amount of precise data, assembled by careful preparations of the juvenile whorls (the spiral-shaped ammonoid shells), Schindewolf used more than 900 pages, including 478 figures, to revise the system of the Mesozoic ammonites, based mostly on sutural ontogenies.

Another field in which Schindewolf worked was corals. As in the ammonoids, he was particularly interested in the phylogeny (evolutionary relationships) of the group and in his studies uncovered relationships by subtle investigations of the development of their skeletons. His major publication on corals was "Zur Kenntnis der Polycoelien und Pterophyllen," published in 1942.

Paralleling his basic studies on diverse material, Schindewolf developed his theoretical concepts. In a pioneering study (1936), he summarized his view on the evolutionary processes, including modern genetics, within 16 theses. He explicitly contradicted the Lamarckian view of evolution, which held that the environment caused physical changes in organisms during their lifetimes; they then passed these changes on to their offspring. This theory was dominant in German paleontology at the time. In two small publications (1945, 1947) and in his magnum opus, *Grundfragen der Paläontologie* (1950), he synthesized his ideas and developed a completely new, comprehensive evolutionary theory, the anti-Darwinian Typostrophe Theory, looking at the large factors at work. Schindewolf's theory was founded on three elements: internalism (change within an organism), saltationism (rapid evolution of new species in a single evolutionary step), and cyclism. In correlating historical developments and evolution, he proposed a three-phased evolutionary cycle (Typostrophe). The first phase, Typogenesis, involved random adaptations in the past that enabled organisms to survive later changes in the present environment. In stage two, Typostasis, slow and gradual developmental processes transform characteristics. Finally, in Typolysis, overspecialization leads to preprogrammed extinction of higher groups. This evolutionary model largely dismisses environmental control and invokes a prominent internal driving force for evolution. Certainly, this was the most controversial of Schindewolf's theories. In the English-speaking scientific communities, the theory was regarded generally as an oddity, but in Germany it was accepted more widely, and elements of it still play a role in evolutionary paleontology.

Schindewolf was a paleontologist with thorough training in geology. Hence, he repeatedly discussed principal questions regarding the interrelationships between geology and paleontology. In a theoretical publication, "Grundlagen und Methoden der paläontologischen Chronologie" (1944), he manifested the primacy of the fossil record as a tool for subdividing time in Earth's geological history. In this article as well as in earlier publications, but especially in later syntheses, such as "Evolution vom Standpunkt eines Paläontologen" (1952), he demonstrated his optimistic view about the state of completeness of the fossil record.

In 1953 the documentation and interpretation of major global faunal breaks (i.e., major extinctions of many groups at the same time) led Schindewolf to the Salt Range of Pakistan to investigate the Permian-Triassic boundary. In his articles "Der Zeitfaktor in Geologie und Paläontologie" (1950) and "Neokatastrophismus?" (1963), he proposed that external factors, such as increased cosmic radiation caused by explosion of supernovae, were responsible for an increase in mutation rate, leading to increases in extinctions.

In spite of his poor health in the years after his retirement as head of the department in Tübingen, Schindewolf did not stop writing. Besides analytical investigations of different topics ("Analyse eines Ammonitengehäuses," 1968; "Über Clymenien und andere Cephalopoden," 1972), he discussed principal problems in systematics (classification) and phylogeny ("Homologie und Taxonomie," 1968; "Über den 'Typus' in morphologischer und phylogenetischer Biologie," 1969), as well as stratigraphy ("Stratigraphie und Stratotypus," 1970). He also engaged philosophical questions in the context of geology and paleontology ("Erdgeschichte und Weltgeschichte," 1964).

Because of Schindewolf's deep insight in all fields of paleontology, gained during his very productive years at Berlin's Prussian Geological Survey in the 1930s and 1940s, and his personal integrity and refusal to collaborate during the Nazi regime, by the 1950s and 1960s he was the leading and doubtlessly most influential German paleontologist. A strong character, Schwindewolf refused to accept the Modern Synthesis, advocating instead his idea of evolution as a largely autonomous process that operated continuously, regardless of any outside influences. He remained steadfast in his opinion of the preeminence of a typological approach for phylogenetic studies and avidly criticized phylogenetic systematics. Nonetheless, he was known to be undogmatic and open-minded about new scientific methods and thoughts. As a tolerant and liberal mentor, he guided more than 60 doctorate students, who went on to investigate numerous different fossil groups and who reflected Schindewolf's own wide range of interest in paleontology.

DIETER KORN

Biography

Born in Hanover, Germany, 7 June 1896. Received Dr. Philo., Marburg University, 1919; habilitation, Marburg University, 1921. Assistant professor, Marburg University, 1927; Preußische Geologische Landesanstalt, Berlin, 1927–47; Humboldt University, Berlin, 1947–48; professor, Tübingen University, 1948–64. Best known for work on ammonoids, corals, evolutionary theory, biostratigraphy, and mass extinction. Died in Tübingen, 10 June 1971.

Major Publications

1921. Versuch einer Paläogeographie des europäischen Oberdevonmeeres. *Zeitschrift der deutschen Geologischen Gesellschaft* 73:137–223.

1923. Beiträge zur Kenntnis des Paläozoikums in Oberfranken, Ostthüringen und dem Sächsischen Vogtlande. 1, Stratigraphie und Ammoneenfauna des Oberdevons von Hof a. S. *Neues Jahrbuch für Mineralogie, Geologie und Paläontologie*, Beilage-Band, 49:250–357, 393–509.

1929. Vergleichende Studien zur Phylogenie, Morphologie und Terminologie der Ammoneen-Lobenlinie. *Abhandlungen der Preußischen Geologischen Landesanstalt*, Neue Folge, 115:1–102.

1933. Vergleichende Morphologie und Phylogenie der Anfangskammern tetrabranchiater Cephalopoden. Eine Studie über Herkunft, Stammesentwicklung und System der niederen Ammoneen. *Abhandlungen der Preußischen Geologischen Landesanstalt*, Neue Folge, 148:1–115.

1936. *Paläontologie, Entwicklungslehre und Genetik: Kritik und Synthese*. Berlin: Borntraeger.

1937. Zur Stratigraphie und Paläontologie der Wocklumer Schichten (Oberdevon). *Abhandlungen der Preußischen Geologischen Landesanstalt*, Neue Folge, 178:1–132.

1942. Zur Kenntnis der Polycoelien und Pleurophyllen: Eine Studie über den Bau der "Tetrakorallen" und ihre Beziehung zu den Madreporarien. *Abhandlungen des Reichsamtes für Bodenforschung*, Neue Folge, 204:1–324.

1944. *Grundlagen und Methoden der paläontologischen Chronologie.* Berlin: Borntraeger.

1945. Darwinismus oder Typostrophismus? *Különnyomat a Magyar Biologiai Kutatóintézet Munkáiból* 16:104–77.

1947. Fragen der Abstammungslehre. *Aufsätze und Reden der Senckenbergischen Naturforschenden Gesellschaft* 1–23.

1950. Grundfragen der Paläontologie. Geologische Zeitmessung. Organische Stammesentwicklung. Biologische Systematik. Stuttgart: Schweizerbart; as *Basic Questions in Paleontology: Geologic Time, Organic Evolution, and Biological Systematics,* Chicago: University of Chicago Press, 1993.

1950. *Der Zeitfaktor in Geologie und Paläontologie.* Stuttgart: Schweizerbart.

1952. Evolution vom Standpunkt eines Paläontologen. *Eclogae Geologicae Helvetiae* 45 (2):374–86.

1960–68. *Studien zur Stammesgeschichte der Ammoniten.* Akademie der Wissenschaften und der Literatur, Abhandlungen der Mathematisch-Naturwissenschaftlichen Klasse. Wiesbaden: Steiner.

1963. Neokatastrophismus? *Zeitschrift der deutschen Geologischen Gesellschaft* 114:430–45.

1964. Erdgeschichte und Weltgeschichte. *Akademie der Wissenschaften und der Literatur, Abhandlungen der Mathematisch-Naturwissenschaftlichen Klasse* 2:53–104.

1968. Homologie und Taxonomie. *Acta Biotheoretica* 18:235–83.

1969. Über den "Typus" in morphologischer und phylogenetischer Biologie. *Akademie der Wissenschaften und der Literatur, Abhandlungen der Mathematisch-Naturwissenschaftlichen Klasse* 4:55–131.

1970. Stratigraphie und Stratotypus. *Akademie der Wissenschaften und der Literatur, Abhandlungen der Mathematisch-Naturwissenschaftlichen Klasse* 2:100–134.

1972. Über Clymenien und andere Cephalopoden. *Akademie der Wissenschaften und der Literatur, Abhandlungen der Mathematisch-Naturwissenschaftlichen Klasse* 3:55–141.

Further Reading

1966. Otto H. Schindewolf. *Neues Jahrbuch für Geologie und Paläontologie, Abhandlungen* 125 (Festband Otto H. Schindewolf):1– 3.

Erben, H.K. 1971. Nachruf auf Otto Heinrich Schindewolf. *Jahrbuch der Akademie der Wissenschaften und der Literatur* 1971:75–86.

Gould, S.J. 1993. Foreword. *In* O.H. Schindewolf, *Basic Questions in Paleontology: Geologic Time, Organic Evolution, and Biological Systematics.* Chicago: Chicago University Press.

Reif, W.-E. 1986. The search for a macroevolutionary theory in German paleontology. *Journal of the History of Biology* 19 (1):79–130.

———. 1993. Afterword. *In* O.H. Schindewolf, *Basic Questions in Paleontology: Geologic Time, Organic Evolution, and Biological Systematics.* Chicago: Chicago University Press.

Teichert, C. 1976. From Karpinsky to Schindewolf: Memories of some great paleontologists. *Journal of Paleontology* 50:1–12.

SCHMALHAUSEN, IVAN FEODOROVICH (JOHANNES THEODORE)

Russian, 1849–94

Ivan Feodorovich Schmalhausen—also known by the Germanized name, Johannes Theodore Schmalhausen—is often considered to be the founder of paleobotany in Russia. He began his career in the 1870s, working with early Russian geological surveys along the newly constructed Trans-Siberian railway. He made important contributions to the classification of Paleozoic, Mesozoic, and Tertiary flora of eastern Europe and the western portion of the Russian empire. He described a Jurassic plant, which previously had been considered as Paleozoic, from Russia's Kiznetsk, Tunguska, and Pechora basins. He also studied the anatomy of the Cretaceous fern *Protopteris.*

Unlike most botanists of late-nineteenth-century Russia, Schmalhausen was interested in the origin of species. He expounded Gregor Mendel's work on hybridization, adding that Charles Darwin had provided the theoretical foundation for viewing hybridization as a mechanism of evolution. (Hybridization is the crossbreeding of organisms in order to encourage offspring with certain characteristics, such as color or strength.) Schmalhausen's son, Ivan Ivanovich Schmalhausen, carried on his father's tradition as a prominent Soviet vertebrate zoologist and evolutionary theorist.

PAUL DAVID POLLY

Biography

Born in St. Petersburg, Russia, 3 April 1849. Received B.S. (1871) and M.S. (1874), St. Petersburg University; studied in Zurich with Oswald Heer and in Strasbourg with De Bary, 1874. Curator, Imperial Botanical Garden, St. Petersburg, 1876; professor of botany and director of botanical garden, Kiev University, 1879-84. Received All City Gold Medal for study of flowering stage of grasses, 1870. Died in Kiev, Ukraine, 7 April 1894.

Major Publications

1877. Beiträge zur Kenntnis der Milchsaftbehälter der Pflanzen. *Akademiia nauk SSSR Mémoires* 25:1–27.

1879. Beiträge zur Jura-Flora Russlands [Review of the Jurassic Flora of Russia]. *Imperatorskaya Akademiia nauk Mémoires* 27:1–96.

1883. Beiträge zur Tertiärflora Südwest-Russlands [Review of the Tertiary flora of Southwestern Russia]. *Palaeontologische Abhandlungen* 1 (4):1–53.

1883. Die Pflanzenreste der Steinkohlenformation am östlichen Abhange des Ural-Gebirges. *Imperatorskaya Akademiia nauk Mémoires* 31:1–19.

1887. Oplsanie ostalkov rastenii Artinskikh I Permskikh otlozhenii [Die Pflanzenreste der artinskischen und permischen Ablagerungen im

Osten des Europäischen Russlands]. *Trudui Commute Geologique* 2 (4):1–42.

1890. Tertiäre Pflanzen der Insel Neusibirien [Tertiary Plants from New Siberia Island]. *Imperatorskaya Akademiia nauk Mémoires* 37:1–22.

1894. *O Devonskikh rasteniyakh Donetzkago kamennoughol'nogo basseina [On the Devonian Plants from the Donetz Basin]*. St. Petersburg: Kommissionery Geologicheskago Komiteta.

Further Reading

Andrews, H.N. 1980. *The Fossil Hunters: In Search of Ancient Plants.* Ithaca, New York, and London: Cornell University Press.

Gudz, Y.P., and O.Y. Pilipchuk. 1991. *Ivan Fedorovich Schmal'gauzen.* Kiev: Science House. [in Ukranian]Krystofovich, A.N. 1956. *History of Paleobotany in the USSR.* Moscow: Academy of Sciences of the USSR.

Turkevich, J. 1963. *Soviet Men of Science: Academicians and Corresponding Members of the Academy of Sciences of the USSR.* Princeton, New Jersey: Van Nostrand.

Vucinich, A. 1988. *Darwin in Russian Thought.* Berkeley: University of California Press.

SCHMALHAUSEN, IVAN IVANOVICH

Ukrainian, 1884–1963

Ivan Ivanovich Schmalhausen, the son of Ivan Feodorovich Schmalhausen, botanist and founder of paleobotany in Russia, was one of the premier evolutionary theorists of the Soviet Union. Ironically, one of the more memorable events in his career was his expulsion from Moscow State University because of his association with Mendelian genetics—a result of the ideological victory of T.D. Lysenko's Lamarckian evolution within the Soviet political hierarchy. However, Schmalhausen was more important for his work on the origin of tetrapods (four-footed, primitive land vertebrates), for his emphasis on the role of organismal integration in evolution and for his contribution of the theory of stabilizing selection.

Schmalhausen began his career as comparative anatomist under A.N. Severtsov, studying the origin of tetrapod limbs and the transition from water to land in vertebrate evolution. Schmalhausen's work was a novel synthesis of embryology, comparative anatomy, and paleontology—a formula he maintained throughout his career. His interest in development and experimental embryology dominated his early career. Growth and morphological (form and structural) differentiation of an organism, Schmalhausen argued, are mathematically related to the rate of growth, and they decrease as an inverse proportion to age. His studies of allometry (the relative growth of a part in relation to the growth of an entire organism) reinforced the idea that organismal integration is an important part of evolution.

Schmalhausen made important contributions to evolutionary theory. He emphasized the connection between heredity and mutation in the process of evolution, pointing out that heredity both prevented change and helped promote evolutionary novelty and that mutation was the source of both novelty and disruption. He also explored the idea that selection can promote evolutionary stability as well as change. Stabilizing selection, he argued, was common, allowing species to accommodate short-term environmental change without compromising their complexly integrated adaptations. Schmalhausen thus reconciled the rather harsh idea of Darwinian selection with the less harsh Lamarckian idea of adaptation through the individual. Schmalhausen also argued that rates of evolution, as evidenced by the fossil record, could be explained best by the organism's position within the environment rather than by climatic factors or by particular features of the organism. Open ecological niches, competition and selection, and evolutionary legacy were particularly important in his explanation.

Following his expulsion from Moscow State University, Schmalhausen retired to the Zoological Institute of the Academy of Sciences of the USSR. Leaving behind the controversial subject of evolutionary mechanisms, he returned to the topic of the transition from water to land in vertebrate evolution. In his last major work, *The Origin of Terrestrial Vertebrates* (1964), he argued that terrestrial vertebrates had a single origin. In particular, Schmalhausen argued that all early Carboniferous tetrapods were derived from a particular group of lobe-finned ancestors and were related only distantly to lungfish. As always, his conclusions were based on a synthesis of paleontological data and comparative embryology.

PAUL DAVID POLLY

Biography

Born in Kiev, Ukraine, 23 April 1884. Received B.S., Physics and Mathematics, 1909; Physics and Mathematics Faculty, Kiev University; assistant to A.N. Severtsov, Kiev University, 1901–11; M.S., Moscow State University, 1914; Ph.D., Moscow State University, 1916; professor, Yuriev University, Tartu, 1916–20; head, Department of Embryology and the Dynamics of Development, Kiev University, 1920–37; academician (1922), director (1941), Biological Institute, Ukrainian Academy of Sciences; academician, Academy of Sciences of the USSR, 1935; director, A.N. Severtsov Institute of Evolutionary Morphology, Moscow, 1936–48; head, Department of Darwinism, Moscow State University, 1939–48; Zoological Institute, Academy of Sciences of the USSR, 1948–63. Died in Moscow, 7 October 1963.

Major Publications

1938. *Organizm kak Tseloe v Individualnom i Istoricheskom Razvitii* [The Organism as a Whole in Individual and Historical Development]. Moscow: Academy of Sciences USSR.

1939. *Puti i Zakonomernosti Evolyutsionogo Protsessa* [Trends of the Evolutionary Process]. Moscow: Academy of Sciences USSR.

1946. *Faktory evolyutsii. Teoria stabiliziruyushchego otbora.* Moscow: Academy of Sciences USSR; as *Factors of Evolution: The Theory of Stabilizing Selection*, Philadelphia: Blakiston, 1949; Chicago: University of Chicago Press, 1986.

1964. *Proiskhozhdenie nazemnhkh pozvonochnykh.* Moscow: Academy of Sciences USSR; as *The Origin of Terrestrial Vertebrates,* New York: Academic Press, 1968.

Further Reading

Blacher, L.J. 1975. Ivan Ivanovich Schmalhausen. *In* C.C. Gillispie (ed.), *Dictionary of Scientific Biography.* New York: Scribner.

Gans, C. 1968. Preface. *In* I.I. Schmalhausen, *The Origin of Terrestrial Vertebrates.* New York: Academic Press.

Turkevich, J. 1963. *Soviet Men of Science: Academicians and Corresponding Members of the Academy of Sciences of the USSR.* Princeton, New Jersey: Van Nostrand.

Vucinich, A. 1988. *Darwin in Russian Thought.* Berkeley: University of California Press.

Wake, D.B. 1986. Forward. *In* I.I. Schmalhausen, *Factors of Evolution: The Theory of Stabilizing Selection.* Chicago: University of Chicago Press.

SEAS, ANCIENT

Shortly after the formation of the Earth, about 4.6 billion years ago, the surface was still molten and water existed only as hot clouds of atmospheric vapor. Within the following 0.5 billion years, the surface of the planet cooled, a continental crust formed, and water vapor condensed into rain. The world ocean formed as the rain water accumulated in the lower elevations. The early seawater became salty because the water and its dissolved carbon dioxide reacted with natural minerals such as clays and carbonates.

About 950 to 700 million years ago, fragments of continental crust were probably moving together to form one great supercontinent. This theoretical landmass has been named "Rodinia," and the corresponding superocean "Mirovia" (McMenamin and McMenamin 1990). During this time, the global climate was cold, and extensive ice sheets were present.

By the late Precambrian, about 600 to 570 million years ago, the climate became warmer, and the ice sheets began to melt. As they did, the sea level rose. At about the same time, the tectonic plates bearing the continental crust began to move apart, creating oceanic spaces between the continental fragments. As movement continued, the mantle (molten rock from deep within Earth) welled up onto the ocean bed through the openings between fragments. Hot mantle material was extruded in the form of huge submarine ridges along the boundaries between plates. The ridges filled areas of the oceanic basin. Continental flooding, which formed large, shallow seas (epicontinental seas), was caused by a combination of ice melt and plate separation.

Although not all scientists agree that a Precambrian supercontinent existed, the concept has received wide acceptance. It is apparent that continuous plate movement has taken place over much of the Earth's history. T.R. Worsley and colleagues (1986) have proposed a "supercontinent megacycle" that consists of four phases: fragmentation, maximum dispersal, assembly, and stasis. The theory suggests that the supercontinent interferes with the escape of heat through the Earth's mantle, causing overheating below, which eventually fragments the supercontinent. The fragments (continents) drift and eventually congregate over an area of colder, downwelling mantle. This sequence has been called the "Wilson Cycle" (after J. Tuzo Wilson). It may have been repeated over time spans of about 500 million years.

The breakup of Rodinia apparently had important consequences for the evolution of multicellular (metazoan) organisms. The newly established epicontinental seas received nutrients from rivers discharging into them. In these shallow waters the nutrients could be recycled by wind-driven currents. Increased vulcanism, which accompanied enhanced plate movement, injected carbon dioxide (CO_2) into the atmosphere. Rising atmospheric CO_2 retained much of the heat that earlier had been lost to space by radiation, so the surface of the Earth became warmer. As simple photosynthetic (planktonic) organisms became more numerous, the oxygen level rose until it reached the threshold required for respiration by metazoan organisms. In an evolutionary sense, the warmer water, increased oxygen, expanded shallow-water habitat, and improved nutrient supply were all positive factors (Briggs 1995).

The first unequivocal metazoan fossils appeared after the global ecosystem recovered from the Precambrian glaciation. These early organisms comprised the Ediacaran Fauna, which developed about 570 million years ago. This simple fauna was succeeded by the "Cambrian Explosion," the evolution of an astounding variety of animal groups comprising as many as 100 different phyla (primary divisions of animal life). As these important biological developments were taking place, the various continental blocks and terranes that once constituted Rodinia became widespread. By the mid-Cambrian, about 530 million years ago, the plates were distributed around the globe (Figure 1).

The continental dispersal apparently continued for about 100 million years. Then the assembly stage of the Wilson Cycle began. From the mid-Silurian to the mid-Triassic, a period of about 200 million years, the plates bearing the various pieces of continental crust moved together until they coalesced into another supercontinent. This most recent assemblage has been called Pangaea (Figure 2). Because Pangaea existed only a little more than 200 million years ago, its configuration and biology is better known that the earlier Rodinia.

The formation of Pangaea was accompanied by a great extinction, during which the ocean lost more than 90 percent of its species diversity. When the continental amalgamation was completed, plate movements ceased, and the ocean basin became relatively quiet. The hot mantle material, which had been extruded in the form of spreading ridges, began to cool and contract. As a result, the ocean basin became deeper and the sea level fell—as much as 280 meters, exposing all of the continental shelves and eliminating almost all shallow-water habitats. Loss of habitat, plus associated climatic and ecological effects, produced the greatest extinction ever recorded (Erwin 1993).

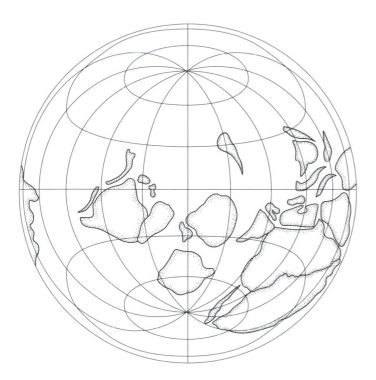

Figure 1. Mid-Cambrian. By this time, the various continental blocks and terranes had undergone considerable dispersal. Illustration by Catherine P. Sexton, after Briggs (1995).

Figure 3. Late Cretaceous. High sea level has resulted in the formation of extensive epicontinental seas. Illustration by Catherine P. Sexton, after Briggs (1995).

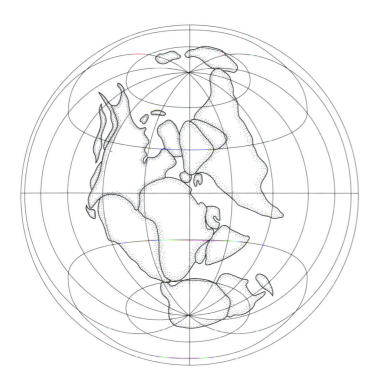

Figure 2. Mid-Triassic. Pangaea is now fully assembled. Illustration by Catherine P. Sexton, after Briggs (1995).

Figure 4. Early Miocene. Africa has contacted Asia via the Arabian Peninsula, eliminating the Tethys Sea and creating the Mediterranean. Illustration by Catherine P. Sexton, after Briggs (1995).

There have been other, less severe historic extinction events. Most were also associated with sea level regressions. Sometimes, as in the Cretaceous/Tertiary event of 65 million years ago, volcanic eruptions or asteroid impacts have also been implicated.

As Pangaea began to break apart, a new Wilson Cycle began. Beginning in the Jurassic, about 200 million years ago, plate movement increased, causing a rise in sea level and more volcanic activity. As earlier, the volcanically-produced CO_2 elevated the temperature of the planet. Extensive inland seas, tropical climate, and high levels of CO_2 produced luxuriant plant growth. Under such conditions, the Earth is considered to be in a "greenhouse" state (Fischer 1984). The greenhouse of the Cretaceous, which produced great dinosaurs and large marine reptiles, lasted more than 60 million years. The extent of continental flooding is apparent on a map of that period (Figure 3).

From the mid-Eocene through the Oligocene, about 45 to 23 million years ago, the Earth underwent another climatic change, from the greenhouse of the Mesozoic and Early Cenozoic to the "icehouse" of the later Cenozoic. By the Early Miocene, about 20 million years ago, dramatic changes in continental relationships had taken place (Figure 4). Australia had moved to the north, India was pushing into southern Asia, the circumtropical Tethys Sea was eliminated, Antarctica was isolated, and the modern Isthmus of Panama was almost completed. As these tectonic changes took place, they altered the ocean current patterns and set the stage for our present climatic regime.

JOHN C. BRIGGS

See also Faunal and Floral Provinces; Ocean Environment; Plate Tectonics and Continental Drift; Trophic Groups and Levels

Works Cited

Briggs, J.C. 1955. *Global Biogeography.* Amsterdam and New York: Elsevier.

Erwin, D.H. 1993. *The Great Paleozoic Crisis.* New York: Columbia University Press.

Fischer, A.G. 1984. The two Phanerozoic supercycles. *In* W.A. Berggren and J.A. Van Couvering (eds.), *Catastrophes and Earth History.* Princeton, New Jersey: Princeton University Press.

McMenamin, M.A.S., and D.L.S. McMenamin. 1990. *The Emergence of Animals: The Cambrian Breakthrough.* New York: Columbia University Press.

Worsley, T.R., R.M. Nance, and J.B. Moody. 1986. Tectonic cycles and the history of the earth's biogeochemical and paleoceanographic record. *Paleoceanography* 1:233–63.

Further Reading

Hallam, A. 1992. *Phanerozoic Sea Level Changes.* New York: Columbia University Press.

Kennett, J.P. 1982. *Marine Geology.* Englewood Cliffs, New Jersey: Prentice-Hall.

Stanley, S.M. 1986. *Earth and Life through Time.* New York: Freeman; 2nd ed., 1989.

SEDGWICK, ADAM

English, 1785–1873

Adam Sedgwick's lifetime work was the study of the Paleozoic strata of England and Wales. His first geological studies were in southwest England, under the tutelage of William Coneybeare, and dealt with the New Red Sandstone, a poorly known unit containing fossils. Sedgwick was regarded as a supreme field geologist, with a flair for interpreting local geology in the context of the larger geographic region. This was illustrated by his first monograph, in which he correlated the Permian Magnesian Limestone in northern England with classic successions of rock strata in Germany. His interpretation of such units as being conformable (representing the same period of deposition), and produced by long-term geological processes was influential in illustrating the great time over which these strata had been deposited. In this he was an ardent ally of geologist Charles Lyell, being highly critical of the "diluvian" views of William Buckland. (The diluvian theory used Noah's flood to explain the presence of unusual fossils in western Europe.) However, Sedgwick took Lyell to task for implying in his *Principles of Geology* that "uniformitarianism" meant geological processes had been absolutely uniform throughout geological history. Sedgwick's background as a field geologist led him to argue that all strata had to be observed and tested in the field to ensure conformity

with uniformitarian views. To him, the complex folding in strata indicated periods of less than "steady state" processes, with periods of "paroxysmal" events that resulting in the formation of mountain ranges.

Sedgwick's most significant geological work was his study of Paleozoic strata, first in Devon and Cornwall and then in North Wales and the Lake District of England, on rocks that he was later to give the name "Cambrian." As the founder of the Cambrian System, he tried to unravel the earliest evidence of life on Earth, as depicted by the fossils that he found in these rocks. In 1831 accompanied by a young Charles Darwin, Sedgwick began his studies of the rock of North Wales. At the same time, Roderick Murchison began his studies of the seemingly younger "Transition" strata in the Welsh Borderlands. (Later, these rocks would be called Silurian.) In a joint six-week field trip to Wales in 1834, it became apparent to both Sedgwick and Murchison that the fossils of Sedgwick's Upper Cambrian Bala Series were similar to those of Murchison's Lower Silurian.

In 1836 Sedgwick and Murchison worked together on unraveling the "Culm Measures" strata in Devon. They discovered that the most ancient rocks upon which the Carboniferous Culm Measures rested were neither Cambrian nor Silurian but were equivalent to the Old Red Sandstone, for which they jointly proposed the term "Devonian."

In the 1840s Sedgwick returned to studying the older Paleozoic rocks in Britain. He believed that his Cambrian rocks contained an older fauna than the Silurian, and the two systems comprised the "Protozoic." However, Murchison argued that his own Lower Silurian included Sedgwick's Upper Cambrian. In fact, Murchison increasingly claimed that more and more of the Cambrian really belonged to his greater Silurian System. Then, when Sedgwick submitted a paper to the geological Society for publication, his stratigraphic nomenclature was changed in accordance with Murchison's views—without consulting Sedgwick first. Sedgwick was furious. As he wrote later (1873), the society "contrived to *change my language, and make me write in a new Silurian tongue*" (Sedgwick's italics). Ultimately, the Council of the Geological Society refused to let Sedgwick bring any paper before them that involved his classification. Sedgwick, in turn, refused to attend further meetings of the society, but he could not bring himself to resign.

The cause of this controversy stemmed from Murchison's error in misinterpreting the older succession of the Lower Silurian in the "type area"—the area where the strata were first identified. Rather than being younger than the Bala Series, they were the same age. Sedgwick also discovered that Murchison had confused Upper with Lower Silurian strata, which made Sedgwick's Upper Cambrian appear to belong to Murchison's system. To make matters worse, because he held a very influential position as head of the Geological Survey, Murchison was reluctant to admit his mistakes. The result was a long-standing, bitter dispute that was not resolved until 1879, when Charles Lapworth showed that Sedgwick's Upper Cambrian and Murchison's Lower Silurian represented a distinct system, the Ordovician.

Although not a paleontologist, Sedgwick developed a great understanding of fossils. As a devout Christian, however, he dismissed Darwin's ideas on natural selection. After reading *The Origin of Species,* Sedgwick wrote to Darwin (Clark and Hughes 1890) that he read the book "with more pain than pleasure." Sedgwick felt that natural selection was a "secondary consequence of supposed, or known, primary facts" and preferred "the will of God" to the "assumptions" of natural selection. Sedgwick was a master of observation and interpretation, not a theorist. Theories that argued for transmutation of species "greatly shocked (his) moral taste." The natural consequence of Darwin's views was that selection equally applied to humans, and Sedgwick could not agree with such an idea. He later wrote, "That Man . . . in the functions and powers of his intellect is absolutely removed from any co-ordination with the lower beings of Nature is, I firmly believe, one of the most certain of well apprehended truths" (Sedgwick 1873).

Although Sedgwick's written output was not immense, as a supreme field geologist and consummate lecturer he had a great impact on his contemporaries and on later generations. He was one of the most distinguished and influential geologists of the nineteenth century, and his work laid the foundation for later studies of Paleozoic strata throughout the world.

KENNETH J. MCNAMARA

Work Cited

Clark, J.W., and T. McKenny Hughes. 1890. *The Life and Letters of the Reverend Adam Sedgwick, LL.D., D.C.L., F.R.S., Fellow of Trinity College, Cambridge, Prebendary of Norwich, Woodwardian Professor of Geology, 1818–1873.* 2 vols. Cambridge: University of Cambridge Press.

Biography

Born in Dent, Yorkshire, 22 March 1785. Educated at Trinity College, Cambridge, graduating in 1808 with distinction in mathematics; elected fellow of Trinity College, 1810; ordained, 1817; Woodwardian Professor of Geology at Cambridge, 1818. Recipient, Wollaston Medal, Geological Society of London, 1851; Copely Medal, Royal Society, 1863; LL.D., Cambridge University, 1866; honorary D.C.L., Oxford University, 1860. Member of numerous scholarly and professional organizations, including British Association (president, 1833; president of geological section, 1837, 1845, 1853, 1860); French Académie des Sciences; Geological Society of London (president, 1829–31); Royal Society (fellow, 1821). Began fieldwork in southwest England, 1818; on the basis of fieldwork in Wales named the Cambrian System; with R.I. Murchison named the Devonian System. Died in Cambridge, 27 January 1873.

Major Publications

1825. On the origin of the Alluvial and Diluvial Formations. *Annals of Philosophy,* new ser., 9:241–47; 10:18–37.

1829. On the geological relations and internal structure of the Magnesian Limestone, and on the lower portions of the New Red Sandstone Series. *Transactions of the Geological Society of London,* 2nd ser., 3, pt. 1:37–124.

1832. With R.I. Murchison. A sketch of the structure of the eastern Alps. *Transactions of the Geological Society of London,* 2nd ser., 3, pt. 2:301–420.

1835a. Introduction to the general structure of the Cumbrian Mountains. *Transactions of the Geological Society of London,* 2nd ser., 4, pt. 1:47–68.

1835b. Remarks on the structure of large mineral masses, and especially on the chemical changes produced in the aggregation of stratified rocks during different periods after their deposition. *Transactions of the Geological Society of London,* 2nd ser., 3 (3):461–86.

1838–41. A synopsis of the English Series of stratified rocks inferior to the Old Red Sandstone. *Proceedings of the Geological Society of London* 2:675–85; Supplement [to the same], 3:541–54.

1840. With R.I. Murchison. On the physical structure of Devonshire, and on the subdivisions and geological relations of the older stratified deposits, etc. *Transactions of the Geological Society of London,* 2nd ser., 5, pt. 3:633–704.

1842a. On the distribution and classification of the older or palaeozoic deposits of the north of Germany and Belgium, and their comparison with formations of the same age in the British Isles. *Transactions of the Geological Society of London* 6 (2):221–301.

1842b. Three letters upon the geology of the Lake District addressed to W. Wordsworth, Esq. *In* J. Hudson (ed.), *A Complete Guide to the Lakes.* London: Wittaker; 4th ed., London: Longman, 1853.

1845. On the older Palaeozoic (Protozoic) rocks of North Wales. *Quarterly Journal of the Geological Society* 1:5–22.

1851–55. *A Synopsis of the Classification of the British Paleozoic Rocks, with a Systematic Description of the British Palaeozoic Fossils in the Geological Museum of the University of Cambridge.* Cambridge: Cambridge University Press.

1852. On the classification and nomenclature of the Lower Palaeozoic rocks of England and Wales. *Quarterly Journal of the Geological Society of London* 8:136–68.

1854. On the May Hill Sandstone, and the Palaeozoic System of England. *Philosophical Magazine,* 4th ser., 8:301–17.

1873. Preface. *In* J.W. Salter (ed.), *A Catalogue of the Collection of Cambrian and Silurian Fossils Contained in the Geological Museum of the University of Cambridge.* Cambridge: University of Cambridge Press.

Further Reading

Clark, J.W., and T. McKenny Hughes. 1890. *The Life and Letters of the Reverend Adam Sedgwick, LL.D., D.C.L., F.R.S., Fellow of Trinity College, Cambridge, Prebendary of Norwich, Woodwardian Professor of Geology, 1818–1873.* 2 vols. Cambridge: University of Cambridge Press.

SEDIMENTOLOGY

Sedimentology is the science concerned with the classification and interpretation of sediments and the rocks they form. This discipline is related to paleontology through interdisciplinary studies of taphonomy (processes of burial and fossilization), paleobiology, and paleoecology. Only a few of the relationships can be discussed here. What follows is an overview of sedimentology and how characters of sedimentary rocks are related to ancient depositional environments. Depositional environments are the places where sediments are deposited, each of which is marked by distinctive physical, chemical, and biological characteristics. We will consider examples of fossiliferous deposits and explore interpretations of their original depositional environments.

Sedimentary rocks are cemented accumulations of particles derived either from preexisting rocks via weathering or chemical precipitation from water. In weathering, particles are broken away by physical forces such as moving wind or precipitation. In chemical precipitation, water reacts with minerals to produce solid particles that settle out (precipitate) from the ambient liquid evironment. Sedimentary rocks cover most of the Earth's land surface, usually topped by a thin veneer of soil. They make up most of the rocks we see around us today. In large depressions called sedimentary basins, layers of sedimentary rocks (strata) can reach thicknesses of several kilometers. The awesome beauty of Grand Canyon National Park, Arizona, is principally owing to the layered nature of sedimentary rocks. The depth of the basin allows us to see the layers along the vertical sides. The study of sedimentology is appropriate for paleontologists, primarily because most known fossil life has been found within sedimentary rocks.

Sedimentary rocks also preserve a suite of characters, among them their fossil contents, which can be used as paleoenvironmental indicators. Researchers use such indicators as clues to reconstruct the original depositional environment of the sediment. For example, a quartz sandstone characterized by well-sorted, medium-grained particles may indicate deposition in any of several possible environments. What environmental indicators can be used to determine if this medium-grained sandstone was deposited in a deltaic (river delta) environment, on a beach, or on the plains of a desert? Four general types of clues can help provide the answer: (1) the fossil content; (2) the sedimentary structures; (3) the lithic characters (those pertaining to the microscopic composition of a rock); and (4) the geometry of a rock deposit.

Fossil content of sedimentary rocks is particularly useful in determining depositional environments. Scholars draw analogies between the fossils and comparable modern organisms that survive only in certain settings. For example, most fishes need a permanent body of water, cacti grow best in dry settings, and the great diversity of molluscs is found in shallow marine waters. A sedimentary rock bearing abundant trilobite (extinct marine arthropods) fossils suggests that it formed in a marine environment but also much more. Depending on the state of knowledge of fossil species and modern analogues, the fossil record also may suggest more about the environment of deposition, including water depth, temperature, and levels of turbidity (amount of suspended sediment) and salinity (Boggs 1987). However, fossil content alone can be misleading. For example, if one is not careful, one could interpret cow bones swept into a stream prior to fossilization, as coming from aquatic animals.

Sedimentary structures are the external and internal geometric shapes of sediments at a macroscopic level (large enough to be seen with the naked eye). Particular structures are associated with specific depositional environments, each of which can be classified in terms of its origin: depositional, erosional, deformational, or biogenic. These categories reflect the effects of basic processes that universally operate on sediments: moving water, wind, gravity, and living organisms (Ricci Lucchi 1995). Depositional structures record the incremental addition of sediment to an area; examples include fine-grained sediments settling slowly to the bottom of a deep lake in thin layers (called cross-bedding), which represents the migration of bedforms such as ripples. Erosional structures preserve evidence of the removal of sediment from one area and its deposition elsewhere, often when a scoured area (such as a channel) becomes filled. Deformational structures may indicate periods of desiccation (drying) or sediment instability, as exhibited by mud cracks and paleoslides (ancient rock slides), respectively. Biogenic structures are those produced by the feeding, locomotion, resting, or burrowing activity of organisms.

Lithic characters pertain to the sedimentary texture of a rock, features that are observed at the scale of individual grains—

lithic characters are much smaller than sedimentary structures. The lithologic composition, size, and shape of grains can be powerful indicators of depositional environment. The composition of a sedimentary rock refers to the origin of the minerals that make up the rock and the types of minerals that constitute the individual grains. Sedimentary grains can be derived either from the weathering and erosion of preexisting rocks (clastic derivation) or through inorganic or organic precipitation (nonclastic derivation).

Common clastic particles are quartz, feldspar, and clay minerals. They are compressed and cemented to form clastic sedimentary rocks, the most abundant of which are sandstone, siltstone, and shale. Nonclastic sedimentary particles form as minerals that precipitate directly from mineral-bearing water. Local chemical conditions (inorganic) or organisms (organic) initiate the precipitation. Inorganic precipitation of minerals, common under conditions in which more water evaporates than falls as, for example, rain or water vapor, may form gypsum, limestone, and rock salt. Organic precipitates have their origins with diverse groups of extinct and extant aquatic (marine and nonmarine) organisms. Corals and microscopic animals such as foraminifera, as well as single-cell algae called coccolithophores, remove calcium carbonate from seawater to form their skeletal structures. Upon death, the carbonate skeletons of these planktonic organisms settle to the ocean floor, eventually becoming cemented as limestone deposits. As a result, although corals are more familiar, foraminifera and coccolithophores (extant groups with extensive fossil records) contribute vast amounts of carbonate sediment to the ocean floor. It should be noted that although clastic and nonclastic grains may form differently, all are transported and deposited by the same physical processes.

Sedimentologists quantify grain size, another lithic character, in several different ways. A commonly used scale lists grains in order of decreasing size: boulder, cobble, pebble, granule, sand, silt, and clay. The size and density of individual grains has a great impact on the ability of such agents as water, ice, wind, and gravity to carry sediment. Simply put, it takes more energy to transport larger or denser particles. While vigorous mountain streams may carry fist-sized cobbles downstream with ease, a quiet river may not shift them at all. Thus, the maximum grain size and density of a sedimentary rock reveals the maximum energy of the depositional medium needed to transport it. Such features can be quantified and verified in laboratory experiments.

R.A. El-Ella and J.M. Coleman (1985) utilized grain-size analyses to discriminate between sediments from several modern depositional environments. (The statistical range of grain sizes contained in a sedimentary rock is termed sorting.) A rock composed of grains of unimodal (the same) size is considered well-sorted, while a rock composed of a wide range of grain sizes (from boulders to clays, for example) is considered poorly sorted. The amount of sorting that a sediment undergoes depends mainly upon the amount of time spent in a depositional environment before consolidation (uniting into a rocky material), perhaps allowing the sediments to be reworked, winnowed, and redeposited several times. For example, desert sands tend to be well-sorted, because sand particles are extensively reworked by eolian (wind) processes.

The shape of individual grains is another lithic clue used to determine the depositional environment of a sedimentary rock. Grain shape is commonly (but not exclusively) measured as the roundness (lack of angular corners) of the particle. An individual grain's roundness is a combined result of the mineral involved, the nature of the transporting agent, the distance of transport, and the degree of weathering. The farther a grain has traveled, the more likely it is to be well rounded.

A related feature of grain shape is grain surface texture, including abrasion patterns, fractures, and other markings, all of which are used to determine the transporting agent. The study of surface textures of quartz grains in modern depositional environments has allowed researchers to distinguish among grains deposited in beach, desert, and glacial settings (Boggs 1987).

In addition to fossil content, sedimentary structures, and lithic characters, larger-scale features, such as the overall shape or geometry of a deposit, may reflect its depositional environment. A beach deposit may preserve a linear geometry that illustrates its presence along an ancient coastline. A single river-channel deposit may retain a sinuous geometry. Rock units neighboring the deposit also must be considered. For example, certain rock units often are found in vertical or horizontal proximity to one another, reflecting side-by-side relationships of active depositional environments to one another. A beach marks the boundary between marine and terrestrial environments. Therefore, a beach sandstone probably will be bordered by marine and terrestrial deposits on opposite sides.

How did earth scientists come to correlate special characteristics of fossils and sediments with unique depositional environments? Principally, they looked at modern environments of deposition, just as paleontologists study modern analogues of extinct organisms to recognize ancient habitats. Sedimentary structures and lithic characters can be correlated with certain transport agents and energy levels in the rocks themselves or in artificial environments such as flume tanks and wind tunnels. Four examples—marine clastic and nonclastic rocks, and terrestrial nonclastic and clastic rocks—illustrate what information is required to correlate features of sedimentary rocks with specific depositional environments.

Today, most sediments are deposited in marine environments. That is partly a reflection of the fact that water covers a large percentage of Earth's surface. But the situation also reflects the significant actions of moving water, Earth's most common transport agent. Marine waters deposit particles in many distinct sedimentary environments, including deltas, beaches, lagoons, reefs, barrier islands, tidal flats, carbonate shelves, and abyssal deeps. Here, we will focus on quiet sedimentary environments, both clastic and nonclastic, which are more likely to lead to fossil preservation.

The Burgess Shale of British Columbia, Canada, is one of the most famous clastic marine deposits, known for its preservation of soft-bodied invertebrate fossils, some of which have been found nowhere else. Soft-body preservation is extremely rare. In part, it is indicative of quick burial in anoxic (oxygen-poor) environments where there are few scavenging organisms. The Burgess Shale is especially important because it provides one of the few records of multicellular life in the Middle Cambrian (about 530 million years ago).

Scholars must do serious detective work in fossil faunas and sedimentary characteristics to determine environments of deposition. Analyzing the Burgess Shale fauna alone suggests that it was marine in origin. Although many of the preserved organisms lack modern analogues, there are representatives of familiar marine invertebrate groups such as brachiopods (clamlike organisms), trilobites, and echinoderms (the group that includes modern starfish and sea cucumbers). Strata of the famous shale are dark, fine-grained clay, which indicates calm, low-energy water conditions. Such conditions are also indicated by the delicate nature of the fossils themselves.

Some sedimentary structures in the Burgess Shale are thin, fining-upward parallel beds (Allison and Brett 1995). The overall geometry of the deposit, and its relationship to other rock units, suggests the most plausible depositional environment. Fine-grained mud of the lower ("basinal") Stephen Formation, the rocks that make up the Burgess Shale, abuts a steep carbonate wall called the Cathedral Escarpment (Whittington 1985). Approximately 530 million years ago, unconsolidated sediments slumped off the top of the Cathedral Escarpment and settled below. Animals living near the edge of the cliff were swept down with the sediments into deeper anoxic waters, where they were quickly covered with mud. Lithified sediments (those that have become rock) of this type, the result of submarine mud flows, are called turbidites. Although some scholars do not agree (Allison and Brett 1995), most interpret strata of the Burgess Shale as turbidites. Interestingly, neither the fauna nor sedimentary structures of the Burgess Shale were sufficiently isolated to establish the depositional context. The crucial evidence in determining the ancient environment leading to the Burgess Shale was derived from the geometry of the deposit, combined with knowledge of the surrounding rocks.

The famous Solnhofen Limestones of southern Germany provides a nonclastic marine example. Quarried for building material and lithographic printing stones, the Solnhofen "Plattenkalke" were formed during the Late Jurassic (about 150 million years ago) by carbonate sedimentation. Dispersed throughout the microcrystalline limestone are fabulously preserved fossils of plants and animals, both marine and terrestrial. Like the Burgess Shale, the Solnhofen deposit is one of only a few known "Lagerstätten," or "fossil mother-lodes," where soft-body preservation is possible. What was the depositional environment of the limestones from Solnhofen?

A diverse fossil assemblage of both marine and terrestrial animals suggests that Solnhofen was once a marine nearshore environment; preservation of the fossils is indicative of a nonturbulent environment. In turbulent waters the sediments would not have settled down so uniformly, nor would the remains have been left undisturbed long enough to be preserved in so pristine a condition. The Solnhofen Lagerstätten are best known for specimens of *Archaeopteryx,* generally accepted as the earliest known bird. The individual carbonate grains surrounding the fossils are of organic origin, including coccolithophore fragments and abrasion products scraped from nearby corals (Barthel et al. 1990). The most common sedimentary structure is parallel bedding, with each bed composed of several fine laminations (layers) (Buisonjé 1985). As with the Burgess Shale, the Solnhofen Limestones were deposited

from suspension in relatively quiet water. (In other words, sedimentary particles were suspended in water, then slowly filtered down to the bottom to cover specimens without disturbing their basic structure.) This process is indicated by the limestones' fine-grained composition and parallel laminations. Unlike the Burgess Shale, the organic strata at Solnhofen preserve some fauna that originated on dry land. These clues suggest that the limestone was deposited in a lagoonal environment. That interpretation is bolstered by the surrounding rocks, which include ancient coral reefs and remnants of carbonate shoals.

Terrestrial deposition (i.e., that on land) occurs in alluvial fans, lakes and rivers, coal swamps, deserts, and glacial environments. Lake (lacustrine) deposits provide particularly interesting examples. Like the marine Lagerstätten, lacustrine deposits are those in which fine-grained particles—clastic or nonclastic—are deposited from suspension, usually with little disturbance from waves or currents. The Middle Eocene shales of ancient Lake Messel in Germany bear well-preserved suites (widely diverse groups that existed in communities) of terrestrial plants and animals (Schaal and Ziegler 1992), as do the deposits of the Green River Formation of Wyoming (Grande 1994).

The Riversleigh limestone of northwestern Queensland, Australia, bear a similarly preserved terrestrial biota (flora and fauna) and is an example of a nonclastic terrestrial sedimentary environment. The "Riversleigh limestone" is a broad term used to group several fossil localities ranging in age from Oligocene to Recent. One of the most productive localities, the Upper Site, preserves a variety of freshwater gastropods (the group including modern clams and snails), fish, insects, lower vertebrates, birds, and mammals of the Miocene (about 20 million years ago). The soft body parts of vertebrates are not preserved, although three-dimensionally preserved insects are present at the Upper Site (Duncan and Briggs 1996). The fauna in general suggests a nonmarine depositional environment, and the non-mammalian vertebrates (snakes, turtles, crocodilians) in particular suggest a tropical environment. Strata consist of limestone, chemically precipitated from restricted water bodies. Although not well documented, sedimentary structures include algal mats (layers of algae bound together and lithified) and iron-enriched bands that may represent anoxic conditions (Archer et al. 1991). The fauna and sedimentary composition of the Upper Site suggest a depositional environment of shallow, lime-rich pools in a tropical rainforest. Animals trapped in the mineral-rich pools drowned, and their bodies settled to the bottom to be covered by limy mud. Here, the fauna and sediment type were the major clues to determining the depositional environment.

The vast majority of terrestrial fossils are preserved in deposits of clastic origin. Among terrestrial deposits, those composed of wind-blown particles may offer the best environments for the preservation of fossils. The sands of ancient Mongolian deserts, for example, preserved exceptional dinosaurian and mammalian fossils over 75 million years ago.

Upper Cretaceous vertebrate fossils of the Mongolian Gobi Desert show outstanding preservation. In general, these fossil localities show better preservation, at least in terms of articulated (intact, organized as in life) skeletons, than known Cretaceous localities anywhere else in the world (Dashzeveg et al.

1995). Fossil localities in the Djadokhta Formation of the famous desert have produced fully articulated skeletons of mammals, lizards, and dinosaurs in fine-grained sandstone. Some of the fossilized skeletons assume lifelike poses, such as standing, indicating rapid burial (Jerzykiewicz et al. 1993). The fine-grained sandstones are well sorted and were deposited in thick beds bearing steep-angle cross-stratification. Both features are correlated with present-day dune sediments. The fossil fauna and its preservation, coupled with the sedimentary characters and structures, indicate that winds preserved the fossils in a desert environment. Animals were quickly entombed as dry desert windstorms deposited sands upon them.

Sedimentology and related fields form a network of scientific subdisciplines, of interest to paleontologists and other earth scientists. Especially relevant to the paleontologist are the methods by which the features of sedimentary rocks are used to reconstruct ancient environments. Fossil content, sedimentary structures, lithic characters, and geometry of deposits are among the many attributes of sedimentary rocks employed for this objective. Earth scientists in general require environmental interpretations of sedimentary environments as background for many types of studies. To paleontologists, recognition of ancient sedimentary environments is crucial to understanding changes in life during the passage of time represented by the rock record.

MICHAEL W. WEBB

See also Atmospheric Environment; Faunal and Floral Provinces; Fossil Record; Global Environment; Ocean Environment; Paleoclimatology; Paleoecology; Seismic and Surface Activity; Stable Isotope Analysis; Terrestrial Environment

Works Cited

Allison, P.A., and C.E. Brett. 1995. In situ benthos and paleo-oxygenation in the Middle Cambrian Burgess Shale, British Columbia, Canada. *Geology* 23:1079–82.

Archer, M., S.J. Hand, and H. Godthelp. 1991. *Riversleigh: The Story of Animals in Ancient Rainforests of Inland Australia.* Balgowlah: Reed.

Barthel, K.W., N.H.M. Swinburne, and S.C. Morris. 1990. *Solnhofen: A Study in Mesozoic Palaeontology.* Cambridge and New York: Cambridge University Press; as *Solnhofen: Ein Blick in die Erdgeschichte,* Thun: Ott, 1978.

Boggs Jr., S. 1987. *Principles of Sedimentology and Stratigraphy.* New York: Macmillan.

Buisonjé, P.H. de. 1985. Climatological conditions during deposition of the Solnhofen limestones. *In* M.K. Hecht, J.H. Ostrom, G. Viohl,

and P. Wellnhofer (eds.), *The Beginnings of Birds: Proceedings of the International Archaeopteryx Conference, Eichstätt 1984.* Eichstätt: Freunde des Jura-Museums Eichstätt.

Dashzeveg, D., M.J. Novacek, M.A. Norell, J.M. Clark, L.M. Chiappe, A. Davidson, M.C. McKenna, L. Dingus, C. Swisher, and P. Altangerel. 1995. Extraordinary preservation in a new vertebrate assemblage from the Late Cretaceous of Mongolia. *Nature* 374:446–49.

Duncan, I.J., and D.E.G. Briggs. 1996. Three-dimensionally preserved insects. *Nature* 381:30–31.

El-Ella, R.A., and J.M. Coleman. 1985. Discrimination between depositional environments using grain-size analyses. *Sedimentology* 32:743–48.

Grande, L. 1994. Studies of paleoenvironments and historical biogeography in the Fossil Butte and Laney members of the Green River Formation. *Contributions to Geology, University of Wyoming* 30:15–32.

Jerzykiewicz, T., P.J. Currie, D.A. Eberth, P.A. Johnston, E.H. Koster, and J.-J. Zheng. 1993. Djadokhta Formation correlative strata in Chinese Inner Mongolia: An overview of the stratigraphy, sedimentary geology, and paleontology and comparisons with the type locality in the pre-Altai Gobi. *Canadian Journal of Earth Sciences* 30:2180–95.

Ricci Lucchi, F.R. 1995. *Sedimentographica: Photographic Atlas of Sedimentary Structures.* 2nd ed., New York and Chichester: Columbia University Press.

Schaal, S., and W. Ziegler (eds.). 1992. *Messel: An Insight into the History of Life and of the Earth.* Oxford: Clarendon Press; New York: Oxford University; as *Messel: Ein Schaufenster in die Geschichte der Erde und des Lebens,* Frankfurt: Kramer, 1988.

Whittington, H.B. 1985. *The Burgess Shale.* New Haven, Connecticut: Yale University Press.

Further Reading

Friedman, G.M., J.E. Sanders, and D.C. Kopaska-Merkel. 1992. *Principles of Sedimentary Deposits.* New York: Macmillan.

Gall, J.-C. 1983. *Ancient Sedimentary Environments and the Habitats of Living Organisms: Introduction to Paleoecology.* Berlin and New York: Springer-Verlag.

Rigby, J.K., and W.K. Hamblin (eds.). 1972. *Recognition of Ancient Sedimentary Environments.* Society of Economic Paleontologists and Mineralogists Special Publication, 16. Tulsa, Oklahoma: Society of Economic Paleontologists and Mineralogists.

Selley, R.C. 1970. *Ancient Sedimentary Environments: A Brief Survey.* New York: Cornell University Press; London: Chapman and Hall; 4th ed., *Ancient Sedimentary Environments and Their Sub-surface Diagnosis,* 1996.

Tucker, M.E., and V.P. Wright. 1990. *Carbonate Sedimentology.* Oxford: Blackwell Scientific.

SEED FERNS

The rise of land plants proceeded from simple form and organization to complex structure and diversity. This evolutionary transition affected plants' vegetative form (leaves, roots, and stems not involved in reproduction) as well as reproductive biology. Early land plant reproduction consisted of a single type of spore (homosporous) that upon germination produced a structure (gametophyte) with both male (antheridium, or sperm-producing structure) and female (archegonium, or egg-producing structure) parts. Characteristically, these spores required water for fertilization, germination, and gametophyte development. This reliance on water during the crucial phases of reproduction restricted early land plants to moist or wet environments. The transition from a morphology (shape and structure) of homospory to heterospory (having two types of different spores) occurred sometime during the Lower Devonian, about 400 million years ago (Gensel and Andrews 1984).

This change allowed land plants some maneuverability within the environment. Like homosporous plants, heterosporous plants relied on water directly from the environment for fertilization and germination, but it was no longer necessary for gametophyte development. Instead of developing as an independent, separate structure, the male and female gametophytes developed within the confines of the spore wall, and fertilization occurred when the two came into contact with each other. (It is widely believed that the seed habit was derived from a heterosporous ancestor.) This new "biological package"—with its larger single functional megaspore (female spore), elaborate mechanism for capturing pollen (male gametophyte), and integument (seed coat)—provided protection, water, and nutrients for fertilization, germination, and gametophyte development. It also allowed for spores to be dispersed within drier and less hospitable environments.

The structure of the earliest ovules (unfertilized seeds) was simple yet highly functional. Ovules typically were surrounded by an outer partial ring of sterile appendages (cupule lobes) and an inner ring of appendages (integumentary lobes). The integumentary lobes and the megasporangium, or nucellus (female spore case), were fused at least one-third the length of the ovule. The apical (free end) portion of the nucellus was modified into a specialized structure (a "lagenostome" and a "pollen chamber") that aided in pollen capture. After pollination the structure sealed itself; in the sealed container fertilization occurred and the embryo developed; this system is referred to as "hydrasperman reproduction" (Rothwell 1986).

The process involved several steps. A thin membranous layer formed the floor of the pollen chamber, and the central area of the floor was occupied by an elongate structure called a "central column." With the aid of the cupule and integumentary lobes, pollen was directed into the lagenostome and settled on the pollen chamber floor. As the apical portion of the megaspore (megagametophyte) expanded, it pushed the central column up, sealing the lagenostome. During this process the pollen chamber floor ruptured, allowing the pollen to come into contact with the megagametophyte. The pollen would germinate, producing sperm, and sperm then would be in direct contact with the megagametophyte. Typically, this would result in fertilization of the eggs within the archegonia. This combination—retaining the megaspore on the parent plant, protecting the megagametophyte within an integument, and developing a unique pollination mechanism—provided ideal conditions for land plants to exploit environments that previously were inaccessible. Seed plants became established firmly and proliferated during the Upper Devonian (approximately 365 million years ago) and Carboniferous (362 to 190 million years ago).

Upper Paleozoic sediments have provided diverse and unusual assemblages composed of several different families and numerous species of seed plants.

During the latter part of the nineteenth century, Grand'Eury (1877) recognized that certain fernlike foliage (Alethopteris, Neuropteris, Odontopteris) was produced on Myeloxylon petioles. (In paleobotany, separate structures are given their own names.) Schenk (1889) and Weber and Sterzel (1896) determined that the petioles assigned to Myeloxylon belonged to the Medullosans (a group of Carboniferous seed ferns). In 1883, Stur noted that a large number of these fern leaves (Alethopteris, Neuropteris, Odontopteris) consistently lacked reproductive structures (sporangia, or spore-producing structures). Based on these observations, Stur concluded that some fern leaves many not belong to ferns but to an unknown group of plants. In 1887 Williamson, who was working on Heterangium and Kaloxylon, realized that these organisms were different from anything living and had features similar to those of both ferns and cycads (early palmlike trees). Using information provided by previous studies, Potonié (1899) proposed the name Cycadofilices. His concept for the group was based exclusively on vegetative anatomical features; nonetheless, he believed that this group was a transitional group between ferns and seed plants.

In 1904 F.W. Oliver and D.H. Scott demonstrated the association between a fernlike frond, petioles, a stem, and—most importantly—an ovule. Although the specimens were not attached to each other physically, they all exhibited common distinctive anatomical features (i.e., capitate glands), suggesting that they belonged together. Based on their study, Oliver and Scott proposed the name Pteridospermae for members of the Cycadofilices that bore seeds. Since the early studies of Oliver and Scott, numerous researchers have uncovered a diverse assemblage of different types of seed ferns spanning many millions of years. These discoveries typically yield only parts of plants, and whole plants seldom are found. Paleobotanists often identify taxa (individual organisms) using these fragmented parts. In many cases the morphology of a particular type of plant organ (i.e., stem, leaf, root) may be common to several different species of plants. Until the relationship of a particular plant part is known (until identification aided by attached or associated reproductive structures), it is assigned to a "form genus." The assignment of a plant part to a form genus allows paleobotanists the opportunity to inform the scientific community of the existence of a particular structure. Without the concept of a form genus, many plant fossils would remain unnamed and unrecognized as entities.

First recognized in Upper Devonian strata (approximately 365 million years ago) and extending into the Lower Cretaceous (approximately 140 million years ago), seed ferns have played a major role in shaping numerous ecosystems. These organisms grew as small shrubby plants, vines, and trees, and typically can be recognized by large or small seeds borne singly or in multiovulate cupules (a cupule is defined as "the unit that encircles or encloses a single space into which one or more ovules protrude"; Rothwell and Scheckler 1988). Also, the pollen organs are aggregated in clusters or organized into large synangiate structures (pollen sacs fused to each other). The leaves are large and fernlike, and the stems have secondary wood and sclerenchyma bands (fibers) within the cortex.

The oldest and most completely known seed fern genus occurs in Upper Devonian (approximately 365 million years ago) sediments of the Hampshire Formation near Elkins, West Virginia. This seed fern, *Elkinsia polymorpha* (Serbet and Rothwell 1992), is hypothesized to be an early colonizer of the Catskill Delta. It occurred with *Rhacophyton* (a zygopterid fern), *Gillespiea* (a stauropterid fern), *Archaeopteris* (a tree-sized progymnosperm), and a small herbaceous lycopod (club moss). *Elkinsia* attained a height of approximately one meter and had fernlike fronds oriented in a single plane and three-dimensional branching axes with terminal cupulate structures. The stem had a three-lobed stele (a vascular cylinder) and fronds with C-shaped vascular strands. *Elkinsia* has provided unequivocal evidence that the earliest seed plants possessed a hydrasperman pollination mechanism. Several other cupulate structures also have been recognized from Upper Devonian sediments of Pennsylvania (*Archaeosperma*), Ireland (*Kerrya*), Great Britain (*Xenotheca*), and Belgium (*Dorinnotheca*, *Moresnetia*). These genera occur as compression fossils (in coal). Some anatomical features are known; however, the exact nature of their pollen-receiving mechanism and their taxonomic affinities remains debatable.

The Lyginopteridaceae is one of the largest groups of seed ferns. Members of this family occur in Carboniferous strata (approximately 355 to 290 million years ago) of the Coal Measures deposits of Britain, equivalent strata of Europe, and the coal basins of North America. Common features found in this family include "eustelic" stems (a ring of vascular tissue with a center of thin-walled cells), axillary branching (a branch situated in the axil, or the angle formed between a stem and a leaf), fernlike foliage, fibers in the cortex, and a hydrasperman pollen chamber. The species *Lyginopteris oldhamia* has been reconstructed as a whole plant, and numerous genera (i.e., stems: *Heterangium*, *Microspermopteris*; pollen organs: *Crossotheca*, *Feraxotheca*; ovules: *Lagenostoma*, *Conostoma*) have been assigned to this group based on shared common features. In this family, the ovules may have partially fused integumentary lobes (partially integumented), like *Genomosperma*, or completely fused integumentary lobes (completely integumented), like *Stamnostoma*. In *Stamnostoma huttonense*, the nucellus and integumentary lobes are completely fused, and the apex of the ovule is modified into a "micropyle." The micropyle functions as a mechanism for receiving and directing pollen and is sealed by the central column as a result of the expanding megagametophyte.

The Medullosan (Medullosaceae) seed ferns are a large and diverse group of organisms. The genus *Medullosa* was established in 1832 by Cotta and has some of the largest known Paleozoic seed ferns. Remains of this family have been uncovered in several states (Ohio, Iowa, Illinois, Kansas), countries in Europe (Germany, France), the United Kingdom (Scotland, England), and in China. The Medullosaceae has been recognized in Carboniferous and Permian sediments (approximately 355 to 250 million years ago), and numerous plant remains (stems, leaves, ovules, pollen organs) have been described and assigned to this family. Members of this group grew as trees, shrubs, and vines. Stems assignable to the Medullosaceae are referred to as *Medullosa*, *Sutcliffia*, and

Quaestora. Fernlike foliage recognized as genera of *Alethopteris* and *Neuropteris* also is assigned to this family. Pollen organs consisted of large complex synangiate structures (*Bernaultia*) and smaller, simpler structures (*Halletheca*).

Medullosan ovules were as large as seven centimeters long (*Pachytesta gigantea*), or as small as one centimeter long (*Stephanospermum*). Unlike the ovules of the Elikinsiaceae and the Lyginopteridaceae, these ovules typically lacked a hydrasperman pollen-receiving mechanism. Medullosan ovules were completely integumented and had a fully functional micropyle. The nucellus was fused to the integument (seed coat) at the base of the ovule and free toward the apex. The upper portion of the nucellus was organized into a pollen chamber floor and walls, and the apex (opening) of the nucellus was modified into a beak-shaped structure (nucellar beak). This beak was situated directly under the micropylar opening. Scholars hypothesize that a pollination droplet or residue was produced at the tip of the ovule (Rothwell and Serbet 1994), trapping pollen. As the liquid dried and shrank, it would draw the pollen grains into the pollen chamber. As the megagametophyte expanded the floor would rupture, allowing the grains to come into contact with the megagametophyte. Subsequent to the germination of the pollen grains, fertilization would occur. The dried liquid at the tip of the nucellus (nucellar beak), in combination with the shrinking of the nucellar beak, would seal the ovule from the external environment.

The Callistophytaceae is one of the most completely understood group of Paleozoic seed ferns. Fossil remains of this family occur in Middle to Upper Pennsylvanian sediments (approximately 320 to 290 million years ago) of the United States and France. *Callistophyton* is depicted as a small, scrambling, shrubby plant. The main stem was up to three centimeters in diameter with fronds arranged in a helix. Within the axil of a frond was a branch, and adventitious roots were common at several nodes (point of attachment of a leaf or leaves). Anatomical features of the stem included a eustelic vascular cylinder with well-developed wood and a cortex with fiber bands.

In *Callistophyton* pollen organs (*Idanothekion*) occur on the lower portions of the fronds and are made up of several pollen sacs fused together at the base. Isolated remains of *Callistophyton* can be recognized by the presence of spherical secretory cavities in the stems, fronds, pollen organs, and seed coats. *Callistophyton*'s ovules (form genus *Callospermarion*) have provided significant insight into the development of these ancient reproductive structures. G.W. Rothwell (1971) documented the growth and development of *Callospermarion* ovules, based on anatomically preserved immature and mature fossil specimens. The study clearly depicts the development of the integument, the nucellus, the pollen chamber, and the megagametophyte. This was one of the first studies of its kind, and it set a precedent for future ontogenetic studies using fossil plant remains.

The pollination mechanism of *Callospermarion* also represents a third step in an evolutionary series. In the earliest-known seed plants (those with hydrasperman reproduction), the upper portion of the nucellus (lagenostome), in combination with the central column, sealed the pollen chamber from the external environment. The pollen chamber sealed whether the ovule was pollinated or not. The ovules of Medullosan seed ferns commonly lacked the central column of hydrasperman ovules, sealing through the shrinkage of the nucellar beak or through a secreted resinous substance. *Callospermarion* ovules were sealed at the micropyle and at the nucellar beak. This pattern of pollen chamber sealing also is recognized among Paleozoic/Mesozoic seed-ferns families, including the Peltaspermaceae, Glossopteridaceae, Corystospermaceae, and Caytoniaceae.

Although the Caytoniaceae, Corystospermaceae, Peltaspermaceae, and Glossopteridaceae are relatively well known, both morphologically and anatomically, their origins and relationships remain a mystery. Typically, they are recognized as the Mesozoic seed ferns because of their geologic age, fernlike foliage, and gymnosperm type of reproduction. Recent analysis of relationships among seed plants has shown that these families (Caytoniaceae, Corystospermaceae, Glossopteridaceae, Peltaspermaceae) are related more closely to each other than to the Paleozoic seed ferns (Elkinsiaceae, Lyginopteridaceae, Medullosaceae, Callistophytaceae) (Rothwell and Serbet 1994). Continuing research on these groups may shed light on their origins and subsequent relationships.

The seed ferns constitute a heterogenous group of organisms that span millions of years of Earth's history. They are recognized by their fernlike foliage, seeds borne in a variety of ways, terminally clustered pollen organs, and by an outer stem cortex composed of longitudinally oriented fibers. The oldest genus, *Elkinsia,* shows a highly derived level of reproductive organization, which enabled it to grow and reproduce in drier, less hospitable environments. Fossil evidence from Carboniferous strata indicates that seed ferns (Lyginopteridaceae, Medullosaceae, Callistophytaceae) underwent an explosive radiation (diversification and geographic spread) at that time. During this period, the seed underwent further structural modifications (e.g., fusion of the lobes that formed an integument and a fully functional micropyle) and became a vital part of gymnosperm reproduction that we recognize in modern plants. Ongoing studies of Mesozoic seed ferns (Caytoniaceae, Corystospermaceae, Glossopteridaceae, Peltaspermaceae) may provide the necessary information to ascertain their relationships to other extinct plants and modern gymnosperms and to establish their origins and evolutionary history.

RUDOLPH SERBET

See also Cycads; Ferns and Their Relatives; Forests, Fossil; Gymnosperms; Progymnosperms

Works Cited

Gensel, P.G., and H.N. Andrews. 1984. *Plant Life in the Devonian.* New York: Praeger.
Rothwell, G.W. 1971. Ontogeny of the Paleozoic ovule, *Callospermarion pusillum. American Journal of Botany* 58:706–15.
———. 1986. Classifying the earliest gymnosperms. *In* R.A. Spicer and B.A. Thomas (eds.), *Systematic and Taxonomic Approaches in Paleobotany.* Systematics Association Special, vol. 31. Oxford: Clarendon; New York: Oxford University Press.
Rothwell, G.W., and S.E. Scheckler. 1988. Biology of ancestral gymnosperms. *In* C.B. Beck (ed.), *Origin and Evolution of Gymnosperms.* New York: Columbia University Press.
Rothwell, G.W., and R. Serbet. 1994. Lignophyte phylogeny and the evolution of spermatophytes: A numerical cladistic analysis. *Systematic Botany* 19:443–82.
Schenk, A. 1889. Über *Medullosa* Cotta und *Tubicaulis* Cotta. *Bandes der Abhandlungen der mathematish-physischen Classe der Königl. Sächsischen Gesellschaft der Wissenschaften* 15:523–58.
Serbet, R., and G.W. Rothwell. 1992. Characterizing the most primitive seed ferns. Part 1, A reconstruction of *Elkinsia polymorpha. International Journal of Plant Sciences* 153:602–21.
Stur, M.D. 1883. Zur morphologie und Systematik der Culm-und Carbonfarne. *Wein Kungl. Akademie der Wissenschaften Sitzungsberichte* 88:633–846.
Taylor, T.N., and E.L. Taylor. 1993. *The Biology and Evolution of Fossil Plants.* Englewood Cliffs, New Jersey: Prentice-Hall.
Weber, O., and J.T. Sterzel. 1869. Beiträge zur Kenntnis der Meddulloseae. *Naturwissenschaftliche gesellschaft zu Chemnitz Bericht* 13:44–143.

Further Reading

Andrews, H.N. 1961. *Studies in Paleobotany.* New York: Wiley.
Arnold, C.A. 1947. *An Introduction to Paleobotany.* New York: McGraw Hill.
Gensel, P.G., and H.N. Andrews. 1984. *Plant Life in the Devonian.* New York: Praeger.
Rothwell, G.W. 1986. Classifying the earliest gymnosperms. *In* R.A. Spicer and B.A. Thomas (eds.), *Systematic and Taxonomic Approaches in Paleobotany.* Systematics Association Special, vol. 31. Oxford: Claredon; New York: Oxford University Press.
Rothwell G.W., and S.E. Scheckler. 1988. Biology of ancestral gymnosperms. *In* C.B. Beck (ed.), *Origin and Evolution of Gymnosperms.* New York: Columbia University Press.
Taylor, T.N., and E.L. Taylor. 1993. *The Biology and Evolution of Fossil Plants.* Englewood Cliffs, New Jersey: Prentice-Hall.
Wilson, W.N., and G.W. Rothwell. 1983. *Paleobotany and the Evolution of Plants.* Cambridge and New York: Cambridge University Press; 2nd ed., 1993.

SEELEY, HARRY GOVIER

English, 1839–1909

From a young age Harry Govier Seeley, the son of Richard Hovell Seeley and Mary Govier, took an interest in geology and paleontology, the two areas of science that would comprise his life's work. Growing up, he was exposed to lectures from such scientists as Sir Richard Owen and William Brayley and was influenced by Charles Lyell's pioneering book *Principles of Geology.* He first became acquainted with vertebrate anatomy by preparing the skeletons of birds, small mammals, and fishes. He spent three years as a reader at the British Museum of Natural History, where he studied under S.P. Woodward and J.E. Gray. Inspired to pursue science in a more formal manner, he entered Sidney Sussex College, Cambridge University, at the age of 20.

Although Seeley never earned a degree from Cambridge, it was during his time there that he caught the eye of the eminent geologist Adam Sedgwick. Citing his "reputation for genius and skill," in 1859 Sedgwick appointed Seeley as his assistant at the Woodwardian Museum at Cambridge (now known as the Sedgwick Museum), where he worked until 1871. In this period of mentorship, Seeley gained the experience and skill in making observations on fossils that would serve as the basis of a prolific scientific career. Among other studies, he eagerly took to an examination of the Cambridge Greensand fauna, which led to his 1869 *Index to the Fossil Remains of Aves, Ornithosauria, and Reptilia,* in which he named nine new genera and 85 new species.

In 1872, shortly before Sedgwick's death, Seeley left the Woodwardian Museum for London. Although he had opportunities to take prestigious positions at the British Museum of Natural History and the Geological Survey of Britain, he turned down both, wanting the freedom to pursue his research interests. Working mostly independently, Seeley became an expert on many groups of fossil vertebrates, including dinosaurs, pterosaurs, marine reptiles, and therapsids (mammal-like reptiles), which comprise a large portion of the approximately 170 publications he produced over his lifetime.

Seeley's major contributions to science were threefold: he split dinosaurs into the groups Saurischia and Ornithischia, he collected and described important therapsids from South Africa, and he described in detail the biology of pterosaurs. The first of these contributions arose from his interest in dinosaurs. As data accumulated after the identification of dinosaurs in 1824, scientists began to notice that dinosaurs showed different degrees of similarity to one another, suggesting that distinct groups had existed. Contemporary paleontologists Edward Drinker Cope, Thomas Henry Huxley, and Othniel Charles Marsh each devised his own system of grouping based on different aspects of dinosaur anatomy. Seeley, however, thought that they were creating groups based on superficial similarity (such as grouping whales and fishes together because both have fins), as opposed to making "natural" groups that reflect true genealogy. Seeley's trained eye led him to believe that the differences in the positioning of the bones of the pelvis among dinosaurs indicated that there had existed two unrelated groups of dinosaur-like animals. In his 1887 paper "On the Classification of the Fossil Animals Commonly Named Dinosauria" he split the Dinosauria into two groups, which he named Saurischia ("lizard-hipped") and Ornithischia ("bird-hipped"). Saurischians, such as *Apatosaurus* and *Tyrannosaurus,* have a pelvis that resembles that of modern reptiles, whereas ornithischians, such as *Stegosaurus* and *Triceratops,* have a pelvis resembling that of modern birds. Although it has been subsequently shown that these two groups actually were closely related, Seeley's Saurischia-Ornithischia dichotomy within the Dinosauria has been universally accepted.

Seeley's second major contribution was his work on Permian and Triassic reptiles of South Africa, particularly of therapsids. Intrigued by the work of Owen and the large amount of material being unearthed by farmers in the Karroo of South Africa, Seeley went there in 1889 to explore and collect. Traveling with Thomas Bain, he discovered a complete skeleton of *Pareiasaurus,* an elephantine member of a basal group of amniotes (known as parareptiles), and many fine therapsid specimens, such as skulls and skeletons of *Cynognathus* and *Diademodon.* Seeley's work on these collections forms a large portion of a series of papers now known as "Researches on the Fossil Reptilia," which firmly set the evolutionary position of therapsids as the ancestors of mammals.

Seeley's life-long interest in pterosaurs (which he referred to as ornithosaurs) led to his third major contribution. Pterosaurs, which are extinct flying vertebrates, were originally considered to have a reptilian physiology. Owen noted that as reptiles, they must have been cold-blooded. Seeley strongly disagreed with this assessment. Based on his studies, he reasoned in his 1901 book *Dragons of the Air* that the only way pterosaurs could maintain active flight was if, like birds, they possessed a physiology that allowed for a high-energy metabolism; from this he concluded that they must have been warm-blooded. To support this contention, Seeley provided strong evidence of birdlike adaptations: pterosaur limb bones were hollow (thus reducing weight) and had openings in them (which, in birds, permit extensions of the lungs to fill the hollow bones). Likewise, pterosaur brains, unlike those of modern reptiles, were large and filled the skull cavity, indicating that they were large enough to accommodate the complex processing involved in active flight. Seeley then postulated that if pterosaurs were warm-blooded, they must have possessed some form of insulation to prevent heat loss, in the form of hair. Evidence supporting this hypothesis was discovered in 1970, when a remarkably preserved pterosaur with structures resembling hair was found in Kazakhstan. Seeley also made other contributions to pterosaur biology—he demonstrated the extreme width to which pterosaurs could open their mouths; he proposed that they could swim based on the webbing between their toes; and he pointed out that at least one of the Cretaceous forms was toothless.

Seeley was not only interested in satisfying his own scientific curiosity, he wanted the public to understand natural history as well; he therefore spent most of his career involved in education. At the Woodwardian Museum, he occasionally lectured in Sedgwick's absence (and later independently), where he learned to convey information to the public in an engaging fashion. He gained academic positions at several institutions, first at King's College in 1876, and later concurrently at Queen's College and the Royal Indian Engineering College. In 1885 he founded the London Geological Field Class, a public summer excursion course that he ran for 25 years and from which he produced the 1891 *Handbook of the London Geological Field Class.*

Seeley was much honored for his work in his lifetime. Among numerous awards, he was made Fellow of the Royal Society of London in 1879 and received the Lyell Medal of the Geological Society of London in 1885. He died in Kensington, London, in 1909.

JOHN J. SOCHA

Biography

Born in London, 18 February 1839. Attended Sidney Sussex College, Cambridge University, 1859. Reader, British Museum (Natural History), 1856–59; assistant to Adam Sedgwick, Woodwardian Museum (now known as the Sedgwick Museum), Cambridge University, 1859–71; professor of geography and lecturer on geology (1876–1908) and professor of geology and mineralogy (1896–1908), King's College; named professor of geography and geology, Queen's College, 1876; lecturer, London Society of the Extension of University Teaching, 1880–90; named dean, Queen's College, 1881; founded the London Geological Field Class, 1885; lecturer (1890) and professor of geology and mineralogy (1891–1905), Royal Indian Engineering College. Fellow (1862), council member (1879–84, 1886–90, 1989–1904), and vice president (1900–2), Geological Society of London, 1862; received award from Murchison Fund, 1875; elected fellow, Royal Society, London, 1879; received Lyell Medal, Geological Society of London, 1885; made a fellow of King's College, 1905; member of numerous foreign scholarly societies, including the Academy of Natural Science of Philadelphia, the South African Philosophical Society, and the Imperial Academy of Science of St. Petersburg. Identified dinosaur groups Ornithischia and Saurischia, 1887; made important contributions to therapsid and pterosaur paleontology. Died in Kensington, London, 8 January 1909.

Major Publications

1869. *Index to the Fossil Remains of Aves, Ornithosauria, and Reptilia.* Cambridge: Deighton, Bell.

1886. *The Freshwater Fishes of Europe: A History of Their Genera, Species, Structure, Habits, and Distribution.* London and New York: Cassell.

1870. *The Ornithosauria.* Cambridge: Deighton, Bell.

1884. *Factors in Life.* London: S.P.C.K.

1885. With Robert Etheridge. Revision of John Phillips' *Manual of Geology.* 2 vols. London: Griffin.

1887. On the classification of the fossil animals commonly named Dinosauria. *Proceedings of the Royal Society of London* 43:165–71.

1887–96. Researches on the structure, organization, and classification of the fossil Reptilia. *Philosophical Transactions of the Royal Society of London,* ser. B, vols. 178–86.

1891. *Handbook of the London Geological Field Class.* London: Philip.

1895. *Story of the Earth in Past Ages.* London: Newnes; New York: Appleton.

1901. *Dragons of the Air: An Account of Extinct Flying Reptiles.* London: Methuen; New York: Appleton.

Further Reading

Anon. 1907. Eminent living geologists: Professor H.G. Seeley. *The Geological Magazine* 4 (6):241–53.

———. 1909. Obituary. *Quarterly Journal of the Geological Society of London* 65:lxx–lxxii.

———. 1910–11. Obituary. *Proceedings of the Royal Society of London,* ser. B, 83:xv–xvii.

Colbert, E.H. 1968. *Men and Dinosaurs: The Search in the Field and Laboratory.* New York: Dutton; London: Evans; 2nd ed., as *The Great Dinosaur Hunters and Their Discoveries,* New York: Dover, 1984.

Desmond, A.J. 1975. *The Hot-Blooded Dinosaurs: A Revolution in Palaeontology.* New York: Dial; London: Blond and Briggs.

Swinton, W.E. 1962. Harry Govier Seeley and the Karroo reptiles. *Bulletin of the British Museum Natural History, Historical Series* 3 (1):39.

Wellnhofer, P. 1991. *The Illustrated Encyclopedia of Pterosaurs.* New York: Crescent; London: Salamander.

SEISMIC AND SURFACE ACTIVITY

Seismic and surface activities include numerous independent and interrelated processes of varying complexity, scale, and duration—processes that are responsible for major alterations to marine and terrestrial landscapes. Such alterations affect virtually every aspect of geological and biological systems. From a paleontological perspective, alterations to marine and terrestrial landscapes over time are important because they modified ecosystems and depositional conditions (those under which sediments were laid down) and either facilitated or limited the fossilization of organisms and entire biotas (collections of biological materials). Among the most conspicuous surface and seismic activities that have influenced these events are mountain building, volcanism, earthquakes, and landslides.

A mountain is a large land mass that projects conspicuously above its surroundings, usually more than about 600 meters. An assemblage of mountains, called a mountain range, can cover many hundreds or thousands of square kilometers. The process of mountain building, called orogenesis, occurs along and just interior to the active margins (edges) of tectonic plates. Orogenesis is the result of complex tectonic processes—such as faulting, folding, and volcanism—initiated and driven by the collision of two plates.

An orogenic episode, called an orogeny, typically lasts for tens of millions of years. Many mountain ranges are the result of several distinct orogenies and other tectonic processes that have occurred over even greater intervals of time. For example, the Appalachian Mountains began forming about 450 million years ago, in the Late Ordovician, and their history includes three Paleozoic orogenies, followed by extensive erosion through the Mesozoic, and a secondary uplift during the Cenozoic. Given their large size, the amount of land they cover, and long life spans, mountain ranges exert tremendous influence on numerous aspects of terrestrial ecosystems and depositional systems (those that govern the deposition of sediments that make up some types of rock).

Mountain ranges are often a barrier to the overland movement of many contemporary (present-day) organisms and undoubtedly have limited the dispersal of terrestrial organisms over time. Conversely, many contemporary plants and animals are restricted to mountainous areas; we expect that this was also the case in the geological past. The evolution of certain groups, such as the lungless salamanders of the family Plethodontidae, was centered in mountainous regions.

Although erosion continuously removes large volumes of rock off mountains, little of this eroded material is retained within mountain ranges, where it might be deposited in lakes, streams, or other environments suitable for burying and preserving plant and animal remains. Consequently, the fossil record of montane (mountain-based) organisms is sparse, and we have relatively little fossil evidence for elucidating the evolution of montane ecosystems. Two kinds of deposits occasionally contain the remains of montane organisms. Caves have yielded a variety of Quaternary-aged fossil and subfossil bones, teeth, scales, arthropod (e.g., insects and crustaceans) fragments, seeds, twigs, and pollen, as well as rare mummified hair and feces. (Subfossils are too young to have completed the fossilization process.) In some cases, these accumulations form layers that are several meters thick and record up to 7,000 years of continuous deposition (Burns 1989). Lake sediments deposited during the Eocene and Oligocene in the mountains of central and northern Colorado preserve an older, but more limited, record of fossil leaves and articulated insects and fish.

Mountains and other regional uplifts are important sources of clastic sediments (those from preexisting rocks). Typically, the large volumes of rock that are eroded annually from mountain ranges are carried away by rivers and deposited in adjacent low-lying areas. These sediments are important for burying and preserving the remains of organisms that live in these low-lying depositional environments. For example, sediments removed from the eastern face of the ancestral Rocky Mountains during the Cretaceous were carried eastward by rivers that eventually emptied into the Western Interior Seaway (this ancient seaway was located in the general area of the Great Plains). As these rivers crossed the broad, low-lying coastal plain that extended between the mountains and the seaway, the rivers slowed down and dropped much of their suspended sediment. This process formed the thick sequence of nonmarine sediment (that which originated from land systems, not ocean systems) that now crops out from southern Alberta and Saskatchewan southwards into Texas and resulted in the rich accumulation of fossils contained in these deposits.

Volcanic eruptions discharge tremendous quantities of gases and volcaniclastics (sediment formed by volcanic activities), with the latter ranging in size from ash flakes to large chunks of rock. These products can adversely affect ecosystems on local, regional, and global scales over varying lengths of time. For example, the 1883 eruption of the volcano on the island of Krakatoa in the Indian Ocean released an estimated 54 cubic kilometers of volcaniclastics and produced a dust plume that rose 32 kilometers into the atmosphere. Within months, the ash cloud blanketed the planet and for the next three years remained sufficiently dense to reduce incoming solar radiation, thus lowering global temperatures by several degrees. This and other isolated volcanic eruptions in historical times suggest that the amount of volcanic debris generated during intense and prolonged episodes of volcanism must have been spectacular. Several episodes of intense volcanism occurred during the Cretaceous and Tertiary in western North America. Not surprisingly, volcanism has been implicated in some of the major extinction events, including the terminal Cretaceous extinction (Rice 1990).

From a paleontological perspective, volcanoes are important for three reasons. First, eruptions produce vast quantities of gases and debris that may kill organisms, either by asphyxiation or burial, and make them available for fossilization. In such events, death can be nearly instantaneous: for instance, grass remains are preserved in the mouths and throats of individuals in a herd of Miocene rhinoceroses from Nevada, implying that these animals were killed instantaneously while grazing (Voorhies and Thomasson 1979). Second, ash can accumulate in sufficient quantities to bury organisms rapidly before they can be disturbed by decay or scavengers. Coverage can be so extensive and rapid that entire fossil biotas may be preserved (Lockley and Rice 1990). Finally, radiometric dating of lava flows and diagenetically altered ash layers, called bentonites, permits scholars to date associated sediments and fossils with considerable accuracy.

An earthquake is a series of shock waves, the vast majority of which occur as a result of faulting (fractures) within the Earth's crust or mantle (Lay and Wallace 1995). Unlike orogenesis and volcanism, an earthquake may last for only a few seconds. The effects of earthquakes, which have been well documented in recent human history, can be extensive, particularly on a local scale. In the terrestrial realm, large earthquakes may produce fault scarps (cliffs), trigger landslides, cause soil liquefaction, offset streams, and produce broad regions of uplift or downdrop (Lay and Wallace 1995). In the marine realm, shock waves generated by an earthquake may trigger submarine landslides and produce gigantic waves called "tsunamis," which are capable of flooding coastal regions catastrophically. While structures produced by earthquakes are identifiable readily in contemporary landscapes, it is generally difficult to demonstrate that similar features preserved in the sedimentary record were formed by an earthquake. For instance, submarine landslides identified in deltaic sandstones of the Upper Cretaceous Blair Formation of Wyoming may have been caused by earthquakes, severe storms, or slope instability (Roehler 1988). Submarine landslides preserved in the Santa Barbara Basin off the coast of California are attributed more reliably to the effects of an earthquake, most likely one that occurred within the last 1000 years (Edwards et al. 1993).

Faulting can have considerable effects on terrestrial ecosystems, particularly aquatic and riparian systems (those along river banks), because faults can alter drainage patterns readily and can establish, drain, or otherwise modify lakes. Rivers and lake basins in areas of extensive faulting may have complex histories, which obviously affects organisms living in and near these water bodies and the depositional histories of these systems. For example, the well-documented incidents of rapid speciation and extinction among snails and cichlid fish inhabiting lakes in the rift valleys of East Africa have been linked to the dynamic histories of these lakes since Miocene times.

"Landslide" is a term that is used informally to describe the downslope movement of material. The volume and time required to move material downslope can vary markedly; factors such as gravity, earthquakes, and storms are among the causes. Some of the largest known terrestrial landslides occurred during the Eocene in the Absaroka Basin of northwestern Wyoming. The most interesting involves a 3,400-square-kilometer field of Paleozoic limestone blocks that were transported downslope along the Heart Mountain Fault (Hague 1993) and now overlie Eocene clastic sediments. The great instability of this vast region during the Eocene, coupled with local volcanism, likely made the area inhospitable to many organisms. In general, however, terrestrial landslides cause only localized disturbances and appear to play no significant role in the long-term alteration of biotas or the preservation of organisms.

Rarely noticed by humankind, submarine landslides can remodel the topography of the ocean floor dramatically and thereby alter water circulation patterns and distributions of marine organisms. Submarine landslides can involve thousands of cubic kilometers of sediment, more than enough for the instantaneous burial and preservation of entire marine communities. The formation of the Middle Cambrian Burgess Shale assemblage—an assemblage that includes tens of thousands of complete specimens, including the soft tissues so rarely preserved—is attributed widely to the downslope transport and rapid burial of marine animals in mud during a submarine landslide (Whittington 1985).

Seismic and surface activities can have diverse effects on ecosystems and their representation in the fossil record. Of particular interest to paleontologists are those processes, such as volcanism and submarine landslides, that promote the preservation of fossil organisms and communities and thereby provide unique snapshots of ancient ecosystems.

MICHAEL W. WEBB AND JAMES D. GARDNER

See also Paleobiography; Plate Tectonics and Continental Drift

Works Cited

Burns, J.A. 1989. Fossil vertebrates from the Rats Nest Cave, Alberta. *Canadian Caverns* 21:41–43.

Edwards, B.D., H.J. Lee, and M.E. Field. 1993. Seismically induced mudflow in Santa Barbara Basin, California. *In* W.C. Schwab, H.J. Lee, and D.C. Twichell (eds.), *Submarine Landslides: Selected Studies in the U.S. Exclusive Economic Zone.* U.S. Geological Survey Bulletin, 2002. Washington, D.C.: U.S. Government Printing Office.

Hague, T.A. 1993. The Heart Mountain detachment: 100 years of controversy. *In* A.W. Snoke, J.R. Steidtmann, and S.M. Roberts (eds.) *Geology of Wyoming.* Geological Survey of Wyoming, Memoir, 5. 2 vols. Laramie: Geological Survey of Wyoming.

Lay, T., and T.C. Wallace. 1995. *Modern Global Seismology.* London and San Diego, California: Academic Press.

Lockley, M.G., and A. Rice (eds.). 1990. *Volcanism and Fossil Biotas.* Geological Society of America Special Paper, 244. Boulder, Colorado: Geological Society of America; Lawrence: University of Kansas.

Rice, A. 1990. The role of volcanism in K/T extinctions. *In* M.G. Lockley and A. Rice (eds.), *Volcanism and Fossil Biotas.* Geological Society of America Special Paper, 244. Boulder, Colorado: Geological Society of America; Lawrence: University of Kansas.

Roehler, H.W. 1988. Submarine slumps in delta-front sandstones of the Upper Cretaceous Blair Formation, Rock Springs Uplift, Wyoming. *U.S. Geological Survey Bulletin* 1699:1–11.

Voorhies, M.R., and J.R. Thomasson. 1979. Fossil grass anthoecia within Miocene rhinoceros skeletons: Diet in an extinct species. *Science* 206:331–33.

Whittington, H.B. 1985. *The Burgess Shale.* New Haven, Connecticut: Yale University Press.

Further Reading

Axelrod, D.I. 1981. *Role of Volcanism in Climate and Evolution.* Geological Society of America Special Paper, 185. Boulder, Colorado: Geological Society of America; Lawrence: University of Kansas.

Behrensmeyer, A.K., and R.W. Hook. 1992. Paleoenvironmental contexts and taphonomic modes. *In* A.K. Behrensmeyer, J.D. Damuth, W.A. DiMichele, R. Potts, H.-D. Sues, and S.L. Wing (eds.), *Terrestrial Ecosystems through Time: Evolutionary Paleoecology of Terrestrial Plants and Animals.* Chicago: University of Chicago Press.

Schwab, W.C., H.J. Lee, and D.C. Twichell (eds.). 1993. *Submarine Landslides: Selected Studies in the U.S. Exclusive Economic Zone.* U.S. Geological Survey Bulletin, 2002. Washington, D.C.: U.S. Government Printing Office.

Stanley, S.M. 1986. *Earth and Life through Time.* New York: Freeman; 2nd ed., 1989.

SELECTION

It may be said that natural selection is daily and hourly scrutinising, throughout the world, every variation, even the slightest; rejecting that which is bad, preserving and adding up all that is good; silently and insensibly working, whenever and wherever opportunity offers, at the improvement of each organic being in relation to its organic and inorganic conditions of life. (Darwin 1859)

Selection is the process by which many evolutionary phenomena—extinction, the origin of new species, morphological change (change in shape or structure), and adaptation—are explained in modern evolutionary theory. While it generally is agreed that selection is a major cause of evolutionary change, many details of its role are not agreed upon. Arguments rage about which features of an organism are subject to selection; about whether selection produces gradual, continuous evolutionary change or whether its effects are sudden and sporadic; about whether selection acts on genes, individuals, populations, or species; and even about whether selection plays an important role in evolution.

Selection works like a filter, removing unfit individuals from a population and leaving those that are more fit to continue on and reproduce (Sober 1993). Amid the variety of individual differences, some organisms, those that are "more fit," are better able to survive and have offspring, which is the definition of "success" in evolutionary theory. Successful individuals pass on to the next generation those features (or combinations of features) that make them more fit (Darwin 1859). Over time, detrimental features are removed systematically from an evolving population, while advantageous features remain. Variation within a population is not lost, however, because mutation adds new features, and sexual reproduction creates new combinations of old features. Because of the mixing of parental traits, the offspring that make up every generation have a new spectrum of traits for selection to act upon.

Selection can both cause and prevent evolutionary change. Directional selection causes evolutionary change by favoring traits that are rare in a population over those that are the norm. Stabilizing selection prevents change by favoring those traits that are the norm in a population over those that are rare (Schmalhausen 1946). Directional selection usually causes either anagenesis (directional change in an evolving lineage, such as lengthening leg bones in horses) or extinction (if the population contains no individuals who can survive the rigors of the selective process). Stabilizing selection prevents evolutionary change by removing extreme variants from a population. The result is stasis. The Red Queen's Hypothesis—which states that there are so many factors causing directional selection, each of which favors different traits, that the end result is constant evolution around a nonchanging norm—can be viewed as another sort of stabilizing selection (Van Valen 1973).

Selection often results in adaptation, which is both the evolutionary process of becoming more fit and the features that are produced by that process. It is easy to imagine that just about any feature of an organism is an adaptation that makes it more fit in its environment—the long horns of *Triceratops* might be an adaptation for protection against *Tyrannosaurus,* and the upright stance of *Australopithecus* might be an adaptation for moving around the savannah while carrying tools.

However, the scientific identification of adaptation is rarely straightforward. In its classic form, selection causes change in a feature that makes an organism better able to survive and reproduce in its environment. However, some features may be selected for because they make an organism more desirable as a mate—this is known as sexual selection. Often several features of an organism are interlinked functionally and developmentally so that selection on one trait affects others. In this case, only those traits on which selection acted can properly be called adaptations. Features also may evolve for reasons that have nothing to do with selection. Some features may exist because the founding members of a species just happened to have them (founder effect), while some new features may be fixed in a species simply because there was no selection *against* them (drift). In some cases, a feature may evolve in response to selection pressure at a given time but might later be coopted for a different use (exaptation) (Gould and Vrba 1982).

An example of the difficulty inherent in identifying adaptations are the enormous horns of the extinct Irish elk, which sometimes spread more than twelve feet. As with all members of the deer family, the horns were grown and shed annually, a process that required a tremendous expenditure of energy and metabolic materials. The evolution of these antlers has been explained as the direct result of selection because they would have allowed their owners to better fend off rivals during the mating process; as the result of sexual selection because females might have preferred males with larger racks; and as an allometric coincidence that was the indirect result of selection for larger body size.

Usually selection is thought of as acting on individual organisms within a population—those organisms that are more fit manage to reproduce. However, there are also arguments that selection acts on genes (Dawkins 1976), demes (a localized group of individuals that reproduce only among themselves) (Wright 1932), species (Stanley 1979), and clades (related groups) (Vrba 1989). R. Dawkins argued that genes themselves are the objects of selection—the organism merely functions as a convenient housing for self-replicating DNA. S. Wright, S.M. Stanley, E.S. Vrba, and others have argued that some groups of individuals—whether they be demes, species, or clades—have defining properties that make them more or less able to survive than other such groups. Through the process known as "species sorting," groups with more favorable features persist and speciate, while groups with less favorable features become extinct. As a result, one can see a large-scale evolutionary trend that is not present within any individual species. All of these ideas have been reviewed and critiqued thoroughly by E. Sober (1993).

How important is selection in evolution? This is one of the main debates among evolutionary theorists today. In the decades following Darwin's *Origin of Species,* evolutionists—notably D.E. Cope and A. Hyatt among paleontologists—rejected natural selection as a primary mechanism of evolution, preferring development-based explanations instead (Bowler 1988). Early twentieth-century scientists of the Modern Synthesis—including the paleontologist G.G. Simpson—revived natural selection as the predominant factor. Evolution was viewed as changing gene frequencies resulting from selection on individual organisms. Since then, some theorists have questioned the importance of organismal selection in evolution. Kimura (1983) has argued that at the molecular level, most evolution is neutral and not the result of selection at all. S.J. Gould and R.C. Lewontin (1979) have popularized the search for other causal factors of evolutionary change. Dawkins (1976) has reduced selection to the level of the gene, while Stanley (1979) and Vrba (1989) have urged paleontologists to look for evolutionary patterns and mechanisms above the species level. Clearly selection remains a timely and vibrant topic in paleontology today.

PAUL DAVID POLLY

See also Adaptation; Coevolutionary Relationships; Diversity; Evolutionary Novelty; Evolutionary Theory; Evolutionary Trends; Extinction; Growth, Development, and Evolution; Speciation and Morphological Change; Systematics; Variation

Works Cited

Bowler, P.J. 1988. *The Non-Darwinian Revolution: Reinterpreting a Historical Myth*. Baltimore, Maryland: Johns Hopkins; London: Johns Hopkins, 1992.

Darwin, C.R. 1859. *The Origin of Species by Means of Natural Selection or the Preservation of Favoured Races in the Struggle for Life*. London: Murray.

Dawkins, R. 1976. *The Selfish Gene*. Oxford and New York: Oxford University Press.

Gould, S.J., and R.C. Lewontin. 1979. The spandrels of San Marco and the Panglossian paradigm: A critique of the adaptationist programme. *Proceedings of the Royal Society London*, ser. B, 205:581–98.

Gould, S.J., and E.S. Vrba. 1982. Exaptation: A missing term in the science of form. *Paleobiology* 8:4–15.

Kimura, M. 1983. *The Neutral Theory of Molecular Evolution*. Cambridge and New York: Cambridge University Press.

Schmalhausen, I.I. 1946. *Faktory evoliutsii. Teoria stabiliziruyushchego otbora*. Moscow: Academy of Sciences USSR; as *Factors of Evolution: The Theory of Stabilizing Selection*, Chicago: University of Chicago Press, 1986.

Sober, E. 1993. *The Nature of Selection: Evolutionary Theory in Philosophical Focus*. Chicago and London: University of Chicago Press.

Stanley, S.M. 1979. *Macroevolution: Pattern and Process*. San Francisco: Freeman.

Van Valen, L. 1973. A new evolutionary law. *Evolutionary Theory* 1:1–30.

Vrba, E.S. 1989. Levels of selection and sorting with special reference to the species level. *Oxford Surveys in Evolutionary Biology* 6:111–68.

Wright, S. 1932. The roles of mutation, inbreeding, crossbreeding, and selection in evolution. *Proceedings of the Sixth International Congress on Genetics* 1:356–66.

Further Reading

Darwin, C.R. 1859. *The Origin of Species by Means of Natural Selection; or, The Preservation of Favoured Races in the Struggle for Life*. London: Murray; 7th ed., London: Murray, 1884; New York: Humboldt, 1884.

Gould, S.J., and R.C. Lewontin. 1979. The spandrels of San Marco and the Panglossian paradigm: A critique of the adaptationist programme. *Proceedings of the Royal Society London*, ser. B, 205:581–98.

Johnson, C. 1976. *Introduction to Natural Selection*. Baltimore, Maryland: University Park.

Sober, E. 1984. *The Nature of Selection: Evolutionary Theory in Philosophical Focus*. Cambridge: Massachusetts Institute of Technology Press; Chicago and London: University of Chicago Press, 1993.

Williams, G.C. 1992. *Natural Selection: Domains, Levels, and Challenges*. New York: Oxford University Press.

SENSORY CAPSULES

During development of living vertebrates, but not "lower" chordates such as sea squirts, capsules for support and protection form around the organs of special sense for smell, vision, and hearing plus equilibrium. These are the nasal, optic, and otic (auditory) capsules. Initially, the nasal and otic capsules consist of cartilage, and they become united with other cartilages of the developing braincase. Later in development, the cartilage of these capsules is usually replaced by bone, in whole or in part, at a variable number of ossification (bone deposition) centers. The bones formed in this fashion may fuse with one another, and they usually become strongly bonded to overlying bones that form in connective tissue. The optic capsule only occasionally includes cartilage, and because the eye must be mobile it does not unite with adjacent parts of the skull.

Nasal Capsule

The developing nasal capsules form around the olfactory sacs, which are inpocketings of ectoderm (outermost germ layer) from the surface of the head. Nerve cells responsive to odors differentiate from ectoderm cells, and their axons (nerve fibers) form the first cranial nerve (the olfactory nerve), connecting to the olfactory bulbs of the brain. If the two nasal capsules are close to one another, there is a thin partition, the nasal septum, between them. In most fishes each capsule has two external nasal openings through which odor-bearing water enters and leaves, and the nasal cavities serve no respiratory function as inlets of water for the gills. In tetrapods (vertebrates with limbs: amphibians, reptiles, birds, and mammals) and their closest relatives among fishes (certain crossopterygians), there are also two openings, but the second one is in the roof of the mouth and is called a choana or internal nasal opening; the nasal passage serves for both olfaction and respiration. Some tetrapods (for example, crocodiles and mammals) have shifted the internal nasal openings posteriorly by developing a secondary palate below the original roof of the mouth to separate the airway from the foodway.

A very different communication between the nasal cavity and the oral (mouth) cavity occurs in some agnathans (jawless vertebrates), namely the living hagfishes and certain ostracoderms (ancient armored fishes). This communication is unpaired, as is the external nasal opening, and the right and left nasal sacs share an unpaired central cavity; this may be the primitive configuration for vertebrates. Other ostracoderms and the living lampreys (which are also agnathans) lack the communication between nasal and oral cavities but are otherwise similar. Gnathostomes (jawed vertebrates) have separate right and left nasal cavities and external nasal openings.

The nasal capsules are extensively ossified in various fishes and ancient amphibians but remain cartilaginous throughout life (and rarely fossilize) in many tetrapods, including living amphibians. Tetrapods have evolved a tear duct (nasolacrimal duct) to carry watery secretion from the space between the eyelids and eyeball to the nasal cavity, and most tetrapods have at least one flat, curved plate (concha or turbinate) projecting into the nasal cavity from the lateral wall of its capsule to increase olfactory surface area. Birds and mammals have several conchae, and those of most mammals are large, delicate, elaborately scrolled structures. Mammals (with a few exceptions, such as whales) have greatly enlarged nasal cavities compared with other vertebrates, partly for olfactory enhancement, partly for air conditioning and to minimize water loss during respiration—these being important functions for animals with high metabolic rates. Posterodorsal (upward and backward) expansion of the nasal cavities of mammals brings them almost into contact with the cavity of the braincase; only the thin cribriform plate of the ethmoid bone intervenes (this bone is an ossified portion of the capsule). The olfactory bulbs of the brain sit on this plate, and the olfactory nerves consist of numerous bundles of axons that pass through numerous holes in the plate to immediately reach the nasal mucous membrane. In more typical vertebrates the bulbs are some distance from the nasal sacs, and the olfactory nerves are long cordlike structures that reach the nasal cavity via canals in the skull.

Expansion of the nasal cavities is very conspicuous in advanced "mammal-like reptiles" (nonmammalian synapsids), especially cynodonts (the group that includes the immediate ancestors of mammals). Whether they possessed elaborate turbinates is unknown, but the fossil remains of such creatures reveal several ridges for turbinate attachment, and it is very probable that complex conchae did exist in life but remained cartilaginous instead of ossifying, as in mammals. No ossified cribriform plate is present in nonmammalian cynodonts, but a cartilaginous plate may well have been present. In mammals there are usually air-filled sinuses that develop by excavation of neighboring bones, such as the maxilla. Large maxillary sinuses are present in some premammalian synapsids. Archosaurs (the group that includes dinosaurs, crocodilians, and birds) also have sinuses of this sort. Most tetrapods have a vomeronasal organ in a special housing on the floor of each nasal cavity; this is an "extra" olfactory organ that often opens into the roof of the mouth and detects odors in the oral cavity. Vomeronasal organs are retained in most mammals but are vestigial in some (such as humans) or entirely eliminated.

Optic Capsule

The optic capsules of the embryo form around the optic cups, which are outpocketings of the developing brain. Light-sensitive cells differentiate in the inner layer of the cup, along with nerve cells whose axons form the second cranial nerve (the optic nerve). The optic capsule should not be confused with the orbital cartilage of the embryonic skull, which lies deeper, or with the orbit, which is a depression in the skull that houses the eye. Usually the optic capsule consists entirely of dense fibrous connective tissue (the fibrous tunic of the eyeball: transparent cornea and translucent or opaque sclera). In primitive vertebrates and some later ones, a ring of bone plates forms within the fibrous sclera to further rigidify the eyeball. Scleral plates are present in some ostracoderms. In primitive bony fishes each eye had four plates, but in later ones the number is reduced to two or zero. Early tetrapods had numerous scleral plates in each eye, and plates are retained in some living reptiles and in birds. They are lost in mammals and their immediate antecedents. Early vertebrates had a third eye—the parietal eye (paired in early ostracoderms but unpaired in later forms)—which occupied a foramen in the middle of the skull roof. Except for lampreys, hagfishes,

and some reptiles, it is lost or converted to a gland in living vertebrates. When present, it has only a fibrous capsule. A parietal eye was retained in all early tetrapods.

Otic Capsule

The developing otic (auditory) capsules form around the otic vesicle, which is derived from an inpocketing of ectoderm. Ectodermal cells differentiate into hair cells responsive to sound and head movement and nerve cells whose axons form the eighth cranial nerve (the vestibulocochlear nerve). The otic capsule of living jawless vertebrates remains cartilaginous throughout life, but in some ostracoderms it was partly ossified. In most jawed vertebrates it becomes largely or completely ossified. In primitive bony fishes a single center of bone formation replaces the cartilaginous capsule, together with adjacent parts of the cartilaginous braincase. In later bony fishes several ossification centers form. Two bones, the prootic anteriorly and the opisthotic posteriorly, are seen in early tetrapods, living reptiles, birds (which add another center dorsally), and early synapsids. Living amphibians usually do not have an opisthotic bone, and mammals have a variable number of ossification centers. When two or more centers occur, they may fuse together in the adult, making the capsule more rigid. In mammals, the centers all unite to form the periotic (petrosal) bone, which may then fuse to the squamosal and tympanic bones, making a composite temporal bone. The medial wall of the otic capsule is virtually nonexistent or unossified in most fishes, early tetrapods, and primitive reptiles, but in birds and mammals a substantial bony wall is present (penetrated by the eighth cranial nerve). Most tetrapods have two "windows" (fenestrae) in the otic capsule, the fenestra vestibuli or ovalis (vestibular or round window) occupied by the base of the sound-conducting stapes, and the fenestra rotunda or cochleae (round or cochlear window) bridged by a membrane. The seventh cranial nerve (facial nerve) may penetrate the capsule anteriorly, and in most mammals it becomes enclosed in a long canal through the periotic bone that leads to an exit called the stylomastoid foramen. During development, the otic capsule of all jawed vertebrates forms connections with adjacent cartilages, including those of the floor and occipital region of the braincase. For auditory reasons, these connections later are eliminated in bats, whales, and sea cows.

EDGAR F. ALLIN

See also Eyes; Hearing and Positional Sense; Lateral Line System; Odor and Pheromone Receptors; Skull

Further Reading

Goodrich, E.S. 1930. *Studies on the Structure and Development of Vertebrates.* London: Macmillan; New York: Dover, 1958.

Hanken, J., and B.K. Hall (eds.). 1993. *The Skull.* Chicago: University of Chicago Press.

Romer, A.S., and T.S. Parsons. 1950. *The Vertebrate Body.* Philadelphia: Saunders; 6th ed., Philadelphia and London: Saunders.

SIMPSON, GEORGE GAYLORD

American, 1902–84

George Gaylord Simpson was born in Chicago on 16 June 1902 and was raised in Denver, Colorado. He attended the University of Colorado for three years, then transferred to Yale, where he received his undergraduate and graduate degrees. Upon receipt of his Ph.D. (1926), Simpson was awarded a National Research Council Fellowship that enabled him to study at the Natural History Museum in London. The result was his outstanding monograph on European Mesozoic mammals (1928). This work, combined with his doctoral thesis on American Mesozoic mammals (published in 1929), established him as a paleontological authority of promise.

In 1927 W.D. Matthew retired from the American Museum of Natural History and Simpson was immediately appointed to succeed him. There, Simpson rose through the ranks, from assistant curator to curator. In 1944 he was appointed chairman of the consolidated Department of Geology and Paleontology. From 1945 to 1959, he was also professor of vertebrate paleontology at Columbia University. With E.H. Colbert, Simpson was appointed to teach and administer the program's graduate course work.

Simpson's long career at the museum was interrupted twice. First came his service in World War II. Secondly, in 1956 while on an expedition to the Amazon in Brazil, Simpson was struck by a falling tree, suffering compound fracture of one leg. He was rushed back to New York, where he endured a long series of operations and lengthy confinements. Yet these two events had only minor effects on his scientific contributions.

Simpson's paleontological career progressed along three parallel paths, each of which complemented the other. First, there were his many expeditions, collecting fossils and studying the geological rock strata in which the fossils were contained. In the field, Simpson was not merely a boss, superintending the pick and shovel work of his assistants. He worked just as long and hard as any members of his field party. Nonetheless, he kept detailed field notebooks, the pages filled with concise descriptions of his observations, augmented by accompanying sketches, stratigraphic sections (the layers of rock in an excavation), and on-the-spot maps. His labors out in the sun and wind, digging, preserving, and plastering the specimens that he had discovered provided the raw data upon which his studies were based.

Second, there were Simpson's empirical studies of the fossils he had collected, as well as innumerable specimens from others' excavations, all housed in museum storage rooms. He published literally hundreds of scientific papers and monographs. These are treasure troves of paleontological facts and analyses, available today in scientific libraries throughout the world. Such publications transformed the fossils from mere objects to significant, three-dimensional records of past life on Earth.

Finally, there were his comprehensive theoretical works, set forth in the books that form the basis of Simpson's reputation as an interpreter of vertebrate evolution. These numerous publications rest to a large degree on the knowledge gained from his empirical descriptions, which in turn rest to a large degree on his labors in the field.

In 1958, after 32 years at the American Museum, Simpson was awarded the position of Alexander Agassiz Professor of Vertebrate Paleontology at the Harvard Museum of Comparative Zoology, a position he held for the next 10 years. In 1967 he moved to Arizona to become professor of geosciences at the University of Arizona. He died in Tucson on 6 October 1984.

EDWIN H. COLBERT

Biography

Born in Chicago, 16 June 1902. Studied at the University of Colorado, 1918–19, 1920–22; Ph.B., Yale University, 1923; Ph.D., Yale University, 1926; scientific staff, American Museum of Natural History, 1927–59; named chair, Department of Geology and Paleontology, American Museum of Natural History, 1944; professor of Vertebrate Paleontology, Columbia University, 1945–59; Agassiz Professor, Harvard University, 1959–70; professor, University of Arizona, 1967–82. Recipient, Lewis Prize, American Philosophical Society, 1942; Thompson Medal, National Academy of Sciences, 1943; Elliott Medal, National Academy of Sciences, 1944, 1961; Penrose Medal, Geological Society of America, 1952; Darwin Medal, Royal Society of London, 1962; National Medal of Science, 1965; International Award, Smithsonian Institution, 1976; honorary degrees from such institutions as Cambridge University, Kenyon College, Oxford University, Princeton University, University of Chicago, University of Colorado, University of Durham, University of Glasgow, University of New Mexico, University of Paris, and Yale University. Member of numerous professional and scholarly associations, including the American Academy of Arts and Sciences; American Association for the Advancement of Science; American Philosophical Society; American Society of Mammalogists; American Society of Zoologists (president); Argentinean National Academy; Brazilian National Academy; Geological Society of America; Italian National Academy (Acadmia de Lincei); National Academy of Sciences; Paleontological Society; Phi Beta Kappa; Royal Society of London; Sigma Xi; Society for the Study of Evolution (president); Society of Systematic Zoology (president); Society of Vertebrate Paleontology (president); Venezuelan National Academy; Zoological Society of London. Collected fossil mammals and made stratigraphic studies in southwestern United States, Florida, Argentina, Brazil, Venezuela; research on fossil vertebrates, particularly primitive mammals from Mesozoic and early Cenozoic horizons; published extensively on extinct mammalian faunas, distributions of mammals through geologic time, taxonomy, principles and mechanisms of evolution, vertebrate evolution, and related subjects. Died in Tucson, Arizona, 6 October 1984.

Major Publications

1928. *Catalogue of the Mesozoic Mammalia in the Geological Department of the British Museum (Natural History).* London: British Museum (Natural History).

1929. *American Mesozoic Mammals. Memoir of the Peabody Museum,* no. 3, pt. 1. New Haven, Connecticut: Peabody Museum, Yale University.

1934. *Attending Marvels: A Patagonian Journal*. New York and London: Macmillan.

1944. *Tempo and Mode in Evolution*. New York: Columbia University Press.

1945. *The Principles of Classification and Classification of Mammals*. American Museum of Natural History Bulletin, 85. New York: American Museum of Natural History.

1948. *The Beginnings of the Age of Mammals in South America*. American Museum of Natural History Bulletin, 91. New York: American Museum of Natural History.

1949. *The Meaning of Evolution: A Study of the History of Life and of Its Significance for Man*. London: Oxford University Press, 2nd ed., New Haven, Connecticut: Yale University Press, 1967.

1953. *The Major Features of Evolution*. New York: Columbia University Press; 3rd ed., 1961.

1961. *Principles of Animal Taxonomy*. New York: Columbia University Press; 3rd ed., 1967.

1964. *This View of Life: The World of an Evolutionist*. New York: Harcourt, Brace, World.

1978. *Concessions to the Improbable: An Unconventional Autobiography*. New Haven, Connecticut: Yale University Press.

1980. *Splendid Isolation: The Curious History of South American Mammals*. New Haven, Connecticut: Yale University Press.

1983. *Fossils and the History of Life*. New York: Scientific American Library.

SIRENIANS

Sirenia is the order of placental mammals comprising modern sea cows (manatees and dugongs) and their extinct relatives. The Sirenia, the Proboscidea (elephants), the extinct orders Desmostylia and Embrithopoda, and possibly the Hyracoidea (hyraces, or hyraxes) together make up a larger group called Tethytheria, whose members (as the name indicates) appear to have evolved in Eurasia along the shores of the ancient Tethys Sea.

The first sirenians appear in the fossil record in the early Eocene and already were diverse by the middle Eocene. They quickly spread along the coasts of the world's shallow tropical seas; in fact, the most primitive sirenian known to date (*Prorastomus*) was found not in the Eastern Hemisphere but in Jamaica. From their beginnings, sirenians were herbivores, and they probably depended on sea grasses and other aquatic angiosperms (flowering plants) for food. To this day, almost all members of the order have remained tropical, marine, and eaters of angiosperms. The manatees (*Trichechus*) live today along the Atlantic coasts and rivers of the Americas and West Africa; one species, the Amazonian manatee, is found only in fresh water. The dugong (*Dugong*) lives in the Indian and southwest Pacific oceans. Steller's sea cow (*Hydrodamalis*), which was exterminated by humans circa A.D. 1768, lived in the temperate to cold waters of the North Pacific Ocean, where it ate kelps and other marine algae (Reynolds and Odell 1991).

The earliest sea cows were pig-sized, four-legged amphibious creatures, but by the end of the Eocene they had taken on their modern, completely aquatic, streamlined body form, featuring flipperlike front legs, no hind legs, and a powerful tail with a horizontal caudal fin that propels them through the water by means of up-and-down movements, as is the case with whales and dolphins. However, sirenians and cetaceans are not closely related; they evolved their outward similarity independently of each other. Being incapable of locomotion on land, sirenians are born in the water and spend their entire lives there. Because they are shallow divers with large lungs, they have heavy skeletons, like a diver's weight belt, to help them stay submerged; their bones are both swollen (pachyostotic) and dense (osteosclerotic), especially the ribs, which are often found as fossils (Domning and de Buffrénil 1991).

Although researchers rely on the cheek teeth to identify species in many other mammalian groups, cheek teeth do not vary much in morphology within the Sirenia, but are almost always low-crowned with two rows of large, rounded cusps. (The most taxonomically informative parts of the sirenian skeleton are the skull and mandible, especially the frontal and other bones of the skull roof.) Except for a pair of tusklike upper incisors seen in many members of the dugong family, front teeth are absent in all but the earliest fossil sirenians. Cheek teeth in adults are typically reduced in number to four or five on each side of each jaw: one or two deciduous premolars, which are never replaced, plus three molars. As described below, however, all three of the Recent genera have departed in different ways from this "typical" pattern.

The Sirenia are divided taxonomically into four families: Prorastomidae, Protosirenidae (both extinct and known only from the Eocene), Dugongidae, and Trichechidae. Sirenians were most diverse during the Oligocene and Miocene, and the vast majority of the population was composed of dungongids.

One major branch of the dugongid family included the well-known fossil genera *Halitherium* and *Metaxytherium*, which were relatively unspecialized sea grass-eaters. They gave rise to the lineage that ended with Steller's sea cow—the largest sirenian that ever lived (up to nine meters or more in length), and the only one to adapt successfully to cold waters and a diet of algae. It was completely toothless, and its abbreviated, clawlike flippers, used for gathering plants and pushing off from rocks, contained no finger bones (phalanges) (Domning 1978, 1987; Domning and Furusawa 1995).

Another branch of the Dugongidae were apparently specialists at digging out and eating the tough, buried rhizomes of sea grasses; for this purpose many of them had large, self-sharpening bladelike tusks (Domning 1994a). The modern dugong is the sole survivor of this group, but it has reduced its once-enameled cheek teeth to simple pegs of dentine and has shifted its diet to more delicate sea grasses.

The manatees (Trichechidae) have a much less complete fossil record than the dugongids; much of their history seems to have been spent in South America, whence they spread to North America and Africa only in the Pliocene or Pleistocene. During the late

Miocene, manatees living in the Amazon basin adapted to a diet of abrasive freshwater grasses by means of an innovation still used by their modern descendants: they continue to add extra teeth to the molar series as long as they live, and as worn teeth fall out at the front, the whole tooth row slowly shifts forward to make room for new ones erupting at the rear. This type of horizontal tooth replacement often has been compared, incorrectly, to that of elephants, but the latter are limited to only three molars. Only one mammal, an Australian rock wallaby, has independently evolved the kind of tooth replacement seen in manatees (Domning 1982, 1983; Domning and Hayek 1984).

Although sirenian fossils have been studied since the earliest days of vertebrate paleontology, and their evolutionary interrelationships are becoming fairly clear (Domning 1994b), their fossil record is still spotty. Most of the well-known species are from Europe and North America, but even in these areas new species and genera of sea cows constantly are being discovered. In the rest of the world, particularly in the Southern Hemisphere and around the Indian Ocean, many extinct taxa of this interesting group doubtless remain to be discovered.

DARYL P. DOMNING

See also Proboscideans

Works Cited

Domning, D.P. 1978. Sirenian evolution in the North Pacific Ocean. *University of California Publications in Geological Sciences* 118:176.
———. 1982. Evolution of manatees: a speculative history. *Journal of Paleontology* 56:599–619.
———. 1983. Marching teeth of the manatee. *Natural History* 92:8, 10–11.
———. 1987. Sea cow family reunion. *National History* 96:64, 66–71.
———. 1994a. West Indian tuskers. *Natural History* 103:72–73.
———. 1994b. A phylogenetic analysis of the Sirenia. *In* A. Berta and T.A. Deméré (eds.), Contributions in marine mammal paleontology honoring Frank C. Whitmore Jr. *Proceedings of the San Diego Society of Natural History* 29:177–89.
Domning, D.P., and V. de Buffrénil. 1991. Hydrostasis in the Sirenia: Quantitative data and functional interpretations. *Marine Mammal Science* 7:331–68.
Domning, D.P., and H. Furusawa. 1995. Summary of taxa and distribution of Sirenia in the North Pacific Ocean. *In* L.G. Barnes, N. Inuzuka, and Y. Hasegawa (eds.), Evolution and biogeography of fossil marine vertebrates in the Pacific realm. *The Island Arc* 3:506–12.
Domning, D.P., and L.C. Hayek. 1984. Horizontal tooth replacement in the Amazonian manatee *(Trichechus inunguis)*. *Mammalia* 48:105–27.
Reynolds, J.E., III, and D.K. Odell. 1991. *Manatees and Dugongs.* New York: Facts on File.

Further Reading

Domning, D.P. 1996. Bibliography and index of the Sirenia and Desmostylia. *Smithsonian Contributions to Paleobiology* 80:1–611.
Packard, J.M., G.B. Rathbun, D.P. Domning, R.C. Best, P.K. Anderson, and T.J. O'Shea. 1984. Sea cows and manatees. *In* D.W. Macdonald (ed.), *The Encyclopedia of Mammals.* New York: Facts on File.
Reynolds, J.E., III, and D.K. Odell. 1991. *Manatees and Dugongs.* New York: Facts on File.
Zeiller, W. 1992. *Introducing the Manatee.* Gainesville: University Press of Florida.

SKELETIZED MICROORGANISMS: ALGAE

Many single-celled protists are autotrophs—they use photosynthesis to manufacture their own food (carbohydrates, such as sugars and starches, and oils) from sunlight, carbon dioxide, and water. (This is in contrast with heterotrophs, which cannot make their own food; they feed on other animals or plants.) For convenience, these organisms usually are grouped as algae because they include a specific type of chlorophyll—chlorophyll *a*—in their photosynthetic process. However, it is becoming increasingly clear that the algae are polyphyletic (have many different origins) and that different autotrophs acquired the ability to photosynthesize at different times. The green algae (as well as their descendants, the higher plants) contain chlorophyll *a* and *b* and carotenoids. (Chlorophylls, carotenoids, and other pigments absorb various sections of the light spectrum.) The brown and golden-brown algae contain chlorophylls *a* and *c* and β-carotene, fucoxanthin, and other carotenoids, and the red algae have chlorophyll *a,* phycobilins, and carotenoids. Chlorophyll *c* and these other pigments broaden the width of the light spectrum, which contributes energy to the photosynthetic process (i.e., more of the spectrum is used for energy production).

Many algae, such as the euglenophytes, are clearly "protistan"—they are single cells with a true nucleus (eukaryotes). Other types of algae are considered colonial—many single cells of the same type join together to form consistent colonial growth forms, for example *Volvox.* Still other algae include large multicellular forms, such as brown algae (including the kelps), red algae (usually calcareous), and multicellular green algae (for example, the sea lettuce *Ulva* and the charophytes). These multicellular algae lack true stems, true leaves, or true roots (i.e., they lack a vascular system). They present many unanswered questions about their evolutionary relationships and relatedness to each other and to other organisms. Some biologists suggest the brown algae and the diatoms comprise a distinctly separate phylum because they have the same types of chlorophyll. Others systematists (those who classify organisms) have suggested that the red algae and the multicellular green algae be placed as independent groups in the plant kingdom.

Pyrrhophyta (Dinoflagellates and Ebridians)

Dinoflagellata

The Class "Dinoflagellata" (Figure 1) have the best-known fossils of the Pyrrhophyta. They typically are small, 20 to 150 micrometers in length, although some are as small as five micrometers, and a few thecate (motile) stages are as large as 2000 micrometers. Dinoflagellates show a remarkable number of ecological adaptations, which have led to a broad distribution in marine and freshwater habitats that receive sunlight (photic). Many are photosynthesizers, others are chemoautotrophs (they use organic or inorganic compounds instead of sunlight for their energy supply), and others are chemoheterotrophs. In addition, dinoflagellates have a number of survival strategies based on complicated life cycles. There is a cyst stage, during which the organism is enclosed in a hard shell. There is a flexible gymnodinioid stage, during which time they may infect other organisms and function as photosymbionts (they form partnerships with other organisms, contributing the products of photosynthesis). And there is a motile (thecate) stage. Dinoflagellate blooms, during which populations can become great enough to produce obvious patches on the surface of water, are associated with nutrient-rich upwelling currents that move up from deep water; the resulting "red-tide" is toxic and can cause mass mortality of fish populations, a phenomenon that is well known along many ocean coasts.

In the motile thecate stage of the life cycle, dinoflagellates have cellulose walls, chlorophylls a and c, and reddish-orange carotenoid pigments. At this stage (Figure 1), they are characterized by two flagella (long, whiplike tails used for propulsion) of unequal length. One occupies a crosswise equatorial groove, or cingulum, and the other a longitudinal groove, or sulcus. The walls of many thecae may be flexible and lack much reinforcement. Other thecae are more rigid and are reinforced with thickened cellulose plates, which are the forms most common in the fossil record. The shape and arrangement of these cellulose plates are consistent within a species and form a useful tool in taxonomy. Although dinoflagellate thecae have a wide range of shapes and many differences in thecal plate size and shape, little is known of the adaptive significance of these differences.

The "cyst stage" is the stage that is preserved most commonly in the fossil record. The cyst forms within the walls of the former motile thecate stage. One type of cyst develops immediately against the walls and plates of the motile cell so that all its morphological features (those of shape and structure) function as molds, and their elements are reproduced as in a casting, commonly with considerable ornamentation. A second type of cyst has a two-layered cyst wall; the layers may be separated to form small cavities. These cavities are thought to aid in buoyancy. A third type of cyst develops in a position that is some distance inside the original thecal wall; short spines (processes) connect the cyst to the thecal wall. These spines are connected to the center of each of the main thecal plates during cyst development, but not to the cingulum or sulcus plates that form the grooves. Cysts usually have a well-defined escape hole, or archeophyle, through which asexually reproduced young leave the cyst to develop and grow in size as a naked gymnodinioid stage.

In some dinoflagellates, the gymnodinioid stage includes most of the known life history, such as the zooxanthellae, which live in symbiotic relations with many shallow-water, tropical-reef protists (such as larger foraminifers) and invertebrates. Other gymnodinioid forms may be predatory or parasitic among the planktonic (drifting) organisms. Many do not have a well-defined thecate stage, lack armor in that stage, or the thecate stage yet has to be identified.

The complete life cycle of only a few dinoflagellates—less than a dozen—has been determined in any detail, so much remains to be learned of the relations among the different parts of the life cycle stages. Because it is not easy to relate individuals in cyst stages to individuals in thecate stages or gymnodinioid stages, different taxonomic classifications have been used for each of the life cycle stages; presently dinoflagellate systematics is certainly not a natural classification.

A Silurian (438 to 408 million years ago) acritarch is the earliest cyst that has been shown to have dinoflagellate features. Other Early and Middle Paleozoic acritarchs may well be dinoflagellate cysts, but so far that fact has not been demonstrated clearly. A few species are reported from the Permian (285 to 250 million years ago) and Triassic (250 to 208 million years ago); however, in the Jurassic (208 to 145 million years ago), they became abundant and diverse, reaching their maximum diversity in the Late Cretaceous. Fossilized marine forms declined in diversity and abundance during the Cenozoic (65 million years ago to Recent). Freshwater dinoflagellates date from the Cenozoic.

Ebridians

Ebridians (Figure 2) are unicellular, marine plankton that have a siliceous endoskeleton (an internal skeleton based upon silica). They differ from silicoflagellates in having solid skeletons with symmetry based upon three or four axes. In addition to two flagella for locomotion, the ebridians use pseudopods (extensions of the cell body) to capture food, usually diatoms. Ebridians lack chloroplasts and are not photosynthesizers; nonetheless, based on structural features, such as their biflagellate locomotion, they usually are placed in either the Pyrrhophyta or the Chrysophyta. Ebridians have a Cenozoic (65 million years ago to Recent) fossil record and were relatively abundant throughout the Miocene, when their diversity and abundance declined abruptly.

Acritarchs

The Acritarcha include a host of mainly marine, organic-walled unicellular vesicle-like structures (Figure 1, 1–7) that are not assigned easily to other established groups. A large number of these forms have a central cavity surrounded by a single-layered wall, about 20 to 50 micrometers in maximum dimension, and many have archeopyle-like openings. They first appeared in the Late Precambrian Riphean Period, reached their greatest diversity in the Lower and Middle Paleozoic, and declined markedly during the later part of the Devonian. They remained at low taxonomic diversity throughout most of the rest of the geologic record, showing only a minor, temporary increase in the Jurassic. They are of considerable evolutionary interest because of their early origin in evolutionary history; however, our current understanding of this group is only suggestive of their significance.

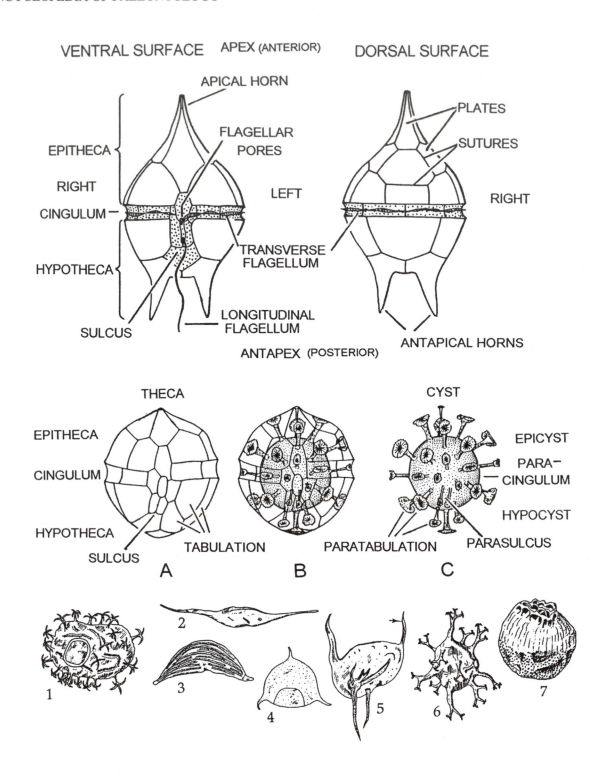

Figure 1. Morphology and features of a peridinialean dinoflagellate. *A, B, C,* the relations between cellulose thecal plates of the active swimming stage and the sporopollenin of the cyst stage. *1–7:* Acritarchs showing various morphological features; *2, Peteinosphaeridium; 3, Leiofusa; 4, Baiomeniscus; 5, Villoscapsula; 6, Sylvanidium; 7, Multiplicisphaeridium; 8, Ooidium; 9, Cymatiosphaera.* Modified from Edwards (1987), adapted from Evitt (1985), courtesy American Association of Stratigraphic Palynologists.

Acritarchs have a central body chamber, or vesicle, from which processes arise. The composition of this chamber wall is similar to that found in plant spores. Most are single-layered; however, some are laminate (layered), and some are radiate and porous. Processes that extend outward from the walls form ridges, ridges with crowns and crests, spines, hairlike tuffs, and even fingerlike projections. The surface of the body chamber may be smooth or variously ornamented with short spines, pits, pores, or

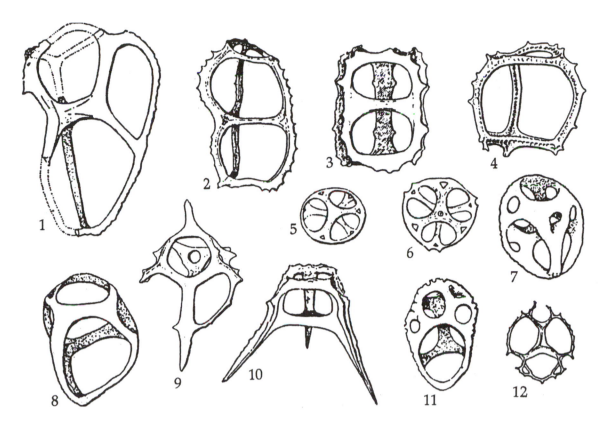

Figure 2. Skeltons of representative ebridians. *1, Micromarsupium; 2, Podamphora; 3, Ammonodochium; 4, Podamphoropsis; 5, Hermesinella; 6, Hermesinum; 7, 8, Ebriopsis; 9, Hermesinopsis; 10, Parathranium; 11, Craniopsis; 12, Ebria.* From McCartney (1987).

other features. A few have what scholars think may be escape sutures or escape holes, like the archaeopyle in dinoflagellates, but these structures are not known widely among the acritarchs.

Because their biological affinities are known so poorly, the acritarchs are classified as artificial "form" genera (names attached to parts of organisms instead of whole organisms). Less than 10 general types are recognized, based on wall structure, escape openings, kinds of processes and crests, and the shape and features of the central body chamber. Several form genera have reasonably distinctive stratigraphic ranges in the Early and Middle Paleozoic (i.e., they are found in very specific rock strata). As a result, they can be used as markers that signal the period during which the rock was originally deposited. Biological groups that may be included within the acritarchs are higher plant spores, algal spores, dinoflagellate cysts, and even invertebrate egg cases, as well as parts of other, still unrecognized, organisms.

Chrysophyta (Silicoflagellates, Chrysomonads, Diatoms, and Coccolithophores)

The golden-brown color of the Chrysophyta results from the combination of chlorophylls *a* and *c*, yellow and brown carotenoids, and xanthophyll pigments in their protoplasm. The combination of chlorophylls and xanthophyll suggests a close relationship with the multicellular brown algae (Phaeophyta), which have a considerably poorer fossil record. Typically, chrysophytes have unicellular biflagellated cells, in which the two flagella are located at one end of the cell near the mouth. These organisms are distributed widely in fresh and marine waters, and some are colonial.

Silicoflagellates

Silicoflagellates (Figure 3) are marine plankton with siliceous (silica-based) skeletons. These organisms are associated with nutrient-rich (and silica-rich) upwelling of cold water in equatorial regions and in cooler, higher latitude silica-rich ocean waters in siliceous-rich sediments. Seasonal blooms are common. Their fossil record, which started in the Cretaceous (145 to 65 million years ago) and peaked in diversity during the Miocene, has been used only sparingly for correlation and paleoecological purposes.

Typically, silicoflagellates have a skeleton of ringlike, hollow opaline silica in circular, quadrate, pentagonal, or hexagonal shape from which spines project. A single flagellum is used for locomotion, and the spines are supports for long strands of pseudopods, which entrap prey. Thus, they are heterotrophic. Complex hemispherical skeletons are common; however, silicoflagellates lack the sphere-within-a-sphere configuration common in the radiolarians, another protist group.

Chrysomonad and Archaeomonad Cysts

The Chrysophyta include a large number of nonmarine (Chry-

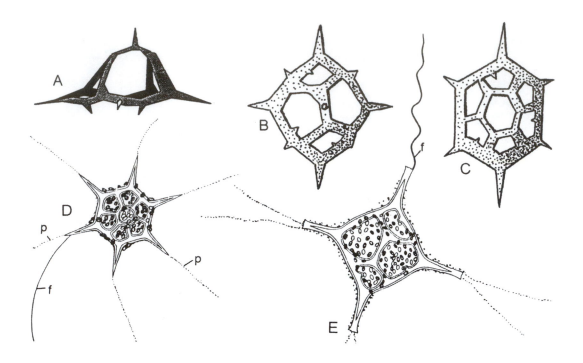

Figure 3. Views of silicoflagellates showing the shape of the skeleton of (A, B) *Dictyocha*; C, *Distephanus*; D, a living *Distephanus*; E, a living *Dictyocha*. Modified from McCartney (1987); modified from H. Tappan's THE PALEOBIOLOGY OF PLANTS PROTISTS © 1980 by W.H. Freeman and Company, used with permission.

somonad) and a few marine (Archaeomonad) forms—phytoplanktonic, unicellular, and colonial—that have left a relatively insignificant fossil record of siliceous "resting" cysts (Figure 4). These small cysts, 3 to 25 micrometers, are subspherical and commonly have a cellulose wall that is impregnated heavily with opaline silica. These structures have a neck and opening with a small plug. They first appeared in the Late Cretaceous and extend into the Recent. A few similar structures were found much earlier, in the Precambrian.

Bacillariophyta (Diatoms)

Diatoms (Figure 5) are yellow or brown in color and are related closely to other algae with brown chloroplasts, such as the Chrysophyta (golden algae) and the Phaeophyta (brown algae). Diatoms inhabit marine and freshwater ecosystems and have an opaline siliceous test (a silica "container"), the frustule" which is formed by two parts that fit together like a box and its lid. Most reproduce asexually, so that each daughter cell receives one of the two parts of the parent's test and regenerates the other half. Thus, the size of the box changes with each generation, although the ornamentation and other surface features of the wall are reproduced faithfully. After a summer of active reproduction, the frustules commonly form long, yellowish-green, stringlike strands with many individuals loosely joined together.

A frustule usually is about 20 to 200 micrometers in size and is circular (centric) or elliptical (pennate). These shapes are used to identify the two diatom orders, the Centrales and Pennales. The test wall is porous, and the pores (punctae) are arranged in distinctive patterns of numerous rows with intervening ridges.

The Centrales, in addition to having frustules that are circular, include forms that are triangular and quadrate. Most are marine plankton; however, some live in brackish water and others in freshwater. Punctae are arranged in ornate rows that radiate from the center of the valve and form patterns that are commonly quite complex. Centrales are recorded from the Cretaceous and became abundant and diverse in the early Cenozoic (65 to 58 million years ago), when they gave rise to the earliest Pennales, and reached their peak diversity in the Miocene.

The Pennales have a bilateral symmetry to their elliptical frustules. A narrow longitudinal groove, called a raphe, extends from pole to pole across the frustule and lacks punctae; however, punctae line the margins of the groove. Some lack a longitudinal groove and instead have a narrow longitudinal area that lacks punctae. At its center the raphe is divided into two parts by a central knob, called a "nodule." Near each pole there is commonly a polar nodule.

Diatoms have adapted to a remarkable number of habitats. They are planktonic (free-floating) in both marine and freshwater and also widespread in benthic habitats (along the seafloor), in streams, ponds, marshes, swamps, oceans, and in wet spots in soil and on trees. Some species form cysts to resist times when conditions are unfavorable (e.g., dry periods). Food is stored as oil (chrysolaminarin) in vascuoles (membrane-bound spaces). Such vacuoles also aid in buoyancy in many species.

A number of studies have used diatoms in stratigraphic correlation in both marine and nonmarine sediments, in interpreting the environmental conditions when the diatoms were deposited, and in studying climate changes during the Pleistocene. For example, in areas of cool marine water, diatoms are common in sediments, and, although present in warm marine water sediments, they tend to be masked by the abundance of other fossil organisms. Marine and freshwater sediments composed solely of accumulations of diatoms are called "diatomites" and are widely used as filters, as an abrasive polish, in toothpaste, and in insulation. Their fine shell structures are used to test the optical resolution of microscopes.

Coccolithophores

Coccolithophores (Figure 6) are small (about 20 micrometers) spherical unicells, with two flagella of the same length and a larger and longer organelle that is whiplike. The cell is coated with minute calcareous plates called coccoliths (about five micrometers in diameter). These calcareous plates are formed within the cell, then are moved to the surface of the cell, where they form an armor. As additional coccoliths are formed, they move to the surface of the cell to displace the existing ones on the surface, which drop off and sink to the ocean floor to form extensive calcareous oozes (at least on ocean floors above the calcium carbonate compensation depth, 4000 to 5000 meters).

Figure 4. Chrysomonads (archaeomonads) showing surface ornamentations (Miocene). From McCartney (1987).

This group of nannophtyoplankton is abundant and provides an important food source for many organisms in the plankton. In aggregate, their photosynthetic activity is enormous, so they are significant in maintaining relatively high oxygen levels in the atmosphere. Because the density of coccolithophores is dependent upon the amount of dissolved mineral concentrations in marine waters, they are most abundant in areas of ocean upwelling and vertical mixing. They have successfully divided their photo-

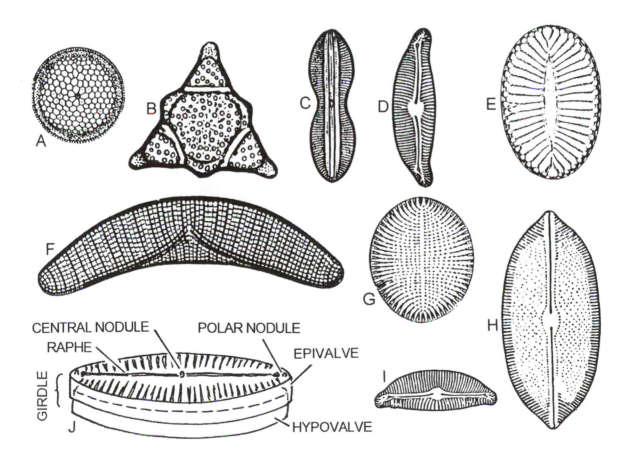

Figure 5. Representatives of diatoms. *A, Thalassiosira; B, Triceratium; C, Diploneis; D, Cymbella; E, Surirella; F, Epithemia; G, Cocconeis; H, Navicula; I, Cymbella; J,* typical features of a diatom frustule. From: *A to I,* modified from Barron (1987); *J,* original.

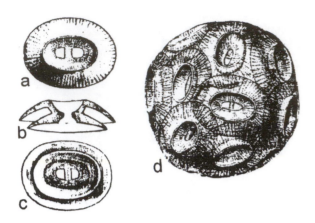

Figure 6. *a, b, c:* three views of a typical coccolith; *d,* a coccosphere of *Cocclithus.* From Siesser and Haq (1987).

synthetic habitats both vertically, by depth, and geographically, by ocean current and water surface temperatures.

In the relatively few coccolithophore life cycles that have been established, some have a rigid shelled, nonmotile form (coccosphere) in addition to the prevalent motile form with a flexible cell wall.

Features of the coccoliths are used to classify these organisms into two basic types (Figure 7). The simplest—and generally smaller—coccoliths are comprised of minute calcite crystal plates arranged in regular, geometrically distinctive patterns. Once they are shed, these fragile plates usually separate along their crystal boundaries. The larger and more complex coccoliths are built from several types of structures, including grains, plates, bars, and rods. These coccoliths are cemented more firmly and make up most of the coccolith fossil record. Although they show diverse geometries and construction, most are discs (shields) formed by radially arranged plates. The central area may be open. This open region may contain one or more crossbars, and the crossbars may unite to form a spine. There are many other variations. Many of the shields have both an outer (distal) and an inner (proximal) layer of radially arranged calcite crystals. Because the crystal sizes of coccolith building blocks are so fine, they are very susceptible to dissolution as they fall through the water column. Most are destroyed by the time they reach depths of 4000 meters. Once on the seafloor and part of the sediments, coccoliths are further susceptible to recrystallization, overgrowths, and other alterations.

Scattered fossils that could possibly be coccoliths are reported from strata as old as Late Precambrian, but the earliest generally accepted fossil forms are from the late Triassic (215 million years ago). These forms show a broad diversification in the Jurassic, reach a peak in the Late Cretaceous, and have lesser diversity peaks in the Eocene (58 to 37 million years ago) and Miocene (24 to 5 million years ago). They are relatively rare in the Pliocene and Pleistocene, presumably because of declining surface temperatures in the world's oceans.

Chlorophyta (Green Algae)

Chlorophytes are characterized by green photosynthetic pigments, including chlorophyll *a* and *b*, and also some β-carotene and various xanthophylls. They usually store food as starches, which are also the building units for the cellulose that many use to construct their cell walls. Although there are a number of classes of chlorophytes, only three are important to paleontology.

One is a single-celled group, the Class Prasinophyceae (Figure 8), which has spherical, thick-walled cells about 500 micrometers in diameter. The wall is composed of polysaccharides. This group first appeared in the Cambrian (540 million years ago), and fossils are common in the Paleozoic; the genus *Tasmanites* formed oily coals that have been distilled for fuel oils.

Members of the Class Chlorophyceae are more diverse in morphology and include unicellular to multicellular forms. They include groups that appear to be immediately ancestral to green vascular plants; scholars believe that this group gave rise to higher plants. One group that usually is placed among the simplest green algae, the "calcispheres," also is claimed by the foraminiferan taxonomists as simple calcareous foraminifers. These fossils first appeared in abundance during the Devonian (408 to 360 million years ago), were common through the Carboniferous, and became rare in the Permian. They typically have a calcareous granular outer wall and a radial calcitic inner wall. Other calcispheres, "radiosphaerids," have a dark organic inner wall surrounded by a granular wall that passes outward into a rugose (wrinkled) outer layer of irregular, crystalline calcite blades. Several simple unicellular algal groups form "algal mats," which are recorded from strata as old as Ordovician (500 to 438 million years ago). These include the freshwater desmids.

Calcareous green algae include two multicellular green algal orders (Figures 8, 9), the Dasycladales and the Siphonales, which have been extensive contributors to warm-water reef and carbonate-based platform deposits since the Cambrian. These two orders of the upper photic zone precipitate calcium carbonate as "aragonitic" needles within the algal cells, apparently as a byproduct of active photosynthesis. (Aragonite is the stable crystal phase of calcium carbonate in warm marine water.) When the cells of many calcareous green algae die, these aragonitic needles are released and form a fine silt-size to clay-size sediment that is transported easily by waves and currents, eventually coming to rest in deeper water as extensive deposits of calcareous mudstones. However, in the dasyclads and siphonales, the aragonitic needles are packed closely between algal cells and become partially cemented together. When the algae die, the internal shape of the cells and the arrangement of cells in the multicelled algae commonly are preserved as molds. Once these needles are part of the sediment, they are likely to be preserved, although they are still susceptible to recrystallization to calcite or dissolution by freshwater in groundwater.

The Dasycladales (Figure 8) are characterized by a central axis from which whorls of branches arise in a regular pattern. Secondary and tertiary branching is common. These algae are attached by rootlike structures called "holdfasts" to the substrate (the surface upon which they grow, e.g., seafloor, underwater rock shelves). Most dasyclads are cylindrical, some are spherical, and others are club-shaped. Some cylindrical forms became quite large (e.g., the receptaculitids).

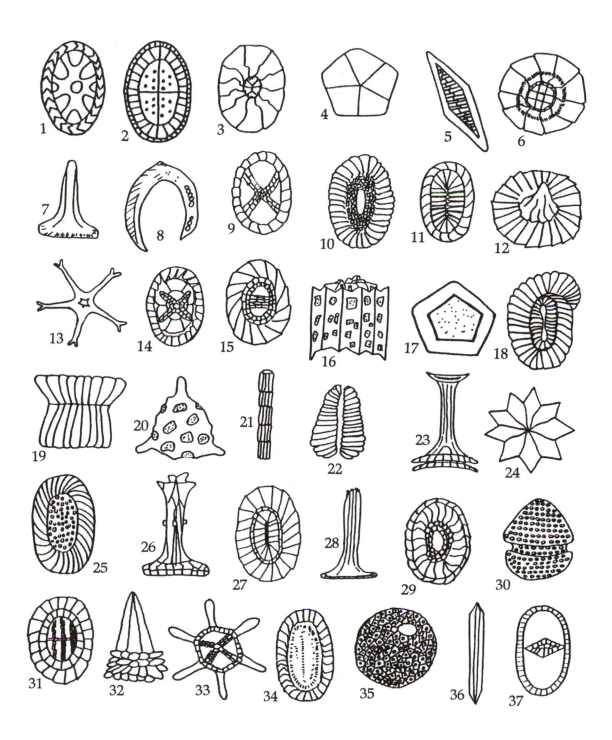

Figure 7. Representative coccolith families. *1*, Ahmuellerellaceae, *Ahmuellerella*; *2*, Arkhangelskiellaceae, *Arkhangelskiella*; *3*, Biscutaceae, *Biscutum*; *4*, Braarudosphaeraceae, *Braarudosphaera*; *5*, Calciosoleniaceae, *Calciosolenia*; *6*, Calyculaceae, *Calyculus*; *7*, Calyptrosphaeraceae, *Calyptrosphaera*; *8*, Ceratolithaceae, *Ceratolithus*; *9*, Chiastozypaceae, *Chiastozygus*; *10*, Coccolithaceae, *Coccolithus*; *11*, Crepidolithaceae, *Crepidolithus*; *12*, Deutschlandiaceae, *Deutschlandia*; *13*, Discoasteraceae, *Discoaster*; *14*, Eiffellithaceaea, *Eiffellithus*; *15*, Ellipsogelosphaeraceaea, *Ellipsagelosphaera*; *16*, Fasciculithaeceae, *Fasciculithus*; *17*, Goniolithaceae, *Goniolithus*; *18*, Helicosphaeraceae, *Helicosphaera*; *19*, Heliolithaceae, *Heliolithus*; *20*, Lithostromationaceae, *Lithostromation*; *21*, Microrhabdulaceae, *Microrhabdulus*; *22*, Nannoconaceae, *Nannoconus*; *23*, Podorhabdaceae, *Podorhabdus*; *24*, Polycyclolithaceae, *Polycyclolithus*; *25*, Pontosphaeraceae, *Pontosphaera*; *26*, Prediscosphaeraceae, *Prediscosphaera*; *27*, Prinsiaceaea, *Prinsius*; *28*, Rhabdosphaeraceae, *Rhabdosphaera*; *29*, Rhagodiscaceae, *Rhagodiscus*; *30*, Schizosphaerellaceae, *Schizosphaerella*; *31*, Sollasitaceae, *Sollasites*; *32*, Sphenolithaceae, *Sphenolithus*; *33*, Stephanolithiaceae, *Stephanolithion*; *34*, Syracosphaeraceae, *Syracosphaera*; *35*, Thoracosphaeraceae, *Thoracosphaera*; *36*, Triquetrorhabdulaceae, *Triquetrorhabdulus*; *37*, Zygodiscaceae, *Zygodiscus*. Modified from Siesser and Haq (1987).

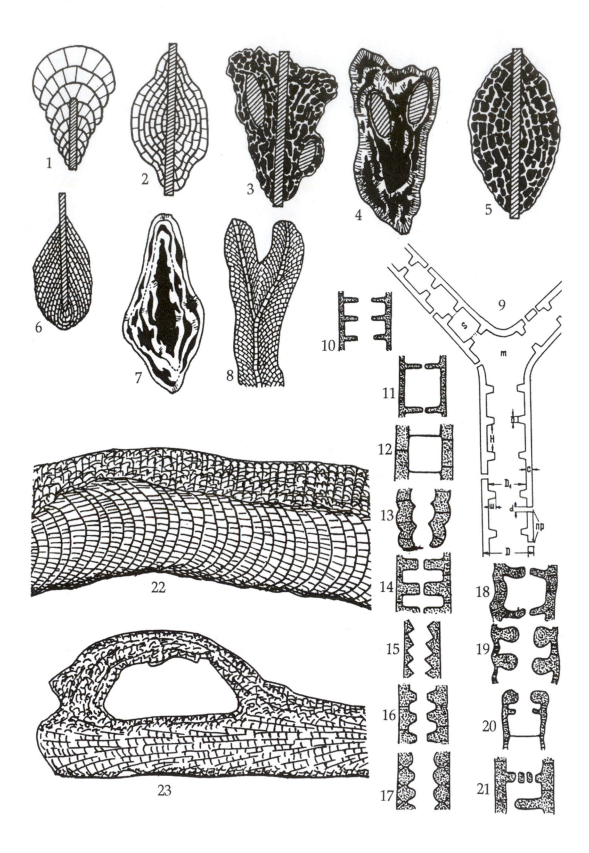

Figure 8. Probable coralline algae: *1, Stacheia; 2, Mametella; 3, Stacheoides; 4, Epistacheoides; 5, Aoujgalia; 6, Fourstonella; 7, Pseudostacheoides; 8, Ungdarella; 9,* growth features used in identifying genera of Palaeobereselleaceae illustrated in *10–21; 10, Kamaena; 11, Kamaenella; 12, Parakamaena; 13, Pseudokamaena; 14, Subkamaena; 15, Stylaella; 16, Palaeoberesella; 17, Exvotarisella; 18, Anthraocoporellopsis; 19, Crassikamaena; 20, Turgajella; 21, Cribrokamaena;* Recent coralline algae showing central and lateral regions of growth: *22, 23, Lithothamnium.* From Bogush et al. (1990).

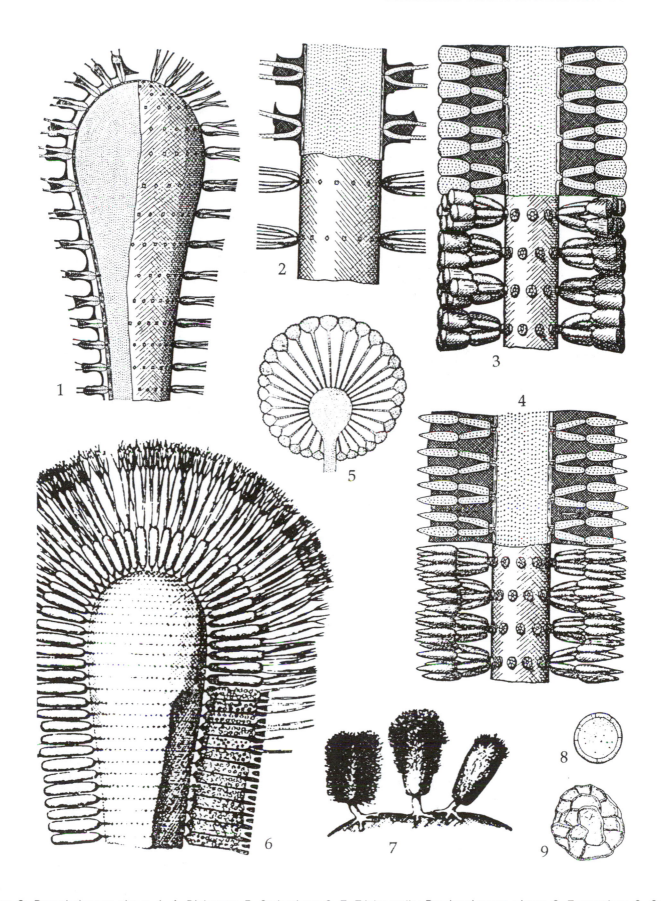

Figure 9. Dasycladacean algae: *1–4, Diplopora; 5, Cyclocrinus; 6, 7, Triploporella;* Prasinophycean algae: *8, Tasmanites; 9, Cymatiosphaera.* Source: *1–7* from Johnson (1961); *8–9* from Mendelson (1987).

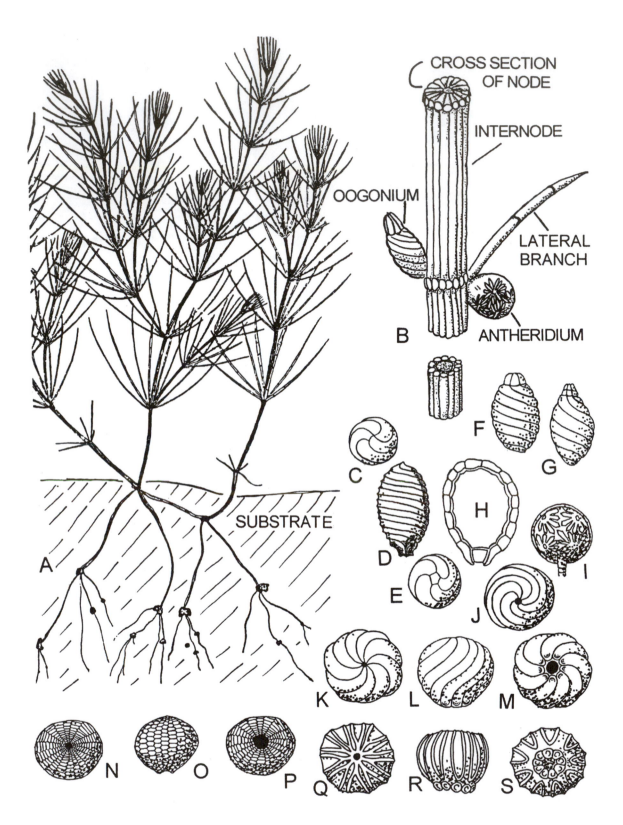

Figure 10. Charophyta. *A,* Recent charophyte with growth form; *B,* enlarged view showing nodes, internodes, lateral branches, and position of the oogonia and antheridia; *C, D, E, Chara* oogonium (apical, lateral, and basal views); *F, Chara* with one-tiered coronal cells; *G, Nitella* with two-tiered coronal cells; *H,* section through an oogonium; *I,* an antheridium; *J,* apical view of *Paleochara* with six cells forming the oogonium; *K, L, M,* a trochiliscacean *Moellerina; N, O, P,* a sycidiacean *Sycidium; Q, R, S,* a chovallacean *Chovanella;* Modified and adapted in part from: *A,* Johnson (1961); *B,* original; *C–S,* retouched from Conkin and Conkin (1977, 1992), courtesy of James E. Conkin.

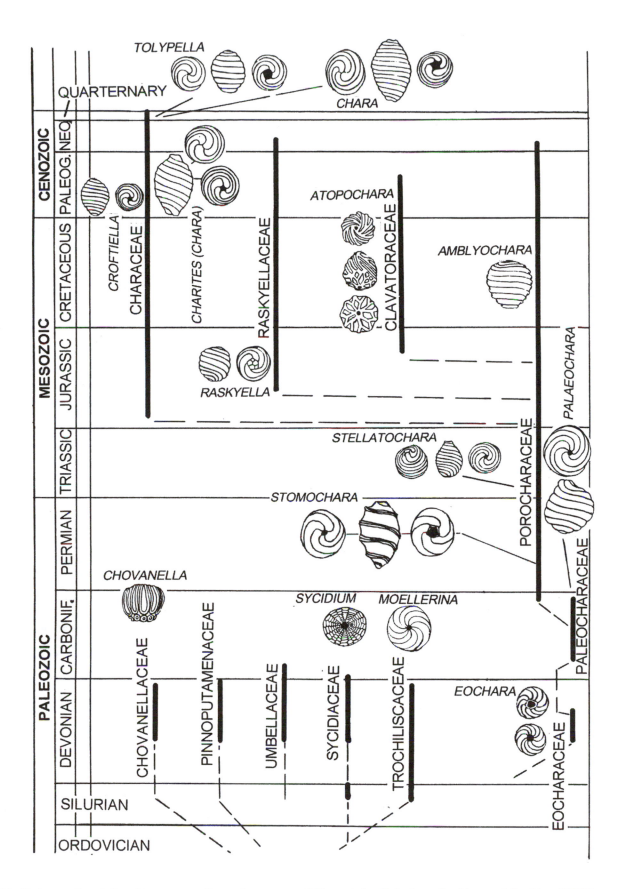

Figure 11. Phylogenetic relationships among the major groups of Charophyta. Data from Conkins and Conkins (1977), courtesy of James E. Conkin; Shaikin (1991).

The Siphonales, mostly of the family Codiaceae (Figure 9), comprise freely branched tubular filaments interwoven into consistent shapes and forms. The organisms may be assembled into plates and articulate branches (e.g., *Halimeda*).

A number of well-known Paleozoic algae are difficult to assign to either of these orders (e.g., the Pennsylvanian and Early Permian "potato chip alga" *Ivanova*, and the Early Devonian *Lancicula* and *Litanaia*).

The Charophyta (Figure 10) is a side branch of the green algae. Since the Pennsylvanian (320 to 285 million years ago), charophytes have been adapted to fresh and slightly brackish water; however, the group first appeared in Late Silurian (410 million years ago) shallow marine and marginal (shoreline) marine sediments, at which time all its characteristic features already were well developed. These algae are composed of a stem consisting of an elongate, central cell that is surrounded by one layer of elongate cortical cells. One set of stem cells is separated from the next set of stem cells by a set of radially arranged node cells. The node cells give rise to branch cells, male antherida (structures that produce male gametes), which grow below the branches, and female oogonia (structures that produce eggs), which grow above the branches. Branches may be a series of branch cells strung end-to-end. The antheridium is composed of many small calcareous plates and, when ripe, sheds many flagellated gametes. The oogonium is a chamber that houses a single egg cell. This chamber is surrounded by long tubular cells that spiral around the oogonial chamber.

The opening at the top of the oogonium is covered by coronal cells and is open when the egg is ready for fertilization. Once fertilized, the cells surrounding the oogonium become strongly calcified, offering protection for the developing embryo. During times of desiccation (drying out) or other environmental stresses, these structures act as resting cysts. In some, the outside of this oogonial structure is enclosed further by an additional set of utricle (pouchlike) cells. Branchlike processes (protrusions) act as holdfasts. Study of the calcified oogonia has demonstrated their usefulness in biostratigraphic correlations.

Seven families of charophyte-like algae are recognized from the Late Silurian and Devonian. Until recently, several were considered foraminifers (e.g., the Chovanellaceae, Pinnoputamenaceae, and Umbellaceae). The family Sycidiaceae is a Late Silurian to Early Mississippian family that has 16 to 20 vertically arranged rows of cells around the oogonium.

The family Trochiliscaceae forms a lineage that started in the Late Silurian and ranged into the Early Mississippian and perhaps extended into the Middle Permian. This family has oogonia with 10 or more cells coiled to the right around the oogonium. Some Late Devonian and Early Mississippian representatives of these genera occur in marine as well as brackish deposits. Some have been mistaken for calcareous foraminifers. The family Eocharaceae is a poorly known group from the Middle Devonian.

In the Characeae, five (six in primitive species) cells spiral to the left to surround the oogonium. This family ranges from the Carboniferous to the Recent. The earliest well-studied genus, *Palaeochara*, is from the early part of the Middle Carboniferous of Nova Scotia and has six cells spiraling to the left. The Middle and Late Carboniferous genus *Stomochara* and the Triassic genus *Stella-*

tochara have five leftward-spiraling cells. In the Jurassic, this family gave rise to the relatively rare Raskellaceae, the Clavatoraceae (with its well-developed utricles), and the essentially modern Characeae. All these families had a major diversification of species and genera in the Cretaceous and have declined through the Cenozoic.

In addition to being used widely in fish aquariums to help maintain the balance between oxygen and carbon dioxide in the water, charophytes are particularly common in slightly alkaline lakes and in temporary lakes of arid regions. Charophytes are important food for many birds, such as ducks and other migratory water fowl, and, as a result, are distributed widely by these migratory birds.

Formed during the Late Jurassic of the western interior of the United States, much of the Morrison Formation is composed of a succession of charophyte-rich lake beds in which many large herbivorous dinosaurs are preserved. This suggests that submerged meadows of charophytes were a readily abundant food source for these huge herbivores. The very fine-grained, freshwater limestones within the Morrison Formation are composed mostly of charophyte debris.

Rhodophyta (Red Algae)

Rhodophytes are mostly marine unicellular to multicellular algae. In addition to chlorophyll *a,* these algae have various amounts of an accessory pigment called phycoerythrin and, in some, a blue pigment called phycocyanin; these pigments give many of the plants a reddish (and even a black) color. These pigments are part of a family of pigments known only from the red algae and the cyanobacteria, permitting these algae to be successful photosynthesizers in the deeper parts of the photic zone (blue and green light spectral range) below the range of green algae. Most red algae are multicellular (Figures 9-22, 9-23); the thalli (stems) of many are filamentous, showing delicate, interwoven patterns of cells. Normally, red algae are sessile and are attached by holdfasts to hard substrates or fragments and to the thalli of other large algae. The life cycle differs from other algae in that the gametes lack flagella and generations commonly alternate between sexual and asexual. Many rhodophytes live in warm tropical and subtropical waters; however, they also are abundant and diverse in cooler waters. Usually, species and genera (groups of species) are correlated closely with specific water temperatures and depth, and depth correlates with available sunlight and clarity of the water.

Rhodophyta of paleobiological interest are included in the Order Cryptonemiales; the families Corallinaceae (Figure 9) (Cretaceous to Recent), Solenoporaceae (Cambrian to Cretaceous), and Gymnocodiaceae (Permian, Cretaceous), and a group of Late Paleozoic red algae of uncertain affinities are geologically significant.

The Corallinacea include nearly all Recent calcareous red algae and are abundant in shallow, well-agitated water typical, for instance, of surf areas. Members of this group are strongly calcified, their calcium carbonate having a high magnesium content. The calcium carbonate is deposited within and between cell walls so that fine details are commonly well-preserved in the fossils. The thallus is differentiated into a "base," that continues into the central portion of the branch (hypothallus), and peripheral portions (perithallus) of the branches. Spore-bearing cavities (sporangia) usually are grouped together in cavities called "conceptacles." Generally, the cells of the hypothallus are large and are arranged regularly, in comparison to much smaller cells of the perithallus. Perithallus cells develop from the top or edge of the hypothallus as a series of cells arranged in a string. In some, the perithallus cells grow in successive layers.

The Solenoporacea lack much, if any, differentiation between hypothallus and perithallus cells, and sporangia are rare or lacking. Most solenoporaceans were rounded, nodular masses, although a few Late Paleozoic and Mesozoic forms were encrusting. On the other hand, gymnocodiaceans (Permian, Cretaceous) typically had porous branching thalli and a tubular growth form with regular constrictions. Segmentation may have been present at the constrictions.

A number of Middle and Late Carboniferous red algae are of stratigraphic interest because they mark consistent stratigraphic intervals; however, they are difficult to assign taxonomically. These diverse forms include *Archaeolithophyllum*, *Cuneiphycus*, *Komia*, and *Ungdarella*.

CHARLES A. ROSS

See also Algae; Microbial Fossils, Precambrian; Skeletized Microorganisms: Protozoans and Chitozoans

Works Cited

Barron, J.A. 1987. Diatoms. *In* J.H. Lipps (ed.), *Fossil Procaryotes and Protists: Notes for a Short Course.* University of Tennessee, Department of Geological Sciences, Studies in Geology 18. Knoxville: University of Tennessee, Department of Geological Sciences.

Bogush, O.I., R.M. Ivanova, and B.A. Luchinina. 1990. *Isbestkobye Vodorosli Verkhnego famena i nizhnego karbona Urala i sibiri.* Akademia Nauk SSSR, Novosibirsk Nauka Sibirskoe otdelenie, Trudy Instituta Geologii i Geophisiki, vypuck 745. Moscow: Akademia Nauk SSSR.

Brasier, M.D. 1980. *Microfossils.* London and Boston: Allen and Unwin.

Conkin, J.E., and B.M. Conkin. 1977. North American primitive Paleozoic Charophytes and descendents. *In* R.C. Romans (ed.), *Geobotany.* New York: Plenum.

———. 1992. *Late Silurian (Ludlovian) Charophyte* Moellerina laufeldi, *n. sp., from the Hamra Beds of the Isle of Gotland, Sweden.* University of Louisville Notes in Paleontology and Stratigraphy,
vol. J. Louiville, Kentucky: Department of Geography and Geosciences, University of Louisville.

Edwards, L.E. 1987. Dinoflagellates. *In* J.H. Lipps (ed.), *Fossil Procaryotes and Protists: Notes for a Short Course.* University of Tennessee, Department of Geological Sciences, Studies in Geology 18. Knoxville: University of Tennessee, Department of Geological Sciences.

Evitt, W.R. 1985. *Sporopollenin Dinoflagellate Cysts: Their Morphology and Interpretation.* Dallas, Texas: American Association of Stratigraphic Palynologists Foundation.

Johnson, J.H. 1961. *Limestone-Building Algae and Algal Limestones.* Golden: Colorado School of Mines.

McCartney, K. 1987. Silicoflagellates, Ebridans, and Archaeomonads. *In* J.H. Lipps (ed.), *Fossil Procaryotes and Protists: Notes for a Short Course.* University of Tennessee, Department of Geological Sciences, Studies in Geology 18. Knoxville: University of Tennessee, Department of Geological Sciences.

Mendelson, C.V. 1987. Acritachs. *In* J.H. Lipps (ed.), *Fossil Procaryotes and Protists: Notes for a Short Course.* University of Tennessee, Department of Geological Sciences, Studies in Geology 18. Knoxville: University of Tennessee, Department of Geological Sciences.

Shaikin, I.M. 1991. Tempy evolutsii kharofitov v fanerozoye. [Rates of evolution of charophytes in the Phanerozoic.] *Paleontologicheskiy zhurnal* 2:3-8.

Siesser, W.A., and B.U. Haq. 1987. Calcareous Nannoplankton. *In* J.H. Lipps (ed.), *Fossil Procaryotes and Protists: Notes for a Short Course.* University of Tennessee, Department of Geological Sciences, Studies in Geology 18. Knoxville: University of Tennessee, Department of Geological Sciences.

Tappan, H. 1980. *The Paleobiology of Plant Protists.* San Francisco: Freeman.

Further Reading

Brasier, M.D. 1980. *Microfossils.* London and Boston: Allen and Unwin.

Conkins, J.E., and B.M. Conkins. 1977. North American primitive Paleozoic Charophytes and descendants. *In* R.C. Romans (ed.), *Geobotany.* New York: Plenum.

Johnson, J.H. 1961. *Limestone-Building Algae and Algal Limestones.* Golden: Colorado School of Mines.

Lipps, J.H. (ed.). 1987. *Fossil Procaryotes and Protists: Notes for a Short Course.* University of Tennessee, Department of Geological Sciences, Studies in Geology 18. Knoxville: University of Tennessee, Department of Geological Sciences.

SKELETIZED MICROORGANISMS: PROTOZOANS AND CHITOZOANS

The world of living organisms is divided into two basic groups—prokaryotes and eukaryotes. Prokaryotes, sometimes called monerans, are the bacteria and archaeans; their cells do not have internal membranes and their DNA is not enclosed within a nucleus. In contrast, the eukaryotes have both internal membranes and DNA enclosed within a nucleus. The eukaryotes include four kingdoms: Plantae, Animalia, Fungi, and Protista.

Kingdom Protista includes most of the single-celled eukaryotes, and in fact most protists are single-celled. However, some are multicellular, such as some species of "algal" protists (the brown algae and some of the red and green algae). These protists have structural organizations comparable in many ways to that of sponges or even plants, where some individual cells become specialized to perform only certain functions. Essentially, then, the protists are a heterogeneous group consisting of all the eukaryotes that do not belong to one of the other three eukaryotic kingdoms.

Scholars still know relatively little about the evolutionary relationships of protist groups, and so they do not yet agree on a single formal classification. Because of this, many scholars still use a traditional classification based on ecology (lifestyle) that divides the protists into three groups according to the way in which they obtain food. First, a large number of phyla have plastids, internal structures enabling them to produce their own food from water and sunlight using chlorophyll; such organisms are called photosynthetic autotrophs. Second, there are many phyla and classes that lack chlorophyll, such as amoebas and ciliates; such organisms, called heterotrophs, consume other organisms for food. Third, a whole range of others survive by living in concert with other organisms (symbiosis). Often such symbionts may have been ingested, they may have entered as infections, or they may be permanent partners. They may also be parasitic, disease-producing organisms.

Then there are those phyla, species, and genera that are both autotrophs and heterotrophs. These protists commonly switch feeding modes as they move from photic (sunlit) to non-photic (dark) environments or change from one life cycle stage to another. (An example would be ocean organisms that spend some time in waters shallow enough to receive filtered sunlight and others in deep dark waters far from the surface.)

To complicate the interpretation of protistan systematic relationships, at different times in the past, some protists have been infected by monerans and other protists, such as dinoflagellates, or have ingested them, some of which have become established in the host's cytoplasm and are passed on from one generation to the next. Many ingested or infectious protists contribute photosynthetic capabilities; this has led to elaborate symbiotic relations and specialization of life cycles of both the hosts and symbionts. Several of the protists' morphological (structural), cytological (cell characteristics), nutritional, and life cycle features have been used in attempts to organize them into a "natural" classification—one based upon common ancestors—with somewhat ambiguous results.

A large number of protists secrete mineralized tests (or skeletons), which are preserved in the fossil record (Figure 1). In gen-

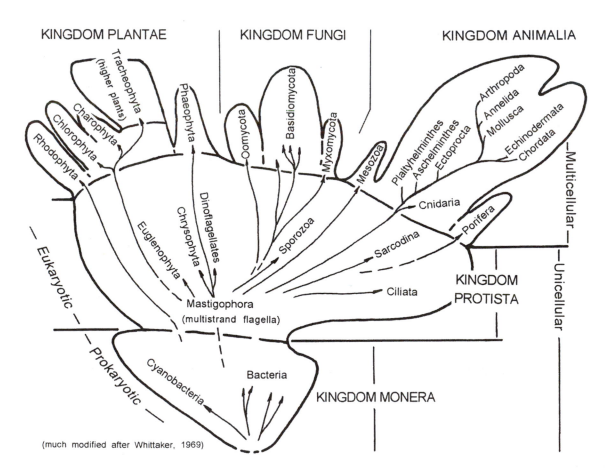

Figure 1. Phylogenetic relations of major groups of protistans and their relationship to multicellular kingdoms. *Left,* includes many protista that contain photosynthetic capabilities. *Right,* includes many protista that either lack photosynthetic capabilities or have acquired photosynthetic symbionts. Modified with permission from Whittaker (1969). Copyright © 1969 American Association for the Advancement of Science.

eral, protists are small and easily altered by diagenesis (shifting and rearrangement) of sediments. As a result, these organisms are not preserved or are preserved very poorly in rocks older than Ordovician. It is assumed that most protistan lineages originated much earlier, at least as early as about the beginning of the Late Precambrian (approximately 1.5 billion years ago). Simple green algae appear in the Late Precambrian (900 million years ago), and red algae appear about 700 million years ago (and possibly as early as 1.1 billion years ago). The first records of two rare groups, foraminifers and radiolarians, are preserved in Late Cambrian sediments (510 million years ago). During this long period of time, protists diverged into distinctive, major lineages. Major protistan lineages that secrete skeletized tests appear to have been in existence since the Cambrian.

Phylum Ciliophora

Class Ciliata, Including Tintinnids and Calpionellids

The ciliophores include those protists that are characterized by having large areas of their outer surface (pellicle) covered with cilia. Cilia are small hairlike structures that are grouped together (in some, they are physically connected) in patterns that allow the cilia to function together so that they produce waves of motion that generate water currents. These currents propel the cell and also create vortices (whirlpool-like water currents) that aid in capturing food, usually other small organisms. Freshwater *Paramecium* and *Stentor* are two well-studied ciliates that are illustrated in many introductory textbooks.

The Suborder Tintinnina of the Order Spirotrichida has a sketchy and not continuous fossil record from the Ordovician to the Recent. Figure 2 illustrates a Recent tintinnid in cross section, showing its various structures. Tintinnids are complex ciliated protists and have a crown of membranelles (small membranes) in addition to rows of cilia. When extended from a protective, sleevelike structure called the lorica, the membranelles aid in swimming and the cilia aid in directing food into the buccal cavity (mouth area) and then to the mouth itself. The tintinnid swims with the caudal appendix (tail structure) pointing forward. Food is typically bacteria and unicellular algae (including green algae, coccolithophores, and dinoflagellates). Two types of cell nucleus are present: a macronucleus, which controls the daily needs of the organism; and one or more micronuclei, which are involved in its reproductive activities. Similar structures are found in *Paramecium* and *Stentor.*

Tintinnids, many of which are widely distributed as marine motile plankton, comprise nearly 40 percent of the known ciliates. They live in a protective lorica (Figure 2). Many form an agglutinated lorica, which they construct by incorporating very fine sand- and silt-size grains (usually derived from the tests of other microorganisms) in their chitin lorica. (That is, the lorica is constructed of a tough, fibrous protein similar to the chitin coating of insects.) The lorica is commonly flexible and is generally elongate and bell-shaped, with an opening, or "aperture," at one end and a closed, pointed to rounded opposite end. Most are 100 to 200 micrometers long, but some are as small as 25 micrometers and others reach 1,000 micrometers. Because most tests are

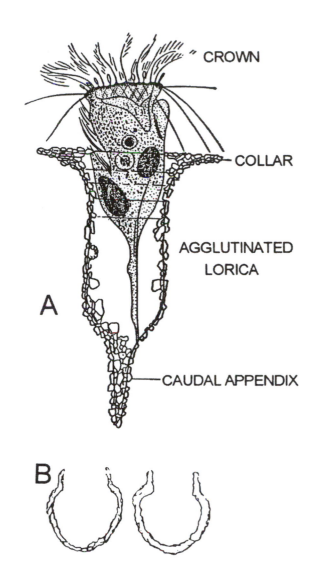

Figure 2. Class Ciliophora: tintinnids and calpionellids: *A*, Recent *Tintinnopsis*; *B*, thin section views of *Calpionella*. Modified from Rauzer-Chernousova and Fursenko (1959).

organic, they are destroyed easily after the death of the individual, so, except for the calpionellids, tintinninids commonly are not preserved.

The Family Calpionellidae (Late Jurassic–Early Cretaceous) had a lorica composed of calcareous (calcium-based) grains that were held together with both calcareous and organic cements. Calpionellids have left an extensive and biostratigraphically useful fossil record (a group of fossils that is used to date rock strata) in deeper water limestone deposits from the later part of the Jurassic through the Mid-Cretaceous. Calpionellids were abundant plankton in warm tropical and subtropical oceans. After the Mid-Cretaceous, their sharp reduction in numbers and distribution probably permitted the great expansion of their principal food supply, the coccolithophores, which, in the later part of the Cretaceous, were responsible for extensive chalk deposits.

Although most scientists who study calpionellids consider them to be a family that is part of the tintinnids, several scholars have considered that their calcareous loricate wall was primary and secreted by the organism. Because such a wall composition is unlike that of any walls in Recent tintinnids, these scholars did not consider the calpionellids to belong to the tintinnids or the ciliates.

Phylum Sarcodina (Foraminifers, Radiolarians, and Heliozoans)

Class Actinopoda: Acantharia and Radiolaria

Acantharians and Radiolarians (Figures 3, 4, and 5) are small, single-celled marine plankton that are 100 to 2,000 micrometers in diameter. In these protists, a porous organic membrane separates the cytoplasm into an inner endoplasm and an outer ectoplasm. The endoplasm contains the nucleus and gives rise to long, thin rays of cytoplasm ("axopoda") that radiate outward through the ectoplasm for feeding. These rays usually have stiffened central fibers. The ectoplasm includes a foam of fatty and gaseous vacuoles. The vacuoles (small cavities) are digestive structures and aid in maintaining bouyancy. Those radiolarians living in the photic zone also may have incorporated another organism, the yellowish photosymbiotic dinoflagellate gymnodinioids (zooxanthellae), in the ectoplasm.

Of particular interest to paleontologists, radiolarians have an internal skeleton of opaline silica, organic-rich opal, or, in the acantharians, strontium sulfate. As they descend through the water column from the photic zone to the ocean floor, the opaline siliceous skeletons are less susceptible to dissolution than the strontium sulfate and organic-rich opal radiolarian skeletons and are considerably less susceptible to dissolution than the calcareous plankton tests. Consequently, the deeper parts of the ocean floors typically have a high percentage of radiolarians and, beneath areas of ocean upwelling and high radiolarian productivity, deposits of radiolarian oozes. Radiolarians are most abundant in tropical warm waters, although some are present in cooler waters of higher latitudes, where they compete with another group, the much more abundant cool-water diatoms. Radiolarians are dependent upon the supply of resources, so the opaline orders compete with diatoms for dissolved silica. Radiolarian population densities fluctuate with the seasonal availability of nutrients. They also divide their planktonic habitats according to ocean water masses (and thus by depth), so that the fossilized species that accumulate together on the ocean floor originally lived at different water-depth levels.

The Subclass Radiolaria (Cambrian to Recent) is divided into three orders. The orders Spumellaria and Nassellaria (Figure 4) have substantial opaline skeletons and comprise most of the fossils. Spumellaria (Cambrian to Recent) have spherical or disk-shaped geometries with latticelike construction. Concentric,

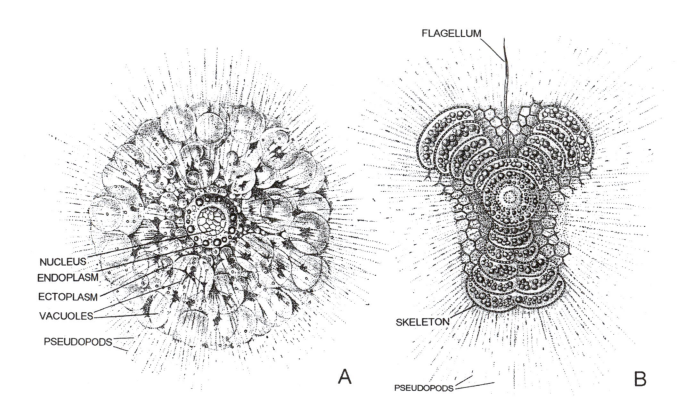

Figure 3. Phylum Sarcodina, Class Actinopoda; an example of the recent Spumellaria genera, A, Thalassophysa; B, Euchitonia. Modified from Rauzer-Chernousova and Fursenko (1959).

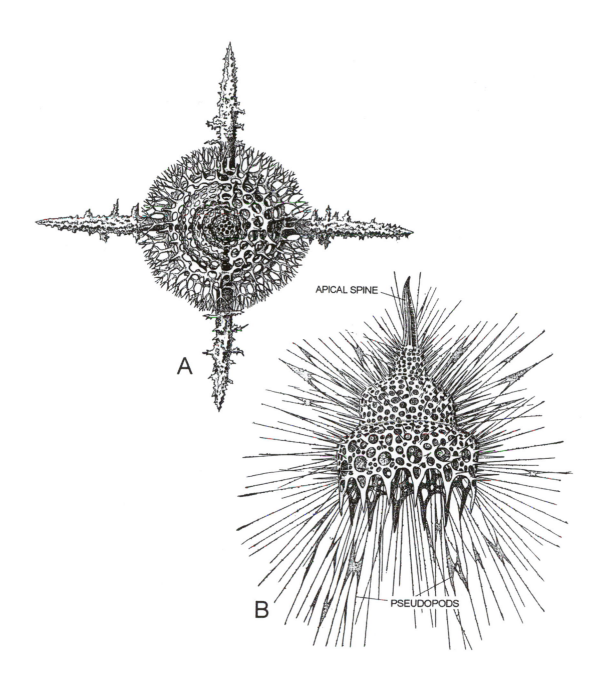

Figure 4. Phylum Sarcodina, Class Actinopoda; Subclass Radiolaria: Skeleton of *A,* Spumellaria genus Staurcarium; *B,* Nassellaria genus Calocyclas. Modified from Rauzer-Chernousova and Fursenko (1959).

spherical skeletons with large and small spines are common but are not the only shapes found in the spumellarines. Nassellaria (Miocene to Recent) have latticelike skeletons. These are usually an expanding envelope that starts with an apical horn and grows around an axis of symmetry. One end may have an aperture.

The order Phaeodaria (Miocene to Recent) have skeletons that are composed of mostly organic material, with only a minor amount of opal as reinforcement. As a result they are not common fossils, and only a few are known from the Miocene to Recent.

Fossils of the Subclass Actinopoda are classified on their skeletal composition and geometric features (Figure 5). The Sub-

class Acantharia (Eocene to Recent) have skeletons composed of strontium sulfate and 20 spines that radiate from a center, having a fourfold symmetry in five planes. These spines generally separate when the organism dies.

Class Heliozoa

Freshwater heliozoans (Pleistocene to Recent) have several similarities to radiolarians. Their cytoplasm, however, is not subdivided by a central capsule membrane. The skeleton is a spherical organic chitinous latticework having only minor opaline strengthening.

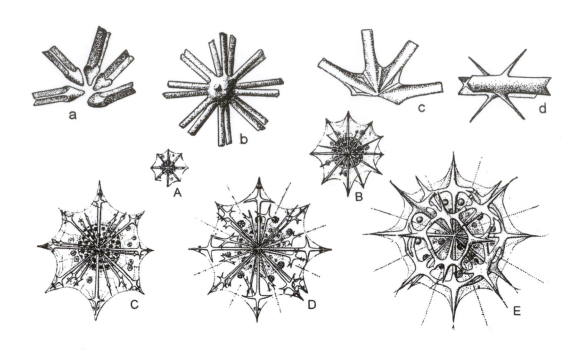

Figure 5. Phylum Sarcodina, Class Actinopoda; Subclass Acantharia. Different stages of development in Pleuraspis. Modified from Rauzer-Chernousova and Fursenko (1959).

Some species can include opaline frustules and spicules (spike-shaped pieces) of other organisms in their walls, but these are poorly cemented to the skeleton and disintegrate upon death.

Class Foraminifera

Foraminifera, which live in marine and brackish waters, are shelled unicells that have streaming pseudopods (long extensions of cytoplasm). Foraminifera have a wide range of sizes, from 100 micrometers to more than 10 centimeters, and are adapted to a wide range of marine habitats. A major part of the marine plankton belongs to this group, as do a variety of encrusting forms, many vagrant benthos (bottom) feeders, and a great diversity of specialized sediment infaunal feeders (those that search for food in the sediment along the bottom). In the marine and benthic photic zones, many foraminifers contain abundant photosynthetic symbionts—either the symbionts have infected the foraminifers or the foraminifers actively have searched out the symbionts and ingested them. They use their pseudopods to capture food, to aid in bouyancy, to aid in adhesion to the substrate (the surface to which they are attached, e.g., seafloor or rocky shelf), to drag the test along on the substrate, or to dig and burrow through the substrate. Foraminifers make use of a great range of foods, including bacteria, other protists, and small invertebrates.

Foraminifers construct resistant tests that are preserved in the stratigraphic record. Although scholars know a great deal about the composition and geometry of foraminiferal tests, we have detailed information about the life cycle of only about a dozen living species. Studies of these groups indicate that many foraminifers are characterized by a life cycle including two distinct stages: One is an asexually produced stage (the gamont), which is haploid (one set of chromosomes per nucleus) and uninucleate (one nucleus per cell); the other is a sexually produced generation (the agamont), which is diploid (two sets of chromosomes per nucleus) and multinucleate (many nuclei per cell) (Figure 6). Many foraminifers repeat the asexual generations several times before undergoing a sexual generation. This "alternation of generations" commonly is visible in that a single species will have one type of test in the asexual generation and another type of test in the sexual generation. The asexually formed generations have a large, or megalospheric, proloculus (attachment structure), but the total size of the entire test is smaller. The sexually formed generation has a much smaller, microspheric proloculus but the total size of the entire test is larger. In a number of species, one or more large brood chambers are formed just before the progeny abandon the parental shell. Much remains to be learned about the biology, functional morphology, nutrition, and microstructure of living foraminifers.

Foraminifers have been largely the domain of micropaleontologists because of extensive studies to determine stratigraphic ages and interpret paleoecological conditions. The classification of foraminifers is based on the composition and geometry of the tests. Current classifications place greatest emphasis on the composition and construction of the test wall. Next in importance is the form and geometry of the tests, then the type and geometry of chambers, followed by number and type of apertures and other openings, external and internal structures in the test, and finally ornamentation. Many foraminifers are studied as whole tests washed from sands and shales, others are concentrated in acid resi-

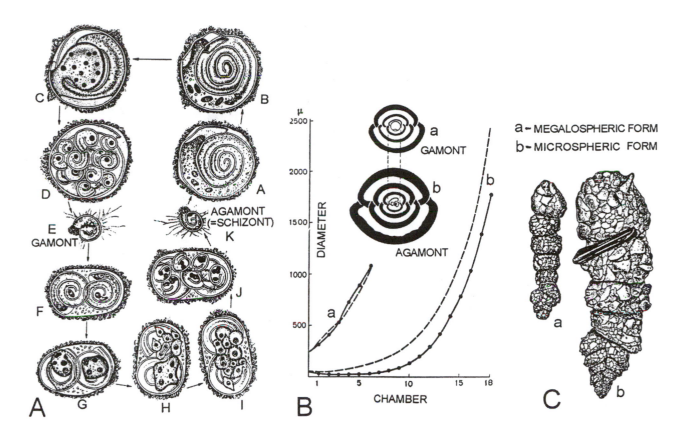

Figure 6. Phylum Sarcodina, Class Foraminifera. *A*, details of the alternation of generations in Spirillina vivipara, showing the gamont, which produces gametes, and the agamont (or schizont), which does not; *B*, microspheric and megalospheric individuals of the miliolinid Pyrgo bradyi; *C*, microspheric and megalospheric individuals of textulariid Bigenerina. Modified from Rauzer-Chernousova and Fursenko (1959).

dues, and still others are studied in rock thin sections where they are viewed in cross sections.

As a result of such careful study, scholars now recognize fifteen orders. Eight first appear in the Paleozoic, of which two became extinct at the end of the Permian and another became extinct during the Triassic. Four orders appear in the Triassic, one in the Jurassic, and two in the Cenozoic, all of which continue into the Recent.

Foraminifers in the Order Allogromiida (Cambrian to Recent) have a flexible, thin tectin wall. This wall of uncertain composition is probably protein-based (proteinaceous) or pseudochitinous (material similar to chitin). In other orders, a similar organic wall lines the interior of the test, separating the outer wall layers from the protoplasm of the organism. In many allogromoids, the exterior of the pseudochitinous wall may have scattered grains of loosely attached sand or silt from the surrounding substrate. Most are unilocular (have only one chamber), and some have minor surface ornamentation. Three orders include those with strongly agglutinated tests: the Astrorhizida, Parathurammida, and Ammodiscida. The Order Astrorhizida (Cambrian?, Ordovician to Recent) are foraminifers with a thick, well-cemented layer of sand (including calcareous sand) and other grains that are embedded into the test wall (Figure 7). These

orders include many saclike spheres with labrynthic internal construction, and even more numerous, irregular tubular and multitubular forms. Free-living or attached members with generally similar features are common.

The Order Parathurammida (Cambrian to Permian) include saclike forms that may have multiple apertures, spines, and, in some, two-layered agglutinated and, perhaps in part, a precipitated wall layer (Figure 7). More complex foraminifers in this order are elongate forms that grow from a clearly identifiable proloculus and have a single aperture. Gradually, through the Late Silurian, Devonian, and Mississippian, these complex forms evolved uniserial protochambers and finally uniserial chambers in the test.

The Order Ammodiscida (Cambrian?, Silurian to Recent) (Figure 8) also began with early members having a proloculus followed by a tubular chamber coiled in one or more planes around the proloculus. Some are planicoiled (to form a flat plane, like the tube of a French horn) some become coiled irregularly around an axis, some are coiled along a vertical axis, others form a complex coiled ball, and still others become attached to a substrate and coil regularly and/or irregularly. More advanced members of the order develop chambers. Internal structures are important in some species. Many species change growth form and geometry as they grow and develop.

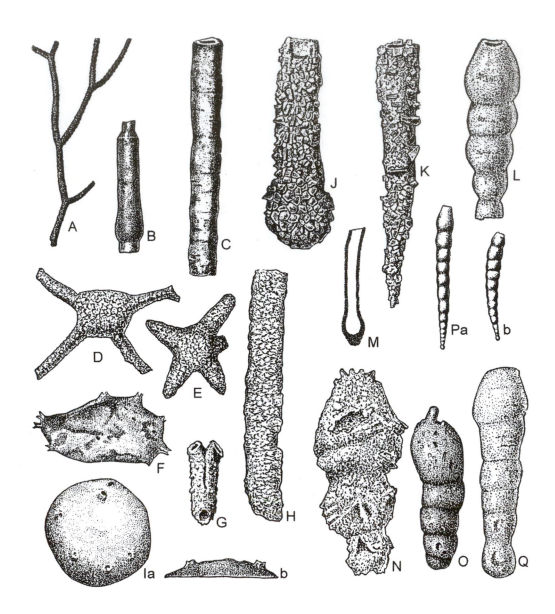

Figure 7. Representatives of the Orders Astrorhizida and Parathurammida. Astrorhizida: *A,* Rhizammina; *B* and *C,* Bathysiphon; *D,* Astrorhiza; *E,* Pseudoastrorhiza; *F* and *G,* Rhaddammina; *H,* Ordovicina; *I,* Archaeochitinia. Parathurammida: *J,* Hyperammina; *K,* Jaculella; *L,* Hyperamminoides; *M,* Earlandia; *N,* Reophax; *O,* Hormosina; *P,* Nodosinella; *Q,* Nodellum. Modified from Rauzer-Chernousova and Fursenko (1959).

Most of the remaining foraminiferal orders have calcareous (calcium-based) walls of one type or another. The simplest of these calcareous walls is in the Order Miliolida (Upper Devonian to Recent) (Figure 9). In their simplest configuration, the walls are comprised of an inner single tilelike layer of flat calcium carbonate plates with a rhombohedral shape. They are oriented flat against the wall. Then there is a thicker layer of randomly oriented calcium carbonate plates and needles scattered in an organic layer of pseudochitin, and an outer single layer of tilelike, flat, calcium carbonate rhombohedral plates oriented flat against the outside of the wall. A pseudochitinous inner lining may be present. In reflected light, these walls look like miniature porcelain china, hence the name porcelaneous wall. In thin sections, these walls are yellowish

amber in color because of the relatively large amount of pseudotectin present in the wall and the random orientation of the calcium carbonate in the thick middle layer. In some, the wall may include some adventitious grains.

Early free-living miliolids have a proloculus around which coils the succeeding tubular, undivided chamber. In some, the coiling is planispiral, but in others it is regular but does not follow the same plane of coiling. Still others are attached and irregularly coiled and shaped. In more advanced miliolids, additional chambers are added, making the geometry of the coiling patterns more complex. One common miliolid pattern has elongate chambers that are one-half coil in length and arranged in varying planes around the proloculus.

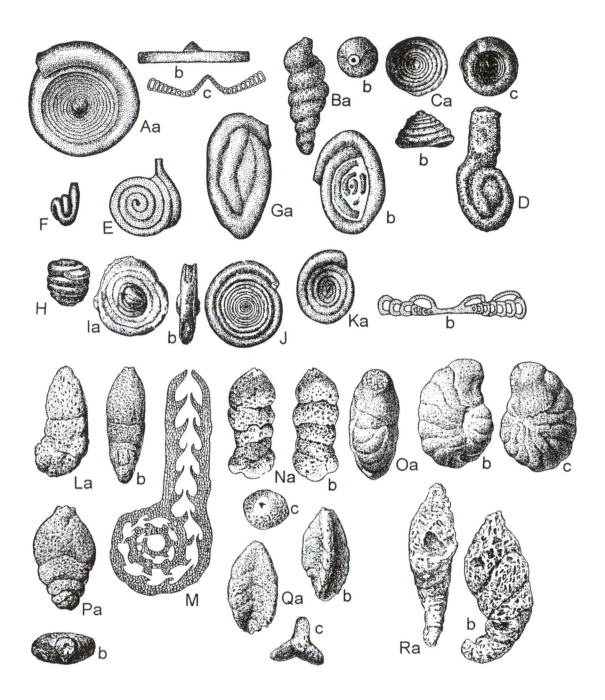

Figure 8. Representatives of the Order Ammodiscida: *Aa–c*, Ammodiscus; *Ba–b*, Turrritellella; *Ca–c*, Arenoturrispirillina; *D*, Lituotuba; *E*, Bifurcammina; *F*, Thalmannina; *Ga–b*, Agathammina; *H*, Glomospira; *Ia–b*, Glomospirella; *J*, Ammodiscus; *K*, Hemidiscus; *L* and *M*, Ammobaculites; *Na–c*, Haplophragmium; *Oa–c*, Lituola; *Pa–b*, Flabellammina; *Qa–c*, Triplasia; *R–b*, Ammotium. Modified from Rauzer-Chernousova and Fursenko (1959).

Some large members of the order have chambers added in near-annular and annular (ring-shaped) patterns. In these genera, chambers are commonly subdivided by internal partitions to form chamberlets, and the outer wall may have multiple apertures. Most tests are disk-shaped, and their outer walls are relatively thin and transparent. These large milioiids are mostly shallow water benthos (live in the ocean floor in shallow water), and typically contain abundant photosynthetic symbionts. A few Late Creta-

ceous and Cenozoic large milioiids are fusiform (have a body tapered at both ends).

The Order Silicoloculinida (Miocene to Recent) (Figure 10) include a small group of foraminifers that are chambered and coiled much like some of the milioloids. However, the silicolocu-linids secrete an imperforate test composed of opaline silica.

Two extinct foraminiferal orders, Endothyrida and Fusulin-ida, have microgranular calcite walls (a few have calcitic fibrous

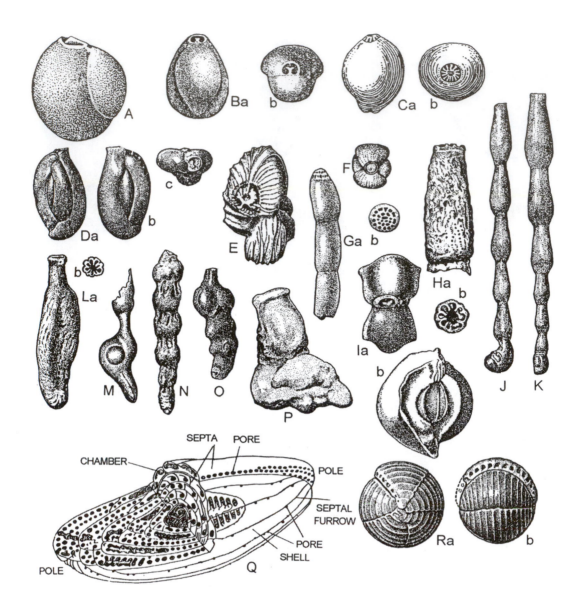

Figure 9. Representatives of the Order Miliolida: *A, Ba, b,* Pyrgo; *Ca, b,* Idalina; *Da–c,* Quinqueloculina; *E,* Cribrolinoides; *F,* Miliola; *Ga, b,* Poroarticulina; *Ha, b, L, M,* Dogielina; *Ia, b,* Flintia; *J, K,* Articulina; *N,* Sarmatiella; *O, P,* Meandroloculina; *Q,* Praealveolina; *Ra, b,* Borelis. Modified from Rauzer-Chernousova and Fursenko (1959).

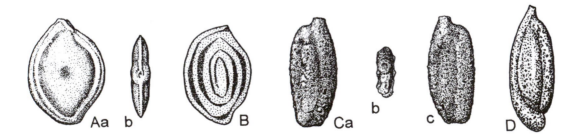

Figure 10. Representative of the Order Silicoloculinida. *Aa, b* and *B,* Rzehakina; *C* and *D,* Miliammina. Modified from Rauzer-Chernousova and Fursenko (1959).

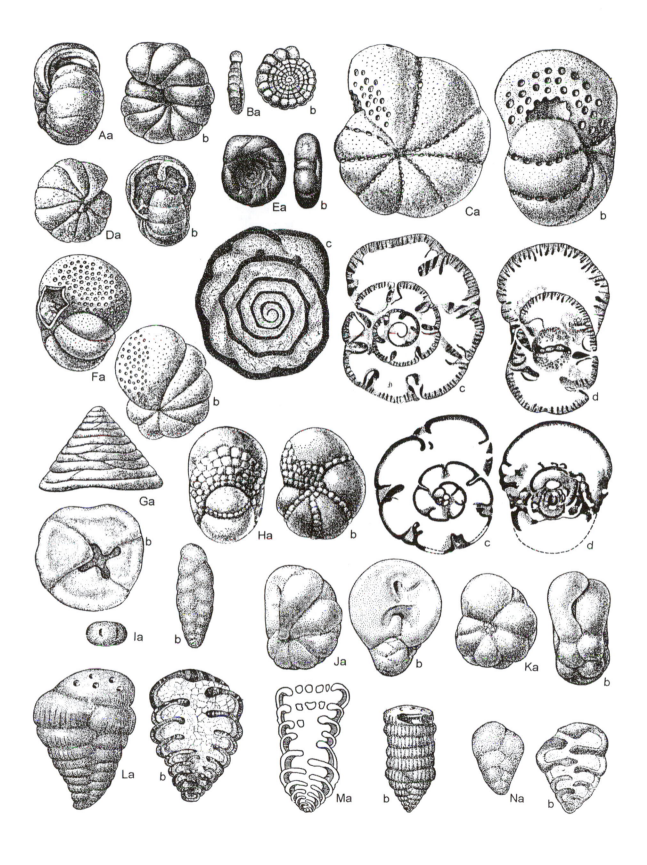

Figure 11. Representatives of the Order Endothyrida. *Aa–b,* Globoendothyra; *Ba–b,* Loeblichia; *Ca–d,* Bradyina; *Da–b,* Endothyranopsis; *Ea–c,* Carbonella; *Fa–b,* Cribospira; *Ga–b,* Tetrataxis; *Ha–d,* Janischewskina; *Ia–b,* Deckerellina; *Ja–b,* Globivalvulina; *Ka–b,* Biseriammina; *La–b,* Cribrostomum; *Ma–b,* Climacammina; *Na–b,* Palaeotextularia.

walls). Endothyrida (Ordovician to Triassic) (Figure 11) commonly have two-layered walls that have fine perforations. Primitive members may have some arenaceous (an alternative calcium compound) material included in the wall. The test chambers are hemispherical, tubular, trochospiral (curved), irregularly coiled, biserial, or uniserial. In some biserial and uniserial endothyrids, the wall has a microgranular outer layer and fibrous calcite inner layer. In the Late Devonian, important members became planispiralled and streptospiralled (spiralled in a twisted manner), and developed chambers along with many distinctive internal structures.

Fusulinida (Late Mississippian to end of Permian) (Figures 12 and 13) became the giants of the Late Paleozoic foraminiferal world, some reaching 10 centimeters or more in length. Early fusulinids included small disk-shaped, planispiralled members. Progressively these expanded along the axis of coiling to form fusiform tests that outwardly look similar to grains of wheat or barley. Some became globular and subspherical; a few were possibly free-floating or planktonic. Their wall structure is layered and consists of 2 types of calcite: one that is darker (owing to a greater content of organic material) and another that is lighter, nearly transparent material. In one family that lived in habitats with shallow, warm water (perhaps slightly hypersaline, i.e., having a high level of salt content), the calcite walls may have a glassy radial fibrous wall structure. In another shallow, warm-water family, the wall is consistently recrystallized to sparry calcite, suggesting these fusulinids originally had a calcite wall with a high level of magnesium. Many of the Late Pennsylvanian and Permian families have relatively thin outer walls, with a "honeycomb" (alveolar) structure that may have been an adaptation to housing photosymbionts. Many other internal test features are used in identification of different families, genera, and species.

The Order Lagenida (Devonian to Recent) (Figure 14) have walls with an organic inner wall (or lining) and an outer wall of one or more clear calcite layers. In most, the calcite crystals are oriented radially, with axes aligned perpendicular to the outer surface of the wall. Early lagenids are composed of a proloculus followed by a single, long, straight or slightly curved second chamber. More advanced forms subdivide the part after the proloculus with constrictions, pseudochambers, true chambers, and even chamberlets. They even may have calcite laminations, or layers that were laid down after initial construction (secondarily).

The Order Involutinida (Triassic to Recent) (Figure 15) have a proloculus followed by an enrolled second chamber. The calcareous wall is perforate, and usually recrystallized to a homogeneous microstructure. Originally the wall was probably aragonite. Pillarlike structures are common in some members.

The Order Spirillinida (Triassic? Jurassic to Recent) (Figure 16) consist of a proloculus followed by an enrolled chamber, or a few chambers per whorl. Some chambers may be divided into chamberlets. The wall is calcite and usually is optically a single cyrstal.

The Order Robertinida (Middle Triassic to Recent) (Figure 17) have planispiral to trochospiral tests; their chambers have internal partitions. The wall is hyaline and perforate and is composed of crystals of aragonitic calcium carbonate oriented with their orthorhombic crystal c-axis perpendicular to the outer wall surface.

Two orders, the planktonic Order Globigerinida (Early Jurassic to Recent) (Figure 18) and the benthic Order Rotaliida (Triassic to Recent) (Figure 19), have hyaline calcite walls with fine pore systems. In the Globigerinida (Figure 18), the calcite optical c-axis is perpendicular to the test surface. Their walls are multilaminate as an additional layer of calcite is deposited with the addition of each new globose chamber. Globigerinids are plankton and extend to water depths of several hundred meters. Those living in the photic zone usually have symbiotic photosynthesizers living in their protoplasm. At the time of reproduction, additional calcite deposits may form on the surface.

The Rotaliida (Figure 19) have multichamber tests that are typically coiled and then become biserial or even uniserial in later growth stages. Some form crusts upon substrates (encrusting) and may form large masses. Chambers are simple to complex, commonly with internal partitions or chamberlets. One or more apertures may be highly specialized and modified. Often, the exterior surface of the wall is highly ornamented, apparently for different ecological adaptations. Rotaliids include a multitude of benthic foraminifers that have successfully subdivided that ecological habitat. These rotaliids have many different coiling patterns and test geometries. In tropical waters, many rotaliids become large and contain abundant photosymbionts. These large tropical foraminifers have been useful in subdividing and correlating Cenozoic carbonate strata.

The Order Carterinida (Eocene, Recent) (Figure 20) include a few foraminifers that have a trochospiral test covered with spined-shaped spicules that are loosely cemented in a chitinous wall. Each spicule is a single calcite crystal and is thought to be secreted by the foraminifer. These walls readily disintegrate. As a result, the caterinid fossil record is poorly preserved.

Chitozoans

Chitozoans (Figure 21) are fossil, flask-shaped, chitinoid, thick-walled vesicles (vessel-shaped structures) with a radial symmetry developed around a longitudinal axis. How they are related to other groups is unknown, and they are included with the protists for convenience. Most are about 150 to 250 micrometers long, although some are as small as 30 micrometers and others as large as 1500 micrometers. The body chamber is composed of two wall layers; usually it has a neck, a lip, and an operculum (cap that covers the opening). In most, the operculum lies near the base of the neck near the body chamber. Many simpler forms have only necks. The outer wall layer of the vesicle may be smooth, but most have some surface ornamentation. Some surfaces are rugose (wrinkled), others are striated or furrowed, and still others have processes that protrude from the outer surface. These protuberances may be hairlike (hispid), spinelike (often split into branches), sleevelike extensions of the basal ends, or other surface ornamentation.

Simple saclike forms (Simplexoperculati) may date back as far as the latest Precambrian. They do have a well-established fossil record in the Ordovician, Silurian, and Devonian (500 to 360 million years ago). Of these, the Desmochitinidae lack a neck and the operculum acts as a simple lid. Several individuals

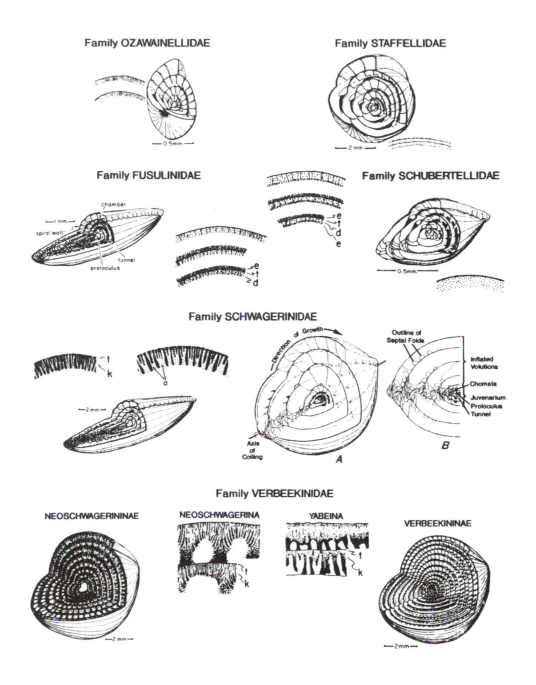

Figure 12. Three-dimensional sketches of representatives of the major families in the order Fusulinida and their typical wall structures. *A*, Ozawainella; *B*, Staffella; *C*, Fusulina; *D*, Schubertella; *E*, Schwagerina (Pseudofusulina); *F*, Pseudoschwagerina; *G*, Neoschwagerina; *H*, Verbeekina. From Ross et al. (1997).

may be clustered together or form chainlike arrangements. They are cemented to one another, usually by the attachment of a vesicle to the operculum of another vesicle. In the Conochitinidae, the operculum is located near the base of a well-developed neck, which may be extended and shaped in various ways. Many groups of simplexoperculate chitozoans became extinct after the Silurian.

More complex forms (Complexoperculati) appear successively through the Ordovician. The Sphaerochitinidae have a cylindrical flange attached to the base of the operculum and a short tube above it. Other complexoperculates (Tanuchitinidae) have more complex apertures, a longer tube above the operculum, and an outer-wall sleeve that projects as a tube around a structure formed from the inner wall (copula). Spine-bearing complexoperculate chitozoans are common in the Silurian and Early and Middle Devonian. Most complexoperculates became extinct after the Middle Devonian, and only a few survived beyond the Devonian. Only a few chitinozoans are reported from beds of Carboniferous and Permian age (360 to 250 million years ago).

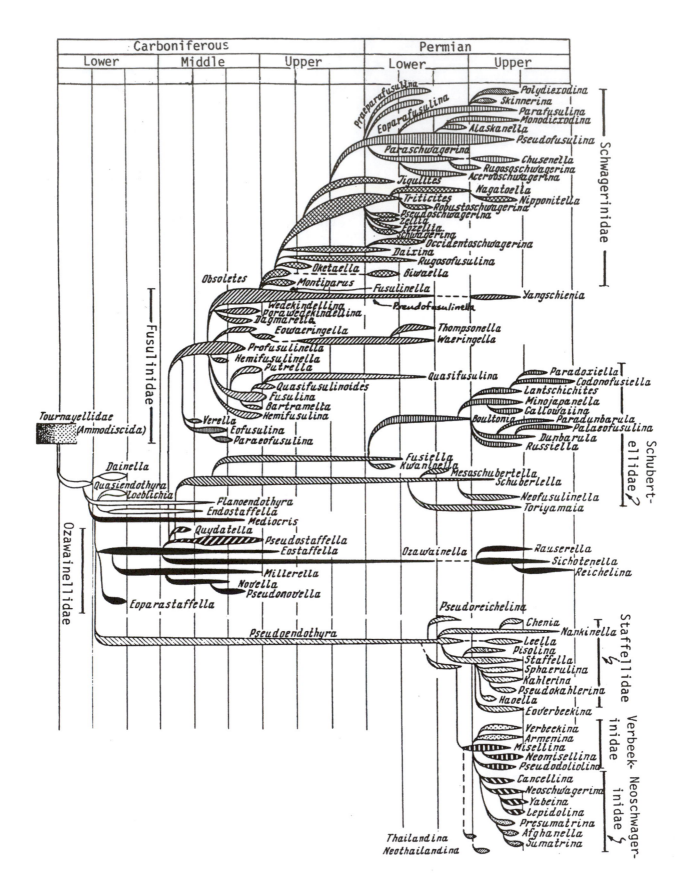

Figure 13. Phylogenetic tree of major genera of Fusulinida illustrating their utility in subdividing the Carboniferous and Permian carbonate successions. From Ross et al. (1997), modified from Rozovskaya (1975).

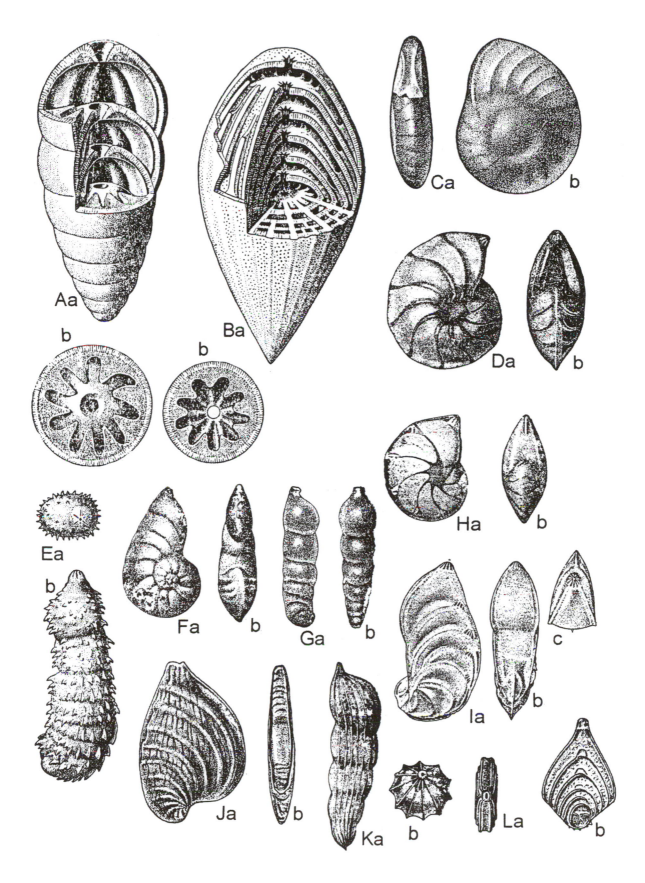

Figure 14. Representative of the Order Lagenida. *Aa–b,* Multiseptida; *Ba–b,* Colaniella; *Ca–b,* Nanicella; *Da–b,* Lenticulina; *Ea–b,* Marginulinopsis; *Fa–b,* Hemicrestellaria; *Ga–b* and *Ka–b,* Marginulina; *Ha–b,* Robulus; *I,* Saracenaria; *J,* Planularia; *La–c,* Neoflabellina. From Rauzer-Chernousova and Fursenko (1959).

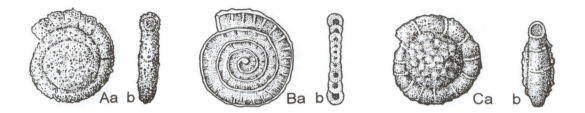

Figure 15. Representative of the Order Involutinida. *Aa–b*, Silicina; *Ba–b*, Involutina; *Ca–b*, Problematica. From Rauzer-Chernousova and Fursenko (1959).

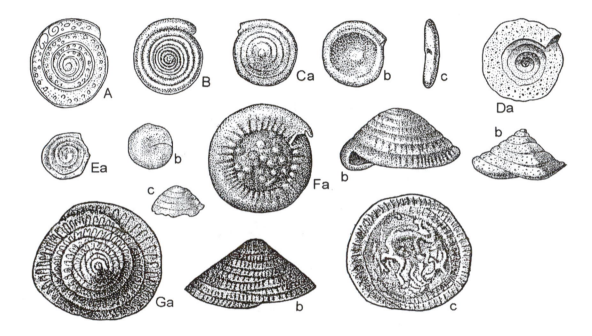

Figure 16. Representatives of the Order Spirillinida. *A* and *Ba–b*, Spirillina; *Ca–b* and *Da–b*, Turrispirillina; *Ea–c*, Conicospirillina; *Fa–c*, Trocholina; *Ga–c*, Patellina. From Rauzer-Chernousova and Fursenko (1959).

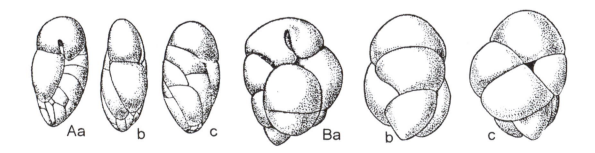

Figure 17. Representatives of the Order Robertinida. *Aa–c*, Robertina; *Ba–c*, Robertinoides. From Rauzer-Chernousova and Fursenko (1959).

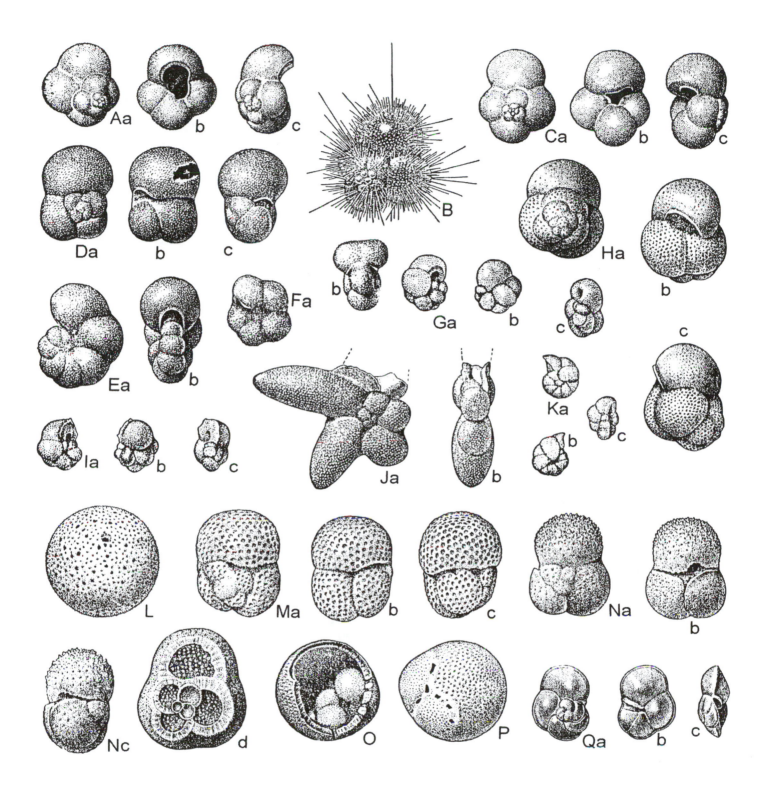

Figure 18. Representatives of the order Globigerinida (living specimen), *Ca* and *Da–c,* Globigerina; *Ea–b,* Globigerinella; *Fa–b,* Biglobigerinella; *Ga–c,* Cassigerinella; *Ha–c, Ia–c,* and *Ka–c,* Globigerinoides; *Ja–b,* Hasterigerinella; *L,* Orbulina; *Ma–c* and *Na–d,* Sphaeroidinella; *O* and *P,* Candorbulina; *Qa–c,* Globorotalia. From Rauzer-Chernousova and Fursenko (1959).

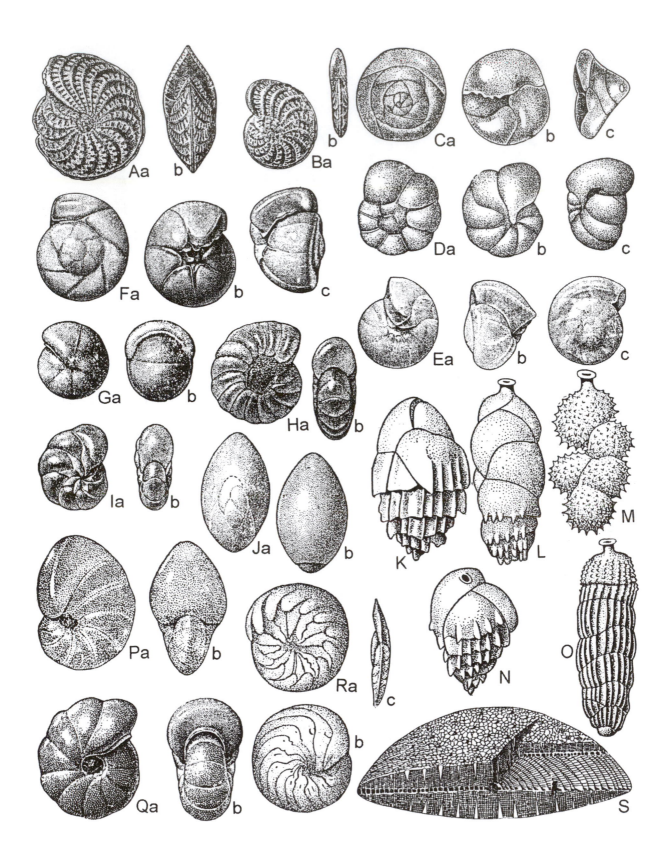

Figure 19. Representatives of the Order Rotaliida. *Aa–b* and *Ba–b,* Elphidium; *Ca–c,* Discorbis; *Da–c,* Valvulineria; *Ea–c,* Gyroidina; *Fa–c,* Gyroidinoides; *Ga–b,* Pullenia; *Ha–b,* Nonion; *Ia–b,* Astrononion; *Ja–b,* Chilostomella; *K, N,* Bulimina; *L, M,* Uvigerina; *O,* Rectuvigerina; *Pa–b,* Nonionella; *Qa–b,* Melonis; *Ra–c,* Amphistegina; *S,* Discocyclina. From Rauzer-Chernousova and Fursenko (1959).

Figure 20. Representative of the Order Carterinida, Carterina. Coiling pattern and development of partitions within chambers are shown as well as a part of the surface composed of minute calcareous spindles.

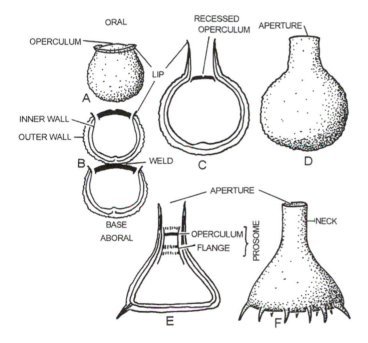

Figure 21. Chitozoans. Examples of: *A, B,* Desmochitina (simplexoperculates); *C, D,* Lagenochitina (simplexoperculates); *E, F,* complexoperculates, Ancyrochitina. Redrawn from Brasier (1980).

The wide distribution of chitozoans in many types of marine sediments suggests they were part of the plankton, living either as free-swimming organisms or attached to floating organisms and debris. Their chitinoid test is very resistant to diagenetic processes in rock cementation and to alteration. They are extracted from rock using techniques developed for extracting fossilized spores from rock.

The affinities of chitozoans remain uncertain. Their chitinoid tests and size suggest some similarities with allogromiinid foraminifers. Budding and secondary thickening of the wall lend support to a protistan affinity. On the other hand, their complexity suggests a possible metazoan (animal) affinity, and different authors have suggested that chitozoans may have been the egg cases of polychaetes, graptolites, or even molluscs. For each of these suggestions, other features cast doubt on such interpretations. Their morphological diversity leaves open the question that chitozoans may be an artificial grouping of disparate organisms.

CHARLES A. ROSS

See also Algae; Microbial Fossils, Precambrian; Problematic Animals; Reefs and Reef-Building Organisms; Skeletized Microorganisms: Algae

Works Cited

Brasier, M.D. 1980. *Microfossils.* London: Allen and Unwin; 3rd ed., London and New York: Chapman and Hall, 1992.

Rauzer-Chernousova, D.M., and A.V. Fursenko. 1959. *Obščaja cast?: Prostejšie.* Osnovy paleontologii 1. Moscow: Akademii Nauk SSSR.

Ross, C.A., J.R.P. Ross, and P.L. Brenckle (eds.). 1997. *Late Paleozoic Foraminifera: Their Biostratigraphy, Evolution, and Paleoecology and the Mid-Carbiniferous Boundary.* Special Publication, 36. Cambridge, Massachusetts: Cushman Foundation for Foraminiferal Research.

Rozovskaya, S.E. 1975. *Composition, Systematics and Phylogeny of the Orders Fusulinida.* Akademia Nauk SSSR, Novosibirsk Nauka Sibirskoe otdelenie, Trudy Instituta Geologii i Geophisiki, vypuck 745. Moscow: Akademii Nauk SSSR.

Whittaker, R.H. 1969. New concepts of kingdoms or organimism. *Science* 163:150–60.

Further Reading

Boltovskoy, E. and R. Wright. 1976. *Recent Foraminifera.* The Hague: Junk; as *Los foraminiferos recientes,* Buenos Aires: Eudeba, 1965.

Brasier, M.D. 1980. *Microfossils.* London: Allen and Unwin; 3rd ed., London and New York: Chapman and Hall, 1992.

Grell, K. 1973. *Protozoology.* New York: Springer-Verlag; as *Protozoologie,* Berlin: Springer-Verlag, 1956.

Hayes, J.R. 1981. *Foraminifera.* New York: Wiley; London: Macmillan.

Lipps, J.H. (ed.). 1987. *Fossil Prokaryotes and Protists, Notes for a Short Course.* Department of Geological Sciences, Studies in Geology 18. Knoxville: University of Tennessee.

Lipps, J.H. (ed.). 1993. *Fossil Prokaryotes and Protists.* Boston: Blackwell Scientific Publications.

Loeblich, A.R., and H. Tappan. 1987. *Foraminiferal Genera and Their Classification.* 2 vols. New York: Van Nostrand Reinhold.

Moore, R.C. (ed.). 1954. *Treatise on Invertebrate Paleontology.* Part D, *Protista 3, Protozea (Chiefly Radiolaria and Tintinnina).* Lawrence: University of Kansas Press; Boulder, Colorado: Geological Society of America.

Phleger, F.B. 1960. *Ecology and Distribution of Recent Foraminifera.* Baltimore, Maryland: Johns Hopkins University Press.

SKELETIZED ORGANISMS AND THE EVOLUTION OF SKELETIZED TISSUES

Skeletized tissues are tissues reinforced by structural materials. Although the uses of skeletons vary widely (e.g., protection, support, locomotion, feeding), the basic functions of skeletization are to make the tissue stiffer (less prone to deformation), tougher (less prone to tearing), or harder (less susceptible to abrasion). These attributes also tend to make skeletons readily fossilizable (soft tissue does not fossilize well—if at all) so that the fossil record is biased heavily toward skeletized tissues.

Scholars often make a distinction between organic and mineralized skeletons, but all skeletons contain some measure of organic material. Structural proteins, such as collagen and keratin, give resilience to purely organic tissues, but collagen also forms the organic groundmass (fine-grained base) of most mineralized skeletons (those embedded with substances such as calcium). Fibrous polysaccharides, such as chitin and cellulose, are the backbone of many resilient tissues, typically in association with other structural organic materials, sometimes also with inorganic minerals.

Stiffness and hardness can be attained in organic skeletons without mineralization, through processes such as protein tanning (as in insect cuticles), the incorporation of metals, or the agglutination of foreign particles (as in sabellid worms). The strongest skeletons, however, are those that incorporate biominerals to some degree.

Organisms can make more than 60 different biominerals, but only a few are used as structural materials in skeletons. The most important ones are two calcium carbonates (calcite and aragonite), three calcium phosphates (hydroxyapatite, francolite, and dahllite), and one silicate, opal. Examples of more rare skeletal minerals are vaterite (a calcium carbonate), celestite (strontium sulphate), and magnetite (ferric oxide). The mechanical properties of the skeletal tissue do not arise from the type of mineral used; rather, these properties depend upon the way it is incorporated into the tissue. The biominerals are typically stiff and hard, but at the same time, they are brittle. The latter deficiency is overcome by combining the minerals with organic matter into "composite materials." For example,

in sponges and octocorals, spicules (star-shaped structural elements) are embedded in a ductile matrix, which increases its stiffness and hardness without sacrificing its resistance to tear. Whereas fossil echinoderm ossicles (bony structures) break quite easily by cracking along the cleavage planes (areas most prone to break in straight facets) of the calcite lattice, this is not the case in those of living echinoderms, in which the calcite forms a meshwork (stereom) interwoven with soft tissue (stroma). Similarly, dry bone has much less resistance to breakage than living bone.

Figure 1. *Cloudina,* the oldest tubular fossil; collected by Yue Zhao in Shaanxi, China; scanning electron micrograph by Stefan Bengtson; cf. Bengtson and Zhao (1992).

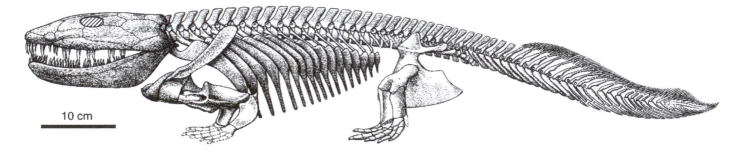

Figure 2. The skeleton of one of the earliest land-living vertebrates, the devonian tetrapod *Ichthyostega;* drawing by Lennart Alex Andersson; reprinted from Jarvik (1996), by permission of Scandinavian University Press.

Figure 3. Reef; photograph by Stefan Bengtson, 1984.

Excluding some possible mineralized skeletons of unicellular protists, spicules are the first skeletal elements to appear in the fossil record, in siliceous (opaline) skeletons of sponges in the Late Proterozoic. Tubular skeletons (those that form an exoskeleton for animals such as worms) appear at the end of the Proterozoic and become dominant in the earliest Cambrian faunas; the tubes may be purely organic, agglutinated, or reinforced with biominerals. In addition, Cambrian marine sediments contain conchs, bivalved shells, primitive supporting skeletons, mineralized cuticles, claw- or toothlike structures, and various sclerites of composite external skeletons, as well as internal ones. These skeletal types comprise basically all types seen today.

This abrupt and overwhelming appearance of skeletons often is referred to as a biomineralization event, but it was part of a general evolutionary event known as the Cambrian Explosion. Animals evolved many different types of organs and tissues, including skeletized ones. In many cases, the primary function appears to have been protective, but other selective pressures led to a variety of uses of skeletons. This variety had particular importance for the subsequent expansion onto land, as most major groups of large terrestrial organisms (arthropods, vertebrates, and vascular plants) owe their success to skeletized tissues for support, locomotion, feeding, protection, mineral storage, and other functions.

Although teeth may constitute only a small part of a vertebrate skeleton, they are commonly found as fossils because of their resistance to decay or breakdown over great periods of time. Throughout the Phanerozoic, many groups of vertebrates are known mainly or exclusively from teeth. Since teeth reflect the animals' eating habits, these structures can give much ecological information.

When organisms started to use biominerals for structural purposes, this action had profound effects on sedimentological environments and biogeochemical cycles (the way chemicals cycle through the biosphere). Practically all of the minerals being formed in modern oceans are biogenic (have a biological origin). When elements such as calcium, silicon, and phosphorous are incorporated in biological tissues and the sediments formed by their skeletons, these materials are out of circulation for longer or shorter periods of geologic time. As a result, the formation and destruction of biogenic minerals are of great importance for the global recycling of elements essential to life.

In addition to producing sedimentary grains, biomineralizing organisms also may build rocks directly, particularly in tropical regions. Tropical reefs can be major deposits of calcium carbonate and have a profound influence on the geology of a region. Reef builders have varied through time; the most prominent ones today are scleractinian corals and calcareous algae.

STEFAN BENGTSON

Work Cited

Bengtson, S., and Y. Zhao. 1992. Predatorial borings in Late Precambrian mineralized exoskeletons. *Science* 257:367–69.

Jarvik, E. 1996. The Devonian tetrapod Ichthyostega. *Fossils and Strata* 40:1–213.

Further Re ading

Allemand, D., and J.-P. Cuif (eds.). 1994. Biomineralization 93. 7th International Symposium on Biomineralization, Monaco, 17–20 November 1993. Session 1, Fundamentals of biomineralization. *Bulletin de l'Institut Océanographique, Monaco,* Numéro spécial 14, vol. 1.

———. 1994. Biomineralization 93. 7th International Symposium on Biomineralization, Monaco, 17–20 November 1993. Session 5, Biomineralization and global oceanology. Session 6, Biomineralization in Environmental studies and aquaculture. Session 7, Biomineralization and fossil data. *Bulletin de l'Institute Océanographique, Monaco,* Numéro spécial 14, vol. 4.

Currey, J.D. 1990. Biomechanics of mineralized skeletons. *In* J.G. Carter (ed.), *Skeletal Biomineralization: Patterns, Processes and Evolutionary Trends.* Vol. 1. New York: Van Nostrand Reinhold.

Lowenstam, H.A., and S. Weiner. 1989. *On Biomineralization.* Oxford: Clarendon; New York: Oxford University Press.

Simkiss, K. 1989. Biomineralization in the context of geological time. *Transactions of the Royal Society of Edinburgh: Earth Sciences* 80:193–99.

Wainwright, S.A., W.D. Biggs, J.D. Currey, and J.M. Gosline. 1976. *Mechanical Design in Organisms.* London: Arnold; New York: Wiley.

SKELETON: AXIAL SKELETON

History

The structure and evolution of the vertebral column and its associated structures has been a central theme in vertebrate paleontology. Early in the twentieth century, the theoretical attempts of Hans Gadow to account for all vertebral structures by modeling them on those of sharks drove the study of the axial skeleton. However, later work by Ernest E. Williams (1959) demonstrated this to be inappropriate. Perhaps the most influential scholar in the field (as well as the study of many other parts of the vertebrate body) was Alfred S. Romer. His textbooks, *The Vertebrate Body* (1949) and *Vertebrate Paleontology* (1933) were benchmark studies that highlighted the importance of vertebral structure in the vertebrate body and its evolution. His landmark *Osteology of the Reptiles* (1956) remains the standard of comparison for studies of vertebrate osteology (study of bones), including the vertebral column. The importance of the skull in systematic studies served to divert attention from studies of the axial skeleton in recent years; however, ongoing research by Robert L. Carroll, Farish A. Jenkins, Robert Holmes, Joshua A. Laerm, and Alec L. Panchen (to name but a few) has demonstrated that there is still much to be learned.

Basic Structure

Among invertebrate chordates, the supporting structure of the body axis is restricted to the notochord, a bendable but incompressible fibrous rod that prevents telescoping of the body. Indeed, the notochord is one of the defining features of chordates. The notochord is located near the dorsal aspect of the body, just beneath and parallel to the neural tube. It is present only in larval stages in members of the Urochordata (tunicates, primitive chordates) but is retained in its entirety throughout life in Cephalochordata (lancelets, primitive chordates). As chordates, vertebrates also possess a notochord for at least some portion of their lifecycle and it is retained to varying degrees in many groups; however, most vertebrates supplement the notochord with a discrete set of repeating, segmental structures (made of bone or cartilage) cumulatively referred to as the vertebral column. The notochord is retained in varying degrees among vertebrates, although it usually is replaced completely or in part by the vertebral column. In more advanced vertebrates the notochord remains only as a component of the intervertebral disc sandwiched between vertebral bodies.

Embryologically, the vertebral column is derived from sclerotomes, subdivisions of the serially repeating mesodermal blocks known as somites. Sclerotomes also contribute to the occipital portion of the braincase and thus to the formation of the occipital condyles—the articulation between the skull and the vertebral column. The most primitive expression of the vertebral column in vertebrates is as a set of dorsal and ventral arches. The dorsal pair protects the neural tube with the aid of intervening intercalary discs (also called "interneural arches"). The dorsal arches support a median neural spine at their apex; ventrally, they and the intercalary discs contact the notochord. The ventral arches abut the ventral surface of the notochord. In posterior sections of the body, ventral projections from these arches may be seen to enclose a space for protection of blood vessels as haemal arches.

More derived examples of individual vertebrae are composed of multiple elements: paired neural arches dorsally surmounted by a median neural spine, and a multipartite vertebral body, also known as the centrum, that variously replaces the notochord of many vertebrates. A significant degree of reorganization of embryonic sclerotomal materials characterizes one component of the vertebral centrum, the pleurocentrum. The centrum also includes the intercentrum, an element that does not appear to be the product of any such embryonic reorganization. The relative sizes of the more cranial intercentrum and the more caudal (tailward) pleurocentrum differ depending on the group considered. Primitively, ribs articulate with intercentrum and the transverse processes of the neural arch in all but the most caudal vertebral segments.

The vertebral column of most fishes are moderately homogeneous in nature; however, those of tetrapods show significant amounts of regional specialization. Amongst primitive tetrapods, the attachment of the pelvic girdle to the specialized sacral vertebrae separates the column into presacral and caudal regions. In more derived forms the presacral region can be subdivided into a cervical region (usually with reduced or small ribs), a thoracic region (characterized by ribs that contribute to the thoracic cage), and a lumbar region between the thoracic region and the sacrum. The first two vertebrae of the cervical region are modified into the specialized atlas-axis complex in most tetrapods. In the thoracic region, ribs may articulate ventrally with a single median element, the sternum. Ribs that articulate with the sternum, either directly or via costal cartilages, are termed true ribs. Those that articulate with one another instead of a sternum are false ribs; those that articulate with nothing ventrally are known as floating ribs.

Survey of Structure

Living agnathans (jawless fishes) exhibit a nearly unmodified notochord and only rudimentary vertebral elements. However, their structure is so derived (or, differently adapted) in other respects that they do not provide a reliable benchmark for interpreting the record of fossil agnathans, often colloquially referred to as "ostracoderms" owing to their frequent possession of a highly ossified exoskeleton. It is possible that the exoskeleton precluded the necessity of a highly ossified endoskeletal vertebral column; alternatively it simply may have obstructed the identification of vertebral elements in ostracoderms. The only evidence of a vertebral column in ostracoderms appears to be impressions of unossified vertebral elements surrounding an essentially unmodified notochord.

Members of the most primitive groups of jawed fishes, the Acanthodii and Placodermi, also retain a completely transsegmental notochord. Placoderms added dorsal and ventral elements of a vertebral column, but they are not conjoined within individual segments. Those of acanthodians are similarly separate, although they are more clearly identifiable as neural arches cranially, and both neural arches and haemal arches caudally.

Perhaps the best-known of fossil cartilaginous fishes includes the shark *Cladoselache* and its relatives. It possessed dorsal elements similar to those of placoderms. However, more recent, and presumably more derived, sharks possess a completely developed vertebral centrum and neural arch. The notochord remains continuous and the nerve cord becomes more completely protected to the presence of interneural arches.

The most primitive of bony fishes in the fossil record, often referred to as paleoniscoids, had patterns of vertebral elements similar to those of acanthodians. More advanced bony fishes demonstrate progressively more completely ossified axial skeletons, including vertebral centra, neural arches and spines, and ribs. However, elements are not necessarily fused into a single immovable unit. Such fusion does occur in many teleost fishes; however, such is not the case in sarcopterygian fishes. Teleost fishes are known for the possession of both dorsal and ventral pairs of ribs.

The pattern and orientation of axial structure is variously expressed in the tail region of fishes. In most fossil groups the vertebral axis is not symmetrical, with the column angling into a more dorsal caudal fin lobe separated from a smaller ventral lobe—a "heterocercal tail." The less common "hypocercal" condition, wherein the vertebral axis angles into the ventral lobe, has been found in a number of ostracoderms. A completely symmetri-

cal "diphycercal" tail is present in fossil lungfishes and the living coelacanth *Latimeria*. Certain groups exhibit what appears to be an externally symmetrical tail, although the internal structures may have a heterocercal axis complemented by accessory structures. This condition often is termed a "homocercal" condition. The earliest known tetrapods (ichthyostegalians) retain a tail fin.

The axial structures of sarcopterygian (lobe-finned) fishes and ichthyostegalians (primitive, Late Devonian amphibians) are remarkably similar in form (Figure 1). Both possess centra that are dominated by a crescentic intercentrum surmounted by a posterodorsally directed neural spine. Small paired pleurocentra are also present, although some scholars have suggested they are more accurately described as intercalary plates. The attachment of muscle blocks via their fibrous partitions, or myosepta, between them is to the intercentra, the neural arches, and the ribs that articulate with them. To the sarcopterygian pattern, tetrapods add a more highly developed neural spine plus paired anterior and posterior zygapophyses (joint processes between the neural arches of adjacent vertebrae) for additional columnar support of the animal's weight out of the water. Cranial zygapophyses are directed dorsally and medially to articulate with the ventral and lateral orientation of posterior zygapophyses. Despite these modifications, myoseptal attachments remain similar to those of sarcopterygians and are useful to determine the position and function of neural arches and intercentra.

Much of the story of the relationships of extinct amphibians is that of the patterns of the vertebral centra. Within the labyrinthodont amphibians, two lineal trends in centrum structure may be identified, each originating from the "rhachitomous" pattern wherein both intercentral and pleurocentral elements are present. One trend led toward more aquatic groups and emphasized the intercentrum as the dominant element of the vertebral centrum. The emphasis on the element not subjected to embryological reorganization likely reflects a retention of aquatic adaptations. Broadly speaking, this lineage is known as the temnospondyl amphibians. Earlier members of this lineage have a large intercentrum but retain pleurocentral elements on either side (exemplified by the rhachitomous temnospondyl *Eryops*). The trend culminated in large stereospondylous amphibians that abandoned the pleurocentrum completely. Some scholars (particularly Bolt 1969) have suggested that modern lissamphibians (including frogs, salamanders, and caecilians) arose from within temnospondyls. Vertebral structure and development of lissamphibians lend little to the resolution of this question. Lissamphibians possess "holospondylous" vertebrae (vertebrae consisting of a single central ossification), but their derivation from the intercentrum or pleurocentrum is not clear (Wake 1970).

In contrast to the temnospondylous vertebral pattern, a more terrestrial "anthrocosaurian" lineage emphasized the development of the pleurocentrum. Primitive (basal) members of this lineage, "embolomerous" amphibians, possessed a relatively larger pleurocentrum (although an intercentrum of nearly equivalent size still was present). The protorogyrinid amphibian *Proterogyrinus* provides a typical example (Figure 1). Successively more derived groupings continued to place proportionally more emphasis on the embryologically reorganized pleurocentrum, particularly in those taxa closely related to amniotes (vertebrates in which their embryos are surrounded by a fluid-filled sac, or amnion). Tradi-

tionally those include the Seymouriamorpha and the Diadectomorpha, the latter of which demonstrate a large pleurocentrum
fused to the neural arch, and only a relatively tiny intercentrum.
These taxa also are characterized by laterally convex (or "swollen")
neural arches. This feature is shared with primitive amniotes and
may have been a feature that provided additional stability to the
individual vertebrae with an arched construction (Sumida 1990).

The other large grouping of amphibians is the Lepospondyli, a taxon that was loosely associated by the common possession of an undivided, spool-shaped holospondylous centrum.
However, the work of Peter P. Vaughn (1972) and Robert L. Carroll and Pamela Gaskill (1978) has pointed out that many so-
called lepospondyls possess discrete intercentra and pleurocentra.
Recently, Michel Laurin and Robert R. Reisz (1997) have suggested that extant lissamphibians are derived from lepospondyls;
among other characters they use to support their argument are
characters of the axial skeleton.

It is among tetrapods that some of the earliest regional specializations of the vertebral column develop. In the region of the
pelvic girdle, large ribs fuse to the neural arches and centrum to
provide the attachment of the ilium as the sacral vertebra(e). The
number of sacral vertebrae is variable. At the cranial end of the
column, the first two postcranial vertebrae are modified as the
atlas-axis complex. Primitively, the components of the atlas-axis
complex (proatlas, atlas intercentrum, atlas pleurocentrum, atlas
neural arches, axis intercentrum, axis pleurocentrum, axis neural
arches, and spine) do not fuse. The axial segment is clearly characterized by an enlarged neural spine for the attachment of dorsal
occipital musculature.

Amniotes continued the emphasis on the pleurocentral component of the vertebral body; further, the neural arch becomes more
firmly fused to the body. Within Amniota, the synapsid lineage that
ultimately led to modern mammals displays progressively greater
degrees of regional specialization. The condition in pelycosaurian-
grade synapsids (primitive mammal-like reptiles) is essentially similar to the primitive amniote condition. Notably, certain pelycosaurian genera developed elongate neural spines that created a large,
dorsally directed, webbed sail. Dorsal sails are known in many genera of two different families of pelycosaurs. The best- known of
these sail-backed pelycosaurs are *Dimetrodon* and *Edaphosaurus*.
Much speculation has surrounded the potential functional significance of the pelycosaurian sail, the most plausible of which is that it
may have been an aid in thermoregulation. More advanced ther-
apsid-grade synapsids show more distinct regionalization: the atlas-
axis complex remains unconsolidated, but a reduction of ribs in the
cervical (neck) and lumbar (lower back) regions is more obvious. In
some taxa the ribs of the thoracic region are marked by overlapping
uncinate (posteriorly projecting, hooklike) processes that may have
aided in the attachment of muscles of ventilation. True mammals
refined the regional specialization of the column. Cervical vertebrae
(with very few exceptions, seven in number) lack distinct, mobile
ribs. Thoracic vertebrae retain movably articulated ribs, whereas
lumbar vertebrae fuse a small part of the rib to the vertebra to create
a more elongate transverse process. Sacral elements (variable in
number) fuse to form a distinct sacrum. Vertebral segments posterior to the sacrum generally are referred to as caudal vertebrae.

As with pelycosaurs, primitive members of the true Reptilia
reflect the primitive amniote condition. This may be stated for
primitive reptilian families such as Captorhinidae and Protorothy-
rididae, as well as basal members of taxa variously assigned to the
Parareptilia (including mesosaurs, parieasaurs, and procolophonids). The latter two groups include some members that
became extremely large with the associated secondary adaptations
of the vertebral column that accompany heavy-bodied animals
(such as a large number of sacral segments, enlarged neural arches,
and stout neural spines). With the exception of protorothyridids
(small, lizardlike reptiles), most basal reptilian groups possessed
laterally expanded neural arches much like those of seymouriamorphs and diadectomorphs (both of which are large-bodies near-
amniote tetrapods). Those taxa that display this condition often
display a distinct alternation in height and structure of the neural
spines, particularly in regions near the limb girdles. This pattern
may have been an adaptation that facilitated the attachment of
longer interspinous muscles (Sumida 1996).

Members of the Araeoscelidia (which include basal diapsid
reptiles) are conservative, or little changed, in a manner similar to
other primitive amniotes; however, they do exhibit a distinct cervical
region in which the vertebrae are markedly elongate. Ultimately, the
myriad expressions of reptilian vertebrae within the Diapsida (all
birds and most reptiles that have two temporal fenestrae, or openings in the skull behind each eye) may be traced to the basal amniote
condition (Romer 1956). Members of the Archosauromorpha,
which includes crocodilians, dinosaurs, and birds, provide some of
the most diverse of such expression. Dinosaurs retain the primitively
multipartite atlas-axis complex but continue to regionalize the vertebral column in a manner that in some cases rivals mammals. Certain lineages of dinosaurs provide excellent examples of adaptations
to large size. In many species, sacral elements enlarge to deal with the
extreme forces imposed by gravity on large size, or the propulsive
forces focused on the pelvic limb owing to the constraints of bipedality. Significantly, the vertebral axis remains nearly parallel to the
substrate, even in bipedal dinosaurs and birds. Only in hominid primate mammals does dorsal lumbar curvature contribute to the
attainment of an upright posture. Certain dinosaurs developed large
sail-like structures in a manner similar to the pelycosaurs of over 100
million years earlier. Many large sauropods and iguanodontid dinosaurs possessed ossified intervertebral ligaments that probably aided
in structural support of these enormous suspensory arches. Finally,
certain sauropods appear to have had points of preferential fusion of
tail segments; these were placed strategically such that certain scholars have suggested they aided female sauropods in elevation and lateral deviation of the tail during mating. The earliest fossil birds
retained the vertebral patterns of theropod dinosaurs; it is not until
much later that the specialized fusions of the vertebral column associated with flight adaptations arose.

The Occipital Condyle

The occipital condyle merits mention. Like vertebrae, it is
derived from sclerotomes; and it articulates with the first element
of the vertebral column. It is a single- or double-faceted surface
that is produced primarily from the basioccipital portion (at the

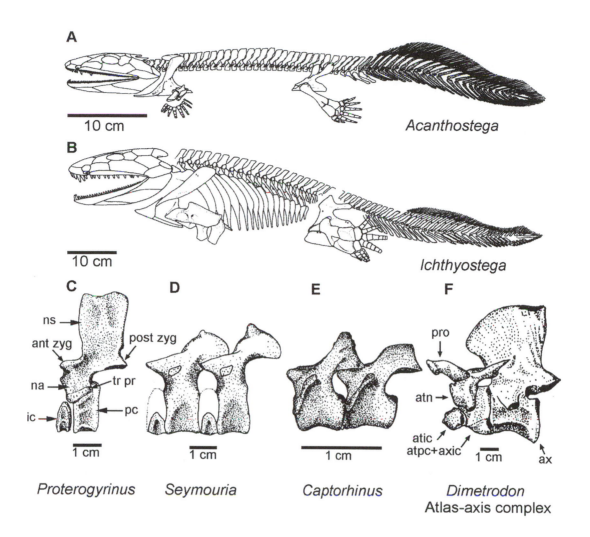

Figure 1. Reconstructions of axial structures in fossil tetrapods; all reconstructions are in left lateral view. *A*, whole body view of the ichthyostegalian amphibian *Acanthostega*; *B*, reconstruction of the ichthyostegalian amphibian *Ichthyostega*; *C*, the proterogyrinid amphibian *Proterogyrinus* demonstrating embolomerous condition; *D*, the seymouriamorph amphibian *Seymouria* demonstrating laterally expanded neural arches; *E*, the primitive reptile *Captorhinus* demonstrating variability in neural spine construction; *F*, the atlas-axis complex of the pelycosaurian-grade synapsid *Dimetrodon*. Abbreviations: *ant zyg*, anterior zygapophysis; *atic*, atlantal intercentrum; *atn*, atlantal neural arch; *atpc+axic*, atlantal pleurocentrum fused to axial intercentrum; *ax*, axis; *ic*, intercentrum; *na*, neural arch; *ns*, neural spine; *pc*, pleurocentrum; *post zyg*, posterior zygapophysis; *pro*, proatlas; *tr pr*, transverse process. *A* and *B* after Coates and Clack (1995); *C* through *F* after Sumida (1996).

lower portion of the foramen magnum) of the braincase, but occasionally with contributions from the paired exoccipitals (portions of the occiptal bone on each side of the foramen magnum). In gnathostome fishes, the occipital articulation generally is characterized by a flattened circular surface that surrounds a variably deep notochordal pit; it looks much like the caudal end of a vertebra. Among labyrinthodont amphibians, the condyle is a single, approximately subcircular structure with a raised rim that surrounds a more concave notochordal pit. This essential pattern of a single condyle is retained throughout the anthrocosaurian lineage, whereas advanced temnospondylous amphibians tend to develop a double-faceted condyle. Lepospondyls exhibit a diversity of occipital constructions: nectridians have paired condyles; lysorophids have a single condyle. The condyle of microsaurs is

particularly distinctive, usually described as a "strap-shaped" double condyle. Primitive amniotes have a single condyle that varies from oval to bean-shaped and often is marked by a notochordal pit. Along the synapsid lineage, a double occipital condyle developed within the Cynodontia and Dicynodontia. Reptiles, on the other hand, retained a single occipital condyle, passing this condition to primitive birds.

The Turtle Shell

Perhaps one of the most extreme specializations of the axial skeleton is the turtle shell. The shell is not completely axial in derivation, some of it being dermal in nature. However, expanded ribs and vertebrae contribute to the shell and its structural integrity, ultimately leading to the unique condition wherein the appendicular skeleton (bones of the limbs) lies internal to the ribcage instead of external to it as in all other vertebrates.

STUART S. SUMIDA

See also Skeleton: Dermal Postcranial Skeleton; Skull

Works Cited

Bolt, J.R. 1969. Lissamphibian origins: Possible protolissamphibian from the Lower Permian of Oklahoma. *Science* 166:888–91.

Carroll, R.L., and P. Gaskill. 1978. The Order Microsauria. *Memoirs of the American Philosophical Society* 126:1–211.

Coates, M.I., and J.A. Clack. 1995. Romer's gap: Tetrapod origins and terrestriality. *Bulletin of the Museum of Natural History, Paris* 17:373–88.

Laurin, M., and R.R. Reisz. 1997. A new perspective on tetrapod phylogeny. *In* S.S. Sumida and K.L.M. Martin (eds.), *Amniote Origins, Completing the Transition to Land.* San Diego, California: Academic Press.

Romer, A.S. 1933. *Vetebrate Paleontology.* Chicago: University of Chicago Press.

———. 1949. *The Vetebrate Body.* Philadelphia and London: Saunders.

———. 1956. *Osteology of the Reptiles.* Chicago: University of Chicago Press.

Sumida, S.S. 1990. Vertebral morphology, alternation of neural spine height, and structure in Permo-Carboniferous tetrapods, and a reappraisal of primitive modes of terrestrial locomotion. *University of California Publications in Zoology* 122:1–133.

———. 1997. Locomotor features of taxa spanning the origin of amniotes. *In* S.S. Sumida and K.L.M. Martin (eds.), *Amniote Origins, Completing the Transition to Land.* San Diego, California: Academic Press.

Vaughn, P.P. 1972. More vertebrates, including a new microsaur from the Upper Pennsylvanian of central Colorado. *Los Angeles County Museum Contributions in Science* 223:1–30.

Wake, D.B. 1970. Aspects of vertebral evolution in the modern Amphibia. *Forma et Functio* 3:33–60.

Williams, E.E. 1959. Gadow's arcualia and the development of tetrapod vertebrae. *Quarterly Review of Biology* 34:1–32.

Further Reading

Jenkins, F.A. 1971. The postcranial skeleton of African cynodonts. *Bulletin of the Peabody Museum of Natural History* 36:1–216.

Kardong, K.V. 1995. *Vertebrates: Comparative Anatomy, Function and Evolution.* Dubuque, Iowa, and Oxford: Brown; 2nd ed., 1997.

Laerm, J.A. 1979. On the origin of rhipidistian vertebrae. *Journal of Paleontology* 53:175–86.

Lauder, G.V. 1980. On the relationship of the myotome to the axial skeleton in vertebrate evolution. *Paleobiology* 6:51–56.

Panchen, A.L. 1977. The origin and early evolution of tetrapod vertebrae. *In* S.M. Andrews, R.S. Miles, and A.D. Walker (eds.), *Problems in Vertebrate Evolution.* Linnean Society Symposium Series, 4. London: Academie Press.

Parrington, F.R. 1967. The vertebrae of early tetrapods. *Colloques Internationaux du Centre National de la Recherche Scientifique, Problèmes Actuels de Paléontologie (Evolution des Vertébrés)* 163:269–79.

Romer, A.S. 1956. *Osteology of the Reptiles.* Chicago: University of Chicago Press.

Sumida, S.S., R.E. Lombard, and D.S. Berman. 1992. Morphology of the atlas-axis complex of the late Palaeozoic tetrapod suborders Diadectomorpha and Seymouriamorpha. *Philosophical Transactions of the Royal Society of London* 336:259–73.

SKELETON: DERMAL POSTCRANIAL SKELETON

Fossils of piscine vertebrates ("fishes") are known mainly through the dermal skeleton, although there are two groups in the early history of Agnathans (jawless vertebrates) that totally lack this feature: hagfishes and lampreys. The dermal skeleton largely is represented by scales and is differentiated generally into a cranial part, which forms part of the skull, and a postcranial (to the back, or rear, of the skull) part. The majority of piscine vertebrates developed large bony plates covering the head. This is not a universal feature, for some jawless fishes (thelodonts) and the cartilaginous fishes (chondrichthyans, which include sharks) do not show that division. In these two groups, there is uniform squamation (scale distribution) all over the head and body, the only differences being the scales' size and the distribution pattern. Various intermediate stages exist in both the jawless and jawed vertebrates. These intermediate forms show tesserae (small bony plates, or platelets) on the skull roof. In the jawless vertebrates the origin of these tesserae is not clear, but in the jawed vertebrates, the tesserae appear to be enlarged or fused scales. Fully developed dermal head shields also appear very early in the history of vertebrates. The earliest true vertebrates, which appeared in the Ordovician from the Southern Hemisphere, possess a large head shield and scales on the rest of the body (Gagnier 1995).

There are three main morphological patterns (those of shape and structure) in the dermal skeleton. In macromery, large plates cover the head, and the rest of the body usually is wrapped in tall, narrow scales. In mesomeric animals, the head is covered with small platelets, and smaller scales cover the rest of the body. Finally, in micromery, tiny scales cover the head and the body. It also should be noted that in the macromeric and mesomeric types, a gradual transition zone exists between the head shield and body scales. Scholars are not sure which of the three patterns was the first to appear, since all appear quite early in the fossil record.

Scales show many important characters that scholars can use when they classify animals. In bony fishes (osteichthyans), several evolutionary trends can be seen. The different types of scales are based mainly on the histological (very fine structural) features. In early bony fishes the scales have three layers—bone, dentine, and a superficial glassy layer of enamel or enameloid. As many lineages arise, the scales become thinner and lighter. The superficial layers tend to disappear, and the underlying bone is reduced to a light platelet. The resulting thin, round scales are called cycloid when the outer surface is smooth and ctenoid when the outer surface bears minute points and ridges. These ridges are often a feature used in classification (diagnosis).

In modern chondrichthyans (neoselachians), teeth show the same structure as the scales. In fact, one could say that teeth are actually modified scales. Both teeth and scales in this group show enamel, dentine, and a bone base around a pulp cavity. The earliest known teeth appear to be from osteichthyans and chondrichthyans, two of the four classes of gnathostomes (jawed vertebrates). The oldest mouth denticles serving as teeth are probably the conodont "elements," which are small, toothlike structures. (Conodont animals are small, elongate, scaleless carnivorous invertebrates with huge terminal eyes.) The shape of phosphatic conodont elements recall the mouth denticles (small, conical teeth) of two agnathan groups, the hagfishes and lampreys, which possess horny teeth. Conodont elements most probably also served as teeth.

The teeth of sharks may be scales that have become elaborated along the margins (edges) of the jaws. Primitive structures, these teeth have an open pulp cavity surrounded by a cone of dentine that is coated with a hard, shiny, enamel-like substance; they are attached to the jaws by connective tissue. As soon as shark teeth are recognizable, they show considerable diversity in the pattern of "cusps" (pointed sections of a tooth). Although these teeth exhibit a great variety in form, they are not very helpful in taxonomy. On the one hand, a tooth pattern may be present in genera that are related only distantly; on the other, and one species may have many shapes of teeth.

The simplest type of scale is found in chondrichthyan fishes. It consists of a cone of dentine capping a pulp cavity. It usually is covered with a hard, shiny, enamel-like tissue. Such elementary scales are called placoid scales, and they probably represent the primitive condition for sharks. Such scales do not grow externally, but internally by infilling of the pulp cavity. As soon as these scales are formed, they have achieved their definite size. Small scales are present on young animals and are replaced by larger scales as the animal grows. Placoidlike scales also exist in a group of jawless fishes called "thelodonts," which tells us that this type of scale apparently has evolved many times in different lineages. Other chondrichthyans are covered by "composite scales" (lepidomoria), which develop by the progressive addition of lepidomorial units.

To a certain degree, the disposition of scales reflects the arrangement of the underlying musculature. The trunk musculature usually is separated into two main parts, below and above the vertebral axis. (An axis is the long general line of a structure; the vertebral axis is the line of the backbone down the fish's body.) It gives the scales an anteriorly (frontward) pointed chevron shape in very early vertebrates. The arrangement in the early jawless vertebrates is more like the cephalochordates (the sister group to vertebrates) than gnathostomes, where the two groups of muscle are separated by a septum (a dividing structure—either membrane or bone).

In the evolution of bony fishes, scales became thinner. Some scholars theorize that this change enabled the trunk and tail to undulate more freely, resulting in improved swimming efficiency. These changes are correlated directly with the reduction of the notochord (a cartilaginous structure that underlies the spine) and increase of the ossification (bone cell content) of the vertebral column to resist increased stresses.

Scholars can assess improvements in swimming ability by studying the structure of the caudal (tail) fin. In primitive jawless vertebrates, the caudal fin is a simple paddle; sometimes there are endoskeletal rays—rodlike structures under the skin—but they are not connected to the musculature. Such rays are especially obvious in a special group of jawless fishes, called osteostracans. This group shows a change in scale orientation on the caudal fin, a change that has been interpreted as reflecting the underlying presence of endoskeletal rays. In bony fishes, endoskeletal rays are extended by fin rays (long spines) derived from scales called lepidotrichia. In jawed fishes, the fins are reinforced by endoskeletal rays that are connected to muscles.

The shape and distribution pattern of the scales on the caudal fin also often reflect the position of the axial support (vertebral column or notochord). An axial support that turns upward is demonstrated by body scales that slant upward; the fin extends below the support. Such a tail is primitive for gnathostomes and is present on sharks, sturgeon, paddlefishes, and some jawless vertebrates. It is called a heterocercal or epicercal caudal fin. When the axial support turns downward it is called a hypocercal caudal fin. Finally, a straight tail is called diphycercal and homocercal. Hypocercal and heterocercal tails represent different trends in evolution, but there is no reason to believe that a diphycercal tail is primitive.

Primitive jawless vertebrates do not have any fin other than the caudal, but often have a crest of scales in the dorsal region (back) and just in front of the anus. Such ridges are present in the cephalochordates. Some groups of jawless fishes have one or two dorsal fins with or without ridge scales. Proper anal fins only develop in some groups of gnathostomes.

The appearance of paired fins is a subject that is highly debated. Many groups of jawless fishes show different structures that have been interpreted as paired fins or structures that preceded paired fins. Pectoral ("chest") fins, when they exist in agnathans (i.e., osteostracans, galeaspids, pitoriaspids), are not in the same position as they are in gnathostomes (jawed fishes), and there is no evidence of internal (endoskeletal) supports. Some agnathans (e.g., anaspids) have paired ventrolateral (sides of the belly) fin folds extending down the body. These folds led to a theory on the origin of the paired fins. It is hypothesized that the foundation evolved a fold of skin extending outward from the body, an internal set of skeletal supports, and, dorsal and ventral to the supports, a sheet of musculature developed to move the fin. All gnathostomes possess two sets of paired fins (pectoral and pelvic). The acanthodian fishes (extinct little Paleozoic spiny fishes) are distinguished from all other primitive fishes by the presence of conspicuous fin spines on all the fins except the caudal; such spines must have provided a very effective defense against predators. Spines, like teeth, are derived from single denticles that became greatly enlarged. In most genera, the base of each spine is deeply inserted in the body. Also, many genera have a number of intermediate spines, mainly between the pectoral and pelvic fins and sometimes in front of the pectoral fins. These intermediate spines are most numerous in the older genera and may be lost entirely in younger forms (Gagnier and Wilson 1996). Even if most intermediate spines do not bear any fins, there is one species where the six pairs of intermediate spines are associated with fins. These intermediate paired spines have been interpreted as remnants of the primitive folds and have been used to bolster the theory that folds were the precursors of fins.

Fin spines are also a prominent feature of sharks. Most sharks have fin spines associated with each of two dorsal fins but not on the paired fins (except in two enigmatic genera). As with acanthodian fishes, the absence of spines represents a specialization. The first dorsal spine is sometimes attached to the head and is used in courtship and copulatory behavior.

With the conquest of land, the postcranial dermal skeleton tends to degenerate and disappear. However, the skin retains the capacity to produce dermal bone. The Paleozoic gave rise to a number of armored amphibians covered with dorsal plates as defense against carnivorous animals. Among the dinosaurs were a number of groups with well-developed dermal armor, such as the stegosaurs with their dorsal plates and the ankylosaurs with an extensive body armor. As in modern crocodilians, the dermal armor of the cervical (neck) and shoulder regions differs considerably in shape and arrangement in ankylosaurs. The cervical armor consists of transverse (crosswise) bands separated by small irregular ossicles (bony structures). This zone of ossicles separates the first band of plates from the skull and permits neck and head movement.

Some reptiles have kept (or re-evolved) vestigial modified ventral bony scales beneath the skin of the belly, termed gastralia. These scales are a series of joint V-shaped rods. They are particularly well developed in a group called the sauropterygians (e.g., placodonts, plesiosaurs). Some placodonts were as heavily armored as turtles, although placodonts have more plates.

In extinct reptiles there are many interesting examples of armor, but that of the turtle body is unequaled for completeness. Beneath the keratinous scutes ("bony" plates made of a tough, hard protein called keratin), most turtles have a stout belly slab termed the plastron. At the sides, the two parts of the shell (plastron and carapace) are connected by a bony bridge. The carapace is open for the head, limbs, and tail.

Essentially, the carapace consists of three sets of plates. At the edge is a set of peripheral marginal plates. There is a set of rectangular plates that run in the midline from the front to the back. Most of these plates are fused to the vertebrae beneath them.

Bound to underlying ribs are eight paired costal plates. All elements of the carapace are fused firmly, to the point that the sutures (places where elements meet) disappear. Often the horny surface scutes are impressed onto the surface of the bony carapace, leaving their lines of separation. The shell is reinforced by the way that the boundaries between the horny scutes of the carapace alternate with the sutures between the bony plates.

The typical turtle plastron consists of a front median element and four paired plates. The front margin is made of the dermal shoulder girdle elements. It has been suggested that gastralia have been incorporated into the plastron, which is partly composed of newly developed elements.

Differences in dermal armor, or osteoderms, have long been used by modern herpetologists in fossil lizard taxonomy (classification). Osteoderms also have proven to be taxonomically useful for other reptiles and for certain mammals such as glyptodonts (armadillos and their extinct relatives). In crocodilians there are rectangular bony plates covered by horny skin. Bony plates only occur in edentates, a group of mammals native to South America. In the armadillos and their extinct relatives, the bony plates form a complete carapace that covers the back and the top of the head and sheaths the tail as well.

PIERRE-YVES GAGNIER

See also Skull; Ornamentation: Vertebrates; Teeth: Earliest Teeth; Vertebrate Hard Tissues

Works Cited

Gagnier, P.-Y. 1995. Ordovician vertebrates and agnathan phylogeny. Proceedings of the Seventh International Symposium on lower vertebrates. *Bulletin du Muséum National d'Histoire Naturelle, Paris,* section C, 4 série, 17 (1–4):1–37.

Gagnier, P.-Y., and M. Wilson. 1996. A revision of Brochoadmones milesi Bernacsek and Dineley 1977, an Acanthodian from Northern Canada. *Modern Geology* 20:235–51.

Further Readings

Carroll, R.L. 1988. *Vertebrate Paleontology and Evolution*. New York: Freeman.

Dorit, R.L., W.F. Walker Jr., and R.D. Barnes. 1991. *Zoology*. Philadelphia: Saunders.

Romer, A.S., and T.S. Parson. 1949. *The Vertebrate Body*. Philadelphia: Saunders; 6th ed., London and Philadelphia: Saunders, 1986.

Walker Jr., W.F. 1987. *Functional Anatomy of the Vertebrates: An Evolutionary Prospective*. Philadelphia: Saunders; 2nd ed., Fort Worth, Texas: Saunders, 1994.

SKULL

In vertebrates, structures that protect the brain and sense organs, based on a complex arrangement of hard tissue elements, are important. Protochordate animals (those from which the vertebrates are derived) had limited sense organs and small brains that had little or no special support or protection. With the development of complex sense organs and a central nervous system to process and use the information received, the skull evolved in the early craniate (vertebrate with a structure that encloses the brain) to cover and protect these specialized organs (Janvier 1995). Other additions to the basic cranial framework of early vertebrates produced jaws and the muscles to operate them, followed by many changes in the parts of the skull associated with respiration and the sense organs.

Evolution of the vertebrate skull is characterized by a series of significant changes, some of which are evident in the fossil record and some of which are not. The skull structure of most adult vertebrates is adapted clearly to the habitat and life of the animal, but remnants of the original pattern are still evident in the embryological development of derived vertebrates.

Skulls of Jawless Vertebrates

Early jawless vertebrates are represented by many different forms, including the cephalaspids, the osteostracans, the heterostracans, and the thelodonts. The process of bone formation in these early vertebrates prefigures similar processes in later vertebrates. Cartilage is a simple tissue that can be a precursor of bone. It consists of cartilage cells that are enclosed in lacunae (spaces); the lacunae are in turn suspended in a clear matrix (a sort of binding, nutritive substance). Two processes change cartilage into bone—calcification and ossification. Both are interrelated.

In calcification, mineral crystals are deposited within the cartilage matrix, which is otherwise unchanged. Calcification may only strengthen cartilage, or it may be part of the process of ossification. Ossification is the process by which calcium phosphate molecules are deposited in cartilage that is formed during the development of an embryo; the bones that result are called endochondral bones. Dermal bones—those that form the skull and body armor in fishes and amphibians, as well as the skulls of other vertebrates—develop within layers or groupings of primitive, undifferentiated (unspecialized) mesenchyme cells lying directly below the skin. Again, the formation of dermal bone involves calcification and ossification.

Bone formation appears early in the cephalaspids. They had head shields (cephalic shields) (Figure 1A) with dermal and chondral ossifications, a visceral (body) skeleton with gill pouches, and ossifications around sense organs and the brain. The internal chondral ossifications reveal details of these soft tissues as endocranial casts—these are casts that are made from the inside of the skull. The dermal shield included canals and other openings of a sense organs that provided the animal with information about its horizontal-vertical position in the water (the lateral line). Cephalaspids had no jaws, but there are traces of arches in the mouth area, in locations that are asso-

ciated with gill arches. Other jawless vertebrates, like osteostracans and heterostracans, are less well preserved. These fishes also had dermal shields, made up of many small elements, that covered a cartilaginous braincase (Figures 1B, 1C). The soft bodies of thelodonts were covered entirely with scales, and the dermal skulls were merely extensions of the scales that surrounded the mouth, gill slits, and openings for sense organs.

The Appearance of Jaws

Jaws develop by modification of the anterior (front) branchial arches. (Branchial arches are structures that ultimately gave rise to gills, as well as jaws.) In jawless vertebrates, such as the Silurian genus *Jaymoytius*, each gill arch is supported by a single cartilaginous rod, all similar in structure (Figure 2A). In vertebrates with jaws, the cartilaginous rods are divided into four parts: pharyngobranchials, epibranchials, ceratobranchials, and hypobranchials (Figures 2B, 2C). The first visceral arch becomes enlarged, and the epibranchial forms the upper jaw (palatoquadrate cartilage). The ceratobranchial forms the lower jaw (mandibular cartilage, also known as Meckel's cartilage).

The second visceral arch, or hyoid arch, changes to support the tongue or the jaw articulation in lower vertebrates; in higher vertebrates it is modified further into an ear ossicle. In fishes and in amphibians with functional gills for respiration in water, the skeleton of the third and subsequent gill arches remains separate from the rest of the head skeleton. In most tetrapods (all vertebrates having four appendages), especially mammals, these elements are modified early in development to form the cartilages of the larynx.

Developmental Framework of the Skull

As a vertebrate embryo develops, the skull forms from three components, the chondrocranium, the dermatocranium, and the splanchnocranium (also known as the "visceral skeleton"). The chondrocranium, based on a template of cartilage in the embryo, partially surrounds the brain and supports the sense organs (Figures 3, 4). This structure may or may not be ossified, depending on the species. The splanchnocranium supports the gill arches of fishes and some amphibians, and their derivatives in higher vertebrates (Figure 3). Like the chondrocranium, the splanchnocranium forms in a template of cartilage and may be mineralized later. The dermatocranium, formed from membrane bones, includes the bones of the skull roof, cheek, and jaws (Figure 5). In every group of jawed vertebrates, these basic components are modified during development, and the structure of the adult skull is a composite of all three components.

Functional Units of the Skull

The vertebrate skull is complex, and elements of the embryonic dermatocranium, chondrocranium, and splanchnocranium are

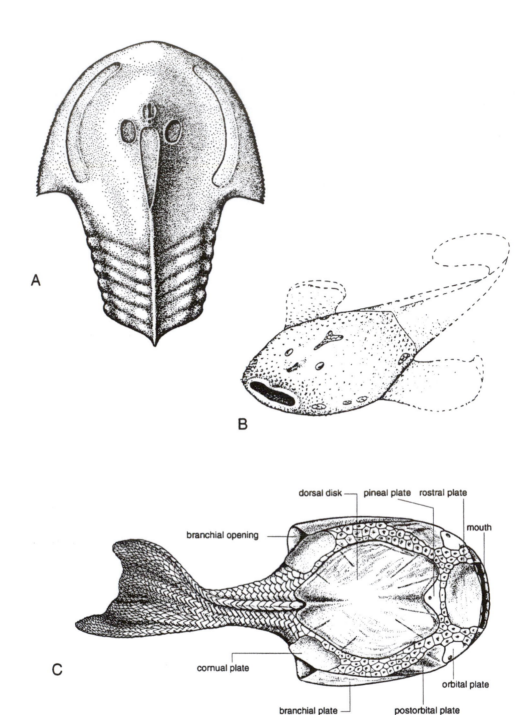

Figure 1. Dermal skulls in jawless vertebrates. *A,* a cephalaspid; *B,* an osteostracan; *C,* a heterostracan. From: *A,* Romer (1966), used by permission of the publisher, The University of Chicago Press, copyright © 1933, 1945, 1966 by The University of Chicago; *B,* Janvier (1995), reproduced by permission of the Palaeontological Association; *C,* figure from PALAEOZOIC FISHES, by R.S. Miles and J.A. Moy-Thomas, copyright © 1971 by Saunders College Publishing, reproduced by permission of the publisher.

blended to produce the adult skull, even in the earliest members of the group. In derived (specialized) vertebrates and in fossil animals, functional units of the adult skull are easier to understand (Romer and Parsons 1986). These units combine elements of the three embryological divisions of chondrocranium, dermatocranium, and splanchnocranium—particularly in advanced vertebrates but also in most of the lower vertebrates as well.

The simplest unit is the dermal skull, consisting entirely of dermal (membrane) bones (Figure 5). The other two units combine dermal and chondral elements. The palate and lower jaw

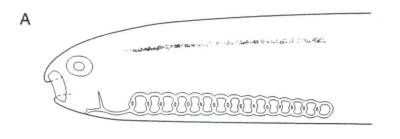

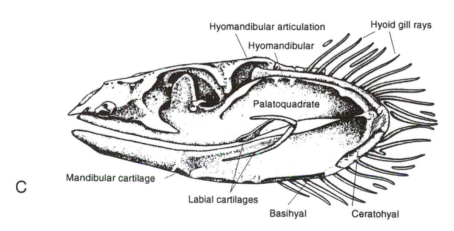

Figure 2. Formation of jaws. *A,* the vis3ceral cranium in a Silurian jawless fish, *Jaymoytius; B,* a series of hypothetical steps in jaw evolution, from the jawless condition, through appearance of palatoquadrate and mandibular cartilages to the condition found in shark jaws; *C,* the chondrocranium of a shark in detail, showing labial cartilages as well as jaws. Figures *A, B,* from PALAEOZOIC FISHES, by R.S. Miles and J.A. Moy-Thomas, copyright © 1971 by Saunders College Publishing; figure *C* from THE VERTEBRATE BODY, Sixth Edition, by A.S. Romer and T.S. Parsons, copyright © 1986 by Saunders College Publishing; all three figures reproduced by permission of the publisher.

have components derived from the dermatocranium and the splanchnocranium. The braincase is mainly chondral in origin but has dermal bone in the roof of the mouth.

Elements of the Braincase

The braincase supports the base of the brain and encloses the ear (Figure 3). This unit consists of chondral elements that remain cartilaginous in elasmobranchs and holocephalans but ossify completely in most bony fish and in tetrapods. At the base of the skull, where the head articulates (joins) with the vertebral column, a ring of four bones develops. These are the occipital bones, and they may have been derived originally from vertebrae. Two separate ossifications surround the inner ear; they are fused in most adult

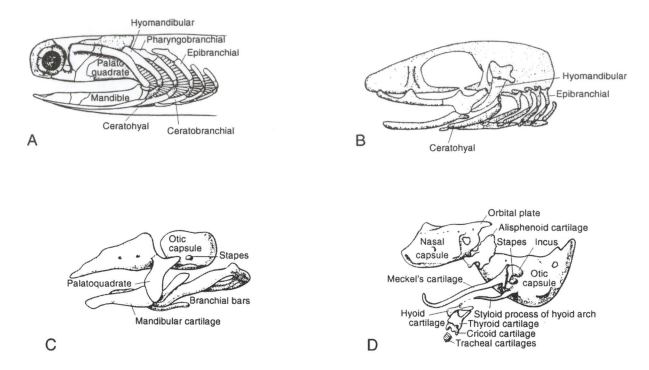

Figure 3. Four levels of evolution of the braincase (chondrocranium) in jawed vertebrates. *A*, the acanthodian *Climatius*; *B*, a teleost fish; *C*, an amphibian; *D*, a primate. Figures from THE VERTEBRATE BODY, Sixth Edition, by A.S. Romer and T.S. Parsons, copyright © 1986 by Saunders College Publishing, reproduced by permission of the publisher.

animals. In front of the otic (ear) bones is the basisphenoid, and in front of this is the sphenethmoid ossification. The dermal element of this functional unit is the parasphenoid, a sheet of dermal bone that forms in the roof of the mouth and covers the ventral (belly-side, or lower) surface of the sphenethmoid and the basisphenoid.

Early development of the braincase follows a similar basic pattern in most vertebrates (Figure 4). First, the parachordal cartilages grow on each side of the embryonic notochord (rigid, fiber-wound rod of connective tissue that lies below the spinal chord) and fuse to produce the basal plate below the brain. Next, two separate trabecular cartilages appear in front of the notochord; the front ends fuse. The trabeculars then join the parachordal cartilages, leaving a medial (center) gap for the pituitary gland. Next, the occipital condyles (actually derived from the first vertebrae) form at the back of the basal plate. Finally, capsules that surround the olfactory organs develop from the trabeculae, and separate cartilaginous capsules surround the vestibular organ or inner ear, later fusing with the basal plate and with the developing quadrate.

In lower vertebrates, the chondrocranium forms around the brain with its cranial nerves and blood supply, enclosing the whole brain and leaving openings (foramina) for nerves and blood vessels. In some groups, such as early dipnoans (lungfishes) and rhipidistians (lobe-finned fishes), the cartilage ossifies. In others, like elasmobranchs (includes sharks, rays, skates, chimeras), holocephalans (cartilaginous marine fishes), and chondrosteans (includes sturgeon, paddlefish), the overall body remains cartilaginous, but the cartilage may calcify. In these early vertebrates, separate cartilages develop around the eyes, within the sclera (the "white" of the eye).

In higher vertebrates, ossification, fusion, and changes in function obliterate much of the initial separation of the different parts.

During evolution, skull structures in lower vertebrates have undergone many changes, most of which can be related to the changing position of other organs in the head, such as the notochord, parts of the brain, cranial nerves, and blood vessels. Further modifications of the braincase occur in land-dwelling tetrapods. One of these changes involves the development of a fenestra (window, or gap) in the otic capsule to improve hearing in air. Another alteration occurs when the orbital cartilage fuses to the anterior lateral (to the front and side) wall of the chondrocranium. Changes in the olfactory or nasal capsules are related to the acquisition of air breathing and the development of a secondary palate. (This structure enables crocodylians and other amphibians to breathe and swallow at the same time.)

Basic Elements of the Dermal Skull

Bones of the dermal skull, called membrane bones, develop below the skin, in templates of a matrix of collagen and calcium secreted into developing mesenchyme cells. These bones are responsible for covering most of the brain. In addition, the dermal skull has openings for the external nares (nostrils), the eyes (orbits), and, in some vertebrates, a third opening for the pineal eye, called the parietal foramen (Figure 5). The ear opens behind the dermal skull, through a notch behind the orbit.

Early in vertebrate evolution, dermal structures of the head skeleton formed a tessera (plate) of small elements, and within the different groups of fishes with dermal skulls, these elements fuse to form larger bones. In sarcopterygians (lobe-finned fishes) this covering of bones over the cranium is thick and strong, particularly where required to protect delicate underlying structures. In rhipidistians, the group closest to the tetrapods, the pattern of skull roofing bones can be traced in the arrangements of bones found in early amphibians (Figure 6).

In the early tetrapods, the dermal skull has two marginal tooth-bearing bones, the maxilla (upper jawbone) and premaxilla (jawbone of the snout), around the border of the upper jaw (Figure 5). A circular series of bones surrounds each eye: the jugal, the lachrymal, the postorbital, prefrontal, and postfrontal. The cheek series includes the squamosal and the quadratojugal. The temporal series has three bones: the tabular, supratemporal, and intertemporal. The median dorsal series of paired bones covering the skull roof includes the nasal, the frontal, the parietal, and the postparietal bones. In derived (specialized) vertebrates, the parietal foramen for the pineal eye lies between the parietal bones. In early vertebrates that have retained an unpaired series of bones in the skull roof, the parietal foramen perforates one of the medial bones.

Elements of the Palate and Mandible

This functional unit of the skull comprises chondral elements of the upper and lower jaws, as well as a covering of dermal bones (Figures 4, 5). The palate may include openings for the olfactory organs (internal nares or choanae), depending on the taxon studied.

Dermal elements of the palate include four bones that form in the roof of the mouth. The pterygoids are the largest and are medial in position, with three bones situated on the lateral surface. These are the vomers, the palatines, and the ectopterygoids. In actinopterygians (including all common fishes, except sharks and skates), these bones may all have teeth, like the maxilla and premaxilla of the dermal skull. The chondral component of the palate is the palatoquadrate cartilage. The back section of this cartilage ossifies to form the quadrate (the joint, or articulation with the mandible, or lower jaw); the front section ossifies as the epipterygoid.

In the mandible, the chondral element is known as Meckel's cartilage. Part of this may ossify as the articular bone (the bone particularly involved in the joint, therefore, in movement). Meckel's cartilage is sheathed by a number of dermal bones. The dentary bone carries teeth, and these occlude (meet) with the teeth of the maxilla and premaxilla. Below the dentary bone are the splenials, the surangular, and the angular bones, on the external surface of the cartilage. On the internal surface of the cartilage, the prearticular and coronoid bones develop. This basic pattern is considerably modified by fusion and loss of bony elements in all major vertebrate groups.

Vertebrates with Jaws

Development of jaws in the early vertebrates permitted a range of adaptations related to feeding, and this fact facilitated an extensive radiation (diversification and geographic spread) of vertebrate life forms. The fossil record of these changes is unfortunately imper-

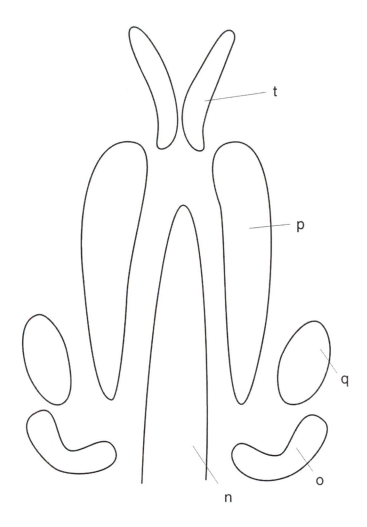

Figure 4. Initial development of the braincase. Key: *n,* notochord; *p,* parachordal cartilages; *q,* quadrate; *o,* otic capsule; *t,* trabeculi cranii.

fect, and some groups, such as the palaeoniscoids, show few transitional forms.

Chondrichthyan (cartilaginous) fishes, such as sharks and holocephalans, have a braincase with a palatoquadrate and mandible but no dermal elements. Eyes are protected by separate scleral cartilages. Labial cartilages are present in the lips around the palatoquadrate and mandibular cartilage, and teeth are attached loosely by connective tissue fibers to all of these cartilages. Fossil chondrichthyans are best known from their teeth, and the skulls are only preserved under exceptional conditions (Lund 1989).

Osteichthyan fishes (true bony fishes), a group that includes the actinopterygians and the sarcopterygians, usually have heavily ossified dermal skulls with many individual bones. The braincase and palatal complex are also well ossified, and the fossil record is extensive for these groups. The dermatocranium of bony fishes consists of a large number of small bones below the skin, reaching back to the pectoral girdle. Bones also protect the operculum (covering over gill slits in bony fishes) and surround the eyes and jaws. The pattern of bones is characteristic of each group of fishes and

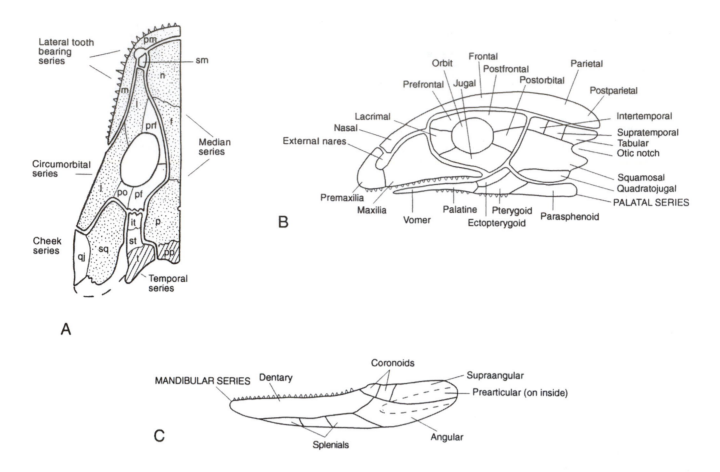

Figure 5. Dermal elements of the skull and jaws. From: *A,* THE VERTEBRATE BODY, Sixth Edition, by A.S. Romer and T.S. Parsons, copyright © 1986 by Saunders College Publishing, reproduced by permission of the publisher; *B, C,* Hildebrand (1995), copyright © John Wiley and Sons, Inc., reprinted by permission of John Wiley and Sons, Inc.

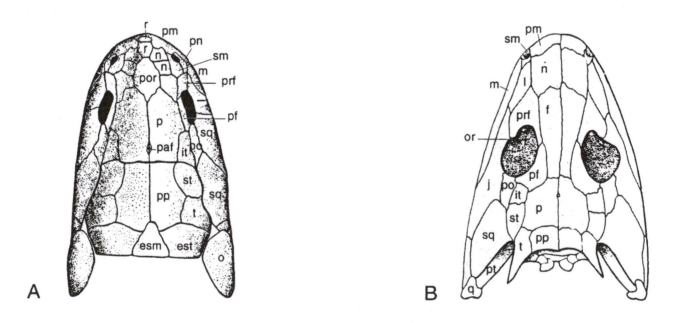

Figure 6. Skull roof. *A,* rhipidistians; *B,* labyrinthodonts. Figures from THE VERTEBRATE BODY, Sixth Edition, by A.S. Romer and T.S. Parsons, copyright © 1986 by Saunders College Publishing, reproduced by permission of the publisher.

not easy to relate to the pattern of bones in higher vertebrates, except in rhipidistians.

Early actinopterygians, including the palaeoniscoids and the modern teleosts, have a tessera of roofing bones. This settles into patterns that are a defining characteristic of the different groups, further modified as the group evolves. Evolution among actinopterygian fishes may have been initiated from the same basic group that produced the sarcopterygians (including lungfishes, coelacanths), but it followed a different course, so later actinopterygians remained bound to the aquatic environment. Changes in feeding and in locomotion produced an enormous variety of adaptations, and the teleost fishes are the most numerous of living vertebrates.

When they first appear in the fossil record, the earliest sarcopterygian fishes (the lungfishes and rhipidistians) are well along the line of evolutionary divergence from the early actinopterygian stock. The lungfishes quickly established unique dental and skull structures, with specific feeding, respiratory, and locomotory adaptations, and surprisingly few characters have changed since. In early dipnoans, fusion between braincase, palate, and dermal skull is complete, but in living dipnoans the dermal bones remain quite separate and are barely attached to the chondrocranium. The pattern of dermal skull bones of early dipnoans such as *Dipnorhynchus* can be traced by a process of fusion, loss, and change in size of the elements to the living *Neoceratodus*.

The pattern of fusion and loss that alters the tessera of dermal bones in dipnoans is difficult to relate to that of tetrapods because in dipnoan evolution the medial unpaired bones remain important. In fact, their skull structure tells scholars that the dipnoans cannot be considered to be the closest sister group of the land animals. The dermal roofing pattern and dentition of dipnoans is unique, and few of the bones can be compared with those of tetrapods. In addition, dipnoans share many characters with sharks, such as a labial cartilage in the upper lip, separate scleral cartilages, and a complete chondrocranium isolated from the dermal skull. Other characters of dipnoans are reminiscent of actinopterygian fishes, such as the tooth-bearing bones (Kemp 1995).

The rhipidistian skull pattern is well established in the earliest known forms. In early species of this group, dermal skulls consisted of a large number of small bones, and modifications in the form of fusions, shape changes, and loss of elements can be traced through the ranks of the rhipidistians and into their closest sister group, the amphibians (Figure 6).

Dermal bones of the rhipidistians and their sister group, the early amphibians, cover the head completely and extend to the shoulder girdle. The evolutionary changes that result in the structures of higher tetrapods (the birds, mammals, and reptiles) have increased the size and degree of ossification of some bones, and reduced others. Still other bones disappear altogether or change in function. Some changes occur as a result of increased brain size, and others are driven by changes in the jaw articulation and musculature or by the development of a secondary palate.

Conquest of the land was not followed immediately by changes in the braincase and dermal skull (Olson 1971). It did affect the remnants of the splanchnocranium (visceral cranium) because gill respiration was lost and the associated gill arches changed their function. Early amphibians are similar in skull and

jaw function to the rhipidistians. Future adaptations to terrestrial life involved changes related to feeding and (to a lesser extent) locomotion and specializations in sense organs. Changes among reptiles were largely related to alterations in the jaw musculature, and some alterations in the function of bones close to the jaw articulation (joint). The brain remained small and unspecialized. Among both archosaurs (including crocodiles, dinosaurs, flying reptiles), which led to modern birds, and synapsids (including extinct mammal-like reptiles), which resulted in mammals, the brain became larger and more complex, resulting in changes in the shape of the cranium. Sense organs also increased in complexity, which involved alterations in the positions of individual sense organs and increased requirements for protection.

Little is known of the intermediate stages in the evolution of the bird skull. Teeth were lost early, but the remains of *Archaeopteryx* (the first fossilized bird) are regarded chiefly as avian because the fossil includes impressions of feathers, not because of any adaptations to the skeleton. In mammal-like reptiles, the fossil record of the changes that led to mammals is a little more complete, but much of the story needs verification from an examination of living animals. Evolution within mammals has centered on studies of teeth and jaws, because these are the parts of the animal that have been preserved most often; they are also the structures that provide most information about the animals.

In the dermal skull of tetrapods, the frequent irregularities in bone shape and arrangement found in fishes largely have disappeared. The median unpaired series of bones present in fishes is not found in tetrapods; in them, the medial bones are paired. An opening for the pineal organ is still present among fossil amphibians and in a few reptiles, but the operculum and the connection of the skull to the pectoral girdle have gone. Numbers of bones in the groups that make up the skull and the jaw are refined by fusions, particularly among the temporal and circumorbital series, and further changes involve the development of fenestrae (spaces in the skull) designed to accommodate the jaw musculature.

Jaw Suspension

Conversion of the first gill arch into jaws, used for capture of prey and for biting and breaking up food, was a major step in vertebrate evolution. The initial change was followed by attempts to strengthen the jaw structure by altering the suspension of the jaws, that is, the relationship of the jaws to the rest of the skull. This has been achieved in several ways by different groups of vertebrates, and a particular form of suspension may have appeared more than once during evolution (Figure 7). For instance, presence of an "autostylic jaw suspension" in four diverse groups of vertebrates does not indicate an evolutionary progression from one to another, nor does the occurrence of an "amphistylic suspension" in sharks and in teleosts indicate a close phylogenetic relationship.

In the simplest jaw suspension system, the autostylic, the epibranchial bone (equivalent to the palatoquadrate), was fused to the chondrocranium, and the rest of the mandibular arch articulated with it as Meckel's cartilage. This type of jaw suspension is found in dipnoans, holocephalans, and placoderms. This system does not involve the second visceral arch (hyoid arch), which

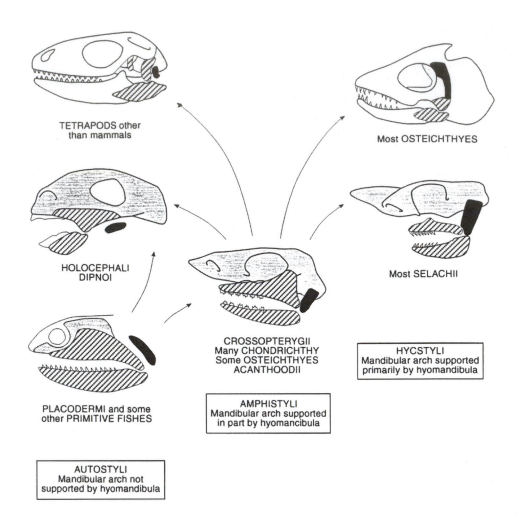

Figure 7. Jaw suspension in vertebrates. Symbols: *black,* derivatives of hyomandibular arch; *hatched,* deirvatives of mandibular arch; *stippled,* derivatives of chondrocranium. Redrawn by Roberto L. Marques after Hildebrand (1955), copyright © 1955 by and by permission of John Wiley and Sons, Inc.

remains separate and has a different function. In rhipidistians, many sharks, acanthodians, and some bony fishes, the jaw suspension is amphistylic. The hyoid arch provides partial support for the jaws. In hyostylic skulls the hyoid arch is responsible for the entire suspension of the jaws, as found in most sharks and bony fishes. Tetrapods have an autostylic arrangement—the hyoid arch is reduced and is not involved in jaw suspension. Additional support for the jaws comes from dermal bones surrounding the jaw articulation. In mammals there have been further changes in the function of the hyoid and the dermal bones present in the reptile jaw.

Jaw Articulation

Over the course of vertebrate evolution, fundamental changes have occurred in the jaw articulation (Figure 8). Most of the changes that take place during the transition from a rhipidistian to an amphibian concern jaw articulation. These involve the development of autostyly, probably independently of the same change

that took place with the holocephalans and dipnoans. The squamosal and quadrate articulate with the mandible without the support of the hyomandibular bone, which becomes an ear ossicle (bone), called the stapes. This little bone acts to enhance transmission of sound to the brain. Other parts of the hyoid arch supported the tongue and still do, but the remaining arches of the visceral cranium become reduced in land-dwelling adult amphibians—although they are retained in the original form in young larvae and in a few salamanders that spend most of their lives in water. In reptiles, birds, and mammals, the remaining cartilages evolved into supporting structures for the larynx, the thyroid, and arytenoid and cricoid cartilages.

Further changes in jaw articulation have occurred in reptiles and birds. Like much of our understanding of vertebrate evolution, this evolutionary sequence was worked out initially using embryology and comparative anatomy, and confirmed using analysis of fossils. In early reptiles, the first mandibular arch still is represented by the quadrate and the articular, but the second hyomandibular arch has become the stapes. In mammal-like rep-

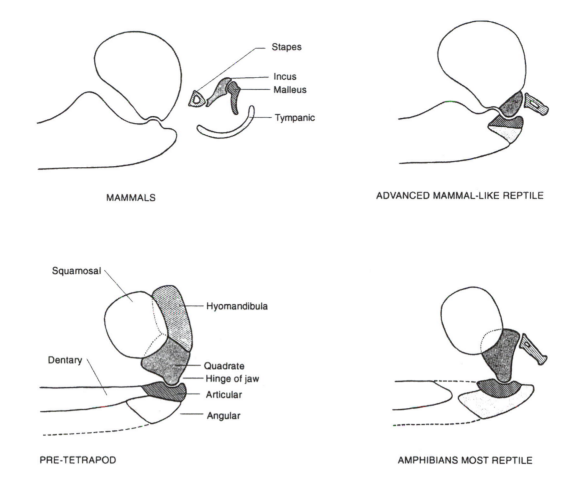

Figure 8. Changes in the jaw articulation in vertebrates. Redrawn by Roberto L. Marques after Hildebrand (1955), copyright © 1955 by and by permission of John Wiley and Sons, Inc.

tiles, the dentary bone in the mandible is enlarged, and the articular reduced. Both articular and quadrate become smaller and evolve into ear ossicles in mammals; the quadrate evolves into the incus and the prearticular and articular evolve into the malleus. The jaw articulation in mammals is between the dentary and the squamosal. Mammals are defined traditionally as having a malleus in the ear, and reptiles as having an articular in the jaw.

Temporal Fenestrae and Emargination

Study of jaw muscles has helped to explain modifications in the dermal bones of amphibians and early reptiles. Amphibians and fishes have the jaw muscles beside the braincase and below the superficial dermal bones of the skull roof. This arrangement also is found in early reptiles. Jaws of derived reptiles are stronger, which places increased stress on different parts of the skull. This resulted in a skull stronger in some areas and weaker in others. As a result, spaces appeared in the skull roof, and jaw muscles became attached to the margins (edges) of the spaces. Among reptiles, this process, called fenestration, or the appearance of spaces, occurred several times in different groups, each time in a different part of the skull (Figure 9).

Very early reptiles had anapsid skulls, with no openings. Being descended from these reptiles, turtles have anapsid skulls too, with no openings apart from the orbit and nasal opening. These animals have evolved a mechanism of accommodating the large jaw muscles: the bones at the back of the skull are emarginated—the edges have become irregular and notched. Synapsid reptiles have a temporal opening, which is bordered by the postorbital, squamosal, and jugal bones. Mammal-like reptiles were synapsid, and the temporal depression behind the orbit of mammalian skulls is a variation of the temporal fenestra of the synapsid skull. Plesiosaurs and ichthyosaurs (giant marine reptiles) have euryapsid skulls, with the temporal opening bordered by the parietal, postorbital, and squamosal bones. There are no living descendants of euryapsid reptiles.

The archosaurs (whose descendants are the crocodiles, dinosaurs, and modern birds) and the lepidosaurs (which gave rise to lizards and snakes) have diapsid skulls with two fenestrae. The upper space is bordered by the postorbital, the squamosal, and the parietal bones, and the lower by the jugal, quadratojugal, postorbital, and squamosal bones. Modern birds have lost the bone between the two openings. Lizards have lost the bone below the

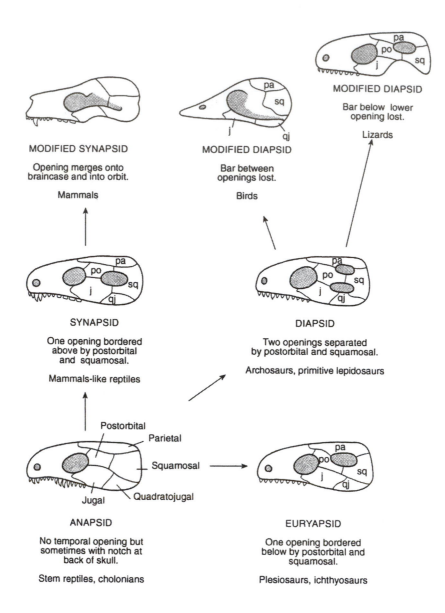

Figure 9. Temporal openings in tetrapod skulls. Redrawn by Roberto L. Marques after Hildebrand (1955), copyright © 1955 by and by permission of John Wiley and Sons, Inc.

lower opening. As a result, both are said to have modified diapsid skulls. Most dinosaurs and crocodiles have retained the basic diapsid arrangement.

Cranial Kinesis

Cranial kinesis refers to movement within the chondrocranium, and among lower vertebrates is usually related to jaw action. Cranial kinesis appears sporadically among vertebrate classes. Acanthodian fishes and early actinopterygians had simple jaws, with a single hinge and a weak bite. Bony fishes have a hinge between the maxilla and the premaxilla, and more anteriorly positioned adductor muscles (those that help close the jaw, are moved toward the front of the jaw). As a result, the jaw is stronger and the gape wider. The maxilla drops down and forward

when the mouth opens, which helps to prevent the escape of prey. Later developments involved movements of the premaxilla, to make the mouth protrusible (able to move forward). Elasmobranchs and holocephalans achieve the same effect, protrusible lips, by using the labial cartilages. Rhipidistians have a joint between the front, trabecular skull and the back, otico-occipital skull to increase the gape and strength of the jaws. Birds and some reptiles can move the palate to and fro on the braincase, using the joint with the quadrate and a hinge between the bones in front of the orbits. This means the upper jaw can be raised when the mandible (lower jaw) is lowered, which increases the size of the gape. It may also make the bite stronger. Mammals do not have cranial kinesis. To achieve the same effects, they vary the form of the jaw articulation, the length of the jaws, and the arrangement and size of the jaw musculature.

Secondary Palates

Lower vertebrates, with few exceptions, swallow food quickly without chewing it. The palate in these fishes, and in early labyrinthodonts, is solid. In amphibians, reptiles, and birds, the palate has openings that make the skull lighter without losing strength. This is sufficient for animals that do not need to grind or crush food items.

More advanced vertebrates, like the mammal-like reptiles, utilize diets that require modification before they are swallowed. However, it is difficult to chew or grind food and breathe at the same time, since the mouth cavity is the same as the breathing cavity. Therefore, mechanisms evolved in some animals to provide a separate passage for air above and behind the mouth cavity, ensuring that breathing and eating can continue at the same time, without conflict.

This process—the development of a secondary palate—required some fundamental changes in the skull (Hildebrand 1995). Some bones in the roof of the mouth, like the parasphenoid, disappeared. The premaxilla loses contact with the internal nares, which merge and move to the back of the mouth (Figure 10). Others moved backwards, like the vomer, or became shorter, like the pterygoids. Shelflike processes (bony protuberances)

developed on the maxilla and palatine bones, which join in the midline. These changes produce a secondary palate, separating the breathing passage from the oral cavity.

A secondary palate evolved more than once during vertebrate history. Some turtles have a short secondary palate. Mammal-like reptiles and mammals have a long secondary palate, partially formed of bone and partly of soft tissue, and crocodiles have a very long, bony secondary palate.

Development of a secondary palate influenced the arrangement of structures associated with the olfactory sense. Nasal structures in mammals are primarily part of the respiratory system, involving not only the nasal bones and cartilage of the septum, along with the secondary palate, but also some delicate scroll-like bones, the turbinates, or conchae. These bones are chondral in origin, and separate each of the paired nasal cavities into three partial passageways: the superior, middle, and inferior meatuses. The bones are concerned mostly with warming and humidifying inspired air (that breathed in) and are significant for mammals that live in marginal environments such as deserts or cold places. The structures are less concerned with the olfactory sense. Olfactory sense cells are positioned in the holes of the "cribriform plate"

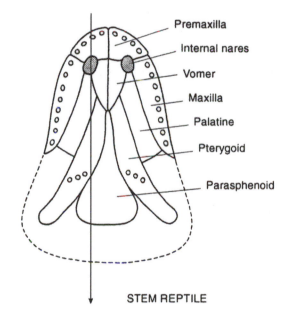

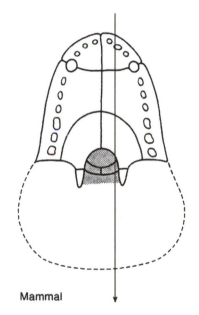

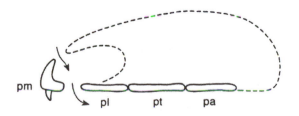

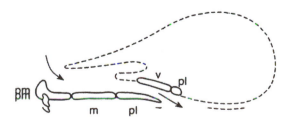

Figure 10. Evolution of the secondary palate. From Hildebrand (1955), copyright © 1995 by John Wiley and Sons, Inc., reprinted by permission of John Wiley and Sons, Inc.

at the back of the nasal cavity, although a few may extend to the epithelium of the turbinate bones.

Modifications in Mammals and Birds

Mammals represent a terminal and simplified state of vertebrate evolution, but the skulls preserve some conservative characters (those that evolved much earlier). Architecture of the cranium, the secondary palate, the jaw suspension, and the ear ossicles is similar to that found in the most advanced mammal-like reptile. Because the brain is larger, dermal and chondral bones of the skull are closely integrated and the space for the brain considerably expanded. Like amphibians, there are two occipital condyles; reptiles and birds have only one. Unlike birds, the cranial sutures are still present in adults, but some bones are fused, like the initially separate occipital bones. Otic bones fuse with the squamosal bones to form the temporal, and the separate sphenoid bones fuse to a single bone. What is more, many bones found in the skulls of amphibians and early reptiles are lost. The prefrontals, postfrontals, postorbitals, quadratojugals, and parasphenoids of reptiles cannot be found in the mammal skull, and the mammalian lower jaw consists of a single bone, the dentary.

The orbit of mammals is often confluent (comes together) with the temporal fenestra (fossa) but may be separated from it by an arch of bone known as the postorbital bar. This may be complete, as in primates and in most herbivores, or partial, as in carnivores. The orbit also varies in position from the lateral (side) surface of the head to the front. Position of the orbit alters the vision of the animal, because the visual fields do not overlap when the orbit is placed on the sides of the head. Generally, the orbits of active carnivorous mammals are front-facing in position, permitting stereoscopic vision; however, the orbit of herbivorous, prey animals is placed on the side of the head, giving two fields of vision over a greater area, extending almost behind the animal.

Mammals and birds have taken different approaches to the development of a light and strong skull. In birds, the bones of the cranial vault are thin and fused so closely that sutures are no longer visible. Mammal skull bones contain sinuses, large vaulted spaces filled with air. Some of these pneumatic bones open into the nasal cavity, and others are closed, like the mastoid process of the temporal bone. Bones with sinuses provide strength without increased weight and may protect animals during fights. The pneumatic bones may also provide resonance for voice production or improve conduction (transmission) of sound.

Development

Early embryologists placed the cells of the developing embryo into categories that reflected their position in the embryo prior to movement of those cells and the formation of defined tissues and organs. Ectodermal cells produce the outer layer of an embryo and are responsible for development of the skin, the nervous system, and derivatives of these tissues. Cells that move into the embryo form the endoderm, producing the intestines, liver, pancreas, and respiratory systems. The mesoderm is responsible for muscular and connective tissues. A specialized derivative of the ectoderm is the neural crest, which consists of cells that appear around the margin of the developing neural plate and migrate into the embryo after the three primary layers have been arranged. The cells then form peripheral nerves and have been implicated in the development of many other tissues as well.

Traditionally, the skull has been regarded as derived entirely from cells of the neural crest. This may well be true in higher vertebrates (Ahlberg 1994). However, it may not be the case in fishes, where the available experimental evidence indicates a role for the neural crest in the formation of parts of the splanchnocranium only in some groups. The development of the vertebrate head is the result of a wide array of complex interactions among many cells. A thorough knowledge of molecular genetics in relation to skeletal development is needed to understand the development of the vertebrate head, as well as the following patterns of induction that occur during epithelial and mesenchymal interactions as embryos develop. Specific genes, induction by nerves entering cellular primordia of skeletal structures, initiation of osteogenic (genes that control bone development) cascades by growth factors, and the effects of stress from muscular action on bones all affect the developing vertebrate skull.

Conclusion

Although much of our information on the evolution of the vertebrate skull is derived from embryology and comparative anatomy of living animals, fossils are essential for complete understanding of vertebrate phylogeny. The fossil record is also important for an analysis of the changes that have occurred during the course of evolution from the early jawless vertebrates to the highly derived mammals and birds.

ANNE KEMP

See also Craniates; Gnathostome; Pharyngeal Arches and Derivatives; Sensory Capsules; Teeth

Works Cited

Ahlberg, P.E. 1994. How to keep a head in order. *Nature* (London) 385:489–90.

Janvier, P. 1995. The dawn of the vertebrates: Characters versus common ascent in the use of current vertebrate phylogenies. *Palaeontology* 39:259–87.

Hildebrand, M. 1995. *Analysis of Vertebrate Structure.* 4th ed., New York: Wiley.

Kemp, A. 1995. Marginal tooth-bearing bones in the lower jaw of the Recent Australian lungfish, *Neoceratodus forsteri* (Osteichthyes, Dipnoi). *Journal of Morphology* 225:345–55.

Lund, R. 1989. New petalodonts (Chondrichthyes) from the Upper Mississipian Bear Gulch Limestone (Namurian E2B) of Montana. *Journal of Vertebrate Paleontology* 9:350–68.

Miles, R.S., and J.A. Moy-Thomas. 1971. *Palaeozoic Fishes.* 2nd ed., London: Chapman and Hall; Philadelphia: Saunders.

Olson, E.C. 1971. *Vertebrate Palaeozoology.* New York: Wiley.

Romer, A.S. 1966. *Vertebrate Paleontology.* 3rd ed,. Chicago: University of Chicago Press.

Romer, A.S., and T.S. Parsons. 1986. *The Vertebrate Body*. 6th ed., Philadelphia: Saunders.

Further Reading

Hanken, J., and B.K. Hall. 1993. *The Skull*. 3 vols. Chicago: University of Chicago Press.

Hildebrand, M. 1974. *Analysis of Vertebrate Structure*. New York: Wiley; 4th ed., 1995.

Olson, E.C. 1971. *Vertebrate Palaeozoology*. New York: Wiley.

Romer, A.S. 1933. *Vertebrate Paleontology*. Chicago: University of Chicago Press; 3rd ed., 1966.

Romer, A.S. 1949. *The Vertebrate Body*. Philadelphia: Saunders; 6th ed. by A.S. Romer and T.S. Parsons, 1986.

SMELL

See Odor and Pheromone Receptors

SMITH, WILLIAM

English, 1769–1839

In Great Britain today, it is possible for persons of quite humble origin to rise to scientific eminence—possible, but still rare. At the beginning of the nineteenth century, such a feat was almost inconceivable. Yet at least one man, William Smith, managed it so successfully that today he is known as the "Father of English Geology."

William Smith was born in the small Oxfordshire village of Churchill on 23 March 1769. His father, a blacksmith, died when William was eight years old. Two years later, when his mother married an innkeeper, his father's eldest brother, a farmer at Over Norton, became William's guardian. It is doubtful whether William had more than a minimum of schooling. Instead, whenever the tasks of the farm permitted, he roamed the countryside, looking at the rocks and collecting the abundant Jurassic fossils of the region—which William and his neighbors named "pundibs," "pound-stones," and "quoit-stones." He began to draw these objects, often in color. Also, in hopes of avoiding a farm laborer's life, he began studying geometry, mathematics, and surveying techniques. As a result, at the age of 18 he was appointed assistant to Edward Webb, Land Surveyor of Stow-on-the-Wold.

At that time, the work of surveyors included many of the tasks today allotted to civil engineers, such as determining the flow rates of water and planning dams, tunnels, and machinery. For all these tasks, Smith was well suited because of his skills in surveying and calculation. Soon he was working quasi-independently, not only undertaking land surveys in Oxfordshire, Gloucestershire, and Warwickshire but also advising on the construction of the Sapperton Tunnel on the Thames and of Severn Canal and examining a boring for coal at Plaitford in the New Forest of Hampshire. In his work, Smith observed how soils controlled the character of the countryside, the trees and plants, and the procedures of farming. Further, he continued to look at the rocks and to notice the fossils they contained.

In 1791 Smith was sent to survey an estate at Stowey, Somersetshire. That county was then a center for coal mining, so the services of surveyors were in high demand. By 1792 Smith was living at Rugborne Farm, near High Littleton, and working for the collieries. He noted:

My subterraneous survey of these coal-veins, with sections which I drew of the strata sunk through in the pits, confirmed my notion of some regularity in their formation; but the colliers would not allow of any regularity in the matter of the hills above the "red-earth," which they were in the habit of sinking through; but on this subject *I began to think for myself.*

At that time, a canal linking Bath, on the River Avon, and Newbury, on the River Kennet, was then under construction. To cut transportation costs, the Somersetshire coal owners decided to construct a local canal that would link with this larger one. Smith was appointed surveyor (1794) and was sent on a tour of other canals in northern England. During the next five years, he guided the Somersetshire Coal Canal project. As the work progressed, Smith observed how the layers of rock, from the "red-earth" (the Triassic New Red Marl) upward, followed one another regularly and in a particular order, "like superposed slices of bread and butter." Furthermore, he perceived that particular beds contained characteristic fossils—bivalves (clams, mussels), brachiopods (clamlike animals), corals, sometimes gastropods (snails), or cephalopods (marine animals with many arms, such as octopuses and squid).

In 1799 Smith attended a momentous meeting in Bath, with two men who were also fossil collectors, the Reverends Benjamin Richardson and Joseph Townsend. Smith not only dictated to them a sequential list of the strata about Bath, complete with their accompanying fossils, but also gave them a map of the Bath district and another of the whole county of Somerset, "coloured geologically." The former survives in the Geological Society collections; the latter is lost.

This earliest table of strata very definitely reflects Smith's practicality and his eye for lithology (study of stone). Approximately 13 units are recognized and characterized by such simple names as "clay," "sand," or "marl"; other names reflected their usage—"freestone" for easy quarrying, and "fullers' earth" for washing sheep fleeces. The difficulty of characterizing Smith had with one unit was made apparent when it was named "Bastard fullers' earth and sundries." For the alternating black clays and argillaceous limestones typical of the Early Jurassic, Smith used the quarrymen's name "Lias," while applying the marketing term "Forest Marble" to another unit. He did not name the fossils he used in identifying the units.

Although this table now seems unimpressive, it attracted considerable attention when circulated by Smith's clerical friends, for it marked the inception—in Britain, at least—of biostratigraphy, the idea that strata formed a definite succession and could be recognized, not merely by lithology but also by the contained fossils. The latter fact had been perceived earlier in France by Abbé Jean Louis Girard Soulavie and was being explored by Georges Cuvier and Alexandre Brongniart in Paris, but it was Smith's wholly independent work that demonstrated this analytical process to the scientific world at large.

One of Smith's earliest "converts" was another land surveyor, John Farey. Smith and Farey first met in 1801, and soon they were going out on geological expeditions together. Not only did Farey publish brief accounts of Smith's discoveries, but he also prepared extended geological sections across southern England, ahead of Smith's own endeavors. Unfortunately, these never were published, so the extent of Farey's contribution to Smith's work cannot be assessed.

After finishing his work for the Coal Canal Company, Smith worked for such people as the great agriculturalist Thomas Coke in Norfolk and the Duke of Bedford at Woburn, examining mines and quarries all over England and Wales. Smith's concerns extended to include such other matters as sea defenses and irrigation. In 1806 he published *Observations on the Utility, Form and Management of Water Meadows, and the Draining and Irrigation of Peat Bogs* and, a year later, a *Description of Norfolk, Its Soils and Substrata.* He also produced reports and prepared plans for his various employers.

Wherever Smith went, he examined the strata and made notes of their fossil content. In 1801, encouraged by his friends, he issued a prospectus for a proposed work on these topics and began preparing a geological map of England and Wales. However, his burgeoning surveying business took up too much of his time; in 1802 he rented an office in Bath, and by 1804 he had moved to London. Following the founding of the Geological Society of London in 1807, some of its members visited Smith's house, where fossils were displayed on sloping shelves. In 1812, a London map publisher and engraver, John Cary, undertook to publish Smith's map, engraving the first plates almost immediately.

Eventually, Smith's monumental work, *A Delineation of the Strata of England and Wales, with Parts of Scotland,* was published in 1815. In all, the plates show 23 different strata at a scale of five miles to the inch; most still are characterized by lithological terms, but four have distinctive names ("Portland Rock," "Oaktree Clay," "Clunch Clay," and "Kelloway's Stone"), two at least of which refer to specific localities. Another, "Cornbrash," is in fact a quarryman's term referring to the similarity in appearance between the rock of that bed and that of corn at an early stage of milling. Each stratum is distinctly colored; the deeper shade at the base of each stratum indicates the general dip. The map was accompanied by a discussion.

A year later the first two parts of Smith's *Strata Identified by Organized Fossils* were issued, containing illustrations of those fossils. Also that year, Smith's collection, arranged stratigraphically, was purchased by the British Museum. Part 3 appeared in 1817, as did *A Geological Section from London to Snowdon* and part 1 of *A Stratigraphical System of Organized Fossils.* (The last was designed to explain the British Museum collection; other parts were planned, but never appeared.)

Smith's work continued steadily. As his knowledge grew, he modified the coloring of his maps. In 1819 Cary published not only part 4 of *Strata* but also Smith's maps of four English counties and his five large *Geological Sections,* which explored different parts of southern England. In 1820, Cary published a smaller, updated version of Smith's original map, at the scale of 15 inches to the mile.

Unfortunately, despite the high scientific importance of these publishing endeavors, they were not profitable for Smith. In 1819 debts caused him to forfeit his London house and most of his possessions (although he did sell his remaining geological collections to the British Museum). During the ensuing five years, he followed a wandering life in the north of England, only rarely visiting London. However, Smith's misfortunes did not hinder his geological work. Instead, he produced even more county maps, eventually covering 21 counties. The map of Yorkshire was detailed enough to require four sheets.

From 1824 to 1828, Smith lived in Scarborough. Thereafter, for almost six years (1828–33), he occupied the position of Resident Land Steward to Sir John V.B. Johnstone in the nearby village of Hackness. During this time, Smith prepared a detailed map of the Hackness estate and surrounding Tabular Hills, at a scale of 6.5 inches to the mile. He then returned to Scarborough, where he lived for the rest of his life, helping to form the Scarborough Philosophical Society and the Scarborough Museum.

Throughout the 1820s, Smith received much assistance in the field from his nephew John Phillips, who would become professor of geology at Oxford and his uncle's first biographer. Together, they presented lectures or courses in geology in Hull, York, Sheffield, and other northern towns. Subsequently, Smith presented papers at meetings of the Yorkshire Geological Society and the British Association for the Advancement of Science. While traveling to an association meeting in Birmingham, he became ill, dying at a friend's house in Northampton on 28 April 1839.

Smith was too practical a person to mull over the question of the causes of earth movements and of the changes of successive faunas. Instead, he furnished his contemporaries with the means for understanding and mapping the sedimentary rocks of their land and singlehandedly made a massive beginning of that task. The title "Father of English Geology," bestowed upon him by Adam Sedgwick, is wholly merited.

WILLIAM A.S. SARJEANT

Biography

Born in Churchill, Oxfordshire, 23 March 1769. Land surveyor; pioneer of geological field mapping techniques; demonstrated the law of superposition of strata; showed that strata could be identified by fossils; identified the first succession of English strata, before 1799; composed first geological map of England and Wales, 1815; also created many county geological maps. Recipient, award of 50 guineas from the Society for the Encouragement of Arts, Manufactures, and Commerce, 1815; first recipient, Wollaston Medal, Geological Society of London, 1831; awarded an annuity of £100 from the British government, 1832; awarded honorary degree of Doctor of Laws, Trinity College, Dublin, 1835. Died in Northampton, 28 April 1839.

Major Publications

1806. *Observations on the Utility, Form and Management of Water Meadows, and the Draining and Irrigating of Peat Bogs, with an Account of Prisley Bog, and Other Extraordinary Improvements, Conducted for His Grace the Duke of Bedford, Thomas William Coke, Esq., M.P. and Others.* Norwich: Longman, Hurst, Rees, and Orne.

1807. *Description of Norfolk, Its Coals and Substrata.* Norwich: privately published.

1815. *A Delineation of the Strata of England and Wales, with Part of Scotland; Exhibiting the Collieries and Mines, the Marshes and Fen Lands Originally Overflowed by the Sea, and the Varieties of Soil According to the Variations of the Substrata, Illustrated by the Most Descriptive Names.* London: Carey. [At least five series were issued, showing additional detail as Smith learned more.]

1816–19. *Strata Identified by Organized Fossils, Containing Prints on Coloured Paper of the Most Characteristic Specimens in Each Stratum.* London: Arding.

1817a. *Geological Section from London to Snowdon: Showing the Varieties of the Strata, and the Correct Altitude of the Hills.* London: Carey.

1817b. *Stratigraphical System of Organized Fossils.* London: Williams.

1819–c. 1824. *A New Geological Map of England and Wales, Showing the Variety of Strata, Collieries, Mines, &c.* London: Carey.

Further Reading

Arkell. W.J. 1933. William Smith and the stratal terms. *In The Jurassic System in Great Britain.* Oxford: Clarendon.

Bather, F.A. 1926. *Address at Bath on 10th July, 1926 after Unveiling a Memorial Tablet to William Smith.* Bath: Bath Royal Literary and Scientific Institution.

Cox, L.R. 1948. *William Smith and the Birth of Stratigraphy.* London: Wightman.

Eyles, J.M. 1969a. William Smith (1769–1839): A bibliography of his published writings, maps and geological sections, printed and lithographed. *Journal of the Society for the Bibliography of Natural History* 5(2):87–109.

———. 1969b. William Smith (1769–1839). A chronology of significant dates in his life. *Proceedings of the Geological Society of London* 1657:173–76.

———. 1979. William Smith: Great discoverer or mere fossil collector? *Open Earth* 2:11–13.

Ford, T.D. 1967. The first detailed geological sections across England, by John Farey, 1806–08. *Mercian Geologist* 2 (1):41–49.

Ford, T.D., and H.S. Torrens. 1989. John Farey (1766–1826), and unrecognized polymath. *In* J. Farey, *General View of the Agriculture and Minerals of Derbyshire.* Vol. 1, Matlock, Derbyshire: Peak District Mines Historical Society.

Phillips, J. 1844. *Memoirs of William Smith, LL.D., Author of the "Map of the Strata of England and Wales."* London: Murray.

Sheppard, T. 1917. *William Smith: His Maps and Memoirs.* Proceedings of the Yorkshire Geological Society, 19. Hull: Brown.

Woodward, H. 1902. William Smith, LL.D., "Father of English Geology." *Proceedings of the Bath Natural History and Antiquarian Field Club* 10 (1):1–14.

SOUTH AMERICA

Since the end of the nineteenth century, the works of the pioneering Argentinean paleontologists Florentino Ameghino and his brother Carlos have documented the peculiar composition of the mammal assemblages from the Cenozoic (65 million years to present) of South America. Later studies by W.B. Scott (1937) and G.G. Simpson (1948, 1951) demonstrated the endemism (i.e., a feature unique to a particular area) of all Tertiary mammals from this continent. During the Cenozoic era, evolution produced many bizarre mammals in South America—*Glyptodon* (a gigantic armadillo-like animal) and related armadillos, diverse ground sloths, a variety of notoungulates (hoofed herbivores), and an outstanding diversity of marsupials and caviomorph rodents (e.g., guinea pigs).

The evolution of these Cenozoic mammals was so different from the evolution of mammals in Laurasia (the supercontinent that included both North America and Europe) and other continents that, when its implications were understood, the whole theory of how biological evolution occurs was enriched substantially. The findings showed that the isolation of a large continent over a long period of geological time may result in quite unique evolutionary products found in no other region in the world.

The study of South American vertebrates from the Mesozoic (from 245 to 65 million years ago) is no less important. In the last 35 years Mesozoic deposits in southern Brazil and several sites in western and southern Argentina have been the subject of significant study and intensive fieldwork. In part, the work was inspired by the research developed in Brazil by the German paleontologist Freidrich von Huene (1942) and in Argentina by the American paleontologist Alfred S. Romer (1966–72). These studies (especially Romer's work) showed that understanding South America's Triassic, Jurassic, and Cretaceous tetrapods (limbed vertebrates) leads to a better understanding of a set of rather complex and puzzling paleontological problems. Perhaps the most important of these is the evolution, paleogeographical distribution, and origin of several groups of tetrapods. Specifically, study of South America's fossil material has concentrated upon (a) the origin of mammals and dinosaurs, (b) the faunal isolation of Laurasia and Gondwana, the two supercontinents through most of the Mesozoic, (c) the evolution of endemic taxa because of this isolation, and (d) numerous unusual kinds of mammals, dinosaurs, crocodiles, and birds.

South America is probably the Gondwanian continent that has supplied most of the paleontological information about that supercontinent. Studying its past has led to a basic understanding of Gondwana's evolutionary and paleobiogeographic history during the Mesozoic. This article concentrates on the more outstanding vertebrates of the Paleozoic, Mesozoic, and Cenozoic of South America.

Paleozoic

South America's record of Paleozoic vertebrates is rather poor. Except for the primitive ray-finned fishes *Tholonosteon santacatarinae* (Beltran 1997), *Tholonotus braziliensis* (Dunkle and Schaeffer 1956), and unpublished species from the state of Santa Catarina (Richter 1991), most of the Paleozoic fishes from South America are based on very incomplete evidence. Bolivia has yielded diverse and well-preserved agnathans (jawless fishes), placoderms, and acanthodians. From Ordovician rocks of Bolivia, P.-Y. Gagnier (1987, 1989) described an interesting, complete specimen of an arandaspid agnathan (a type of jawless fish) *Sacabambaspis janvieri*, which is considered to be the oldest, most complete specimen of a vertebrate, not only from South America but from the whole world. M. Richter (1985) discussed various types of early fishes—acanthodians ("spiny sharks"), chondrichthyans (sharks and their relatives), paleonisciforms (primitive ray-finned fishes), and crossopterygians (lobe-finned fishes)—from Devonian, Carboniferous, and Permian sites in Brazil. However, these finds usually have been very fragmentary. In 1996 G. Arratia and A. Cione (1996) discussed the record of fossil fishes of southern South America.

Except for some footprints made by a Middle-Upper Devonian ichthyostegalian amphibian (a very primitive type of tetrapod) (Leonardi 1983) from Ponta Grossa Formation (Paraná State, Brazil), Paleozoic tetrapods of South America are represented only by Late Permian amphibians and reptiles. Marine or brackish-water mesosaurs (a group of very primitive reptiles) are very well known through large collections from the Iratí Formation (southeastern Brazil); these finds date from the Upper Permian, approximately 260 million years ago. Anatomical and comparative studies on hundreds of complete specimens (Araújo 1976; Oelofsen and Araújo 1987) demonstrated the presence of three genera, each represented by a single species: *Mesosaurus braziliensis*, *Brazilosaurus sanpaulensis*, and *Stereosternum tumidum* (the latter also recorded in South Africa). The relationship between mesosaurs and other reptiles remains unclear.

In 1948 L.I. Price described a long-snouted archegosaurid temnospondyl (a type of amphibian) called *Prionosuchus plummeri* from Early to Middle Permian beds of the Maranhao state (northeastern Brazil). The animal is represented by fossils of most of the preorbital region of the skull (the region between the eyes and the snout) and a femur (thigh bone).

Tetrapods, both amphibians and reptiles, are found in the Upper Permian Rio do Rasto Formation (Paraná and Rio Grande do Sul states) of southeastern Brazil. The specimens include several incomplete temnospondyl amphibians assigned to the Rhinesuchoid group. The forms include one with a short snout, *Rastosuchus*, and one with a long snout, *Australerpeton consgriffi*. Comparisons made with South African *Cistecephalus*-Zone temnospondyls suggest the groups on the two continents actually are closely related.

The reptiles of the Rio do Rasto Formation also include the therapsid (mammal-like reptiles) *Endothiodon*, which is represented by most of the skull and jaws (Barberena et al. 1985), and the parareptile *Pareiasaurus americanus* (Araújo 1982), which is represented by skull, jaws, and good portions of the postcranium. Comparative data drawn from both temnospondyls and reptiles indicate close affinities with taxa from the *Cistecephalus* and *Daptocephalus* zones of the Lower Beaufort Series of South Africa.

Triassic

The Triassic fossil record of South America covers most of the period (245 to 205 million years ago), with successive assemblages in the Early, Middle, and Late Triassic. However, stratigraphic hiatuses occur between the three periods. M.C.F.S. Lima and colleagues (1984) reported on fragmentary remains of paleonisciforms and cleitrolepiforms fishes (two groups of primitive ray-finned fishes) from Middle and Upper Triassic beds of the Santa María Formation (Brazil). The similarly aged Las Cabras, Portrerillos, and Cacheuta Formations of western Argentina have revealed three genera belonging to the actinopterygian family Perleidae, and 16 other actinopterygian genera.

Early Triassic

From the Early Triassic, two assemblages of tetrapods have been recognized that seem to be similar to those of the *Lystrosaurus* zone of South Africa: First, the Zanga do Cabral assemblage (southern Brazil) bears temnospondyls such as the *Deltasaurus pustulatus* and a lydekkerinid genus, as well as vertebrae from a Protorosauria-like archosauromorph; also found were numerous but fragmentary remains of *Procolophon* (a parareptile). Second, the Puesto Viejo Inferior assemblage (Mendoza Province) bears the remains of a primitive archosauromorph called a proterosuchid (a crocodile-like reptile), and skulls of a dicynodont (an herbivorous, turtle-beaked group of therapsids).

Two Early Triassic assemblages in the Mendoza Province (Argentina)—the Upper Puesto Viejo and the Río Mendoza assemblages—probably correlate with the *Cynognathus* Zone of South Africa. The Upper Puesto Viejo assemblage produced complete skulls and jaws of the dicynodont *Kannemeyeria argentinensis* and two cynodonts (the most advanced therapsid group), *Cynognathus minor* and the primitive traversodontid *Pascualgnathus polanskii* (Bonaparte 1969a, 1969b, 1971). The Río Mendoza assemblage produced complete skulls and lower jaws of the primitive traversodontid cynodonts *Andescynodon mendozensis* and *Rusconiodon mignonei* (Bonaparte 1972); a lower jaw of the galesaurid cynodont *Cromptodon mamiferoides*; and the kannemeyeriid dicynodont *Vinceria andina*.

Middle Triassic

Only one locality in South America unambiguously dates to the Middle Triassic age, Los Chañares (Argentina). However, in the lower Santa María Formation (southern Brazil) is probably close in age, as it shares several genera with Los Chañares (Barberena et al. 1985). Perhaps the more notable significance of the Middle Triassic tetrapods concerns the origin of mammals, dinosaurs, and crocodiles. The Middle Triassic tetrapods of South America show a strong radiation (diversification) of new adaptive types, both in archosaurs (group including dinosaurs, pterosaurs, and crocodiles) and therapsids. The Los Chañares Fauna, discovered and studied primarily by Romer (1966–72) of Harvard, is made up of the taxa presented in Table 1. Asterisked forms also have been found in southern Brazil.

Late Triassic

The Los Chañares Fauna is more primitive than the Ischigualasto Fauna, which dates from early in the Late Triassic. Two other formations—the Cacheuta Formation, Mendoza (Argentina), and the *Scaphonyx* Assemblage Zone (southern Brazil)—are approximately the same age. This period of the Late Triassic saw the oldest saurischian ("lizard-hipped") dinosaurs. In the Ischigualasto beds, which are more than 400 meters thick, are fossils of *Herrerasaurus* and other related theropod genera, and in Brazil are fossils of the saurischians *Staurikosaurus* and *Guaibasaurus*. In addition, the oldest known ornithischian ("bird-hipped") dinosaur *Pisanosaurus,* was also found in Ischigualasto.

All these dinosaurs were part of a faunal assemblage still dominated by therapsids. Using information gathered from the lower Ischigualasto beds through the uppermost levels, J.F. Bonaparte (1982) has summarized some significant information on the replacement of the Therapsid Fauna by the Archosaur Fauna. In most cases, the taxa recorded at Ischigualasto (Table 2) are represented by good and complete specimens. The Casheuta assemblage of vertebrates (Table 3) is dominated by actinopterygian fishes and themnospondyls, with only one genus of a primitive archosaur.

Trying to correlate the assemblages of the Santa María and Ischigualasto formations has proven rather confusing. M.C. Barberena and colleagues stated that the *Scaphonyx* Assemblage (Brazil) may be contemporary with the lower Ischigualasto strata, while the younger Caturrita Formation fauna corresponds to the middle and late Ischigualasto strata. The tetrapods from both of these Brazilian assemblages are presented in Table 4.

Two late Late Triassic assemblages are located in northwestern and southern Argentina in the provinces of La Rioja and Santa Cruz. In the Los Colorados Formation the dominance of prosauropod dinosaurs and archosauromorphs over the few surviving therapsids is remarkable. At the same time, this period marks the first stage of dominance of the saurischians over the rest of the nondinosaur archosaurs. The upper levels of Los Colorados Formation have produced prosauropods and archosauromorphs, as well as the oldest known protosuchian crocodile and an advanced trithelodontid cynodont *Chaliminia.* (*Chaliminia* is a genus that is somewhat more primitive than *Pachygenelus,* from the Early Jurassic of South Africa.)

The chelonians (turtles) are represented by several complete skeletons and carapaces (shells) of the primitive australochelid *Palaeochersis* (Rougier et al. 1995). These finds afford new evidence for the early diversification of turtles. Table 5 presents the tetrapods from the upper section of the Los Colorados Formation.

Table 1. Middle Triassic Taxa (Los Chañares Fauna, Argentina)

Archosauromorphs
- *Chanaresuchus bonapartei**
- *Gracilisuchus stipanicicorum*
- *Gualosuchus reigi*
- *Lagosuchus talampayensis*
- *Lewisuchus admixtus*
- *Luperosuchus fractus*
- *Marasuchus lilloensis*
- "*Pseudolagosuchus major*"
- *Tropidosuchus romeri*

Cynodonts
- *Massetognathus major*
- *Massetognathus pascualii**
- *Massetognathus terugii*
- *Megagomphodon oligodens*
- *Probainognathus jenseni*
- *Probelesodon lewisi**
- *Probelesodon minor*

Dicynodonts
- *Chanaria platyceps*
- *Dinodontosaurus brevirostris**
- *Dinodontosaurus platygnathus*
- kannemeyeriid indet.

Note: Asterisk indicates a genus also found in southern Brazil.

Table 2. Late Triassic Taxa (Ischigualasto Fauna, Argentina)

Temnospondyls
- *Pelorocephalus, Promastodonsaurus*

Archosauromorphs
- *Aetosauroides, Proterochampsa, Saurosuchus, Trialestes, Venaticosuchus*

Rhynchosaurs
- *Scaphonyx*

Ornithischians
- *Pisanosaurus*

Saurischians
- *Eoraptor, Frenguellisaurus, Herrerasaurus, Ischisaurus*

Dicynodonts
- *Ischigualastia*

Cynodonts
- *Chiniquodon, Exaeretodon, Ischignathus, Probainognathus*

Table 3. Late Triassic Taxa (Cacheuta Formation Assemblage)

Actinopterygians
- *Cenechoia, Challaia, Eurynotus, Guaymallenia, ?Gyrolepidoides, Neochallaia, ?Pholidophorus, ?Rhadinychthys*

Temnospondyls
- *Chigutisaurus, ?Icanosaurus, Pelorocephalus*

Archosauromorphs
- *Cuyosuchus*

Table 4. Late Triassic Taxa
(*Scaphonyx* and Caturrita Assemblages, Brazil)

Archosauromorphs
       Aetosauroides, Cerritosaurus, Hoplitosuchus,
         Proterochampsa, Rauisuchus, Rhadinosuchus
Rhynchosaurs
       Scaphonyx
Saurischians
       Guaibasaurus, Staurikosaurus
Dicynodonts
       Jachaleria
Cynodonts
       Exaeretodon, Gomphodonthosuchus, Therioherpeton

Table 5. Late Triassic Taxa (Los Colorados Formation)

Chelonians
       Palaeochersis
Archosauromorphs
       Fasolasuchus, Neoaetosauroides, Pseudhesperosuchus,
         Riojasuchus
Crocodilians
       Hemiprotosuchus
Saurischians
       Coloradisaurus, Riojasaurus, Theropoda indet.
Cynodonts
       Chaliminia, Trytilodontidae indet.

Table 6. Jurassic Taxa

Actinopterygians
    Chondrostei
        Coccolepis
    Teleostei
        Antofagastaichthys, Bobbichthys,
          Chongichthys, Domeykos, Luisinella,
          Protoclupea, "Tharrias," Varasichthys
Anurans
    Ascaphidae
        Notobatrachus, Vieraella
Ornithischians
        Ornithopoda indet.
Sauropods
    Cetiosauridae
        Amygdalodon, Patagosaurus, Wolkheimeria
Theropods
    Allosauridae
        Piatnitzkysaurus

In southern Santa Cruz Province of Argentina there is a rich site from late in the Late Triassic (or Earliest Jurassic) that has been worked extensively. It has yielded only prosauropod remains, but the specimens range in size from 15 centimeters long (hatchlings) up to six meters long, which produces interesting information

about the group's ontogeny (developmental history). The only known genus is *Mussaurus,* based on juvenile specimens from a prosauropod nest. R.M. Casamiquela (1981) ascribed the adult specimens to the European genus *Plateosaurus.* However, the morphology (shape, structure) of the cervical (neck) vertebrae does not confirm such interpretation.

Comments on the Triassic Tetrapods

The Triassic record of South American tetrapods is particularly rich in therapsids and archosaurs of Middle and Late Triassic age, groups that are seldom as well represented in other regions of the world. Important events, such as the faunal replacement marking the beginning of archosaur dominance in the Late Triassic, are documented fairly well along the Ischigualasto beds.

Based on discoveries of very well-preserved juvenile specimens in the lower Ischigualasto beds, scholars have hypothesized that mammals originated from advanced carnivorous cynodonts by means of heterochronic processes (changes in developmental timing). Finally, the origin of saurischian dinosaurs was clarified by the discovery of lagosuchid dinosauromorphs (sister taxa of dinosaurs) from the Middle Triassic beds.

Besides these crucial problems of general vertebrate paleontology, South American Triassic collections have added to our knowledge about some additional, rather more restricted subjects: (a) the evolution of traversodontid cynodonts; (b) the diversification of Middle Triassic archosaurs; (c) the evolution of Triassic crocodiles; (d) the origin and dominance of the prosauropod dinosaurs; (e) the systematics (evolutionary relationships) of the Proterochampsidae (a family of possibly aquatic archosauromorphs); and (f) the postcranial adaptations of the rauisuchids (a group of large predatory archosauromorphs).

Jurassic

Few stages of the Jurassic are represented by South American vertebrates, but some are of special significance. For instance, the oldest known anuran (frog), *Vieraella,* dating from the Hettangian epoch (205 to 201 million years ago), was found in the Roca Blanca Formation (Reig 1961). Among the fishes found in the Domeyko mountains of Chile, some are preserved with three-dimensional muscles intact. Marine reptiles such as the plesiosaurs from the Bajocian (176 to 170 million years ago) and the metriorhynchids (a family of marine crocodilians) afford significant paleobiogeographical and evolutionary information. Table 6 presents the most significant groups.

The Middle Jurassic dinosaur assemblage (Bonaparte 1986b) is made up of cetiosaurid sauropods and an allosaurid theropod. These remains provide good evidence of relationships with other groups and further an understanding of the complex evolution of the sauropod presacral vertebrae (trunk vertebrae).

Footprints

Late Jurassic footprints (trace fossils) of small dinosaurs and mammals give the first evidence that in this age the gondwanatheres (supposed multituberculates) had a "ricochetal" style of running (i.e., hopping, as seen in kangaroo rats).

One interesting Late Jurassic footprint site was discovered by Casamiquela (1961) in the Patagonian Santa Cruz Province (Table 7). Another footprint locality, the Araraquara assemblage from the São Paulo State (Brazil) is a rich collection of small prints left by animals that resembled therapsids and coelurosaurian theropods (Leonardi 1976). They may be similar in age to the Late Jurassic footprints found in Patagonia.

Table 7. Jurassic Footprints from Santa Cruz Province
Ornithischians
Delatorrichnus
Theropods
Sarmientichnus, Wildeichnus
Multituberculates
Gondwanatheria
Ameghinichnus

Cretaceous

The best of South America's Cretaceous deposits are found in Argentina and Brazil; minor deposits are found elsewhere on the continent. In Argentina the Cretaceous record covers most of the period, although there are important gaps between one faunal assemblage and another. Dinosaurs and associated fauna have been collected, and most of them have been described.

Neocomian

The only Neocomian site with significant vertebrate remains is La Amarga Formation, Neuquén Province (Argentina). It has produced three incomplete specimens of the bizarre sauropod *Amargasaurus cazaui*. The holotype (specimen first used to define the species) of *Amargasaurus* is represented by articulated vertebrae from the presacral and sacral areas, the temporal and basicranial portion of the skull, girdles, and limb bones. A second, unpublished specimen affords good information on the caudal (tail) vertebrae, as well as the pubis and ischium (two of the three bones in the pelvis) not preserved in the holotype.

Amargasaurus is a sauropod very closely related to the Late Jurassic *Dicraeosaurus* from the Tendaguru beds of East Africa, but *Amargasaurus* has more developed neural spines along the cervical vertebrae and more dorsal vertebrae bearing bifurcated (split in two) neural spines. A second, undescribed sauropod from La Amarga Formation is represented by a dorsal vertebrae with a morphotype similar to that of *Rebbachisaurus* from Africa; the similarities suggests a primitive rebbachisaurid coexisted with the more frequently found dicraeosaurid.

Theropod remains testify to the presence of a rather large species represented by a slender tibia (shin bone), a 25-centimeter-long metatarsal (foot bone between the ankle and the toes), and some isolated teeth. So far, this animal is undescribed. A second, small theropod, *Ligabueino andesi* (Bonaparte 1996), is represented by a few diagnostic bones: some complete neural arches (which help form the spinal canal) and caudal vertebrae, an ilium, an incomplete pubis, one femur, and foot phalanges. The only known specimen suggests it is a ceratosaurian, possibly of the family Noasauridae.

The Stegosauria (order of ornithischian dinosaurs with erect plates or spines along the back) is represented only by incomplete cervical vertebrae and some dermal plates, indicating some affinities with *Kentrosaurus* from the Tendaguru beds of East Africa. However, further material is necessary for a definitive identification. Unidentified pterosaurs (flying archosaurs) are recorded in the La Amarga assemblage by a femur and a possible radius (one of the forearm bones). Scholars also have described a small crocodile, *Amargasuchus,* on the basis of an incomplete maxilla (upper jaw) bearing some diagnostic characters.

Finally, a well-preserved pretribosphenic mammal, *Vincelestes neuquenianus* (Bonaparte 1986b), was found at La Amarga. It is represented by six skulls, 12 lower jaws, and several disarticulated postcranial remains, all collected in a small place. The very derived (specialized) postcanine teeth consist of two premolars and three molars, the last one very reduced in size. The protocone (internal cusp) on the upper molar is tiny, reflecting an early stage in its evolution. The glenoid cavity (jaw joint) is bisected by the suture between the jugal ("cheek bone") and squamosal bones. The lateral wall of the braincase is formed by equal contributions of two bones there, the petrosal and alisphenoid. The cochlea (inner ear diverticulum responsible for hearing) is twisted only 180 degrees. G.W. Rougier (1993) studied *Vincelestes* in detail.

Aptian Deposits

The most complete and fascinating Aptian locality in South America is found in the Chapada de Araripe, or Araripe Basin of Brazil, where the Crato and Santana Formations are located (Brito 1990). The finds, characterized by abundant and exceptionally preserved organisms, include several taxa of molluscs, echinoderms, crustaceans, insects, spiders, fish, frogs, crocodilians, pterosaurs, turtles, dinosaurs, and birds (Maisey 1991). In addition, pollen, spores, and intact plant remains of gymnosperms and angiosperms have led to the discovery of several plant species (Martill et al. 1993).

The stratigraphy of the basin corresponds to fluvial (floodplain), lacustrine (lake bed), and coastal marine paleoenvironments. Pterosaurs of rather large size are recorded in the Romualdo Member of the Santana Formation, as well as fishes, turtles, crocodiles, and scarce dinosaurs. Table 8 lists the fossil vertebrates from the Crato and Santana Formations (Martill et al. 1993).

In Argentina the Aptian beds with vertebrates correspond to the Lohan Cura Formation in Neuquén Province, which probably represents paleoenvironments formed by river deltas. The few materials collected there suggest the presence of two new, undescribed sauropods, both of which are represented by incomplete skeletons. One of them is quite unique, as it bears thin, large dermal plates above the vertebral column. The second is distinguished by the morphology of cervical and caudal vertebrae and of the ischium.

Table 8. Aptian Deposits
CRATO FORMATION
Actinopterygians
?Araripelepidotes, Cladocyclus, Dastilbe, ?Tharrias
Amphibians
Anura (undescribed)
Birds
An isolated feather; family indeterminate
SANTANA FORMATION
Chondrichthyans
"Rhinoblatos," Tribodus
Actinopterygians
Araripelepidotes, Araripichthys, Brannerion,
Cladocyclus, Clupeiformes indet., *Enneles, Iemanja,*
"Leptolepis," Neoproscinetes, Notelops, Obaichthys,
Oshunia, Paraelops, Rhacolepis, Tharrias, Vinctifer
Coelacanths
Axelrodichthys, Mawsonia
Turtles
Araripemys
Crocodilians
Araripesuchus, Itasuchus
Pterosaurs
Anhanguera, Araripedactylus, Araripesaurus,
Brasilodactylus, Cearadactylus, Santanadactylus,
Tapejara, Tropeognathus, Tupuxuara
Saurischians
Fragmentary material of two undescribed genera
Theropods
Irritator, represented by an incomplete skull

Table 9. Late Cretaceous Taxa (Río Colorado Formation)
Snakes
Dinilysia
Crocodilians
Comahuesuchus, Cynodontosuchus, Lomasuchus,
Notosuchus, Pierosaurus
Ornithopods
Gasparinisaura
Sauropods (titanosaurs)
Antarctosaurus, Neuquensaurus, Titanosaurus
Theropods
Alvarezsaurus, Velocisaurus
Birds
Neuquenornis, Patagopteryx

Albian-Cenomanian

The only South American Albian-Cenomanian beds that bear vertebrates are exposed in Neuquén Province (Argentina) and are part of the Río Limay Formation. The fossiliferous beds occur in the Candeleros and Huincul members. Both have yielded spectacular dinosaurs. The most bizarre, tentatively considered Albian (107–95 million years), is *Carnotaurus,* a theropod with extremely shortened forelimbs and two frontal horns.

The Candeleros Member beds are exposed widely around the lake of El Chocón dam. The site yielded a number of finds: *Andesaurus,* of the family Andesauridae, is a primitive titanosaur (sauropod) represented by an incomplete skeleton without a skull. "Rebbachisaurus" is based on an almost complete skeleton collected by J.F. Bonaparte and assistants in 1989. *Giganotosaurus,* a giant abelisaurian theropod, is represented by most of the skeleton and by the skull and jaws. In addition, scholars have collected undescribed frogs, crocodiles, and turtles. A significant assemblage of footprints was also revealed (Calvo 1991).

The Huincul Member beds outcrop around Plaza Huincul city. These yielded the gigantic titanosaur sauropod *Argentinosaurus,* which is the largest Cretaceous dinosaur known to date. Huge sauropods have also been recorded in Aptian, Albian, and Turonian beds (114 to 88 million years ago) of Neuquén Province, but *Argentinosaurus* is the better known genus; its femur alone measured 2.5 meters. As far as is known, a wave of gigan-

tism in South American saurischians lasted from the Aptian through approximately Turonian times and probably was limited to titanosaurs and theropods.

Late Cretaceous

Deposits from the Late Cretaceous are found primarily in four succeeding faunal assemblages that have been recorded in northern Patagonia. Some partially synchronous deposits exist in southern Patagonia, northern Argentina, and Brazil.

Lisandro Member

The Lisandro Member is the upper section of the Río Limay Formation. Good fossiliferous sites have been discovered some 15 kilometers south of Plaza Huincul, where R.A. Coria (with Salgado 1996) collected well-preserved remains of an iguanodontid-like ornithischian. At present Coria is excavating three specimens of abelisaurian-like theropods. These beds are estimated to be from 95 to 91 million years old.

Portezuelo Member

The relative age of the Portezuelo Member and its theropod fauna is probably Turonian (91 to 88 million years ago). The Portezuelo Member makes up the lower section of the Río Neuquén Formation. West of Plaza Huincul are exposed fossiliferous beds where F.E. Novas (1997) discovered three taxa of theropod dinosaurs. Novas interpreted *Patagonykus* as related to the birdlike *Mononykus* from Mongolia. Anatomically, scholars have considered *Unenlagia,* with its *Archaeopteryx*-like pelvis, very close to birds. A third large theropod, represented by a few bones, is yet to be described.

Río Colorado Formation

More significant is the assemblage of vertebrates from the lower section of the Rio Colorado Formation, recorded on the campus grounds of the Universidad Nacional del Comahue in the northeastern section of Neuquén City. The faunal assemblage (Bonaparte 1991) consists of rather small species of crocodiles, theropods, snakes, and birds. Table 9 lists the taxa recorded at the campus and from a few other sites in the Neuquén and Río Negro provinces. Table 10 lists the groups recovered from other fossil sites located in central Patagonia and northern Argentina, all of approximately the same age.

Los Alamitos Formation

The Los Alamitos Formation in northeastern Patagonia yielded South America's first well-dated assemblage of Late Cretaceous mammals. They were associated with fishes, turtles, and saurischian and ornithischian dinosaurs. During the Late Cretaceous the paleoenvironment of the Los Alamitos Formation alternated between a plain near the seacoast and a lake not far from the ocean. Along the coast of the lake, the bones were worked strongly by waves. The mammals from this site include a number of derived therians, mostly dryolestoids. Table 11 presents the faunal list of vertebrates from this site.

The relative age of the Los Alamitos fauna is Late Campanian-Early Maastrichtian (83 to 65 million years ago). Possibly the most important aspect of the Los Alamitos Assemblage are the unique nontribosphenic mammals (e.g., gondwanatheres), animals that do not possess the triangular upper molars of therian mammals. This endemism indicates that Los Alamitos mammals evolved along unexpected paths not recorded in Laurasia.

Allen Formation (and Equivalent Levels)

The Allen Formation, of Maastrichtian age, crops out eastward from Neuquén City. Outcrops of this formation are found in Río Negro Province, in depressed areas called "bajos." The outcrops include numerous dinosaur nests, most of which were probably constructed by sauropods. The same areas hold abundant remains of titanosaurids, hadrosaurids, and turtles. The only recorded theropod is the abelisaur *Abelisaurus*. The faunal list is given in Table 12. The Allen Formation was probably deposited about the same time as the Lecho Formation of Salta (northern Argentina). Table 13 lists the taxa are recorded from the Lecho Formation.

As far as vertebrates are concerned, the end of the Cretaceous is not recorded well in South America. There is no information, no clue to explain whether the extinction was gradual or sudden or to show which taxa survived until the very end of the period. The Cretaceous-Tertiary (K-T) boundary in Patagonia, the richest paleontological region of South America, is represented by marine paleoenvironments created by an Atlantic transgression (rise in sea level). The transgression created a body of water that covered most of Patagonia approximately 3 to 5 million years before the K-T boundary. The last Cretaceous mammals are recorded from the Late Campanian-Early Maastrichtian fossil beds, formed approximately 8 million years before the boundary.

The sea covering Patagonia finally withdrew in late in the Early Paleocene, some 4 million years after the end of the K-T boundary. The terrestrial faunal of this time was quite different from that of the latest Cretaceous. There were no saurischian or ornithischian dinosaurs, nor triconodonts, symmetrodonts, docodonts, and dryolestoid mammals. Several groups did survive the

Table 10. Late Cretaceous Taxa (Synchronous with Río Colorado Taxa)
Frogs
Saltenia
Turtles
Pelomedusidae indet.
Sauropods
Epachthosaurus
Theropods
Xenotarsosaurus

great extinction, such as the leptodactylid and pipid frogs, the chelid and meiolanid turtles, the boid snakes, the sebecosuchian crocodiles, and the multituberculate mammals.

Cenozoic

Most of the paleobiogeographical and evolutionary information about the continental Cenozoic vertebrates of South America concerns mammals, and it is preserved in Argentina, Bolivia, Colombia, Uruguay, and Chile. Fishes, amphibians, reptiles, and birds also are important, but they are represented by fewer number of species than the mammals.

Some of the Early Cenozoic tetrapods are amphibians, turtles, some crocodiles, and multituberculate mammals that existed in the Late Cretaceous and that survived beyond the K-T boundary. Except for multituberculates and a platypus, all the known mammals correspond to immigrant Metatheria (marsupials) and Eutheria (placentals) that had moved into South America from Central and North America. These immigrants radiated throughout South America, giving rise to many endemic groups, some of them very bizarre.

An important migratory event from Africa occurred by the Late Eocene, bringing the ancestors of caviomorph rodents (e.g., guinea pigs) and ceboid monkeys. Finally, in the Pliocene the land bridge between North and South America was formed. Now animals on the two continents could migrate from one continent to the other, an activity called the "Great American Interchange." It was completed by the Middle Pleistocene. Humans arrived in South America some time in the Late Pleistocene.

Paleocene

Early Paleocene. Fossil sites in Tiupampa (Bolivia), Punta Peligro, Las Flores, and Río Chico (Argentina), and Itaboraí (Brazil) represent the Early Paleocene. The oldest site is Tiupampa (Marshall and De Muizon 1988), which probably dates back to the earliest Paleocene. Tiupampa yielded marsupials and eutherians that are closely related to families in North America, suggesting that the immigrant groups had arrived relatively recently.

Although originally the Tiupampa assemblage was considered to date to the Late Cretaceous, at present scholars interpret it as Early Paleocene and correlate its characteristics with the North American assemblage of the Puerco Formation. Table 14 lists the recorded groups of vertebrates (mammals excluded).

Table 11. Late Cretaceous Taxa (Los Alamitos Formation)

Chondrichthyans		Batoidei indet.
Actinopterygians		Aridae indet., *Atractosteus*, Diplomistidae indet., Lepisosteidae indet., Percoidei indet.
Lungfishes		*Ceratodus*
Frogs		Leptodactylidae indet., *Xenopus*
Turtles		Chelidae indet., *Niolania*
Snakes		*Alamitophis, Patagoniophis, Rionegrophis*
Ornithischians	Ornithipoda	*Kritosaurus*
Sauropods	Titanosauridae	*Aeolosaurus*
Mammals	Docodonts?	Reigitherium
	Dryolestids	*Alamitherium, Barberenia, Brandonia, Casamiquelia, Groebertherium, Leonardus, Paraungulatum, Quirogatherium, Rougietherium*
	Multituberculates	*Ferugliotherium, Gondwanatherium*
	Symmetrodonts	*Bondesius*
	Triconodonta	*Austrotriconodon*

Table 12. Late Cretaceous Taxa (Allen Formation)

Chondrichthyans		Batoidei indet.
Lungfishes		Ceratodus
Frogs		Leptodactylidae indet.
Turtles		Chelydae indet.
Snakes		Booidae indet.
Ornithischians	Ornithipoda	Lambeosaurinae indet.
Sauropods	Titanosauridae	*Neuquensaurus, Titanosaurus*
Theropods	Abelisauridae	*Abelisaurus*

Table 13. Late Cretaceous Taxa (Lecho Formation)

Sauropods	Titanosauridae	*Saltasaurus*
Theropods	Abelisauria	*Noasaurus*
Aves	Enantiornithes	*Enantiornis, Lectavis, Soroavis, Yungavolucris*

The fossil record of mammals from Tiupampa (Table 15) is highly significant because of its variety, because it provides key information for understanding the very early steps of diversification of metatherians and eutherians, and because it aids understanding where immigrants to South America came from and when they arrived.

Punta Peligro, in southern Patagonia, is an interesting fossil locality for frogs, turtles, crocodiles, multituberculates, platypuses, metatherians, and placental mammals (Table 16). The deposits date from the Early Paleocene, but because they are younger than Tiupampa, the animals there probably correlate with North American mammals of Torrejonian age. At Punta Peligro the stratigraphy indicates that as the Salamanquian Sea regressed, continental vertebrates colonized the emerging areas.

Leptodactylid frogs, chelid turtles, and multituberculates represent surviving groups from the Late Cretaceous of Patagonia. However, eusuchian crocodiles, marsupials, and eutherian mammals are taxa that originated in North America, groups that have no previous record in South America. Several significant facts stand out about the few mammals from Punta Peligro: (a) the first endemic family of ungulates (hoofed animals), the Peligrotheriidae, appeared; (b) the first monotremes appeared outside of Australia; (c) the most primitive prelitoptern (another endemic South American ungulate) appeared; (d) mammals increased in size and moved into new and diversified ecological niches, a trend not found in Tiupampa or in any Late Cretaceous assemblage.

Middle Paleocene. The Middle Paleocene is represented by the vertebrate assemblage of Itaboraí (near Rio de Janeiro, Brazil) and Las Flores (Chubut Province, Argentina). Perhaps the most interesting characteristics of this mammalian fauna are the outstanding diversity of marsupials; the appearance of most of the primitive, endemic groups of ungulates; and the (presumed) extinction of the multituberculates and monotremes that had arisen during the Early Paleocene. The fossil record of Itaboraí (Table 17) is better known than that of Las Flores, although in both assemblages the diversity of marsupials is high.

Middle to Late Paleocene (Río Chico Formation). The rich Middle to Late Paleocene fauna of continental vertebrates is made almost entirely of mammals, recorded primarily in the Río Chico Formation (central Patagonia), and to a lesser degree in the Mealla Formation (northwestern Argentina). In this Paleocene assemblage the endemic characters of all the recorded mammals are well established, and the typical South American orders of marsupials and ungulates are defined clearly. After 8 million years of isolated evolution in South America, the condylarth (archaic ungulates) and didelphimorph (early marsupials) immigrants evolved into several endemic groups that characterized the whole Cenozoic history of mammals of this continent. The recorded families are listed in Table 18.

Eocene-Oligocene

The geographic and faunal isolation of South America since the latest Cretaceous resulted in the evolution of unique orders of ungulates and marsupials. This faunal isolation and evolution, lasting approximately 35 million years, was interrupted in the Late Eocene by the arrival of monkeys and rodents from Africa, possibly across a relatively narrow ocean gap between northeastern Brazil and Sierra Leone (west Africa). Diversification of the platyrrhine monkeys and the caviomorphs rodents (whose fossil records begin in the Oligocene), dramatically changed the faunal makeup of South America. The families of South American rodents and monkeys recorded in the Late Oligocene are listed in Table 19.

Table 14. Early Paleocene Taxa (Tiupampa)

Chondrichthyans
Batoidea, (Dasyatidae)

Actinopterygians
Ariidae, Characidae, Enchodontidae, Erythrinidae, Hiodontidae, Ictaluridae, Lepisosteidae, Osteoglossidae, Percichthydae, Serrasalmidae, Siluriformes

Lungfishes
Ceratodontidae, Lepidosirenidae

Frogs
Leptodactylidae

Turtles
Pelomedusidae

Lizards
indet.

Snakes
Aniliidae, Booidae

Crocodilians
Sebecosuchia, ?Dyrosauridae

Birds
indet.

Table 15. Mammals of Tiupampa

Marsupials
Sparassodonta, Hathliacinidae
Didelphimorphia, Didelphidae, Family indet.
Peradectia, Peradectidae
Microbiotheria, Microbiotheriidae
Paucituberculata, Kollpaniidae
Order indet., Family indet.

Placentals
Leptictida
Palaeoryctidae?
"Condylarths," Mioclaenidae, Periptychidae
Pantodonta

Table 16. Early Paleocene Taxa (Punta Peligro)

Frogs
Leptodactylidae, ?Pipidae

Turtles
Chelidae

Crocodilians
Alligatoridae, Crocodylidae

Monotremes
Ornithorhynchidae

Multituberculates
Sudamericidae

Metatherians
indet.

Eutherians
Mioclaenidae, Peligrotheriidae

Table 17. Fossils of Itaboraí		
Marsupials	Polydolopidae	
	Caroloameghiniidae	
	Peradectidae	
	Hathliacynidae	
	Didelphidae	
	Protodidelphidae	
	Microbiotheriidae	
	Pediomydae	
Placentals	Astrapotheria	Trigonostylopidae
	Notoungulata	Oldfieldthomasidae
	Xenungulata	Carodniidae
	Litopterna	"Proterotheriidae"

Table 18. Fossils of Río Chico		
Marsupials	?Bonapartheriidae	
	Borhyaenidae	
	Caroloameghinidae	
	Didelphidae	
	Polydolopidae	
	Prepidolopidae	
Placentals	Xenarthra	Dasypodidae
	"Condylarths"	Didolodontidae
	Litopterna	Proterotheriidae
	Notoungulata	Archaeopithecidae
		Interatheriidae
		Henricosborniidae
		Notostylopidae
		Oldfieldthomasidae
		Sparnotheriodontidae
	Astrapotheria	Astrapotheriidae
		Trigonostylopidae
	Xenungulata	Carodniidae

While the fauna of the Eocene is represented primarily in Argentine Patagonia (and to a lesser degree in northwestern Argentina), Oligocene deposits that bear mammals are distributed more widely over South America. These sites are found in Argentine Patagonia, in La Salla (Bolivia), and not far from São Paulo, Brazil (in the locality of Tremembé). The last has provided a rich assemblage of teleost fishes, turtles, crocodiles, birds, and mammals. Included in the last category are marsupials, rodents, bats, glyptodonts (large armadillo-like animals), and three orders of endemic ungulates: astrapotheres, notoungulates, and litopterns. The most typical and bizarre South American mammals, the order Xenarthra (e.g., armadillos, anteaters, and sloths), appears for the first time in the Early Eocene in the form of armadillo fossils (family Dasypodidae). By the Late Oligocene, glyptodonts and megalonychid ground sloths are well represented.

In the Oligocene the archaic ungulates—the condylarths—decline, but several endemic families prosper. At this time we see the origin and diversification of the litoptern families Proterotheriidae and Macrauchenidae; these persisted until the Late Cenozoic. Other orders that appear in the Eocene include the Pyrotheria (which lasts until the Oligocene), and the Astrapotheria (which persists into the Pliocene).

Miocene-Pliocene

As far as scholars know, the Miocene of South America, abundantly represented in southern Patagonia and central Colombia, marks the time of the highest diversity of fossil mammals, birds, and reptiles. The richness of South America's fauna may have been the result of the continent's temperate and subtropical climate. For instance, remains of several Miocene ceboid monkeys and numerous caviomorph rodents have been found from southern Patagonia (Santa Cruz Province) up to as far as Colombia, which suggests that a temperate forest extended along most of the western side of South America. Later in the Pliocene, those favorable conditions deteriorated.

During the Miocene-Pliocene, ungulate diversity shrank to only the litoptern families Proterotheriidae and Macrauchenidae. The Astrapotheria became extinct in the Late Miocene, and the Toxodontia (large, lumbering herbivores) survived until the latest

Table 19. Eocene-Oligocene Taxa
Caviomorph Rodents
Eocardidae
Chinchillidae
Octodontidae
Dasyproctidae
Echimyidae
Erethizontidae
Cephalomyidae
Platyrrhine Monkeys
Cebinae
Branizellinae
Atelinae
Pithecinae

Table 20. Immigrants from South America to North America
Phorusrhachidae (large predaceous birds)
Didelphidae (opossums)
Dasypodidae (armadillos)
Glyptodontidae (large armadillo relatives)
Megalonichidae (ground sloths)
Megatheriidae (ground sloths)
Mylodontidae (ground sloths)
Myrmecophagidae (anteaters)
Toxodontidae (a notoungulate family)
Trichechidae (manatees)
Erethizontidae (porcupines)
Hydrochoeridae (capybaras)
Camelidae (camels)

Pleistocene. Armadillos and ground sloths were diversified, with several genera belonging to the families Dasypodidae, Glyptodontidae, Megatheriidae, and Megalonichidae. The diversified marsupials produced a notable sabertoothed borhyaenid called *Thylacosmilus,* which bears outstanding anatomical convergences with the placental sabertooth carnivorans.

The typical South American crocodiles, the Sebecidae, with their deep and narrow skulls, are recorded for the last time in the Miocene of Colombia. Gavialids (narrow-snouted, fish-eating crocodilians) were distributed widely throughout South America—they are recorded in Argentina, Brazil, Colombia, and Venezuela. Alligatorid and nettosuchid crocodiles are known from the Urumaco Formation (Venezuela). An outstanding record of gigantic crocodiles is known from Accre (Brazil). Members of the families Alligatoridae and Nettosuchidae, these reptiles had skulls that measured 1.8 meters long.

Late in the Pliocene the first signs of the "Great American Faunal Interchange" are documented: fossils of procyonids (raccoon family) and cricetid rodents (muskrat family), both native to North America.

The Late Cenozoic Faunal Interchange Between the Americas

Central America and South America were isolated through most of the Tertiary. However, beginning approximately 9 million years ago, a series of temporary land bridges and later a permanent one connected the two. Temporary bridges were created by tectonic processes in Central America and drops in the sea level, and they enabled terrestrial vertebrates to travel from the south to the north and vice versa. The first wave of migration, limited in size, occurred in the Late Pliocene, some 8 to 9 million years ago. The raccoon family, Procyonidae, traveled south from Central America. At the same time, representatives of two ground sloth families—Megalonychidae and Mylodontidae—colonized North America.

A more significant wave of migration occurred between 3 million and possibly less than 1 million years ago, reaching its greatest intensity approximately 2.5 million years ago. Among the animals that moved south from North America were rodents,

insectivorans (e.g., shrews, moles), bats, peccaries, weasels, tapirs, cats, dogs, bears, camels, deer, horses, and proboscideans called gomphotheres.

A total of 29 families of mammals originated in Central and North America and went on to colonize South America. Some limited themselves to northern South America, but a great majority of them covered most of the continent. On the other hand, 14 families of mammals migrated north from South America, most becoming distributed in southern Central America, Mexico, and the United States (Table 20). Only one caviomorph rodent genus reached Canada. Some migrations went back and forth. Camels arose in North America, invaded South America, diversified there, and then reentered North America. A family of giant, predatory, flightless birds, the Phorusrhachidae, also migrated north.

The biological dynamic of the faunal interchange was very complex. It involved problems of direct and indirect competition, of adaptation to new environments, and possibly decimation of some populations infected by pathogens introduced by the various newcomers.

Available evidence suggests that some 20 or 25 thousand years ago, humans reached South America. They may have played a significant role in the faunal extinction at the end of the Pleistocene. Climactic variations that included very dry periods contributed to the extinction. What we see today in the complex fauna of South America are the surviving native groups plus the groups of North American origin, groups that colonized South America 3 million years ago.

JOSÉ F. BONAPARTE

See also Placentals: Endemic South American Ungulates

Works Cited

Ameghino, F., and C. Ameghino. 1813–36. *Obras Completas y Correspondencia Científica.* A. Torcelli (ed.). 24 vols. La Plata: Taller de Impresiones Oficiales.

Araújo, D.C. 1976. *Taxonomía e Relaçoes dos Proganosauria da Bacia do Paraná.* Anais Academia Brasileira de Ciencius 48 (1):92–116.

———. 1982. *Estudo do Material de Pareiasauroidea (Reptilia, Anapsida, Cotylo-Sauria, Procolophonia) do Neopermiano do Estado do Rio Grande do Sul, Brasil.* Porto Alegre: Universidade Federal do Rio Grande do Sul, Curso de Pós-Graduação em Geociência.

Arratia, G., and A. Cione. 1996. The record of fossil fishes of southern South America. *Münchner Geowissenschaftliche Abhandlungen* 30 (A):9–72.

Barberena, M.C., D.C. Araújo, and E.L. Lavina. 1985. Later Permian and Triassic tetrapods of southern Brasil. *National Geographic Research* 1 (Winter):5–20.

Beltran, L. 1997. Découverte d'une ichthyofaune dans le Carbonifère supérieur d'Uruguay Rapports avec, les faunes ichthyologiques contempordines des austres régions du Gondwana. *Annals Societé Geologique du Nord* 97:351–55.

Bonaparte, J.F. 1969a. Dos nuevas "faunas" de reptiles Triásicos de Argentina. *I Simposio internacional sobre estatigrafía y paleontología del Gondwana, Mar del Plata, 1967.* Mar del Plata: Asociación Geológica Argentina.

———. 1969b. Cynognathus minor (Therapsida-Cynodontia), nueva evidencia de la vinculacíon faunística Afro-Sudamericana a princípio del Triásico. *I Simposio internacional sobre estatigrafía y paleontología del Gondwana, Mar del Plata, 1967.* Mar del Plata: Asociación Geológica Argentina.

———. 1971. Annotated list of the South American Triassic Tetrapods. *Second Gondwana Symposium, South Africa, July to August 1970: Proceedings and Papers.* Protoria: Council For Scientific and Indistrial Research.

———. 1972. Cromptodon mamíferoides gen. et sp. nov., Galesauridae de la Formación Río Mendoza, Mendoza, Argentina. (Therapsida-Cynodontia). *Revista de la Asociación Paleontológica Argentina* 9 (4):343–53.

———. 1979. A Jurassic assemblage from Patagonia. *Association for the Advancement of Science* 205:1377–79.

———. 1982. Faunal replacement in the Triassic of South America. *Journal of Vertebrate Paleontology* 2 (3):362–71.

———. 1986a. Sobre Mesungulatum houssayi y nuevos mamíferous Cretácicos de Patagónia, Argentina. *IV Congreso Argentino de Paleontología y Bioestratigrafía: Actas 4, Mendoza, Argentina.* Mendoza: Congreso Argentino de Paleontología y Bioestratigrafía.

———. 1986b. Les dinosaures (carnotaures, allosauridés, sauropodes, cétio-sauridés) du Jurassique Moyen de Cerro Cóndor (Chubut, Argentine). *Annales de Paléontologie (vert.-invert.)* 72 (4): 325–86.

———. 1991. Los vertebrados fósiles de la Formación Río Colorado, de la cuidad de Neuquén y cercanías, Cretácico Superior, Argentina. *Revista del Museo Argentina de Ciencias Naturales "B. Rivadavia"* 4 (3):17–123.

———. 1996. Cretaceous tetrapods of Argentina. *Münchner Geowissenschaftliche Abhandlungen* 30 (A):73–130.

Brito, I.M. 1990. *O cretáceo e sua importância na geologia do Brasil.* Rio de Janeiro: Editora UFRJ.

Calvo, J.O. 1991. Huellas de dinosaurios en la Formación Río Limay (Albiano-Cenomania no), Picún Leufú, Prov. de Neuquén, Rep. Argentina (Ornithischia-saurischia: Sauropoda-theropoda). *Ameghiniana (Revista Assoc. Paleontologica Argentina)* 28 (3–4):241–58.

Casamiquela, R.M. 1961. Sobre la presencia de un mamífero en el primer elenco (Icnológico) de vertebrados del Jurásico de la Patagonia. *PHYSIS* 22 (63):225–33.

———. 1980. La presencia del género Platerosaurus (prosauropoda) en el Tri-Ásico Superior de la Formación El Traquilo, Patagónia. *Actas de Segundo Congreso Argntino de Paleontología y Bioestratigrafía y Primer Congreso Latinoamericano de Paleontología.* Bueno Aires: Asociación Paleontologica Argentina.

Coria, R.A., and L. Salgado. 1996. A basal Inguanodontia (Ornithischia: ornithopoda) from the Late Cretaceous of South America. *Journal of Vertebrate Paleontology* 16 (3):445–57.

Dunkle, D.H., and B. Schaeffer. 1956. Preliminary description of a Palaeoniscoid fish from the Late Paleozoic of Brasil. *Boletím da Faculadade da Filosofia, Ciências e Letras da Universidade de São Paulo (geol.), São Paulo* 13:5–22.

Gagnier, P.-Y. 1987. Sacabambaspis janvieri, heterostraceo del Ordovícico Superior de Bolivia. *Acta del IV Congreso Latinoamericano de Paleontología.* Vol. 2, Santa Cruz de la Sierra: Asociación Paleontologica Argentina.

———. 1989. Forum: The oldest vertebrate: A 470-million-year-old jawless fish, Sacabambaspis janvieri, from the Ordovician of Bolivia. *National Geographic Research* 5 (2):250–53.

Huene, F. von. 1942. *Die fossilen Reptilien des Sudamerikanischen Gondwanalandes.* Munich: Beck.

Leonardi, G. 1976. On the discovery of an abundant ichno-fauna (vertebrates and invertebrates) in the Botucatu Formation s. s in Araraquara, São Paulo, Brasil. *Anais Academia Brasileira de Ciencias* 52 (3):559–67.

———. 1983. Notopus petri nov. gen., nov. sp.: Une empreinte D'Amphibien du Dévonien au Parana (Bresil). *Geobios* 16 (2):233–39.

Lima, M.C.F.S., M. Richter, and E.L. Lavina. 1984. Paleoictiología da Formação Santa María (Grupo Rosário do Sul), Rio Grande, so Sul, Brasil. *Congresso Brasilerio de Geología, 33. Anais Sociadade Brasileira de Geología* 2:563–77.

Maisey, J.G. (ed.). 1991. *Santana Fossils: An Illustrated Atlas.* Neptune City, New Jersey: T.F.H. Publications.

Marshall, L.G., and C. de Muizon. 1988. The dawn of the age of mammals in South America. *National Geographic Research* 4 (1):23–55.

Martill, D.M., A.R.I. Cruickshank, E. Frey, P.G. Small, and M. Clark. 1993. A new crested maniraptoran dinosaur from the Santana Formation (Lower Cretaceous) of Brazil. *Journal of the Geological Society* 153 (1):5–8.

Novas, F.E. 1997. Anatomy of Patagonykus puertai (Theropoda, Avialae, Alvarezsuridae) from the Late Cretaceous of Patagonia. *Journal of Vertebrate Paleontology* 17 (1):137–66.

Oelofsen, B.W., and D.C. Araújo. 1987. Two mesosurid reptiles (Mesosaurus tenuidens and Stereosternum tumidum) in Permian Gondwana of Southern Africa and South America. *Journal of Sciences* 83 (6):370–72.

Price, L.I. 1948. Um anfibio Labirintodonte da Formação Pedra de Fogo, Estado do Maranhão. *Ministério da Agricultura, Divisão de Geología e Mineralogía Boletim* 124:7–32.

Reig, O.A. 1961. Noticia sobre un nuevo anuro fósil del Jurásico de Santa Cruz (Patagonia). *Ameghiniana* 2:73–78.

Richter, M. 1985. Situação da pesquisa paleoictiológica no Paleozoico Brasileiro. *Coletânea de Trabalhos Paleontológicos: Trabalhos apresentados no. III Congreso Brasileiro de Paleontología, 1983.* Brasilia: Ministerio das Minas e Energía, Departamento Nacional da Producao Mineral.

———. 1991. A new marine ichthyofaune from the Permian of the Parana Basin of southern Brazil. Ph.D. diss., King's College, London.

Romer, A.S. 1966–72. The Chañares (Argentina) Triassic reptile Fauna. *Brevoria* 247, 264, 295, 373, 377–79, 385, 390, 394–96, 401.

Rougier, G.W. 1993. *Vincelestes neuquenianus* Bonaparte (Mammalia, theria) un primitivo mamífero del Cretácico inferior de la Cuenca Neuquina. Ph.D. diss., Universidad Nacional de Buenos Aires.

Rougier, G.W., M.S. de la Fuente, and A.B. Arcucci. 1995. Late Triassic turtles from South America. *American Association for the Advancement of Science* 268:855–58.

Scott, W.B. 1937. *A History of Land Mammals in the Western Hemisphere.* Rev. ed., New York: Macmillan.

Simpson, G.G. 1948. The beginning of the Age of Mammals in South America. *Bulletin of the American Museum of Natural History* 85:1–350.

———. 1951. History of the fauna of Latin America. *In* G.A. Baitsell (ed.), *Science in Progress.* 7th Series. New Haven, Connecticut: Yale University Press; London: Oxford University Press.

Further Reading

Arratia, G., and A. Cione. 1996. The record of fossil fishes of southern South America. *Münchner Geowissenschaftliche Abhandlungen* 30 (A):9–72.

Patterson, B., and R. Pascual. 1972. The fossil mammal fauna of South America. *In* A. Keast, F.C. Erk, and B. Glass (eds.), *Evolution, Mammals, and Southern Continents.* Albany: State University of New York Press.

SOUTHEAST ASIA

Southeast Asia consists of Burma, Thailand, Laos, Vietnam, Cambodia, Malaysia, Singapore, Indonesia, Brunei, and the Philippines. The region has had a complicated political history that has influenced paleontological research within its boundaries. By the end of the nineteenth century, all the above areas, with the single exception of Thailand, had become colonies of western powers. Some of the first paleontological discoveries in the region were side products of political or military missions. In 1826, for instance, when sailing up the Irrawady River to the Burmese capital of Ava, Sir John Crawfurd collected a large number of fossil bones of Pleistocene mammals, which he sent to England. There, they were studied by William Buckland. Subsequently, the early paleontological exploration of Southeast Asia was largely the work of geological surveys established by the colonial powers (Britain in Burma and Malaysia, France in Indochina, the Netherlands in Indonesia). In Thailand, too, early paleontological studies were carried out by foreigners working either independently or for the Siamese government.

In many cases, paleontological discoveries were a by-product of geological mapping and the search for mineral resources. Few purely paleontological expeditions of a large scale were conducted in Southeast Asia. There were exceptions. Eugene Dubois conducted expeditions to Java in search of Pleistocene hominids and the accompanying fauna; he discovered *Pithecanthropus* (now *Homo*) *erectus* there in 1891. Later expeditions were headed by Lenore Selenka (1907–8) and Ralph von Koenigswald (1930s). In 1922 the American Museum of Natural History in New York also sent an expedition, led by Barnum Brown, to Burma to collect Tertiary mammals. Admittedly, the tropical climate and dense plant cover did not encourage the kind of collecting that was possible in the arid regions of western North America or Central Asia. Local paleontologists generally had to wait to develop their own paleontological research until after World War II, when the former colonies gained their independence. Even then, in many places the work continued to be hindered by war and political unrest. In quieter countries such as Thailand, paleontological research developed during the 1960s and 1970s, in cooperation with Japanese and western experts. Today, such research is conducted largely by paleontologists affiliated with national geological surveys or local universities, but collaboration with paleontologists from Europe, North America, or Japan still plays an important role.

The geological history of Southeast Asia is a complicated one. Mainland Southeast Asia consists of several "microcontinents," or terranes, which are assumed to have originally been part of the northern rim of the southern supercontinent Gondwana (together with northern and southern China). During the Paleozoic these continental blocks rifted apart from Gondwana and began to drift northward, eventually colliding with each other and with Eurasia. In the Tertiary, the Indian subcontinent collided with mainland Asia, reorganizing the Southeast Asian region, with large-scale displacements and rotations of continental blocks.

Today, Australia is drifting toward Asia, causing complex collision phenomena in the region of the Philippines and eastern Indonesia. This movement is responsible for the present biogeographic patterns observed in Southeast Asia (with, notably, Wallace's Line, which separates the Oriental and Australasian regions across Indonesia). This long and complex geological history has had far-reaching consequences for the evolutionary history of the floras and faunas that inhabited the Southeast Asian blocks. As a result, scholars use fossils from the various regions of Southeast Asia to trace the paleogeological history of the different terranes, reconstructing their floral and faunal affinities (with Gondwana or with Laurasia) at different periods of geological time. This is an arduous task, which is far from completed. One of the results of Southeast Asia's geological history is that some land areas are much older than others. Parts of Thailand, Laos, and Cambodia have been dry land since the Late Triassic, some 220 million years ago, whereas the islands of some of the archipelagos (such as the Philippines or eastern Indonesia) were formed much more recently, during the Tertiary. This means that the fossil records of the various parts of Southeast Asia can be very different, depending on the geological history of the region in question.

Paleozoic

Early Paleozoic fossils are known from several areas of mainland Southeast Asia, especially western Thailand (Wongwanich and Burrett 1983) and Vietnam. Late Cambrian trilobites (early arthropods) have been found in the Tarutao Sandstone on Tarutao Island, off the western coast of southern Thailand. Fossils of the same age have been found on nearby Langkawi Island, in Malaysia. In the northern part of Vietnam, Middle and Late Cambrian trilobites also occur.

Ordovician fossils are found not only on Tarutao Island, but also on the southern peninsula and parts of western and northern Thailand. The Ordovician assemblages (groupings of a wide variety of species) from Thailand include conodonts (the earliest jawless vertebrates), brachiopods (clamlike invertebrates), shelled nautiloids, trilobites, and graptolites (extinct colonial organisms). Ordovician fossils are found also in Malaysia. Ordovician nautiloids and other fossils from western Thailand and Malaysia show close affinities with Australian forms, suggesting that these parts of Southeast Asia belonged to Gondwana during the Early Palaeozoic (Burrett and Stait 1985).

Silurian fossils occur in western, northern, and northeast Thailand, with graptolites, conodonts, brachiopods, corals, trilobites, and crinoids (cup-shaped animals with feathery arms). Fossiliferous beds of Silurian age are widespread in Vietnam, where they contain graptolites, trilobites, brachiopods, and echinoids (e.g., sea urchins). In Malaysia, the Kuala Lumpur Limestone contains a rich Middle-to-Late Silurian fauna.

Marine Early and Middle Devonian fossils are abundant in northern and central Vietnam. They include foraminifera (tiny organisms that form calcium-based shells), conodonts, brachiopods, corals, tentaculites, and trilobites. Late Devonian fossils also have been reported from many localities in northern and central Vietnam. Devonian plant remains from marine or coastal deposits in Vietnam represent two distinct assemblages, one from the Early Devonian and another from the Middle Devonian. Vietnam also has a good record of Devonian fishes, including ostracoderms and antiarchs (armored, jawless fishes). In northern Vietnam, which was part of the South China block in the Devonian, a characteristic Early Devonian assemblage containing galeaspids (another type of armored jawless fishes that superficially resembles horseshoe crabs) (Janvier et al. 1993), antiarchs, and sarcopterygians (lobe-finned fishes) has been found. The Middle Devonian fish fauna from central Vietnam, which was part of the Indochina block, contains a peculiar placoderm, *Lyhoalepis* (Tong-Dzuy et al. 1995). In Thailand, marine Devonian fossils, including trilobites, conodonts, brachiopods, gastropods (clams, snails, sea stars), and graptolites have been found in the western, northern, and northeastern parts of the country. A few Late Devonian fish remains have been reported from northern Thailand.

Marine Carboniferous fossils are abundant in many parts of Thailand. The assemblages range in age from Early to Latest Carboniferous and include algae, foraminifera, corals, conodonts, brachiopods, pelecypods (clams, oysters, mussels), ammonoids (shelled animals), and trilobites. Foram-bearing limestones are widespread in Southeast Asia throughout the Carboniferous deposits. Interesting late Early Carboniferous floras have been reported from coal mines in northeastern Thailand (Laveine et al. 1993). They include large *Lepidodendron* (a fossil plant) specimens and various seed ferns. The occurrence of the typical Euramerican form *Paripteris* is especially important from a paleobiogeographical point of view, since it shows that Indochina was in contact with South China as early as the Early Carboniferous. As in Thailand, Vietnam and Laos contain abundant Carboniferous marine fossils. In Malaysia, Carboniferous corals are reported from Sumatra.

Fossiliferous Permian limestones, representing all stages of the Permian (Ingavat-Helmcke 1994), are widespread in many parts of Southeast Asia. The area contains abundant foraminifera (tiny organisms that form calcium-based shells), as well as corals, brachiopods, crinoids, and algae. Such assemblages are known from Thailand, Vietnam, Sumatra, and Malaysia. Detailed studies on the Permian faunas of Thailand have shown that in the Early Permian most of Thailand was characterized by subtropical assemblages. On the other hand, what are assumed to be glacio-marine deposits with a "cold" fauna occur in the Phuket area of the southern peninsula. Scholars hypothesize that this region was situated close to glacier-covered areas in Gondwana during the Late Carboniferous and Early Permian. By the Late Permian the northward drift of the Phuket block brought it near the equator. Interesting continental vertebrates of the Late Permian have been found near Luang Prabang in northern Laos (Battail et al. 1995). They include amphibians and mammal-like reptiles, the latter belonging to two distinct species of *Dicyodon*, a plant-eating genus found throughout Pangaea, indicating that in the Late Permian the Indochina Block no longer was isolated from other land masses.

Mesozoic

Marine Triassic fossils, such as pelecypods, cephalopods, gastropods, brachiopods, and corals are abundant in the northern part of Vietnam. Pelecypods are especially abundant and can be used for biostratigraphic purposes; when they are found, different types indicate the presence of Early, Middle, and Late Triassic. In northern Thailand, fossils from the marine Triassic Lampang Group also include abundant pelecypods; organisms with coiled shells, called ammonoids, also occur. Triassic marine fossils are found in Laos, too. In southern Thailand, limestones dated as Early Triassic on the basis of conodonts have yielded a skeleton of one of the most primitive known ichthyosaurs (long-snouted, fish-shaped marine reptiles), *Thaisaurus chonglakmanii* (Mazin et al. 1991). In northeastern Thailand, Late Triassic nonmarine sediments contain vertebrate remains. Nonmarine environments include terrestrial, lake, river, or lagoon settings. The Huai Hin Lat Formation, which was once the site of a lake, has yielded Norian lungfishes, temnospondyl amphibians (possible ancestors of present-day frogs and toads), turtles, and phytosaurs (crocodilelike, semi-aquatic reptiles). The overlying, latest Triassic Nam Phong Formation has yielded the oldest known Southeast Asian dinosaur, a prosauropod. Marine Triassic fossils are found in central Malaya; they include algae, foraminifers, conodonts, corals, pelecypods, and ammonoids. Several Indonesian islands have yielded marine Triassic fossils. The best record is from Timor, with especially rich ammonoid faunas. Timor also has produced a few remains of Triassic marine reptiles.

During the Jurassic, the central part of the Indochina Block was a land area, so the nonmarine sediments contain remains of continental vertebrates. Marine deposition prevailed in the surrounding areas, so that marine invertebrates, including ammonites, are found in western Thailand in the west, and from Laos and southern Vietnam in the east. The Lower Jurassic of southern Laos also has yielded a few fish and reptile remains. In northeastern Thailand, the presumably Late Jurassic Phu Kradung Formation contains remains of nonmarine vertebrates, such as temnospondyl amphibians, turtles, crocodilians, and two types of types of saurischian ("lizard-hipped") dinosaurs: theropods (gracile, bipedal carnivores, e.g., tyrannosaurs), and sauropods (the massive quadripedal herbivores with very long necks and tails). Nonmarine Jurassic sediments in the southern peninsula of Thailand contain palynomorphs, conchostracans, insects, fishes, temnospondyl amphibians (Buffetaut et al. 1994), turtles, and crocodilians. In the islands of Southeast Asia, the Jurassic is mainly marine, so they are the site of Jurassic ammonites, especially several Indonesian islands, as well as the Philippines.

The Cretaceous of mainland Southeast Asia is largely continental and has yielded a number of nonmarine invertebrates and vertebrates. The best record is found in northeastern Thailand. Its Khorat Group is a thick series of nonmarine sediments dated mainly from the Early Cretaceous on the basis of palynology, the study of fossilized pollen, spores, and seeds. Nonmarine pelecypods are abundant in some areas. Vertebrates are represented by dinosaur footprints and abundant skeletal remains of fishes, turtles, crocodilians, and dinosaurs (Suteethorn et al. 1995). The best dinosaur assemblage is from the Sao Khua Formation, which corresponds to the early part of the Early Cretaceous. It includes the sauropod *Phuwiangosaurus*, the early tyrannosaurid *Siamotyrannus* (Buffetaut et al. 1996), ornithomimosaur (a small, two-legged dinosaur), and the possible spinosaurid *Siamosaurus* (a two-legged dinosaur with a large crest, or "sail" running down the back). The Aptian-Albian Khok Kruat Formation has yielded the freshwater shark *Thaiodus*, also known from Tibet (Cappetta et al. 1990), turtles, crocodilians, the ceratopsian *Psittacosaurus* (the so-called parrot-beaked dinosaur), iguanodontids, and theropods. Fossil beds of apparently the same age in Laos have yielded bones of sauropods and iguanodontids, as well as dinosaur footprints. In Cambodia and in Malaya, nonmarine Cretaceous beds contain plant fossils. Marine Cretaceous fossils occur in other parts of Southeast Asia. Cretaceous ammonites are known, for instance, from Burma and from the Philippines.

Cenozoic

Paleogene marine fossils, including nummulites (tiny organisms that incorporate lime into protective shells), corals, and molluscs, are know from many parts of insular Southeast Asia, including the Philippines and Indonesia. Abundant plant and fish remains are found in possibly Oligocene lacustrine (lake) oil shales in the Padang Highlands of Sumatra. Important Paleogene nonmarine vertebrate sites are found in mainland Southeast Asia. The Late Eocene Pondaung fauna of Burma (Colbert 1938) includes carnivores, abundant anthracotheres (hippopotamus-like mammals), brontotheres (rhinoceros-like mammals with bony knobs on the skull),

and rhinoceroses, and the primates *Amphipithecus* and *Pondaungia*, which are interpreted as early anthropoids (group including monkeys, apes, and humans). In southern Thailand, abundant vertebrate remains have been found in coal-bearing beds of Late Eocene age at Krabi (Ducrocq et al. 1995). The fauna includes turtles, crocodilians, snakes, and mammals. The mammal assemblage is remarkably rich, including insectivores (e.g., hedgehogs, shrews, and moles), dermopterans ("flying lemurs"), bats, carnivores, rodents, pigs, various anthracotheres, tragulids (small, hornless ancestors of modern deer, cows, and giraffes), perissodactyls (e.g., horses, tapirs), and primates. Among the latter, *Siamopithecus eocaenus* is considered an early anthropoid, probably related to *Pondaungia* (Chaimanee et al. 1997). These Burmese and Thai Eocene primates suggest that Southeast Asia played a key role in the early evolution of anthropoids. A few Paleogene mammal remains, including pigs and anthracotheres, have also been reported from Borneo.

Neogene fossils from mainland Southeast Asia are mainly from continental lake deposits, although there are some coastal and lagoonal deposits. In northern Vietnam, there are abundant plant remains from the Miocene and Pliocene. Neogene lignite-bearing (lignite is a type of fossil wood) lacustrine deposits occur in many intermontane (between mountains) basins in northwestern Thailand. Several have yielded vertebrate remains (Ducrocq et al. 1995), including fishes, turtles, snakes, birds, bats, tree shrews, rodents, carnivores, pigs, anthracotheres, rhinoceroses, mastodons, *Dendropithecus* and primates (*Tarsius* and the hominoid *Dendropithecus orientalis*). The composition of these faunas indicates that the basins date back to the Middle Miocene.

Pleistocene marine fossils occur in coastal deposits along the coasts of Southeast Asia. Pleistocene vertebrates discovered mainly in river deposits from caves, and fissure-fillings (deposits formed when sediment fills cracks in rock and later itself becomes lithified). Remains of large Pleistocene mammals have been found in deposits where streams merge with the great rivers of Southeast Asia, such as the Irrawady in Burma, the Chao Phraya in Thailand, and the Mekong. However, the most famous vertebrate-bearing river deposits in the region are the Early and Middle Pleistocene ones in Java, where fairly abundant remains of *Homo erectus* have been found, together with a diverse vertebrate assemblage comprising tortoises, crocodilians, deer, bovids, elephants, and hippopotami. During the Pleistocene glaciations, sea levels dropped, turning large parts of what is now Indonesia into an extension of the Asian mainland. This change enabled Asian land vertebrates to spread to Indonesia. On some very isolated islands, however, dwarf populations of otherwise large mammals could evolve, as shown by the pygmy forms of the proboscidean *Stegodon* found on Timor, Flores, and Sulawesi (Hooijer 1970). Many caves in the limestone areas of Southeast Asia contain fossil-rich sediments. In Vietnam, caves have yielded the Middle Pleistocene *Stegodon/Ailuropoda* assemblage (also found in southern China), as well as remains of the giant ape *Gigantopithecus*. In Thailand, rodent remains have been used to date the sediments from caves and fissures, thus revealing a succession of faunas ranging from the Late Pleistocene to Holocene (Chaimanee et al. 1993).

ERIC BUFFETAUT

Works Cited

Battail, B., J. Dejax, P. Richir, P. Taquet, and M. Veran. 1995. New data on the continental Upper Permian in the area of Luang-Prabang, Laos. *Journal of Geology, Hanoi* B 5–6:11–15.

Buffetaut, E., L. Raksaskulwong, V. Suteethorn, and H. Tong. 1994. First post-Triassic temnospondyl amphibians from the Shan-Thai block: Intercentra from the Jurassic of peninsular Thailand. *Geological Magazine* 131:837–39.

Buffetaut, E., V. Suteethorn, and H. Tong. 1996. The earliest known tyrannosaur from the Lower Cretaceous of Thailand. *Nature* 381:689–91.

Burrett, C., and B. Stait. 1985. South East Asia as a part of an Ordovician Gondwanaland: A palaeobiogeographic test of a tectonic hypothesis. *Earth and Planetary Science Letters* 75:184–90.

Cappetta, H., E. Buffetaut, and V. Suteethorn. 1990. A new hybodont shark from the Lower Cretaceous of Thailand. *Neues Jahrbuch für Geologie and Paläontologie, Monatshefte* 11:659–66.

Chaimanee, Y., J.J. Jaeger, and V. Suteethorn. 1993. Pleistocene microvertebrates from fissure-fillings in Thailand. *Journal of Southeast Asian Earth Science* 8:45–48.

Chaimanee, Y., V. Suteethorn, J.J. Jaeger, and S. Ducrocq. 1997. A new Late Eocene anthropoid primate from Thailand. *Nature* 385:429–31.

Colbert, E.H. 1938. Fossil mammals from Burma in the American Museum of Natural History. *Bulletin of the American Museum of Natural History* 74:255–436.

Ducrocq, S., Y. Chaimanee, V. Suteethorn, and J.J. Jaeger. 1995. Mammalian faunas and the ages of the continental Tertiary fossiliferous localities from Thailand. *Journal of Southeast Asian Earth Sciences* 12:65–78.

Hooijer, D.A. 1970. Pleistocene South-east Asiatic pygmy stegodonts. *Nature* 225:474–75.

Ingavat-Helmcke, R. 1994. Paleozoic paleontological evidence of Thailand. *In* P. Angsuwathana, T. Wongwanich, W. Tansathien, S. Wongsomak, and J. Tulyatid (eds.), *Proceedings of the International Symposium on Stratigraphic Correlation of Southeast Asia.* Bangkok: Department of Mineral Resources.

Janvier, P., T. Tong-Dzuy, and P. Ta Hoa. 1993. A new Early Devonian galeaspid from Bac Thai Province, Vietnam. *Palaeontology* 36:297–309.

Laveine, J.P., B. Ratanasthien, and S. Sithirach. 1993. The Carboniferous flora of northeastern Thailand: Its paleogeographic importance. *Comptes Rendus de l'Académie des Sciences* 2, 317:279–85.

Mazin, J.M., V. Suteethorn, E. Buffetaut, J.J. Jaeger, and R. Helmcke-Ingavat. 1991. Preliminary description of *Thaisaurus chonglakmanii* n.g., n.sp., a new ichthyopterygian (Reptilia) from the Early Triassic of Thailand. *Comptes Rendus de l'Académie des Sciences* 2, 313:1207–12.

Suteethorn, V., E. Buffetaut, V. Martin, Y. Chaimanee, H. Tong, and S. Triamwichanon. 1995. Thai dinosaurs: An updated review. *In* A. Sun and Y. Wang (eds.), *Sixth Symposium on Mesozoic Terrestrial Ecosystems and Biota, Short Papers* Beijing: China Ocean.

Tong-Dzuy, T., P. Janvier, and T. Doan-Nhat. 1995. Première découverte d'un Placoderme (Vertebrata) dans le Dévonien du bloc Indochinois (Trung Bo, Viêt-Nam central). *Bulletin du Muséum National d'Histoire Naturelle de Paris* C, 16:258–79.

Wongwanich, T., and C. Burrett. 1983. The Lower Palaeozoic of Thailand. *Journal of the Geological Society of Thailand* 6:21–29.

Further Reading

Hutchinson, C.S. 1989. *Geological Evolution of South-east Asia.* Oxford: Clarendon; New York: Oxford University Press.

Kobayashi, T., R. Toriyama, and W. Hashimoto (eds.). 1964–84. *Geology and Palaeontology of Southeast Asia.* 25 vols. Tokyo: University of Tokyo Press.

Whitmore, T.C. (ed.). 1981. *Wallace's Line and Plate Techtonics.* Oxford: Clarendon; New York: Oxford University Press.

———. (ed.). 1987. *Biogeographical Evolution of the Malay Archipelago.* Oxford: Clarendon; New York: Oxford University Press.

SPECIATION AND MORPHOLOGICAL CHANGE

Species play a fundamental role in evolutionary paleontology and biology because species are the entities that evolve. Species are also the unit of measure to assess the diversity or similarity of biological communities and fossil assemblages in ecology and paleoecology. They are the smallest biological category for reconstructing a genetic history and for classification. Speciation (evolution of new species) is a major area of research on modern populations.

Reconciling the rate of evolutionary change and its processes in modern species (microevolution) with patterns of long-term evolution above the species level (macroevolution) in the fossil record is an enduring problem, dating back to Darwin's *Origin of Species* (1859). Darwin envisioned gradual transitions from one species to another through an accumulation of minor differences brought about through the influence of natural selection. Geneticists of the early twentieth century challenged this view, proposing that transitions between species occur in a single jump (saltation) when one genetic variant (allele) is replaced by a new, mutant allele that has major effects upon the individual. In the mid-twentieth century, the neo-Darwinian synthesis refuted this proposal. Then, the emergence of the theory called punctuated equilibria (Eldredge and Gould 1972) raised new questions about whether species evolved gradually. Punctuated equilibria holds that during speciation, differences between species in physical properties (e.g., morphology, physiology, behavior) evolve rapidly. (These changes are called phenotypic changes because they affect the physical manifestation—the phenotype—of some sort of change in the genetic inheritance. Genotype refers to the organism's genetic makeup; some changes in genes do not affect the phenotype.) During the time between speciation events, there is no significant evolution.

Recognizing and naming species is a fundamental human activity that assumes special importance and formality in science. Thus, there is a long history of scientific debate, known as the "species problem," on how to define species. Different concepts are appropriate for different purposes, and fossil species present special problems of their own. The effects of environmental factors and biological properties of organisms on the tendency for new species to form and the rate of formation are important subjects in evolutionary biology.

Species Concepts

Many species concepts have been proposed; they can be placed in four major groups: typological (essentialist), nominalistic, biological, and evolutionary (Mayr and Ashlock 1991; Smith 1994).

Typological Concepts

Typological concepts concern the phenotypic product of evolution. They emphasize morphological (structural) similarities within species and dissimilarities among them. Implicitly, typological concepts assume that species are phenotypically homogeneous and stable entities. However, these qualities create theoretical and practical problems. Virtually all species contain conspicuous variation within populations and between populations. For instance, only consider the wide variety within humans and between human populations. Conversely, "sibling species"—species that are closely related, such as horses and asses—are indistinguishable using conventional morphological criteria but are separate evolutionary units. Thus, morphological differences may evolve without resulting in speciation, and speciation may not entail obvious morphological change. Nonetheless, typological concepts treat variation among individuals of a species as accidental departures from unchanging ideal properties of a species. As a result, typological concepts belong to the philosophical tradition of essentialism and are incompatible with the principle of evolution.

Nevertheless, in general, in the Linnean system of classification, which is the foundation of modern biological classification, typological species are the most basic classification group, and the rules for naming new species depend on typology. Although there is no longer any doubt that species have to evolve and give rise to new species, and although relying on morphological similarity and discontinuity creates practical problems, the typological species concept is embedded firmly in naming and classifying modern and fossil organisms. Typological species are necessary to create a stable and reliable nomenclature.

Nominalistic Concepts

Nominalistic concepts are of largely historical interest and have few adherents today. They treat only individual specimens as real objects. Species, on the other hand, are viewed as imaginary groups created to allow scholars to use collective names. Although individuals of a species are real objects, they collectively form the temporary repository of genetic information (gene pool) that determines the long-term identity and fate of species. Therefore, species are a real evolutionary unit; individual specimens are not.

Biological Concepts

The biological species concept, which has its roots in eighteenth-century natural history, plays a central role in the study of evolutionary processes in living populations. During the mid-1900s, E. Mayr and T. Dobzhansky integrated ideas from natural history, phylogeny (evolutionary history), and Darwinian theory with new developments on the genetics of natural populations. The theory that grew out of this synthesis is called "neo-Darwinian" or "synthetic" theory, and one of its cornerstones is the biological species concept. It focuses on processes that unite members of the same species and that isolate them from members of other species. Biological species are defined as "groups of actually or potentially interbreeding natural populations that are reproductively isolated from other such groups" (Mayr 1963). Thus, members of a species form a reproductive community within which interbreeding takes place under natural conditions. Consequently biological species form a distinct genetic unit.

Members of a biological species also form an ecological unit that interacts with the environment in a characteristic way. The biological species concept does not refer directly to phenotypes, but phenotypic similarity among individuals, the basis for typological species, should result from the ecological unity and genetic integration of biological species. Consequently, there is a general correspondence between biological and typological species, and processes that characterize biological species should help account for properties of modern and fossil typological species.

Evolutionary Concepts

The evolutionary species concept was proposed to meet the unique needs of paleontology. The biological species concept emphasizes reproductive compatibility and genetic cohesion, which is difficult to apply to modern species and all but impossible for fossils. Furthermore, it does not address the enormous expanses of geological time encompassed by the fossil record.

In 1961, G.G. Simpson proposed the evolutionary concept: "An evolutionary species is a lineage (an ancestral-descendant sequence of populations) evolving separately from others and with its own unitary evolutionary role and tendencies" (Simpson 1961). This concept does recognize persistence of species (independent lineages) over long periods of geological time. However, it also presents serious conceptual problems. Although the concept addresses both cohesion within species and their evolutionary independence from each other, it does not address the causes for cohesion and independence. Nor does this concept specify where in a lineage an ancestral species ends and a descendant species begins. This limitation presents particular problems for anagenic speciation—the transformation within a single lineage of one species throughout its entire range (the region throughout which the members are found) into a new species.

Two solutions to this problem have been proposed (Mayr and Ashlock 1991). Simpson himself suggested that transitions between evolutionary species be inferred from the magnitude of morphological differences between them. However, this "solution" has its own serious problem. At a sufficiently fine timescale, transitions between species generally should be formed by a gradient of small morphological changes; major differences may simply result from gaps in the fossil record. Alternatively, W. Hennig (1966) argued that at a branch point in phylogeny (i.e., cladogenesis), neither of the species derived from their common ancestors could represent the ancestral species that was present before the lineage split. In this concept, evolutionary species would be defined by the occurrence of cladogenesis. However, Hennig's proposal is inconsistent with ample evidence that one species can evolve from another without the ancestor evolving significantly or going extinct (e.g., Eldredge and Cracraft 1980; Williams 1992). In such cases, one member of the pair of species present after a branch point in phylogeny may be the common ancestor of both. Hennig's proposal also ignores the possibility of species-level anagenic change within lineages. As a result, using either the magnitude of morphological differences or branch points in phylogeny as criteria for evolutionary species may be unsatisfactory.

All in all, despite its limitations, the typological species concept is the most useful in most paleontological work. Both biological and evolutionary species concepts do include ideas that apply to paleontology. The biological species concept depends on criteria that are rarely observable in fossils (see Schneider and Kennett 1996 for an interesting exception), and dividing fossil lineages into discrete evolutionary species is problematical. In practice, most fossil species are defined by morphological criteria based on analogy with related modern typological species. They are typological species.

Biological Nomenclature

The scientific names of species are an integral part of scientific communication (e.g., Savory 1962; Mayr and Ashlock 1991). Although formal codes differ somewhat among major groups (notably animals, plants, and bacteria), the codes do insure that nomenclature is universal, stable, and practical. Scientific names of species consist of the generic name followed by the trivial name (e.g., *Tyrannosaurus,* generic; *rex,* trivial) and are always italicized.

To name new species, several general rules must be followed. The species description must be published in printed form. It must include a diagnosis (analysis of the nature of a thing), spelling out those character states (variants of traits) that distinguish the new species from all species described previously. However, diagnoses may be incomplete or may fail to distinguish a new species from species discovered later, so a type specimen—a representative specimen—must be deposited in a museum to serve as the ultimate standard for a species' scientific name. A verbal description of the new species provides more information than the diagnosis and must be accompanied by an adequate illustration. All new species must be assigned to a genus in the original description.

Sometimes more than one name is published for what later proves to be the same species. In such cases, the description published on an earlier date or even on an earlier page of the same publication is the senior synonym and is adopted as the valid name. This rule applies even if the later name is more accurate. The most famous application of this rule of priority is replacement of "eohippus" (which accurately portrays the close relationship of this fossil to the ancestry of horses) by its senior synonym, *Hyracotherium,* which does not reflect its relationships. The scientific names of species change when the name of its genus (the larger group to which several species belong; plural, genera) changes due to priority or new interpretations of evolutionary relationships. Names published prior to 1753 (or 1758 for animals), when Linnaeus founded the current system of biological nomenclature, are ignored.

In paleontology, describing synonymous species and assigning specimens to the wrong existing species are particular problems. Fossils are often fragmentary, and even complete specimens of the same species may be different enough to be assigned incorrectly to separate species. For example (Aldridge and Purnell 1996), isolated conodont (early jawless vertebrate) elements are extremely abundant in Paleozoic marine rocks and have been known since the 1840s. However, it was not discovered until the 1930s that individual conodont animals possessed several different kinds of elements that had previously been assigned to different species. The soft-bodied conodont animals themselves were not discovered until 1982.

Similarly, because of ignorance of relationships between dissimilar members of the same species, scholars can assign males and females, different age classes (especially adults and larvae), and major genetic or developmental variants to different species. For instance, differences in the size of males and females (sexual dimorphism) is so common and striking in ammonites (extinct, spiral-shelled invertebrates) that the males and females of several species apparently have been placed in separate genera (Smith 1994). Fossilized burrows and tracks (icnofossils) of fossil species are difficult to associate with the species that made them, so scholars may use separate systems of nomenclature to avoid creating synonymous names. Similarly, paleobotanists refer to macrofloras (large groupings) based on leaf macrofossil species, and palynofloras, based on palynomorph (pollen) species. Although the usual rules of biological nomenclature apply to fossils, they often present special difficulties requiring special naming conventions. With fossils, there are ambiguities and errors in naming new species and identifying specimens that do not have parallels in the study of extant organisms.

Speciation

Biological species are defined by possession of reproductive isolating mechanisms (Mayr 1963; Otte and Endler 1989). These mechanisms prevent mating, and, as a result, prevent substantial hybridization and genetic exchange between distinct species that occur in one area (sympatric species).

It is important to distinguish between premating and postmating isolating mechanisms because natural selection favors the evolution of premating mechanisms but cannot favor postmating mechanisms. Premating mechanisms prevent individuals from wasting time, energy, and other resources on hybrid offspring; such offspring may be unable to survive, sterile, or otherwise of low quality. In contrast, natural selection cannot favor postmating mechanisms because they take effect after the parents already have wasted resources on hybrid offspring. Consequently, postmating isolating mechanisms generally must evolve by chance or because selection favors some other trait.

Premating mechanisms include the following: (1) ecological or habitat isolation; (2) seasonal or temporal isolation; (3) ethological or sexual isolation owing to reduced attraction between the sexes; (4) mechanical isolation, usually owing to structural incompatibly of genitalia; and (5) gametic isolation, owing to the failure of the sex cells to unite. Postmating isolation results from (1) hybrid inviability, (2) hybrid sterility, and (3) hybrid breakdown, which occurs when the hybrid's offspring cannot survive or is sterile.

There are two major areas of research in speciation: the geographical setting and genetic basis for evolution of isolating mechanisms, and the role of adaptation in evolution of premating isolation (Otte and Endler 1989). Understanding the evolution of ecological differences between ancestral and descendant species is also important, because ecological differentiation is necessary for reproductively isolated populations (i.e., species) to coexist in the same area.

Speciation may occur within a range of temporal and spatial settings (Mayr and Ashlock 1991). New species may form instantaneously when related species have hybrid offspring that are polyploid (i.e., with more than the usual two sets of chromosomes per nucleus). Often these offspring are tetraploid, having four sets of chromosomes in each nucleus. Such offspring can breed successfully among themselves but not with members of either parental species. This mode of speciation instantly produces a reproductively isolated, hybrid species that has a phenotype that is generally intermediate between the parental species. Because polyploid hybrids generally cannot reproduce with members of either parental species, there is no exchange of genes between the two groups. That means that the parental species retain the status of a separate species. Speciation by polyploidy may have important macroevolutionary implications, but it is uncommon.

Gradual speciation, the evolution of isolating mechanisms and other phenotypic differences by accumulation of small genetic differences over many generations, may occur under a variety of circumstances. Sympatric speciation requires formation of two species within a deme—a single population of interbreeding individuals. For this to occur, isolating mechanisms and ecological differences between groups of individuals within the population must evolve gradually. Although there is great interest in sympatric speciation, theoretical analyses show that this type of speciation requires improbable genetic and ecological conditions.

Parapatry refers to populations that are located next to each other and that experience ongoing genetic exchange (gene flow) through interbreeding. Parapatric populations of a species typically exhibit phenotypic differentiation, which can often be attributed to environmental variation. Scholars postulate that parapatric speciation occurs when isolating mechanisms evolve along the ecological and phenotypic boundaries (clines) between divergent populations in adjacent habitats, despite migration between them. Theoretical objections to parapatric speciation are also formidable, and evidence for its occurrence is equivocal.

The most likely process for species formation is geographic, or allopatric, speciation. Under this model of speciation, individuals from different populations of a species cannot mate because of a geographical barrier that severely limits or prevents migration. Such separated populations are called allopatric (occurring in different areas). The separation allows phenotypes to arise that cause ecological differences, reproductive isolation, or both to evolve in each group. If the two groups had interacted, gene flow would have retarded speciation (Mayr 1963). Allopatry may result from division of an ancestral species' range into two large areas by fragmentation of water, land masses, or other habitat patches. Or, it may result when a few individuals cross a dispersal barrier (e.g., mountain range, isthmus, channel) to colonize an already-isolated habitat patch. This process is called peripatric speciation and is especially interesting because it may be common, and it has the potential to cause sweeping genetic reorganization in the isolated population.

Peripatric speciation may involve colonization by a small founding population. In the original population, the frequency of certain alleles may be fairly stable. (Alleles are slightly different versions of a gene, such as the gene that controls eye color in certain flies. It is possible to determine the frequency of the various alleles in a populations—say version A occurs 5 times of 9, version B occurs 3 of 18, version C occurs 3 of 18, and version D occurs 1 of 9.) However, the smaller the number of colonists, the more likely it is that this new population will, by chance, have different allele frequencies than the original population. The new colony may even lose alleles that were present in the source population. If separate genes interact strongly (epistasis), random changes of allele frequencies of some genes may cause natural selection to favor changes in other frequencies. A cascade of such interactions between genes, called a "genetic revolution," could lead to formation of new combinations of "coadapted" genes—genes that function harmoniously together but in the original population are incompatible. This process could lead directly or indirectly to isolating mechanisms between the new colony and the original population.

The new genetic equilibrium formed after a genetic revolution might also alter the new species' response to natural selection for traits related to reproductive and ecological properties, further enhancing divergence. In a small, isolated habitat, ecological conditions may also differ in important ways from those in the habitat of the original population of the species. Thus, each of these conditions—genetic changes owing to chance, altered responses to environmental selection, and contrasting ecological conditions experienced by an isolate—can contribute to peripatric speciation. N. Eldredge and S.J. Gould (1972) proposed that the peripatric model of speciation can account for punctuated equilibria in the fossil record.

Punctuated Equilibria

In 1972 Eldredge and Gould proposed punctuated equilibria to reconcile patterns of change through time in the fossil record with the theoretical expectations for the fossil record based on natural selection. Darwin (1859) believed that natural selection should produce gradual transitions (phyletic gradualism) between species in the fossil record. In Chapter 9 of *The Origin of Species,* "On The

Imperfection of the Geological Record," Darwin explained his expectation for phyletic gradualism—and its absence from the fossil record—as follows:

> But just in proportion as this process of extinction has acted on an enormous scale, so must the number of intermediate varieties, which have formerly existed on the earth, be truly enormous. Why then is not every geological formation and every stratum full of such intermediate links? Geology assuredly does not reveal any such finely graduated organic chain; and this perhaps is the most obvious and gravest objection which can be urged against my theory [of natural selection]. The explanation lies, as I believe, in the extreme imperfection of the geological record.

Eldredge and Gould argued that in the 110 years since publication of *The Origin of Species,* paleontological research had failed to produce the abundance of phyletic gradualism demanded by Darwin as validation for the role of natural selection in macroevolution. Instead, the fossil record seemed to be dominated by long periods of evolutionary stasis, "equilibria," during which no morphological intermediates (transitional stages in evolution) occur. Eldredge and Gould called these transitional periods "punctuations" and argued that stasis dominates the fossil record. Eldredge and Gould argued that paleontologists rarely report such stasis because they expect phyletic gradualism and attribute observed stasis to an incomplete fossil record.

Rather than accepting Darwin's requirement of phyletic gradualism, Eldredge and Gould argued that punctuated equilibria is a logical consequence of Mayr's model of peripatric speciation extended through geological time. If species form rapidly in small, isolated populations, both their small size and the high speed of change would greatly reduce the chances of observing speciation in the fossil record. Furthermore, if genetic revolutions during speciation form new complexes of coadapted genes, once formed, such complexes would tend to be disrupted by any further changes in the frequencies of alleles, gradual or not. Thus, after completion of speciation, the evolutionary response to natural selection should be constrained severely by the adverse effects of any change on interactions among coadapted genes. While Darwin's natural selection seemed to require phyletic gradualism in the fossil record, peripatric speciation and genetic coadaptation of neo-Darwinian theory seemed to require punctuated equilibria. Failure to detect punctuations could be attributed to their high speed and restriction to small populations. Thus, research on punctuated equilibria has emphasized testing biostratigraphic sequences (rock strata) for stasis.

Many detailed analyses of the fossil sequences have been performed since 1972, and they have produced mixed results. P.D. Gingerich has offered compelling evidence for phyletic gradualism of tooth size in biostratigraphic sequences of several Early Cenozoic North American mammals (1980). The most extensive and detailed evidence for punctuated equilibria comes from Cheetham's analyses of Late Tertiary encrusting marine inverte-

brates called bryozoans (1986). Studies on patterns of change in the fossil record have produced roughly equal numbers of cases interpreted by their authors as punctuated equilibrium and phyletic gradualism (Erwin and Anstey 1995). Thus, the focus of research has now shifted away from whether evolution is either gradual or punctuated. Recent scholars now investigate questions about relative gene frequencies and distributions among geological time intervals, population structures, taxonomic groups, stages in the diversification of a group, and environments. Resolving these problems will require many careful analyses using numerous large samples made at fine, evenly spaced stratigraphic intervals distributed over long time periods.

Punctuated equilibria began as an attempt to reconcile patterns of change in the fossil record with neo-Darwinian theory. Later, however, "punctuationist" ideas were developed as a challenge to neo-Darwinian theory, and two opposing camps emerged. One camp, composed mostly of evolutionary theorists and population biologists, claimed that neo-Darwinian theory is substantially complete, requiring only minor modification (Charlesworth et al. 1982). In contrast, punctuationists, comprising mostly invertebrate paleontologists, argued that new mechanisms are needed to account for the differences between mechanisms observed in modern species and patterns of change in the fossil record (Gould 1980).

In some cases, the new mechanisms are really reformulations or minor modifications of neo-Darwinian theory. Others, however, represent more radical departures. Chief among them is the proposal that the genetic basis for variation within species is fundamentally different from that for speciation. The complexities of epistasis and developmental processes are invoked both to provide novel genetic variation (macromutations) for seemingly instantaneous, saltational change during punctuations and to account for stasis in the fossil record. However, theoretical analyses using reasonable assumptions suggest that natural selection on small differences among individuals can account for stasis and also can cause such high rates of evolution (i.e., speciation within 10^2 and 10^3 generations) that only the finest possible stratigraphic resolution, which is rarely available, could reveal the gradation of small evolutionary steps between species postulated for phyletic gradualism.

Important corollaries of punctuated equilibria are "species selection" and related proposals that selective extinction and speciation are needed to account for long-term trends in the fossil record. If it is true that significant evolution occurs only during peripatric speciation, natural selection alone could not cause long-term evolutionary trends. During peripatric speciation, evolution is influenced strongly by random genetic change and adaptation to local conditions. Thus, phenotypic change during a sequence of parapatric speciation events in a lineage is unlikely to allow the lineage to evolve adaptations to long-term, widespread environmental changes. Rather, tracking such environmental trends would require selective extinction of species that fail to fit the trend or excess production of species that fit it.

Punctuated equilibria also has focused attention on the dominance of stasis (equilibria) in the fossil record, encouraging paleontologists to document it when it is encountered and theorists to attempt to account for it in terms of microevolutionary processes. Punctuated equilibria has spawned many controversies, but it has added theoretical vigor to paleontology, encouraged objective analysis of biostratigraphic sequences, and has enriched evolutionary theory with paleontological data.

Adaptive or Evolutionary Radiation

A group of species and their common ancestor form a clade. Many clades have experienced episodes of rapid increase in the number of species and their range of phenotypic variation. Expansions of this kind, known as "adaptive radiations," have provided important evidence for the development of evolutionary thought (Mayr 1963; Eldredge and Cracraft 1980; Bell and Andrews 1997; Carroll 1997). Darwin's observation of a small radiation of "Darwin's finches" on the Galapagos Islands strongly influenced his thinking on adaptive radiation. The Early Tertiary radiation of mammals is a classic example of a major radiation, but many others have been documented in the fossil record (Taylor and Larwood 1990).

Adaptive radiations clearly depend on speciation, but the causes of their elevated speciation rates are obscure. New ecological opportunities, which may appear after mass extinctions, radical environmental change, or colonization of a new area appear to trigger adaptive radiations. It is unclear, however, why one group radiates while another does not. Radiating groups may possess phenotypic novelties (key innovations) that allow their species to specialize in response to a wide variety of ecological resources. Or, reproductive isolating mechanisms may evolve more readily in some groups than others. Qualities that may have triggered an adaptive radiation are recognizable only in hindsight, making it difficult to determine whether those qualities, some other property of the radiating group, or chance alone were really responsible for the group's radiation.

MICHAEL A. BELL

See also Adaptation; Coevolutionary Relationships; Diversity; Evolutionary Novelty; Evolutionary Trends; Extinction; Faunal Change and Turnover; Growth, Development, and Evolution, Paleobiogeography; Selection; Systematics; Variation

Works Cited

Aldridge, R.J., and M.A. Purnell. 1996. The conodont controversies. *Trends in Ecology and Evolution* 11:463–68.

Bell, M.A., and C.A. Andrews. 1997. Evolutionary consequences of postglacial colonization of fresh water by primitively anadromous fishes. *In* B. Streit, T. Städler, and C.M. Lively (eds.), *Evolutionary Ecology of Freshwater Animals*. Basel and Boston: Birkhauser Verlag.

Carroll, R.L. 1997. *Patterns and Processes of Vertebrate Evolution*. New York: Cambridge University Press.

Charlesworth, B., R. Lande, and M. Slatkin. 1982. A neo-Darwinian commentary on punctuated equilibria. *Evolution* 36:474–98.

Cheetham, A.H. 1986. Tempo of evolution in a Neogene bryozoan: Rates of morphologic change within and across species boundaries. *Paleobiology* 12:190–202.

Darwin, C.R. 1859. *The Origin of Species by Means of Natural Selection; or, The Preservation of Favored Races in the Struggle for Life*. London: Murray; New York: Appleton, 1860.

Eldredge, N., and J. Cracraft. 1980. *Phylogenetic Patterns and the Evolutionary Process*. New York: Columbia University Press.

Eldredge, N., and S.J. Gould. 1972. Punctuated equilibria: An alternative to phyletic gradualism. *In* T.J.M. Schopf (ed.), *Models in Paleobiology*. San Francisco: Freeman Cooper.

Erwin, D.H., and R.L. Anstey. 1995. *New Approaches to Speciation in the Fossil Record*. New York: Columbia University Press.

Gingerich, P.D. 1980. Evolutionary patterns in early Cenozoic mammals. *Annual Review of Earth and Planetary Sciences* 8:407–24.

Gould, S.J. 1980. Is a new and general theory of evolution emerging? *Paleobiology* 6:119–30.

Hennig, W. 1966. *Phylogenetic Systematics*. D.D. Davis and R. Zangerl (trans.). Urbana: University of Illinois Press; as *Phylogenetische Systematik*, Berlin: Parey, 1982.

Mayr, E. 1963. *Animal Species and Evolution*. Cambridge, Massachusetts: Belknap Press of Harvard University.

Mayr, E., and P.D. Ashlock. 1991. *Principles of Systematic Zoology*. 2nd ed., New York: McGraw-Hill.

Otte, D., and J.A. Endler. 1989. *Speciation and Its Consequences*. Sunderland, Massachusetts: Sinauer.

Savory, T. 1962. *Naming the Living World*. New York: Wiley; London: English Universities Press.

Schneider, C.E., and J.P. Kennett. 1996. Isotopic evidence for interspecies habitat differences during evolution of the Neogene planktonic foraminiferal clade *Globoconella*. *Paleobiology* 22:282–303.

Simpson, G.G. 1961. *Principles of Animal Taxonomy*. New York: Columbia University Press.

Smith, A.B. 1994. *Systematics and the Fossil Record*. Oxford and Cambridge, Massachusetts: Blackwell.

Taylor, P.D., and G.P. Larwood (eds.). 1990. *Major Evolutionary Radiations*. Oxford: Clarendon Press; New York: Oxford University Press.

Williams, G.C. 1992. *Natural Selection: Domains, Levels, and Challenges*. Oxford Series in Ecology and Evolution, 4. New York: Oxford University Press.

Further Reading

Carroll, R.L. 1997. *Patterns and Processes of Vertebrate Evolution*. New York: Cambridge University Press.

Eldredge, N., and J. Cracraft. 1980. *Phylogenetic Patterns and the Evolutionary Process*. New York: Columbia University Press.

Erwin, D.H., and R.L. Anstey. 1995. *New Approaches to Speciation in the Fossil Record*. New York: Columbia University Press.

Futuyma, D.J. 1979. *Evolutionary Biology*. Sunderland, Massachusetts: Sinauer; 3rd ed., 1997.

Mayr, E. 1963. *Animal Species and Evolution*. Cambridge, Massachusetts: Belknap Press of Harvard University.

Otte, D., and J.A. Endler. 1989. *Speciation and Its Consequences*. Sunderland, Massachusetts: Sinauer.

Skelton, P. (ed.). 1993. *Evolution: A Biological and Palaeontological Approach*. Worthingham: Longman; Reading, Massachusetts: Addison-Wesley.

SPONGES AND SPONGELIKE ORGANISMS

An early branching event in the history of animals separated the sponges from other metazoans (animals). As one would expect based on their phylogenetic position (evolutionary relationship to other animals), fossil sponges are among the oldest known animal fossils, dating from the Late Precambrian. Since then, sponges have been conspicuous members of many fossil communities; the number of described fossil genera exceeds 900. The approximately 5,000 living sponge species are classified in the phylum Porifera, which is composed of three distinct groups, the Hexactinellida (glass sponges), the Demospongia, and the Calcarea (calcareous sponges). Sponges are characterized by a feeding system unique among animals. Flagella line the surface of chambers that are connected by a series of canals. The beating of the flagella (long, whiplike structures) directs water through the chambers where food particles are filtered out. Sponge cells perform a variety of bodily functions and appear to be more independent of each other than are the cells of other animals.

Sponge Phylogeny and Systematics

At one time, a diagnostic feature (distinguishing characteristic) of the Porifera was the presence of specialized structures called spicules, which are slender, often pointed structures that provide support to a sponge's body. As a result, certain fossil groups whose organization was consistent with that of living sponges were not placed within the phylum Porifera. In particular, groups with a solid calcareous (calcium-embedded) skeleton (i.e., the Archaeocyatha, chaetetids, sphinctozoans, and stromatoporoids) were problematic. A great deal of insight into the phylogenetic affinities of these groups was gained with the discovery of more than 15 extant (present-day) species of sponges having a solid calcareous skeleton. These species are diverse in form and would be classified with the chaetetids, sphinctozoans, and stromatoporoids if found as fossils. However, with the living material in hand, scholars could observe histological (tissue), cytological (cell), and larval characteristics. This information suggests that these 15 species readily can be placed within the Calcarea and the Demospongia (Vacelet 1985). This discovery radically changes our view of poriferan phylogeny.

It is accepted widely among poriferan biologists that the Calcarea and the Demospongia are more closely related to each other than either is to the Hexactinellida (Reitner and Mehl 1996). With the discovery of living chaetetids, stromatoporoids, and sphinctozoans, a fourth class was erected for these so-called sclerosponges. However, the Sclerospongia is not a natural monophyletic grouping (one with a single common ancestor), so it is being abandoned (Vacelet 1985; Reitner 1990). The abundant fossil chaetetids, stromatoporoids, and sphinctozoans probably are part of the classes Demospongia and Calcarea, although some uncertainty still remains. The Archaeocyatha pose a special case. No living representative of this group has been discovered. Their organization is consistent with that of living sponges (Debrenne and Vacelet 1984; Kruse 1990; Savarese 1992). The one phyloge-

netic analysis that included archaeocyaths with other sponges grouped them as sisters to the demosponges (Reitner 1990). Therefore, although the taxonomic term Archaeocyatha is often accorded phylum status, it is likely a subgroup of the phylum Porifera, thereby violating the ranking system. A hypothesis for the phylogeny of sponges and spongelike organisms is presented at the bottom of Figure 1.

Sponge Ecology

Sponges are predominantly marine (salt-water based), with the notable exception of the family Spongillidae, an extant group of freshwater demosponges whose fossil record begins in the Cretaceous. Sponges are ubiquitous benthic creatures, found at all latitudes beneath the world's oceans, and from the intertidal (in the zone affected by the rise and fall of tides) to the deep sea. Generally, they are sessile, although it has been shown that some are able to move slowly (up to four millimeters per day) within aquaria (Bond and Harris 1988). It is as yet unknown whether this movement is important for sponge ecology under natural conditions. Some sponges bore into the shells of bivalves, gastropods, and the colonial skeletons of corals by slowly etching away chips of calcareous material.

Water flowing through sponges provides food and oxygen, as well as a means for waste removal. This flow is generated actively by the beating of flagella. The water movement through some sponges is aided by ambient (surrounding) currents passing over raised excurrent openings (those through which water flows out of the sponge). This moving water creates an area of low pressure above the excurrent openings, assisting in drawing water out of the sponge. Sponges can regulate the amount of flow through their bodies by constricting various openings. The volume of water passing through a sponge can be enormous—up to 20,000 times its volume in a single 24-hour period. In general, sponges feed by filtering bacteria from the water that passes through them. Many sponges, however, harbor symbionts—they provide a home for single-celled photosynthetic organisms such as dinoflagellates or cyanobacteria, from which the sponges also derive nutrients. (This is a symbiotic relationship, as both organisms benefit.) Sponges of the family Cladorhizidae are especially unusual in that they typically feed by capturing and digesting whole animals (Vacelet and Boury-Esnault 1996; Vacelet et al. 1996).

Sponges reproduce by both asexual and sexual means. Most poriferans that reproduce by sexual means are hermaphroditic (include both male and female reproductive structures) and produce eggs and sperm at different times. Sperm are released in the excurrent flow of male individuals and are subsequently captured by females of the same species housing eggs. Fertilization happens internally, and the larvae can develop inside the sponge body or in the water column. Sponges that reproduce asexually produce "buds" or, more often, gemmules, which are packets of several cells of various types inside a protective covering. Freshwater sponges of

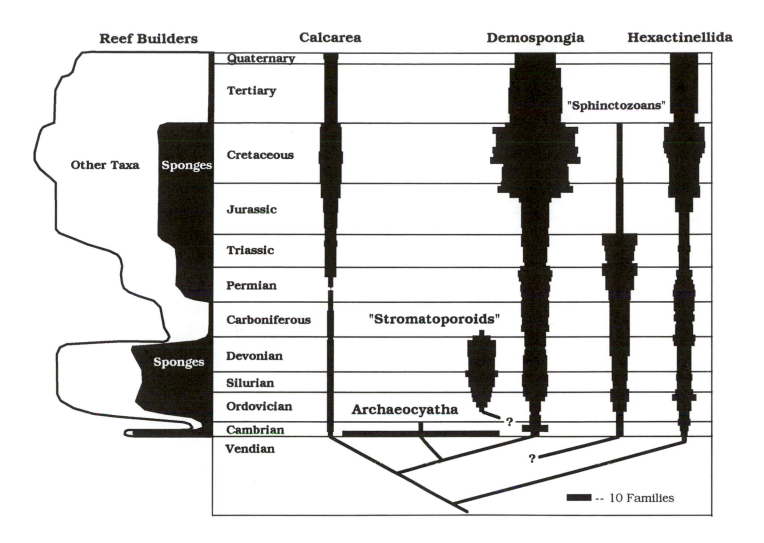

Figure 1. Composite diagram of the history of sponges. A phylogenetic hypothesis for Porifera is shown at the bottom (modified from Reitner 1990). To the left is a cartoon representing the contribution of sponges to carbonate reef buildups through the Phanerozoic (derived from Rowland and Gangloff 1988 and Kauffman and Fagerstrom 1993). The remaining section shows the known fossil record of sponge families (tabulated from Rigby et al. 1993). Note that the illustrated number of archaeocythan families present during the Lower Cambrian is roughly one half of the actual number known (an astonishing 120) due to space limitations.

the Spongillidae often produce gemmules prior to winter. These then develop into adult sponges at the beginning of the following spring.

Sponge Morphology

Sponge bodies are diverse in form (morphology), ranging from encrusting sheets, to volcano-shaped mounds, to tubes as small as one millimeter or as large as one meter, to upright sheets reminiscent of elephant ears. Often, scholars distinguish between sponges according to the level of complexity exhibited by their bodies. The simplest form—called ascon—consists of a single tube two cell-layers thick. The interior is lined by choanocytes (cells with a central flagellum surrounded by a collar of microvilli, or tiny fleshy projections), while the exterior is covered by dermal cells termed pinacocytes. Between the two layers is a thin space called mesohyl

or mesenchyme, consisting of a protein-rich matrix, some cells, and spicules. Poriferans with this type of architecture are necessarily very small, due to surface area-to-volume constraints. In order for a sponge to attain greater size, the sponge wall must be folded in on itself. A simple folding of the wall yields a sponge body with sycon organization. The vast majority of sponges are organized in a more complex way, the leucon condition, with folds upon folds, resulting in a series of flagellated chambers connected by canals. Ascon, sycon, and leucon are levels of complexity that grade one into the other. Figure 2 shows a scanning electron microscope (SEM) image of the choanocyte chambers, tubular in shape, of a demosponge that falls somewhere between the sycon and leucon grades of organization.

Sponges do not possess any structures that can be considered organs. Instead, sponge cells of various types are responsible for bodily functions (e.g., choanocytes generate water currents and

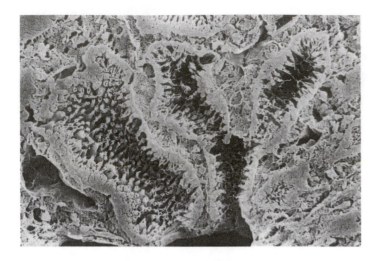

Figure 2. Scanning electron micrograph of the demosponge *Halisarca dujardini,* showing two choanocyte chambers. To the left is a tubular chamber roughly 100 micrometers in length, while on the right is a Y-shaped chamber. The organizational pattern of these chambers is more complex than the typical sycon condition and less complex than the classic leucon condition. From De Vos et al. (1991), courtesy of L. De Vos, K. Rützler, N. Boury-Esnault, C. Donadey, and J. Vacelet.

capture food; archeocytes digest food; sclerocytes secrete spicules; archeocytes and choanocytes produce gametes). As a whole, sponges have diverse skeletal elements, including calcareous laminae (thin plates), organic filaments, and siliceous and calcareous spicules. Spicules come in an array of beautiful shapes, as seen in the SEM images on Figures 3 and 4, and are often categorized by size, the larger being "megascleres" and the smaller "microscleres."

Sponge Fossil Record

As the basal (most archaic) branch of the metazoans, poriferans have long been expected to be among the earliest undoubted animal fossils, those of the Vendian (or Ediacaran) period. Until recently, however, no sponge body fossils had been identified or described from this fauna. Then, in 1996, J.G. Gehling and J.K. Rigby identified and described the first probable sponge, *Paleophragmodictya,* from the Ediacara of Australia (Gehling and Rigby 1996). Their specimens revealed a reticulating (interconnected) net in the body wall quite reminiscent of that in the hexactinellid sponges of the family Dictyospongiidae, previously known from the Ordovician to the Permian.

Since the Precambrian, sponges have been numerous in the seas, a fact reflected in their record as fossils. Throughout most of the Phanerozoic, sponges have been major contributors to reef formation (Rowland and Gangloff 1988; Kauffman and Fagerstrom 1993). A generalized cartoon of sponge contribution to the formation of reef carbonates is shown on the left of Figure 1. It illustrates that, historically speaking, the present situation, where scleractinian corals dominate, is more of an exception than a rule. Today, sponges are important ecological constituents of reef communities, but they commonly do not contribute to the construction of reef frame-

works. However, sponges did play such a role during most of their history. The fossil record of sponges suggests that their greatest diversity was achieved during the Cretaceous (Rigby et al. 1993). Figure 1 shows estimates of family diversity, based on first and last occurrences, for each of the major sponge groups through time. It should be noted that charts such as these, known as spindle diagrams, do not account for the biases of the fossil record.

Archaeocyatha

The first archaeocyath fossils appear roughly 530 million years ago, at the base of the Tommotian stage of the Lower Cambrian. During the subsequent 10 million years, the archaeocyaths were incredibly successful, diversifying into an amazing array of forms and playing a dominant role in the construction of the Earth's first reefs. As fantastic as their diversification was, their demise was just as dramatic. By the end of that 10-million-year period, the reef builders had all but disappeared. The last recorded archaeocyath is a single species from the Upper Cambrian of Antarctica.

The major subdivisions among the Archaeocyatha are based on early ontogenetic features (those that occur in early development). Lower taxonomic categories are determined by characters exhibited later in development. Accordingly, the two main groups of Archaeocyatha, the Regulares and the Irregulares, are distinguished on the basis of presence or absence of a character expressed in the very earliest stage of growth. Similarly, superfamilies and families are based on outer and inner wall characters, respectively. This results in a neat classification scheme, although it probably does not approximate the phylogenetic history of the group. By the current scheme, the phylum Archaeocyatha is split into 2 classes, 6 orders, 12 suborders, 120 families, and nearly 300 genera (Debrenne et al. 1990; Debrenne and Zhuravlev 1992).

The Archaeocyatha was generally a shallow-water tropical group. Fossils are nearly always found with photosynthesizing cyanobacteria (bacteria that are capable of photosynthesis), possibly symbiotically, and thus the group is thought to have lived within the region of seawater that receives sunlight (photic zone). The distribution of archaeocyath fossils, and the characteristics of the rock strata that contain them, suggest that the group was restricted largely to warm, shallow waters near the equator (Debrenne and Zhuravlev 1996). Although not as massive as reefs that existed later in the Phanerozoic, substantial carbonate build-ups comprised largely of the remains of archaeocyath skeletons formed the earliest known reefs.

While archaeocyaths display a variety of growth forms, from disklike to branching (Figure 5), the typical archaeocyath skeleton resembles two ice-cream cones, one inside the other, connected by vertical and sometimes horizontal plates called "septa" and "tabula" respectively (Figure 6). The entire space between the inner and outer walls is termed the "intervallum," while each section of the intervallum set off by two septae is called a "loculus." Nearly all of the primary skeletal elements (e.g., inner walls, outer walls, septae, and tabulae) are perforated by small pores. Archaeocyaths were attached to the substrate (the surface—e.g., seafloor, rocks—on which organisms grow) by a "holdfast" consisting of several prongs or, more commonly, a solid mass. Archaeocyath fossils

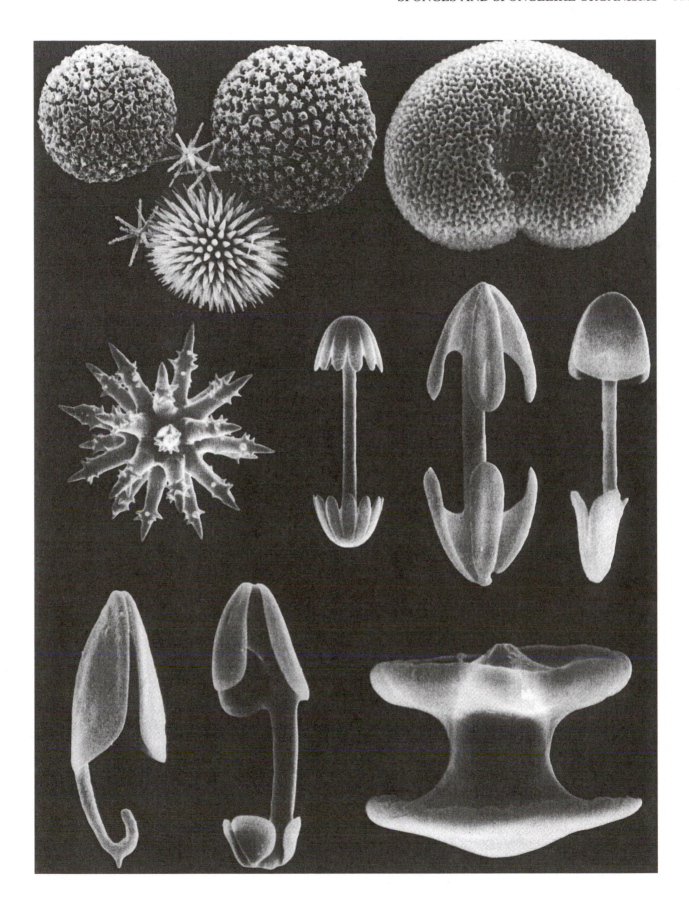

Figure 3. Scanning electron micrograph of various siliceous microscleres from demosponges. These microscleres range in size from 15 to 70 micrometers. From De Vos et al. (1991), courtesy of L. De Vos, K. Rützler, N. Boury-Esnault, C. Donadey, and J. Vacelet.

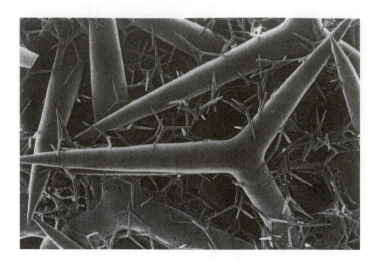

Figure 4. Scanning electron micrograph of three-rayed calcareous spicules of the calcarean sponge *Leucetta imberbis*. Rays of the larger spicules are nearly one millimeter in length, while those of the smaller spicules are roughly 100 micrometers. From De Vos et al. (1991), courtesy of L. De Vos, K. Rützler, N. Boury-Esnault, C. Donadey, and J. Vacelet.

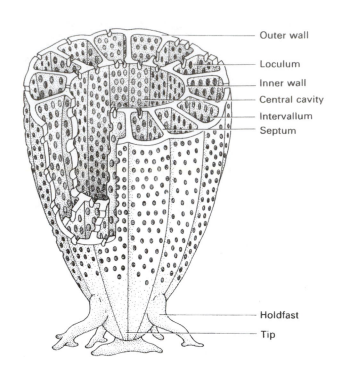

Figure 6. Typical two-walled skeleton of Archaeocyatha. From Boardman et al. (1987)

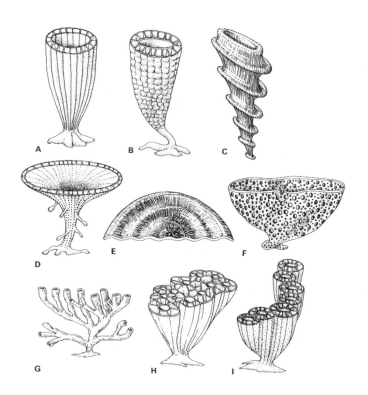

Figure 5. The variety in body form displayed by archaeocyathans. From Boardman et al. (1987).

range in size from as small as one millimeter to well over 0.5 meters, but typically they are on the order of one to three centimeters. Skeletal material consists of interlocked microgranular polyhedra of calcium carbonate (presumably calcite) with randomly oriented axes (long planes). Spicules are lacking.

Hexactinellida

The hexactinellids, or glass sponges, are characterized by siliceous (silicon-based) spicules consisting of six rays intersecting at right angles, as seen in Figure 7. Hexactinellids are viewed widely as an early branch within the Porifera because there are major differences between extant hexactinellids and other sponges. In particular, hexactinellid tissues are largely syncitial (have multinucleate cells), although some discrete cell types do exist, including archeocytes. Furthermore, whereas other sponges possess the ability to contract, hexactinellids do not. Moreover, hexactinellids possess a unique system for rapidly conducting electrical impulses across their bodies, allowing them to react quickly to external stimuli. As mentioned earlier, the oldest fossil sponge is a hexactinellid from the Vendian (or Ediacaran). By the Cambrian, relatively simple forms are known worldwide. Hexactinellid fossils exhibit a pattern of increasing complexity throughout their history. The group probably achieved its maximum diversity during the Cretaceous (Figure 1). Roughly 300 fossil genera are known.

Hexactinellids are exclusively marine. Today, the roughly 500 species are found mostly in deeper waters, 200 to 2,000 meters. Many modern hexactinellids are found living on soft substrates. Fossil hexactinellids often are found in strata of fine-grained limestones and shales, suggesting that for its entire history the group has been associated with quiet waters upon which soft sediments slowly accumulate. Although hexactinellids are most common at great depths today, they are more abundant and diverse at shallower depths of the polar regions. In Antarctica they are the most conspicuous form of benthic life. It appears that some hexactinellids may be important in structuring diversity on the continental slopes, as well as on the continental shelf of Antarctica (Barthel 1992; Bett and Rice 1992). Large mats of their spicules provide a hard substratum that may allow for a greater number of species to exist in a given area.

The six-rayed spicules, called hexactines (Figure 7) give the hexactinellids their name. However, some early members of the group only possess spicules with four rays that intersect at right angles in a single plane, "stauractins." These may represent reduced hexactines or the primitive spicule type for hexactinellids. Hexactinellid megascleres have hollow canals in their center that are square in cross section. The overall body shape of hexactinellids is more regular than that of other sponges, although no clear symmetries exist. Often, long tufts of spicules grow at the base of the sponge body, acting as an anchor to the substrate. Presumably, these tufts are important in allowing hexactinellids to live on soft sediments. The body of hexactinellids is vaselike and contains both syncitial and cellular tissues. Syncitia predominate, and all surfaces that contact water are syncitial. Syncitia with collars and flagella (choanosyncitia) line the chambers where flagellar beating creates water flow through the body.

The Hexactinellida is split into two major groups, the Hexasterophora and the Amphidiscophora, based on the presence or absence, respectively, of six-rayed microscleres called "hexasters." The Amphidiscophora is the older of the two groups; one of its subgroups, the Reticulosa, is found from the Vendian through the Permian. The Reticulosa includes the most simple hexactinellids, the Protospongoidea, who possessed just a single dermal layer of spicules. A second amphidiscophoran group, the Hemidiscosa, consisting of just a couple of genera, is known from the Carboniferous and the Cretaceous. A third order of the Amphidiscophora, the Amphidiscosa, is known from the Ordovician, and is still present today.

The Hexasterophora appeared in the Ordovician and is composed of three orders—the Lyssacinosa, the Hexactinosa, and the Lychniscosa—all of which have living representatives in the seas today. The members of all three of these groups have skeletons composed of overlapping six-rayed spicules (as shown in Figure 7), but they can be differentiated by the extent of fusion of adjacent spicules. The three groups appear sequentially in the fossil record. The least fused group, the Lyssacinosa, appears in the Ordovician, while the intermediate group, the Hexactinosa, is known from the Devonian. Finally, the Lychniscosa, with the most tightly interlocking spicules, is first found in rocks of Triassic age. Having noted this possible example of a progressive evolutionary trend toward greater complexity, it should be mentioned that neither of the more simple groups has become extinct, making it difficult to argue that greater complexity has been selected for.

Calcarea

Members of the group Calcarea are the only sponges that possess spicules composed of calcium carbonate. There are only mega-

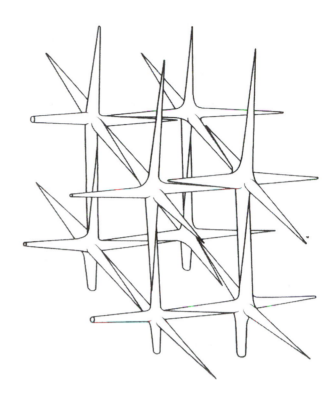

Figure 7. The characteristic spicule of hexactinellids, with six rays and three axes at right angles. From Boardman et al. (1987).

scleres, and these spicules do not have hollow axial canals. The Calcarea first appears at the base of the Lower Cambrian and has persisted until the present. More than 100 fossil genera are known. Figure 1 suggests that the Calcarea, like the Hexactinellida and the Demospongia, was at their most diverse during the Cretaceous. Today, diversity of the calcarean sponges is greatest in the tropics, as is the case with most marine groups. They are predominantly found in shallow waters, although at least one species is known from a depth of 4,000 meters. The fossil record of the Calcarea indicates that it has always been more abundant in near-shore shallow water settings.

The basal group of the Calcarea is the Heteractinida (Reitner and Mehl 1996). The heteractinids, characterized by eight-rayed calcareous spicules, or derivative forms, are known from the base of the Lower Cambrian. The group never achieved great diversity and was extinct by the end of the Paleozoic. The other two primary groups of calcarean sponges, the Calcinea and Calcaronea, share a more recent common ancestor and are characterized by regular three-rayed and four-rayed spicules. The Calcinea is difficult to characterize, and thus may be paraphyletic (Reitner and Mehl 1996). The Calcaronea is more likely a monophyletic group of sponges, since they share characteristic larvae and choanocytes, presumably due to common ancestry (Reitner and Mehl 1996). The Calcinea is known from the Permian, while probable calcaronean fossils have been identified from the Cambrian. Both groups persist with many representatives in today's oceans.

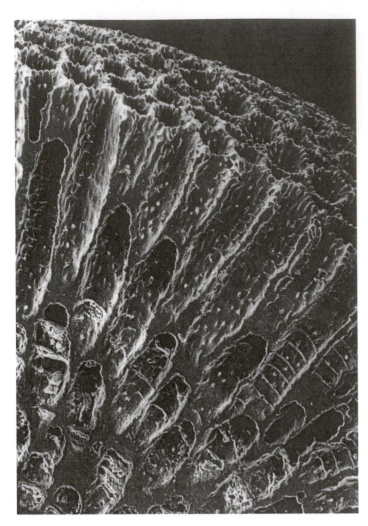

Figure 8. Scanning electron micrograph of the calcareous skeleton of the living chaetetid, *Acanthochaetetes wellsi.* Note the closely packed tubes (approximately 250 micrometers across) with tabulae. From De Vos et al. (1991), courtesy of L. De Vos, K. Rützler, N. Boury-Esnault, C. Donadey, and J. Vacelet.

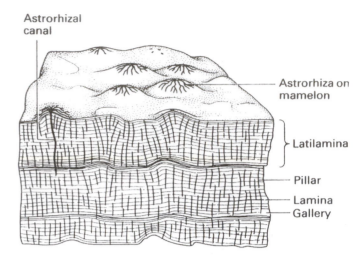

Figure 9. Typical laminar growth form displayed by the stromatoporoids. From Boardman et al. (1987).

Demospongia

The Demospongia is by far the most diverse sponge group. Greater than 90 percent of the 5,000 known living sponge species are demosponges. This ratio is not maintained in the fossil record, where less than half of the known genera and families are demosponges. However, the vast majority of living demosponges do not possess skeletons that would fossilize easily, thus their fossil diversity, which peaks in the Cretaceous, is probably an enormous underestimate of their actual diversity. As their great number of species would suggest, demosponges are found in many different environments, from warm, high-energy, intertidal settings to quiet, cold, abyssal depths. Indeed, all of the known freshwater poriferans are demosponges.

Demosponge skeletons are composed of flexible spongin fibers and/or siliceous spicules, although one genus *(Oscarella)* has neither. Demosponge spicules, if present, are siliceous, have one to four rays not at right angles, and axial canals that are triangular in

cross section. Demosponges take on a variety of growth forms, from encrusting sheets living beneath stones to branching stalks upright in the water column. They tend to be large and only exhibit the leucon grade of organization.

Demosponge systematics (study of evolutionary relationships) is an active area of research, and much is still to be learned. However, some rudimentary outlines can be made. The basal clade of the Demospongia is the Homoscleromorpha, characterized by the possession of a larva more reminiscent of that of the Calcarea than that of the rest of the Demospongia. Demosponges other than the Homoscleromorpha are split into two major groups, the Tetractinomorpha and the Ceractinomorpha. These two groups share characters that indicate common descent, such as a distinctive larval type and the presence of spongin (Reitner and Mehl 1996). Currently, the two groups are each characterized by distinctive types of microscleres, although some doubt still remains as to whether the distinctive microsclere types evolved only once in each group. Fossils of each of these groups are known from the Cambrian, suggesting an early radiation of the major lineages of demosponges. The Lithistida, a taxonomic grouping into which many of the fossil demosponges fall, is most certainly polyphyletic, with members in both the Tetractinomorpha and the Ceractinomorpha (Kelly-Borges and Pomponi 1994).

Other Sponge Groups

Three important fossil groups that most certainly belong within the Porifera are the sphinctozoans, the chaetetids, and the stromatoporoids. Sphinctozoans are sponges that grow as a series of chambers, one on top of the next. Most have no spicules, including the living representative *Vaceletia crypta.* However, a few Mesozoic forms contain triradiate calcareous spicules embedded in the body wall. This suggests that the sphinctozoans may be related to the calcareans. On the other hand, soft parts of *V. crypta* indicate that it shares a common ancestor with the ceractinomorph demosponges (Vacelet 1985). The sphinctozoan growth form probably has evolved independently within the Calcarea and the Demospongia, making the grouping polyphyletic (Reitner 1990). Thus, they cannot be thought of as a natural evolutionary group. Fossil "sphinctozoan" families for which calcarean or demosponge affinities cannot be determined are known from the Cambrian to the Cretaceous, as presented in Figure 1.

The chaetetids compose a small group that most often was presumed to be corals, allied to the Tabulata. Prior to the discovery of a living representative, chaetetids were known from the Ordovician to the Miocene. The overall body form varied from flat encrusting to upright columns. Some achieved a size of over three meters. Their fossil record suggests that they were mostly warm, shallow-water organisms often associated with photosynthetic algae, and that they apparently required hard substrates for settlement and the onset of growth. The chaetetids contributed to the development of reefs during the Paleozoic and Mesozoic, both overgrowing and serving as substrate for other reef-associated organisms. The general chaetetid growth form can be described as a cluster of closely packed tubes with floors or tabulae. The rigid skeleton is calcareous. Figure 8 is a scanning electron micrograph image of the skeleton of a living chaetetid, *Acanthochaetetes wellsi*. This species possesses siliceous spicules and soft parts that clearly place it within the demosponges (Vacelet 1985). Spicules rarely are preserved in fossil chaetetids. It is unknown if chaetetids form a monophyletic grouping, although the hypothesis of monophyly has not been disproven at this point in time.

The stromatoporoids had massive calcareous skeletons that are preserved as rather conspicuous fossils during two distinct time periods. Some formed domes more than five meters in diameter. The record of the earlier group begins in the Ordovician and persists until the Early Carboniferous, as shown in Figure 1. After their appearance, the Paleozoic stromatoporoids quickly became dominant reef builders, persisting as such for over 100 million years. Then, between the Early Carboniferous and the Late Permian, stromatoporoids are absent in the fossil record. The members of these two eras may represent two distinct groups. The Mesozoic stromatoporoids are again important contributors to reef formation, especially during the Cretaceous. Several living sponges would be classified as stromatoporoids if found as fossils, and these can be assigned to the Demospongia based on soft parts (Vacelet 1985). To reflect this, Figure 1 incorporates the Mesozoic stromatoporoids within the Demospongia. The affinities of the Paleozoic stromatoporoids are still unknown.

The basic stromatoporoid skeleton is shown in Figure 9. The stromatoporoid grew by secreting calcareous sheets. This growth process resulted in layers (laminae) parallel to the substrate, with rodlike pillars perpendicular to the laminae. Growth may have been episodic, resulting in occasional thicker laminae called "latilaminae." The spaces between laminae and pillars are termed "galleries." Galleries near the surface of the skeleton probably contained living tissue, while commonly those away from the surface appear to have been back-filled with calcite. The surface of the skeleton, where most of the living tissue resided, has raised structures called "mamelons," presumably serving as sites for excurrent openings. Associated with mamelons are astrorhizae and astrorhizal canals. Very similar structures, observed on the extant sponges of the genus *Astrosclera*, represent excurrent canal systems. This is strong evidence that fossil stromatoporoids were poriferans.

ALLEN G. COLLINS

See also Problematic Animals; Reefs and Reef-Building Organisms

Works Cited

Barthel, D. 1992. Do hexactinellids structure Antarctic sponge associations? *Ophelia* 36 (2):111–18.

Bett, B.J., and A.L. Rice. 1992. The influence of hexactinellid sponge (*Pheronema carpenteri*) spicules on the patchy distribution of macrobenthos in the Porcupine Seabight (bathyal NE Atlantic). *Ophelia* 36 (3):217–26.

Boardman, R.S., A.H. Cheetham, and A.J. Rowell (eds.). 1987. *Fossil Invertebrates*. Palo Alto, California: Blackwell Scientific.

Bond, C., and A.K. Harris. 1988. Locomotion of sponges and its physical mechanism. *Journal of Experimental Zoology* 246:271–84.

Debrenne, F., A. Rozanov, and A. Zhuravlev. 1990. *Regular Archaeocyaths: Morphology, Systematics, Biostratigraphy, Paleogeography Biological Affinities*. Paris: Centre National de la Recherche Scientifique.

Debrenne, F., and J. Vacelet. 1984. Archaeocyatha: Is the sponge model consistent with their structural organization? *Palaeontographica Americana* 54:358–69.

Debrenne, F., and A. Zhuravlev. 1992. *Irregular Archaeocyaths: Morphology, Ontogeny, Systematics, Biostratigraphy, Palaeoecology*. Paris: Centre National de la Recherche Scientifique.

———. 1996. Archaeocyatha, palaeoecology: A Cambrian sessile fauna. *In* A. Cherchi (ed.), *Autecology of Selected Fossil Organisms: Achievements and Problems*. Bollettino della Società Paleontologica Italiana, special vol. 3. Modena: Mucchi.

De Vos, L., K. Rützler, N. Boury-Esnault, C. Donadey, and J. Vacelet. 1991. *Atlas of Sponge Morphology*. Washington, D.C.: Smithsonian Institution.

Gehling, J.G., and J.K. Rigby. 1996. Long expected sponges from the neoproterozoic ediacara fauna of South Australia. *Journal of Paleontology* 70 (2):185–95.

Kauffman, E.G., and J.A. Fagerstrom. 1993. The phanerozoic evolution of reef diversity. *In* R.E. Ricklefs and D. Schluter (eds.), *Species Diversity in Ecological Communities: Historical and Geographical Perspectives*. Chicago: University of Chicago Press.

Kelly-Borges, M., and S.A. Pomponi. 1994. Phylogeny and classification of lithistid sponges (Porifera: Demospongiae): A preliminary assessment using ribosomal DNA sequence comparisons. *Molecular Marine Biology and Biotechnology* 3 (2):87–103.

Kruse, P.D. 1990. Are archaeocyaths sponges, or are sponges archaeocyaths? *Geological Society of Australia Special Publication* 16:311–23.

Reitner, J. 1990. Polyphyletic origin of the "Sphinctozoans." *In* K. Rutzler (ed.), *New Perspectives in Sponge Biology, Papers Contributed to Third International Conference on the Biology of Sponges (Woods Hole, Massachusetts, 17–23 November 1985)*. Washington, D.C.: Smithsonian Institution.

Reitner, J., and D. Mehl. 1996. Monophyly of the Porifera. *Verhandlungen des Naturwissenschaftlichen Vereins in Hamburg* 36:5–32.

Rigby, J.K., G.E. Budd, R.A. Wood, and F. Debrenne. 1993. Porifera. *In* M.J. Benton (ed.), *The Fossil Record 2.* London and New York: Chapman and Hall.

Rowland, S.M., and R.A. Gangloff. 1988. Structure and Paleoecology of Lower Cambrian Reefs. *Palaios* 3:111–35.

Savarese, M. 1992. Functional analysis of archaeocyathan skeletal morphology and its paleobiological implications. *Paleobiology* 18 (4):464–80.

Vacelet, J. 1985. Coralline sponges and the evolution of the Porifera. *In* S. Conway Morris, J.D. George, R. Gibson, and H.M. Platt (eds.), *The Origins and Relationships of Lower Invertebrates.* Systematics Association, spec. vol. 28. Oxford: Clarendon; New York: Oxford University Press.

Vacelet, J., and N. Boury-Esnault. 1996. A new species of carnivorous sponge (Demospongiae; Cladorhizidae) from a Mediterranean cave. *Bulletin de l'Institut Royal des Sciences Naturelles de Belgique Biologie* 66 (suppl.):109–15.

Vacelet, J., A. Fiala-Medioni, C.R. Fisher, and N. Boury-Esnault. 1996. Symbiosis between methane-oxidizing bacteria and a deep-sea carnivorous cladorhizid sponge. *Marine Ecology Progress Series* 145 (1–3):77–85.

Further Reading

Barnes, R.D. 1963. Sponges and Placozoans. *In* R.D. Barnes, *Invertebrate Zoology.* Philadelphia: Saunders; 6th ed., with E.E. Rupert, Fort Worth, Texas: Saunders College, 1994.

Bergquist, P.R. 1978. *Sponges.* London: Hutchinson; Berkeley: University of California Press.

Broadhead, T.W. 1983. *Sponges and Spongiomorphs, Notes for a Short Course.* Knoxville: University of Tennessee.

De Vos, L., K. Rutzler, N. Boury-Esnault, C. Donadey, and J. Vacelet. 1991. *Atlas of Sponge Morphology.* Washington, D.C.: Smithsonian Institution.

Rigby, J.K. 1987. Phylum Porifera. *In* R.S. Boardman, A.H. Cheetham, and A.J. Rowell (eds.), *Fossil Invertebrates.* Palo Alto, California: Blackwell Scientific.

STABLE ISOTOPE ANALYSIS

Following H. Urey's researches, isotope paleontology began when it was realized that the oxygen isotope composition of calcium carbonate was related to the water temperature at which it crystallizes. Thus, the isotope composition of carbonate fossil shells could be used as a paleotemperature scale (Urey et al. 1951). Since then, several elements—hydrogen (H), carbon (C), nitrogen (N), sulfur (S), silicon (Si), magnesium (Mg), and calcium (Ca)—from different biominerals (opal of diatoms and radiolarians, calcium phosphate of vertebrates) were found to provide additional biological and environmental informations. Among them, oxygen (O), carbon, and nitrogen have been the most widely employed.

The isotopic composition of elements having low atomic numbers—hydrogen, oxygen, carbon, nitrogen, sulfur, silicon, magnesium, and calcium—are variable in natural compounds because of a mass-dependent fractionation (separation) occurring between isotopes of the same element during chemical and physical processes. Since differences in natural isotopic abundances are slight, they are expressed in δ notation that represents the deviation per mil (thousand) of the isotopic ratio ($^{18}O/^{16}O$ for O) of the sample versus the same ratio in the international standard.

Isotopic paleontology first was developed in marine environments. The oxygen isotopic composition of calcium carbonate is not only temperature dependent but is also controlled by $\delta^{18}O$ of water ($\delta^{18}Ow$) from which the carbonate has precipitated. $\delta^{18}Ow$ is strongly related to the amount of ice water stored on the continents in the form of glacial ice. Because $H_2{}^{16}O$ molecules are preferentially removed by evaporation, oceans are enriched with ^{18}O with respect to rain water, snow, and continental ice. The quantity of water trapped into ice also influences ocean salinity. On the other hand, the $\delta^{13}C$ of calcium carbonate precipitated from aqueous solutions is mainly controlled by that of the inorganic carbon reserve, called the dissolved inorganic carbon (DIC).

Photosynthesis leads to an enrichment in ^{13}C into organic matter. As a consequence, photosynthesis causes an increase of the $\delta^{13}C$ of DIC in the photic zone (that penetrated by light) of the ocean. After the death of organisms, organic matter is oxidized and sinks, leading to a decrease of DIC $\delta^{13}C$ in the deeper layers of the ocean.

The isotopic variation in shells of organisms, such as foraminifera sampled in long cores of deep-sea sediments, have been used in the determination of climatic fluctuations throughout geological time. The history of surface temperatures during the Mesozoic and Cenozoic eras have been reconstructed and shows significant variations (Savin 1977). The data obtained also reflect the formation of the continental ice sheet on Antarctica during the Miocene epoch, and the glaciation-deglaciation fluctuations that occurred during Pleistocene times (Woodruff et al. 1981).

The study of the $\delta^{13}C$ and $\delta^{18}C$ of both planktonic and benthic (sea-bottom dwelling) species provides information about oceanic conditions both from the water surface and from the seafloor. Anomalies or even collapse in the surface-to-bottom carbon isotope gradient of ancient oceanic water indicate disturbances in photosynthesis and thus in biological productivity. Such a crisis is found at the Cretaceous-Tertiary boundary (Hsü and McKenzie 1985). The isotopic signatures of water masses allow their characterization (such as characterization of bottom deepwater by paleosalinity) and permit the reconstruction of their circulation in the oceans.

Since ocean chemistry and circulation control the atmospheric carbon dioxide level of the greenhouse effect gas, carbon dioxide, this leads to a better understanding of the global atmospheric environment.

From a geological point of view, comparison of the chemostratigraphic data (ordering rocks based on their chemistry) with biostratigraphic data (ordering rocks based on their contained fossils) and magnetostratigraphic information (ordering rocks based on their magnetic signals) provides a tool for the calibration of biostratigraphic events on a global scale. Once an isotopic signal is shown to be global, it can be used for testing the synchroneity of paleontological data in various regions. Instead of studying changes in isotope composition throughout successions of sediments, an alternative approach is to sample successive growth layers of fossil skeletons and to trace temperature fluctuations associated with seasons.

Isotope analysis can be used in terrestrial environmental investigations, although these are limited by gaps in sedimentary record. Moreover, temperature reconstructions are restricted by the determination of $\delta^{18}Ow$ of meteoric water, which varies between wide limits. On the other hand, $\delta^{13}C$ allows a discrimination between oceanic and continental environments: because of the presence of CO_2 derived from the decay of plant debris in soils, freshwater carbonates are enriched in ^{12}C as compared with marine carbonates.

Isotopic approaches also have been used successfully in paleodietary investigations, considering that isotopic composition of an animal reflects that of its diet. Both mineral (apatite) and organic (bone and dentin collagen) remains of vertebrates, mainly mammals, have been used for this purpose. Whereas the carbon isotopic compositions of an animal and its diet are very similar, the animal is enriched in ^{15}N compared to its food supplies; thus the amount of ^{15}N increases at each step of the food chain. Measuring isotope signals in vertebrate remains allows inference of the biological sources and the relationships between organisms of the ecological setting in which they lived. $\delta^{15}N$ signal used alone or linked to strontium-calcium ratio in mineral parts (strontium-calcium ratio presents an opposite trend of depletion from the bottom to the top of the food chain) has been useful, for example, in determining the degree to which the prehistoric human diet was carnivorous, or in distinguishing herbivorous from carnivorous diets of extinct species, when the comparative and functional morphology of teeth and jaws could not lead to obvious conclusions (Bocherens et al. 1995).

$\delta^{13}C$ values permit a discrimination between the two major photosynthetic pathways of terrestrial plants: C_3 plants (all trees, most shrubs and herbs in cold and temperate climates) and C_4 plants (tropical grasses and herbs from savanna). The conservative transfer of carbon to the animal from its diet has been useful in tracing C_3 or C_4 input in food chains, such as corn (C_4) in the diet of prehistoric humans or in the distinction between grazing (C_3 feeders) and browsing (C_4 feeders) herbivores.

Such biological information can assist in the creation of local or global environmental and climatic reconstructions. In closed woodlands, ^{13}C composition of leaves near the forest floor is depleted relative to the leaves at the top of the canopy owing to the incorporation of respiratory CO_2 which is ^{13}C depleted. Thus, forest floor plant consumers with more negative ^{13}C values than those of other herbivores indicate a dense forest in the past. Because C_4 and C_3 plants display different ecologic and climatic preferences, the proportion of C_4 grasses to C_3 grasses in a region is sensitive to temperature and humidity and allows the tracing of

floral transitions and climatic evolutions (Quade et al. 1992). Climatic informations also can be inferred from the ^{15}N composition of bone collagen, which is related to water stress and trace aridity.

Thus, isotope analysis of fossil remains offers various useful answers for the study of the evolution of oceanological, climatological, and ecological conditions in the past. However, many postmortem processes can modify the initial isotopic composition of fossils; to reach relevant conclusions the quality of preservation of the fossil remains, the absence of diagenetic alteration (i.e., chemial alteration/degradation of bone) and the absence of disturbance in sedimentary sequence, must be checked thoroughly.

ELISE DUFOUR

See also Atmospheric Environment; Ocean Environment; Paleoclimatology; Terrestrial Environment; Trace Element Analysis

Works Cited

Bocherans H., S.D. Emslie, D. Billiou, and A. Mariotti. 1995. Stable isotopes (^{13}C, ^{15}N) and paleodiet of the giant short-faced bear (*Artodus simus*). *Comptes Rendus de l'Académie des Sciences*, 2nd ser. 323:779–84.

Hsü, K.J., and J.A. McKenzie. 1985. A "strangelove" ocean in the earliest Tertiary. In E.T. Sundquist and W.S. Broecker (eds.), *The Carbon Cycle and Atmospheric COb2s: Natural Variations Archean to Present*. Washington, D.C.: American Geophysical Union.

Quade, J., T.E. Cerling, J.C. Barry, M.E. Morgan, D.R. Pilbeam, A.R. Chivas, J.A. Lee-Thorp, and N.J. van der Merwe. 1992. A 16-Ma record of paleodiet using carbon and oxygen isotopes in fossil teeth from Pakistan. *Chemical Geology* 94:183–92.

Savin, S.M. 1977. The history of the Earth's surface temperature during the past 100 million years. *Annual Review of Earth and Planetary Science* 5:319–44.

Urey, H.C., H.A. Lowestam, S. Epstein, and C.R. McKinney. 1951. Measurement of paleotemperatures and temperatures of the upper Cretaceous of England, Denmark, and the Southeastern United States. *Bulletin of the Geological Society of America* 62:399–416.

Woodruff, R., S.M. Savin, and R.E. Douglas. 1981. Miocene stable isotope record: A detailed deep Pacific Ocean study and its paleoclimatic implications. *Science* 212:665–68.

Further Reading

Brand, U., and J.O. Morrison. 1987. Paleoscene #6: Biogeochemistry of fossil marine invertebrates. *Geoscience Canada* 14:85–107.

DeNiro, M.J. 1987. Stable isotopy and archaeology. *American Scientist* 75:182–91.

Faure, G. 1986. *Principles of Isotope Geology*. New York: Wiley.

Koch, P.L., M.L. Fogel, and N. Tuross. 1994. Tracing the diets of fossil animals using stable isotopes. In K. Lajtha and R.H. Michener (eds.), *Stable Isotopes in Ecology and Environmental Science*. Oxford and Boston: Blackwell Scientific.

Wefer, G., and W.H. Berger. 1991. Isotope paleontology: Growth and composition of extant calcareous species. *Marine Geology* 100:207–48.

STATISTICAL TECHNIQUES

Statistics is the science of collecting, describing, and inferring things from data. Data are the facts and numbers that describe things. In paleontology, data may include such things as the morphology (shape and structure) of fossils, the relative abundance of different species at different locales or times, the probability of two species always occurring together, and the frequency of rounder versus more elongate body shapes in varied ecologies. Statistical techniques guide the process of asking and answering questions of the data. Such questions may concern similarity or difference among traits and among the populations of fossil organisms that show the traits.

Descriptive statistics involves methods of finding and expressing values that accurately represent the sample of organisms for the selected variables or traits. The central tendency (the dominant characteristic) and its surrounding scatter (the amount of variation around the measure of central tendency) are the most universal of descriptive statistical parameters. For example, assume you are measuring the length of the cranium of a mouse species. You gather measurements from a number of animals. The measure of central tendency is usually the mean (average) but also could be the midpoint. Describing dispersion for such fossil measurements, you can estimate how much actual measurements vary around the mean. If you are measuring something "countable," or a qualitative ("nominal") variable—such as presence or absence of a fenestra (openings) in the cranium—the central tendency would be the frequency (proportion) of the presence of the fenestra.

Although these descriptive parameters are critical to scientific communication, scholars in paleontology in particular must remember that the accuracy of the parameters depends on the randomness and representativeness of the sample of organisms upon which the variables were measured. Fossilization is not a random process, and statistical techniques cannot really adjust for nonrandom sampling.

For decades, descriptive statistics—for instance, average length of the earliest whales—have been very important to the analysis of fossils, and they are more readily understood, exchanged, and replicated among many scholars than more subjective and qualitative impressions that characterized an earlier age. From Darwin's time, scholars have recognized that variation is a universal zoological phenomenon. Finger length or the width of a wing will be different from one individual to the next. Scholars have also recognized that natural selection acts upon variations in shapes and structures. That is why one cannot inflexibly rely upon a single type specimen to characterize a species.

When comparing data about a sample with data for a known group, scholars are setting out a "null hypothesis." This says that an observed difference (between skull size, for instance) is due to chance alone, not to truly significant distinction (i.e., the differences are those between species). Inferential statistical methods rely on extrapolation. From the description of the sample, one infers the characteristics that are probably found in the parent population from which the sample (ostensibly randomly) came. An attached probability statement spells out the probable level of accuracy of the inferences. Then you use one of the various models of the distribution, such as the normal ("bell-shaped" mathematical) curve, one can answer the key question: What is the probability that this sample is a member of some theoretical target population? For example, suppose you have measured the mean cranium length in a certain fossil group. How often could that mean be found in a certain population that has a mean that is already known? If the probability is critically low, say less than 5 percent, one would usually infer that the sample did not belong to the same family as the known population.

The t test is the most common inferential test for the null hypothesis that a measured variable in two fossil samples could reasonably represent the same parent population. This test compares the differences between two sample means in comparison to the common amount of variability. The more variable a trait is—for instance, leg length in early horses—the more likely it is that you could have substantially different means every time you take a new random sample from the same statistical population. If a large probability value results from a t test, then the null hypothesis might be sound (i.e., the variation is due to chance). However, if the probabilities are low (from higher t values), the investigator might conclude that the discrepancies between the populations represented by the samples are enough to be significant. However, the common extension of this reasoning, that the samples come from two different species (because, for example, their leg lengths differ significantly), may be hazardous. The differences could be owing to any number of factors in the parent populations, such as sexes, seasons of fossilization, or even how the calipers (very sensitive measuring devices) are held by two different investigators. Similarly, it is incorrect to infer two samples represent the same species when the data do not reject null hypothesis. This merely establishes that the investigator has failed to reject that hypothesis. The results could be owing to any number of experimental errors, including unavoidable ones of insufficient sample size.

The chi-square test is the most frequently encountered inferential method for counted (i.e., present/absent) data. It compiles the differences between observed frequencies of a trait in samples and a mathematical frequency that represents no differences between samples.

There are many statistical techniques that do not depend on so many assumptions about a variable's probability distribution. Some rely on calculating the exact probabilities for observed differences in rank-ordered character states (e.g., from smallest to largest). For instance, what is the probability that group A of fossils (containing the first, second, third, seventh, eighth, and ninth smallest cranial breadths) could be sampled from the same parent population as group B (containing the fourth, fifth, sixth, tenth, eleventh, and twelfth ranks)? Perhaps unexpectedly, the probability that such differences are random is well under one in ten.

In recent years a family of methods known as resampling methods has emerged as a major challenge to all the classical approaches that require preexisting knowledge about distributions. Best known among resampling techniques is the "bootstrap." It is based upon the theorem that a finite sample, if random and distributed in a manner representative of its parent population, can itself be randomly resampled a large number of times, and the distributions that result will approximate what one would find if one constantly took new samples of equivalent size from the parent population (the latter is difficult to do in paleontology because parent populations of fossils are limited). Using a random number generator to bootstrap a sample, any sort of comparison of parameters can be approached, and there is but one assumption, that of random sampling. Much more will undoubtedly be heard from the versatile bootstrap in paleontological analyses. Some predict it will generally replace the classical, distribution-dependent methods in both research and teaching (Peterson 1991).

Many further methods exist to compare samples over more than one variable at a time (Sokal and Rohlf 1987). The simplest extension is to "bivariate analysis," such as a correlation that determines the proportion of jointly shared variability between two characters. "Multivariate techniques" employ three or more variables to test whether difference compounded over all variables is large enough to reject the null hypothesis.

Many such methods also produce a useful measure of that overall difference (statistical "distance"), apart from the attached probability that yields the inferential decision. Such summary measures can be used in the process of pattern recognition (technically a different process from inferential statistics), such as determining whether samples A and B are more similar (less distant) than either is to sample C. The pattern recognition properties of multivariate statistics rely considerably less upon complicated (and, admittedly, probably never naturally justified) assumptions about multidimensional distributional characteristics of biological data. The complexity of the computations and distributions involved in multivariate techniques has led more than one authority to conclude that this method has resulted in more misuse than insight in the paleontological literature. The bootstrap approach, which can be used equally well with multivariate as with univariate questions, might alleviate the number of faulty conclusions that have arisen because unsophisticated scholars have misused or misunderstood classically based (and indiscriminately available) multivariate statistical computer programs.

ROBERT S. CORRUCCINI

See also Computer Applications in Paleontology; Systematics; Variation

Works Cited

Peterson, I. 1991. Pick a sample. *Science News* 140:56–58.
Sokal, R.R., and F.J. Rohlf. 1987. *Introduction to Biostatistics*. 2nd ed., New York: Freeman.

Further Reading

Beerbower, J.R. 1960. *Search for the Past: An Introduction to Paleontology.* Englewood Cliffs, New Jersey: Prentice-Hall; 2nd. ed., 1968.
Gonick, L., and W. Smith. 1993. *The Cartoon Guide to Statistics.* New York: HarperPerennial.
Sokal, R.R., and F.J. Rohlf. 1973. *Introduction to Biostatistics*. San Francisco: Freeman; 2nd ed., New York: Freeman, 1987.

STEGOSAURS

In 1877 Othniel Charles Marsh of Yale College proposed the name Stegosauria for a new order of large extinct reptiles from the Upper Jurassic of Morrison, Colorado. He considered that the back of *Stegosaurus armatus* (Greek *stege,* roof; *saurus,* reptile; Latin *armatus,* armed) was covered by large osteoderms, or dermal plates (some more than a meter in length), that were completely embedded in the skin, as found in some large aquatic turtles. The discovery of an almost complete skeleton with the plates and spines preserved so that the arrangement of bones was intact showed that all the plates of *Stegosaurus* were held vertically and that the tail bore spines (Marsh 1887). The first skeletal reconstruction of *Stegosaurus* showed the plates in a single row down the center of the back plus four pairs of tail spines (Figure 1A) (Marsh 1891, 1896; see Czerkas 1987 for more details on subsequent restorations; see also under "Anatomy," below).

Systematics

In the 1980s, the group name Thyreophora ("shield bearers") of Franz Baron Nopcsa (1915) was set up to include the Stegosauria (now known as "plated dinosaurs") and Ankylosauria (now known as "armored dinosaurs"). The very early thyreophorans (Coombs et al. 1990) include three genera (groups; singular, genus) from the Lower Jurassic: the quadrupedal *Scelidosaurus* from England (Figure 1E) (Owen 1861, 1863), the bipedal and more lightly built *Scutellosaurus* from Arizona (Colbert 1981), and the recently described skull and fragmentary postcrania (body skeleton) of *Emausaurus* from Germany (Haubold 1990). Thyreophorans are united by having a transversely broad bar behind the orbit (eye sockets) (Figure 2A, C, E) and dermal armor consisting of parallel rows of low-keeled scutes (bony armor plates) extending from the head to the tail along the back and sides (Figure 1D, E) (Sereno 1986).

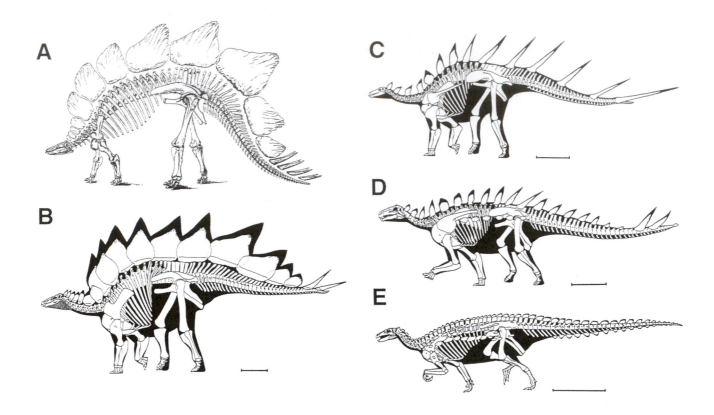

Figure 1. Skeletal reconstructions of stegosaurs *(A–D)* and *Scelidosaurus (E). A,* stegosaurid *Stegosaurus* (Upper Jurassic of the western United States), first published composite reconstruction of a stegosaur (Marsh 1891), with vertebrae, girdles, limbs, and four pairs of tail spines based on specimens of *Stegosaurus ungulatus* (Peabody Museum of Natural History 1853, 1854, 1858); skull and dermal armor based on *S. stenops* (United States National Museum 4934) [of the 17 plates, four anterior plates were paired but not indicated as such on the reconstruction (Marsh 1896); plate 17 omitted to make room for the two extra pairs of tail spines in *S. ungulatus* (Czerkas 1987)]. *B, Stegosaurus stenops,* mostly based on two specimens at the United States National Museum—primarily specimen 4934, specimen 4714 for last half of tail and a tail spine. *C,* stegosaurid *Kentrosaurus* (Upper Jurassic of Tanzania, East Africa), based on mounted skeleton in Humboldt Museum für Naturkunde (Janensch 1925). *D,* huayangosaurid *Huayangosaurus* (Middle Jurassic of China), based on Zigong Dinosaur Museum T7001 (Zhou 1984); parasacral spine after Sereno and Dong (1992). *E,* early thyreophoran *Scelidosaurus* (Lower Jurassic of England), from Paul (1987). Scale: line represents 50 centimeters. From Galton (1997); copyright for Figures *B–E* retained by Gregory S. Paul; reproduced by permission of Indiana University Press, Bloomington.

Scelidosaurus has a characteristic sinuous curve to the lower tooth row, which is found on the dentary bone, and a bone above the eye is incorporated into the skull roof to form part of the upper edge of the orbit (Figure 2E, F) (Sereno 1986). These characteristics show that *Scelidosaurus* is the sister group (closest relative) of the Eurypoda, the group from which Stegosauria arises.

The derived (unique) characters of the Eurypoda are also primitive characters for the Stegosauria (and Ankylosauria). In the skull three supraorbitals are located above the orbit, no distinct notch exists for the upper part of the eardrum, and a deep median keel (central ridge) extends the length of the palate (Figure 2A–D). The forefoot has relatively short metacarpals (bones between the wrist and "fingers") and the last bone in each digit ("finger") is hooflike. The ilium (upper hip bone, plural ilia) (Figure 1A–D) has a very short postacetabular process (bony structure to the rear of the hip bone) and a very long preacetabular process (bony structure in front of the hip joint), directed at least 35 degrees to the side. In adults the tibia and fibula (shin bones) are fused with the

astragalus and calcaneum (ankle bones). The hind foot has short, spreading metatarsals (bones within the foot, between the ankle and toes), and the last bone (ungual) of the digit is, again, hooflike. The osteoderms or dermal armor, include elevated spines (Figure 1A–D).

The Stegosauria are medium-sized to large animals (up to nine meters in total body length), quadrupedal ornithischians ("bird-hipped" reptiles) with an extensive system of erect plates and spines running down the back along the middle of the back and tail (Figure 1A–D) (Dong 1990; Galton 1990; Sereno and Dong 1992; Olshevsky and Ford 1993).

The Huayangosauridae (*Huayangosaurus* and *Regnosaurus*) is the sister taxon to the Stegosauridae (all other stegosaurs). The stegosaurids differ from the huayangosaurids in a number of ways. Teeth are gone from the bone that forms the upper snout, and the row of scutes along either side of the trunk are gone. The pelvic region has changed: The edges of the sacral ribs, near the spine, are fused to form a nearly solid plate between the ilia (closing up what

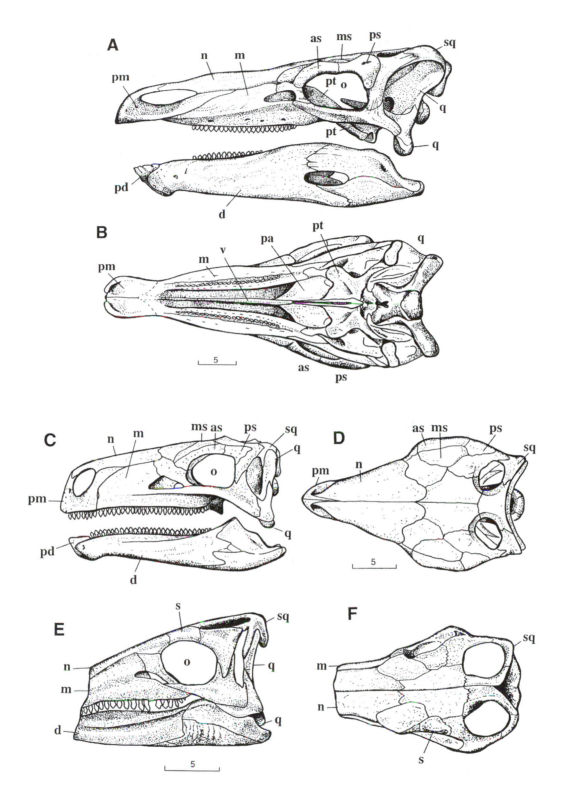

Figure 2. Skulls of stegosaurs and *Scelidosaurus*. *A,* stegosaurid *Stegosaurus stenops* from the Upper Jurassic of Colorado (left lateral view); *B, Stegosaurus stenops* (ventral view, without lower jaw); *C,* huayangosaurid *Huayangosaurus* from the Middle Jurassic of China (left lateral view); *D, Huayangosaurus* (dorsal view); *E,* early thyreophoran *Scelidosaurus* from the Lower Jurassic of England (left lateral view); *F, Scelidosaurus* (dorsal view). Abbreviations: *as,* anterior supraorbital; *d,* dentary; *m,* maxilla; *ms,* medial supraorbital; *n,* nasal; *o,* orbit; *pa,* palatine; *pd,* predentary; *pm,* premaxilla; *ps,* posterior supraorbital; *pt,* pterygoid; *q,* quadrate; *s,* supraorbital; *sq,* squamosal. Scale: line equals 50 millimeters. After: *A, B, C, D,* Sereno and Dong (1992); *E, F,* Coombs et al. (1990). From Galton (1997); reproduced by permission of Indiana University Press, Bloomington.

otherwise would be large, empty spaces between the ribs); the front bony projection of the pubis has increased in length; and the femur (thigh bone) is at least 1.5 times the length of the humerus (the bone of the upper arm; in *Huayangosaurus* the femur and humerus are the same length) (Figure 1A–D). The systematic relationships among the more derived (specialized) stegosaurids remain unclear (Sereno and Dong 1992).

Distribution

Almost complete skeletons with skulls of *Huayangosaurus* (Figures 1D, 2C, 2D) have been found in the Middle Jurassic of the People's Republic of China (Zhou 1984; Sereno and Dong 1992); the only older record is fragmentary material from the Lower Bathonian of England (Galton and Powell 1983). The best stegosaurs are found in the Upper Jurassic, with articulated (intact, organized) skeletons (most lack skulls) for many of the genera. Two from England (Galton 1985)—*Dacentrurus* from the Kimmeridge Clay and *Lexovisaurus* Hoffstetter from the older Lower Oxford Clay—also are found in France and Portugal. Abundant bones of *Kentrosaurus* (Figure 1C) were excavated in what is now Tanzania (Hennig 1924; Janensch 1925). A partial skeleton of *Chialingosaurus* was described by Chung Chien Young (1959) from the Shangshaximiao Formation of Sichuan, China, and, since then, this formation has produced the skeletons of two additional genera, *Tuojiangosaurus* and *Chungkingosaurus*) (Dong et al. 1983). The People's Republic of China now has the longest and most diverse fossil record for stegosaurs (see Dong 1990; Galton 1990; Olshevsky and Ford 1993).

Stegosaurs are rare in the Cretaceous (Galton 1981). The first Cretaceous stegosaurs were described from the Lower Cretaceous of England. They were represented by a partial lower jaw of *Regnosaurus* (Mantell 1841) and the partial neural arch of a dorsal vertebra of *Craterosaurus* (Seeley 1874). (The neural arch is the top half of the vertebra.) Other finds of this age include the partial skull of *Paranthodon* from South Africa (Galton 1981) and partial skeletons of *Wuerhosaurus* from the People's Republic of China (Dong 1990). The most recent record is a partial skeleton of *Dravidosaurus* from the Upper Cretaceous of India (Yadagari and Ayyasami 1979).

Anatomy

Compared to the skull of *Huayangosaurus,* that of *Stegosaurus* (and probably all other stegosaurids) is shallower, and the skull roof above the orbits is narrower relative to skull length (Figure 1A–D). As in other ornithischians, the tips of the anterior bones of the skull, which form the snout (the upper premaxillae and the lower predentary), were covered by rhamphothecae (horny sheaths) used to crop vegetation. There are seven teeth in the premaxilla of *Huayangosaurus* but none in the Stegosauridae, in which the rhamphothecae were proportionally larger (Figure 2A–C). A horny sheath is a good cropping structure because it always has a continuous, self-sharpening edge, it can have a cutting edge and/or a flat crushing area, and it is rapidly replaced as it is worn away. In *Stegosaurus* (but not in *Huayangosaurus*) there is an edentulous (toothless) gap, or

diastema, between the rhampothecae and the rows of cheek teeth. The cheek tooth crowns are simple in form and show a few places where tooth-to-tooth contact has created worn spots (wear facets).

As in other ornithischians, stegosaurs have a space outside the tooth rows that is roofed by a prominent horizontal ridge on the maxilla (upper jaw) and floored by the massive dentary (lower jaw) (Figure 2A, C). The cheeklike structure attached to these ridges is bordered by a space that receives any chewed food that ends up outside the lower teeth (Galton 1973). The long, narrow-based, slender tongue scooped up this residual food and returned it to the mouth to be chewed again.

A deep keel along the length of the palate (Figure 2B) probably provided support for a soft secondary palate that was supported along the sides by the maxillae. This palate separates the nasal passages from the oral cavity so that stegosaurs can continue to breathe while chewing food.

The lower jaw is jointed to the quadrate bone, the upper end of which is fused to the squamosal bone in adult individuals (Figure 2A). The skull forms a solid box and, because the quadrate is fixed, when the jaw closes during the chewing cycle, the teeth of the lower jaw move up against those of the upper jaw, a much less complex system than that found in the Ornithopoda.

The dorsal vertebrae (those along the back) of all stegosaurs are tall. The increase in height is in the region between the centrum (the major structure of the vertebra, on the side away from the skin) and the diapophyses (transverse processes that carry ribs). This structure increases the height of the body cavity, providing more room for inner organs. In other dinosaurs with tall dorsals, the increased height is owing to elongation of the neural spines on the skin side of the vertebrae. In stegosaurs, the increased height may have provided additional attachment surfaces needed to maintain trunk rigidity, since these animals had lost the ossified tendons found in all other ornithischian dinosaurs (Sereno and Dong 1992). In the vertebrae at the center of the back, the diapophyses are directed upward and angle to the side by as much as 50 to 60 degrees from horizontal. This increased angle would have provided better support for the overlying osteoderms, which, because of the way they are arranged parallel to the spine, would have concentrated their weight along the region adjacent to the ends of the diapophyses. This region is also supported by the shafts of the ribs, which have a T-shaped cross section.

In the Stegosauridae, the diapophyses and the sacral T-shaped ribs fuse together to form an almost solid plate between the neural spines of the vertebrae and the flat surface of the ilium bone of the pelvis. This plate strengthens the sacrum (lower back), and appears to be associated with the long femur. It elevates the hip joint well above the shoulder joint, so the femur supports much of the body weight.

The neural canal of the sacrum is extremely dilated to form what is called an "endosacral enlargement" (see Giffin 1991). Marsh described this region as a "posterior brain case" (1881); hence, the popular misconception of Stegosaurus having "two sets of brains, one in his head, the usual place, and the other at his spinal base." Actually, the front part of this "sacral brain" was occupied by an enlarged spinal cord associated with the increased size of a network of nerves that then supplies nerves to the large hind limbs. In addition, the rear part of the endosacral enlargement housed nerves that ran to the caudifemoral muscle, which pulled the hind limb backward during walking and moved the tail with its osteoderms. The rest of the space was probably occupied by a glycogen body (as in birds), the function of which is unclear. A similar but smaller enlargement of the neural canal is located in the lower cervical vertebrae; this enlargement accommodates the brachial enlargement, which supplied nerves to the muscles of the massive forelimbs (Lull 1917).

The ends of the neural spines of the anterior caudal vertebrae are expanded to the sides, and the centra of the posterior caudal vertebrae are almost square (Figure 1A–D). These modifications help support the weight of the caudal osteoderms.

The lower part of the scapula (shoulder blade) forms a broad plate, and the humerus (upper arm bone) is short but massive, with expanded ends (Figure 1A–D), providing plenty of room for the attachment of powerful shoulder and pectoral muscles needed to support the weight of the front of the body. The forefoot is quite elephant-like, being short and relatively inflexible. Five short and robust metacarpals bear short digits, at least two of which terminate in a hooflike ungual. The pubis has a relatively long bony projection to the front (at least 40 percent of length of the bony projection to the rear) and an oval-shaped socket for the hipbone, which is directed to the side (Sereno and Dong 1992). Viewed from the side, the femur is slender, but viewed from the front it is broad, with a straight shaft of nearly uniform width. In all stegosaurs except *Huayangosaurus,* the femur is longer than the humerus (and than the tibia) (Figure 1A–D). This, and the stocky proportions of the hind foot, are characteristics of a "graviportal" (elephantine) mode of locomotion (see below, under "Paleobiology and Behavior"). The three central weight-supporting digits are robust, bearing hooflike unguals, whereas the first digit is lost, and the fifth digit is small and nonfunctional. This arrangement results in a foot that is relatively symmetrical about the third digit.

Huayangosaurus has low-keeled, lateral (side) osteoderms that are similar to those of *Scelidosaurus,* but these are lost in the Stegosauridae (Figure 1). In *Huayangosaurus, Tuojiangosaurus, Kentrosaurus,* and *Lexovisaurus,* a pair of low-angled spines are present adjacent to the shoulder region, but these spines were lost in *Stegosaurus* (Figure 1B–D). The rest of the osteoderms of stegosaurs are situated above the vertebral column, rather than being spread over the back as a whole, and are angled upwards and slightly outwards. Viewed from the side, the osteoderms of most stegosaurs form a series that grade from short, erect plates near the head to longer spines that are angled toward the tail (Figures 1C, D). In all stegosaurs, the series ends with a proportionally narrow pair of spines that continue beyond the last tail vertebra (Figure 1A–D). In all stegosaurs except *Stegosaurus stenops,* the dorsal osteoderms are all paired and go through a gradual transition in size from head to tail, from small to larger plates, ending in the spines that cover most of the tail (Figure 1C, D). In *Stegosaurus armatus* there is at least one pair of large plates that are the same size and shape (Ostrom and McIntosh 1966), so all of the plates may have been arranged in pairs in this species (Paul 1987); it also has four pairs of tail spines (Figure 1A) (Marsh 1891, 1896;

Ostrom and McIntosh 1966). However, in articulated skeletons of *Stegosaurus stenops,* the dermal armor consists of a series of 17 erect, thin plates of varying sizes, extending along most of the tail, with only two pairs of spines at the end of the tail. No two plates have exactly the same shape or size and all are preserved in an alternating pattern (Figure 1B) (Gilmore 1914; Paul 1992; Carpenter and Small 1993).

Taphonomy and Paleoecology

The Tendaguru fauna of Tanzania occurs in nearshore deposits that came from land subjected to a warm climate with periodic droughts. *Kentrosaurus* is a relatively minor element of the fauna. The preservation of partly articulated and partly sorted remains of medium-sized individuals was favored in the main stegosaur quarry (Hennig 1924; Russell et al. 1980).

In the Morrison Formation, *Stegosaurus* occurs more frequently in channel sands comprised of a concentration of bones from animals that probably spent much of their lives on floodplain (Dodson et al. 1980). However, *Stegosaurus* was probably somewhat separated ecologically from sauropods (long-necked, land-based dinosaurs) because it may have inhabited areas farther from sources of water. *Stegosaurus* occurs only occasionally as an articulated skeleton. Usually it is part of an accumulation of 20 to 60 skeletons of other dinosaurs with only moderate to low degrees of articulation. This is because carcasses typically decomposed in open, dry areas or spent a considerable time in channels prior to being covered with sediment.

Several skeletons of stegosaurs from Sichuan, China, include skulls, and because the degree of articulation of the skeletons is greater than those from the Morrison Formation, the carcasses must have been buried more rapidly. *Huayangosaurus* occurs in sandstones of the Xiashaximiao Formation, which were deposited in a lakeshore, shallow-bank environment that experienced little disturbance (Xia et al. 1984).

Paleobiology and Behavior

Stegosaurs were graviportal, or elephantine, in their locomotion (Coombs 1978). As with elephants, stegosaurs did not use the occasional, more upright, bipedal pose, with the body supported by the tail, for feeding (Alexander 1985; Bakker 1986). Consequently, stegosaurs were probably important low-level browsers up to about the height of one meter, the maximum "comfortable" height that could be reached while on all fours.

The encephalization quotient (ratio of measured brain size to "expected" brain size for dinosaurs of identical body size) of stegosaurs is comparable to that of ankylosaurs and less than that of all other dinosaurs except sauropods. This low value probably resulted from their reliance on defensive armor and tail weapons rather than speedy flight to cope with predators (Hopson 1980). The tail spines of stegosaurs originally were covered with horn and would have been formidable weapons, especially if the spines were driven into the body of an attacker (Bakker 1986).

The armor of all stegosaurs is ideally arranged for maximum effect during a lateral display (Spassov 1982), and each species has its own characteristic overall pattern of the plates and spines (Figure 1B–D). Lee Shiovich Davitashvili (1961) suggested that the erect osteoderms originally developed for the recognition of other members of the same species and for sexual display.

Recent studies of the histology (minute structures) of the plates of *Stegosaurus* by Vivian de Buffrénil et al. (1986) suggest that the plates were held upright. This version contrasts with the theory that muscles lifted the plates suddenly from a horizontal, defensive position to a vertical one, either to startle and deter an attacker or to ward off attack from above, as originally suggested by Nicholas Hotton (1963) and elaborated on by Robert Bakker (1986). In support of his theory, Buffrénil notes that surface markings on the basal third of the plates indicate that they were embedded symmetrically in the thick, tough skin. Furthermore, the plates of *Stegosaurus* were unlikely to have functioned as armor because they do not consist of thick, compact bone.

The plates of *Stegosaurus* (and *Lexovisaurus*) also could have functioned in temperature regulation. The plates formed a scaffolding for a rich supply of blood vessels, enabling them to function as efficient heat exchange structures. In an alternating arrangement, the plates functioned as a forced convection fin to dissipate heat and possibly as heat absorbers for solar radiation (Farlow et al. 1976; Buffrénil et al. 1986).

If *Stegosaurus* was an ectotherm (i.e., was "cold-blooded"), then the plates performed a heat-absorbing role, but if *Stegosaurus* was to any degree endothermic ("warm-blooded"), then heat loss by radiation or forced convection would have been useful (Buffrénil et al. 1986). However, in other stegosaurs display was probably the main function of the plates.

PETER M. GALTON

See also Skeleton: Dermal Postcranial Skeleton

Works Cited

Alexander, R.M. 1985. Mechanics of posture and gait of some large dinosaurs. *Zoological Journal of the Linnean Society* 83:1–25.

Bakker, R.T. 1986. *The Dinosaur Heresies: New Theories Unlocking the Mystery of the Dinosaurs and Their Extinction.* New York: William Morrow.

Buffrénil, V. de, J.O. Farlow, and A. de Ricqlès. 1986. Growth and function of *Stegosaurus* plates. Evidence from bone histology. *Paleobiology* 12:459–73.

Carpenter, K., and B. Small. 1993. New evidence for plate arrangement in *Stegosaurus stenops. Journal of Vertebrate Paleontology* 13 (Supplement to 3):28A–29A.

Colbert, E.H. 1981. A primitive ornithischian dinosaur from the Kayenta Formation of Arizona. *Museum of Northern Arizona Bulletin* 53:1–61.

Coombs Jr., W.P. 1978. Theoretical aspects of cursorial adaptations in dinosaurs. *Quarterly Review of Biology* 53:393–418.

Coombs Jr., W.P., D.B. Weishampel, and L.M. Witmer. 1990. Basal Thyreophora. *In* D.B. Weishampel, P. Dodson, and H. Osmólska (eds.), *The Dinosauria.* Berkeley: University of California Press.

Czerkas, S.A. 1987. A reevaluation of the plate arrangement on *Stegosaurus stenops. In* S.J. Czerkas and E.C. Olson (eds.),

Dinosaurs Past and Present. Vol. 2, Los Angeles and Seattle: Natural History Museum of Los Angeles County, with University of Washington Press.

Davitashvili, L. 1961. *Teoriia polovogo otbora [The Theory of Sexual Selection].* Moscow: Izdatel'stvo Akademia Nauk SSSR.

Dodson, P., A.K. Behrensmeyer, R.T. Bakker, and J.S. McIntosh. 1980. Taphonomy and paleoecology of the Upper Jurassic Morrison Formation. *Paleobiology* 6:208–32.

Dong, Z. 1990. Stegosaurs of Asia. *In* K. Carpenter and P.J. Currie (eds.), *Dinosaur Systematics: Approaches and Perspectives.* Cambridge and New York: Cambridge University Press.

Dong, Z., S.W. Zhou, and Y.H. Chang. 1983. The dinosaur remains from Sichuan Basin, China. *Palaeontologica Sinica* 162 (C) 23:1–166 [in Chinese; English summary].

Farlow, J.O., C.V. Thompson, and D.E. Rosner. 1976. Plates of the dinosaur *Stegosaurus:* Forced convection heat loss fins? *Science Nature (London)* 192:1123–25.

Galton, P.M. 1973. The cheeks of ornithischian dinosaurs. *Lethaia* 6:67–89.

———. 1981. *Craterosaurus pottonensis* Seeley, a stegosaurian dinosaur from the Lower Cretaceous of England, and a review of Cretaceous stegosaurs. *Neues Jahrbuch für Geologie und Paläontologie, Abhandlungen* 161:28–46.

———. 1985. British plated dinosaurs (Ornithischia, Stegosauria). *Journal of Vertebrate Paleontology* 5:211–54.

———. 1990. Stegosauria. *In* D.B. Weishampel, P. Dodson, and H. Osmólska (eds.), *The Dinosauria.* Berkeley: University of California Press.

———. 1997. Stegosaurs. *In* J.O. Farlow and M.K. Brett-Surman (eds.), *The Complete Dinosaur.* Bloomington: University of Indiana Press.

Galton, P.M., and H.P. Powell. 1983. Stegosaurian dinosaurs from the Bathonian (Middle Jurassic) of England, the earliest record of the Stegosauridae. *Géobios* 16:219–29.

Giffin, E.B. 1991. Endosacral enlargements in dinosaurs. *Modern Geology* 16:101–12.

Gilmore, C.W. 1914. Osteology of the armored dinosaurs in the United States National Museum, with special reference to the genus *Stegosaurus. Bulletin of the United States National Museum* 89:1–136.

Haubold, H. 1990. Ein neuer Dinosaurier (Ornithischia, Thyreophora) aus dem unteren Jura des nördlichen Mitteleuropa. *Revue de Paléobiologie* 9:149–77.

Hennig, E. 1924. *Kentrurosaurus aethiopicus,* die Stegosaurier-Funde von Tendaguru, Deutsch-Ostafrika. *Palaeontographica,* Supplement 7 (1, 1):103–254.

Hoffstetter, R. 1957. Quelques observations sur les Stégosaurinés. *Bulletin de Muséum National d'Histoire Naturelle de Paris* 29 (2):537–47.

Hopson, J.A. 1980. Relative brain size in dinosaurs—implications for dinosaurian endothermy. *In* R.D.K. Thomas and E.C. Olson (eds.), *A Cold Look at the Warm-Blooded Dinosaurs.* Selected Symposium 28. Boulder, Colorado: Westview Press, American Association for the Advancement of Science.

Hotton III, N. 1963. *Dinosaurs.* New York: Pyramid.

Huene, F. 1956. *Paläontologie und Phylogenie der Niederen Tetrapoden.* Jena: Fischer.

Hulke, J.W. 1887. Note on some dinosaurian remains in the collection of A. Leeds, Esq., of Eyebury, Northamptonshire. *Quarterly Journal of the Geological Society of London* 43:695–702.

Janensch, W. 1925. Ein aufgestelltes Skelett des Stegosauriers *Kentrurosaurus aethiopicus* E. Hennig aus den Tendaguru-Schichten Deutsch-Ostafrikas. *Palaeontographica,* Supplement 7 (1, 1):257–76.

Lucas, F.A. 1902. Paleontological notes: The generic name *Omosaurus*. *Science* 19:435.

Lull, R.S. 1917. On the functions of the "sacral brain" in dinosaurs. *American Journal of Science* 44:471–77.

Mantell, G.A. 1841. Memoir on a portion of the lower jaw of the *Iguanodon*, and on the remains of the *Hylaeosaurus* and other saurians, discovered in the strata of Tilgate Forest, in Sussex. *Philosophical Transactions of the Royal Society of London* 131:131–51.

Marsh, O.C. 1877. New order of extinct Reptilia (Stegosauria) from the Jurassic of the Rocky Mountains. *American Journal of Science* 14:513–14.

———. 1880. Principal characters of American Jurassic dinosaurs. Part 3. *American Journal of Science* 19:253–59.

———. 1881. Principal characters of American Jurassic dinosaurs. Part 4, Spinal cord, pelvis and limbs of *Stegosaurus*. *American Journal of Science* 21:167–70.

———. 1887. Principal characters of American Jurassic dinosaurs. Part 9, The skull and dermal armor of *Stegosaurus*. *American Journal of Science* 34:413–17.

———. 1891. Restoration of *Stegosaurus*. *American Journal of Science* 42:179–81.

———. 1896. Dinosaurs of North America. *16th Annual Report of the United States Geological Survey 1894–95*. Washington, D.C.: U.S. Government Printing Office.

Nopsca, F. 1915. Die Dinosaurier der siebenbürgischen Landesteile Ungarns. *Mittheilungen aus dem Jahrbuch der Ungarischen Geologischen Reichsanstalt* 23:1–26.

Olshevsky, G., and T. Ford. 1993. The origin and evolution of the stegosaurs. *Gakken Mook* 4:65–103 [in Japanese].

Ostrom, J.H., and J.S. McIntosh. 1966. *Marsh's Dinosaurs: The Collections from Como Bluff*. New Haven: Yale University Press.

Owen, R. 1861. A monograph of the fossil Reptilia of the Lias formations. 1, *Scelidosaurus harrisonii*. *Palaeontographical Society Monographs* 13:1–14.

———. 1863. A monograph of the fossil Reptilia of the Lias formations. 2, *Scelidosaurus harrisonii* Owen of the lower Lias. *Palaeontographical Society Monographs* 14:1–26.

———. 1875. Monographs of the fossil Reptilia of the Mesozoic Formations. Parts 2 and 3, Genera *Bothriospondylus, Cetiosaurus, Omosaurus*. *Palaeontographical Society Monographs* 29:15–94.

Paul, G.S. 1987. The science and art of restoring the life appearance of dinosaurs and their relatives. *In* S.J. Czerkas and E.C. Olson (eds.), *Dinosaurs Past and Present*. Vol. 2, Los Angeles and Seattle: Natural History Museum of Los Angeles County, with University of Washington Press.

———. 1992. The arrangement of plates in the first complete *Stegosaurus*, from Garden Park. *Garden Park Paleontological Society, Tracks in Time* 3(1):1–2.

Russell, D., P. Béland, and J.S. McIntosh. 1980. Paleoecology of the dinosaurs of Tendaguru (Tanzania). *Mémoires de la Société Géologique de France*, ns, 139:169–75.

Seeley, H.G. 1874. On the base of a large lacertian cranium from the Potton Sands, presumably dinosaurian. *Quarterly Journal of the Geological Society of London* 30:690–92.

Sereno, P.C. 1986. Phylogeny of the bird-hipped dinosaurs (Order Ornithischia). *National Geographic Research* 2:234–56.

Sereno, P.C., and Z. Dong. 1992. The skull of the basal stegosaur *Huayangosaurus taibaii* and a cladistic analysis of Stegosauria. *Journal of Vertebrate Paleontology* 12:318–43.

Spassov, N.B. 1982. The bizarre dorsal plates of *Stegosaurus*: Ethological approach. *Comptes Rendus de l'Academie Bulgare des Sciences* 35:367–70.

Xia, W., X. Li, and Z. Yi. 1984. The burial environment of dinosaur fauna in Lower Shaximiao Formation of Middle Jurassic at Dashanpu, Zigong, Sichuan. *Chengdu College of Geology, Journal* 2:46–59 [in Chinese; English summary].

Yadagiri, P., and K. Ayyasami. 1979. A new stegosaurian dinosaur from Upper Cretaceous sediments of south India. *Journal of the Geological Society of India* 20:521–30.

Young, C.C. 1959. On a new Stegosauria from Szechuan, China. *Vertebrata PalAsiatica* 3:1–8.

Zhou, S.W. 1984. *The Middle Jurassic Dinosaurian Fauna from Dashanpu, Zigong, Sichuan*. Vol. 2, *Stegosaurs*. Chongqing: Chongqing Sichuan Scientific and Technical Publishing House [in Chinese; English summary].

Further Reading

Bakker, R.T. 1986. *The Dinosaur Heresies: New Theories Unlocking the Mystery of the Dinosaurs and Their Extinction*. New York: William.

Carpenter, K., and P.J. Currie (eds.). 1990. *Dinosaur Systematics: Approaches and Perspectives*. Cambridge and New York: Cambridge University Press.

Czerkas, S.J., and E.C. Olson (eds.). 1987. *Dinosaurs Past and Present*. 2 vols. Los Angeles and Seattle: Natural History Museum of Los Angeles County, with University of Washington Press.

Farlow, J.O., and M.K. Brett-Surman (eds.). 1997. *The Complete Dinosaur*. Bloomington: University of Indiana Press.

Ostrom, J.H., and J.S. McIntosh. 1966. *Marsh's Dinosaurs: The Collections from Como Bluff*. New Haven, Connecticut: Yale University Press.

Weishampel, D.B., P. Dodson, and H. Osmólska (eds.). 1990. *The Dinosauria*. Berkeley: University of California Press.

STEHLIN, HANS GEORG

Swiss, 1870–1941

Hans Georg Stehlin was born in Basel, Switzerland on 13 January 1870. Following secondary schooling, Stehlin studied a variety of scholarly topics, ranging from the natural and medical sciences to art and philosophy. Although he successfully passed the medical examination, Stehlin decided to concentrate on the natural sciences, and under the tutelage of Professor Ludwig Rütimeyer he received his doctorate in 1893 for work on an important thesis dealing with postembyonic changes of the skulls of ruminant mammals.

Stehlin pursued his professional scientific training through extensive traveling and scientific excursions to paleontological sites and collections in Bonn, Germany, France, Spain, and the Canary Islands. In 1896, Stehlin was appointed assistant at the Natural

History Museum of Basel, and following Rütimeyer's death a year later, he took over the study of the museum's rich fossil collection. In 1898, Stehlin became a member of the Museum Commission of Basel and curator of the section on Comparative Anatomy and Paleontology of mammals. During his 43-year tenure at the museum, Stehlin is credited with considerably enlarging this aspect of its collection.

From 1912 to 1918, Stehlin served as editor of *Verhandlungen der Baselr Naturforschenden Gesellschaft.* Then, in 1920, he succeeded Dr. Fritz Sarasin as director of the Natural History Museum of Basel, a post which he dutifully held until 1940. The following year, in 1921, Stehlin was appointed chairman of the editing committee of the *Abhandlungen der Schweizerischen Paläontologischen Gesellschaft,* of which he had been a member since 1912. That same year, he founded the Swiss Paleontological Society.

Having systematically refused any kind of teaching activity, Stehlin devoted all of his time and energy to research and publication in the field of paleontology. As a result of this dedication, he acquired an immense and surprising knowledge of the fossil mammalian fauna of the European Tertiary and published more than 100 major monographs dealing with various stratigraphical, taxonomical, or morphological aspects of mammals. In these monographs, Stehlin examined various aspects of Switzerland (Eocene molasse formation, glacial deposits of Birtal, Basel-Delémont, Cotencher Cave, and Neuchâtel), France (Upper Pliocene of Senèze and Haute-Loire), and southern Germany. His vast experience and intense study of fossil material from all over Western Europe, combined with the collaborations he developed with colleagues abroad, contributed to his precise definition of the local stratigraphy within a continental scheme during the Tertiary period. Furthermore, Stehlin's international contacts provided him with the opportunity to examine mammals from around the world, including Venezuela, Java, and Persia. Hans Georg Stehlin died in Basel, Switzerland on 19 November 1941.

EDOUARD L. BONÉ AND BRIAN CALLENDER

Biography

Born in Basel, Switzerland, 13 January 1870. Received Ph.D, Natural History Museum of Basel, 1893. Appointed assistant, Natural History Museum of Basel, 1896; member, Museum Commission of Basel, 1898; curator of comparative anatomy and paleontology of mammals, Natural History Museum of Basel, 1898; member, editing committee, *Abhandlungen der Schweizerischen Paläontologischen Gesellschaft,* 1912; editor, *Verhandlungen der Baseler Naturforschenden Gesellschaft,* 1912–18; director, Natural History Museum of Basel, 1920; chairman, editing committee, *Abhandlungen der Schweizerischen Paläontologischen Gesellschaft,* 1921; founded Swiss Paleontological Society, 1921. Died in Basel, Switzerland, 19 November 1941.

Major Publications

1892. Zur Kenntniss der postembryonalen Schädelmetamorphosen bei Wiederkauern. Ph.D. dis., University of Basel; Basel: Schwabe, 1893.

1899–1900. *Über die Geschichte des Suiden-Gebisses.* Abhandlungen der Schweizerischen Paläontologischen Gesellschaft, 26–27. Zurich: Druck von Zucher und Furrer.

1903–8. *Die Säugetiere des Schweizerischen Eocaens: Critischer Catalog der Materialien.* Abhandlungen der Schweizerischen Paläontologischen Gesellschaft, 30–35. Zurich: Druck von Zucher und Furrer.

1914. *Übersicht über die Säugetiere der Schweizerischen Molasseformation.* Verhandlungen der Naturforschende Gesellschaft, 25.

1917. *Geschichte der Naturforschenden Gesellschaft in Basel 1817–1917.* Verhandlungen der Naturforschende Gesellschaft, 28.

1923. *Die Oberpliocaene Fauna von Senèze (Haute Loire).* Eclogae Geologicae Helvetiae, 18. Basel: Birkenhaeuser.

1930. *Die Säugetierfauna von Leffe (Prov. Bergamo).* Eclogae Geologicae Helvetiae, 23. Basel: Birkenhaeuser.

1940. *Zur Stammesgeschichte der Soriciden.* Eclogae Geologicae Helvetiae, 33. Basel: Birkenhaeuser.

Further Reading

Peyer, B. 1942. Hans Georg Stehlin (1878–1941). *Verhandlugen der Schweizerischen Naturforschenden Gesellschaft in Basel* 319–325.

Revilliod, P. 1942. Hans Georg Stehlin, 1870–1941. *Compte Rendu des Séances de la Société de Physique et d'Histoire Naturelle de Genève* 59:17–25.

Schaub, S. 1943. Hans Georg Stehlin, 1870–1941. *Verhandlugen der Schweizerischen Naturforschenden Gesellschaft in Basel* 54:183–221.

STENSIÖ, ERIK

Swedish, 1891–1984

Erik Helge Osvald Andersson was born in 1891, in the village of Stensjö in southeastern Sweden. While still at school he developed a keen interest in natural history and chemistry and later graduated from Uppsala University in zoology. Between 1912 and 1918 he led six expeditions to Spitsbergen, a Norwegian archipelago in the Arctic Ocean, and began research on the Triassic fishes of those islands. Because the family name Andersson is confusingly prevalent in Sweden, at some point around 1917 he adopted the name Stensiö, after his birthplace.

Stensiö traveled fearlessly, and not without incident, during World War I to study and to visit leading paleontologists in England, Germany, Italy, and Switzerland. In 1923, Stensiö became professor and head of the Paleozoology Department in the Swedish Museum of Natural History. Apart from a short interval between 1933 and 1935, when he took leave of absence to occupy the Chair of Geology and Historical Geology at Uppsala University, Stensiö remained at the Swedish museum for the rest of his career, building an outstanding team of scientists and technicians and publishing a stream of works that revolutionized vertebrate paleontology.

In 1921, Stensiö completed his doctoral thesis on Triassic fishes from Spitsbergen. In this, his first major work, he demonstrated the extraordinary qualities that made him the outstanding paleontologist of his generation: his profound knowledge of the subject (geology, paleontology, comparative anatomy), his painstaking attention to detail, and his treatment of fossils as anatomical specimens to be dissected and interpreted as though they were modern specimens. Throughout his work, Stensiö self-consciously maintained the traditions of nineteenth century German *Morphologie,* particularly in the detailed anatomical descriptions and beautifully executed illustrations that grace his publications. This tradition is powerfully evident in the paper that resulted from a visit to the United States and Canada in 1922. In Chicago he spent 10 days carefully removing rock from the braincase of *Macropetalichthys* and was able, as a result of his "dissection," to describe in great detail the brain cavity and nerves and blood vessels of the head. Demonstrating the force of his approach, he concluded that this hitherto enigmatic Devonian fish was related to sharks and rays.

But Stensiö reserved the most powerful demonstration of his genius for a study of the minute cephalaspid "fishes" that had been collected by Norwegian expeditions in late Silurian and early Devonian rocks in Spitsbergen between 1909 and 1912. Published in 1927, this work established him as the world's leading paleontologist. Here he adopted the method of serial grinding (and enlarged wax-plate model building) to reinforce careful dissection with needles under powerful lights and a binocular microscope. Despite employing highly skilled preparators and artists, Stensiö found that the work was time-consuming and called for great reserves of patience and skill. One dissection of *Kiaeraspis* alone took more than two months to complete. Stensiö's methods revealed such details of cranial anatomy that some comparative anatomists simply refused to believe in his work. But his results as a whole have stood the test of time, including his radical conclusion that the cephalaspids are jawless vertebrates related to modern lampreys.

With this milestone piece of research, Stensiö perfected his working tools, including the "Stensio mallet," a small rock drill developed with the help of his dentist from a standard dental drill. He also perfected the research routine (prepare, photograph, draw, describe, compare, and interpret) that was to serve him for the next 50 years. At his death in 1984, he had well over 50 publications to his name, many of them of substantial length, including several more than 300 pages long, and two more than 600 pages. These include works on Triassic and Devonian fishes from Greenland, including an exemplary monograph on *Bothriolepis* (perhaps, like Darwin, Stensiö felt the need to prove his worth in a substantial work on an extended family history). Other subjects included outstanding studies on the shoulder girdles and heads of placoderms (a group of ancient jawed fishes), a major contribution on agnathans (jawless fishes) to the *Traité de Zoologie,* and two separate contributions on agnathans and placoderms to the *Traité de Paléontologie.* Stensiö summarized much of his life's work in these late articles in the *Traité de Paléontologie,* which were published with the help of Jean-Pierre Lehman, a former student who had created the Laboratory of Paleontology in Paris.

Stensiö founded a laboratory in Stockholm that all students of lower vertebrates aspired to visit, to learn firsthand of his extraordinary achievements and discover the secrets of his success. Among his many outstanding students were Gunnar Säve-Söderbergh (1910–48, first to describe *Ichthyostega,* the earliest known tetrapod), Eigel Nielsen (1910–68, who used the serial grinding method to describe Triassic fishes from Greenland), Eric Jarvik (who based much of his research on *Eusthenopteron* specimens that Stensiö obtained following his 1922 trip to North America), and Tor Ørvig (a founder of modern paleohistology). Jarvik was Stensiö's successor at the museum in Stockholm and was in turn succeeded by Ørvig.

Stensiö's approach does have a weakness. It lies in the need for Recent models that form the basis of detailed anatomical interpretations. If there is no independent evidence of a relationship between model and fossil, the analysis can lead to circular reasoning. Thus Stensiö interpreted heterostracans (for which we have little fossil evidence of soft anatomy) after modern hagfishes, and *then* concluded, on the basis of his interpretation, that heterostracans were hagfish ancestors. Nevertheless, we may say that Stensiö's influence rightly endures in the example he set as an adventurous and exacting comparative anatomist.

Stensiö received many honors in his lifetime, tokens of both respect and affection for a great man of science. These embrace membership in 26 academies and learned societies, including the Royal Swedish Academy and the Royal Society of London. He also received 17 medals and orders, including Knight Commander of the First Class in the Royal Order of the North Star; the Daniel Elliot Giraud Medal of the National Academy of Sciences, USA; the Nansen Medal of the Norwegian Academy of Sciences; and the Linné and Lovén Medals of the Royal Swedish Academy of Sciences.

ROGER MILES

Biography

Born in the village of Stensjö, southeastern Sweden, 2 October 1891. Entered Uppsala University, 1912; Ph.D., Uppsala University, 1921. Swedish expeditions to Spitsbergen 1912, 1913, 1915, 1916, 1917, and 1918; English-Norwegian-Swedish Spitsbergen expedition, 1939; head of the Paleozoology department, Swedish Museum of Natural History, 1923–59; elected to the Royal Swedish Academy, 1927; chair of Geology and Historical Geology, University of Uppsala, 1933–35; elected as Foreign Member of the Royal Society of London, 1946; genus names *Erikodus* Nielsen, *Stensioella* Broili, *Stensionotus* Lehman, and *Stensiopelta* Denison chosen to honor him, as well as many species names. Died in Danderyd, Sweden, 11 January 1984.

Major Publications

1921. *Triassic Fishes from Spitzbergen,* Part 1. Vienna: Holzhausen.

1925. On the head of the macropetalichthyids, with certain remarks on the head of the other arthrodires. *Publications of the Field Museum of Natural History, Geological Series* 4 (4):87–197.

1927. *The Downtonian and Devonian vertebrates of Spitsbergen.* Part 1, *Family Cephalaspidae.* Skrifter om Svalbard og Nordishavet, 12. Oslo: I Kommisjon hos. J. Dybwad.

1964. Cyclostomes fossiles ou ostracoderms. *In* J. Piveteau (ed.), *Traité de Paléontologie*. Vol. 4, no. 1, Paris: Masson.

1969. Arthrodires. *In* J. Piveteau (ed.), *Traité de Paléontologie*. Vol. 4, no. 2, Paris: Masson.

Further Reading

Patterson, C. 1990. Erik Helge Osvald Stensiö. *Bibliographic Memoires of Fellows of the Royal Society* 35:361–80.

STERNBERG, CHARLES HAZELIUS

American, 1850–1943

Although Charles Hazelius Sternberg studied briefly at the Kansas State Agricultural College (now Kansas State University), he did not complete college training. Instead, he applied for a position with fossil-hunter E.D. Cope. A childhood injury had left Sternberg so lame that the first time they met, Cope wondered whether Sternberg could even ride a horse. But Sternberg proved he was more than capable. As part of Cope's team, he collected mosasaurs and pterosaur fossils in the Cretaceous Niobrara Chalk of western Kansas (Rogers 1991), covering large areas on foot and working under the difficult conditions in what was then very definitely the "Wild West." Sternberg transported finds by horse and, in the early years, had to dodge problems with Native Americans. One time, they interrupted his work in the John Day beds in Oregon (he boxed and hid some fossil specimens). On one expedition, Cope and Sternberg were collecting within 150 miles of the site of Custer's death at the Little Bighorn, which had occurred only six weeks earlier. They camped near a gathering of 2,000 Crow, some of whom Cope charmed by taking out his false teeth to wash them (1909).

Later, Sternberg became part of another type of team. In 1882 his oldest son George (age nine) found his first fossil (Rogers 1991). By 1908 Sternberg and his three sons had become a potent fossil-hunting team. Conditions for the Sternbergs' field work were always difficult—bad weather and poor (sometimes scarce) food. One of the team's most spectacular finds was a petrified hadrosaur mummy from eastern Wyoming. George found it while he and his brother Levi stayed at the site while their father and brother Charlie took the buckboard to town to get supplies. The hadrosaur is now displayed at the American Museum of Natural History.

In 1912 Sternberg began working, often with his sons, in the badlands of the Red Deer River, under contract with the Geological Survey of Canada. The Sternbergs reached these difficult-to-access badlands by traveling by flatboat up the river (1917). This area has now become Dinosaur Provincial Park; the spectacular Tyrrell Museum, rich in dinosaur displays, is associated with the park. In 1954 Sternberg's son Charlie served as consultant to the park during its early stages of development (Rogers 1991).

After 1917 the Sternbergs went their separate ways. The two younger sons remained in Canada; George returned to the United States, then went on two expeditions to Patagonia to collect a wide variety of vertebrates (Rogers 1991). On his return, George returned to Kansas, where his father had a workshop. George eventually joined the staff of Kansas State Teachers College (now Fort Hays State University), founding its fledgling museum and serving as curator (Rogers 1991). George continued to collect for the rest of his life, reserving choice specimens for the museum—

such as the "fish-in-a-fish" fossil from the Kansas chalk, in which a 5.2 meter fish contains one that is 1.8 meters long (Rogers 1991). In 1970 the museum was renamed the Sternberg Memorial Museum to honor not only George, but his father and brothers.

During most of his career, Charles Hazelius Sternberg had maintained a workshop in Lawrence, Kansas. He concentrated his collecting in several geographical regions. From the Cretaceous of western Kansas, he produced plesiosaurs and mosasaurs (large marine reptiles), giant marine turtles, and the large fish *Portheus*. The Cretaceous of Wyoming yielded *Triceratops* and hadrosaurs; the Oligocene of Wyoming yielded large mammals such as titanotheres; the Permian of Texas yielded pelycosaurs; the Red Deer River Cretaceous area in Alberta, Canada, yielded *Albertosaurus*, *Stegoceras*, and *Styracosaurus* (Rogers 1991). Sternberg also did significant work in the Miocene of Kansas and Nebraska and in the Pleistocene of California. Many of his finds now reside in museums in 22 states and four European countries.

Sternberg's real-life adventures, described in his autobiographical work, contains many fascinating passages in which he views or walks among animals of the past, reconstructed in his lively imagination. As Henry Fairfield Osborn, then president of the American Museum of Natural History, said in the introduction to Sternberg's first autobiography, "the fossil hunter is always seeking to bring extinct animals back to life. This revivification of the past . . . is attended with as great fascination as the quest of live game, and to my mind is a still more honorable and noble pursuit" (1909). Although some of Sternberg's ideas are now out of date, all are interesting and insightful. His books foreshadow popular works on fossil collecting expeditions, such as those of Roy Chapman Andrews.

JUDITH A. SCHIEBOUT

Work Cited

Rogers, K. 1991. *The Sternberg Fossil Hunters, a Dinosaur Dynasty*. Missoula, Montana: Mountain Press.

Biography

Born in New York state, near Cooperstown, 1850. Attended Kansas State Agricultural College, 1868–69. Professional vertebrate fossil collector, pioneered collecting in the North American west; collected mammal, dinosaur, plant, and invertebrate remains that are currently housed in major museums in the United States, Canada, and Europe; prepared many specimens he collected; pioneered the method of removing fossils from the field in protective casts; trained paleontologists such as J. Wortman and J.B.

Hatcher; worked as a team with his three sons (George, Levi, and Charles), amassing impressive finds. Member, American Association for the Advancement of Science; Kansas Academy of Science; Society of American Vertebrate Paleontologists. Died in Toronto, 21 July 1943.

Major Publications

1909. *The Life of a Fossil Hunter.* New York: Holt; revised, 1931.

1917. *Hunting Dinosaurs in the Bad Lands of the Red Deer River, Alberta, Canada.* Lawrence, Kansas: Sternberg.

Further Reading

Colbert, E.H. 1968. *Men and Dinosaurs.* Chicago: Dutton.
Lessem, D. 1992. *Kings of Creation.* New York: Simon and Schuster.
Rogers, K. 1991. *The Sternberg Fossil Hunters: A Dinosaur Dynasty.* Missoula, Montana: Mountain Press.

STIRTON, RUBEN ARTHUR

American, 1901–66

Ruben Arthur Stirton made significant contributions to our knowledge of the Cenozoic vertebrate faunas of western North America, northern South America, and Australia. His monographic study of the evolution of the Equidae (1940), the family including horses and their kin, was a major contribution. It served as a foundation for our current, detailed understanding of the evolution of the horses and is cited in discussions of patterns and processes of evolution in most modern biology textbooks.

Stirton's interests in vertebrates of the Southern Hemisphere possibly were sparked while he was an undergraduate at the University of Kansas. During those years H.T. Martin, curator of the university's Museum of Natural History, led field trips to Patagonia, bringing back large collections of fossil vertebrates to Kansas. In 1925 and 1927 Stirton worked as a mammalogist on the Donald R. Dickey Expeditions to El Salvador, a country to which he would return in 1940–41 to collect the remains of *Eremotherium,* a gigantic ground sloth, as well as other late Pleistocene vertebrates.

In 1927, Stirton entered the graduate program at the University of California and became an assistant to William Diller Matthew, who had come to Berkeley from the American Museum of Natural History in New York. In the three years before Matthew's death in 1930, the two collaborated on studies of Tertiary mammals and coauthored papers on fossil horses from Texas and on *Borophagus,* hyaena-like dogs that once ranged over most of North America.

Through the 1930s Stirton continued an active research program, building on Matthew's legacy. In addition to the study of horses, Stirton published a review of beaver evolution; contributed to the description of Cenozoic faunas from California, Nevada, Nebraska, and Texas; and participated in research to establish the relative ages of these faunas. Although Stirton remained interested in North American Cenozoic faunas throughout his life, the primary focus of his research shifted in 1944, when he initiated fieldwork in Colombia.

The first remains of fossil vertebrates had been collected in the valley of the Magdalena River, Colombia, in the 1920s. During the following decades, oil exploration began, and more fossils were discovered. In 1944, Stirton received a Guggenheim Fellowship and began field research in Colombia, in collaboration with geologist José Royo y Gómez, a member of the Servicio Geológico National de Colombia. In this project, which continued until 1950, Stirton, others from Berkeley (including his students R.W. Fields and D.E. Savage), and Colombian colleagues made extensive collections, documenting the La Venta Fauna. The diverse mammals and other vertebrates of the La Venta Fauna inhabited Colombia from about 13.6 to 11.6 million years ago. This fauna provides a significant benchmark, documenting the terrestrial inhabitants of northern South America before animals began moving between South and North America. That interchange began a few million years later, when the Central America land bridge was established (Madden et al. 1997).

At the beginning of the 1950s, little was known of the evolution of the prehistoric terrestrial fauna of Australia. Sediments that filled caves and fissures, as well as some floodplain deposits, had yielded records of its diverse Pleistocene terrestrial fauna, including many species that became extinct only a few thousand years ago. Almost nothing was known of their ancestral stocks. In 1953, supported by Fulbright scholarships, Stirton and his graduate student, R.H. Tedford, spent nine months in Australia. Their goal was to find records of the earlier Australian terrestrial fauna. The two men were about to return essentially empty handed, when, on their last field reconnaissance with colleagues from the South Australian Museum and the University of Adelaide, they discovered the rich series of fossil-laden deposits exposed in the bluffs around Lake Palankarinna, east of Lake Eyre in northern South Australia (Tedford 1991). This find began a continuing series of field investigations that expanded northward, first in the valleys between great linear sand dunes east of Lake Eyre, then farther into the Northern Territory, as well as into other regions of the continent.

The work of Stirton, his students and colleagues from Berkeley, and colleagues from Australian museums and universities produced collections that now document the evolution of Australia's terrestrial vertebrate fauna over at least the last 15 million years. The finds record the evolutionary diversification of the terrestrial vertebrate fauna, including the kangaroos and their kin. These relatives include animals such as a group of large, rhinoceros-size herbivorous marsupials (diprotodonts) which were among the lineages that became extinct a few thousand years ago.

Beyond their contribution to the fossil record, the discoveries at Lake Palankarinna and other central Australian sites fostered student exchanges and collaborative research projects involving paleontologists and geologists at Australian and American universities. In turn, this research has been instrumental in the flowering of the field of vertebrate paleontology in Australian universities and museums.

Throughout his career at the University of California, Stirton was associated with the Museum of Paleontology. In addition to his own research, he supported projects of other members of the staff, faculty, and their students. The success of these endeavors is reflected in the museum's extensive collections, among the largest and most diverse in North America, and the many publications based on them. In the fall of 1966, Stirton died unexpectedly while he was attending the Forty-Sixth Annual Meeting of the American Society of Mammalogists. He was there to give a paper on an aspect of his studies of the evolutionary relationships of Australian mammals.

W.A. CLEMENS

Works Cited

Madden, R.H., D.E. Savage, and R.W. Fields. 1997. A history of vertebrate paleontology in the Magdalena Valley. *In* R.F. Kay, R.H. Madden, R.L. Cifelli, and J.J. Flynn (eds.), *Vertebrate Paleontology in the Neotropics: The Miocene Fauna of La Venta, Colombia.* Washington and London: Smithsonian Institution.

Tedford, R.H. 1991. Vertebrate Palaeontology in Australia: The American contribution. *In* P. Vickers-Rich, J.M. Monaghan, R.F. Baird, and T.H. Rich (eds.), *Vertebrate Palaeontology of Australasia.* Lilydale, Victoria: Monash University Publications.

Biography

Born near Muscotah, Kansas, 20 August 1901. Received A.B., University of Kansas, 1925; M.A., University of California, Berkeley, 1931; Ph.D. University of California, Berkeley, 1940; Guggenheim Fellow, 1944–45; Fulbright awardee, 1953. Mammalogist, Donald R. Dickey expeditions, El Salvador, 1925, 1927; faculty, University of California, Berkeley 1930–66; research on Cenozoic vertebrate faunas of western North America (1928–66), Colombia, South America (1944–53), Australia and Papua New Guinea (1953–66). Died in Santa Monica, California, 14 June 1966.

Major Publications

1940. Phylogeny of North American Equidae. *University of California Publication, Bulletin, Department of Geological Sciences* 25:165–98.

1961. With R.H. Tedford and A.H. Miller. Cenozoic stratigraphy and vertebrate paleontology of the Tirari Desert, South Australia. *Records, South Australian Museum* 14:19–61.

Further Reading

Camp, C.L., W.A. Clemens, J.T. Gregory, and D.E. Savage. 1967. Ruben Arthur Stirton. 1901–1966. *Journal of Mammalogy* 48:298–305.

SUPERPHYLA

Carl Linnaeus' original system of animal nomenclature, devised in the eighteenth century and still recognized as the starting point for modern zoological names, did not use the phylum rank at all. Linnaeus provided for six classes within the Kingdom Animalia: Mammalia, Aves (birds), Amphibia, Pisces (fishes), Insecta (mostly arthropods), and Vermes (all other invertebrates). The shortcomings of this system became obvious as zoologists learned more about invertebrate animals, so various scientists proposed major reforms. In 1812 Georges Cuvier created a new rank above the class level, the *embranchement* (branch). He divided the animals into four *embranchements:* Vertebrata, Articulata (segmented invertebrates, such as arthropods and annelids), Mollusca (including many unsegmented invertebrates, besides the Mollusca as defined now), and Radiata (radially symmetrical animals). Although this fourfold taxonomic scheme was championed by eminent scientists such as Louis Agassiz (e.g., Agassiz 1859), it also proved inadequate (Winsor 1976). As Cuvier's old *embranchements* were divided up, the *phylum* (Greek, *tribe*) came into use as the highest rank in zoological classification.

Hyman (1940) gave a working definition of a phylum: "closely allied animals distinguishable from any other phylum by well-defined positive characteristics, some of which do not exist in other phyla or not in that particular combination. Any group of animals, however small, having such distinct characters, should be regarded as a separate phylum until evidence shall be forthcoming showing its relationship to some other phylum." Most biologists would give a similar definition: a phylum is a group of organisms that share a distinctive "general plan" or "distinctive set of characters" by common descent. Hyman (1940) listed 22 animal phyla, while most authors today accept between 30 and 40 living animal phyla (Table 1).

As biologists have become aware that the phyla of older schemes included very different organisms, the older phyla have been split up. Cuvier's Radiata, for example, included all animals with a radially symmetrical body plan; it has long been split into the phyla Cnidaria (e.g., anemones, jellyfishes), Ctenophora (comb jellies), and Echinodermata (e.g., sea stars, crinoids) (Winsor 1976). New and unusual animals are still being discovered and ranked in new phyla. The most recently proposed living phyla, all of which include only microscopic animals, are the Loricifera (Kristensen 1983), Lobatocerebromorpha (Haszprunar et al. 1991), and Cycliophora (Funch and Kristensen 1995).

Several fossil groups also have been put forth—if not universally accepted—as phyla. These include the Agmata, for some conical shelly fossils from the Cambrian period (Yochelson 1977); Archaeocyatha, for archaeocyathids (Hill 1972); Petal-

Table 1.

List of the generally accepted animal phyla.

		Mesozoa	mesozoans
		Placozoa	placozoans
		Porifera	sponges
		Cnidaria	cnidarians
		Ctenophora	comb jellies
DEUTEROSTOMIA			
		Echinodermata	echinoderms
		Hemichordata	hemichordates
		Urochordata	tunicates
		Cephalochordata	amphioxus
		Chordata	chordates
PROTOSTOMIA			
		Platyhelminthes	flatworms
		Gnathostomulida	gnathostomulids
		Rotifera	rotifers
		Gastrotricha	gastrotrichs
		Chaetognatha	arrow worms
		Cycliophora	cycliophorans
		Entoprocta	entoprocts
	Ecdysozoa		
		Nematoda	roundworms
		Nematomorpha	horsehair worms
		Priapulida	priapulid worms
		Kinorhyncha	kinorhynchs
		Loricifera	loriciferans
		Tardigrada	water bears
		Onychophora	velvet worms
		Arthropoda	arthropods
	Lophotrochozoa		
		Brachiopoda	brachiopods
		Bryozoa	bryozoans
		Phoronida	phoronids
		Annelida	segmented worms
		Echiura	spoon worms
		Pogonophora	beard worms
		Vestimentifera	giant rift worms
		Nemertea	ribbon worms
		Mollusca	molluscs
		Sipuncula	peanut worms

Note that most do not have common names. Boldface indicates phylum with an extensive fossil record.

onamae, for some of the Ediacaran organisms (enigmatic animals of the Late Precambrian) (Pflug 1972); Conulariida, for conulariids (Babcock 1991); Conodontophora, for the animals with simple cone-shaped teeth (Briggs et al. 1983; but see Aldridge and Purnell 1996; Pridmore et al. 1997); and Procoelomata, for hypothetical crawling organisms close to the common ancestry of most living phyla (Bergström 1989). One author even proposed seven separate phyla—most of which contain only one species—

to cover some of the "oddballs" of the Burgess Shale, a deposit in which soft-bodied organisms of the Cambrian Explosion are preserved (Anderson 1993).

As the number of phyla has grown, so has the number of taxonomic schemes for clustering phyla together in even higher, more inclusive taxa. Classification in "superphyla" is useful for two reasons. Any classification needs to serve as a practical basis for information storage; thus, as the number of phyla grows, superphyla become a very convenient and practical way to refer to groups of related phyla. Furthermore, almost all systematists now believe that the classification of organisms should reflect their evolutionary history. Superphyla, as groupings above the phylum level, provide a framework for discussing major events in animal evolution.

There is no real consensus as to what the ranks above the phylum level should be called or how many should be established between kingdom and phylum. In fact, although Hyman's definition might seem clear, in practice there is real ambiguity in defining just what a phylum is (Bengtson 1986). For instance, in what sense is the Phylum Cycliophora—which currently includes exactly one described species, found only on the mouthparts of lobsters—equivalent to the Phylum Arthropoda, with several million species living in almost every habitat imaginable? Is it even useful to have a phylum with only one species in it? The single species Phylum Cycliophora is, by any standard, quite different from species in any other phylum. On the other hand, an octopus, a giant clam, and a slug are extremely different from each other, yet all three are in the Phylum Mollusca. How different do two organisms have to be in order to be placed in separate phyla, and how should such differences be defined and quantified? How does one define the "general plan" shared by all members of a phylum? Hyman's definition of a phylum also implies that the closest relatives of that phylum aren't known (if they were, they'd be grouped together in the same phylum). Therefore, a phylum is a statement of ignorance of evolutionary relationships (Bengtson 1986). So, on what grounds can phyla be classified together in superphyla?

There are no simple answers to these questions, which could be debated endlessly. Many important groupings of phyla have never had a formal rank assigned to them. In fact, a number of systematists have proposed that taxonomic rank should be done away with entirely, and that names should be used simply to denote clades (groupings of all descendants of a common ancestor), without the added connotations of a rank (e.g., De Quieroz and Gauthier 1992). This article will simply treat various schemes of taxonomy within the Kingdom Animalia, concentrating on those above the level of the traditional phylum.

Divisions of the Animalia

The Protozoa, which included most non-plantlike protists, once were grouped together as a single phylum within the Kingdom Animalia. All animals other than the Protozoa were classified in the subkingdom Metazoa (e.g., Hyman 1940). We now know that most "protozoa" are not related closely at all to the animals. The organisms in the old "Phylum Protozoa" now are placed together

in a separate kingdom, or in several kingdoms (e.g., Cavalier-Smith 1993). A few systematists have retained one group of "protozoa" in the Animalia. These are the Choanoflagellata, single-celled or colonial protists that are extremely similar to the "collar cells" of sponges and that almost certainly are close to the root of animal evolution (Nielsen 1985). Most systematists, however, do not include any protists in the Animalia, making a formal distinction between Animalia and Metazoa unnecessary. The term "Metazoa" is used still, more or less as a synonym for Animalia.

Some biologists have proposed a major division of the Metazoa between the sponges (Parazoa or Enantiozoa) and all other animals, the Eumetazoa (Hyman 1940; Bergquist 1978). The major difference between parazoans and eumetazoans is that parazoans lack organs. Sponges are loose aggregates of cells, and all cells of a sponge retain the ability to move within the sponge's body. A cellular sponge actually can be broken up into its component cells by passing it through fine cloth, and afterward the cells will rejoin and reform a new sponge (Bergquist 1978). In contrast, Eumetazoan bodies are more organized and integrated, and eumetazoan cells are bound more tightly together. The organizational difference is so great that sponges once were considered to have an independent origin, completely separate from all other animals (e.g., Hadzi 1963). However, the underlying similarities outweigh the differences, and sponges now are considered to be true animals.

Metazoan Superphyla

Except for the sponges, cnidarians, ctenophores, and a few minor phyla, all animals are composed of tissues derived from three layers of cells ("germ layers") in the embryo. The ectoderm makes up the outer covering or skin; the endoderm forms the gut and its derivatives. Derived in early development from one or both of these layers, the third layer, the mesoderm, fills the space in between the other two and forms muscle and various organs. Animals with three germ layers are called triploblasts and sometimes are classified in the Triploblasta. A more common name for this group is the Bilateria, since all its members are bilaterally symmetrical (two-sided) or are evolved from bilaterally symmetrical ancestors.

In addition to the gut, many animals have a fluid-filled cavity enclosed within the mesoderm, which surrounds the gut. The general term for such a cavity is coelom. In the usual definition of a true coelom, the gut is surrounded completely by sheets of mesoderm and is suspended within the coelom by sheets of mesodermal tissue, the mesenteries. A common scheme is to divide the Bilateria into those animals with no coelom and those with a true coelom. A third group can consist of those phyla whose members have a fluid-filled space surrounding the gut but no surrounding mesoderm and no true mesenteries. These three groups have been named the Acoelomata, Coelomata, and Pseudocoelomata respectively. Acoelomata includes the flatworms (phylum Platyhelminthes), while Pseudocoelomata includes roundworms (phylum Nematoda), rotifers (phylum Rotifera), horsehair worms (phylum Nematomorpha), priapulid worms (phylum Priapulida), and several others, which are less well known (Figures 1–4). Another common name for the pseudocoelomates is the Aschelminthes.

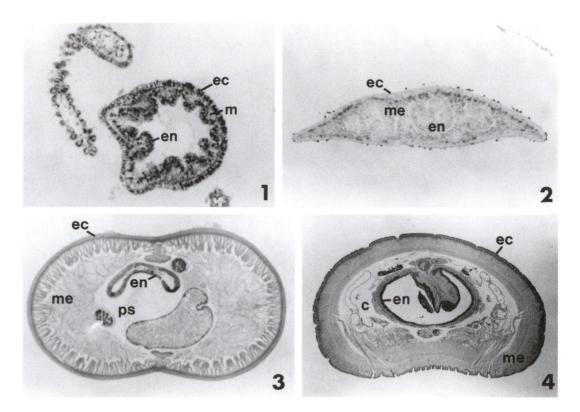

Figure 1. Cross section through a freshwater polyp, *Hydra* (phylum Cnidaria). Key: *ec*, ectoderm; *en*, endoderm; *m*, mesoglea (jellylike material between ectoderm and endoderm, not considered a true tissue layer).

Figure 2. Cross section through a flatworm, *Dugesia* (phylum Platyhelminthes), showing the acoelomate type of body. Key: *ec*, ectoderm; *me*, mesoderm; *en*, endoderm; *g*, gut branches.

Figure 3. Cross section through a human intestinal roundworm, *Ascaris* (phylum Nematoda), showing the pseudocoelomate body type. Key: *ec*, ectoderm; *me*, mesoderm; *en*, endoderm; *ps*, pseudocoel.

Figure 4. Cross section through an earthworm, *Lumbricus* (phylum Annelida), showing the true coelomate body type. Key: *ec*, ectoderm; *me*, mesoderm; *en*, endoderm; *c*, coelom.

This triple division is standard fare in biology textbooks, but it probably does not represent the real evolutionary relationships of the animal phyla. It has become apparent that coeloms may develop in many different ways (Ruppert 1991). Technically, the Nemertea (ribbon worms) are acoelomate, but actually they are related more closely to certain coelomates than to the acoelomate flatworms (Turbeville et al. 1992; Winnepenninckx et al. 1995a). Furthermore, although some systematists retain the Aschelminthes (Nielsen 1995), molecular phylogeny and careful studies of anatomy strongly suggest that the aschelminths are not monophyletic (do not descend from a single ancestor). They include at least three separate evolutionary lineages and thus should not be classified together (Winnepenninckx et al. 1995b; Aguinaldo et al. 1997). The names "acoelomate," "coelomate," and "pseudocoelomate" are useful as descriptions of anatomical types, but do not represent monophyletic taxa.

Coelomate Superphyla

The most generally accepted groupings of metazoan coelomate phyla are the Protostomia and Deuterostomia (Grobben 1908) (Figure 5). Protostomes ("mouth first") include molluscs, arthro-pods, annelids, and a host of minor phyla. During the embryological development of typical members of these phyla, either the mouth forms before the anus or the mouth and anus form at the same time. Deuterostomes ("mouth second") include the chordates, echinoderms, tunicates, and their kin. In these phyla, the anus develops before the mouth.

However, the differences between the two groups run deeper. When protostome embryos first begin dividing, the latitudinal rows of cells typically assume a spiraling pattern, "spiral cleavage," in which each horizontal circlet of cells is offset with respect to the circlet below. Deuterostomes typically show a different pattern, "radial cleavage," in which circlets of cells are aligned with each other. As adults, most protostomes have a ventral (belly-side) nerve cord (or pair of nerve cords) and a dorsal (back-side) main blood vessel. This pattern is reversed in deuterostomes, which typically have a dorsal nerve cord and a ventral blood vessel. It must be said that there are plenty of exceptions to all these generalizations. The larvae of various animals may differ radically from the generalized pattern. However, the distinction has held up under scrutiny: molecular phylogeny (evolutionary relationships inferred from DNA information) agrees with traditional morphology in separating the deuterostomes and the protostomes (e.g., Wada and Satoh 1994).

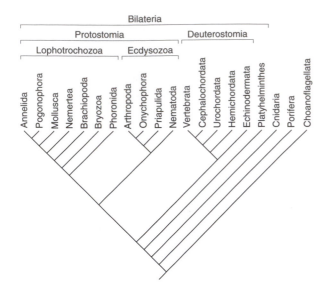

Figure 5. Tree showing a plausible (though by no means certain) hypothesis of the relationships among prominent animal phyla. Some of the proposed groups above the phylum level are shown.

The members of one traditional superphylum-level group do not fit neatly into either the Protostomia or the Deuterostomia. The Lophophorata (sometimes called Tentaculata) are characterized by a looped gut, with the anus opening near the mouth, and a "lophophore," a ring of ciliated feeding tentacles around the mouth. The tentacles contain extensions of the coelom. The group includes two phyla with extensive fossil records, the Brachiopoda and Bryozoa. It also includes the small phylum Phoronida, with no direct fossil record and fewer than 15 living species of wormlike organisms. Lophophorates show mixtures of "classical" protostome and deuterostome characters. Traditionally, they have been separated from both categories and often are considered closer to deuterostomes than to protostomes. However, molecular evidence consistently places the lophophorates within the protostomes (Halanych et al. 1995; Conway Morris et al. 1996; Mackey et al. 1996).

Protostome Relationships

Two of the most prominent protostome phyla are the Annelida and the Arthropoda. These two are externally segmented, and both arthropods and polychaeta annelids have well-developed heads and numerous appendages. For a long time it was usual to group them together, sometimes in the taxon Annulata or Annulosa. Recent analyses, however, are overturning this traditional view. Instead, the Arthropoda and related phyla appear closest to some of the "aschelminth" phyla, notably the priapulids and nematodes (Eernisse et al. 1992; Winnepenninckx et al. 1995a; Waggoner 1996). This grouping recently has been called the Ecdysozoa, or "molting animals," because its members have a cuticle (outermost skin) that is typically molted several times during the animal's life (Aguinaldo et al. 1997) (Figure 5).

Annelids and molluscs now seem to be more closely related to each other, together with several phyla of unsegmented worms such as the Pogonophora (deep-sea beard worms) and Echiura (innkeeper worms and spoon worms). All of these have similar free-swimming ciliated larvae known as "trochophores," and the name Eutrochozoa has been proposed for this group. The Lophotrochozoa, another proposed group, would include these phyla plus the lophophorates (Halanych et al. 1995), but as of yet, exact phylogenetic patterns within the Lophotrochozoa are not well resolved.

Final Note

By now, this article may seem like a boring and befuddling parade of long Greek names and biological trivia. But these names are not nearly as important as what they represent—our changing evaluations of how the 100 million or more animal species that have ever lived are related to each other. Charles Darwin wrote that, when evolution became accepted, "our classifications will come to be, as far as they can so be made, genealogies ... " (Darwin 1859). A classification based on evolutionary relationships has been the goal of most practicing systematists ever since. The past few decades have seen great floods of new data on animal relationships: new fossil finds, new discoveries of living organisms, and new techniques, such as electron microscopy and gene sequencing. The chaotic state of nomenclature may be daunting, but this chaos reflects the intense activity and excitement in the study of animal evolution.

Paleontology has contributed a great deal to this excitement. To cite a famous example, the fossils of the Burgess Shale, of Middle Cambrian age, include several forms that do not belong to any known phylum (Briggs et al. 1983). A growing number of other sites around the world, from the latest Precambrian and Cambrian, also have yielded fossil forms that do not fit into any living phylum. The study of these "weird wonders" is beginning to shed light on the evolutionary relationships among established phyla, although much remains to be done (e.g., Conway Morris 1993; Conway Morris and Peel 1995; Waggoner 1996).

BEN WAGGONER

See also Ediacaran Biota; Metazoan Phyla, Minor; Problematic Animals: Phanerozoic Problematica

Works Cited

Agassiz, L. 1859. *An Essay on Classification.* London: Longman, Brown Green, Longman, and Roberts.

Aguinaldo, A.M.A., J.M. Turbeville, L.S. Rivera, M.C. Linford, J.R. Garey, R.A. Raff, and J.A. Lake. 1997. Evidence for a clade of nematodes, arthropods and other moulting animals. *Nature* 387:489–93.

Aldridge, R.J., and M.A. Purnell. 1996. The conodont controversies. *Trends in Ecology and Evolution* 11:463–68.

Anderson, C. 1993. Classification of organisms: Living and fossil. *BioSystems* 31:99–109.

Babcock, L.E. 1991. The enigma of conulariid affinities. *In* A.M. Simonetta and S. Conway Morris (eds.), *The Early Evolution of Metazoa and the Significance of Problematic Taxa.* Cambridge and New York: Cambridge University Press.

Bengtson, S. 1986. Introduction: The problem of the Problematica. *In* A. Hoffman and M.H. Nitecki (eds.), *Problematic Fossil Taxa.* Oxford: Clarendon; New York: Oxford University Press.

Bergquist, P.R. 1978. *Sponges.* Berkeley: University of California Press; London: Hutchinson.

Bergström, J. 1989. The origin of animal phyla and the new phylum Procoelomata. *Lethaia* 22:259–69.

Briggs, D.E.G., E.N.K. Clarkson, and R.J. Aldridge. 1983. The conodont animal. *Lethaia* 16:1–14.

Cavalier-Smith, T. 1993. Kingdom Protista and its 18 phyla. *Microbiological Reviews* 57:953–94.

Conway Morris, S. 1993. The fossil record and the early evolution of the Metazoa. *Nature* 361:219–25.

Conway Morris, S., B.L. Cohen, A.B. Gawthrop, T. Cavalier-Smith, and B. Winnepenninckx. 1996. Lophophorate phylogeny. *Science* 272:282–83.

Conway Morris, S., and J.S. Peel. 1995. Articulated halkieriids from the Lower Cambrian of North Greenland and their role in early protostome evolution. *Philosophical Transactions of the Royal Society of London,* ser. B, 347:305–58.

Darwin, C. 1859. *On the Origin of Species.* London: John Murray; New York: Humboldt.

de Quieroz, K., and J. Gauthier. 1992. Phylogenetic taxonomy. *Annual Review of Ecology and Systematics* 23:449–80.

Eernisse, D.J., J.S. Albert, and F.E. Anderson. 1992. Annelida and Arthropoda are not sister taxa: A phylogenetic analysis of spiralian metazoan morphology. *Systematic Biology* 41:305–30.

Funch, P., and R.M. Kristensen. 1995. Cycliophora is a new phylum with affinities to Entoprocta and Ectoprocta. *Nature* 378:711–14.

Grobben, K. 1908. Die systematische Einteilung des Tierreiches. *Verhandlungen der Königlichen Zoologisch-Botanischen Gesellschaft in Wien* 58:491–511.

Hadzi, J. 1963. *The Evolution of the Metazoa.* Oxford: Pergamon; New York: Macmillan.

Halanych, K.M., J.D. Bacheller, A.M.A. Aguinaldo, S.M. Liva, D.M. Hillis, and J.A. Lake. 1995. Evidence from 18*S* ribosomal DNA that the lophophorates are protostome animals. *Science* 267:1641–43.

Haszprunar, G., R.M. Rieger, and P. Schuchert. 1991. Extant "Problematica" within or near the Metazoa. *In* A.M. Simonetta and S. Conway Morris (eds.), *The Early Evolution of Metazoa and the Significance of Problematic Taxa.* Cambridge and New York: Cambridge University Press.

Hill, D. 1972. *Treatise on Invertebrate Paleontology.* Part E, vol. 1, *Archaeocyatha.* 2nd ed., Boulder, Colorado: Geological Society of America; Lawrence, Kansas: University of Kansas Press.

Hyman, L.H. 1940. *The Invertebrates: Protozoa through Ctenophora.* New York: McGraw-Hill.

Kristensen, R.M. 1983. Loricifera, a new phylum with Aschelminthes characters from the meiobenthos. *Zeitschrift für Zoologische Systematik-und Evolutionforschung* 21:163–80.

Mackey, L.Y., B. Winnepenninckx, R. De Wachter, T. Backeljau, P. Emschermann, and J.R. Garey. 1996. 18S rRNA suggests that Entoprocta are protostomes, unrelated to Ectoprocta. *Journal of Molecular Evolution* 42:552–59.

Nielsen, C. 1985. Animal phylogeny in light of the trochaea theory. *Biological Journal of the Linnean Society of London* 25:243–99.

———. 1995. *Animal Evolution: Interrelationships of the Living Phyla.* Oxford: Clarendon; New York: Oxford University Press.

Pflug, H.D. 1972. Systematik der jung-Präkambrischen Petalonamae Pflug 1970. *Paläontologische Zeitschrift* 46:56–67.

Pridmore, P.A., R.E. Barwick, and R.S. Nicoll. 1997. Soft anatomy and the affinities of conodonts. *Lethaia* 29:317–28.

Ruppert, E.E. 1991. Introduction to the aschelminth phyla: A consideration of mesoderm, body cavities, and cuticle. *In* F.W. Harrison and E.E. Ruppert (eds.), *Microscopic Anatomy of Invertebrates.* Vol. 4, *Aschelminthes.* New York and Chichester: Wiley-Liss.

Turbeville, J.M., K.G. Field, and R.A. Raff. 1992. Phylogenetic position of Phylum Nemertini, inferred from 18S rRNA sequences: Molecular data as a test of morphological character homology. *Molecular Biology and Evolution* 9 (2):235–49.

Wada, H., and N. Satoh. 1994. Details of the evolutionary history from invertebrates to vertebrates, as deduced from the sequences of 18S rDNA. *Proceedings of the National Academy of Sciences* 91:1801–4.

Waggoner, B.M. 1996. Phylogenetic hypotheses of the relationships of arthropods to problematic Vendian and Cambrian organisms. *Systematic Biology* 45:190–222.

Winnepenninckx, B., T. Backeljau, and R. De Wachter. 1995a. Phylogeny of protostome worms derived from 18S rRNA sequences. *Molecular Biology and Evolution* 12:641–49.

Winnepenninckx, B., T. Backeljau, L.Y. Mackey, J.M. Brooks, R. De Wachter, S. Kumar, and J.R. Garey. 1995b. 18S rRNA data indicate that aschelminthes are polyphyletic in origin and consist of at least three distinct clades. *Molecular Biology and Evolution* 12:1132–37.

Winsor, M.P. 1976. *Starfish, Jellyfish, and the Order of Life.* New Haven, Connecticut, and London: Yale University Press.

Yochelson, E. 1977. Agmata, a proposed extinct phylum of early Cambrian age. *Journal of Paleontology* 51:437–54.

SYNAPSIDS

The Synapsida is the vertebrate group that includes mammals and their fossil antecedents, the so-called mammal-like reptiles. Although traditionally classified as a subclass within the Class Reptilia (Romer 1966; Carroll 1988), the currently accepted definition of Synapsida includes mammals within the group, making it strictly monophyletic (all members having evolved from a common ances-tor) in a cladistic sense (cladistics being the school of systematics that determines evolutionary relationships based on the presence of shared derived features) (Hopson and Barghusen 1986). Thus, at present, Synapsida is technically defined as the most-inclusive clade of amniote vertebrates that includes mammals but not living reptiles and birds (the latter falling within its sister clade, the Sauropsida).

Between 1925 and the mid–1980s, the synapsids were divided into two subgroups, the more primitive Pelycosauria and the more mammal-like Therapsida (Carroll 1988). J.A. Hopson and H.R. Barghusen (1986) made both the Synapsida and Therapsida strictly monophyletic by extending their formal definitions to include mammals. The term Pelycosauria, on the other hand, characterizes a paraphyletic group (one that includes some, but not all, descendants) because it does not include its therapsid (including mammalian) descendants; were it to include therapsids, the resulting group would have the same contents as that covered by the name Synapsida. As a result, Pelycosauria has been discarded as a formal name, though "pelycosaur" continues to be used as an informal term (as it is here) for the primitive, non-therapsid synapsids.

All synapsids, from the most ancient fossil species to modern mammals, are characterized by the possession of an opening in the side of the skull behind the eye socket, the lateral temporal fenestra. This opening, sealed in life by a membrane, functions as an attachment site for jaw-closing muscles. Synapsids also have an enlarged canine tooth near the anterior (front) part of the maxillary bone of the upper jaw. A major trend within synapsids has been to improve predatory ability by enlarging upper and lower canine teeth, the main weapons for capturing and killing prey, and expanding the temporal opening so as to increase the mass of jaw-closing musculature that could attach around its margins. Shifts to a plant diet (herbivory) have occurred repeatedly in synapsid history, leading to reduction or loss of canines and modification of the cheek teeth for breaking down plant tissues.

Discovery and Early Research on Synapsids

The first descriptions of non-mammalian synapsid fossils were published in 1838 by S.S. Kutorga, who believed they pertained to mammals; it would be nearly 40 years before these fragmentary specimens from the Late Permian of Russia were recognized by Sir Richard Owen (1876b) as primitive therapsids. About the same year that Kutorgu published "Mammals," Andrew Geddes Bain, road builder and self-taught geologist, began collecting complete therapsid skulls and skeletal parts from Permian and Triassic rocks in the Karoo Basin of South Africa. These he sent to London where, from 1845 to 1887, they were described by Owen in a long series of publications. The first named Karoo therapsid was *Dicynodon lacerticeps,* a short-faced, near-toothless, presumably plant-eating, animal with a pair of large tusks in the upper jaw. Owen (1860) later grouped this and similar forms together in a group he called "Anomodontia" (from the Greek for "different tooth"). He also described a great variety of carnivorous therapsids that he grouped as the Theriodontia (Greek for "beast tooth"), which he acknowledged showed resemblances to mammals (Owen 1876a). However, the American paleontologist Edward Drinker Cope (1878b) was the first to explicitly associate these South African fossils with the ancestry of mammals.

The first pelycosaur to be described was *Bathygnathus borealis,* based on a fragmentary maxilla containing seven teeth from the Late Pennsylvanian of Prince Edward Island in eastern Canada. This specimen originally was described by J. Leidy (1854) as a lower jaw of Triassic age, and Leidy compared its large bladelike teeth to those of dinosaurs. Owen (1876b), however, recognized the specimen as an upper jaw and compared it with carnivorous therapsids from the Karoo. Not until 1905 was *Bathygnathus* correctly interpreted as a sphenacodontid pelycosaur, similar to the familiar sail-backed *Dimetrodon* (Romer and Price 1940).

In the 1870s Cope described Dimetrodon and related forms that he grouped as the Pelycosauria (Cope 1878a). He noted their resemblance to Russian and South African therapsids and subsequently (Cope 1878b) united them all in the order Theromorpha (Greek for "beast form"), which, he suggested, was the ancestral group from which mammals were derived. He later advocated the derivation of mammals directly from pelycosaurs (Cope 1884),

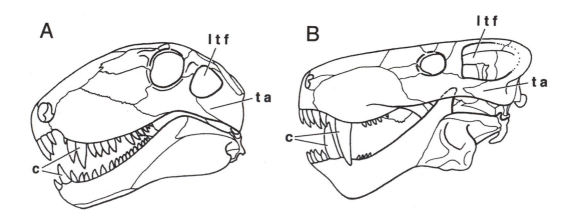

Figure 1. *A,* skull of a primitive synapsid, the Early Permian pelycosaur *Dimetrodon,* showing moderately enlarged canines and a small lateral temporal fenestra. *B,* skull of an early therapsid, the Late Permian gorgonopsian *Leontocephalus,* showing greatly enlarged canines and an expanded temporal fenestra. The temporal opening in the therapsid was filled with jaw-closing musculature, which attached around its rim. Abbreviations: *c,* canines; *ltf,* lateral temporal fenestra; *ta,* temporal arch. From Hopson (1994; by permission of the Paleontological Society).

even as evidence was mounting for their direct descent from therapsids (Osborn 1898).

The name "Synapsida" was created by H.F. Osborn (1903) for reptiles with a single temporal arch—that is, with a single bony bar below the temporal opening (Figure 1), as opposed to the two bars and two temporal openings seen in Diapsida (lizards, crocodiles, and their relatives). In his Synapsida Osborn included species that are now placed in the Therapsida (a name coined by Robert Broom in 1905), but, ignoring Cope's earlier association of pelycosaurs with therapsids, he placed the Pelycosauria in the Diapsida. However, R. Broom (1910) compared the skulls of pelycosaurs and therapsids and demonstrated that Cope was indeed correct.

Samuel W. Williston (1925) was the first to restrict the contents of the Synapsida to pelycosaurs and therapsids, a view that was universally accepted for the next 60 years (Carroll 1988). Then, in the mid–1980s, mammals were added to the Synapsida, thus making it strictly monophyletic.

Synapsid Diversity and Distribution in Time and Space

The most primitive (basal) synapsids of pelycosaurian grades were reptilian in their anatomy and presumed physiology. Members are placed in six families, with the Sphenacodontidae being most closely allied to the Therapsida. Pelycosaurs are first known from the Late Pennsylvanian of Nova Scotia, Canada (about 310 million years ago), and they are most diverse in the Early Permian (until about 275 million years ago), especially in the redbed deposits of the American Southwest. Two families survive into the early part of the Late Permian.

Non-mammalian therapsids span the anatomical, and presumably the physiological, range separating pelycosaurs from mammals. The group appears in the early part of the Late Permian (about 268 million years ago) of Russia and shortly thereafter in South Africa and China. Through the rest of the Permian and into the early part of the Middle Triassic (until about 240 million years ago), there is a continuous record of therapsids, primarily from the Karoo beds. During most of the Middle and Late Triassic, therapsids are well-represented in other parts of the world, particularly in South America, where a nearly continuous Triassic record occurs in Argentina. The oldest true mammals appear in the Late Triassic, about 225 million years ago. Early Jurassic faunas containing both mammals and non-mammalian therapsids are well represented in southern Africa, China, Western Europe, and southwestern United States. The last non-mammalian therapsids, the rodentlike tritylodontids, occur in the early Late Jurassic of China. Mesozoic mammalian faunas are discussed in the section on early mammals.

JAMES A. HOPSON

See also Pelycosaus; Therapsids

Works Cited

Broom, R. 1905. On the use of the term Anomodontia. *Records of the Albany Museum* 1:266–69.

———. 1910. A comparison of the Permian reptiles of North America with those of South Africa. *Bulletin of the American Museum of Natural History* 28:197–234.
Carroll, R.L. 1988. *Vertebrate Paleontology and Evolution.* New York: Freeman.
Cope, E.D. 1878a. Descriptions of extinct Batrachia and Reptilia from the Permian formations of Texas. *Proceedings of the American Philosophical Society* 17:505–30.
———. 1878b. The theromorphous Reptilia. *American Naturalist* 12:829–30.
———. 1884. The relations between the theromorphous reptiles and the monotreme Mammalia. *Proceedings of the American Association for the Advancement of Science* 33:471–82.
Hopson, J.A. 1987. The mammal-like reptiles: A study of transitional fossils. *American Biology Teacher* 49:16–26.
———. 1994. Synapsid evolution and the radiation of non-therian mammals. *In* D.R. Prothero and R.M. Schoch (eds.), *Major Features of Vertebrate Evolution* (Short Courses in Paleontology, no. 7). Knoxville: University of Tennessee Press.
Hopson, J.A., and H.R. Barghusen. 1986. An analysis of therapsid relationships. *In* N. Hotton III, P.D. MacLean, J.J. Roth, and E.C. Roth (eds.), *The Ecology and Biology of Mammal-Like Reptiles.* Washington, D.C.: Smithsonian Institution Press; London, 1987.
Leidy, J. 1854. On *Bathygnathus borealis,* an extinct saurian of the New Red Sandstone of Prince Edward's Island. *American Journal of Science,* ser. 2, 19:444–46.
Osborn, H.F. 1898. The origin of the Mammalia. *American Naturalist* 32:309–34.
———. 1903. The reptilian subclasses Diapsida and Synapsida and the early history of the Diaptosauria. *Memoire of the American Museum of Natural History* 1:449–507.
Owen, R. 1860. On the orders of fossil and recent Reptilia, and their distribution in time. *Report of the British Association for the Advancement of Science* (29th meeting, 1859). London: British Association for the Advancement of Science.
———. 1876a. Evidence of a carnivorous reptile (*Cynodraco major,* Ow.) about the size of a lion, with remarks thereon. *Quarterly Journal of the Geological Society of London* 32:95–102.
———. 1876b. Evidences of theriodonts in Permian deposits elsewhere than in South Africa. *Quarterly Journal of the Geological Society of London* 32:352–63.
Romer, A.S. 1966. *Vertebrate Paleontology.* 3rd ed., Chicago: University of Chicago Press.
Romer, A.S., and L.I. Price. 1940. Review of the Pelycosauria. *Special Papers of the Geological Society of America* 28:1–538; New York: Arnop, 1980.
Williston, S.W. 1925. *The Osteology of the Reptiles.* Cambridge, Massachusetts: Harvard University Press.

Further Reading

Aulie, R.P. 1974–75. The origin of the idea of the mammal-like reptile. *American Biology Teacher* 36:476–85, 545–53; 37:21–32.
Bowler, P.J. 1996. *Life's Splendid Drama.* Chicago: University of Chicago Press.
Hopson, J.A. 1987. The mammal-like reptiles: A study of transitional fossils. *American Biology Teacher* 49:16–26.
———. 1994. Synapsid evolution and the radiation of non-therian mammals. *In* D.R. Prothero and R.M. Schoch (eds.), *Major Features of Vertebrate Evolution.* Short Courses in Paleontology, no. 7. Knoxville: University of Tennessee Press.

SYSTEMATICS

Systematics is the science of the diversity of organisms and all relationships between them. Its core consists of taxonomy, or the science of biological classification, but systematics also includes determining evolutionary relationships (phylogeny) and determining geographic relationships (biogeography). A systematist uses the comparative approach to the diversity of life to understand all patterns and relationships that explain how life came to be the way it is. Systematics deals with such questions as these: How are species grouped into larger categories? How are classification schemes set up, and what do they mean? Systematics is more than just naming and describing new species, because species and higher taxa reflect evolution. Systematists are interested in comparing different species, deciding how they are related, and ultimately in deciphering their evolutionary history. This perspective looks at the diversity of organisms in time and space and tries to understand the large-scale patterns of nature. Systematists look at the present and past geographic distributions of organisms and try to determine how they got there. In short, systematics involves looking at the total pattern of natural diversity and trying to understand how it came to be.

Systematics provides the framework of understanding and interconnection upon which all the rest of biology and paleobiology are based. Without it, each organism is a random particle in space, and what we learn about it has no relevance to anything else in the living world. One of the most important issues on this planet today—biodiversity—is within the domain of systematics.

Taxonomy

There are many ways to classify things. Some classification schemes attempt to have a logical basis or structure to make them easier to use. For a long time, the Dewey Decimal system was the most widely used means of cataloging books, until it was replaced in many libraries by the Library of Congress system. Both try to cluster books by natural groups (such as a category for science books, which then are subdivided into physics, chemistry, biology, geology, and so on), but the Library of Congress system apparently is more flexible at handling larger numbers of books. Both natural classification schemes attempt to organize the same array of objects, but apparently one is more successful than the other.

Modern classification techniques began with the Swedish botanist Carolus Linnaeus (1707–78). His *Systema Naturae, Regnum Animale* (the system of nature, animal kingdom) was first published in 1735, and its tenth edition (1758) is now regarded as the starting point of modern systematic zoology. As thousands of new species were described since 1758, Linnaeus' original classification became outdated, but his fundamental system still is used. Each species is given a binomen (two-part name), consisting of the genus name (always italicized or underlined, and always capitalized) and the trivial name indicating the species (always italicized or underlined but never capitalized). For example, our genus is *Homo* (Latin, *human*) and our trivial name is

sapiens (Latin, *thinking*), so our species name is *Homo sapiens* (abbreviated *H. sapiens*). The trivial name can never stand by itself (as they are repeated over and over in taxonomy), but must always accompany its genus. To prevent confusion, a species name can never be used for any other organism in the same kingdom, and a genus name can only be used to name species that are closely related (there are few generic names that are reused for different animals and plants).

Genera then are grouped into higher categories, such as the family (always capitalized, but never underlined or italicized, and with the "-idae" ending in animals, the "-aceae" ending in plants), then orders, classes, divisions (for plants) or phyla (for animals), and kingdoms. For example, humans are members of the Kingdom Animalia (there are also kingdoms for plants, fungi, and single-celled organisms), the Phylum Chordata (including all other backboned animals), the Class Mammalia (mammals), the Order Primates (including lemurs, monkeys, apes, and ourselves), the Family Hominidae (including our own genus and the extinct *Australopithecus, Ardipithecus,* and *Paranthropus*), the genus *Homo* (including other extinct species such as *Homo habilis* and *H. erectus*), and our species *H. sapiens.*

The Linnaean classification scheme is hierarchical. Each rank is grouped into larger ranks, so that there may be several species in a genus, several genera in a family, and so on. The reason for the success of Linnaeus' scheme is this flexibility inherent in clustering groups hierarchically—there is infinite room for expansion as new species are discovered. The Latinized binomen is also very flexible and is universally recognizable in science. Universal terms are important in communication. Local vernacular names in a single language may vary greatly. For instance, in English the word "gopher" refers to both a tortoise and a burrowing rodent, and every other language uses completely different names for the same animals. But in all languages, the scientific name always is based on Latin or Greek (since these were the languages of scholars in Linnaeus' time) or on a Latinized version of other words. A scientist can pick up a publication in some unfamiliar (to most scientists) alphabet, such as Cyrillic or Hebrew or Chinese, and not recognize a word except the scientific names. These universal terms stand out and can communicate the essential content of the paper.

To Charles Darwin, clustering organisms into groups within groups to form a hierarchical, nested, branching structure of life only made sense if life had descended from common ancestry in a branching fashion. Darwin transformed the goals of classification from an arbitrary system of arranging things into pigeonholes to a system that also had evolutionary meaning. Taxonomists were trying to create natural groups that reflected evolutionary history, not just convenience. Although these goals are not contradictory, they do not always agree, either. Some taxonomists view organisms of similar descent and ecology, such as the fishes, as a formal group, "Pisces." But in evolutionary terms, not all fish are created equal. Lungfishes, for example, are related more closely to four-legged land vertebrates (tetrapods) than they are to a shark or a tuna. In other words, a lungfish and a cow are related more closely to each other than a lungfish and a tuna. Here we see a clear tension between ecological groupings, or evolutionary grades, such as "fish," and natural evolutionary lineages, or "clades," such as the lungfish-tetrapod group (known as the Sarcopterygii). Which is better? The different priorities and goals of taxonomists has led to much debate over the proper methods of classification.

What is the proper way to classify organisms? That question had been the center of a very intense scientific debate since the 1960s. As D. Hull (1988) points out, the debate reveals almost as much about the sociology of science as it does about the science itself. In the late 1950s, there was relatively little argument, since the majority of taxonomists practiced a vaguely formulated method later called "evolutionary taxonomy," exemplified by G.G. Simpson's (1961) *Principles of Animal Taxonomy* or E. Mayr's (1966) *Principles of Systematic Zoology.* This mainstream, orthodox school of taxonomy was challenged by two upstarts in the 1960s and 1970s, "phenetics" (or numerical taxonomy) and "cladistics" (or phylogenetic taxonomy). Both schools of thought followed very different basic assumptions and used new jargon to distinguish themselves from the old style of classification. Sometimes practitioners took very extreme positions, so that they could be seen as different and not be absorbed into the mainstream as a minor variant. Later practitioners may have moderated those extremes as the controversies died down, but such positions were important in the early phases of the movements.

Phenetics

Numerical taxonomy was precipitated by several factors: the availability of the first practical computers; an increase in interest in statistical methods, and a widespread dissatisfaction with conventional taxonomy as being an intuitive, arbitrary "art" that was only valid and reproducible in the mind of the taxonomist. To get away from this subjectivity, the numerical taxonomists argued that classification should be a purely objective, statistical exercise that can be coded and deciphered by a computer. Numerical taxonomists concluded that since classifications cannot reflect both evolutionary history and degree of overall similarity, we should forget trying to make our classifications reflect historic relationships and instead base them on objective statistical similarities and differences, or overall phenetic similarity. These scientists judged a "natural" classification by how successfully it clusters groups with the most in common and how well it creates stable classification schemes that are maximally useful to scientists. Typically, this is accomplished by measuring and coding numerous anatomical features, or "characters," in each specimen or taxon (called "OTUs," or "operational taxonomic units") to create a large data matrix of OTUs versus characters. Next, a computer program sorts the data and finds clusters of OTUs that have the most characters in common. When the computer analysis is finished, a branching diagram of similarity is produced.

A few years after numerical taxonomy became popular, it went into decline. The majority of systematists never accepted the fundamental goals of phenetics. Most still wanted classification to reflect evolutionary relationships in some way, even if this was a difficult task. The most serious blows came when a number of

studies showed that the "objectivity" of phenetics was a myth. No one can code and weigh the importance of the characters in the data matrix objectively. When one systematist decides that a wing represents a single character state and another subdivides it into numerous character states, which approach is correct? Once again, the "art" of systematic judgment comes into play. Ultimately, taxonomists must decide what is a character, and that decision is filtered through their own prejudices. Even more serious were studies that showed that the same data matrix gave different results with different computer programs—occasionally even with the same computer program. If the methods were not truly objective and reproducible and, at the same time, gave up on the whole idea of evolutionary classification, then what was the advantage? If a purely phenetic classification placed unrelated animals such as whales and fish together, then what good was it?

Cladistics

The other primary reason for the decline of phenetics was competition from an even more radical school of systematics, cladistics. In many ways, cladistic methods are the opposite extreme from phenetics. Rather than abandoning the evolutionary meaning behind taxonomy, cladists argued that classification should reflect *only* evolutionary history and ignore overall phenetic similarity. Rather than throwing all the characters, unweighted, into a computer, cladists argued that not all characters are created equal. The only characters that are useful in a given problem are those that are shared evolutionary novelties, or shared derived characters ("synapomorphies," in cladistic terminology). For example, the presence of hair and mammary glands is a shared specialization of all mammals, unique to them and found nowhere else in the animal kingdom. Those characters are "synapomorphies" that help define the taxon Mammalia. Characters such as the presence of four limbs, or a backbone, would not be very useful in distinguishing mammals from other vertebrates, because they are found in reptiles, birds, and amphibians; they are shared primitive characters (they predate the origin of these various groups), or "symplesiomorphies." Taxa are recognized and defined only by their unique evolutionary novelties. Characters already found in their near relatives and ancestors are considered "primitive" and, therefore, irrelevant to the problem of the evolutionary relationships within their group.

Whether a character is primitive or derived depends upon how it is used. For example, within the Mammalia, hair and mammary glands are the primitive state; scholars cannot use them to decide the relationships of different groups of mammals. If a systematist wanted to find shared derived characters that unite monkeys, apes, and humans, he or she would use unique specializations, such as the opposable thumb and stereovision, not primitive features found in all other mammals, such as hair and mammary glands. This means that hair and mammary glands are derived characters at the level of Class Mammalia, where they can be used to distinguish between it and other related groups such as Class Reptilia; at the level of the orders and families within the Mammalia, however, these characters are primitive.

To analyze these characters, the systematist draws a branching diagram known as a "cladogram" (Figure 1). At the tip of each

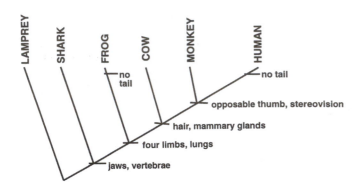

Figure 1. Cladogram showing the evolutionary relationships of some vertebrates. The unique evolutionary novelties, or "shared derived characters" ("synapomorphies"), that support these relationships are shown on the branching points (nodes) of the cladogram.

branch are the taxa, and the branching geometry shows which taxa are related more closely to each other. In Figure 1, the cladogram shows that monkeys and humans are related more closely to each other than either is to anything else in the diagram. Monkeys, humans, and cows, as mammals, are related more closely to each other than they are to any non-mammal. Frogs, cows, monkeys, and humans, as four-legged tetrapods, are related more closely to each other than they are to any non-tetrapod, such as a shark. Notice that the fork of each branch (the node) represents the common ancestor of the organisms at the tip of the branch, and the node (where lines separate) is defined by the shared derived characters that unite those taxa. For example, opposable thumbs and stereovision are derived characters that define the node uniting monkeys and humans; hair and mammary glands are derived characters that define the node Mammalia; the presence of derived characters such as four legs and lungs define the tetrapods and distinguish them from other vertebrates.

Cladogram Construction

How is a cladogram constructed? Typically, the systematist sets up a data matrix of characters and taxa, just as in phenetics. However, instead of relying on the computer to cluster these characters for overall similarity, the cladist evaluates each character and decides which state is primitive and which is derived. The best way to do this is to examine more primitive relatives, known as outgroups, and see what character state they possess. For example, hair and mammary glands are not found in mammal outgroups such as the frog, shark, or lamprey; therefore, these features are derived for the mammals. The absence of four limbs, lungs, or hands and feet instead of fins (as found in sharks and lamprey) shows that those characters are derived for tetrapods. Once the derived character states have been decided upon, then the systematist (or a computer) clusters only the derived character states to see which taxa have the most shared specializations in common and which have fewer. Ideally, this process generates a branching cladogram.

Sometimes there are several possible character states within an array of organisms. For example, the anatomy of the digestive tract of vertebrates ranges from the simple tubelike gut of some fish, to those with complex spiral intestines (as in sharks), to guts with a separate stomach and intestines (as in most vertebrates), to highly complex digestive tracts with a four-part stomach (as in ruminants, such as cows and sheep). This spectrum of morphologies forms a morphocline of character states. Although, in this case, it seems obvious which is the primitive or derived end of the morphocline, in most cases it is not so apparent. Cladists use a variety of criteria (such as outgroup comparison, or developmental transformation series) to identify the primitive and the derived characteristics in a morphocline.

Although a cladogram superficially looks like an evolutionary tree, it is not. A cladogram shows a nested pattern of evolutionary specializations within diverse taxa. It works with any three or more taxa, no matter how distant their relationships. (A family tree works only with immediate ancestors and descendants.) The nodes in a cladogram summarize the derived character states of the hypothetical common ancestor, not real ancestors. Cladists avoid naming real ancestors for several reasons. Because the fossil record is so incomplete, it is very unlikely that we actually have a true ancestor. Another problem is that ancestors have nothing but primitive character states compared to their descendants. It is impossible to tell if a potentially ancestral fossil was truly an ancestor, because it has no unique evolutionary specializations that link it with another taxon. At a more fundamental level, cladists abhor searching for ancestors because this search emphasizes primitive characters and may ignore important derived characters. In many cases, troubling long-standing phylogenetic problems were solved when the systematists stopped looking for ancestors and instead discovered a remarkable pattern of shared derived similarities that long had been neglected. Instead of ancestors and descendants, cladograms show only that two taxa are closely related sister groups. For example, monkeys and humans are sister groups, compared to cows or other non-primates.

Therefore, a cladogram is simply a branching diagram of relationships, supported by unique shared derived characters states. This arrangement makes no statements about ancestry. This minimalist approach to systematics has a major advantage: it is testable. Each cladogram is a scientific hypothesis; to test it, the systematist can look at additional character states or additional taxa (especially more outgroups). Cladists find this very appealing, because one of their central philosophical tenets is that all science must be testable. Family trees with ancestors may be more interesting, but because there is no way of testing their more complicated hypotheses and assumptions, these trees fall outside this narrow definition of science.

One of the great advantages of the cladistic method is that it provides a simple, straightforward set of rules that any systematist can follow, and each phylogenetic hypothesis can be tested immediately and rejected if better data emerge. In the old school of "evolutionary taxonomy," on the other hand, phylogenetic trees had no characters at the nodes, so they could not be tested. Trees came out of the intuition and experience of the systematist, and since there was no way of evaluating them or seeing how they were constructed or supported, there was no way to criticize them. In a cladogram, it is apparent immediately if there are few or no derived characters to support a node. If the characters have been incorrectly coded or evaluated, that too is clear. Systematists can no longer hide behind the foggy obscurity of phylogenetic trees but have to suffer immediate criticism if their work does not hold up. A lot of early cladograms were overturned, but eventually, as fewer and fewer problems were found, the cladograms began to converge upon consistent and often surprising answers to long-standing phylogenetic problems.

Construction Difficulties

If nature were ideally cooperative, all character data matrices would give a single, unique cladogram of life, and there would be no doubts. But the real world is much more complex than this. Although life has had a single evolutionary pathway, character states have changed more than once, and in confusing ways— sometimes they have reverted back to the ancestral state. In Figure 1, for example, humans and frogs could be united by the loss of a tail. If we were basing our cladogram on just that one character, humans and frogs would be related more closely than humans and monkeys. However, many more characters support human-monkey relationships, so it is simpler (or more parsimonious) to suggest that humans and frogs independently and secondarily have lost their tails (especially since both have tails in their embryonic state). The loss of a tail is considered an evolutionary convergence. Convergence occurs when a characteristic evolves in two or more groups independently.

The criterion of simplicity, or parsimony, may not work in every case, but most problems are resolved without too many conflicts of this type. This concept is especially useful when a difficult problem appears. For example, a superficial analysis might suggest that whales, ichthyosaurs (marine reptiles), and fish share many similarities, such as fins, a paddle tail, a streamlined body, and other features related to swimming in water. But a more detailed analysis incorporating nonaquatic animals would find many more shared derived features (mostly concerning internal anatomy, which is unrelated to swimming) that overwhelmingly show that whales are mammals, ichthyosaurs are reptiles, and fish are more primitive than either. All of their phenetic similarities are due to convergence.

When cladistics burst upon the scene in the early 1970s, paleontologists were among the harshest critics. The denial of ancestors certainly alienated them, as did another extreme claim: stratigraphic order (the order in which fossils are found in rock strata) is of no relevance when deciding whether a character is primitive or derived. Most cladists felt that the stratigraphic record was too full of gaps, and that fossils were too incomplete, to ever use them reliably in determining derived character states (Schaeffer et al. 1972; Patterson 1981). This extreme position was partly a response to previous generations of paleontologists, who stacked fossils in stratigraphic order and "connected the dots" without conducting any independent anatomical analysis of the character states.

In some ways, the cladists were correct. It is true that there are many gaps in the fossil record. Some fossil species may appear earlier than their presumed ancestor. And most fossils are much less complete than living specimens for the purposes of phylogenetic analysis. As a result, since these initial debates, a number of paleontologists (Fortey and Jefferies 1982; Lazarus and Prothero 1984; Huelsenbeck 1994; Smith 1994; Hitchin and Benton 1997; Huelsenbeck and Rannala 1997) have developed methods of rigorously analyzing stratigraphic data so they can be incorporated into a cladistic analysis with some degree of testability. One such method is called "stratocladistics" (Fisher 1994; Clyde and Fisher 1997). It uses probability methods to assess the reliability of stratigraphic sequence of fossils, as well as the reliability of the character polarities.

Cladistics and Classification

Many traditional systematists agree that cladistics is an effective method for inferring phylogenetic relationships but draw the line at another issue: cladistic classification. As we mentioned earlier, some cladists argue that classification should be a strict reflection of phylogeny and nothing else. Once the branching sequence has been determined, it dictates the ranks and clustering of higher taxa. Although traditional evolutionary systematists also try to reflect phylogeny in classification, they mix in a bit of ecology and phenetic divergence as well. For example, a cladist might say that since birds are descended from theropod dinosaurs, they should be a subgroup within the Theropoda. Traditional taxonomists argue that since birds have undergone a huge evolutionary radiation (diversification and geographic spread), with their own specialized ecological niches, they deserve their own higher rank, Class Aves. A traditional classification (Figure 2) divides the vertebrates into five or more classes of equal rank: birds, mammals, reptiles, amphibians, and one or more classes of fishes. The cladistic classification is not nearly as simple, since it requires multiple ranks of taxa to reflect the fact that birds are descendants of reptiles, reptiles are lower-ranking taxon within amphibians, amphibians within lobe-finned fishes, and so on.

Figure 3 shows the cladogram of higher primates. There is little disagreement over the geometry of their relationships. Traditionally, the human-ape clade was divided into two families: the Hominidae for ourselves, and the Pongidae for all the nonhuman apes. This classification scheme reflected both the huge divergence between ourselves and the rest of the apes and also our own egotism and anthropocentrism. Such distinctions are unacceptable to a strict cladist. The Hominidae are a natural group with shared derived characters that support it (a monophyletic group), but the Pongidae becomes a "wastebasket" taxon of all the apes that don't happen to be human. The Pongidae have some shared derived characters (such as the loss of a tail) that define them (but so do hominids). As long as Hominidae is a separate but equal family, the Pongidae is defined partially by the lack of the characters that define Hominidae. In cladistic terms, a group that does not include all its descendants is a paraphyletic group, defined by the absence of synapomorphies.

There are many such unnatural, wastebasket groups in classification schemes, such as the "invertebrates" (defined by the

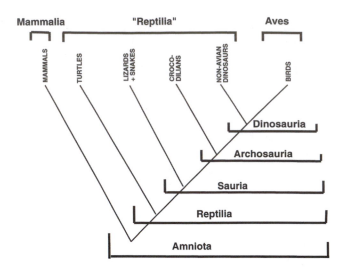

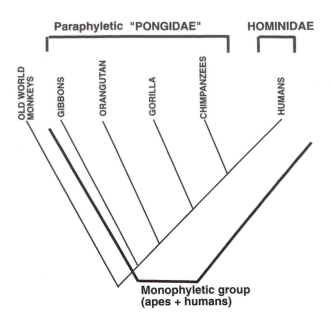

Figure 2. Different ways of classifying the same groups of organisms. *Top brackets,* traditional classifications emphasize the large morphological divergence and explosive evolutionary radiations of birds and mammals. The two are placed in their own classes, equal in rank to the rest of the amniotes, which are lumped in the paraphyletic "Reptilia." *Bottom brackets,* a cladistic classification does not permit mixing of phylogeny with other factors, such as evolutionary divergence. Instead, each group is monophyletic and defined strictly by evolutionary branching sequence. In this view, birds are a subgroup of dinosaurs, archosaurs, saurians, and reptiles.

Figure 3. Traditional classifications emphasize the differences between humans and other apes by placing humans in a separate family Hominidae and placing the rest of the apes in a paraphyletic wastebasket taxon "Pongidae." To a cladist, humans must be included in the group that includes the apes. This could mean expanding the Hominidae to include all the apes, or placing the Hominidae within the Pongidae.

absence of a derived character, the vertebral column) (Figure 4). If Reptilia does not include birds, then Reptilia is paraphyletic. If Amphibia does not include all higher vertebrates descended from them, then Amphibia becomes paraphyletic—and so on. In rare cases, taxa converge from very different parts of the cladogram and might be put in a group together, forming a polyphyletic group (Figure 5). These are clearly unnatural, and few systematists would defend them once their polyphyly is revealed.

Once again, this debate is not merely an argument over semantics; it represents two fundamentally different ways of looking at the world. Traditional systematists don't mind mixing a little bit of ecology or phenetics into the classification, such as when they place Class Aves in an equal rank with Class Reptilia; in such a case, the evolutionary relationship is no longer apparent in the classification. Cladists say that mixing two or more data types in the classification is confusing. How can the nonspecialist recognize which groups are strictly based on phylogeny (monophyletic) and which ones mix phylogeny with ecology (paraphyletic or polyphyletic)? Traditional systematists complain that the larger, more cumbersome classification schemes demanded by cladistics are harder to learn than the simple, parallel taxa of equal rank in the old system. But cladists would argue that if the old system was a confusing and inconsistent mixture of natural and unnatural groups, why are we using it in the first place?

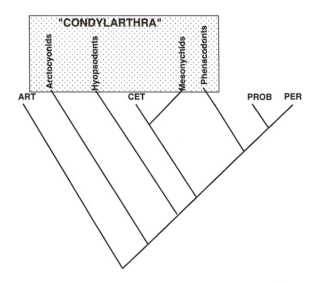

Figure 4. The taxon "Condylarthra" (shaded box) was long used as a wastebasket for all extinct hoofed mammals that clearly were not members of living orders. It is an example of a polyphyletic group, because it includes many different groups of hoofed mammals with widely different origins. These include the primitive arctocyonids and hyposodonts, the mesonychids (which are closer to whales), and the phenacodonts (which are closer to horses, rhinos, and elephants). Key: *Art,* artiodactyls (even-toed hoofed mammals); *Cet,* cetaceans (whales); *Prob,* proboscideans (elephants); *Per,* perissodactyls (odd-toed hoofed mammals).

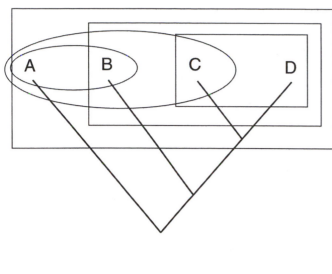

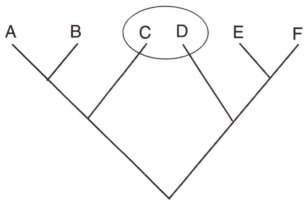

Figure 5. A "monophyletic group" includes all the descendants of a common ancestor, while a "paraphyletic group" excludes some of those descendants. *Top,* monophyletic groups, outlined by rectangles, include all descendants of a common ancestor; paraphyletic groups (in ovals) exclude at least one descendant (group D). *Bottom,* a "polyphyletic taxon" is composed of taxa from two or more unrelated lineages. In the lower figure, the grouping of C and D is polyphyletic, since these two groups are from very different lineages.

Conclusion

Although the 1960s and 1970s were marked by noisy controversies over systematics, since about the mid–1980s most systematists have followed cladistic methods in determining evolutionary relationships. The classification of organisms, however, has not changed to reflect this new systematic philosophy. Many biologists and paleontologists still prefer to use convenient but unnatural groups, such as "fishes," "amphibians," "reptiles," "apes" (as conventionally defined), and have not yet abandoned these terms for those representing natural monophyletic clades, such as "gnathostomes," "tetrapods," "amniotes," "archosaurs" that would replace them in a cladistic classification. In part, this resistance is owing to inertia and familiarity with the old system. Also, the current generation of biologists does not wish to surrender the convenience of

paraphyletic groups that are composite of both phylogeny and ecology for groups that do not serve their purposes as well. However, in some parts of the animal kingdom, cladistic classification is now the accepted norm, so the next generation of biologists may find the rigor of cladistic classification preferable to the established tradition and convenience of the older classification schemes (de Queiroz and Gauthier 1992, 1994).

DONALD R. PROTHERO

See also Adaptation; Diversity; Evolutionary Novelty; Evolutionary Theory; Homology; Speciation and Morphological Change

Works Cited

Clyde, W.C., and D.C. Fisher. 1997. Comparing the fit of stratigraphic and morphologic data in phylogenetic analysis. *Paleobiology* 23:1–19.
de Queiroz, K., and J. Gauthier. 1992. Phylogenetic taxonomy. *Annual Reviews of Ecology and Systematics* 23:449–80.
———. 1994. Toward a phylogenetic system of biological nomenclature. *Trends in Ecology and Evolution* 9:27–31.
Fisher, D.C. 1994. Stratocladistics: Morphological and temporal patterns and their relation to phylogenetic process. *In* L. Grande and O. Rieppel (eds.), *Interpreting the Hierarchy of Nature*. San Diego, California: Academic Press.
Fortey, R.A., and R.P.S. Jefferies. 1982. Fossils and phylogeny: A compromise approach. *Systematics Association Special Volume* 21:197–234.
Hitchin, R., and M.J. Benton. 1997. Congruence between parsimony and stratigraphy: Comparisons of three indices. *Paleobiology* 23:20–32.
Huelsenbeck, J.P. 1994. Comparing the stratigraphic record to estimates of phylogeny. *Paleobiology* 20:470–83.
Huelsenbeck, J.P., and B. Rannala. 1997. Maximum likelihood estimation of phylogeny using stratigraphic data. *Paleobiology* 23:174–80.
Hull, D. 1988. *Science as a Process*. Chicago: University of Chicago Press.
Lazarus, D.B., and D.R. Prothero. 1984. The role of stratigraphic and morphologic data in phylogeny reconstruction. *Journal of Paleontology* 58:163–72.
Mayr, E. 1969. *Principles of Systematic Zoology*. New York: McGraw-Hill.
Patterson, C. 1981. Significance of fossils in determining evolutionary relationships. *Annual Review of Ecology and Systematics* 12:195–223.
Schaeffer, B., M.K. Hecht, and N. Eldredge. 1972. Phylogeny and paleontology. *Evolutionary Biology* 6:31–46.
Simpson, G.G. 1961. *Principles of Animal Taxonomy*. New York: Columbia University Press.
Smith, A.B. 1994. *Systematics and the Fossil Record: Documenting Evolutionary Patterns*. Oxford and Cambridge, Massachusetts: Blackwell Scientific.

Further Reading

Eldredge, N., and J. Cracraft. 1980. *Phylogenetic Patterns and the Evolutionary Process*. New York: Columbia University Press.
Hennig, W. 1966. *Phylogenetic Systematics*. Urbana: University of Illinois Press.

Hull, D. 1988. *Science as a Process.* Chicago: University of Chicago Press.

Mayr, E. 1969. *Principles of Systematic Zoology.* New York: McGraw-Hill; 2nd ed., E. Mayr and P.D. Ashlock (eds.), 1991.

Padian, K., D.R. Lindberg, and P.D. Polly. 1994. Cladistics and the fossil record—the uses of history. *Annual Reviews of Earth and Planetary Sciences* 22:63–91.

Schoch, R.M. 1986. *Phylogeny Reconstruction in Paleontology.* New York: Van Nostrand Reinhold.

Simpson, G.G. 1961. *Principles of Animal Taxonomy.* New York: Columbia University Press.

Smith, A.B. 1994. *Systematics and the Fossil Record: Documenting Evolutionary Patterns.* Oxford and Cambridge, Massachusetts: Blackwell Scientific.

Sokal, R.R., and P.H.A. Sneath. 1963. *Principles of Numerical Taxonomy.* San Francisco: Freeman.

Wiley, E.O. 1981. *Phylogenetics: The Theory and Practice of Phylogenetic Systematics.* New York: Wiley.

Wiley, E.O., D. Siegel-Causey, D.R. Brooks, and V.A. Funk. 1991. *The Compleat Cladist: A Primer of Phylogenetic Procedures.* University of Kansas Museum of Natural History Special Publication, 19. Lawrence: University of Kansas Press.

T

TAPHONOMY

The science of taphonomy is still in its infancy. The term taphonomy was coined by I.A. Efremov (1940) from the Greek *tajoz* (*taphos,* meaning burial) and *nomoz* (*nomos,* meaning laws). However, the foundations of modern taphonomic research were laid down with the foundations of paleontology. When describing fossil organisms, most paleontologists made observations and formulated theories on how the organisms might have become fossils. These early workers focused on interpreting fossil deposits in terms of postmortem processes that were observable in the modern natural environment. Many of these studies were performed in Germany between the two world wars, including the monographic works by J. Weigelt (1989) and R. Richter (1928) on the death, decay, disarticulation, and burial of vertebrate carcasses. It was Richter (1928) who coined the term *"aktuopaläontologie"* ("actual paleontology") for the study of postmortem processes on modern organisms and their relevance to the form of fossil assemblages. This concept of the present being the key to the past is known as uniformitarianism and is still regarded as one of the key parameters in taphonomic research.

However, taphonomy was not recognized as a separate study until after the defining work of Efremov (1940). Efremov recognized that diagenetic factors, as well as biostratinomic effects (transport and burial processes) and necrolytic effects (postmortem decay and disarticulation), also bore relevance to fossil accumulations. Much of the work undertaken from the 1950s to the 1970s analyzed the effects of taphonomic bias or losses in the fossil record and investigated how to compensate for such processes in paleoecological reconstructions.

Actualistic studies became fashionable in the late 1960s and 1970s, especially with the onset of the ideas that taphonomy potentially could make a contribution to both archaeological and paleontological research. Investigations included work on transportation, disarticulation, and weathering of modern animal skeletons (e.g., Behrensmeyer and Hill 1980). However, it is important to note that most of these studies refer to large mammalian vertebrate remains. The period from the 1950s to the 1970s also saw the application of statistical techniques to taphonomic investigations, including the estimates of original numbers of living organisms and the modeling of large-scale biases in the fossil record.

For a more comprehensive review of the early literature of taphonomic research, the reader is directed to papers in Donovan (1991) and Allison and Briggs (1991), and specifically for vertebrate taphonomy, Shipman (1981), Behrensmeyer and Hill (1980), and Lyman (1994).

Over the 1980s and 1990s the number of taphonomic studies has grown exponentially. In most cases paleontological investigations are not considered to be complete without some mention of preservational styles and possible taphonomic histories (e.g., Davis 1996). Indeed, it was in the mid-1980s that the concept of fossils possessing a taphonomic history was first defined, although preliminary schemes were illustrated as early as the mid-1960s. Taphonomic histories are now understood to be complex and cumulative: the effects of a late taphonomic process upon a fossil are often related to those that had occurred early in its history. It also has been recognized that a taphonomic history may be determined by lifestyle considerations, for example the preference of certain habitats or diets (Shipman 1981).

Most modern taphonomic studies focus on the positive contributions that fossils and fossil assemblages can provide to our understanding of the biotic record, rather than being solely concerned with taphonomic losses. Specific topics being researched include taphonomy's contribution to our knowledge of past ecosystems, depositional environments, the interaction of organisms and sediments, time-averaging and relative rates of sedimentation, and processes of fossilization.

Many modern taphonomic studies rely heavily on actualistic observational, experimental, and analytical approaches. They also incorporate sedimentological and stratigraphic data, providing information about depositional environment and burial profiles. Experimental studies have included analyses of mechanical rounding and sorting by transport in simulated fluvial (river or stream) or marine conditions. Other studies have included observations on the decay of organisms under strict laboratory settings or closely monitored natural conditions (e.g., Davis and Briggs 1995, 1998). There has been a plethora of taphonomic theories based upon observations of hard-part modification by predation and scavenging, biogenic corrosion (Davis 1997), and the effects of weathering and trampling. Some of these studies have incorporated experimental investigations in order to demonstrate the processes leading to the formation of fossil concentrations. Understanding the processes of post-burial modification and eventual fossilization has become a major theme of research in the 1990s, with experimental techniques being pioneered in understanding processes such as phosphatization, pyritization, charring, and calcification of organisms.

The scope of some of these studies is often quite limited, taxonomically or in terms of the variables used to define a certain taphonomic parameter, and they can be rather simplistic in the application of results from laboratory or controlled experiments to the fossil record. For instance, much of the research concerning disarticulation, transport, and abrasion of vertebrate remains in fluvial regimes was carried out upon large mammalian skeletons and cannot be applied readily to accumulations of extinct non-mammalian microvertebrates. Other studies rely heavily upon uniformitarianism. For example, understanding and recognition of modern predator activity is extremely useful, but how relevant is it to extinct faunas? The concepts and problems in applying actualistic procedures are further discussed and reviewed in detail by R.L. Lyman (1994).

PAUL G. DAVIS

See also Biomass and Productivity Estimates; Fossilization Processes; Fossil Record; Mortality and Survivorship; Sedimentology

Works Cited

Allison, P.A., and Briggs, D.E.G. (eds.). 1991. *Taphonomy: Releasing the Data Locked in the Fossil Record.* Topics in Geobiology, 9. New York: Plenum.

Behrensmeyer, A.K., and A.P. Hill (eds.). 1980. *Fossils in the Making: Vertebrate Taphonomy and Paleoecology.* Chicago: University of Chicago Press.

Davis, P.G. 1996. The taphonomy of *Archaeopteryx lithographica. Bulletin of the National Science Museum,* ser. C (Geology and Palaeontology), 22 (3–4):91–106.

———. 1997. The bioerosion of bird bones. *International Journal of Osteoarchaeology* 7:388–401.

Davis, P.G., and D.E.G. Briggs. 1995. The fossilization of feathers. *Geology* 23 (9):783–86.

———. 1998. The impact of decay and disarticulation on the preservation of fossil birds. *Palaios* 13 (1):3–13.

Donovan, S.K. (ed.). 1991. *The Processes of Fossilization.* New York: Columbia University Press.

Efremov, I.A. 1940. Taphonomy: A new branch of palaeontology. *Pan-American Geologist* 74:81–93.

Lyman, R.L. 1994. *Vertebrate Taphonomy.* Cambridge Manuals in Archaeology. Cambridge and New York: Cambridge University Press.

Richter, R. 1928. Aktuopaläontologie und paläobiologie, eine Abgrenzung. *Senkenbergiana* 19.

Shipman, P. 1981. *Life History of a Fossil: An Introduction to Taphonomy and Paleoecology.* Cambridge, Massachusetts: Harvard University Press.

Weigelt, J. 1989. *Recent Vertebrate Carcases and Their Palaeobiological Implications.* Chicago: University of Chicago Press; as *Rezente Wirbeltierleichen und ihre paläobiologische Bedeutung,* Leipzig: Weg, 1927.

Further Reading

Allison, P.A., and Briggs, D.E.G. (eds.). 1991. *Taphonomy: Releasing the Data Locked in the Fossil Record.* Topics in Geobiology, 9. New York: Plenum.

Behrensmeyer, A.K., and A.P. Hill (eds.). 1980. *Fossils in the Making: Vertebrate Taphonomy and Paleoecology.* Chicago: University of Chicago Press.

Donovan, S.K. (ed.). 1990. *The Processes of Fossilization.* New York: Columbia University Press.

Lyman, R.L. 1994. *Vertebrate Taphonomy.* Cambridge Manuals in Archaeology. Cambridge: Cambridge University Press.

Shipman, P. 1981. *Life History of a Fossil: An Introduction to Taphonomy and Paleoecology.* Cambridge, Massachusetts: Harvard University Press.

TEETH: CLASSIFICATION OF TEETH

Before considering the various terms used to classify and describe the teeth of vertebrates, it is first pertinent to consider what constitutes a tooth. The need for a strict definition arises because the histologies (minute structures) of teeth and mineralized dermal scales of fishes are indistinguishable. In fact, in some groups, such as some ray-finned fishes, cartilaginous fishes, and some fossil jawless fishes, the oral cavity is lined with scales that have toothlike functions. The most common distinction between teeth and scales is that teeth only occur within a jaw, although many fossil fish exhibit a gradual transition in morphology (shape and structure) from teeth that are actual parts of the jaw, to teeth that develop along the edge of the jaw, to teeth that line the oral cavity. More recently, there has been a change to the definition based on the place where teeth and scales form. Whereas scales develop superficially, directly at the interface between the epithelium (top layer of skin) and underlying mesenchyme derived from ectoderm, W.E. Reif (1982) contended that teeth are formed within a deep epidermal invagination (hollow) called the "dental lamina," where they are prefabricated for replacement. When considering fossil taxa, this definition is potentially problematic.

Assuming that you are dealing with a true tooth, there are a number of complementary terms of classification that together convey a morphological description. The relationship between tooth and jaw falls into three basic categories. As Figure 1 shows,

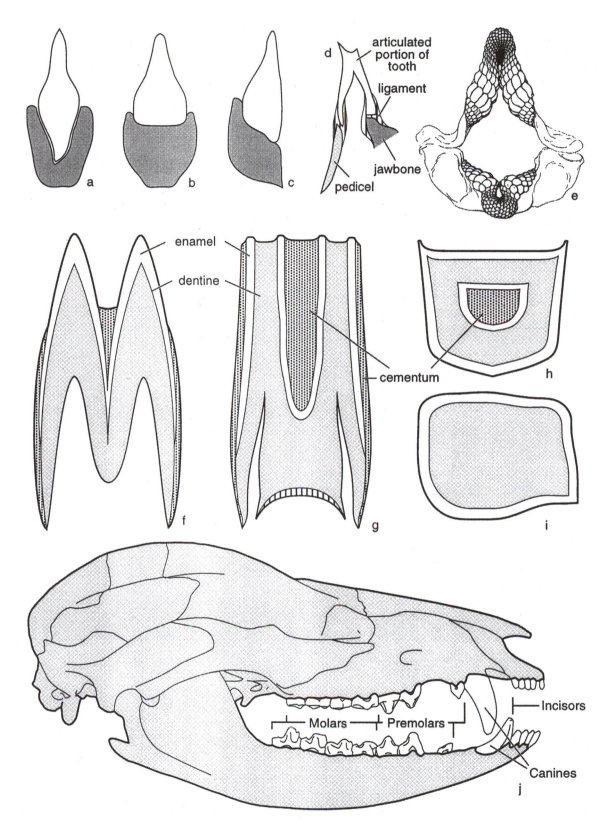

Figure 1. Teeth structure. *a–d,* classification of teeth according to locale and type of attachment to the jaw; *a,* thecodont condition; *b,* acrodont condition; *c,* pleurodont condition; *d,* a pedicellate tooth; *e,* heterodont dentition in *Heterodontus; f–i,* hypsodont dentition; *f,* unworn; *g,* worn; *h,* selenodont; *i,* lophodont; *j,* classification of teeth in mammals according to position. *e,* from Peyer (1968).

teeth are either (a) socketed, or "thecodont"; (b) situated in a shallow groove on the crest of the jaw bone, or "acrodont"; or (c) attached to the inner face of the jaw, or "pleurodont." In addition, a tooth can be held in place either by a mineralized union between jaw and bone ("ankylosis"), or attached by fibers to the jaw ("fibrous attachment"). Fibrous attachment allows for a degree of flexibility in the tooth-jaw junction. Some apparently loosely attached teeth can be deflected inwards but not outwards, which prevents the escape of prey (e.g., the teeth of the upper jaw of *Lophius,* the angler fish). Pedicellate teeth (Figure 1d), which occur only in lissamphibians (e.g., frogs and salamanders), are attached to both the jaw and an underlying bony structure known as the "pedicel." The tooth is attached by flexible ligaments, which allow it to articulate (move about) on the pedicel.

Although some animals, such as lungfishes, sometimes have only one set of teeth (permanent dentition), it is more common for teeth to be shed and replaced in successive generations (deciduous dentition). Deciduous teeth can occur in many generations (polyphyodont) or only two, as in our own (diphyodont).

In many cases, all teeth in the jaw will be morphologically invariable (homodont); in others, the shape and function varies (heterodont) (Figure 1e). Heterodonty is particularly prevalent among more derived (specialized) vertebrates, such as mammals. Where there is morphological variation, scholars can use it to classify teeth further, in terms of their position within the mouth. Such schemes are used most widely among mammals, where teeth are divided into front incisors, adjacent canines, premolars at the sides of the mouth, and molars farthest to the back (Figure 1j). For an individual species, the dentition can be described as a dental formula that summaries the number of each tooth type on one side of the head. The dental formula for the mammal in Figure 1j would be:

$$I\ 5/4,\ C\ 1/1,\ PM\ 3/3,\ M\ 4/4$$

This means that there are five upper and four lower incisors, one upper and one lower canine, three upper and three lower premolars, and four upper and four lower molars. If specific tooth categories are absent, they are indicated by a zero.

Terms also exist for the classification of the discrete morphological types of tooth, such as "brachydont," where the crowns of the teeth are low in the mouth, and "hypsodont," where crowns are high (Figure 1f). The surfaces where hypsodont teeth come together (occlusal surfaces) characteristically undergo extensive wear. As a result, a series of alternating ridges and troughs are developed owing to the differences in the degree of wear between dentine and the relatively more resistant enamel. One can see this in the molars of many herbivorous mammals, including elephants, mammoths, domestic cattle, and sheep (Figure 1g). The exact pattern of ridges that form from such wear depend upon the original arrangement of the cusps (points on grinding surfaces). Cusps drawn out into ridges result in a "lophodont" pattern (Figure 1h), whereas cusps that originally were crescent-shaped produce a "selenodont" pattern (Figure 1i). The occlusal surfaces of teeth tell us most about feeding behavior. For example, omnivores typically bear teeth with cusps that form blunt peaks, a condition known as "bunodont." In many carnivorous mammals, the fourth upper premolar and first lower molar have adapted to form a scissorlike pair of shearing blades. These teeth are known as "carnassials" and are used to slice through flesh and bone. Carnassials represent the current acme of "sectorial tooth development," a morphological group of teeth found only in carnivores and specifically designed for slicing.

PHILIP C.J. DONOGHUE

See also Enamel Microstructure; Gnathostomes; Teeth: Earliest Teeth; Teeth: Evolution of Complex Teeth; Teeth: Evolution of Mammalian Teeth; Teeth: Tooth Eruption Patterns

Works Cited and Further Reading

Peyer, B. 1968. *Comparative Odontology.* R. Zangerl (trans.). Chicago: University of Chicago Press.
Reif, W.-E. 1982. Evolution of the dermal skeleton and dentition in vertebrates: The odontode regulation theory. *Evolutionary Biology* 15:287–368.

TEETH: EARLIEST TEETH

Mineralized skeletal components form the majority of fossils, and vertebrates are no exception: bones and teeth represent the most commonly recovered evidence for the history of vertebrate evolution. The vertebrate skeleton can be divided into two types: the endoskeleton (internal bones such as limb bones, backbone, and ribs), and the exoskeleton, including the dermal skeleton. The dermal skeleton is largely represented by teeth and skin scales. The same developmental pathways produce both structures, so the two are considered homologous. Skin scales and teeth are generally referred to as "odontodes," although true teeth have an intimate association with a fold in the "skin" that covers the inside of the mouth (the dental lamina) and also have a food processing func-

tion (Reif 1982). In terms of composition, odontode tissues are formed from a substance called hydroxyfluorapatite and are constructed with a variety of vertebrate hard tissue types, including enamel, enameloid, dentine, bone, and cartilage. Commonly, microfossils, toothlike in shape, are found early in the vertebrate fossil record. However, although often similar in morphology to true teeth, these microfossils may have been formed either in the animal's skin or in the mucous membrane of the oral cavity, independent of a dental lamina.

The extant (present-day) jawless fishes, lampreys and hagfishes, lack mineralized odontodes but do possess keratin-based conical toothlets around their mouths. (Keratin is a fibrous pro-

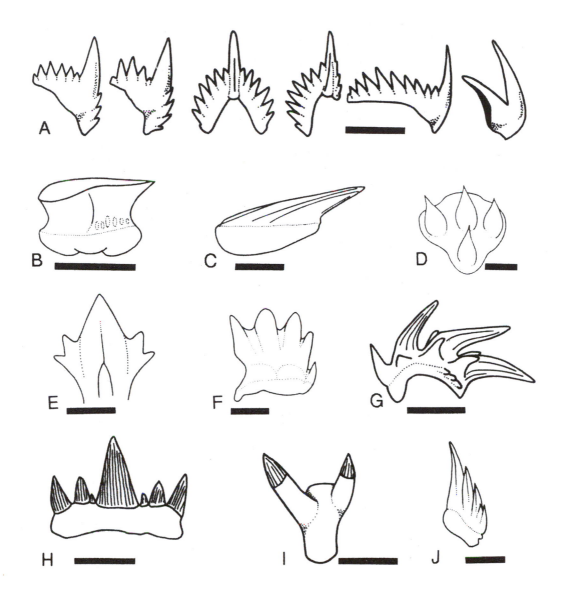

Figure 1. Primitive vertebrate teeth and toothlike structures. *A,* oral toothlike elements of the Middle Ordovician conodont *Microoozarkodina;* scale bar equals 0.5 millimeters. *B, C,* thelodont skin scales; scales bar equals 0.5 millimeters. *D,* thelodont oral denticles; scale bar equals 0.01 millimeter. *E, F,* actinopterygian teeth; scale bar equals 0.5 millimeters. *G,* actinopterygian tooth whorl; scale bar equals 1.0 millimeters. *H, I,* primitive chondrichthyan teeth; scale bar equals 1 to 2 millimeters. *J,* chondrichthyan mucous membrane denticle; scale bar equals 0.5 millimeters.

tein that also forms hair and nails.) The toothlets of the fossil hagfishes and lampreys from the Upper Carboniferous of Illinois are preserved as molds (the form or impressions are preserved but not the actual item), and thus we cannot be completely sure that they were keratinous. The toothlets of both hagfishes and lampreys are found on a protrusible tongue and are used to grasp and rasp flesh. The disc surrounding the oral opening of lampreys is studded with additional "horny teeth," which are used to gain purchase on their prey. Although they share similar functions and morphology, the toothlets of hagfishes and lampreys and true teeth of other vertebrates are derived from quite separate and distinct developmental pathways (Smith and Hall 1990).

Conodonts (literally "cone-teeth") are relatively abundant in marine rocks from the Late Cambrian to end-Triassic and recently have been identified as belonging to naked, eel-like animals (Aldridge et al. 1993). Their relationships to other phyla have been the subject of considerable debate in the scientific literature, although the presence of a notochord, ray-supported tail, paired sensory organs, and hard tissues, such as enamel and dentine, strongly supports their classification among the vertebrates. They possess a complex, bilaterally arranged (left-right symmetry), multicomponent feeding apparatus in the oral region, the front elements of which are probably analogous to the horny "toothlets" on the protrusible tongue of hagfishes and lampreys. Individual elements of this apparatus can be up to one centimeter in total length, although the majority are only a tenth of that size. The elements of a single apparatus often show a wide range of morphologies (shapes and structures) (Figure 1A), suggesting that the "teeth" of this apparatus were able to perform complex grasping, biting, and slicing functions (Jeppsson 1979).

The Late Cambrian similarly provides the earliest record of vertebrate dermal armor. *Anatolepis,* from the Late Cambrian–Early Ordovician deposits in North America, Greenland, and Spitzbergen (Norway), is considered to be the oldest armored fish. It has small tubercles (protrusions), less than 0.5 millimeters across, connected by a sheet of dermal armor. Frustratingly, little else is known about *Anatolepis,* since it has only been recorded from scraps of skin armor (Smith et al. 1996).

The Ordovician and Silurian periods saw the appearance of a number of major groups of fishes, the majority of which also are known largely from fragments of dermal armor. These fishes included the heavily armored heterostracans (an order of early jawless armored fishes—agnathans—with a common gill slit opening on each side behind the main armor plates), thelodonts (another agnathan group), and sharklike fishes, the latter two having minute, toothlike "denticles" in their skin.

As well as having skin covered with minute denticles (Figures 1B, 1C), certain thelodonts from the Upper Silurian of Scotland recently have been described with similar structures (Figure 1D) lining the oral and nasal cavity and the branchial (gill) regions. It seems likely that these internal structures are, at least in part, equivalent to the denticles of chondrichthyan fishes, which arise from the mucous membrane.

Minute, toothlike denticles are found in the skin of modern-day sharks, giving the skin its characteristic rough texture; similar structures also line their oral mucous membranes. Morphologically similar denticles have been recovered from the fossil record (Figure 1J). True shark teeth are recorded from the Lower Devonian (Figures 1H, 1I), although what appear to be shark scales first appear in the Ordovician of North America (Sansom et al. 1996). Teeth have not, so far, been found with these early scales, and it has been suggested that the scales represent jawless "proto-sharks."

The earliest true teeth come from jawed Silurian acanthodian ("spiny shark") and actinopterygian (ray-finned) fish. Many advanced acanthodian taxa (groups; singular, taxon) lack teeth, although primitive forms possess simple teeth attached to the jaw cartilage (Figures 1E, 1F) and/or tooth whorls (Figure 1G). Early actinopterygians possessed simple, conical teeth that were fused directly to the jaw; later forms developed attachment to bone, to secure the tooth firmly in the jaw.

The jawbones of placoderms (heavily armored jawed fish also found first during the Silurian) have oral surfaces sculpted into toothlike structures. They appear to lack recognizable true teeth, although oral denticles are sometimes present on elements of the palate.

The appearance of teeth in the fossil record seems to reflect a shift in feeding strategy among the vertebrates, from a filter-feeding and mud-munching lifestyle to one of active predation, which entailed the need to be able to grasp, bite, and slice prey.

IVAN J. SANSOM

See also Diet; Feeding Adaptations: Vertebrates; Gnathostomes; Skeletized Organisms and the Evolution of Skeletized Tissues; Skeleton: Dermal Postcranial Skeleton; Vertebrate Hard Tissues: Mineralized Tissues

Works Cited

Aldridge, R.J., D.E.G. Briggs, M.P. Smith, E.N.K. Clarkson, and N.D.L. Clark. 1993. The anatomy of conodonts. *Philosophical Transactions of the Royal Society of London,* ser. B, 338:405–21.

Jeppsson, L. 1979. Conodont element function. *Lethaia* 12:153–71.

Reif, W.-E. 1982. Evolution of dermal skeleton and dentition in vertebrates: The odontode-regulation theory. *Evolutionary Biology* 15:287–368.

Sansom, I.J., M.M. Smith, and M.P. Smith. 1996. Scales of thelodont and shark-like fishes from the Ordovician of Colorado. *Nature* 379:628–30.

Smith, M.M., and B.K. Hall. 1990. Development and evolutionary origins of vertebrate skeletogenic and odontogenic tissues. *Biological Review of the Cambridge Philosophical Society* 65:277–373.

Smith, M.P., I.J. Sansom, and J.E. Repetski. 1996. Histology of the first fish. *Nature* 380:702–4.

Further Reading

Janvier, P. 1996. The dawn of the vertebrates: Characters versus common ascent in the rise of current vertebrate phylogenies. *Palaeontology* 39:259–87.

———. 1996. *Early Vertebrates.* Oxford Monographs on Geology and Geophysics, 33. Oxford: Clarendon Press; New York: Oxford University Press.

Long, J.A. 1995. *The Rise of Fishes: 500 Million Years of Evolution.* Baltimore, Maryland: Johns Hopkins University Press.

Maisey, J.G. 1996. *Discovering Fossil Fishes.* New York: Holt.

Moy-Thomas, J.A. 1939. *Palaeozoic Fishes.* London: Methuen; New York: Chemical Publishing; 2nd ed., with R.S. Miles, Philadelphia: Saunders; London: Chapman and Hall, 1971.

TEETH: EVOLUTION OF COMPLEX TEETH

It is generally thought that the complexity of life has increased over time as more complex organisms have evolved from simpler organisms. Complexity, however, is a difficult property to measure directly; therefore, biological complexity must be estimated, as either the number of parts in an organism, the amount of differentiation among those parts, or the degree of functional interaction among those parts (McShea 1996). For example, there is good evidence that multicellular animals became more complex—at least as measured by number of cell types—during the Early Phanerozoic (Valentine et al. 1994). In serial structures such as teeth or vertebrae, complexity increases with differentiation. By this measure, mammals have more complex vertebral columns than either reptiles or fishes (McShea 1993). Structures that interact with each other, such as the occluding molars (molars that meet each other) of mammals, are more complex than structures that do not, such as the nonoccluding conical teeth of most reptiles. The complexity of vertebrate teeth varies greatly in terms of the shape of individual teeth, the microscopic structure of hard tissues, differentiation along the tooth row (e.g., between molars and incisors), and degree of functional interaction between teeth (Figure 1). This essay reviews the evolution of various kinds of complex teeth in vertebrates, arranged by taxonomic group, and asks whether complexity in teeth has increased over time.

Conodonts

Conodonts were a diverse group of Cambrian-to-Triassic soft-bodied marine animals with phosphatic mouth parts called "conodont elements." Recent discoveries of complete conodont animals have revealed that these elements were part of a feeding apparatus and that conodonts possessed many characters in common with vertebrates (Aldridge and Purnell 1996). If conodont elements are homologous with vertebrate teeth, then teeth may be the earliest form of mineralized skeleton in vertebrates (Smith and Hall 1993). Conodont elements possess hard tissues similar to those in vertebrate teeth—enamel and dentine—as well as additional tissues. Each element is composed of a crown—made of an enamel homolog and, in some forms, an underlying "white matter" of cellular bone—and a basal body made variably of dentine or calcified cartilage (Sansom et al. 1992, 1994).

Conodont elements certainly functioned as teeth and evolved many complex shapes. Conodont elements were arranged in rough bilateral symmetry (Figure 2), with anterior (front) S and M elements and posterior (rear) P elements, each covered with denticles (Purnell and von Bitter 1992; Purnell 1993). P elements range widely in shape including conical, bladelike, and molarlike platform structures. Wear facets are present on matching surfaces of left and right P elements; they appear similar to wear facets found on mammalian teeth. This similarity suggests that right and left P elements occluded (Purnell 1995). Fine striations, which suggest shearing, commonly occur on the conical and bladelike elements, but broad pits, which suggest compression, typically

occur on the platform elements. Nevertheless, conodonts lacked supportive jaws for their mouth parts, and it is unknown how conodonts could have controlled their mouth parts without jaws (Aldridge and Purnell 1996).

Fishes and Early Tetrapods

Teeth are found throughout the gnathostomes (jawed fishes), where they are associated with the jaws, palate, and branchial arches (gill support) surrounding the pharynx. Both true enamel and enameloid—a hard tissue formed in development by two types of cells, ameloblasts and odontoblasts—occur in the teeth of fishes and larval amphibians (Smith 1992). Diverse forms of dentine, which form a continuum between true dentine and bone, occur in the teeth, denticles, and scales of Paleozoic fishes (Smith and Hall 1993).

Although modern sharks typically have simple sharp teeth, many Paleozoic sharks (Figure 3A) possessed more complex teeth, with multiple cusps (Schaeffer 1967; Zangerl 1981). Hybodont sharks possessed anterior high-cusped teeth and posterior low-cusped teeth. Although modern elasmobranchs (sharks, skates, and rays) typically replace their teeth multiple times in "tooth whorls," bradyodont elasmobranchs had continuously growing teeth with limited replacement. Tooth plates of flattened, abutting teeth evolved independently in sharks, rays, ratfishes, and other elasmobranchs.

In teleost fishes (higher bony fishes), pharyngeal teeth—anchored to the palate and branchial arches—typically are well developed (Figure 3B), but oral teeth may be reduced or lost. Pharyngeal teeth in cichlid fishes are of particular interest because specialized pharyngeal jaws may have contributed to the diversification of this group (Galis and Drucker 1996). Cichlid pharyngeal teeth include blunt columns in mollusc-eating species, flat compressive surfaces in algae-eating ones, serrated blades in fish-eating ones, and barbed hooks in scale-eating ones (Liem 1973). Among lobe-finned fishes, lungfishes evolved batteries of flattened, abutting teeth. Rhipidistean fishes and the earliest tetrapods (limbed vertebrates) share derived "labyrinthodont" teeth, characterized by complex foldings of dentine (Schultze 1970).

Diapsid Reptiles

With some exceptions (Edmund 1969), diapsid reptiles have simple teeth and little differentiation along the tooth row. Heterodonty (more than one type of tooth) among reptiles is most conspicuous in snakes, with their elongate maxillary fangs for transporting venom (Figure 4A). Among lizards, heterodonty can result through tooth replacement when blunt molariform teeth erupt at the back of the jaw, replacing sharp teeth (Figure 4B). Many heterodont lizards are omnivores (eating both plants and animals), and a change in diet may accompany ontogenetic change in the dentition (Estes and Williams 1984). Although the

Figure 1. Types of complex teeth in vertebrates. Complexity in teeth can be measured in terms of (a) tooth shape: the number of parts (e.g., cusps) found on a single tooth; (b) hard tissues: heterogeneity in tooth microstructure; (c) heterodonty: degree of differentiation between teeth in a dentition; or (d) function: the degree of interaction between teeth.

	Tooth Shape	Hard Tissues	Heterodonty	Function
Conodonts	multiple denticles conical, bladelike, and platform P elements	crown—enamel(?) and sometimes bone basal body—dentine or calcified cartilage	anterior (S and M) and posterior (P) elements	shear(?) compression(?)
Fishes and early tetrapods	multiple cusps in Paleozoic sharks diverse pharyngeal teeth in cichlids	diverse forms of dentine both enamel and emaneloid labyrinthodont teeth in rhipidistians and early tetrapods	crown height variation in hybodont sharks oral and pharyngeal teeth in bony fishes	compression between dental batteries
Diapsid reptiles	multiple cusps in some crocodilians chisel-shaped teeth in heterodontosaurids	prismatic enamel in *Uromastix*	snake maxillary fangs molariforms in some lizards and crocodilians	shear and compression(?) between dental batteries in ceratopsians and hadrosaurs
Synapsid reptiles	multiple cusps in some therapsids multiple roots in tritylodontids gomphodont postcanines in traversodontids	prismatic enamel in *Pachygenelus*	incisors, precanines, canines, and postcanines postcanine differentiation in some cynodonts (esp. *Diademodon*)	shear and compression incisor interlock in dinocephalians postcanine occlusion in bauriamorphs and advanced cynodonts
Mammals	multiple cusps, crests, and roots diverse molar types	prismatic enamel and prism decussation	incisors, canines, premolars, and molars	shear and compression precise occlusion

teeth of diapsid reptiles usually have simple hard tissues, the lizard *Uromastix* evolved prismatic enamel similar to that of mammals (Cooper and Poole 1973).

Generally crocodilians also have simple teeth, with some forms having posterior blunt teeth (Edmund 1969). However, an Early Cretaceous crocodilian from Malawi (Figure 4C) possessed a well-differentiated dentition, with anterior caniniforms and posterior molariforms, each with a massive central cusp surrounded on three sides by a ring of enamel with smaller cusps (a cingulum) (Clark et al. 1989). *Chimaerosuchus,* an Early Cretaceous crocodilian from China (Figure 4D), also possessed differentiated caniniforms and molariforms, but each molariform had three rows of multiple cusps (Wu et al. 1995). Similar teeth occur in tritylodontid cynodonts (a group of advanced therapsids), multituberculate mammals, the marsupial *Ektopodon,* and myomorph rodents, all known or presumed to be omnivorous or herbivorous. The Malawi crocodilian and *Chimaerosuchus* probably utilized a forward jaw motion, powered by reptilian pterygoid muscles, to slide their teeth back and forth past each other, as does the living Tuatara.

The teeth of dinosaurs are varied in shape and degree of differentiation. The ornithischian (bird-hipped) heterodontosaurids were named after their dentition—"heterodont" means "varied teeth." Their dentitions featured anterior caniniforms and posterior chisel-shaped teeth (Weishampel and Witmer 1990). The dental batteries that evolved in hadrosaurs (duck-billed dinosaurs) and ceratopsians (horned dinosaurs) featured rows of hexagonally packed teeth that wore against occluding teeth to produce a rough occlusal surface. In ceratopsians, the dental batteries wore down nearly vertically as they sheared past each other on closing the jaw (Ostrom 1966). In hadrosaurs with kinetic (moveable) skulls, the dental batteries sheared past each other more obliquely, with slight lateral movements of the maxillae (Weishampel 1983). Juveniles of the hadrosaur *Maiasaura* (Hunter 1989), some adult hadrosaurs (Weishampel 1984), and *Leptoceratops* (Ostrom 1966) also wore their dental batteries somewhat horizontally along their buccal edge (facing the cheek), suggesting that compression as well as shear could occur between dental batteries.

Synapsid Reptiles and Early Mammals

Mammals and mammal-like reptiles belong to the amniote group Synapsida, which first appeared in the Pennsylvanian Period. The teeth of primitive synapsids—pelycosaurs such as *Dimetrodon*—were simple and nearly homodont (all alike), except for the presence of enlarged canine teeth, which divided the tooth row into classes: incisors (in the premaxilla), precanines (in the maxilla), canines, and postcanines. Postcanines are specialized in different pelycosaurs suggesting diversification in diet. Small forms, such as the insectivorous *Ianthasaurus,* possessed numerous, pointed teeth (Hopson 1994). *Edaphosaurus* and other large herbivores had stout, rounded teeth, and *Dimetrodon* and other large carnivores possessed sharp, recurved (backwardly curved) teeth (Kemp 1982). Upper and lower teeth of pelycosaurs did not contact one

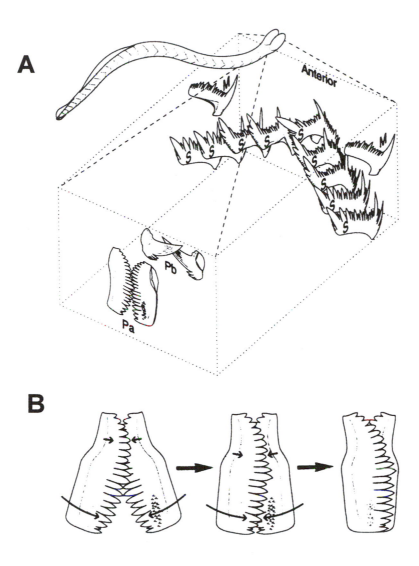

Figure 2. Complex "teeth" in conodonts. *A,* arrangement of conodont elements; *B,* operation of P elements. From Purnell and Bitter (1992), reprinted by permission of *Nature,* copyright © 1992, Macmillan Magazines Ltd.

another in any regular manner. Pelycosaurs retained palatal teeth as well as teeth on the jaws themselves.

Greater differentiation among tooth classes evolved in therapsids, advanced synapsid reptiles descended from the pelycosaurs (Kemp 1982). In dinocephalians and gorgonopsians, upper and lower incisors interlocked. In the titanosuchid dinocephalians, internal heels in the back of the teeth served to lengthen cutting blades on the incisors. In the herbivorous tapinocephalid dinocephalians, both incisors and postcanines interlocked, and the internal heels functioned in compression as well as cutting (Figure 5A). Posterior extension of the incisor interlock mechanism to the postcanines is an early example of the extension of a morphologic gradient from one part of the dentition to another, similar to molarization of the premolars in mammals (Butler 1978). The postcanines of many therapsids became reduced or lost altogether. For example, in the herbivorous dicynodonts horny pads replaced incisors and later postcanines. In some therocephalians—*Bauria* (Figure 5B) and its

relatives—the postcanine teeth expanded transversely (from side to side), with uppers meeting lowers directly in a simple kind of occlusion (Crompton 1962; Gow 1978).

In cynodont therapsids, the most advanced of the mammal-like reptiles, complexity increased in both tooth shape and differentiation. Primitive cynodonts, such as *Thrinaxodon,* possessed nonoccluding postcanine teeth that differed in shape along the jaw: anterior simple teeth with one cusp, posterior complex teeth with a main cusp and accessory cusps, and teeth of intermediate complexity in between (Crompton 1972). In the lineage of *Cynognathus* and the herbivorous cynodonts (Hopson 1994), there evolved complex, more differentiated postcanines and precise occlusion. *Diademodon,* an early omnivorous or herbivorous cynodont, possessed differentiated postcanines with anterior conical teeth, posterior sectorial (slicing) teeth, and gomphodont (crushing) teeth with transverse blades that interlocked as the lower jaw was brought upward (Crompton 1972; Grine 1977).

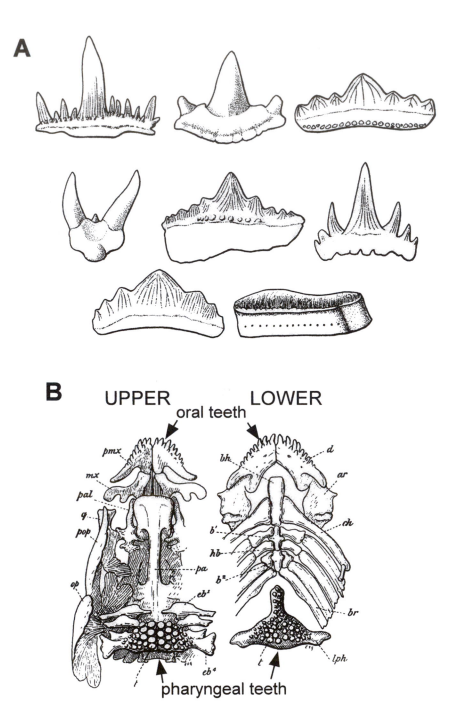

Figure 3. Complex teeth in fishes. *A,* Paleozoic shark teeth; *B,* upper and lower dentition of the teleost *Labrus.* From: *A,* Schaeffer (1967); *B,* Peyer (1968). *B,* Peyer (1968), used by permission of the publisher, The University of Chicago Press, copyright © 1968 by The University of Chicago.

Traversodontids, possibly descended from *Diademodon,* reduced the conical and sectorial teeth but elaborated the gomphodont teeth, which interlocked as the lower jaw was brought upwards and backwards (Crompton 1972). Further, a posterior shelf on the lower postcanines occluded with a cusp on the upper postcanines (Figure 5C), allowing both shear and compression to occur on the same teeth, a condition that evolved separately (convergently) in the tribosphenic molars of therian mammals. In the mammal-like tritylodontids (Figure 5D), probable descendants of traversodontids, longitudinal rows of cusps evolved, and postcanines occluded as the lower jaw was drawn backwards (Crompton 1972). Tritylodontids also evolved multiple tooth roots conver-

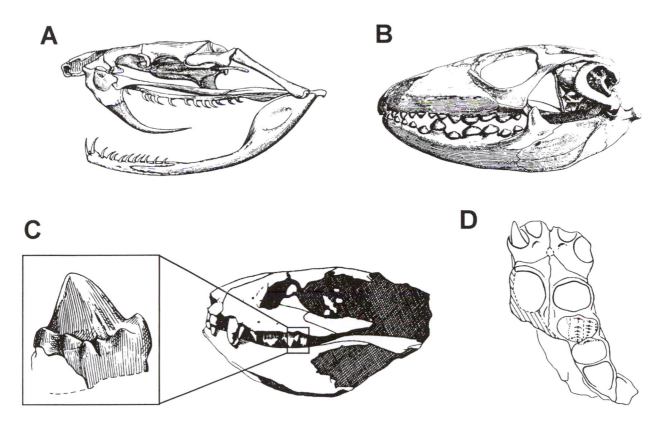

Figure 4. Complex teeth in diapsid reptiles. *A,* skull of a pit viper and *B,* skull of the heterodont lizard *Dracaena; C,* molariform tooth and skull of the Malawi crocodilian; *D,* snout of *Chimaerosuchus.* From: *A, B,* Peyer (1968), used by permission of the publisher, The University of Chicago Press, copyright © 1968 by The University of Chicago; *C,* reprinted with permission from Clark et al. (1989), copyright © 1989 American Association for the Advancement of Science; *D,* Wu et al. (1995), reprinted with permission from *Nature,* copyright © 1995, Macmillan Magazines Ltd.

gently with mammals. Among herbivorous cynodonts, the complexity of individual postcanines increased through time (Hopson 1994), but differentiation among postcanines declined.

In the lineage of carnivorous cynodonts and mammals (Hopson 1994), the postcanine teeth remained more primitive. Only in advanced tritheledontids (Crompton 1995) and perhaps in chiniquodontids (Crompton 1972) did upper and lower teeth occlude, enabling the teeth to shear food. Jaw movement was primarily upwards in tritheledontids, with some rotation of the mandible about a longitudinal axis due to a mobile mandibular symphysis (anterior midline joint) (Crompton 1995). At least one tritheledontid, *Pachygenelus,* possessed prismatic enamel (Grine et al. 1979), whereas other synapsid reptiles and the most primitive mammals possessed prismless "synapsid columnar enamel" (Sander 1997).

In early mammals—the morganucodontids (Crompton 1995) and the haramiyids (Jenkins et al. 1997)—the postcanine tooth row is differentiated enough that molars and premolars are discernible. In morganucodontids, occlusion occurred with an upward, medial, and rotatory jaw motion (Crompton 1995), but in haramiyids occlusion occurred with a power stroke that moved upward (Jenkins et al. 1997) and perhaps backwards (Butler and MacIntyre 1994). The cynodont-mammal transition is compli-

cated, however, by the primitive mammal *Sinoconodon,* which lacked precise occlusion altogether and had undifferentiated postcanines (Crompton 1995), suggesting that complex occlusion evolved convergently in herbivorous cynodonts, tritheledontids, and mammals (Luo 1994).

Mesozoic Mammals

The earliest mammals with precise occlusion, such as *Morganucodon,* had to wear down their molars considerably before uppers and lowers fit well (Crompton 1995). Later mammals possessed molars with more closely matching surfaces, requiring less wear to function, but this change was accomplished differently in different lineages. In multituberculates, extra rows of cusps evolved, and molars met directly, with cusp rows interdigitated and a backward power stroke (Krause 1982). In early therian mammals (symmetrodonts and eupantotheres), the cusps present in morganucodontids became arranged in triangles, and each lower molar occluded between two uppers with an upward and medial power stroke (Crompton 1971). A third lineage of Mesozoic mammals, the docodonts, expanded a cuspidate cingulum (marginal ridge), bringing upper and lower molars into direct opposition (Butler 1988). It is not clear, however, whether docodont teeth evolved

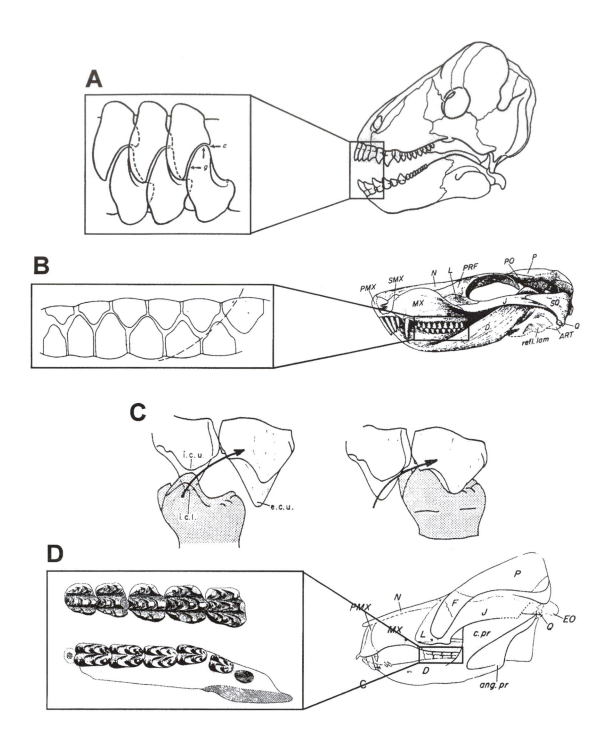

Figure 5. Complex teeth in synapsid reptiles. *A*, incisors and skull of a tapinocephalid dinocephalian; *B*, postcanines and skull of *Bauria*; *C*, postcanine occlusion in *Scalenodon hischsoni*, a traversodontid; *D*, postcanine dentition and skull of *Oligokyphus*, a tritylodontid. After *A*, Kemp (1982) and Hopson (1994); *B*, Kemp (1982); *C*, Crompton (1972); *D*, Kemp (1982).

from teeth with cusps in a line, as in morganucodontids (Crompton and Jenkins 1968), or with cusps in a triangle, as in early therians (Butler 1997). Several mammalian lineages evolved prismatic enamel during the Mesozoic (Clemens 1997), concomitant with the evolution of more accurate occlusion.

Among therian mammals, the major innovation during the Mesozoic was the addition of a "talonid basin" at the back of the lower molars, which occluded with a new lingual (tongue-side) cusp called the protocone, on the upper molars. Such "tribosphenic molars" evolved gradually from symmetrodont molars through the Jurassic and Early Cretaceous, documented by several transitional stages (Crompton 1971; Butler 1990). The protocone initially sheared past a bladelike talonid, but later the tip of the protocone contacted a basined talonid (Crompton 1971). Tri-

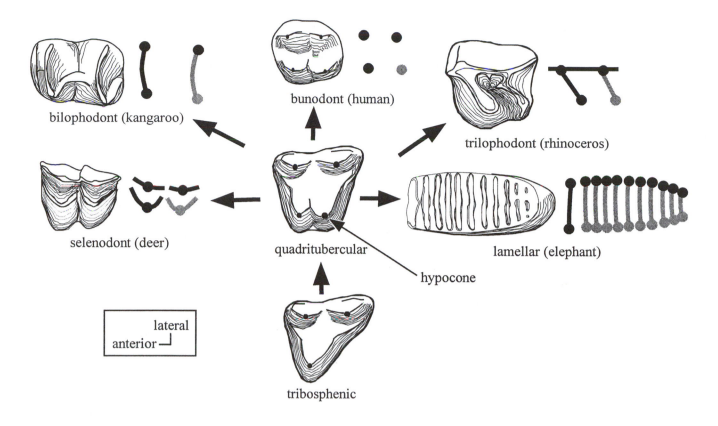

Figure 6. Derivation of complex mammalian upper molars through tribosphenic and quadritubercular stages. After Hunter and Jernvall (1995) and Jernvall (1995).

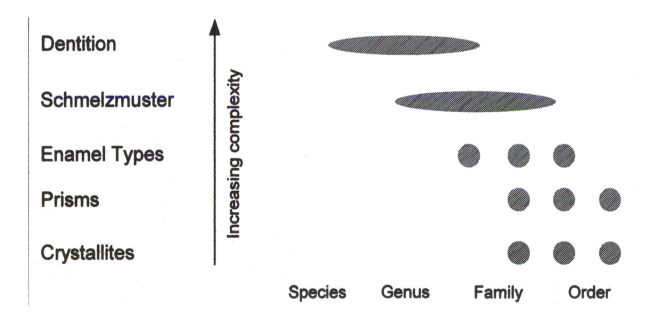

Figure 7. Levels of structural complexity in the enamel of mammals and the taxonomic rank at which each level is believed to be the most important. From Koenigswald and Clemens (1992).

bosphenic molars combine shearing and compressive functions on the same tooth and are convergent on the gomphodont teeth of traversodontids (Crompton 1972), the bulbous molars of docodonts (Butler 1988), and the molars of *Shuotherium,* an unusual therian with a "pseudotalonid" at the anterior end of the lower molars (Chow and Rich 1982).

Cenozoic Mammals

The evolutionary radiation of marsupial and placental mammals resulted in a great diversification in molar shape, derived from the basic plan of the tribosphenic molar. This radiation was underway during the Late Cretaceous, when numerous variations on the tribosphenic molar evolved (Crompton and Kielan-Jaworowska 1978; Butler 1990). However, radical departures from the tribosphenic molar did not evolve until the Cenozoic. A critical early event was the convergent evolution in many mammalian lineages of the hypocone (a cusp on the rear, lingual corner of a now-squared upper molar), with reduction of the paraconid on the lower molars (Hunter and Jernvall 1995). The hypocone appears to be an adaptation for a generalized diet but a prerequisite for specialized herbivory, implying that the quadritubercular molar (i.e., one with a hypocone) is a necessary transitional stage in the evolution of derived molar types found among mammalian herbivores (Figure 6).

During the Cenozoic, many derived molar types evolved convergently. Bunodont molars with blunt cusps and thick enamel (Figure 6) evolved in bears, pigs, primates, marsupial groups, and others. Among herbivores, lophed (bladed) molars evolved in several ways. In the bilophodont molars (Figure 6) of arsinotheres, some primates, extant tapirs, kangaroos, listriodontid pigs, and manatees, transverse blades interdigitate, two on each upper and lower molar (Janis and Fortelius 1988). In the trilophodont molars of rhinoceroses, hyraxes, and notoungulates, the transverse blades on the upper molars are supplemented by a longitudinal loph on the buccal side of the crown. Selenodont molars, with cusps compressed into longitudinal blades, evolved in ruminant artiodactyls and the koala.

Blades on the teeth of carnivorous mammals can occupy most of the crown and are used with an upward and slightly medial jaw movement. In carnivorous eutherians (carnivorans and creodonts), teeth remain roughly in the same position in the jaw after eruption, and one or more bladed "carnassial" teeth differentiate (Butler 1946). In carnivorous marsupials, each molar functions in turn as the primary carnassial tooth, and each molar, therefore, must be equally carnassiform (Werdelin 1987). However, in the marsupial "lion" *Thylacoleo,* a bladed premolar that remained in roughly the same position along the jaw with growth became elaborated into a carnassial-like tooth (Werdelin 1988).

Heterodonty is characteristic of mammals. Nevertheless, the shape of each tooth is not completely independent of the shape of its neighbors, and each tooth may resemble adjacent teeth to some degree (Butler 1978). Such resemblance also can increase over evolutionary time, as in the phenomenon among herbivores known as "molarization" of the premolars (Butler 1952). These observations suggest that the shape of individual teeth, even in a heterodont den-

tition, may be controlled in development by a few underlying factors (Van Valen 1970). The mechanistic basis of this phenomenon remains elusive, but it is likely that homeobox-containing genes (a family of regulatory genes) are involved (Weiss et al. 1994).

Among mammals, enamel internal structure may be complex. Enamel prisms can decussate, alternating with prisms with different orientations. Decussation probably enhances the durability of teeth (Koenigswald and Pfretzschner 1991), and vertical decussation is well developed in the enamel crests of mammalian herbivores where occlusal stress is high (Fortelius 1984). Horizontal decussation is more widespread among mammals but is particularly well-developed in the gnawing incisors of rodents (Martin 1993). The internal fabric of enamel imparted by its particular pattern of decussation is its "Schmelzmuster" (Koenigswald 1980).

Enamel can vary in complexity at several spatial scales, from enamel crystallite orientation to differentiation in Schmelzmuster along the tooth row. Systematists are interested in how, and at what spatial scale, enamel characters can contribute to taxonomic (classification) studies (Figure 7) (Koenigswald and Clemens 1992). An emerging generalization is that differences in enamel complexity at a small spatial scale (i.e., crystallites) seem to characterize taxonomic differences at high rank (the more inclusive levels of classification), for example, between derived (specialized) mammals, which have prismatic enamel, and synapsid reptiles and early mammals, which have prismless "synapsid columnar enamel" (Sander 1997). Similarly, differences in enamel complexity at a larger spatial scale (i.e., Schmelzmuster) seem to characterize taxonomic differences at low taxonomic rank (most specific levels of classification), for example, between genera of rodents with different Schmelzmuster of the incisor enamel (Martin 1993). Enamel structure seems to be conservative (changes little over time) at a small scale but adapts to functional demands at a large scale.

Has Complexity in Teeth Increased?

Overall complexity in the teeth of vertebrates probably has increased over time, but the trend has not been straightforward. Although mammalian teeth are probably more complex—in shape, enamel structure, differentiation, and function—than those other vertebrates, complex teeth have evolved in many ways in other vertebrate groups (Figure 1). The origin of mammalian teeth occurred along with the convergent evolution of complex teeth and occlusion in several synapsid lineages, with a variety of jaw movements. Enamel complexity probably peaked late in vertebrate history (in mammals), but dentine complexity may have peaked earlier, among Paleozoic fishes. A rich and varied adaptive radiation of form occurred among mammalian teeth in the Cenozoic, but a similar radiation may have occurred among conodonts in the Paleozoic. Mammalian herbivores have some of the most complexly shaped molars, but their postcanines may become relatively homodont as the premolars undergo molarization, a process bringing the development of molars and premolars under common control. Thus, even complex teeth can occur within a simple (i.e., homodont) dentition.

JOHN P. HUNTER

See also Enamel Microstructure; Feeding Adaptations: Vertebrates; Teeth: Classification of Teeth; Teeth: Earliest Teeth; Teeth: Evolution of Complex Teeth; Teeth: Tooth Eruption Patterns

Works Cited

Aldridge, R.J., and M.A. Purnell. 1996. The conodont controversies. *Trends in Ecology and Evolution* 11:463–68.

Butler, P.M. 1946. The evolution of carnassial dentitions in the Mammalia. *Proceedings of the Zoological Society, London* 116:198–220.

———. 1952. Molarization of the premolars in the Perissodactyla. *Proceedings of the Zoological Society, London* 121:819–43.

———. 1978. The ontogeny of mammalian heterodonty. *Journal de Biologie Buccale* 6:217–27.

———. 1988. Docodont molars as tribosphenic analogues. *Memoires du Museum National d'Histoire Naturelle, Paris,* ser. C, 53:329–40.

———. 1990. Early trends in the evolution of tribosphenic molars. *Biological Reviews of the Cambridge Philosophical Society* 65:529–52.

———. 1997. An alternative hypothesis on the origin of docodont molar teeth. *Journal of Vertebrate Paleontology* 17:435–39.

Butler, P.M., and G.T. MacIntyre. 1994. Review of the British Haramiyidae (?Mammalia, Allotheria), their molar occlusion and relationships. *Philosophical Transactions of the Royal Society of London,* ser. B, 345:433–58.

Chow, M., and T.H. Rich. 1982. *Shuotherium dongi,* n. gen. and sp., a therian with pseudotribosphenic molars from the Jurassic of Sichuan, China. *Australian Mammalogy* 5:127–42.

Clark, J.M., L.L. Jacobs, and W.R. Downs. 1989. Mammal-like dentition in a Mesozoic crocodylian. *Science* 244:1064–66.

Clemens, W.A. 1997. Characterization of enamel microstructure and application of the origins of prismatic structures in systematic analyses. *In* W. Koenigswald and P.M. Sander (eds.), *Tooth Enamel Microstructure.* Rotterdam and Brookfield, Vermont: Balkema.

Cooper, J.S., and D.F.G. Poole. 1973. The dentition and dental tissues of the agamid lizard, *Uromastix. Journal of Zoology, London* 169:85–100.

Crompton, A.W. 1962. On the dentition and tooth replacement in two bauriamorph reptiles. *Annals of the South African Museum* 46:231–55.

———. 1971. The origin of the tribosphenic molar. *Zoological Journal of the Linnean Society Supplement* 50:65–87.

———. 1972. Postcanine occlusion in cynodonts and tritylodonts. *Bulletin of the British Museum of Natural History (Geology)* 21:21–71.

———. 1995. Masticatory function in nonmammalian cynodonts and early mammals. *In* J. Thomason (ed.), *Functional Morphology in Vertebrate Paleontology.* Cambridge and New York: Cambridge University Press.

Crompton, A.W., and F.A. Jenkins Jr. 1968. Molar occlusion in Late Triassic mammals. *Biological Reviews* 43:427–58.

Crompton, A.W., and Z. Kielan-Jaworowska. 1978. Molar structure and occlusion in Cretaceous therian mammals. *In* P.M. Butler and K.A. Joysey (eds.), *Development, Function and Evolution of Teeth.* London and New York: Academic Press.

Edmund, A.G. 1969. Dentition. *In* C. Gans (ed.), *Biology of the Reptilia.* Vol. 1, *Morphology A.* London and New York: Academic Press.

Estes, R., and E.E. Williams. 1984. Ontogenetic variation in the molariform teeth of lizards. *Journal of Vertebrate Paleontology* 4:96–107.

Fortelius, M. 1984. Vertical decussation of enamel prisms in lophodont ungulates. *In* R.W. Fearnhead and S. Suga (eds.), *Tooth Enamel IV.* Amsterdam, Oxford, and New York: Elsevier Science.

Galis, F., and E.G. Drucker. 1996. Pharyngeal biting mechanisms in centrarchid and cichlid fishes: Insights into a key evolutionary innovation. *Journal of Evolutionary Biology* 9:641–70.

Gow, C.E. 1978. The advent of herbivory in certain reptilian lineages during the Triassic. *Palaeontologia Africana* 21:133–41.

Grine, F.E. 1977. Postcanine tooth function and jaw movement in the gomphodont cynodont *Diademodon* (Reptilia, Therapsida). *Palaeontologia Africana* 20:123–35.

Grine, F.E., C.E. Gow, and J.W. Kitching. 1979. Enamel structure in the cynodonts *Pachygenelus* and *Tritylodon. Proceedings, Electron Microscopy Society of Southern Africa* 9:99–100.

Hopson, J.A. 1994. Synapsid evolution and the radiation of non-eutherian mammals. *In* D.R. Prothero and R.M. Schoch (eds.), *Major Features of Vertebrate Evolution.* The Paleontological Society and the University of Tennessee, Knoxville. Knoxville: University of Tennessee Press.

Hunter, J.P. 1989. Tooth wear in juvenile and adult hadrosaurs (Ornithischia, Dinosauria). A.B. Honors Thesis. Brown University, Providence, Rhode Island.

Hunter, J.P., and J. Jernvall. 1995. The hypocone as a key innovation in mammalian evolution. *Proceedings of the National Academy of Sciences, USA* 92:10718–22.

Janis, C.M., and M. Fortelius. 1988. On the means whereby mammals achieve increased functional durability of their dentitions, with special reference to limiting factors. *Biological Reviews* 63:197–230.

Jenkins Jr., F.A., S.M. Gatesy, N.H. Shubin, and W.W. Amaral. 1997. Haramiyids and Triassic mammalian evolution. *Nature* 385:715–18.

Jernvall, J. 1995. Mammalian molar cusp patterns: Developmental mechanisms of diversity. *Acta Zoologica Fennica* 198:1–61.

Kemp, T.S. 1982. *Mammal-like Reptiles and the Origin of Mammals.* London and New York: Academic Press.

Koenigswald, W. 1980. Schmelzmuster und morphologie in den molaren der Arvicolidae (Rodentia, Mammalia). *Abhandlungen der senckenbergischen naturforschenden Gesellschaft* 539:1–129.

Koenigswald, W., and W.A. Clemens. 1992. Levels of complexity in the microstructure of mammalian enamel and their application in studies of systematics. *Scanning Microscopy* 6:195–218.

Koenigswald, W., and H.-U. Pfretzschner. 1991. Biomechanics in the enamel of mammalian teeth. *In* N. Schmidt-Kittler and K. Vogel (eds.), *Constructional Morphology and Evolution.* Berlin and New York: Springer-Verlag.

Krause, D.W. 1982. Jaw movement, dental function, and diet in the Paleocene multituberculate *Ptilodus. Paleobiology* 8:265–81.

Liem, K.F. 1973. Evolutionary strategies and morphological innovations: Cichlid pharyngeal jaws. *Systematic Zoology* 22:425–41.

Luo, Z. 1994. Sister-group relationships of mammals and transformations of diagnostic mammalian characters. *In* N.C. Fraser and H.-D. Sues (eds.), *In the Shadow of the Dinosaurs: Early Mesozoic Tetrapods.* Cambridge and New York: Cambridge University Press.

Martin, T. 1993. Early rodent incisor enamel evolution: Phylogenetic implications. *Journal of Mammalian Evolution* 1:227–54.

McShea, D.W. 1993. Evolutionary change in the morphological complexity of the mammalian vertebral column. *Evolution* 47:730–40.

———. 1996. Perspective: Metazoan complexity and Evolution: Is there a trend? *Evolution* 50:477–92.

Ostrom, J.H. 1966. Functional morphology and evolution of the ceratopsian dinosaurs. *Evolution* 20:290–308.

Peyer, B. 1968. *Comparative Odontology.* Chicago: University of Chicago Press.

Purnell, M.A. 1993. Feeding mechanisms in conodonts and the function of the earliest vertebrate hard tissues. *Geology* 21:375–77.

———. 1995. Microwear on conodont elements and macrophagy in the first vertebrates. *Nature* 374:798–800.

Purnell, M.A., and Bitter, P.H. von. 1992. Blade-shaped conodont elements functioned as cutting teeth. *Nature* 359:629–31.

Sander, P.M. 1997. Non-mammalian synapsid enamel and the origin of mammalian enamel prisms: The bottom-up perspective. *In* W. Koenigswald and P.M. Sander (eds.), *Tooth Enamel Microstructure.* Rotterdam and Brookfield, Vermont: Balkema.

Sansom, I.J., M.P. Smith, H.A. Armstrong, and M.M. Smith. 1992. Presence of the earliest vertebrate hard tissues in conodonts. *Science* 256:1308–11.

Sansom, I.J., M.P. Smith, and M.M. Smith. 1994. Dentine in conodonts. *Nature* 308:591.

Schaeffer, B. 1967. Comments on elasmobranch evolution. *In* P.W. Gilbert, R.F. Mathewson, and D.P. Rall (eds.), *Sharks, Skates and Rays.* Baltimore, Maryland: Johns Hopkins Press.

Schultze, H.-P. 1970. Folded teeth and the monophyletic origin of tetrapods. *American Museum Novitates* 2408:1–10.

Smith, M.M. 1992. Microstructure and evolution of enamel amongst osteichyan fishes and early tetrapods. *In* P. Smith and E. Tchernov (eds.), *Structure, Function and Evolution of Teeth.* London: Freund.

Smith, M.M., and B.K. Hall. 1993. A developmental model for evolution of the vertebrate exoskeleton and teeth. *Evolutionary Biology* 27:387–488.

Valentine, J.W., A.G. Collins, and C.P. Meyer. 1994. Morphological complexity increase in metazoans. *Paleobiology* 20:131–42.

Van Valen, L.M. 1970. An analysis of developmental fields. *Developmental Biology* 23:456–77.

Weishampel, D.B. 1983. Hadrosaurid jaw mechanics. *Acta Palaeontologica Polonica* 28:271–80.

———. 1984. The evolution of jaw mechanisms in ornithopod dinosaurs. *Advances in Anatomy, Embryology and Cell Biology* 87:1–110.

Weishampel, D.B., and L.M. Witmer. 1990. Heterodontosauridae. *In* D.B. Weishampel, P. Dodson, and H. Osmólska (eds.), *The Dinosauria.* Berkeley: University of California Press.

Weiss, K.M., J. Bollekens, F.H. Ruddle, and K. Takashita. 1994. Distal-less and other homeobox genes in the development of the dentition. *Journal of Experimental Zoology* 270:273–84.

Werdelin, L. 1987. Jaw geometry and molar morphology in marsupial carnivores: Analysis of a constraint and its macroevolutionary consequences. *Paleobiology* 13:342–50.

———. 1988. Circumventing a constraint: The case of *Thylacoleo* (Marsupialia: Thylacoleonidae). *Australian Journal of Zoology* 36:565–71.

Wu, X.-C., H.-D. Sues, and A. Sun. 1995. A plant-eating crocodyliform reptile from the Cretaceous of China. *Nature* 376:678–80.

Zangerl, R. 1981. *Chondrichthyes. I. Paleozoic elasmobranchii.* Stuttgart and New York: Fischer.

Further Reading

Alexander, R.M. 1994. *Bones: The Unity of Form and Function.* New York: Macmillan; London: Weidenfeld and Nicholson.

Butler, P.M. 1983. Evolution and mammalian dental morphology. *Journal de Biologie Buccale* 11:285–302.

———. 1995. Ontogenetic aspects of dental evolution. *International Journal of Developmental Biology* 39:25–34.

Fortelius, M. 1985. Ungulate cheek teeth: Developmental, functional, and evolutionary interrelations. *Acta Zoologica Fennica* 180:1–76.

———. 1990. The mammalian dentition, a "tangled" view. *Netherlands Journal of Zoology* 40:312–28.

Hillson, S. 1986. *Teeth.* Cambridge and New York: Cambridge University Press.

Koenigswald, W., and P.M. Sander (eds.) 1997. *Tooth Enamel Microstructure.* Rotterdam and Brookfield, Vermont: Balkema.

Patterson, B. 1956. Early Cretaceous mammals and the evolution of mammalian molar teeth. *Fieldiana: Geology* 13:1–105.

Van Valen, L.M. 1994. Serial homology: The crests and cusps of mammalian teeth. *Acta Palaeontologica Polonica* 38:145–58.

TEETH: EVOLUTION OF MAMMALIAN TEETH

Living and ancient mammals can be divided into two major groups, broadly termed "nontherians" and "therians." Nontherian mammals (also known as prototherians) form a diverse group composed of members of the extinct orders Triconodonta, Docodonta, and Multituberculata, and the extant (living) order Monotremata (egg-laying mammals). The basic dental features of prototherians vary widely, as opposed to the single basic form found in therians. Therian mammals are represented in the fossil record by members of the extinct orders Symmetrodonta and Eupantotheria and the extant placental and marsupial mammals. The evolution of mammalian dental features is best illustrated by the therian mammals, recognized as fossils by their "reversed triangle" dentition. This pattern consists of opposed, alternating triangles (upper and lower molars in a tooth row) that shear past each other in a zigzag pattern, similar to the two blades in a pair of pinking shears. Reverse triangle dentition is advantageous because it increases the total length of the shearing edges along the tooth row without requiring additional teeth.

More advanced therian mammals possess a "tribosphenic dentition," a pattern established by the Early Cretaceous in the therians *Pappotherium* and *Aegialodon*. The enamel crowns of tribosphenic molars are complex and share a derived (specialized) pattern of cusps (points on the grinding surface) and connecting crests (ridges). This complexity makes tribosphenic molars excellent models for studying the evolution of mammals; many fossil mammals can be identified as specifically as the species level on the basis of their dentitions alone. Molar teeth are relatively unaffected by growth of the animal or by sexual dimorphism (physical distinctions between males and females) (Gingerich 1976), contributing to their uniformity within a species. It is fortunate that tooth enamel is the hardest vertebrate tissue, because this characteristic allows teeth to be preserved commonly as fossils. The following discussion describes the basic tribosphenic dentition diagrammatically, followed by a brief look at its origin and some examples of subsequent modification. The emphasis here is upon the basics of tooth morphology. More detailed descriptions and terminology can be found in Crompton (1971) and Bown and Kraus (1979).

Throughout the discussion, numbers indicating tooth features are keyed to the definitions in Figure 1.

Basic Tooth Structures

A tribosphenic upper molar can be viewed as a basic triangle (called the trigon), with one point oriented down (Figure 1A). This tooth (a left upper molar) is oriented so that the left side of the tooth is toward the front (anterior) of the mouth, and the top of the tooth is toward the lips (labial). The bottom apex of the triangle points toward the tongue (lingual). This basic tooth orientation commonly is indicated by a pair of perpendicular arrows indicating anterior and labial (Figure 1A). The triangle serves as a platform upon which three main cusps, also known as cones, are placed. The paracone (1) is near the upper left (anterolabial) corner, the metacone (2) near the upper right (posterolabial) corner, and the protocone (3) is near the bottom (lingual) corner. A depression centered among the three main cusps is termed the trigon basin (9). The function of the main cones is to puncture and grind food during chewing.

In addition to the three main cones, smaller cusps termed the paraconule (protoconule) and metaconule (5 and 6, respectively) commonly develop lingual to the paracone and metacone, respectively. Around the triangular platform of the tooth, at the base of the tooth crown, lies a variably developed set of shelves, or cingula (singular cingulum). A hypocone (4) may develop posterior to the protocone on the postcingulum (8), while less commonly, a pericone may develop anterior to the protocone on the precingulum (7). The area labial to the paracone and metacone, termed the stylar shelf, also may bear up to five small cusps. Commonly denoted A to E from front to rear, they are stylar cusp A (parastyle), stylar cusp B (stylocone), stylar cusp C, stylar cusp D, and stylar cusp E (metastyle). All five stylar cusps may be present in some extinct marsupials, but placental mammals commonly bear only the parastyle and metastyle. Stylar cusps usually do not exist as isolated points on the crown; they form a network connected by crests, or cristae (singular crista). Food is sliced as cristae on the upper and lower molars slide past one another.

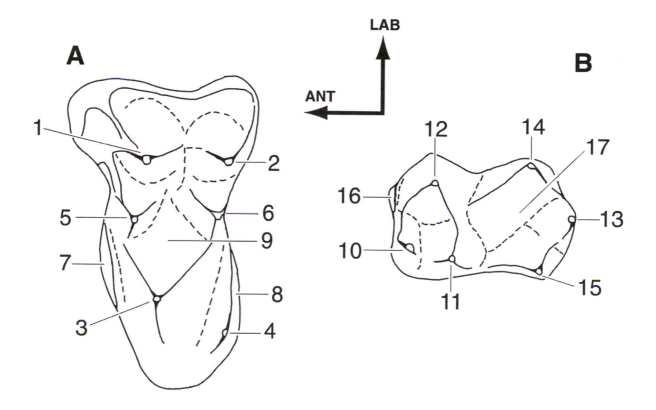

Figure 1. Occlusal views of generalized tribosphenic molars. *A*, left upper; *B*, right lower. Perpendicular arrows indicate directions: *ANT*, anterior; *LAB*, labial. Important features are labelled with the following numbering scheme: *1*, paracone; *2*, metacone; *3*, protocone; *4*, hypocone; *5*, paraconule; *6*, metaconule; *7*, precingulum; *8*, postcingulum; *9*, trigon basin; *10*, paraconid; *11*, metaconid; *12*, protoconid; *13*, hypoconulid; *14*, hypoconid; *15*, entoconid; *16*, precingulid; *17*, talonid basin. Modified and redrawn from Kay and Hiiemäe (1974).

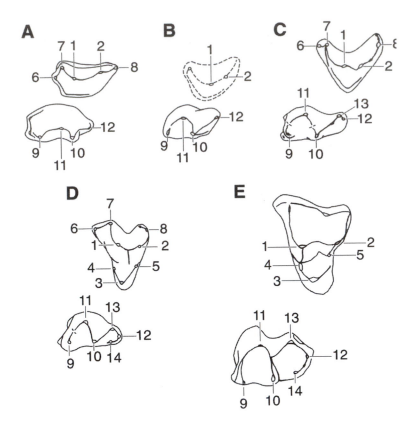

Figure 2. Occlusal views of therian molars showing important stages in the evolution of tribosphenic molars. In *A* and *B*, upper teeth are above, lowers below. View corresponds to Figure 1. *A, Kuehneotherium praecursoris; B, Amphitherium prevostii* (upper molar hypothetical); *C, Peramus tenuirostris; D,* upper molar of *Pappotherium pattersoni,* lower molar of *Aegialodon dawsoni; E, Didelphodus* sp. Important features are labelled with the following numbering scheme: *1,* paracone; *2,* metacone; *3,* protocone; *4,* paraconule; *5,* metaconule; *6,* parastyle; *7,* stylocone; *8,* metastyle; *9,* paraconid; *10,* metaconid; *11,* protoconid; *12,* hypoconulid; *13,* hypoconid; *14,* entoconid. Modified and redrawn from Crompton (1971).

As with the upper molar, a tribosphenic lower molar can be viewed as a basic equilateral triangle with one point up. However, in addition to the triangle (trigonid), lower molars bear a variably developed heel (talonid) attached to the back of the trigonid (Figure 1B). The illustrated tooth, a right lower molar, is oriented so that its left side is toward the front of the mouth (anterior), and the top of the tooth is toward the lips (labial). The trigonid, like the trigon, bears three main cusps. The protoconid (12) is near the top of the triangle (labial), the paraconid (10) is near the bottom left corner, and the metaconid (11) is near the bottom right corner. In clockwise fashion, the three major talonid cusps are the hypoconid (14: near 12 o'clock), the hypoconulid (13: near 3 o'clock), and the entoconid (15: near 6 o'clock). These three talonid cusps enclose a second depression, termed the talonid basin (17). As in upper molars, cusps are connected by cristae, and cingula border the base of the crown.

Evolution of the Tribosphenic Molar

Evolution of the tribosphenic molar can be traced from the earliest known symmetrodonts (e.g., *Kuehneotherium*), which lived in the Early Jurassic. However, the teeth of mammals did not become truly tribosphenic until the Early Cretaceous, when they evolved a protocone on the upper molars and a fully basined talonid on the lower molars. These two structures function in mortar-and-pestle fashion, adding a new crushing ability to teeth that previously functioned only as shearing blades. These two characteristics were first established in Early Cretaceous mammals that are difficult to classify (e.g., *Pappotherium* and *Aegialodon*) because they possess characters of both marsupial and placental mammals. Thus, their relationships to later forms are ambiguous. Studying the evolution of the tribosphenic molar shows that several genera of fossil mammals represent various evolutionary steps. A survey of these genera helps outline important stages of evolution toward the tribosphenic molar.

Kuehneotherium

Kuehneotherium, a primitive Early Jurassic mammal, is among the most primitive known therians, representing an early stage in the evolution of the tribosphenic molar. Owing to its generalized morphology, tribosphenic terminology is difficult to apply to mam-

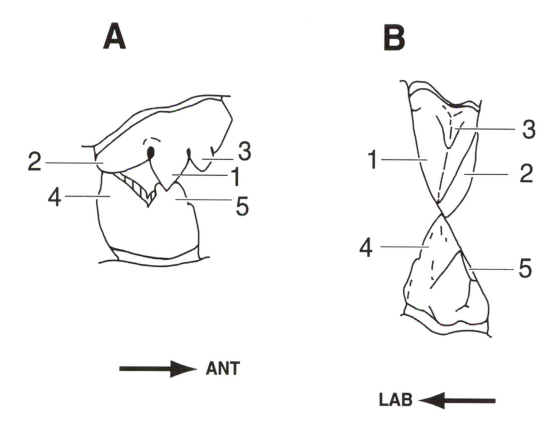

Figure 3. *Smilodon* carnassials (from the right side of jaw). *A*, lateral view; *B*, anterior view. Arrows indicate directions: *ANT*, anterior; *LAB*, labial. Actual length of the last upper premolar (P4) is approximately 4 centimeters. Important features are labelled with the following numbering scheme: *1*, paracone; *2*, metacone; *3*, parastyle; *4*, protoconid; *5*, paraconid. Modified and redrawn from Bryant and Russell (1995).

mals as archaic as *Kuehneotherium*. Some authors resort to naming cusps with a series of upper- and lower-case letters, for upper and lower molars, respectively.

The cheek teeth of *Kuehneotherium* show the earliest trend toward a triangular outline but possess neither a protocone nor a basined talonid (Figure 2A). A trigonlike basin is formed by the paracone (1), metacone (2), and stylocone (7), instead of the protocone. The trigonid consists of cusps typical of tribosphenic lower molars. The talonid is merely a small heel that bears a single cusp, arguably a hypoconulid (12). Molars of *Kuehneotherium* functioned primarily as shearing devices, having little crushing ability. Wear patterns show that shear was confined to front parts of the trigon (prevallum) and back parts of the trigonid (postvallid). Such prevallum-postvallid shear is often revealed by a prominent "wear facet." This is a flat plane on a tooth in one jaw that shows how it rubs against a corresponding tooth in the other jaw. Prevallum-postvallid shear is the primary shearing mechanism in tribosphenic mammals, and it persists in most modern mammals. *Kuehneotherium* has two more pairs of wear facets on molars, indicating two additional shearing surfaces. (See Crompton 1971 for a more detailed discussion of wear facets and their importance in the study of tooth form and function.)

Symmetrodonts and Later Forms

Later Jurassic and Cretaceous symmetrodonts show further advancements toward tribosphenic morphology. The surface angles in trigons and trigonids become more acute than in the obtuse-angled *Kuehneotherium*, but no new cusps evolve. Further advancements are represented by the Middle Jurassic *Amphitherium*, a member of the extinct order Eupantotheria. Eupantotheres represent the main lines toward modern therian mammals, the marsupials and placentals. *Amphitherium* possesses a larger talonid than *Kuehneotherium*, but the hypoconulid (12) remains the sole talonid cusp (Figure 2B). The metacone (2) is enlarged, and its lingual surface forms a new wear facet with the posterolabial edge of the talonid. Early development of the talonid correlated with development of an additional shearing plane. Only later did the talonid become basined, which modified it into a crushing tool.

Novel cusps appear in later members of the eupantotherian lineage, as illustrated by the Late Jurassic *Peramus. Peramus* (Figure 2C) possesses a still larger metacone (2), and the hypoconid (13) joins the hypoconulid (12) on the talonid. *Peramus* also exhibits an expanded lingual cingulum, which provided the foundation for development of the protocone, the major next step in therian evolution.

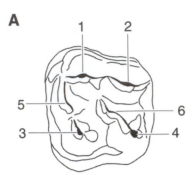

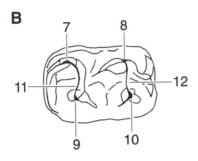

Figure 4. Occlusal views of second molars of *Hyracotherium*. *A*, upper; *B*, lower. View corresponds to Figure 1. Actual length of the second lower molar (m2) is approximately 0.7 centimeter. Important features are labelled with the following numbering scheme: *1*, paracone; *2*, metacone; *3*, protocone; *4*, hypocone; *5*, protoloph; *6*, metaloph; *7*, protoconid; *8*, hypoconid; *9*, metaconid; *10*, entoconid; *11*, protolophid; *12*, hypolophid. Modified and redrawn from Radinsky (1969).

The problematic Cretaceous therians *Pappotherium* and *Aegialodon* represent the oldest known tribosphenic upper and lower molars, respectively. These therians from the Early and Middle Cretaceous are known only from isolated molars, not from jaws in which the teeth were set. Nonetheless, these teeth often are paired for purposes of comparison, to help visualize structures of the earliest upper and lower tribosphenic molars. The upper molar of *Pappotherium* (Figure 2D) possesses a true protocone (3), and the lower molar of *Aegialodon* bears a fully basined talonid. An additional talonid cusp, the entoconid (14), serves to fully encircle the talonid basin. The protocone and its occlusion (primary contact) with the talonid basin are the primary defining characters of an almost modern tribosphenic dentition. The physical contact between the front part of the protocone and the front section of the talonid basin results in another wear facet.

The Final Stage
The final stage in development of the tribosphenic dentition is represented by the living marsupial (opossum) *Didelphis* and the early Cenozoic eutherian *Didelphodus* (Figure 2E). In such mammals, the upper molars develop distinct conules lingual to the

paracone (1) and metacone (2), while the talonid basin increases in size. At this point, another wear facet is added via wear between the back part of the protocone and the posterolingual corner of the talonid basin.

Adaptations in Carnivores and Herbivores
During Cenozoic time, tribosphenic molars have been modified substantially in many mammalian lineages. In some groups, the crown pattern in premolars closely resembles that of molars. Carnivores have emphasized shear to slice prey into manageable pieces. In contrast, several groups of herbivores independently developed molar teeth that emphasize grinding of plant material. Many mammals, including our own order Primates, have developed molar patterns necessitated by an omnivorous diet.

Carnivores
Specializations for meat eating have appeared in many groups of mammals since the early Tertiary. Some true carnivorans, members of the order Carnivora, emphasize prevallum-postvallid shear in their cheek teeth at the expense of all other functions. In a specialized adaptation in carnivorans, shear across the tooth row is concentrated at the "carnassial pair," the last upper premolar (P4) and the first lower molar (m1). This is especially true in cats (families Felidae and Nimravidae), where crushing molars are lost and the carnassials are emphasized through enlargement and anteroposterior alignment of shearing crests. *Smilodon*, the well-known Pleistocene "saber-toothed" cat, is best known for its enlarged canines, but its array of shearing teeth also is of interest. The upper first molar of *Smilodon* is absent, as are more upper molars farther back, making way for the large, bladelike fourth upper premolar. The P4 (Figure 3A) consists of three anteroposteriorly aligned shearing blades, modified from a laterally compressed anterior parastyle (3), a central paracone (1), and a posterior metacone (2), or metastylar blade. The protocone and metastyle are separated by a V-shaped valley called the "carnassial notch." The lower first molar is the sole molar of the lower tooth row, more posterior molars having been lost. This molar is also a bladelike structure, with the shearing surface formed by a laterally compressed anterior paraconid (5) and a posterior protoconid (4), separated by a carnassial notch. Flesh caught between the carnassials was efficiently sheared in a scissorlike motion (Figure 3B).

Herbivores
Several groups of mammals have molar and premolar teeth specialized for grinding tough plant material. Evolution of these teeth is perhaps best illustrated by the well-studied lineage of the modern horse. The early Eocene *Hyracotherium* (formerly known as *Eohippus*) is the best-known primitive member of the order Perissodactyla, a once-diverse order represented today only by horses, tapirs, and rhinoceroses. The molar teeth of *Hyracotherium* are low-crowned (brachyodont), unlike those of the modern horse. However, the molar teeth of *Hyracotherium* show the initial stages of a "lophodont dentition." Here, the connecting crests

between cusps are emphasized to such a degree that the cusps become ill-defined, forming tooth structures called "lophs." They function as crushing and grinding mills for tough plant material, such as leaves and stems. The upper molars of *Hyracotherium* (Figure 4A) are generally rectangular, as the hypocone (4) becomes a significant addition to the tooth crown. Two transverse crossing crests extend across the crown: from the paracone (1) lingual to the protocone (protoloph, 5), and from the metacone (2) lingual to the hypocone (metaloph, 6). The crowns of the lower molars of *Hyracotherium* also bear two main transverse lophs (Figure 4B). The paraconid is lost, and the anterior loph (protolophid, 11) extends from the metaconid (9) labially to the protoconid (7). Posteriorly, a loph (hypolophid, 12) reaches from the entoconid (10) to the hypoconid (8). Later members of the horse lineage accentuated the lophodont nature of the molars and premolars and developed high-crowned (hypsodont) teeth in order to compensate for tooth wear produced by an abrasive diet of silica-rich grasses.

Tribosphenic dentition also can be found relatively unaltered both in fossil and living groups. Some extinct and living insectivores, tree shrews, and primates bear relatively unspecialized dentitions, as do the modern opossum *Didelphis* and its extinct relatives. The so-called primitive (more accurately described as generalized) molar pattern of these animals is advantageous for opportunistic feeding on a wide variety of food items.

Although this essay has focused on development of molar teeth, it is important to note that cheek teeth do not work in isolation. They are part of a complete tooth row consisting of teeth that function in nipping, piercing, slicing, grinding, and even communicating. Upper and lower tooth rows must occlude precisely to function properly. The tooth rows, in turn, are part of a more inclusive and intricate system for capturing food and processing it initially. Essential components of this complex system include the jaw joint, tongue, mandibles, jaw muscles, and the nervous system that coordinates biting, slicing, and chewing motions.

MICHAEL W. WEBB

See also Diet; Diversity; Enamel Microstructure; Teeth: Classification of Teeth; Teeth: Earliest Teeth; Teeth: Evolution of Complex Teeth; Teeth: Tooth Eruption Patterns

Works Cited

Bown, T.M., and M.J. Kraus. 1979. Origin of the tribosphenic molar and metatherian and eutherian dental formulae. *In* J.A. Lillegraven, Z. Kielan-Jaworowska, and W.A. Clemens (eds.), *Mesozoic Mammals: The First Two-Thirds of Mammalian History*. Berkeley: University of California Press.

Bryant, H.N., and A.P. Russell. 1995. Carnassial functioning in nimravid and felid sabertooths: Theoretical basis and robustness of inferences. *In* J.J. Thomason (ed.), *Functional Morphology in Vertebrate Paleontology*. Cambridge and New York: Cambridge University Press.

Crompton, A.W. 1971. The origin of the tribosphenic molar. *In* D.M. Kermack and K.A. Kermack (eds.), *Early Mammals*. Zoological Journal of the Linnean Society, 50. London: Academic Press.

Gingerich, P.D. 1976. *Cranial Anatomy and Evolution of Early Tertiary Plesiadapidae*. University of Michigan Papers on Paleontology, 15. Ann Arbor: Museum of Paleontology, University of Michigan.

Kay, R.F., and K.M. Hiiemäe. 1974. Jaw movement and tooth use in recent and fossil primates. *American Journal of Physical Anthropology* 40:227–56.

Radinsky, L.B. 1969. The early evolution of the Perissodactyla. *Evolution* 23:308–28.

Further Reading

Kermack, D.M., and K.A. Kermack (eds.). 1971. *Early Mammals*. Zoological Journal of the Linnean Society, 50. London: Academic Press.

———. 1984. *The Evolution of Mammalian Characters*. Washington, D.C.: Kapitan Szabo; London: Croom Helm.

Lillegraven, J.A., Z. Kielan-Jaworowska, and W.A. Clemens (eds.). 1979. *Mesozoic Mammals: The First Two-Thirds of Mammalian History*. Berkeley: University of California Press.

TEETH: TOOTH ERUPTION PATTERNS

All vertebrates possess morphological structures that allow them to procure food. Excluding the cyclostomes (lampreys and hagfishes), all modern vertebrates use jaws for this purpose. Among their many advantages, the evolution of jaws allowed animals access to a much wider variety of food items previously denied to jawless organisms. Jaws are, perhaps, the most significant advancement in the evolution of vertebrates.

Teeth, in their most basic sense, are hard structures associated with the jaws to enhance food processing. As tools for food capture and initial processing, teeth function as a unit. The harmony of a functional tooth row may be disrupted during an animal's life as teeth are lost during growth or incidents of trauma. Disruption of function is minimized through a pattern of tooth replacement unique to a specific organism or shared among several related taxa.

The focus of this article is the marginal teeth of gnathostome vertebrates (i.e., jawed fishes and tetrapods). Since teeth can arise on several bones associated with the oral cavity, only marginal teeth are discussed. In all gnathostome groups except the elasmobranchs (sharks and rays), marginal teeth are those associated with the maxilla and premaxilla in the upper jaw, and dentary in the lower jaw. Marginal tooth eruption and replacement patterns of some major gnathostome groups are illustrated.

Most gnathostomes are polyphyodont. Polyphyodont vertebrates exhibit continuous replacement of older teeth by younger successors. Some of the oldest known fossils to show evidence of continuous tooth replacement are members of the elasmobranchs. Polyphyodonty in elasmobranchs is first recorded in the Devonian (over 360 million years ago) and is still seen today (Carroll 1988). The marginal teeth of elasmobranchs form on cartilaginous tissues that are not homologous (related through shared ancestry) with the maxilla, premaxilla, or dentary. In most elasmobranchs, a functional tooth at a single spot occupies the jaw margin while several successive tooth generations form on the inside of the jaw margin, medial to the functional tooth row. Each successor is similar in shape to its predecessor, but slightly larger in order to fill the progressively growing jaw. Except in groups where more than one tooth generation is functional at any one time, a new tooth will only become functional after its predecessor has been shed.

Like elasmobranchs, most other lower vertebrates (bony fishes, amphibians, and reptiles) possess a continuous tooth eruption and replacement pattern. Of interest to researchers has been the order and timing of tooth replacement. An alternating pattern of tooth replacement predominates in gnathostomes; alternating (even and odd) teeth are commonly at different developmental stages, each group replaced as a series more or less independently of the other (Edmund 1960). Less well understood is the pattern in which one series, say one containing all odd-numbered teeth, is replaced. Edmund's survey of reptilian modes of tooth replacement focused on anteriorly migrating zahnreihen, or waves of tooth eruption along a jaw, the teeth of several zahnreihen forming the functional tooth row at any one time. Edmund's work initiated many studies on zahnreihen and tooth replacement, resulting in the recognition of several different types of tooth replacement waves (Bolt and DeMar 1986). At this time, there is no consensus on a single general pattern of continuous tooth replacement common to lower vertebrates.

Some dinosaurian groups provide exceptions and modifications to the continuous tooth replacement pattern that are of special interest to biologists and paleontologists. Most carnivorous dinosaurs retain the simple teeth and replacement patterns of their ancestors. However, Late Cretaceous (about 95 to 65 million years ago) hadrosaurian dinosaurs multiplied their tooth numbers, consolidating teeth of several generations into unified structures called dental batteries. A dental battery is formed by numerous teeth in rising vertical series (representing more than one tooth generation) supporting each other in a tightly-packed framework, a modification for the initial processing of tough plant matter (Weishampel and Horner 1990). Older teeth near the top of the dental battery are not sloughed off, but efficiently worn down, roots and all. The growth of new teeth from below replenishes the dental battery, counteracting tooth wear.

Mammals differ from other gnathostomes in being diphyodont: they possess only two reduced sets of teeth, deciduous (or milk) and permanent. Diphyodonty is a key development in the evolution of efficient tooth occlusion characteristic of the Mammalia (Carroll 1988). Mammals are also heterodont (except where this condition is lost secondarily): they possess a variety of tooth morphologies along the functional tooth row. This allows teeth to be grouped anteroposteriorly (from front to back) as incisors, canines, premolars, and molars.

Living mammals include marsupials and placentals. While marsupials after birth replace only the most posterior premolar, all teeth except for the molars are replaced by placental mammals. The permanent teeth of an adult mammal is therefore composed of parts of two dental series. The marsupial pattern of tooth replacement that we see today was established as early as the Late Cretaceous and is correlated with nipple fixation during early postnatal life (Cifelli et al. 1996). All marsupial teeth belong to the first dental series except the permanent third premolar, which is part of the second series. The placental pattern of tooth replacement, replacing all teeth except for the molars, is decidedly more primitive as it more closely approaches the polyphyodont condition. The molars are affiliated with the first dental series, while the more anterior teeth belong to the second dental series. In both groups of mammals, tooth eruption and replacement proceeds anteroposteriorly.

Among the placentals, fossil elephants demonstrate a uniquely modified tooth replacement pattern. Members of the Elephantidae (including the modern elephants and extinct mammoths), ranging in time from Miocene to Recent, possess only three premolars and three molars in their short jaws. The six grinding teeth erupt sequentially, with the sixth tooth erupting well into adulthood; each tooth is substantially larger than its predecessor in order to accommodate jaw growth. Teeth move forward in the jaw as they wear, drop out when totally worn, and are replaced from behind by their successors. Rarely are more than two teeth functional in any one jaw quadrant at a time (Haynes 1991). In contrast with other mammals, tooth replacement occurs in both childhood and adult life, and replacement teeth erupt behind, not beneath, the functional teeth.

Gnathostome vertebrates do not replace teeth in random fashion. Rather, replacement proceeds in regular patterns in response to growth and injury. The most basic replacement pattern is one based on the polyphyodont dentitions of sharks, reptiles, and other lower vertebrates. In these groups, alternate teeth are continuously and regularly replaced by waves of tooth eruption. Mammals, being diphyodont, have greatly reduced tooth replacement; placental and marsupial adult dentitions are composed of parts of only two tooth waves. In light of the array of tooth forms and functions, it is interesting to note that this diversity is based upon only a few basic tooth replacement patterns. Tooth replacement patterns are as ancient as teeth themselves and are crucial for the maintenance of properly functioning dentitions.

MICHAEL W. WEBB

See also Feeding Adaptations: Vertebrates; Growth, Development, and Evolution; Teeth: Classification of Teeth; Teeth: Earliest Teeth; Teeth: Evolution of Complex Teeth; Teeth: Evolution of Mammalian Teeth

Works Cited

Bolt, J.R., and R.E. DeMar. 1986. Computer simulation of tooth replacement with growth in lower tetrapods. *Journal of Vertebrate Paleontology* 6:233–50.
Carroll, R.L. 1988. *Vertebrate paleontology and evolution*. New York: Freeman.

Cifelli, R.L., T.B. Rowe, W.P. Luckett, J. Banta, R. Reyes, and R.I. Howes. 1996. Fossil evidence for the origin of the marsupial pattern of tooth replacement. *Nature* 379:715–18.

Edmund, A.G. 1960. *Tooth Replacement Phenomena in the Lower Vertebrates.* Toronto: Life Sciences Division Royal Ontario Museum.

Haynes, G. 1991. *Mammoths, Mastodonts, and Elephants: Biology, Behavior, and the Fossil Record.* Cambridge and New York: Cambridge University Press.

Weishampel, D.B., and J.R. Horner. 1990. Hadrosauridae. *In* D.B. Weishampel, P. Dodson, and H. Osmólska (eds.), *The Dinosauria.* Berkeley: University of California Press.

Ziegler, A.C. 1971. A theory of the evolution of therian dental formulas and replacement patterns. *Quarterly Review of Biology* 46:226–49.

Further Reading

Butler, P.M., and K.A. Joysey (eds.). 1978. *Development, Function, and Evolution of Teeth.* London and New York: Academic Press.

Kurtén, B. (ed.). 1982. *Teeth: Form, Function, and Evolution.* New York: Columbia University Press.

Peyer, B. 1968. *Comparative Odontology.* Chicago: University of Chicago Press.

TEILHARD DE CHARDIN, PIERRE

French, 1881–1955

Pierre Teilhard de Chardin's background in both the sciences and theology proved instrumental in the development of his synthesis of a distinctly Christian evolutionary theory. Born in Sarcenat, France, on 1 May 1881, he received his early education at the Jesuit college of Mongré (Rhône), and he entered the Society of Jesus in 1899. He was ordained a priest in 1911. His interests soon turned to natural history, and after further study in England he began work in the field of paleontology at the Museum of Natural History in Paris in 1912, under the direction of Marcellin Boule. Interrupted in his studies and scientific training by World War I, Teilhard de Chardin chose to become a stretcher bearer in the French army, not a chaplain, and he was decorated for courage. Upon his return from the war, he completed his doctoral thesis *Les Mammifères de l'Eocène inférieur français et leurs gisements* and successfully defended it at the Sorbonne in 1922.

Teilhard taught geology for a brief period at the Catholic Institute of Paris, but soon he left for China, joining paleontological teams (among which was the *Croisière Jaune*, organized by Citroën). He resided in Shanghai and Peking until 1943, sharing the responsibility of the Geobiological Institute. There, as a consultant to the Geological Survey, he focused his study and attention on the stratigraphy and paleontology of northern China and Asia. In this capacity he collaborated in the excavations at Zhoukoudian near Beijing and in the discovery of *Sinantropus pekinensis* (Peking Man, *Homo erectus*). He also participated in numerous expeditions in Central Asia, India, Burma, and Java. Kept under house arrest by the Japanese during their occupation of China, he was able to pursue his intense paleontological activity through much of World War II.

From 1946 until his death, first in France and then in New York as a fellow of the Wenner-Gren Foundation for Anthropological Research, he devoted himself to the elaboration of an anthropogenesis, a kind of new anthropology, a scientific and philosophical effort to describe the real "place of mankind" in the universe. The foundation sent him on two different occasions to South Africa to evaluate the recent discoveries of Australopithecines and coordinate expeditions concerning the origin of human life in sub-Saharan Africa.

Teilhard's specific contribution to paleontology and stratigraphy appears in the 170 or so articles and technical papers he published, which added substantially to the knowledge of sedimentary deposits and the history of life in Asia (particularly the history of Cenozoic mammals and human evolution). His studies have proven most helpful in dating the fossilized breccia at Zhoukoudian and correlating it with the Paleolithic strata of the entire continent. His interest in the evolution of man dominates his research in these technical fields.

Teilhard's influence moves beyond strict paleontological science, however, and concerns what might be called natural philosophy. He envisions mankind in its totality as a phenomenon to be described and analyzed as any other phenomenon: it and all its manifestations, including human history and values, are proper objects for scientific study. His *Phénomene humaine* (1955) proposes a threefold synthesis: first, of the material and physical world with the world of mind and spirit; second, of the past with the future; and third, of variety with unity, the many with the one. He achieved this synthesis by examining every subject of his investigation with reference to its development in time and its evolutionary position. The universe as a whole must be regarded as one gigantic process of becoming, of attaining new levels of organization, which properly can be called an ongoing becoming: cosmogenesis, biogenesis, noogenesis (gradual evolution of mind and mental properties). As lucidly expressed by Sir Julian Huxley in his English-language introduction to the work (translated as *The Phenomenon of Man*, 1959), evolutionary processes cannot be evaluated solely in terms of their origins: they are better defined by their direction, their inherent dynamism and possibilities and their deducible future trends.

Teilhard coined the concept of the "noosphere," the new "thinking layer" or membrane on the Earth's surface, superposed on the living layer (biosphere) and the lifeless layer of inorganic matter (lithosphere). Obeying the "law of complexification/conscience," the entire universe undergoes a process of "convergent integration" and tends to a final state of concentration, the "point Omega" where the noosphere will be intensely unified and will have achieved a "hyperpersonal" organization. Teilhard equates this future hyperpersonal psychological organization with an emergent divinity. This effort to reconcile the supernatural elements in Christianity (he writes of the trend as a "Christogenesis") with the facts and implications of evolution raises difficult questions about Teilhard's methodology and epistemology, but it in no way detracts from the positive value of his naturalistic general approach. His "natural philosophy" was developed through 40 years of meditation and proposed in many essays, both published and unpublished, all of which were assembled after his death in some 15 volumes.

Teilhard has been characterized as one of the great minds of the twentieth century. Despite reservations and criticisms, his visionary and somewhat prophetic perspectives, as well as his seductive and global interpretation of the universe, where matter and spirit, body and soul, science and faith find their unity, have raised considerable interest and are still being studied among scientists, philosophers, sociologists, and theologians.

EDOUARD L. BONÉ

Biography

Born in Sarcenat, Orcine, department Puy-de-Dôme, 1 May 1881. Educated at the Jesuit college of Mongré (Rhône); entered the Society of Jesus, Province of Lyons, 1899; studied philosophy at Jersey, theology at Hastings (southern England), 1908–12; ordained as a priest in 1911; received Ph.D., Sorbonne, Paris, 1922. Taught physics and chemistry, Cairo, Egypt, 1905–8; began work in paleontology at the Muséum d'Histoire Naturelle, Paris, 1912; served as stretcher bearer during World War II, earning membership in the Légion d'Honneur; assistant professor of geology, Institut Catholique de Paris, 1920–23; spent considerable time doing research in China, 1923–45; appointed scientific adviser (1929) and, later, acting director, Chinese Geological Society; director of research, Centre National des Recherches Scientifiques, 1947; became member, Académie Française, 1947; fellow, Wenner-Gren Foundation for Anthropological Research, New York, 1952–55. Best known as the discoverer of Peking Man (*Homo erectus,* 1929) and as the proponent of a synthesis of the evolutionary perspective of modern science with the Christian worldview. Died in New York City, 10 April, 1955.

Major Publications

1916–21. *Les Mammifères de l'Eocène inférieur français et leurs gisements.* Paris: Masson.

1955a. *Le phénomene humain.* Paris: Seuil; as *The Phenomenon of Man,* New York: Harper, 1959; London: Collins, 1959.

1955b. *Oeuvres de Pierre Teilhard de Chardin.* 15 vols. Paris: Seuil. [Vol. 13, *Le coeur de la matière,* contains a complete bibliography.]

1956. *Lettres de voyage, 1923–1939.* Paris: Grasset.

1957. *Nouvelles lettres de voyage, 1939–1955.* Paris: Grasset; translated (with *Lettres de voyage, 1923–1939*) as *Letters from a Traveller,* New York: Harper, 1962; London: Collins, 1962.

1971. N. Schmitz-Moormann and K. Schmitz-Moormann (eds.). *Pierre Teilhard de Chardin: L'oeuvre scientifique.* 10 vols. Munich: Walter-Verlag.

Further Reading

Barbour, G. 1965. *In the Field with Teilhard de Chardin.* New York: Herder and Herder.

Cuénot, C. 1965. *Teilhard de Chardin: A Biographical Study.* Baltimore, Maryland: Helicon; London: Burns and Oates; as *Pierre Teilhard de Chardin: Les grandes étapes de son évolution.* Paris: Plon, 1958.

Delfgaauw, B. 1969. *Evolution: The Theory of Teilhard de Chardin.* New York: Harper and Row; London: Collins; as *Teilhard de Chardin,* Baarn: Wereldvenster, 1961.

McCarthy, Joseph M. 1981. *Pierre Teilhard de Chardin: A Comprehensive Bibliography.* New York: Garland.

TERRESTRIAL ENVIRONMENT

Paleoenvironmental reconstructions typically combine studies by sedimentologists, stratigraphers, taphonomists, geochemists, and paleontologists to interpret ancient environments and to understand how environments changed through time. Sedimentary rocks contain a record of ancient environments, but reading this record is a complex puzzle that must combine many different kinds of information. Each depositional environment leaves behind sediment bodies that have distinct geometries and internal characteristics. Organisms that live in different environments can disrupt (bioturbate) sediments in distinct ways; such organisms are commonly preserved as fossils in the environments in which they lived. The chemistry of certain types of sediments also provides clues to environmental change. Scientists reconstructing ancient environments generally need detailed knowledge of depositional processes in modern environments and the habitats preferred by different types of organisms. If we understand what is laid down in modern settings, we can look for sim-

ilar features in ancient sediments for clues to environments of the past.

In order for sedimentary rocks to form, large volumes of sediments must accumulate over long periods of time. The most continuous records of ancient terrestrial environments form in major sedimentary basins next to mountain belts, in areas of rifting (where tectonic plates are splitting), and at shorelines where rivers enter the sea. Sediments can also accumulate in subsiding desert areas, where winds build large sand dunes, and when continental glaciers retreat, leaving till (mix of clay, sand, gravel, and boulders) to be reworked by winds into sheets of silt and by rivers into coarse-grained outwash deposits. Many terrestrial environments are rarely preserved in the ancient geologic record. Alpine areas, high plateaus, and other landscapes being eroded by rivers tend to be represented in the rock record only as major erosion surfaces.

Sedimentary rocks contain many internal structures that indicate the type and the energy of depositional mechanisms that operated in the environment where they formed. Relationships between sedimentary structures and depositional processes were defined by studying modern environments and by making scale models in artificial water courses. Recognition and interpretation of these sedimentary features provide the basic building blocks for any interpretation of depositional environments. For example, the grain size of a sedimentary rock generally reflects the strength of currents in which it was deposited. Deposits of coarse-grained gravel or sand form where currents are fast, whereas fine-grained muds can only settle in quiet water. Migration of ripples and dunes in rivers, under ocean waves, or on the desert floor produces cross-stratification (sets of inclined laminations, bounded by relatively horizontal surfaces). Details of such cross-stratification can indicate current speed and whether depositional currents consistently flowed in one direction, fluctuated due to tides, or oscillated under the influence of waves. There are many types of sedimentary structures preserved within ancient rocks, and subtle differences within each type. Those interested in the details should consult any introductory sedimentology text book (e.g., Allen 1985; Boggs 1995).

Major terrestrial environments include riverine, glacial, desert, and coastal environments. Within each environment, various subenvironments can be identified, such as floodplains and channels in the riverine case. Different depositional processes operate in each subenvironment; therefore, associated deposits have different characteristics. For example, coarse-grained, cross-stratified deposits accumulate in the river channel, whereas finer-grained deposits accumulate on the floodplain, where they are subsequently bioturbated by vegetation and burrowing organisms. The set of sedimentary features that makes a particular unit of sedimentary rock distinctive from the rocks around it is called a sedimentary "facies." The spatial organization of facies within sedimentary rocks records the changing processes of deposition within subenvironments and the shifting position of subenvironments during sediment accumulation. By studying characteristic facies associations formed by different depositional processes, geologists have developed "facies models" that summarize the facies produced in numerous terrestrial environments and their typical lateral and vertical distribution. Geologists examine sedimentary rocks, describe their character and distribution, and interpret depositional environments by comparing observed facies associations with facies models. Facies models for a few common terrestrial environments are very briefly summarized below, to provide a flavor of what these models entail. There are several good introductory textbooks summarizing facies models of different environments for those interested in delving deeper into the literature (e.g., Walker and James 1992; Reading 1996).

In riverine environments, sandy channel deposits are incised into muddy floodplain deposits. Channels typically leave long ribbon-like sandstones, elongated down the course of the river. The exact shape of these sandstones depends on (1) how sinuous the river becomes as it migrates and (2) whether the river was single channel or highly braided. Channel deposits generally become finer grained, reflecting slower currents where sediments accumulate on the inside of river bends and faster flows in deeper water near the outside of river bends. Large-scale inclined bedding forms

as channels migrate, and internal cross-stratification can be used to reconstruct the size and discharge of ancient rivers (e.g., Willis 1993). Channels with low-velocity flows and muddy fills can be excellent sites for fossil accumulation, whereas fossils tend to be abraded and destroyed in fast-flowing rivers carrying loads of abrasive, coarse-grained sediment. Overbank deposits form when water overtops the channel and spreads thin lobes or sheets of sand and mud across the floodplain. The sandier sediments tend to be deposited next to the channel, forming leeves, whereas muds tend to settle out in swamps and local floodplain ponds, in low areas farther away from the river channel.

Most overbank sediments are deposited during rare major floods and thus do not record "normal" environments on the floodplain. In contrast, ancient soils (paleosols) provide an indication of the floodplain environments in which the now-fossilized fauna and flora lived. Where the water table was high and the ground swampy, organic matter tends to be preserved in soils rather than to decompose completely. These become dark gray paleosols or coals when they are buried and lithified. Well-drained areas of the floodplain tend to have soils with leached, oxidized upper horizons that decompose organic matter and, where the climate is dry enough, an underlying horizon of carbonate nodules. Soils in these areas tend to become bright red-orange paleosols that lack organic matter. The isotopic composition of carbonate nodules in these well-drained soils can provide an important record of the types of vegetation that grew on the floodplain (Cerling et al. 1989). In the best-preserved examples, paleosols have all the rich features and horizons of modern soils, which allows for fairly detailed comparisons with the soil science literature. G.J. Retallack (1990) provides an introductory text to paleosol interpretation. If the soil chemistry is suitable for bone preservation, paleosols can be rich fossil sites, but they can be barren when it is not.

Deltas form where a river enters a standing body of water, such as a lake or ocean. As river currents enter the sea, they decelerate and rapidly drop their sediment load to form a thick lobe of sediment that thins and becomes finer-grained basinward. As the delta grows, coarser-grained deposits near the shore extend out over finer-grained deposits formed in deeper areas of the basin. Thus, as one moves upward within delta deposits, sediments become coarser-grained. Delta deposits typically are divided into three parts: "Topset deposits" are formed in sandy distributary channels, swamps, and muddy interdistributary bays on the subaerially exposed top of the delta; "foreset deposits" are steeply inclined interbedded sands and shales that dip seaward; and "bottomset deposits" are mostly laminated mud beds in front of the delta that are parallel with the sea floor. Delta deposits can be quite variable, depending on the extent that sediments delivered by the river are subsequently reworked by waves and tides. Marine fossils can accumulate at the edge of the delta, mixed with terrestrial material transported to the delta front by rivers. Deposits in areas more open to the sea tend to be bioturbated by a richer diversity of burrows than deposits laid down in brackish and freshwater environments.

Barrier beaches are typically long, thin sand bodies that parallel the coast and form away from major rivers. Here, wave currents dominate deposition. The waves build a sandy island separated from land by a shallow lagoon. In contrast to deltas, which can have a complex intermixing of sand and mud, the sandstone of barrier islands tends to be clean. Sands are transported and deposited by high-energy waves along the shore, but muds remain suspended until they are carried farther out to sea. When barrier islands grow seaward over the muddy seafloor, they form an upward-coarsening deposit. Generally, marine muds change upward to wave-deposited cross-stratified sands, and finally to planar, laminated beach sands. As tidal channels cut barriers, the moving water can rework sands both seaward and landward into the lagoon, producing relatively small ebb and flood tidal deltas, respectively. The lagoon muds behind the barrier tend to be black with organic materials and contain thin sand sheets, which formed as unusually large hurricane waves washed sands over the top of the barrier island.

Estuaries form in bays that can amplify tidal currents. When tides are strong, sand bars can migrate along the length of the estuary. Elongate tidal sand bodies are concentrated along the estuary axis, whereas extensive muddy tidal flats form along its margins. Where waves are strong at the mouth of the estuary, a barrier island can form to produce a protected estuary bay filled with bioturbated mudstones. Bayhead deltas occur at the landward end of many estuaries. Bayhead deltas can prograde gradually, eventually filling the estuary and protruding from the coastline into the sea as a normal delta.

Terrestrial environments have changed dramatically over 4.6 billion years of geologic history. A particularly important change occurred in the Devonian (360–400 million years ago), when plants first emerged from the sea and then covered the landscape. However, throughout geologic history major changes in terrestrial environments have occurred as plants continued to evolve, climates changed, sea level fluctuated, tectonic plates drifted to different latitudes, and mountain belts uplifted and eroded. In the simplest scenario, as sediments fill in a subsiding basin and environments shift seaward, a record of the changing environments across an ancient landscape is preserved. In such a case, the vertical stacking of different rock types records the lateral distribution of environments across an ancient land surface. For example, a vertical progression from marine mudstones, to deltaic sandstones, and finally to river deposits can be taken to record the normal distribution of paleoenvironments along a transect perpendicular to the shoreline.

In reality, the geologic record is more complex because environments are constantly evolving in both space and time, and deposits from some spatially linked environments might not be preserved. For example, it has been observed in some systems that when the sea level falls, river deposits are incised by valleys, and deltas become dominated by rivers as the rivers rapidly prograde seaward. When sea levels subsequently rise, valleys become flooded by rising waters, and retrograding deltas tend to be more influenced by wave action. In this case, placement of esturine deposits over the base of a river valley, or of wave-dominated delta over river-dominated delta deposits, does not represent the vertical stacking of laterally linked environments. Rather, the environments have changed over time as the sediments aggraded. The valley represents the long period of time when sediment was bypassed basinward. Similarly, marine erosion surfaces and hiatus hard-

grounds can form as sea level rises and deposition shifts landward. Such lateral shifts in deposition are important because they indicate that similar thicknesses of sediment do not represent similar amounts of time. A thin erosion surface in one succession may represent the same period of time as a thick succession of sandstone in the next. Ideally paleoenvironmental reconstructions should cover a wide enough area to document lateral shifts in facies across the basin, to distinguish spatially shifting paleoenviroments from the evolution of paleoenvironments through time.

As the area of investigation gets larger, the problems of correlating isolated outcrops to reconstruct ancient environments becomes more consequential. Unlike many marine strata, where rapidly evolving microfossils are relatively common and widespread, terrestrial strata seldom have high enough biostratigraphic resolution to significantly improve lithostratigraphic cor-relations. Magneto-stratigraphy allows moderately high resolution correlation of some terrestrial successions deposited during times when Earth's magnetic polarity switched rapidly. Similarly, some terrestrial successions contain numerous ash beds that can be correlated and dated. In the end, all available information must be used in paleoenvironmental reconstructions (e.g., a comparison of two integrated studies of long terrestrial successions is given in Badgley and Behrensmeyer 1995). Important bedding surfaces and facies changes must be traced and correlated as far as possible. The depositional history of the sediments, subsequent bioturbation (including pedogenesis), and interpreted habitats of enclosed fossils allow interpretations of the local environment. Finally, changes in lateral and vertical facies, important stratigraphic erosion and hiatus surfaces, and any other interdependent methods of correlation are used to interpret the evolution of environments in space and time.

BRIAN J. WILLIS

See also Atmospheric Environment; Faunal and Floral Provinces; Global Environment; Ocean Environment; Paleoclimatology; Palynology; Sedimentology; Seismic and Surface Activity; Stable Isotope Analysis

Works Cited

Allen, J.R.L. 1985. *Principles of Physical Sedimentology.* London and Boston: Allen and Unwin.

Badgley, C., and A.K. Behrensmeyer (eds.). 1995. Long records of continental ecosystems. *Paleogeography, Paleoclimatology, Paleoecology* Special issue, 115.

Boggs, S. 1995. *Principles of Sedimentology and Stratigraphy.* 2nd ed., Englewood Cliffs, New Jersey: Prentice-Hall.

Cerling, T., J. Quade, W. Yang, and J. Bowman. 1989. Soil and paleosols as ecologic and paleoecologic indicators. *Nature* 341:138–39.

Reading, H.G. (ed.). 1996. *Sedimentary Environments: Processes, Facies and Stratigraphy.* 3rd ed., Oxford and Cambridge, Massachusetts: Blackwell.

Retallack, G.J. 1990. *Soils of the Past.* Boston: Unwin-Hyman; London: Harper Collins Academic.

Walker, R.G., and N.P. James (ed.). 1992. *Facies Models: Response to Sea*

Level Change. St. John's, Newfoundland: Geological Association of Canada.

Willis, B.J. 1993. Ancient river systems in the Himalayan foredeep, Chinji Village area, northern Pakistan. *Sedimentary Geology* 88:1–76.

Further Reading

Allen, J.R.L. 1985. *Principles of Physical Sedimentology*. London and Boston: Allen and Unwin.

Boggs, S. 1987. *Principles of Sedimentology and Stratigraphy*. New York: Macmillan; 2nd ed., Englewood Cliffs, New Jersey: Prentice-Hall, 1995.

Reading, H.G. (ed.). 1978. *Sedimentary Environments: Processes, Facies and Stratigraphy*. New York: Elsevier; as *Sedimentary Environments and Facies,* Oxford: Blackwell; 3rd ed., Oxford and Cambridge, Massachusetts: Blackwell.

Retallack, G.J. 1990. *Soils of the Past*. Boston: Unwin-Hyman; London: Harper Collins Academic.

TERRESTRIALIZATION OF ANIMALS

Establishing which animals first set foot on land is heavily constrained by the nature of the fossil record. While an aqueous environment is likely to be conducive to fossilization, the bare, hostile land surface on which these early animals walked was not. The land, lacking an extensive plant cover, would have been whipped by winds, water courses would have shifted constantly, and sandstorms repeatedly would have covered, uncovered, and moved dead bodies. However, at a few localities, a combination of serendipitous factors has produced exceptional preservation. This has been either in the form of actual body fossils, sometimes exquisitely preserved, or as trace fossils that detail the behavior of many of these early terrestrial colonizers.

Both lines of evidence point to arthropods as having been the first metazoans to achieve terrestrialization. Despite being very well preadapted to terrestrialization, such early arthropod land pioneers would have faced immense physiological problems in making the transition from an aqueous to a dry environment. The major problems centered on inhabiting an environment where daily temperatures could be much higher or much lower than in the aquatic environment. Moreover, the much greater diurnal (daytime) changes presented the problem of desiccation (drying out). There was also the requirement to respire (breathe) in another medium: air. Consequently, different methods of gas exchange were needed. The evolution of lungs may have occurred, in the case of tetrapods, in fishes that became adapted to living in freshwater environments under very low oxygen conditions. However, the major limiting factor in the transition from an aquatic environment to an air-breathing one is the problem of carbon dioxide excretion in air (Selden and Edwards 1989).

One of the main reasons for the success of arthropods lay in their tough, crusty outer shell, which evolved at the beginning of the Cambrian period. This preadapted arthropods to a life on land. In addition to providing defense against predators, it gave strength to the body for locomotion and feeding. Moreover, it helped overcome the dragging effects of gravity, a major problem to organisms used to the buoyant effects of water. Without such prestrengthened legs, terrestrial locomotion would have posed many problems. This is emphasized by the fact that land arthropods today can still be vulnerable to mechanical failure following molting, while their new cuticle is hardening. Arthropods also possessed the ability, like land plants, to secrete a waterproof outer covering on their shell to stop water loss.

Among the earliest indications of animal activity on land are trace fossils found in Late Ordovician fossil soils in Pennsylvania (Retallack and Feakes 1987). Within these ancient soils, there are vertical burrows up to 20 millimeters in diameter that have been interpreted as possibly having been made by millipedes. The suggestion that millipedes were very early terrestrial colonizers implies that they may have overcome high temperature and the problems of desiccation by burrowing in the soil, or hiding in any crevices they could find, much as they do today. Other indirect evidence for animals on land comes from Late Silurian deposits in Sweden, where M.A. Sherwood-Pyke and J. Gray (1985) have described what they interpret as fossilized fecal pellets. Containing fungal hyphae (threadlike processes), they indicate the existence of fungi-eating microarthropods, perhaps mites or millipedes. If so, this implies that some of the earliest land animals occupied a decomposer niche. As such, they would have played an important role in the establishment of soils, reworking the upper layers and increasing nitrate and phosphate levels. This would have provided a necessary habitat to allow subsequent colonization by vascular plants.

Support for the indication of early millipede colonization of the land comes from fossil trackways attributed to these arthropods found in Middle Ordovician rocks in the Lake District, England (Johnson et al. 1994). The nature of the preservation of the tracks indicates that they were made in a subaerial environment. A rich arthropod trace fossil fauna from Late Silurian rocks in the Murchison River region in Western Australia provides evidence that a diverse fauna of large arthropods was present on land by this time (Trewin and McNamara 1995). Trackways, up to 30 centimeters across, indicated that eurypterids, possibly giant scorpions, centipedes, and euthycarcinoids, and a range of other unknown arthropods, were walking on land. A single body fossil of the euthycarcinoid arthropod *Kalbarria brimmellae* represents the oldest known fossil of a land animal (McNamara and Trewin 1993).

One of the earliest sites to provide evidence of the rich community of arthropods that first colonized the land is the early Devonian Rhynie Chert in Aberdeenshire, Scotland. Three hundred ninety-five million years ago, what is now a small field in Aberdeenshire looked more like modern-day New Zealand, with hot springs, belching fumaroles, and geysers. Here, animals were trapped in small pools of hot silica-rich water, so providing an intimate insight into the first life on land. Crawling through an undergrowth of early simple vascular plants, algae, fungi, and lichens was a rich fauna dominated by arthropods. These include the fairy shrimp *Lepidocaris;* three species of spiderlike trigonotarbids; the mite *Protocarus;* and the earliest hexapod *Rhyniella.* The presence of book lungs (paired respiratory structures arranged like pages in a book) in one trigonotarbid, *Palaeocharinus,* provides firm evidence that the animal had achieved a major step of terrestrialization: the ability to respire on land.

New fossil finds made in recent years provide evidence that early terrestrial arthropods were predominantly carnivores. Processing of a muddy siltstone from just above the famous Late Silurian Ludlow Bone Bed in Shropshire has revealed a large quantity of arthropod cuticle, representing at least two types of centipedes, the trigonotarbid arachnid *Eotarbus jerami,* an arthropleurid, and a probable terrestrial scorpion (Jeram et al. 1990).

Slightly younger Middle Devonian remains from Gilboa in New York State have yielded a similar arthropod-dominated terrestrial fauna of millipedes, mites, pseudoscorpions, and arachnids, including the earliest known spider (Shear et al. 1984). Like modern spiders, this tiny animal, between half and about one centimeter long, called *Attercopus fimbriunguis,* is equipped with a spinneret, providing evidence that even the earliest spiders were able to spin webs (Selden et al. 1991). It also was endowed with fangs and a poison gland. Within the same deposit occurs the earliest known pseudoscorpion *Dracochela.* This is surprisingly similar to living pseudoscorpions and can be accommodated within a living superfamily.

Like arthropods from Rhynie and Ludlow, those from Gilboa were mainly predators, with a few detritivores (debris eaters). Herbivores are unknown. The predators probably fed mainly on the microarthropod detritivores such as mites and millipedes. Although rarely preserved, they probably comprised a major part of the litter fauna. There is little evidence for herbivorous arthropods in the fossil record until well into the Carboniferous period. W.A. Shear (1991) has suggested that by-products from the synthesis of lignin, which was present in early vascular plants, may have been toxic to early terrestrial animals. He has suggested that true herbivory may only have become established when animals had evolved enzymes along with a gut microflora of symbiotic bacteria. Then they would have been able to break down fresh plant material directly without the need for external decomposers.

However, fossil coprolites (feces) from the Late Silurian deposits in Shropshire indicate that animals were feeding on some form of plant matter at this time. These ancient droppings are composed largely of undigested land-plant spores. The question is, therefore, were the droppings from detritivores (such as millipedes) that had been feeding on dead plants, or was another arthropod eating fresh material? It is most likely that detritivores were feeding on litter that was rich in spores.

Among other metazoan groups, there are no fossil records of terrestrial planarians, nematodes, or nemerteans. The oldest fossil remains of oligochaete annelids (earthworms) are in the Carboniferous (Selden and Edwards 1989). Likewise, terrestrial

pulmonate and helicinid prosobranch gastropods (snails) appeared in the Upper Carboniferous. The earliest terrestrial crustaceans are isopods found in the Eocene, although aquatic forms are known from as far back as the Carboniferous. Terrestrialization of crabs did not occur until the Late Neogene. Despite having a fossil record of marine forms back to the Early Cambrian, it is not known when onychophorans (velvet worms) became terrestrial.

Vertebrate terrestrialization occurred some time after arthropod invasion of the land. The earliest tetrapod remains are amphibians. Before 1975 only two fossil amphibians were known from the Devonian: *Ichthyostega* and *Acanthostega,* both from the Late Devonian of eastern Greenland. In 1977 the lower jawbone of an amphibian named *Metaxygnathus* was described from the Late Devonian of central New South Wales, Australia. This was thought to be slightly older than the eastern Greenland amphibians. Fossil trackways attributed to amphibians found in Victoria, Australia, provide evidence that the group was widespread by that time. In 1984, a fossilized amphibian forelimb was found in the Late Devonian in Russia and named *Tulerpeton.* Surprisingly, it was found to possess six digits on each hand, rather than the conventional pattern of five present on most tetrapod hands and feet.

In 1990 fossilized trackways attributed to land-walking tetrapods were found in Late Devonian rocks in Scotland and southwestern Ireland. These fossil trackways show that tetrapods were widespread in the Late Devonian. These trackways show that some of these early tetrapods walked with digits pointing outward from the axis of the body, not facing forward as would be expected for a primitive fishlike limb.

Recent detailed work on the limbs of *Acanthostega* and *Ichthyostega* has revealed that neither amphibian had five digits, as was previously supposed (Coates and Clack 1990). *Ichthyostega* had seven digits on the foot, whereas *Acanthostega* had eight on the hands and feet. It has been suggested that this "polydactylous condition" (i.e., having more than five digits per limb) was probably an adaptation for swimming, rather than for walking on land, casting doubt on the terrestrial ability of these tetrapods. The picture is now emerging, from studies of the stapes (ear bone), the braincase, the limb skeletons, and the presence of gill arches, that these early amphibians were little more than fishes with slightly modified skull patterns, and digits, rather than fins, on the ends of their limbs. More than likely they still lived highly aquatic lifestyles, with only *Ichthyostega* possibly venturing onto land for short periods.

The oldest tetrapod remains are much more incomplete and occur in the upper Frasnian (early Late Devonian) Scat Craig deposit, near Elgin, Scotland (Ahlberg 1991). These bones have been named *Elginerpeton.* This amphibian also was very fishlike in its anatomy and, presumably, in its behavior. The fish-tetrapod transition generally is viewed as a complex transition involving a large degree of morphological change. These changes include the development of the ability to breathe air, rather than gill-breathing in water; the ability to walk on land, rather than swim; the ability to hear, as opposed to sensing with a lateral line system; the ability to retain body moisture; and the ability to reproduce out of water. If, as seems likely, these steps were taken one at a time, it is not surprising that the first tetrapods did not rush out of the water, but emerged fully equipped and pre-adapted for a life on land.

Selection pressure that "drove" vertebrates onto land may well have related to predation. Panderichthyid fishes, from which tetrapods are considered to have evolved, are thought to have been predators, possessing very large heads relative to their body size, large fangs, and the ability to open their mouths wide. The well-developed hands and feet, if not initially adaptations for locomotion on land, may well have been adaptations for improving swimming speed. However, they would have been preadapted for helping to support the animals' body weight out of water. The positioning of eyes on top of the skull meant that they were perfectly suited to viewing a new, terrestrial world.

The first tetrapods possessed a long, fishlike tail that was practically unchanged from the panderichthyid fish tail. Even after the more advanced amphibians developed improved limb girdles that allowed them to walk freely on land, the tail remained as the important propulsive device for aquatic forays. Finally, the first amphibians retained a body covered by fishlike scales. It has been argued (Coates 1996) that as they began to invade the terrestrial habitat, equipped with limbs of limited terrestrial locomotory capability, the presence of a scale cover over the belly would have provided an important protection for the animals' ventral surface when dragging themselves across the ground. It also would have assisted in preventing moisture loss on land.

Consequently, one of the great steps in evolution, the invasion of land by vertebrates, probably did not arise until well after the first tetrapods had evolved from fishes. The refinement of their limb skeletons and vertebral columns took place during the Carboniferous period, the age when the first reptiles evolved. These animals acquired a great evolutionary novelty: a hard-shelled amniote egg. This broke the shackles, so that tetrapods no longer were tied to water. They were therefore able to venture away from the rivers and lakes of the humid Carboniferous world and invade inland habitats.

KENNETH J. MCNAMARA

See also Annelids; Arthropods: Overview; Metazoan Phyla, Minor; Molluscs: Overview; Tetrapods: Overview

Works Cited

Ahlberg, P.E. 1991. Tetrapod or near tetrapod fossils from the Upper Devonian of Scotland. *Nature* 354:298–301.

Coates, M.I. 1996. The Devonian tetrapod *Acanthostega gunnarit* Jarvik: Postcranial anatomy, basal tetrapod interrelationships and patterns of skeletal evolution. *Transactions of the Royal Society of Edinburgh: Earth Sciences* 87:363–421.

Coates, M.I., and J.A. Clack. 1990. Polydactyly in the earliest known tetrapod limbs. *Nature* 347:66–69.

Jeram, A.J., P.A. Selden, and D. Edwards. 1990. Land animals in the Silurian: Arachnids and myriapods from Shropshire, England. *Science* 250:658–61.

Johnson, E.W., D.E.G. Briggs, R.J. Suthren, J.L. Wright, and S.P. Tunnicliff. 1994. Non-marine arthropod traces from the subaerial Ordovician Borrowdale Volcanic Group, English Lake District. *Geological Magazine* 131:395–406.

McNamara, K.J., and N.H. Trewin. 1993. A euthycarcinoid arthropod from the Silurian of Western Australia. *Palaeontology* 36:319–35.

Retallack, G.J., and C.R. Feakes. 1987. Trace fossil evidence for Late Ordovician animals on land. *Science* 235:61–63.

Selden, P.A., and D. Edwards. 1989. Colonisation of the land. *In* K.C. Allen and D.E.G. Briggs (eds.), *Evolution and the Fossil Record.* London: Belhaven Press; Washington, D.C.: Smithsonian Institution Press, 1990.

Selden, P.A., W.A. Shear, and P.M. Bonamo. 1991. A spider and other arachnids from the Devonian of New York, and reinterpretations of Devonian Araneae. *Palaeontology* 34:241–81.

Shear, W.A. 1991. The early development of terrestrial ecosystems. *Nature* 351:283–89.

Shear, W.A., P.M. Bonamo, J.D. Grierson, W.D.I. Rolfe, E.L. Smith, and R.A. Norton. 1984. Early land animals in North America: Evidence from Devonian age arthropods from Gilboa, New York. *Science* 224:492–94.

Sherwood-Pyke, M.A., and J. Gray. 1985. Silurian fungal remains: Probable records of the class Ascomycetes. *Lethaia* 18:1–20.

Trewin, N.H., and K.J. McNamara. 1995. Arthropods invade the land: Trace fossils and palaeoenvironments of the Tumblagooda Sandstone (?late Silurian) of Kalbarri, Western Australia. *Transactions of the Royal Society of Edinburgh: Earth Sciences* 85:177–210.

TERRESTRIAL LOCOMOTION IN VERTEBRATES

A wide variety of forms of terrestrial vertebrates can be found on Earth. Morphological differences (those of shape and structure) have evolved in different ecological niches, or differences simply result from constructions found in the ancestors (preconstructions). For a given task, like running fast, accelerating the body forward, or climbing a tree, however, physical and physiological constraints limit the possible constructions of vertebrates. Such constraints might become obvious if forms that are not closely related phylogenetically (in terms of evolutionary history) share traits, like columnar limbs found in both large mammals and large dinosaurs.

Mechanical Principles

Animal locomotion is governed by the laws of mechanics. At rest, the total force (interaction between a body and its environment)

acting on an animal's body must be zero. The weight of the body (force due to gravity) has to be counterbalanced by forces acting from the surface (substrate)—be that soil, rocky shelf, ocean bottom, or coral reef—on the body parts that have contact with the ground. According to Newton's third law of mechanics, these ground reaction forces are of equal magnitude and opposite direction as the forces exerted by the animal against the substrate. The resultant torque (twisting) experienced by the body also must be zero. Unless tension is exchanged between supporting body parts and the substrate (as happens during climbing), zero torque can be achieved only if the center of mass *(CM)* is located above the area of support; this area is limited by the outlines of the body parts placed on the ground and the tangential lines connecting them (Figure 1). During steady-state locomotion, in which speed fluctuates only slightly around a constant value, the resultant force also fluctuates, but when averaged over a longer period must be zero. The same is true for the resultant torque, as long as the average orientation of the body in space remains the same. During slow locomotion, only small deviations from equilibrium are possible, because even small resultant forces or torques evoke large shifts when acting in the same direction over a long period.

During accelerations of the whole body or of a body part, a net force has to act in the direction of the acceleration. According to Newton's second law of mechanics, the "force" *(F)* is given by "mass" *(m)* times "acceleration" *(a)*:

$$F = m \cdot a$$

During curvilinear accelerations (e.g., during the swinging of a limb around its proximal joint), different segments experience different accelerations. Acceleration is higher in segments that are farther away from the axis of rotation. The resistance of a body or a body part to angular accelerations is called "moment of inertia" *(I)*. For an animal that has to reorientate its body quickly, concentrating the body mass toward the axis of rotation is advantageous. A toad, with its bulky body, can turn quickly to the side, and some bipedal hoppers can accomplish a 180-degree turn during a jump around a more or less vertically oriented trunk, using a long tail with a high moment of inertia about the vertical body axis for the countermovement. With a "torque" *(T)* acting about the axis of rotation, an "angular acceleration" (α) results according to

$$T = I \cdot \alpha$$

The "in-torque" *(T_i)* that a muscle produces at a certain joint is given by "muscle force" (in-force, F_i) times "lever arm" (in-lever, l_i, the shortest distance between the line of action of the muscle force and the axis of rotation of the joint):

$$T_i = F_i \cdot l_i$$

In equilibrium, the "out-force" *(F_0)* with the "out-lever" *(l_0)* is counterbalanced by the muscle force (Figure 2):

or

$$F_i \cdot l_i = F_o \cdot l_o$$

$$F_i / F_o = l_o / l_i$$

The speed of shortening of the muscle (v_i) is transformed to the speed (v_0) at the distance (l_0) from the axis of rotation:

$$v_o / v_i = l_o / l_i$$

With a longer lever arm *(l_i)* of a muscle, less force is necessary to produce a certain out-torque. On the other hand, more and faster shortening of the muscle is necessary in order to achieve a certain angular displacement or a certain angular velocity, respectively, about the joint. Since the maximum rates of shortening of muscle fibers seem to be physiologically limited, relatively high ratios l_0/l_i can be observed if fast movements are important, as in the limbs of fast-running animals, while low ratios l_0/l_i occur where high out-forces are important, as in the limbs of diggers. With the basic physical principles outlined above, it is usually not difficult to understand the mechanical construction of a terrestrial vertebrate.

Limb Posture

The first terrestrial tetrapods inherited from their aquatic ancestors two pairs of extremities and the ability to undulate the long body axis laterally (side to side). In terrestrial locomotion these features can be utilized by adopting a sprawling limb posture. Limbs that are splayed to the side can serve as lever arms to rotate hip and shoulder girdles horizontally, motions that occur during lateral undulations of the body (Figure 3). Additional limb movements forward and back relative to shoulder and hip girdles increase the length of a stride and the speed of locomotion; such movement becomes increasingly important with the ability to attain high speeds in fast-running lizards. Limb movements that can be used for propulsion are circular rotations of the upper limbs (as in monotremes, or egg-laying mammals), retracting the upper limbs, and stretching the limbs during retractions.

A sprawling limb posture might be regarded as a primitive characteristic, since it is the starting point for all later developments in the limb construction of terrestrial vertebrates. Nonetheless, being primitive does not make it inferior to a more erect posture. From some hundred million years ago, all the way up to today, numerous amphibians and reptiles, and even a few mammals (monotremes) successfully have adopted a sprawling limb posture. Some small- and medium-sized lizards attain maximum speeds that are no lower than those of fast mammals with a similar body mass. A sprawling limb posture carries the center of mass close above the substrate, a condition that is very suitable for high and quickly repeated accelerations, and, together with the large area of support, facilitates locomotion on inclined substrates. Scholars have measured the energy needed for animals to carry a unit of body mass over a given distance. The results indicate that, at least at low or moderate speeds, locomotion with sprawling limbs is no less economical—requires no more energy—than loco-

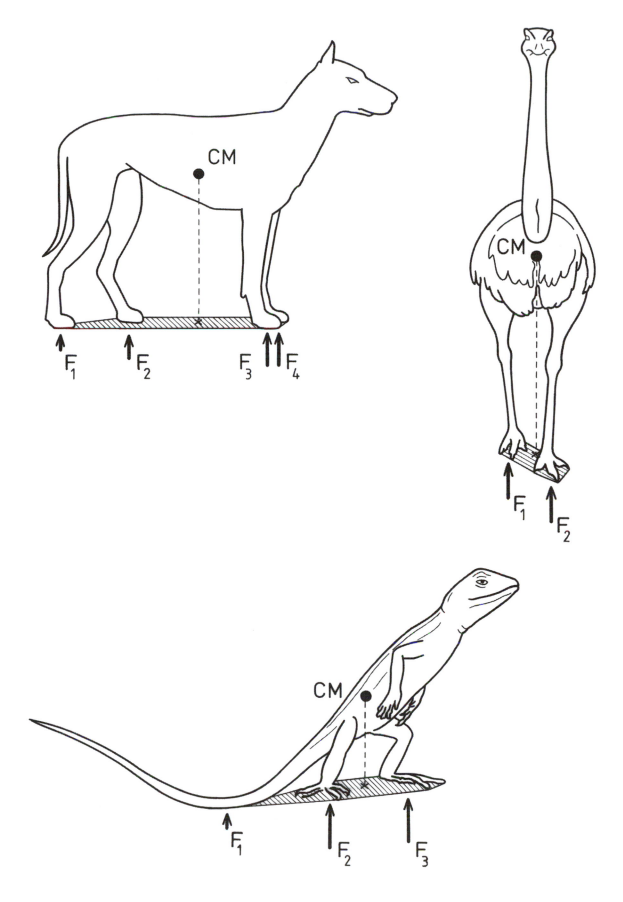

Figure 1. Areas of support (shaded area) in different standing vertebrates.

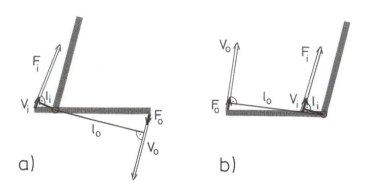

Figure 2. Two different types of levers. *A*, in-force (F_i) and out-force (F_o) acting on different sides of the joint; *B*, in-force (F_i) and out-force (F_o) acting on the same side of the joint. Key: l_i, in-lever; l_o, out-lever; v_i, in-velocity; v_o, out-velocity.

Figure 3. Salamander walking.

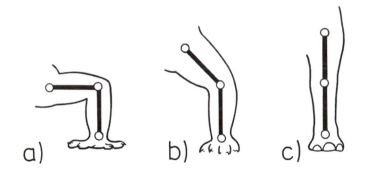

Figure 4. Different limb postures. *a*, sprawling; *b*, semierect; *c*, erect.

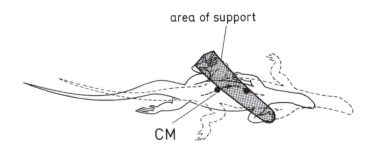

Figure 5. Area of support in a trotting lizard. Key: *CM*, center of mass.

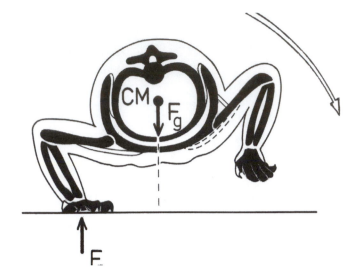

Figure 6. With limbs on only one side of the body on the ground, a sprawler would quickly turn over to the opposite side. Key: F_r, ground reaction force; F_g, weight force; *CM*, center of mass.

motion with limbs that are positioned under the trunk (Bakker 1972; Taylor 1977). For small animals that depend on high sprint speeds, quick accelerations, and the ability to move over a variety of surfaces, locomotion with sprawling limbs and lateral undulations of the body must be regarded as highly effective.

In large, heavy vertebrates, however, a sprawling posture entails static and dynamic problems (Christian and Garland 1996). To sustain the high loads, the limbs either must be very forceful and, therefore, very massive (which results in high moments of inertia), or the limbs must be short in order to reduce the out-levers at the limb joints. In any case, fast locomotion is impeded. This constraint might have triggered the evolution towards an erect limb posture among therapsids (the mammal-like reptiles that immediately precede mammals). Furthermore, lateral undulations of the body impede breathing (Carrier 1987), so that maintaining fast locomotion over a long distance seems to be difficult.

Large monitor lizards and crocodilians are known to adopt a semierect limb posture (Figure 4), when ground reaction forces are highest during fast locomotion. This posture decreases the out-levers at the limb joints. A semierect limb posture, however, does not shift energy efficiently from a laterally undulating body axis and onto the limbs. Nor does a semierect limb posture give much of the dynamic benefits of a fully erect limb posture. Therefore, it is not surprising that most walking or running vertebrates assume either a sprawling or a fairly erect limb posture.

Birds, nearly all mammals, most dinosaurs, and various other extinct vertebrates are characterized by a fully erect limb posture (Figure 4). Erect limbs are rotated towards the body with the elbows pointing forward and the knees pointing backward, placing the feet beneath the body. The degree of flexion in the limb joints is very variable. During locomotion, limb swinging is more or less confined to movement parallel to the body midline (parasaggital planes), though some lateral excursions might occur. Several therapsids and some dinosaurs might have combined erect

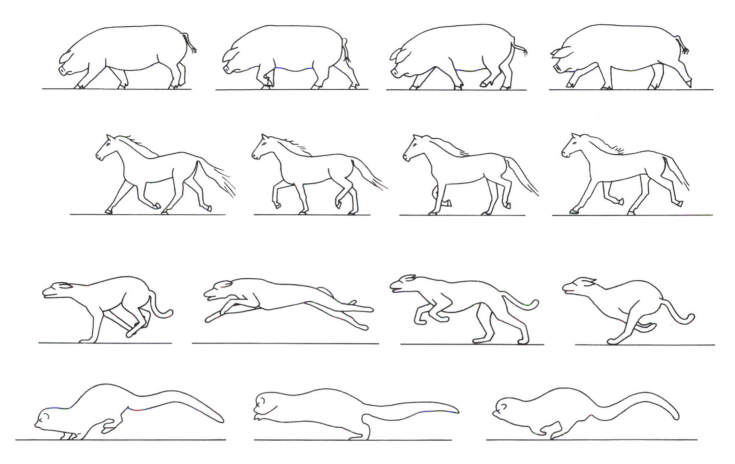

Figure 7. Different gaits in quadrupedal vertebrates; pig walking, horse trotting, dog galloping, and prosimian bounding.

hind limbs with forelimbs that, at least occasionally, could be splayed somewhat to the sides.

The evolution of an erect limb posture is accompanied by marked morphological changes. The muscles that prevent sprawlers from sagging down in between their limbs can be much reduced. Consequently, below the hip and shoulder joints there is no need for large bony areas that provide attachment points of forceful adductor muscles. The shoulder girdle might be reduced so much that the scapula (shoulder blade) is able to perform ample movements on the ribcage. Especially in fast-running mammals, rotations of scapula and pelvic girdle in the sagittal (median—central axis running from head to tail) plane increase the effective limb length and the speed of the swinging limbs. In these forms, the pelvis appears rather rodlike if seen from the side, and a portion of the spine anterior to (to the front of) the pelvis (lumbar spine) is free from ribs which facilitate flexion in the sagittal plane. On the other hand, the backbone loses much of its ability to flex horizontally.

The forces exerted by humerus and femur against the facets of shoulder and joints are in the parasagittal plane (parallel to the sagittal plane) instead of pointing inward, as in a sprawler. The consequence is best visible in the bony structure of the acetabulum (hip joint), which is medially closed in animals with a sprawling posture, but frequently forms an open ring that is reinforced at the upper rim in animals with an erect posture.

With a sprawling posture, in order to keep feet flat on the sur-face, limbs must rotate around the long axes of the lower limbs if hip or shoulder joint, respectively, move forward during locomotion. With a fully erect limb posture, such lower limb pronations as well as the muscles to manage such movement and attachment points for those muscles are not necessary. Instead, in all limb joints, rotation can take place around a transverse (crosswise, i.e., perpendicular to the sagittal plane of the animal) axis, providing the possibility for a less complicated construction of lower limbs and feet.

In a sprawling or semierect limb posture the femur (thigh bone) usually is shaped like an "S," with the two condyles (bony knobs) of the knee joint facing downward, and the femoral (the rounded end that fits into the hip) head protruding more or less upward. In an erect limb, the femur appears to have shifted about 90 degrees around its long axis so that the head protrudes medially (toward the center of the body). Similar changes have occurred in the humerus (upper arm) during the change from a sprawling to an erect limb posture.

With an erect limb posture, the tail loses its function in assist-ing the lateral undulation of the long body axis. During the evolu-tion toward mammals, the tail seems to have been reduced about the time when the hind limbs became erect. Bipedal dinosaurs kept the tail to be a counterweight or a weapon, to balance the body, to facil-itate turning to the side, or as a heat exchanger. In several mammals, a long tail has evolved again to serve various functions.

Gaits

Vertebrates usually travel on even ground by repeating identical sequences of movements called "strides." Sprawlers are essentially confined to placing contralateral limbs (opposing front and back legs, e.g., right front leg and left back leg) on the ground at the same time. This strategy maintains the center of mass above the area of support. If sprawlers placed just one limb or both limbs of the same side on the ground, the body would quickly turn over toward the opposite side (Figure 6).

In contrast, erect limb posture allows a choice of very different gaits (Figure 7). Gaits can be compared with the gears of machines, each providing a different relationship between out-levers and in-levers and functioning most effectively in a certain speed range (Hoyt and Taylor 1981).

During slow movement vertebrates usually use a walking gait, placing each foot on the ground for more than half the duration of a stride. In quadrupeds, three feet often touch the ground at the same time. The speed of locomotion *(v)* is given by the distance covered during one stride, the stride length *(s)*, times the number of strides per unit of time, the stride frequency *(f)*:

$$v = s \cdot f$$

With their short limbs, small mammals only can reach slow walking speeds before they must increase the stride frequency (Preuschoft et al. 1996). Walking is more effective in large vertebrates, which may travel with only moderately flexed supporting limbs. This position keeps out-levers at the limb joints short while stride length is long. The forward swinging limbs behave similar to pendulums driven by gravity and by accelerations of the hip and shoulder joints (Mochon and McMahon 1980; Hildebrand 1985).

Both stride frequency and stride length must increase in order to increase speed. Owing to the maximum speed of muscle contractions and to the maximum force that can be generated by muscles, stride frequency cannot exceed a certain limit. Therefore, in faster gaits the fraction of time a foot is placed on the ground ("duty factor") decreases, which increases the ground reaction forces. At medium speeds, many quadrupedal vertebrates use a trot, placing contralateral feet on the ground simultaneously, as in sprawlers. Some long-limbed mammals like giraffes, camels, or elephants might walk fast or run with both limbs of one side of the body swinging simultaneously (pace), preventing the limbs from interfering with each other but providing worse body support than the trot. Gaits like walk, trot, and pace, in which both limbs of a pair, fore or hind, move alternately, are called "symmetrical."

To reach even higher speeds, asymmetrical gaits are chosen, in which both hind limbs and both forelimbs swing together more or less simultaneously. This introduces one or two extended intervals to each stride when the body is unsupported—when it is extended and when it is flexed. This considerably increases the stride length. Stride length also benefits from the flexion of the trunk (Figure 8), which changes the distance between shoulder and hip girdles and leads to rotations of scapulae and pelvis paral-

Figure 8. Flexion of the spine in a running hare.

lel to the direction of the body. This adds to the angular excursions of the limbs. Furthermore, adding the trunk musculature to that of the limbs facilitates an increase in stride frequency. In the gallop, typical for horses and other hoofed animals, ground contact by forefeet and hind feet is extended by placing forefeet and hind feet not-exactly simultaneously on the ground, in contrast to the bound of many small mammals (Preuschoft et al. 1996). Small mammals often use the half-bound, with the hind limbs swinging strictly together and the forelimbs moving not simultaneously. The "pronk," in which all four limbs are placed on the ground at the same time (seen, for instance, in some antelopes) is less common.

In many small vertebrates that depend on quick, forward accelerations, the hind limbs are much longer and more forceful than the forelimbs and, therefore, are better suited for running at high speeds. Consequently, many fast-running small vertebrates change to a bipedal gait at their highest speeds of locomotion (provided that a well-developed tail exists for balancing the body). Bipedally running lizards keep the alternating mode of hind limb swinging as during quadrupedal locomotion. Mammals that shift from quadrupedal to bipedal locomotion at high speeds hop with simultaneous swinging hind limbs ("ricochetal locomotion"). In the short support phases, hoppers may store a considerable amount of energy in tendons, which recoil during the take-offs, releasing the stored energy for reaccelerating the body.

Bipedality

Numerous vertebrates habitually or even exclusively walk and run only on the hind limbs (Figure 9). In many forms, like bipedal dinosaurs, birds, or kangaroos, the body is shaped more or less like a "T." Frequently, there is a long tail, which counterbalances the weight of head, neck, trunk, and forelimbs. In all bipedal vertebrates (except humans) that walk and run with alternately swinging hind limbs, the body is horizontally oriented along the long body axis. This structure provides for a high moment of horizontal inertia, passively counteracting large angular displacements of the long body axis due to the twisting produced by the swinging hind limbs. In humans, these torques are counteracted by swinging each arm in the opposite direction of the limb of the same side. Hoppers might choose a more vertical orientation of the trunk. In bipeds, a long horizontal extension of the body entails high bending moments, especially close to the hips. In some heavy bipeds,

Figure 9. Examples for bipedal locomotion. *a*, human; *b*, kangaroo rat; *c*, basilisk; *d*, theropod dinosaur; *e*, ostrich.

like large ornithopod dinosaurs, a large portion of the vertebral column was stabilized conspicuously against bending in the sagittal plane by long spinal processes (bony extensions) of the vertebrae (which increased the lever arms of back muscles), by ossified (strengthened with bony materials) tendons, and by a long sacrum (pelvic bone of the spinal column, a fusion of the last few lumbar vertebrae), which passively immobilized the section of the spine close to the hip joints.

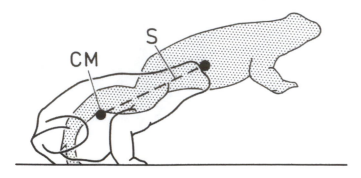

Figure 11. Different foot postures. *a*, plantigrade (bear); *b*, digitigrade (theropod dinosaur); *c*, unguligrade (horse).

Figure 10. Jumping toad during takeoff. Nearly the full length of the limb contributes to the distance of acceleration.

Jumping and Leaping

Hopping and leaping vertebrates are said to be "saltatorial." In contrast to hopping, jumping or leaping usually ends by bringing the body to a complete rest, like in a jumping frog, so that little mechanical energy can be stored for the next leap. To reach a sufficiently high initial speed for a long or high jump, the body must be accelerated with a sufficiently high force over a sufficiently long distance. In small leapers, the mechanical challenge is to provide a long distance for the acceleration. In large leapers, with their longer hind limbs, the challenge is to produce sufficiently high forces (Preuschoft et al. 1996). Small leapers usually have relatively long hind limbs with high out-lever/in-lever ratios, particularly at the most distal joints (those farthest from the body). An additional joint in the feet may increase the takeoff speed. Nearly the full possible hind limb extension is used for the takeoff (Figure 10). In large leapers, like several primates with a body mass of more than one kilogram, the distance over which they accelerate is long, even if they do not use the full length of the hind limbs. In these forms the takeoff starts from a less crouched posture, which lowers the out-lever/in-lever ratios, so that with a given muscle force more out-force is produced. Small leapers usually initiate the takeoff from a crouched position by accelerating the upper body parts first, prestretching muscles and tendons that control the distal limb joints before the leap takes place. The energy stored in elastic tissues can be released quickly at the end of the takeoff, when a high power output is needed.

The impact of the body at landing often leads to forces that are even higher than those during the takeoff. In leaping primates the forceful hind limbs serve as shock absorbers; in anurans (e.g., frogs, toads), forelimbs and shoulder girdle absorb the first impact.

Cursorial Adaptations

Animals that travel fast or over a long distance are called "cursorial." Attaining a high speed is facilitated with limbs that are long in relation to other body parts, providing long out-levers, and a low moment of inertia. This means that these limbs can be accelerated quickly and economically. Therefore, in many vertebrates, especially in cursorial mammals and birds, the limb mass is shifted to the proximal end (closest to the body). This is mostly accomplished by lengthening the limb segments farthest from the body (i.e., the "forearm" and "calf") more than the proximal ones, which carry more muscle mass. The lower limbs and the feet, especially the metacarpals and metatarsals (bones of the proximal portions of the front and back foot) are lengthened in relation to the upper limbs (Coombs 1978; Garland and Janis 1993). Elongate feet cannot be used effectively to increase speed if the feet are placed on the ground so that the complete sole touches the ground ("plantigrade foot posture") (Figure 11). This posture is found in humans or bears. Most cursorial animals contact the substrate with the fingers and toes only ("digitigrade posture"), such as recent carnivores, birds, and many dinosaurs. Some walk only upon the tips of the toes ("unguligrade posture"), as in ungulates such as horses and cattle. Apes might walk on the knuckles of their hands (gorillas, chimpanzees) or on the fist (orangutans), thereby utilizing versatile hands to increase the arm length.

In some forms such as ungulates, the moments of inertia of the limbs are further decreased by reducing the number of bones in the lower leg, ankle, and foot. This allows higher bone strength with less bone mass and less muscle mass for controlling the movements of the distal bones. Instead, joint movements tend to be passively restricted (e.g., by grooves that guide the movements of tendons and adjacent bones). The trade-off is reduced versatility of the limbs.

Size Effects

In geometrically similar animals body weight generally scales with the third power of linear dimensions (e.g., body weight increases at the rate equal to the cube of the increase in total body length), while the ability of bones, tendons, ligaments, and muscles to sustain forces scales only with the second power of linear dimensions. Double body length would entail eightfold loads on the supportive tissues but just fourfold in strength. Similarly, the torques produced at the joint would increase less with size than the moments of inertia of body segments. Therefore, it is relatively more difficult for large animals to carry their body weight and to accelerate body parts than smaller ones. Large vertebrates adapt to this condition in various ways. Supportive tissues tend to be relatively stronger, in-levers tend to be relatively longer, and out-levers tend to be relatively shorter, as in smaller forms that adopt a sprawling or crouched posture. This arrangement is more suitable for quick

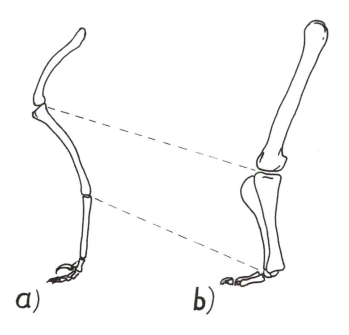

Figure 12. Limb proportions. *Left,* a small fast theropod *(Deinonychus); right,* a large graviportal sauropod *(Brachiosaurus).*

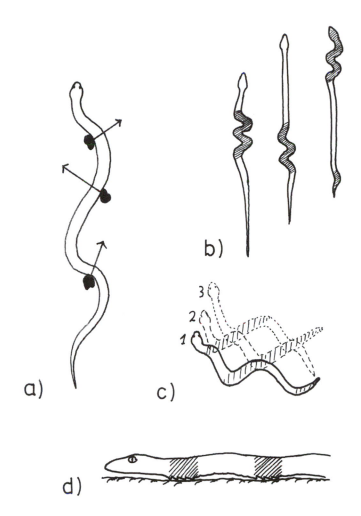

Figure 13. Different methods of limbless locomotion. *a,* lateral undulations *(arrows,* horizontal reaction forces exerted on the body by obstacles); *b,* concertina movement; *c,* sidewinding; *d,* rectilinear movement. Shading: in *b, c, d,* indicates body segments that are supported by the ground.

accelerations (Alexander 1985; Biewener 1990). During locomotion, larger vertebrates generally tend to keep limb excursions and flexion of the limb joints comparatively low.

If adaptations for carrying a high body weight dominate a vertebrate's construction, it is said to be graviportal (e.g., many dinosaurs and several living and extinct mammalian giants). Typically, these animals reduce the lever arms of the ground reaction forces about their limb joints by adopting a columnlike limb posture with vertically oriented limbs. The bone shafts are straight; the joint surfaces are in line with the shafts. Broad feet distribute the weight. In contrast to cursorials, distal limb segments are relatively short, proximal segments are long (Figure 12). Gaits with extended unsupported phases are avoided, the spine is kept rather stiff, and limb excursions are comparatively smaller.

Limbless Locomotion

Among amphibians and lizards limbless locomotions has evolved several times, and it is used by some thousand recent vertebrates (Gans 1975) (Figure 13). The most common way of traveling without limbs is to throw the body in loops by lateral undulations. The loops travel backwards along the animal's body but remain at the same place relative to the ground, anchored by objects against which the body presses sideward and backward. The forward components of the reaction forces push the animal against the friction over the ground. If at least three objects are used to anchor the body, the sideward force components will be balanced, preventing the body from shifting sideways or rotating.

Many snakes, caecilians (wormlike amphibians), and amphisbaenians (serpents)—particularly those that climb and bur-

row—wedge the body by one or more S-shaped coils against an obstacle (e.g., the walls of a tunnel or a crevice). By pressing rear coils downward and backward, the front of the body is pushed forward, since friction prevents the coils from slipping. Then, the anterior body part is wedged by coils, and the posterior part can be drawn up to repeat the cycle. This type of movement is called "concertina movement."

In "sidewinding," a snake contacts the ground with two or three parts of the body at parallel lines lifting the body in between these lines. The body parts on the ground are stationary, those in between are moving. The snake leaves a characteristic track of parallel lines. Sidewinding can be used for moving rapidly on sandy soil.

Limbless progression can be achieved without any lateral excursions of the body at all. During rectilinear movement (i.e., movement in a straight line) used by various amphisbaenians and snakes, the body is anchored by several regions of the body where the ventral scutes are gathered, so that they overlap and prevent

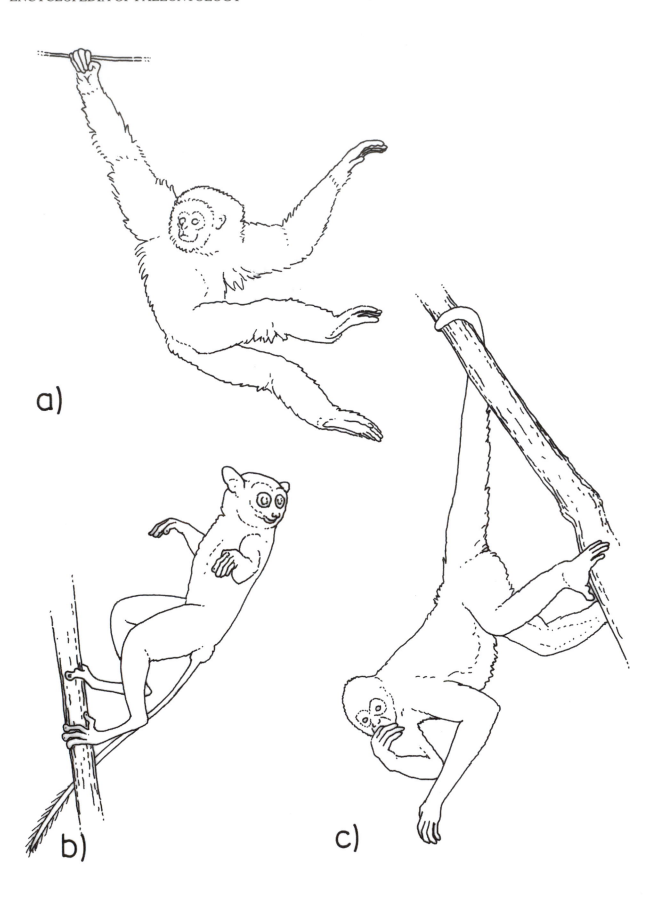

Figure 14. Some examples of how primates use the three-dimensional surface of a forest's roof for body support during rest and movement. *a, Hylobates; b, Tarsius; c, Ateles.*

slipping back. During progression, these regions remain stationary on the ground and push backward along the animal's body. The body parts in between these regions are lifted clear of the ground. This slow way of limbless locomotion is useful in narrow tunnels or for stalking prey.

Subterranean Locomotion

A variety of vertebrates spend part or most of their lives under the ground, moving about by different ways of digging. Some vertebrates simply cover themselves with soft soil ("cover-up digging"), such as some anurans or some desert lizards, which submerge by body vibrations. These animals usually do not show marked morphological adaptations for digging.

If animals possess traits that can be understood as adaptations for digging, these animals are said to be "fossorial." Long and slender forms with reduced or absent limbs might crawl through loose soil using a firm head as digging device ("soil-crawling"). Many mammals, some turtles, and some birds dig by alternately flexing and extending limbs ("scratch-digging"). Other diggers, like the true moles, get the power for digging with the forelimbs from rotations of the humerus around its longitudinal axis ("humeral-rotation digging"); in this method, in contrast to scratch-diggers, the elbow does not provide forceful strokes. Several rodents use their large incisors and powerful jaws to loosen even hard soil; the soil is then removed with their heads or feet ("chisel-tooth digging"). In hook-and-pull digging, used by anteaters, long claws dislodge soil as hard as a termite hill. Some rodents and golden moles build tunnels by head-lift digging.

A fossorial lifestyle favors a slender, streamlined body with short limbs or no limbs at all. If the head is involved actively in digging activities, it has to be built strongly and attached to a short, forceful neck. Feet used to move soil must be shovel-like. Limbs used for digging must be able to produce high out-forces. In contrast to cursorials, distal limb segments of diggers are shorter than proximal segments. The out-levers are short, and lever arms of the very forceful limb muscles are long. Due to the reinforced and large areas required for the origin and attachment of muscles, the limb bones get a rugged appearance. A long scapula provides large areas for muscle attachment, and a solid, extended sacrum is capable of sustaining high stress in forms that use the hind limbs for bracing during digging.

Climbing and Traveling above the Ground

Many amphibians, reptiles, birds, and mammals are capable of climbing rocks or trees. Vertebrates with the ability to climb are said to be "scansorial," animals living in trees are called "arboreal" (Figure 14).

A three-dimensional, discontinuous surface, such as the roof of a forest, opens many possibilities for moving in different directions but makes body support critical. In order to cling or move on a steeply inclined surface, friction and tensile forces (forces caused by extension and elastic stress) become essential. A variety of adaptations can be found that prevent scansorial vertebrates from falling. Many arboreal forms, like primates and chameleons, establish a firm

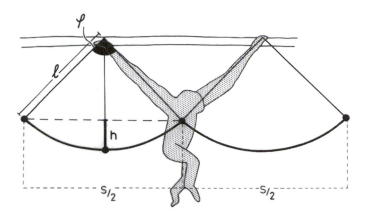

Figure 15. Arm-swinging gibbon. The length of a full cycle (s) depends on pendulum length (l) and angle of excursion (φ). Depending on the maximum height difference (h) during each half-cycle, potential energy is transformed into kinetic energy, and vice versa.

grip around twigs and thin branches with their feet. The tail of many new-world monkeys is an additional grasping device. Squirrels and lizards splay their limbs to the sides, using the whole span of the extremities for grasping; this posture reduces the load on the body by keeping the center of mass close to the surface of the trunks and branches. Snakes can even use their whole body to loop around a branch. A firm grip around a branch not only allows them to exert tensile forces; it also serves to prevent slipping by increasing friction. "Interlocking" between the animal's surface and the surface of the substrate also prevents slipping by increasing friction. Interlocking might be established by hooking a bill (birds) or claws (lizards, birds, or small mammals) into a crevice. The feathers on the tail of woodpeckers, the scales on the feet of lizards, and the ridges on the finger balls of primates have a similar function. Tree frogs bond their finger balls with the help of sticky secretions on the substrate. In geckos, adhesion is secured by up to 150,000 hairlike setae (bristles) on the toes, each branching into numerous smaller bristles with endplates measuring just 0.2 micrometers in diameter, causing microscopic bonds when the toe is pressed against the substrate. Some bats fix their knuckles and ankles with suction cups.

Further widespread specializations for an arboreal lifestyle are highly mobile and versatile limbs, long extremities for reaching far, long feet that give a wide grip, and a long tail to balance the body when moving or adjusting the orientation of the body by swift movements during a jump, as in leaping primates such as tarsiers and galagos.

As in moving over even ground, walking, running, and jumping might be used to move through an arboreal habitat. Leaping is quite common, since it enables animals to cover the distance between branches in all directions. Large gaps might also be covered by bridging them with a long body (snakes) or by reaching with long extremities (large primates). Orangutans, sloths, and others move through the forest's roof by reaching and pulling from one support to another. A special way of arboreal locomotion is the arm-swinging ("brachiation") of several primates, especially gibbons and siamangs. The animals swing like a pendulum under a support, switching from one supporting arm to the next (Figure 15). In fast locomotion, short air-borne phases might be introduced between the support phases. Arm-swinging is most efficient if the animal swings with a frequency that matches the natural pendulum frequency of its body. While the frequency decreases with the square root of the pendulum length, the distance covered by each cycle increases in proportion to the length of the pendulum, so the speed of locomotion increases with the square root of the pendulum length. Arm-swinging is restricted to animals of a narrow size range. In small forms, speed of locomotion would be too low; in large forms, external forces would be too large (Preuschoft and Demes 1985).

ANDREAS CHRISTIAN

See also Biomechanics; Fundamental Morphology; Fins and Limbs, Paired

Works Cited

Alexander, R.McN. 1985. Body support, scaling, and allometry. *In* M. Hildebrand, D.M. Bramble, K.F. Liem, and D.W. Wake (eds.), *Functional Vertebrate Morphology.* Cambridge, Massachusetts: Harvard University Press.

Bakker, R.T. 1972. Locomotor energetics of lizards and mammals compared. *Physiologist* 15:278.

Biewener, A.A. 1990. Biomechanics of mammalian terrestrial locomotion. *Science* 250:1097–103.

Carrier, D.R. 1987. The evolution of locomotor stamina in tetrapods: Circumventing a mechanical constraint. *Paleobiology* 13:326–41.

Christian, A., and T. Garland Jr. 1996. Scaling of limb proportions in monitor lizards (squamata: varanidae). *Journal of Herpetology* 30 (2):219–30.

Coombs Jr., W.P. 1978. Theoretical aspects of cursorial adaptations in dinosaurs. *Quarterly Review of Biology* 53:393–418.

Gans, C. 1975. Tetrapod limblessness: Evolution and functional corollaries. *American Zoologist* 15:455–67.

Garland Jr., T., and C.M. Janis. 1993. Does metatarsal/femur ratio predict maximal running speed in cursorial mammals? *Journal of Zoology, London* 229:133–51.

Hildebrand, M. 1985. Walking and running. *In* M. Hildebrand, D.M. Bramble, K.F. Liem, and D.W. Wake (eds.), *Functional Vertebrate Morphology.* Cambridge, Massachusetts: Harvard University Press.

Hoyt, D.F., and C.R. Taylor. 1981. Gait and the energetics of locomotion in horses. *Nature* 292:239–40.

Mochon, S., and T.A. McMahon. 1980. Ballistic walking. *Journal of Biomechanics* 3:49–57.

Preuschoft, H., and B. Demes. 1985. Influence of size and proportions on the biomechanics of brachiation. *In* W.L. Jungers (ed.), *Size and Scaling in Primate Biology.* New York: Plenum.

Preuschoft, H., H. Witte, A. Christian, and M.S. Fischer. 1996. Size influences on primate locomotion and body shape, with particular emphasis on the locomotion of "small mammals." *Folia Primatologica* 66:93–112.

Taylor, C.R. 1977. The energetics of terrestrial locomotion and body size in vertebrates. *In* T.J. Pedley (ed.), *Scale Effects in Animal Locomotion.* New York and London: Academic Press.

Further Reading

Alexander, R.McN. 1982. *Locomotion of Animals.* New York: Wiley; London: Blackie.

———. 1989. *Dynamics of Dinosaurs and Other Extinct Giants.* New York: Columbia University Press.

Hildebrand, M. 1974. *Analysis of Vertebrate Structure.* New York: Wiley; 4th ed., 1995.

Howell, A.B. 1944. *Speed in Animals.* Chicago: University of Chicago Press.

McMahon, T.A., and J.T. Bonner. 1983. *On Size and Life.* New York: Scientific American Books.

Muybridge, E. 1957. *Animals in Motion.* New York: Dover.

Thulborn, R.A. 1990. *Dinosaur Tracks.* London and New York: Chapman and Hall.

TETRAPODS: OVERVIEW

Four-legged vertebrates, or tetrapods, are an evolutionarily successful group that includes, among other taxa, more than 5,000 amphibian species and more than 20,000 amniote species (amniotes are tetrapods that lay shelled eggs). The transition from fish to tetrapod occurred during the Middle or Late Devonian, approximately 380 million years ago. By the Early Carboniferous (Mississippian), early tetrapods had diversified into a number of major taxa, all of which are extinct. These include the colosteids, palaeostegalids, adelogyrinids, aïstopods, nectrideans, baphetids, proto-anthracosaurs, anthracosaurs, and diadectomorphs. As clearly as the Devonian is the "age of fishes," the end of the Paleozoic could be considered the "age of early tetrapods."

Taxonomically diverse, tetrapods also embrace a wide variety of sizes, shapes, behaviors, and adaptations. Both extremes of the tet-rapod size range are living on Earth today: the Brazilian frog *Psyllophryne didactyla* is the smallest tetrapod, measuring 9.8 millimeters, whereas the blue whale *Balaenoptera musculus* is definitely the largest, with its 33-meter-long and 145,000-kilogram body. Contrary to popular belief, dinosaurs are not the largest tetrapods ever to have lived on Earth (with the possible exception of the sauropods *Ultrasaurus* and *Seismosaurus*). Tetrapods conquered most of the biosphere's inhabitable environments during the past 350 million years. Although the great majority of tetrapods are walking, four-legged terrestrial sarcopterygians (lobe-finned fish), other locomotor patterns have emerged. Some tetrapods glide or fly (weigeltisaurs, kuehneosaurs, pterosaurs, birds, and bats); some jump (frogs, kangaroos, and some small rodents); some are bipedal (some archosauromorphs, many dinosaurs, birds, kangaroos, and hominids);

some are limbless (aïstopods, caecilians, snakes, and amphisbaenid lizards); and some are aquatic (most early tetrapods, some capitosaurs, some salamanders, some nectrideans, adelogyrinids, mesosaurs, turtles, nothosaurs, plesiosaurs, placodonts, mosasaurs, ichthyosaurs, some crocodilians, pinnepeds, and cetaceans).

Origin of Tetrapods

The transition between fishes and tetrapods during the Late Devonian is one of the most significant events in the history of vertebrates. Animals previously dependent on the water for survival had to undergo radical changes in anatomy, physiology, and behavior in order to move, breathe, and feed on land. Less than 50 years ago, it was said that amphibians originated from fishes and were the first vertebrates to walk on land. However, as our knowledge of early tetrapods increased, it became clear that amphibians are a derived (specialized) group of tetrapods that originated after the Devonian diversification; that the first tetrapods were still aquatic; and that among fishes, a peculiar group of advanced lobe-finned fishes were of special interest.

Over the past 30 years, the relationships between the various groups of sarcopterygians, as well as the origin of tetrapods, has generated much debate among students of systematics (the study of evolutionary relationships). Various groups of piscine sarcopterygians have been suggested as the ancestor or sister group of tetrapods. Candidates have included coelacanths, lungfishes, osteolepiforms, and elpistostegalians (previously known as panderichthyids). For over a century, the tristichopterid osteolepiform fish *Eusthenopteron foordi,* from the Upper Devonian Escuminac Formation of Miguasha in eastern Québec, Canada, was idealized as the transitional link between fishes and tetrapods. In 1892 the North American vertebrate paleontologist Edward Drinker Cope made the first attempt to position *Eusthenopteron* in an evolutionary framework by comparing the internal skeleton of the paired fins with that of Carboniferous amphibians. As a result of efforts that spanned most of his life, the famous Swedish paleoichthyologist Erik Jarvik compiled a large amount of data about the anatomy of *Eusthenopteron.* Numerous features of this fish were said to be similar to that of early tetrapods. These included (1) the presence of an internal nostril on the palate (choana); (2) elaborately infolded "labyrinthodont" dentine on the larger teeth; (3) a well-defined forelimb with humerus, radius and ulna; (4) entepicondylar and ectepicondylar foramina (holes for the passage of nerves and blood vessels) at the distal end of the humerus; (5) processes (raised areas for muscle attachment) on the humerus (e.g., supinator, deltoid, entepicondylar, and ectepicondylar processes); and (6) vertebral bodies that were composed of a large median intercentrum and smaller, paired pleurocentra.

In 1981 the assumed close relationship between osteolepiforms and tetrapods was challenged by a group of four cladists (cladistics is the most widely used method of systematics): the North American ichthyologist Donn E. Rosen, and the British paleontologists Peter L. Forey, Brian G. Gardiner, and Colin Patterson. They advanced the idea that lungfishes were the closest relatives of tetrapods. They compiled a list of shared-derived character states (synapomorphies) that they claimed supported a sister-

group relationship between tetrapods and lungfishes. Although subsequent rebuttals eliminated many features that Rosen and his coauthors used (Schultze 1981; Cloutier and Ahlberg 1996), their work, coupled with some timely discoveries of new taxa, were key factors in generating a wealth of interest in the fish-tetrapod transition. There is no agreement at present as to which living taxa—lungfishes, coelacanths, or both groups together—are the closest relatives of tetrapods. Among extinct taxa, another group of Late Devonian lobe-finned fishes, the elpistostegalians, display a melange of tetrapod-like and osteolepiform-like features.

A few years after the discovery of the first Devonian tetrapods, the British paleontologist T. Stanley Westoll described a single partial skull roof from the Escuminac Formation of Québec as "a perfect transition between Crossopterygian and Ichthyostegid patterns of dermal bones" (Westoll 1938). As a result, this middle Frasnian fish, *Elpistostege watsoni,* was considered to be a primtive tetrapod. This interpretation remained in the literature until new material was discovered (Schultze and Arsenault 1985). In 1970, the German paleoichthyologist Hans-Peter Schultze, from the Museum für Naturkunde in Berlin, placed the rhipidistian fish *Panderichthys* as the closest relative to the basal tetrapod *Ichthyostega* based on tooth structure. The Russian paleoichthyologist Emilia I. Vorobyeva corroborated the link between *Panderichthys* and tetrapods in her description of complete specimens of the early Frasnian *Panderichthys rhombolepis* from the Lode Quarry of Latvia. Her work proved that *Panderichthys* and *Elpistostege* were close relatives and confirmed the very fishlike nature of these animals. Among the piscine sarcopterygians, the Late Devonian elpistostegalians are clearly the closest relatives of tetrapods (Cloutier and Ahlberg 1996). They share with the early tetrapods a similar skull roof pattern, including the presence of a pair of frontal bones. Another similarity with tetrapods is the absence of dorsal and anal fins.

Although the relationship between the Elpistostegalia and the Tetrapoda is well-corroborated, the phylogenetic relationships among the so-called osteolepiforms remain unclear. Morphological conservatism, a high degree of intraspecific variation, and major stratigraphic gaps in the Devonian fossil record are some of the reasons why phylogenetic resolution among these groups is so poor. However, the tristichopterid osteolepiforms (the Givetian *Tristichopterus* from Scotland, the Frasnian *Eusthenopteron* from Europe and North America, and the Famennian *Eusthenodon* from Greenland) are among the most advanced osteolepiform fishes. Finally, a low-diversity but geographically widespread group of sarcopterygyian fishes, the Rhizodontida, is considered by a few paleontologists to be one of the most advanced groups. Most recently Edward B. Daeschler and Neil H. Shubin (1998) described a rhizodontid pectoral fin that had eight jointed fingers.

Definition of Tetrapods

The Swedish anatomist Neils Holmgren (1933) introduced the idea of a diphyletic origin of tetrapods, meaning that they arose from two different lineages of fishes. Holmgren proposed that urodeles (salamanders) arose from dipnoans (lungfishes) whereas frogs arose from osteolepiforms. Jarvik (1942) regarded the lungfishlike porolepiforms as the ancestors of urodeles and thought that all other tetrapods arose from osteolepiforms such as *Eusthenopteron*. Since the 1960s there has been an effort to demonstrate that tetrapods are monophyletic, in other words that they share a single common ancestor. As part of this effort, numerous attempts have been made to identify shared-derived character states that define Tetrapoda.

Traditionally, tetrapods were defined by the presence of four legs (hence their name), and also by the loss of the gill cover, the freeing of the shoulder girdle from the skull, and a pelvic girdle firmly attached to the spine and forming a solid ring around the viscera. However, these morphological traits were subsequently redefined in the face of new fossil discoveries. In 1979 the North American paleoherpetologist Eugene S. Gaffney, from the American Museum of Natural History in New York, proposed a precise definition of the group based on nine derived features. However, fossil discoveries made over the subsequent two decades demonstrated that some of these features are valid only for a subset of tetrapods.

Out of the nine features Gaffney listed, six were cranial. First, he noted that the tetrapod braincase is solid, while that of sarcopterygian fishes (with the exception of lungfishes) is divided into an anterior ethmosphenoid component and a posterior otico-occipital component. It is now known that the braincase of the basal tetrapods *Ichthyostega* and *Acanthostega* is divided. A second, apparently still valid character, is the back of the tetrapod skull's anteroposterior compression (i.e., it is shortened in a fore-aft direction) compared to that of sarcopterygian fishes. Third, basal tetrapods have an otic notch, a V-shaped embayment at the posterior margin of the skull roof between the tabular and squamosal bones that was originally thought to have housed a tympanum (eardrum). However, this structure might be homologous to the spiracular notch described in elpistostegalians and might even have retained an aquatic respiratory function (Coates and Clack 1991). Fourth, tetrapods have a single pair of large nasal bones located anterior to the frontal bones and that thus form part of the anterior region of the skull roof.

Along with the otic notch, Gaffney proposed two other derived cranial features related to hearing. The first is the presence of a stapes devoted exclusively to an acoustic role; the second is the presence of a fenestra ovalis (oval window). In recent amphibians (modern lissamphibians) the stapes (columella) crosses the air-filled middle ear and transmits sounds from the ear drum to the fenestra ovalis. Airborne vibrations are thus carried to the fluid-filled labyrinth of the inner ear, which is located in the otic capsule. The stapes, which is homologous to the hyomandibular bone of fishes, has an acoustic function, while its primitive piscine homologue functions in respiration and jaw suspension. Now it appears that the stapes of *Acanthostega* might have controlled palatal and spiracular movements in breathing. Furthermore, there is no convincing evidence that basal tetrapods had an oval window (this lack of evidence is, however, due in part to poor preservation of the neurocranium).

As one might expect, the postcranial skeleton of tetrapods is loaded with evolutionary novelties. The presence of digits in the fore- and hind limbs along with definite wrist and ankle joints were thought to be among the most distinctive tetrapod novelties.

The pectoral skeleton is freed from the skull, resulting in the loss of three dermal bones associated with the dorsal part of the shoulder girdle: the posttemporal, the supracleithrum, and the anocleithrum. It is now known that *Acanthostega* retains an anocleithrum and its wrists and ankles were relatively inflexible. The tetrapod pelvis is also distinctive. First the pelvis has a well-ossified iliac blade that extends dorsally to the level of the vertebral column and attaches to the latter by at least one ossified sacral rib. Furthermore, the pelvis is characterized by a well-developed puboischiadic ramus and a well-developed pubic symphysis (midline articulation between left and right pelvises). Ossified ribs are well developed and directed ventrally, in contrast to osteolepiforms, which bear weak ribs that are dorsally oriented.

It is evident from the foregoing that formulating a stable definition for tetrapods that is valid for all basal forms is not an easy task. Some of Gaffney's character states have held up while others are valid only for more restricted groups of tetrapods. In the course of his study of the Carboniferous colosteid *Greererpeton burkemorani* from West Virginia, Canadian paleontologist Stephen J. Godfrey (1989) compiled a list of 41 shared-derived character states that were believed to define all tetrapods. According to Godfrey, tetrapods modify the median series of skull roof bones so that the parietals are longer than the frontals and the postparietals are shorter than the parietals. In the cheek region the jugal bone forms at least half of the ventral margin of the orbit. A number of dermal cranial bones are lost, including the posterior postparietals, extracapulars, operculum, suboperculum, submandibulars, and median gulars. The dermal sculpturing of the external cranial bones consists of deep polygonal pits or troughs surrounded by raised ridges. In the pectoral girdle the cleithrum is shaftlike, and the ventral part of the girdle includes a large interclavicle with a ventral exposure that is longer than the ventral exposure of either the clavicle or the scapulocoracoid. Well-developed articular processes extending from the anterior and posterior sides of the neural arch (pre- and postzygapophyses) create a stronger connection between adjacent vertebrae. Finally, ribs extend from the neural arch of the first cervical (neck) vertebra all the way to the fifth or sixth caudal (tail) vertebra. Until recently, Godfrey's character list was capable of defining all existing tetrapod fossils. Then the discovery of fragmentary tetrapods even more primitive than *Acanthostega* necessitated revision of even this list.

In 1995 Swedish paleontologist Per Erik Ahlberg, from the Natural History Museum in London, redefined the Tetrapoda based on new characters from the lower jaw, in order to accommodate some new basal tetrapods from Scotland. One of the features is the presence of a tooth row on a small parasymphysial plate located on the inner side of the lower jaw on either side of the symphysis (the midline joint). While sarcopterygian fishes share a parasymphysial plate with this early tetrapod, theirs is studded with denticles on the buccal (outer) surface. Associated with the posterior part of the parasymphysial plate are two relatively large parasymphysial foramina piercing the inner side of the lower jaw. In these Scottish tetrapods the Meckelian bone (the ossified anterior portion of Meckel's cartilage, the original gnathostome lower jaw), which lies against the inner surface of the lower jaw, is not exposed dorsal to the prearticular bone.

Although they were quite different internally, primitive tetrapods looked like large salamanders except with heavily ossified skulls and dermal scales covering part of the trunk. Basal tetrapods retained some generalized osteichthyan or sarcopterygian features that have been modified or lost in all other tetrapods. These features include a ventral fissure in the braincase, a relatively mobile cheek and palatoquadrate bone (the original gnathostome upper jaw), and sensory lines partly enclosed in canals. *Ichthyostega* and *Acanthostega* have the lateral line canals of the skull completely enclosed in tubes, in contrast with the more open grooves of more advanced tetrapods. The branchial (gill) skeleton of *Acanthostega* is fishlike—the ceratohyal (an element of the second branchial arch) is expanded proximally and the ceratobranchials (more posterior arch elements) are large and carry grooves left by the aortic arches. The shoulder girdle bears a postbranchial lamina along the anterior margin; in fishes this supports the posterior wall of the opercular chamber, which surrounds the gills. Contrary to popular belief, pentadactyly—the presence of five digits at the end of each limb—is not a tetrapod characteristic. In fact, the number of digits varies among early tetrapods (Coates and Clack 1990): *Ichthyostega* has six toes, *Acanthostega* has eight fingers and seven toes, and *Tulerpeton* has seven toes. The tails of *Ichthyostega* and *Acanthostega* possess endoskeletal radials, dermal fin rays, and scales, just as those of fishes.

In numerous basal tetrapods, the vertebral centrum (the ossified ring surrounding the notochord) consists of three elements, as is the case in advanced sarcopterygians. A single median intercentrum occupies an anteroventral position; more posteriorly and lying in a dorsolateral position are paired pleurocentra (the latter usually support the neural arch). Different lineages tend to emphasize one or the other component later in tetrapod history, often to the eventual exclusion of the minor one. For example, mammals only retain the pleurocentra (which are secondarily fused). Another pervasive trend is the fusion of vertebral elements; for example, the neural arches of aïstopods and nectrideans are fused to their centra.

Extant tetrapods modify a number of soft anatomical features as an adaptation to life on land. Since they rely on pulmonary respiration and can excrete ammonia through their kidneys, external gills are lost. Pulmonary circulation is improved, and the separation between oxygenated blood and deoxygenated blood is enhanced by the presence of a complete interauricular septum (wall) in the anterior chamber of the heart. Eyelids protect the eyes against desiccation, and the outermost layer of the skin—the stratum corneum—performs the same function for the rest of the body. Nasolacrimal (tear) ducts keep the eyes moist. Some of these features might have been present relatively early in the evolution of terrestrial tetrapods; however, none of these characteristics are documented in the fossil record.

Higher-Level Tetrapod Relationships

Throughout the nineteenth, anatomists studied the morphology and development of the vertebrae of fossil and living fishes and tetrapods in the belief that this supplied reliable information about evolutionary relationships (Gardiner 1983). In the 1800s, higher taxa were named on the basis of vertebral morphology: Lepospondyli (*lepis,* husk; *spondylos,* vertebra: spool-shaped centra), Phyllospondyli (*phyllon,* leaf: vertebrae with fused neural arches), Rhachitomi (*rhachis,* spine; *tome,* cutting: arches not fused with centra), Stereospondyli (*stereos,* solid: single-element centra), and Temnospondyli (*temnein,* to cut: vertebrae not fused). Owing to the work of two famous vertebrate paleontologists, the British David Meredith Seare Watson and the North American Alfred Sherwood Romer, the classification and evolutionary relationships of so-called amphibians were based on vertebral morphology. A number of taxa created on this basis have now been reassigned to classic groups of non-amniote tetrapods such as the Capitosauroidea, Colosteidae, Aïstopoda, Nectridea, Microsauria, Baphetidea, and Anthracosauria. Although the pattern of vertebral construction among non-amniote tetrapods is quite diverse, it has proven to be an inadequate criterion for establishing phylogenetic relationships among primitive tetrapods.

Tetrapod systematics was given a new direction in 1988 with the publication of a new phylogeny of amniotes authored by Jacques A. Gauthier, Arnold G. Kluge, and Timothy Rowe. They used a wide spectrum of anatomical characters instead of relying on vertebral features alone and analyzed their data using cladistic methodology. Since then, other researchers (Milner 1988, 1990, 1993; Panchen and Smithson 1988; Trueb and Cloutier 1991; Lombard and Sumida 1992; Carroll 1995; Laurin and Reisz 1997) have undertaken cladistic analyses of basal tetrapod relationships. Lomard and Sumida (1992) generated a cladogram that affirmed most commonly accepted relationships, whereas Laurin and Reisz (1997) proposed a radically different phylogeny of basal tetrapods.

Interrelationships among basal tetrapods are difficult to investigate due to the patchy nature of the fossil record and the often fragmentary nature of the fossils themselves. The Frasnian elginerpetontids (*Elginerpeton* and *Obruchevichthys*) are the oldest and most primitive tetrapods. With the possible exception of *Tulerpeton* from Russia, all Devonian genera branched off before the split between amphibians and reptiliomorphs. Phylogenetic trees that include Devonian tetrapods have been presented by Ahlberg and Milner (1994), Ahlberg (1995), and Lebedev and Coates (1995).

Three major tetrapod clades emerged from the Late Devonian diversification. These are the lepospondyls, the temnospondyls, and the reptiliomorphs. If the Carboniferous colosteids are temnospondyls, then the term Amphibia becomes synonymous with Temnospondyli. If *Tulerpeton* is a reptiliomorph, as suggested by Lebedev and Coates (1995), it implies a very early origin for the other two groups.

A great deal of controversy concerns the relationships of lissamphibians (frogs, salamanders, caecilians, and the extinct albanerpetontids) and amniotes to other groups of tetrapods. In fact, so much effort has been directed toward these two groups that the interrelationships of most other taxa have been neglected.

In contrast to traditional views that separated temnospondyls and lissamphibians, it is now believed that lissamphibians are simply derived temnospondyls closely related to branchiosauroids (Trueb and Cloutier 1991). Earlier studies suggested close relationships between lissamphibians and dissorophids (another temnospondyl family), or between lissamphibians and various groups of lepospondyls (microsaurs, lysorophids, and nectrideans). The first cladistic analysis of temnospondyls was performed by Gardiner (1983).

Lepospondyls are placed either within the Amphibia or the Reptiliomorpha, or in between. Lepospondyli includes the following groups: Adelospondyli, Aïstopoda, Nectridea, Microsauria, and Lysorophia. Although the exact phylogenetic position of the group is unresolved, Carboniferous and Permian lepospondyls seem to form a natural group. However, it is still possible that Lepospondyli will ultimately prove to be polyphyletic (having at least two separate origins).

Reptiliomorphs include the palaeostegalian *Crassygirinus,* the proto-anthracosaur *Whatcheeria,* the anthracosaurs, seymouriamorphs, and diadectomorphs. Gauthier and colleagues (1988) discovered a number of shared-derived character states linking amniotes to the reptiliomorphs.

New fossil discoveries, advances in cladistic methodology, and the use of computer-aided analysis have all helped improve our knowledge of early tetrapod evolution. However, much remains to be learned, and we are many years from anything resembling a consensus.

RICHARD CLOUTIER

See also Evolutionary Novelty; Fins and Limbs, Paired; Lepospondyls; Lissamphibians; Sarcopterygians; Tetrapods: Basal Tetrapods; Tetrapods: Near-Amniote Tetrapods

Works Cited

Ahlberg, P.E. 1995. *Elginerpeton pancheni* and the earliest tetrapod clade. *Nature* 373:420–25.

Ahlberg, P.E., and A.R. Milner. 1994. The origin and early diversification of tetrapods. *Nature* 368:507–14.

Carroll, R.L. 1995. Problems of the phylogenetic analysis of Paleozoic choanates. *Bulletin du Muséum National d'Histoire Naturelle, Paris* 4e série, 17, section C:389–445.

Clack, J.A. 1989. Discovery of the earliest-known tetrapod stapes. *Nature* 342:425–26.

Cloutier, R., and P.E. Ahlberg. 1996. Morphology, characters, and the interrelationships of basal sarcopterygians. *In* M.L.J. Stiassny, L.R. Parenti, and G.D. Johnson (eds.), *Interrelationships of Fishes.* San Diego, California: Academic Press.

Coates, M.I., and J.A. Clack. 1990. Polydactyly in the earliest known tetrapod limbs. *Nature* 347:66–69.

———. 1991. Fish-like gills and breathing in the earliest known tetrapod. *Nature* 352:234–36.

Cope, E.D. 1892. On the phylogeny of the Vertebrata. *Proceedings of the American Philosophical Society* 30:278–81.

Daeschler, E.B., and N.H. Shubin. 1998. Fish with fingers? *Nature* 391:133.

Gaffney, E.S. 1979. Tetrapod monophyly: A phylogenetic analysis. *Bulletin of Carnegie Museum of Natural History* 13:92–105.

Gardiner, B.G. 1983. Gnathostome vertebrae and the classification of the Amphibia. *Zoological Journal of the Linnean Society* 79:1–59.

Gauthier, J.A., A.G. Kluge, and T. Rowe. 1988. Amniote phylogeny and the importance of fossils. *Cladistics* 4:105–209.

Godfrey, S.J. 1989. The postcranial skeletal anatomy of the Carboniferous tetrapod *Greererpeton burkemorani* Romer, 1969. *Philosophical Transactions of the Royal Society of London, Biological Sciences,* ser. B, 323:75–153.

Holmgren, N. 1933. On the origin of the tetrapod limb. *Acta Zoologica, Stockholm* 14:185–295.

Jarvik, E. 1942. On the structure of the snout of crossopterygians and lower gnathostomes in general. *Zoologiska Bidrag fran Uppsala* 21:235–675.

Laurin, M., and R.R. Reisz. 1997. A new perspective on tetrapod phylogeny. *In* S.S. Sumida and K.L.M. Martin (eds.), *Amniote Origins: Completing the Transition to Land.* San Diego, California: Academic Press.

Lebedev, O.A., and M.I. Coates. 1995. The postcranial skeleton of the Devonian tetrapod *Tulerpeton curtum* Lebedev. *Zoological Journal of the Linnean Society* 112:307–48.

Lombard, R.E., and S.S. Sumida. 1992. Recent progress in understanding early tetrapods. *American Zoologist* 32:609–22.

Milner, A.R. 1988. The relationships and origin of living amphibians. *In* M.J. Benton (ed.), *The Phylogeny and Classification of the Tetrapods.* Vol. 1, *Amphibians, Reptiles, Birds.* Systematics Association Special Volume 35A. Oxford: Clarendon; New York: Oxford University Press.

———. 1990. The radiations of temnospondyl amphibians. *In* P.D. Taylor and G.P. Larwood (eds.), *Major Evolutionary Radiations.* Oxford: Clarendon; New York: Oxford University Press.

———. 1993. The Paleozoic relatives of lissamphibians. *In* D. Cannatella and D. Hillis (eds.), Amphibian relationships: Phylogenetic analysis of morphology and molecules. *Herpetological Monograph* 7:8–27.

Panchen, A., and T.R. Smithson. 1987. Character diagnosis, fossils and the origin of tetrapods. *Biological Reviews of the Cambridge Philosophical Society* 62:341–438.

———. 1988. The relationships of the earliest tetrapods. *In* M.J. Benton (ed.), *The Phylogeny and Classification of the Tetrapods.* Vol. 1, *Amphibians, Reptiles, Birds.* Systematics Association Special Volume 35A. Oxford: Clarendon; New York: Oxford University Press.

Rosen, D.E., P.L. Forey, B.G. Gardiner, and C. Patterson. 1981. Lungfishes, tetrapods, paleontology and plesiomorphy. *Bulletin of the American Museum of Natural History* 167:159–276.

Schultze, H.-P. 1970. Folded teeth and the monophyletic origin of tetrapods. *American Museum Novitates* 2408:1–10.

———. 1981. Hennig und der Ursprung der Tetrapoda. *Paläontologische Zeitschrift* 55:71–86.

Schultze, H.-P., and M. Arsenault. 1985. The panderichthyid fish *Elpistostege:* A close relative of tetrapods? *Palaeontology* 28:293–309.

Trueb, L., and R. Cloutier. 1991. A phylogenetic investigation of the inter- and intrarelationships of the Lissamphibia (Amphibia: Temnospondyli). *In* H.-P. Schultze and L. Trueb (eds.), *Origins of Higher Groups of Tetrapods: Controversies and Consensus.* Ithaca, New York: Cornell University Press.

Westoll, T.S. 1938. Ancestry of the tetrapods. *Nature* 141:127–28.

Further Reading

Sumida, S.S., and K.L.M. Martin (eds.). 1997. *Amniote Origins: Completing the Transition to Land.* San Diego, California: Academic Press.

TETRAPODS: BASAL TETRAPODS

Already at the beginning of the 1800s, all land vertebrates with four legs were designated as "Tetrapoda." At that time, this classification included living taxa, almost exclusively. In 1726 German naturalist J.J. Scheuchzer described the first fossil amphibian, a Miocene salamander, although he did identify it wrongly, saying it was a human fossil, *Homo diluvii testis*. Between 1824 and 1854, scholars did discover and describe a series of European fossil amphibians. As the German paleontologist Karl A. von Zittel said in the last edition of his *Text-Book of Palaeontology* (1932), "The four Classes of Vertebrates above *Pisces* [*Amphibia, Reptilia, Aves,* and *Mammalia*] are grouped sometimes under the name *Tetrapoda* (four-footed), sometimes as *Stapedifera* (bearing a *stapes* or ear bone, which is equivalent to the hyomandibular bone of *Pisces*)." Of all these classifications, only the term Tetrapoda is still in use, and even it did not represent a formal taxon until quite recently.

Nowadays, tetrapods account for some 23,500 living species and a variety of extinct forms. Eight genera represent basal (archaic) forms from the Late Devonian: *Elginerpeton* and *Obruchevichthys* from the Late Frasnian; *Metaxygnathus* and *Hynerpeton* from the Early to Middle Famennian; and *Ventastega, Acanthostega, Ichthyostega,* and *Tulerpeton* from the Late Famennian. Tetrapoda also includes more than 5,000 amphibians, including approximately 4,000 extant (present-day) and approximately 200 extinct lissamphibian species (lissamphibians include frogs, salamanders, and caecelians). There are also approximately 25 microsaurs (lasting from the Carboniferous to the Permian), and approximately 20 genera of anthracosaurs. Finally, there are thousands of amniotes and related taxa, including approximately 18,100 living species of mammals, birds, crocodiles, sphenodontids, lizards, snakes, and turtles. Traditionally, all non-amniote tetrapods (those that do not lay shelled eggs), were designated as amphibians. The famous eighteenth-century Swedish naturalist Carl von Linné (1707–78), founder of the modern system of binomial nomenclature, created Amphibia to house what we classify today as amphibians, some reptiles, and even some fishes. Although the term "amphibian" is still widely used, its meaning varies from author to author. Popular usage is quite different from scientific usage. As a result, the term "amphibian" has taken on a relatively narrow, but precise, meaning for modern systematists. Three groups are now considered to belong to the Amphibia. These are the Lepospondyli (encompassing the Aïstopoda and Nectridea of the Carboniferous and Permian periods), the Baphetidae of the Carboniferous, and the Temnospondyli (Lissamphibia is nested within the Temnospondyli). Features that unite these groups as amphibians include the dorsal orientation of the stapes and the reduction of the number of digits in the hand to four.

The heavily ossified skull observed in early tetrapods led the North American paleontologist Edward Drinker Cope (1840–97) to embrace a variety of Carboniferous to Triassic fossils under the group name, Stegocephali. Subsequently, stego-cephalians were said to be divided into the robust labyrinthodonts and the gracile phyllospondyls (the original members of which are now assigned to two groups—the branchiosaurids and the micromelerpetontids). Only the taxon Labyrinthodontia enjoyed long-term acceptance, but its eventual recognition as a wastebasket housing primitive forms caused its relatively recent abandonment.

Labyrinthodontia was customarily subdivided into three orders: the Ichthyostegalia (restricted to Devonian genera); the Temnospondyli (excluding lissamphibians); and the Anthracosauria. The term "labyrinthodont" refers to the complex infolding of the dentine seen in their teeth. This type of dentine (called "plici-dentine") is now known to be a primitive feature found in rhipidistian fish—the ancestors of tetrapods.

In his "Review of the Labyrinthodontia" (1947), the North American vertebrate paleontologist Alfred Sherwood Romer (1894–1973) diagnosed this group based on vertebral characteristics: "Primitive aspidospondyls in which centra are formed by arch elements (pleurocentra or intercentra or both) and anuran specializations are lacking." Such a diagnosis was so broadly defined that it was uninformative. British paleoherpetologist Alex L. Panchen (1980) explained that "labyrinthodonts" do not form a homogeneous and monophyletic group, which means that while the group has a common ancestor, it does not embrace all its descendants.

Basal Tetrapods: The Devonian Diversification

Although the fossil record of Devonian tetrapods is fairly scarce, it is most important in order to understand the transition from the aquatic to the terrestrial environment—the conquest of the land. The history of the discoveries of Devonian tetrapods dates back only to the 1930s, and the greatest diversity of species has been found within only the past 10 years. Until 1932, the oldest tetrapods were from the uppermost Early Carboniferous, some 325 million years ago. With the exception of the famous *Acanthostega* and *Ichthyostega*, Late Devonian tetrapods are known exclusively from isolated elements or only partly articulated specimens. Some genera are known only from cranial fragments (*Metaxygnathus, Obruchevichthys, Elginerpeton,* and *Ventastega*), isolated postcranial bones (Tetrapoda indet. from Scotland), or a few disarticulated cranial and postcranial elements (*Hynerpeton* and *Tulerpeton*).

All skeletal remains of Devonian tetrapods range from the Middle Frasnian to the Late Famennian, between 370 and 355 million years, whereas trace fossils interpreted to have been made by Devonian tetrapods range in time from the Middle Devonian to the Famennian, and have been found in Australia, Scotland, and Ireland. The Mid to Late Devonian trackways from Valentia Island, in southwestern Ireland, consisting of several hundred footprints, are the most impressive.

In a crucial paper published in 1932, the Swedish paleoichthyologist D. Gunnar Säve-Söderbergh (1910–48) described six species of Late Devonian tetrapods from East Greenland (Upper Famennien, Celsius Bjerg Group). At the time, they were referred to as "primitive labyrinthodont stegocephalians." In a single publication, Säve-Söderbergh pushed the origin of tetrapods back in time by some 20 million years and increased the morphological diversity of early tetrapods. *Ichthyostega* was the first Devonian tetrapod genus to be discovered, and the species *I. stensioei* was until recently the best-known Devonian tetrapod. Säve-Söderbergh originally described five species of *Ichthyostega* in 1932: *I. stensioei*, *I. watsoni*, *I. ? kochi*, *I. eigili*, and *I. ? sp. b*. Another tetrapod was named *Ichthyostegopsis wimani*; however, it is most likely that this species corresponds to *Ichthyostega stensioei*. Numerous specimens of *Ichthyostega* were found in the supposed fluvial deposit of the Britta Dal Formation (Sederholm Bjerg and Wiman Bjerg). This fossil material allowed another famous Swedish paleoichthyologist, Erik Jarvik (1908–98), also from the Naturhistoriska Riksmuseet in Stockholm, to describe the complete morphology of this tetrapod, with the exception of the hand, which remains unknown. He described a fishlike tail, robust ribs, and rachitomous vertebrae like those of a rhipidistian fish. In his exhaustive monograph Jarvik (1997) provided a photographic atlas and a description of *Ichthyostega* based on more than 200 specimens collected by Danish expeditions between 1929 and 1955. Out of the four species recognized by Säve-Söderbergh, Jarvik (1997) recognized solely the validity of the type species.

The Upper Devonian of East Greenland did not only yield *Ichthyostega*, but also complete specimens of another genus, *Acanthostega*. Jarvik (1952) identified this new form of primitive tetrapods based on two incomplete skulls. For the past 10 years, owing to the study of new material by British vertebrate paleontologists Jenny A. Clack and Michael I. Coates, *Acanthostega gunnari* has replaced *Ichthyostega* as the best known Devonian tetrapod. This 60-centimeter-long animal comes from the Britta Dal (Wiman Bjerg) and Aina Dal Formations (Upper Famennian). Although this species is unequivocally a tetrapod, it retains primitive features found in osteolepiform and elpistostegalian fishes (the latter being the nearest sister taxon to tetrapods) that have been lost in more derived tetrapods. While only some of the anatomy of *Acanthostega* has been described in great detail, what we know about it is quite revealing. *Acanthostega* has a well-ossified skull with a neurocranium (endochondral braincase) that resembles those of a sarcopterygian (lobe-finned) fish. The neurocranium is divided into two parts ventrally; it thus stands halfway between the completely divided neurocranium of sarcopterygians and the undivided braincase of more advanced tetrapods. The branchial and hyoid apparatus are like that of a lungfish (Coates and Clack 1991), and there is a stout stapes that would have functioned in ventilation rather than hearing. The pectoral (shoulder) girdle is free from the skull (a derived feature of tetrapods), and from it extend paddlelike forelimbs with eight fingers (Coates and Clack 1990). In contrast to Jarvik's reconstruction of *Ichthyostega* as a fully quadrupedal land vertebrate, the newly reconstructed *Acanthostega* reveals a four-legged sarcopterygian adapted for an aquatic mode of locomotion.

In addition to the two best-known Devonian tetrapods, a series of recently described taxa have filled some of the gaps in the group's early history. A number of these transitional fossils were identified alternately as advanced fishes (mainly elpistostegalians) or basal tetrapods. In 1933, the German vertebrate paleontologist Walter Gross (1903–1974), founder of modern paleohistology, described some Late Famennian teeth and scales of a so-called osteolepiform fish (a group of lobe-finned fishes) from Latvia under the name *Polyplocodus wenjukovi*. A few years later, he reinterpreted these remains as those of an elpistostegalid fish (another group of lobe-finned fishes), *Panderichthys bystrowi*. Finally, additional material allowed Ahlberg and colleagues (1994) to reassign these fossils to that of a basal tetrapod, which they named *Ventastega curonica*. Cranial bones as well as pectoral and pelvic girdle elements of *Ventastega* came from Pavāri and Ketleri in Latvia. *Ventastega* appears to be a tetrapod that is more primitive than *Ichthyostega* and *Acanthostega*.

Another problematic fossil consists of a single half of a lower jaw from the Lower Famennian Cloghnan Formation of New South Wales, Australia. Some paleoichthynlogists questioned the original description of *Metaxygnathus denticulus* as a primitive amphibian similar to *Ichthyostega;* however, the animal is still considered to be a basal tetrapod. This partial lower jaw is the only skeletal evidence of Devonian tetrapods from Gondwana (the southern supercontinent); however, older trackways are known from western Victoria, Australia.

In 1991 Swedish paleontologist Per E. Ahlberg, working now at the Natural History Museum in London, described a number of tetrapod-like mandibular and postcranial (tibia and humerus) fragments from the Upper Frasnian of Scat Craig, near Elgin, in Scotland. These had lain unrecognized in various British collections for more than a century. The Scat Craig tibia represents the earliest known tetrapod-like hind limb. Within the basal diversification of tetrapods, the Late Frasnian *Elginerpeton pancheni* and *Obruchevichthys gracilis* are the oldest known at the moment. Furthermore, they are considered to be the sister group of the remaining tetrapods (Ahlberg 1995). The family Elginerpetontidae was created to unite the two genera, based on bones of the lower jaw. The large-sized *Elginerpeton*, known solely from disarticulated cranial bones, comes from the Upper Devonian of Scat Craig in Scotland. It is likely that some of the postcranial bones found in the same locality belong to the same animal. Originally identified as an elpistostegalian fish, *Obruchevichthys* most recently was reinterpreted as a Devonian tetrapod (Ahlberg 1995). Only two incomplete lower jaws coming from Latvia and Russia are assigned to this taxon.

Tulerpeton curtum is one of only three Devonian tetrapods for which articulated material has been found and described. The discovery of *Tulerpeton* by the Russian paleoichthyologist Oleg A. Lebedev was to change our idea about the anatomy of a primitive limb—the forelimb he described bears six digits. Additional bones were subsequently discovered at the original locality of Toula in central Russia (Lebedev and Coates 1995); all these fossils were found in deposits that lie close to the Devonian-Carboniferous boundary.

In 1993 a shoulder girdle was found in sandstones from the Catskill Formation in Pennsylvania, by a field expedition led by Edward B. Daeschler from the Academy of Natural Sciences of Philadelphia and the University of Pennsylvania. This specimen turned out to be the oldest tetrapod from North America, the

Famennian *Hynerpeton bassetti*. Little is known about this tetrapod, since only a pectoral girdle and a lower jaw have been found (Daeschler et al. 1994).

The oldest tetrapods predate by some 25 million years the origin of the first terrestrial vertebrates. Most Devonian tetrapods were adapted for an aquatic mode of life, suggesting that the transition from aquatic to terrestrial vertebrates occurred during the Early Carboniferous (Clack and Coates 1995). Unfortunately, knowledge of the fossil record during the Early Carboniferous remains incomplete, with the exception of a few sites, and we have only brief glimpses of a large number of diverging lineages, for which few relationships are adequately established. The current hypothesis is that tetrapods arose during the Frasnian and diversified rapidly during the Famennian and Tournaisian. However, a 30-million-year gap in the fossil record hides the early history of terrestrial tetrapods, from the base of the Tournaisian to the Viséan (Carroll 1997). This gap, known as "Romer's Gap," in honor of the American paleontologist Alfred S. Romer (Coates and Clack 1995), corresponds to the period of diversification during which most major tetrapod taxa arose. A few isolated bones (humeri, neural arches, interclavicles, clavicles, and femurs) and trackways belonging to three types of early tetrapods have been collected from the Mid-Tournaisian Horton Bluff site in Nova Scotia, eastern Canada (Carroll 1997). Middle Viséan to Early Namurian tetrapod assemblages are known from the United States (West Virginia, Iowa, Illinois, and Utah), Canada (Nova Scotia), and Scotland.

A Diverse Group: The Temnospondyli

In 1947, Alfred S. Romer defined the Temnospondyli on what we would now consider to be primitive tetrapod characters. Temnospondyl amphibians are the largest group of non-amniote tetrapods represented in the fossil record from the Carboniferous to the Recent. According to different classifications, temnospondyls either include (Trueb and Cloutier 1991) or exclude (Laurin and Reisz 1997) extinct and extant lissamphibians. Excluding the lissamphibians, Carboniferous to Early Cretaceous temnospondyls include approximately 160 genera divided into 40 families. One of the most distinctive temnospondyl features concerns a paired opening in the palate referred to as the "interpterygoid vacuity." This large and rounded vacuity is essentially defined by the medial margin of the pterygoid, a dermal palatal bone involved with bracing the maxilla (upper jawbone) and suspensorium (jaw suspension) against the braincase.

In terms of morphology and ecology, the temnospondyls are a diverse group including lightly and heavily built species and demonstrating aquatic to terrestrial behavior and burrowing to saltatory (leaping) adaptations. The Carboniferous *Dendrerpeton* from Nova Scotia, Canada, can be considered a generalized temnospondyl, whereas forms such as the crocodile-like Triassic marine *Trematosaurus* and the Triassic helmet-headed *Plagiosuchus* show the group's great morphological diversity. A series of small Permian temnospondyls often referred to as "dissorophoids" (such as the doleserpetontid *Doleserpeton* from Oklahoma, the dissorophid *Dissorophus* from Texas, and the branchiosaurid *Apateon*

from Europe) links the modern lissamphibians to the heavily ossified forms such as *Edops* and *Eryops* (Trueb and Cloutier 1991).

Colosteids (*Colosteus*, *Greererpeton*, and *Pholidogaster*) generally are considered to be primitive temnospondyls. Among colosteids, the Late Carboniferous *Greererpeton* is thought to be a primitive genus. A Mid-Tournaisian colosteid, recently discovered in Nova Scotia by R.L. Carroll, is the oldest record of this group, as well as one of the oldest temnospondyls. Over the past 30 years, discoveries of well-preserved skeletons of the Westphalian *Greererpeton burkemorani* at Greer, West Virginia, have allowed a few paleoherpetologists to reassess the cranial and postcranial anatomy of this 1.4-meter-long temnospondyl. The deeply domed skull with flexible cheek was slightly elongate, with grooved sensory canals and deeply sculptured bones. The stapes is interpreted essentially as a bracing and stabilizing element with the braincase. As with numerous early tetrapods, the limbs were relatively short and had five digits; the trunk was elongate, as exhibited by the large number of presacral vertebrae (41 vertebrae anterior to the pelvis); and the body was covered completely with imbricated (overlapping), bony scales. The anteriormost vertebrae, the atlas and the axis, were differentiated, allowing the salamander-like animal to rotate its head.

During the Permian, the diversification of temnospondyls began to decline while amniotes became dominant. Nevertheless, during the Triassic capitosauroids and lissamphibians started to diversify. The Permo-Triassic, non-lissamphibian temnospondyls are divided into three groups—the trematosaurs, the capitosaurs, and the aberrant plagiosaurs. The Mid-Permian capitosaurid *Rhinesuchus* and *Rhinesuchoides* from South Africa are the oldest Capitosauroidea. Some of the families extended into the Jurassic (Brachyopidae, Chigutisauridae, and possibly the Capitosauridae), and even into the Cretaceous (Plagiosauridae) (Milner 1990). All these taxa once were referred to as the Stereospondyli, based on the structure of the vertebrae. Among them there is a general trend to increase the size of the median component of the vertebral centrum—the intercentrum. In some taxa the paired pleurocentra are lost, leaving the intercentrum as the sole element forming the centrum.

Numerous species are described solely based on fragmentary skulls, whereas very little is known of the postcranium. The head morphology of the capitosauroids is characterized by a flattening of the whole skull, an enlargement of the external nares (nostrils), an elongation of the preorbital region, and a posterior position of the orbits. Furthermore, the dorsal surface of the skull is sculptured with large, open-grooved sensory canals found in adult specimens, a feature related to their aquatic mode of life. Capitosauroids are mainly aquatic, and they represent the only group of amphibians to have penetrated the marine habitat with the trematosaurids (such as the Early Triassic *Trematosuchus* from South Africa) and the rhytidosteids (such as the Early Triassic *Deltasaurus* from Australia and Tasmania). Capitosauroids are most common in Triassic red-beds of Australia, Tasmania, South Africa, Russia, Greenland, and Spitzbergen, although they have been found in Europe (Germany, England, and France), the United States, Asia (China, Thailand, and India), Africa (Madagascar, Zambia, Lesotho, and Morocco), and Antarctica.

Modern amphibian orders, the Lissamphibia, can be traced back to the Triassic or the Jurassic. The oldest Salientia (frogs), *Triadobatrachus,* is from the Lower Triassic of Madagascar. Recently, the oldest caecilian (limbless, burrowing amphibians), the Early Jurassic *Eocaecilia,* was discovered in Arizona; in contrast to the remaining limbless gymnophionans, this primitive form still retains small limbs. The earliest undoubted urodeles (salamanders) on record are Middle (*Albanerpeton* from western Canada) and Late Jurassic (*Karaurus* from Russia and *Comonecturoides* from the United States); a Late Triassic specimen from Uzbekhistan was questionably identified as a larval urodele.

The Primitive Carboniferous Baphetidae (Loxommatidae)

According to various paleontologists, baphetids (*Baphetes, Megalocephalus, Spathicephalus,* and *Loxomma*) have been considered to be closely related to either temnospondyls, anthracosaurs, amniotes, *Crassigyrinus,* or basal tetrapods. Most members of the baphetid group are known exclusively from their skulls; a new articulated specimen from the Upper Carboniferous of Lancashire, England, as well as a new, small baphetid from Nyrany in the Czech Republic, offer the first chance to study the postcranial anatomy of a baphetid. The orbit is coalescent with a large anterior opening of questionable function (the antorbital vacuity), giving the distinctive keyhole shape to the orbit of this primitive group of Late Viséan-to-Westphalian tetrapods.

Long-Bodied Adelospondyli

Adelogyrinids (*Adelogyrinus, Dolichopareias, Adelospondylus,* and *Palaeomolgophis*) are restricted to a short time span in the Viséan and Namurian and are known only from a restricted area near Edinburgh in Scotland. *Palaeomolgophis* is the oldest member of the group. The chisel-tipped marginal dentition is highly characteristic of the group. The hyoid apparatus is extremely well-ossified in all mature adelogyrinids. Although they have lost their limbs and pelvic girdle, the dermal shoulder girdle is retained. Adelospondyls have a long body characterized by at least 70 trunk vertebrae. The elongate body, the vertebrae with cylindrical centra, and the animal's possible lack of limbs are features similar to those of eel-like fishes, suggesting that these animals were most likely slow swimmers in midwater.

The Palaeostegalia: The Enigmatic Viséan-Namurian *Crassigyrinus*

Crassigyrinus scoticus is considered by many paleontologists to be a primitive and aberrant early tetrapod. This large tetrapod is known from three Carboniferous localities, two not far from Edinburgh in Scotland, and a third locality in eastern Canada. The Canadian remains are tentatively identified as *Crassigyrinus.* The first specimen of *Crassigyrinus* apparently was collected in the 1850s by Hugh Miller (1802–56), the Scottish stonemason, geologist, journalist, and preacher. In 1890 R. Lydekker named the specimen and in 1929, the English paleontologist D.M.S. Watson (1886–1973) described it. This original specimen consists of the right side of a massive skull from snout to jaw articulation, on a block of iron-stone. A second specimen, discovered by the famous fossil collector, Stanley Wood, allowed an almost complete description of the anatomy of this curious, 130-centimeter-long tetrapod. The skull, the pectoral skeleton, the trunk, the pelvic girdle, the sacral rib, and the hind limb are known. The bizarre specializations of this aquatic predator include the reduced size of the forelimbs combined with a mixture of primitive features (the morphology of the palate) and features that are advanced (the form of the tabular horns).

The elongate body shape, the large size of the orbits, the unspecialized nature of the atlas-axis complex, and the extreme reduction of the forelimb suggest that this animal was a permanently aquatic form that lived in the larger, deeper pools of a coal swamp environment. In terms of external appearance, *Crassigyrinus* has been compared with the living eel-like salamanders *Amphiuma* and *Siren.*

The phylogenetic position of this Carboniferous creature remains problematic. The cheek region retains some primitive characters, such as a large preopercular bone, seen in osteolepiform fishes such as the Late Devonian *Eusthenopteron.* Nevertheless, the animal shares some features comparable to those of anthracosaurs: the dermal ornamentation of the skull roof, the way in which the back of the skull roof extends posteriorly (to the rear) into tabular horns, and the dark dentine of the teeth.

Carboniferous to Permian Anthracosauria (or Anthracoauroidea)

In 1934 Säve-Söderbergh created the group Anthracosauria, which included all taxa more closely related to amniotes than to lissamphibians. The content of the group was modified over the years, and paleontologists suggested a close relationship to either *Crassigyrinus,* the Seymouriamorpha, or the Amniota. It was accepted for some time that the most "reptilelike" tetrapods were the anthracosaurs (also referred to as batrachosaurs) of the Carboniferous and Permian. Today, Carboniferous anthracosaurs are widely accepted as stem-amniotes. Some of the features shared by anthracosaurs and more advanced taxa (i.e., Seymouriamorpha, Diadectomorpha, and Amniota) include the contact between the tabular and the parietal bones in the posterior part of the skull table, and a foot with a characteristic number of phalanges for each toe (two in the first toe or hallux, three in the second, four in the third, five in the fourth, and four or five in the fifth toe).

Anthracosaurs include three major groups—the Herpetospondyli, the aquatic Embolomeri, and the terrestrial Gephyrostegoidea. The Herpetospondyli was proposed to include two early anthracosaurs: *Proterogyrinus* from the Viséan of West Virginia, and *Eoherpeton* from contemporary Scottish Gilmerton Ironstone of the Edinburgh area in Scotland. The Embolomeri of the Upper Carboniferous Coal Measures and Lower Permian are divided into Anthracosauridae (solely the British *Anthracosaurus*), Archeriidae (solely the American *Archeria*), and Eogyrinidae. And finally, the Gephyrostegoidea accomodates several relatively small, generalized tetrapods from the Upper Carboniferous. Recently, O.A. Lebedev and M.J. Coates (1995) argued that the Devonian *Tulerpeton,* the Carboniferous *Crassigyrinus,* and the Viséan *Westlothiana* were anthracosaurs.

The best known of the early anthracosaurs is *Proterogyrinus scheelei* from the Upper Viséan from Greer in West Virginia. *Proterogyrinus* is a medium-sized anthracosaur measuring approximately one meter long with a semiaquatic mode of life. The limbs are well-ossified and the trunk, shorter than most other anthracosaurs, has only 31 presacral vertebrae. The rare *Proterogyrinus* is found in association with the more abundant colosteid temnospondyl *Greererpeton*. Although they are not as completely preserved as *Proterogyrinus*, the Viséan small-sized *Silvanerpeton miripedes* and *Eldeceeon rolfei* from East Kirkton Quarry in Scotland are the earliest members of the group (Rolfe et al. 1994). It is likely that a Mid-Tournaisian anthracosaur is present in the Horton Bluff tetrapod assemblage of Nova Scotia, Canada (Carroll 1997).

Embolomere anthracosaurs were among the earliest amphibians to be described from the Carboniferous and were once thought to occupy a central position in the radiation of tetrapods. These animals are long-snouted, crocodile-like, long-bodied anthracosaurs, with around 40 presacral vertebrae and small limbs. In this group, both the intercentrum and the pleurocentrum are complete rings, forming a "double" centrum. Embolomeres were among the largest predators of the Euramerican Late Carboniferous coal swamps, lakes, and estuaries.

An Early Carboniferous tetrapod from Delta, Iowa, was described as a "proto-anthracosaur," occupying a phylogenetic position between *Crassigyrinus* and the anthracosaurs. The so-called proto-anthracosaur *Whatcheeria deltae* from the Viséan St. Louis Formation is represented by about 50 partial skeletons and some nearly complete, articulated skeletons. *Whatcheeria* retains a number of surprisingly primitive characteristics that are lost in most of the earliest tetrapods. The skull table of this one-meter-long, near-amniote tetrapod retains an intertemporal bone, but lacks a contact between the tabular and parietal bones; a tabular horn of anthracosaur-type is present, the cheek retains a preoperculum, and the anatomy of the inner side of the lower jaw retains primitive osteolepiform characters (Lombard and Bolt 1995).

Discoveries of Some Important Devonian and Early Carboniferous Sites

Devonian tetrapods attained a virtually global equatorial distribution. Sites that yield these fossils are located in the northeastern United States, Scotland, East Greenland, Ireland, Latvia, Russia, and Australia. The center of radiation (the area where the group originated) cannot be determined, although some paleontologists have suggested Gondwana and others have proposed the Old Red Sandstone Continent. Among these Devonian localities, the history of the exploration of East Greenland is the most interesting.

At the end of the nineteenth century during an expedition to the east coast of Greenland, the geologist A.G. Nothorst found several bones on the side of a mountain he named Celsius Bjerg, in honor of the eighteenth-century Swedish astronomer. The bones were those of a fish that was 360 million years old. In East Greenland, the Upper Devonian outcrops in a few localities surrounding Kejser Franz Josephs Fjord, an area about 500 miles north of the Arctic Circle. Fossil localities also were found in places near mountains named in honor of European paleontologists: Smith Wood-

wards Bjerg, after Arthur Smith Woodward (1864–1944) of England, and Stensiös Bjerg, after Erik Anderson Stensiö (1891–1984) of Sweden. In 1929 the first ichthyostegalids—represented by an imperfect three-dimensional skull and a few articulated thoracic ribs—were collected during an expedition led by Danish geologist Lauge Koch (1892–1964). These East Greenland fossils, studied by Säve-Söderbergh in 1932, shed new light on the early history of tetrapods. During the early 1930s, Danish, Swedish, and British geologists returned to East Greenland. The largest collection of *Ichthyostega* material is housed in the Department of Palaeozoology of the Naturhistoriska Riksmuseet in Stockholm, Sweden. E. Jarvik studied the material after Säve-Söderbergh's initial description.

In 1970, John Nicholson collected *Acanthostega* material during one of a series of geological expeditions organized by Peter Friend from the University of Cambridge. Specimens of *Acanthostega* and *Ichthyostega,* including articulated limbs and skulls, were also collected in 1987 by a Cambridge-Copenhagen expedition to East Greenland. The fossils are curated by the Geological Museum of the University of Copenhagen.

The Scottish East Kirkton and Canadian Joggins localities are among the few Carboniferous sites providing evidence of tetrapod diversity. The Lower Carboniferous East Kirkton locality, near Bathgate in Scotland, is a 15-meter-thick sequence of limestones, shales, cherts, and tuffs that resulted from the activities of volcanoes and hot springs. By their very nature, terrestrial fossil assemblages are rare in the geological record; however, East Kirkton is among the few exceptional sites that provide early evidence of a fauna associated with fully terrestrial tetrapods. This Late Viséan age, approximately 335 million years old, represents one of the oldest Carboniferous tetrapod assemblages. Since the early nineteenth century, occasional fossils of tetrapods had been found here. From 1984 on, Stanley P. Wood, a Scottish commercial collector from Edinburgh, uncovered an important series of tetrapods and other terrestrial fossils. In a collective work titled *Volcanism and Early Terrestrial Biotas,* Rolf and colleagues (1994) revised the fauna and flora of East Kirkton in a series of papers. These dealt with temnospondyls (*Balanerpeton woodi* and a large temnospondyl indet.), aïstopods *(Ophiderpeton kirktonense),* anthracosaurs (*Eldeceeon rolfei* and *Silvanerpeton miripedes*), *Westlothiana lizziae,* and a possible nectridean. Nicknamed "Lizzy," the 30-centimeter-long *Westlothiana* is generally considered to be a stem-group amniote, although it was originally identified as a primitive reptile. *Westlothiana* lacks two important amniote characteristics—the pterygoid flange in the palate and the huckle-bone astragalus.

In 1871, Sir Charles Lyell (1797–1875), the father of geology, described the coastal cliffs near Joggins, in northwestern Nova Scotia, Canada, as "the finest example in the world" of Carboniferous rocks. These rocks include the 2,745-meter-thick Upper Carboniferous Cumberland Group. At Joggins, the skeletal remains of Westphalian terrestrial vertebrate faunas are found. As early as 1845, the Canadian Sir William E. Logan (1798–1875), founder of the Geological Survey of Canada, reported remains of early tetrapods found in the stumps of upright tree trunks of the lycopsid *Sigillaria*. Among these trapped tetrapods was *Dendrerpeton acadianum,* described by the British anatomist Richard Owen (1804–92) based on material collected by Charles Lyell and William Dawson in 1852.

From 1860 to 1882, the Canadian paleontologist and paleobotanist Sir J. William Dawson (1820–99) from McGill University, Montreal, described tetrapods from Joggins. In his 1863 monograph entitled *The Air-Breathers of the Coal Period in Nova Scotia,* Dawson describes the disarticulated Joggins material, including among others, the temnospondyl *Dendrerpeton acadianum,* the stem-amniote *Hylonomus lyelli,* and the microsaur *Hylerpeton dawsoni.* The 20-centimeter-long, lizardlike *Hylonomus,* discovered at the end of the nineteenth century in the Mid-Carboniferous basin of Nova Scotia, was thought to be the earliest reptile. Already at the end of the last century, *Hylonomus* was considered "as a type of the higher Carboniferous Amphibia approaching to Reptilia" (Dawson 1891). The cotylosaur *Archerpeton anthracos,* the pelycosaur *Protoclepsydrops haplous,* and the microsaur *Trachystegos megalodon* figure among the Joggins tetrapods that Carroll (1997) described. In addition to these oft-cited tetrapods, a few microsaurs (*Novascoticus multidens, Ricnodon* sp., *Leiocephalikon problematicum, Asaphestera intermedia, A. platyris*), the embolomere anthracosaur *Calligenethlon watsoni,* and possibly "*Baphetes*" *minor* were living in the Carboniferous swamps of Joggins.

RICHARD CLOUTIER

See also Evolutionary Novelty; Fins and Limbs, Paired; Lepospondyls; Lissamphibians; Sarcopterygians; Tetrapods: Overview

Works Cited

Ahlberg, P.E. 1991. Tetrapod or near-tetrapod fossils from the Upper Devonian of Scotland. *Nature* 354:298–301.

———. 1995. *Elginerpeton pancheni* and the earliest tetrapod clade. *Nature* 373:420–25.

Ahlberg, P.E., E. Luksevics, and O. Lebedev. 1994. The first tetrapod finds from the Devonian (Upper Famennian) of Latvia. *Philosophical Transactions of the Royal Society of London,* ser. B, 343:303–28.

Carroll, R.L. 1997. The earliest Carboniferous tetrapods from North America. *Journal of Vertebrate Paleontology* 17 (supplement):36A.

Clack, J.A. 1989. Discovery of the earliest-known tetrapod stapes. *Nature* 342:425–26.

Clack, J.A., and M.I. Coates. 1995. *Acanthostega gunnari,* a primitive, aquatic tetrapod? *Bulletin du Muséum National d'Histoire Naturelle, Paris* 4e série, 17, section C:373–88.

Coates, M.I., and J.A. Clack. 1990. Polydactyly in the earliest known tetrapod limbs. *Nature* 347:66–69.

———. 1991. Fish-like gills and breathing in the earliest known tetrapod. *Nature* 352:234–36.

———. 1995. Romer's gap: Tetrapod origins and terrestriality. *Bulletin du Muséum National d'Histoire Naturelle, Paris* 4e série, 17, section C:373–88.

Daeschler, E.B., N.H. Shubin, K.S. Thomson, and W.W. Amaral. 1994. A Devonian tetrapod from North America. *Science* 265:639–42.

Dawson, J.W. 1863. *Air-Breathers of the Coal Period: A Descriptive Account of the Remains of Land Animals Found in the Coal Formation of Nova Scotia, with Remarks on Their Bearing on Theories of the Formation of Coal and of the Origin of Species.* Montreal: Dawson Brothers; New York: Baillieve.

———. 1891. On new specimens of *Dendrerpeton Acadianum,* with remarks on other Carboniferous amphibians. *Geological Magazine* Decade 3, 8:145–56.

Jarvik, E. 1952. On the fish-like tail in the ichthyostegid stegocephalians with descriptions of a new stegocephalian and a new crossopterygian from the Upper Devonian of East Greenland. *Meddelelser om Grønland* 114:1–90.

———. 1997. The Devonian tetrapod *Ichthyostega. Palaeogeography, Palaeoclimatology, Palaeoecology* 40:1–213.

Laurin, M., and R.R. Reisz. 1997. A new perspective on tetrapod phylogeny. *In* S.S. Sumida and K.L.M. Martin (eds.), *Amniote Origins: Completing the Transition to Land.* San Diego, California: Academic Press.

Lebedev, O.A., and M.I. Coates. 1995. The postcranial skeleton of the Devonian tetrapod *Tulerpeton curtum* Lebedev. *Zoological Journal of the Linnean Society* 114 (3):307–48.

Lombard, E.R., and J.R. Bolt. 1995. A new primitive tetrapod, *Whatcheeria deltae,* from the Lower Carboniferous of Iowa. *Palaeontology* 38:471–94.

Milner, A.R. 1990. The radiations of temnospondyl amphibians. *In* P.D. Taylor and G.P. Larwood (eds.), *Major Evolutionary Radiations.* Oxford: Clarendon.

Panchen, A.L. 1980. The origin and relationships of the anthracosaur Amphibia from the Late Palaeozoic. *In* A.L. Panchen (ed.), *The Terrestrial Environment and the Origin of Land Vertebrates: Proceedings of an International Symposium Held at the University of Newcastle upon Tyne.* Systematics Association Special Volume 15. London and New York: Academic Press.

Rolfe, W.D.I., G.P. Durant, W.J. Baird, and C. Chaplin. 1994. The East Kirkton Limestone, Visean, of West Lothian, Scotland: Introduction and stratigraphy. *Transactions of the Royal Society of Edinburgh, Earth Sciences.* Special Issues: Volcanism and Early Terrestrial Biotas, 84 (3–4).

Romer, A.S. 1947. Review of the Labyrinthodontia. *Bulletin of the Museum of Comparative Zoology, Harvard College* 99:1–368.

Säve-Söderbergh, G. 1932. Preliminary note on Devonian stegocephalians from East Greenland. *Meddelelser om Grønland* 94:1–107.

———. 1934. Some points of view concerning the evolution of the vertebrates and the classification of this group. *Arkiv för Zoologi* 26A:1–20.

Trueb, L., and R. Cloutier. 1991. A phylogenetic investigation of the inter- and intrarelationships of the Lissamphibia (Amphibia: Temnospondyli). *In* H.-P. Schultze and L. Trueb (eds.), *Origins of the Higher Groups of Tetrapods: Controversy and Consensus.* Ithaca, New York: Comstock.

Zittel, Karl A. 1932. *Text-Book of Palaeontology.* C.R. Eastman (ed. and trans.), revised by A.S. Woodward. 3 vols. London and New York: Macmillan; adapted from *Grundzüge der Paläontologie,* Munich and Berlin: Oldenbourg, 1895.

Further Reading

Ahlberg, P.E., and A.R. Milner. 1994. The origin and early diversification of tetrapods. *Nature* 368:507–14.

Carroll, R.L. 1992. The primary radiation of terrestrial vertebrates. *Annual Review of Earth and Planetary Sciences* 20:45–84.

Panchen, A.L. (ed.). *The Terrestrial Environment and the Origin of Land Vertebrates: Proceedings of an International Symposium Held at the University of Newcastle upon Tyne.* Systematics Association Special Volume 15. London and New York: Academic Press.

Zimmer, C. 1995. Coming onto the land. *Discover* 16 (6):118–27.

TETRAPODS: NEAR-AMNIOTE TETRAPODS

Amniota are classified together because of their common possession of a specialized, shelled cleidoic egg with its four associated extraembryonic membranes, namely, chorion, allantois, amnion, and yolk sac. The extinct non-amniote sister taxa of the Amniota, however, are necessarily defined on the basis of osteological (bony) characters. This has engendered some debate regarding the potential closest relatives of the amniotes, as osteological features allow only speculation as to the presence of embryonic structures. Further, the history of discovery and description of the nearest relatives of amniotes have produced some confusion. Edward D. Cope and Ermine C. Case championed the concept of the "Cotylosauria" in the early part of the twentieth century, including within it both primitive amniotes and many of their close relatives. This led to the description of many of the taxa currently implicated as near-amniote relatives—particularly taxa currently included within the Diadectomorpha, which are among the largest of Lower Permian tetrapods. Alfred S. Romer (1933) was perhaps the most pivotal figure studying primitive amniotes and their anamniote relatives in the middle of the century. Subsequently one of his students, Robert L. Carroll, pursued the study of amniote ancestors. Although some elements of his work have been contested, he was among the first to recognize the importance of solenodonsaurids in the consideration of near amniote relatives. Most recently, significant work in this area has been pursued by Malcolm Heaton, David S. Berman, Stuart S. Sumida, and again by Robert Carroll. Most of the work on the sister lineages of the Amniota has centered on specimens from North America. However, the recent work of Berman and Sumida in central Europe has complemented some of Carroll's work in suggesting a much more global perspective and distribution of the taxa in question.

Members of the tetrapod grouping Diadectomorpha are generally considered to be the nearest sister group to Amniota. However, more distant sister taxa have been the subject of much debate. The majority of published analyses suggest that Seymouriamorpha (another group of relatively large-bodied near-amniote tetrapods) and perhaps solenodonsaurids include more primitive sister taxa to the Diadectomorpha plus Amniota (still referred to by many as "Cotylosauria"). However, R.L. Carroll (1995) and M. Laurin and R.R. Reisz (1992) have proposed that the Lepospondyli (a grouping including microsaurs, nectridians, adelogyrinids, lysorophids, and aïstopods, whose vertebrae typically have only a single central element similar to modern salamanders) is the more likely sister group of Cotylosauria. Furthermore, they include the extant Lissamphibia within the Lepospondyli. This hypothesis suggests that the living frogs, salamanders, and caecilians may provide a better model of near-amniote relatives than previously thought.

Seymouriamorpha

Seymouriamorphs are a widespread group of Late Paleozoic choanates (with internally opening nasal passages). Small specimens with aquatic larvae are known to be seymouriamorphs, but adults appear to be completely terrestrial. Skull size ranges from a minute six millimeters to as much as 15 centimeters in mature adults. *Seymouria* and *Kotlassia* are among the best understood of seymouriamorphs and are known from terrestrial specimens only. Other genera of the group are represented by larval and postmetamorphic specimens. Previously, these were collectively described as "discosauriscids," but it is now considered an unnatural grouping. Recent discoveries of large specimens of the discosauriscid *Ariekanerpeton* and very small specimens of the seymouriid *Seymouria* have bridged the gap. Seymouriamorphs retained the complete complement of skull roofing bones that also were found in more primitive taxa; significantly, this includes the intertemporal bone. Most, if not all seymouriamorphs possessed a transverse flange of the pterygoid (a bone at the base of the skull, a feature previously thought to pertain only to amniotes). All seymouriamorphs possess a very small posttemporal fenestra—an opening on the occipital surface for the entrance of blood vessels into the skull. The body was short and stout, usually including 24 to 28 trunk vertebrae. Limb bones were short but well ossified.

In an analysis of the phylogenetic relationships of the Seymouriamorpha, Michel Laurin (1995) has proposed that the species of *Seymouria* form a natural taxon, although the grouping of *Ariekanerpeton, Discosauriscus,* and *Seymouria* form an unresolvable trichotomy within the Seymouriamorpha by Laurin's estimation. Berman and his coworkers (Berman et al. 1996) have gone further and suggested that "discosauriscids" gave rise to, and were replaced by, *Seymouria,* the earliest occurring and morphologically most primitive member of the family Seymouriidae.

Lepospondyli

Members of the Lepospondyli present a remarkable range of morphologies. Only among the Microsauria (studied extensively by Carroll and his colleague Pamela Gaskill) are organisms that display significant similarities to the Seymouriamorpha, Diadectomorpha, or Amniota found. Even within the Microsauria there exists a large range of morphological variability. The number of vertebrae is extremely variable between genera. Most have short limbs. Generally they are smaller than seymouriamorphs, diadectomorphs, and most primitive amniotes; however they are comparable in size to at least certain primitive amniotes (such as captorhinids and protorothyridids) and this may have prompted the comparison of this group to amniotes despite their generally accepted amphibian assignment. They are most commonly united by the similarity of their cylindrically shaped vertebral bodies. Curiously, they also lack an intertemporal bone, though the arrangement of the adjacent temporal series of bones appears to indicate that the intertemporal was not lost via incorporation into the parietal as a lateral lappet (as seen in diadectomorphs and primitive amniotes), but rather fused to another bone (possibly the tabular bone). Another feature apparently shared with diadectomorphs and amniotes is the possession of an ossified supratem poral bone. Perhaps one of the most interesting hypotheses regarding microsaurs is that of Carroll (1995) and Laurin and Reisz (1997), who suggest that not only are microsaurs closely related to diadectomorphs and amniotes, but that they are the group from which extant lissamphibians (including frogs, salamanders, and caecilians) are derived. If this is correct, extant lissamphibians might prove to be more useful for sister-group comparisons with amniotes than was previously thought, providing functional models for physiologists and morphologists alike.

Diadectomorpha

A number of independent phylogenetic analyses (e.g., Laurin and Reisz 1995, 1997; Lee and Spencer 1997) have supported the hypothesis that they form the nearest sister group to Amniota. One analysis (Berman et al. 1992) has gone so far as to suggest that they may even be amniotes themselves. The Diadectomorpha includes three families of primitive reptiles: Limnoscelidae, Tseajaiidae, and Diadectidae (see Figure 1). This group was the center of what had long been something of a taxonomic trash basket of taxa collectively known as the "Cotylosauria." More recently, Cotylosauria has been more restrictively defined as Diadectomorpha plus Amniota. Characters that support the unity of the Diadectomorpha include: (1) a single postparietal bone; (2) a broad, convex basioccipital condyle; (3) a supraoccipital that extends laterally beyond the margin of the otic capsule; and (4) an anteroventral process of the axial intercentra. Diadectomorphs demonstrate a suite of postcranial features that are suggestive of extreme terrestriality. Although these features are not necessarily exclusive to them taxonomically, they are characteristics that might be expected of amniote relatives. They include vertebral elements that include accessory articulations that aid in the structural integrity of the column, extremely well ossified limb elements, and well-developed processes for the attachment of locomotor musculature. Perhaps most significantly, a large number of shared, derived characters unite the Diadectomorpha and Amniota. Lee and Spencer (1997) identified 23 different shared, derived characters that united the two. Some of them include: absence of lateral line grooves on the skull; the location of both the tabular and postparietal bones on the occipital surface of the skull; loss of the presplenial and first coronoid bones; and positioning of the atlas pleurocentrum directly dorsal to the axial intercentrum. One of the most telling features is their mutual loss of an independent intertemporal bone. It appears to have been incorporated as a lateral flange of the parietal bone. This condition was previously thought to be a shared, derived feature of amniotes exclusively. Berman and colleagues (1992) have pointed out the mutual possession of an otic trough (a stout rectangular flange of the opisthotic that projects ventrally from the posterior border of the fenestra ovalis with a deep trough-like basin on its anterior surface) by diadectomorphs and primitive synapsids, the basal lineage of Amniota.

Within the Diadectomorpha, Tseajaiidae and Diadectidae generally are considered to share a more recent common ancestor with one another than with Limnoscelidae. The relatively more primitive dentition and postcranial skeleton in *Limnoscelis* may indicate that it is a more basal (primitive) member of the group when compared to *Tseajaia* or diadectids (that are predominantly adapted for a herbivorous lifestyle). It is noteworthy that a recently discovered diadectid from Germany appears to exhibit an intermediate morphology, with a diadectid-like pattern of cranial bones but more typical laterally compressed teeth.

Temporal, Geographic, and Paleogeographic Context

Most estimates of the origin of amniotes place the earliest amniote approximately in the middle Pennsylvanian. Thus, the sister taxa of amniotes must have lived at least as early or earlier. In fact, the actual fossil record for near-amniote relatives of amniotes is clearly concentrated in Late Pennsylvanian and Early Permian. With the possible exception of some Asian discosauriscids (members of the Seymouriamorpha), all of the Late Pennsylvanian (Late Carboniferous) and Early Permian tetrapod groups in question are distributed within a narrow belt of approximately 10 degrees north and south of the paleoequator, where presumably a warm, humid, tropical climate existed. The distribution extended across the southern region of Euramerica, with the southern extent being bounded by the prominent Appalachian-Maurettinide-Viscarian mountain chain of central Pangaea that marks the continental union with Gondwana. Present-day distributions of fossil localities extend across terrestrial and semiterrestrial deposits of the United States, southwestern United States, to southern Oklahoma and north-central Texas, to the tristate area of Ohio, West Virginia, and Pennsylvania. European localities are somewhat more scattered but include deposits in present-day England, France, and Germany. Terrestrial tetrapods have not been recorded during this time in the several regions of terrestrial deposits found in Russia, India, South America, and South Africa that were distributed between approximately 10 and 30 degrees north and 10 and 60 degrees south of the paleoequator. Within the groups surveyed only a few exceptions can be noted that do not exhibit a widespread, Euramerican distribution during the Late Pennsylvanian and Early Permian. Evidence of widespread distributions of Late Pennsylvanian–Early Permian Euramerican relatives of amniotes has been bolstered greatly by the recent discovery of the highly terrestrial genus *Diadectes* in Germany in addition to its wide distribution throughout North America. Presumably, the highly terrestrial relatives of amniotes encountered no significant biogeographic barriers to dispersal during these times.

Biology and Behavior

Soft tissue physiology is difficult to estimate on the basis of osteological features alone; however, some lifestyle characteristics may be estimated. Within the Seymouriamorpha, discosauriscids appear to have been primarily aquatic organisms, but their closest relatives— the seymouriids—demonstrate no apparent aquatic phases in their ontogeny (embryonic development and growth). Stout construction of the vertebral column and limbs indicates that seymouriids were at least semiterrestrial, and perhaps nearly completely terrestrial. They were adapted for effective, albeit not rapid, terrestrial locomotion. Scholars can only speculate about their feeding behav-

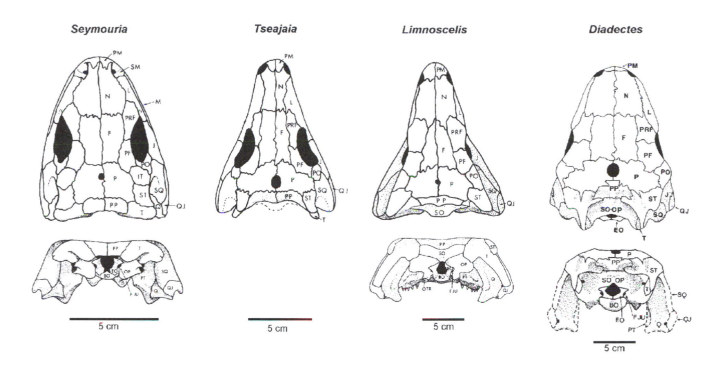

Figure 1. Cranial anatomy in dorsal and occipital views of taxa near the anamniote to amniote transition. From left to right: the semouriamorph *Seymouria*, the diadectomorph *Limnoscelis*, the diadectomorph *Tseajaia*, the diadectomorph *Diadectes*. Abbreviations: *BO*, basioccipital; *EO*, exoccipital; *F*, frontal; *F JU*, jugular foramen; *L*, lacrimal; *M*, maxilla; *N*, nasal; *OP*, opisthotic; *O TR*, otic trough; *P*, parietal; *PF*, postfrontal; *PM*, premaxilla; *PO*, postorbital; *PP*, postparietal; *PRF*, prefrontal; *PS*, parasphenoid; *PT*, pterygoid; *Q*, quadrate; *QJ*, quadratojugal; *SM*, septomaxilla; *SO*, supraoccipital; *SO OP*, fused supraoccipital-opisthotic; *SQ*, squamosal; *ST*, supratemporal; *T*, tabular.

ior, although seymouriamorphs likely were omnivorous. The possession of a transverse pterygoid flange has long been held as a shared, derived feature of amniotes; however, the description of a transverse flange of the pterygoid bone in *Seymouria* suggests that it may have been capable of feeding strategies normally ascribed to amniotes, namely, a diet of plants and hard-shelled invertebrates. The osteology of *Solenodonsaurus* is not known adequately to speculate on its physiological attributes. If the hypothesis that lepospondyls are closely related to amniotes bears out, it should be noted that many members of the group do not appear to be highly terrestrially adapted. However, some microsaurs show a suite of terrestrial adaptations including well-developed limbs, highly consolidated skulls, and a dentition adapted for an omnivorous diet.

Diadectomorphs are even more terrestrially adapted than seymouriamorphs, lepospondyls, or *Solenodonsaurus*. They are larger than seymouriamorphs, and appear to have been highly terrestrial. All members of the group have well ossified limbs and vertebral columns. Muscular processes on the limb elements are highly developed. Vertebral bodies, neural arches, and neural spines are all firmly sutured to one another in mature forms. Tseajaiids and limnoscelids present a dentition that is indicative of either flesh-eating or perhaps a diet of animal and plant substances. This appears to be the case for the most primitive of diadectids as well. However, the Late Pennsylvanian *Desmatodon*, and the Early Permian *Diadectes* possess

remarkably modified teeth. They are laterally expanded and cuspate, which some scholars suggest indicate a diet of molluscs or shellfish. More recent hypotheses are much more convincing: the dentition and jaw mechanics allow the hypothesis that they were among the first high-fiber herbivores. It is noteworthy that other than amniotes, only diadectids display morphological adaptations found in herbivores. Some scholars including S.P. Modesto (1992) and Laurin and Reisz (1997) have argued that this may be an indication of an amniote level of reproduction in this group (although it cannot be proven with fossils).

The Cleidoic Egg

Lee and Spencer (1997) have suggested that diadectomorphs (and perhaps solenodonsaurids) share so many features with amniotes that they may very well have had laid cleidoic eggs. Laurin and Reisz (1997) have pointed out that the fossil record does not allow exact determination of the origin of the cleidoic egg. They do suggest, however, that the hypothesis of an intermediate stage in which anamniotic eggs were laid on land is no better a theory than the suggestion that extraembryonic membranes evolved to facilitate extended egg retention.

STUART S. SUMIDA

Works Cited

Berman, D.S., S.S. Sumida, and R.E. Lombard. 1992. Reinterpretation of the temporal and occipital regions in *Diadectes* and the relationships of the diadectomorphs. *Journal of Paleontology* 66:481–99.

———. 1997. Biogeography of primitive amniotes. *In* S.S. Sumida and K.L.M. Martin (eds.), *Amniote Origins, Completing the Transition to Land*. San Diego, California: Academic Press.

Carroll, R.L. 1995. Phylogenetic analysis of Paleozoic choanates. *Bulletin du Muséum National d'Histoire Naturelle de Paris* 4, 17:389–445.

Laurin, M. 1995. Comparative cranial anatomy of *Seymouria sanjuanensis* (Tetrapoda: Batrachosauria) from the Lower Permian of Utah and New Mexico. *PaleoBios* 16:1–8.

Laurin, M., and R.R. Reisz. 1995. A reevaluation of early amniote phylogeny. *Zoological Journal of the Linnean Society* 113:165–223.

———. 1997. A new perspective on tetrapod phylogeny. *In* S.S. Sumida and K.L.M. Martin (eds.), *Amniote Origins, Completing the Transition to Land*. San Diego, California: Academic Press.

Lee, M.Y.S., and P.S. Spencer. 1997. Crown-clades, key characters and taxonomic stability: when is an amniote not an amniote? *In* S.S. Sumida and K.L.M. Martin (eds.), *Amniote Origins, Completing the Transition to Land*. San Diego, California: Academic Press.

Modesto, S.P. 1992. Did herbivory foster early amniote diversification? *Journal of Vertebrate Paleontology* 12:44A.

Romer, A.S. 1933. *Vertebrate Paleontology*. Chicago: University of Chicago Press; 3rd ed., 1968.

Further Reading

Czerkas, S.J., and S.A. Czerkas. 1990. *Dinosaurs, a Global View*. Mallard, 1991; rev. ed., Limpsfield, Surrey: Dragon's World; New York: Barnes and Noble, 1995.

Lombard, R.E., and S.S. Sumida. 1992. Recent progress in understanding early tetrapods. *American Zoologist* 32:609–22.

Sumida, S.S., and K.L.M. Martin (eds.). 1997. *Amniote Origins, Completing the Transition to Land*. San Diego, California: Academic Press.

THERAPSIDS

Therapsida is a subgroup of Synapsida, the group of amniote vertebrates to which the living mammals belong. Although traditionally known as "mammal-like reptiles" and placed in the class Reptilia as the paraphyletic group ancestral to the class Mammalia, the Therapsida has been redefined as a strictly monophyletic group of synapsids by including mammals within it (Hopson and Barghusen 1986). Therapsida may be defined technically as the most inclusive clade of synapsids, one that includes Mammalia but not Sphenacodontidae (its primitive sister group; see Figure 1). This definition excludes all pelycosaurs and includes all of the traditional therapsids plus mammals (for a comparable definition, see Laurin and Reisz 1996). Most of the characteristic features that distinguish therapsids from sphenacodontids represent modifications in the direction of a more mammal-like structure and, presumably, a more mammal-like physiology and ecology than seen with pelycosaurs. This article deals primarily with the non-mammalian therapsids.

The fossil record of non-mammalian therapsids spans a time period of about 110 million years, from the early part of the Late Permian (about 268 million years ago) to the late Middle Jurassic or early Late Jurassic (about 159 million years ago) (Figure 2). Whereas more primitive synapsids (pelycosaurs) are known primarily from North America and Western Europe, early therapsids are best known from Russia west of the Urals and the Karoo Basin of South Africa (although recently new finds of comparable age have been described from China). Later, in the Triassic, more advanced therapsids are found in many parts of the world, notably in southern and eastern Africa and South America (Brazil and Argentina) but also in Russia, China, North America, Antarctica, India, Madagascar, and Australia. By the end of the Triassic and into the Jurassic, therapsids attained a worldwide distribution, with notable faunas in southern Africa, China, Great Britain, eastern Canada, and southwestern United States. The earliest undoubted mammals appear in the Late Triassic (about 215 million years ago), although specimens that may be mammals occur some 10 million years earlier (Lucas and Luo 1993).

Distribution and Characteristics of Primitive Therapsids

The oldest undoubted therapsids are from the Ocher faunal assemblage (Zone I) of early Late Permian age of Russia (Figure 2), although fossils of similar age have been discovered recently in China and South Africa (Li et al. 1996; Rubidge 1994). Poorly preserved specimens from the late Early Permian of Texas and Oklahoma were once described as therapsids (Olson 1962, 1974), but recently they have been shown to belong with the pelycosaurs (Sidor and Hopson 1995). Another early synapsid, *Tetraceratops insignis*, from the Early Permian of Texas, has been interpreted as a basal therapsid by M. Laurin and R.R. Reisz (1990, 1996), although its state of preservation is so poor that its therapsid status must be considered uncertain.

The most primitive therapsid known from adequate material is *Biarmosuchus* from Ocher (Figure 3A), which, although possessing some unique specializations, may be considered representative of the ancestral therapsid stock (Sigogneau and Tchudinov 1972). It is smaller and considerably more lightly built than typical sphenacodontid pelycosaurs such as *Dimetrodon*. The skull of early therapsids has a general resemblance to that of sphenacodontids, except that the snout is relatively longer and lower, and the temporal region is shorter. The temporal fenestra (opening) is deeper, and a small muscle scar on the margin of the postorbital bar indicates that a portion of the jaw-closing musculature passed out through the opening to attach to the outer surface of the skull. The maxilla (the main tooth-bearing bone of the upper jaw) is much deeper than in sphenacodontids, contacting the prefrontal and excluding the lacrimal from its primitive contact with the nasal. Functionally, this change is related to the greater length of the root of the upper canine tooth. Five small upper incisors and four lower incisors seem to be primitive for therapsids. The upper canine forms a long serrated blade, but the lower canine is relatively short and incisor-like. The postcanine teeth are uniformly small and bladelike.

The skull of therapsids is sutured together more solidly than that of pelycosaurs, so intracranial movements were no longer possible. The palate is fixed firmly to the braincase, but otherwise its structure is generally primitive, with elongated internal narial (nasal) openings lying far forward between the canines and anterior cheek teeth. In the slender lower jaw, the bone at the lower rear corner, the angular, is deeply notched. The part below the notch is called the reflected lamina. In therapsids the reflected lamina stands out as a distinct process, and its outer surface is marked by a characteristic pattern of radiating ridges.

In the postcranial skeleton, the limb girdles are much less massive than those of pelycosaurs, and the limb bones are more slender. The shoulder joint faces down and back rather than outward, and the head of the humerus (the upper arm bone) is rounded. These features indicate a less sprawling posture and much greater freedom of movement than was possible in pelycosaurs. The humerus was oriented obliquely down, back, and somewhat outward, rather than extending straight out to the side. The acetabulum (hip socket) is a circular hollow, deeper than that of pelycosaurs, and the femur (upper leg bone) has a distinct inturned head, suggesting that the thigh was oriented downward and forward. The fingers and toes are more uniform in length due to the reduction of certain phalanges (digital bones) to short discs.

The modifications of the skeleton and dentition in primitive therapsids indicate that the carnivorous adaptations first seen in the sphenacodontids were becoming more specialized. The greatly enlarged upper canine and serrated teeth provided a more effective mechanism for killing prey. In therapsids, the expansion of the temporal fenestra suggests an increase in mass of the jaw-closing muscles (Barghusen 1968). The girdles and limbs of therapsids were more lightly built and the elbows and knees were more inturned, suggesting a more upright stance and improved locomotion. All of these changes suggest that therapsids actively hunted for their food, foraging widely in their search for prey (Hopson 1987).

Therapsid Diversity

In the first half of the twentieth century, the non-mammalian therapsids were placed in five major groups, based on well-known South African fossils: Dinocephalia, Dicynodontia, Gorgonopsia, Therocephalia, and Cynodontia. These were, in turn, placed within two higher-level groups: Anomodontia, for the herbivorous Dicynodontia and (perhaps) the Dinocephalia; and Theriodontia, for the remaining three, primarily carnivorous, groups (Romer 1966). Eventually the affinities of two poorly understood taxa, the Dromasauria and Bauriamorpha, were resolved; the

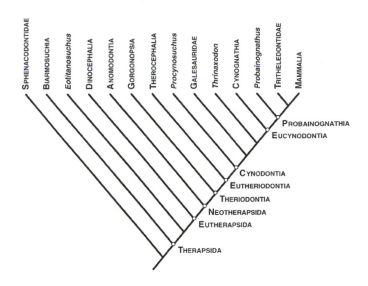

Figure 1. Cladogram of Therapsida, with its sister taxon, the family Sphenacodontidae, also indicated. Cynognathia includes two subgroups, Cynognathidae and Gomphodontia (see Figure 2).

former group was merged into the Anomodontia (Watson and Romer 1956) and the latter into the Therocephalia (Hopson and Barghusen 1986).

Later, as knowledge of older therapsid faunas from Russia improved, it became evident that many early therapsids (such as *Phthinosuchus, Biarmosuchus,* and *Eotitanosuchus*) were too primitive (sphenacodontid-like) to fit into any of the groups that were based on later fossils that came primarily from South Africa. To accommodate these basal therapsids, A.S. Romer (1961) created a new group that he called the Phthinosuchia, and L.D. Boonstra (1963) independently created a comparable group under the name Eotitanosuchia. However, because the position of *Phthinosuchus* is uncertain, Phthinosuchia now includes only this genus and a few closely related forms (Sigogneau-Russell 1989). Likewise, because *Eotitanosuchus* appears related more closely to advanced therapsids than to *Biarmosuchus,* Eotitanosuchia includes only *Eotitanosuchus* (Hopson and Barghusen 1986; Sigogneau-Russell 1989). The remaining basal therapsids, *Biarmosuchus* and its close relatives, are now included in a new group, the Biarmosuchia (Sigogneau-Russell 1989; Hopson 1991). In the following sections, the major therapsid groups are characterized and briefly described.

Biarmosuchia

The primitive Russian genus *Biarmosuchus* is related to several later taxa: *Proburnetia* from the younger Kotel'nich assemblage of Russia (Tatarinov 1974) and a variety of South African genera (e.g., *Hipposaurus, Ictidorhinus, Burnetia*). (The latter often are grouped in the family Ictidorhinidae, from younger faunas of Late Permian age.) All of these taxa share a few specializations that set

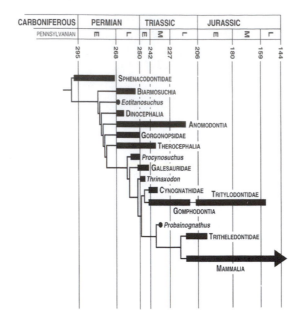

Figure 2. Geological timescale showing the temporal ranges of Sphenacodontidae (sister group of Therapsida) and the subgroups of therapsids

them off as a distinct group (Hopson 1991). The back of the skull is rotated anteroventrally (forward and downward) so that the jaw joint lies below the rear border of the skull roof rather than behind it; this indicates that the head was tilted downward on the neck. The postcanine teeth are swollen, with coarsely serrated margins, and certain wrist bones (carpals 4 and 5) are fused to form a single large element. Biarmosuchians are always rare elements of the faunas in which they occur.

Eotitanosuchia

Eotitanosuchus from the Ocher assemblage of Russia is a large carnivore (skull length 35 centimeters) known from a single skull that lacks the lower jaw (Figure 3B). It is more advanced than biarmosuchians in having a much larger temporal fenestra, in which the upper margin flares back and out. As a result, a large area for jaw muscle attachment formerly lying beneath the temporal roof now is exposed laterally and dorsally on the postorbital and squamosal bones. The bladelike upper canine is very long and robust. Unlike biarmosuchians, the rear of the skull slopes down and back as it does in most later therapsids, indicating that the head was held in line with the horizontal neck rather than being tilted downward.

Advanced Therapsids—The Eutherapsida

The Dinocephalia, Anomodontia, Gorgonopsia, Therocephalia, and Cynodontia (with mammals as a subgroup of cynodonts) were united as the Eutherapsida (Figure 1) by J.A. Hopson (1994). They are more advanced than biarmosuchians and, with less certainty, than the inadequately known *Eotitanosuchus*. Two skeletal differences from biarmosuchians are: the great reduction in size of the olecranon process on the ulna (elbow knob) and the loss of a disc-like phalanx from the fifth digit of the hind foot. In all eutherapsids, the cheek region flares more, and the intertemporal roof usually is narrower, so that the temporal fenestra has a much greater exposure from above than in *Eotitanosuchus* and biarmosuchians.

Formerly, dinocephalians were considered to be anomodonts (Romer 1966; King 1988; but see Hopson 1991; Grine 1997), but now they generally are recognized as the most primitive eutherapsids, the sister group to the anomodonts and theriodonts (Rowe 1988; Hopson 1994). The latter two groups are united here as the Neotherapsida (Figure 1) and defined as the most inclusive clade that includes Anomodontia and Theriodontia but not Dinocephalia.

Dinocephalia

Dinocephalians are the most primitive group of eutherapsids, representing the earliest as well as the most short-lived major adaptive radiation of therapsids. They were medium to large in size (about the size of a grizzly bear), stoutly built carnivores and herbivores known from the oldest Russian, Chinese, and South African therapsid faunas. Although abundant in the *Tapinocephalus* assemblage zone of the early Late Permian of South Africa, they did not survive into later times.

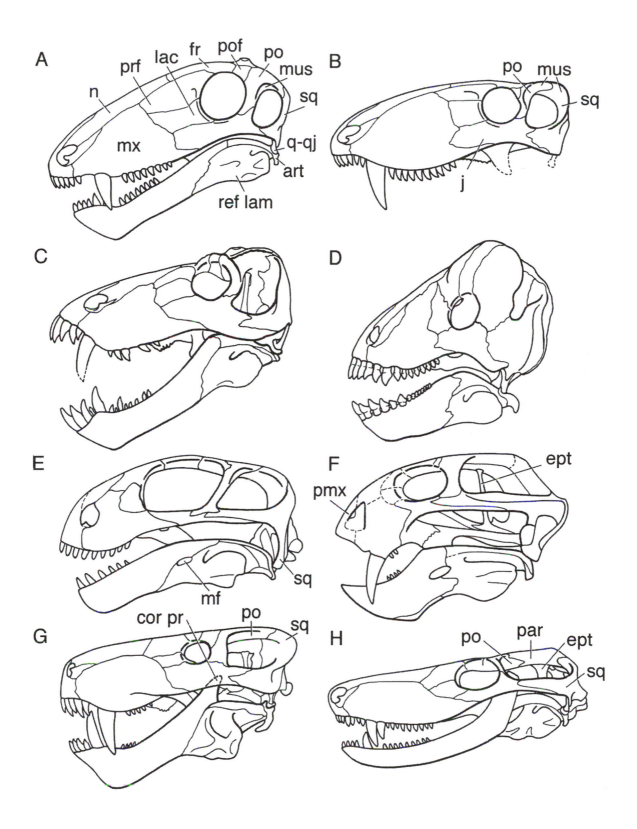

Figure 3. Skulls of non-cynodont therapsids. *A,* the basal therapsid *Biarmosuchus; B, Eotitanosuchus; C,* the anteosaurian dinocephalian *Titanophoneus; D,* the tapinocephalid dinocephalian *Ulemosaurus; E,* the basal anomodont *Patranomodon; F,* the early dicynodont anomodont *Eodicynodon; G,* the gorgonopsian *Leontocephalus; H,* the early baurioid therocephalian *Ictidosuchoides.* Abbreviations: *art,* articular; *cor pr,* coronoid process; *ept,* epipterygoid; *fr,* frontal; *j,* jugal; *lac,* lacrimal; *mf,* mandibular fenestra; *mus,* muscle attachment site; *n,* nasal; *par,* parietal; *pmx,* premaxilla; *po,* postorbital; *pof,* postfrontal; *prf,* prefrontal; *q-qj,* quadrate-quadratojugal complex; *ref lam,* reflected lamina of angular; *sq,* squamosal. Modified from Hopson (1994), by permission of the Paleontological Society.

The most characteristic feature of dinocephalians is the precise intermeshing of the upper and lower incisor teeth; this is such a striking specialization that the monophyly of the group rarely has been questioned. The incisors of most dinocephalians also possess distinct posterior heels. As in biarmosuchians, the jaw joint of all dinocephalians is rotated forward, and the face is turned downward with respect to the plane of the occiput, most prominently in the herbivorous forms. In the hand and foot, the number of phalanges is (from digit 1 to digit 5): 2-3-3-3-3; this phalangeal formula, indicating the number of bones in each digit, characterizes mammals and was later evolved independently in several groups of neotherapsids.

Hopson and H.R. Barghusen (1986) divided dinocephalians into two subgroups: one is carnivorous, the Anteosauria, and includes a single family, the Anteosauridae. The other is herbivorous, the Tapinocephalia, and includes four families, the Estemmenosuchidae, Titanosuchidae, Tapinocephalidae, and Styracocephalidae (the last being very poorly known).

The Anteosauridae includes earlier, more primitive, forms from Russia (such as *Syodon*, *Titanophoneus* (Figure 3C), and *Doliosauriscus* (Orlov 1958) of South Africa *(Australosyodon)* (Rubidge 1994). Most are of moderate size (skulls range from 25 to 60 centimeters long), although the later, highly specialized *Anteosaurus*, from South Africa, was an enormous animal with a skull nearly a meter long. The alveolar margin (toothed) of the premaxilla shows a pronounced upward tilt in order to accommodate very large forwardly inclined incisors. *Doliosauriscus* shows a thickening of the cranial bones (pachyostosis) that is developed even further in *Anteosaurus*. The latter, armed with extremely long pointed incisors with reduced heels, was presumably the major predator on the large herbivorous dinocephalians.

The herbivorous dinocephalians of the families Estemmenosuchidae, Titanosuchidae, and Tapinocephalidae (and probably the poorly known Styracocephalidae) are grouped as the Tapinocephalia on the basis of many specializations of the skull (Hopson and Barghusen 1986). The tip of the lower canine passes external to the maxilla and the cheek dentition is a long row of small, spatulate, coarsely serrated teeth. Tapinocephalians are all very large animals; the skull of *Estemmenosuchus* is 80 centimeters long, and the titanosuchid *Jonkeria* has a skull about 50 centimeters in length and a total body length of four meters. Estemmenosuchids, from the Ocher fauna of Russia, combine apparently primitive dinocephalian features, such as a broad intertemporal roof, with unique hornlike outgrowths on the skull. Titanosuchids, exemplified by *Jonkeria*, and tapinocephalids, exemplified by *Struthiocephalus* and *Moschops*, are almost exclusively South African groups, with only the tapinocephalid *Ulemosaurus* (Figure 3D) from Russian Zone II occurring elsewhere. They possess large heels on the incisors that form crushing surfaces when these teeth are intermeshed. The titanosuchid *Jonkeria* has a long low face with well-developed canines and spatulate cheek teeth. In the more diverse tapinocephalids, the canines and anterior cheek teeth are incisorlike and interdigitate with the teeth in the opposing jaw, thus forming a cutting and crushing battery for breaking down vegetation. The most notable feature of the tapinocephalids is the pachyostosis of the bones of the cranial roof and postorbital bar. Barghusen (1975) has demonstrated convincingly

that the thick-boned tapinocephalid skull and the somewhat less specialized skulls of *Anteosaurus* and *Estemmenosuchus* were adapted for head-to-head ramming and shoving contests between members of the same species, much as occurs today in mountain sheep and other ungulates.

Anomodontia

Following the dinocephalians, the second great radiation of early therapsids was that of the anomodonts, the dominant herbivores of the latest Permian and the first half of the Triassic. The oldest known anomodont, *Otsheria*, is from the Ocher assemblage (Zone I) of Russia and is, thus, a contemporary of the most primitive undoubted therapsids and the earliest dinocephalians. In South Africa, an even more primitive anomodont, *Patranomodon* (Figure 3E), occurs in the slightly younger *Eodicynodon* Assemblage Zone at the base of the Beaufort Group (Rubidge and Hopson 1990, 1996).

The name Anomodontia is used here to include only the dicynodonts and their close relatives, the so-called dromasaurs and venyukovioids. Anomodonts are characterized by a slender, dorsally arched zygomatic (cheek) arch, a short face, the absence of true canines, and a mandibular fenestra between the dentary and the angular bones of the lower jawbone. Recent discoveries of primitive anomodonts in both South Africa and Russia indicate that the Dromasauria and Venyukovioidea earlier classifications are paraphyletic taxa and so cannot be recognized as valid taxonomic groups.

Patranomodon was a small, lightly built animal, with a delicate skull about six centimeters in length, elongate slender limbs with large-clawed toes, and (presumably) a long tail. The face is short, and the temporal fenestra somewhat smaller than the orbit. The squamosal has a characteristic anomodont morphology—a thin zygomatic process that lies well above the base of the skull and a deep vertical posteroventral process that supports the quadrate and quadratojugal. The quadrate (the bone that forms the upper half of the jaw joint) has a hingelike, rather than sliding, articulation with the lower jaw. The upper and lower dentition consists of a small number of peg-like teeth, rounded in cross section, and there is no indication of a canine in either jaw.

Successively more dicynodont-like evolutionary stages are represented by *Otsheria* from Zone I of Russia, *Galeops* from the *Tapinocephalus* Assemblage Zone of South Africa, and *Ulemica* and *Suminia* from Russian Zone II. In the last three taxa the jaw articulation forms a fore-aft sliding surface. *Galeops* also approaches dicynodonts in the reduction in size of the teeth and the development of a lateral ridge, possibly horn-covered, on the jaw margins.

Ulemica (formerly included in the genus *Venyukovia*; see Ivakhnenko 1996) of Russian Zone II is very dicynodont-like in many respects, although it is uniquely specialized in the great enlargement of the incisor teeth, the bulbous nature of the remaining teeth, and the development of bony knobs and ridges on the lower jaw. As noted above, the more primitive anomodonts lack enlarged canines, but in *Ulemica* the bulbous fourth maxillary tooth is much larger than the adjacent teeth, suggesting an early stage in the development of the long maxillary caniniform of dicynodonts. In *Ulemica* and *Suminia,* as in dicynodonts, the descending flange of the squamosal has a lateral depression for the origin of a new outer slip of the main jaw-closing muscle.

Dicynodonts were by far the most abundant terrestrial vertebrates of the Late Permian and Early Triassic, in terms both of species and of individuals (King 1988). They were found throughout the supercontinent of Pangaea in the Late Permian and throughout the Triassic, becoming extinct in the Late Triassic (Parrish et al. 1986). The skull and lower jaws are extremely modified for an herbivorous diet, but this stereotyped dicynodont morphology shows a wide diversity of feeding specializations (Hotton 1986). The facial region of dicynodonts is extremely short, and the temporal region long. The premaxilla and front of the dentary are always toothless. Often an enlarged upper caniniform and a few postcanines are all that remains of the dentition. The pattern of numerous vascular foramina (openings for blood vessels) on the snout, palate, and dentary indicates that in life these animals had a turtlelike horny beak that formed a cutting edge at the front of the mouth. The dicynodont jaw joint is specialized for extensive fore-aft sliding (Crompton and Hotton 1967). In the palate, the premaxilla is expanded greatly backwards and, with the palatine, forms a secondary bony palate, which moves the internal nasal opening toward the rear of the mouth. (The secondary palate separates the nasal cavity from the mouth.)

The postcranial skeleton of dicynodonts is strikingly different from that of primitive anomodonts. The trunk in smaller dicynodonts is elongate and the limbs short—the animal looked rather like a dachshund. Larger dicynodonts have barrel-like trunks and longer, more massive limbs. The tail is always short. The hand and foot are short and broad, the digits subequal in length with broad flat claws. Smaller dicynodonts such as *Diictodon* are sometimes found in corkscrew-shaped burrows (Smith 1987).

The earliest and most primitive dicynodont is *Eodicynodon* (Figure 3F) from the *Eodicynodon* Assemblage Zone of South Africa (Rubidge 1990). It is a typical dicynodont in most features, but it differs from all other dicynodonts in having completely fused premaxillae, separate vomers, and well-developed pterygoid flanges.

In the later Permian, dicynodonts become immensely abundant, both in number of species (Cluver and King 1983) and of individuals. The most primitive of the advanced dicynodonts are the endothiodonts, characterized by a long row of cheek teeth but without a caniniform. Endothiodonts were large animals (skull length more than 50 centimeters), which occur in the *Cistecephalus* Assemblage Zone of South Africa and in beds of equivalent age in East Africa, Brazil, and India. In the remaining dicynodonts, the cheek teeth are greatly reduced in both size and number. Included here are a diverse array of Late Permian forms ranging from the small, tusked *Pristerodon,* which possesses cheek teeth, through the medium-sized, tusked *Dicynodon,* which lacks cheek teeth, to the very large, totally edentulous (toothless) *Rhachiocephalus.*

At the end of the Permian, the great radiation of dicynodonts dwindled nearly to extinction, to be replaced in the Triassic by a new radiation of primarily large-bodied forms. Although rare in the latest Permian, the genus *Lystrosaurus,* characterized by a deep, near-vertical snout, was extraordinarily abundant and widespread in the earliest Triassic. It ranged through the southern supercontinent of Gondwana, as evidenced by fossils found in South Africa, India, Antarctica, and possibly Australia. It also inhabited the northern supercontinent of Laurasia, as shown by fossils recovered from China, Russia, and possibly Laos (Parrish et al. 1986). The later Triassic was dominated by a worldwide radiation of very large dicynodonts, including *Placerias* from North America, one of the last known dicynodonts.

Theriodontia

The remaining therapsids—the Gorgonopsia, Therocephalia, and Cynodontia—are placed in the Theriodontia (Figure 1), a group of primitively carnivorous forms that includes the Mammalia as the most derived subgroup (Hopson and Barghusen 1986). A feature unique to theriodonts is the coronoid process, a protrusion at the upper edge of the dentary bone (Figure 3G). The lower canine is greatly elongated with respect to the lower incisors, unlike the condition in more primitive therapsids. In addition, the quadrate is reduced in height and lies in a depression on the anterior face of the squamosal. The shape of the theriodont skull is also characteristic, having a relatively low, flat dorsal profile and a snout that is wider than high in cross section.

Gorgonopsians. Among the theriodonts, the gorgonopsians retain the greatest number of primitive therapsid features. They show little morphological diversity, with only a single family, the Gorgonopsidae. They are medium to large in size (one to three meters total length) and are carnivores, with relatively long robust limbs and well-clawed feet. The appendicular skeleton shows evidence of a semi-erect posture. The fingers and toes are of nearly equal length, with disclike phalanges in the third and fourth digits.

The gorgonopsian skull is that of a highly specialized predator, with very long, laterally compressed and serrated canines, large, serrated incisors, and a short row of small postcanine teeth (Figure 3G). The skull is specialized to permit a very wide gape, required to allow sufficient clearance of the canines and a powerful bite (Parrington 1955; Kemp 1969). Although the temporal roof is wide, the temporal fenestra is relatively large due to the outward and backward flaring of the squamosal (Figure 4A). This morphology indicates that the jaw-closing muscles were large and pulled strongly backward as well as upward.

Gorgonopsians appear in the *Eodicynodon* Assemblage Zone of South Africa and are known from the later Permian of South and East Africa and Russia. They became extinct at the end of the Permian.

Therocephalia. Currently, therocephalians and cynodonts are recognized as sister groups, united as the Eutheriodontia (Figure 1) by Hopson and Barghusen (1986) on the basis of several shared characters: the reduction in width of the temporal roof so that it overlies only the braincase; a shortened postorbital that does not contact the squamosal on the medial side of the temporal opening; posterior elongation of the parietal behind the parietal foramen to form a prominent sagittal (midline) crest for attachment of jaw-closing muscles (Figures 4B, C); and anteroposterior expansion of

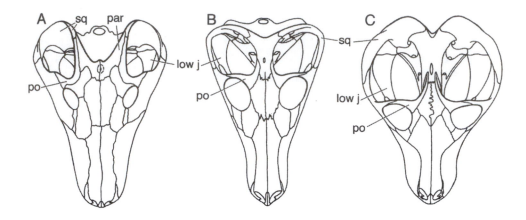

Figure 4. The skulls of theriodont therapsids in dorsal view. *A*, a gorgonopsian showing a broad temporal roof and very short parietal; *B*, a primitive therocephalian, *Ictidosuchoides*, showing the eutheriodont condition of a narrow temporal roof and long sagittal crest on the parietal behind the parietal foramen; *C*, the early cynodont *Procynosuchus*, showing flaring of the zygomatic arches to create a wide gap between the cheekbones and the lower jaw for passage of the incipient masseter muscle to the outer surface of the dentary. Abbreviations: *low j*, lower jaw; *par*, parietal; *po*, postorbital; *sq*, squamosal. Modified from Hopson (1987).

the epipterygoid in the side wall of the braincase. Of the two groups of eutheriodonts, therocephalians are the less modified, but they are characterized uniquely by the presence of suborbital vacuities, openings in the palate bounded by the palatines, pterygoids, and ectopterygoids (Figure 5A).

Early therocephalians superficially resemble gorgonopsians, but later forms show a great diversity in size and skull morphology. The oldest therocephalian is from the *Eodicynodon* Assemblage Zone in South Africa (Rubidge et al. 1983). In the later Permian, advanced therocephalians are known in great variety from South Africa, with some of the same genera known from East Africa and related forms from Russia (Parrish et al. 1986). Therocephalians survived in much lower diversity through the Early Triassic and into the Middle Triassic in southern Africa and China (Sigogneau-Russell and Sun 1981).

The early therocephalians of the Lower Beaufort belong to two families, the Lycosuchidae and Scylacosauridae (van den Heever 1994). Both groups are convergent on gorgonopsians in having large serrated canines, with the lower canine inserting into the internal narial opening, and relatively few, small postcanines. *Lycosuchus* is the most primitive known therocephalian, whereas scylacosaurids appear to be closer to more derived therocephalians (called Eutherocephalia by Hopson and Barghusen 1986), sharing with them specializations of the braincase and a ridge on the maxilla that indicates the beginning of a secondary palate (van den Heever 1994).

The eutherocephalians (families Hofmeyriidae, Whaitsiidae, and Akidnognathidae, and superfamily Baurioidea) are characterized by a posterior expansion of the dentary that broadly overlaps the postdentary bones (convergent on the condition in cynodonts), rounded incisors bearing longitudinal ridges, completely fused vomers, and loss of the postfrontal bone. Of several families,

the most interesting are those in the superfamily Baurioidea. Within this group we see all stages in the development of a complete secondary bony palate formed by plates of maxillae and palatines (Mendrez 1975) (Figure 5A). The baurioids are one of two groups of eutherocephalians that survived into the Triassic. The most derived are the bauriids, notable for developing expanded cheek teeth that meet to form crushing surfaces and a complete secondary palate formed by the maxillary plates contacting on the midline. Bauriids survive into the Middle Triassic of South Africa, Namibia, and China.

Cynodonts. Under current systems of classification, mammals are included within the Cynodontia as the most specialized and only surviving members of the group (Figure 1). First known from rocks of latest Permian age (about 247 million years ago), cynodonts radiated extensively in the Triassic and gave rise to the mammals about 225 million years ago in the Late Triassic. Among the non-mammalian cynodonts, tritylodontids survived into the late Middle or early Late Jurassic. The evolutionary significance of cynodonts lies in the fact that they are ideal structural intermediates between the earliest synapsids, which are at a reptilian level of organization, and modern mammals. The history of cynodonts in the Permian and Triassic demonstrates how many uniquely mammalian features were derived from reptile-like antecedents.

Evolutionary Trends in Cynodonts. Cynodonts are characterized by a very large number of unique features, which are already observed in the Late Permian *Procynosuchus* (Figures 4C, 5B, 6A). Many of these are in the head and relate to the shift from a more reptilian to a more mammalian mode of processing food. The dentary is expanded backwards and the coronoid process bears a lateral depression that presumably served as the attachment site for a new jaw-closing muscle (the homolog of the mammalian masseter) that extended from the main adductor (jaw-closing) muscle mass down

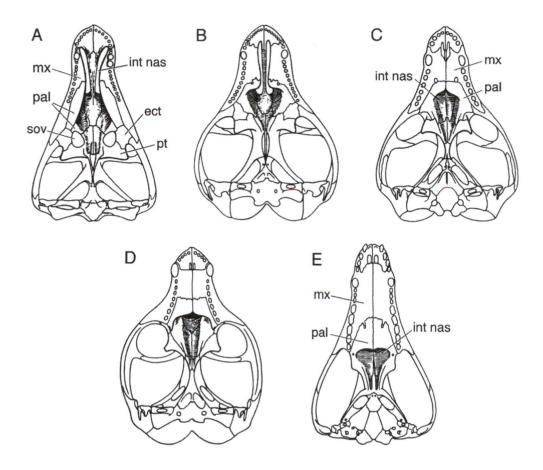

Figure 5. The skulls of therapsids (ventral view), showing the development of the bony secondary palate. *A*, the therocephalian *Icti-dosuchoides*, showing development of medial plates on the maxillary and palatine bones partially closing the internal nasal passage off from the mouth cavity; *B*, the early cynodont *Procynosuchus*, showing further development of the maxillary and palatine plates; *C*, the later cynodont *Thrinaxodon*, in which the plates contact on the midline to form a complete but short bony secondary palate; *D*, the advanced cynodont *Probainognathus*, in which the secondary palate has been elongated posteriorly; *E*, the early mammaliaform *Mor-ganucodon*, with a fully mammalian bony secondary palate. Abbreviations: *ect*, ectopterygoid; *int nas*, internal nasal opening; *mx*, max-illa; *pal*, palatine; *pt*, pterygoid; *sov*, suborbital vacuity. Modified from Hopson (1987).

to the cheek region. To make space for the developing masseter mus-cle to pass between the lower jaw and the zygomatic arch, the latter is bowed strongly outward. The remaining part of the adductor muscle mass forms another new mammalian jaw muscle, the tem-poralis. This muscle attaches to the upper border of the coronoid process and to the high sagittal crest on the skull roof.

The teeth also changed. Unlike earlier therapsids, in which the teeth behind the large canines are simple points adapted only for grasping prey, the cheek teeth of cynodonts are molarlike. There is a small accessory cusp anterior and posterior to the main cusp, suggesting that cynodonts chewed food to some extent rather than swallowing it whole. Food broken into small bits by chewing is digested quickly so that its energy is delivered rapidly to the body. In the palate, plates formed by the maxillae and palatines extend in toward the midline below the air passage to form an incipient secondary bony palate. This arrangement shifted the internal nasal opening further back in the skull, serving to separate inhaled air from the mouth cavity. The mammal-like

ability to breathe without interruption while processing food in the mouth suggests that early cynodonts needed a continuous, uninterrupted supply of oxygen to the body tissues. Changes in the jaws, teeth, and palate all suggest that cynodonts were develop-ing a more mammalian (endothermic, or "warm-blooded") physi-ology than existed in earlier therapsids.

Through the Triassic, the dentary continued to increase in size, especially the areas for muscle attachment on the coronoid process and along its lower border (Figures 6B–H). In the molar-like cheek teeth, shearing contacts developed between upper and lower teeth in order to cut up food more effectively. The second-ary palate became completely closed by meeting of the palatal plates on the midline and the palatal opening of the air passage came to lie behind the tooth row (Figures 5C–E).

As the dentary became progressively larger, the postdentary bones of the lower jaw became progressively reduced in size (Fig-ures 6B–D); this trend included the bones that form the jaw joint: the articular in the lower jaw and the quadrate in the skull. In the

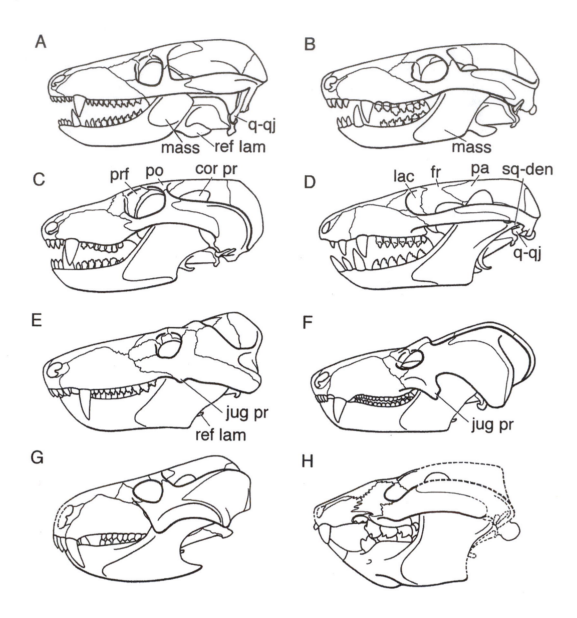

Figure 6. Skulls of cynodont therapsids. *A*, the Late Permian basal cynodont *Procynosuchus. B*, the Early Triassic *Thrinaxodon.* C–D: Probainognathian eucynodonts: *C*, the Middle Triassic *Probainognathus; D*, the Early Jurassic tritheledontid *Pachygenelus.* E–H: Cynognathian eucynodonts: *E*, the Early/Middle Traissic cynognathid *Cynognathus; F*, the early Early/Middle Triassic gomphodont *Diademodon; G*, the Late Triassic gomphodont *Exaeretodon; H*, the Early or Middle Jurassic tritylodontid *Bocatherium.* Abbreviations: *cor pr,* coronoid process of dentary; *fr,* frontal; *j pr,* suborbital process of jugal; *lac,* lacrimal; *mass,* fossa for attachment of masseter muscle; *pa,* parietal; *po,* postorbital; *prf,* prefrontal; *q-qj,* quadrate-quadratojugal complex; *ref lam,* reflected lamina of angular; *sq-den,* squamosal-dentary contact. Modified from Hopson (1994), by permission of the Paleontological Society.

Late Triassic, the rear of the dentary made a new contact with the squamosal bone of the skull, creating a new, uniquely mammalian jaw joint (Figure 6D). In the earliest mammals, the old articular-quadrate joint is retained alongside the new dentary-squamosal joint, but by Mid-Jurassic times the postdentary bones lose their attachment to the dentary and several of them form a series of sound-conducting elements in the mammalian middle ear (Allin and Hopson 1992).

The limbs of cynodonts show progressive changes from a more sprawling to a more upright posture and the backbone shows changes indicating a shift from the side-to-side bending characteristic of reptilian locomotion to the more up-and-down bending of the spine seen in running mammals. The postcranial skeleton of certain late non-mammalian cynodonts, tritheledontids (ictidosaurs) and tritylodontids, is almost indistinguishable from those of early mammals.

Cynodont Diversity. The cat-sized *Procynosuchus* of the very Late Permian appears to be close to the morphological ancestor of all later cynodonts. It ranged widely through Africa and into Europe. In the earliest Triassic, the more progressive cynodonts

Galesaurus and *Thrinaxodon* (Figures 5C, 6B) are common in the *Lystrosaurus* Assemblage Zone of South Africa, and *Thrinaxodon* also occurs in similar rocks in Antarctica. In the later part of the Early Triassic appeared a major group of much more mammal-like cynodonts, the Eucynodontia (Kemp 1982; see Figure 1). In these animals the large dentary nearly reaches the jaw joint, the postdentary bones are reduced to a slender rod, and the reflected lamina of the angular is reduced to a small hooklike process. By the end of the Triassic, eucynodonts achieved a worldwide distribution.

A major subgroup of eucynodonts, the Cynognathia (Hopson and Barghusen 1986), radiated extensively in the Middle and Late Triassic and Jurassic; it included a large carnivore, *Cynognathus* (family Cynognathidae) (Figure 6E), and a diversity of plant-eating forms collectively known as gomphodonts (Figures 6F–H). When viewed from above, the skull of cynognathians is triangular in shape and there is a very deep zygomatic arch typically bearing a process on the jugal, below the eye socket. Gomphodonts are characterized by transversely expanded cheek teeth that meet crown to crown, like the molars of herbivorous mammals.

The oldest gomphodonts were contemporaries of *Cynognathus,* occurring in the late Early Triassic of South African and Argentina. Through the Middle and Late Triassic the gomphodonts were abundant in Africa and South America, and also occurred in Madagascar, India, North America, and Europe. A group of very specialized gomphodonts, the tritylodontids (Figure 6H), appeared in the Early Jurassic (Kühne 1956; Clark and Hopson 1885; Sues 1986) (see Figure 2). Superficially, tritylodontids are rodentlike, with a pair of enlarged upper and lower incisors and complex multicusped cheek teeth. Tritylodontids were the latest surviving cynognathians, becoming extinct in the Middle or Late Jurassic.

The second major subgroup of eucynodonts consisted of persistently small insect- and meat-eaters, the Probainognathia (Hopson 1990), including *Probainognathus* (Figures 5D, 6C) of the Middle Triassic. Probainognathians are characterized by the loss of the parietal (pineal) foramen in the skull roof and a trend toward elongation of the secondary palate behind the level of the tooth row. Tritheledontids (also called ictidosaurs) (Figure 6D) are extremely mammal-like probainognathians of the latest Triassic and Early Jurassic. The members of this group have lost the postorbital bar and have enlarged the dentary to the point that it appears to have contacted the squamosal bone of the skull, although a well-defined dentary-squamosal jaw joint, as seen in mammals, cannot be distinguished (Crompton 1958). The probainognathian lineage gave rise to mammals no later than the early Late Triassic.

JAMES A. HOPSON

See also Mammals, Mesozoic and Non-Therian; Thermoregulation

Works Cited

Allin, E.F., and J.A. Hopson. 1992. Evolution of the auditory system in Synapsida ("mammal-like reptiles" and primitive mammals) as seen in the fossil record. *In* D.B. Webster, R.R. Fay, and A.N. Popper (eds.), *The Evolutionary Biology of Hearing*. New York: Springer-Verlag.

Barghusen, H.R. 1968. The lower jaw of cynodonts (Reptilia, Therapsida) and the evolutionary origin of mammal-like adductor jaw musculature. *Postilla* 116:1–49.

———. 1975. A review of fighting adaptations in dinocephalians (Reptilia, Therapsida). *Paleobiology* 1:295–311.

Boonstra, L.D. 1963. Early dichotomies in the therapsids. *South African Journal of Science* 59:176–95.

Clark, J.M., and J.A. Hopson. 1985. Distinctive mammal-like reptile from Mexico and its bearing on the phylogeny of the Tritylodontidae. *Nature* 315:398–400.

Cluver, M.A., and G.M. King. 1983. A reassessment of the relationships of Permian Dicynodontia (Reptilia, Therapsida) and a new classification of dicynodonts. *Annals of the South African Museum* 91:195–273.

Crompton, A.W. 1958. The cranial morphology of a new genus and species of ictidosaurian. *Proceedings of the Zoological Society of London* 130:183–216.

Crompton, A.W., and N. Hotton III. 1967. Functional morphology of the masticatory apparatus of two dicynodonts (Reptilia, Therapsida). *Postilla* 109:1–51.

Grine, F.E. 1997. Dinocephalians are not anomodonts. *Journal of Vertebrate Paleontology* 17:177–83.

Hopson, J.A. 1987. Synapsid phylogeny and the origin of mammalian endothermy. *Journal of Vertebrate Paleontology* 7 (3 supplement):18A.

———. 1990. Cladistic analysis of therapsid relationships. *Journal of Vertebrate Paleontology* 10 (3 supplement):28A.

———. 1991. Systematics of the nonmammalian Synapsida and implications for patterns of evolution in synapsids. *In* H.-P. Schultze and L. Trueb (eds.), *Origins of the Higher Groups of Tetrapods: Controversy and Consensus*. Ithaca, New York: Comstock.

———. 1994. Synapsid evolution and the radiation of non-therian mammals. *In* D.R. Prothero and R.M. Schoch (eds.), *Major Features of Vertebrate Evolution*. Short Courses in Paleontology, No. 7. Knoxville, Tennessee: University of Tennessee Paleontological Society.

Hopson, J.A., and H.R. Barghusen. 1986. An analysis of therapsid relationships. *In* N. Hotton III, P.D. MacLean, J.J. Roth, and E.C. Roth (eds.), *The Ecology and Biology of Mammal-Like Reptiles*. Washington, D.C.: Smithsonian Institution Press; London: Smithsonian Institution Press, 1987.

Hotton III, N. 1986. Dicynodonts and their role as primary consumers. *In* N. Hotton III, P.D. MacLean, J.J. Roth, and E.C. Roth (eds.), *The Ecology and Biology of Mammal-Like Reptiles*. Washington, D.C.: Smithsonian Institution Press; London: Smithsonian Institution Press, 1987.

Ivakhnenko, M.F. 1996. Primitive anomodonts, venyukoviids, from the Late Permian of Eastern Europe. *Paleontological Journal* 30:575–82.

Kemp, T.S. 1969. On the functional morphology of the gorgonopsid skull. *Philosophical Transactions of the Royal Society of London*, ser. B, 256:1–83.

———. 1982. *Mammal-Like Reptiles and the Origin of Mammals*. London and New York: Academic Press.

King, G.M. 1988. Anomodontia. *In* P. Wellnhofer (ed.), *Encyclopedia of Paleoherpetology*, part 17C. Stuttgart and New York: Fischer-Verlag.

Kühne, W.G. 1956. *The Liassic Therapsid Oligokyphus*. London: Trustees of the British Museum.

Laurin, M., and R.R. Reisz. 1990. *Tetraceratops* is the oldest known therapsid. *Nature* 345:249–50.

———. 1996. The osteology and relationships of *Tetraceratops insignis*, the oldest known therapsid. *Journal of Vertebrate Paleontology* 16:95–102.

Li, J., B.S. Rubidge, and Z. Cheng. 1996. A primitive anteosaurid dinocephalian from China: Implications for the distribution of earliest therapsid faunas. *South African Journal of Science* 92:252–53.

Lucas, S.G., and Z. Luo. 1993. *Adelobasileus* from the Upper Triassic of West Texas: The oldest mammal. *Journal of Vertebrate Paleontology* 13:309–34.

Mendrez, C.H. 1975. Principales variations du palais chez les thérocéphales sud-africains (Pristerosauria et Scaloposauria) au cours du Permien Supérieur et du Trias Inférieur [Principal variations in the palates of the South African Therapsida (Pristerosauria and Scaloposauria) during the Upper Permian and Lower Triassic]. *Colloque International du Centre National de la Recherche Scientifique* 218:379–408.

Olson, E.C. 1962. Late Permian terrestrial vertebrates, U.S.A. and U.S.S.R. *Transactions of the American Philosophical Society* 52:3–224.

———. 1974. On the source of the therapsids. *Annals of the South African Museum* 64:27–46.

Orlov, J.A. 1958. The carnivorous dinocephalians of the Isheevo fauna (titanosuchians). *Transactions of the Academy of Sciences U.S.S.R.* 72:3–113. [In Russian]

Parrington, F.R. 1955. On the cranial anatomy of some gorgonopsids and the synapsid middle ear. *Proceedings of the Zoological Society of London* 125:1–40.

Parrish, J.M, J.T. Parrish, and A.M. Ziegler. 1986. Permian-Triassic paleogeography and paleoclimatology and implications for therapsid distribution. *In* N. Hotton III, P.D. MacLean, J.J. Roth, and E.C. Roth (eds.), *The Ecology and Biology of Mammal-Like Reptiles*. Washington, D.C.: Smithsonian Institution Press; London: Smithsonian Institution Press, 1987.

Romer, A.S. 1961. Synapsid evolution and dentition. *In* G. Vandebroek (ed.), *Koninklijke Vlaamse Academie voor Wetenschappen, Letteren en Schone Kunsten van Belgie, Klasse der Wetenschappen: International Colloquium on the Evolution of Lower and Non-Specialized Mammals*. Brussels: Paleis der Academien.

———. 1966. *Vertebrate Paleontology*. 3rd ed. Chicago: University of Chicago Press.

Rowe, T. 1988. Definition, diagnosis, and origin of Mammalia. *Journal of Vertebrate Paleontology* 8:241–64.

Rubidge, B.S. 1990. Redescription of the cranial anatomy of *Eodicynodon oosthuiseni* (Therapsida: Dicynodontia). *Navorsinge van die Nasionale Museum Bloemfontein* 7:1–25.

———. 1994. *Australosyodon*, the first primitive anteosaurid dinocephalian from the Upper Permian of Gondwana. *Palaeontology* 37:579–94

Rubidge, B.S., and J.A. Hopson. 1990. A new anomodont therapsid from South Africa and its bearing on the ancestry of Dicynodontia. *South African Journal of Science* 86:43–45.

———. 1996. A primitive anomodont therapsid from the base of the Beaufort Group (Upper Permian) of South Africa. *Zoological Journal of the Linnean Society* 117:115–39.

Rubidge, B.S., J.W. Kitching, and J.A. van den Heever. 1983. First record of a therocephalian (Therapsida: Pristerognathidae) from the Ecca of South Africa. *Navorsinge van die Nasionale Museum Bloemfontein* 4:229–35.

Sidor, C.A., and J.A. Hopson. 1995. The taxonomic status of the Upper Permian eotheriodont therapsids of the San Angelo Formation (Guadalupian), Texas. *Journal of Vertebrate Paleontology* 15 (3 supplement):53A.

Sigogneau, D., and P.K. Tchudinov. 1972. Reflections on some Russian eotheriodonts. *Palaeovertebrata* 5:79–109.

Sigogneau-Russel, D. 1989. Theriodontia I. *In* P. Wellnhofer (ed.), *Encyclopedia of Paleoherpetology*, part 17B/I. Stuttgart and New York: Fischer-Verlag.

Sigogneau-Russel, D., and A.-L. Sun. 1981. A brief review of Chinese synapsids. *Geobios* 14:275–79.

Smith, R.M.H. 1987. Helical burrow casts of therapsid origin from the Beaufort Group (Permian) of South Africa. *Palaeogeography, Palaeoclimatology, Palaeoecology* 60:155–70.

Sues, H.-D. 1986. The skull and dentition of two tritylodontid synapsids from the Lower Jurassic of western North America. *Bulletin of the Museum of Comparative Zoology* 151:217–68.

Tatarinov, L.P. 1974. Teriodonty SSSR [Theriodonts of U.S.S.R.]. *Transactions of the Academy of Sciences U.S.S.R.* 143:5–250.

Van den Heever, J.A. 1994. The cranial anatomy of the early Therocephalia (Amniota: Therapsida). *Universiteit van Stellenbosch Annale* 1994 (1):1–59.

Watson, D.M.S., and A.S. Romer. 1956. A classification of therapsid reptiles. *Bulletin of the Museum of Comparative Zoology* 114:37–89.

Further Reading

Benton, M.J. 1990. *Vertebrate Paleontology*. London and Boston: Unwin Hyman; 2nd ed., London and New York: Chapman and Hall, 1997.

Cluver, M.A. 1978. *Fossil Reptiles of the South African Karoo*. Cape Town: South African Museum; 2nd ed., 1991.

Hopson, J.A. 1987. The mammal-like reptiles: A study of transitional fossils. *American Biology Teacher* 49:16–26.

Hotton III, N., P.D. MacLean, J.J. Roth, and E.C. Roth (eds.). 1986. *The Ecology and Biology of Mammal-Like Reptiles*. Washington, D.C.: Smithsonian Institution Press; London: Smithsonian Institution Press, 1987.

Kitching, J.W. 1977. The distribution of the Karroo vertebrate fauna. *Bernard Price Institute for Palaeontological Research Memoir* 1:1–31

THERMOREGULATION

Modern Animals

Animals often expend considerable effort and energy to regulate their body temperatures (thermoregulation) within a relatively narrow range. This is because most physiological attributes (e.g., muscle contraction, nerve conduction, hormone function) are thermally sensitive—they usually proceed most efficiently within a relatively narrow range of body temperatures.

In most vertebrates, internal heat production (heat produced by the body itself) is insufficient to alter body temperature, so internal heat must be derived primarily from the environment ("ectothermy"). In these forms, body temperature often corresponds to the temperature of the environment ("poikilothermy"). Poikilothermy usually does not disrupt physiological processes in thermally homogenous environments such as many marine and freshwater ecosystems. Genetic adaptation and phenotypic acclimation to typical temperature changes maintain normal physiological function.

Air does not conduct heat well, so many ectothermic terrestrial species are surprisingly adept at regulating their temperatures in daytime through behavior, such as basking (for solar radiation) and microhabitat selection, choosing shady or sunlit spaces as needed. Although they are essentially nocturnal thermoconformers, a number of lizards seasonally maintain relatively constant daytime body temperature, that is often significantly higher than the temperatures around them—in fact, often similar to that of many birds and mammals. Some particularly large tropical lizards (e.g., *Varanus komodoensis,* the Komodo dragon) even achieve near-homeothermy (thermal stability) because the ratio of the skin surface area to the body's volume is relatively small; as a result, there is a correspondingly low rate of nocturnal heat loss (inertial homeothermy). It is quite possible that many of the earliest (Paleozoic) reptiles maintained diurnal (daytime) temperatures similar to those of their living descendants, including birds and mammals.

The ability to maintain continuous, metabolically based, high, and relatively stable body temperatures in the face of greatly fluctuating ambient temperatures (temperature of the surrounding air) is among the most remarkable attributes of mammals and birds. Such "warmbloodedness," or more correctly "endothermic homeothermy," generally results from two characteristics: high, aerobically supported heat production rates when resting (about five- to tenfold greater than that of reptiles) in virtually all soft tissues; and enough insulation (e.g., hair feathers) to retard excessive heat loss. As a consequence, in birds and mammals many temperature-sensitive physiological processes proceed at relatively stable rates over a wide range of ambient temperatures.

Birds and mammals maintain constant deep body temperatures largely by (1) minimizing heat loss with fur or feathers and, in some cases, by storing significant amounts of fat just below the skin surface (reptiles maintain most fat stores internally) and (2) sustaining metabolic heat production at a rate that equals the rate at which body heat is lost to the environment. To compensate for particularly high rates of heat loss, oxygen consumption increases at cold ambient temperatures; this supports increased metabolic activity and, therefore, heat production. There is also a range of ambient temperatures over which heat production rates are minimal (BMR, or basal metabolic rate) and constant (Ruben 1995).

Avian and mammalian endothermy is tightly linked to greatly expanded aerobic (oxygen-consuming) capacities during activity. Consequently, most birds and mammals can carry on much higher levels of sustained activity than ectotherms. With some noteworthy exceptions, ectotherms such as reptiles typically rely on non-sustainable, anaerobic metabolism (metabolism that does not rely on oxygen) for all activities beyond relatively slow movements. Although capable of often spectacular bursts of intense exercise, ectotherms generally fatigue rapidly because anaerobic metabolism produces an accumulation of lactic acid. Aerobic exercise does not produce this by-product. As a result, endotherms are able to sustain even relatively high levels of activity for extended periods of time, enabling these animals to forage widely and to migrate over extensive distances. The capacity of bats and birds to sustain long-distance powered flight is far beyond the capabilities of modern ectotherms (Bennett 1991).

A few snakes (e.g., *Python*) and some large-sized fish (including some billfish, tunas, and lamnid sharks) can maintain somewhat greater than ambient core, or "deep body," temperatures. When brooding their eggs, female pythons enhance heat production via powerful, spasmodic contractions of their body muscles. Fish combine high activity levels with well-developed vascular countercurrent heat exchange ("rete mirabile") systems; some taxa utilize highly specialized "heater" cells that help to elevate central nervous system temperatures (Block 1991).

However, "endothermy" in these unusual taxa is not truly comparable to that of birds and mammals. In the absence of constant heat-generating skeletal muscle contractions, it is unlikely that sufficient heat is generated to maintain elevated whole-body temperatures. In any case, body temperature in these taxa does not exceed ambient temperature by more than about 10 degrees to 25 degrees centigrade. Thus, the source and magnitude of the caloric expenditure, as well as the stability and marked elevation of body temperature associated with avian and mammalian endothermy, is truly unique among animals.

Low resting metabolic rates of extant reptiles are not necessarily associated with minimal body temperature or unsophisticated temperature-sensing mechanisms. As in endotherms, part of the forebrain (the hypothalamus) is the primary thermostatic control center, and many lizards use behavior to thermoregulate during extended periods of diurnal activity at body temperatures that overlap those of endotherms. Accordingly, the evolution of avian or mammalian metabolic status need not have involved a radical modification of ancestral thermostatic sensors or body temperature set-points.

Interpreting Metabolic and Thermoregulatory Physiology in Fossil Vertebrates

Like their modern counterparts, most fossil fish, amphibians, and reptiles were almost certainly ectotherms. Similarly, it is reasonable to expect that most extinct ectotherms were adept behavioral thermoregulators and may well have maintained body temperatures similar to those in many living ectotherms. In this context, it is noteworthy that a variety of large, extinct probable ectotherms (e.g., pelycosaurs, stegosaurs) possessed peculiar anatomical features that might have facilitated behavioral thermoregulation. These were primarily flat, well-vascularized, saillike or platelike structures, ideally suited for absorbing infrared radiation or dissipating heat (Bennett 1996).

Although endothermy is widely agreed to have evolved independently in birds and mammals, the evolutionary history of endothermy has been the subject of considerable speculation and debate. In the past few decades, many paleontologists have flailed away with largely futile efforts to demonstrate the endothermic status of various extinct Mesozoic era reptilian and avian taxa, including especially dinosaurs, and therapsids (the ancestors of mammals). From time to time, other candidates for possible endothermy have included pterosaurs, ichthyosaurs, rhynchosaurs, early crocodilians, and the earliest bird, *Archaeopteryx*.

Deciphering the evolutionary history of tetrapod endothermy has not been straightforward. Potential signals of endothermy—such as elevated blood-oxygen carrying capacity, complex lungs, and a high number of mitochondria in cells—are not preserved in fossils. Consequently, most conjecture that extinct vertebrates may have been endothermic has relied primarily on weakly supported correlations of metabolic rate with a variety of far-flung criteria. They include (but are not limited to) features such as predator-prey ratios, upright posture, trackways (fossilized "footprints" in ancient riverbeds), brain size, and geographic distribution. Close scrutiny has revealed that virtually all of these correlations are, at best, equivocal (Farlow 1990; Farlow et al. 1995). Some scholars have attempted to associate supposedly high overall growth rate in endotherms with hypothesized fast growth and endothermy in some dinosaurs. However, growth rates in a variety of extant endotherms and several dinosaurs overlap broadly with some ectotherms. More recently, the ratio of oxygen isotopes in fossilized bones was purported to demonstrate endothermy in some dinosaurs. However, a variety of geological and physiological evidence is broadly at odds with major assumptions underlying these studies, and fossilized bone oxygen isotope ratios in dinosaurs are likely to reveal little, if anything, about their thermoregulatory or metabolic physiology (Ruben 1995).

Perhaps most importantly, almost all of the arguments were based predominantly on similarities to the mammalian or the avian condition. There was no clear functional correlation to endothermic processes themselves. Until recently, no studies described a preservable structure that was functionally related unambiguously and exclusively to endothermy. This situation changed with the discovery that the nasal respiratory turbinate bones (scroll-shaped bones) in mammals, and possibly birds, are tightly and causally linked to high ventilation rates (rates of breathing) and endothermy in these taxa. Evidence of the presence or absence of these structures is often preserved in fossils of long-extinct species, so the discovery of a tie between turbinate bones and endothermy promises exciting new insight into the chronology and selective factors associated with evolution of endothermy.

Respiratory Turbinates: Structure and Function

Turbinate bones, or cartilages, are scroll- or baffle-like elements located in the nasal cavity of virtually all reptiles, birds, and mammals. In most mammals and birds, these usually consist of two distinct sets of mucous membrane-lined structures that protrude directly into either the main nasal airway, or into blind "alley-ways," immediately adjacent to the main respiratory airway. Respiratory turbinates are situated directly within the nasal passage proper. They are thin, complex structures lined with moist respiratory epithelia. Olfactory turbinates (lateral sphenoids, naso- or ethmoturbinates) are located just out of the main path of respired air, usually above and behind the respiratory turbinates. Olfactory turbinates are lined with olfactory (sensory) epithelia and are the primary centers for the sense of smell. They occur in all reptiles, birds, and mammals and have no particular association with the maintenance of endothermy.

Only the respiratory turbinates have a strong functional association with endothermy. In both birds and mammals, endothermy is tightly linked to high levels of oxygen consumption and elevated breathing rates. In the laboratory, breathing rates of birds and mammals exceed those of similar size reptiles by 3.5 to 5 times. In the field, avian and mammalian pulmonary ventilation rates undoubtedly exceed reptilian rates by about 20 times. In mammals and birds, the respiratory turbinates are essential for moderating what would be unacceptably high rates of water and heat loss associated with elevated rates of breathing.

Respiratory turbinates facilitate an exchange of respiratory heat and water between respired air and the moist linings of the turbinates. Briefly, as cool external air is inhaled, it absorbs heat and moisture from the turbinate linings and carries them to the lungs. This process keeps the lungs from drying out, cools the respiratory epithelia, and creates a thermal gradient along the turbinates. During exhalation, the process is reversed: warm air from the lungs, now fully saturated with water vapor, is cooled as it once again passes over the respiratory turbinates. The cooled air becomes supersaturated, and "excess" water vapor condenses on the turbinate surfaces, where it can be reclaimed and recycled. Over time, a substantial amount of water and heat can thus be saved rather than lost to the environment. In the absence of respiratory turbinates, continuously high rates of oxidative metabolism and endothermy might well be unsustainable—respiratory water loss rates would frequently exceed tolerable levels, even in species living in nondesert environments.

Although often similar in overall appearance, the embryological development of mammalian and avian respiratory turbinates indicates that these structures evolved independently in the ancestors of living birds and mammals. This finding emphasizes the independent evolution of avian and mammalian endothermy and underlines the necessity for all endotherms to restrict high rates of respiratory water loss that could result from their high lung ventilation rates. Alternately, the reptilian nasal cavity (or the nasal cavity of any extant ectotherm) has no structures specifically designed to recover respiratory water vapor, nor are they as likely to be needed. Reptilian lung ventilation rates are sufficiently low that water loss rates seldom create significant problems, even for desert species.

To summarize, physiological data imply that independent selection for endothermy in birds, mammals, and their ancestors was tightly associated with the convergent (independent) evolution of respiratory turbinates. In the absence of these structures, unacceptably high rates of pulmonary water loss would probably always have posed a chronic obstacle to maintaining bulk lung ventilation consistent with endothermy, or with metabolic rates approaching endothermy. Consequently, the confirmed presence or absence of respiratory turbinates are likely bellwether indicators of lung ventilation and metabolic rates in virtually all terrestrial taxa, living or extinct (Hillenius 1992; Ruben 1996).

The Evolution of Endothermy in Mammals, Birds, and Their Ancestors

Mammalia evolved from cynodont therapsids, or "mammal-like" reptiles, by sometime late in the Triassic Period (approximately 200 million years ago) and based on the presence of a secondary palate and upright posture in Triassic era cynodonts, it long has been suggested that late therapsids had achieved at least near-endothermy. However, rudimentary ridges for support of respiratory turbinate (specifically, maxillo-turbinate) bones first appeared in some late Paleozoic era theriodont therapsids, for example *Glanosuchus,* a wolf-like pristerognathid therocephalian.

Accordingly, initial phases in the evolution of "mammalian" oxygen consumption rates may have begun as early as the Late Permian period (250 million years ago), some 40 to 50 million years prior to the origin of the Mammalia. By the Lower to Middle Triassic, cynodonts such as the galesaurid *Thrinaxodon* and the traversodontid *Massetognathus,* as well as the earliest mammals (e.g., the Late Triassic *Morganucodon* and the Early Jurassic *Docodon*), present evidence that their maxillo-turbinates were as well developed as those of extant mammals, presumably with a similar capacity for respiratory water recovery. This finding represents the first compelling evidence that ventilation rates, and by extension, metabolic rates of the earliest mammals and at least some late mammal-like reptiles, may have been near or equal to those of extant mammals (Hillenius 1994).

In the dinosaur-bird assemblage, several problems complicate the study of the evolutionary history of turbinates. Most notably, although respiratory turbinates ossify or calcify in many mammals, these structures often remain cartilaginous in birds, which significantly decreases their chances for fossil preservation. Fortunately, the presence of respiratory turbinates in extant endotherms is associated with marked expansion of the size of the cross-sectional area of the nasal cavity proper. Such an increase in endotherms probably accommodates both elevated lung ventilation rates and provides increased nasal volume to house the respiratory turbinates. Significantly, the nasal passage diameter in a sequence of successively more recent, increasingly mammal-like therapsids, approaches and (in the very mammal-like *Thrinaxodon*), even attains the proportions of the mammalian/avian nasal passage.

Recently, computed axial tomography, or CT scans, have been used to study paleontological specimens. The process has greatly facilitated studying the fine details of the nasal region in fossilized specimens, especially those that have been "incompletely" prepared (i.e., the nasal passage is still filled with rock matrix). Some CT scans of particularly well-preserved specimens have revealed delicate remnants of calcified, cartilaginous, and lightly calcified cartilaginous structures. In the tyrannosaurid *Nanotyrannus,* CT scans clearly demonstrate that in life, this animal probably boasted well-developed olfactory turbinates but probably had no respiratory turbinates. They are absent from the fossil, and, most importantly, nasal passage cross-sectional dimensions are virtually identical to those in extant ectotherms. Additionally, CT scans of the nasal regions of another theropod dinosaur, the ornithomimid *Ornithomimus,* as well as the ornithischian dinosaur *Hypacrosaurus,* also indicate the presence of narrow, ectotherm-like nasal cavities, unlikely to have housed respiratory turbinates. Again, this condition is strikingly similar to the nasal region of many extant reptiles (e.g., *Crocodylus*) and is strong evidence for low lung ventilation rates and ectothermy, or near-ectothermy, in these dinosaurs (Ruben et al. 1996).

Other structural evidence also adds to the debate. The almost varanid lizard-like arrangement of the nostrils and choanae (internal nasal openings) in some dromaeosaurs (e.g., the "raptors" *Deinonychus, Dromaeosaurus*) is also strongly suggestive that respiratory turbinates were unlikely to have been present in these theropod taxa.

The absence of respiratory turbinates in the varied taxa presented here suggests that ectothermic, or near-ectothermic, rates of lung ventilation and metabolism were possibly widespread in dinosaurs during periods of routine activity. Nevertheless, it would be erroneous to then conclude that dinosaurs were necessarily similar in lifestyle to most modern, temperate-latitude reptiles (i.e., sluggish herbivores or "sit-and-wait" predators). The dynamic skeletal structure of many dinosaurs strongly suggests they possessed bird- or mammal-like capacity for at least sharp bursts of activity. Moreover, even if they were fully ectothermic, had dinosaurs possessed aerobic metabolic capacities and predatory habits equivalent to those of some modern varanid lizards of the tropics (such as the Komodo dragon of the South Pacific), they may have maintained large home ranges, actively pursued and killed large prey, and defended themselves fiercely when cornered.

Finally, if the dinosaurian ancestors of birds were not endotherms, it is possible that the earliest Mesozoic era birds (e.g., *Archaeopteryx, Sinornis*) also maintained metabolic rates that were lower than those of modern birds. This scenario for the ectothermic, or near-ectothermic, metabolic status of the earliest birds is also consistent with the presence of reptile-like annular growth rings in the long bones of some Early Cretaceous birds. Consequently, it is reasonable to suggest that not only were the earliest birds ectothermic, or near-ectothermic, but that complete avian endothermy may not have been achieved until mid-late Cretaceous times, perhaps 50 million years after the appearance of *Archaeopteryx* (Ruben 1991, 1996).

JOHN RUBEN

See also Paleoethology; Growth, Development, and Evolution; Growth, Postembryonic; Ornamentation: Vertebrates; Respiration; Sensory Capsules

Works Cited

Bennett, A.F. 1991. The evolution of activity capacity. *Journal of Experimental Biology* 160:1–23.

Bennett, S.C. 1996. Aerodynamic and thermoregulatory function of the dorsal sail of edaphosaurs. *Paleobiology* 22:496–506.

Block, B.A. 1991. Endothermy in fish: Thermogenesis, ecology and evolution. *In* P.W. Hochachka and T. Mommsen (eds.), *Biochemistry and Molecular Biology of Fishes.* Vol. 1, Amsterdam and New York: Elsevier Science.

Farlow, J.O. 1990. Dinosaur energetics and thermal biology. *In* D.B. Weishampel, P. Dodson, and O. Halszka (eds.), *The Dinosauria*. Berkeley: University of California Press.

Farlow, J.O., P. Dodson, and A. Chinsamy. 1995. Dinosaur biology. *Annual Review of Ecology and Systematics* 26:445–71.

Hillenius, W.J. 1992. The evolution of nasal turbinates and mammalian endothermy. *Paleobiology* 18:17–29.

———. 1994. Turbinates in therapsids: Evidence for Late Permian origins of mammalian endothermy. *Evolution* 48:207–29.

Ruben, J.A. 1991. Reptilian physiology and the flight capacity of *Archaeopteryx. Evolution* 45:1–17.

———. 1993. Powered flight in *Archaeopteryx:* Response to Speakman. *Evolution* 47:935–38.

———. 1995. The evolution of endothermy: From physiology to fossils. *Annual Review of Physiology* 57:69–95.

———. 1996. The evolution of endothermy in mammals, birds and their ancestors. *In* I.A. Johnston and A.F. Bennett (eds.), *Animals and Temperature*. Cambridge and New York: Cambridge University Press.

Ruben, J.A., W.J. Hillenius, N.R. Geist, A. Leitch, T.D. Jones, P.J. Currie, J.R. Horner, and G. Espe. 1996. The metabolic status of some Late Cretaceous dinosaurs. *Science* 273:1204–7.

THEROPODS

The name Theropoda ("beast foot") was first coined by O.C. Marsh in 1881 as a general group that encompassed all of the meat-eating dinosaurs known at the time. Today, Theropoda contains a diverse assemblage of dinosaurs, virtually all of which are carnivores, ranging in size from the one-meter long *Eoraptor* to the recently discovered *Giganotosaurus,* an incompletely known 12- to 13-meters long behemoth that might challenge *Tyrannosaurus* for the title of the largest theropod discovered to date. The remains of theropods have been found on every continent, but they are especially abundant in North America and Asia. The time span of the theropods far exceeds that of any other dinosaur group, because the most derived (specialized) members of the clade (related group), Aves (birds), are alive today. Even ignoring birds, theropods have an enormous range through time, with the first members of the group, *Herrerasaurus* and *Eoraptor,* appearing in the Late Triassic, approximately 225 million years ago, and the last theropods, such as *Tyrannosaurus* and *Albertosaurus,* perishing during the final extinction of the dinosaurs at the end of the Cretaceous, 65 million years ago.

Theropoda and its sister group Sauropodomorpha comprise Saurischia, which is one of the two great clades of dinosaurs. Members of the Theropoda are partitioned into a variety of hierarchical groupings such as Ceratosauria, Tetanurae, Coelurosauria, and Maniraptora, but all possess a number of specialized skeletal characters unique to the group. These include exposure of the lacrimal (the bone that forms the front of the eye socket) on the skull roof (Figure 1); development of a joint in the middle of the lower jaw; unique modifications of neck and tail vertebrae; long, narrow scapulae (shoulder blade) (Figure 2); shortened upper arms with the humerus less than half the length of the femur (thigh bone); elongation of the hand with reduction or loss of the outer two fingers (Figure 3); enlargement of part of the pubis bone (the "boot") in the pelvis; development of a crest of bone near the head of the femur for muscle attachment; and a thin, narrow fibula, attached to a crest on the side of the tibia (one of the two bones in the lower leg) (Figure 4). The Theropoda is composed of the common ancestor of all of the members of these hierarchical groupings and all of that ancestor's descendants, including Aves.

All theropods were bipedal, walking and running on strong hind limbs. They share a number of other defining characteristics, although the following are not unique to Theropoda. The limb bones are hollow, and many bones of the skull and skeleton are pneumatic (possess air spaces). "Pneumaticity" is evident in the bones in front of and around the eye socket in most theropods, while more advanced genera (groupings; singular, genus), including birds, exhibit pneumaticity in the bones of the braincase. Pneumaticity of the skeleton usually is confined to the cervical vertebrae and their ribs, but in some genera it can extend as far back as the tail. The center of gravity was located over the hips, and a long tail acted as a counterweight to the head and body. Many theropods show another modification to the pelvis, in addition to the presence of a boot on the pubis: The ischium bone (the rear-most pelvic bone) has been modified so that the obturator foramen (a hole that allowed passage of nerves and blood vessels) is open, forming an obturator notch above an obturator process (Figure 5).

The hind limbs were long and slender in smaller forms but often very powerfully built in the larger species. Later theropods possessed relatively longer hind limbs because of elongation of the lower leg. In many later genera, the elongation of the tibia (shin) and fibula was accompanied by elongation of the metatarsus (the bones between the ankle and the toes). This elongation of the lower leg, relative to the femur (upper leg bone), increased the length and efficiency of the animal's stride, facilitating faster running. Higher speeds would generate instability, so a portion of the astragalus (one of the ankle bones) ascends along the tibia to brace the lower leg during movement at elevated speeds (Figure 4). The forelimbs of theropods run the gamut in terms of size and functionality. Members of the clade Maniraptora had long, agile hands with mobile wrists, such as those seen in *Deinonychus;* some of the larger theropods, such as *Carnotaurus,* had short, relatively immobile, and seemingly useless arms. Most theropods had large hands, with elongate fingers and recurved (curved back), pointed claws (Figure 3). The elongate, clawed hands probably were used during predation in many theropod species. Virtually all theropods were carnivores, with pointed and often laterally compressed (narrow), bladelike teeth. In most genera the teeth bear a series of serrations on the front and back edge, allowing them to act like small steak knives slicing through flesh.

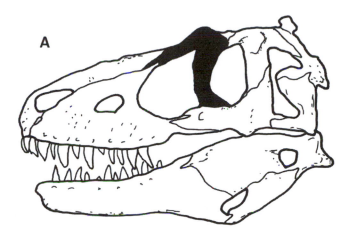

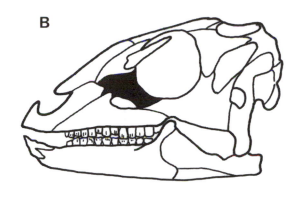

Figure 1. Position of the lacrimal bone (shaded area). *A*, the tyrannosaurid theropod *Daspletosaurus*; *B*, the ornithopod *Dryosaurus*.

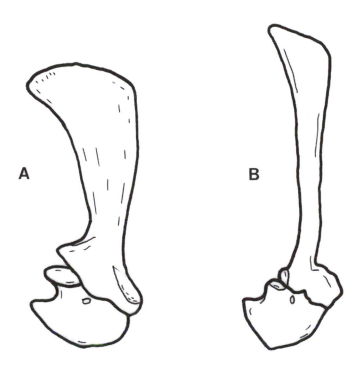

Figure 2. The scapulocoracoid. *A*, the ornithopod *Hypsilophodon*; *B*, the theropod *Albertosaurus*. Note the much more slender scapular blade in *B*.

Discoveries

The first theropod and the first dinosaur to be described was *Megalosaurus*. It was recovered from Middle Jurassic rocks in Oxfordshire, England, by the Rev. William Buckland in 1818 and described by him six years later. Little material referable to *Megalosaurus* has been uncovered since Buckland's initial discovery, but *Megalosaurus* will always be notable because it is one of the three dinosaurs used by Richard Owen to establish the Dinosauria in 1841.

Another early and highly notable European discovery, made in Bavaria in the 1850s, consisted of a near-complete specimen of *Compsognathus* in a lithographic (very fine-grained) limestone very similar to the deposit that yielded remains of the protobird *Archaeopteryx*. But most of the early discoveries of theropod dinosaurs were made in North America. The earliest included *Allosaurus* and *Dryptosaurus* (originally named *Laelaps* by E.D. Cope in 1866, but renamed by O.C. Marsh in 1877 because the name Laelaps had already been assigned to an insect). The end of the 1800s were marked by the discovery of *Ceratosaurus, Coelophysis,* and *Ornithomimus*. Of these early discoveries, *Allosaurus* and *Coelophysis* have since become two of the best-known of all theropods.

The theropod discoveries of the twentieth century were much more numerous and distinctly more cosmopolitan (widespread), with specimens recovered from all over the world. The majority of finds were made in North America (for example, *Albertosaurus, Deinonychus, Dilophosaurus, Struthiomimus, Tyrannosaurus*) and Asia (*Deinocheirus, Oviraptor, Sinraptor, Tarbosaurus, Velociraptor*), but important specimens were recovered from Antarctica (*Cryolophosaurus*), Argentina (*Abelisaurus, Carnotaurus, Eoraptor, Herrerasaurus*), Egypt (*Carcharodontosaurus, Spinosaurus*), England (*Baryonx*), Niger (*Afrovenator*), and Zimbabwe (*Syntarsus*). Only recently, in the latter half of this decade, a number of interesting and potentially very significant discoveries have been made. A few examples include an embryo of *Oviraptor* and two embryo-sized skulls of a theropod similar to *Velociraptor* (Norell et al. 1994), a 140 million-year-old theropod embryo in an egg from France, a complete skull of an abelisaurid theropod from Madagascar, and fragmentary remains of a huge maniraptoran from Argentina. Most spectacular and interesting are specimens of *Sinosauropteryx* from China, a "feathered" theropod, and *Unenlagia* from the Late Cretaceous of Patagonia. *Unenlagia* possesses a mixture of theropod and avian features that may provide further support for the ancestor-descendant link between theropods and birds (Novas and Puerta 1997).

Theropods are the most compelling of all dinosaurs, capturing the imagination of the public more than any other group. The widespread fascination for theropods has been shared by many

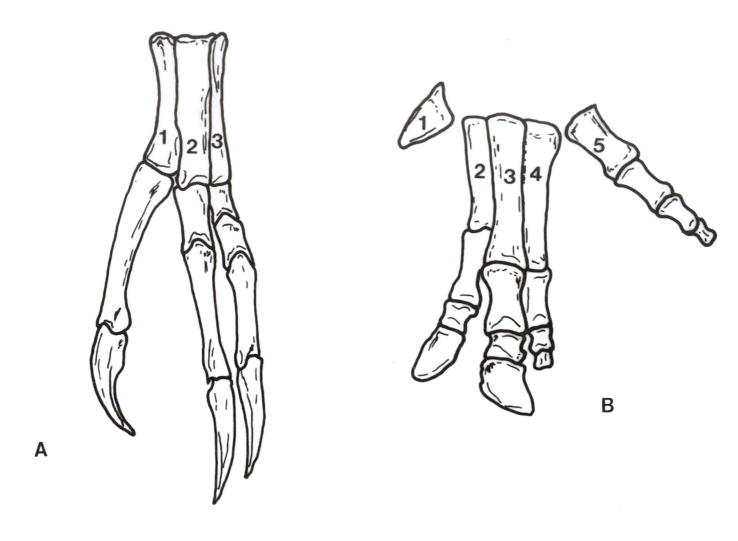

Figure 3. Left manus (hand) of two dinosaurs to illustrate the reduction/loss of digits 4 and 5. *A*, the theropod *Struthiomimus; B*, the ornithopod *Iguanodon*.

noted paleontologists over the years, beginning with Owen, Marsh, and Cope in the 1800s, then H.F. Osborn, L.M. Lambe, and W.A. Parks in the early 1900s. More recently, theropods have been collected and described by J.H. Ostrom, Z.-M. Dong, J.H. Madsen, D.A. Russell, P.C. Sereno, and P.J. Currie, among many others.

Systematics

The classification of theropods is in a state of constant change, reflecting the continual addition of new information as new specimens are discovered, analyzed, then reanalyzed in the light of new knowledge. J. Gauthier provided the basic structure of theropod classification in 1986 with a comprehensive, ground-breaking analysis of saurischian dinosaurs and the origin of birds. Modifications of Gauthier's work followed (e.g., Holtz 1994, 1996; Russell and Dong 1993; Sereno 1997; Sereno et al. 1994, 1996), and while the general organization of the clade remains reasonably constant throughout the various analyses (Figure 6), scholars still do not agree on the details.

Early Theropods

The first theropods are, by coincidence, the oldest dinosaurs known from complete skeletons. *Eoraptor* and *Herrerasaurus* (Figure 7), both from the Late Triassic Ischigualasto Formation of Argentina, are regarded as basal (archaic) theropods (Sereno 1997). *Herrerasaurus* is more advanced than the smaller form, *Eoraptor*. Particularly important in *Herrerasaurus* is the presence of the intramandibular joint in the middle of the lower jaw and an expanded pubis, a character seen in almost all other nonavian theropods and primitive birds. (*Eoraptor* does not possess the intramandibular joint seen in *Herrerasaurus* and all other theropods—except for a few genera in which the joint has been fused secondarily—and this is one of the reasons why some scholars, such as Holtz, in 1995, do not include *Eoraptor* in the Theropoda.) *Herrerasaurus* is closely related to Late Triassic genera *Staurikosaurus* (Brazil) and *Chindesaurus* (North America) and probably is related to *Agrosaurus* (Australia), suggesting a global distribution of the first theropods (Sereno 1997). Above these basal theropods, there are two major divisions of theropods, the Ceratosauria and the Tetanurae (Figure 6).

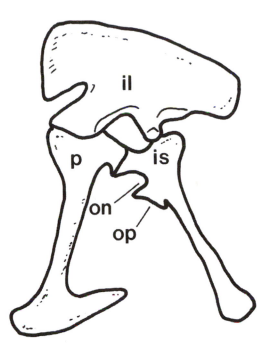

Figure 4. Tibia, fibula, and astragalus of the oviraptor *Ingenia*. Key: *a*, astragalus; *f*, fibula; *t*, tibia. Redrawn from Barsbold et al. (1990).

Figure 5. Pelvis of *Allosaurus* in left lateral view. Key: *il*, ilium; *is*, ischium; *on*, obturator notch; *op*, obturator process; *p*, pubis.

Ceratosauria

Members of the Ceratosauria, named for *Ceratosaurus* (Late Jurassic, United States), are characterized by specializations of a few of the cervical (neck) vertebrae, fusion between sacral (pelvic) vertebrae and their ribs, and fusion of ankle bones. Ceratosaurids were distributed all over the globe and ranged in time from the Late Triassic to the Late Cretaceous. Relationships within Ceratosauria are not understood well because only limited information is available from key specimens, but there are sufficient defining characteristics to allow the Ceratosaurids to be split into two groups: Coelophysoidea and Ceratosauroids (Figure 6).

Coelophysoidea. The group Coelophysoidea (Holtz 1994) is named for *Coelophysis,* the small theropod from the Late Triassic Chinle Formation of Arizona, and subsumes other small theropods such as *Syntarsus* (Early Jurassic, Zimbabwe) and *Procompsognathus* (Early Jurassic, Germany), in addition to two medium-sized animals, *Dilophosaurus* (Early Jurassic, Arizona) and *Liliensternus* (Late Triassic, Germany). Coelophysoidea are united by modifications of the vertebrae, a loose contact between the premaxilla (at the tip of snout) and the maxilla (the tooth-bearing bones that form most of the upper jaw), and premaxillary teeth that are subcircular in cross section and unserrated. Typically, coelophysoids have long, delicate skulls on long necks, and they bear large claws on three fingers of each hand. *Dilophosaurus* and *Syntarsus* each possess paired thin crests on their skulls, which were used most likely for sexual display.

Ceratosauroids. The Ceratosauroids are thought to consist of *Ceratosaurus* (Late Jurassic, North America), *Elaphrosaurus* (Late Jurassic, Tanzania), and all members of the Abelisauridae, a family of unusual theropods confined to the Late Cretaceous. The Abelisauridae includes *Carnotaurus* and *Abelisaurus* (Argentina), *Indosuchus* (India), and a genus found only on the island of Madagascar. *Carnotaurus* is a bizarre animal by any standard. Its skull is very high and short, unlike that of any other large theropod, and it bears two large frontal horns (Figure 8). The frontal horns are particularly notable because they project laterally (to the sides) over the eyes and beyond the margins (edges) of the skull. Another striking feature in *Carnotaurus* is the extreme reduction of the forelimb, in which the radius and ulna (the bones of the forearm) are short and squat, almost like two fat finger bones. Such a diminished forearm probably resulted in a practically useless pair of limbs.

Tetanurae

All remaining theropods are designated as members of the Tetanurae (Figure 6). The term tetanurae means "stiff tails"; the back half of the tail of all members of the group is stiffened by the interlocking of bony projections that extend from each caudal (tail) vertebra. Tetanurae consists of birds and all theropods closer to birds than Ceratosauria. The members are linked by increased pneumaticity of the skull, shortening of the maxillary tooth row, three-fingered hands, and further modifications of the pelvis and lower

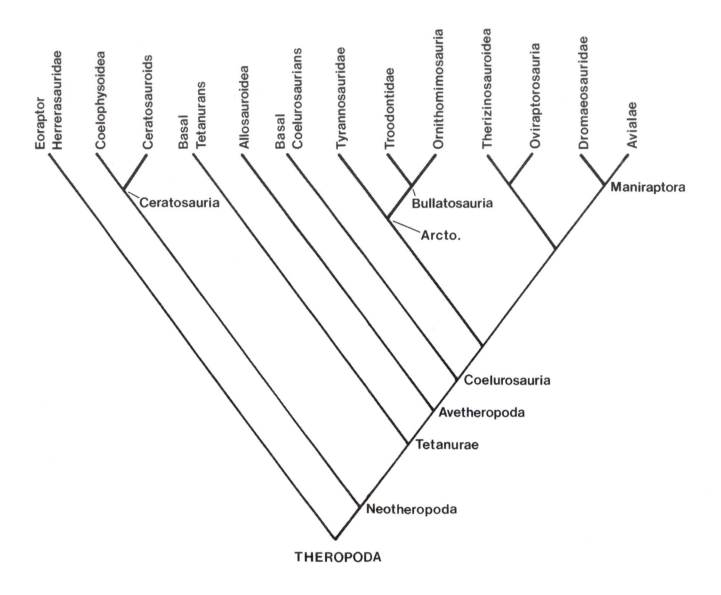

Figure 6. Generalized cladogram of Theropoda. Key: *Arcto,* Arctometatarsalia.

leg. A group of basal tetanurans—which might include *Compsognathus* (Late Jurassic, Germany); torvosaurids, named for the genus *Torvosaurus* (Late Jurassic, United States); and possibly the spinosaurids—are excluded from the next hierarchical grouping, the Avetheropoda (Holtz 1994). The spinosaurids, named for *Spinosaurus* (Late Cretaceous, Egypt), are unusual theropods because they are envisaged as fish-eaters, based upon specializations of the skull and teeth. The most notorious spinosaurid is the English form *Baryonyx* (Early Cretaceous), with a vicious 30-centimeters long claw on each hand, thought to be used for skewering fish. Other genera that also show what probably are adaptations for a piscivorous diet are being recovered from Morocco and Brazil (Kellner and Campos 1996; Milner 1996).

Above these basal tetanurans, all remaining theropods are referred to as Avetheropoda. The Avetheropoda is split into the Carnosauria and a much larger assemblage, Coelurosauria (Figure 6). Carnosauria and Coelurosauria were named by F. von Huene in the early 1900s to effect a separation between small, slender theropods (coelurosaurs) and large theropods with massive skulls and large teeth (carnosaurs), although most authors today prefer the term "Allosauroidea" instead of Carnosauria.

Allosauroidea. The Allosauroidea encompasses a diverse collection of large theropods, linked by only a few specializations of the skull. Typical allosauroids are *Acrocanthosaurus* (Early Cretaceous, United States), *Allosaurus* (Late Jurassic, United States), *Carcharodontosaurus* (Mid-Cretaceous, Egypt), *Giganotosaurus* (Late Cretaceous, Argentina), and *Sinraptor* (Late Jurassic, China) (Figure 9a). The group also includes the Antarctica theropod *Cryolophosaurus* (Early Jurassic) and a crested form from the mid-Jurassic of China, *Monolophosaurus* (Figure 9b). *Allosaurus* is particularly well known because it has been found in a mass accumulation at the Cleveland-Lloyd Quarry in Utah and because virtually every bone of the skull and post-cranial skeleton is known in great detail (Madsen 1976). Allosauroids include some of the largest of all theropods. Partial remains of *Saurophaganax* (Late Jurassic, United States), *Acrocanthosaurus*, and isolated large bones of *Allosaurus* indicate that some adults of these species were approximately 12 meters in length, rivaling *Tyrannosaurus*. R.A. Coria and L. Salgado (1995) have reconstructed a partial skeleton of another allosauroid, *Giganotosaurus,* to a length of 12.5 meters, making it one of the largest predatory dinosaur ever discovered. A few genera within Allosauroidea have unusual skull features. *Monolophosaurus* has a large, centrally positioned crest that runs the length of the skull (Figure 9b), while *Cryolophosaurus* bears a unique transverse (crosswise) crest of bone, situated on the skull roof just in front of the eyes, a crest that projects vertically and slightly forwards.

Coelurosauria. Coelurosauria consists of a number of basal genera that are excluded from several higher subdivisions of the group. The basal members may include *Coelurus* and *Ornitholestes* (Late Jurassic, United States), *Deltadromeus* (Late Cretaceous, Morocco), and *Dryptosaurus* (Late Cretaceous, United States). However, fossils are made up of such fragmentary material, yielding such limited information, that definite resolution of the relationships is not yet possible. All coelurosaurs are linked by several refinements of the skull and skeleton, including a larger circular eye socket, modifications of neck and tail vertebrae, and many alterations in the bones of the pelvis. Above the basal genera, the partitioning of remaining coelurosaurs into successively more specialized groups is an area of theropod systematics that is especially unstable and open to different interpretations.

Major Groups within Coelurosauria

Coelurosaurs above the basal genera include therizinosauroids, ornithomimosaurs, tyrannosaurids, oviraptorosaurs, troodontids, dromaeosaurids, and birds (Figure 6). Various combinations of these groups have been established by different authors, using different lines of evidence, and given names such as Arctometatarsalia, Bullatosauria, Deinonychosauria, Maniraptora, Oviraptorosauria, and Paraves. For example, Arctometatarsalia ("compressed metatarsal") was erected to unite all theropods with a pinched third metatarsal (ornithomimosaurs, troodontids, tyrannosaurids, and others) (Figure 10). However, the definition of the group now has been changed to *Ornithomimus* and all theropods closer to *Ornithomimus* than to birds (Holtz 1994, 1996). Another example is Maniraptora ("seizing hand"), introduced by Gauthier (1986) to aggregate those theropods in the possession of a modified forelimb that includes a long, mobile, raptorial hand (Figure 3). Again, there has been some modification of the group (Holtz 1996), but Maniraptora stands today as the group that includes birds and their ancestors.

Therizinosauroidea

The therizinosauroids are some of the most unusual of all theropods. In fact, their status as theropods was in doubt until only recently. The group consists of a primitive form, *Alxasaurus,* and the Therizinosauridae, formerly known as Segnosauridae. Therizinosauroids have small heads on short necks and a shortened tail. They

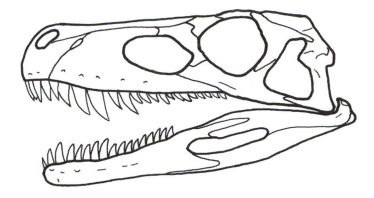

Figure 7. Skull of the basal theropod *Herrerasaurus*.

possess an opisthopubic pelvis (one in which the ischium and pubis parallel each other, projecting down and back) and a foot that is not modified into the typical, three-toed theropod condition. They also have cheeks and a beak, features that are characteristic of ornithischian, rather than saurischian, dinosaurs. The teeth are reduced, and it may be that therizinosauroids were at least partially herbivorous. The body was bulky and bore similarities to that of a prosauropod. This unique and eccentric combination of characters has puzzled paleontologists for almost 30 years, beginning with Perle's description of *Segnosaurus* as a theropod in 1979 and his naming of the family Segnosauridae. Barsbold (1979) also considered the segnosaurs to be theropods, but other paleontologists proposed closer ties to the Sauropodomorpha (e.g., Gauthier 1986). A recent analysis of the first well-preserved skull for the group details the priority of the family name Therizinosauridae over Segnosauridae and details the morphological characters of the skull that justify Perle and Barsbold's designation of therizinosaurs as theropods (Clark et al. 1994).

Ornithomimosauria

The ornithomimosaurs also are an unusual group, consisting of several genera that share several defining characters, such as a relatively small, lightly built skull on a long neck, with a long, low snout, loss of the upper teeth, substantive or complete loss of the lower teeth, and large orbits (eye sockets) (Figure 11). The peculiar skull also bears a relatively large antorbital opening (a large cavity on each side positioned between the eye socket and nostril). Typical, well-known genera include *Ornithomimus, Struthiomimus,* and *Gallimimus* (Late Cretaceous, United States). All possess modifications of the fore- and hind limbs, including elongation of the hand and foot, and bear a resemblance to large extant (present-day) birds. In fact, the name ornithomimosaur translates to "bird mimic reptile," and the same etymology was employed for *Struthiomimus* ("ostrich mimic") and *Dromiceiomimus* ("emu mimic"). Ornithomimosaurs are atypical theropods in a variety of ways but most distinctly so in their greatly reduced, or absent, dentition. It

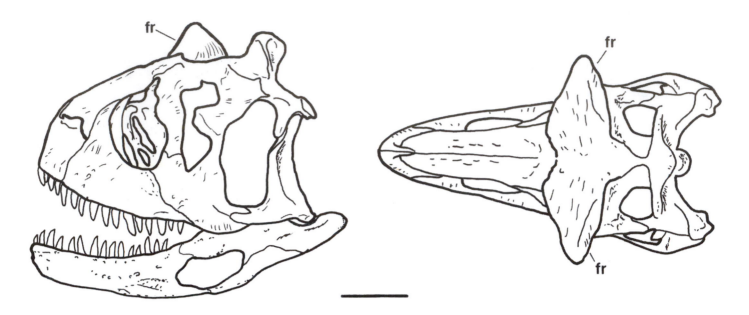

Figure 8. Skull of the abelisaurid *Carnotaurus*. Scale bar, 10 centimeters. Key: *fr,* frontal. Redrawn from Bonaparte et al. (1990).

has been proposed that ornithomimosaurs had an omnivorous diet, possibly consisting of insects, larvae, eggs, and small vertebrates (Barsbold and Osmolska 1990).

Tyrannosauridae

Tyrannosaurids are large theropods characterized by characters such as premaxillary teeth that are D-shaped in cross section, greatly reduced forelimbs, and loss of the third finger. All tyrannosaurids lived during the Late Cretaceous. The defining member of the group—and for many the defining member of Dinosauria—is *Tyrannosaurus rex* (North America), one of the most widely recognized of all biological organisms. Other well-known examples of tyrannosaurids include the North American forms *Albertosaurus* (Figure 12a) and *Daspletosaurus* and the Asian tyrannosaurid *Tarbosaurus.* Tyrannosaurids are known for their massively constructed skulls and large, daggerlike teeth. This morphological development is most evident in *Tyrannosaurus* (Figure 12b). Its skull is over 1.5 meters long and contains more than 50 serrated teeth, some of which measure up to 15 centimeters in length. When combined with heavily muscled jaws, the teeth comprised a formidable weaponry for taking down prey animals. Tyrannosaurids possessed large eyes and stereoscopic vision, a relatively large brain, and the ratio of the length of upper to lower leg bones indicates that it could obtain speeds of up to 20 or 30 miles per hour (Farlow et al. 1995). Accordingly, *Tyrannosaurus* has always been pictured as an immensely powerful, intimidating, fearless killer, a depiction unaltered by recent unconvincing speculations that it might have been better suited for scavenging.

Oviraptorosauria

Oviraptorosaurs are yet another group of unusual theropods, known mostly from the Upper Cretaceous of Asia but also from North America. The group consists of the poorly known North American group, the caenagnathids, and the Mongolian oviraptorids. The oviraptorids are extraordinary animals. Their edentulous (toothless) skulls are extremely distinctive because of the high position of the external nares (nostrils) and a large, very prominent premaxillary and nasal crest in front of and above the nares (Figure 13). Oviraptorids also possess a ventrally positioned palate, and a lower jaw in which the substantial mandibles are fused where they meet in front. The quadrate (a bone on each side at the back of the skull that acts as a hinge for the lower jaw) is also distinctive because in addition to its articulation (joint) with the squamosal bone at the back of the skull, typical of dinosaurs, it has an additional articulation with the braincase. This double-headed contact is typical of birds, suggesting that oviraptorosaurs might be close to the origin of birds. The typical oviraptorid skull is best characterized as extraordinary, and if it were not for the more characteristic postcranial (body) skeleton, it might be hard to envisage oviraptorids as theropods, or even as dinosaurs.

Troodontidae

Troodontids were named for the North American genus *Troodon* and consists of at least four genera that share highly derived characters of the skull and foot. *Troodon* ("wounding tooth") was first named in 1856, based on an isolated tooth collected the year before in Alberta, but it wasn't until more than 100 years later that the skull and skeleton of *Troodon* could be reconstructed with confidence. The most notable feature of troodontids is their highly modified skull, which includes an enlarged braincase, a well-developed middle ear, pervasive pneumaticity (similar to that seen in modern birds), and an increased tooth count. Also unusual is the greatly reduced fibula that tapers to a terminal point short of the ankle. Troodontids possess a large sickle claw on the second toe, just like

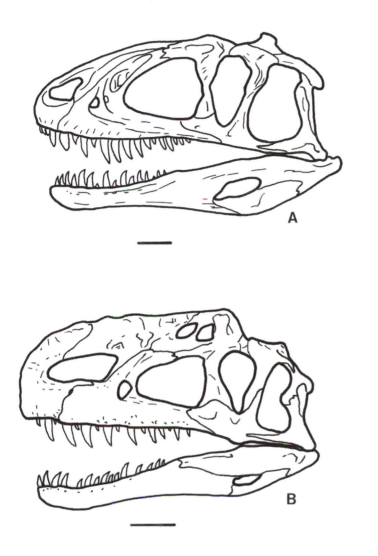

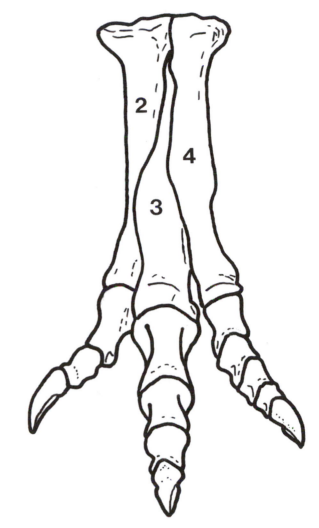

Figure 9. Skull of the allosauroids. *A, Sinraptor; B, Monolophosaurus.* Scale bar, 10 centimeters. Redrawn from: *A,* Currie and Zhao (1993); *B,* Zhao and Currie (1993).

Figure 10. Simplified sketch of the right pes (foot) of a tyrannosaurid to illustrate the pinched third metatarsal.

that seen in dromaeosaurids (Figure 14), and some scholars use this feature, and others, including a tail stiffened by unusual chevrons (bony rods that extend from the underside of vertebrae) and a functionally didactyl (two-toed) foot, to link troodontids and dromaeosaurids in the Deinonychosauria (e.g., Sereno 1997). The consensus view, however, is that troodontids are related more closely to ornithomimids than dromaeosaurids (e.g., Holtz 1994).

The positioning of troodontids is yet another example of the plentiful and contradictory interpretations of the phylogeny (evolutionary history) of the tetanurans and coelurosaurs. Groups and subgroups are placed together under different names, the name usually reflecting the character that individual scholars have chosen to designate defining the group. The subjectivity involved in assigning biological entities to pigeonholes often results in the creation of artificial assemblages that usually are refined or often rendered redundant by new discoveries and reinterpretations. But, in spite of the inevitable changes, the most important aspect of any

classification of theropods is likely to remain that dromaeosaurids enjoy a close relationship with *Archaeopteryx* and all other birds (Figure 6). This has been the case ever since John Ostrom's 1969 description of *Deinonychus* and his illumination of the similarities between *Deinonychus* and *Archaeopteryx* (Ostrom 1975, 1976). It is accepted almost universally that birds are descended from theropod dinosaurs (e.g., Chiappe 1995; Gauthier 1986; Sereno 1997). Analyses that purport to debunk this relationship are not always notable for their scientific rigor, and some scholars seem content to discard an overwhelming body of evidence for the theropod-bird link without explanation, preferring to utilize a limited database and prevaricant reasoning to support their proclivities.

Dromaeosauridae

The theropod group closest to birds, the dromaeosaurids, are named for the Canadian genus *Dromaeosaurus* (Late Cretaceous, Alberta).

The group includes *Deinonychus* (Early Cretaceous, United States), one of the most important dinosaurs ever discovered, and *Velociraptor* (Late Cretaceous, Mongolia), one of the most famous (largely because of recent media exposure). Another well-known member of the group is the giant *Utahraptor* (Early Cretaceous, United States). All dromaeosaurids possessed enlarged trenchant claws on the second toe (Figure 14), cervical vertebrae with sloping articular surfaces (surfaces where they meet) that ensured that the head was carried well above the trunk, and further modification of the tetanuran condition of the tail into a rigid beam, achieved by long and overlapping chevrons that span up to ten vertebrae, bracing the tail. The specialized tail probably acted as a dynamic stabilizer, counterbalancing the weight of the trunk and head as the animal leapt at its prey. In fact, the species name for *Deinonychus* is *antirrhopus*, meaning "counter balancing." Dromaeosaurids are known in Europe, North America, Mongolia, and Japan.

The dromaeosaurid *Deinonychus* is perhaps the most significant dinosaur ever discovered (Figure 15). It forced paleontologists to think of dinosaurs as active, agile, intelligent animals, much closer to warm-bloodedness than suspected previously, and it allowed Prof. John Ostrom to compare dinosaurs and birds in a new light and reestablish and substantiate earlier theories of bird origins (Ostrom 1969, 1975, 1976). The significance of the discovery of *Deinonychus,* and Ostrom's seminal work on the genus, cannot be overstated.

The public is more familiar with *Velociraptor,* which is essentially a smaller version of *Deinonychus* but with a more flattened skull. It is famous for its recent movie appearances, but more legitimately for the preservation of one specimen locked in combat with a herbivorous *Protoceratops.* The specimens are known collectively as "the fighting dinosaurs" and truly constitute one of the wonders of the paleontological world.

Recent Discoveries

Three of the most recent discoveries of theropods have generated a great deal of interest because of their potential significance in illuminating further the ancestor-descendant relationship between theropods and birds. A truly spectacular theropod recovered in 1996 from Early to Mid-Cretaceous sediments in Liaoning Province, China, was preserved flattened on its side with a distinct frill of structures that at first were thought to be feathers. Named *Sinosauropteryx* ("Chinese reptile wing"), the specimen was subjected to detailed examination, and the consensus is that the structures are not feathers, but they do have a fiberlike construction. A similarity between the frill of *Sinosauropteryx* and that of some modern lizards has led to the postulate that the frill was designed as an aid for swimming, but the rest of the specimen shows no swimming adaptations. Subsequent to the discovery of *Sinosauropteryx,* another equally intriguing theropod specimen was recovered from the same area. Named *Protoarchaeopteryx* ("first ancient wing"), the specimen has traces of featherlike structures around its tail and is also extraordinary for the fact that the specimen appears to have two eggs preserved in an oviduct.

The third new theropod of great interest was described recently by F.E. Novas and P.F. Puerta (1997). Collected from Late

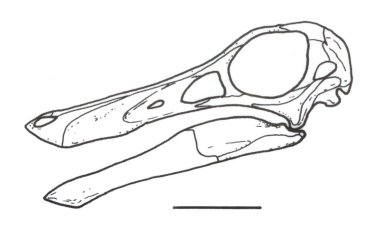

Figure 11. Skull of the ornithomimid *Gallimimus*. Scale bar, 10 centimeters.

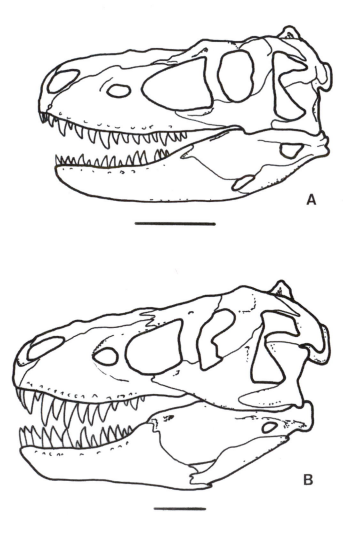

Figure 12. Skulls of the tyrannosaurids. *A, Albertosaurus; B, Tyrannosaurus.* Scale bar, 30 centimeters.

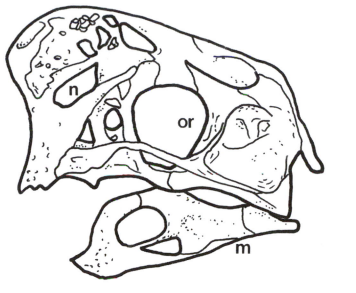

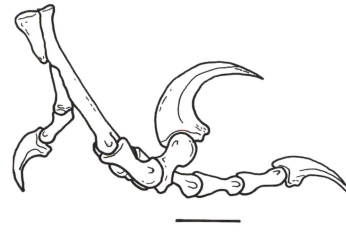

Figure 13. Skull of the oviraptor *Oviraptor* in left lateral view. Scale bar, five centimeters. Key: *m*, mandible (lower jaw); *n*, naris (nostril); *or*, orbit (eye socket).

Figure 14. Medial view of the left pes (foot) of *Deinonychus*, showing the enlarged, trenchant ungual (claw) on the second toe. Scale bar, five centimeters. Redrawn from Ostrom (1969).

Cretaceous sediments in Patagonia, *Unenlagia* ("half bird") is described as a sister taxon to Aves, slotting in phylogenetically as a transition group between Dromaeosauridae and *Archaeopteryx*. *Unenlagia* is known from one incomplete specimen, consisting of the pelvis, hind limb, and scapula, and the preserved elements appear to possess an even mixture of coelurosaurian and avian characters. This mixture of characters is seen in the bones of the pelvis and in the orientation of the glenoid cavity (the shoulder socket). Novas and Puerta (1997) describe it as facing laterally, as it does in birds, not down and back as it does in other dinosaurs. This structure would have allowed *Unenlagia* to raise its forelimb, perhaps preparatory to an effective downstroke. The conclusion that the forelimb was usable as a wing is tempered by the facts that no feathers were preserved in the specimen. Body proportions also suggest that *Unenlagia* was flightless, but it is an important specimen nonetheless, bearing testimony to the transition between theropods and birds.

Feeding

A carnivorous diet can be assigned with confidence to virtually all theropods. In fact, the skeletal adaptations to enhance successful prey procurement are often the most notable characteristics of theropod skeletal morphology. For example, most theropods possessed enlarged hands with elongate first, second, and third fingers, each of which was equipped with a claw. Various skull designs within Theropoda reflect their function, ranging from the low, sleek skull of *Troodon* with forwardly directed orbits (eye sockets) and many small, serrated ripping teeth, to the massively

constructed skulls of allosauroids and tyrannosaurids with huge, relatively blunt, stabbing teeth. Some theropods possessed specialized weaponry on their feet, or hands, or both, while others evidently had heightened senses for locating or tracking prey.

Behavior

It is mere speculation to reconstruct a behavioral repertoire for any dinosaur, but there is some circumstantial evidence for various behaviors in different theropods. Ostrom's discovery of the associated remains of four individuals of *Deinonychus* and one *Tenontosaurus* led him to speculate that the *Deinonychus* were gregarious and acting as members of a pack. In this attack upon the much larger *Tenontosaurus*, four had perished in the effort (Ostrom 1969). The predators would leap at the prey, grasping it with their hands, biting into the flesh, kicking and slashing with the large claws on the foot. The stiffened tail would have served to balance *Deinonychus* during this maneuver.

Evidence for gregarious behavior in other theropods is equally circumstantial, with perhaps the best example involving more than one thousand individuals of *Coelophysis* preserved at the famous Ghost Ranch locality in Arizona (Colbert 1989). Water transported the carcasses to the area, but it seems likely that drought-related stress brought the large number of individuals together prior to death (Schwartz and Gillette 1994). Two other substantial aggregates of theropods involve *Syntarsus*, a close relative of *Coelophysis*, and *Allosaurus*. Whereas the assemblages of *Syntarsus* and *Coelophysis* are virtually monospecific (no other dinosaurs are represented), the Cleveland-Lloyd quarry contains

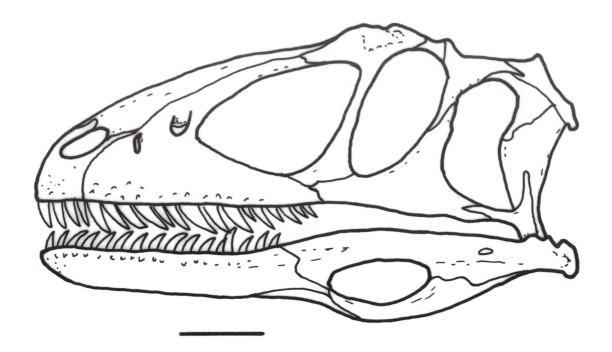

Figure 15. Skull of *Deinonychus* in left lateral view. Scale bar, five centimeters. Modified from Ostrom (1969).

the remains of more than 60 individuals of *Allosaurus,* and thousands of bones of at least ten other dinosaur genera. The C-L quarry probably represents some form of a trap in which various animals became ensnared, with a similar fate awaiting the allosaurs that came to feed on them.

Other behaviors that may be inferred for theropods include cannibalism and nesting. Preserved stomach contents illustrate that *Coelophysis* cannibalized its own young (Colbert 1989), and it is not out of the question that other theropods may have been opportunistic cannibals. Nesting behavior is suggested strongly by the many remarkable occurrences in Mongolia of an individual *Oviraptor* preserved on top of a clutch of eggs, apparently brooding, with its forelimbs spread out to protect the eggs (Dong and Currie 1996; Norell et al. 1996).

We presume almost all theropods were predators, but no unequivocal evidence of predatory behavior is preserved in the fossil record. The circumstantial evidence for predatory behavior in *Deinonychus* is mentioned above. Beyond that, we can not be sure that the cannibalism exhibited by *Coelophysis* represents predation rather than scavenging, and the same is true of an extraordinary fossil occurrence of a complete lizard in the stomach of a specimen of *Compsognathus* (Ostrom 1978). Similarly it is not certain that the "fighting dinosaurs" represent a *Velociraptor* preying on a *Protoceratops.* It is possible, no matter how unlikely, that the presumed prey animal actually was protecting some interest of its own and attacked the presumed predator. The largest predatory theropod *Tyrannosaurus* has left its teeth impressions in many bones of the plant eaters *Triceratops* and *Edmontosaurus* (Erickson and Olson, 1996), but again there is no way to differentiate between the marks of predation and scavenging.

Intelligence

Some of the behaviors attributed to theropods would suggest heightened mental capacity, but such capacity cannot be measured. The size of the brain cavity in some theropods, such as *Troodon* and the ornithomimosaurs, is relatively large and close to that of birds, but the size of the cavity is not a reliable indicator of intelligence. We simply can speculate that the more specialized theropods might have possessed increased mental ability, perhaps similar to that of birds.

Environment

Theropods have been recovered from sediments across the globe, representing a wide range of environments, from floodplains and coastal shorelines (e.g., *Albertosaurs, Acrocanthosaurus, Troodon*) to much more harsh desert environments (e.g., *Tarbosaurus, Velociraptor*). The fossils of theropod dinosaurs are relatively rare, but it is obvious from their worldwide distribution and their presence in a wide range of habitats that they formed an omnipresent and important component of dinosaurian communities through the 160 million years of their existence.

W. Desmond Maxwell

See also Birds; Thermoregulation

Works Cited

Barsbold, R. 1979. Opisthopubic pelvis in the carnivorous dinosaurs. *Nature* 279:792–93.

Barsbold, R., and H. Osmolska. 1990. Ornithomimosauria. *In* D.B. Weishampel, P. Dodson, and H. Osmolska (eds.), *The Dinosauria.* Berkeley: University of California Press.

Barsbold, R., T. Maryanska, and H. Osmolska. 1990. Oviraptorosauria. *In* D.B. Weishampel, P. Dodson, and H. Osmolska (eds.), *The Dinosauria.* Berkeley: University of California Press.

Bonaparte, J.F., F.E. Novas, and R.A. Coria. 1990. *Carnotaurus sastrei,* the horned, lightly built carnosaur from the middle Cretaceous of Patagonia. *Contributions in Science, Natural History Museum of Los Angeles County* 416:1–41.

Chiappe, L.M. 1995. The first 85 million years of avian evolution. *Nature* 378:349–55.

Clark, J.M., P. Altangerel, and M.A. Norell. 1994. *The Skull of* Erlicosaurus andrewsi, *a Late Cretaceous "Segnosaur" (Theropoda: Therizinosauridae) from Mongolia.* American Museum Novitates, 3115. New York: American Museum of Natural History.

Colbert, E.H. 1989. *The Triassic Dinosaur* Coelophysis. Museum of Northern Arizona Bulletin, 57. Flagstaff: Museum of Northern Arizona Press.

Coria, R.A., and L. Salgado. 1995. A new giant carnivorous dinosaur from the Cretaceous of Patagonia. *Nature* 377:224–26.

Currie, P.J., and X.-J. Zhao. 1993. A new carnosaur (Dinosauria, Theropoda) from the Jurassic of Xinjiang, People's Republic of China. *Canadian Journal of Earth Sciences* 30 (10): 2037–81.

Dong, Z.-M., and P.J. Currie. 1996. On the discovery of an oviraptorid skeleton on a nest of eggs at Bayan Mandahu, Inner Mongolia, People's Republic of China. *Canadian Journal of Earth Sciences* 33 (4):631–36.

Erickson, G.M., and K.H. Olson. 1996. Bite marks attributable to *Tyrannosaurus rex:* Preliminary description and implications. *Journal of Vertebrate Paleontology* 16 (1):175–78.

Farlow, J.O., M.B. Smith, and J.M. Robinson. 1995. Body mass, bone "strength indicator," and cursorial potential of *Tyrannosaurus rex. Journal of Vertebrate Paleontology* 15 (4):713–25.

Gauthier, J. 1986. Saurischian monophyly and the origin of birds. *Memoir of the California Academy of Sciences* 8:1–55.

Holtz Jr., T.R. 1994. The phylogenetic position of the Tyrannosauridae: Implications for theropod systematics. *Journal of Paleontology* 68 (5):1100–17.

———. 1995. A new phylogeny of the Theropoda. *Journal of Vertebrate Paleontology* 15 (3):Supplement 35A.

———. 1996. Phylogenetic taxonomy of the Coelurosauria (Dinosauria: Theropoda). *Journal of Paleontology* 70:536–38.

Kellner, A.W.A., and D. de A. Campos. 1996. First Early Cretaceous theropod dinosaur from Brazil with comments on Spinosauridae. *Neues Jahrbuch für Geologie und Paläontologie, Abhandlungen* 199 (2):151–66.

Madsen Jr., J.H. 1976. Allosaurus Fragilis: *A revised osteology.* Bulletin of the Utah Geological and Mineral Survey, 109. Salt Lake City: Utah Geological and Mineral Survey.

Milner, A.C. 1996. Morphology, relationships and ecology of spinosaurs, aberrant long-snouted Cretaceous theropods. *Journal of Vertebrate Paleontology* 16 (3): Supplement 53A.

Norell, M.A., J.M. Clark, D. Demberelyin, B. Rhinchen, L.M. Chiappe, A.R. Davidson, M.C. McKenna, P. Altangerel, and M.J. Novacek. 1994. A theropod dinosaur embryo and the affinities of the Flaming Cliffs dinosaur eggs. *Science* 266:779–82.

Norell, M.A., J.M. Clark, L.M. Chiappe, and D. Dashzeveg. 1995. A nesting dinosaur. *Nature* 378:774–76; erratum, 1996, Nature 379:186.

Novas, F.E., and P.F. Puerta. 1997. New evidence concerning avian origins from the Late Cretaceous of Patagonia. *Nature* 387:390–92.

Ostrom, J.H. 1969. Osteology of *Deinonychus antirrhopus,* an unusual theropod from the Lower Cretaceous of Montana. *Bulletin, Peabody Museum of Natural History* 30:1–165.

———. 1975. The origin of birds. *Annual Reviews of Earth and Planetary Science* 3:55–77.

———. 1976. *Archaeopteryx* and the origin of birds. *Biological Journal of the Linnean Society* 8:91–182.

———. 1978. The osteology of *Compsognathus longipes* Wagner. *Zitteliana* 4:73–118.

———. 1990. Dromaeosauridae. *In* D.B. Weishampel, P. Dodson, and H. Osmolska, (eds.), *The Dinosauria.* Berkeley: University of California Press.

Russell, D.A., and Z.-M. Dong. 1993. The affinities of a new theropod from the Alxa Desert, Inner Mongolia, People's Republic of China. *Canadian Journal of Earth Sciences* 30:2107–27.

Schwartz, H.L., and D.D. Gillette. 1994. Geology and taphonomy of the *Coelophysis* quarry, Upper Triassic Chinle Formation, Ghost Ranch, New Mexico. *Journal of Paleontology* 68 (5):1118–30.

Sereno, P.C. 1997. The origin and evolution of dinosaurs. *Annual Reviews of Earth and Planetary Science* 25:435–389.

Sereno, P.C., J.A. Wilson, H.C.E. Larsson, D.B. Dutheil, and H.-D. Sues. 1994. Early Cretaceous dinosaurs from the Sahara. *Science* 266:267–70.

Sereno, P.C., D.B. Dutheil, M. Larochene, H.C.E. Larsson, G.H. Lyon, P.M. Magwene, C.A. Sidor, D.J. Varricchio, and J.A. Wilson. 1996. Predatory dinosaurs from the Sahara and Late Cretaceous faunal differentiation. *Science* 272:986–91.

Zhao, X.-J., and P.J. Currie. 1993. A large crested theropod from the Jurassic of Xinjiang, People's Republic of China. *Canadian Journal of Earth Sciences* 30 (10):2027–36.

Further Reading

Currie, P.J., Z.M. Dong, and D.A. Russell. 1993. Results from the Sino-Canadian dinosaur project. *Canadian Journal of Earth Sciences* 30:1997–2272.

Farlow, J.O. 1993. On the rareness of big, fierce animals: Speculations about the body sizes, population densities, and geographic ranges of predatory mammals and large carnivorous dinosaurs. *American Journal of Science* 293A:167–99.

Fastovsky, D.E., and D.B. Weishampel. 1996. Theropoda I: Nature red in tooth and claw. *In* D.E. Fastovsky and D.B. Weishampel (eds.), *The Evolution and Extinction of the Dinosaurs.* Cambridge and New York: Cambridge University Press.

Maxwell, W.D., and J.H. Ostrom. 1995. Taphonomy and paleobiological implications of *Tenontosaurus-Deinonychus* associations. *Journal of Vertebrate Paleontology* 15 (4):707–12.

Norell, M.A., J.M. Clark, D. Demberelyin, B. Rhinchen, L.M. Chiappe, A. Davidson, R. McKenna, M.C.P. Altangerel, and M.J. Novacek. 1994. A theropod dinosaur embryo and the affinities of the Flaming Cliffs dinosaur eggs. *Science* 266:779–82.

Paul, G.S. 1988. *Predatory Dinosaurs of the World.* New York: Simon and Schuster.

Sereno, P.C., and F.E. Novas. 1993. The skull and neck of the basal theropod *Herrerasaurus ischigualastensis. Journal of Vertebrate Paleontology* 13:451–76.

Weishampel, D.B., P. Dodson, and H. Osmolska (eds.). 1990. *The Dinosauria.* Berkeley: University of California Press.

TRACE ELEMENT ANALYSIS

Trace element analysis of ancient calcified tissue has become a valuable tool in environmental and dietary studies during the last three decades of the twentieth century in the fields of archeology and, to a lesser extent, paleontology. It is most meritoriously utilized when considered within an interdisciplinary context that takes into account aspects of physiology, biochemistry, geochemistry, and, perhaps most importantly, calcified tissue biology. If human samples are the focus of the study, the disciplines of anthropology and human ecology are of significance as well.

Two alkaline earth minerals, strontium (Sr) and barium (Ba), have been demonstrated to provide dietary information on both physiological and geochemical grounds; a number of other elements, such as zinc (Zn) and sodium (Na), have purported to provide similar lines of evidence, but there is no sound scientific basis for such claims (see Ezzo 1994a, 1994b for a review of this literature). Strontium and barium resemble calcium (Ca) structurally and can substitute for calcium in certain physiological and biochemical contexts, most conspicuously fixation in the crystalline lattice of hydroxyapatite, $Ca_{10}(PO_4)_6(OH)_2$, the predominate mineral of calcified tissues (in the previous example, P stands for phosphorus and H stands for hydrogen). Strontium and barium have no known physiological function, and the body processes them similarly to calcium. As calcium is biopurified through each level of the food web, strontium and barium are fractionated (discriminated) such that their ratios to calcium decrease from bedrock to soil to plants to herbivores to carnivores in a given environment.

In paleodietary analysis, strontium and barium most commonly are expressed as ratios to calcium. This helps to account for the normal variations in calcium bone levels as well as diagenesis, or chemical degradation/alteration of bone; the bone levels of strontium and barium are not proportional simply to the amount of strontium and barium in the diet, but to the mean strontium/barium and barium/calcium ratios of the diet. In other words, it is the amount of strontium and barium relative to the total amount of available bone-forming ions ($Ca+Sr+Ba+Pb \approx Ca$, where Pb stands for lead) that determine the percentage of bone mineral that is represented by strontium or barium (Burton and Wright 1995). A third ratio, barium/strontium, has proven effective in characterizing the nature of ancient environments and accompanying diets (Burton and Price 1990). Because of the insolubility of barium in seawater (occurring primarily as barite, $BaSO_4$), marine diets (referred to as the marine signature) have very low barium/strontium ratios, whereas the barium/strontium ratios of terrestrial diets/signatures approach unity. Estuary, desert, and aquatic diets/signatures fall in-between. Elements such as magnesium, iron, and fluoride occur in fossil bone primarily as contaminants, and can, depending on the geochemical context, provide information on the soil solution in which the calcified tissue was buried. Extreme cases of lead poisoning may be detected by measuring lead content of bone, although lead isotope analysis is required

to determine the source of lead (Kowal et al. 1990). Under certain pathological conditions, the zinc content of calcified tissues may provide information about remodeling rates of bone mineral (Blondiaux et al. 1992). Phosphorous levels in bone mineral are necessary to determine the structure of hydroxyapatite through use of the calcium/phosphorus ratio (the theoretical mass Ca/P being 2.15). In summary, use of multiple elements is essential to understanding the nature of tissue preservation and the environment in which it was buried, and, by extension, the dietary signature.

Trace element analysis has been applied to a wide range of paleontological and archeological samples, from Lower Miocene fauna from Nebraska (Toots and Voorheis 1965) to early hominids such as *Australopithecus robustus* from Swartkrans, South Africa (Sillen 1992) to historical period human remains (Schoeninger 1989). The majority of studies have been archaeological in nature, focusing on prehistoric human remains. Sillen and Kavanaugh (1982); Price, Schoeninger, and Armelagos (1985); and Aufderheide (1989) have provided overviews of such studies.

Controlled studies in the form of feeding experiments, simulations of processes of degradation of bone under different environmental conditions, and techniques for removing contaminants from ancient samples constitute a large portion of the archaeological trace element literature. Particularly important feeding experiments that have provided information on the pathways of strontium and barium from diet to bone include Price, Connor, and Parsen (1985); Price and colleagues (1986); and Lambert and Weydert-Homeyer (1993). Particularly important studies of bone degradation designed to understand physiochemical changes that calcified tissues undergo in the postmortem environment include Grupe (1988), Grupe and Piepenbrink (1988), Pate and colleagues (1989), Hedges and Millard (1995), Child (1995), and Newesley (1988, 1989). Bone-cleaning experiments have focused on removal of physical contaminants through mechanical abrasion and removal of diagenetic effects (postburial changes) through sequential acid or buffered acid washing. Among the more salient contributions in this area of research are Sillen (1986, 1989, 1992), Sillen and LeGeros (1991), Sillen and Sealy (1995), Lambert and colleagues (1990, 1991), Price (1989), Price and colleagues (1992), and Ezzo and colleagues (1995).

As with all scientific endeavors, the analytical strength of trace element data derived from ancient calcified tissues is enhanced by parallel lines of data. Techniques that can complement trace element analysis in paleodietary studies include stable carbon ($^{13}C/^{12}C$) and nitrogen ($^{15}N/^{14}N$) isotope analysis of calcified tissues (see, for example, Ezzo 1992; Schoeninger 1989), strontium isotope ($^{87}Sr/^{86}Sr$) analysis of calcified tissue (Sealy et al. 1991), paleopathology (Ezzo et al. 1995), analysis of associated faunal and paleobotanical remains, and coprolite (paleofeces) analysis.

JOSEPH A. EZZO

See also Diet; Stable Isotope Analysis

Works Cited

Aufderheide, A.C. 1989. Chemical analysis of skeletal remains. *In* M.Y. Iscan and K.A.R. Kennedy (eds.), *Reconstruction of Life from the Skeleton.* New York: Liss.

Blondiaux, J.A., C.A. Baud, N. Boscher-Barré, C. Dardenne, N. Deschamps, P. Trocellier, and L. Buchet. 1992. Trace elements in paleopathology: Quantitative analysis of a case of hypertrophic osteoarthropathy by instrumental neutron activation analysis. *International Journal of Osteoarchaeology* 2:241–44.

Burton, J.H., and T.D. Price. 1990. The ratio of barium to strontium as a paleodietary indicator of consumption of marine resources. *Journal of Archaeological Science* 17:547–57.

Burton, J.H., and L. Wright. 1995. Nonlinearity in the relationship between bone Sr/Ca ratios and dietary ratios: Paleodietary implications. *American Journal of Physical Anthropology* 96:273–82.

Child, A.M. 1995. Towards an understanding of the microbial decomposition of archaeological bone in the burial environment. *Journal of Archaeological Science* 22:165–74.

Ezzo, J.A. 1992. Dietary change and variability at Grasshopper Pueblo, Arizona. *Journal of Anthropological Archaeology* 11:219–89.

———. 1994a. Putting the "chemistry" back into bone chemistry analysis: Modeling potential dietary indicators. *Journal of Anthropological Archaeology* 13:1–34.

———.1994b. Zinc as a paleodietary indicator: An issue of theoretical validity in bone chemistry analysis. *American Antiquity* 59:606–21.

Ezzo, J.A., C.S. Larsen, and J.H. Burton. 1995. Elemental signatures of archaeological bone from the Georgia Bight. *American Journal of Physical Anthropology* 98:471–81.

Grupe, G. 1988. Impact of the choice of bone samples on trace element data in excavated human skeletons. *Journal of Archaeological Science* 15:123–29.

Grupe, G., and H. Piepenbrink. 1988. Trace element contaminations in excavated bones by microorganisms. *In* G. Grupe and B. Herrmann (eds.), *Trace Elements in Environmental History.* Berlin and New York: Springer-Verlag.

Hedges, R.E.M., and A.R. Millard. 1995. Bones and groundwater: Towards the modelling of diagenetic processes. *Journal of Archaeological Science* 22:155–64.

Kowal, W.A., P.M. Krahn, and O.B. Beattie. 1990. Lead levels of human tissues from the Franklin Forensic Project. *International Journal of Environmental Analytical Chemistry* 35:119–26.

Lambert, J.B., J.M. Weydert, S.R. Williams, and J.E. Buikstra. 1990. Comparison of methods for the removal of diagenetic material in buried bone. *Journal of Archaeological Science* 17:453–68.

Lambert, J.B., L. Xue, and J.E. Buikstra. 1991. Inorganic analysis of excavated human bone after surface removal. *Journal of Archaeological Science* 18:363–83.

Lambert, J.B., and J. Weydert-Homeyer. 1993. The fundamental relationship between ancient diet and the inorganic constituents of bone as derived from feeding experiments. *Archaeometry* 35:279–94.

Newesly, H. 1988. Chemical stability of hydroxyapatite under different conditions. *In* G. Grupe and B. Herrmann (eds.), *Trace Elements in Environmental History.* Berlin and New York: Springer-Verlag.

———. 1989. Fossil bone apatite. *Applied Geochemistry* 4:233–45.

Pate, F.D., J.T. Hutton, and K. Norrish. 1989. Ionic exchange between soil solution and bone: Toward a predictive model. *Applied Geochemistry* 4:303–16.

Price, T.D. 1989. Multielement studies of diagenesis in prehistoric bone. *In* T.D. Price (ed.), *The Chemistry of Prehistoric Human Bone.* Cambridge and New York: Cambridge University Press.

Price, T.D., M. Connor, and J.D. Parsen. 1985. Bone strontium analysis and the reconstruction of diet: Strontium discrimination in white-tailed deer. *Journal of Archaeological Science* 12:419–42.

Price, T.D., M.J. Schoeninger, and G.J. Armelagos. 1985. Bone chemistry and past behavior: An overview. *Journal of Human Evolution* 14:419–47.

Price, T.D., R.W. Swick, and E.P. Chase. 1986. Bone chemistry and prehistoric diet: Strontium studies of laboratory rats. *American Journal of Physical Anthropology* 70:365–75.

Price, T.D., J. Blitz, J.H. Burton, and J.A. Ezzo. 1992. Diagenesis in prehistoric bone: Problems and solutions. *Journal of Archaeological Science* 19:513–29.

Schoeninger, M.J. 1989. Reconstructing prehistoric human diet. *In* T.D. Price (ed.), *The Chemistry of Prehistoric Human Bone.* Cambridge and New York: Cambridge University Press.

Sealy, J.C., N.J. van der Merwe, A. Sillen, F.J. Kruger, and H.W. Krueger. 1991. $^{87}Sr/^{86}Sr$ as a dietary indicator in modern and archaeological bone. *Journal of Archaeological Science* 18:399–416.

Sillen, A. 1986. Biogenetic and diagenetic Sr/Ca in Plio-Pleistocene fossils of the Omo Shunguru Formation. *Paleobiology* 12:311–23.

———. 1989. Diagenesis of the inorganic phase of cortical bone. *In* T.D. Price (ed.), *The Chemistry of Prehistoric Human Bone.* Cambridge and New York: Cambridge University Press.

———. 1992. Strontium-calcium ratios (Sr/Ca) of *Australopithecus robustus* and associated fauna from Swartkrans. *Journal of Human Evolution* 23:495–516.

Sillen, A., and M. Kavanaugh, 1982. Strontium and paleodietary research: A review. *Yearbook of Physical Anthropology* 25:67–90.

Sillen, A., and R. LeGeros. 1991. Solubility profiles of synthetic apatites and of modern and fossil bones. *Journal of Archaeological Science* 18:385–97.

Sillen, A., and J.C. Sealy. 1995. Diagenesis of strontium in fossil bone: A reconsideration of Nelseon et al. (1986). *Journal of Archaeological Science* 22:313–20.

Toots, H., and M.R. Voorheis. 1965. Strontium in fossil bones and the reconstruction of food chains. *Science* 149:854–55.

Further Reading

Aufderheide, A.C., 1989. Chemical analysis of skeletal remains. *In* M.Y. Iscan and K.A.R. Kennedy (eds.), *Reconstruction of Life from the Skeleton.* New York: Liss.

Ezzo, J.A. 1994. Putting the "chemistry" back into bone chemistry analysis: Modeling potential dietary indicators. *Journal of Anthropological Archaeology* 13:1–34.

Grupe, G., and B. Herrmann (eds.). 1988. *Trace Elements in Environmental History.* Berlin and New York: Springer-Verlag.

Price, T.D. (ed.). 1989. *The Chemistry of Prehistoric Bone.* Cambridge and New York: Cambridge University Press.

TRACE FOSSILS

In a broad sense, trace fossils can be defined as any evidence of the existence of an extinct organism that does not include fossilized remains of the actual organism itself. Examples of trace fossils are fossilized trackways, burrows, egg shells, and coprolites (fossil dung). Most studies tend to use a narrower definition of trace fossils as the fossilized structures produced in unlithified sediment, sedimentary rock, or a biogenic substrate (e.g., wood or shell) by the activity and/or growth of an extinct organism.

The study of trace fossils is termed ichnology—from the Greek *ichnos,* meaning a trace—and can provide very important paleoecological and paleoenvironmental information. In particular, they can shed light on environmental parameters such as salinity, oxygen level, and water depth, which are often difficult to deduce from sedimentological studies alone. Unlike body fossils, the vast majority of trace fossils cannot be transported and so are found in the exact location where they were formed. Often, they are the only record of the activities of soft-bodied organisms that rarely get fossilized.

Trace fossils are important in many other areas of geological study, such as stratigraphy (especially the correlation of "unfossiliferous" strata), sequence stratigraphy, evolutionary studies, and sediment lithification and diagenesis. Recent reviews of trace fossils and their geological applications can be found in Bromley (1990), Pemberton and colleagues (1992), and Donovan (1994).

Classification

There are three main classification schemes that can be applied to trace fossils.

Taxonomic

Originally, trace fossils were thought to be the fossilized remains of marine algae and so were classified as species and genera. Although this system of naming trace fossils is still used today, it is recognized that no phylogenetic relationship exists between "species" of trace fossils. Indeed, a single trace fossil taxon could be produced by many different benthic (deep-sea) species, and different species may produce very similar traces. In order to avoid confusion we refer to *ichno*species and *ichno*genera when classifying trace fossils. Problems concerning the taxonomy of trace fossils are discussed in detail by R.K. Pickerill (1994).

Ethological

Trace fossils are the product of the interaction between organism and substrate and hence record the behavior of extinct organisms. Nine behavioral categories are recognized: (1) traces produced by stationary organisms *(cubichnia);* (2) locomotion traces *(repichnia);* (3) horizontal grazing traces composed of meandering or spiral trails *(pascichnia);* (4) deposit-feeding traces *(fodichnia);* (5) permanent or semipermanent dwelling structures *(domichnia);* (6) burrows that

were either built as traps for migrating organisms or as "gardens" for the culture of microbes *(agrichnia);* (7) structures that formed through predatory behavior *(praedichnia);* (8) structures formed by infaunal organisms (those that are embedded in the substrate) as they change position to keep pace with erosion or aggradation of the surrounding sediment *(equilibrichnia);* and (9) traces produced as organisms try to escape from predation or sudden burial *(fugichnia).* This classification scheme is very useful for paleoecological studies, although not all ichnogenera are easy to interpret.

Preservational

Trace fossils also can be classified according to their relationship with the surrounding rock (Figure 1). This can be important for paleoenvironmental reconstruction. For example, traces preserved as endichnia (within a bed) were formed after that unit was deposited, whereas those preserved as semirelief hypichnia (on the base of the bed) were formed during deposition of the *previous* unit.

The Ichnofacies Concept

Trace fossils do not occur randomly in the rock record but often are found in recurring assemblages. These distinctive assemblages allow geologists to recognize different facies solely on the basis of the ichnofossils that are present (i.e., ichnofacies). Currently, nine of these ichnofacies have been recognized, and each one is named for a representative ichnogenus: *Scoyenia, Trypanites, Teredolites, Glossifungites, Psilonichnus, Skolithos, Cruziana, Zoophycos,* and *Nereites.* However, it should be noted that the ichnofacies still can be recognized even if a representative ichnogenus is absent. For example, even though the ichnogenus *Cruziana* is absent from Mesozoic and younger rocks owing to the extinction of the trace-making organisms (trilobites) in the Late Palaeozoic, the *Cruziana* ichnofacies can still be recognized. Also, some ichnotaxa are not facies-specific and may be found in a number of different assemblages (e.g., *Skolithos, Planolites*).

Each characteristic assemblage, each ichnofacies, represents a specific suite of environmental parameters (such as substrate consistency, light, and nutrient levels) that was present when the trace-making organisms were alive. Many of these parameters change progressively with increasing water depth, and one of the first uses of ichnofacies was as paleo-depth indicators (Figure 2).

The *Scoyenia* ichnofacies traditionally characterizes continental red-bed deposits and is dominated by traces produced by terrestrial arthropods. At present, it is the only fully terrestrial ichnofacies that is recognized. However, it is clear that the terrestrial realm can be subdivided still further and that certain (as yet unnamed) ichnofossil assemblages characterize fluvial (river), desert, and lake environments, for example.

The *Psilonichnus* ichnofacies characterizes the peritidal-supratidal environment (for example, beaches and sand dunes). This is a harsh and fluctuating environment where few creatures actually choose to live. Hence, this ichnofacies is a low-diversity, low-abundance assemblage dominated by the repichnia of invertebrate and vertebrate scavengers. Occasional, small domichnia of insects or crustaceans also may be present.

The *Skolithos* ichnofacies represents fully marine conditions, generally in a high-energy setting with a sandy, shifting substrate. This type of environment favors the preservation of deep burrows, particularly those formed by stationary suspension feeders. The trace fossil assemblage is characterized by vertical domichnia and equilibrichnia, which often have strengthened walls (e.g., *Ophiomorpha*). Diversity is low, but abundance may be high. An example of this is piperock, which is formed by shallow marine, monospecific assemblages of *Skolithos* and which is particularly common in Cambrian strata.

The *Cruziana* ichnofacies characterizes shallow marine environments above the storm wave base, but below the fair-weather wave base. It represents a lower-energy environment than the *Skolithos* ichnofacies, although occasional higher-energy storm layers are present, and it includes a mixture of vertical and horizontal burrows formed by mobile deposit feeders. A wide range of behaviors may be represented by the ichnofauna, including cubichnia, fodichnia, domichnia, and pascichnia.

The *Nereites* ichnofacies characterizes very deep (i.e., bathyal-abyssal), low-energy marine environments. The assemblage is usually diverse and tends to be dominated by horizontal grazing traces (pascichnia) and farming traces (agrichnia). Typically these trace fossils are preserved as hypichnial traces on the soles of turbidite beds.

The *Zoophycos* ichnofacies contains a low-diversity, often high-abundance assemblage of fodichnia or pascichnia produced by deposit-feeding organisms. It is said to characterize low-energy environments, below storm wave base, that are affected by intervals of oxygen restriction. This produces environmental stress that reduces the diversity of burrowing organisms and hence trace fossils. *Zoophycos* itself is often thought of as an indicator of low oxygen conditions, but this is probably only true for Mesozoic and Cenozoic times. Several authors have expressed doubt about the validity of this ichnofacies (e.g., Bromley 1990).

The *Glossifungites* ichnofacies characterizes sediments that were firm, but unlithified, at the time of colonization. A typical example would be a shallow marine mud layer that had been buried (and hence compacted) and then exhumed by an erosive episode (e.g., storm activity). The firm ground is difficult to burrow through, and so the assemblage is dominated by the domichnia of filter feeders, rather than the fodichnia or pascichnia of deposit feeders.

The remaining two ichnofacies are characteristic of hard substrates and hence involve boring activity rather than burrowing. The *Trypanites* ichnofacies characterizes fully lithified marine substrates and usually represents a break in deposition (i.e., a marine hiatus). The *Teredolites* ichnofacies results from borings into woody substrate (e.g., a floating tree trunk).

Tiering

Within any community of infaunal organisms, different animals will occupy different levels within the sediment. In ancient sediments this phenomenon is known as tiering. As each level will have different organisms and different environmental conditions (such as pH and oxygen concentration), trace fossils within the sediment will also exhibit tiering. Knowing the tiering structure of trace fossil assemblages is often of great importance in paleoecological studies.

The original tiering pattern is rarely observed in ancient sediments because of the effect of sediment accumulation. As sediment is deposited, the tiers migrate upward in order to remain at the same depth relative to the surface. This means that the burrows of deeper-tier organisms may crosscut those of shallower-tier animals that have since migrated upwards. Eventually, this process will lead to a complex arrangement of burrows within a trace fossil assemblage (Figure 3a). In order to reconstruct the original tiering pattern, it is necessary to determine the crosscutting relationships between the burrows: the deepest burrows will crosscut all the others, the shallowest will be crosscut by all the others (Figure 3b). Reconstruction of the tiering relationships in ancient sediments has shown how the burrowing community have evolved through time (e.g., Bottjer and Droser 1994 and references therein).

Trace Fossils and Paleo-Oxygen Levels

The concentration of dissolved oxygen is a fundamental control on the diversity and abundance of marine benthic communities and hence the character of the trace fossil assemblages. In general, the amount and depth of bioturbation, the average and maximum burrow diameters, and the diversity of the trace fossil assemblage all decrease with decreasing oxygen concentrations. Eventually, oxygen levels will sink so low that a burrowing infauna is completely absent. In modern environments this occurs with oxygen concentrations of less than 0.1 ml per liter of water. These anaerobic conditions can lead to the preservation of organic matter within the sediments, which later may produce petroleum. For this reason, the study of trace fossils has important economic value.

In addition to the general changes in the ichnofossil assemblage with decreasing oxygen levels, several authors have suggested that certain trace fossils are characteristic of oxygen-deficient environments. Examples include *Chondrites* and *Zoophycos*. However, it should be noted that these hypotheses are based on studies of Cretaceous and Tertiary sediments and may not apply to older strata. In any given assemblage, one would expect organisms producing the deepest tier trace fossil to be most tolerant to low oxygen concentrations.

Trace Fossils and Mass Extinctions

The examination of links between trace fossils and extinction events is a relatively new and exciting field of study. Changes in trace fossil assemblages through extinction events may reflect environmental change (which has some bearing on the cause of the extinction) or extinction of the soft-bodied infauna. Trace fossils may prove very important in documenting the extinction of soft-bodied organisms that are not usually preserved.

Earlier studies suggest that ichnogeneric diversity has remained almost constant since the Ordovician, and that trace fossils have not been affected by any of the recognized Phanerozoic mass extinctions. However, recent studies suggest that mass extinctions do affect ichnofossil assemblages. For example, during the end-Permian mass extinction, development of oxygen-restricted facies in shallow environments led to a reduction in tiering, diversity, and burrow diameter (Twitchett and Wignall 1996). In addition, the ichnogenus *Zoophycos* disappeared from very shallow environments during this time. Does this represent the loss of the *Zoophycos*-producing behavior in shallow settings, or extinction of the shallow-water *Zoophycos* trace-maker?

RICHARD J. TWITCHETT

See also Diet; Feeding Adaptations: Invertebrates; Paleoecology; Paleoethology

Works Cited

Bottjer, D.J., and M.L. Droser. 1994. The history of Phanerozoic bioturbation. *In* S.K. Donovan (ed.), *The Palaeobiology of Trace Fossils.* Chichester: Wiley; Baltimore, Maryland: Johns Hopkins University Press.

Bromley, R.G. 1990. *Trace Fossils: Biology and Taphonomy.* Special Topics in Palaeontology No. 3. London and Boston: Unwin Hyman.

Donovan, S.K. (ed.). 1994. *The Palaeobiology of Trace Fossils.* Chichester: Wiley.

Pemberton, S.G., J.A. MacEarchen, and R.W. Frey. 1992. Trace fossil facies models. *In* R.G. Walker and N.P. James (eds.), *Facies Models: Response to Sea Level Change.* St. John's, New Foundland: Geological Association of Canada.

Pickerill, R.K. 1994. Nomenclature and taxonomy of invertebrate trace fossils. *In* S.K. Donovan (ed.), *The Palaeobiology of Trace Fossils.* Chichester: Wiley.

Twitchett, R.J., and P.B. Wignall. 1996. Trace fossils and the aftermath of the Permo-Triassic mass extinction: Evidence from northern Italy. *Palaeogeography, Palaeoclimatology, Palaeoecology* 124:137–51.

Further Reading

Bromley, R.G. 1990. *Trace Fossils: Biology and Taphonomy.* Special Topics in Palaeontology No. 3. London and Boston: Unwin Hyman; 2nd ed., London and New York: Chapman and Hall, 1996.

Donovan, S.K. (ed.). 1994. *The Palaeobiology of Trace Fossils.* Chichester: Wiley; Baltimore, Maryland: Johns Hopkins University Press.

TREE SHREWS

The order Scandentia includes only one family, Tupaiidae. Tupaiids, or tree shrews, are small (45 to 350 grams), squirrel-like mammals inhabiting the forests of South and Southeast Asia, from western India to Mindanao and the Philippines and from southern China through Java and Indonesia. Their diet consists of mainly insects and fruit, but they also eat other plant material and small animals. All are diurnal except for the nocturnal *Ptilocercus lowii.*

The family Tupaiidae consists of six extant (present-day) genera and eighteen species and is split into two subfamilies, Ptilocercinae and Tupaiinae. Ptilocercinae contains the single genus *Ptilocercus* (one species), and Tupaiinae consists of the genera *Anathana* (one species), *Dendrogale* (two species), *Lyonogale* (two species), *Tupaia* (eleven species), and *Urogale* (one species).

Tupaiid molars have high, sharp cusps (pointed sections), reflecting their insectivorous diet. Their lower incisors are closely aligned and project forward, enabling them to be used as a tooth-comb (for grooming). Their orbits (openings for the eyes) face to the side (laterally) (except for the arboreal *Ptilocercus,* whose orbits face forward) and are encircled in bone (postorbital bar). All scandentians possess claws on their fingers and toes.

Tupaiid lifestyle varies from completely arboreal (tree-based) to predominantly terrestrial (land-based), and this variety is reflected in their anatomy. For instance, *Ptilocercus* and *Tupaia minor* are both arboreal and are smaller in size and have longer tails than terrestrial tupaiids, presumably for balance on branches. Similarly, terrestrial tupaiids (e.g., *Lyonogale* and *Urogale*) have longer snouts and better developed claws than arboreal species, presumably for rooting in leaf litter (Martin 1990).

The tupaiid fossil record is extremely poor. Although several early Tertiary groups—including *Entomolestes, Tupaiodon,* and *Anagale* of the family Anagalidae—have been considered to be tupaiids or tupaiid relatives, all have since been rejected as such (e.g., McKenna 1963). Erroneous references of fossils to the Tupaiidae may be due to the fact that most are based on cheek tooth morphology (shape and structure). Tupaiid cheek teeth appear to have evolved along similar paths (convergently) to those of many early Tertiary mammals. Since these similarities probably arose independently, the similarities probably do not indicate that the two groups are related.

The majority of tupaiid fossils probably come from the Siwaliks of India and Pakistan. A.K. Dutta (1975) reported the discovery of a complete rib cage that may represent *Tupaia* from the upper Siwaliks of India (Pliocene in age). However, this specimen never has been described properly or figured (drawn), making its status as a tupaiid difficult to evaluate. In 1979, S.R.K. Chopra and colleagues, and Chopra and R.N.T. Vasishat described a skull fragment, a left maxillary fragment (upper jawbone), and a lower right second molar from the middle Siwaliks of India (Miocene in age). These fossils were attributed to a new taxon, *Palaeotupaia sivalicus,* within the subfamily Tupaiinae. The skull fragment is most similar to *Tupaia* and is the size of *T. minor* (45 grams). W.P. Luckett and L.L. Jacobs (1980), while agreeing that these specimens are tupaiids, argued that they are virtually indistinguishable from *Tupaia* and therefore should not be allocated to a new genus.

Jacobs (1980) described additional tupaiid fossils of Miocene age (approximately ten million years old) from the Siwaliks of Pakistan (further west than the distribution of living tupaiids). These specimens, consisting of a skull fragment, a lower left first molar, and a lower molar talonid, probably represent new taxa. The skull fragment is distinct from living genera but is similar in size to that of *T. glis* (160 grams), while the size of the lower molar is more similar to that of *T. minor*. The larger size of the skull fragment relative to that of the lower molar (as well as to that of the Indian specimens) indicates that these specimens probably represent separate species. Due to their limited number, Jacobs did not make generic or specific allocations for these specimens, but Chopra and Vasishat suggested that they may be assigned to *Palaeotupaia sivalicus*. This potential assignment, however, probably would have been premature, considering the differences in size (and morphology) between the Pakistani and Indian skull fragments. Z. Qiu (1986) argued that all the Siwalik fossils cannot be allocated to *Palaeotupaia* and may represent as many as three new tupaiid taxa.

The first tupaiid fossils recovered outside the Siwaliks were discovered in Miocene beds at Lufeng, China. Qiu (1986) described seventeen isolated teeth and attributed them to a new taxon, *Prodendrogale yunnanica*, based on similarities to *Dendrogale* in morphology and size. Qiu concluded that these taxa probably represent one another's closest relatives. The earliest fossil tupaiids ever discovered, described by Y. Tong (1988), are from Eocene beds at Henan, China. Consisting of an upper left molar, upper right first and third molars, and two lower molar talonids (flat extension at the rear portion of a molar), these isolated teeth are similar to those of *Dendrogale* and were assigned to the new taxon *Eodendrogale parvum*.

The evolutionary relationships of tupaiids have long been debated, and relatedness is confounded by their poor fossil record. Originally, tupaiids were included in the Insectivora and subsequently were combined with macroscelidids (elephant shrews) into the insectivoran suborder Menotyphla. In 1910, Gregory proposed the superorder Archonta, which included Menotyphla, Chiroptera (bats), Dermoptera (flying lemurs), and Primates. In 1922, Carlsson included tupaiids in the order Primates, an action that was supported further by the work of Le Gros Clark in the 1920s and Simpson in 1945 (although he believed Archonta to be an unnatural group). Tupaiids were removed from Primates in the 1960s, when it was deemed that most similarities between the two groups were either erroneous observations, shared primitive (very ancient) characters, or convergences found only in derived (specialized) representatives of the groups (e.g., Van Valen 1965). In 1972, Butler classified tupaiids as an independent order, Scandentia. In 1975, McKenna accepted this classification and excluded macroscelidids from the Archonta. This revised Archonta hypothesis remains controversial today and since has been supported by some studies and

rejected or revised by others. Several molecular studies, for example, have supported a group that includes Scandentia, Primates, and Dermoptera, but excludes Chiroptera. There has also been much recent debate about which group is the closest relative of tupaiids: Primates, Euprimates, or Lagomorpha. In summary, the existence of the Archonta has not been agreed upon, and scandentian supraordinal relationships remain poorly understood.

ERIC J. SARGIS

See also Insectivorans; Placentals: Minor Placental Orders of Small Body Size

Works Cited

Chopra, S.R.K., S. Kaul, and R.N. Vasishat. 1979. Miocene tree shrews from the Indian Sivaliks. *Nature* 281:213–14.

Chopra, S.R.K., and R.N. Vasishat. 1979. Sivalik fossil tree shrew from Haritalyangar, India. *Nature* 281:214–15.

Dutta, A.K. 1975. Micromammals from Siwaliks. *Indian Minerals* 29:76–77.

Jacobs, L.L. 1980. Siwalik fossil tree shrews. *In* W.P. Luckett (ed.), *Comparative Biology and Evolutionary Relationships of Tree Shrews.* New York, Plenum.

Luckett, W.P., and L.L. Jacobs. 1980. Proposed fossil tree shrew genus *Palaeotupaia*. *Nature* 288:104.

Martin, R.D. 1990. *Primate Origins and Evolution.* Princeton, New Jersey: Princeton University Press; London: Chapman and Hall.

McKenna, M.C. 1963. New evidence against tupaioid affinities of the mammalian family Anagalidae. *American Museum Novitates* 2158:1–16.

Qiu, Z. 1986. Fossil tupaiid from the hominoid locality of Lufeng, Yunnan. *Vertebrata PalAsiatica* 24:308–19.

Tong, Y. 1988. Fossil tree shrews from the Eocene Hetaoyuan Formation of Xichuan, Henan. *Vertebrata PalAsiatica* 26:214–20.

Van Valen, L.M. 1965. Tree shrews, primates, and fossils. *Evolution* 19:137–51.

Further Reading

Luckett, W.P. (ed.). 1980. *Comparative Biology and Evolutionary Relationships of Tree Shrews.* New York: Plenum.

Lyon, M.W. 1913. Tree shrews: An account of the mammalian family Tupaiidae. *Proceedings of the United States National Museum* 45:1–188.

MacPhee, R.D.E. (ed.). 1993. *Primates and Their Relatives in Phylogenetic Perspective.* New York: Plenum.

Martin, R.D. 1982. Et tu, tree shrew? *Natural History* 8:26–33.

Martin, R.D. 1984. Tree shrews. *In* D. Macdonald (ed.), *The Encyclopedia of Mammals.* New York: Facts on File.

TRILOBITES

At Arcy-sur-Cur, France, an archaeological site 15,000 years old, a trilobite was found with an artificial perforation suggesting that it had been worn as a decoration or as an amulet. Some Australian aboriginal tribes are known to have collected trilobites, as did the Pahvant Utes of Utah. The Utes wore the abundant Middle Cambrian trilobite *Elrathia kingi* (which they called *timpe khanitza pachavee* or "little water bug in a stone house") as amulets against sickness and against white settlers' bullets. As one Ute told a questioner, "At least it work[ed] for a time" (Taylor and Robison 1976; Gunther and Gunther 1981; Robison and Kaesler 1987). Today, although their ability to stop bullets is questionable, trilobites remain among the most distinctive, best known, most recognizable, and most highly prized of all invertebrate fossils.

Morphology

Adult trilobites ranged from a few millimeters to 70 centimeters in length, but most were between 1 and 10 centimeters long. Like all arthropods trilobites were segmented animals, with an exoskeleton that was molted periodically over the animal's life. Most trilobite dorsal exoskeletons were highly calcified, giving them a good chance to become fossilized. The underside and the appendages, however, were not calcified, so they rarely appear in fossils (Figure 1). The term "trilobite," meaning "three-lobed," refers to the division of the trilobite thorax (midsection) into three parallel longitudinal structure: a central "axial ring," containing the gut and other organs, and two "pleural lobes," one on either side of the axial lobe. The pleural lobes were composed of "pleurae," which overlapped to form an armored layer covering over the appendages. In some species the ends of the pleurae formed long spines. This three-part division is also seen on the "cephalon," or headshield, and on a group of fused segments at the tail, called the "pygidium." After molting, trilobites left behind discarded exoskeletons, or "exuviae," that soon fell apart; as a result, complete fossils are less common—and more highly prized—than separate exoskeletal pieces (Figure 2). Very rarely, specimens may show traces of spotted or banded color patterns (Babcock 1982).

Some trilobites were blind or had highly reduced eyes, but most trilobites bore a pair of compound eyes on the cephalon. Like all arthropod compound eyes, trilobite eyes were clusters of simpler elements called "ommatidia." The outer parts of the ommatidia, the "corneal lenses," were made of transparent crystalline calcite, and are often preserved in fossils. A number of different eye constructions are known. "Holochroal" trilobite eyes had close packing of the lenses, while in "schizochroal" eyes, the lenses were separated (Figure 11). Some trilobites with schizochroal eyes had evolved doublet corneal lenses that corrected for spherical aberration; this unusual innovation enabled the animals to produce sharply focused images under water (Levi-Setti 1993).

Between the eyes lay the "glabella," a bulge that usually was divided into lobes by shallow furrows. Most trilobites bore "sutures" on the cephalon—lines of weakness, along which the cephalon split when the trilobite molted. The sutures divide the cephalon into the central portion, or "cranidium," and the "librigenae," or "free cheeks"; the position and shape of these sutures is important for identifying species. Often, spines are found at the posterior (rear) corners of the cephalon ("genal spines") and may be present elsewhere on the cephalon as well. Beneath the head, lying over the mouth like an "upper lip," was a small plate, the "hypostome."

Thanks to a few rare cases of unusually good fossil preservation (e.g., Whittington 1975; Cisne 1981; Müller and Walossek 1987), scholars know a good deal about the anatomy of the softer parts of trilobites. All trilobites whose appendages are known bore a pair of "uniramous" (single-branched) antennae on the head and a series of appendages on the head and body that were "biramous," bearing an inner branch specialized for walking and an outer, fringelike branch that functioned as a gill. Typically, four of these biramous appendages were borne on the head, behind the mouth. The functional specialization so characteristic of most living arthropods—the modification of some appendages for defense, mating, feeding, swimming, and so on, is rarely seen in trilobites. There were no specialized mouthparts, but in some trilobites the "coxae," the first joints of the legs, were large and spiny, indicating that they probably were used in processing food.

The mouth was on the ventral side (underside) of the head, and the J-shaped gut ran forward ventrally and then looped back on the dorsal (top) side. The glabella marked the position of an expanded stomach. Highly branched organs, probably digestive glands, lay under the cephalon and were connected to the stomach. The gut ran back along the central axis and ended at an anus at the end of the pygidium. Traces of the circulatory and muscular systems are also known; in general they resemble those of primitive living arthropods (Figure 1).

Major Groups of Trilobites

There continues to be debate over how trilobites should be classified. What is presented here will not find favor with all paleontologists, but is a pragmatic compromise among competing viewpoints.

Polymerida

About 95 percent of all trilobite species fall into one major group, the Polymerida (Figures 1–3, 5–10, 12–13). With a few exceptions, polymerids had five or more thoracic segments, prominent eyes, and a pygidium smaller than the cephalon (this is referred to as being "anisopygous"). A common scheme divides the Polymerida into nine suborders: Olenellida, Redlichiida, Asaphida, Proetida, Solenopleurida, Illaenida, Phacopida, Odontopleurida, and Lichida (Levi-Setti 1993) (Figure 14). The Olenellida, the dominant Lower Cambrian trilobites of North America, Argentina, and much of

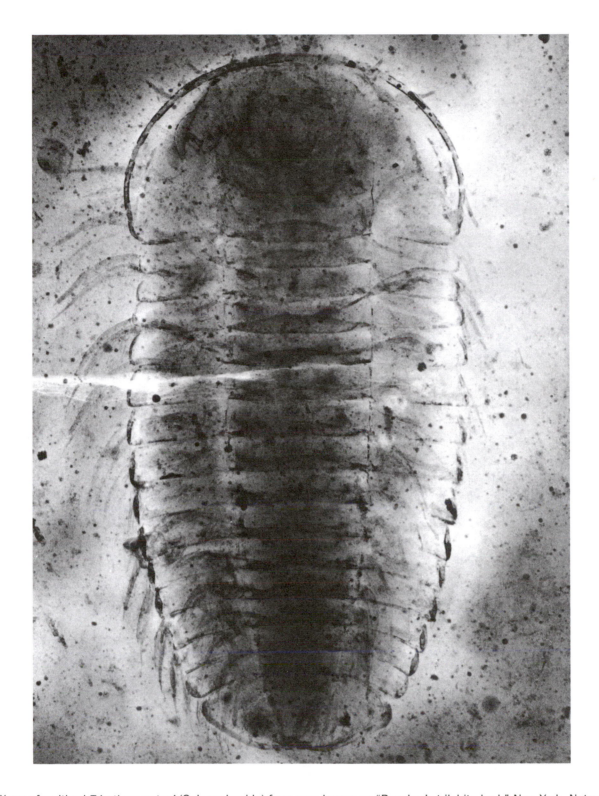

Figure 1. X ray of pyritized *Triarthrus eatoni* (Solenopleurida) from area known as "Beecher's trilobite bed," New York. Note remarkably preserved details of antennae, appendages, and gut. Scale: *bar,* one centimeter. From Cisne (1981).

Europe, differ from all other trilobites in that they lack cephalic sutures and have a tiny pygidium. On this basis, K.-E. Lauterbach (1980) placed olenellids closer to chelicerates than to the rest of the trilobites. This placement is not widely accepted now (Fortey 1990), but olenellids appear to be the most primitve trilobite group, as well as one of the earliest in time. In fact, the Polymerida may well by "paraphyletic"—the last common ancestor of all polymerids, which was also ancestral to the next group, the Agnostida.

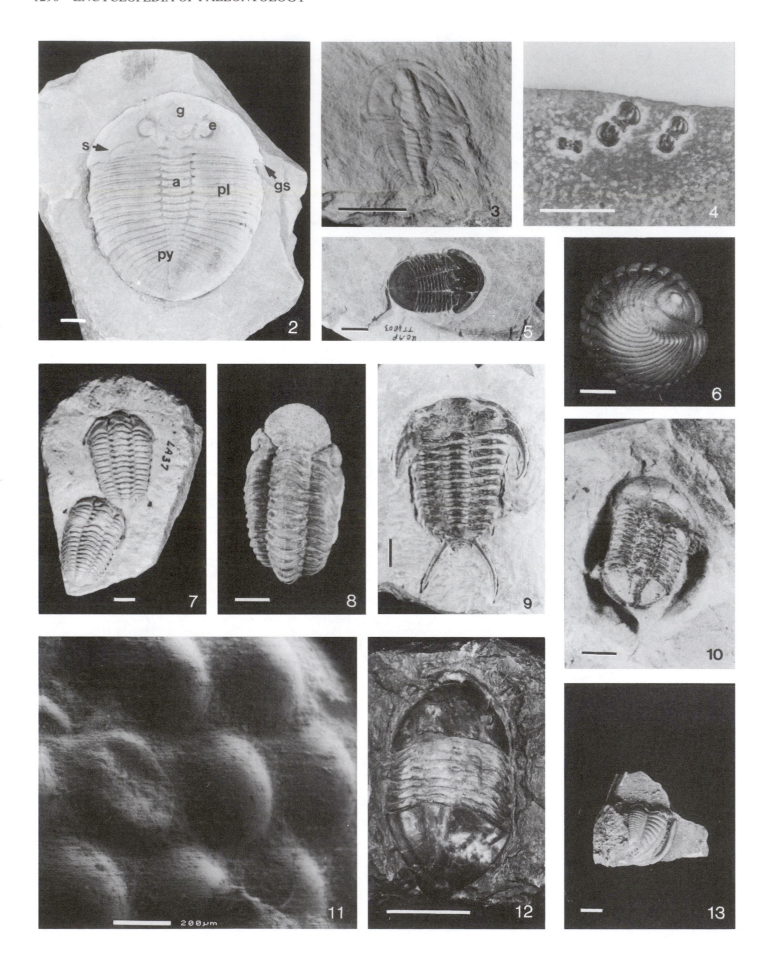

Figure 2. *Ogygiocarella debuchii* (Asaphida), with parts of exoskeleton labeled. (Middle Ordovician; Powys, Wales.) Key: *e*, eye; *g*, glabella; *py*, pygidium; *a*, axial ring; *pl*, pleurae; *s*, suture; *gs*, genal spine (not prominent in this species). Scale: *bar*, one centimeter. From University of California Museum of Paleontology collection.

Figure 3. *Nevadella* sp. (Olenellida). Note lack of cephalic sutures. (Lower Cambrian; Silver Peak Range, County, Nevada.) Scale: *bar*, one centimeter. From University of Central Arkansas collection.

Figure 4. *Peronopsis* sp. (Agnostida). (Middle Cambrian; House Range, Utah.) Scale: *bar*, one centimeter. From University of California Museum of Paleontology collection.

Figure 5. *Asaphiscus wheeleri* (Solenopleurida). Note lack of genal spines. (Middle Cambrian; House Range, Utah.) Scale: *bar*, one centimeter. From University of California Museum of Paleontology collection.

Figure 6. *Pliomera fischeri* (Phacopida), lateral view showing enrollment. (Ordovician; St. Petersburg region, Russia.) Scale: *bar*, one centimeter. From University of Central Arkansas collection.

Figure 7. Two specimens of *Calymene niagarensis* (Solenopleurida; often included in the Phacopida of the Silurian; Milwaukee, Wisconsin.) Scale: *bar*, one centimeter. From University of California Museum of Paleontology collection.

Figure 8. *Phacops rana* (Phacopida). (Devonian; Geneseo, New York.) Scale: *bar*, one centimeter. From University of California Museum of Paleontology collection.

Figure 9. *Gabriceraurus* sp. (Phacopida). Note long genal spines and pair of pygidial spines. (Middle Ordovician; Bowmanville, Ontario, Canada.) Scale: *bar*, one centimeter.

Figure 10. *Ductina vietnami* (Phacopida) showing secondary evolutionary loss of the eyes. (Devonian; Hunan, China.) Scale: *bar*, one centimeter. From University of California Museum of Paleontology collection.

Figure 11. Scanning electron micrograph (SEM) of the schizochroal compound eyes of *Reedops* sp. Each lens is circular, distinct, and separated from the others by the sclera. (Phacopida, Devonian.) Scale: *bar*, 200 millimeters. From University of California Museum of Paleontology collection.

Figure 12. *Isotelus* sp. (Asaphida). Note that the pygidium is nearly the same size as the cephalon; this trilobite is nearly isopygous. (Ordovician; Ohio.) Scale: *bar*, five centimeters. From University of California Museum of Paleontology collection.

Figure 13. The tail end of the trilobites, in more ways than one: an enrolled specimen of *Anisopyge* (Proetida), one of the last trilobites. Note the edge of the cephalon beneath the pygidium. (Middle Permian; Glass Mountains, Texas.) Scale: *bar*, one centimeter. From University of California Museum of Paleontology collection.

Agnostida

Restricted to the Cambrian and Ordovician, agnostid trilobites are unusually small, most less than 15 millimeters long (Figure 5). The cephalon and pygidium are of equal size (said to be "isopygous"), there are only two or three body segments, and the eyes and sutures are either lacking (Agnostina) or highly reduced (Eodiscacea). Agnostid appendages also differ notably from the polymerid pattern (Müller and Walossek 1987). Their anatomy is unusual enough that a few paleontologists have suggested that agnostids, or at least the eyeless Agnostina, should not be called trilobites at all (e.g., Bergström 1992). However, most paleontologists continue to group the agnostids in the Trilobita proper (e.g., Fortey and Theron 1994).

Related Taxa

The fossil *Naraoia compacta*, first described from the Burgess Shale, is the best-known member of a Cambrian taxon of trilobite-like arthropods often referred to as the Nektaspida, or sometimes as the Naraoiidae. Other species of *Naraoia* and similar genera are known from sites in Poland, the United States, South Africa, Russia, and China (e.g., Robison 1984; Fortey and Theron 1994). Nektaspids lacked thoracic segments entirely, bearing only a large, featureless cephalon and a pygidium. They lacked eyes, and their exoskeletons were not mineralized. Nevertheless, their appendages, trilobation, and internal anatomy show them to be quite close to the Trilobita (e.g., Delle Cave and Simonetta 1991). Whether the Nektaspida are "true trilobites" is largely a matter of definition; some paleontologists have placed them within the Trilobita, while others have left them out.

Various other Cambrian arthropods superficially look like trilobites, but they lack calcification as well as some of the distinctive features of trilobite anatomy. These were once grouped in the "Trilobitoidea," which is now considered a "wastebasket" of unusual forms. Some "trilobitoids," however, are still probably closer to trilobites than to any other major arthropod group. These include Burgess Shale taxa such as *Habelia*, *Tegopelte*, and *Helmetia* (Delle Cave and Simonetta 1991; Briggs et al. 1994), as well as some recently described Early Cambrian Chinese forms

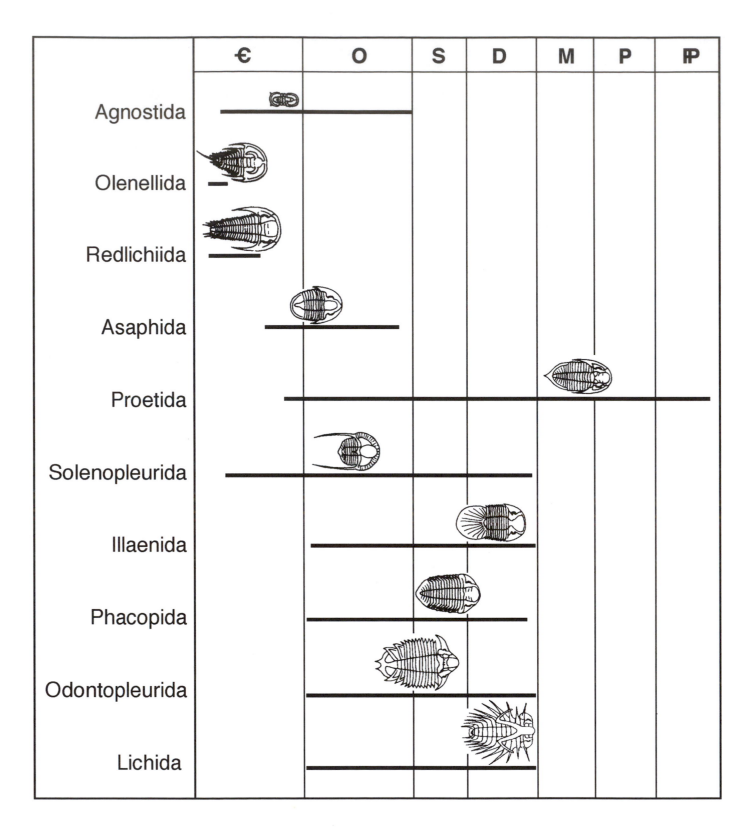

Figure 14. Chart of the time ranges of the trilobite taxa discussed in this article, with drawings of representatives of each taxon. Modified from Clarkson (1986) and Levi-Setti (1993).

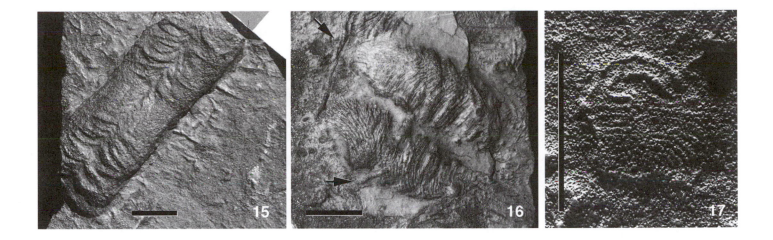

Figure 15. *Cruziana*, a trail left by an unknown trilobite. (Lower Cambrian; White-Inyo Mountains, California.) Scale: *bar*, one centimeter. Photo courtesy of James W. Hagadorn.

Figure 16. *Rusophycus*, a fossil trilobite burrow. Note its proximity to fossil worm burrows *(arrows)*, whose makers the trilobite may have been hunting. (Lower Cambrian; White-Inyo Mountains, California.) Scale: *bar*, one centimeter. Photo courtesy of James W. Hagadorn.

Figure 17. An as yet unnamed fossil resembling an unmineralized trilobite. (Late Precambrian; Ediacara Hills, Australia.) Scale: *bar*, one centimeter. Photo courtesy of James Gehling.

such as *Xandarella, Cindarella,* and *Saperion* (Hou and Bergström 1991; Hou et al. 1991; Ramsköld et al. 1997; Edgecombe 1997), and an unusual north Greenland form, *Kleptothule* (Budd 1995). The relationships and higher taxonomy of these arthropods have not been settled, but the informal taxon "Trilobitomorpha" has been proposed to incorporate true trilobites plus all non-trilobite relatives. Within the arthropods, the chelicerates are the closest living group to the trilobites; "Arachnomorpha" and "Arachnata" are proposed names for a taxon excluding crustaceans and including all trilobites, all chelicerates, and their relatives (Wills et al. 1994).

Paleoecology
Growth and Development
The life cycles are known for a number of trilobite species. Possible trilobite embryos have been found in Middle Cambrian rocks of south China (Zhang and Pratt 1994). However, the earliest stage with a calcified exoskeleton was the "protaspid" larva, whose exoskeleton consisted of only a single dorsal plate. The "meraspid" juvenile developed a separate cephalon and pygidium, and as the meraspid molted, thoracic segments appeared. Some trilobites, but not all, changed their form dramatically between the protaspid and meraspid stages, probably indicating an ecological shift from a free-floating lifestyle (planktonic) to one lived on the ocean bottom (benthic) (Speyer and Chatterton 1990). Eventually, the number of thoracic segments stabilized, marking the "holaspid," or adult, phase; a few trilobites, however, continued to add segments throughout adult life.

There are instances in the fossil record in which great swarms belonging to a single trilobite species all are preserved together on one bedding plane; some of these may have been mating swarms, not unlike the seasonal swarms of horseshoe crabs. Trilobites lacked specialized copulatory organs; they probably shed their eggs and sperm freely into the water.

Lifestyles
Most polymerid trilobites were benthic; their walking trails and burrows have been preserved as trace fossils (Figures 16, 17). Some, however, were probably nektonic. Agnostids have often been considered planktonic (free-swimming); this fact is supported by the fact that many species are distributed worldwide in deep-water sediments, as might be expected for organisms living in the open ocean. However, K.J. Müller and D. Walossek (1987) reconstructed the agnostid *Agnostus pisiformis* as nekto-benthic, living in a flocculent zone just above the sediment surface.

Some trilobites bore unusually large, spiny gnathobases and were probably predators. In fact, trace fossils have been found that show trilobite trails intercepting worm burrows, recording the moment of prey capture (Jensen 1990) (Figure 16). However, many trilobites probably scavenged or fed on small particles. Trilobites were also prey for other organisms. Throughout their time range, trilobites have been found with bites taken out of the pleurae by unknown predators (e.g., Babcock 1993). The post-Cambrian declines in trilobite abundance and diversity may have been related to the rise of predators at about the same time, notably eurypterids (large chelicerntes), large cephalopods (e.g., ammonoids, nautiloids squid and octopuses), and later, jawed fishes. Many trilobites could roll up as a defensive maneuver (e.g.,

Figures 6, 13), and some were armored with spines that may have been useful in defense.

Fossil History and Localities

A few arthropod-like fossils have been found in the Vendian (latest Precambrian) that had an unmineralized exoskeleton but showed a crescent-shaped head and segmented body. These are not true trilobites, but they may represent early lineages of trilobite relatives (Waggoner 1996). Recently, a very trilobite-like fossil, still not formally described, has been reported from the Precambrian rocks of the Ediacara Hills, southern Australia (Gehling 1991; Jenkins 1992) (Figure 17).

True trilobites first appear in the Atdabanian stage of the Lower Cambrian; they then rapidly diversified all through the Cambrian. Cambrian trilobites are abundant at certain sites in the western United States, such as the Early Cambrian Latham Shale at Cadiz, California (e.g., Mount 1980), and Middle Cambrian sites in Utah, near the towns of Logan and Delta (e.g., Gunther and Gunther 1981). The Burgess Shale has 19 species of trilobite, including three whose appendages have been preserved, as well as *Naraoia* and other "trilobitomorph" arthropods (Briggs et al. 1994). The Upper Cambrian orsten limestone of southern Sweden has yielded millimeter-sized juveniles of the agnostid *Agnostus pisiformis,* with their undersides and appendages preserved by replacement with phosphate (Müller and Walossek 1987). By the end of the Cambrian, trilobites were as diverse as they ever would be: there were well over 300 genera.

Proetids, phacopids, and lichids first appeared in the Ordovician. However, the Olenellida and Redlichiida disappeared at the end of the Cambrian, and trilobite species diversity began dropping in the Ordovician. Famous Ordovician sites include "Beecher's Trilobite Bed" near Rome, New York, where specimens of *Triarthrus eatoni* have been replaced by pyrite (Beecher 1893). The pyrite preserves details of the internal organs and appendages, and since it is opaque to X rays, internal detail can be studied by X-raying the fossils (Cisne 1981) (Figure 1).

There was a modest resurgence of trilobite diversity in the Silurian and Devonian. Several Silurian and Devonian sites in New York, Ohio, and Oklahoma are well known for magnificent trilobite specimens. The Hunsrück Slate from the Devonian of Germany also preserves complete trilobites. Like those from "Beecher's Trilobite Bed," these specimens are pyritized, and their anatomy can be studied by using X rays (Levi-Setti 1993). Only a few families survived past the Devonian, all members of one order (Proetida) and most restricted to reef habitats. The last trilobites died out in the Late Permian (but before the very end of the Permian), when reef ecosystems in general were hit hard. Permian rocks of Thailand and west Texas are among the places where these last trilobites have been found (Brezinski 1992) (Figure 13).

History of Trilobite Paleontology

It would be impossible to list every paleontologist who has contributed to our knowledge of trilobites; only a few can even be mentioned here. Aside from the animal's appearance in archaeol-

ogy and folk tradition, Western scientists, beginning with the Welsh naturalist Edward Lhwyd in 1698, variously classified trilobites as vertebrates, worms, or molluscs. C. Linnaeus was among the first to classify the trilobites with the rest of the arthropods, grouping several species under the name *Entomolithus paradoxus,* "paradoxical stone insect"—or should it be translated "little water bug in stone house" (Harrington et al. 1959; St. John 1997)?

The French expatriate Joachim Barrande was the first to describe trilobite larvae, in 1852; he also published extensively on Silurian trilobites and other fossils from around his adopted hometown of Prague (Harrington et al. 1959). Before 1870, trilobite appendages were unknown, and the affinities of trilobites within the Arthropoda were very uncertain. In 1876, American paleontologist Charles Walcott first published observations on trilobite appendages, and went on to show that trilobites could not be true crustaceans, and must represent a separate class of arthropods (Walcott 1918). Walcott also studied Cambrian trilobites extensively. His contemporary Charles Beecher also studied trilobite appendages and anatomy and worked on their larval development (e.g., Beecher 1893, 1902). Contemporary experts on trilobites and their kin include Euan Clarkson, Richard Fortey, and Harry Whittington in Great Britain; Brian D.E. Chatterton, Rolf Ludvigsen, and Brian Pratt in Canada; Loren Babcock, Niles Eldredge, Nigel Hughes, Riccardo Levi-Setti, Bruce Liebermann, and Alison R. "Pete" Palmer in the United States; Gregory Edgecombe in Australia; David Bruton in Norway; Jan Bergström and Lars Ramsköld in Sweden; Andrei Ivantsov and Lada Repina in Russia; and Hou Xianguang and Zhou Zhiyi in China.

BEN WAGGONER

Works Cited

Babcock, L.E. 1982. Original and diagenetic color patterns in two phacopid trilobites from the Devonian of New York. *Third North American Paleontological Convention, Proceedings* 1:17–22.

———. 1993. Trilobite malformations and the record of behavioral asymmetry. *Journal of Paleontology* 67:217–29.

Beecher, C.E. 1893. On the thoracic legs of Triarthrus. *American Journal of Science,* 3rd ser., 46:467–70.

———. 1902. The ventral integument of trilobites. *American Journal of Science,* 4th ser., 13:165–74.

Bergström, J. 1992. The oldest arthropods and the origin of the Crustacea. *Acta Zoologica* 73:287–91.

Brezinski, D.K. 1992. Permian trilobites from west Texas. *Journal of Paleontology* 66:924–43.

Briggs, D.E.G., D.H. Erwin, and F.J. Collier. 1994. *The Fossils of the Burgess Shale.* Washington, D.C.: Smithsonian Institution.

Budd, G.E. 1995. *Kleptothule rasmusseni* gen. et sp. nov.: An ?olenellinid-like trilobite from the Sirius Passet fauna (Buen Formation, Lower Cambrian, North Greenland). *Transactions of the Royal Society of Edinburgh: Earth Sciences:* 1–12.

Cisne, J.L. 1981. *Triarthrus eatoni* (Trilobita): Anatomy of its exoskeletal, skeletomuscular, and digestive systems. *Palaeontographica Americana* 9 (53):99–140.

Clarkson, E.N.K. 1986. *Invertebrate Palaeontology and Evolution.* 2nd ed., London and Boston: Allen and Unwin.

Delle Cave, L., and A.M. Simonetta. 1991. Early Palaeozoic arthropods and problems of arthropod phylogeny; with some notes on taxa of doubtful affinities. *In* A.M. Simonetta and S. Conway Morris (eds.), *The Early Evolution of Metazoa and the Significance of Problematic Taxa.* Cambridge and New York: Cambridge University Press.

Edgecombe, G.D. 1997. Phylogenetic relationships of trilobite-allied Arachnata. Second International Trilobite Conference, St. Catharines, Ontario, Canada.

Fortey, R.A. 1990. Trilobite evolution and systematics. *In* D.G. Mikulic (ed.), *Arthropod Paleobiology. Paleontological Society Short Courses in Paleontology* 3:44–65.

Fortey, R.A., and J.N. Theron. 1994. A new Ordovician arthropod, *Soomaspis*, and the agnostid problem. *Palaeontology* 37:841–61.

Gehling, J.G. 1991. The case for Ediacaran fossil roots to the metazoan tree. *Memoirs of the Geological Society of India* 20:181–223.

Gunther, L.F., and V.D. Gunther. 1981. Some Middle Cambrian fossils of Utah. *Brigham Young University Geology Studies* 28 (1):1–87.

Harrington, H.J., G. Hennigsmoen, B.F. Howell, V. Jaanuson, C. Lochman-Balk, R.C. Moore, C. Poulsen, F. Rasetti, E. Richter, R. Richter, H. Schmidt, K. Sdzuy, W. Struve, L. Størmer, C.J. Stubblefield, R. Tripp, J.M. Weller, and H.B. Whittington. 1959. *Treatise on Invertebrate Paleontology.* Part O, Volume 1, *Arthropoda.* Boulder, Colorado: Geological Society of America; Lawrence: University of Kansas Press.

Hou, X., and J. Bergström. 1991. The arthropods of the Lower Cambrian Chengjiang fauna, with relationships and evolutionary significance. *In* A.M. Simonetta and S. Conway Morris (eds.), *The Early Evolution of Metazoa and the Significance of Problematic Taxa.* Cambridge and New York: Cambridge University Press.

Hou X., L. Ramsköld, and J. Bergström. 1991. Composition and preservation of the Chengjiang fauna—a Lower Cambrian soft-bodied biota. *Zoological Scripta* 20:395–411.

Jenkins, R.J.F. 1992. Functional and ecological aspects of Ediacarian assemblages. *In* J.H. Lipps and P.W. Signor (eds.), *Origin and Early Evolution of the Metazoa.* New York: Plenum.

Jensen, S. 1990. Predation by Early Cambrian trilobites on infaunal worms: Evidence from the Swedish Mickwitzia Sandstone. *Lethaia* 23:29–42.

Lauterbach, K.-E. 1980. Schlüsselereignisse in der Evolution des Grundplans der Arachnata (Arthropoda). *Abhandlungen des Naturwissenschaftlichen Vereins in Hamburg* 23:163–327.

Levi-Setti, R. 1993. *Trilobites.* 2nd ed. Chicago: University of Chicago Press.

Mount, J.D. 1980. Characteristics of Early Cambrian faunas from eastern San Bernardino County, California. *Southern California Paleontological Society, Special Publication* 2:19–29.

Müller, K.J., and D. Walossek. 1987. Morphology, ontogeny, and life habit of *Agnostus pisiformis* from the Upper Cambrian of Sweden. *Fossils and Strata* 19:1–124.

Ramsköld, L., J. Chen, G.D. Edgecombe, and G. Zhou. 1997. *Cindarella* and the arachnate clade Xandarellida (Arthropoda, Early Cambrian) from China. *Transactions of the Royal Society of Edinburgh: Earth Sciences* 88:19–38.

Robison, R.A. 1984. New occurrences of the unusual trilobite *Naraoia* from the Cambrian of Idaho and Utah. *University of Kansas Paleontological Contributions* 112:1–8.

Robison, R.A., and R.B. Kaesler. 1987. Phylum Arthropoda. *In* R.S. Boardman, A.H. Cheetham, and A.J. Rowell (eds.), *Fossil Invertebrates.* Palo Alto, California: Blackwell Scientific.

Speyer, S.E., and B.D.E. Chatterton. 1990. Trilobite larvae, larval ecology and developmental paleobiology. *In* D.G. Mikulic (ed.), *Arthropod Paleobiology. Paleontological Society Short Courses in Paleontology* 3:137–56.

St. John, J. 1997. Understanding the search for affinities: The history of research on trilobites from antiquity to the 1820s. Second International Trilobite Conference, St. Catharines, Ontario, Canada.

Taylor, M.E., and R.A. Robison. 1976. Trilobites in Utah folklore. *Brigham Young University Research Studies,* Geological Ser. 23 (2):1–6.

Waggoner, B.M. 1996. Phylogenetic hypotheses of the relationships of arthropods to problematic Vendian and Cambrian organisms. *Systematic Biology* 42:190–223.

Walcott, C.D. 1918. Appendages of trilobites. Cambrian Geology and Palaeontology, 4. *Smithsonian Miscellaneous Collections* 67:115–216.

Whittington, H.B. 1975. Trilobites with appendages from the Middle Cambrian, Burgess Shale, British Columbia. *Fossils and Strata* 4:97–136.

Wills, M.A., D.E.G. Briggs, and R.A. Fortey. 1994. Disparity as an evolutionary index: A comparison of Cambrian and Recent arthropods. *Paleobiology* 20:93–130.

Zhang, X.-G., and B.R. Pratt. 1994. Middle Cambrian arthropod embryos with blastomeres. *Science* 266:637–39.

Further Reading

Harrington, H.J., G. Hennigsmoen, B.F. Howell, V. Jaanuson, C. Lochman-Balk, R.C. Moore, C. Poulsen, F. Rasetti, E. Richter, R. Richter, H. Schmidt, K. Sdzuy, W. Struve, L. Størmer, C.J. Stubblefield, R. Tripp, J.M. Weller, and H.B. Whittington. 1959. *Treatise on Invertebrate Paleontology.* Part O, Volume 1, *Arthropoda.* Boulder, Colorado: Geological Society of America; Lawrence: University of Kansas Press.

Kaesler, R. (ed.). 1997. *Treatise on Invertebrate Paleontology.* Part O, Volume 1, *Revised: Trilobita.* Boulder, Colerado: Geological Society of America; Lawrence: University of Kansas Press.

Levi-Setti, R. 1975. *Trilobites: A Photographic Atlas.* Chicago: University of Chicago Press; 2nd ed., 1993.

TROPHIC GROUPS AND LEVELS

Trophic groups (Greek, *trophe,* food, nourishment) refers to the organization of ecosystems based upon the feeding relationships of organisms in food chains, webs, or pyramids—this perspective categorizes according to what organisms eat, and how they go about it.

This applies to terrestrial (land-based) food chains as well as marine. At the most basic level, all living organisms can be divided into two trophic categories. "Autotrophs" (or producers) are those that convert elements or compounds into organic matter using solar (photoautotrophic) or chemical (chemoautotrophic) energy; examples are cyanobacteria, algae, and vascular plants. "Heterotrophs" (or consumers) are those that live on pre-existing organic matter; this group includes most animals. Some consumers may be partial heterotrophs—organisms that supplement their energy by living symbiotically with autotrophs. (The fungi that is joined with an alga to form the organism called "lichen" is one example.) This role has been suggested for one of the earliest animal communities, the soft or firm-bodied Ediacaran or Vendian fauna of the latest Precambrian (approximately 570 to 544 million years ago), and for organisms that live in cold or hot vent communities of the deep sea.

To bundle all consumers into one bag does little to explain the resourcefulness of organisms trying to find a meal. Therefore, consumers have commonly been subdivided into smaller units that identify how and what they eat. To do this, scholars divide consumers into trophic groups by feeding techniques. For example, in marine environments, "filter feeders" are those that selectively filter their food from the water mass (e.g., sponges). "Suspension feeders" are those that capture their food from the water mass above (e.g., brachiopods, some molluscs). This group may be divided further according to the tools they use to capture food (e.g., lophophorate, ciliate, tentaculate; some scholars argue that suspension feeding includes filterers). "Diffusion feeders" take up nutrients through their cell wall membranes (e.g., perhaps the vendoblont). "Grazers-browsers" move along the bottom digesting biofilms, microbial mats, or plants (e.g., some snails); "deposit feeders" swallow sediment to extract nutrients (e.g., some arthropods). "Predators" make an active search for live prey, and "scavengers" are those seeking usually dead or decomposing matter. Many organisms may use more than one feeding method for survival, switching daily, seasonally, or through their life cycle (adopting one mode when immature—as larvae—and another as adults).

Another overlapping or interchangeable way of grouping is sorting organisms by food type: "Planktivores" are those that seek out floating microorganisms (zoo- or phytoplankton), "detritivores" are those that seek out organic detritus (dead plant or animal material) from sediment or the water mass (includes deposit feeders), "herbivores" seek out plant matter or microbial mats, "carnivores" require animal prey, and "omnivores" are those that live on mixed diets. "Planktotrophic larvae" are those that feed on plankton or organic detritus in suspension; "lecthotrophic larvae" are those using an egg yolk (Greek, *lecythus*, flask) for their planktic life stage, and thus need not rely on plankton at the time. These two feeding styles of larvae separate major groups of organisms and their food source, perhaps making each group differentially vulnerable to mass extinction episodes or serious shifts in the global environment. It has been suggested that detritus feeding may have given organisms a better chance of survival following mass extinctions, when large amounts of dead detritus was available, and the ecosystem had not yet restructured its food chains. Thus, trophic structure has evolutionary and extinction implications.

"Trophic levels" normally refers to the biological level at which organisms feed in food chains or food webs. This usually is visualized best by looking at a food pyramid, with the autotroph producers at the base forming quantitatively (either by weight or volume) the largest biomass, and successive, smaller consumer levels above this feeding on the layers below. For example, herbivores (first level consumers) are preyed upon by carnivores (second level consumers) at higher levels. The size of each level (the number of individuals and their aggregated mass) is usually less than 10 percent of the level below it, so trophic levels are a broad, idealized reflection of the transfer and loss of energy and efficiency in the ecosystem. Organisms can shortcut this system in the pyramid by skipping a level, something some giant whales have done by strainer feeding on zooplankton or humans by converting to vegetarian diets.

Some scholars also have used trophic levels as a means of denoting the level above the seafloor at which organisms feed—low-level suspension feeders being those that feed in the lowest 5 centimeters of watermass above the seafloor, intermediate level at 5 to 25 centimeters, and high level those obtaining their nutrients at above 25 centimeters. However, these physical levels of feeding are now usually referred to as trophic tiering—the tiers above the seafloor at which nutrition is obtained.

PAUL COPPER

See also Biomass and Productivity Estimates; Feeding Adaptations: Invertebrates; Paleoecology; Population Dynamics; Predation

Further Reading

Little, C. 1990. *The Terrestrial Invasion*. Cambridge and New York: Cambridge University Press.

McCall, P.L., and M.J.S. Tevesz (eds.). 1982. *Animal-Sediment Relations*. New York: Plenum.

Panchen, A.L. 1980. *The Terrestrial Environment and the Origin of Land Vertebrates*. Systematics Association Special Volume 15. London and New York: Academic Press.

Tevesz, M.J.S., and P.L. McCall (eds.). 1983. *Biotic Interactions in Recent and Fossil Communities*. New York: Plenum.

Valentine, J.W. (ed.). 1985. *Phanerozoic Diversity Patterns*. Princeton, New Jersey: Princeton University Press; San Francisco: American Association for the Advancement of Science.

TUBULIDENTATES
See Aardvarks

TURTLES

Turtles (Testudines or Chelonia) are among the most distinct vertebrates. They are the last group of anapsid-grade reptiles to appear in the fossil record and have survived largely unchanged since the Late Triassic. Their unique armored body plan almost certainly contributed to this success: turtles differ from all other tetrapods in exhibiting striking morphological specializations that involve not just the shell, but also associated modifications of the vertebrae, limbs, and skull.

The turtle shell (Figure 1) is a boxlike structure consisting of a dorsal carapace (back shield) and a ventral plastron (belly shield), joined laterally by the "bridge." It is open anteriorly (at the front) for the head and forelimbs and posteriorly (at the back) for the tail and hind limbs. The shell is unique among tetrapods in incorporating both dermal armor and internal skeletal elements. It is covered by large keratinous (horny) scutes. These usually do not fossilize, but their boundaries are usually visible as grooves on the external bony surface. The junctions between the bony elements, and between the scutes, alternate rather than coincide, resulting in added strength. The shell is secondarily reduced in certain forms, especially aquatic taxa such as sea turtles and soft-shell turtles.

The carapace is domed and incorporates dermal armor, vertebrae, and ribs. There is a median row of neural plates, fused to the underlying vertebrae. In front of the neurals, there is a nuchal plate (just behind the head), and behind, one or more pygal plates (just in front of the tail). The nuchal and pygal are not fused to vertebrae. From each median plate, a pair of long costal plates extends laterally, each fused to the underlying rib. The edges of the carapace are formed by the marginal plates, which are not associated with any internal skeletal elements.

The plastron is flat and incorporates dermal armor and elements from the shoulder girdle. Anteriorly, there are a pair of epiplastra and a median entoplastron, representing modified clavicles and interclavicles respectively. The rest of the plastron consists solely of dermal armor; typically, there are three pairs of large plates (hyoplastra, hypoplastra, and xiphiplastra).

The vertebral column in turtles is highly modified. There are eight cervical (neck) vertebrae, ten dorsal (back) vertebrae, and usually fewer than 30 tail (caudal) vertebrae. Typical primitive reptiles have approximately five cervicals, 20 dorsals, and more than 40 caudals. Thus, in turtles, the neck is lengthened, resulting in greater mobility of the head, while the body and tail are shortened to fit within the confines of the shell. The dorsal vertebrae and ribs of turtles are immobile, being completely fused to the inside of the carapace.

The limb girdles of turtles are unique in lying within (rather than outside) the ribcage, inside the protective shell. The shoulder girdle is triradiate (having three prongs), the dorsal prong (the scapula blade) contacts the carapace, the anteroventral prong (the acromion process) contacts the plastron, and the posterior prong (coracoid) projects freely. The pelvic girdle is also triradiate; the ilium projects dorsally to contact the sacral ribs, while the pubis

and ischium project ventrally. In all pleurodires and some other primitive turtles, the three prongs of the pelvis are fused immovably to the shell. The limbs project horizontally through the anterior and posterior shell openings, resulting in a low, sprawling stance and broad trackway. The digits are short; there are usually fewer than three phalanges in each digit. The movements of the limbs are constrained by the limits of the shell openings, and stride length is consequently short. Except in marine turtles, the limbs can be retracted into the shell.

The skull of turtles is also highly modified and very different from that of other anapsid-grade reptiles. All teeth on the jaw margins are lost and replaced by keratinous beaks (rhamphothecae). However, some primitive turtles retain small teeth on the palate. The orbits (eye openings) are positioned anteriorly, resulting in a short facial region and a long cheek region. The embayment (notch) for the eardrum is very deep. Turtles have lost the pineal foramen and several skull bones found in other primitive reptiles (tabular, postparietal, postfrontal, septomaxilla). In all primitive turtles, the cheeks are solid walls. However, extensive emarginations (scooped-out areas) along the posterior and ventral cheek margins have evolved within pleurodires and within cryptodires.

Turtles are so different from all other amniotes (animals that lay shelled eggs) that their origins and affinities have long been problematical. Most recent studies have placed them within a group of mainly Paleozoic reptiles called "parareptiles" (Laurin and Reisz 1995). Within parareptiles, the large herbivorous pareiasaurs appear to be the nearest relatives, if not the actual ancestors, of turtles (Lee 1996). Nevertheless, there remains a substantial stratigraphic gap between the last pareiasaurs (Upper Permian) and the earliest turtles (Late Triassic). This gap is even more puzzling because turtles have an otherwise excellent fossil record. Their tough shells fossilize readily and are easily identifiable even from fragmentary remains. O. Rieppel and M. deBraga (1996), however, have recently suggested that turtles have affinities with advanced diapsids. If true, this would explain why turtles do not appear until the Late Triassic.

The relationships between the major groups of turtles, and derived features supporting this arrangement, are shown in Figure 2. The most primitive turtles are *Proganochelys* from the Upper Triassic, and the australochelids, from the Upper Triassic and Lower Jurassic (Gaffney 1990; Rougier et al. 1995; Figure 3A). They are large, terrestrial herbivores with robust legs and extremely short digits. They are superficially similar to large modern land tortoises but could not retract their heads into the shell. Instead, the vulnerable neck region was protected by loose armor plates in *Proganochelys* and by an anterior expansion of the carapace in australochelids (Rougier et al. 1995). Both groups are more primitive than all other turtles ("casichelydians") in retaining several features found in their parareptilian ancestors: lacrimal and supratemporal bones in the skull, a median opening in the roof of the mouth (interpterygoid vacuity), separate rather than fused external nostril openings, and a very weakly developed acromion

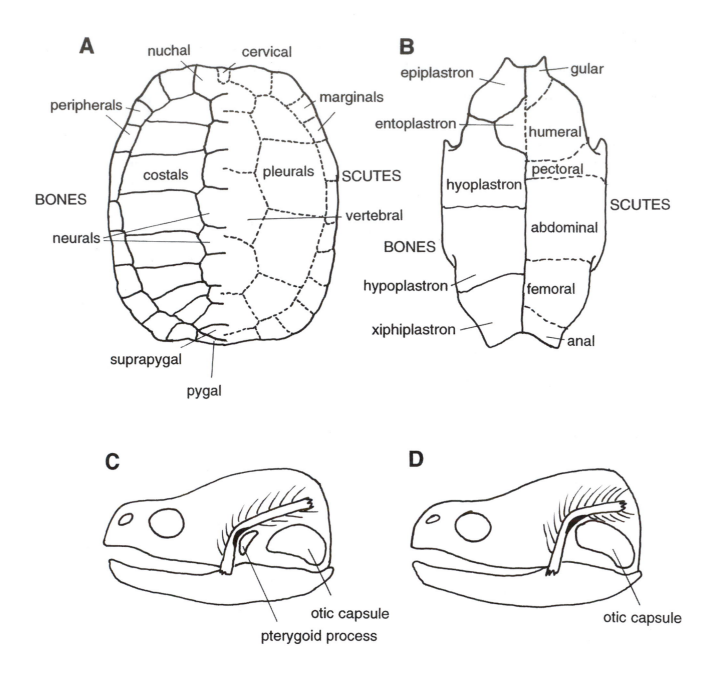

Figure 1. Turtle shell in (A) dorsal and (B) ventral view. The boundaries between different bones are shown in solid lines, boundaries between the overlying keratinous scutes are shown in dotted lines. Bones are labeled on the left of each view, scutes are labeled on the right. The trochlear (pulley) system for the jaw adductor muscles in (C) a pleurodire, and (D) a cryptodire.

process on the shoulder girdle. The remaining turtles (which include all living forms) have the advanced condition in all these features, and fall into two large groups, pleurodires and cryptodires (Figure 2).

Advanced pleurodires retract their heads by lateral bending of the neck. They also have a unique arrangement of jaw muscles, where the main jaw-closing muscle (adductor mandibulae) passes over a trochlea (pulleylike structure) formed by the pterygoid, a bone in the roof of the mouth (Gaffney 1975; Figure 1C). These traits have not been confirmed in the primitive "pleurodires" *Platy-*

chelys and *Notoemys*, but other features of the shell unite these forms with true pleurodires. Scholars previously believed fusion of the pelvis with the shell to be unique to and diagnostic of pleurodires; however, recent work suggests that this feature might be more widespread (Rougier et al. 1995). The Late Triassic *Proterochersis*, known only from shell remains, was formerly assigned to the Pleurodira based on this dubious character. This leaves the Late Jurassic *Platychelys* and *Notoemys* as the earliest undoubted pleurodires. Apart from these poorly known genera, all other pleurodires fall into two families with living representatives: pelomedusids and chelids (Figure 3B). Both families are now restricted to freshwater habitats of the southern hemisphere. All living representatives are "terrapin-like" in general morphology (form and structure). However, pelomedusids had a cosmopolitan (worldwide) distribution during the Late Cretaceous and Early Tertiary and included forms with high-domed shells suggesting terrestrial habits.

Advanced cryptodires (but not primitive forms) retract their heads by folding the neck in the vertical plane. Like pleurodires, the jaw muscles pass over a trochlea: however, in all cryptodires this is formed by a lateral expansion of the otic capsule, part of the braincase (Gaffney 1975; Figure 1D). The earliest and most primitive cryptodire is the Lower Jurassic *Kayentachelys,* which, based on the flattened streamlined shell, is the oldest known highly aquatic turtle (Gaffney et al. 1987). The baenids are another primitive cryptodire group (Brinkman and Nicholls 1991). These generalized turtles are abundant from the Late Cretaceous to the Late Eocene and can be recognized by the unique shape of the cutting surface of the upper jaw: narrow anteriorly and broad posteriorly (Gaffney and Meylan 1988). Meiolaniids, known from the Early Tertiary to the Pleistocene, are large terrestrial forms, with highly domed shells, stubby toes, and wide, horned skulls up to 50 centimeters across. Many characters suggest that they, too, are primitive cryptodires (Figure 2). However, they retain some surprisingly primitive features that raise the possibility that, despite their late occurrence, meiolaniids are actually a much more primitive group of turtles than currently thought. Like *Proganochelys,* meiolaniids have an opening in the palate (interpterygoid vacuity), ribs in the neck region, dermal armor covering the tail, and a tail club.

All these archaic "cryptodire" groups lack the diagnostic neck modifications found in "true" cryptodires (including all living forms) and presumably could not retract the head into the shell. However, they can be allied with "true" cryptodires on the basis of possession of the pulleylike specialization of the braincase.

All other cryptodires are united by the common possession of the vertical neck joint. They fall into four major groups, all with living representatives: chelydrids, chelonioids, trionychoids, and testudinoids. Chelydrids (snapping turtles) are first known from the Late Cretaceous and are primarily sedentary freshwater ambush predators. The chelonioids (sea turtles) are known from the early Cretaceous onward, but were most diverse during Late Cretaceous. They are all specialized marine forms characterized by limbs modified into flippers (Figure 3C). The forelimbs are enlarged and used in underwater flight. Unlike typical turtles, they rely partly on speed to escape predators. Accordingly, they have lost the ability to retract the skull and limbs, and reduced the shell. Large holes (fontanelles) are present near the shell margin in all species. The buoyancy afforded by water has allowed some sea turtles to reach gigantic proportions. The living leatherback turtle (*Dermochelys*) and the related Cretaceous forms *Protostega* and *Archelon* reach nearly four meters in length and are the largest known turtles (Zangerl 1953).

The trionychoids (Late Cretaceous onward) are unusual in that the last dorsal vertebra is not fused to the shell (Meylan 1987). They include the living soft-shelled turtles (Figure 3D), which are highly aquatic, predatory freshwater forms. These are fast swimmers and rely primarily on speed to escape predators; the

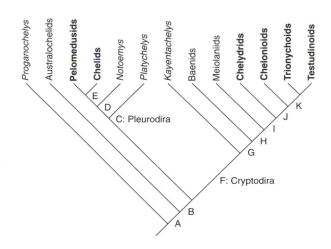

Figure 2. Phylogenetic relationships of the major groups of turtles; groups with living representatives are shown in **bold.** Some derived characters diagnosing the indicated clades are as follows: A, loss of teeth on palatine and vomer, slender hearing ossicle (stapes), braincase strongly fused to cheek elements (squamosal and quadrate); B, loss of lacrimal and supratemporal bones in the skull, closure of interpterygoid vacuity in the palate, fusion of external nostril openings, acromion process on the shoulder girdle extended as a long rod; C, mesoplastra not united along midline; D, loss of supramarginal scutes, first pair of thoracic ribs reduced; E, pterygoid forms trochlear (pulley) for jaw muscles, horizontal flexion of neck (both not yet known in *Platychelys* and *Notoemys*), mesoplastra missing or equidimensional; F, trochlear process (pulley) for jaw muscles formed by braincase, prefrontal (on skull roof) contacts vomer (on palate); G, posterior emargination of cheek separates parietal and squamosal bones; H, posterior position of the *foramen posterius canalis carotici interni* (Gaffney and Meylan 1988); I, vertical ("cryptodire") neck joint; J, tails with reduced haemal spines; K, postorbital and squamosal bones on skull roof do not meet.

shell is thus reduced and highly streamlined, being very flat and covered in smooth skin.

The testudinoids (Late Cretaceous onward) are a highly diverse group that includes most remaining living turtles, including familiar forms such as the semiaquatic freshwater terrapins (e.g., *Emys, Chrysemys*) and the highly terrestrial land tortoises with robust, highly domed shells (e.g., *Testudo, Terrapene, Geochelone;* Figure 3E). Testudinoids are united mainly by specializations of the shell (Gaffney and Meylan 1988).

Since their appearance in the late Triassic, turtles have diversified steadily until the present. The early groups with non-retractile heads ("amphichelydians") are all now extinct and have been replaced by pleurodires and cryptodires. The increasing representation of the latter groups in the turtle fauna has been attributed to a design superiority. Amphichelydians were unable to retract their heads and were more vulnerable to predators. M.L. Rosenzweig and R.D. McCord (1991) noted five independent instances where amphichelydians were replaced by turtles with retractile heads. They noted that replacement was not gradual—

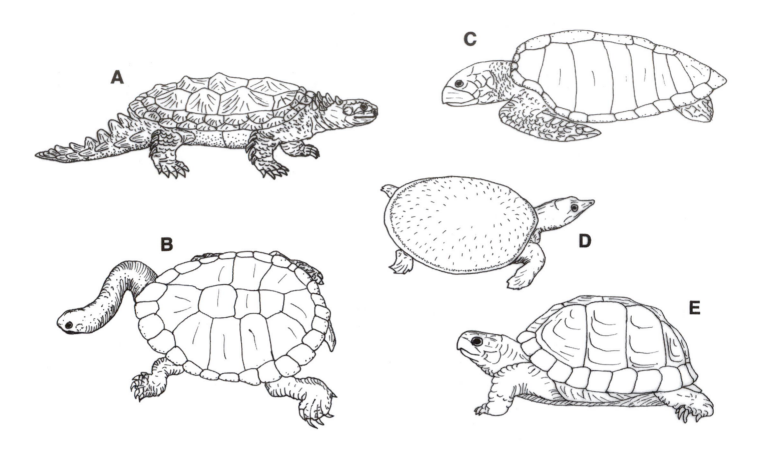

Figure 3. Representative turtles. *A, Proganochelys,* a primitive Triassic form; *B, Chelodina,* a living chelid; *C, Caretta,* a living chelonoid; *D, Trionyx,* a living trionychoid; *E, Terrapene,* a living testudinoid.

rather, it was accelerated during times of mass extinction—and developed a model to explain this. During times of normal (low) extinction rates, the design superiority of pleurodires and cryptodires could not usually be exploited. Incumbent amphichelydian turtles were adapted to their niches by "fine scale local adaptations." Pleurodires and cryptodires, despite their superiority in neck design, occupied other habitats and lacked these adaptations. Thus they could not displace the incumbent amphichelydians from these niches. However, after mass extinctions eliminated these amphichelydians, other amphichelydians, along with pleurodires and cryptodires, all attempted to radiate into the vacant niche. These other amphichelydians, unlike their extinct predecessors, lacked the advantage of the fine scale local adaptations to this niche. Thus, pleurodires and cryptodires, with their superior neck design, now prevailed and managed to occupy the niche. Rosenzweig and McCord termed this process "incumbent replacement" and suggest that it is responsible for long-term evolutionary progress.

MICHAEL S.Y. LEE

See also Aquatic Locomotion; Aquatic Reptiles; Skeleton: Dermal Postcranial Skeleton

Works Cited

Brinkman, D.B., and E.L. Nicholls. 1991. Anatomy and relationships of the turtle *Boremys pulchra* (Testudines: Baenidae). *Journal of Vertebrate Paleontology* 11:302–15.

Gaffney, E.S. 1975. A phylogeny and classification of the higher categories of turtles. *Bulletin of the American Museum of Natural History* 155:387–436.

———. 1990. The comparative osteology of the Triassic turtle *Proganochelys. Bulletin of the American Museum of Natural History* 194:1–263.

Gaffney, E.S., J.H. Hutchison, F.A. Jenkins, Jr., and L.J. Meeker. 1987. Modern turtle origins: The oldest known cryptodire. *Science* 237:289–91.

Gaffney, E.S., and P.A. Meylan. 1988. A phylogeny of turtles. *In* M.J. Benton (ed.), *The Phylogeny and Classification of Tetrapods,* vol. 1. Oxford: Clarendon; New York: Oxford University Press.

Laurin, M., and R.R. Reisz. 1995. A reevaluation of early amniote phylogeny. *Zoological Journal of the Linnean Society* 113:165–223.

Lee, M.S.Y. 1996. Correlated progression and the origin of turtles. *Nature* 379:812–15.

Meylan, P. 1987. The phylogenetic relationships of soft-shelled turtles. *Bulletin of the American Museum of Natural History* 186:1–101.

Rieppel, O., and M. deBraga. 1996. Turtles as diapsid reptiles. *Nature* 384:453–55.

Rosenzweig, M.L., and R.D. McCord. 1991. Incumbent replacement: Evidence for long-term evolutionary progress. *Paleobiology* 17:202–12.

Rougier, G.W., M.S. de la Fuente, and A.B. Arcucci. 1995. Late Triassic turtles from South America. *Science* 268:855–58.

Zangerl, R. 1953. The vertebrate fauna of the Selma formation of Alabama. Part 3, The turtles of the family Protostegidae; Part 4, 379:812–15.

The turtles of the family Toxochelyidae. *Fieldiana, Geology Memoirs* 3:61–277.

Further Reading

Alderton, D. 1988. *Turtles and Tortoises of the World*. London: Blandford Press; New York: Facts on File.

U

UNGULATES, ARCHAIC

The ungulates, or hoofed animals, include most of the extinct and living large-bodied herbivorous mammals (Figure 1). They make up over one-third of the known genera (groups, singular genus) and families of mammals, outnumbering even the rodents. Ungulates include the even-toed artiodactyls (pigs, hippos, peccaries, camels, deer, cattle, antelope, sheep, giraffes, and their extinct relatives), the odd-toed perissodactyls (horses, rhinos, tapirs, hyraxes, and their extinct relatives), the tethytheres (the proboscideans, or elephants, plus manatees, and their extinct relatives), and surprisingly, the cetaceans (whales) and their extinct relatives, the mesonychids. The largest known animal (the blue whale), the largest known land mammal (the extinct rhinoceros *Paraceratherium*), and the largest living land mammal (the African elephant) are all ungulates.

Ungulates dominate the large herbivore niche in most ecosystems, but they were much more ecologically diverse. Some groups were probably bearlike omnivores, while the whales and their relatives feed on fish, squid, or plankton. Although ungulates are partially defined as having hooves on their toes, several groups (including the whales and manatees) have evolved further to become aquatic and have not only lost their hooves but even their hind limbs; their arms have become flippers. Some ungulates (such as elephants and several extinct groups) became huge, with thick, stocky limbs, while others became adapted for running (especially horses, antelopes, and many extinct ungulates). One group is even adapted for climbing trees.

The earliest ungulates were only the size of rats and showed no obvious signs of evolving into horses, elephants, cows, or whales. Discovered in Late Cretaceous (85-million-year-old) rocks in Uzbekistan in central Asia, these earliest ungulates (called the "zhelestids") already showed the characteristic ungulate teeth, with low rounded cusps for grinding vegetation. By the end of the age of dinosaurs, 65 million years ago, ungulates were represented by a rat-sized animal known as *Protungulatum* ("first ungulate"), which had not only plant-eating molar teeth but also a highly distinctive foot and ankle structure that distinguished ungulates from primates, insectivores (such as moles and shrews), and other mammals that lived in a world dominated by *Tyrannosaurus* and *Triceratops*.

After the extinction of the dinosaurs, hoofed mammals evolved rapidly to fill the niche of large-bodied herbivores and have dominated that role ever since. Almost 70 percent of the mammals that arose during the Early Paleocene (the time immediately after the extinction of the dinosaurs) are ungulates. The earliest group to evolve from *Protungulatum* were the arctocyonids. Although these animals had low-crowned, blunt molar teeth for eating an omnivorous diet and hooves on their fingers and toes, they were similar in size and ecology to raccoons. The largest members of this group, such as *Claenodon* and *Arctocyon,* date from the Late Paleocene (60 to 56 million years ago) in Europe and North America. These animals were the size of small bears, and given their large canine teeth and low-crowned molars for eating a wide variety of foods, they probably also lived and fed much like bears.

One of the earliest groups to branch off from this ancestral ungulate stock were the even-toed hoofed mammals, or artiodactyls. The next major group of archaic ungulates include the periptychids and the hyopsodonts. Periptychids were particularly common in the Early Paleocene, some 60 to 65 million years ago. The periptychid *Ectoconus* was a large (2 meters long), clumsy, unspecialized animal, with broad five-toed feet and a long tail. Periptychids have few specializations except for their teeth, which have a peculiarly wrinkled enamel surface that is immediately recognizable. They were extinct by the end of the Paleocene, about 55 million years ago.

Although closely related to periptychids, hyopsodonts were much smaller animals having the size and proportions of a dachshund. These animals were particularly common in the Late Paleocene and Early Eocene, between 58 and 50 million years ago. Hyopsodont molars have high crowns with numerous cusps, sometimes forming half-moon-shaped crests that vaguely resemble the teeth of artiodactyls, but apparently this is the result of evolutionary convergence (they evolved independently). Although hyopsodonts became increasing rare after the Early Eocene, they straggled on until the late Middle Eocene, about 45 million years ago. They were the last of the archaic ungulate groups to become extinct.

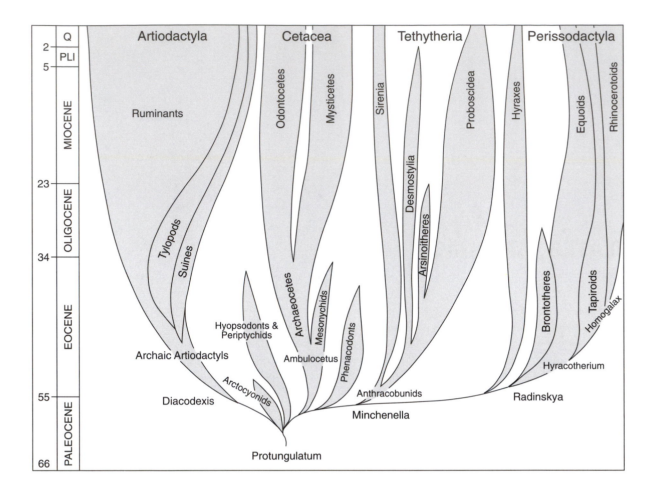

Figure 1. Family tree of the ungulates, or hoofed mammals; the various archaic lineages at the base of the radiation (such as the arctocyonids, periptychids plus hyopsodonts, phenacodonts, and mesonychids) were once placed in a "wastebasket" order "Condylarthra." Illustration by Catherine P. Sexton, after Prothero and Schoch (1998).

After the early divergence of artiodactyls, and the hyopsodont-periptychid group from the archaic arctocyonids, the next major group to branch off was the whales and their extinct relatives, called the mesonychids. Finally, the higher ungulates (perissodactyls, tethytheres, and their extinct relatives) diverged from the common ungulate stock. The most primitive group in the perissodactyl-tethythere lineage is known as "phenacodonts." They were common animals of the Late Paleocene and Early Eocene, but their abundance and diversity decreased rapidly during the Middle Eocene until their final extinction about 47 million years ago. The sheep-sized *Phenacodus* had relatively long toes and limbs and a long tail. Its ankles were specialized for front-to-back running and had restricted ability to move side-to-side. The molar teeth were highly squared off and flattened for eating vegetation, and the canines were relatively reduced.

For many years, paleontologists thought that the phenacodonts were ancestors of the perissodactyls, since the resemblance between Late Paleocene phenacodonts such as *Tetraclaenodon* and the earliest perissodactyls is quite close. However, that notion has been discredited by the discovery of fossils much closer to perisso-

dactyls, such as *Radinskya,* dating from the Late Paleocene of China. Another group from the Late Paleocene and Early Eocene, the meniscotheres, developed molars with half-moon-shaped crests on their crowns very early, but these are apparently convergent on the molars of artiodactyls and hyopsodonts. Meniscotheres are now considered a subgroup of the phenacodonts.

For over a century, some archaic hoofed mammals (arctocyonids, periptychids, hyopsodonts, phenacodonts, meniscotheres, and mesonychids) were not clearly related to the living perissodactyls, artiodactyls, tethytheres, or whales. These "orphan" groups were placed in a taxonomic "wastebasket," the order "Condylarthra." The name "condylarth" is completely meaningless, except as a convenient term for hoofed mammals that were not clearly members of living groups. Since 1988, however, the phylogenetic relationships of the ungulates have become much clearer, so the term "condylarth" is obsolete and has no further use. It is disappearing from paleontology, since it obscures evolutionary relationships.

DONALD R. PROTHERO

See also Artiodactyls; Hyraxes; Mesonychids; Perissodactyls; Proboscideans; Sirenians; Whales

Further Reading

Archibald, J.D. 1996. Fossil evidence for a Late Cretaceous origin of "hoofed" mammals. *Science* 272:1150–53.

———. 1998. Archaic ungulates ("Condylarthra"). *In* C.M. Janis, K.M. Scott, and L.L. Jacobs (eds.), *Evolution of Tertiary Mammals of North America.* Cambridge and New York: Cambridge University Press.

Prothero, D.R. 1993. Ungulate phylogeny: Molecular versus morphological evidence. *In* F.S. Szalay, M.J. Novacek, and M.C. McKenna (eds.), *Mammal Phylogeny.* Vol. 2, *Placentals.* New York and London: Springer-Verlag.

Prothero, D.R., E. Manning, and M. Fisher. 1988. The phylogeny of the ungulates. *In* M.J. Benton (ed.), *The Phylogeny and Classification of the Tetrapods.* Oxford: Clarendon; New York: Oxford University Press.

Prothero, D.R., and R.M. Schoch. 1998. *Horns, Tusks, Hooves, and Flippers: The Evolution of Hoofed Mammals and Their Relatives.* Baltimore, Maryland: Johns Hopkins University Press; Princeton, New Jersey: Princeton University Press.

Savage, R.J.G., and M.R. Long. 1986. *Mammal Evolution: An Illustrated Guide.* London: British Museum (Natural History); New York: Facts-on-File.

UNITED STATES, CONTINENTAL

In a sense, the history of vertebrate paleontology in the United States had its beginnings thousands of years ago, when primitive people discovered and saved fossil bones as curious objects, to be examined, discussed, and wondered at. This is more than mere conjecture; some proof is to be seen in portions of a skull with teeth of the Eocene mammal, *Phenacodus primaevus,* discovered in a pit house in New Mexico, dated 700–900 A.D. Part of a lower jaw of a fossil carnivore also was found in this thousand-year-old dwelling.

The Eocene fossils collected by the early pre-Columbian natives were probably curiosities, nothing more. But a thousand years later, when European settlers were digging into the earth to plant their crops, extract minerals, or push canals across the landscape, more fossils were found, many of which needed explanations concerning their natures and relationships. In the late eighteenth century such fossils were often the remains of proboscideans (Pleistocene mastodonts and mammoths) of large size and frequently well-preserved. There were the fossils discovered in 1739 south of Lake Erie by Charles Le Mayne, second baron de Longuevil, and by George Croghan in 1765, probably in the vicinity of a famous fossil site near the Ohio River in Kentucky, a locality subsequently and aptly to be named Big Bone Lick. Fossil mammals were so abundant at Big Bone Lick that the locality was exploited by many people, not the least of whom was President Thomas Jefferson.

It should be said that Jefferson's interest in fossil vertebrates antedated his involvement with Big Bone Lick by a decade; in 1796, a week after his inauguration as vice president (an office he was to hold for four years before ascending to the presidency), he read a paper at the American Philosophical Society concerning fossils from a cave in what is now West Virginia. Among the fossils was a huge claw that Jefferson named *Megalonyx,* a creature that he assumed must still be living in the vast, unknown western regions of the North American continent. The identity of *Megalonyx* as a giant ground sloth subsequently was established by Desmarest in 1822.

In the meantime Jefferson had launched the remarkable Lewis and Clark expedition up the Missouri River and on to the west coast. During the course of this epochal venture, fossils were recovered and sent back to Jefferson, one of which was a fish described by Dr. Richard Harlan as *Saurocephalus lanciformis.*

Such incidental discoveries whetted Jefferson's paleontological appetite, so in 1807, after the conclusion of the Lewis and Clark expedition, the president lured Clark to collect fossils from Big Bone Lick. These fossils and others acquired by Jefferson were housed in one room of the newly constructed executive mansion (later to be known as the White House), where they were studied by Dr. Caspar Wistar of Philadelphia.

Perhaps the culmination of early collecting activities and research on fossil vertebrates in the United States is to be found in the incredibly energetic career of Charles Willson Peale, an American Renaissance man who was an accomplished professional artist, a student of natural history, a fossil collector, a founder of the Peale Museum (which for some years was housed in Independence Hall, Philadelphia), and the father of a large brood of children, all of whom were named after famous artists such as Rembrandt, Titian, and Rubens. Some of his children were excellent artists in their own right.

In 1801 Peale excavated a complete mastodon skeleton, now know as the "Peale Mastodon," in upper New York State and celebrated the event in his large painting, *Excavating the Mastodon.* The painting includes full figure portraits of Charles Willson and Titian and Rembrandt Peale, and it depicts a detailed representation of a large excavation, carefully organized.

A Time of Transition

The initial period of collecting and interpretation of fossil vertebrates in the United States, extending from colonial days into the early years of the nineteenth century, was a time of haphazard amateur efforts, dominated by chance discoveries and uninformed attempts to make sense out of the fossils that had come to light. Some of the explanations concerning the nature of newly discovered bones and teeth were very naive, as might be expected. Others were unexpectedly shrewd. Frequently the determination of what the fossils might be were submitted to the wisdom of medical practitioners—in those days the only people who had a firsthand knowledge of bones. As often as not, the medical people made bad guesses, so information about fossil remains accumulated slowly.

Then came a time, lasting from the early years of the nineteenth century until the U.S. Civil War, when fossils were discovered more abundantly, and when competent, serious-minded scholars saw fossils as keys to the past, rather than curious objects.

An outstanding figure during the early nineteenth century was Dr. Richard Harlan of Philadelphia, who, according to George Simpson, was the first American "who may be said to have had a career as a vertebrate paleontologist." He was trained in medicine at the University of Pennsylvania, and he soon followed Caspar Wistar as an authority on fossil vertebrates. Furthermore, his high position as a student of extinct vertebrates was based upon research prosecuted through many years, from 1823 until 1842. During this time he described and analyzed extinct reptiles and mammals ranging in geologic age from the Cretaceous into the Pleistocene. Furthermore, he described extinct faunas as well as individual species. He was an acute observer, and he appreciated the evidence for the succession of vertebrate faunas within the stratigraphic deposits of North America.

Although Harlan preceded Charles Darwin's theory of natural selection, he lived at a time when the broader concept of evolution was in the air. He was familiar with the works of Erasmus Darwin (Charles Darwin's grandfather) and Lamarck, as well as other scholars of those days. In short, he was a distinguished forerunner of the paleontological giants who were to arise in North America during the later years of the nineteenth century.

Several other students of fossil vertebrates shared the paleontological stage with Harlan during the early nineteenth century, but for the most part their descriptions were occasional and unfocused, evidently based upon specimens that came into their hands from various sources. There would seem to have been few long-term collecting and research programs; these were to develop in later years. This was still a time when much attention was devoted to the bones and teeth of the American mastodon, probably because such fossils were often well preserved and widely collected.

Mention might be made of a few "specialists" among these early nineteenth-century paleontologists. Edward Hitchcock, president of Amherst College, devoted many years to the collecting and study of Triassic dinosaur footprints found in the valley of the Connecticut River. Ironically, Hitchcock never realized that he was describing early dinosaur trackways; to the day of his death he thought the fossil footprints had been made by early ground-living birds, some of gigantic size. Then there was W.C. Redfield, who directed his efforts toward the description of early fossil fishes, found in the eastern states. Another student of fossil fishes was S.G. Morton.

Vertebrate paleontology was a scientific discipline continued through the first half of the nineteenth century as a predominantly part-time occupation for most people who made the effort to collect and study the extinct vertebrates of North America. The days of well-established museums, independently organized or within universities, laboratories, libraries, and publication programs, were still to come, particularly in the years following the Civil War.

The Age of Giants

The Civil War cut across the middle of the nineteenth century, from 1861 to 1865, overwhelming Americans north and south and largely suppressing the pursuits of peaceful people. Thus the development of American vertebrate paleontology can be seen as having been bifurcated into a prewar period of haphazard growth and practice and a postwar period of unprecedented development, organization, and accomplishment. It was a century marked by prewar paleontological fumbling and part-time prescientific attention, followed by postwar sophisticated fieldwork and research, resulting in a golden age of collections and distinguished publications.

In the United States three giants dominated the field of postwar vertebrate paleontology: Joseph Leidy, professor of anatomy in the medical school of the University of Pennsylvania and for many years president of the Philadelphia Academy of Natural Science; Edward Drinker Cope, an independent freelance paleontologist with certain ties to the Philadelphia Academy; and Othniel Charles Marsh of Yale University, first director of the Yale Peabody Museum.

Leidy, who experienced the closing years of the transitional period of American vertebrate paleontology, lived to become an almost Jovian figure during the onset of modern paleontological science in the late nineteenth century. From 1847 to 1891, he dominated the study of fossil vertebrates with a continuous flood of well-researched publications, his prodigious output of scientific knowledge being contained in some 220 monographs and papers describing Cretaceous and Tertiary vertebrates, largely from the western territories. Among his accomplishments was his description of *Hadrosaurus foulki,* probably the first dinosaur to be made known from a reasonably complete skeleton, the initial portions of which were found in 1856 in Cretaceous sediments across the river from Philadelphia.

Leidy was not a field man; his preeminence assured that fossils were brought *to* him, many of them supplied by fur traders and travelers from the vast lands of the Mississippi River. In his later years he became associated with the Hayden Survey, one of the four territorial surveys established by the federal government after the Civil War.

It was not only the Civil War that cut across the history of the nineteenth century in the United States, for in 1859 there appeared Darwin's revolutionary opus *The Origin of Species by Means of Natural Selection,* which altered mankind's concept of the natural world and of mankind itself. Leidy readily accepted organic evolution and its newly realized significance in the interpretation of fossil vertebrates as solid records of the development of life through the ages.

Another of the three paleontological giants here being considered was Alfred Drinker Cope, a Philadelphian about 20 years younger then Leidy. The son of a wealthy shipowner, Cope can only be described as a genius. He was also precocious, opinionated, and in spite of belonging to a respectable family of Friends, or Quakers, was very belligerent. Cope was an independent worker; he used money from the family fortune to finance his fieldwork and research.

In contrast to Leidy, Cope was a vigorous field collector, spending months each year working in the Mesozoic and Cenozoic sediments of the western United States. He and his assistants amassed a large collection of fossil vertebrates, which he described in an amazing number of monographs and papers; his bibliography totaled more than 1,400 titles.

Cope worked hard, he engaged in numerous scientific feuds (most notably with Marsh), and in the end he squandered the family fortune on ill-fated silver mines in Mexico. He died, his health worn down, his energy worn out, at the age of 57, one of the most remarkable characters in the history of American science.

Cope's contemporary and rival, Othniel Charles Marsh, the third of the giants here being considered, was as remarkable as Cope (but in a different way). He was born in Lockport, New York. His mother died when he was three years old, and Marsh lived a rather confused life as a boy, spending time with various relatives. In 1852 he came of age and received money from his mother's dowry. Then the brother of his mother came to the rescue. George Peabody was a wealthy businessman, a partner of Julius Spencer Morgan, founder of the great firm of Morgan. Peabody, a bachelor, lived in London; he was a generous philanthropist, a friend of Queen Victoria. His motto was "Education: a debt due from present to future generations." So in keeping with this sentiment he financed Marsh's education, which included some years at Yale. Marsh in time induced Peabody to build a museum at Yale—the Peabody Museum—with Marsh established as director and professor of paleontology.

Marsh did not have Cope's brilliance, but he was an adept organizer, often ruthless in practice. Through the years he amassed superb collections of fossil vertebrates, principally from the western states and territories. These fossil were housed and displayed at the Peabody Museum.

The American Museum of Natural History, established in 1869, acquired Cope's collection through the munificence of J.P. Morgan and the urgings of Henry Fairfield Osborn, Morgan's nephew, who founded the paleontological program at the museum. Osborn, a Cope disciple, inaugurated a well-conceived and vigorous field program that was continued through the years by his colleagues and successors, notably William Diller Matthew, William King Gregory, Walter Granger, Barnum Brown, and George Gaylord Simpson.

There is no need here to repeat the well-known story of the Marsh-Cope "war," a result of one of the most bitter and disgraceful rivalries in the history of science. Sufficient to say that the competitive efforts of these two men resulted in the accumulation of two great collections, one in New Haven and one in Philadelphia.

The Years of Growth

However vicious the rivalry between Cope and Marsh may have been, it stimulated the collection of and research on fossil vertebrates at a scale far greater than anything imagined by the pioneer protagonists of science. By the final years of the nineteenth century, it was becoming evident that comprehensive programs of collecting, preparation, and research, which are expensive activities, could best be pursued by institutions rather than by individuals. Thus there was a remarkable growth of museums or museum departments dedicated to the discipline of vertebrate paleontology.

A leader in the growth of vertebrate paleontology has been and continues to be the American Museum of Natural History in New York. Its predominance in this field, established by the leadership of Osborn, was exemplified early by the development of the famous Bone Cabin in Wyoming.

At Bone Cabin, not far from the Como Bluff excavations of Marsh, a large field crew labored for several seasons, excavating skeletons and miscellaneous bones of gigantic Upper Jurassic dinosaurs, found in the Morrison Formation. These fossils, properly protected by plaster jackets as they were removed from the enclosing rock, were shipped to New York, where a group of excellently trained preparators freed them from their jackets and prepared them for research and exhibition. At a site known as Quarry Nine, not far from Bone Cabin, were found the fossil remains of tiny mammals—specimens of incalculable value for the interpretation of mammalian evolution.

Other institutions soon followed suit in what may be called the institutionalization of vertebrate paleontology, whereby fossils were no longer the possessions of individuals but rather of established museums and universities, to be properly curated, studied, and housed in permanent quarters.

The growth of vertebrate paleontological institutions and institutional departments, which began about the turn of the century and has continued to present days, has been phenomenal. In the days of Cope and Marsh, only a handful of scientists and technicians were engaged in this science; today the annual meetings of the Society of Vertebrate Paleontology are attended by upwards of a thousand individuals representing hundreds of museums throughout the United States and Canada. The museums are government and private nonprofit institutions, as well as university and college museums, which are particularly numerous. Vertebrate paleontology today is a very lively science, engaging the attention of millions of interested spectators of all ages.

The Modern Period

Just as the beginnings of vertebrate paleontology in the nineteenth century were brought to a standstill by the American Civil War, so the modern development of the science was interrupted in the twentieth century by the First and Second World Wars, but particularly by the latter. There was a marked hiatus in fieldwork, which was made almost impossible by wartime restrictions, and in research, which could be prosecuted only on a reduced level of activity. But at the end of World War II the pace of work on fossil vertebrates in the United States was resumed and increased. The years from 1945 to the present may be thought of as the modern period of vertebrate paleontology, although the boundary between prewar and postwar developments in the science is admittedly very fuzzy. The period of growth, which had started in the late nineteenth century, truly has continued to the present day, while the modern period was in fact vigorously under way during the time between the two great wars. However, the modern period when seen as being defined since the end of the Second World War has been marked by some notable advances in discoveries and techniques.

As noted above, the intellectual development of vertebrate paleontology in the United States, as elsewhere in the world, was profoundly influenced by the publication of Darwin's *The Origin of Species by Means of Natural Selection* in 1859. In a parallel manner, the concept of vertebrate evolution throughout the world has been enriched by an understanding of the stupendous movements of landmasses through geologic time, now designated as plate tectonics, formerly called continental drift.

According to plate tectonics evidence, our present continents are the displaced fragments of what was once a single huge supercontinent known as Pangaea. Although the Pangaean supercontinent formed a great terrestrial block extending north and south from pole to pole, and east and west across more than 150 degrees of longitude, it nevertheless was clearly composed of several subdivisions. North of the ancient equator was that part of Pangaea designated as Laurasia, made up of what eventually became North America and Eurasia minus peninsular India. South of the equator was Gondwanaland, consisting of the future South America, Africa, Australia, and Antarctica, with peninsular India squeezed between Africa and Antarctica. Contact zones between the future continents were close and extended, except for a seaway, the Tethys Sea, between the northern edge of future Africa and the southern edge of Laurasia—an ancient coast that eventually was to be occupied in part by the collision of peninsular India with the Asian landmass.

Pangaea was intact during Paleozoic time, but with the advent of Mesozoic history it began to break apart, so that eventually its several fragments (our present continents) migrated to the positions they occupy today. Such tremendous movements must have affected the evolution of life across the globe.

During the Mesozoic era, North America, once an integral part of Pangaea, became increasingly separated from the other Pangaean blocks, except for the retention of an extended contact zone with western Europe. By Late Cenozoic and Recent times North America was a distinct continental block, intermittently connected to Europe by way of an Icelandic-Greenland passage, to Asia by way of the Beringian bridge, and to South America by way of the Panamanian isthmus.

These varying Mesozoic and Cenozoic connections of North America with other continental areas necessarily affected the nature of evolving vertebrate faunas, primarily the continental faunas but the aquatic ones as well, in this part of the world.

The Succession of Fossil Vertebrates in the United States

The collections of fossil vertebrates found in the United States—numerous, of vast size, and housed in many museums—provide a visible evolutionary record probably unequaled elsewhere. It would indeed be futile to attempt a summary, within the limits of this essay, of the exceedingly complex paleontological testimony before us. However, a necessarily brief account of the paleontological sequence contained within the rocks will be presented here.

Our knowledge commences sketchily with the earliest fossils, the scales of very primitive freshwater "fishes" found in the Ordovician Harding sandstone of Colorado. The story begins in detail with the fossil of agnathous or jawless fishes, found in Devonian sediments throughout the world. These fossils are found abundantly in the black shales around Cleveland, Ohio, along with early sharks and gigantic armored fishes known as arthrodires. In Devonian times fishes with jaws, ancestral to the bony fishes that so dominated the waters of later ages, also had made their debut on the evolutionary stage.

The emergence of vertebrates from life in the water to life on land took place in Late Devonian times when an ancestral amphibian, *Ichthyostega*—partly aquatic, partly terrestrial—made its appearance in what is now Greenland. The conquest of the land proceeded with geological rapidity, so that by Lower Carboniferous (or Mississipian) times landscapes throughout a still-intact Pangaea were the homes of early amphibians and reptiles. From later Carboniferous (or Pennsylvanian) deposits reptiles were becoming increasingly dominant, and as this trend continued into the Permian period the land-living reptiles ruled the still-intact Pangaean supercontinent. In the North American segment of Pangaea, the sequence is admirably preserved in the "Red Beds" of Texas and adjacent areas. Varied reptilian-amphibian faunas are found here in a succession of Carboniferous and Permian rocks, ranging from older to younger sediments, specifically through the Wichita–Clear Fork–Hennessey–San Angelo–Flower Pot and Pease River Formations.

During the transition from Permian to Triassic times, there were widespread extinctions of vertebrates, marked by the disappearance of many of the amphibians and reptiles so characteristic of Late Paleozoic faunas, to be replaced by new and very different tetrapods that were destined to dominate Mesozoic landscapes. There was a great reduction of the labyrinthodont amphibians, to be largely replaced by the frogs and other amphibians of our modern world. The mammal-like reptiles, so dominant in Permian faunas, gave way to their descendants, the early mammals, and to a vigorous new line of reptilian evolution, the archosaurs, which included the ancestors of the dinosaurs.

The events here listed are found in American Triassic formations, ranging along the eastern seaboard as a sequence of formations known as the Newark Series, and in the western and southwestern states as the Chinle and related beds. Numerous faunas, dominated by archosaurian reptiles, have been recovered from these sediments.

During the Jurassic and Cretaceous periods the various blocks that had constituted Pangaea were becoming increasingly defined and were drifting to the positions they occupy today. Although a strong connection persisted between northeastern North America and western Europe, the American landmass was moving toward its eventual position.

This was the age of dinosaurs, and perhaps nowhere in the world do the dinosaurs occur so widely and so varied as in North America. The Upper Jurassic Morrrison Formation, widely exposed in the western states, has yielded an abundant harvest of varied dinosaurs, including the gigantic long-necked sauropods. More familiar reptiles accompany these dinosaurs: crocodilians, lizards and snakes, and turtles. And here, as mentioned above, are some of the early mammals, insignificant in size but destined to be progenitors of the ruling mammals.

Evolution of the dinosaurs continued and became increasingly rich during the Cretaceous Period. Lower Cretaceous dinosaurs were not well known in past years, but today intensive work in the Cloverly Formation and other Lower Cretaceous horizons is yielding many new dinosaurs.

With the advent of the Cretaceous Period there was a paleobotanical "explosion" of great significance. This was the appearance of the angiosperms—the flowering plants—which established a rich new food supply for plant-eating animals.

So it was that there occurred a resultant "explosion" of plant-eating dinosaurs. Many new lines of herbivorous dinosaurs made their appearance: the iguanodonts, the hadrosaurs or duckbilled dinosaurs, the armored dinosaurs, and the horned ceratopsians. Dinosaurian faunas were abundant and varied, and the great array of plant-eating dinosaurs was accompanied by numerous crocodilians and other reptiles, and significantly by increasingly numerous mammals. Moreover, the birds, having arisen probably in Jurassic times as descendants from the dinosaurs (or as descendants from an ancestry shared with the dinosaurs), were appearing as major occupants of the North American continent.

This series of great evolutionary events is recorded in the United States in the Lower Cretaceous Cloverly and related formations, and in the Upper Cretaceous Niobrara–Pierre–Kirtland–Two Medicine–Aguja–Judith River–Mesa Verde–Hell Creek–Lance formations in the western states and in the Raritan–Magothy–Matawan–Monmouth formations along the eastern tier of states.

Then came the great extinction that took place at the end of the Cretaceous period. It was the time when all of the dinosaurs vanished, and much has been made of this event. Perhaps too much. For whatever may have been the cause of the Cretaceous extinction, it was peculiarly along zoological lines. For some reason the dinosaurs failed to cross the boundary between Mesozoic and Cenozoic times, but hordes of other animals made the crossing quite successfully. Such were the frogs and other amphibians that grace our modern world, such were the turtles, the lizards and snakes, the crocodilians, and the birds. Such were the early mammals.

The mammals, which would seem to have been repressed by the dominant dinosaurs, now evolved along many lines on and around the several continents, now free of Pangaean linkages. The future United States became the site of varied evolved mammalian faunas; indeed certain mammalian lineages were overwhelmingly or even totally of American heritage. Such to a large degree were the rodents, the carnivores, and the proboscideans—especially the tertiary mastodonts. Such particularly were various ungulates and hoofed mammals—the horse and their large cousins, the titanotheres, the camels, and the very American oreodonts.

All in all, mammalian evolution is richly represented in the Cenozoic sequence in America. This sequence has its origin in the Lower Paleocene Puerco and Torrejon Formations in the U.S. southwest. The Upper Paleocene is represented especially by the western Tiffany and Clark Fork Formations. The story is continued in the Eocene Wasatch, Bridger, and Uinta Formations of the Rocky Mountain region.

The impressive White River badlands of South Dakota, consisting of the Chadron Formation and, above it, the Brulé Formation, form a treasure trove of Oligocene mammalian faunas; the region has been explored since the early years of the nineteenth century.

The record of mammalian evolution during Miocene and Pliocene times is abundantly preserved in the High Plains of Texas and California. Here may be mentioned the Arikaree–Harrison–Snake Creek–Hemingford–Sheep Creek–Marsland–Pawnee Creek–Valentine–Burge–Ash Hollow beds of Nebraska and adjacent regions, the Barstow–Clarendon–Hemphill beds of California and Texas, and the Santa Fe Formation of New Mexico. This is but a sampling of the mammal-bearing sediments in western America.

This brings us to the American Pleistocene deposits, which are found throughout the extent of the United States. And it brings us back to where we started with some remarks concerning the pioneers of vertebrate paleontology in America, men who made those early tentative explorations in the superficially deposited Ice Age sediments, where the bones and teeth of mastodonts and mammoths, of giant ground sloths and other mammals that lived, geologically speaking, in the Recent past, were interred within deposits as young as 10,000 years of age.

Conclusion

The account of American vertebrate paleontology, as set forth above, has been made possible because of almost two centuries of work by hundreds of people. Thus it is a compendium of knowledge that has accumulated through time. This needs to be emphasized.

Such knowledge is based upon three lines of endeavor on the part of paleontologists. First there is discovery and excavation, the paleontological activities that are most interesting and exciting to the general public. Second there is preparation of the fossils in the laboratory, work that requires special knowledge and skills. It may not be as exciting, but it is crucial if the fossils are to be protected against the ravages of time and the stress of handling. Finally there must be research, perhaps the most protracted and exacting phase of the science, if the fossils are to have any real meaning.

It often has been said that a fossil does not exist until it has been described in a scientific publication. This statement may not apply to common, well-known fossils such as mastodon teeth. (Yet even such fossils may yield crucial new knowledge.) But it is certainly true for new, hitherto unknown fossils.

So it is that what we know about the fossil vertebrates of America, as about fossils from all over the world, is contained in publications that are available to the paleontologists and to interested citizens of all lands and cultures. That is how we know what fossils are: the visible remains of former life on the Earth.

EDWIN H. COLBERT

Further Reading

Colbert, E.H., and M. Morales. 1955. *Evolution of the Vertebrates: A History of the Backboned Animals through Time*. New York: Wiley; 4th ed., 1991.

Matthew, W.D. 1915. *Climate and Evolution.* Annals of the New York
    Academy of Sciences, 24. New York: New York Academy of
    Sciences.
Romer, A.S. 1933. *Vertebrate Paleontology.* Chicago: University of Chicago
    Press; 3rd ed., 1966.

Scott, W.B. 1927. Development of American paleontology. *American
    Philosophical Society, Proceedings* 66:409–29.
Simpson, G.G. 1942. The beginnings of vertebrate paleontology in
    North America. *American Philosophical Society, Proceedings* 86
    (1):130–88.

UROCHORDATES

The phylum Chordata consists of three subphyla: the familiar
vertebrates and two invertebrate groups, the urochordates and the
cephalochordates. The urochordates, more commonly known as
tunicates, are conspicuous members of the marine realm, including about 1,250 described species. There are three classes of tunicates: the sessile (attached at the base) ascidians, the pelagic (open-
sea) thaliaceans, and the pelagic larvaceans. All three classes have at
some point in their life cycle the defining chordate characters: a
notochord, a dorsal hollow nerve cord, an endostyle, gill slits, and
a dorsal postanal tail.

Ascidians, also known as sea squirts, are the most common
urochordate. They are found throughout the world's oceans, usually in shallow waters attached to a hard substratum (e.g., rocks,
sand, and shells), but a few have been collected from depths
greater than several hundred meters. There are both solitary and
colonial forms; solitary forms range in size from about 1 millimeter to 18 centimeters, and colonies can range from centimeters to
over a meter in diameter and several centimeters in thickness.
The chordate affinity of the adult ascidian is not easily recognized; in fact they were thought to be molluscs until the larva was
known, because the adult animal is basically a bag-shaped organism surrounded by a tough and sometimes leathery tunic that
occasionally contains calcareous spicules (slender, supporting
structures).

The anatomy of ascidians is best described using a solitary
form (Figure 1). Opposite the surface attached to the substratum
there are two openings: the buccal and atrial siphons. Water
enters the buccal siphon, where it passes over the buccal tentacles
on its way to the pharynx. The pharynx is perforated with gill
slits, allowing water to pass out of the pharynx into the atrium.
Most ascidians are filter feeders and use mucus produced by the
endostyle to capture food particles. Cilia on the pharynx then
transport this mucus to the dorsal lamina, where it is conveyed to
the esophagus. The esophagus then leads to the stomach and the
intestine. Attached to the anterior intestine is the pyloric
gland(s), which is (are) secretory in nature but whose function is
not well understood. Undigested food is passed to the rectum and
exits via the anus. The anus opens into the atrium, and fecal matter, water from the pharynx, and the gametes all exit the atrium
via the atrial siphon.

Ascidians have a well-developed circulatory system, an
unusual feature of which is heartbeat reversal: the blood will flow
in one direction, then the heart arrests, and then the blood flows
in the opposite direction. Another unusual feature is that the
blood contains morula cells, which have the ability to concentrate

heavy metals such as iron and vanadium. Ascidians are able to
concentrate vanadium by a 100 million-fold increase with respect
to the vanadium concentration in the surrounding sea water. Furthermore, vanadium, as found in ascidians, is stable at a pH of less
than two, which necessitates the presence of sulfuric acid in the
cellular vesicles of vanadium-containing morula cells. It is believed
that ascidians use vanadium for the synthesis of the tunic and,
because of its toxicity, as an antipredatory device. The excretory
system is unusual in that many of the waste products are not
excreted but stored in specialized organs and released upon death
of the organism. The nervous system of the adult is simple and
consists of a cerebral ganglion between the two siphons with
nerves innervating the various components of the body. There are
no specialized sense organs, but sensory cells are present around
the siphons.

Ascidians use both asexual and sexual development, with
the former prevalent in colonial ascidians. Most ascidians are hermaphrodites (i.e., both female and male sex organs are present in
the same individual). There is usually a single testis and a single
ovary near the stomach, and both open via ducts to the atrium.
Fertilization is external and development follows the typical deuterostome pattern leading to the formation of the tadpole in
many ascidian species (Figure 2). The tadpole larva has a well-
defined tail region with both a notochord and dorsal hollow nervous system. The larva does not feed but merely settles to the
bottom on an appropriate substrate and then commences metamorphosis. Metamorphosis is radical: the tail and its associated
organs (e.g., notochord) degenerate, and the body rotates by 180
degrees, bringing both the mouth and anus away from the substrate. The gill slits rapidly increase in number, and the juvenile
begins to feed.

Thaliaceans and larvaceans are both planktonic urochordates. Thaliaceans (Figure 3) are very much like ascidians in their
anatomy, except that the buccal and atrial siphons are on opposite
ends of the body, which allows for the water current to be used as a
propulsion agent. There are only about six genera, but they are
cosmopolitan (worldwide) in their distribution, with most found
in tropical and subtropical areas. Larvaceans (Figure 4) are structured very similarly to the tadpole of ascidians; the adult retains a
tail containing a notochord. There are about 70 species of larvaceans, which also are cosmopolitan, and they can occur in very
large numbers in a small area of water. Larvaceans are unusual in
that they build a "house" made of a gelatinous material around
themselves. These houses are used to screen plankton, and only
the smallest particles are able to enter the body proper.

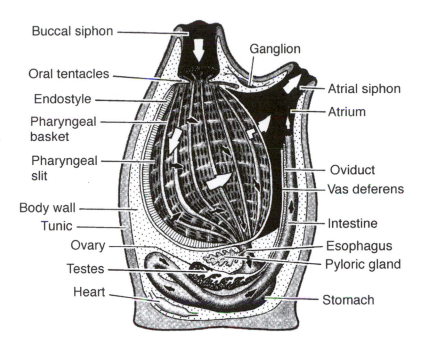

Figure 1. General anatomy of a solitary ascidian. *Large arrows* show the path of water flow; *small arrows* show the path of the mucus-laden food net. Modified from INVERTEBRATE ZOOLOGY, Sixth Edition, by E.E. Ruppert and R.D. Barnes, copyright © 1994 by Saunders College Publishing, by permission of the publisher.

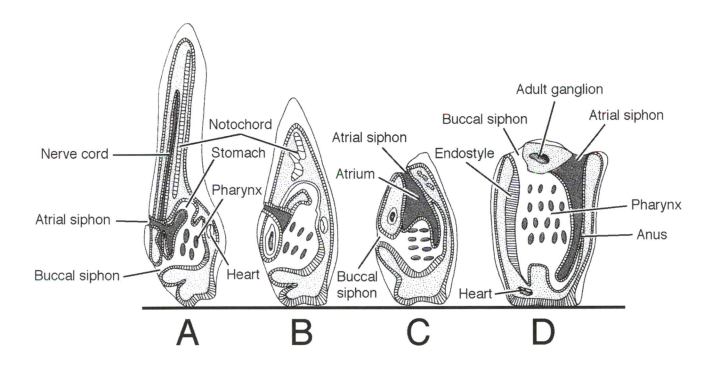

Figure 2. Morphology of an ascidian larva and metamorphosis. *A,* at the beginning of metamorphosis, the tunicate tadpole settles on its anterior end; *B–C,* larval–specific structures (e.g., the tail) begin to degenerate and the body begins to rotate; *D,* with the completion of degeneration and body rotation, as well as replication of the gill slits, the young juvenile begins to feed. Modified from INVERTE-BRATE ZOOLOGY, Sixth Edition, by E.E. Ruppert and R.D. Barnes, copyright © 1994 by Saunders College Publishing, by permission of the publisher.

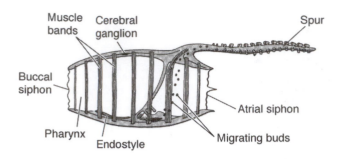

Figure 3. Morphology of a thaliacean. Modified from INVERTEBRATE ZOOLOGY, Sixth Edition, by E.E. Ruppert and R.D. Barnes, copyright © 1994 by Saunders College Publishing, by permission of the publisher.

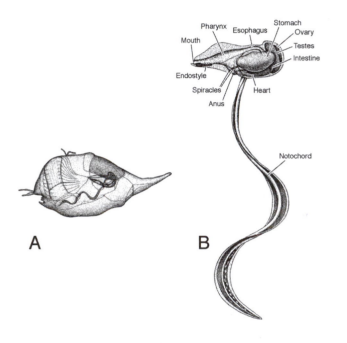

Figure 4. Morphology of a larvacean. *A,* a larvacean shown in its mucus house; *B,* anatomy of the larvacean removed from its house. *A* from Nielsen (1995); *B* modified from INVERTEBRATE ZOOLOGY, Sixth Edition, by E.E. Ruppert and R.D. Barnes, copyright © 1994 by Saunders College Publishing, by permission of the publisher.

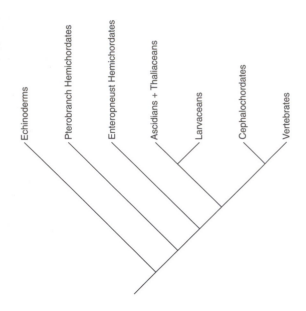

Figure 5. Phylogenetic relationships among deuterostomes based on both morphological and molecular studies. Note that the studies of Holland (1989) indicate that thaliaceans may not be a natural group of organisms; some thaliaceans are related to one group of ascidians, whereas other thaliaceans are related to a different group of ascidians.

Morphological analyses of urochordate sperm (Holland 1989) and molecular studies (Wada and Satoh 1994) both support the phylogenetic (evolutionary) relationships shown in Figure 5. An important point with respect to this phylogeny is the basal position of larvaceans within the urochordates. Many earlier scholars assumed that the ascidian life cycle was primitive not only for urochordates, but for chordates as a whole. W. Garstang (1928), for example, proposed that both larvaceans and the latest common ancestor of cephalochordates and vertebrates originated from sessile tunicate-like ancestors by a process of neoteny, whereby the tunicate tadpole stage became the reproductive stage. This new phylogenetic information suggests that chordates in general, and urochordates in particular, were primitively free-living, planktonic animals.

The fossil record of urochordates is meager at best. Two ascidian fossils have been described, but their urochordate affinity is questionable. *Ainiktozoon loganense* from the Silurian of Scotland was assigned tentatively to the Ascidiacea by A. Ritchie (1985), but new specimens have convinced W. van der Brugghen and colleagues (1997) that *Ainiktozoon* is a crustacean arthropod. K.J. Müller (1977) described *Palaeobotryllus taylori* from the Upper Cambrian of Nevada and allied it to the Ascidiacea. They are small phosphatic fossils with what Müller described as colonies of ascidians very similar to the modern *Botryllus*. However, as no known ascidian has a phosphate skeleton, and there are no unequivocal ascidian or urochordate characters present when one adds the problems enumerated by R.P.S. Jefferies (1986), the ascidian status of *Palaeobotryllus* is dubious. Ascidian spicules have, however, been found in Cenozoic-aged rocks from several localities including the Miocene of Australia and the Pliocene of France (Müller 1977; Jefferies 1986). A. Zhang (1987) discussed some interesting fossils from the Early Cambrian of China that he assigned to the Larvacea. They appear to be tadpole-shaped organisms within a "house" that seem to show a similar morphology to the houses of modern larvaceans. Nonetheless, a serious discussion of this animal must await the publication of a proper description of these forms. No fossil thaliacean has been described. Jefferies (1986), in accord with his "calcichordate theory," has described (or discussed) a group of calcitic fossils that he assigns to the Urochordata. However, it appears that these forms, along with the remaining "calcichordates," are, in fact, echinoderms (Peterson 1995).

KEVIN J. PETERSON

See also Cephalochordates; Craniates

Works Cited

Brusca, R.C., and G.J. Brusca. 1990. *Invertebrates.* Sunderland, Massachusetts: Sinauer.

Garstang, W. 1928. The morphology of the Tunicata and its bearing on the phylogeny of the Chordata. *Quarterly Journal of Microscopical Science* 72:51–87.

Holland, L.Z. 1989. Fine structure of spermatids and sperm of *Dolioletta gegenbauri* and *Doliolum nationalis* (Tunicata: Thaliacea): Implications for tunicate phylogeny. *Marine Biology* 101:83–95.

Jefferies, R.P.S. 1986. *The Ancestry of the Vertebrates.* Cambridge and New York: Cambridge University Press.

Müller, K.J. 1977. *Palaeobotryllus* from the Upper Cambrian of Nevada: A probable ascidian. *Lethaia* 10:107–18.

Nielsen, C. 1995. *Animal Evolution: Interrelationships of the Living Phyla.* Oxford and New York: Oxford University Press.

Peterson, K.J. 1995. A phylogenetic test of the calcichordate scenario. *Lethaia* 28:25–38.

Ritchie, A. 1985. *Ainiktozoon loganense* Scourfield, a protochordate? from the Silurian of Scotland. *Alcheringa* 9:117–42.

Ruppert, E.E., and R.D. Barnes. 1994. *Invertebrate Zoology.* 6th ed., Fort Worth, Texas: Saunders.

van der Brugghen, W., F.R. Schram, and D.M. Martill. 1997. The fossil *Ainiktozoon* is an arthropod. *Nature* 385:589–90.

Wada, H., and N. Satoh. 1994. Details of the evolutionary history from invertebrates to vertebrates, as deduced from the sequences of 18S rDNA. *Proceedings of the National Academy of Sciences, USA* 91:1801–4.

Zhang, A. 1987. Fossil appendicularians in the Early Cambrian. *Scientia Sinica,* ser. B, 30:888–96.

Further Reading

Barrington, E.J.W. 1965. *The Biology of Hemichordata and Protochordata.* Edinburgh and London: Oliver and Boyd; San Francisco: Freeman.

Berrill, N.J. 1955. *The Origin of Vertebrates.* Oxford: Clarendon.

Holland, L.Z., G. Gorsky, and R. Fenaux. 1988. Fertilization in *Oikopleura dioica* (Tunicata, Appendicularia): Acrosome reaction, cortical reaction and sperm-egg fusion. *Zoomorphology* 108:229–43.

Katz, M.J. 1983. Comparative anatomy of the tunicate tadpole, *Ciona intestinalis. The Biological Bulletin* 164:1–27.

Swalla, B.J., and W.R. Jeffery. 1996. Requirement of the Manx gene for expression of chordate features in a tailless ascidian larva. *Science* 274:1205–8.

V

VARIATION

The fossil record spans billions of years and encompasses perhaps tens of millions of species, most of which no longer exist. Geological strata preserve remains of organisms as tiny as bacteria (in Canada's gunflint cherts) and as enormous as dinosaurs, some of which weighed many tons (the remains of which are found on most continents). Against the background of such paleontological diversity it would be quite natural to feel that, just as certain organisms no longer exist, perhaps the forces that produced them have changed in our own time as well. Countering this ready (but unnecessary) assumption is one of the most important operating principles in paleontology, uniformitarianism, the idea that the same general set of factors that have shaped the Earth in the past—from the falling of rain and freezing of water through glacial and volcanic activity to the shifting of continents over the Earth's surface—continue to operate at present.

Within this context, the most important perspective to bear in mind about variation in the fossil record is that, at the base, it results from exactly the same phenomena that shape the variation seen in living organisms: interaction of genes inherited from preceding generations with environmental influences (climate, food, and so on) that shape the expression of those genes. Furthermore, with just one important exception, variation preserved in the fossil record reflects the same kinds and degrees of difference that we see among populations of living organisms—differences owing to age, sex, and geographic distribution, as well as some individual idiosyncrasies arising from accidents during development. The one exception is that variation in the fossil record encompasses the added dimension of time, which, under the influence of forces of evolution such as natural selection, allows small genetic differences between generations to compound amazingly over millions of years. Consequently, even if a single lineage is sampled from the fossil record, it can be expected to include much more variation than a comparable single extant species (Sheldon 1987).

A more formal framework for analysis of variation will be elaborated below, but initially we will establish a basis for understanding by starting with something familiar: domestic dogs. Because elaboration of various breeds by artificial selection has taken place extremely rapidly over the last several thousand years, and because so many intermediate breeds have been preserved, when we survey existing canine variation it seems almost as if time has been foreshortened, thereby creating a microcosm of the evolutionary processes involved in the generation and preservation of variation.

Imagine that a family owns an adult male and female of the same breed, such as an Australian kelpie, acquired from different kennels to reduce the probability of inbreeding, and has mated them. After the puppies are born we can consider the sources of variation in the group. First there are the differences between the adult male and female; these usually are referred to under the term sexual dimorphism. Taking the kelpie as an example, on average males are 18 to 20 inches tall at the shoulder, while females are 17 to 19 inches. Males range in weight from 25 to 30 pounds, while females are 20 to 25 pounds. Males are, therefore, very approximately 25 percent heavier than females. In addition to being generally more robust, males also have slightly larger and more projecting canine teeth. These contrasts are scarcely evident at birth, appearing only during the course of maturation under the developmental influences of hormones, diet, and exercise. The capacity for sexual dimorphism is encoded genetically, but its degree of expression is developmentally mediated and thus open to some environmental influence.

Among the dogs in our small family sample there would also be variation owing to age. Puppies weigh only a few ounces at birth, so the adults are roughly 100-fold larger; but the puppies would differ in appearance from adults in more than mere size. Their legs would be shorter and feet larger in proportion to body size than in adults; their faces would be shorter as well. At first their jaws would be toothless, then around weaning age the deciduous or milk teeth would appear, only to be lost later as the larger and more numerous permanent teeth erupt into muzzles that had lengthened to accommodate them.

Variation can arise from other influences as well. In every litter some individuals are smaller than others, either from slight genetic differences or from environmental factors such as being crowded in the womb during gestation. Such size differences, whatever their original causes, can become exaggerated further after birth as smaller, less vigorous offspring compete less effectively, first for milk and later for solid food. Developmental interactions, however complex, can leave their marks on the characteristics of adults whose skeletons might be preserved in the fossil record, along with those of immature specimens.

All of the differences mentioned so far are observable within a single family group, but there are other factors as well. Animal species that are distributed over a wide area exhibit systematic patterns of geographic variation. For example, in warm-blooded vertebrates such as birds and mammals, body size varies inversely with environmental temperature (Bergmann's rule), so animals living in colder areas tend to be larger on average than those living in warmer regions. Similarly, warm-blooded species living in colder climates generally have shorter extremities (limbs, ears) than those in warmer climates (Allen's rule). Like much variation among present and past organisms, these patterns have functional explanations: Larger bodies and shorter appendages conserve body heat in colder areas, while smaller bodies and longer appendages dissipate heat in warmer environments. Resultant geographic variation in size and shape persists in the face of gene flow among the populations because of differences in the adaptive values of the underlying genes in respective areas. The observable patterns of distribution are referred to as clines, a term borrowed from meteorology. Clines are gradients in the frequency or degree of expression of genes or visible characters, the distributions of which usually change gradually and continuously over wide areas in the case of spatial clines, or spans of time in the case of temporal clines.

Geographic variation in natural populations has an approximate counterpart in differences among dogs mentioned earlier. Breeds recognized by the American Kennel Club are closed populations that are not supposed to exchange genes; puppies of mixed ancestry cannot be registered. However, the resultant artificial barriers to gene flow have not resulted in the separation of dog breeds into separate species. The several hundred known breeds are interfertile with each other and with wolves, the surviving wild ancestors from which domestic dogs have descended. Because of the extreme levels of selection practiced by humans, who have identified and preserved sporadic mutations and certain more complex genetic combinations, there still exists an enormous pool of variation represented by over three hundred breeds.

Among all of these populations it is possible to see a series ranging from some that are rather wolflike in appearance (such as German shepherds, Alaskan malamutes, Siberian huskies) through medium-sized working dogs (border collies) to various extremes (dachshunds that combine stubby legs with elongate bodies, Mexican hairless dogs that are virtually bald, and Chihuahuas, which weigh no more than two to five pounds fully grown). In the case of the kelpie, it is known that the breed is the result of a mix between the border collie brought to Australia by Europeans and the dingo brought by the Australian Aborigines who preceded them. The dingo, in turn, is relatively similar to its wolflike ancestors, so we have here a case in which it is possible to see little-changed representatives of ancestral populations existing simultaneously with their highly derived descendants and surviving intermediates as well—and all interfertile despite their distinctive appearances.

Suppose all existing domestic dogs, young and old, male and female, Chihuahuas through German shepherds, were to die in some common disaster and their skeletons to be preserved in the fossil record in substantial numbers. Imagining an incident of this sort is not unreasonable; similar events have occurred episodically in the history of life on Earth. Suppose further that the canine fossils were studied by some future paleontologist who knew nothing about dogs except what could be inferred from their bones and teeth. Faced with such a problem, our hypothetical scientist probably would attempt to partition the variation present in the sample into separate taxa (groups; singular, taxon), in the process reasoning that the collection contained numerous species, perhaps a minimum of several dozen. Yet we know that more than one species never had existed.

An exercise of this sort illustrates the fallacy of typological reasoning, in which taxonomic diversity is inferred from morphological discontinuity, and is believed to reflect substantial underlying genetic differences as well. One of the most convincing demonstrations of the extent to which morphological appearance can be a misleading guide to genetic relationship was provided by M. King and A.C. Wilson (1975), who compiled data demonstrating that chimpanzees (*Pan troglodytes*) and humans (*Homo sapiens*) differ by much less in genotype, the inherited set of DNA-based instructions for building each organism in an environment compatible with its survival, than they do in phenotype, or observable appearance. For example, chimpanzees differ from humans in only about 1 percent of their genetic material, but on average modern human brains are approximately three times the size of chimpanzee brains.

When we make comparisons of this sort, contrasting patterns of variation at the genetic level (which are virtually undetectable in the fossil record) with those at the phenotypic levels of anatomy or morphology (which can be read from bones or other hard tissues), another set of considerations arise: How the variation is packaged or distributed in the population. For example, DNA sequences vary in discontinuous ways. A particular nucleotide must be either present or absent at a given position; similarly, serological features such as blood groups are determined by alleles occupying particular loci that govern production of distinguishable alternative antigens. Because several discrete categories can exist in a population, the resultant distribution is referred to as a polymorphism (combining the roots "poly" for many, "morph" for form).

In contrast, a great many morphological features are distributed continuously; their phenotypes grade smoothly from one individual to another rather than being marked by sharp contrasts. From our own experience we know that in living organisms such continuous distributions are the norm for anatomical characteristics including body weight and length (or stature), and for components of size such as masses of various muscles as well as lengths and diameters of the bones that comprise the skeleton.

As a general rule, discretely distributed characters are under the control of loci at which a limited number of genotype combinations tend to express themselves rather invariantly, with little influence from environmental perturbations on their expression. Continuously distributed characters commonly are under the joint influence of multiple independently inherited (polygenic) loci that in combination can generate very large numbers of genotypes that produce phenotypes differing in expression only by small degrees, and exhibiting greater developmental lability to differences in nutrients, temperature, and other environmental influences.

Single-locus discrete traits and multilocus continuous traits do not account for all observed patterns of variation among either present or past populations. There also are quasi-continuous variants such as meristic traits, in which individuals might differ incrementally, as in numbers of serially repeated bones, or in numbers of foramina (openings) or other discrete structures. For example, in the lower back, most humans (72 percent) have five sacral vertebrae, but in rare instances there may be as few as three or as many as seven. By way of comparison, in chimpanzees the modal number of sacral vertebrae is six (found in 55 percent of individuals), with a range from four to eight (Schultz 1968). While generalizations about patterns of variation are based chiefly on studies of living populations, as for the distributions just described, a uniformitarian perspective underlies the operating assumption that differences exhibited by organisms in the fossil record must have been generated by comparable causal and developmental mechanisms.

Knowledge about patterns of variation in living taxa can aid in interpreting correctly the phyletic position of fossil finds. Illustrative of this point is a recent case in which S. Moyà Solà and M. Köhler (1993) reported the discovery in Spain of a cranium (specimen number CLL-18000) representing the hominoid primate *Dryopithecus laietanus*. The investigators assigned this taxon to a *Pongo* clade, signaling their belief that *D. laietanus* was ancestral to various fossil and living Asian ape taxa including the orangutan (*Pongo pygmaeus*) but not to the group that includes the extant (present-day) African apes (*Pan* and *Gorilla*) as well as all of the human populations descended from the common ancestor shared with them. A key feature that influenced this phylogenetic arrangement was that CLL-18000 possessed a maxillary bone rugose (roughened) on its superior portion, with three zygomaxillary foramina located high on its frontal process. Solà and Köhler maintained that these features can be observed only in *Pongo,* in which they are functionally related to the presence of large cheek pads. In fact, individuals with three zygomaxillary facial foramina occur not only in *Pongo* but also are common in all other extant hominoid taxa including *Pan, Gorilla, Symphalangus,* and *Hylobates.* Notably, in this feature *Pongo* itself exhibits very extensive numerical variation, with a range from one to eight foramina; individual specimens of *Pongo* with three foramina actually are less common than those with either fewer than three (one or two) or more than three (four through eight). On the basis of these

very particular observations (Eckhardt 1994) two important inferences can be drawn. First, the primitive condition that was present in ancestral hominoids was the same as now is encountered in the extant taxa that are closely related to them: A polymorphism of considerable phenotypic and ontogenetic complexity. Second, and of greater general significance, polymorphism is pervasive in mammals (Howard 1988), and detailed knowledge of this and other patterns of variation is critical to understanding and interpreting the paleontological record.

ROBERT B. ECKHARDT

See also Adaptation; Evolutionary Novelty; Evolutionary Theory; Growth, Development, and Evolution; Selection; Speciation and Morphological Change

Works Cited

Eckhardt, R.B. 1994. Ape family tree. *Nature* 372:326–27.

Howard, J.C. 1988. How old is a polymorphism? *Nature* 332:588–90.

King, M., and A.C. Wilson. 1975. Evolution at two levels in humans and chimpanzees. *Science* 188:107–16.

Moyà Solà, S., and M. Köhler. 1993. Recent discoveries of *Dryopithecus* shed new light on evolution of great apes. *Nature* 365:543–45.

Schultz, A.H. 1968. The Recent hominoid primates. *In* S.W. Washburn and P. Jay (eds.), *Perspectives on Human Evolution.* 2 vols. New York: Holt, Rinehart and Winston.

Sheldon, P.R. 1987. Parallel gradual evolution of Ordovician trilobites. *Nature* 330:561–63.

Further Reading

Eckhardt, R.B. 1989. Evolutionary morphology of human skeletal characteristics. *Anthropologischer Anzeiger* 47:193–228.

Hauser, G., and G.F. De Stefano. 1989. *Epigenetic Variants of the Human Skull.* Stuttgart: Schweizerbart.

Huxley, J.S. 1942. *Evolution: The Modern Synthesis.* London: Allen and Unwin; New York: Harper; 3rd ed., London: Allen and Unwin, 1974; New York: Hufner, 1974.

Levinton, J. 1988. *Genetics, Paleontology, and Macroevolution.* Cambridge and New York: Cambridge University Press.

Shea, B.T., S.R. Leigh, and C.P. Groves. 1993. Multivariate craniometric variation in chimpanzees: Implications for species identification. *In* W.H. Kimbel and Y. Rak (eds.), *Species, Species Concepts, and Primate Evolution.* New York: Plenum Press.

VASCULAR PLANTS, EARLIEST

An important aspect of biochemical evolution is the development of ligninlike compounds, as well as starch and cellulose—all important elements of vital land plant tissues. Some authors

think that this development had to take place before the mosaiclike steps could lead to the evolution of land plants and thus vascular plants. The main features of vascular plants are the possession of (1) tissues that prevent evaporation or surface membranes that repel water (cuticles), (2) pores that control water balance (stomata), (3) organs that anchor and that assimilate nutrients (rhizoids or roots), (4) consolidating and conducting tissue with secondary wall thickenings (hydroids or tracheids), and (5) the development of sporangia (spore-bearing structures) with trilete (three-sided) spores through the cell division process called meiosis. Trilete spores, cuticle-like sheets of tissue, and various types of tubelike cells are known from Cambrian-Ordovician times on. These remains indicate the presence of land plants, even perhaps vascular plants. The first undoubted vascular plant, *Cooksonia pertoni,* dates from the Silurian. It shows all the elements of vascular plants (Edwards et al. 1979).

That vascular plants evolved from algae is generally accepted; the debate is over the specific group of algae involved and the environmental changes that occurred during successive evolutionary steps. There are four hypotheses for vascular plant ancestors and their environment: (1) origin from highly organized brown algae, with later groups invading the terrestrial habitat from marine environments via the tidal region; (2) origin from highly organized brown algae, with later groups invading the terrestrial habitat from lagoonal and brackish water environments; (3) origin from highly organized red or green algae (Charales), with later groups invading the terrestrial habitat via limnic (freshwater) environments; (4) origin of vascular plants directly in terrestrial habitat from specialized green algae (Chaetophorales); and (5) origin of vascular plants in terrestrial habitat from bryophytes (mosses and liverworts).

The theory that vascular plants originated from brown algae was based upon similar morphological (shape and structural) features of *Taeniocrada* and related Early Devonian plants, whereas the hypothesis of the origin from red algae was based on the way its spores develop in groups of four (tetraspores). New finds made it evident that the first possible vascular plants in the Silurian ranged from millimeters to centimeters tall. Even in the Early Devonian they attained a height of only about 20 to 25 centimeters. These multicellular, tiny, specialized first vascular plants, with their flattened shape, are so small that it is unlikely that well-developed and highly organized algae led to higher land plants.

Today, most researchers assume that freshwater or terrestrial green algae are the ancestors of land plants. Some authors even suppose that higher plants have multiple origins (polyphy-letic origins). For instance, H.J. Sluiman (1985) posits that several algal ancestors acquired archegonia (female sex organs) and terminated in meiosis, a process essential to sexual reproduction (Taylor 1988). Nevertheless, judging from basic similarities with known vascular plants, most researchers believe that land plants originated from one particular group of green algae. Based on biochemical studies of living representatives, the Charophyceae seem to be most closely related to land plants. Biological factors also support this heritage—growth from the tips of structures (apical growth), multicellular sexual organs, and complex vegetative development (e.g., specialized structures, such as nodes with rhizoids).

For a long time, most paleobotanists have accepted *Cooksonia* as the oldest vascular plant (Figure 1). The genus ranges worldwide from Middle Silurian to Early Devonian (415 to 385 million years ago). The erect, dichotomous-branched axes (stems) of this plant

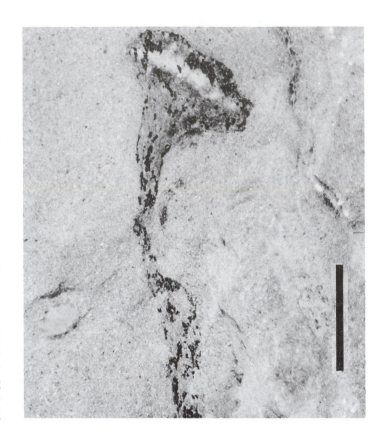

Figure 1. *Cooksonia caledonica* Edwards, a plant thought to be one of the first tracheophytes, Pragian (Early Devonian), Horm near Düren, Germany. Scale bar equals 2 millimeters.

terminate in sporangia. The sporangia bear trilete spores produced by meiosis, and no less than one species shows convincing tracheids, which are lignified structures for transporting materials. These plants are not differentiated into stems, leaves, and roots. The weight of the growing upright axes pushes down on the basal parts on the ground, initiating the growth of rhizoids.

Once the first important step in developing land plants was made, there was a burst of diversification of higher organized plants (Figure 2). These plants (i.e., *Cooksonia* and related plants of the early Paleozoic) are pooled in the taxon Rhyniophytina, which became extinct in the Middle Devonian. Their main morphological criteria are the erect, bifurcate (split into two equal structures) axes that terminate in a variety of shapes of sporangia. The biological basis and the definition of this taxon are based on hypothetical features with little corroborating evidence and, thus, are very doubtful. Already in the Silurian, the Zosterophyllophytina and the Lycophyta should have split off from the early Rhyniophytina.

The zosterophylls lack vascularized enations (outgrowths, such as microphylls or leaves) and roots. Branching often is k-shaped in rhizomes. The sporangia are roundish to kidney-shaped and are arranged along the sides of small stalks, suggesting a close relationship to the Lycophyta. The oldest, fully developed, and best-known vascular plant is the Early Devonian *Asteroxylon* (Figure 3) from the Rhynie Chert in Scotland. This plant is

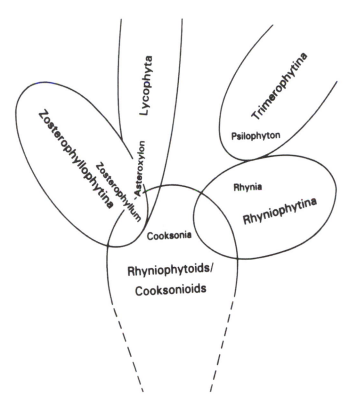

Figure 2. Schematic representation of possible relationships of early vascular plants.

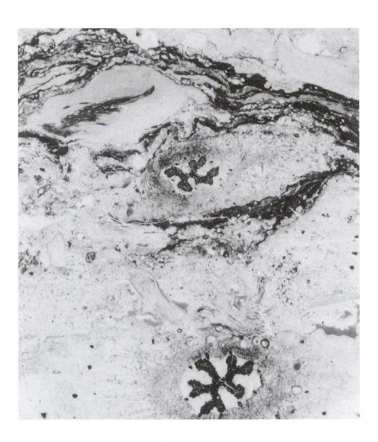

Figure 3. *Asteroxylon mackiei* Kidston and Lang. Cross sections through the deeply lobed actinostele of this prelycopod, Pragian to Emsian (Early Devonian), Rhynie, Great Britain.

already highly developed with its naked rhizome, roots, and an aerial shoot system densely covered with leaflike enations. Sporangia are borne along the sides of short stalks, between the leaflets, and the vascular tissue is organized as a deeply lobed actinostele (specialized stele with armlike projections of certain vascular tissues). These features approach the characteristics of lycopods. Therefore, lycopods seem to be descendants or a sister taxon (closely related group) of the zosterophylls and are the most ancient group of vascular plants still found today.

While the Rhyniophytina and their descendants spread rapidly all over the world, the trimerophytes—which led to seed plants and ferns—evolved from a particular type of Lower Devonian Rhyniophytina (possibly from Rhyniaceae) that had cylindrically shaped sporangia. The first well-established representative of this group is *Psilophyton* (Figure 4), found in many Lower Devonian localities all over the world. The branches of the plant develop through apical growth without bifurcation, and the side branches form in twos or threes. The terminal, spindle-shaped (fusiform) sporangia are aggregated to clusters; they originate from definite fertile branches. The large, centrarch stele shows tracheids with scalariform- (ladderlike) to circular-bordered pits. These plants are considered to be ancestors of some ferns and seed plants that developed at the end of the Devonian, 360 million years ago. By the Middle Devonian, many representatives of these plant groups were as large as middle-sized shrubs. Their size was restricted because stems without secondary growth could not achieve very great diameter. The evolution of secondary wood gave a further evolutionary push to the growth of trees and the build-up of storied forests. By the end of the Devonian, all the important elements of modern vascular plants (i.e., leaves, seeds, secondary wood) had developed except flowers and fruits.

Parallel to the evolution of vascular plants was the evolution of groups of nonvascular plants, which also were developing strategies to colonize the terrestrial environment. Some of these fossils—to date most of them collectively referred to the group "nematophytes"—once were thought to belong to the ancestors of vascular plants. They include the biggest plants in Silurian–Early Devonian times, such as *Prototaxites,* which ranged from Late Silurian to Late Devonian. Fossils of this plant appear as large logs up to 90 centimeters in diameter. The stems typically consist of longitudinal tubes of two sizes, with tissue organized much like ground tissue. (In vascular plants, ground tissue gives rise to many primary tissues.) Scholars now are debating the relationship between this group and a number of others, incl;luding green algae, as a member of the vascular plant lineage, brown algae (Niklas 1976), fungi, or lichens. The Late Devonian *Protosalvinia,* previously interpreted as brown alga, forms a flattened, creeping, thalloid (undifferentiated) body bearing small upright shoots. Spores develop just below the surface as tetraspores. This organization resembles that of F.E. Fritsch's concept of the first land plants (1945). The plant is known only from the Albany Shale (Upper Devonian) and cannot be a direct ancestor of higher land plants.

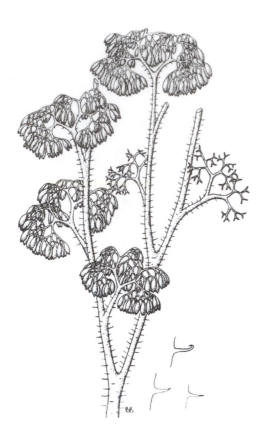

Figure 4. *Psilophyton charientos* Gensel, trimerophyte from the Emsian (Early Devonian) of New Brunswick, Canada. Restoration after Gensel (1979).

Figure 5. *Sporogonites exuberans* Halle, a tentative bryophyte, Pragian (Early Devonian), Horm near Düren, Germany.

These and other Silurian-Devonian genera found worldwide are interpreted as enigmatic plants of uncertain affinities that independently developed strategies to invade terrestrial habitats.

Discussions of the colonization of terrestrial habitats and the origin of vascular plants generally ignore the bryophytes. *Sporogonites* (Figure 5), found in Devonian strata in Europe, South America, and Australia, is regarded as a bryophyte because sporangial stalks grow up from a thalluslike region. The sporangium is multilayered, and a columella (straight central stem) may develop. There is no evidence of conducting tissue. The bryophytic affinities of some other Early Devonian plant fossils are still more conjectural.

All the data mentioned above are based mainly on findings from the Northern Hemisphere. In recent years more information about Early Paleozoic strata in China, Australia, and Africa became available, and it raises new questions. Whereas the Lower Silurian of South China has produced a plant with algal morphology and tracheidal structures, the Late Silurian flora of China looks similar to the *Cooksonia*-dominated floras of Europe and North America. But in the Early Devonian the character of the Chinese flora changed, with more than 10 well-established genera like *Discalis* and *Hsüa*. In Australia the relatively advanced lycopod (club moss relative) *Baragwanathia* (Figure 6) with broad, helically attached leaves, vascular tissue, and sporangia in leaf axils occurs in the Late Silurian, contemporary to the cooksonioid floras of the Northern Hemisphere. In the Early Devonian such possibly

endemic genera as *Hedeia, Yarravia,* and *Pluricaulis* give a very special phenotypic touch to the Australian flora. One can assume that the early flora had a higher diversity than seen from their outer appearance and that the ancestors of vascular plants may have arisen in the Ordovician rather than in the Silurian.

Most of our knowledge about early land plants is based on material from few localities. One of the most exciting sites is Rhynie in Scotland. Under a meadow, an Early Devonian chert deposit yielded over 20 species of terrestrial plant fossils. The silica petrifactions, which preserve also finest details of anatomy, include the best-known land plants, such as *Rhynia, Aglaophyton,* and *Asteroxylon,* but also fungi, algae, and lichens. It is the oldest in situ fossilized plant community in a special volcanic environment with high stress factors. Between 1917 and 1921, Robert Kidston and William H. Lang published a monograph on the Rhynie flora, which still is the basis of all research on the chert of Rhynie.

Other famous and important Lower Devonian localities lie on the Gaspé Peninsula in Quebec and in northern New Brunswick (Canada). These outcrops in northeastern Canada yielded compression fossils and petrifactions known from several other localities in the world, but the diversity of the flora is unique. Closely involved in the paleontology of this region is Sir J. William Dawson, an active geologist and pioneer in studying Devonian fossils. He demonstrated the value and legitimacy of paleobotany in interpreting and solving geological problems.

Figure 6. *Baragwanathia longifolia* Lang and Cookson, one of the oldest lycophytes, *thomasi*-zone, Middle Pragian (Early Devonian), Yarra Track, Victoria, Australia. Arrows point to sporangia.

many endemic genera has been carried out since 1977 by the geologist Xingxue Li, one of the initiators of early land plant paleobotany in China.

STEPHAN SCHULTKA

See also Algae; Bryophytes; Fungi; Plants: Overview; Plants: Mechanical Plant Design; Plants: Vegetative Features; Plants: Adaptive Strategies; Reproductive Strategies: Plants; Terrestrialization of Animals

Works Cited

Edwards, D., M.G. Basset, and E.C.W. Rogerson. 1979. The earliest vascular land plants: Continuing the search for proof. *Lethaia* 12:313–24.

Fritsch, F.E. 1945. Studies in the comparative morphology of the algae. 4, Algae and archegoniate plants. *Annals of Botany*, new ser., 9:1–29.

Gensel, P.G. 1979. Two Psilophyton species from the Lower Devonian of eastern Canada with a discussion of morphological variation within the genus. *Palaeontographica* 168B:81–99.

Niklas, K.J. 1976. Chemotaxonomy of Prototaxites and evidence for possible terrestrial adaptation. *Review of Palaeobotany and Palynology* 22:1–17.

Taylor, T.N. 1988. The origin of land plants: Some answers, more questions. *Taxon* 37:805–33.

Sluiman, H.J. 1985. A cladistic evaluation of the lower and higher green plants (Viridiplantae). *Plant Systematics and Evolution* 149:217–32.

Walter, M.R. 1983. Archean stromatolites: Evidence of earth's earliest benthos. *In* J.W. Schopf (ed.), *Earth's Earliest Biosphere: Its Origin and Evolution*. Princeton, New Jersey: Princeton University Press.

Further Reading

Gensel, P.G., and H.N. Andrews. 1984. *Plant Life in the Devonian*. New York: Praeger Scientific.

Kenrick, P., and P.R. Crane. 1997. *The Origin and Early Diversification of Land Plants: A Cladistic Study*. Washington, D.C., and London: Smithsonian Institution Press.

Meien, S.V. 1987. *Fundamentals of Palaeobotany*. London and New York: Chapman and Hall.

Stewart, W.N., and G.W. Rothwell. 1983. *Paleobotany and the Evolution of Plants*. Cambridge and New York: Cambridge University Press; 2nd. ed., 1993.

Taylor, T.N., and E.L. Taylor. 1993. *The Biology and Evolution of Fossil Plants*. Englewood Cliffs, New Jersey: Prentice-Hall.

Encouraged by the diversity of Early Devonian plants in the Wahnbachtal near Bonn (Germany), Richard Kräusel and Hermann Weyland described many compression fossils and tried to reconstruct Devonian plant associations of the Rhenish slate mountains.

The landscape around Yea in Victoria (Australia) became famous because of a Late Silurian flora of high diversity containing the lycopod *Baragwanathia*. In conjunction with William H. Lang, the paleobotanist Isabell Cookson worked on this compression flora, which is most important for evolutionary questions. Also, there are many interesting localities of Early Devonian floras in China; the most important are those of Quging and Wenshan, in the province of Yunnan. Basic research on these floras with

VENT AND SEEP FAUNAS

Modern hydrothermal vent and cold-seep marine invertebrate communities are biologically unique because the base of the vent-seep food chain is fueled by bacterial chemosynthesis (the process by which organisms derive energy from chemical reactions, not from sunlight, to synthesize food). Bacteria occur in these environments both as free-living mats (surface crusts) and as especially adapted endosymbionts (a symbiont, or organism, that lives within the cells of its partner) housed within tissues of larger invertebrates, such as the giant white clam *Calyptogena,* or the luxuriant white vestimentiferan tube worms (long worms that live within a

Figure 1. *Peregrinnella whitneyi,* a fossil brachiopod abundant in Early Cretaceous cold-seep limestone mounds (approximately 135 million years old) that formed in association with undersea serpentine diapirs, northern California. The genus *Peregrinella* is the largest of all Mesozoic articulate brachiopods worldwide, and appears to have been restricted to hydrocarbon seep paleoenvironments across the ancient Tethys Seaway, from California to Europe to Tibet.

hollow tube) with red plumes at their tips. Hydrothermal vent fluids and cold-seep fluids contained reduced chemicals such as dissolved hydrogen sulfide (H_2S, the essence of rotten eggs) and methane (CH_4, natural gas). Chemosynthetic bacteria transform (biochemically oxidize) these chemicals to support the growth of dense, localized, benthic (bottom-dwelling) communities in an otherwise food-poor deep sea.

Chemosymbiotic vent-seep invertebrates comprise certain tube worms (vestimentiferans, pogonophorans), bivalves (clamlike families Lucinidae, Thyasiridae, Solemyidae, Vesicomyidae, Mytilidae), gastropods (snail-like family Provannidae), and polychaetes (e.g., family Alvinellidae, with *exo*symbiotic bacteria on their epidermis, or "skin"). Other non-chemosymbiotic organisms reported from these settings include several types of crabs, shrimp, fishes, barnacles, brittle stars, sea stars, anemones, soft corals, sponges, copepods, benthic foraminifera, and various other worms, snails, and clams. Many of the species in these groupings are restricted to hydrothermal vent, cold-seep, or other sedimentary environments in the world's oceans.

Vent-seep fluids discharge at the seafloor in specific geologic settings that have a preservation history from the present day back to the Archean (more than 2.5 billion years ago). For example, modern hydrothermal vents are found at deep ocean locations that are centers for volcanic spreading, where tectonic plates pull apart and seawater comes into contact with hot, rising, molten magma (e.g., mid-Atlantic Ridge). Today, hydrocarbon-rich cold-seeps generally are found in two types of plate tectonic settings. Many are generated along the edges of actively converging plates, where a plate that lies under the ocean subducts (dives) beneath a continental plate (e.g., eastern Pacific margin offshore of Oregon, Costa Rica, and Peru). In

the process, fluids are squeezed out of the sediments that lie on top of the seafloor. Cold-seeps also occur along passive continental margins, where diapirs (buoyantly rising mud and brine) carry fluids to the surface from the deep waters (e.g., the Gulf of Mexico). Ancient vent-seep paleoenvironments can be traced back through Earth history by their unusual fauna and by their associated ore and sedimentary deposits (such as barium sulfate and iron sulfide minerals, or geochemically distinctive limestone).

Early vent-seep paleoenvironments of the Archean probably supported microorganisms, since some deposits have included structures that were possible stromatolites (round-shaped rocky deposits built up by bacteria) or individual bacteria-like shapes. In addition, a 3.2-billion-year-old hydrothermal vent deposit in South Africa contains organic compounds that indicate microorganism activity. What is more, because the most ancestral bacterium alive today is well adapted to live in thermal springs, many scientists have suggested that early life on Earth was microbial and thrived in hot water. The oldest, definite larger invertebrates yet known from vent-seep deposits include nondescript tubes, primitive molluscs (monoplacophorans), and brachiopods (clamlike organisms that were fastened to the seafloor by a stalk). These date from Silurian age (414-million-year-old) sulfide ores in the southern Ural Mountains of Russia. Throughout Paleozoic and Mesozoic times (from approximately 414 to 135 million years ago), many seep-vent invertebrate paleocommunities were dominated by worm tubes and brachiopods, the latter which were common benthos (bottom-dwelling organisms) in Early Phanerozoic seas. ("Phanerozoic" refers to the interval of Earth history during which many fossils were formed because life was copious.)

Vent-seep faunas began to take on a more "modern" aspect in the Late Jurassic (approximately 150 million years ago), when chemosymbiotic bivalves entered these paleoenvironments. Fossil representatives in the same family groups as living chemosymbiotic bivalves are well represented world-wide in Jurassic–Pliocene age (approximately 135- to 5-million-year-old) vent-seep deposits. At the same time, fossil brachiopods appear to have declined in chemosynthetic settings since the Mesozoic. In Mesozoic and Cenozoic deposits of the eastern Pacific (western North American sites), collectors have found fossil cold-seep gastropods that are related to living western Pacific vent snails of the Fiji, Lau, and Mariana oceanic basins.

Owing to the very specialized conditions required for fossilization (preservational biases), the soft-bodied invertebrates and bacterial mats that flourish at many modern vent-seep sites are not well represented in comparable ancient deposits. In addition, geographic differences in invertebrate faunas have been identified among vents and seeps in modern oceans. For instance, communities are dominated by shrimp in the Atlantic; by tube worms, polychaetes, and bivalves in the eastern Pacific; and by gastropods in the western Pacific. Studies of ancient diversities and abundances of vent-seep fossils in the geologic record are only just beginning. With the expected, continuing discoveries of additional and older hydrothermal vent and cold-seep deposits, the potential exists for us to peer more deeply into the environmental origins of life on Earth and track better the paleobiogeography and evolution of chemosynthetic communities through geologic time. It remains to be seen whether their history is similar to or different from that of photosynthetic paleocommunities across the great radiations and mass extinctions of the Phanerozoic.

KATHLEEN A. CAMPBELL

See also Origin of Life; Trophic Groups and Levels

Further Reading

Campbell, K.A., and D.J. Bottjer. 1995. Brachiopods and chemosymbiotic bivalves in Phanerozoic hydrothermal vent and cold-seep environments. *Geology* 23:321–24.

de Ronde, C.E.J., and T.W. Ebbesen. 1996. 3.2. by of organic compound formation near sea-floor hot springs. *Geology* 24:791–94.
Goode, J.A., G.R. Bock, and M.R. Walter. 1996. *Evolution of Hydrothermal Ecosystems on Earth (and Mars?).* Ciba Foundation Symposium, 202. Chicester and New York: Wiley.
Humphris, S.E., R.A. Zierenberg, L.S. Mullineaux, and R.E. Thompson (eds.). 1995. *Seafloor Hydrothermal Systems: Physical, Chemical, Biological, and Geological Interactions.* Geophysical Monograph, 91. Washington, D.C.: American Geophysical Union.
Little, C.T.S., R.J. Herrington, V.V. Maslennikov, N.J. Morris, and V.V. Zaykov. 1997. Silurian hydrothermal-vent community from the southern Urals, Russia. *Nature* (London) 385:146–48.
Lutz, R.A., and M.J. Kennish. 1993. Ecology of deep-sea hydrothermal vent communities: A review. *Reviews of Geophysics* 31:211–42.

VERTEBRATE HARD TISSUES: KERATINOUS TISSUES

Tetrapods (all vertebrates normally having four appendages) have evolved a number of external body coverings, serving several functions related to regulation of body temperature, protection from the environment or from predators, attack, and behavioral displays. In higher vertebrates these structures originate in the epidermis (outer layer of skin) and are based on the protein keratin. Lower vertebrates have scales or dermal armor, formed by an interaction between the epithelial ("skin") and underlying mesenchymal (undifferentiated, unspecialized) tissues, and, like the dentition and elements of the dermal skull of early fishes, are based on complex dentines, enamel, enameloid, and bone.

Scales of Lower Vertebrates

The body surface of most fishes is covered in scales or dermal denticles (small, toothlike structures), under the epithelium. In sharks these denticles emerge from the outer layer of skin, making the surface rough. They actually are arranged in a way that reduces turbulence as the shark swims. Holocephalans (cartilaginous marine fishes, e.g., chimaeras, ratfishes) have a reduced number of denticles that have similar form and origin. Dermal denticles are also found on the pelvic and head claspers of holocephalans, and on the pelvic claspers of sharks. (Claspers are structures involved in copulation.) Dermal denticles are simple in structure. Layers of enameloid (hard coating material) cover a core of dentine (a matrix of collagen, usually mineralized with calcium hydroxapatite). The base of the denticle is embedded in the deeper layer of the skin, the dermis (Figure 2A).

The scales and dermal armor of early fossil fishes include many different forms of dentine and enameloid (Figure 1) and the tissues and their arrangements are important in classifying these animals (Ørvig 1967). This is an active field of research, which still is producing new descriptions of hard tissues.

In all forms of osteostracans (ancient jawless fishes) and acanthodians (first jawed fishes), scales have a base of bone; this bone may be cellular (bone cells are enclosed in openings within a miner-alized matrix) or acellular (cells are not enclosed and often lie outside the mineralized matrix). The bone bases are covered by a specialized layer of dentine and enameloid (Figure 1A, 1D). Acanthodian teeth are simpler, with bone, a simple form of dentine, and enameloid. The heterostraci have a dermal skeleton of bone covered by dentine; in some forms the bone skeleton is covered with enameloid (Figure 1B). Arthrodires and thelodonts have scales containing semidentine (Figures 1C, 1E); in thelodonts scales develop on a base of aspidin, a form of acellular bone (Figure 1C). Actinopterygians have bone and dentine covered by enamel (Figure 3A). Placoderms have scales made up of layers of two types of bone, and have a layer of semidentine covered by enameloid.

In sarcopterygians (the large group that includes present-day lungfishes and coelacanths), thick scales form in epithelial pockets embedded in the dermis of the fish. The scales have a base that consists of layers of lightly mineralized, netlike (reticular) collagen; then a more superficial layer of dentine, covered finally by a layer of thin enamel (cosmine). Part of surface of the cosmine is ornamented by spines (Figure 2B). Palaeoniscoids (early ray-finned fishes) have thick, interlocking rhomboid scales consisting of layers of ganoin (a form of enamel) that cover a base of dentine over layers of bone. Modern teleosts (including most modern bony fishes) have thin bony scales, with a ctenoid or cycloid shape (Figure 3A).

Scale shape, ornament, and fine structure vary in different groups of fishes, and these characters are useful for taxonomy (classification), particularly among fossil fishes. Such characters are less helpful in assessing the age of the fish, because the incremental lines found in the scales reflect the nutrition available in past seasons; they cannot be viewed solely as annual growth lines.

Supporting Tissues of the Fins of Fishes

The fins of fishes are supported by internal hard tissues of different types (Hildebrand 1995). "Ceratotrichia" are the fin rays of cartilaginous fishes. The name means "horn and hair," and such rays are not segmented. They are composed of a hornlike secretion of

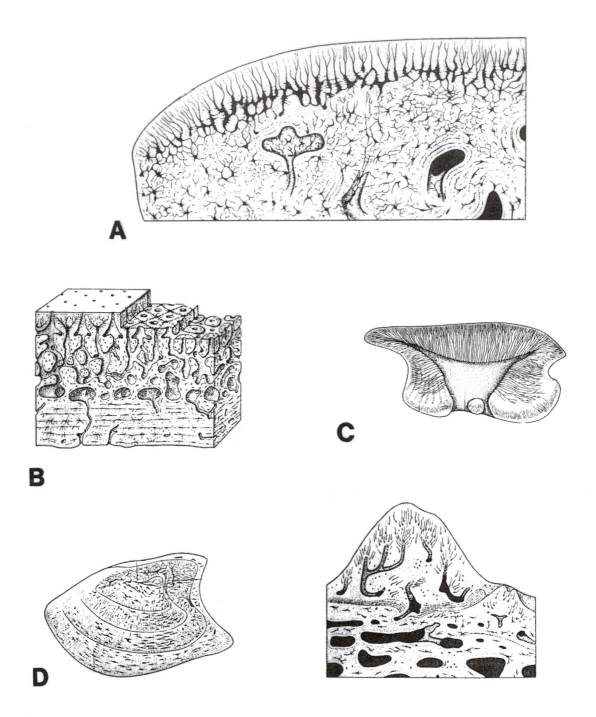

Figure 1. Scales of early vertebrates. *A*, osteostracan; *B*, heterostracan; *C*, thelodont; *D*, acanthodian; *E*, arthrodire. From: *A, B, E,* Ørvig (1967); *C, D,* Miles and Moy-Thomas (1971).

the epidermal cells and are slender, like hairs. The "lepidotrichia" of bony fishes are fin rays derived from scales, are segmented, and are made of bone. The name means "scale and hair." True hair is not involved in the formation of either structure.

Scales and Skin of Amphibians

Early amphibians had overlapping bony scales like fishes. In the fossil *Eryops,* these scales have been reduced to bony plates in the skin (Figure 4A), but in *Trimerorhachis* they resemble overlapping scales (Figure 4B). These scales were lost in most amphibians as the skin became modified into a keratinized epithelium—the skin is impregnated with long, fibrous, sulfur-containing proteins that form a hardened structure—although living caecilians (limbless, tropical amphibians) have bony ossicles in the skin. Apart from this small group of modern amphibians, derived amphibians have a keratinized epithelium, free of scales but having a surface coating of mucus to help to prevent desiccation (drying out). The changes in amphibian skin occurred *after* the conquest of land, not because of it (Olson 1971).

Later developments in the skin of higher vertebrates—the scales of reptiles and birds, the hair of mammals, the feathers of birds, as well as hooves, horns, and claws—are not derived from the hard tissues of fishes and early amphibians. They are separate structures formed from epithelial tissues.

Scales of Reptiles

Few examples of reptilian scales or scutes (bony plates) are preserved in the fossil record. The outer surface of reptile skin consists of heavily keratinized epithelium that forms flexible scales (Hildebrand 1995). The scales are joined by a hinge (Figure 3B) and are shed when the reptile molts to allow for growth. Crocodiles and turtles carry scutes, thick keratinous plates, on the outer surface of their scales. The scutes are not shed to allow for growth. Instead, they show incremental lines as rings of new material are added around the margin (edges) as the animal grows. Part of the turtle shell is made up of scutes that cover "osteoderms," and part is formed by enlarged ribs. (Osteoderms are plates of bone in the skin, below the horny scutes. Gastralia are bones in the ventral abdomen of crocodiles.)

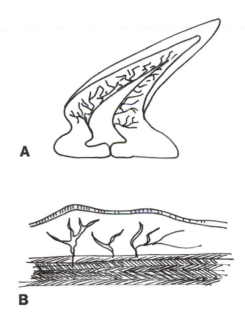

Figure 2. Scales of derived fishes. *A*, dermal denticle, shark; *B*, part of a dipnoan scale.

Scales and Feathers of Birds

The body surface of birds is a thin skin that is covered almost completely with keratinized feathers. Feathers consist of a hollow quill continuous with a shaft or "rachis" (Figure 5A). Barbs branch from the shaft on both sides, forming the "vane." Barbs are linked loosely by means of interlocking structures on the barbules. This results in a light flexible configuration of the feather that can be repaired easily by preening.

Birds have "contour feathers" (those that follow the general shape of structures) over most of the body, modified into "flight feathers" on the tail and wings. Below the contour feathers are "down feathers," which have no shafts. Bristles are modified contour feathers; the vane is removed, forming a short, stiff feather used to protect the eyes or the nostrils, or to increase the size of the gape (the size of the open mouth). Feathers are so rare in the fossil record that instances when they occur become famous, such as the feathers preserved with the skeleton of *Archaeopteryx* and the celebrated single feather from Koonwarra in Gippsland, Australia. Birds also have scales, which cover the legs and feet. These scales are similar to those of reptile skin. The toes have claws as well.

Epidermal Structures in Mammals

Mammals have a thick keratinized epithelium, which in some groups may take the form of scales. Rodent tails are scaly, and the body armor of armadillos and pangolins is derived from scales. Hair may have arisen from sensory receptors of reptiles, which are located between scales. Evidence for this connection is seen in the fact that when hair and scales occur together in mammals (e.g., the pangolin), the hairs occur between the scales. A thick covering of hair provides good insulation and protects the skin from solar

radiation. Each hair is attached by a small muscle to the underlying dermis. This means that the hair can be elevated to increase the thickness of the insulating layer, and to increase the apparent size of the animal during threat or fright displays.

A hair is a flexible strand. Produced by a hair follicle (a "pocket" in the skin), hair is made of layers of keratin and is derived from fused keratinized epithelial cells. The shaft projects from the skin, and the root is embedded in the hair follicle (Figure 5B). The inner medulla (core) is covered by thick pigmented cortex, overlaid by a cuticle derived from single cells. Hairs are shed and replaced throughout an animal's life. Most hairs are fine and soft and form a thick fur. They are found in groups surrounding a long, thick guard hair. The strongest hairs are sensory and are known as "vibrissae." Quills in porcupines are derived from hairs.

Claws are present in most mammals, but some groups (e.g., horses, cattle) have developed hooves. Claws consist of hardened keratin secreted by epithelial cells. Like claws, hooves also are keratinized structures—they develop from the epithelium around the terminal bones of digits but are thicker and more complex, with the keratin arranged in a tubular fashion. Claws and hooves rarely are preserved in the fossil record, except in very recent deposits.

Horns and antlers are epidermal or dermal in origin depending on the taxon (group; plural, taxa) (Hildebrand 1995). Rhinoceros horn consists of keratinized fibers pressed into a permanent solid structure. This structure grows from dermal papillae at the base, similar to the horn tubules of an equine hoof. Deer antlers are outgrowths of bone from the skull and initially are covered by velvet (skin); the antlers are shed every year. Pronghorns develop a horn cap instead of skin over the horn; the horny cap is shed every year. The true horns of cattle, antelopes, and some dinosaurs have vascular cores (ones well-supplied with blood ves-

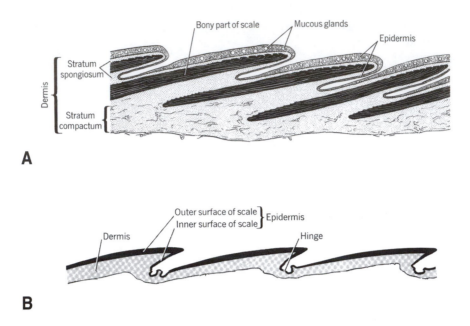

Figure 3. Relationships of scales and skin in fishes and reptiles. *A,* teleost fish; *B,* reptile. From Hildebrand (1995). Copyright © 1995 John Wiley and Sons, Inc., reprinted by permission of John Wiley and Sons, Inc.

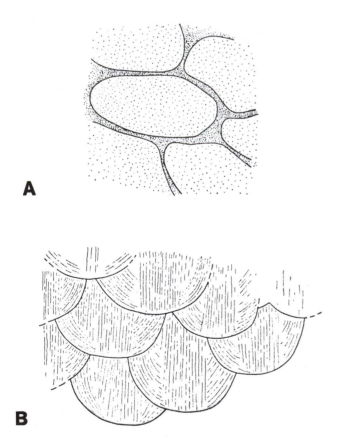

Figure 4. Scales of early amphibians. *A,* Eryops; *B,* Trimerorachis. From Olson (1971). Copyright © 1971 John Wiley and Sons, Inc., reprinted by permission of John Wiley and Sons, Inc.

sels) of bone covered by horny sheaths that grow continuously, and have incremental growth lines.

Phylogeny

Although it is possible to trace the changes in scales of fishes and early amphibians during the course of evolution, it is more difficult to construct similar phylogenies for higher vertebrates based on their epidermal and dermal structures. Few traces of these structures are preserved in the fossil record, except in recent fossils. Those that are present tell us little of the phylogenetic development of the structures. The few known fossil feathers are surprisingly modern in design, and evolutionary changes between birds and reptiles actually are inferred from skeletal structures, not from the feathers. Among these hard-tissue structures, adaptation and convergence (independent evolution) have confused the issues significantly. Hard tissue structures in the skin of vertebrates may be analogous (similar), but they are not often homologous (having arisen through connected genetic pathways).

ANNE KEMP

See also Ornamentation: Vertebrates; Vertebrate Hard Tissues: Mineralized Tissues

Works Cited

Hildebrand, M. 1995. *Analysis of Vertebrate Structure.* 4th ed., New York: Wiley.

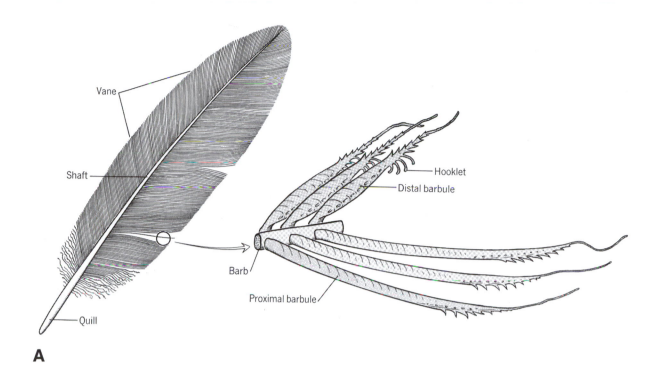

A

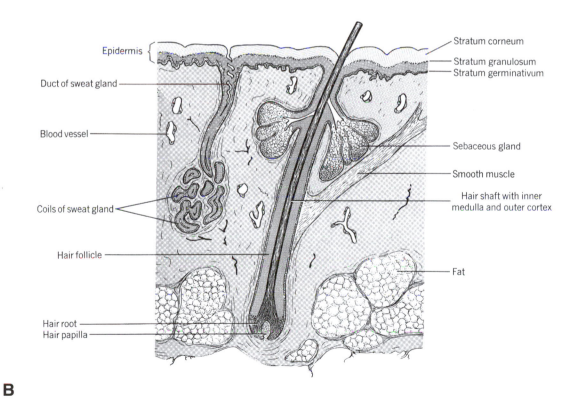

B

Figure 5. Feathers and hair. *A,* contour feather of a bird; *B,* hair of a mammal. From Hildebrand (1995). Copyright © 1995 John Wiley and Sons, Inc., reprinted by permission of John Wiley and Sons, Inc.

Miles, R.S., and J.A. Moy-Thomas. 1971. *Palaeozoic Fishes*. 2nd ed., London: Chapman and Hall; Philadelphia: Saunders.

Olson, E.C. 1971. *Vertebrate Palaeolozoology*. New York: Wiley-Interscience.

Ørvig, T. 1967. Phylogeny of tooth tissues: Evolution of some calcified tissues in early vertebrates. *In* A.E.W. Miles (ed.), *Structural and Chemical Organisation of Teeth*. Vol. 1, New York: Academic Press.

Smith, M.P., I.J. Sansom, and J.E. Repetski. Histology of the first fish. *Nature* 380:702–4.

VERTEBRATE HARD TISSUES: MINERALIZED TISSUES

Vertebrates have developed a number of internal hard tissues, skeletal structures that support the animal and serve as sites for muscle attachment, as well as permitting the movement of joints. In addition, these tissues protect vital organs and are used for capturing and processing food. They are involved in attack and defense of the animal, and their structures are sufficiently versatile to allow for growth and to enclose blood-forming tissues. The hard tissues include several forms of bone and cartilage as well as a large number of dentines and several forms of enamel or enameloid.

Diversity of hard tissue structure in vertebrates is exceptionally wide, but it does not include the hard tissues of conodont elements, small, toothlike fossils from pelagic marine invertebrates (those living in open ocean waters). Occasionally, scholars see an apparent similarity of fine structures in certain conodont elements to histology (minute structures) of hard tissues of some vertebrates; however, these similarities occur in conodonts only from particular localities but not consistently in one species of conodont. The structures are not found in well-preserved conodonts of the same species from other localities. In fact, similarities to vertebrate hard tissues are related to the conditions of preservation of the conodont elements; similarities are not indicative of vertebrate affinities for conodonts. Well-preserved and unaltered conodont elements do not have histological structures that resemble vertebrate bone, dentine, cartilage, or enamel.

The Basics of Cartilage and Bone

Cartilage

Cartilage forms the skeleton of all vertebrate animals while they are embryos and persists in parts of the skeleton in adults. It is not exclusively a vertebrate tissue—it also is found in cephalopod molluscs. Cartilage is preserved in fossils only under exceptional circumstances, as is the case with the chondrichthyan fishes of the Upper Mississipian Bear Gulch Limestones of Montana (Lund 1989).

The cartilage of all young vertebrates is hyaline cartilage, a simple tissue consisting of a clear sulfate matrix that surrounds cells enclosed in lacunae (spaces) (Figure 1A). The matrix includes some collagen fibrils (binding fibrous protein material). In adult higher vertebrates, hyaline cartilage is found in the trachea and larynx; this substance also covers the articular surfaces of bones (those areas on bones—e.g., the ball and socket region of the leg

and hip—directly involved in a joint). In adults of many lower vertebrates, hyaline cartilage forms a major part of the skeleton. Hyaline cartilage has no blood supply, so the cartilage cells, completely surrounded by matrix, rely on diffusion (the passive movement of materials in and out of cells) for nutrient supply and waste exchange.

Mineralized forms of cartilage are common among vertebrates. Sharks and holocephalans, or ghost sharks, with skeletons based on cartilage, produce several different types of calcified cartilage. Many sharks develop globular calcified cartilage in the skull. The external and internal layers of cartilage calcify in small spheres that retain enclosed cells just as in the original cartilage (Figure 1B). Vertebrae of these fishes develop linear calcifications, possibly along lines of stress, that do not enclose cells (Figure 1C). Linear calcifications may also develop in the cartilage of holocephalans. Normally, higher vertebrates do not form calcified cartilage except in the laryngeal and costal cartilages (which links the ribs and sternum), where linear calcification develops as part of a degenerating process in older individuals. Calcification (the deposition of calcium hydroxyapatite in cartilage) is also a part of endochondral ossification, the process that changes cartilage to bone (Figure 1F).

There are two additional ways of strengthening cartilage that do not involve depositing mineral in the tissue. The matrix of fibrous cartilage includes many collagen fibrils; these components provide tensile strength (the ability to stretch) with the capacity to absorb compressive shock, as in discs between vertebrae (Figure 1D). Elastic cartilage has a matrix with many elastic fibers; it is flexible but maintains the shape of a structure, as in the pinna (external ear) (Figure 1E). These two forms of cartilage have cellular structures similar to those of hyaline cartilage.

Bone

Bone is a strong skeletal tissue found only in vertebrate animals and adapted to withstand both compressive and tensile stresses. It is based on an organic matrix of collagen mineralized with calcium hydroxyapatite. Although characteristic of most vertebrate animals, bone is absent from some groups, notably sharks and holocephalans. Bone is classified under several headings, based upon histological structure and developmental history.

Bone may be cellular, with osteocytes (bone cells) enclosed in lacunae within the mineralized matrix, or acellular, with no enclosed cells. Cells associated with the latter lie outside the min-

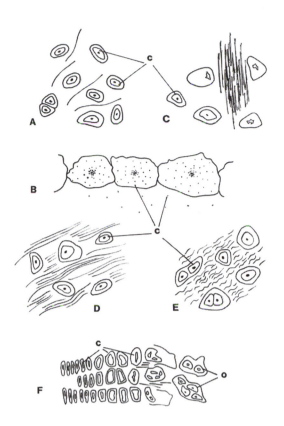

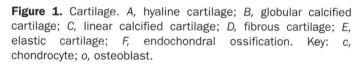

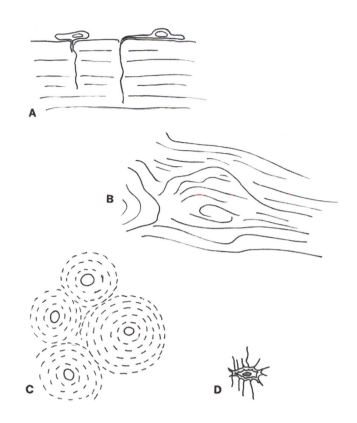

Figure 1. Cartilage. *A*, hyaline cartilage; *B*, globular calcified cartilage; *C*, linear calcified cartilage; *D*, fibrous cartilage; *E*, elastic cartilage; *F*, endochondral ossification. Key: *c*, chondrocyte; *o*, osteoblast.

Figure 2. Bone. *A*, acellular bone of teleost fish; *B*, aspidin; *C*, cellular bone of tetrapods (Haversian systems); *D*, tetrapod osteocyte in lacuna.

eralized matrix and extend long processes (extensions) into the tissue (Figure 2A). Acellular bone is characteristic of derived (advanced) bony fish and early agnathans (jawless fishes). In the latter group, the acellular bone is known as "aspidin," and the cells are presumed to have withdrawn into vascular spaces (Figure 2B). It has been derived from a form of cellular bone. The acellular bone of teleost fishes developed independently from the aspidin of early fishes (Halstead 1968).

The cellular bone of sarcopterygian fishes and tetrapods (all vertebrates normally having four appendages) develops in one of several ways. Most bones are endochondral bones, formed by replacing the cartilaginous templates of the embryonic skeleton (Figure 1F). Bones of the skull in derived vertebrates and bones of the skull and body armor in fishes and amphibians develop within mesenchyme cells below the skin (dermis). As a result, these bones are known as dermal bones. Despite the differences in origin, any fully developed bone has the same histological structure. A third form of bone, termed perichondral bone, develops below the perichondrium, the outer membrane covering a cartilaginous element.

Cellular bone in higher vertebrates is organized into osteons, or "Haversian canals" (Figure 2C). These are columns of cellular hard tissue that surround a canal containing nerves and blood vessels. The hard tissue matrix is arranged in layers known as lamellae, which contain lacunae that enclose bone cells, or osteocytes. Unlike the lacunae of cartilage, the lacunae of bone

have numerous canaliculi (minute canals) for cell processes (Figure 2D). Osteocytes are active cells and obtain their nutrients by means of the canaliculi. The surrounding mineralized matrix serves as a store of calcium and phosphates.

Bone is formed by osteoblasts (bone-forming cells); they proliferate from the tissue that covers each bone, the highly vascular periosteum. Bones grow in young individuals and are remodeled continually, even in old individuals. This process is mediated by osteoclasts, cells derived in mammals from blood-forming cells called "monocytic macrophages." Osteoclasts are capable of selectively breaking bone down so that osteoblasts can form new bone in the spaces left behind.

Ossification and Calcification

There are two processes that result in mineralization of a tissue: ossification and calcification. In calcification, mineral crystals are deposited within the extracellular matrix of cartilage, which is otherwise unchanged. In ossification, a cartilaginous template is transformed into bone, and the process follows a series of specific steps (Figure 1F). Ossification is associated with the development and growth of chondral bones. While more superficial cartilage cells continue to divide and form new cartilage, deeper cells become enlarged, and the surrounding matrix calcifies. As a result, the enclosed cartilage cells are deprived of nutrients and the matrix

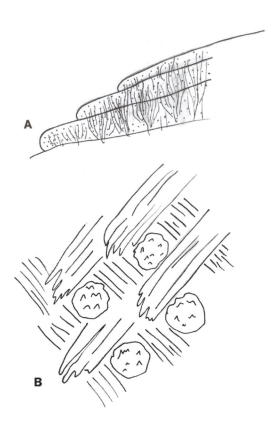

Figure 3. Enamel. *A*, dipnoan enamel with radial crystallites and amelogenin granules; *B*, enamel prisms in *Microtia*. Drawn from a scanning electron micrograph in von Koenigswald (1988).

begins to deteriorate. Osteoblasts invade the areas where matrix has been destroyed and deposit bone matrix. Subsequently, this material is organized into osteons.

Dental Histology

Teeth consist of combinations of several basic hard tissues. Softer dentine surrounds the pulp cavity and is covered by the more durable enamel or enameloid. The structure of the teeth of early vertebrates reaches an extraordinary level of complexity. Some of their teeth had different forms of dentine or more than one layer of enameloid. Dental structure is simplified considerably in derived vertebrates.

Enamel

Enamel is mineralized with calcium hydroxyapatite, as are most other vertebrate hard tissues, and the mineral is arranged in radial crystallites, which develop perpendicular to the surface of the tooth. However, the organic matrix of enamel differs from that of other vertebrate hard tissues because it is based, not on collagen, but on proteins known as enamelin, amelogenin, and tuftelin. Enamelins are secreted by cells in the inner dental lamina called ameloblasts; they persist in mature enamelin as a network bound to the hydroxyapatite crystals (Ten Cate 1989). Amelogenin, also

secreted by ameloblasts, but in the form of granules, is broken down, or removed, as the enamel mineralizes. In mammals, this activity is mediated by Tomes processes, which are cytoplasmic extensions from the ameloblasts that enter the developing enamel. Tuftelin is a protein found between the enamel and dentine, secreted in some groups, like dipnoans (lungfishes), by cells of the dental papilla (neural crest of a toothbud, which forms dentine).

Enamel is characteristic of tetrapods like reptiles, amphibians, and mammals. It also occurs in the teeth and scales of sarcopterygian (lobe-finned fishes) and in the scales of some actinopterygians (ray-finned fishes) (Figure 3). Below the mammalian level of organization, the enamel is less complex, although still based on radial crystallites, still having incremental lines (Figure 3A) and in some groups prismatic or protoprismatic as well. In dental structures, the ameloblasts arise from the oral epithelium (skin that lines the oral cavity). In such cases, the ameloblasts are arranged as an inner dental epithelium within a dental lamina. In scales, cells of the external epithelium are responsible for enamel formation (Figure 3B).

Sarcopterygian fishes, like tetrapods, have true enamel. The enamel of dipnoans is simple, consisting of layers of amelogenin mineralized with radial crystallites of hydroxyapatite (Figure 3A). Details of the formation of dipnoan enamel are not completely known, but the material is based on small spheres of hard tissue, not prisms, and there are no Tomes processes. The enamel of actinistians (coelacanths) also is layered and has radial crystallites. Later actinistians, and their sister group the labyrinthodont amphibians (extinct group resembling salamanders or crocodiles), have teeth consisting of intricate folds of dentine and enamel (Figure 4C). The enamel of palaeoniscoid (primitive ray-finned fishes) scales, and the ganoin of other actinopterygian (all common fish except sharks and skates) scales, is formed in thick layers (Figure 4A). The cosmine of sarcopterygian (including lungfishes and coelacanths) dermal armor and scales, also a form of enamel, develops in thin layers (Figure 4B) and covers the underlying dentine and bone. The term "cosmine" has been used to describe a complex of three hard tissues: an outer layer, consisting of enamel, covering a form of dentine with enclosed sensory structures, supported by a base of dermal bone (Bemis and Northcutt 1991). This is not an appropriate use of the word, because it does not convey the complexity of the hard tissues that make up the dermal armor of sarcopterygians (Meinke 1987). The term "cosmine" should be reserved for the outer enamel layer of the structure.

The enamel of mammalian teeth is arranged in complex prisms, deposited by epithelial ameloblasts in incremental layers (Figure 3B). Most mammals have simple teeth, with the basic arrangement of inner orthodentine and outer enamel (Figure 4D), anchored to the underlying bone by cementum, a form of bone. Herbivorous mammals of several groups have developed complex infolding of the enamel and dentine, with cementum included in the crown of the tooth as well.

Enameloid

Most vertebrates below the tetrapod level of organization have teeth covered with "enameloid" instead of enamel. This hard tissue

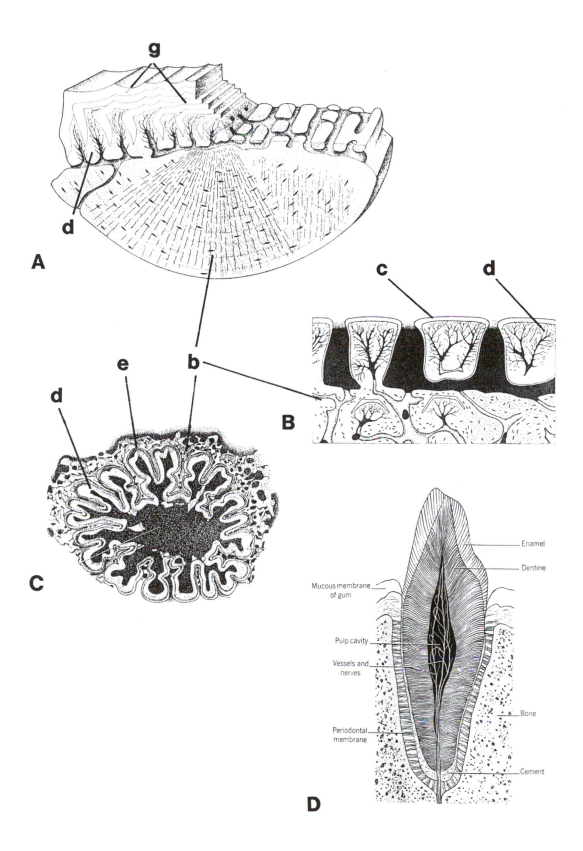

Figure 4. Complex hard tissue structures with enamel. *A,* scale of *Cheirolepis,* showing ganoin (enamel), dentine, and bone; *B,* cosmine, dentine, and bone in an actinistian fish; *C,* infolded enamel and dentine in a tooth of Eusthenopteron; *D,* mammalian tooth. Key: *e,* enamel; *d,* dentine; *c,* cosmine; *b,* bone. From: *A, B,* Ørvig (1967); *C,* from PALAEOZOIC FISHES, by R.S. Miles and J.A. Moy-Thomas, copyright © 1971 by Saunders College Publishing, reproduced by permission of the publisher; *D,* Hildebrand (1995), copyright © 1995 John Wiley and Sons, Inc., reprinted by permission of John Wiley and Sons, Inc.

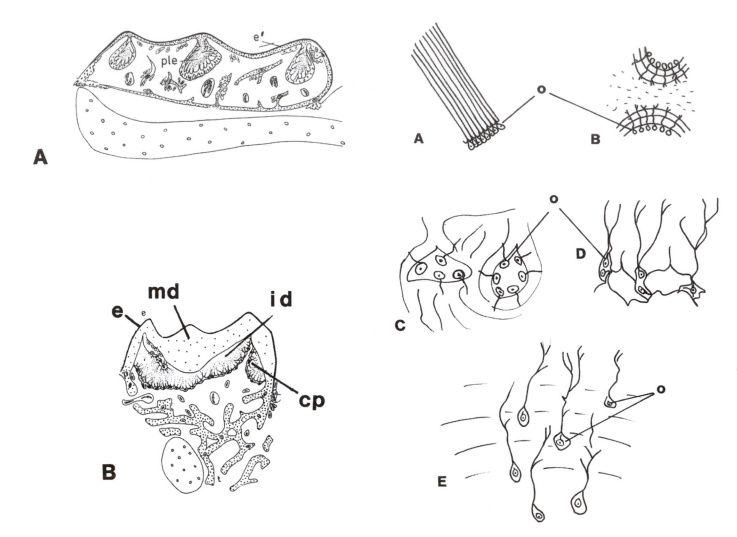

Figure 5. Complex hard tissue structures with several dentines. *A,* holocephalan; *B,* dipnoan. Key: *e,* enamel; *e',* enameloid; *od,* odontoblast; *md,* mantle dentine; *cp,* circumpulpar dentine; *id,* interdenteonal dentine; *ple,* pleromin. From Kemp (1984), *Proceedings of the Linnean Society of New South Wales.*

Figure 6. Dentine. *A,* orthodentine; *B,* osteodentine; *C,* vasodentine; *D,* mesodentine; *E,* semidentine. Key: *o,* odontocytes. After Ørvig (1967).

differs from enamel in several ways: in development, in the mineralization patterns of the organic components, and particularly in the detailed histological structures found in different groups (Lund et al. 1992). Enameloid forms as a result of interaction between ameloblasts and cells of the dermal mesenchymal primordium, but the enamelin matrix mineralizes before dentine does, and the tissue may contain more than one structurally distinctive layer. Enameloid is a simple, mineralized tissue that contains rod-like crystallites that lie parallel to the tooth surface, as in holocephalan tooth plates. In sharks, the tissue may have two additional layers, a parallel-fibered enameloid below the terminal membrane enameloid and an innermost zone having tangled collagen fibers. In teleosts, enameloid is also complex and has multiple layers. As in sharks, enameloid here includes collagen fibrils contributed by the odontoblasts. Enameloid may be mineralized with the substances hydroxyapatite or fluorapatite.

Dentine

Most dentines are associated with cells that lie outside the mineralized tissue and are not enclosed in lacunae but send processes into the dentine. This generalization is not always true, and forms of dentine with enclosed cells—dentines intermediate between bone and dentine—are known. Despite having diverse histology, dentines share certain characteristics. Dentines are based on an extracellular matrix of collagen mineralized with calcium hydroxyapatite. (The exception is pleromin, the specialized hard tissue of holocephalan teeth, that contains a substance called whitlockite.) Dentine is produced by odontoblasts, which secrete collagen fibrils that later mineralize. The odontoblasts then retreat, leaving a process enclosed by the dentine. Lower vertebrate teeth contain many different forms of dentine, but in tetrapods the tissues are simplified.

Mantle, or primary dentine, is the form of dentine first deposited in developing teeth. It consists of a thin layer of coarse collagen bundles formed just below the enamel-dentine junction. Mantle is secreted by odontoblasts with short, irregular processes. This form of dentine is found in many vertebrate teeth at an early stage of development and persists in the continually growing tooth plates of lungfishes (Figure 5B).

Despite their derived position in the evolutionary hierarchy, the dentine of mammalian teeth is orthodentine, the simplest and commonest form of dentine (Figure 5A). Orthodentine is organized around an open pulp cavity containing odontoblasts and blood vessels and nerves. Each odontoblast sends a single, long, fine process into a canaliculus in the dentine. Processes and canaliculi are parallel and may pass through the dentine-enamel junction into the enamel. Orthodentine is deposited initially as predentine, a layer of newly secreted dentine inside the mineralized tissue. This type of dentine is found in the teeth of tetrapods and in many fishes but is not present in holocephalans, dipnoans, and some placoderms and acanthodians.

Osteodentine is found in the teeth of many fishes. There is no distinct pulp cavity, but the dentine contains numerous wide canals containing vascular pulp (Figure 6B). The canals anastomose (join) with each other and accommodate the osteodontocytes. This dentine contains denteons, which are similar to the osteons of bone but less regular.

Vasodentine is found in members of some osteichthyan families (Figure 6C). This dentine contains passages for blood capillaries, but no tubules for long odontoblast processes (Lund et al. 1992). Mesodentine has large lacunae, each of which contains several cells (Figure 6D). Mesodentine contains cells intermediate between osteoblasts and odontoblasts, with many centrifugally directed processes. These may be enclosed or retracted to the walls of vascular canals. Mesodentine is found in the teeth and scales of Osteostraci (an order of ostracoderms with bony body armor) (Orvig 1967). In semidentine, the odontoblasts have single centrifugally directed processes, and the cells may be enclosed, in vascular canals, or in a pulp cavity (Figure 6E). This tissue occurs in arthrodire (extinct order of heavily armored jawed fishes) teeth and odontodes (toothlike complex of tissues).

Two groups of fishes have continuously growing tooth plates with specialized dentines. Ptyctodont arthrodires (a group of placoderms resembling modern fishes), holocephalans (extinct forms of rat-fishes), and cochliodonts have tooth plates that grow from the margin of the tooth plate (Figure 5A). Although they contain complex dentines, these teeth are not compound teeth—they do not form by fusion of smaller elements. Most dipnoans (lungfishes) have tooth plates as well; these are compound because they develop from fusion of initially separate denticles. The tooth plates grow continuously from below.

The tooth plates of holocephalans develop within a shell of trabecular dentine, which is covered by terminal membrane enameloid and containing tritural columns of pleromin, mineralized with whitlockite. ("Pleromin" means a hard tissue that fills in a space in a tooth plate.) In young specimens the pleromin contains long, branching cell processes from the cells that surround the hard tissue, but these grow less prominent as the tissue grows older. Denteons form within the mass of pleromin, but there is no distinct layer of dentine.

Derived dipnoan tooth plates, as found in fossil species of *Ceratodus* and *Neoceratodus,* are based on a shell of mantle dentine covered in a thin layer of radial crystallite enamel (Figure 5B). Within the enamel and mantle dentine shell, denteons develop, with "circumpulpar dentine" surrounded by "interdenteonal dentine." (Circumpulpar dentine is soft, high in collagen, and has many cell processes. Interdenteonal dentine is hard, low in collagen, and has few, branching cell processes.) The denteon contains a capillary loop and nerve fibers extending from the pulp cavity. Devonian dipnoans like *Chirodipterus* and *Dipterus* have a less organized form of interdenteonal dentine, associated with circumpulpar dentine, also growing in a shell of mantle dentine. A number of derived dipnoans, like species of *Mioceratodus* and *Gnathorhiza,* include blocks and columns of a highly mineralized dentine called petrodentine. This is based, like the other dentines, on collagen fibers and is not found in other fishes.

Development

Enamel, enameloid, and dentines develop as a result of complex interactions of epithelial and mesenchymal cells; bone and cartilage develop as a result of interactions within mesenchyme cells in deeper tissues. Details of these processes are not understood completely. Ameloblasts of the inner dental epithelium induce the development of dentine above the dental papilla, and enamel formation follows the initial deposition of dentine. However, cells of the dental papilla determine the form of the tooth. Bone and cartilage form in deeper layers, remote from effects of epithelial cells, and develop under the control of agents such as growth factors.

Cells of developing embryos are categorized according to their position in the embryo before those cells move and form defined tissues and organs. This is the germ layer theory, which divided embryonic cells into three types: ectoderm, endoderm, and mesoderm. "Ectodermal cells" form the outer layer of an embryo and are responsible for development of the skin, the nervous system, and derivatives of these tissues.

Cells that move into the embryo form the endoderm, which produces the intestines, liver, pancreas, and respiratory system; and mesoderm, which is responsible for muscular and connective tissues. Neural crest is a specialized cell type that arises from the ectoderm and migrates out of the neural tube after the three primary layers have been arranged. In the body and head, the neural crest gives rise to peripheral nerves and pigment cells. In the head region only, the neural crest gives rise to skeletal structures. There is some evidence that Hox genes are involved in the patterning of these head structures.

Conclusion

Hard tissue structure is not helpful for understanding vertebrate evolution as a whole, although within groups of organisms evolutionary trends are evident. Examples are the gradual refinement of tooth plate structures within holocephalans or dipnoans and the increasing complexity of molar structure within herbivorous mammals. This is not to deny the importance of analysis of hard tissues in vertebrate animals, because this research provides useful insights into the relationships among some vertebrate groups and can help identify problematic material or poorly preserved fossil fragments.

ANNE KEMP

See also Ornamentation: Vertebrates; Skeletized Organisms and the Evolution of Skeletized Tissues; Skeleton; Skull; Teeth; Vertebrate Hard Tissues: Keratinous Tissues

Works Cited

Bemis, W.E., and R.G. Northcutt. 1991. Skin and blood vessels of the snout of the Australian lungfish, *Neoceratodus forsteri,* and their significance for interpreting the cosmine of Devonian lungfishes. *Acta Zoologica (Stockholm)* 73:115–39.

Halstead, L.B. 1968. *The Pattern of Vertebrate Evolution.* San Francisco: Freeman; Edinburgh: Oliver and Boyd, 1969.

Hildebrand, M. 1995. *Analysis of Vertebrate Structure.* 4th ed., New York: Wiley.

Kemp, A. 1984. A comparison of the developing dentitions of *Neoceratodus fosteri* and *Callorhynchus milii. Proceedings of the Linnean Society of New South Wales* 107:245–62.

Lund, R. 1989. New petalodonts (Chondrichthyes) from the Upper Mississippian Bear Gulch Limestone (Namurian E2B) of Montana. *Journal of Vertebrate Paleontology* 9:350–68.

Lund, R., P. Bartholomew, and A. Kemp. 1992. The composition of the dental hard tissues of fishes. In P. Smith, E. Tchernov (eds.), *Structure, Function and Evolution of Teeth.* London: Freund.

Meinke, D.K. 1987. Morphology and evolution of the dermal skeleton in lungfishes. *Journal of Morphology,* Supplement 1:133–49.

Miles, R.S., and J.A. Moy-Thomas. 1971. *Palaeozoic Fishes.* 2nd ed., London: Chapman and Hall; Philadelphia: Saunders.

Ørvig, T. 1967. Phylogeny of tooth tissues: Evolution of some calcified tissues in early vertebrates. In A.E.W. Miles (ed.), *Structural and Chemical Organisation of Teeth.* New York: Academic Press.

Ten Cate, A.R. 1989. *Oral Histology: Development, Structure and Function.* 3rd ed., St. Louis, Missouri: Mosby.

von Koenigswald, W. 1988. Enamel modification in the enlarged front teeth among mammals and the various possible reinforcements of the enamel. *In* D.E. Russell, J.-P. Santoro, and D. Sigogneau-Russell (eds.), *Bulletin du Muséum National d'Histoire Naturelle, Paris,* ser. C, 53:147–67.

Further Reading

Halstead, L.B. 1968. *The Pattern of Vertebrate Evolution.* San Francisco: Freeman; Edinburgh: Oliver and Boyd, 1969.

Miles, A.E.W. (ed.). 1967. *Structural and Chemical Organisation of Teeth.* New York: Academic Press.

Smith, P., and E. Tchernov (eds.). 1992. *Structure, Function and Evolution of Teeth.* London: Freund.

Ten Cate, A.R. 1980. *Oral Histology: Development, Structure and Function.* St. Louis, Missouri: Mosby; 4th ed., 1994.

VERTEBRATES

See Burrowing Adaptations in Vertebrates; Chordate and Vertebrate Body Structure; Craniates; Eyes: Vertebrates; Feeding Adaptations: Vertebrates; Micropaleontology, Vertebrate; Ornamentation: Vertebrates; Reproductive Strategies: Vertebrates; Terrestrial Locomotion in Vertebrates; Vertebrate Hard Tissues

WALCOTT, CHARLES DOOLITTLE

American, 1850–1927

Charles D. Walcott was a commanding figure in his prime: tall, athletic, with a manner that left no doubt about who was in charge of any enterprise he was engaged upon. Before he was 20, he had decided to dedicate his life to science, with a particular interest in the fossils of the Cambrian period, the time when fossils first became abundant in sedimentary rocks. As a schoolboy he collected natural history specimens, and a chance meeting with the paleontologist Colonel E. Jewett—and the loan of a number of books—gave Walcott inspiration, advice, and encouragement.

After a short, promising career in business, Walcott went to work on a farm near Trenton Falls, in the Mohawk Valley of New York State. From the limestones and shales in the nearby river gorges, he amassed a large and unique collection of fossils, which formed the basis of his first articles on trilobites. One of these articles announced the discovery of traces of biramous (two-branched) limbs in enrolled trilobites, the first ever found, in thin, transparent sections cut from fossils. Walcott would return to trilobite limbs several times, including his description of the remarkably preserved specimens he recovered from the Burgess Shale (1918). His early activities brought Walcott to the notice of James Hall, state geologist and paleontologist of New York. In 1876, Walcott went to Albany to become Hall's assistant. In 1879 the United States Geological Survey was established, and Walcott, recommended by Hall, was appointed to it.

During his years on the Geological Survey, Walcott discovered thousands of Cambrian fossils and the sequences (strata, or layers) of rocks in which they occurred in all parts of the United States. His first major work in paleontology described Cambrian brachiopods (clamlike invertebrates) and trilobites, and younger Paleozoic fossils from the Eureka district, Nevada (1884). Walcott's discoveries of the *Olenellus* fauna, in the oldest Cambrian rocks, set forth in his 1890 report, established him internationally as a leader in his field. In his investigations in the northeastern States and eastern Canada, he already had found that this fauna was indeed that of the earliest Cambrian (as it was known to be in Europe), a major conclusion that helped to settle a long-standing controversy among geologists working in the northeastern States.

Walcott described and collected trilobites of the Middle and Upper Cambrian, the most abundant fossils and reliable indicators of stratigraphical age, but he did not neglect other fossils. Shorter papers on Cambrian brachiopods were followed by his great monograph (1912). More enigmatic were the fossils (or supposed fossils) that he dealt with in his monograph on Cambrian Medusae (1898), an important work drawing attention to problematic structures. Walcott was an early student of trace fossils, collecting and describing tracks and trails ascribed to trilobites, and a pioneer in searching for Precambrian fossils and gathering information on stromatolites (the earliest plantlike lifeforms). In 1893 his acute observation skills enabled him to recognize tiny fragments of bony scales in a Middle Ordovician sandstone, among the oldest known of such material.

Walcott's energy and drive enabled him to make these great additions to knowledge, while at the same time his vision and ability led to an increasing administrative burden as he became chief paleontologist, then director of the Geological Survey. He was most successful in enlarging the Geological Survey and expanding its activities into the conservation of national resources.

Walcott had long had a connection with the Smithsonian Institution, because the paleontologists of the Geological Survey, with their collections, worked in a special section of the institution (the United States National Museum), alongside the museum's own staff. Walcott had become assistant secretary of the Smithsonian Institution in 1896, in charge of the National Museum, although he remained with the Geological Survey. Then in 1907, Walcott was persuaded to leave the Survey to become secretary of the Smithsonian Institution. At the age of 57, he began a new and highly productive phase of his scientific career. Busy as he was administering the Smithsonian—promoting and fostering the Carnegie Institution, supporting aeronautics, and promoting what became the National Park Service—he still reserved time for scientific work in the laboratory and in the field in the Canadian Rocky Mountains. His long series of articles on Cambrian stratigraphy, trilobites, brachiopods, and other fossils (1908–28) fill some 2,500 pages (plus many accompanying plates of photographs) of the institution's periodical, the Smithsonian Miscellaneous Collections. These, with his Geological Survey publications, constitute a huge body of information on the Cambrian of North America and China (based upon collections made by a Carnegie expedition) resulting from extended field collections and observations of Walcott and his assistants. Today, this information and the collections housed in the National Museum form an essential basis for continuing studies by scientists in all parts of the world.

After more than 40 years of searching for Cambrian fossils all over North America, Walcott's greatest discovery came in 1909, when he found loose blocks of the Burgess Shale. These were not the usual Cambrian fossils—the mineralized shells, which are the hard parts of animals preserved under common conditions—but rather extraordinary preservations of both shell and soft parts and of entirely soft-bodied animals, such as worms (1911). Realizing the importance of his find, Walcott returned the next year, located the rock strata that was the source of the loose materials, and began to quarry them. Quarrying continued over the next two years and again in 1917. The result was a collection of more than 60,000 of these unique fossils (Yochelson 1996). Walcott was 59 when he made his discovery, and his outstanding energy and devotion enabled him to continue the quarrying and also to make his finds known in a series of short articles published between 1911 and 1924, illustrated by good photographs. Zoologists as well as paleontologists were amazed at the revelation of the complexity and variety of Cambrian marine organisms, particularly when nothing remotely similar had been found in older, Precambrian strata. Walcott discussed the problem posed by the rapid diversification of marine animals in the Cambrian. He was also well aware that he had been able to make no more than preliminary investigations of his own great find. As work in the last 30 years has shown (Whittington 1985), Walcott bequeathed a major legacy to science in his Burgess Shale collection. His career shows how effective dedication to science may be, without the formal university preparation required today and despite a heavy administrative burden.

H.B. WHITTINGTON

Works Cited

Whittington, H.B. 1985. *The Burgess Shale*. New Haven, Connecticut: Yale University Press.

Yochelson, E.L. 1996. Discovery, Collection and Description of the Middle Cambrian Burgess Shale Biota by Charles Doolittle Walcott. *Proceedings of the American Philosophical Society* 140:469–545.

Biography

Born in Oneida County, New York, 31 March 1850. Attended school in Utica until age 18. Assistant to James Hall, New York State Geological Survey, 1876; became member (1879), chief paleontologist (1892), and director (1894), U.S. Geological Survey; secretary, Smithsonian Institution, 1907. Recipient of numerous awards, including Bigsby Medal, Geological Society of London; Gaudry Prize, Geological Society of France; Hayden Memorial Geology Award, Academy of Natural Sciences of Philadelphia; Mary Clark Thompson Medal, National Academy of Sciences; Wollaston Medal, Geological Society of London. Member and officer of numerous scholarly and professional associations, including the Academy of Natural Sciences of Philadelphia; Academy of Sciences of Bologna; American Academy of Arts and Sciences; French Academy of Sciences; French Geological Society; Geological Society of London; Imperial Society of Naturalists, Moscow; National Academy of Sciences (president, 1917–23); National Research Council (founder); Royal Swedish Academic Society; Washington Archaeological Society (president). Received honorary degrees from institutions including Cambridge University, Christiana University, Harvard University, Johns Hopkins University, Royal Fredericks University, University of Chicago, University of Pennsylvania, University of Pittsburgh, and University of St. Andrews. Discovered traces of limbs in trilobites, 1876; demonstrated that fossils of the Lower and Middle Cambrian in North America occurred in same sequence as those in Europe, 1888; continued field and laboratory work on Cambrian strata and fossils in United States and in Rocky Mountains of western Canada, from 1907 on; discovered Burgess Shale, 1909; quarried site and amassed over 60,000 fossils, 1910–17. Died in Washington, D.C., 9 February 1927.

Major Publications

1881. The trilobite: New and old evidence relating to its organization. *Harvard University Museum of Comparative Zoology Bulletin* 8 (10):191–230.

1884a. *On the Cambrian Faunas of North America: Preliminary Studies.* U.S. Geological Survey Bulletin, 10. Washington, D.C.: U.S. Government Printing Office.

1884b. *Paleontology of the Eureka District.* United States Geological Survey, Monograph 8. Washington, D.C.: U.S. Government Printing Office.

1886. *Second Contribution to the Study on the Cambrian Faunas of North America: Preliminary Studies.* U.S. Geological Survey Bulletin, 30. Washington, D.C.: U.S. Government Printing Office.

1890. The fauna of the Lower Cambrian or *Olenellus* zone. *United States Geological Survey, 10th Annual Report,* Part 1. Washington, D.C.: U.S. Government Printing Office.

1898. *Fossil Medusae.* United States Geological Survey, Monograph 30. Washington, D.C.: U.S. Government Printing Office.

1906. Cambrian faunas of China. *Proceedings of the United States National Museum* 30:563–595.

1911. Middle Cambrian Annelids. Cambrian Geology and Paleontology, 2. *Smithsonian Miscellaneous Collections* 57 (5):109–44.

1912. *Cambrian Brachiopoda.* 2 vols. United States Geological Survey, Monograph 51. Washington, D.C.: U.S. Government Printing Office.

1914a. *Problems of American Geology.* New Haven, Connecticut: Yale University Press.

1914b. Pre-Cambrian Algonkian algal flora. *Smithsonian Miscellaneous Collections* 64 (2):77–156.

1916. Evidences of primitive life. *Smithsonian Institution Annual Report, 1915.* Washington, D.C.: Smithsonian Institution.

1918. Appendages of trilobites. Cambrian Geology and Palaeontology, 4. *Smithsonian Miscellaneous Collections* 67 (4):115–216.

Further Reading

Darton, N.H. 1928. Memorial of Charles Doolittle Walcott. *Bulletin of the Geological Society of America* 39:80–116.

Schuchert, C. 1927. Charles Doolittle Walcott, paleontologist, 1850–1927. *Fort Hayes Studies, Science Series* 65:455–58.

Whittington, H.B. 1985. *The Burgess Shale*. New Haven, Connecticut: Yale University Press.

Yochelson, E.L. 1967. Charles Doolittle Walcott, 1850–1927. *Biographical Memoirs*, National Academy of Science of the United States. Vol. 39. New York: Columbia University Press.

———. 1996. Discovery, Collection and Description of the Middle Cambrian Burgess Shale Biota by Charles Doolittle Walcott. *Proceedings of the American Philosophical Society* 140:469–545.

WATSON, DAVID MEREDITH SEARES

English, 1886–1973

As a child, Watson was introduced to geology by his father, the metallurgist David Watson. He enrolled at the University of Manchester to study chemistry and prepare himself for a job in industry, but he soon became interested in Carboniferous coal balls and their petrifactions and switched to geology as his main subject of study. Watson published several papers on Carboniferous plants even before his graduation. He became a demonstrator at Manchester after receiving his Master's degree in 1909. Through his work on coal ball fossils, Watson became acquainted with an amateur geologist named Sutcliffe who also had collected a Liassic plesiosaur from Whitby. The two men recovered another plesiosaurian skeleton, and Watson switched his interest to fossil reptiles. Between 1908 and 1910 Watson worked in the rich collections of fossil vertebrates housed at the British Museum (Natural History) in London. He became especially interested in the tetrapods, especially therapsids, from the Permo-Triassic continental strata of the Karoo in South Africa. This interest led Watson to visit South Africa in 1911 for the purpose of making extensive collections, which formed the material basis for many of his research projects in subsequent years. In 1912 he started lecturing on vertebrate paleontology at University College, London. After several years of travel, including an extended stay in Australia, followed by military service during World War I, Watson returned to University College and, in 1921, was appointed Jodrell Professor of Zoology and Comparative Anatomy. He worked at University College for the remainder of his research career with the exception of service as secretary of the Scientific Subcommittee of the Food Policy Committee of the British War Cabinet during World War II and a year as visiting Alexander Agassiz Professor of Zoology at Harvard University.

Watson made many important contributions to the anatomy and phylogeny of fossil vertebrates, ranging from jawless fishlike vertebrates to derived therapsids. He is now best known for his studies on Paleozoic fishes, labyrinthodont amphibians, and therapsids. His only book, *Paleontology and Modern Biology* (1951), was based on his Silliman Lectures at Yale University in 1937 and presents a useful summary of some of Watson's major research projects. For his anatomical studies, Watson frequently broke apart specimens preserved in hard rock to work out in great detail critical anatomical features that otherwise would have been inaccessible owing to the very limited possibilities for preparation of fossils at that time. He usually did not content himself with mere morphological description but also considered the functional implications of anatomical structures as well as the broader relationships of the animals in question. Along with W.K. Gregory, Watson was an early supporter of the Gaupp-Reichert theory, which postulates the homology of the ossicles of the mammalian middle ear with the postdentary bones of the lower jaw of reptiles, and, together with Robert Broom, argued persuasively for the theriodont (a therapsid group) origin of mammals. Watson was also among the first researchers to demonstrate that tetrapods are more closely related to rhipidistian fishes such as *Osteolepis* than to lungfishes.

Watson's scientific contributions were recognized by numerous awards and several honorary degrees. He was elected Fellow of the Royal Society of London in 1922, Foreign Correspondent of the Academy of Sciences of the U.S.S.R. in 1931, Honorary Fellow of University College London in 1948, and Fellow of the Royal Society of Edinburgh in 1949. Watson also served as a Trustee of the British Museum.

HANS-DIETER SUES

Biography

Born in Higher Broughton, near Salford, Lancashire, 18 June 1886. Received B.Sc. with first-class honors in geology, University of Manchester, 1907; M.Sc., University of Manchester, 1909. Demonstrator, University of Manchester, 1909–10; lecturer on vertebrate paleontology, University College, London, 1912–21; Jodrell Professor of Zoology and Comparative Anatomy, University College, London, 1921–25; secretary, Scientific Subcommittee, Food Policy Committee, British War Cabinet, 1940–43; Visiting Alexander Agassiz Professor of Zoology, Harvard University, 1951–52. Elected fellow, Royal Society, London, 1922; elected foreign correspondent, Academy of the Sciences of the U.S.S.R., 1931; received Lyell Medal (1935) and Wollaston Medal (1965), Geological Society of London; received Makdoughal Medal and Prize, Royal Society of Edinburgh, 1939; received Thompson Medal, National Academy of Sciences, 1941; received Darwin Medal, Royal Society, London, 1942; named honorary fellow, University College, London, 1948; elected fellow of the Royal Society of Edinburgh, 1949; received Linnean Medal (1949) and Darwin-Wallace Medal (1958), Linnean Society of London; trustee, British Museum (Natural History); received honorary degrees from Cape Town, Manchester, Reading, Wales, Aberdeen, and Witwatersrand. Made many important contributions to anatomy and phylogeny of Paleozoic and Mesozoic fishes and tetrapods, especially amphibians and synapsids. Died in Harrow, England, 23 July 1973.

Major Publications

1916. The monotreme skull: A contribution to mammalian morphogenesis. *Philosophical Transactions of the Royal Society of London*, ser. B, 207:311–74.

1919. The structure, evolution and origin of the Amphibia: The "orders" Rachitomi and Stereospondyli. *Philosophical Transactions of the Royal Society of London*, ser. B, 209:1–73.

1926. The evolution and origin of the Amphibia. *Philosophical Transactions of the Royal Society of London*, ser. B, 214:189–257.

1951. *Paleontology and Modern Biology*. New Haven, Connecticut: Yale University Press.

1957. On *Millerosaurus* and the early history of the sauropsid reptiles. *Philosophical Transactions of the Royal Society of London*, ser. B, 240:325–400.

Further Reading

Parrington, F.R., and T.S. Westoll. 1974. David Meredith Seares Watson 1886–1973. *Biographical Memoirs of Fellows of the Royal Society* 20:483–504.

WESTOLL, THOMAS STANLEY

English, 1912–95

Westoll made original contributions to our knowledge of the structure and relationships of early vertebrates, especially by clarifying concepts of dermal bone homologies (similarity of structures due to common ancestry) in the sarcopterygians (crossopterygians, dipnoans) and tetrapods. Many of Westoll's works are characterized by a particular interest in the evolution of major structures and the construction of transformational theories. He introduced new views on the origin of pectoral fins and the evolution of the tetrapods. Westoll was an early follower of Alfred Lothar Wegener and believed in continental drift long before the geophysicists made it respectable and fashionable. Under his guidance and inspiration, an important school of vertebrate paleontology was established in the 1960s at the University of Newcastle-upon-Tyne in the north of England. His wider interests extended to sedimentation in Devonian and Carboniferous times and to problems of structural geology.

Born in West Hartlepool in the north of England, Stanley Westoll was a keen naturalist as a child; his interest in geology dated from his tenth birthday, when a favorite uncle gave him a book on rocks and fossils. Within weeks, on a family holiday at Whitby, he had collected a better specimen of *Dactylioceras* than that figured in the book (possibly A. Morley Davies' *Introduction to Palaeontology* of 1920) and became a keen collector. His interest in mineralogy and microscopy was encouraged at school, and as a teenager he won commendation in the prestigious local Hancock Museum/Northumberland Natural History Society Prize for his essay "The Geology of the District around West Hartlepool."

At Armstrong College (later King's College, originally of the University of Durham and then the University of Newcastle-upon-Tyne), he received a good grounding in geology under the mentorship of Professor George Hickling, who later fostered his interest in fossil vertebrates. This encouragement led to his doctoral research on the rare complete Permian paleoniscoid fishes of northeast England that provided the foundation for later major works on actinopterygians from the Carboniferous and Permian in Europe and America (e.g., Westoll 1937a, 1937c; 1941a, 1941c; 1944). He related the fishes to their structure and function and postulated lifestyles. Westoll's major monograph on haplolepid fishes (later published 1944), gained Westoll an honorable mention in the New York Academy of Science's A. Cressy Morrison Prize competition of 1942.

Professor Edwin Sherbon Hills (pioneer Devonian fish scholar in Australia) spoke with affection of sharing a room with Westoll in 1936 when they were both studying under D.M.S. Watson at University College, London. Westoll was then recipient of a DSIR Senior Research Award, which he had taken up in 1934. Here he began in earnest the researches on Paleozoic and especially Old Red Sandstone fishes, which were to be the focus of much of his professional life. Watson was his adviser for three years, and Westoll benefited from the magnificent comparative material and knowledge of the important Carboniferous amphibians and fishes that "DMS" had amassed over many years. In the next 40 years Westoll dedicated much of his time to elucidating the nature and use of Paleozoic fishes in biostratigraphy; he became an expert on Paleozoic fish localities in Scotland and the north of England. The DSIR award made it possible for him to visit many European museums and institutes; with the help of grants from the J.B. Tyrrell Fund of the Geological Society of London and the Royal Society in 1937, he was able to visit Canada, where, in conjunction with W.E. Graham-Smith, he made field collections at the Late Devonian (Frasnian) Escuminac site of Quebec (Lemieux 1996). This work resulted in papers on the lungfish *Fleurantia* (1937), earlier collected by Graham-Smith, and his discovery of a purported tetrapod at Miguasha, *Elpistostege* (1938), which greatly enhanced interest in the Escuminac site. The early Canadian work continued in later life and provided the basis for a body of his work and that of his students until the 1970s with papers on *Eusthenopteron foordi* (1970) and *Cheirolepis canadensis* (1979). Following up on his work on Permian coelacanths (1939), he was due to go to South Africa in 1939 to help J.L.B. Smith analyze the newly found *Latimeria*, but the outbreak of World War II foiled this plan.

The study of the patterns of dermal bones of the skull roof have played an important part in the elucidation of early vertebrate phylogeny and evolution, and Westoll was among those to put forward plans to demonstrate the homology between the bones of sarcopterygians and tetrapods. His conclusion (1943a) that the parietals are invariably the bones that flank the pineal foramen in early vertebrates has held good (except in dipnomorphs; Janvier 1996). We owe to him the current idea that lungfishes are merely derived sarcopterygians and are closely allied to porolepiforms (Janvier 1996). In 1952 Westoll described *Dipno-*

rhynchus lehmanni from the Lower Devonian of Germany, then one of the oldest lungfishes known, from material collected by W. Lehmann of Nahe. He returned to dipnorhynchid lungfish skull roofs in his last major paper (1989), maintaining a sister-group relationship between lungfishes and osteolepids.

The nature and possible phylogeny of agnathan (jawless) fishes was the subject of his 1945 paper, which included the first discussion since Traquair's at the turn of the century of thelodont branchial morphology. His conclusions on the paraphyletic nature of thelodonts are still favored by some today (e.g., Janvier 1996). He did accept *Turinia pagei* as a "coelolepid" (i.e., true thelodont) but thought it possible that various "thelodonts" were juveniles of other ostracoderms (an idea that Turner 1991 has refuted).

The 1948 International Geological Congress had the first ever vertebrate paleontology section on the correlation of continental vertebrate-bearing rocks, and Westoll delivered a seminal paper there on the vertebrate-bearing rocks of Scotland (1948b). He personally led the northern leg of the IGC Excursion held in Britain in 1948, visiting classic Silurian (Lesmahagow/Hagshaw), "Downtonian" (Stonehaven), Devonian (Scottish Midland Valley, Forfar, and Caithness), and Carboniferous (Glancartholm and Tarras Foot) sites, as well as other Permian and Triassic sites (1948a, 1948b). Around this time he was collecting and developing his work on the Achanarras and Banniskirk material that eventually led to a complete description of the Mid-Devonian *Coccoteus cuspidatus* (Miles and Westoll 1968) and other placoderms. His work on the Achanarras fauna was financially supported by the DSIR, which enabled him to acquire the Murray-Threipland family collections made over two generations, as well as by utilizing the *Dipterus* collections of Sir Clive Forster-Cooper (Westoll 1949).

Westoll also did work on the origin of paired limbs, in particular on the lateral fin-fold theory and the pectoral fins of ostracoderms and early fishes. Westoll pointed out that there is a strong trend in several ostracoderms for development of paired ventrolateral balancing structures along the flanks; finny extensions were presumed to have formed independently in a number of cases. His and Miles' study of *Gemeundina* was important in evaluating the nature of primitive placoderms and whether their fins are homologous with those of higher vertebrates.

P.H. Greenwood (1978) noted in his foreword to the Linnean Society of London's Festschrift for Westoll that "there was not a single major group of fish-like vertebrates, gnathous or agnathous, that he had not investigated at some time or another." His early work on the cosmine covering of dermal bones and scales of *Osteolepis* and *Dipterus* (1936) spurred later studies on cosmine resorption in dipnoans and osteolepids and clarified former taxonomic difficulties. Westoll brought a biological background to solve paleontological problems. Eventually he was to be honored scientifically with the term "Westoll-Lines" (undulating concentric zones separating areas of growth in cosmine; Westoll 1936; Bystrow 1942).

Westoll maintained close associations with North America, gaining the Geological Society of London's Daniel Pidgeon Fund in 1939 for an opportunity to study further the fish localities in eastern Canada. He crossed the Atlantic again with D.M.S. Watson to attend the International Conference on Genetics, Paleontology, and Evolution held during Princeton's bicentennial celebration in January 1947 and gave talks on evolution of fishes at Yale, the Museum of Comparative Zoology (Harvard), and the American Museum of Natural History (New York). One aim of the GPE meeting was to "stimulate young scientists to explore new areas and methods of research"; here he talked on the origin of the Dipnoi. Joining the Society of Vertebrate Paleontology in 1943, he was able to attend several meetings: at Chicago in 1946; at Cambridge in 1952; while serving as the Visiting Alexander Agassiz Professor at Harvard University in 1959; in Los Angeles in 1977; and in Toronto in 1978. He also visited Australia in the winter of 1959–60 to attend the centenary of the Royal Society of New South Wales.

After a period as lecturer at the University of Aberdeen, Westoll became J.B. Simpson Professor of Geology at the University of Newcastle-upon-Tyne (formerly King's College, Newcastle-upon-Tyne, University of Durham). His next decade was taken up with the administrative duties and the arduous task of creating a new and modern geology department, and his research slowed accordingly. In 1952, however, he became a fellow of the Royal Society at the comparatively young age of 39. At this time he cooperated with Rex Parrington in work on the evolution of the ear, enlisting the support also of an Aberdeen ear surgeon, John Gerrie. A visit to Oslo and Stockholm in the summer of 1961 did much to revive his interest in publishing, resulting in the *Nature* paper on ptyctodonts and holocephalans (Westoll 1962). During his professorship he initiated extremely important work on the nature of coal, which was carried out in his department and fostered during the thirteenth Inter-University Geological Congress in January 1965 (Murchison and Westoll 1968). During his 29 years as head of the department, he delighted and inspired students with his lectures.

In Miles and Westoll (1968), he and student Roger Miles attacked the classic placoderm fish *Coccosteus cuspidatus* from the Middle Old Red Sandstone of Scotland, utilizing the collections made by Westoll at Achannarras and checking all known forms in Britain and elsewhere referred to as *Coccosteus,* synonymizing many taxa. They already had created two new taxa *Watsonosteus* and *Dickosteus* (Miles and Westoll 1963) for other former "*Coccosteus*" species. The 1968 paper is a model of its kind, illustrating many examples of each plate and even postcranial and postthoracic scales.

From the mid-1950s Westoll had nurtured several vertebrate palaeontologists: Alick D. Walker, who began to work on the enigmatic *Stagonolepis,* and S. Mahala Andrews, an enthusiastic DSIR granted-research assistant in the 1960s with whom he began to unravel the postcranial skeleton of sarcopterygians. They were able to reconstruct musculature of the pectoral fin skeleton of the key rhipidistian *Eusthenopteron foordi* and make close comparison with the tetrapod limb. Westoll undertook important placoderm and later lungfish studies with Roger S. Miles. He also worked with Peter Zaborski, who took on the coelacanth acquired from the Comoros through the auspices of the Royal Society in 1972; with D. Mike Pearson, who worked on primitive ray-finned fishes; with Angela Brown (née Swonnell), who completed a major thesis on *Holoptychius;* with Bobbie Paton, who was originally Westoll's research assistant and became Alick Walker's student; with Maggie Rowlands on cephalaspids; and with Susan Turner, who completed her Ph.D. on thelodonts under his wing. Westoll's geological students included Noel Donovan and Nigel Trewin, who worked on the nature of the Orcadian Basin.

Westoll hosted several major symposia, notably the 1972 NATO conference "Implications of Continental Drift to the Earth Science" at the time when he was president of the Geological Society. Another key event at this time was the acquisition in 1972 of a specimen of the extant coelacanth, *Latimeria chalumnae,* through the good offices and with the aid of the Royal Society. This specimen is housed at the Hancock Museum in Newcastle and was destined for dissection by Westoll's student, Peter Zaborski; it was cast by Stuart Baldwin, and that cast was on display until quite recently with the new renovation of the Geology Gallery.

Westoll will be remembered for his love of travel, breadth of knowledge, and scholarship, as well as his sense of humor and his many anecdotes. He was a man of considerable influence and was held in high regard by the scientific community of zoologists and paleontologists. Many contributed to the Festschrift volume edited by his students, Andrews, Miles, and Walker (with the help of Kim Dennis) entitled "Problems in Vertebrate Evolution." The associated symposium was held at the Linnean Society of London to commemorate Professor Westoll's retirement from the J.B. Simpson Chair. Westoll's many accomplishments support the claim that he was one of this century's foremost paleoichthyologists.

Most of Westoll's papers were thought-provoking and are regarded as milestones in the field. As Westoll himself concluded on the occasion of receiving the Murchison Medal from the Geological Society of London (1968), "I can only hope, as any scientist must, to be like them [his medal predecessors] a link in the chain that binds the past, through the present, with the future."

SUSAN TURNER

Works Cited

Bystrow, A.P. 1942. Deckknochen und Zähne der *Osteolepis* und *Dipterus.* *Acta Zoologica* 23:263–89.

Dunham, K.C. 1968. The president presented the Murchison Medal to Professor T.S. Westoll. *Proceedings of the Geological Society of London* 1644:281–82.

Greenwood, P.H. 1979. Foreword. *In* S.M. Andrews, R.S. Miles, and A.D. Walker (eds.), *Problems in Vertebrate Evolution.* Linnean Society Symposium Series No. 4. London and New York: Academic Press.

Janvier, P. 1996. *Early Vertebrates.* Oxford: Clarendon; New York: Oxford University Press.

Lemieux, P. 1996. The Fossil Lagerstätte Miguasha: Its past and present history. *In* H.-P. Schultze and R. Cloutier (eds.), *Devonian Fishes and Plants of Miguasha, Quebec, Canada.* Munich: Verlag Dr. Friedrich Pfeil.

Murchison, D. 1996. Thomas Stanley Westoll (1912–1995). *Geological Society Annual Report* 1996:22–23.

Turner, S. 1991. Monophyly and interrelationship of the Thelodonti. *In* M.-M. Chang, Y.-H. Liu, and G.R. Zhang (eds.), *Early Vertebrates and Related Problems of Evolutionary Biology.* Symposium on Early Vertebrates, September 1987. Beijing: Science Press.

Biography

Born 3 July 1912 in West Hartlepool, England. Awarded open entrance scholarship to Armstrong College (later known as King's College, originally of the University of Durham and then the University of Newcastle-upon-Tyne), 1929; received B.Sc., Armstrong College, 1932; received Ph.D., Armstrong College, 1935. Lecturer in geology, University of Aberdeen, 1937–48; named J.B. Simpson Professor of Geology, University of Newcastle-upon-Tyne, 1948; Alexander Agassiz Visiting Professor of Vertebrate Palaeontology, Harvard University 1952; Huxley Lecturer, University of Birmingham, 1967; retired as Professor Emeritus, University of Newcastle-upon-Tyne, 1977. Recipient, DSIR Senior Research Award, 1934–37; grant recipient, J.B. Tyrrell Fund, Geological Society of London, 1937; grant recipient, Daniel Pidgeon Fund, Geological Society of London, 1939; elected fellow, Royal Society of Edinburgh, 1943; elected to the Society of Vertebrate Paleontologists, 1943; elected fellow, Royal Society (London), 1952; received D.Sc., University of Aberdeen, 1952; member, Council of the Royal Society, 1966–68; president, Palaeontological Association, 1966–68; elected fellow, Geological Society of London; awarded Murchison Medal, Geological Society of London, 1967; president, Geological Society of London, 1972–74; elected fellow, Linnean Society of London, 1976; elected Honorary Life Member, Society of Vertebrate Paleontologists, 1976; recipient, Clough Medal Edinburgh, Geological Society; held Leverhulme Emeritus Research Fellow Award 1977–79; awarded Linnean Society of London Gold Medal (Zoology), 1978; received Hon. LLD., University of Aberdeen, 1979; chairman of University Convocation, University of Aberdeen,1979–89. Died 19 September 1995 in Newcastle-upon-Tyne.

Major Publications

1936. On the structure of the dermal ethmoid shield of *Osteolepis. Geological Magazine* 73:157–71.

1937a. The Old Red Sandstone fishes of the North of Scotland, particularly of Orkney and Shetland. *Proceedings of the Geological Association* 48:13–45.

1937b. On a remarkable fish from the Lower Permian of Autun, France. *Annual Magazine of Natural History* 10 (19):553–78.

1937c. On a specimen of *Eusthenopteron* from the Old Red Sandstone of Scotland. *Geological Magazine* 74:507–24.

1937d. On the cheek bones in teleostome fishes. *Journal of Anatomy* 71 (3):362–82.

1937e. With W. Graham-Smith. On a new long-headed Dipnoan from the Upper Devonian of the Scaumenac Bay, P.Q., Canada. *Transactions of the Royal Society of Edinburgh* 59:241–56.

1938. Ancestry of the tetrapods. *Nature* (London) 141:127–28.

1939. On *Spermatodus pustulosus* Cope, a coelacanth from the "Permian" of Texas. *American Museum Novitiates* 1017:1–23.

1940a. New Scottish material of *Eusthenopteron. Geological Magazine* 77:65–73.

1940b. With F.R. Parrington. On the evolution of the mammalian palate. *Philosophical Transactions of the Royal Society of London* 230:305–55.

1941a. The age of certain Permian fish-bearing beds. *Geological Magazine* 78:37–44.

1941b. Latero-sensory canals and dermal bones. *Nature* (London) 148:168.

1941c. The Permian fishes *Dorypterus* and *Lekanichthys. Proceedings of the Zoological Society of London,* ser. B, 111:39–58.

1942. Relationships of some primitive tetrapods. *Nature* (London) 150:121.

1943a. The origin of the primitive tetrapod limb. *Proceedings of the Royal Society of London,* ser. B, 131:373–93.

1943b. The hyomandibular of *Eusthenopteron* and the tetrapod middle ear. *Proceedings of the Royal Society of London,* ser. B, 131:393–414.

1943c. The origin of the tetrapods. *Biology Review* 18:78–98.

1944. The Haplolepidae, a new family of Late Carboniferous bony fishes: A study in taxonomy and evolution. *Bulletin of the American Museum of Natural History* 83:1–122.

1945a. A new cephalaspid fish from the Downtonian (Silurian) of Scotland, with notes on the structure and classification of Ostracoderms. *Transactions of the Royal Society of Edinburgh* 61:341–57.

1945b. The paired fins of placoderms. *Transactions of the Royal Society of Edinburgh* 61:81–398.

1948a. Scotland. *In* 18th International Geological Congress, *Guide Excursion C 16.* London: International Geological Congress.

1948b. The vertebrate-bearing strata of Scotland. *In* 18th International Geological Congress, *Abstract 18.* London: International Geological Congress.

1949. On the evolution of the Dipnoi. *In* G.L. Jepson, E. Mayr, and G.G. Simpson (eds.), *Genetics, Palaeontology and Evolution.* Princeton, New Jersey: Princeton University Press.

1951. The vertebrate-bearing strata of Scotland. *In* W.E. Swinton (ed.), *The Correlation of Continental Vertebrate-bearing Rocks.* Report of the 18th Session of the International Geological Congress, 1948. Pt. 11, sect. K. London: International Geological Congress.

1952. With W. Lehmann. A primitive dipnoan fish from the Lower Devonian of Germany. *Proceedings of the Royal Society of London,* ser. B, 140:403–21.

1954. Mountain revolutions and organic evolution. *In* J. Huxley, A.C. Hardy, and E.B. Ford (eds.), *Evolution as a Process.* London: Allen and Unwin; 2nd ed., London: Allen and Unwin, 1958; New York: Collier, 1963.

1958. (Ed.). *Studies on Fossil Vertebrates Presented to David Meredith Seares Watson.* London: Athlone. (*Includes* The lateral fin-fold theory and the pectoral fins of ostracoderms and early fishes.)

1961. A crucial stage in vertebrate evolution: Fish to land animal. *Proceedings of the Royal Institution of Great Britain* 38:600–18.

1962. Ptyctodontid fishes and the ancestry of Holocephali. *Nature* (London) 194:949–52.

1963. With R.S. Miles. Two new genera of Coccosteid Arthrodira from the Middle Old Red Sandstone of Scotland and their stratigraphical distribution. *Transactions of the Royal Society of Edinburgh* 65:179–210.

1967. *Radotina* and other tesserate fishes. *In* C. Patterson and I.E. White (eds.), Fossil Vertebrates. *Journal of the Linnean Society of London (Zoology)* 47:83–98.

1968. With R.S. Miles. The placoderm fish *Coccosteus cuspidatus* Miller ex Agassiz from the Middle Old Red Sandstone of Scotland. Part 1, Descriptive morphology. *Transactions of the Royal Society of Edinburgh* 67:373–476.

1968. With D.G. Murchison (eds.). Coal and coal-bearing strata. Edinburgh and London: Oliver and Boyd; New York: American Elsevier. (*Includes* Sedimentary rhythms in coal-bearing strata; Vertebrate faunas of coal-bearing strata.)

1970. With S.M. Andrews. The postcranial skeleton of *Eusthenopteron foordi* Whiteaves. *Transactions of the Royal Society of Edinburgh* 68:207–329.

1972. Devonian fish. *In* D.H. Tarling and S.K. Runcorn (eds.), *Implications of Continental Drift to the Earth Sciences.* Vol. 1. London and New York: Academic Press.

1979. Devonian fish biostratigraphy. *In* M.R. House, C.T. Scrutton, and M.G. Bassett (eds.), The Devonian System. *Special Papers in Palaeontology* 23:341–53.

1979. With D.M. Pearson. The Devonian Actinopterygian *Cheirolepis* Agassiz. *Transactions of the Royal Society of Edinburgh* 70:337–99.

1989. A new interpretation of the dermal skull of the Australian Devonian lungfish *Dipnorhynchus. In* R.W. Le Maitre (ed.), *Pathways in Geology: Essays in Honour of Edwin Sherbon Hills.* Carlton (Australia): Blackwell Scientific; Melbourne: Hills Memorial Volume Committee.

Further Reading

Greenwood, P.H. 1979. Foreword, *In* S.M. Andrews, R.S. Miles, and A.D. Walker (eds.), *Problems in Vertebrate Evolution.* Linnean Society Symposium Series No. 4. London and New York: Academic Press.

Murchison, D. 1995. Professor Stanley Westoll. *The Independent,* 11 November.

———. 1996. Thomas Stanley Westoll (1912–1995). *Annual Report of the Geological Society of London* 1996:22–23.

———. 1998. Thomas Stanley Westoll, BSc, PhD (Dunelm), DSc, LLD (Aberd), FRS, FGS. *Yearbook of the Royal Society of Edinburgh* 1998:151–53.

Turner, S. 1995. Professor Thomas Stanley Westoll, Ph.D., D.Sc., F.R.S., F.R.S.E. 1912–1995. *Ichthyolith Issues* 16:16–19.

———. 1997. Professor Thomas Stanley Westoll, Ph.D., D.Sc., Hon. LL.D., F.G.S., F.L.S., F.R.S.E., F.R.S., 1912–1995. *News Bulletin, Society of Vertebrate Paleontology* 169:86–89.

WHALES

The mammalian order Cetacea includes modern whales, dolphins, and porpoises. Cetaceans are among the most specialized mammals, all of which are obligate aquatic animals—they cannot live outside the water. They have retained many characters that show their mammalian heritage. Their lower jaw consists of a single bone (the dentary); the upper jaw (maxilla) is immovably fused to the skull. There are two bony knobs at the back of the skull for articulation with the first neck vertebra and three bones in the ear. Cetaceans breath air with lungs and have a four-chambered heart. The dorsal fin lacks skeletal support. And, finally, fetuses are attached to the mother's uterus by means of a placenta, and infants are nursed with milk produced by the mother.

On the other hand, modern cetaceans have greatly modified their morphology (form) and are very different from primitive mammals. Cetaceans do not chew their food, they either have teeth that lack the complicated relief (surface contours) found in the teeth of other mammals or lack teeth altogether. Their nose opening has shifted to the top of the head, and their ear and jaw are modified for hearing underwater. Their forelimbs are modified into flippers, their hind limbs are absent, the tail is expanded to form a horizontal fluke, and they have lost their fur, replacing it with an insulating layer of fat below the skin (blubber). R. Kellogg (1928) and L.G. Barnes and E.D. Mitchell (1978) have discussed cetacean morphology in more detail. Cetaceans did not acquire all these changes simultaneously; the fossil record shows a gradual acquisition of characters related to aquatic life. The origin of cetaceans is one of the best paleontologically documented examples of major morphological change in vertebrate history.

Mesonychids, the Ancestors of Cetaceans

Mesonychia are a group of archaic ungulates that are commonly held to be ancestral to cetaceans. Mesonychid fossils date from Paleocene through Oligocene deposits of Asia, Europe, and North America. Mesonychids are diverse (O'Leary and Rose 1995; Zhou et al. 1995); the smallest are no larger than a weasel, and the largest, *Andrewsarchus*, may have been the size of a grizzly bear (only a skull has been found for this animal, so its size cannot be estimated with confidence). Mesonychids are thought to be closely related to cetaceans because of the morphology of the teeth. Primitively, molars of placental mammals are tribosphenic (with three primary cusps arranged in a triangle) (Simpson 1936). They consist of a few large cusps (points) and a number of accessory cusps, crests, and basins. In both mesonychids and early cetacaeans, the dental morphology is reduced, consisting of little more than the large cusps. Individual mesonychid species may have lived very differently, but it's clear that some were runners. Their diet may have included vertebrate flesh or carrion.

Pakicetids, the Earliest Cetaceans

Pakicetids are the oldest known and most primitive cetaceans (Thewissen 1994). They are only known from the Eocene (around 52 million years ago) of India and Pakistan, and it is likely that cetaceans originated on this continent. Pakicetids are found in

freshwater deposits only, and until recently, only dental and skull material has been described for them.

Three specializations are unique to cetaceans and can be used to distinguish them from other mammals. The first feature is a bony crest (the sigmoid process) on the outer side of one of the bones of the ear, the tympanic. Second is the involucrum, the enormous thickening on the medial side of the tympanic. Third, the proportions of the incus, one of the bones involved in sound transmission, are modified. It is likely that these changes are related to hearing in a new environment. Early whales may have been especially sensitive to vibrations of the substrate (soil, water) and less to airborne sound. Pakicetids are more primitive than other cetaceans; their nasal opening is still over the incisors, and their mandible is not linked to the ear as in later cetaceans.

Ambulocetids, the Oldest Marine Whales

Ambulocetids are known from early-to-middle Eocene (approximately 50 million year old) littoral (coastal) sediments of Pakistan (Figure 1). Most of the skeleton is known for *Ambulocetus*. Ecologically, *Ambulocetus* may have resembled a crocodile, hunting live prey by lurching at it from shallow water (Thewissen et al. 1996a). *Ambulocetus*, and most later whales, have a cavity in the mandible that opens at a large foramen (hole) in the back of the jaw. In modern toothed whales, this cavity houses a fat pad that extends from the mandible to the ear region and transmits sounds. This system of sound transmission is probably especially efficient in underwater hearing.

The skeleton of *Ambulocetus* shows that it swam in different ways from modern cetaceans. Modern whales swim by pushing their fluke through the water by means of flexing their vertebral column vertically. *Ambulocetus* probably had a long tail but lacked a fluke. Instead it probably swam with its large feet, powering them by bending the vertebral column in a manner similar to the way modern cetaceans power the tail fluke.

Ambulocetus lived in near-shore marine environments, but oxygen isotopes in its teeth show that it probably drank freshwater, as did pakicetids. It is possible that the early whales that moved from freshwater to near-shore marine environments were unable to handle the salt load caused by drinking seawater (Thewissen et al. 1996b). So, these early whales may have employed a strategy

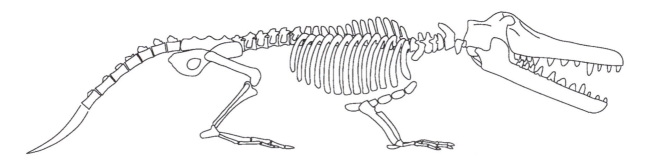

Figure 1. Reconstruction of *Ambulocetus natans*, the walking and swimming whale. Approximately 50 million years old, from the Kala Chitta Hills of northern Pakistan. From Thewissen et al. (1996a), courtesy of the Senckenberg Research Institute and Natural History Museum, Frankfurt A.M.

similar to manatees, which live in near-shore marine environments: offsetting salt intake by drinking fresh water from rivers.

Protocetids, Independence from Freshwater
Protocetids, which lived during the Middle and Late Eocene (48 to 42 million years ago) (Barnes et al. 1985), inhabited tropical and subtropical regions of the entire world. A diverse group, some retain a large sacrum and pelvis, implying that they had large hind limbs. In other protocetids (e.g., *Rodhocetus* from Pakistan) (Gingerich et al. 1994), the pelvis is reduced and tail-based locomotion (with a fluke) may have evolved. Protocetids are found in sediments that indicate fully marine environments. Oxygen isotope analyses indicate that *Indocetus,* a protocetid from the middle Eocene of India, drank seawater. This adaptation made protocetids significantly more independent from land than their relatives and may have helped them colonize the world. Protocetids differ from more primitive whales in two ways. The nasal opening has a more posterior position, and a supraorbital shield, a flat bony shelf on the forehead, has developed, causing the eyes to face to the side.

Basilosaurids, Last of the Archaic Whales
The late Eocene is dominated by two subfamilies of cetaceans, Basilosaurinae and Dorudontinae, both of which are usually included in Basilosauridae (Kellogg 1936). The best basilosaurid skeletons were found in Egypt and North America. Their skeletons are characterized by many long vertebrae, indicating that the vertebral column was very mobile. The hind limbs and pelvic girdle of basilosaurines are greatly reduced, and the hip bones are not attached to the vertebral column, suggesting that the hind limbs are not weight-bearing limbs (Gingerich et al. 1992). Femur and tibia (leg bones) are short, and the hind limbs probably protruded only slightly from the abdomen. Unlike later whales, basilosaurids retained a distinction between premolars and molars in their teeth, and the molars are multicuspid. Basilosaurines were large (up to 15 meters) and had long, snakelike bodies. Dorudontines were much smaller and may have been dolphinlike in appearance.

Odontocetes: Toothed Whales, Dolphins, and Porpoises
Odontocetes originated in the early Oligocene (approximately 35 million years ago). Unlike the more archaic cetaceans, all teeth of a typical odontocete are very similar. Also, in odontocetes the bones of the face are rearranged—bones at the front are shifted backward over the forehead. The most striking specialization of odontocetes is echolocation. Odontocetes produce clicks (usually at a high frequency) and determine the shape of their surroundings by listening to the reflections (echoes) of these sounds. To make this possible, odontocetes have greatly modified skulls. The sound-producing organ is in the nose and these sounds are focused by an expanded fat pad (the "melon") that makes up much of the forehead. The bones of the forehead are flat or dished to accommodate the melon. Returning echoes are received by the ear, which

has become isolated from the rest of the skull to varying degrees. Today, odontocetes include, among others, sperm whales, beaked whales, freshwater dolphins, marine dolphins, and porpoises.

Odontocetes originated in the sea, but a number of them have returned to freshwater. These are commonly grouped with a number of marine relatives as platanistoids. Some of the freshwater forms are similar in many aspects of morphology, and are very different from marine dolphins (e.g., *Platanista* from the Ganges and Indus, and *Inia* from South America). Most scholars consider that these groups evolved such similar adaptations to life in rivers independently (Muizon 1987). Among the strangest cetaceans is *Odobenocetops,* a relative of narwhals and belugas, which lived on the coast of Peru in the Pliocene. This cetacean had greatly asymmetrical tusks and a very short snout; it probably dug in the seafloor for food, much like modern walruses (Muizon 1993).

Mysticetes, Baleen Whales
Mysticetes originated in the Late Eocene. The early forms (such as Llanocetidae and Aetocetidae) retain teeth. However, later baleen whales do not—they replace them with "baleen." These are plates of a hornlike substance that hangs from the upper jaw on the side of the mouth. Mysticetes use the baleen to strain water, filtering out small organisms (such as krill) for food. Filterfeeding in mysticetes originated as the Earth's continents were rearranging themselves. These tectonic changes caused the ocean circulation to change, creating areas of upwelling and thus high productivity that could sustain these large filterfeeders (Fordyce 1980).

Mysticetes are characterized by rearranged skull bones. The bones nearest the back greatly overlap bones in front of them (Kellogg 1928). These animals include the largest vertebrates that ever lived—including *Balaenoptera musculus,* the Blue Whale, which may weigh as much as 485,000 kilograms. Gigantism was a late trend within mysticetes—the oldest balaenopterids date from the Middle Miocene, approximately 14 million years ago. Among odontocetes, large sperm whales are known from the Early Miocene. Fordyce and Barnes (1996) reviewed the fossil history of cetaceans in some detail.

J.G.M. THEWISSEN

See also Aquatic Locomotion; Mesonychids

Works Cited
Barnes, L.G., and E.D. Mitchell. 1978. Cetacea. *In* V.J. Maglio and H.B.S. Cooke (eds.), *Evolution of African Mammals.* Cambridge, Massachusetts: Harvard University Press.
Barnes, L.G., D.P. Domning, and C.E. Ray. 1985. Status of studies on fossil marine mammals. *Marine Mammal Science* 1:15–53.
Fordyce, R.E. 1980. Whale evolution and Oligocene southern ocean environments. *Palaeogeography, Palaeoclimatology, Palaeoecology* 31:319–36.
Fordyce, R.E., and L.G. Barnes. 1994. The evolutionary history of whales and dolphins. *Annual Review of the Earth and Planetary Sciences* 22:419–55.

Gingerich, P.D., B.H. Smith, and E.L. Simons. 1992. Hindlimbs of Eocene Basilosaurus: Evidence of feet in whales. *Science* 249:154–57.

Gingerich, P.D., M.D. Raza, M. Arif, M. Anwar, and X. Zhou. 1994. New whale from the Eocene of Pakistan and the origin of cetacean swimming. *Nature* 368:844–47.

Kellogg, R. 1928. The history of whales: Their adaptation to life in the water. *Quarterly Review of Biology* 3:29–76, 174–208.

———. 1936. A review of the Archaeoceti. *Carnegie Institution of Washington Publication* 482:1–366.

Muizon, C. de. 1987. *The Affinities of Notocetus Vanbenedeni, and Early Miocene Platanistoid (Cetacea, Mammalia) from Patagonia, Southern Argentina.* American Museum Novitates. New York: American Museum of Natural History.

———. 1993. Walrus-like feeding adaptation in a new cetacean from the Pliocene of Peru. *Nature* 365:745–48.

O'Leary, M., and K.D. Rose. 1995. Postcranial skeleton of the early Eocene mesonychid Pachyaena. *Journal of Vertebrate Paleontology* 15:401–30.

Simpson, G.G. 1936. Studies of the earliest mammalian dentitions. *Dental Cosmos* 78.

Thewissen, J.G.M. 1994. Phylogenetic aspects of cetacean origins: A morphologic perspective. *Journal of Mammalian Evolution* 2:157–84.

Thewissen, J.G.M., S.I. Madar, and S.T. Hussain. 1996a. Ambulocetus natans, an Eocene cetacean (Mammalia) from Pakistan. *Courier Forschungs-Institut Senckenberg* 190:1–86.

Thewissen, J.G.M., L.J. Roe, J.R. O'Neil, S.T. Hussain, A. Sahni, and A. Bajpai. 1996b. Evolution of cetacean osmoregulation. *Nature* 381:379–80.

Zhou, X., R. Zhai, P.D. Gingerich, and L. Chen. 1995. Skull of a new mesonychid (Mammalia, Mesonychia) from the Paleocene of China. *Journal of Vertebrate Paleontology* 15:431–42.

WILSON, ALICE EVELYN

Canadian, 1881–1964

If one encounters illnesses in childhood but endures them under favorable circumstances, with books amply available, the result can be beneficial—the development of a strong personality and of an unusual degree of intellectual curiosity. Alice Evelyn Wilson well exemplifies this. Alice was born on 26 August 1881. Her father, Dr. John Wilson, was professor of classics at Victoria University, Coburg, Ontario. In his household, scholarship was respected, but physical activity also was encouraged vigorously. Although she had two healthy brothers, she herself was plagued by illness during her earlier years. Her family's outdoor interests—tramping, camping, swimming, and canoeing—not only brought Wilson to better health but also aroused her interest in nature. In particular, she collected fossils from the Paleozoic limestones around Coburg and minerals from the lake country farther north in Ontario.

Even so, when Wilson enrolled at the University of Toronto in 1901, it was to study languages. A breakdown in her final year prevented her from completing her degree and enforced a long convalescence. When she regained her health, she found employment as an assistant in the University's Museum of Mineralogy—and discovered her true vocation. In November 1909, she gained a second temporary appointment as a clerk in the invertebrate paleontology section of the Geological Survey of Canada in Ottawa.

Wilson's work involved cataloging, arranging, and labeling collections in the new Victoria Memorial Museum. In addition, her knowledge of languages enabled her to aid Percy Raymond, who was preparing a chapter on trilobites for the Eastman edition of Zittel's *Textbook of Palaeontology.* Raymond took a liking to Wilson and in 1910 persuaded her to take a leave of absence from the Survey in order to finish her degree. Returning to the Survey in April 1911, she was granted a permanent appointment at level IIB (skilled technician as technical staff) but with a salary just $50 a year greater than she had earned before.

With Raymond's encouragement, Wilson developed her interest in fossils of the Ordovician strata of Ontario. Her first paper (1913) reported a new brachiopod (extinct stalked animal with a head surrounded by feathery tentacles), and a second (1915) reported a new bivalve. Unfortunately, when Raymond left to teach at Harvard, Wilson's other male colleagues proved less friendly, firmly excluding her from their scientific circle. Matters were made worse when in February 1916 the central block of the Parliament Buildings burned down and the Victoria Memorial Museum was requisitioned by the "homeless" politicians. After assisting in packing up specimens for storage, Wilson found service with the Canadian equivalent of the Women's Land Army until after the end of World War I.

By 1920 the Geological Survey of Canada was back in the Victoria Museum, and Wilson was an Assistant Paleontologist. While her new chief, Edward M. Kindle, was friendly, other colleagues were less so, blocking her attempts to obtain a leave for doctoral studies. Their doubts about her were increased, and her own finances set back, by a serious illness during the years 1921–22. Her illness sent her to the Clifton Springs sanatorium in New York state and caused her colleagues to view her as a poor prospect for long-term service in the survey. Not until 1926, and then only through the intercession of the Federation of University Women, was Wilson granted the leave she sought.

Wilson worked on her doctorate at the University of Chicago, at first under the supervision of Stuart Weller, then, after Weller's premature death, with Carey Croneis. Both men emphasized the stratigraphy (study of rock strata) and paleontology of the region around Cornwall, Ontario. After gaining her doctorate in 1929, Wilson's work was to be of great practical value during the construction of the Saint Lawrence Seaway.

Back in Ottawa, there were fresh tasks. As Canada entered the Depression years, Wilson was ordered to set aside her work in Ontario and study instead the Devonian strata of the petroleum-rich west. In addition she undertook the identification of Paleozoic invertebrates from all parts of Canada, putting in order the National Type Collection, a collection that provided samples of every group of living things found in the country.

Although her gender was considered to prohibit her from participation in extended field work, Wilson repeatedly obtained funding for shorter field trips on foot, by bicycle, or by car. Her companions found her so enthusiastic and knowledgeable that several became firm converts to geology. (One of them, Madeline Fritz, actually gained her doctorate in 1926, three years before Wilson did.)

Promotion, however, was slow in coming for Wilson—slower than it would have been for a male geologist or, for that matter, for a nonpaleontologist. Only when she had been awarded the Order of the British Empire in 1935 did her superiors embarrassedly upgrade her—not to Associate Paleontologist, as she anticipated, but to Assistant Geologist. In 1938, she was one of the first women elected to Fellowship of the Royal Society of Canada. Two years later, she was appointed Associate Geologist. Despite certain reports to the contrary, salary records show this was the highest rank she attained.

Wilson's retirement in 1946 brought little change in lifestyle. She would go to her office on most days, except when engaged in fieldwork, and continued to write regular accounts of the Paleozoic geology and fossils of Ontario—brachiopods, gastropods (clams, snails, and sea stars), and bivalves in particular. She wrote a geological textbook for children, *The Earth Beneath Our Feet* (1947); a series of five articles, "Life comes to a planet," for the *Canadian Mineralogy Journal* (1948–49); and an account of "Life in the Proterozoic" for a Royal Society of Canada publication, *The Proterozoic in Canada* (1957). She had always enjoyed travel, visiting the Bahama Islands and British Guiana (now Guyana) in 1932; retirement brought greater opportunities, with visits to Brazil and Mexico. By then Wilson had gained renown as one of Canada's first professional woman scientists. Her career was the subject of articles in leading newspapers and of a National Film Board photo story (1952). Another consequence was her appointment as a part-time lecturer in Paleontology at Carleton University, Ottawa, where she was awarded an honorary degree of Doctor of Laws (1960).

Early in 1964 Wilson informed the Director of the Geological Survey that she would be vacating her office, since "my work is done." She died on 15 April and was honored posthumously when a meeting-room in the Survey's Booth Street headquarters was named Alice Wilson Hall. Alice Wilson will be remembered not only for her work on Canadian Paleozoic geology and invertebrate fossils but also as one of the first women to achieve recognition in a male-dominated scientific world.

WILLIAM A.S. SARJEANT

Biography

Born in Coburg, Ontario, 26 August 1881. Received B.A., University of Toronto, 1911; Ph.D., University of Chicago, 1929; Hon. LL.D., Carleton University, 1960. Member, Geological Survey of Canada, 1909–46. Awarded Order of the British Empire, 1935; elected member, Fellowship of the Royal Society of Canada, 1938. Known for studies of the Lower Paleozoic stratigraphy and invertebrate fossils of Canada, especially Ontario and Quebec. Died in Ottawa, 15 April 1964.

Major Publications

1926. An upper Ordovician fauna from the Rocky Mountains, British Columbia. *Bulletin of the Geological Survey of Canada* 44:1–34.

1932. Ordovician fossils from the region of Cornwall, Ontario. *Transactions of the Royal Society of Canada*, ser. 3, 26 (4):373–408.

1947. *The Earth Beneath Our Feet.* Toronto: Macmillan.

1948–49. Life comes to a planet. *Canadian Mineralogy Journal,* Part 1, 69 (7):57–65; Part 2, 69 (9):60–69; Part 3, 69 (11):69–82; Part 4, 70 (1):77–88; Part 5, 70 (3):79–88.

1956. A guide to the geology of the Ottawa district [Ontario-Quebec]. *Canadian Field Naturalist* 70 (1):1–68.

1957. Life in the Proterozoic. In *The Proterozoic in Canada.* Royal Society of Canada Special Publications, 2. Toronto: University of Toronto Press; London: Oxford University Press.

Further Reading

Meadowcroft, B. 1990. Alice Wilson, 1881–1964: Explorer of the Earth beneath her feet. *In* G.M. Ainley (ed.), *Despite the Odds: Essays on Canadian Women and Science.* Montreal and Buffalo, New York: Véhicule.

Montagnes, A. 1966. Alice Wilson, 1881–1964. *In* M.Q. Innis (ed.), *The Clear Spirit: Twenty Canadian Women and Their Times.* Toronto: University of Toronto Press, for Canadian Federation of University Women; Buffalo, New York: University of Toronto Press, 1981.

Sarjeant, W.A.S. 1993. Alice Wilson, first woman geologist with the Geological Survey of Canada. *Earth Sciences History* 12 (2):122–28.

Sinclair, G.W. 1966. Memorial to Alice E. Wilson (1881–1964). *Geological Society of America Bulletin* 77:215–18.

Webb, M. 1991. *Alice Wilson: Telling the Earth's Story.* Mississauga, Ontario: Copp Clark Pitman.

Zaslow, M. 1975. *Reading the Rocks.* Ottawa: MacMillan, in association with the Department of Energy, Mines and Resources and Information Canada.

WOODWARD, ARTHUR SMITH

English, 1864–1944

During his lifetime, Arthur Smith Woodward was renowned as a vertebrate paleontologist and mineralogist and as an international authority in fossil fishes of the Late Jurassic and Cretaceous. He wrote copiously, publishing papers and monographs in learned journals—after his death, his bibliography occupied 24 pages (Forster-Cooper 1945). As a later writer noted, he was "an intensely busy man, completely without humour" (Miller 1972). That may explain why he was taken in by the Piltdown hoax. The idea that someone had falsified fossils found in Sussex, England, as an elaborate joke was probably totally foreign to Woodward.

Woodward was a paleontological prodigy. At the age of 13, using his own press, he printed an account of the natural history and geology of North Wales, the result of a holiday taken there. Although not a specialist in human paleontology, when Charles Dawson reported the finding of allegedly fossil human bones buried in gravel beds near Piltdown, Sussex, England, Woodward was appointed to be Dawson's scientific advisor. The two men communicated their findings to the Geological Society, and Woodward categorized the Piltdown fragments as belonging to the genus *Eoanthropus dawsoni*.

For the rest of his life, Woodward was much involved with the Piltdown bones and the site from which they came. As a result, he is remembered more for this unfortunate incident than for his prodigious work on the fossil fishes. Although his reconstruction of the Piltdown skull fragments was criticized, to the end of his life he believed that the chimpanzee jaw and the relatively modern human skull were the genuine remains of a Middle Pleistocene hominid. His final account of the Piltdown "discoveries" was published posthumously.

Woodward never lived to witness the exposure of the Piltdown hoax by modern chemical analyses of the specimens (Weiner et al. 1953). The results showed that the fragments had been impregnated with chromate to give the bones stains that were similar to the natural stains caused by flints found in the gravel. Since the materials obviously were impregnated before the bones had been placed surreptitiously in the gravel, no one ever suspected that Woodward perpetrated the fraud. He simply was present when one of the skull fragments was found. The Piltdown Hoax has perhaps unfairly colored Woodward's other work. He also named the human remains from Broken Hill, Zambia, as *Homo rhodesiensis*. He died at Haywards Heath, Sussex, England, 2 September 1944.

J.J. WYMER

Works Cited and Further Reading

Forster-Cooper, C. 1945. Sir Arthur Smith Woodward. *Obituary Notices of Fellows of the Royal Society* 1945–1948:79–112.

Miller, R. 1972. *The Piltdown Men: A Case of Archaeological Fraud.* St. Albans: Paladin.

Weiner, J.S., K.P. Oakley, and W.E. Le Gros Clark. 1953. The solution of the Piltdown problem. *Bulletin of the British Museum (Natural History) Geology* 2:141–46.

Biography

Born in Macclesfield, 23 May 1864. Educated at Owen's College, University of Manchester; King's College, University of London. Assistant in the Department of Geology at the British Museum (Natural History), 1882; assistant keeper, then keeper, British Museum, 1892–1924; fellow, Geological Society of London, 1885; Lyell Medal, 1896; president, Geologists' Association, 1904–6; vice president, Geological Society of London, 1908; president, Geological Society of London, 1914–16; knighted, 1924. Died at Haywards Heath, Sussex, 2 September 1944.

Major Publications

1948. *The Earliest Englishman.* London: Watts.

1890. With C.D. Sherborn. *A Catalogue of British Fossil Vertebrata.* London: Dulau.

1913. With C. Dawson. On the discovery of a Palaeolithic human skull and mandible in a flint-bearing gravel overlying the Wealden (Hastings Beds) at Piltdown (Fletching) Sussex. *Quarterly Journal of the Geological Society of London* 69:117–51.

X

XENARTHRANS

The continent of South America completed its separation from Africa and North America during the Late Cretaceous period, approximately 75 to 80 million years ago, effectively isolating itself from all other continental land masses until the rise of the Isthmus of Panama, which took place 3 million years ago. The initial separation began a great evolutionary experiment that yielded a mammalian fauna unlike that found in any other part of the globe. A host of unusual endemic (native to an area) groups of mammals characterize the Cenozoic fossil record of South America, but perhaps none are more unusual than the members of the mammalian order Xenarthra.

In modern-day South and Central America, the xenarthrans are represented by three strange and somewhat disparate types of animals. The armadillos are the only armored mammals, with a flexible mosaic of bony plates embedded in their skin, covered by a layer of horny scales. This armor covers the animal's tail, back, sides, and the top of the head. The 20 living species of armadillos are specialized diggers. They exhibit a range of diets, from strict insectivores feeding on ants and termites to omnivores that feed on a variety of plant material, insects, carrion, and small vertebrates. The anteaters are represented by four living species. Although these toothless mammals range in size and habitat from large terrestrial (living on land) denizens of open grasslands to smaller arboreal (living in trees) or semi-arboreal inhabitants of rain forests, all are specialized for feeding on ants and termites. The five living species of tree sloths are long-limbed arboreal mammals that suspend themselves beneath tree branches and crawl slowly, hand over hand, through the canopy of tropical rain forests. These peculiar leaf-eating creatures have a chambered, fermentative stomach like that of a cow, and they grow algae on the surface of their hair.

As odd an assemblage as the living xenarthrans may seem, the extinct forms are even more unusual. Indeed, fossil xenarthrans include some of the most bizarre mammals ever to have existed. Numbered among these extinct xenarthrans are the pampatheres, giant armadillo-like herbivores that were up to three meters in length (Montgomery 1985); the glyptodonts, enor-

mous grazing animals that were covered by a thick, domed bony shell and often trailing a spiked or clublike tail, animals that were up to four meters long (Gillette and Ray 1981); and the ground sloths, hulking terrestrial cousins to the tree sloths, some of which grew to the size of modern-day elephants and could rear up on their hind limbs to a height of four to five meters. These three types of large herbivorous xenarthrans include over 100 described genera (groups; singular, genus), making them one of the most diverse, successful, and characteristic elements of the Cenozoic mammalian fauna of South America (Hoffstetter 1958). When the Panamanian isthmus arose, all three herbivorous groups successfully invaded North America and dwelled there for some three million years. Along with many other large mammals, the big xenarthran herbivores finally became extinct soon after the glaciers retreated at the end of the Pleistocene epoch in both North and South America.

Fossil xenarthrans have figured importantly in the history of paleontology. A skeleton of the gigantic Pleistocene ground sloth *Megatherium* was unearthed in the late eighteenth century in present-day Argentina. The bones were sent to Spain and eventually were described by the great French anatomist Georges Cuvier, considered by many to be the father of paleontology. For Cuvier, these bones, clearly allied to living sloths yet so radically different from the extant (living today) species, constituted one of the first definitive proofs that species can and do go extinct, an idea still very much in debate at the time. Charles Darwin also uncovered the bones of fossil xenarthrans during his voyages along the coast of South America in the 1830s. These bones later were to become an important piece of evidence supporting Darwin's case for the evolution of species. The similarity of the fossil bones to skeletons of xenarthrans currently living in the same area suggested to Darwin that the living forms were modified descendants of the fossilized animals and had undergone a gradual process of evolutionary change *in situ* (in the place of origin). The discovery of fossil ground sloth bones in a cave in western Virginia in the 1790s signaled the beginning of vertebrate paleontology in the United States. These bones were described by

Figure 1. *Holmesina* sp. (Xenarthra, Pampatheriinae) fossil giant armadillos of North America. *Top,* life restoration; *bottom,* skeletal reconstruction. From Edmund (1985).

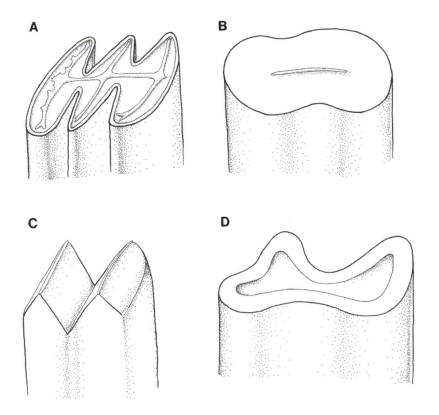

Figure 2. Fossil xenarthran "molariform" teeth. *A, Glyptotherium arizonae* (Xenarthra, Glyptodontidae); *B, Holmesina* sp. (Xenarthra, Pampatheriinae); *C, Megatherium* sp. (Xenarthra, Megatheriidae); *D, Paramylodon harlani* (Xenarthra, Mylodontidae).

none other than Thomas Jefferson. He named the animal *Megalonyx* ("great claw"), but unfortunately misidentified it as some type of large lion. The bones were later identified correctly by Caspar Wistar.

The Xenarthra continues to be of great interest to modern-day paleontologists. This group has played a key role in recent analyses attempting to unravel the explosive pattern of diversification of the major orders of placental mammals. In 1975 Dr. Malcolm McKenna of the American Museum of Natural History suggested that the Xenarthra may represent the first group to diverge from primitive placental mammals. Subsequent studies have supported McKenna's idea, although it remains controversial (Novacek 1994). Xenarthrans also may share a close relationship with several specific groups of living and fossil mammals from other parts of the globe. These include the living group Pholidota (the pangolins or scaly anteaters of Africa and Asia), the extinct group Palaeanodonta (an assemblage of digging specialists from Early Tertiary deposits of North America and Europe), *Eurotamandua* (a purported anteater from the famed mid-Eocene Messel deposits of Germany), and *Ernanodon* (a slothlike creature from the Paleocene of China) (Rose and Emry 1993; Novacek 1994). Resolving these relationships could contribute much to our modern understanding of the biological and geographic origin of the mammalian orders and the patterns of mammalian migration during the earliest stages of the Cenozoic era.

Notwithstanding their significance to paleontologists, the xenarthrans are an important group of animals in their own right. They are represented by a great diversity of body, locomotory, and dietary types. The group has played a significant role in the evolution of the mammals of the Western Hemisphere. Hence, the xenarthrans have attracted a great deal of interest from researchers in a wide variety of disciplines, including paleontologists, and will continue to play a prominent role in studies of mammalian biology in the future.

Armadillos, Pampatheres, and Glyptodonts

The armadillos are the first xenarthran group to appear in the fossil record. Isolated armadillo scutes (individual bony armor plates) and isolated foot bones are known from the Middle Paleocene faunas from São José de Itaboraí in Brazil (Pascual et al. 1985). The oldest well-preserved xenarthran skeletal material is also from an armadillo, *Utaetus,* from the Early Eocene (approximately 55 to 50 million years ago) of Patagonia in what is today southern Argentina. These early remains of *Utaetus* include parts of the skull and postcranial (body below the skull) skeleton. However, *Utaetus* is most remarkable for its teeth, which retain a thin coating of enamel. Enamel is lost in all other known xenarthrans.

Armadillo skeletal remains do not become common until the Miocene epoch. The Miocene Santa Cruz Formation of Patagonia contains the first precursors of the two major types of modern armadillos, the euphractans (*Prozaedius*) and the dasypodans (*Stegotherium*), as well as the peculiar *Peltephilus*. The last genus bears two "horns" on its snout in the form of modified scutes applied to the surface of the skull. It has sharp, pointed teeth that differ strongly from the small peglike teeth of other armadillos and

may have had a scavenging or even carnivorous diet. Armadillos are relatively common in subsequent South American deposits. The first living genera made their appearance in the Pliocene epoch (Pascual et al. 1985). At least one species dispersed to southern North America during the Pleistocene.

Superficially, the pampatheres resemble large armadillos, with "bucklers" of fused armor plates covering the shoulder and hip regions connected by flexible rows of armor attached to the underlying skin (Figure 1). However, scholars believe that pampatheres are apparently more closely related to the glyptodonts, based upon their large body size, certain detailed similarities in cranial anatomy, and their shared possession of lobate teeth, lobe-shaped teeth that are made up of a central area of hard dentine surrounded by a zone of softer dentine (Montgomery 1985) (Figures 2A, B). These teeth indicate that, like the glyptodonts, pampatheres were likely herbivorous mammals. The pampatheres do not enter the fossil record until the Early Eocene, when they are represented only by the isolated scutes and teeth of the genus *Machlydotherium* (Hoffstetter 1958). Relatively complete skeletal remains are unknown prior to the mid-Miocene La Venta fauna of Colombia. Pampatheres are well represented in Pliocene and Pleistocene faunas, in both South America and North America. Some of these later Plio-Pleistocene forms reached gigantic proportions, rivalling the large glyptodonts in size.

The glyptodonts are the mammalian equivalent of the turtle. They differ from other armored xenarthrans ("cingulates") because their armor is nearly or completely inflexible. Its component scutes are fused into a single carapace ("shell") that lacks any mobile bands in the middle. The carapace is tall and domed, giving the largest forms somewhat the appearance of a Volkswagen Beetle with legs (Figure 3). The scutes themselves are often much thicker than those of other cingulates. Even in large pampatheres, scutes are typically less than 1.3 centimeters thick. Individual glyptodont scutes may be more than five centimeters thick (Gillette and Ray 1981). Such thick scutes must have made the carapace enormously heavy. To support such a burden, the glyptodont skeleton is drastically modified. The feet are elephant-like, with broad, short toes and hooflike nails. The limbs are heavy and thick. The pelvis is fused to the undersurface of the carapace. The backbone is largely solidified into a single, fused bony rod. Movable spinal joints are found only in the neck and in the tail (Figure 3). In some South American forms the armored tail is tipped with a bony club, which may have a variable number of horny spikes, as is the case in the genus *Doedicurus*. The glyptodont skull is short and massive with lobate, continuously growing teeth that are used to grind up plant material (Figure 2A). Glyptodonts carried their heads low to the ground, suggesting that they were grazers that fed on grasses and low-lying shrubs. This idea is further confirmed by the fact that glyptodont fossil remains are usually found in deposits of lowland grassy or marshy sediments (Gillette and Ray 1981).

The first glyptodont scutes do not appear until the Middle Eocene (Pascual et al. 1985). As with the armadillos, the oldest well-preserved glyptodont skeletal remains are Miocene in age. These early glyptodonts, including the well-known *Propalaeohoplophorus,* are relatively small-bodied forms. The more abun-

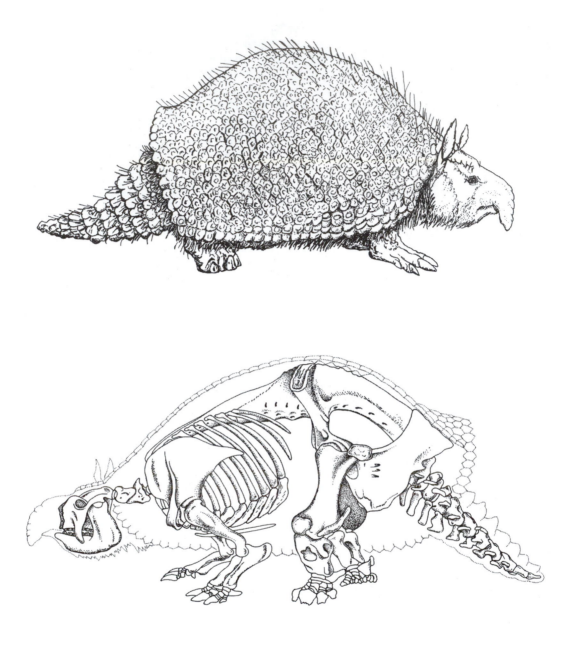

Figure 3. *Glyptotherium arizonae* (Xenarthra, Glyptodontidae). *Top,* life restoration; *bottom,* skeletal reconstruction. From Gillette and Ray (1981), used by permission of the publisher, the Smithsonian Institution Press.

dant remains from the Pliocene and Pleistocene of South America include several very large forms that approach four meters in total body length. The Plio-Pleistocene radiation (diversification and geographic spread) of South American glyptodonts is quite extensive, encompassing three subfamilies that contain nearly 50 genera (Hoffstetter 1958), and glyptodonts are exceedingly common in these fossil beds. Glyptodonts (genus *Glyptotherium*) also are known from Plio-Pleistocene deposits in the southernmost parts of North America, but they are never common (Gillette and Ray 1981).

Anteaters

The anteaters have a very sketchy fossil record. There are no definitive records of the group prior to the Miocene. The purported Eocene anteater *Eurotamandua* from the Messel deposits of Germany has several similarities to undoubted anteaters, not the least of which is the complete absence of teeth. Yet several features that are considered hallmarks of the Xenarthra—for instance, the extra joints in the backbone (which gave the order its name: *xenos,* strange, *arthron,* joint, Greek)—either are not present or are at the very least difficult to verify (Rose and Emry 1993). The only

Figure 4. *Nothrotheriops shastense*. Life restoration by Charles R. Knight. From Stock (1925), courtesy of Carnegie Institute of Washington.

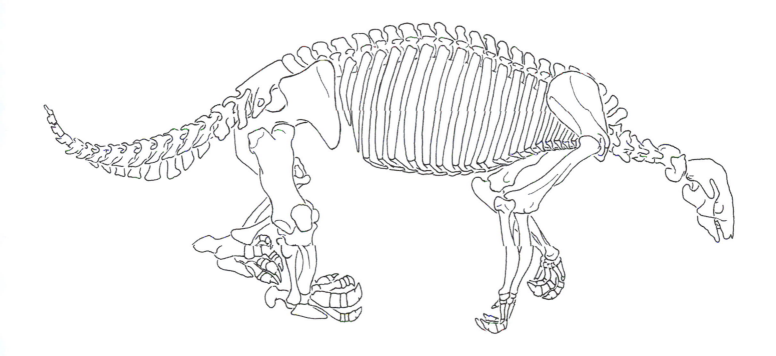

Figure 5. *Pronothrotherium typicum* (Xenarthra, Nothrotheriidae). Skeletal reconstruction. Based on FMNH P14503.

undoubted anteater fossils are restricted geographically to fossil beds in Argentina. The oldest anteater is an undescribed skeleton from the Early Miocene of Patagonia. Several skulls and partial skeletons of the genus *Protamandua* date from slightly later in the Miocene (Patterson et al. 1992). A few isolated, incomplete anteater remains also are known from Pliocene and Pleistocene rock strata.

Sloths

The ground sloths are arguably the most diverse group of extinct xenarthrans, with more than 50 genera divided into four separate families. More is known about their appearance and habits than any other group of extinct xenarthrans. In fact, the biology of ground sloths is better understood than that of almost any other group of extinct mammals. Mummified remains of these sloths, including dried remnants of muscles, ligaments, cartilage, and, most notably, attached pieces of hairy skin have been found in dry caves in both the southwestern United States and in Patagonia. These caves often contain hundreds of pieces of sloth dung, which look like large mudballs filled with ground up plant stems and which reach up to 0.18 meters in diameter. Footprints from ground sloths have been identified in both North and South American deposits (Stock 1925).

Both the southwestern United States cave-dwelling sloth *Nothrotheriops shastense* (the so-called Shasta ground sloth) (Figure 4) and the Patagonian cave-dweller *Mylodon darwinii* were covered by a coat of long, yellowish-brown hair. Some evidence suggests that *Nothrotheriops* may have grown algae in its hair like the living tree sloths. *Mylodon's* skin was underlaid by a pavement of bony structures similar to the scutes of armadillos, except that *Mylodon's* are not connected to one another. Such structures are also known in *Mylodon's* North American relative *Paramylodon*, from the famed La Brea tar pits in Los Angeles (Stock 1925), as well as in the gigantic ground sloth *Eremotherium*. Analysis of plant parts in the sloth dung show that *Nothrotheriops* was a browsing animal that fed on typical desert shrubbery such as globemallow, mormontea, cactus, yucca, and agave. *Mylodon*, on the other hand, was more of a grazing animal, with a high percentage of grasses, small herbs, and perhaps even some roots in its diet.

The foot structure in many ground sloths was peculiar. The hind feet often were turned inward, soles facing one another, so that the animal walked on the outside edges of its feet. Also, sloths often walked on the knuckles of their forefeet, with the claws curled upward toward the palm (Hoffstetter 1958) (Figure 5). Both positions appear to be adaptations to keep their large, sharp claws from contacting the ground, thus preventing them from becoming dulled. Footprints reveal that *Megatherium*, a large terrestrial sloth and a close relative of *Eremotherium*, could walk either bipedally (on two feet) or quadrupedally (on four feet). Studies of limb morphology (shape and structure) demonstrate that the slow terrestrial amble of *Megatherium* was not the only mode of locomotion represented within this group. Some of the smaller "ground" sloths were climbers, and some may even have been suspensory, like modern tree sloths.

The oldest ground sloth remains include isolated teeth, claws, and ankle bones from the Eocene of Patagonia and Antarctica,

which was connected briefly to South America during the Early Tertiary (Pascual et al. 1985). More complete skeletons are first available in the Late Oligocene (Hoffstetter 1958). They belong to the family Mylodontidae, a group of large-bodied grazing sloths characterized by their irregularly lobate teeth, similar to those in glyptodonts, but with a depressed core of soft dentine rather than a raised core of hard dentine (Figure 2D). By the end of the Miocene, all four families of ground sloths are represented in the fossil record.

In Early Miocene deposits, Mylodontids are joined by the families Megalonychidae and Nothrotheriidae. The former is characterized by enlarged front teeth that look much like canine teeth or rodent incisors. These teeth were used presumably to crop vegetation from bushes and trees and for defensive purposes. The latter family has square back teeth with elevated crests made of hard dentine running across them (Figure 2C). Nothrotheriids also had elongate forelimbs and were likely bipedal and/or semi-arboreal (Figures 4, 5).

The Megatheriidae are very large-bodied browsing terrestrial sloths that look superficially like the nothrotheres. Megatheriids make their first appearance in sediments of the Middle Miocene. By the Pleistocene, they reached gigantic proportions. The largest, *Eremotherium*, had a body length of nearly six meters and an estimated body mass approaching four metric tons. This is nearly as massive as modern-day African elephants. These large megatheres likely fed as do modern elephants, consuming entire tree branches and at times entire trees.

All four ground sloth families enjoyed successful radiations in South America in the Pliocene and Pleistocene. All four spread to North America either just prior to or at the same time as the emergence of the Isthmus of Panama. The megalonychids are absent or poorly known in South America after the Pliocene but were particularly successful in North America. The genus *Megalonyx* spread northward as far as the north slope of Alaska (Montgomery 1985). The megalonychids also gave rise to a large radiation of sloths in the West Indies, a radiation from which the modern two-toed sloth *Choloepus* may be derived (Patterson et al. 1992). The living three-toed sloth is apparently unrelated, representing an early tree-dwelling offshoot of early sloths that left no fossil record.

The ground sloths became extinct in both South and North America only relatively recently. Remains have been found associated with human remains and artifacts in caves in South America and the West Indies. In addition, there is some evidence that humans butchered and ate ground sloths. Although many large mammals became extinct in North and South America at the end of the last ice age, human predation may have played a particularly important role in the demise of this group.

TIMOTHY J. GAUDIN

See also Burrowing Adaptations in Vertebrates; Paleanodonts; Pangolins; Skeleton: Dermal Postcranial Skeleton

Works Cited

Edmund, A.G. 1985. The fossil giant armadillos of North America (Pampatheriinae, Xanartha-Edentata). *In* G.G. Montgomery (ed.),

The Evolution and Ecology of Armadillos, Sloths, and Vermilinguas. Washington, D.C.: Smithsonian Institution Press.

Gillette, D.D., and C.E. Ray. 1981. *Glyptodonts of North America.* Smithsonian Contributions to Paleobiology, 40. Washington, D.C.: Smithsonian Institution Press.

Hansen, R.M. 1978. Shasta ground sloth food habit, Rampart Cave, Arizona. *Paleobiology* 4 (3):303.

Hoffstetter, R. 1958. Xenarthra. *In* J. Piveteau (ed.), *Traité de Paléontologie.* Paris, France: Masson.

Montgomery, G.G. 1985. *The Evolution and Ecology of Armadillos, Sloths, and Vermilinguas.* Washington, D.C.: Smithsonian Institution Press.

Novacek, M.J. 1994. The radiation of placental mammals. *In* D.R. Prothero and R.M. Schoch (eds.), *Major Features of Vertebrate Evolution.* Knoxville: University of Tennessee Press.

Pascual, R., M.G. Vucetich, G.J. Scillato-Yané, and M. Bond. 1985. Main pathways of mammalian diversification in South America. *In* F.G. Stehli and S.D. Webb (eds.), *The Great American Biotic Interchange.* New York: Plenum.

Patterson, B., W. Segall, W.D. Turnbull, and T.J. Gaudin. 1992. The ear region in xanarthrans (=Edentata, Mammalia). Part 2, Pilosa (sloths, anteaters), palaeanodonts, and a miscellany. *Fieldiana, Geology,* new ser., 24:1–79.

Rose, K.D., and R.J. Emry. 1993. Relationships of Xenarthra, Pholidota, and fossil "edentates": The morphological evidence. *In* F.S. Szalay, M.J. Novacek, and M.C. McKenna (eds.), *Mammal Phylogeny.* New York and London: Springer-Verlag.

Stock, C. 1925. *Cenozoic Gravigrade Edentates of Western North America.* Carnegie Institute of Washington Publications, 331. Washington, D.C.: Carnegie Institution of Washington.

Further Reading

Kurten, B., and E. Anderson. 1980. *Pleistocene Mammals of North America.* New York: Columbia University Press.

Montgomery, G.G. 1985. *The Evolution and Ecology of Armadillos, Sloths, and Vermilinguas.* Washington, D.C.: Smithsonian Institution Press.

Schaal, S., et al. 1992. *Messel: An Insight into the History of Life and of the Earth.* Oxford: Clarendon; New York: Oxford University Press; as *Messel: Ein Schaufenster in die Geschichte der Erde und des Lebens,* Frankfurt am Main: Kramer, 1988.

Simpson, 2G.G. 1980. *Splendid Isolation: The Curious History of South American Mammals.* New Haven, Connecticut: Yale University Press.

Y

YANG ZHUNGJIAN (CHUNG CHIEN YOUNG)

Chinese, 1897–1979

Yang Zhungjian, also known as Chung Chien Young (following another transliteration of Chinese characters), was the founder of the Chinese school of vertebrate paleontology. Born into a family of teachers at Huaxian, in Shaanxi Province, he entered the Faculty of Geology at Peking University in 1917. After earning a degree there, he left for Germany in 1923 to study vertebrate paleontology at the University of Munich under Max Schlosser and Ferdinand Broili. In 1927 he obtained his doctorate for his thesis on fossil rodents of northern China, and in 1928 he returned home, where he began a career in paleontological research and teaching that was to last 50 years. Until then, practically all research in vertebrate paleontology in China had been the work of foreigners, so Yang can be considered as the first Chinese vertebrate paleontologist.

When he came back to China, Yang became the head of the Cenozoic Research Laboratory, which was in charge of the excavations at the "Peking Man" site at Zhoukoudian. At this site many important remains of *Homo erectus* were found in the 1920s and 1930s. Yang and the paleoanthropologist Pei Weizhong were the main Chinese investigators at Zhoukoudian, and in the early 1930s he published several papers on the fauna associated with early man at that famous site. Yang also produced studies on Late Cenozoic mammals from North China, some of which he coauthored with Pierre Teilhard de Chardin.

During the 1930s Yang turned his attention more and more toward older fossil vertebrates, especially reptiles, and he extended the scope of his fieldwork to northwestern and southern China. He described dicynodonts (mammal-like reptiles) from the Triassic of Xinjiang and dinosaurs from the Cretaceous of various parts of northwestern China. In 1938 he started excavations with Bien Meinian, near the village of Lufeng, in the southern province of Yunnan. The Lufeng excavations, which lasted until 1950, yielded a vast assemblage of animals of Late Triassic to Early Jurassic age. The area came to be known as the Lufeng Saurischian Fauna and was described in a succession of monographs by Yang and others. As its name implies, this fauna (or succession of faunas) was dominated by saurischian (lizard-hipped) dinosaurs, among which prosauropods were the most numerous. In 1941 while the war against

the Japanese was raging, Yang was in Chongqing, Sichuan Province, supervising the mounting of the first dinosaur skeleton to be displayed in China, a prosauropod he described as *Lufengosaurus huenei*. Besides various prosauropod and theropod dinosaurs, the Lufeng Beds yielded a rich vertebrate assemblage, including amphibians, turtles, pseudosuchians, protosuchian crocodiles, mammal-like reptiles, and early mammals.

Just after World War II, Yang traveled extensively in Europe and the United States. After the founding of the People's Republic of China in 1949, he became the head of the Laboratory of Vertebrate Paleontology of the Academia Sinica, which in 1957 was renamed the Institute of Vertebrate Paleontology and Paleoanthropology and is the major Chinese research institution in its field. Also in 1957, *Vertebrata PalAsiatica* was launched and soon became a major paleontological journal, devoted mainly to Chinese fossil vertebrates. In 1959 Yang helped found the Beijing Natural History Museum, of which he became the director.

During the 1950s and early 1960s, Yang published extensively on Mesozoic reptiles, including marine reptiles, mammal-like reptiles, pterosaurs (notably *Dsungaripterus* and *Noripterus*), pseudosuchians (extinct reptiles related to crocodiles), and dinosaurs. Among the dinosaurs he described were the extremely long-necked sauropod *Mamenchisaurus* from the Jurassic of Sichuan, a new species of the Early Cretaceous ceratopsian *Psittacosaurus* from Shandong, and the bizarre hadrosaur *Tsintaosaurus*, with its hollow bony spike above the orbits (eye sockets), from the Upper Cretaceous of Shandong. Yang also pioneered the study of dinosaur footprints and eggs in China.

During the late 1960s, Yang's research activity was severely curtailed by the Cultural Revolution, but he began again in the 1970s and continued until his death in 1979. His last papers were devoted mainly to fossil reptiles, from dinosaurs to pterosaurs, crocodilians and tritylodonts (highly specialized plant-eating reptiles very closely related to mammals).

Yang Zhungjian's contribution to the development of vertebrate paleontology in China was considerable. He published more than 500 papers on that topic and erected more than 200 new groups of fossil vertebrates (which, admittedly, may not all be valid).

The most important point, however, is that when he returned from Germany in 1928, research on fossil vertebrates in China was almost exclusively the work of foreign scientists from Sweden, Austria, France, or the United States. By the time of his death in 1979, there was an active school of Chinese vertebrate paleontology, and our knowledge of Chinese fossil vertebrates had increased enormously. China is now one of the leading countries in the field of vertebrate paleontology. The bases for this prominence were laid by Yang Zhungjian and his coworkers and followers.

HAIYAN TONG AND ERIC BUFFETAUT

Biography

Born in Huaxian, Shaanxi, 1 June 1897. Received M.Sc., Faculty of Geology, Peking University, 1923; Ph.D., University of Munich, 1927. Participated in the excavations of the "Peking Man" site at Zhoukoudian, late 1920s, early 1930s; excavated dinosaur sites, Lufeng, Yunnan, 1938; became head of the Laboratory of Vertebrate Paleontology, the Academia Sinica, 1953; head, Institute of Vertebrate Paleontology and Paleoanthropology, 1957; excavated Cretaceous dinosaurs, near Laiyang, Shandong, 1951–1953; described *Lufengosaurus huenei* (1941), *Mamenchisaurus constructus* (1954), *Tsintaosaurus spinorhinus* (1957), *Dsungaripterus weii* (1964). Died 15 January 1979 in Beijing.

Major Publications

1927. *Fossile Nagetiere aus Nord-China.* Palaeontologia Sinica, C, 5. Pei-ching: Ko hsueh chu pan she.

1933. With D. Black, P. Teilhard de Chardin, and W.C. Pei. *Fossil Man in China. The Choukoutien Cave Deposits with a Synopsis of our Present Knowledge of the Late Cenozoic in China.* Memoirs of the Geological Survey of China, A. Peiping: Geological Survey of China.

1941. *A Complete Osteology of* Lufengosaurus huenei *Young (gen. et sp. nov.) from Lufeng, Yunnan, China.* Palaeontologia Sinica, C, 7. Pei-ching: Ko hsueh chu pan she.

1958. *The Dinosaurian Remains of Laiyang, Shantung.* Palaeontologia Sinica, C, 16. Pei-ching: Ko hsueh chu pan she.

1964a. On a new pterosaurian from Sinkiang, China. *Vertebrate Palasiatica* 8:221–56.

1964b. *The Pseudosuchians in China.* Palaeontologia Sinica, C, 19. Pei-ching: Ko hsueh chu pan she.

Further Reading

Tung, Chih-Ming. 1992. *Dinosaurian Faunas of China.* Berlin and New York: Springer-Verlag.

Yang, Z. 1982. *Yang Chung-chien wen chi: Selected Works of Yang Zhungjian.* Pei-ching: Ko hsueh chu pan she; Beijing: Science Press.

APPENDIX

PALEONTOLOGICAL JOURNALS

Compiled by Ronald G. Wolff

These select journals, among the best known and most widely available, publish studies from all areas of paleontology. Entries include the year of first publication, publisher, city and country of publication, language (if other than or in addition to English), focus, and affiliated organization.

Acta Palaeobotanica. 1960. Polish Academy of Sciences, W. Szafer Institute of Botany, Krakow, Poland. English, French, German. Paleobotany, paleoecology, palynology.

Acta Palaeontologica Polonica. 1956. Polish Academy of Sciences, Institute of Paleobiology, Warsaw, Poland. English; Polish summaries. General paleontology.

Acta Palaeontologica Sinica (Gushengwu Xuebao). 1950. Chinese Academy of Sciences, Nanjing Institute of Geology and Paleontology, Nanjing, China. Chinese; English summaries. General paleontology.

Alcheringa. 1976. Geological Society of Australia, Association of Australasian Palaeontologists, Sydney, Australia. Geology and paleontology, general paleontology.

Amegheniana. Revista de la Asociación Paleontólogica Argentina. 1957. Asociación Paleontológica Argentina, Buenos Aires, Argentina. Spanish, English; English summaries. General paleontology.

American Journal of Botany. 1914. Botanical Society of America, Columbus, U.S.A. Botany, including paleobotany.

Ancient Biomolecules. 1996. Gordon and Breach, Harwood Academic, Amsterdam, Netherlands. Fossil molecules.

Annalen des Naturhistorischen Museums in Wien. Ser. A für Mineralogie und Petrographie, Geologie und Paläontologie, Anthropologie und Prähistorie. 1980. Natural History Museum of Vienna, Austria. German. Mineralogy, petrography, geology, paleontology, anthropology, and prehistory.

Annales de Paléontologie. 1906. Masson Périodiques, Paris, France. French; English summaries. General paleontology.

The Auk. A Quarterly Journal of Ornithology. 1884. American Ornithologists' Union, Washington, D.C., U.S.A. The biology of birds, including fossil birds.

Géobios—Paléontologie, Stratigraphie, Paléoécologie. 1968. Université de Lyon, Villeurbanne, France. English, French. General paleontology, stratigraphy, and paleoecology. Association Eurolypal.

Geologica et Palaeontologica. 1967. Philips-Universität, Geologisch-Paläontologisches Institut, Marburg, Germany. German. General paleontology and geology.

Grana. An International Journal of Palynology and Aerobiology. 1954. Scandinavian University Press, Oslo, Norway. Pollen, spores, and other air-borne organisms. Scandinavian Palynological Collegium, International Association for Aerobiology.

Historical Biology. An International Journal of Paleobiology. 1988. Gordon and Breach-Harwood Academic, Amsterdam, Netherlands. General paleontology.

Ichnos: The Study of Plant and Animal Traces. 1990. Gordon and Breach-Harwood Academic, Amsterdam, Netherlands. Trace fossils.

International Journal of Plant Science. 1875. University of Chicago, Chicago, U.S.A. Plant science, including paleobotany.

Journal of Micropalaeontology. 1982. British Micropalaeontological Society, Geological Society Publishing House, Bath, England. Microfossils, biostratigraphy, evolution, paleobiology, paleoecology.

Journal of Paleontology. 1927. Paleontological Society, Lawrence, Kansas, U.S.A. General taxonomic paleontology and its implications to paleobiology and stratigraphic paleontology.

Journal of Vertebrate Paleontology. 1981. Society of Vertebrate Paleontology, Lincoln, Nebraska, U.S.A. General vertebrate paleontology.

Lethaia. An International Journal of Palaeontology and Stratigraphy. 1968. Scandinavian University Press, Oslo, Norway/Stockholm, Sweden. English, German, French. General paleontology and biostratigraphy. International Palaeontological Association.

Marine Micropaleontology. 1976. Elsevier Science, Amsterdam, Netherlands. General marine micropaleontology.

Micropaleontology. 1954. Micropaleontology Press, American Museum of Natural History, New York City, U.S.A. General micropaleontology.

Nature (London). 1869. Macmillan Journals, London, England. Various topics, including general paleontology.

Neues Jahrbuch für Geologie und Paläontologie, Abhandlungen. 1950. E. Schweizerbart'sche Verlagsbuchhandlung, Stuttgart, Germany. German. Geology and general paleontology.

Nipponites/Quarterly Journal of Palaeontology. 1935. Palaeontological Society of Japan, Tokyo, Japan. English; Japanese summaries. General paleontology.

The Palaeobotanist. 1952. Birbal Sahni Institute of Palaeobotany, Lucknow, India. Paleobotany.

Palaeogeography, Palaeoclimatology, Palaeoecology: An International Journal for the Geo-Sciences. 1965. Elsevier Science, Amsterdam, Netherlands. English, French, German. Paleogeography, paleoclimatology, and paleoecology.

Palaeontographica. Beiträge zur Naturgeschichte der Vorzeit. Abteilung A: Paläozoologie, Stratigraphie. 1846. E. Schweizerbart'sche Verlagsbuchhandlung, Stuttgart, Germany. English, German; English, French, German summaries. General paleozoology and stratigraphy.

Palaeontographica. Beiträge zur Naturgeschichte der Vorzeit. Abteilung B: Paläophytologie. 1846. E. Schweizerbart'sche Verlagsbuchhandlung, Stuttgart, Germany. English, French, German; English, French, German summaries. General paleobotany.

Palaeontologia Africana. 1953. Bernard Price Institute for Palaeontological Research, University of Witwatersrand, Johannesburg, South Africa. General African paleontology.

Palaeontologia Electronica. 1998. Coquina Press, Texas A&M University, Texas, U.S.A. (http://www-odp.tamu.edu/paleo/index.htm). General paleontology. Paleontological Society, Paleontological Association, Cushman Society, Sociedad Española de Paleontología, British Micropalaeontological Society, Society of Vertebrate Paleontology. English, Spanish. Mirror sites: Texas, U.S.A. (http://www-odp.tamu.edu/paleo/toc.htm); Canada (http://www.earthsci.carleton.ca/paleo/toc.htm); Switzerland (http://www.erdw.ethz.ch/~pe/toc.htm); California, U.S.A. (http://gs.ucsd.edu/paleo/toc.htm); Oklahoma, U.S.A. (http://www.omnh.ou.edu/paleo/toc.htm); Spain (http://www.uv.es/~pardomv/pe/toc.htm).

Paläontologische Zeitschrift. 1913. E. Schweizerbart'sche Verlagsbuchhandlung, Stuttgart, Germany. English, German; English, French summaries. General paleontology. Paläontologische Gesellschaft.

Palaeontology. 1957. Blackwell Scientific, Oxford, England. General paleontology. Palaeontological Association.

Palaeovertebrata. 1967. Laboratoires de Paléontologie, École Pratique des Hautes Ètudes, and Université des Sciences et Techniques du Languedoc, Montpellier, France. English, French, German, Spanish. General vertebrate paleontology.

Palaios. 1986. Society of Economic Paleontologists and Mineralogists, Tulsa, U.S.A. Paleontology, stratigraphy, sedimentology, paleogeography, paleoecology, paleobiology, and astrobiology.

Paleobiology. 1975. Paleontological Society, Lawrence, Kansas, U.S.A. Paleobiological processes and patterns.

Paleontological Journal (Official translation of *Paleontologicheskiy Zhurnal*, Russia). 1967. Interperiodica, Birmingham, Alabama, U.S.A. General paleontology, especially of eastern Europe and Asia.

Palynology. 1977. American Association of Stratigraphic Palynologists Foundation, College Station, Texas, U.S.A. Pollen and spores.

Quaternaria Nova. 1990. Istituto Italiano di Paleontologia Umana, Rome, Italy. English, French, German, Italian, Spanish; English, French abstracts. Natural and cultural history of the Quaternary (prehistory, paleontology, geology).

Review of Palaeobotany and Palynology: An International Journal. 1967. Elsevier Science, Amsterdam, Netherlands. English, French, German. General paleobotany, pollen, and spores.

Revista Española de Micropaleontología. 1997. Instituto Tecnológico Geominero de España, Madrid, Spain. Spanish, English, French, Italian; Spanish, English summaries. General micropaleontology.

Rivista Italiana di Paleontologia e Stratigrafia. 1895. Università degli Studi di Milano, Milan, Italy. Italian. General paleontology and stratigraphy.

Science (Washington, D.C.). 1883. American Association for the Advancement of Science, Washington, D.C., U.S.A. Various science topics, including general paleontology.

Senckenbergiana Lethaea. 1919. Senckenbergische Naturforschende Gesellschaft, Frankfurt-am-Main, Germany. English, French, German. General paleontology.

Vertebrata PalAsiatica (Gu Jizhui Dongwu Xuebao). 1959. Academia Sinica, Institute of Vertebrate Paleontology and Paleoanthropology, Beijing, China. Chinese; English summaries. General vertebrate paleontology and paleoanthropology.

INDEXES

TAXONOMIC INDEX

Page numbers in **boldface** indicate subjects with their own entries. Page numbers in *italics* indicate illustrations.

GENERAL INDEX

This is a general subject index of people, places, and things related to paleontology. As subjects of articles, a few broad taxonomic names appear here, but coverage of most taxonomic terms is located in the Taxonomic Index. Page numbers in **bold-face** indicate subjects with their own entries. Page numbers in *italics* indicate illustrations.

CONTRIBUTOR AND ADVISER ADDRESSES

CONTRIBUTOR AND ADVISER ADDRESSES

Alcover, Josep Antoni. Institut Mediterrani d'Estudis Avençats, Carretera de Valldemossa km 7.5, 07071 Ciutat de Mallorca, Balears, Spain. **Essay:** Oceanic Islands.

Alexander, R. McNeill. Department of Pure and Applied Biology, University of Leeds, Leeds, LS2 9JT, UK. **Essay:** Biomechanics.

Aller, Josephine Y. Marine Sciences Research Center, SUNY at Stony Brook, Stony Brook, NY, 11794-5000, USA. **Essay:** Mortality and Survivorship.

Allin, Edgar F. Department of Anatomy, Midwestern University, 555 31st Street, Downer's Grove, IL, 60515, USA. **Essays:** Hearing and Positional Sense; Sensory Capsules.

Asher, Robert. Doctoral Program in Anthropological Sciences, SUNY at Stony Brook, Stony Brook, NY, 11794, USA. **Essays:** Insectivorans; Placentals: Minor Placental Orders of Small Body Size.

Badgley, Catherine. Museum of Paleontology, University of Michigan, 1109 Geddes Road, Ann Arbor, MI, 48109-1079, USA. **Essay:** Paleoecology.

Beaupre, Steven. Department of Anthropology, University of Arkansas, Old Main 330, Fayetteville, AR, 72701, USA. **Essay:** Feeding Adaptations: Vertebrates.

Bell, Michael A. Department of Ecology and Evolution, State University of New York at Stony Brook, Stony Brook, NY, 11794, USA. **Essays:** Olson, Everett C.; Speciation and Morphological Change.

Bengtson, Stefan. Department of Palaeozoology, Swedish Museum of Natural History, Box 50007, SE-104 05 Stockholm, Sweden. **Essay:** Skeletized Organisms and the Evolution of Skeletized Tissues.

Bennett, S. Christopher. Natural History Museum, University of Kansas, Lawrence, KS, 66045-2454, USA. **Essays:** Aerial Locomotion; Pterosaurs.

Bishop, Gale A. Department of Geology and Geography, Georgia Southern University, P.O. Box 8149, Statesboro, GA, 30460, USA. **Essay:** Crustaceans.

Bonaparte, José F. Paleontologia Vertebrados, Museo Argentino De Ciencias Naturales, Avenida A. Gallardo 470, 1405 Buenos Aires, Argentina. **Essay:** South America.

Boné, Edouard L. TECO, Université Catholique de Louvain, Coll. A. Descamps, Grand-Place, 45, 1348 Louvain-la-Neuve, Belgium. **Essays:** Abel, Othenio; Agassiz, Jean Louis Rudolphe; Boule, Marcellin; Breuil, Henri Édouard Prosper; Brongniart, Alexandre; Dollo, Louis Antoine Marie Joseph; Europe: Western Europe; Gaudry, Albert Jean; Geoffroy, Saint-Hilaire Étienne; Hürzeler, Johannes; Linnaeus, Carolus (Carl von Linné); Orbigny, Alcide Charles Victor Dessalines d'; Stehlin, Hans Georg; Teilhard de Chardin, Pierre.

Brainerd, Elizabeth L. Department of Biology, University of Massachusetts, Amherst, MA, 01003-5810, USA. **Essay:** Respiration.

Brandt, Danita S. Department of Geological Sciences, Michigan State University, East Lansing, MI, 48824-1115, USA. **Essay:** Aquatic Invertebrates, Adaptive Strategies of.

Braun, Christopher B. Parmly Hearing Institute, Loyola University Chicago, 6525 North Sheridan Road, Damen Hall, Room 141, Chicago, IL, 60626, USA. **Essay:** Brain and Cranial Nerves.

Bray, Emily S. Geology Section, University of Colorado Museum, University of Colorado, Campus Box 315, Boulder, CO, 80309-0315, USA. **Essay:** Egg, Amniote.

Briggs, Derek E.G. Department of Earth Sciences, University of Bristol, Wills Memorial Building, Queens Road, Bristol, BS8 1RJ, UK. **Essays:** Arthropods: Miscellaneous Arthropods; Arthropods: Overview.

Briggs, John C. Zoological Collections, Museum of Natural History, University of Georgia, Athens, GA, 30602, USA. **Essays:** Faunal and Floral Provinces; Seas, Ancient.

Britt, Brooks B. Natural History Division, Museum of Western Colorado, Box 20000-5020, Grand Junction, CO, 81501-5020, USA. **Essay:** Pneumatic Spaces.

Brochu, Christopher A. Department of Geology, Field Museum of Natural History, Lake Shore Drive at Roosevelt Road, Chicago, IL, 60605, USA. **Essays:** Crocodylians; Crocodylomorphs.

Buatois, Luis. Instituto Superior de Correlacion Geologica, Universidad Nacional de Tucuman, Casilla de Correo 1 (CC), 4.000-San Miguel de Tucuman, Argentina. **Essay:** Feeding Adaptations: Invertebrates.

Buffetaut, Eric. Centre National de la Recherche Scientifique, 16 cour du Liegat, 75013 Paris, France. **Essays:** Buckland, William; Leidy, Joseph; Marsh, Othniel Charles; Meyer, Christian Erich Hermann von; Southeast Asia; Yang Zhungjian (Chung Chien Young).

Burnham, Robyn J. Museum of Paleontology, University of Michigan, 1109 Geddes Road, Ann Arbor, MI, 48109-1079, USA. **Essay:** Plants: Adaptive Strategies.

Burrow, Carole J. Department of Zoology, University of Queensland, St. Lucia, QLD 4072, Australia. **Essay:** Micropaleontology, Vertebrate.

Callaway, Jack M. Department of Geology, Laredo College, West End Washington Street, Laredo, TX, 78040-4395, USA. **Essay:** Ichthyosaurs.

Callender, Brian. 9 South 310 Aero Drive, Naperville, IL, 60564, USA. (University of Chicago) **Essays:** Abel, Othenio; Agassiz, Jean Louis Rudolphe; Boule, Marcellin; Breuil, Henri Édouard Prosper; Brongniart, Alexandre; Dollo, Louis Antoine Marie Joseph; Gaudry, Albert Jean; Geoffroy, Saint-Hilaire Étienne; Linnaeus, Carolus (Carl von Linné); Orbigny, Alcide Charles Victor Dessalines d'; Stehlin, Hans Georg.

Campbell, Kathleen A. Department of Geology, The University of Auckland, Private Bag 92019, Auckland, New Zealand. **Essay:** Vent and Seep Faunas.

Carpenter, Kenneth. Department of Earth Sciences, Denver Museum of Natural History, 2001 Colorado Blvd., Denver, CO, 80205, USA. **Essays:** Ankylosaurs; Sauropterygians.

Carrano, Matthew T. Department of Organismal Biology and Anatomy, University of Chicago, 1027 East 57th Street, Chicago, IL, 60637, USA. **Essay:** Saurischians.

Chinsamy, Anusuya. South African Museum, P.O. Box 61, Cape Town 8000, South Africa. **Essay:** Growth, Postembryonic.

Christian, Andreas. Bildungswissenschaftliche Hochschule Flensburg - Universität Institut für Biologie und Sachunterricht und ihre Didaktik, Mürwiker Str. 77, 24943 Flensburg, Germany. **Essay:** Terrestrial Locomotion in Vertebrates.

Churcher, Charles S. Box 12, Site 42, RR 1, Gabriola Island, BC, V0R 1X0, Canada.

Cipriani, Roberto. Department of Geophysical Sciences, University of Chicago, 5734 South Ellis Ave., Chicago, IL, 60637, USA. **Essay:** Haeckel, Ernst Heinrich.

Clarkson, E.N.K. Department of Geology and Geophysics, University of Edinburgh, West Mains Road, Edinburgh, EH9 3JW, UK. **Essay:** Eyes: Invertebrates.

Clemens, W.A. Museum of Paleontology, University of California-Berkeley, Berkeley, CA, 94720-4780, USA. **Essays:** Extinction; Stirton, Ruben Arthur.

Cloutier, Richard. Parc de Miguasha, CP 183, Nouvelle, Québec, G0C 2E0, Canada. *and* UPRESA 8014 du CNRS, Université des Sciences et Technologies de Lille, 59655 Villeneuve d'Ascq, France. **Essays:** Actinopterygians; Osteichthyans; Tetrapods: Basal Tetrapods; Tetrapods: Overview.

Colbert, Edwin H. Department of Geology, Museum of Northern Arizona, 3101 North Fort Valley Road, Flagstaff, AZ, 86001, USA. **Essays:** Cope, Edward Drinker; Granger, Walter Willis; Gregory, William King; Matthew, William Diller; Osborn, Henry Fairfield; Simpson, George Gaylord; United States, Continental.

Collins, Allen G. Department of Integrative Biology, University of California-Berkeley, Berkeley, CA, 94720, USA. **Essays:** Evolutionary Trends; Sponges and Spongelike Organisms.

Cooke, H. B.S. 2133, 154 Street, White Rock (South Surrey), BC, V4A 4S5, Canada. **Essay:** Leakey, Louis Seymour Bazett.

Copper, Paul. Department of Earth Sciences, Laurentian University, Ramsey Lake Road, Sudbury, ON, P3E 2C6, Canada. **Essays:** Reefs and Reef-Building Organisms; Trophic Groups and Levels.

Coria, Rodolfo A. Museo "Carmen Funes," 8318 Plaza Huincul, Municipalidad de Plaza Huincul, Provincia del Neuquén, Argentina. **Essay:** Ornithischians.

Corruccini, Robert S. Department of Anthropology, Southern Illinois University, Carbondale, IL, 62901-4502, USA. **Essay:** Statistical Techniques.

Craig, Robert Samuel. School of Applied Geology, Curtin University of Technology, Earth and Planetary Sciences, Perth, WA 6001, Australia. **Essay:** Brachiopods.

Croft, Darin A. Department of Organismal Biology and Anatomy, University of Chicago, 1027 East 57th Street, Chicago, IL, 60637, USA. **Essay:** Placentals: Endemic South American Ungulates.

Cuffey, Roger J. Department of Geosciences, Pennsylvania State University, University Park, PA, 16802, USA. **Essay:** Bryozoans.

Cuny, Gilles. Department of Geology, University of Bristol, Wills Memorial Building, Queens Road, Bristol, B58 1RJ, UK. **Essay:** Chondrichthyans.

Czarniecki, Stanislaw. Polish Academy of Sciences, Institute of Geological Sciences, ul. Senacka 1, 31-002 Krakow, Poland. **Essay:** Europe: Eastern Europe.

Davis, Paul G. Department of Geology, University of Portsmouth, Burnaby Road, Portsmouth, PO1 2UP, UK. **Essays:** Birds; Fossilization Processes; Taphonomy.

Dawson, Mary R. Section of Vertebrate Paleontology, Carnegie Museum of Natural History, 4400 Forbes Avenue, Pittsburgh, PA, 15213-4080, USA. **Essay:** Glires.

Delson, Eric. Department of Anthropology, American Museum of Natural History, Central Park West at 79th Street, New York, NY, 10024-5192, USA. **Essay:** Primates.

Diamond, Michael K. 3100 37th Street, Rock Island, IL, 61201, USA. **Essays:** Circulatory Patterns; Evolutionary Theory; Growth, Development, and Evolution.

Dilcher, David. Florida Museum of Natural History, University of Florida, Paleobotany Laboratory, Department of Natural Sciences, Gainesville, FL, 32611-2035, USA. **Essay:** Forests, Fossil.

Dilkes, David W. Redpath Museum, McGill University, 859 Sherbrooke Street West, Montreal, PQ, H3A 2K6, Canada. **Essay:** Amniotes.

DiMichele, William A. Department of Paleobiology, MRC 121, National Museum of Natural History, Smithsonian Institution, Washington, DC, 20560, USA. **Essay:** Biomass and Productivity Estimates.

Domning, Daryl P. Department of Anatomy, Howard University, 520 West Street NW, Washington, DC, 20059, USA. **Essay:** Sirenians.

Donoghue, Philip C.J. School of Earth Sciences, University of Birmingham, Edgbaston, Birmingham, B15 2TT, UK. **Essay:** Teeth: Classification of Teeth.

Donovan, Stephen K. British Museum (Natural History), London, WC1B 3DG, UK. **Essay:** Cephalopods.

Doyle, James A. Section of Evolution and Ecology, University of California, Storer Hall, Davis, CA, 95616, USA. **Essay:** Angiosperms.

Dufour, Elise. CNRS Laboratoire de Biogéochemie Isotopique, Tour 26, Case 120, Université Pierre et Marie Curie (Paris 6), 4 Place Jussieu, 75252 Paris, France. **Essay:** Stable Isotope Analysis.

Dyke, Gareth J. Department of Earth Sciences, University of Bristol, Wills Memorial Building, Queens Road, Bristol, BS8 1RJ, UK. **Essay:** Birds.

Eckhardt, Robert B. College of Health and Human Development, The Pennsylvania State University, University Park, PA, 16802, USA. **Essay:** Variation.

Elias, Scott A. Institute of Arctic and Alpine Research, University of Colorado, 1560 30th Street, Campus Box 450, Boulder, CO, 80309-0450, USA. **Essay:** Global Environment.

Englander, Julie. 25862 Fairmount Blvd., Cleveland, OH, 44122, USA. **Essay:** Broom, Robert.

Enter, Janie A. Los Alamos National Library, MS J514, Los Alamos, NM, 87545, USA. **Essay:** Gastroliths.

Ezzo, Joseph A. 840 North Alvernon #203, Tucson, AZ, 85751-1811, USA. **Essay:** Trace Element Analysis.

Fastovsky, David E. Department of Geology, University of Rhode Island, Kingston, RI, 02881-0807, USA. **Essay:** Dinosaurs.

Flynn, Lawrence J. Peabody Museum of Archaeology and Ethnology, Harvard University, 11 Divinity Ave., Cambridge, MA, 02138, USA. **Essay:** Indian Subcontinent.

Ford, Susan M. Department of Anthropology, #4502, Southern Illinois University, Carbondale, IL, 62901-4502, USA. **Essay:** Phyletic Dwarfism and Gigantism.

Forsten, Ann. Zoological Museum, Vertebrates Division, Finnish Museum of Natural History, P.O. Box 17 (P. Rautatiekatu 13, FIN-00014, University of Helsinki, Helsinki, Finland. **Essay:** Kowalevsky, Vladimir (Woldemar) Onufrievich.

Forster, Catherine A. Department of Anatomical Sciences, State University of New York at Stony Brook, Health Sciences Center, Stony Brook, NY, 11794, USA. **Essays:** Ceratopsians; Field Techniques.

Gagnier, Pierre-Yves. Grande Galérie d'Évolution, Muséum National d'Histoire Naturelle, 8, rue Buffon, Paris 75005, France. **Essays:** Eyes: Vertebrates; Ornamentation: Vertebrates; Skeleton: Dermal Postcranial Skeleton.

Galton, Peter M. College of Naturopathic Medicine, University of Bridgeport, 60 Lafayette Street, Bridgeport, CT, 06601-2449, USA. **Essay:** Stegosaurs.

Gardner, James D. Laboratory for Vertebrate Paleontology and Department of Biological Sciences, University of Alberta, Edmonton, AB, T6G 2E9, Canada. **Essay:** Seismic and Surface Activity.

Gaudin, Timothy J. Department of Biological and Environmental Sciences, University of Tennessee at Chattanooga, 615 McCallie Avenue, Chattanooga, TN, 37403-2598, USA. **Essays:** Palaeanodonts; Pangolins; Xenarthrans.

Geary, Dana H. Department of Geology and Geophysics, University of Wisconsin-Madison, 1215 West Dayton Street, Madison, WI, 53706, USA. **Essay:** Predation.

Geist, Nicholas R. Department of Zoology, 3029 Cordley Hall, Oregon State University, Corvallis, OR, 97331-2914, USA. **Essays:** Paleoethology; Reproductive Strategies: Vertebrates.

Gensel, Patricia G. Department of Biology, University of North Carolina, 405 Coker, Campus Box 3280, Chapel Hill, NC, 27599-3280, USA. **Essay:** Bryophytes.

Geraads, Denis. UMR 152 du CNRS, Musée de l'Homme, place du Trocadéro, F-75116 Paris, France. **Essay:** Africa: North Africa and the Middle East.

Geyer, Gerd. Institut für Paläontologie, Universität Würzburg, Pleicherwall 1, D-97070 Würzburg, Germany. **Essay:** Gastropods.

Gheerbrant, Emmanuel. Laboratoire de Paléontologie, URA 12 CNRS, Muséum National d'Histoire Naturelle, 8, rue Buffon, F-75005 Paris, France. **Essay:** Arambourg, Camille Louis Joseph.

Hammer, William R. Department of Geology, Augustana College, Rock Island, IL, 61201, USA. **Essay:** Antarctica.

Hancox, P.J. Department of Geology, University of Witwatersrand, Private Bag 3, Wits 2050, South Africa. **Essay:** Africa: Sub-Saharan Africa.

Harper, David A.T. Department of Geography, National University of Ireland, Galway, The Concourse, Distillery Road, Galway, Ireland. **Essay:** Computer Applications in Paleontology.

Hedges, S. Blair. Department of Biology, Pennsylvania State University, 208 Mueller Lab, University Park, PA, 16802, USA. **Essay:** Molecular Paleontology.

Hill, Robert S. Department of Plant Science, University of Tasmania, GPO Box 252-55, Hobart, Tasmania, 7001, Australia. **Essay:** Australia: Paleobotany.

Hopson, James A. Department of Organismal Biology and Anatomy, University of Chicago, 1027 East 57th Street, Chicago, IL, 60637, USA. **Essays:** Mammals, Mesozoic and Non-Therian; Synapsids; Therapsids.

Hua, Stéphane. CNRS Laboratoire de Paléontologie des Vertébrés, Tour 15, Case 106, Université Pierre et Marie Curie (Paris 6), 4 Place Jussieu, 75252 Paris, France. **Essay:** Aquatic Locomotion.

Hunter, John P. Department of Anatomy, New York College of Osteopathic Medicine, Old Westbury, NY, 11568, USA. **Essays:** Diversity; Teeth: Evolution of Complex Teeth.

Janis, Christine. Department of Ecology and Evolutionary Biology, Brown University, Box G-B207, Providence, RI, 02912, USA. **Essay:** Artiodactyls.

Janvier, Philippe. Laboratoire de Paléontologie, URA 12 du CNRS, Muséum National d'Histoire Naturelle, 8, rue Buffon, F-75005 Paris, France. **Essay:** Craniates.

Johnston, Paul A. Department of Paleontology, Royal Tyrell Museum, Box 7500, Drumheller, AB, T0J 0Y0, Canada. **Essay:** Bivalves.

Johnston, Roger G. Chemical Laser Science Division, Los Alamos National Laboratory, P.O. Box 1663, Mail Stop J565, Los Alamos, NM, 87545, USA. **Essay:** Gastroliths.

Kemp, Anne. Department of Anatomical Sciences, University of Queensland, St. Lucia, QLD 4072, Australia. **Essays:** Odor and Pheromone Receptors; Skull; Vertebrate Hard Tissues: Keratinous Tissues; Vertebrate Hard Tissues: Mineralized Tissues.

Knaus, Margaret Jane. Physics Department, Southwest Texas State University, 100 Science Building, San Marcos, TX, 78666-4604, USA. **Essay:** Problematic Plants.

Koppelhus, Eva Bundgaard. Tyrell Museum of Palaeontology, Box 7500, Drumheller, AB, T0J 0Y0, Canada. **Essays:** Cycads; Horsetails and Their Relatives.

Korn, Dieter. Institüt und Museum für Geologie und Paläontolgie, Eberhard-Karls-Universität Tübingen, Sigwartstrasse 10, Tübingen D-72076, Germany. **Essay:** Schindewolf, Otto Heinrich.

Krause, David W. Department of Anatomical Sciences, State University of New York at Stony Brook, Stony Brook, NY, 11794-8081, USA. **Essay:** Madagascar.

Kürschner, Wolfram Michael. Laboratory of Palaeobotany and Palynology, Utrecht University, Budapestlaan 4, 3584 CD Utrecht, Netherlands. **Essay:** Plants: Vegetative Features.

Labandeira, Conrad C. Department of Paleontology, National Museum of Natural History, Smithsonian Institution, MRC-121, Washington, DC, 20560, USA. **Essays:** Insects and Other Hexapods; Myriapods.

Lambert, W. David. Department of Biology, St. Peter's College, Kennedy Blvd., Jersey City, NJ, 07306, USA. **Essay:** Proboscideans.

Lange-Badré, Brigitte. CNRS Laboratoire de Paléontologie des Vertébrés, Université Pierre et Marie Curie (Paris 6), Tour 25-15, Case 106, 4 Place Jussieu, 75252 Paris, France. **Essay:** Piveteau, Jean.

Lee, Michael S.Y. School of Biological Sciences, University of Sydney, Building A08, Sydney, NSW 2006, Australia. **Essays:** Aquatic Reptiles; Parareptiles; Turtles.

LePage, Ben A. Department of Geology, University of Pennsylvania, 240 South 33rd Street, Philadelphia, PA, 19104-6316, USA. **Essays:** Coniferophytes; Ginkgos; Gymnosperms; Plants: Overview.

Lewis, Margaret E. Biology Program, NAMS, The Richard Stockton College of New Jersey, Pomona, NJ, 08240-0195, USA. **Essay:** Carnivorans.

Lézine, Anne-Marie. CNRS Laboratoire de Paléontologie et Stratigraphie, Case 106, Université Pierre et Marie Curie (Paris 6), Jussieu-Boite 106-Tour 26/16-4 étage, 75252 Paris, France. **Essay:** Palynology.

Long, John A. Western Australian Museum, Francis Street, Perth, WA, 6000, Australia. **Essays:** Gnathostomes; Placoderms.

Lucas, Spencer G. New Mexico Museum of Natural History, 1801 Mountain Road NW, Albuquerque, NM, 87104, USA. **Essays:** Andrews, Roy Chapman; Dating Methods; Geological Timescale; Paleomagnetism.

MacPhee, R.D.E. Department of Mammalogy, Chairman and Curator, American Museum of Natural History, 79th Street and Central Park West, New York, NY, 10024, USA. **Essay:** Aardvarks.

Maisch, Michael W. Institüt und Museum für Geologie und Paläontolgie, Universität Tübingen, Sigwartstrasse 10, Tübingen D-72076, Germany. **Essays:** Huene, Friedrich Freiherr von; Kuhn-Schnyder, Emil.

Mallatt, Jon. Department of Zoology, Washington State University, Pullman, WA, 99164-4236, USA. **Essay:** Pharyngeal Arches and Derivatives.

Mángano, M. Gabriela. Instituto Superior de Correlacion Geologica, Instituto Nacional de Tucuman, Casilla de Correo 1 (CC), 4.000-San Miguel de Tucuman, Argentina. **Essay:** Feeding Adaptations: Invertebrates.

Martin, John. Leicester City Museums, The Rowans, College Street, Leicester, LE1 7EA, UK. **Essay:** Sauropodomorphs.

Martin, Thomas. Institut für Paläontolgie, Freie Universität Berlin, Malteserstrasse 74-100, Haus D, D-12249 Berlin, Germany. **Essay:** Enamel Microstructure.

Martin-Rolland, Valérie. Musee des Dinosaures, 12260 Esperaza, France. **Essay:** Sauropodomorphs.

Massare, Judy A. Department of the Earth Sciences, State University of New York at Brockport, 350 New Campus Drive, Brockport, NY, 14420, USA. **Essay:** Ichthyosaurs.

Maxwell, W. Desmond. Department of Biological Sciences, University of the Pacific, Stockton, CA, 95211, USA. **Essays:** Adaptation; Ornithopods; Theropods.

McElwain, Jenny C. Department of Animal and Plant Sciences, University of Sheffield, Sheffield, S10 2TN, UK. **Essay:** Atmospheric Environment.

McKinney, Michael L. Department of Geology, University of Tennessee, Knoxville, TN, 37996, USA. **Essay:** Population Dynamics.

McMenamin, Mark A.S. Department of Geography and Geology, Mount Holyoke College, South Hadley, MA, 01075 USA. **Essays:** Problematic Animals: Overview; Problematic Animals: Phanerozoic; Problematic Animals: Poorly Characterized.

McNamara, Kenneth J. Western Australian Museum, Francis Street, Perth, WA 6000, Australia. **Essays:** Australia: Invertebrate Paleontology; Echinoderms; Sedgwick, Adam; Terrestrialization of Animals.

McRoberts, Christopher A. Department of Geological Sciences and Environmental Studies, State University of New York at Cortland, P.O. Box 6000, Binghamton, NY, 13902-6000, USA. **Essay:** Faunal Change and Turnover.

Metcalf, Sara J. Humber Estuary Discovery Centre, North East Lincolnshire Council Leisure Services, Knoll Street, Cleethorpes, DN35 4LN, UK. **Essay:** Paleoclimatology.

Miao, Desui. Museum of Natural History, University of Kansas, Lawrence, KS, 66045-2454, USA. **Essay:** China.

Miles, Roger. 3 Eagle Lane, London, E11 1PF, UK. **Essay:** Stensiö, Erik.

Milner, Angela C. Department of Palaeontology, The Natural History Museum, Cromwell Road, London, SW7 5BD, UK. **Essay:** Lepospondyls.

Montellano-Ballesteros, Marisol. Departamento de Paleontología, Insituto de Geología, Universidad Nacional Autónoma de México, Ciudad Universitaria, Delegación Coyoacán, 04510 Mexico City, D.F., México. **Essay:** Mexico and Central America.

Nambudiri, E.M.V. Department of Biology, Nipissing University, 100 College Drive, Box 5002, North Bay, ON, P1B 8L7, Canada. **Essay:** Club Mosses and Their Relatives.

Niklas, Karl J. Section of Plant Biology, Cornell University, Plant Science Building, Ithaca, NY, 14853-5908, USA. **Essay:** Plants: Mechanical Plant Design.

Northcutt, R. Glenn. Neurosciences 0201, University of California San Diego, La Jolla, CA, 92093-0204, USA. **Essays:** Brain and Cranial Nerves; Lateral Line System.

Novacek, Michael J. Department of Vertebrate Paleontology, American Museum of Natural History, Central Park West at 79th Street, New York, NY, 10024-5192, USA. **Essay:** Placentals: Overview.

Parrish, J. Michael. Department of Biological Sciences, Northern Illinois University, DeKalb, IL, 60115, USA. **Essay:** Archosauromorphs.

Peterson, Kevin J. Division of Biology, Mail Code 156-29, California Institute of Technology, Pasadena, CA, 91125, USA. **Essays:** Cephalochordates; Urochordates.

Polly, Paul David. Department of Biomedical Sciences, Queen Mary and Westfield College, Mile End Road, Room Number BMS 2.36, London, E1 4NS, UK. **Essays:** Creodonts; Hyatt, Alpheus; Schmalhausen, Ivan Feodorovich; Schmalhausen, Ivan Ivanovich; Selection.

Poteet, Mary F. Department of Integrative Biology, University of California at Berkeley, Berkeley, CA, 94720, USA. **Essay:** Coevolutionary Relationships.

Prothero, Donald R. Department of Geology, Occidental College, Los Angeles, CA, 90041, USA. **Essays:** Fossil Record; Mesonychids; Paleobiogeography; Paleontology: Overview; Perissodactyls; Plate Tectonics and Continental Drift; Systematics; Ungulates, Archaic.

Purnell, Mark A. Department of Geology, University of Leicester, University Road, Leicester, LE1 7RH, UK. **Essay:** Diet.

Rage, Jean-Claude. CNRS Laboratoire de Paléontologie des Vertébrés, Tour 15 Case 106, Université Pierre et Marie Curie (Paris 6), 4 Place Jussieu, 75252 Paris, France. **Essay:** Lissamphibians.

Rasmussen, D. Tab. Department of Anthropology, Washington University, Campus Box 1114, St. Louis, MO, 63130, USA. **Essay:** Hyraxes.

Reisz, Robert R. Department of Biology, University of Toronto, Erindale College, 3359 Mississauga Rd., Mississauga, ON, L5L 1C6, Canada. **Essays:** Pelycosaurs; Sauropsids.

Rich, Thomas H. National Museum of Victoria, 285-321 Russell Street, Melbourne, VIC, 3001, Australia. **Essay:** Australia: Vertebrate Paleontology.

Rieppel, Olivier. Department of Geology, Field Museum of Natural History, Roosevelt Road at Lake Shore Drive, Chicago, IL, 60605-2496, USA. **Essay:** Lepidosauromorphs.

Rose, Kenneth D. Department of Cell Biology and Anatomy, The Johns Hopkins University, School of Medicine, 725 North Wolfe Street, Baltimore, MD, 21205, USA. **Essay:** Burrowing Adaptations in Vertebrates.

Ross, Charles A. Department of Geology, MS 9080, Western Washington University, Bellingham, WA, 98225, USA. **Essays:** Skeletized Microorganisms: Algae; Skeletized Microorganisms: Protozoans and Chitozoans.

Rothwell, Gar W. Department of Environmental and Plant Biology, Ohio University, Porter Hall, Room 401e, Athens, OH, 45701-2979, USA. **Essay:** Gnetophytes.

Ruben, John. Zoology Department, Oregon State University, 3029 Cordley Hall, Corvallis, OR, 97331-2914, USA. **Essay:** Thermoregulation.

Ruddat, Manfred. Department of Ecology and Evolution, University of Chicago, Erman Biology Center, EPC 10, 1103 East 57th Street, Chicago, IL, 60637, USA. **Essays:** Defensive Structures: Plants; Reproductive Strategies: Plants.

Ruse, Michael. Department of Philosophy, University of Guelph, Guelph, ON, N1G 2W1, Canada. **Essays:** Buffon, Georges-Louis Leclerc, Comte de; Cuvier, Georges; Darwin, Charles Robert; Huxley, Thomas Henry; Lyell, Charles; Owen, Richard; Phillips, John.

Sampson, Scott D. Department of Anatomy, New York College of Osteopathic Medicine, Old Westbury, NY, 11568, USA. **Essay:** Pachycephalosaurs.

Sansom, Ivan J. School of Earth Sciences, University of Birmingham, Edgbaston, Birmingham, B15 2TT, UK. **Essay:** Teeth: Earliest Teeth.

Sargis, Eric J. Department of Anthropology, Hunter College, City University of New York, 695 Park Avenue, New York, NY, 10021, USA. **Essays:** Bats; Tree Shrews.

Sarjeant, William A.S. Department of Geological Sciences, University of Saskatchewan, 114 Science Place, Saskatoon, SK, S7N 5E2, Canada. **Essays:** Deflandre, Georges Victor; Ehrenberg, Christian Gottfried; Eisenack, Alfred; Erdtman, Otto Gunnar Elias; Halstead, Lambert Beverly; Smith, William; Wilson, Alice Evelyn.

Scheckler, Stephen E. Department of Biology, Virginia Polytechnic Institute and State University, 3016 Derring, Blacksburg, VA, 24061-0406, USA. **Essay:** Progymnosperms.

Schiebout, Judith A. Louisiana State University Museum of

Natural Science, Louisiana State University, 354 Howe-Russel Hall, Baton Rouge, LA, 70803, USA. **Essays:** Placentals: Minor Placental Orders of Large Body Size; Sternberg, Charles Hazelius.

Schoch, Robert M. College of General Studies, Boston University, 871 Commonwealth Avenue, Boston, MA, 02215, USA. **Essays:** Hoaxes and Errors; Paleontology: History of Paleontology.

Schultka, Stephan. Museum für Naturkunde, Institut für Paläontologie, Invalidenstrasse 43, D-10115 Berlin, Germany. **Essay:** Vascular Plants, Earliest.

Schultze, Hans-Peter. Institut für Paläontologie, Museum für Naturkunde, Humboldt-Universität, D-10115 Berlin, Germany. **Essays:** Denison, Robert Howland; Gross, Walter Robert; Sarcopterygians.

Schweitzer, Mary H. Department of Biology and Microbiology and Museum of the Rockies, Montana State University, Office CL 5B, Bozeman, MT, 59717, USA. **Essay:** Molecular Paleontology.

Scillato-Yané, Gustavo J. Departmento Cientifico Paleontologia de Vertebrados, Facultad de Ciencias Naturales y Museo, Universidad Nacional de la Plata, Paseo del Bosque, 1900 La Plata, Conicet, Argentina. **Essays:** Ameghino, Carlos; Ameghino, Florentino.

Scrutton, Colin T. Department of Geological Sciences, University of Durham, South Road, Durham, DH1 3LE, UK. **Essays:** Anthozoans; Coelenterates.

Seilacher, Adolf. Geology and Geophysics, Yale University, PM 203, New Haven, CT, 06520, USA. **Essay:** Ediacaran Biota.

Serbet, Rudolph. Museum of Natural History, University of Kansas, Lawrence, KS, 66045-2454, USA. **Essay:** Seed Ferns.

Shea, Brian T. Department of CMS Biology, Northwestern University, 303 East Chicago Ave., Office # 7-334 w-7195, Chicago, IL, 60611, USA. **Essays:** Allometry; Heterochrony.

Shu, Degan. Early Life Institute, Department of Geology, Northwest University, 710069 Xi'an, China. **Essay:** Hemichordates.

Shubin, Neil H. Department of Biology, University of Pennsylvania, Philadelphia, PA, 19104-6017, USA. **Essays:** Evolutionary Novelty; Fins and Limbs, Paired.

Skog, Judith E. Department of Biology 3E1, George Mason University, 4400 University Drive, Fairfax, VA, 22030-4444, USA. **Essay:** Ferns and Their Relatives.

Smith, Gerald R. Museum of Paleontology, University of Michigan, Ann Arbor, MI, 48109, USA. **Essay:** Hibbard, Claude W.

Smith, Giles. Department of Geology, University of Bristol, Wills Memorial Building, Queens Road, Bristol, BS8 1RJ, UK. **Essay:** Chondrichthyans.

Smith, Jodie E. Department of Geology, McMaster University, Hamilton, ON, L8S 4M1, Canada. **Essay:** Ocean Environment.

Socha, John J. Department of Organismal Biology, University of Chicago, 1027 East 57th Street, Chicago, IL, 60637, USA. **Essays:** Anning, Mary; Seeley, Harry Govier.

Spalding, David A.E. 1105 Ogden Road, R.R. #1, Pender Island, British Columbia, V0N 2M1, Canada. (Professional Associate, Department of Geological Sciences, University of Saskatchewan) **Essays:** Bird, Roland Thaxter; Brown, Barnum; Dawson, John William; Fossil Resource Management; Parks, William Arthur.

Speer, Brian R. Museum of Paleontology, University of California, Valley Life Sciences Building, Berkeley, CA, 94720, USA. **Essay:** Algae.

Spoor, Fred. Department of Anatomy and Developmental Biology, University College London, Rockefeller Building, London, WC1E 6JJ, UK. **Essay:** Radiological Imaging and Associated Techniques.

Stafford, Brian J. Division of Mammals, National Museum of Natural History, Smithsonian Institution, NHB 390, MRC 108, Washington, DC, 20560, USA. **Essays:** Bats; Dermopterans.

Storrs, Glenn W. Geier Collections and Research, Cincinnati Museum Center, 1720 Gilbert Ave., Cincinnati, OH, 45202, USA. **Essay:** Placodonts.

Sues, Hans-Dieter. Department of Vertebrate Palaeontology, Royal Ontario Museum, 100 Queen's Park, Toronto, ON, M5S 2C6, Canada. **Essays:** Romer, Alfred Sherwood; Watson, David Meredith Seares.

Sumida, Stuart S. Department of Biology, California State University San Bernardino, 5500 University Parkway, San Bernardino, CA, 92407-2307, USA. **Essays:** Skeleton: Axial Skeleton; Tetrapods: Near-Amniote Tetrapods.

Szalay, Frederick S. Department of Anthropology, Hunter College, City University of New York, 695 Park Avenue, New York, NY, 10021, USA. **Essay:** Marsupials.

Tattersall, Ian. Department of Anthropology, American Museum of Natural History, Central Park West at 79th Street, New York, NY, 10024-5192, USA. **Essay:** Primates.

Theunissen, Bert. Institute for the History of Science, Nieuwegracht 187, 3512 LM Utrecht, Netherlands. **Essay:** Dubois, Marie Eugène François Thomas.

Thewissen, J.G.M. Department of Anatomy, NEOUCOM, 4209 State Route 44, P.O. Box 95, Rootstown, OH, 44272, USA. **Essay:** Whales.

Thomason, Jeff. Department of Biomedical Sciences, Ontario Veterinary College, University of Guelph, Guelph, ON, N1G 2W1, Canada. **Essay:** Functional Morphology.

Ting, Suyin. Louisiana State University Museum of Natural Sciences, Louisiana State University, 119 Foster Hall, Baton Rouge, LA, 70803, USA. **Essay:** Placentals: Minor Placental Orders of Large Body Size.

Tobias, Phillip V. Medical School, Department of Anatomical Sciences, University of the Witwatersrand, 7 York Road, Parktown, Johannesburg, 2193, South Africa. **Essay:** Dart, Raymond Arthur.

Tokaryk, Tim T. Eastend Fossil Research Station, Royal Saskatchewan Museum, Box 460, Eastend, Saskatchewan, S0N 0T0, Canada. **Essays:** Canada and Alaska; Preparation Techniques.

Tong, Haiyan. 16 Cour du Liegat, 75013 Paris, France. **Essay:** Yang Zhungjian (Chung Chien Young).

Turner, Susan. Queensland Museum, P.O. Box 3300, South Brisbane, QLD, 4101, Australia. **Essays:** Hooijer, Dirk Albert; Jawless Fishes; Micropaleontology, Vertebrate; Westoll, Thomas Stanley.

Tuttle, Russell H. Department of Anthropology, University of Chicago, 1126 East 59th Street, Chicago, IL, 60637-1587, USA. **Essay:** Hominids.

Twitchett, Richard J. Department of Earth Sciences, University of Leeds, Leeds, LS2 9JT, UK. **Essay:** Trace Fossils.

Ungar, Peter S. Department of Anthropology, University of Arkansas, Old Main 343, Fayetteville, AR, 72701, USA. **Essay:** Feeding Adaptations: Vertebrates.

Utgaard, John E. Department of Geology, Southern Illinois University, Carbondale, IL, 62901-4324, USA. **Essay:** Bryozoans.

van der Burgh, Johan. Laboratory of Palaeobotany and Palynology, Utrecht University, Budapestlaan 4, 3584 CD Utrecht, Netherlands. **Essay:** Plants: Vegetative Features.

Vizcaíno, Sergio F. Departamento Científico Paleontología de Vertebrados, Museo de La Plata, Paseo del Bosque s/n, 1900 La Plata, Argentina. **Essays:** Ameghino, Carlos; Ameghino, Florentino.

Vorobyeva, Emilia I. Corr.-Member of RAS, Institute of Palaeontology, Moscow, Provsoyuznaja 113, Russia. **Essay:** Russia and the Former Soviet Union.

Waggoner, Ben. Department of Biology, University of Central Arkansas, Conway, AR, 72035-0001, USA. **Essays:** Chelicerates; Fungi; Lichens; Microbial Fossils, Precambrian; Miller, Hugh; Origin of Life; Superphyla; Trilobites.

Webb, Michael W. Department of Geology and Geophysics, University of Wyoming, P.O. Box 3006, Laramie, WY, 82071-3006, USA. **Essays:** Sedimentology; Seismic and Surface Activity; Teeth: Evolution of Mammalian Teeth; Teeth: Tooth Eruption Patterns.

Werdelin, Lars. Department of Palaeozoology, Swedish Museum of Natural History, Box 50007, S-104 05 Stockholm, Sweden. **Essay:** Kurtén, Björn.

Whittington, H.B. Department of Earth Sciences, Sedgwick Museum, University of Cambridge, Downing Street, Cambridge, CB2 3EQ, UK. **Essays:** Lapworth, Charles; Walcott, Charles Doolittle.

Williams, Nic A. School of Animal and Microbial Sciences, The University of Reading, Whiteknights, Reading, RG6 6AJ, UK. **Essay:** Homology.

Willis, Brian J. Bureau of Economic Geology, University of Texas at Austin, University Station, Campus Mail Code E0630, Austin, TX, 78713-8924, USA. **Essay:** Terrestrial Environment.

Wills, Matthew A. Oxford University Museum of Natural History, Oxford University, Parks Road, Oxford, OX1 3PW, UK. **Essays:** Annelids; Arthropods: Miscellaneous Arthropods; Arthropods: Overview; Metazoan Phyla, Minor.

Wing, Scott L. Department of Paleobiology, NHB 121, Smithsonian Institution, Washington, DC, 20560, USA. **Essay:** Biomass and Productivity Estimates.

Wolff, Ronald G. Department of Zoology, University of Florida, POB 118525, Gainesville, FL, 32611-8525, USA. **Essays:** Chordate and Vertebrate Body Structure; Chordates; Comparative Anatomy; Paleontology: Careers for Paleontologists; Photographic Techniques; Appendix: Paleontological Journals.

Wright, Anthony D. School of Geosciences, The Queen's University of Belfast, Belfast, Northern Ireland, BT7 1NN, UK. **Essays:** Defensive Structures: Invertebrates; Exoskeletal Design; Ornamentation: Invertebrates.

Wymer, J.J. Wessex Archaeology, The Vines, Great Cressingham, Thetford, Norfolk, IP25 6NL, UK. **Essays:** Murchison, Roderick Impey; Woodward, Arthur Smith.

Yochelson, Ellis L. Department of Paleobiology, National Museum of Natural History, Smithsonian Institution, Washington, DC, 20560, USA. **Essays:** Molluscs: Minor Molluscan Classes; Molluscs: Overview.

Young, Gavin C. Geology Department, Faculty of Science, Australian National University, Canberra, ACT, 0200, Australia. **Essay:** Acanthodians.